Dictionary of Quotations

The Wordsworth
Dictionary of Quotations

Edited by Connie Robertson

Wordsworth Reference

This edition published 1996 by Wordsworth Editions Ltd.
Cumberland House, Crib Street, Ware, Hertfordshire SG12 9ET.

ISBN 1-85326-379-6

Printed and bound in Great Britain by Mackays of Chatham PLC.

Editor's Introduction

THE AIM of this edition is to provide the reader with, firstly, the means of finding a half-remembered phrase or reference; secondly, examples of what has been said by the famous, the not so famous and the infamous on a particular subject; and thirdly, when using the dictionary alphabetically by author, a representation of statements made by the author or speaker which have become memorable or remarkable. Whilst aiming to fulfil these criteria it is hoped that this book will also provide a ready source of amusement and diversion for the browser.

The obvious sources of established quotations, such as the Bible, the Classical authors, Shakespeare and the great poets, are all represented here, but these sections have been deliberately pruned to provide only the more useful and relevant quotations since more extensive selections can be found in specialized dictionaries. Instead we have hoped to include contemporary quotations which will be relevant to our particular time and its readers.

Arrangement of Entries

Entries have been arranged alphabetically by author and also indexed by keywords (usually at least two) so that if the originator is not known it should not prove difficult to find a quotation by using the index. The Keyword Index opens at p.593.

Authors are listed under their most commonly used name, for example where a pseudonym or titled form is the best known version. Where joint authors are responsible for a quote, they are listed under the first name by which the pairing is commonly known, but this is not intended to diminish the importance of the contribution of the other author.

Foreign language quotations are given together with the English where they are well known, otherwise only the translation appears.

The source of the quotation is shown where it is known to come from a published work by that author. Where the source is a part-work such as a story or poem within a larger work, it is given within single quotation marks. Notes which clarify the context of the quotation are shown in brackets. Film quotations are given under the name of the actor who spoke the lines but since they are not the words of that particular person but of the character which they are playing, the lines are given in double quotation marks.

I hope you find it both a useful and informative addition to your reference shelf, and fun to read.

Connie Robertson
June 1996

Acknowledgements

The Publisher and Editor wish to thank Mervyn Edwards, Sheila Mudge and Ena Richards for their invaluable contribution to the making of this dictionary.

Contents

Dictionary of Quotations

ABBEY Edward
1
Growth for the sake of growth is the ideology of the cancer cell.

ABSE Dannie 1923-
2 `Pathology of Colours'
I know the colour rose, and it is lovely,
But not when it ripens in a tumour;
And healing greens,leaves and grass, so springlike,
In limbs that fester are not springlike.

3 'Pathology of Colours'
So in the simple blessing of a rainbow,
In the bevelled edge of a sunlit mirror,
I have seen visible, Death's artifact
Like soldier's ribbon on a tunic tacked.

ACE Goodman
4
The best cure for hypochondria is to forget about your own body and get interested in someone else's.

ACE Jane
5
Doctor, feel my purse.

6
Time wounds all heels.

ACHESON Dean 1893-1971
7
The future comes one day at a time.

8
Negotiation in the classic diplomatic sense assumes parties more anxious to agree than to disagree.

9
Great Britain has lost an Empire and has not yet found a role.

10
The first requirement of a statesman is that he be dull.

11
A memorandum is written not to inform the reader but to protect the writer.

ACTON Lord 1834-1902
12
Truth is the only merit that gives dignity and worth to history.

13
The most certain test by which we judge whether a country is really free is the amount of security enjoyed by minorities.

14
There is no worse heresy than that the office sanctifies the holder of it.

15 Historical Essays and Studies
Power tends to corrupt, and absolute power corrupts absolutely. Great men are almost always bad men.

ADAMOV Arthur 1908-1970
16
The only thing to know is how to use your neuroses.

ADAMS Abigail 1744-1818
17
These are times in which a genius would like to live. It is not in the still calm of life, or the repose of a pacific station, that great characters are formed...Great necessities call out great virtues.

ADAMS Cindy
18
Success has made failures of many men.

ADAMS Douglas 1952-
19 The Hitch Hiker's Guide to the Galaxy
The Answer to the great Question of...Life, the Universe and Everything...is Forty-two.

ADAMS Frank and HOUGH Will H.
20
I wonder who's kissing her now.

ADAMS Franklin P. 1881-1960
21
Christmas is over, and Business is Business.

22
Health is the thing that makes you feel that now is the best time of the year.

23
There are plenty of good five-cent cigars in the country. The trouble is they cost a quarter. What the country really needs is a good five-cent nickel.

24 *Nods and Becks*
Years ago we discovered the exact point, the dead centre of middle age. It occurs when you are too young to take up golf and too old to rush up to the net.

25 *Nods and Becks*
Elections are won by men and women chiefly because most people vote against somebody rather than for somebody.

ADAMS Henry Brooks 1838-1918
26 *The Education of Henry Adams*
Nothing in education is so astonishing as the amount of ignorance it accumulates in the form of inert facts.

27 *The Education of Henry Adams*
They know enough who know how to learn.

28 *The Education of Henry Adams*
Politics, as a practice, whatever its professions, has always been the systematic organization of hatreds.

29 *The Education of Henry Adams*
Accident counts for much in companionship as in marriage.

30 *The Education of Henry Adams*
A friend in power is a friend lost.

31 *The Education of Henry Adams*
The effect of power and publicity on all men is the aggravation of self, a sort of tumour that ends by killing the victim's sympathies.

32 *The Education of Henry Adams*
Chaos often breeds life, when order breeds habit.

33 *The Education of Henry Adams*
A teacher affects eternity; he can never tell where his influence stops.

34 *The Education of Henry Adams*
One friend in a lifetime is much; two are many; three are hardly possible.
Friendship needs a certain parellelism of life, a community of thought, a rivalry of aim.

35 *The Education of Henry Adams*
Morality is a private and costly luxury.

36 *The Education of Henry Adams*
Practical politics consists in ignoring facts.

37 *The Education of Henry Adams*
No one means all he says, and yet very few say all they mean, for words are slippery and thought is viscous.

ADAMS Joey
38
Bankruptcy is a legal proceeding in which you put your money in your pants pocket and give your coat to your creditors.

ADAMS John 1735-1826
39
There is a danger from all men. The only maxim of a free Government ought to be to trust no man living with power to endanger the public liberty.

40 *(letter to Horacio Gates)*
In politics the middle way is none at all.

41 *(letter to Thomas Jefferson)*
You and I ought not to die before we have explained ourselves to each other.

42 `Novanglus'papers*
A government of laws, and not of men.

43 *(on his presidency)*
The four most miserable years of my life ...

44 *Thoughts on Government*
The happiness of society is the end of government.

45 *Thoughts on Government*
Fear is the foundation of most governments.

ADAMS John Quincy 1767-1848
46
In esse I am nothing; in posse I am everything.

47
If I were to go over my life again, I would be a shoemaker rather than an American Statesman.

48
Had I been chosen president again, I am certain I could not have lived another year.

ADAMSON Harold 1906-1980

49

Comin' in on a wing and a pray'r.

ADCOCK Sir Frank 1886-1968

50

That typically English characteristic for which there is no English name - *esprit de corps.*

ADDISON Joseph 1672-1719

51

Nothing that is not a real crime makes a man appear so contemptible and little in the eyes of the world as inconsistency.

52

A man should always consider how much he has more than he wants, and how much more unhappy he might be than he really is.

53

Young men soon give, and soon forget affronts,

Old age is slow in both.

54

As vivacity is the gift of women, gravity is that of men.

55

A perfect tragedy is the noblest production of human nature.

56

Sunday clears away the rust of the whole week.

57

I have often thought, says Sir Roger, it happens very well that Christmas should fall out in the Middle of Winter.

58

We have in England a particular bashfulness in everything that regards religion.

59 *Ancient Medals*

Pray consider what a figure a man would make in the republic of letters.

60 *The Campaign*

And those who paint 'em truest praise 'em most.

61 *Cato*

What pity is it

That we can die but once to serve our country!

62 *Cato*

From hence, let fierce contending nations know

What dire effects from civil discord flow.

63 *Cato*

The woman that deliberates is lost.

64 *(of Cowley)*

He more had pleased us, had he pleased us less.

65 *The Drummer*

There is nothing more requisite in business than dispatch.

66 *(dying words)*

See in what peace a Christian can die.

67 `A Song for St Cecilia's Day'

Music, the greatest good that mortals know

And all of heaven we have below.

68 *The Spectator*

The hand that makes us divine

69 *The Spectator*

Sir Roger told them, with the air of a man who would not give his judgement rashly, that much might be said on both sides.

70 *The Spectator*

If we may believe our logicians, man is distinguished from all other creatures by the faculty of laughter.

71 *The Spectator*

A woman seldom asks advice until she has bought her wedding clothes.

ADE George 1866-1944

72

He had been kicked in the head by a mule when young, and believed everything he read in the Sunday papers.

73

In uplifting, get underneath.

74

One man's poison ivy is another man's spinach.

75
A people so primitive that they did not know how to get money except by working for it.

76 *Fables in Slang*
After being turned down by numerous publishers, he had decided to write for posterity.

77 *'The Steel Box'*
`Whom are you?' he asked, for he had attended business college.

78 *The Sultan of Sulu.*
R-E-M-O-R-S-E.
Those dry Martinis did the work for me;
Last night at twelve I felt immense,
Today I feel like thirty cents.

ADENAUER Konrad 1876-1967
79
The good Lord set definite limits on man's wisdom, but set no limits on his stupidity - and that's just not fair.

80
A thick skin is a gift from God.

81
I havn't asked you to make me young again. All I want is to go on getting older.

82
A dead man
Who never caused others to die
Seldom rates a statue.

ADLER Alfred 1870-1937
83
Trust only movement. Life happens at the level of events not of words.

84
The feeling of inferiority rules the mental life and can be clearly recognized as the sense of incompleteness and unfulfillment, and in the uninterrupted struggle both of individuals and of humanity.

85 *The problems of Neurosis*
The truth is often a terrible weapon of aggression. It is possible to lie, and even to murder, for the truth.

ADLER Mortimer J. 1902-
86
The telephone book is full of facts but it doesn't contain a single idea.

87
In the case of good books, the point is not to see how many of them you can get through, but rather how many can get through to you.

ADLER Polly 1900-1962
88
A House in not a Home.

ADLER Renata 1938-
89
The nice sense of measure is certainly not one of nature's gifts to her English children ... we have all of us yielded to infatuation at some moment of our lives.

ADY Thomas fl. 1655
90 *A Candle in the Dark*
Matthew, Mark, Luke and John,
The bed be blest that I lie on,
Four angels round my head,
One to watch, and one to pray,
And two to bear my soul away.

AESCHYLUS c.525-456 BC
91
It is always in season for old men to learn.

92
Words are the physicians of a mind diseased.

93 *(of Helen)*
Hell to ships, hell to men, hell to cities.

AESOP c.550 BC
94 *Fables 'The Dog and the Shadow'*
Good judgement comes from experience, and experience - well, that comes from poor judgement.

95 *Fables 'Hercules and the Waggoner'*
The gods help them that help themselves.

96 *Fables `The Milkmaid and her Pail'*
Don't count your chickens before they are hatched.

97 *Fables `The Wolf in Sheep's Clothing'*
The lamb that belonged to the sheep whose skin the wolf was wearing began to

follow the wolf in the sheep's clothing.

AGA KHAN III 1877-1957
98 *(defending his taste for alcohol)*
There is no such thing as a little garlic.

AGAR Herbert 1897-1980
99
To eat is human, to digest, divine.

100 *A Time for Greatness*
There are some people that if they don't
know, you can't tell 'em.

AGATE James 1877-1947
101
Long experience has taught me that in
England nobody goes to the theatre unless
he or she has bronchitis.

102
The English instinctively admire any man
who has no talent and is modest about it.

103 *Ego 6*
My mind is not a bed to be made and re-
made.

AGATHON c.445-400 BC
104
Even God cannot change the past.

AGNEW Spiro T. 1918-
105
To some extent if you've seen one city
slum you've seen them all.

106
The only thing to know is how to use your
neuroses.

AHMAD Iqbal
107
When you give the reins to reason then the
imagination is repressed.

AHMANSON Howard
108
I'm so happy to be rich, I'm willing to take
all the consequences.

AKINS Zoë 1886-1958
109
The Greeks had a word for it.

ALAIN (Émile-Auguste Chartier) 1868-
1951
110

Time must needs call the tune and man
must follow it.

111 *Propos sur la religion*
Nothing is more dangerous than an idea,
when you have only one idea.

ALAIN-FOURNIER (Henri Alban) 1886-
1914
112
Life on the farm is a school of patience;
you can't hurry the crops or make an ox in
two days.

113 *Le Grand Meaulnes*
There is so much good in the worst of us,
and so much bad in the best of us, that it's
rather hard to tell which of us ought to
reform the rest of us.

114 *Le Grand Meaulnes*
How can a man who has once strayed into
Heaven ever hope to make terms with the
earth!

ALBEE Edward 1928-
115 *Who's afraid of Virginia Woolf?*
I have a fine sense of the ridiculous, but no
sense of humour.

**ALBERT Prince (Consort to Queen
Victoria)** 1819-1861
116 *(of the French)*
I clearly forsee the day when this
vainglorious and immoral people will have
to be put down.

ALBERTI Leon Battista 1404-1472
117
Beauty - the adjustment of all parts
proportionately so that one cannot add or
subtract or change without impairing the
harmony of the whole.

ALCOTT Louisa May 1832-1888
118 *Little Women*
When you're as great as I am, it's hard to
be humble.

ALDEN Robert
119
A man should always consider how much
he has more than he wants, and how much
more unhappy he might be than he really
is.

ALDINGTON Richard 1892-1962
120 *The Colonel's Daughter*
Hell is truth seen too late.

ALDISS Brian 1925-
121 *Barefoot in the Head*
Keep violence in the mind
Where it belongs.

ALDRICH Henry 1647-1710
122 *A Catch*
If all be true that I do think,
There are five reasons we should drink;
Good wine, a friend, or being dry,
Or lest we should be by and by;
Or any other reason why.

ALDRICH Thomas Bailey 1836-1907
123
The man who suspects his own
tediousness has yet to be born.

124
The possession of gold has ruined fewer
men than the lack of it.

ALDRIN 'Buzz' 1930-
125 *(on successful moon landing of Apollo XI)*
Houston, Tranquillity Base here. The Eagle
has landed.

ALEXANDER Cecil Frances 1818-1895
126 *`All things bright and beautiful'*
All things bright and beautiful,
All creatures great and small,
All things wise and wonderful
The Lord God made them all.

127 *`There is a green hill far away'*
There is a green hill far away,
Without a city wall,
Where the Dear Lord was crucified,
Who died to save us all.

128 *`Once in Royal David's city'*
Once in Royal David's City
Stood a lowly cattle shed,
Where a mother laid her baby,
In a manger for its bed:
Mary was that mother mild,
Jesus Christ her little child.

ALEXANDER The Great 356-323 BC
129
I am dying with the help of too many
physicians.

ALFVÉN Hannes 1872-1960
130
What's a cult? It just means not enough
people to make a minority.

ALGREN Nelson 1909-1981
131
A walk on the wild side.

132 *A Walk on the Wild Side*
Young men soon give, and soon forget
affronts,
Old age is slow in both.

ALI Muhammad (Cassius Clay) 1942-
133
When you're as great as I am, it's hard to
be humble.

134
A man only understands what is akin to
something already existing in himself.

135 *(announcing his retirement)*
I want to get out with my greatness intact.

136 *(motto)*
The law locks up both man and woman
Who steals the goose from off the
common,
But lets the great felon loose
Who steals the common from the goose.

137 *(his slogan from c.1963)*
I am the greatest.

ALLAINVAL, Abbé d' 1700-1753
138
L'embarras des richesses
The embarrassment of riches

ALLEN Fred 1894-1956
139
Every woman's man, and every man's
woman.

140
(A gentleman) is any man who wouldn't
hit a woman with his hat on.

141 *(attributed)*
Committee - a group of men who
individually can do nothing but as a group
decide that nothing can be done.

ALLEN George 1902-1989
142
Winning can be defined as the science of being totally prepared.

143
Every time you win, you're reborn; when you lose you die a little.

ALLEN Marty
144
A study of economics usually reveals that the best time to buy anything is last year.

ALLEN William 1889-1949
145
America - the best poor man's country in the world.

ALLEN Woody 1935-
146
Showing up is eighty percent of life.

147
I don't want to achieve immortality through my work. I want to achieve immortality through not dying.

148 *All You Ever Wanted to Know About Sex*
If a man can remember what he worried about last week, he has a very good memory.

149 *Annie Hall*
[Sex] was the most fun I ever had without laughing.

150 *Annie Hall (of masturbation)*
Don't knock it. It's sex with someone you love.

151 *Clown Prince of American Humour*
I want to tell you this terrific story about contraception. I asked this girl to sleep with me, and she said no.

152 *Without Feathers*
I'm not afraid to die. I just don't want to be there when it happens.

153 *Without Feathers*
Money is better than poverty, if only for financial reasons.

154 *'Notebooks'*
If only God would give me some clear sign! Like making a large deposit in my name at a Swiss bank.

155 `My Philosophy', *Getting Even*
Not only is there no God, but try getting a plumber on weekends.

156 *Sleeper*
My Brain? It's my second favourite organ.

ALLINGHAM Margery 1904-1966
157 *Flowers for the Judge*
Once sex rears its ugly 'ead it's time to steer clear.

ALLINGHAM William 1828-1899
158 *The Fairies*
Up the airy mountain,
Down the rushy glen,
We daren't go a-hunting,
For fear of little men.

ALTMAN Robert 1925-
159
What's a cult? It just means not enough people to make a minority.

AMERY Leo 1873-1955
160 *(of Herbert Asquith)*
For twenty years he has held a season-ticket on the line of least resistance and has gone wherever the train of events has carried him, lucidly justifying his position at whatever point he has happened to find himself.

161 *(in House of Commons)*
Speak for England.

AMES Adelbert
162
The things we see are the mind's best bet as to what is out front.

AMES Fisher 1758-1808
163
A monarchy is a merchantman, which sails well, but will sometimes strike on a rock and go to the bottom, whilst a republic is a raft which will never sink, but then your feet are always in the water.

AMHERST Earl 1773-1857
164
In the bad old days, there were three easy ways of losing money - racing being the quickest, women the pleasantest and

farming the most certain.

AMIEL Henri Frédéric 1821-1881

165
For purposes of action nothing is more useful than narrowness of thought combined with energy of will.

166
To know how to grow old is the master-work of wisdom, and one of the most difficult chapters in the great art of living.

167
Every life is a possession of faith, and exercises an inevitable and silent propaganda.

168
Analysis kills spontaneity. The grain once ground into flour springs and germinates no more.

169
Doing easily what others find is difficult is talent; doing what is impossible for talent is genius.

170
A man only understands what is akin to something already existing in himself.

171
The man who has no inner life is the slave of his surroundings.

172
Man *becomes* man only by the intelligence, but he is man only by the heart.

173
A thousand things advance; nine hundred and ninety-nine retreat; that is progress.

AMIS Sir Kingsley 1922-1995

174
The delusion that there are thousands of young people about who are capable of benefiting from university training, but have somehow failed to find their way there, is...a necessary component of the expansionist case...More will mean worse.

175 `A Bookshop idyll'
We men have got love well weighed up; our stuff
Can get by without it.

Women don't seem to think that's good enough;
They write about it.

176 `A Bookshop idyll'
Man *becomes* man only by the intelligence, but he is man only by the heart.

177 `Delivery Guaranteed'
Life on the farm is a school of patience; you can't hurry the crops or make an ox in two days.

178 *One Fat Englishman*
Outside every fat man there was an even fatter man trying to close in.

179 *One Fat Englishman*
He was of the faith chiefly in the sense that the church he currently did not attend was Catholic.

180 *Lucky Jim*
I really believe there are things nobody would see if I didn't photograph them.

AMSTERDAM Maury

181
Our Congressman are the finest body of men money can buy.

ANDERSON Judith

182
There is nothing enduring in life for a woman except what she builds in a man's heart.

ANDERSON Patrick

183
Power is like a woman you want to stay in bed with forever.

ANDERSON Robert 1917-

184 *Tea and Sympathy*
All you're supposed to do is every once in a while give the boys a little tea and sympathy.

ANDREW Prince, The Duke of York 1960-

185 *(on his engagement)*
(I am) over the moon ... We are both over the moon, and will be even more so when this is over.

ANDREWES Bishop Lancelot 1555-1626
186 *Of the Nativity*
The nearer the Church the further from
God.

ANNE Princess, The Princess Royal 1950-
187 *(attributed)*
When I appear in public, people expect me
to neigh, grind my teeth and swish my tail.

188 *(on her first encounter with a horse)*
One was presented with a small hairy
individual and out of general curiosity, one
climbed on.

189 *(on pregnancy)*
It's a very boring time. I am not
particularly maternal - it's an occupational
hazard of being a wife.

ANONYMOUS
190
All glory comes from daring to begin.

191
There are two reasons for doing things - a
very good reason and the real reason.

192
'Mean to' don't pick no cotton.

193
There is little serenity comparable to the
serenity of the inexperienced giving advice
to the experienced.

194
Middle age is when you have a choice of
two temptations and choose the one that
will get you home earlier.

195
The United States was born in the country
and moved to the city in the nineteenth
century.

196
There is a difference between a pyschopath
and a neurotic. A pyschopath thinks two
and two are five. A neurotic knows that
two and two are four, but he worries about
it.

197
Art is all that cannot be suppressed.

198
Book lovers never go to bed alone.

199
If a cluttered desk is an indication of a
cluttered mind, what is indicated by an
empty desk?

200
Inflation is defined as the quality that
makes balloons larger and candy bars
smaller.

201
Who buys has need of two eyes
But one's enough to sell the stuff.

202
A fair price for oil is whatever you can get
plus ten to twenty per cent.

203
What costs nothing is worth nothing.

204
To dream of the person you would like to
be is to waste the person you are.

205
Character is like a tree, and reputation like
its shadow. The shadow is what we think
of it; the tree is the real thing.

206
A camel is a horse designed by a
committee.

207
Conscience is a cur that will let you get
past it but that you cannot keep from
barking.

208
A dead man
Who never caused others to die
Seldom rates a statue.

209
Death is terrible to Cicero, desirable to
Cato, and indifferent to Socrates.

210
To lose
Is to learn.

211
No one in this world needs a mink coat
but a mink.

212
Good judgement comes from experience, and experience - well, that comes from poor judgement.

213
The final test of fame is to have a crazy person imagine he is you.

214
There is no such thing as a little garlic.

215
To eat is human, to digest, divine.

216
A little nonsense now and then is relished by the wisest men.

217
The parting genius is with sighing sent.

218
The nature of God is a circle of which the centre is everywhere and the circumference is nowhere.

219
If God lived on earth, people would break his windows.

220
He who would do good to another, must do it in minute particulars.

221
There is so much good in the worst of us and so much bad in the best of us, that it's rather hard to tell which of us ought to reform the rest of us.

222
Hell is truth seen too late.

223
A genealogist is one who traces your family back as far as your money will go.

224
The past is a foreign country; they do things differently there.

225
Each man is his own absolute lawgiver and dispenser of glory or gloom to himself, the maker of his life, his reward, his punishment.

226
Honour follows those who flee it.

227
Wit is far more often a shield than a lance.

228
He who laughs, lasts.

229
Every time a man puts a new idea across he finds ten men who thought of it before he did - but they only thought of it.

230
Little wit in the head makes much work for the feet.

231
Ne'er of the living can the living judge - Too blind the affection, or too fresh the grudge.

232
Any fool can make a rule, and every fool will mind it.

233
The law locks up both man and woman Who steals the goose from off the common, But lets the great felon loose Who steals the common from the goose.

234
Literature is a power to be possessed, not a body of objects to be studied.

235
Good children's literature appeals not only to the child in the adult, but to the adult in the child.

236
In the act of loving someone you arm them against you.

237
A husband always prefers his wife's mother-in-law to his own.

238
If every man would mend a man, then all the world would be mended.

239
Nostalgia ain't what it used to be.

240
If a man can remember what he worried about last week, he has a very good memory.

241
There is nothing wrong with making mistakes. Just don't respond with encores.

242
Things could be worse. Suppose your errors were counted and published every day, like those of a baseball player.

243
When you want really big money, you usually find yourself talking to people who didn't go to Eton.

244
Even moderation ought not to be practised to excess.

245
Oboe - an ill woodwind that nobody blows good.

246
Harpists spend half their life tuning and the other half playing out of tune.

247
Keep a thing seven years and you will find a use for it.

248
Anything which parents have not learned from experience they can now learn from their children.

249
A mother is a person who if she is not there when you get home from school you wouldn't know how to get your dinner, and you wouldn't feel like eating it anyway.

250
The French have a passion for revolution but an abhorrence of change.

251
Her face looks as if it had worn out two bodies.

252
Deep down he is shallow.

253
What men usually ask of God when they pray is that two and two not make four.

254
Modern kitchen - where the pot calls the kettle chartreuse.

255
Every year it takes less time to fly across the Atlantic, and more time to drive to the office.

256
Psychiatry is the care of the id by the odd.

257
The four-letter word for psychotherapy is 'talk'.

258
He wouldn't give a duck a drink if he owned Lake Michigan.

259
Alimony: the cash surrender value of a husband.

260
His shortcoming is his long staying.

261
If there were any justice in the world, people would be able to fly over pigeons for a change.

262
There's a wonderful family called Stein,
There's Gert, and there's Epp and there's Ein:
Gert's poems are bunk,
Epp's statues are junk,
And no one can understand Ein.

263
Coffee in England is just toasted milk.

264
'Tis better than riches
To scratch when it itches.

265
He'd give the devil ulcers.

266
The Church of England is the Tory party at prayer.

267
Let's all give God a great big hand. I've seen the last page of the Bible and it's all going to turn out all right.

268
The sea hath no king but God alone.

269
Every April, God rewrites the Book of Genesis.

270
If you really do put a small value upon yourself, rest assured that the world will not raise your price.

271
Gentleman: one who never hurts anyone's feelings unintentionally.

272
It takes time to be a success, but time is all it takes.

273
Success is not so much what you are, but rather what you appear to be.

274
Tact is the intelligence of the heart.

275
A distinguished diplomat could hold his tongue in ten languages.

276
The Eiffel Tower is the Empire State Building after taxes.

277
If the student fails to learn the teacher fails to teach.

278
The secret of teaching is to appear to have known all your life what you learned this afternoon.

279
A bred-in-the-bone Boston lady, when asked why she never travelled, said 'Why should I? I'm already there.'

280
The early North American Indians made a great mistake by not having an immigration bureau.

281
Old men and far travellers may lie with authority.

282
Some people handle the truth carelessly; others never touch it at all.

283
Truth is the daughter of time.

284
Pretty much all the honest truthtelling there is in the world is done by children.

285
Violence is, essentially, a confession of ultimate inarticulateness.

286
War does not determine who is right - only who is left.

287
A word to the wise is infuriating.

288
Some women blush when they are kissed; some call for the police; some swear; some bite. But the worst are those who laugh.

289
The average girl would rather have beauty than brains because she knows the average man can see much better than he can think.

290
The cleverest woman finds a need for foolish admirers.

291
A hobby is hard work you wouldn't do for a living.

292
The beginning is easy; what happens next is much harder.

293
Write something, even if it's just a suicide note.

294
Young men think old men fools and old men know young men to be so.

295
This is a youth-oriented society, and the joke is on them because youth is a disease from which we all recover.

296
One boy's a boy, two boys are half a boy; three boys are no boy at all.

297
The bigger they are, the further they fall.

298
The bible tells us to forgive our enemies; not our friends.

299
Confirmation at Eton: like a huge garden party, faintly over-shadowed by a sense of religion.

300
A committee is a group of the unwilling, chosen from the unfit, to do the necessary.

301
I married my husband for life, not for lunch.

302
Liberty is always unfinished business.

303
There is a green hill far away,
Without a city wall,
Where the Dear Lord was crucified,
Who died to save us all.

304
A walk on the wild side.

305
The nearest thing to death in life
Is David Patrick Maxwell Fyfe,
Though underneath that gloomy shell
He does himself extremely well.

306
The delusion that there are thousands of young people about who are capable of benefiting from university training, but have somehow failed to find their way there, is...a necessary component of the expansionist case...More will mean worse.

307
No more Latin, no more French,
No more sitting on a hard board bench.
No more beetles in my tea,
Making googly eyes at me;
No more spiders in my bath
Trying hard to make me laugh.

308
He was of the faith chiefly in the sense that the church he currently did not attend was Catholic.

309
We men have got love well weighed up;
our stuff
Can get by without it.
Women don't seem to think that's good enough;
They write about it.

310
Tempora mutantur, et nos mutamur in illis.
Times change, and we change with them.

311
If all the world were paper,
And all the sea were ink,
And all the trees were bread and cheese
What should we do for drink.

312
In his chamber weak and dying,
While the Norman Baron lay.
Loud, wihtout, his men were crying
'Shorter hours and better pay'.

313
He that fights and runs away,
May live to fight another day.

314
There was an old lady from Riga
Who rode with a smile on a tiger
They returned from the ride
With the lady inside
And a smile on the face of the tiger.

315
Expletive deleted.

316
Give me a child for the first seven years, and I'll give you the man.

317

An Intelligent Russian once remarked to us, `Every country has its own constitution; ours is absolutism moderated by assassination'.

318

Muscular Christianity.

319

Hail Caesar, those who are about to die salute you.

320

I married my husband for life, not for lunch.

321

Lloyd George knew my father,
My father knew Lloyd George.

322

There was a young lady from Kent,
Who said she knew what men meant
When they asked her to dine;
Private room, champagne, wine -
She knew what they meant and she went.

323

Baby faced people suffer job discrimination like other minorities.

324

A smile is a curve that can set things straight.

325

Absence makes the heart grow fonder.

326

A-roving! A-roving!
Since roving's been my ru-i-n
I'll go no more a-roving
With you fair maid.

327

Early one morning, just as the sun was rising,
I heard a maid sing in the valley below:
'Oh, don't deceive me; Oh, never leave me!
How could you use a poor maiden so?'

328

Power to the people.

329

I feel no pain dear mother now
But oh, I am so dry!
O take me to a brewery
And leave me there to die.

330

Lizzie Borden took an axe
And gave her mother forty whacks;
When she saw what she had done
She gave her father forty-one!

331

The rabbit has a charming face:
Its private life is a disgrace.
I really dare not name to you
The awful things that rabbits do.

332

There is a tavern in the town,
And there my dear love sits him down,
And drinks his wine 'mid laughter free,
And never, never thinks of me.
Fare thee well, for I must leave thee,
Do not let this parting grieve thee,
And remember that the best of friends must part.

333

There was a faith-healer from Deal
Who said, 'Although pain isn't real,
If I sit on a pin
And it punctures my skin,
I dislike what I fancy I feel'.

334

Where is the man who has the power and skill
To stem the torrent of a woman's will?
For if she will, she will, you may depend on't;
And if she won't, she won't; so there's an end on't.

335

Whilst Adam slept, Eve from his side arose;
Strange his first sleep should be his last repose.

336

Yankee Doodle came to town
Riding on a pony;
Stuck a feather in his cap
And called it macaroni.

337
The world is full of fools, and he who would not see it should live alone and smash his mirror.

338
Tempora mutantur, et nos mutamur in illis.
Times change, and we change with them.

339
Ad majorem Dei gloriam.
To the greater glory of God.

340
After you've heard two eyewitness accounts of an auto accident it makes you wonder about history.

341 *(1940s saying)*
If it moves, salute it; if it doesn't move, pick it up; and if you can't pick it up, paint it white.

342 *(at 1972 Only One Earth Conference)*
We have forgotten how to be good guests, how to walk lightly on the earth as other creatures do.

343 *(advertisement)*
What did you do in the Great War, daddy?

344 *(advertisement for Doan's Backache Kidney Pills)*
Every picture tells a story.

345 *American Declaration of Independence*
So poetry is something more philosophical and more worthy of serious attention than history.

346 *(by an American Lawyer)*
Obscenity is whatever gives a judge an erection.

347 *(American life insurance slogan)*
Death [is] nature's way of telling you to slow down.

348 *(annotation to a ministerial brief)*
This is a rotten argument, but it should be good enough for their lordships on a hot summer afternoon.

349 *Articles of War*
Any Officer who shall behave in a scandalous manner, unbecoming the character of an officer and a gentleman

shall....be cashiered.

350 *(Audi motors advertising slogan)*
Vorsprung durch Technik.
Progress through Technology.

351 *(Black Extremist slogan)*
Burn, Baby, Burn.

352 *(on the British monarchy)*
At certain times of grave national stress, when that rag-bag called the British Constitution is in grave danger of coming unstuck, thank heaven for the big safety-pin at the top that keeps it together.

353 *(British pacifist slogan)*
A bayonet is a weapon with a worker at each end.

354 *(Charles E. Wilson's defence policy)*
A bigger bang for a buck.

355 *(colloquial axiom)*
There's no such thing as a free lunch.

356 *(on the construction of Dreadnoughts)*
We want eight, and we won't wait.

357 *(said during the coronation of a new Pope)*
Sic transit gloria mundi.
Thus passes the glory of the world.

358 *(of David Lloyd George)*
He uses figures as if they were adjectives.

359 *(Decca Recording Company rejecting The Beatles)*
We don't like their sound, and guitar music is on the way out.

360 *(definition of a lie)*
Pray consider what a figure a man would make in the republic of letters.

361 *(on Edward VII's accession to the throne)*
We shall not pretend that there is nothing in his long career which those who respect and admire him would wish otherwise.

362 *(epitaph for Alexander the Great)*
A tomb now suffices him for whom the whole world was not sufficient.

363 *Everyman*
Everyman, I will go with thee, and be thy guide,
In thy most need to go by thy side.

364 *(forecasting advance of science in 1949)*
Computers in the future will weigh no more than 1.5 tons.

365 *(of the French Foreign Legion)*
They were never defeated, they were only killed.

366 *(of G.B. Shaw)*
John the Baptist pretending to be Karl Marx.

367 *(graffito found on a London Underground)*
Life is a sexually transmitted disease.

368 *(on the Gunpowder Plot)*
Please to remember the fifth of November,
Gunpowder Treason and Plot.
We know no reason
Why gunpowder treason
Should ever be forgot.

369 *(IBM engineer on the microchip in 1968)*
But what...is it good for?

370 *(Illinois Institute of Technology)*
After an eight-hour day, workers require three overtime hours to produce two regular hours of results.

371 *(on impartiality)*
Like Caesar's wife, all things to all men.

372 *(inscription on one of Columbus' caravels)*
Following the sun we left the old world.

373 *(inscription Dachau concentration camp gates)*
Work liberates.

374 *(inscription at Delphi)*
Know thyself.

375 *(inscription at Delphi)*
Nothing in excess.

376 *(inscription on a sundial)*
Time wastes our bodies and our wits;
But we waste time, so we are quits.

377 *(on investing in the radio in 1920s)*
`Whom are you?' he asked, for he had attended business college.

378 *(Jacobite toast)*
The King over the water.

379 *(Jaws 2: film advertising copy)*
Just when you thought it was safe to go back in the water.

380 *(Jesuit maxim- attributed)*
Give me a child for the first seven years, and I'll give you the man.

381 *(of Julius Ceasar)*
Every woman's man, and every man's woman.

382 *(keyboard checking exercise)*
The quick brown fox jumped over the lazy dog.

383 *King's Regulations*
All present and correct.

384 *(labour and civil rights song)*
We shall not be moved.

385 *(Labour party pamphlet on parenting)*
Children are luxuries rather than investments.

386 *The Masque of Balliol*
My name is George Nathaniel Curzon, I am a most superior person.

387 *(on microbes)*
Adam
Had'em.

388 *(motto, at US Air Force test base)*
Ad Inexplorate.
Toward the Unknown.

389 *(motto of the British SAS regiment)*
Who dares wins.

390 *(motto of the Crown of Scotland)*
Nemo me impune lacessit.
No one provokes me with impunity.

391 *(motto of the French Revolution)*
Liberté! Égalité! Fraternité!
Freedom! Equality! Brotherhood!

392 *(motto of the Mulvany family)*
Per ardua ad astra.
Through struggle to the stars.

393 *(motto of the Olympic Games)*
Citius, altius, fortius.
Swifter, higher, stronger.

394 *(motto of the Order of the Garter)*
Honi soit qui mal y pense.
Evil be to him who evil thinks.

395 *(motto of the State of Kansas)*
Ad astra per aspera.
To the stars through hardship.

396 *(motto of Volunteers Movement)*
An Intelligent Russian once remarked to
us, `Every country has its own
constitution; ours is absolutism moderated
by assassination'.

397 *(Muslim Creed)*
I believe there is no god but Allah alone
and Muhammed is his prophet.

398 *(Nazi party slogan)*
Ein reich, ein volk, ein Führer.
One realm, one people, one leader.

399 *(negro spiritual)*
God gave Noah the rainbow sign,
No more water, the fire next time.

400 *(negro spritual)*
Swing low, sweet chariot
Comin' for to carry me home;
I looked over Jordan and what did I see?
A band of angels comin' after me
Comin' for to carry me home.

401 *(news headline)*
Whose finger do you want on the trigger?

402 *(news headline on evolution findings)*
Hail Caesar, those who are about to die
salute you.

403 *(notice in a dancing saloon)*
Please do not shoot the pianist. He is doing
his best.

404 *(notice in an English doctor's waiting-
room)*
To avoid delay, please have all your
symptoms ready.

405 *(oil drillers in 1859)*
Drill for oil? You mean drill into the
ground to try and find oil? You're crazy.

406 *(overheard at a performance of Cleopatra)*
How different, how very different from the
home life of our own very dear Queen!

407 *(pacifist slogan)*
War will cease when men refuse to fight.

408 *(pamphlet from Chinese Family Planning
Centre)*
Marriage is not a finished affair. No
matter to what age you live, love must be
continuously consolidated. Being
considerate, thoughtful and respectful
without ulterior motives is the key to a
satisfactory marriage.

409 *Passing By*
There is a lady sweet and kind,
Was never a face so pleased my mind;
I did but see her passing by
And yet I love her till I die.

410 *(Post Office inscription, Washington D.C.)*
Messenger of sympathy and love, servant
of parted friends, consoler of the lonely,
bond of the scattered family, enlarger of
the common life.

411 *(report to Admiralty)*
We shelled the Turks from 9 to 11: and
then, it being Sunday, had Divine Service.

412 *(Rugby Football rules in Toronto)*
If a player continues transgressing the
rules, his side shall lose him.

413 *(Scottish toast)*
Here's tae us; wha's like us? Gey few, and
they're a'deid.

414 *(sign on the desk of President Harry S.
Truman)*
The buck stops here.

415 *(sign on lawn, University of Iowa)*
If allowed to survive, this grass will
produce enough oxygen for two students
to breathe for one semester.

416 *(slogan)*
There was a young lady from Kent,
Who said she knew what men meant
When they asked her to dine;
Private room, champagne, wine -
She knew what they meant and she went.

417 *(slogan of American civil rights
campaigners)*
Black is beautiful.

418 *(slogan of the Black Panther movement)*
Power to the people.

419 *(slogan of nuclear disarmament campaigners)*
Better red than dead.

420 *(slogan, World Whores Congress)*
Good girls go to heaven. Bad girls go everywhere.

421 *(song)*
O Death, where is thy sting-a-ling-a-ling
O grave, thy victory?
The bells of hell go ting-a-ling-a-ling
For you but not for me.

422 *(song)*
It's love that makes the world go round.

423 *(song)*
Old soldiers never die;
They only fade away.

424 *(song)*
We're here because we're here because we're here because we're here.

425 *(song)*
John Brown's body lies a mould'ring in the grave
His soul is marching on.

426 *(song)*
It is good to be merry and wise,
It is good to be honest and true,
It is best to be off with the old love,
Before you are on with the new.

427 *Stevins MS*
Thirty days hath September,
April, June and November;
All the rest have thirty-one,
Excepting February alone,
And that has twenty-eight days clear,
And twenty-nine in a leap year.

428 *(submission of recorded Presidential Conversations)*
Expletive deleted.

429 *(title of BBC Television series)*
Not So Much a Programme, More a Way of Life.

430 *(title of a song)*
We Shall Overcome.

431 *(tomb inscription)*
Et in Arcadia ego.
And I too am in Arcadia.

432 *(two-line comic song)*
Lloyd George knew my father,
My father knew Lloyd George.

433 *Universal Declaration of Human Rights*
All human beings are born free and equal in dignity and rights.

434 *(weaver's Song)*
Now I am a bachelor, I live by myself and I work at the weaving trade,
And the only thing that I ever did wrong
Was to woo a fair young maid.
She sighed, she cried, she damned near died:
She said 'What shall I do?'
So I took her into bed and covered up her head
Just to save her from the foggy, foggy dew.

435 *(Weller's Law)*
Nothing is impossible for the person who doesn't have to do it.

436 *(Western Union memo, 1876)*
Time wastes our bodies and our wits;
But we waste time, so we are quits.

437 *(West Indian calypso)*
The singer not the song.

438 *(of the Winchester Cathedral organ)*
Audible at five miles, painful at three, and lethal at one.

439 *(World War II health slogan)*
All human beings are born free and equal in dignity and rights.

440 *(World War II security slogan)*
Careless talk costs lives.

ANOUILH Jean 1910-1987
441
A good actor must never be in love with anyone but himself.

442
When you are forty, half of you belongs to the past ... And when you are seventy, nearly all of you.

443
We poison our lives with fear of burglary and shipwreck, and, ask anyone, the house is never burgled, and the ship never goes down.

444
Things are beautiful if you love them.

445
Man dies when he wants, as he wants, of what he chooses.

446
Every man thinks God is on his side. The rich and powerful know he is.

447
What you get free costs too much.

448
Oh, love is real enough, you will find it some day, but it has one arch-enemy - and that is life.

449
Love is, above all, the gift of oneself.

ANTHONY Metropolitan of Sourozh 1914-
450 Beginning to Pray
So often when we say, 'I love you,' we say it with a huge 'I' and a little 'you'.

ANTHONY Susan B. 1820-1906
451
The only question left to be settled now is, are women persons?

452
There is a tavern in the town,
And there my dear love sits him down,
And drinks his wine 'mid laughter free,
And never, never thinks of me.
Fare thee well, for I must leave thee,
Do not let this parting grieve thee,
And remember that the best of friends must part.

453 Motto, The Revolution
Men their rights and nothing more;
Women their rights and nothing less.

ANTISTHENES c.445-c.370 BC
454
The investigation of the meaning of words is the beginning of education.

ANTOINETTE Marie 1755-1793
455 (on the way to the guillotine)
Courage! I have shown it for years; think you I shall lose it at the moment when my sufferings are to end?

ANTRIM Minna 1861-
456 Naked Truth and Veiled Allusions
Experience is a good teacher, but she sends in terrific bills.

457 Naked Truth and Veiled Allusions
Where is the man who has the power and skill
To stem the torrent of a woman's will?
For if she will, she will, you may depend on't;
And if she won't, she won't; so there's an end on't.

APPLETON Sir Edward 1892-1965
458
I do not mind what language an opera is sung in so long as it is a language I don't understand.

APPLETON Thomas Gold 1812-1884
459
Good Americans, when they die, go to Paris.

460
A Boston man is the east wind made flesh.

APPLEY Lawrence
461
Management is now where the medical profession was when it decided that working in a drug store was not sufficient training to become a doctor.

AQUINAS St. Thomas 1225-1274
462
The End of every maker is himself.

463 Summa Theologicae
Therefore it is necessary to arrive at a prime mover, put in motion by no other; and this everyone understands to be God.

464 Summa Theologicae
If all evil were prevented, much good would be absent from the universe.

The ARABIAN NIGHTS
465 *The History of Ali Baba*
Open Sesame!

ARBUS Diane 1923-1971
466
You see someone on the street, and
essentially what you notice about them is
the flaw.

467
I really believe there are things nobody
would see if I didn't photograph them.

468
My favourite thing is to go where I've
never been.

ARBUTHNOT John 1667-1735
469
Biography is one of the new terrors of
death.

470 *The History of John Bull*
Law is a bottomless pit.

ARCHIMEDES 287-212 BC
471 *(on making a discovery)*
Eureka!
I have got it!

472 *(on the lever)*
Give me a firm spot on which to stand,
and I will move the earth.

ARDREY Robert
473
Human war has been the most successful
of all our cultural traditions.

ARENDT Hannah 1906-1975
474
Ideas, as distinguished from events, are
never unprecedented.

475
Equality is the result of human
organization. We are not born equal.

476
The most radical revolutionary will
become a conservative on the day after a
revolution.

477
Under conditions of tyranny it is far easier
to act than to think.

ARETINO Pietro 1492-1556
478
Age has a good mind and sorry shanks.

ARISTOTLE 384-322 BC
479
Art not only imitates nature, but also
completes its deficiencies.

480
To enjoy the things we ought, and to hate
the things we ought, has the greatest
bearing on excellence of character.

481
Without friends no one would choose to
live, though he had all other goods.

482
Dignity does not consist in possessing
honours, but in deserving them.

483
Humour is the only test of gravity, and
gravity of humour, for a subject which will
not bear raillery is suspicious, and a jest
which will not bear serious examination is
false wit.

484
It is Homer who has chiefly taught other
poets the art of telling lies skilfully.

485
Inferiors revolt in order that they may be
equal, and equals that they may be
superior.

486
Melancholy men are of all others the most
witty.

487
The worst form of inequality is to try to
make unequal things equal.

488 *Nicomachean Ethics*
We make war that we may live in peace.

489 *Poetics*
So poetry is something more philosophical
and more worthy of serious attention than
history.

490 *Poetics*
Probable impossibilities are to be preferred
to improbable possibilities.

491 *Politics*
Man is by nature a political animal.

492 *Politics*
He who is unable to live in society, or who has no need because he is sufficient for himself, must be either a beast or a god.

493 *Politics*
Nature does nothing without purpose or uselessly.

494 *Politics*
Where some people are very wealthy and others have nothing, the result will be either extreme democracy or absolute oligarchy, or despotism will come from either of those excesses.

ARMISTEAD Lewis Addison 1817-1863
495 *(during the American Civil War)*
Give them the cold steel, boys!

ARMOUR J. Ogden
496
The young man who wants to marry happily should pick out a good mother and marry one of her daughters - any one will do.

ARMSTRONG Louis 1901-1971
497
There are some people that if they don't know, you can't tell 'em.

498
What we play is life.

499
All music is folk music, I ain't never heard no horse sing a song.

ARMSTRONG Neil 1930-
500
Fear is not an unknown emotion to us.

501 *(on becoming the first man to walk on the Moon)*
That's one small step for man, one giant leap for mankind.

ARMSTRONG Sir Robert 1927-
502 *(during `Spycatcher' trial)*
It contains a misleading impression, not a lie. It was being economical with the truth.

ARNE T. Augustine 1710-1778
503
Britain's best bulwarks are her wooden walls.

ARNOLD George 1834-1865
504 `The Jolly Old Pedagone'
The living need charity more than the dead.

ARNOLD Matthew 1822-1888
505
The nice sense of measure is certainly not one of nature's gifts to her English children ... we have all of us yielded to infatuation at some moment of our lives.

506
Nature, with equal mind,
Sees all her sons at play,
Sees man control the wind,
The wind sweep man away.

507
Journalism is literature in a hurry.

508
The same heart beats in every human breast.

509 `Parting'
Say, has some wet bird-haunted English lawn
Lent it the music of its trees at dawn?

510
Tired of knocking at Preferment's door.

511
This strange disease of modern life.

512
Culture is the passion for sweetness and light, and (what is more) the passion for making them prevail.

513
Conduct is three-fourths of our life and its largest concern.

514 *Absence*
And we forget because we must
And not because we will.

515 *Culture and Anarchy*
The men of culture are the true apostles of equality.

516 *Culture and Anarchy*
When I want to distinguish clearly the
aristocratic class from the Philistines
proper or middle class, I name the former,
in my own mind the Barbarians.

517 *Dover Beach*
Ah, love, let us be true
To one another.

518 *Empedocles on Etna*
Is it so small a thing
To have enjoyed the sun,
To have lived light in the spring,
To have loved to have thought, to have
done.

519 *Essays in Criticism*
[Oxford] whispering from her towers the
last enchantments of the Middle Ages...
Home of lost causes, and forsaken beliefs,
and unpopular names, and impossible
loyalties!

520 *Essays in Criticsm*
Poetry is at bottom a criticism of life.

521 `Isolation. To Marguerite'
This truth - to prove, and make thine own:
`Thou hast been, shalt be, art, alone'.

522 *Letters of Matthew Arnold*
I am past thirty, and three parts iced over.

523 *Morality*
We cannot kindle when we will
The fire which in the heart resides,
The spirit bloweth and is still
In mystery our soul abides.

524 'Philomela'
Hark! ah, the Nightingale!
The tawny-throated!
Hark! from that moonlit cedar what a
burst!
What triumph! hark - what pain!

525 `Philomela'
Eternal Passion!
Eternal Pain!

526 `The Scholar-Gipsy'
Go, for they call you, Shepherd, from the
hill.

527 `The Scholar-Gipsy'
Still nursing the unconquerable hope, still
Clutching the inviolable shade.

528 `Self-Dependence'
Resolve to be thyself: and know, that he
Who finds himself, loses his misery.

529 `Thyrsis'
And that sweet City with her dreaming
spires,
She needs not June for beauty's
heightening.

530 `Youth's Agitations'
And sigh that one thing only has been lent
To youth and age in common - discontent.

ARNOLD Samuel J. 1774-1852
531 *The Death of Nelson*
For England, home and beauty.

ARNOLD Thomas 1795-1842
532
My object will be, if possible, to form
Christian men for Christian boys I can
scarcely hope to make.

533 *(address to his scholars at Rugby)*
What we must look for here is, first,
religious and moral principles; secondly,
gentlemanly conduct; thirdly, intellectual
ability.

ASAF George 1880-1951
534 *'Pack up your Troubles in Your Old Kit
Bag'*
What's the use of worrying?
It never was worth while,
So pack up your troubles in your old kit
bag,
And smile, smile, smile.

ASCH Sholem 1880-1957
535
Not the power to remember, but its very
opposite, the power to forget, is a
necessary condition for our existence.

536
It has been said that writing comes more
easily if you have something to say.

ASHBURTON Lord 1731-1783
537 *(motion in the House of Commons)*
The power of the Crown has increased, is

increasing, and ought to be diminished.

ASHFORD Daisy 1881-1972
538
I am very fond of fresh air and royalties.

ASHRAWI Hanan
539
Women in politics are more honest and
forthright. We are not in it for the ego
gratification.

ASHTON-WARNER Sylvia
540
I tore myself away from the safe comfort of
certainties through my love for truth; and
truth rewarded me.

ASIMOV Isaac 1920-1992
541
Our lifetime may be the last that will be
lived out in a technological society.

ASNAS Max
542
Money is something you got to make in
case you don't die.

ASQUITH Herbert H. 1852-1928
543
You should read it, though there is much
that is skip-worthy.

544
Greatness is a zigzag streak of lightning in
the brain.

545
It is fitting that we should have buried the
Unknown Prime Minister [Bonar Law] by
the side of the unknown Soldier.

546
[The War office kept three sets of figures:]
one to mislead the public, another to
mislead the Cabinet, and the third to
mislead itself.

547 *(phrase used repeatedly in speeches)*
We had better wait and see.

ASQUITH Margot 1865-1945
548 *(of David Lloyd George)*
He can't see a belt without hitting below it.

549 *(of F.E. Smith)*
He's very clever, but sometimes his brains
go to his head.

550 *(of her husband)*
His modesty amounts to deformity.

551 *(to Jean Harlow, correcting the
mispronunciation of her name)*
The `T' is silent - as in `Harlow'.

552 *(of Lady Desborough)*
She tells enough white lies to ice a
wedding cake.

553 *(of Lord Kitchener)*
If Kitchener is not a great man, he is, at
least, a great poster.

554 *(of a politician)*
He always has his arm round your waist
and his eye on the clock.

555 *(of Sir Stafford Cripps)*
He has a brilliant mind until he makes it
up.

ASSISI St Francis of 1181-1226
556 *'Prayer of St Francis'*
Lord, make me an instrument of Your
peace!
Where there is hatred let me sow love;
Where there is injury, pardon;
Where there is doubt, faith;
Where there is despair, hope;
Where there is darkness, light;
Where there is sadness, joy.

O divine Master, grant that I may not so
much seek
To be consoled as to console;
To be understood as to understand;
To be loved as to love.
For it is in giving that we receive;
It is in pardoning that we are pardoned;
And it is in dying that we are born to
eternal life.

ASTAIRE Fred 1899-1987
557
The hardest job kids face today is learning
good manners without seeing any.

ASTLEY Sir Jacob 1579-1652
558 *Prayer before the battle of Edgehill*
O Lord! thou knowest how busy I must be

this day: if I forget thee, do not thou forget me.

ASTOR Lady 1879-1964

559

The main dangers in this life are the people who want to change everything - or nothing.

560

My vigour, vitality and cheek repel me. I am the kind of woman I would run from.

561

I married beneath me. All women do.

ATKINS Eileen 1934-

562

Fame means absolutely nothing except a good table at a restaurant.

ATKINSON Brooks 1894-1984

563

Every man with an idea has at least two or three followers.

564

Life is seldom as unendurable as, to judge by the facts, it logically ought to be.

565

The virtue of the camera is not the power it has to transform the photographer into an artist, but the impulse it gives him to keep on looking.

566 *Once around the Sun*

After each war there is a little less democracy to save.

567 *Once Around The Sun*

We cheerfully assume that, in some mystic way, love conquers all; that good outweighs evil in the just balances of the universe, and that at the 11th hour, something gloriously triumphant will prevent the worst before it happens.

ATKINSON E.L. and GARRARD Apsley Cherry 1882-1929 and 1882-

568 *(inscription on the burial-place of Captain Oates)*

A very gallant gentleman.....he walked willingly to his death in a blizzard to try to save his comrades beset by hardships.

ATTLEE Clement 1883-1967

569

I think the British have the distinction above all other nations of being able to put new wine into old bottles without bursting them.

570

Winston Churchill - fifty per cent genius, fifty per cent bloody fool.

571 *(on himself)*

Few thought he was even a starter.
There were many who thought themselves smarter.
But he ended PM, CH and OM.
An Earl and a Knight of the Garter.

572

The voice we heard was that of Mr. Churchill but the mind was that of Lord Beaverbrook.

573

[Russian Communism is] the illegitimate child of Karl Marx and Catherine the Great.

574

Democracy means government by discussion, but it is only effective if you can stop people talking.

ATWOOD Margaret 1939-

575

If the national mental illness of the United States is megalomania, that of Canada is paranoid schizophrenia.

576

Fear has a smell, as
Love does.

577

The answers you get from literature depend upon the questions you pose.

578

A divorce is like an amputation; you survive, but there's less of you.

AUBREY John 1626-1697

579 *Brief Lives `John Milton'*

Oval face. His eye a dark grey. He had auburn hair. His complexion exceeding fair - he was so fair that they called him the lady of Christ's College.

AUDEN W. H. 1907-1973

580
Let us humour if we can
The vertical man
Though we value none
But the horizontal one.

581
Geniuses are the luckiest of mortals
because what they must do is the same as
what they most want to do.

582
We are all here on earth to help others;
what on earth the others are here for I
don't know.

583
It is nonsense to speak of 'higher' and
'lower' pleasures. To a hungry man it is,
rightly, more important that he eat than
that he philosophize.

584
Almost all of our relationships begin, and
most of them continue, as forms of mutual
exploitation, a mental or physical barter, to
be terminated when one or both parties
run out of goods.

585
Any marriage, happy or unhappy, is
infinitely more interesting and significant
than any romance, however passionate.

586
My poetry doesn't change from place to
place - it changes with the years. It's very
important to be one's age. You get ideas
you have to turn down - 'I'm sorry, no
longer', 'I'm sorry, not yet.'

587
The ear tends to be lazy, craves the familiar
and is shocked by the unexpected; the eye,
on the other hand, tends to be impatient,
craves the novel and is bored by repetition.

588
When we do evil,
We and our victims
Are equally bewildered.

589
A professor is one who talks in someone
else's sleep.

590 *(of himself)*
My face looks like a wedding-cake left out
in the rain.

591
Art is born of humiliation.

592
To ask the hard question is simple.

593 *A Certain World*
All sin tends to be addictive, and the
terminal point of addiction is what is
called damnation.

594 *Dog Beneath the Skin*
Happy the hare at morning, for she cannot
read
The Hunter's waking thoughts.

595 *The Dyer's Hand*
Among those whom I like, I can find no
common denominator, but among those
whom I love, I can: all of them make me
laugh.

596 *The Dyer's Hand*
Man is a history-making creature who can
neither repeat his past nor leave it behind.

597 *The Dyer's Hand `Reading'*
Some books are undeservedly forgotten;
none are undeservedly remembered.

598 *'Epitaph for the Unknown Soldier'*
To save your world you asked this man to
die:
Would this man, could he see you now, ask
why?

599 *'The Love Feast'*
In an upper room at midnight
See us gathered on behalf
Of love according to the gospel
Of the radio-phonograph.

600 *'Lullaby'*
Lay your sleeping head, my love,
Human on my faithless arm.

601 *'This Lunar Beauty'*
Love shall not near
The sweetness here,

Nor sorrow take
His endless look.

602 *'In memory of Sigmund Freud'*
To us he is no more a person
now but a whole climate of opinion.

603 *`In memory of W.B.Yeats'*
Earth, receive an honoured guest:
Willam Yeats is laid to rest.
Let the Irish vessel lie
Emptied of its poetry.

604 *`In memory of W.B.Yeats'*
In the deserts of the heart
Let the healing fountain start
In the prison of his days
Teach the free man how to praise.

605 *'New Year letter'*
To the man-in-the-street, who, I'm sorry to say,
Is a keen observer of life,
The word `Intellectual' suggests straight away
A man who's untrue to his wife.

606 *`Night train'*
This is the night mail crossing the Border,
Bringing the cheque and the postal order,
Letters for the rich, letters for the poor.
The shop on the corner, the girl next door.

607 *'Orators'*
Private faces in public places
Are wiser and nicer
Than public faces in private places.

608 *'September 1, 1939'*
I, and the public know
What all schoolchildren learn
Those to whom evil is done
Do evil in return.

609 *'September 1, 1939'*
There is no such thing as the State
And no one exists alone;
Hunger allows no choice
To the citizen or the police;
We must love one another or die.

610 *'Stop All the Clocks'*
He was my North, my South, my East and West,
My working week and my Sunday rest,
My noon, my midnight, my talk, my song;

I thought that love would last forever: I was wrong.

611 *'The Unknown Citizen'*
Our researchers into Public Opinion are content
That he held the proper opinions for the time of year;
When there was peace, he was for peace;
when there was war, he went.

612 *'As I Walked Out One Evening'*
The years shall run like rabbits,
For in my arms I hold
The Flower of the Ages,
And the first love of the world.

613 *'The Witnesses'*
The sky is darkening like a stain;
Something is going to fall like rain,
And it won't be flowers.

AUGUSTINE St. 354-430
614
Lord, who art always the same, give that I know myself, give that I know Thee.

615
Charity is no substitute for justice withheld.

616
We make ourselves a ladder out of vices if we trample the vices themselves underfoot.

617
There is no salvation outside the church.

618 *Confessions*
Give me chastity and continence, but not yet.

619 *Contra Epistolam Parmeniani*
The verdict of the world is final.

620 *De Duabus Animabus*
Hear the other side.

621 *(on the Good of Marriage)*
To many, total abstinence is easier than perfect moderation.

622 *Joannis*
Love and do what you like.

623 *Sermons*
Rome has spoken; the case is concluded.

AUGUSTUS 63 BC-AD 14

624
Festina lente.
Make haste slowly.

625 *(of Rome)*
He could boast that he inherited it brick
and left it marble.

AURELIUS Marcus 121-180

626
There is no man so blessed that some who
stand by his deathbed won't hail the
occasion with delight.

627
Whatever the universal nature assigns to
any man at any time is for the good of that
man at that time.

628
Never let the future disturb you. You will
meet it, if you have to, with the same
weapons of reason which today arm you
against the present.

629
Life is a stranger's sojourn, a night at an
inn.

630
The art of living is more like that of
wrestling than of dancing. The main thing
is to stand firm and be ready for an
unforeseen attack.

631
Time is a sort of river of passing events,
and strong is its current; no sooner is a
thing brought to sight than it is swept by
and another takes its place, and this too
will be swept away.

632
Every instant of time is a pinprick of
eternity. All things are petty, easily
changed, vanishing away.

633
To change your mind and to follow him
who sets you right is to be nonetheless the
free agent that you were before.

634
Whatever may happen to you was
prepared for you from all eternity; and the
implication of causes was from eternity
spinning the thread of your being.

635
Remember that no man loses any other life
than this which he now lives, nor lives any
other than this which he now loses.

636
All things from eternity are like forms and
come round in circles.

637
The Universe is transformation; our life is
what our thoughts make it.

638
Nothing happens to any man that he is not
formed by nature to bear.

AUSTEN Jane 1775-1817

639
There is nothing like staying at home for
real comfort.

640
I have been a selfish being all my life, in
practice, though not in principle.

641 *Emma*
An egg boiled very soft is not
unwholesome.

642 *Emma*
One half of the world cannot understand
the pleasures of the other.

643 *Emma*
With men he can be rational and
unaffected, but when he has ladies to
please, every feature works.

644 *Emma*
The sooner every party breaks up the
better.

645 *Emma*
Surprises are foolish things. The pleasure
is not enhanced, and the inconvenience is
often considerable.

646 *Emma*
One has great hopes from Birmingham. I
always say there is something direful in
the sound.

27

647 *Emma*
Business, you know, may bring money, but friendship hardly ever does.

648 *Emma*
Why not seize the pleasure at once? How often is happiness destroyed by preparation, foolish preparation?

649 *Letter to Fanny Knight*
Single women have a dreadful propensity for being poor - which is one very strong argument in favour of matrimony.

650 *Letters*
What dreadful hot weather we have! It keeps me in a continual state of inelegance.

651 *Letters*
I do not want people to be very agreeable, as it saves me the trouble of liking them a great deal.

652 *Letters*
In nine cases out of ten, a woman had better show more affection than she feels.

653 *Letters*
Men are all so good for nothing, and hardly any women at all.

654 *Mansfield Park*
A large income is the best recipe for happiness I ever heard of. It certainly may secure all the myrtle and turkey part of it.

655 *Northanger Abbey*
Oh! who can ever be tired of Bath!

656 *Northanger Abbey*
From politics, it was an easy step to silence.

657 *Persuasion*
She had been forced into prudence in her youth, she learned romance as she grew older - the natural sequel of an unnatural beginning.

658 *Persuasion*
Next to being married, a girl likes to be crossed in love a little now and then.

659 *Persuasion*
My sore throats are always worse than anyone's.

660 *Persuasion*
All the privilege I claim for my own sex ... is that of loving longest, when existence or when hope is gone.

661 *Pride and Prejudice*
It is a truth universally acknowledged, that a single man in possession of a good fortune, must be in want of a wife.

662 *Pride and Prejudice*
She was a woman of mean understanding, little information, and uncertain temper.

663 *Pride and Prejudice*
Loss of virtue in a female is irretrievable...one false step involves her in endless ruin.

664 *Pride and Prejudice*
A lady's imagination is very rapid; it jumps from admiration to love, from love to matrimony in a moment.

665 *Sense and Sensibility*
An annuity is a very serious business.

AUSTIN Alfred 1835-1913
666 *(attributed: on illness of the Prince of Wales)*
Across the wires the electric message came: `He is not better, he is much the same'.

AUSTIN Warren R. 1877-1962
667 *(in a debate on the Middle East)*
[Jews and Arabs should settle their differences] like good Christians.

AVERY Milton 1893-1965
668
The idea is in my head; to put it down is nothing.

AVOT Pirke
669
If I am not myself, who will be?

AWDRY Revd W. V. 1911-
670 *Thomas the Tank Engine*
You've a lot to learn about trucks, little Thomas. They are silly things and must be kept in their place. After pushing them about here for a few weeks you'll know almost as much about them as Edward. Then you'll be a Really Useful Engine.

AXELROD George 1922-
671
The Seven Year Itch.

AYCKBOURN Alan 1939-
672 *Bedroom Farce*
My mother used to say, Delia, if S-E-X ever rears its ugly head, close your eyes before you see the rest of it.

673 *How the Other Half Loves*
Do you realize, Mrs Foster, the hours I've put into that woman? When I met her, you know, she was nothing. Nothing at all. With my own hands I have built her up. Encouraging her to join the public library and make use of her non-fiction tickets.

674 *Table Manners*
I always feel with Norman that I have him on loan from somewhere. Like one of his library books.

AYER A. J. 1910-1989
675
No morality can be founded on authority, even if the authority were divine.

676 *(attributed)*
Why should you mind being wrong if someone can show you that you are?

677 *Language, Truth and Logic*
We offer the theist the same comfort as we gave to the moralist. His assertions cannot possibly be valid, but they cannot be invalid either....It is only when the theist claims that in asserting the existence of a transcendent god he is expressing a genuine proposition that we are entitled to disagree with him.

AYRES Pam 1947-
678 `Oh no, I got a cold'
Medicinal discovery,
It moves in mighty leaps,
It leaps straight past the common cold,
And gives it us for keeps.

AYTOUN Sir Robert 1570-1638
679 `To an Inconstant Mistress'
I loved thee once, I'll love no more,
Thine be the grief, as is the blame;
Thou art not what thou wast before,
What reason I should be the same?

BACALL Lauren 1924-
680
Stardom isn't a profession; it's an accident.

BACH George R.
681
Anger cannot be dishonest.

BACON Francis 1561-1626
682
The virtue of prosperity is temperance; the virtue of adversity is fortitude, which in morals is the heroical virtue.

683
There is no excellent beauty that hath not some strangeness in the proportion.

684
As the births of living creatures at first are ill-shapen, so are all innovations, which are the births of time.

685
All rising to great places is by a winding stair.

686
Knowledge is power.

687
Atheism is rather in the lip than in the heart of Man.

688
Truth emerges more readily from error than from confusion.

689
A man that is young in years may be old in hours, if he has lost no time.

690
That all things are changed, and that nothing really perishes, and that the sum of matter remains exactly the same, is sufficiently certain.

691
Universities incline wits to sophistry and affectation.

692
I would live to study, and not study to live.

693
Hope is a good breakfast, but it is a bad supper.

694
Anger makes dull men witty, but it keeps them poor.

695 *The Advancement of Learning*
For all knowledge and wonder (which is the seed of knowledge) is an impression of pleasure in itself.

696 *The Advancement of Learning*
So let great authors have their due, as time, which is the author of authors, be not deprived of his due, which is further and further to discover truth.

697 *The Advancement of Learning*
If a man will begin with certainties, he shall end in doubts; but if he will be content to begin with doubts, he shall end in certainties.

698 *The Advancement of Learning*
[Knowledge is] a rich storehouse for the glory of the Creator and the relief of man's estate.

699 *The Advancement of Learning*
Antiquities are history defaced, or some remnants of history which have casually escaped the shipwreck of time.

700 *The Advancement of Learning*
Poesy was ever thought to have some participation of divineness, because it doth raise and erect the mind, by submitting the shows of things to the desires of the mind; whereas reason doth buckle and bow the mind unto the nature of things.

701 *The Advancement of Learning*
The knowledge of man is as the waters, some descending from above, and some springing from beneath; the one informed by the light of nature, the other inspired by divine revelation.

702 *The Advancement of Learning*
They are ill discoverers that think there is no land, when they can see nothing but sea.

703 *The Advancement of Learning*
But men must know, that in this theatre of man's life it is reserved only for God and angels to be lookers on.

704 '*The Antitheta of Things*'
Riches are a good handmaid, but the worst mistress.

705 '*The Antitheta of Things*'
Silence is the virtue of fools.

706 *The Elements of the Common Law*
I hold every man a debtor to his profession.

707 *Essays*
Some books are to be tasted, others to be swallowed, and some few to be chewed and digested.

708 *Essays*
They do best who, if they cannot but admit Love, yet make it keep quarter; and sever it wholly from their serious affairs and actions of life.

709 *Essays 'Of Adversity'*
Prosperity is the blessing of the Old Testament, adversity is the blessing of the New.

710 *Essays 'Of Adversity'*
Prosperity is not without many fears and distastes; and adversity is not without comforts and hopes.

711 *Essays 'Of Adversity'*
Prosperity doth best discover vice, but adversity doth best discover virtue.

712 *Essays 'Of Atheism'*
A little philosophy inclineth man's mind to atheism, but depth in philosophy bringeth men's minds about to religion.

713 *Essays 'Of Atheism'*
They that deny a God destroy man's nobility; for certainly man is of kin to the beasts by his body; and, if he be not of kin to God by his spirit, he is a base and ignoble creature.

714 *Essays 'Of Beauty'*
That is the best part of beauty, which a picture cannot express.

715 *Essays 'Of Ceremonies and Respects'*
Light gains make heavy purses.

716 Essays 'Of Ceremonies and Respects'
He that is too much in anything, so that he giveth another occasion of satiety, maketh himself cheap.

717 Essays 'Of Counsel'
Books will speak plain when counsellors blanch.

718 Essays 'Of Cunning'
I knew one that when he wrote a letter he would put that which was most material in the postscript, as if it had been a bymatter.

719 Essays 'Of Cunning'
Nothing doth more hurt in a state than that cunning men pass for wise.

720 Essays 'Of Death'
Men fear death as children fear to go in the dark; and as that natural fear in children is increased with tales, so is the other.

721 Essays 'Of Death'
There is no passion in the mind of man so weak, but it mates and masters the fear of death. And therefore death is no such terrible enemy, when a man hath so many attendants about him that can win the combat of him. Revenge triumphs over death; love slights it; honour aspireth to it; grief flieth to it.

722 Essays 'Of Death'
It is as natural to die as to be born; and to a little infant, perhaps, the one is as painful as the other.

723 Essays 'Of Death'
Above all, believe it, the sweetest canticle is Nunc dimittis, when a man hath obtained worthy ends and expectations. Death hath this also, that it openeth the gate to good fame, and extinguisheth envy.

724 Essays 'Of Dispatch'
To choose time is to save time.

725 Essays 'Of Expense'
Riches are for spending.

726 Essays 'Of Expense'
A man ought warily to begin charges which once begun will continue.

727 Essays 'Of Followers and Friends'
There is little friendship in the world, and least of all between equals.

728 Essays 'Of Fortune'
Chiefly the mould of a man's fortune is in his own hands.

729 Essays 'Of Fortune'
If a man look sharply, and attentively, he shall see Fortune: for though she be blind, yet she is not invisible.

730 Essays 'Of Friendship'
A crowd is not company, and faces are but a gallery of pictures, and talk but a tinkling cymbal, where there is no love.

731 Essays 'Of Friendship'
It redoubleth joys, and cutteth griefs in halves.

732 Essays 'Of Gardens'
God Almighty first planted a garden; and indeed, it is the purest of human pleasures.

733 Essays 'Of Great Place'
Men in great place are thrice servants; servants of the sovereign or state, servants of fame, and servants of business.

734 Essays 'Of Great Place'
It is a strange desire to seek power and to lose liberty.

735 Essays 'Of Great Place'
Severity breedeth fear, but roughness breedeth hate.

736 Essays 'Of Innovations'
He that will not apply new remedies must expect new evils; for time is the greatest innovator.

737 Essays 'Of Love'
It has been well said that 'the arch-flatterer with whom all the petty flatterers have intelligence is a man's self'.

738 Essays 'Of Marriage and the Single Life'
He that hath wife and children hath given hostages to fortune; for they are impediments to great enterprises, either of virtue or mischief.

739 *Essays 'Of Marriage and the Single Life'*
Wives are young men's mistresses, companions for middle age, and old men's nurses.

740 *Essays 'Of Marriage and the Single Life'*
He was reputed one of the wise men that made answer to the question when a man should marry? 'A young man not yet, an elder man not at all.'

741 *Essays 'Of Negotiating'*
It is generally better to deal by speech than by letter.

742 *Essays 'Of Nobility'*
New nobility is but the act of power, but ancient nobility is the act of time.

743 *Essays 'Of Nobility'*
Nobility of birth commonly abateth industry.

744 *Essays 'Of Parents and Children'*
The joys of parents are secret, and so are their griefs and fears.

745 *Essays 'Of Parents and Children'*
Children sweeten labours, but they make misfortunes more bitter.

746 *Essays 'Of Praise'*
Fame is like a river, that beareth up things light and swollen, and drowns things weighty and solid.

747 *Essays 'Of Regimen of Health'*
Age will not be defied.

748 *Essays 'Of Revenge'*
Revenge is a kind of wild justice, which the more man's nature runs to, the more ought law to weed it out.

749 *Essays 'Of Revenge'*
A man that studieth revenge keeps his own wounds green.

750 *Essays 'Of Seditions and Troubles'*
Money is like muck, not good except it be spread.

751 *Essays 'Of Seditions and Troubles'*
The remedy is worse than the disease.

752 *Essays 'Of Seeming Wise'*
The French are wiser than they seem, and the Spaniards seem wiser than they are.

753 *Essays 'Of Studies'*
To spend too much time in studies is sloth.

754 *Essays 'Of Studies'*
They perfect nature and are perfected by experience.

755 *Essays 'Of Studies'*
Read not to contradict and confute, nor to believe and take for granted, nor to find talk and discourse, but to weigh and consider.

756 *Essays 'Of Studies'*
Reading maketh a full man; conference a ready man; and writing an exact man.

757 *Essays 'Of Studies'*
Histories make men wise; poets, witty; the mathematics, subtile; natural philosophy, deep; moral, grave; logic and rhetoric, able to contend.

758 *Essays 'Of Superstition'*
There is a superstition in avoiding superstition.

759 *Essays 'Of Suspicion'*
There is nothing makes a man suspect much, more than to know little.

760 *Essays 'Of Suspicion'*
Suspicions amongst thoughts are like bats amongst birds, they ever fly by twilight.

761 *Essays 'Of Travel'*
Travel, in the younger sort, is a part of education; in the elder, a part of experience. He that travelleth into a country before he hath some entrance into the language, goeth to school, and not to travel.

762 *Essays 'Of the True Greatness of Kingdoms'*
Neither will it be, that a people overlaid with taxes should ever become valiant and martial.

763 *Essays 'Of Truth'*
A mixture of a lie doth ever add pleasure.

764 *Essays 'Of Vicissitude of Things'*
In the youth of a state arms do flourish; in the middle age of a state, learning; and then both of them together for a time; in the declining age of a state, mechanical

arts and merchandise.

765 *Essays 'Of Wisdom for a Man's Self'*
Be so true to thyself as thou be not false to others.

766 *Essays 'Of Wisdom for a Man's Self'*
It is the wisdom of the crocodiles, that shed tears when they would devour.

767 *Essays 'Of Youth and Age'*
Young men are fitter to invent than to judge, fitter for execution than for counsel, and fitter for new projects than for settled business.

768 *'A Letter of Advice to the Duke of Buckingham'*
I have rather studied books than men.

769 *'A Letter of Advice to the Earl of Essex'*
Opportunity makes a thief.

770 *'To My Lord Treasurer Burghley'*
I have taken all knowledge to be my province.

771 *Meditationes Sacrae 'Of Heresies'*
For also knowledge itself is power.

772 *New Atlantis*
God's first Creature, which was Light.

773 *Novum Organum*
For what a man would like to be true, that he more readily believes.

774 *Novum Organum*
Nature cannot be ordered about, except by obeying her.

775 *Resuscitatio*
Books must follow sciences, and not sciences books.

776 *The World*
What is it then to have or have no wife,
But single thraldom, or a double strife?

BADEN-POWELL Robert 1857-1941
777 *Scouting for Boys*
The scouts' motto is founded on my initials, it is: BE PREPARED, which means, you are always to be in a state of readiness in mind and body to do your DUTY.

BAECK Leo 1873-1956
778
The mark of a mature man is the ability to give love and receive it joyously and without guilt.

BAEDEKER Karl 1801-1859
779 *Great Britain - Route 30*
Oxford is on the whole more attractive than Cambridge to the ordinary visitor; and the traveller is therefore recommended to visit Cambridge first, or to omit it altogether if he cannnot visit both.

BAEZ Joan 1941-
780
The only thing that's been a worse flop than the organization of non-violence has been the organization of violence.

781 *(of 60s contemporaries)*
Everyone is either bald or dead or looks like a plum pudding.

BAGEHOT Walter 1826-1877
782
Business is really more agreeable than pleasure; it interests the whole mind ... more deeply. But it does not look as if it did.

783
To a great experience one thing is essential - an experiencing nature.

784
The best reason why monarchy is a strong government is that it is an intelligible government: the mass of mankind understand it, and they hardly anywhere in the world understand any other.

785
The great pleasure in life is doing what people say you cannot do.

786
Poverty is an anomaly to rich people: it is very difficult to make out why people who want dinner do not ring the bell.

787 *The English Constitution 'Its History'*
As soon as we see that England is a disguised republic we must see too that the classes for whom the disguise is necessary must be tenderly dealt with.

788 *The English Constitution*
Women - one half of the human race at least - care fifty times more for a marriage than a ministry.

789 *The English Constitution 'The Cabinet'*
The mystic reverence, the religious allegiance, which are essential to a true monarchy, are imaginative sentiments that no legislature can manufacture in any people.

790 *The English Constitution 'The Cabinet'*
In such constitutions [as England's] there are two parts ... first, those which excite and preserve the reverence of the population - the dignified parts ... and next, the efficient parts - those by which it, in fact, works and rules.

791 *The English Constitution 'The Cabinet'*
A cabinet is a combining committee - a hyphen which joins, a buckle which fastens, the legislative part of the state to the executive part of the state.

792 *The English Constitution 'The Cabinet'*
It has been said that England invented the phrase, 'Her Majesty's Opposition'; that it was the first government which made a criticism of administration as much a part of the polity as adminstration itself. This critical opposition is the consequence of cabinet govenment.

793 *The English Constitution 'The Cabinet'*
'The Times' has made many ministries.

794 *The English Constitution 'Checks & Balances'*
It has been said, not truly, but with a possible approximation to truth, that in 1802 every hereditary monarch was insane.

795 *The English Constitution 'The Monarchy'*
Above all things our royalty is to be reverenced, and if you begin to poke about it you cannot reverence it ... Its mystery is its life. We must not let in daylight upon magic.

796 *The English Constitution 'The Monarchy'*
The Sovereign has, under a constitutional monarchy such as ours, three rights - the right to be consulted, the right to encourage, the right to warn.

797 *Estimates of some Englishmen and Scotchmen*
No real English gentleman, in his secret soul, was ever sorry for the death of a political economist.

798 *Estimates of some Englishmen and Scotchmen*
Writers, like teeth, are divided into incisors and grinders.

BAILEY John
799
Politics is not a good location or a vocation for anyone lazy, thin-skinned or lacking a sense of humour.

BAILEY Philip James 1816-1902
800
Art is man's nature; nature is God's art.

801
Hell is more bearable than nothingness.

802 *Festus*
America, thou half-brother of the world;
With something good and bad of every land.

BAILLIE Joanna 1762-1851
803 *Basil*
But woman's grief is like a summer storm,
Short as it violent is.

BAINBRIDGE Beryl 1934-
804 *A Weekend with Cloud*
He is, after all, the reflection of the tenderness I bear for myself. It is always ourselves we love.

BAIRNSFATHER Bruce 1888-1959
805 *Fragments from France*
Well, if you knows of a better 'ole, go to it.

BAKER Bobby
806
Shopping is the perfect model for the Quest.

BAKER Russell
807
I've had an unhappy life, thank God.

808
Happiness is a small and unworthy goal for something as big and fancy as a whole lifetime, and should be taken in small

doses.

BALANCHINE George 1904-1983
809
I am a choreographer. A choreographer is a poet. I do not create. God creates. I assemble, and I will steal from everywhere to do it.

BALDWIN James 1924-1987
810
All art is a kind of confession, more or less oblique. All artists, if they are to survive, are forced, at last, to tell the whole story; to vomit the anguish up.

811
Children have never been very good at listening to their elders, but they have never failed to imitate them.

812
Education is indoctrination, if you're white - subjugation if you're black.

813
Experience, which destroys innocence, also leads one back to it.

814
Most people in action are not worth very much; and yet every human being is an unprecedented miracle.

815
This world is white no longer, and it will never be white again.

816
We take our shape, it is true, within and against that cage of reality bequeathed us at our birth, and yet it is precisely through our dependence on this reality that we are most endlessly betrayed.

817
I met a lot of people in Europe. I even encountered myself.

818
Money, it turned out, was exactly like sex, you thought of nothing else if you didn't have it and thought of other things if you did.

819
It comes as a great shock around the age of 5, 6 or 7 to discover that the flag to which you have pledged allegiance, along with everybody else, has not pledged allegiance to you. It comes as a great shock to see Gary Cooper killing off the Indians and, although you are rooting for Gary Cooper, that the Indians are you.

820 *Another Country*
The face of a lover is unknown, precisely because it is invested with so much of oneself. It is a mystery, containing, like all mysteries, the possibility of torment.

821 *Nobody Knows My Name*
Anyone who has ever struggled with poverty knows how extremely expensive it is to be poor.

822 *Nobody Knows My Name*
Freedom is not something that anybody can be given; freedom is something people take and people are as free as they want to be.

BALDWIN Roger
823
I always felt from the beginning that you had to defend people you disliked and feared as well as those you admired.

BALDWIN Stanley 1867-1947
824
War would end if the dead could return.

825
A platitude is simply a truth repeated until people get tired of hearing it.

826
I think it is well also for the man in the street to realize that there is no power on earth that can protect him from being bombed. Whatever people may tell him, the bomber will always get through. The only defence is in offence, which means that you have to kill more women and children more quickly than the enemy if you want to save yourselves.

827
Since the day of the air, the old frontiers are gone. When you think of the defence of England you no longer think of the

chalk cliffs of Dover; you think of the Rhine. That is where our frontier lies.

828
There are three classes which need sanctuary more than others - birds, wild flowers, and Prime Ministers.

829
The intelligent are to the intelligentsia what a gentleman is to a gent.

830 *Economic Consequences of the Peace*
They [parliament] are a lot of hard-faced men who look as if they had done very well out of the war.

BALFOUR Arthur James 1848-1930
831
Winston has written four volumes about himself and called it 'World Crisis'.

832
Society, dead or alive, can have no charm without intimacy and no intimacy without an interest in trifles.

833 *Letter to Mrs. Drew*
It is unfortunate, considering that enthusiasm moves the world, that so few enthusiasts can be trusted to speak the truth.

BALL George W.
834
Nostalgia is a seductive liar.

BALL John d. 1381
835 *Sermon*
When Adam delved, and Eve span,
Who was then a gentleman?

BALL Lucille 1911-1989
836
I think knowing what you cannot do is more important than knowing what you can do.

BALLOU Hosea 1771-1852
837
Hatred is self-punishment.

BALMAIN Pierre 1914-1982
838
The trick of wearing mink is to look as though you were wearing a cloth coat. The trick of wearing a cloth coat is to look as though you are wearing mink.

BALZAC Honoré De 1799-1850
839
Bureaucracy is a giant mechanism operated by pygmies.

840
The majority of husbands remind me of an orang-utan trying to play the violin.

841
A mother who is really a mother is never free.

842
Manners are the hypocrisy of a nation.

843
All happiness depends on courage and work. I have had many periods of wretchedness, but with energy and above all with illusions, I pulled through them all.

844 *Le Peau de Chagrin*
To kill the emotions and so live to old age, or to accept the martyrdom of our passions and die young is our doom.

BANKHEAD Tallulah 1903-1968
845
I'd rather be strongly wrong than weakly right.

BANZINI Luigi
846
A gentleman does things no gentleman should do in a way only a gentleman can.

BARAKA Imamu Amiri 1934-
847 *Midstream*
God has been replaced, as he has all over the West, with respectability and air-conditioning.

848 *'Tokenism'*
A man is either free or he is not. There cannot be any apprenticeship for freedom.

BARBER James David
849
Trying to make the presidency work these days is like trying to sew buttons on a custard pie.

BARHAM R.H. ('Thomas Ingoldsby')
1788-1845
850 *The Ingoldsby Legends*
So put that in your pipe, my Lord Otto,
and smoke it.

BARING Maurice 1874-1945
851
If you would know what the Lord God
thinks of money, you have only to look at
those to whom he gives it.

852 *Outline of Russian Literature*
In Mozart and Salieri we see the contrast
between the genius which does what it
must and the talent which does what it
can.

BARING-GOULD Sabine 1834-1924
853 *'Onward, Christian Soldiers'*
Onward, Christian soldiers,
Marching as to war,
With the cross of Jesus
Going on before.

BARKER J.M.
854
Only an incompetent mind is content to
express itself incompetently.

855
It is a sobering thought that each of us
gives his hearers and his readers a chance
to look into the inner working of his mind
when he speaks or writes.

BARNARD Christian 1922-
856
The prime goal is to alleviate suffering,
and not to prolong life. And if your
treatment does not alleviate suffering, but
only prolongs life, that treatment should
be stopped.

BARNARD Frederick R.
857 *Printers' Ink*
One picture is worth ten thousand words.

BARNES Clive 1927-
858
Television is the first truly democratic
culture - the first culture available to
everybody and entirely governed by what
the people want. The most terrifying thing
is what people do want.

BARNES Djuna 1892-1982
859
We are adhering to life now with our last
muscle - the heart.

BARNES Julian 1946-
860 *Flaubert's Parrot*
What does this journey seem like to those
who aren't British - as they head towards
the land of embarrassment and breakfast?

861 *Flaubert's Parrot*
Do not imagine that Art is something
which is designed to give gentle uplift and
self-confidence. Art is not a brassiere. At
least, not in the English sense. But do not
forget that brassiere is the French for life-
jacket.

862 *Flaubert's Parrot*
Books say: she did this because. Life says:
she did this. Books are where things are
explained to you; life is where things aren't
... Books make sense of life. The only
problem is that the lives they make sense
of are other people's lives, never your
own.

863 *A History of the World in 10½ Chapters*
Does history repeat itself, the first time as
tragedy, the second time as farce? No,
that's too grand, too considered a process.
History just burps, and we taste again that
raw onion sandwich it swallowed
centuries ago.

864 *Talking It Over*
Love is just a system for getting someone
to call you darling after sex.

BARNES Peter 1931-
865 *The Ruling Class*
CLAIRE: How do you know you're ...
God?
EARL OF GURNEY: Simple. When I pray
to Him I find I'm talking to myself.

BARNUM Phineas T. 1810-1891
866
Every crowd has a silver lining.

867 *(attributed)*
There's a sucker born every minute.

BARRAULT Jean-Louis 1910-1994
868
Acting consists of the ability to keep an audience from coughing.

BARRIE J.M. 1860-1937
869
The secret of happiness is not in doing what one likes, but in liking what one has to do.

870
Heaven for climate, hell for company.

871
God gave us memories that we might have roses in December.

872 *The Admirable Crichton*
His lordship may compel us to be equal upstairs, but there will never be equality in the servants' hall.

873 *Peter Pan*
When the first baby laughed for the first time, the laugh broke into a thousand pieces and they all went skipping about, and that was the beginning of fairies.

874 *Peter Pan*
Every time a child says 'I don't believe in fairies' there is a little fairy somewhere that falls down dead.

875 *Peter Pan*
To die will be an awfully big adventure.

876 *What Every Woman Knows*
There are few more impressive sights in the world than a Scotsman on the make.

877 *What Every Woman Knows*
It's a sort of bloom on a woman. If you have it, you don't need to have anything else; and if you don't have it, it doesn't much matter what else you have.

BARRYMORE John 1882-1942
878
I want him ('Hamlet') to be so male that when I come out on the stage, they can hear my balls clank.

BARTH John 1930-
879
'Tis e'er the wont of simple folk to prize the deed and overlook the motive, and of learned folk to discount the deed and lay open the soul of the doer.

880
More history's made by secret handshakes than by battles, bills and proclamations.

BARTH Joseph
881
Marriage is our last, best chance to grow up.

BARTH Karl 1886-1968
882
Laughter is the closest thing to the grace of God.

BARTHES Roland 1915-1980
883
Flaubert had infinite correction to perform.

884 *Mythologies 'La nouvelle Citroën'*
I think that cars today are almost the exact equivalent of the great Gothic cathedrals: I mean the supreme creation of an era, conceived with passion by unknown artists, and consumed in image if not in usage by a whole population which appropriates them as a purely magical object.

BARUCH Bernard 1870-1965
885
To me, old age is always fifteen years older than I am.

886
The greatest blessing of our democracy is freedom. But in the last analysis, our only freedom is the freedom to discipline ourselves.

887
Age is only a number, a cipher for the records. A man can't retire his experience. He must use it. Experience achieves more with less energy and time.

888
Vote for the man who promises least; he'll be the least disappointing.

889
Let us not be deceived - we are today in the midst of a cold war.

BARZUN Jacques 1907-
890
Whoever wants to know the hearts and minds of America had better learn baseball.

891
The test and the use of man's education is that he finds pleasure in the exercise of his mind.

892
In any assembly the simplest way to stop transacting business and split the ranks is to appeal to a principle.

893
Teaching is not a lost art, but the regard for it is a lost tradition.

BASHO Matsuo 1644-1694
894
Do not seek to follow in the footsteps of the men of old; seek what they sought.

BASINGER Kim
895
The more flesh you show, the further up the ladder you go.

BATES Marston
896
Research is the process of going up alleys to see if they are blind.

BAUDELAIRE Charles 1821-1867
897
Genius is childhood recaptured.

898
We love women in proportion to their degree of strangeness to us.

899
As a remedy against all ills - poverty, sickness, and melancholy - only one thing is absolutely necessary: a liking for work.

900
How many years of fatigue and punishment it takes to learn the simple truth that work, that disagreeable thing, is the only way of not suffering in life, or at all events, of suffering less.

901
I have cultivated my hysteria with joy and terror.

BAUER Gerard
902
The voice is a second face.

BAUGHMAN M. Dale
903
You can never hope to become a skilled conversationalist until you learn how to put your foot tactfully through the television set.

BAX Sir Arnold 1883-1953
904
You should make a point of trying every experience once, excepting incest and folk-dancing.

BAYLY Thomas Haynes 1797-1839
905 *Isle of Beauty*
Absence makes the heart grow fonder, Isle of Beauty, Fare thee well!

BEADLE E.R.
906
Half the work that is done in the world is to make things appear what they are not.

BEARD Charles A. 1874-1948
907
When it is dark enough, you can see the stars.

BEATON Sir Cecil 1904-1980
908
After twenty annual visits, I am still surprised each time I return to see this giant asparagus bed of alabaster and rose and green skyscrapers.

BEATTY David 1871-1936
909 *(at the Battle of Jutland)*
There's something wrong with our bloody ships today, Chatfield.

BEAUMARCHAIS Pierre-Augustin Caron de 1732-1799
910
It is not necessary to understand things in order to argue about them.

911
Vilify! Vilify! Some of it will always stick.

912
Nature says to a woman: 'Be beautiful if
you can, wise if you want to, but be
respected, that is essential.'

913 *The Barber of Seville*
Drinking when we are not thirsty and
making love all year round, madam; that is
all there is to distinguish us from the other
animals.

BEAUMONT Francis 1584-1616
914 *The Maid's Tragedy*
Those have most power to hurt us, that we
love.

915 *The Scornful Lady*
Kiss till the cow comes home.

BEAVERBROOK Lord 1879-1964
916
Business is more exciting than any game.

917 *(attributed)*
Buy old masters. They fetch a better price
than old mistresses.

918 *The Decline and Fall of Lloyd George*
[He] did not seem to care which way he
travelled providing he was in the driver's
seat.

919 *(about Edward VIII)*
Our cock won't fight.

BECKER Carl 1873-1945
920 *Progress and Power*
The significance of man is that he is that
part of the universe that asks the question,'
What is the significance of man? 'He alone
can stand apart imaginatively and,
regarding himself and the universe in their
eternal aspects, pronounce a judgement:
'The significance of man is that he is
insignificant and is aware of it.'

BECKER Ernest
921
Men use one another to assure their
personal victory over death.

BECKER May Lamberton
922
We grow neither better nor worse as we
get old, but more like ourselves.

BECKETT Samuel 1906-1989
923
There's never an end for the sea.

924 *Malone Dies*
If I had the use of my body I would throw
it out of the window.

925 *Waiting for Godot*
One of the thieves was saved. (Pause) It's a
reasonable percentage.

926 *Waiting for Godot*
ESTRAGON: Charming spot. Inspiring
prospects. Let's go.
VLADIMIR: We can't.
ESTRAGON: Why not?
VLADIMIR: We're waiting for Godot.

927 *Waiting for Godot*
We all are born mad. Some remain so.

BECON Thomas 1523-1567
928 *Catechism*
For commonly, wheresoever God buildeth
a church, the devil will build a chapel just
by.

BEDFORD Harry and SULLIVAN Terry
929 *(song written for Marie Lloyd)*
I'm a bit of a ruin that Cromwell knocked
about a bit.

BEECHAM Sir Thomas 1879-1961
930
The English may not like music, but they
absolutely love the noise it makes.

931
Music first and last should sound well,
should allure and enchant the ear. Never
mind the inner significance.

932 *Beecham Stories*
There are two golden rules for an
orchestra: start together and finish
together. The public doesn't give a damn
what goes on in between.

933 *Beecham Stories (describing the
harpsichord)*
Like two skeletons copulating on a
corrugated tin roof.

934 *Beecham Stories (of Herbert von Karajan)*
A kind of musical Malcolm Sargent.

935 *(to a cellist - attributed)*
Madam, you have between your legs an
instrument capable of giving pleasure to
thousands - and all you can do is scratch it.

936 *Wit of Music*
Why do we have to have all these third-
rate foreign conductors around - when we
have so many second-rate ones of our
own?

BEECHER Henry Ward 1813-1887
937
Never forget what a man says to you when
he is angry.

938
The dog is the god of frolic.

939
Where is human nature so weak as in the
bookstore?

940
A Christian is nothing but a sinful man
who has put himself to school for Christ
for the honest purpose of becoming better.

941
Do not be afraid of defeat. You are never
so near to victory as when defeated in a
good cause.

942
You never know till you try to reach them
how accessible men are; but you must
approach each man by the right door.

943
The worst thing in this world, next to
anarchy, is government.

944
Mirthfulness is in the mind and you
cannot get it out. It is just as good in its
place as conscience or veneration.

945
Flowers have an expression of countenance
as much as men or animals. Some seem to
smile, some have a sad expression, some
are pensive and diffident, others again are
plain, honest and upright.

946
What the mother sings to the cradle goes
all the way down to the coffin.

947
Clothes and manners do not make the
man; but, when he is made, they greatly
improve his appearance.

948
The philosophy of one century is the
common sense of the next.

949
The meanest, most contemptible kind of
praise is that which first speaks well of a
man, and then qualifies it with a 'but'.

950
It is not well for a man to pray cream and
live skim milk.

951
The difference between perseverance and
obstinacy is that one often comes from a
strong will, and the other from a strong
won't.

BEECHER John
952
Strength is a matter of the made-up mind.

BEERBOHM Sir Max 1872-1956
953
You cannot make a man by standing a
sheep on its hind legs. But by standing a
flock of sheep in that position you can
make a crowd of men.

954
The past is a work of art, free of
irrelevancies and loose ends.

955
To mankind in general Macbeth and Lady
Macbeth stand out as the supreme type of
all that a host and hostess should not be.

956 *(attributed)*
I belong to the generation that says
goodbye at the front door.

957 *A Defence of Cosmetics*
Most women are not so young as they are
painted.

958 *And Even Now 'Hosts and Guests'*
Mankind is divisible into two great classes:
hosts and guests.

959 *More 'Going Back to School'*
I was not unpopular [at school] ... It is
Oxford that has made me insufferable.

960 *More 'Going Back to School'*
Undergraduates owe their happiness
chiefly to the consciousness that they are
no longer at school. The nonsense which
was knocked out of them at school is all
put gently back at Oxford or Cambridge.

961 *Zuleika Dobson*
The fading signals and grey eternal walls
of that antique station, which, familiar to
them and insignificant, does yet whisper to
the tourist the last enchantments of the
Middle Age.

962 *Zuleika Dobson*
The dullard's envy of brilliant men is
always assuaged by the suspicion that they
will come to a bad end.

963 *Zuleika Dobson*
Women who love the same man have a
kind of bitter freemasonry.

BEETON Mrs 1836-1865
964 *The Book of Household Management*
A place for everything and everything in
its place.

BEGLEY Louis
965
The test of the ultimate validity of what
you think about is whether you can write
it down.

BEHAN Brendan 1923-1964
966
A Torontonian is a man who leaves culture
to his wife.

967
Critics are like eunuchs in a harem: they
know how it's done, they've seen it done
every day, but they're unable to do it
themselves.

968
It's not that the Irish are cynical. It's rather
that they have a wonderful lack of respect
for everything and everybody.

969
We had gone out there to pass the
beautiful day of high summer like true
Irishmen - locked in the dark Snug of a
public house.

970
What the hell difference does it make, left
or right? There were good men lost on
both sides.

971 *My Brother Brendan (by Dominic Behan)*
There's no such thing as bad publicity
except your own obituary.

972 *The Hostage*
PAT: He was an Anglo-Irishman.
MEG: In the blessed name of God what's
that?
PAT: A Protestant with a horse.

973 *The Hostage*
When I came back to Dublin, I was court-
martialled in my absence and sentenced to
death in my absence, so I said they could
shoot me in my absence.

974 *The Hostage*
We're here because we're queer
Because we're queer because we're here.

BEHN Aphra 1640-1689
975 *The Emperor of the Moon*
Oh, what a dear ravishing thing is the
beginning of an Amour!

976 *The Lover's Watch: Four o'clock*
Love ceases to be a pleasure, when it
ceases to be a secret.

977 *Lycidus*
Since man with that inconstancy was born,
To love the absent, and the present scorn,
Why do we deck, why do we dress
For such a short-lived happiness?
Why do we put attraction on,
Since either way 'tis we must be undone?

978 *The Rover*
Variety is the soul of pleasure.

979 *The Rover*
Come away; poverty's catching.

980 *The Rover*
Money speaks sense in a language all
nations understand.

BELL Clive 1881-1964

981 *Art*

Art and Religion are means to similar states of mind.

982 *Civilization*

Only reason can convince us of those three fundamental truths without a recognition of which there can be no effective liberty: that what we believe is not necessarily true; that what we like is not necessarily good; and that all questions are open.

BELLOC Hilaire 1870-1953

983

The Llama is a woolly sort of fleecy hairy goat
With an indolent expression and an undulating throat
Like an unsuccessful literary man.

984

Just as there is nothing between the admirable omelette and the intolerable, so with autobiography.

985 *A Bad Child's Book of Beasts 'The Tiger'*

The Tiger, on the other hand, is kittenish and mild,
He makes a pretty play fellow for any little child;
And mothers of large families (who claim to common sense)
Will find a Tiger well repay the trouble and expense.

986 *A Bad Child's Book of Beasts - dedication*

Child! do not throw this book about;
Refrain from the unholy pleasure
Of cutting all the pictures out!
Preserve it as your chiefest treasure.

987 *'To the Balliol Men Still in Africa'*

Balliol made me, Balliol fed me,
Whatever I had she gave me again:
And the best of Balliol loved and led me.
God be with you, Balliol men.

988 *More Beasts for Worse Children 'The Microbe'*

The Microbe is so very small
You cannot make him out at all.
But many sanguine people hope
To see him through a microscope.

989 *More Beasts for Worse Children 'The Microbe'*

Oh! let us never, never doubt
What nobody is sure about!

990 *'On His Books'*

When I am dead, I hope it may be said:
'His sins were scarlet, but his books were read.'

991 *Cautionary Tales 'Henry King'*

Physicians of the Utmost Fame
Were called at once; but when they came
They answered, as they took their Fees,
'There is no Cure for this Disease'.

992 *Cautionary Tales 'Jim'*

And always keep a-hold of Nurse
For fear of finding something worse.

993 *Cautionary Tales 'Lord Lundy'*

In my opinion, Butlers ought
To know their place, and not to play
The Old Retainer night and day.

994 *Cautionary Tales 'Lord Lundy'*

Sir! you have disappointed us!
We had intended you to be
The next Prime Minister but three:
The stocks were sold; the Press was squared.
The Middle Class was quite prepared.
But as it is! ... My language fails!
Go out and govern New South Wales!

995 *Cautionary Tales 'Matilda'*

For every time She shouted 'Fire!'
They only answered 'Little Liar!'
And therefore when her Aunt returned,
Matilda, and the House, were Burned.

996 *Cautionary Tales 'Rebecca'*

A Trick that everyone abhors
In Little Girls is slamming Doors.

997 *Fatigue*

I'm tired of Love: I'm still more tired of Rhyme.
But money gives me pleasure all the Time.

998 *'On a Great Election'*

The accursed power which stands on Privilege
(And goes with Women, and Champagne, and Bridge)
Broke - and Democracy resumed her reign:

(Which goes with Bridge, and Women and Champagne).

999 *'Heroic Poem upon Wine'*
Strong brother in God and last companion, Wine.

1000 *Life of Hilaire Belloc*
Gentlemen, I am a Catholic ... If you reject me on account of my religion, I shall thank God that He has spared me the indignity of being your representative.

1001 *The Modern Traveller*
Whatever happens we have got
The Maxim Gun, and they have not.

1002 *New Cautionary Tales 'About John'*
Like many of the Upper Class
He liked the Sound of Broken Glass

1003 *New Cautionary Tales 'Peter Goole'*
And even now, at twenty-five,
He has to WORK to keep alive!
Yes! All day long from 10 till 4!
For half the year or even more;
With but an hour or two to spend
At luncheon with a city friend.

1004 *'Newdigate Poem'*
A smell of burning fills the startled Air -
The Electrician is no longer there!

1005 *On Nothing 'On Tea'*
Is there no Latin word for Tea? Upon my soul, if I had known that I would have let the vulgar stuff alone.

1006 *More Peers 'Lord Finchley'*
Lord Finchley tried to mend the Electric Light
Himself. It struck him dead: And serve him right!
It is the business of the wealthy man
To give employment to the artisan.

1007 *'On a Sundial'*
I am a sundial, and I make a botch
Of what is done much better by a watch.

1008 *Verses 'Dedicatory Ode'*
From quiet homes and first beginning,
Out to the undiscovered ends,
There's nothing worth the wear of winning,
But laughter and the love of friends.

BELLOW Saul 1915-
1009
A man is only as good as what he loves.

1010
The truth is, we've not really developed a fiction that can accommodate the full tumult, the zaniness and crazed quality of modern experience.

1011
All a writer has to do to get a woman is to say he's a writer. It's an aphrodisiac.

1012
Our society, like decadent Rome, has turned into an amusement society, with writers chief among the court jesters - not so much above the clatter as part of it.

1013
I have never turned over a fig leaf yet that didn't have a price tag on the other side.

1014 *Writers at Work*
Art has something to do with the achievement of stillness in the midst of chaos. A stillness which characterizes prayer, too, and the eye of the storm ... an arrest of attention in the midst of distraction.

BELLUSCH Pietro
1015
To be truly free, it takes more determination, courage, introspection and restraint than to be in shackles.

BELTAIRE Mark
1016
The nicest thing about the promise of spring is that sooner or later she'll have to keep it.

BENCHLEY Robert 1889-1945
1017
Anyone can do any amount of work provided it isn't the work he is supposed to be doing at that moment.

1018 *Chips off the old Benchley 'Safety Second'*
My only solution for the problem of habitual accidents ... is to stay in bed all day. Even then, there is always the chance that you will fall out.

1019 *Pluck and Luck*
In America there are two classes of travel -
first class, and with children.

1020 *Robert Benchley*
It took me fifteen years to discover that I
had no talent for writing, but I couldn't
give it up because by that time I was too
famous.

1021 *Wits End 'Robert Benchley' on Venice*
Streets Flooded. Please advise.

BENEDICT Francis G.
1022
The extra calories needed for one hour of
intense mental effort would be completely
met by eating one oyster cracker or one
half of a salted peanut.

BENÉT Stephen Vincent 1898-1943
1023
As for what you're calling hard luck - well,
we made New England out of it. That and
codfish.

1024
Honesty is as rare as a man without self-
pity.

1025
He could fiddle all the bugs off a sweet-
potato vine.

1026
(Abraham Lincoln's) weathered face was
homely as a plowed field.

1027 *'American Names'*
I shall not rest quiet in Montparnasse.
I shall not lie easy at Winchelsea.
You may bury my body in Sussex grass,
You may bury my tongue at Champmédy.
I shall not be there, I shall rise and pass.
Bury my heart at Wounded Knee.

BENN Tony 1925-
1028
In developing our industrial strategy for
the period ahead, we have the benefit of
much experience. Almost everything has
been tried at least once.

1029
Bookshops are the one University
everyone can enter.

1030
If you file your wastepaper basket for 50
years you build a public library.

1031 *The Benn Heresy 'Interview with Tony
Benn'*
It is as wholly wrong to blame Marx for
what was done in his name, as it is to
blame Jesus for what was done in his.

BENNARD George 1873-1958
1032 *'The Old Rugged Cross'*
I will cling to the old rugged cross,
And exchange it some day for a crown.

BENNETT Alan 1934-
1033 *'Place Names of China'*
Here I sit, alone and sixty,
Bald, and fat, and full of sin,
Cold the seat and loud the cistern,
As I read the Harpic tin.

1034 *Dinner at Noon*
What keeps us in our place is
embarrassment.

1035 *Enjoy*
I don't want to give you the idea I'm
trying to hide anything, or that anything
unorthodox goes on between my wife and
me. It doesn't. Nothing goes on at all ...
No foreplay. No afterplay. And fuck all in
between.

1036 *Forty Years On*
HEADMASTER: Of course they're out of
date. Standards are always out of date.
That is what makes them standards.

1037 *Getting On*
We started off trying to set up a small
anarchist community, but people wouldn't
obey the rules.

1038 *The Old Country*
We were put to Dickens as children but it
never quite took. That unremitting
humanity soon had me cheesed off.

BENNETT Arnold 1867-1931
1039
A man of sixty has spent twenty years in
bed and over three years in eating.

1040 *The Card*
His opinion of himself, having once risen, remained at 'set fair'.

1041 *Things that have Interested Me*
The price of justice is eternal publicity.

1042 *(attributed to his tailor)*
Trousers should shiver on the shoe, but not break.

1043 *The Title*
Being a husband is a whole-time job. That is why so many husbands fail. They cannot give their entire attention to it.

BENNETT James Gordon 1795-1872
1044
Remember, son, many a good story has been ruined by over-verification.

BENNETT Jill 1931-1990
1045
Never marry a man who hates his mother, because he'll end up hating you.

BENNETT W.A.C.
1046
Yes, I'm 68, but when I was a boy I was too poor to smoke, so knock off ten years. That makes me 58. And since I never developed the drinking habit, you can knock off ten more years. So I'm 48 - in the prime of my life. Retire? Retire to what?

BENOIT Madame
1047
I feel a recipe is only a theme, which an intelligent cook can play each time with a variation.

BENSON A.C. 1862-1925
1048
I have known some quite good people who were unhappy, but never an interested person who was unhappy.

1049 *Finale to Elgar's Coronation Ode*
Land of Hope and Glory, Mother of the Free,
How shall we extol thee who are born of thee?
Wider still and wider shall they bounds be set;
God who made thee mighty, make thee

mightier yet.

BENSON Stella 1892-1933
1050 *This is the End*
Call no man foe, but never love a stranger.

BENTHAM Jeremy 1748-1832
1051 *Anarchical Fallacies*
Natural rights is simple nonsense: natural and imprescriptible rights, rhetorical nonsense - nonsense upon stilts.

1052 *The Commonplace Book*
The greatest happiness of the greatest number is the foundation of morals and legislation.

1053 *Principles of Morals and Legislation*
All punishment is mischief: all punishment in itself is evil.

BENTLEY E. C. 1875-1956
1054 *Biography for Beginners 'Sir Christopher Wren'*
Sir Christopher Wren
Said, 'I am going to dine with some men.
If anybody calls
Say I am designing St. Paul's.'

1055 *Biography for Beginners 'Clive'*
What I like about Clive
Is that he is no longer alive.
There is a great deal to be said
For being dead.

1056 *Biography for Beginners - Introduction*
The Art of Biography
Is different from Geography.
Geography is about Maps,
But Biography is about Chaps.

1057 *More Biography 'George the Third'*
George the Third
Ought never to have occurred.
One can only wonder
At so grotesque a blunder.

BENTLEY Eric 1916-
1058
Fashion, which elevates the bad to the level of the good, subsequently turns its back on bad and good alike.

1059
Ours is the age of substitutes: instead of language, we have jargon; instead of

46

principles, slogans; and, instead of genuine ideas, Bright Ideas.

BENTLEY John
1060
Making money is fun, but it's pointless if you don't use the power it brings.

BENTLEY Richard 1662-1742
1061 *Bentley, his judgement on claret*
It would be port if it could.

1062 *The Works of Samuel Johnson*
It is a pretty poem, Mr. Pope, but you must not call it Homer.

BENTLEY Thomas 1730-1780
1063
No man is demolished but by himself.

BERENSON Bernhard 1865-1919
1064
Consistency requires you to be as ignorant today as you were a year ago.

1065
Enemies could become the best companions. Companionship is based on a common interest, and the greater the interest the closer the companionship. What makes enemies of people, if not the eagerness, the passion for the same thing?

1066
We define genius as the capacity for productive reaction against one's training.

1067
Governments last as long as the undertaxed can defend themselves against the overtaxed.

1068
A complete life may be one ending in so full an identification with the not-self that there is no self left to die.

BERESFORD Lord Charles 1846-1919
1069 *The World of Fashion 1837-1922*
Very sorry can't come. Lie follows by post.

BERGLER Edmund
1070
Every writer, without exception, is a masochist, a sadist, a peeping Tom, an exhibitionist, a narcissist, an injustice collector and a depressed person

constantly haunted by fears of unproductivity.

BERGSON Henri 1859-1941
1071
Art has no other object than to set aside the symbols of practical utility, the generalities that are conventionally and socially accepted, everything in fact which masks reality from us, in order to set us face to face with reality itself.

BERKELEY George 1685-1753
1072 *Concerning the Principles of Human Knowledge*
We have first raised a dust and then complain we cannot see.

1073 *Concerning the Principles of Human Knowledge*
All the choir of heaven and furniture of earth - in a word, all those bodies which compose the mighty frame of the world - have not any subsistence without a mind.

1074 *Oration at Plymouth*
Westward the course of empire takes its way;
The first four acts already past,
A fifth shall close the drama with the day:
Time's noblest offspring is the last.

1075 *Siris*
Truth is the cry of all, but the game of the few.

1076 *Three Dialogues between Hylas and Philonous*
The same principles which at first lead to scepticism, pursued to a certain point bring men back to common sense.

BERLIN Irving 1888-1989
1077
The toughest thing about success is that you've got to keep on being a success.

1078 *Annie Get Your Gun*
There's no business like show business.

1079 *Carefree 'Change Partners'*
Must you dance ev'ry dance
With the same fortunate man?
You have danced with him since the music began.
Won't you change partners and dance with

me?

1080 *Follow the Fleet 'Let's Face the Music and Dance'*
There may be trouble ahead,
But while there's moonlight and music and love and romance,
Let's face the music and dance.

1081 *'God Bless America'*
God bless America,
Land that I love,
Stand beside her and guide her
Thru the night with a light from above.
From the mountains to the prairies,
To the oceans white with foam,
God bless America,
My home sweet home.

1082 *Holiday Inn 'White Christmas'*
I'm dreaming of a white Christmas,
Just like the ones I used to know,
Where the tree-tops glisten
And children listen
To hear sleigh bells in the snow.

1083 *Top Hat 'Cheek-to-Cheek'*
Heaven - I'm in Heaven - And my heart beats so that I can hardly speak;
And I seem to find the happiness I seek
When we're out together dancing cheek-to-cheek.

BERLIN Sir Isaiah 1909-
1084
Rousseau was the first militant lowbrow.

1085 *Two Concepts of Liberty*
Liberty is liberty, not equality or fairness or justice or human happiness or a quiet conscience.

BERLIOZ Hector 1803-1869
1086
The luck of having talent is not enough; one must also have a talent for luck.

1087
Time is a great teacher, but unfortunately it kills all its pupils.

BERNANOS Georges 1888-1948
1088
Hell, madame, is to love no longer.

1089 *Journal d'un curé de campagne*
The wish for prayer is a prayer in itself.

BERNARD Claude 1812-1878
1090
Art is I, science is we.

BERNARD Dorothy
1091
Courage - fear that has said its prayers.

BERNE Eric 1910-1970
1092
Games people play: the psychology of human relationships.

BERRA Yogi 1925-
1093
You can observe a lot just by watching.

1094
You can't think and hit at the same time.

1095
The game isn't over until it's over.

1096
Ninety per cent of this game is half-mental.

BERRIGAN Daniel 1921-
1097
There are no makers of peace because the making of peace is at least as costly as the making of war - at least as exigent.

BERRYMAN John 1914-1972
1098 *'A Point of Age'*
We must travel in the direction of our fear.

BETJEMAN Sir John 1906-1984
1099 *'Death of King George V'*
Old men who never cheated, never doubted,
Communicated monthly, sit and stare
At the new suburb stretched beyond the run-way
Where a young man lands hatless from the air.

1100 *'Death in Leamington'*
Oh! Chintzy, Chintzy cheeriness,
Half dead and half alive!

1101 *'Henley-on-Thames'*
Oh shall I see the Thames again?
The prow-promoted gems again,
As beefy ATS

Without their hats
Come shooting through the bridge?
And 'cheerioh' or 'cheeri-bye'
Across the waste of waters die
And low the mists of evening lie
And lightly skims the midge.

1102 *'How to get on in Society'*
Phone for the fish-knives, Norman
As Cook is a little unnerved;
You kiddies have crumpled the serviettes
And I must have things daintily served.

1103 *'Middlesex'*
Gaily into Ruislip Gardens
Runs the red electric train,
With a thousand Ta's and Pardon's
Daintily alights Elaine;
Hurries down the concrete station
With a frown of concentration,
Out into the outskirt's edges
Where a few surviving hedges
Keep alive our lost Elysium - rural
Middlesex again.

1104 *'Slough'*
Come friendly bombs, and fall on Slough!
It isn't fit for humans now,
There isn't grass to graze a cow.
Swarm over, Death!

1105 *'A Subaltern's Love-Song'*
Miss J. Hunter Dunn, Miss J. Hunter Dunn,
Furnish'd and burnish'd by Aldershot sun,
What strenuous singles we played after tea,
We in the tournament - you against me.

1106 *'A Subaltern's Love-song'*
Around us are Rovers and Austins afar,
Above us, the intimate roof of the car,
And here on my right is the girl of my choice,
With the tilt of her nose and the chime of her voice.

1107 *Summoned by Bells*
The dread of beatings! Dread of being late!
And, greatest dread of all, the dread of games!

BETTI Ugo 1882-1954
1108
A vague uneasiness; the police. It's like when you suddenly understand you have

to undress in front of the doctor.

1109
This free-will business is a bit terrifying anyway. It's almost pleasanter to obey, and make the most of it.

BEUDOIN Patricia C.
1110
The toughest thing about being a housewife is you have no place to stay home from.

BEVAN Aneurin 1897-1960
1111
I have never regarded politics as the arena of morals. It is the arena of interests.

1112
No amount of cajolery, and no attempts at ethical or social seduction, can eradicate from my heart a deep burning hatred for the Tory Party ... So far as I am concerned they are lower than vermin.

1113
The language of priorities is the religion of Socialism.

1114
We know what happens to people who stay in the middle of the road. They get run down.

1115 *Aneurin Bevan*
Damn it all, you can't have the crown of thorns and the thirty pieces of silver.

1116 *(debate on Suez crisis)*
I am not going to spend any time whatsoever in attacking the Foreign Secretary ... If we complain about the tune, there is no reason to attack the monkey when the organ grinder is present.

1117 *The Doctors*
I stuffed their mouths with gold.

1118 *(of Robert Boothby)*
Why read the crystal when he can read the book?

1119 *(speech at Blackpool)*
This island is made mainly of coal and surrounded by fish. Only an organizing genius could produce a shortage of coal and fish at the same time.

1120 *(on unilateral disarmament)*
If you carry this resolution you will send
Britain's Foreign Secretary naked into the
conference chamber.

BEVERIDGE Karl
1121
My favourite example (of ex-patriotism) is
James Joyce, who left Ireland at nineteen
and never came back. But he spent the rest
of his life writing about Ireland from the
perspective of living in Paris.

BEVERIDGE William Henry 1879-1963
1122 *Social Insurance and Allied Services*
The object of government in peace and in
war is not the glory of rulers or of races,
but the happiness of the common man.

1123 *Voluntary Action*
The state is or can be master of money, but
in a free society it is master of very little
else.

BEVIN Ernest 1881-1951
1124
The most conservative man in this world is
the British Trade Unionist when you want
to change him.

1125
There never has been a war yet which, if
the facts had been put calmly before the
ordinary folk, could not have been
prevented ... The common man, I think, is
the great protection against war.

1126
My [foreign] policy is to be able to take a
ticket at Victoria Station and go anywhere I
damn well please.

1127 *Ernest Bevin and the Foreign Office*
If you open that Pandora's Box, you never
know what Trojan 'orses will jump out.

The BIBLE (Authorized Version)
1128 *New Testament: Acts of the Apostles ch.9
v.5*
It is hard for thee to kick against the
pricks.

1129 *New Testament: Acts of the Apostles
ch.10 v.34*
God is no respecter of persons.

1130 *New Testament: I Corinthians ch.8 v.1*
Knowledge puffeth up, but charity
edifieth.

1131 *New Testament: I Corinthians ch.13 v.1*
When I was a child, I spake as a child, I
understood as a child, I thought as a child:
but when I became a man, I put away
childish things.
For now we see through a glass, darkly;
but then face to face: now I know in part;
but then shall I know even as also I am
known.
And now abideth faith, hope, charity, these
three; but the greatest of these is charity.

1132 *New Testament: I Corinthians ch.15 v.26*
The last enemy that shall be destroyed is
death.

1133 *New Testament: I Corinthians ch.15 v.55*
O death, where is thy sting? O grave,
where is thy victory?

1134 *New Testament: Ephesians ch.4 v.25*
We are members one of another.

1135 *New Testament: Ephesians ch.4 v.26*
Be ye angry and sin not: let not the sun go
down upon your wrath.

1136 *New Testament: Galatians ch.6 v.5*
Every man shall bear his own burden.

1137 *New Testament: Hebrews ch.11 v.1*
Faith is the substance of things hoped for,
the evidence of things not seen.

1138 *New Testament: James ch.5 v.3*
Behold, we count them happy which
endure. Ye have heard of the patience of
Job.

1139 *New Testament: James ch.5 v.12*
Let your yea be yea; and your nay, nay.

1140 *New Testament: I John ch.4 v.18*
There is no fear in love; but perfect love
casteth out fear.

1141 *New Testament: Revelation ch.1 v.7*
I am Alpha and Omega, the beginning and
the ending, saith the Lord.

1142 *New Testament: Revelation ch.21 v.4*
And God shall wipe away all tears from
their eyes; and there shall be no more

death, neither sorrow, nor crying, neither shall there be any more pain: for the former things are passed away.

1143 *New Testament: Romans ch.4 v.15*
For where no law is, there is no transgression.

1144 *New Testament: Romans ch.6 v.23*
The wages of sin is death.

1145 *New Testament: Romans ch.12 v.19*
Vengeance is mine; I will repay, saith the Lord.

1146 *New Testament: St John ch.1 v.1*
In the beginning was the Word, and the Word was with God, and the Word was God.

1147 *New Testament: St John ch.1 v.3*
All things were made by him; and without him was not any thing made that was made.

1148 *New Testament: St John ch.4 v.48*
Except ye see signs and wonders, ye will not believe.

1149 *New Testament: St John ch.8 v.7*
He that is without sin among you, let him first cast a stone.

1150 *New Testament: St John ch.8 v.32*
And ye shall know the truth, and the truth shall make you free.

1151 *New Testament: St John ch.10 v.11*
I am the good shepherd: the good shepherd giveth his life for the sheep.

1152 *New Testament: St John ch.14 v.2*
In my Father's house are many mansions ... I go to prepare a place for you.

1153 *New Testament: St John ch.14 v.6*
I am the way, the truth, and the life: no man cometh unto the Father, but by me.

1154 *New Testament: St John ch.15 v.13*
Greater love hath no man than this, that a man lay down his life for his friends.

1155 *New Testament: St Luke ch.4 v.23*
Physician, heal thyself.

1156 *New Testament: St Luke ch.6 v.27*
Love your enemies, do good to them which hate you.

1157 *New Testament: St Luke ch.15 v.7*
Joy shall be in heaven over one sinner that repenteth, more than over ninety and nine just persons, which need no repentance.

1158 *New Testament: St Luke ch.17 v.21*
The kingdom of God is within you.

1159 *New Testament: St Luke ch.23 v.34*
Father, forgive them: for they know not what they do.

1160 *New Testament: St Mark ch.2 v.27*
The sabbath was made for man, and not man for the sabbath.

1161 *New Testament: St Mark ch.3 v.25*
If a house be divided against itself, that house cannot stand.

1162 *New Testament: St Mark ch.4 v.9*
He that hath ears to hear, let him hear.

1163 *New Testament: St Mark ch.4 v.24*
With what measure ye mete, it shall be measured to you.

1164 *New Testament: St Mark ch.8 v.36 St Matthew ch.16 v.26*
For what shall it profit a man, if he shall gain the whole world, and lose his own soul?

1165 *New Testament: St Matthew ch.5 v.3*
Blessed are the poor in spirit: for theirs is the kingdom of heaven.
Blessed are they that mourn: for they shall be comforted.
Blessed are the meek: for they shall inherit the earth.
Blessed are they which do hunger and thirst after righteousness: for they shall be filled.
Blessed are the merciful: for they shall obtain mercy.
Blessed are the pure in heart: for they shall see God.
Blessed are the peacemakers: for they shall be called the children of God.

1166 *New Testament: St Matthew ch.5 v.13*
Ye are the salt of the earth: but if the salt
have lost his savour, wherewith shall it be
salted?

1167 *New Testament: St Matthew ch.5 v.16*
Let your light so shine before men, that
they may see your good works.

1168 *New Testament: St Matthew ch.5 v.39*
Resist not evil: but whosoever shall smite
thee on thy right cheek, turn to him the
other also.

1169 *New Testament: St Matthew ch.6 v.3*
When thou doest alms, let not thy left
hand know what thy right hand doeth.

1170 *New Testament: St Matthew ch.6 v.24*
No man can serve two masters ... Ye
cannot serve God and mammon.

1171 *New Testament: St Matthew ch.6 v.33*
Seek ye first the kingdom of God, and his
righteousness; and all these things shall be
added unto you.

1172 *New Testament: St Matthew ch.7 v.1*
Judge not, that ye be not judged.

1173 *New Testament: St Matthew ch.7 v.7*
Ask, and it shall be given you; seek, and ye
shall find; knock, and it shall be opened
unto you.

1174 *New Testament: St Matthew ch.7 v.15*
Beware of false prophets, which come to
you in sheep's clothing, but inwardly they
are ravening wolves.

1175 *New Testament: St Matthew ch.8 v.12*
But the children of the kingdom shall be
cast out into outer darkness: there shall be
weeping and gnashing of teeth.

1176 *New Testament: St Matthew ch.8 v.22*
Let the dead bury their dead.

1177 *New Testament: St Matthew ch.9 v.13*
I am not come to call the righteous, but
sinners to repentance.

1178 *New Testament: St Matthew ch.10 v.8*
Freely ye have received, freely give.

1179 *New Testament: St Matthew ch.11 v.28*
Come unto me, all ye that labour and are
heavy laden, and I will give you rest.

1180 *New Testament: St Matthew ch.12 v.30*
St Luke ch.11 v.23
He that is not with me is against me.

1181 *New Testament: St Matthew ch.16 v.23*
Get thee behind me, Satan.

1182 *New Testament: St Matthew ch.18 v.3*
Except ye be converted, and become as
little children, ye shall not enter into the
kingdom of heaven.

1183 *New Testament: St Matthew ch.18 v.20*
For where two or three are gathered
together in my name, there am I in the
midst of them.

1184 *New Testament: St Matthew ch.19 v.6*
What therefore God hath joined together,
let not man put asunder.

1185 *New Testament: St Matthew ch.19 v.30*
But many that are first shall be last; and
the last shall be first.

1186 *New Testament: St Matthew ch.22 v.14*
For many are called, but few are chosen.

1187 *New Testament: St Matthew ch.22 v.21*
Render therefore unto Caesar the things
which are Caesar's; and unto God the
things that are God's.

1188 *New Testament: St Matthew ch.24 v.35*
Heaven and earth shall pass away, but my
words shall not pass away.

1189 *New Testament: St Matthew ch.26 v.39*
If it be possible, let this cup pass from me.

1190 *New Testament: St Matthew ch.13 v.57*
A prophet is not without honour save in
his own country.

1191 *New Testament: II Thessalonians ch.3
v.10*
If any would not work, neither should he
eat.

1192 *New Testament: I Timothy ch.6 v.7*
For we brought nothing into this world,
and it is certain we can carry nothing out.

1193 *New Testament: I Timothy ch.6 v.10*
The love of money is the root of all evil.

1194 *Old Testament: Amos ch.3 v.3*
Can two walk together, except they be
agreed?

1195 *Old Testament: Apocrypha Ecclesiasticus
ch.5 v.15*
Be not ignorant of any thing in a great
matter or a small.

1196 *Old Testament: Apocrypha Ecclesiasticus
ch.6 v.1*
A faithful friend is the medicine of life.

1197 *Old Testament: Apocrypha Ecclesiasticus
ch.18 v.25*
When thou hast enough, remember the
time of hunger.

1198 *Old Testament: Apocrypha Ecclesiasticus
ch.28 v.18*
Many have fallen by the edge of the
sword: but not so many as have fallen by
the tongue.

1199 *Old Testament: Apocrypha Ecclesiasticus
ch.30 v.24*
Envy and wrath shorten the life.

1200 *Old Testament: Apocrypha Ecclesiasticus
ch.31 v.17*
Leave off first for manners' sake.

1201 *Old Testament: Apocrypha Ecclesiasticus
ch.44 v.1*
Let us now praise famous men, and our
fathers that begat us.

1202 *Old Testament: Numbers ch.32 v.23*
Be sure your sin will find you out.

1203 *Old Testament: Deuteronomy ch.6 v.4*
Hear, O Israel: The Lord our God is one
Lord.

1204 *Old Testament: Deuteronomy ch.32 v.10*
He kept him as the apple of his eye.

1205 *Old Testament: Ecclesiastes ch.1 v.2*
Vanity of vanities, saith the Preacher,
vanity of vanities; all is vanity.

1206 *Old Testament: Ecclesiastes ch.1 v.7*
All the rivers run into the sea; yet the sea is
not full.

1207 *Old Testament: Ecclesiastes ch.3 v.1*
To every thing there is a season, and a time
to every purpose under the heaven.

1208 *Old Testament: Ecclesiastes ch.8 v.15*
A man hath no better thing under the sun,
than to eat, and to drink, and to be merry.

1209 *Old Testament: Ecclesiastes ch.9 v.11*
The race is not to the swift, nor the battle
to the strong.

1210 *Old Testament: Ecclesiastes ch.10 v.8*
He that diggeth a pit shall fall into it.

1211 *Old Testament: Ecclesiasticus ch.3 v.22*
Seek not out the things that are too hard
for thee, neither search the things that are
above thy strength.

1212 *Old Testament: Ecclesiasticus ch.44 v.7*
All these were honoured in their
generations and were the glory of their
times.

1213 *Old Testament: Ecclesiastes ch.1 v.9*
There is nothing new under the sun.

1214 *Old Testament: Ecclesiastes ch.1 v.18*
In much wisdom is much grief: and he that
increaseth knowledge increaseth sorrow.

1215 *Old Testament: Ecclesiastes: ch.10 v.19*
Wine maketh merry: but money answereth
all things.

1216 *Old Testament: Exodus ch.3 v.5*
Put off thy shoes from off thy feet, for the
place whereon thou standest is holy
ground.

1217 *Old Testament: Exodus ch.3 v.8*
A land flowing with milk and honey.

1218 *Old Testament: Exodus ch.21 v.23*
Life for life,
Eye for eye, tooth for tooth, hand for hand,
foot for foot,
Burning for burning, wound for wound,
stripe for stripe.

1219 *Old Testament: Genesis ch.2 v.23*
This is now bone of my bones, and flesh of
my flesh: she shall be called Woman,
because she was taken out of man.

1220 *Old Testament: Genesis ch.2 v.24*
Therefore shall a man leave his father and
his mother, and shall cleave unto his wife:
and they shall be one flesh.

1221 *Old Testament: Genesis ch.3 v.13*
The serpent beguiled me, and I did eat.

1222 *Old Testament: Genesis ch.3 v.16*
In sorrow thou shalt bring forth children.

1223 *Old Testament: Genesis ch.3 v.19*
For dust thou art, and unto dust shalt thou return.

1224 *Old Testament: Genesis ch.9 v.6*
Whoso sheddeth man's blood, by man shall his blood be shed.

1225 *Old Testament: Hosea ch.8 v.7*
They have sown the wind, and they shall reap the whirlwind.

1226 *Old Testament: Isaiah ch.22 v.13*
Let us eat and drink; for tomorrow we shall die.

1227 *Old Testament: Isaiah ch.40 v.15*
The nations are as a drop of a bucket, and are counted as the small dust of the balance:

1228 *Old Testament: Jeremiah ch.13 v.23*
Can the Ethiopian change his skin, or the leopard his spots?

1229 *Old Testament: Job ch.12 v.8*
Speak to the earth, and it shall teach thee.

1230 *Old Testament: Job ch.19 v.20*
I am escaped with the skin of my teeth.

1231 *Old Testament: Job ch.1 v.21*
The Lord gave, and the Lord hath taken away; blessed be the name of the Lord.

1232 *Old Testament: Job ch.28 v.18*
The price of wisdom is above rubies.

1233 *Old Testament: Job ch.32 v.9*
Great men are not always wise.

1234 *Old Testament: Job ch.5 v.7*
Man is born unto trouble, as the sparks fly upward.

1235 *Old Testament: Joel ch.2 v.28*
Your old men shall dream dreams, your young men shall see visions.

1236 *Old Testament: Proverbs ch.10 v.1*
A wise son maketh a glad father: but a foolish son is the heaviness of his mother.

1237 *Old Testament: Proverbs ch.12 v.4*
A virtuous woman is a crown to her husband.

1238 *Old Testament: Proverbs ch.13 v.19*
The desire accomplished is sweet to the soul.

1239 *Old Testament: Proverbs ch.13 v.24*
He that spareth his rod hateth his son.

1240 *Old Testament: Proverbs ch.14 v.23*
In all labour there is profit.

1241 *Old Testament: Proverbs ch.15 v.1*
A soft answer turneth away wrath.

1242 *Old Testament: Proverbs ch.16 v.18*
Pride goeth before destruction, and an haughty spirit before a fall.

1243 *Old Testament: Proverbs ch.16 v.32*
He that is slow to anger is better than the mighty; and he that ruleth his spirit than he that taketh a city.

1244 *Old Testament: Proverbs ch.17 v.22*
A merry heart doeth good like a medicine.

1245 *Old Testament: Proverbs ch.20 v.11*
Even a child is known by his doings.

1246 *Old Testament: Proverbs ch.21 v.9*
It is better to dwell in a corner of the housetop, than with a brawling woman in a wide house.

1247 *Old Testament: Proverbs ch.22 v.6*
Train up a child in the way he should go: and when he is old, he will not depart from it.

1248 *Old Testament: Proverbs ch.24 v.3*
Through wisdom a house is built and through understanding it is established.

1249 *Old Testament: Proverbs ch.28 v.20*
He that maketh haste to be rich shall not be innocent.

1250 *Old Testament: Proverbs ch.31 v.6*
Give strong drink unto him that is ready to perish, and wine unto those that be of heavy hearts.

1251 *Old Testament: Revelation ch.7 v.3*
Hurt not the earth, neither the sea, nor the trees.

1252 *Old Testament: I Samuel ch.13 v.14*
A man after his own heart.

BIDAULT Georges 1899-1983
1253
The weak have one weapon: the errors of those who think they are strong.

BIERCE Ambrose 1842-c.1914
1254 *The Devil's Dictionary*
Acquaintance, n: a person whom we know well enough to borrow from, but not well enough to lend to.

1255 *The Devil's Dictionary*
Apologize, v: to lay the foundation for a future offence.

1256 *The Devil's Dictionary*
Christian, n: one who believes that the New Testament is a divinely inspired book admirably suited to the spiritual needs of his neighbour.

1257 *The Devil's Dictionary*
Commendation, n: the tribute that we pay to achievements that resemble, but do not equal, our own.

1258 *The Devil's Dictionary*
Cynic, n: a blackguard whose faulty vision sees things as they are, not as they ought to be.

1259 *The Devil's Dictionary*
Destiny, n: a tyrant's authority for crime and a fool's excuse for failure.

1260 *The Devil's Dictionary*
Debauche, n: one who has so earnestly pursued pleasure that he has had the misfortune to overtake it.

1261 *The Devil's Dictionary*
Education, n: that which discloses to the wise and disguises from the foolish their lack of understanding.

1262 *The Devil's Dictionary*
Epitaph, n: an inscription on a tomb showing that virtues acquired by death have a retroactive effect.

1263 *The Devil's Dictionary*
History, n: an account mostly false, of events, mostly unimportant, which are brought about by rulers, mostly knaves, and soldiers, mostly fools.

1264 *The Devil's Dictionary*
Idiot, n: a member of a large and powerful tribe whose influence in human affairs has always been dominant and controlling.

1265 *The Devil's Dictionary*
Ignoramus, n: a person unacquainted with certain kinds of knowledge familiar to yourself, and having certain other kinds that you know nothing about.

1266 *The Devil's Dictionary*
Infidel, n: in New York, one who does not believe in the Christian religion; in Constantinople, one who does.

1267 *The Devil's Dictionary*
Litigant, n: a person about to give up his skin for the hope of retaining his bone.

1268 *The Devil's Dictionary*
Mausoleum, n: the final and funniest folly of the rich.

1269 *The Devil's Dictionary*
Marriage, n: the state or condition of a community consisting of a master, a mistress, and two slaves, making, in all, two.

1270 *The Devil's Dictionary*
Painting, n: the art of protecting flat surfaces from the weather and exposing them to the critic.

1271 *The Devil's Dictionary*
Peace, n: in international affairs, a period of cheating between two periods of fighting.

1272 *The Devil's Dictionary*
Philanthropist, n: a rich (and usually bald) old gentleman who has trained himself to grin while his conscience is picking his pocket.

1273 *The Devil's Dictionary*
Piracy, n: commerce without its folly-swaddles - just as God made it.

1274 *The Devil's Dictionary*
To be positive: to be mistaken at the top of one's voice.

1275 *The Devil's Dictionary*
Pray, v: to ask that the laws of the universe be annulled in behalf of a single petitioner - confessedly unworthy.

BIGOD Roger, Earl of Norfolk 1245-1306
1276 *The Chronicle of Walter of Guisbrough*
By God, O King, I will neither go nor hang!

BILLINGS Josh 1818-1885
1277
Adversity has the same effect on a man that severe training has on the pugilist - it reduces him to his fighting weight.

1278
When a man comes to me for advice, I find out the kind of advice he wants, and I give it to him.

1279
The happiest time in any man's life is when he is in red-hot pursuit of a dollar with a reasonable prospect of overtaking it.

1280
Every man has his follies - and often they are the most interesting things he has got.

1281
As a general thing, when a woman wears the pants in a family, she has a good right to them.

1282
Nature never makes any blunders; when she makes a fool she means it.

1283
Pity costs nothin' and ain't worth nothin'.

1284
Laughter is the sensation of feeling good all over, and showing it principally in one spot.

1285
The trouble ain't that people are ignorant: it's that they know so much that ain't so.

1286
The truly innocent are those who not only are guiltless themselves, but who think others are.

1287
My advice to those who are about to begin, in earnest, the journey of life, is to take their heart in one hand and a club in the other.

1288
Most men would rather be charged with malice than with making a blunder.

1289
To bring up a child in the way he should go, travel that way yourself once in a while.

1290
There are some people so addicted to exaggeration that they can't tell the truth without lying.

1291
It is a very delicate job to forgive a man, without lowering him in his estimation, and yours too.

1292
It is not only the most difficult thing to know oneself, but the most inconvenient one, too.

1293
When a man gets talking about himself, he seldom fails to be eloquent and often reaches the sublime.

1294
As scarce as truth is, the supply has always been in excess of the demand.

1295
There are many people who mistake their imagination for their memory.

1296 *Josh Billings' Wit and Humour*
'Vote early and vote often' is the Politishun's golden rule.

BINGER William
1297
A man is a person who will pay two dollars for a one-dollar item he wants. A woman will pay one dollar for a two-dollar item she doesn't want.

BINYON Laurence 1869-1943
1298 *'For the Fallen'*
They shall grow not old, as we that are left

grow old.
Age shall not weary them, nor the years
condemn.
At the going down of the sun and in the
morning
We will remember them.

BIRNEY Earle 1904-
1299
The essentials of poetry are rhythm, dance
and the human voice.

BIRRELL Augustine 1850-1933
1300 *Obiter Dicta 'Carlyle'*
The great dust-heap called 'history'.

BIRT John 1944-
1301
Politicians have a higher claim to speak for
the people than journalists.

BISMARCK Prince Otto von 1815-1898
1302
Politics is the art of the possible.

1303
Place in the hands of the King of Prussia
the strongest possible military power, then
he will be able to carry out the policy you
wish; this policy cannot succeed through
speeches, and shooting-matches, and
songs; it can only be carried out through
blood and iron.

1304
If there is ever another war in Europe, it
will come out of some damned silly thing
in the Balkans.

1305
When you say that you agree to a thing in
principle, you mean that you have not the
slightest intention of carrying it out.

1306
Prussia needs only one ally: the German
people.

1307
You can trust all Englishmen except those
who speak French.

BLACK Conrad 1944-
1308
Humility is a good quality, but it can be
overdone.

BLACKBURN Tony
1309
Why should the Pope be any closer to God
than I am?

BLACKER Valentine 1728-1823
1310 *'Oliver's Advice'*
Put your trust in God, my boys, and keep
your powder dry.

BLACKSTONE Sir William 1723-1780
1311 *Commentaries on the Laws of England*
The king never dies.

1312 *Commentaries on the Laws of England*
The Royal Navy of England hath ever been
its greatest defence and ornament; its
ancient and natural strength; the floating
bulwark of the island.

1313 *Commentaries on the Laws of England*
That the king can do no wrong, is a
necessary and fundamental principle of the
English constitution.

1314 *Commentaries on the Laws of England*
It is better that ten guilty persons escape
than one innocent suffer.

BLADE Toledo
1315
A great many open minds should be
closed for repairs.

BLAIR Tony 1953-
1316
Attendance at school is non-negotiable.

BLAKE Eubie 1883-1983
1317 *(on reaching 100)*
If I'd known I was gonna live this long, I'd
have taken better care of myself.

BLAKE William 1757-1827
1318
He who desires, but acts not, breeds
pestilence.

1319
The Old and New Testaments are the Great
Code of Art.

1320
Some are born to sweet delight,
Some are born to endless night.

1321
Improvement makes straight roads; but the crooked roads without improvement are roads of genius.

1322 *(attributed)*
I love fun, but too much is abominable.

1323 *'Auguries of Innocence'*
To see a world in a grain of sand
And a heaven in a wild flower
Hold infinity in the palm of your hand
And eternity in an hour.

1324 *'Auguries of Innocence'*
A robin red breast in a cage
Puts all Heaven in a rage.

1325 *'Auguries of Innocence'*
He who shall hurt the little wren
Shall never be beloved by men
He who the ox to wrath has moved
Shall never be by woman loved.

1326 *'Auguries of Innocence'*
A truth that's told with bad intent
Beats all the lies you can invent.

1327 *Book of Thel*
Can Wisdom be put in a silver rod,
Or Love in a golden bowl?

1328 *'A Divine Image'*
Cruelty has a human heart,
And Jealousy a human face;
Terror the human form divine,
And Secrecy the human dress.

1329 *The Everlasting Gospel*
Was Jesus gentle or did he
Give any marks of gentility
When twelve years old he ran away
And left his parents in dismay.

1330 *Jerusalem*
Ever weeping Paddington.

1331 *Jerusalem*
He who would do good to another, must do it in minute particulars
General good is the plea of the scoundrel, hypocrite and flatterer.

1332 *Jerusalem 'To the Jews'*
The fields from Islington to Marybone,
To Primrose Hill and Saint John's Wood
Were builded over with pillars of gold;

And there Jerusalem's pillars stood.

1333 *The Marriage of Heaven and Hell*
Without contraries is no progression.
Attraction and repulsion, reason and energy, love and hate, are necessary to human existence.

1334 *The Marriage of Heaven and Hell*
Energy is Eternal Delight.

1335 *The Marriage of Heaven and Hell*
The road of excess leads to the palace of wisdom.

1336 *The Marriage of Heaven and Hell*
Prudence is a rich, ugly, old maid courted by incapacity.

1337 *The Marriage of Heaven and Hell*
A fool sees not the same tree that a wise man sees.

1338 *The Marriage of Heaven and Hell*
If the fool would persist in his folly he would become wise.

1339 *The Marriage of Heaven and Hell*
Prisons are built with stones of Law, brothels with bricks of Religion.

1340 *The Marriage of Heaven and Hell*
The pride of the peacock is the glory of God.
The lust of the goat is the bounty of God.
The wrath of the lion is the wisdom of God.
The nakedness of woman is the work of God.

1341 *The Marriage of Heaven and Hell*
Damn braces: Bless relaxes.

1342 *The Marriage of Heaven and Hell*
Exuberance is beauty.

1343 *The Marriage of Heaven and Hell*
If the doors of perception were cleansed everything would appear to man as it is, infinite.

1344 *Milton [preface]*
And did those feet in ancient time
Walk upon England's mountains green?
And was the holy Lamb of God
On England's pleasant pastures seen?

And did the Countenance Divine
Shine forth upon our clouded hills?
And was Jerusalem builded here
Among these dark Satanic mills?

1345 *Milton [preface]*
Bring me my bow of burning gold:
Bring me my arrows of desire:
Bring me my spear: O clouds, unfold!
Bring me my chariot of fire.

1346 *Milton [preface]*
I will not cease from mental fight,
Nor shall my sword sleep in my hand,
Till we have built Jerusalem,
In England's green and pleasant land.

1347 *MS Note-Book*
The errors of a wise man make your rule
Rather than the perfections of a fool.

1348 *MS Note-Book*
Great things are done when men and
mountains meet
This is not done by jostling in the street.

1349 *Note-book*
Never seek to tell thy love, Love that never
told can be.

1350 *Note-book*
What is it men in women do require?
The lineaments of gratified desire.
What is it women do in men require?
The lineaments of gratified desire.

1351 *For the Sexes: The Gates of Paradise*
[prologue]
Mutual Forgiveness of each vice,
Such are the Gates of Paradise.

1352 *'The Smile'*
There is a Smile of Love,
And there is a Smile of Deceit,
And there is a Smile of Smiles
In which these two Smiles meet.

1353 *Songs of Experience 'The Clod and the
Pebble'*
Love seeketh not itself to please,
Nor for itself hath any care;
But for another gives its ease,
And builds a Heaven in Hell's despair.

1354 *Songs of Experience 'The Clod and the
Pebble'*
Love seeketh only Self to please,
To bind another to its delight,
Joys in another's loss of ease,
And builds a Hell in Heaven's despite.

1355 *Songs of Experience 'Infant Sorrow'*
My mother groaned! my father wept.
Into the dangerous world I leapt:
Helpless, naked, piping loud;
Like a fiend hid in a cloud.

1356 *Songs of Experience 'A Poison Tree'*
I was angry with my friend;
I told my wrath, my wrath did end.
I was angry with my foe:
I told it not, my wrath did grow.

1357 *Songs of Experience 'The Tiger'*
Tyger Tyger, burning bright,
In the forests of the night;
What immortal hand or eye,
Could frame thy fearful symmetry?

1358 *Songs of Innocence 'On Another's
Sorrow'*
Can I see another's woe,
And not be in sorrow too.
Can I see another's grief,
And not seek for kind relief.

1359 *Songs of Innocence 'The Divine Image'*
To Mercy Pity Peace and Love,
All pray in their distress.

1360 *Songs of Innocence 'The Divine Image'*
For Mercy has a human heart
Pity a human face:
And Love, the human form divine,
And peace, the human dress.

BLANCH Lesley 1907-
1361 *The Wilder Shores of Love*
She was an Amazon. Her whole life was
spent riding at breakneck speed towards
the wilder shores of love.

BLESSINGTON Lady 1789-1849
1362
Religion converts despair, which destroys,
into resignation, which submits.

BLIXEN Karen 1885-1962
1363
In the mind and nature of a man a secret is

an ugly thing, like a hidden physical defect.

1364 *Out of Africa*
A herd of elephant ... pacing along as if they had an appointment at the end of the world.

1365 *Seven Gothic Tales 'The Dreamers'*
What is man, when you come to think upon him, but a minutely set, ingenious machine for turning, with infinite artfulness, the red wine of Shiraz into urine?

BLOCH Arthur
1366
A conclusion is the place where you got tired of thinking.

BLOOMFIELD Harold H.
1367
The irony of love is that it guarantees some degree of anger, fear and criticism.

BLUM Norbert
1368
Politics is like football - it doesn't matter whether you win 3-1 or 1-0, you still get 2 points.

BLUNDEN Edmund 1896-1974
1369 *'The Kiss'*
I am for the woods against the world,
But are the woods for me?

1370 *'Report on Experience'*
I have been young, and now am not too old;
And I have seen the righteous forsaken,
His health, his honour and his quality taken.
This is not what we were formerly told.

1371 *'The Resignation'*
This was my country and it may be yet,
But something flew between me and the sun.

BLY Robert 1926-
1372 *'Driving Through Minnesota During Hanoi Bombings'*
Terror just before death,
Shoulders torn, shot
From helicopters, the boy
Tortured with the telephone generator,

'I felt sorry for him
And blew his head off with a shotgun.'

BLYTHE Ronald 1922-
1373 *The Age of Illusion*
As for the British churchman, he goes to church as he goes to the bathroom, with the minimum of fuss and with no explanation if he can help it.

BODENHEIM Maxwell 1893-1954
1374
Poetry is the impish attempt to paint the colour of the wind.

BOESE Paul
1375
Nature thrives on patience; man on impatience.

BOETHIUS 476-524
1376 *De Consolatione Philosophiae*
Who can give a law to lovers? Love is a greater law unto itself.

1377 *De Consolatione Philosophiae*
For in every ill-turn of fortune the most unhappy sort of unfortunate man is the one who has been happy.

BOGART Humphrey 1899-1957
1378
The whole world is about three drinks behind.

1379 *in Casablanca*
"Of all the gin joints in all the towns in all the world, she walks into mine."

1380 *in Casablanca*
"Here's looking at you, kid."

1381 *in In A Lonely Place*
"I was born when you kissed me. I died when you left me. I lived a few weeks while you loved me."

1382 *in The Maltese Falcon*
"You're an angel. I'll wait for you. If they hang you, I'll always remember you."

BOHR Niels 1885-1962
1383
One of the favourite maxims of my father was the distinction between the two sorts of truths, profound truths recognized by the fact that the opposite is also a

profound truth, in contrast to trivialities where opposites are obviously absurd.

1384
The opposite of a correct statement is a false statement. But the opposite of a profound truth may well be another profound truth.

BOILEAU Nicolas 1636-1711
1385
Hasten slowly, and without losing heart, put your work twenty times upon the anvil.

1386 *L'Art poétique*
A fool can always find a greater fool to admire him.

1387 *Satire (2) A M.Molière*
Of every four words I write, I strike out three.

BOK Derek 1930-
1388
If you think education is expensive - try ignorance.

BOLINGBROKE 1st Viscount 1678-1751
1389 *Observations, Anecdotes, and Characters*
The great mistake is that of looking upon men as virtuous, or thinking that they can be made so by laws.

1390 *Observations, Anecdotes, and Characters*
The greatest art of a politician is to render vice serviceable to the cause of virtue.

BOLITHO William
1391
A very beautiful woman hardly ever leaves a clear-cut impression of features and shape in the memory: usually there remains only an aura of living colour.

BOLT Robert 1924-1995
1392 *A Man for All Seasons*
Morality's not practical. Morality's a gesture.
A complicated gesture learned from books.

1393 *A Man for All Seasons*
It profits a man nothing to give his soul for the whole world ... But for Wales - !

BOLTON Robert
1394
A belief is not merely an idea the mind possesses; it is an idea that possesses the mind.

BOMBECK Erma 1927-
1395
Guilt: the gift that goes on giving.

BONAPARTE Napoleon 1822-1891
1396
There are only two forces that unite men - fear and interest.

1397
The first virtue in a soldier is endurance of fatigue; courage is only the second virtue.

1398
As to moral courage, I have very rarely met with the two o'clock in the morning kind. I mean unprepared courage, that which is necessary on an unexpected occasion, and which, in spite of the most unforeseen events, leaves full freedom of judgement and decision.

1399
All celebrated people lose dignity on a close view.

1400
Fashion condemns us to many follies; the greatest is to make oneself its slave.

1401
The art of governing consists in not letting men grow old in their jobs.

1402
A leader is a dealer in hope.

1403
How many really capable men are children more than once during the day?

1404
My downfall raises me to infinite heights.

1405
If they want peace, nations should avoid the pinpricks that precede cannon shots.

1406
Riches do not consist in the possession of treasures, but in the use made of them.

1407
If you start to take Vienna - take Vienna.

BOND Edward 1934-
1408
Law and order is one of the steps taken to
maintain injustice.

BONHOEFFER Dietrich 1906-1945
1409
One's task is not to turn the world upside
down, but to do what is necessary at the
given place and with a due consideration
of reality.

The BOOK of COMMON PRAYER
1410 *Articles of Religion no.37*
The Bishop of Rome hath no jurisdiction in
this Realm of England.

1411 *The Burial of the Dead, First Anthem*
Man that is born of a woman hath but a
short time to live, and is full of misery.

1412 *The Burial of the Dead, First Anthem*
In the midst of life we are in death.

1413 *The Burial of the Dead, Interment*
Forasmuch as it hath pleased Almighty
God of his great mercy to take unto
himself the soul of our dear brother here
departed, we therefore commit his body to
the ground; earth to earth, ashes to ashes,
dust to dust; in sure and certain hope of
the Resurrection to eternal life, through
our Lord Jesus Christ.

1414 *The Litany*
From all evil and mischief; from sin, from
the crafts and assaults of the devil; from
thy wrath, and from everlasting
damnation,
Good Lord, deliver us.

1415 *Morning Prayer, General Confession*
We have erred, and strayed from thy ways
like lost sheep. We have followed too
much the devices and desires of our own
hearts.

1416 *Morning Prayer, General Confession*
We have left undone those things which
we ought to have done; And we have done
those things which we ought not to have
done; And there is no health in us.

1417 *Morning Prayer, The Third Collect, for
Grace*
Grant that this day we fall into no sin,
neither run into any kind of danger.

1418 *Morning Prayer, Versicle*
Give peace in our time, O Lord.

1419 *Psalm 23 v.1*
The Lord is my shepherd: therefore can I
lack nothing.

1420 *Psalm 23 v.4*
Yea, though I walk through the valley of
the shadow of death, I will fear no evil: for
thou art with me; thy rod and thy staff
comfort me.

1421 *Psalm 25 v.6*
O remember not the sins and offences of
my youth.

1422 *Psalm 37 v.11*
The meek-spirited shall possess the earth.

1423 *Psalm 46 v.1*
God is our hope and strength: a very
present help in trouble.

1424 *Psalm 71 v.8*
Cast me not away in the time of age:
forsake me not when my strength faileth
me.

1425 *Psalm 90 v.4*
For a thousand years in thy sight are but as
yesterday: seeing that is past as a watch in
the night.

1426 *Psalm 90 v.12*
So teach us to number our days: that we
may apply our hearts unto wisdom.

1427 *Psalm 93 v.1*
He hath made the round world so sure:
that it cannot be moved.

1428 *Psalm 98 v.1*
O sing unto the Lord a new song: for he
hath done marvellous things.

1429 *Psalm 100 v.1*
Be ye sure that the Lord he is God: it is he
that hath made us, and not we ourselves;
we are his people, the sheep of his pasture.

1430 *Psalm 122 v.1*
I was glad when they said unto me: We
will go into the house of the Lord.

1431 *Psalm 136 v.1*
O give thanks unto the Lord, for he is
gracious: and his mercy endureth for ever.

1432 *Psalm 137 v.1*
By the waters of Babylon we sat down and
wept: when we remembered thee, O Sion.

1433 *Psalm 139 v.13*
I will give thanks unto thee, for I am
fearfully and wonderfully made.

1434 *Solemnization of Matrimony, Wedding*
With this Ring I thee wed, with my body I
thee worship, and with all my worldly
goods I thee endow.

1435 *Solemnization of Matrimony, Wedding*
Those whom God hath joined together let
no man put asunder.

BOORSTIN Daniel J. 1914-
1436
The deeper problems connected with
advertising come less from the
unscrupulousness of our 'deceivers' than
from our pleasure in being deceived; less
from the desire to seduce than from the
desire to be seduced.

1437
Best-sellerism is the star system of the
book world. A (best-seller) is a celebrity
among books. It is a book known
primarily (sometimes exclusively) for its
well-knowness.

1438
A sign of a celebrity is often that his name
is worth more than his services.

1439
Some are born great, some achieve
greatness, and some hire public relations
officers.

1440 *The Image*
A best-seller was a book which somehow
sold well simply because it was selling
well.

BOOTH Edwin 1833-1893
1441
An actor is a sculptor who carves in snow.

BOOTH John Wilkes 1838-1865
1442 *(having shot President Lincoln)*
The South is avenged.

BOREN James H. 1925-
1443
Guidelines for bureaucrats:
(1) When in charge, ponder.
(2) When in trouble, delegate.
(3) When in doubt, mumble.

BORGE Victor 1909-
1444
Laughter is the shortest distance between
two people.

1445 *(playing to a half-filled house)*
Flint must be an extremely wealthy town; I
see that each of you bought two or three
seats.

BORGES Jorge Luis 1899-1986
1446
The Falklands thing was a fight between
two bald men over a comb.

1447
What you really value is what you miss,
not what you have.

BORGIA Cesare 1476-1507
1448 *(Motto inscribed on his sword)*
Caesar or nothing.

BORLAND Hal
1449
Summer ends, and Autumn comes, and he
who would have it otherwise would have
high tide always and a full moon every
night.

BÖRNE Ludwig 1786-1837
1450
Women are most adorable when they are
afraid; that's why they frighten so easily.

BORROW George 1803-1881
1451 *Lavengro*
A losing trade, I assure you, sir: literature
is a drug.

1452 *Lavengro*
Youth will be served, every dog has his day, and mine has been a fine one.

1453 *Lavengro [preface]*
There are no countries in the world less known by the British than these selfsame British Islands.

BORSODI Ralph
1454
There is less leisure now than in the Middle Ages, when one third of the year consisted of holidays and festivals.

BOSQUET Pierre 1810-1861
1455 *(of the Charge of the Light Brigade at Balaclava)*
It is magnificent, but it is not war.

BOSSIDY John Collins 1860-1928
1456 *(at Holy Cross College)*
And this is good old Boston,
The home of the bean and the cod,
Where the Lowells talk to the Cabots
And the Cabots talk only to God.

BOSSUET Jacques-Bénigne 1627-1704
1457
The inexorable boredom that is at the core of life.

BOSWELL James 1740-1795
1458 *Boswell's London Journal*
We may be in some degree whatever character we choose.

1459 *Journal of a Tour to the Hebrides*
We [Boswell and Johnson] are both Tories; both convinced of the utility of monarchical power, and both lovers of that reverence and affection for a sovereign which constitute loyalty, a principle which I take to be absolutely extinguished in Britain.

1460 *Journal of a Tour to the Hebrides*
A page of my Journal is like a cake of portable soup. A little may be diffused into a considerable portion.

1461 *The Life of Samuel Johnson*
JOHNSON: Well, we had a good talk.
BOSWELL: Yes Sir; you tossed and gored several persons.

1462 *The Life of Samuel Johnson*
A man, indeed, is not genteel when he gets drunk; but most vices may be committed very genteelly: a man may debauch his friend's wife genteelly: he may cheat at cards genteelly.

BOTTOMLEY Gordon 1874-1948
1463 *'To Ironfounders and Others'*
Your worship is your furnaces,
Which, like old idols, lost obscenes,
Have molten bowels; your vision is
Machines for making more machines.

BOTTOMLEY Horatio 1860-1933
1464 *(Speech at the Oxford Union)*
Gentlemen: I have not had your advantages. What poor education I have received has been gained in the University of Life.

BOTTOMLEY Virginia 1948-
1465
Smoking is a dying habit.

BOUCICAULT Dion c.1820-1890
1466
I wish Adam had died with all his ribs in his body.

BOULDING Kenneth
1467
In any evolutionary process, even in the arts, the search for novelty becomes corrupting.

1468
Canada has no cultural unity, no linguistic unity, no religious unity, no economic unity, no geographic unity. All it has is unity.

1469
Nothing fails like success because we don't learn from it. We learn only from failure.

BOULEZ Pierre 1925-
1470
The function of pop music is to be consumed.

1471
Populism - as we all know - frequently transforms itself into fascism.

BOULTON Sir Harold Edwin 1859-1935
1472 *'Glorious Devon'*
When Adam and Eve were dispossessed
Of the garden hard by Heaven,
They planted another one down in the
west,
'Twas Devon, glorious Devon!

1473 *'Skye Boat Song'*
Speed, bonnie boat, like a bird on the
wing,
'Onward,' the sailors cry;
Carry the lad that's born to be king,
Over the sea to Skye.

BOURDILLON F.W. 1852-1921
1474 *Among the Flowers 'Light'*
The night has a thousand eyes,
And the day but one;
Yet the light of the bright world dies,
With the dying sun.

The mind has a thousand eyes,
And the heart but one;
Yet the light of a whole life dies,
When love is done.

BOURJAILY Vance
1475
Every man, even the most blessed, needs a
little more than average luck to survive
this world.

BOWEN Catherine Drinker
1476
Chamber music - a conversation between
friends.

BOWEN E.E. 1836-1901
1477 *'Forty Years On' (Harrow School Song)*
Forty years on, when afar and asunder
Parted are those who are singing to-day.

1478 *'Forty Years On' (Harrow School Song)*
Follow up! Follow up! Follow up! Follow
up! Follow up!
Till the field ring again and again,
With the tramp of the twenty-two men,
Follow up!

BOWEN Elizabeth 1899-1973
1479
With three or more people there is
something bold in the air: direct things get
said which would frighten two people

alone and conscious of each inch of their
nearness to one another. To be three is to
be in public - you feel safe.

1480
Each of us keeps, battened down inside
himself, a sort of lunatic giant - impossible
socially, but full-scale. It's the knockings
and batterings we sometimes hear in each
other that keep our intercourse from utter
banality.

1481
In big houses in which things are done
properly, there is always the religious
element. The diurnal cycle is observed
with more feeling when there are servants
to do the work.

1482 *The Death of the Heart*
The innocent are so few that two of them
seldom meet - when they do, their victims
lie strewn around.

1483 *The Death of the Heart*
It is about five o'clock in an evening that
the first hour of spring strikes - autumn
arrives in the early morning, but spring at
the close of a winter day.

1484 *The Death of the Heart*
Some people are moulded by their
admirations, others by their hostilities.

1485 *(of Edith Sitwell)*
A high altar on the move.

1486 *The House in Paris*
Fate is not an eagle, it creeps like a rat.

BOWEN Ezra
1487
If thee marries for money, thee surely will
earn it.

BOWEN Lord 1835-1894
1488
When I hear of an 'equity' in a case like
this, I am reminded of a blind man in a
dark room - looking for a black hat - which
isn't there.

1489
The rain, it raineth on the just
And also on the unjust fella:
But chiefly on the just, because

The unjust steals the just's umbrella.

BOWER Walter
1490
The wolf was sick, he vowed a monk to be;
But when he got well, a wolf once more
was he.

BOWERING George
1491
nobody
belongs anywhere,
even the
Rocky Mountains
are still
moving.

BOWIE David 1947-
1492 *'Space Oddity'*
Ground control to Major Tom.

BOWMAN Louis Nelson
1493
Another thing about capitalism -
everybody knows who's in Grant's tomb.

BOWMAN Peter
1494
Only man, among living things, says
prayers. Or needs to.

BOWRA Sir Maurice 1898-1971
1495 *John Betjeman Summoned by Bells*
I'm a man more dined against than dining.

BOYD-ORR Lord 1880-1971
1496
If people have to choose between freedom
and sandwiches they will take sandwiches.

BOYER Charles 1899-1978
1497
A French woman, when double-crossed,
will kill her rival. The Italian woman
would rather kill her deceitful lover. The
Englishwoman simply breaks off relations
- but they will all console themselves with
another man.

BOYSE J.F.
1498
It would be a great advantage to some
schoolmasters if they would steal two
hours a day from their pupils, and give
their own minds the benefit of the robbery.

BRACKELL Fogg
1499
Facts in books, statistics in encyclopedias,
the ability to use them in men's heads.

BRADBURY Malcolm 1932-
1500 *Eating People is Wrong*
The English have the most rigid code of
immorality in the world.

BRADFORD John c.1510-1555
1501 *(on seeing a group of criminals led to
execution)*
But for the grace of God there goes John
Bradford.

BRADLEE Benjamin 1921-
1502
News is the first rough draft of history.

BRADLEY Bill
1503
Becoming number one is easier than
remaining number one.

BRADLEY F.H. 1846-1924
1504
In all of us, the excited amateur has to die
before the artist can be born.

1505
Few people would not be the worse for
complete sincerity.

1506 *Appearance and Reality [preface]*
Where everthing is bad it must be good to
know the worst.

BRADLEY Omar 1893-1981
1507
The world has achieved brilliance without
wisdom, power without conscience. Ours
is a world of nuclear giants and ethical
infants.

1508
We have grasped the mystery of the atom,
and rejected the Sermon on the Mount.

BRADSHAW John 1602-1659
1509 *(at the trial of Charles I)*
Rebellion to tyrants is obedience to God.

BRADSTREET Anne c.1612-1672
1510 *'The Prologue'*
Let Greeks be Greeks, and Women what
they are,

Men have precedency, and still excel.

1511 'The Prologue'
This mean and unrefinèd stuff of mine,
Will make your glistering gold but more to
shine.

BRAMAH Ernest 1868-1942
1512 *The Wallet of Kai Lung*
The whole narrative is permeated with the
odour of joss-sticks and honourable high-
mindedness.

BRAMSTON James c.1694-1744
1513 *The Art of Politics*
What's not destroyed by Time's devouring
hand?
Where's Troy, and where's the Maypole in
the Strand?

BRANCUSI Constantin 1876-1957
1514
Architecture is inhabited sculpture.

BRANDEIS Louis Dembitz 1856-1941
1515
The most important office is that of private
citizen.

1516
We can have democracy in this country or
we can have great wealth concentrated in
the hands of a few, but we can't have both.

BRANDEN Nathaniel
1517
For the rational, psychologically healthy
man, the desire for pleasure is the desire to
celebrate his control over reality. For the
neurotic, the desire for pleasure is the
desire to escape from reality.

BRANDO Marlon 1924-
1518
An actor's a guy who, if you ain't talking
about him, ain't listening.

1519 *in On The Waterfront*
"I coulda been a contender. I coulda had
class and been somebody."

BRAQUE Georges 1882-1963
1520 *Le Jour et la nuit: Cahiers*
Art is meant to disturb, science reassures.

1521 *Le Jour et la nuit: Cahiers*
Truth exists; only lies are invented.

**BRATTON John W. and KENNEDY
James B.**
1522 *'The Teddy Bear's Picnic'*
If you go down in the woods today
You're sure of a big surprise
If you go down in the woods today
You'd better go in disguise
For every Bear that ever there was
Will gather there for certain because,
Today's the day the Teddy Bears have their
Picnic.

BRAUN Wernher von 1912-1977
1523
Everything in space obeys the laws of
physics. If you know these laws, and obey
them, space will treat you kindly. And
don't tell me man doesn't belong out there.
Man belongs wherever he wants to go -
and he'll do plenty well when he gets
there.

1524
Basic research is when I'm doing what I
don't know what I'm doing.

BRECHT Bertholt 1898-1956
1525
The resistible rise of Arturo Ui.

1526
Fearful is the seductive power of goodness.

1527
People are too durable, that's their main
trouble. They can do too much to
themselves, they last too long.

1528
Poverty makes you sad as well as wise.

1529
Today every invention is received with a
cry of triumph which soon turns into a cry
of fear.

1530
What happens to the hole when the cheese
is gone?

1531 *Mother Courage*
Peace is nothing but slovenliness, only war
creates order.

1532 *Mother Courage*
Don't tell me peace has broken out, when I've just bought some new supplies.

1533 *Mother Courage*
War is like love. It always finds a way.

1534 *The Threepenny Opera*
Food comes first, then morals.

1535 *The Threepenny Opera*
What is robbing a bank compared with founding a bank?

BRENAN Gerald 1894-1987
1536 *Thoughts in a Dry Season*
Those who have some means think that the most important thing in the world is love. The poor know that it is money.

1537 *Thoughts in a Dry Season*
Religions are kept alive by heresies, which are really sudden explosions of faith.

1538 *Thoughts in a Dry Season*
In a happy marriage, it is the wife who provides the climate, the husband the landscape.

BRENNAN Lynne
1539
Aggression is showing people you are out of control.

BRIDGE Ann N.
1540
In any relationship we feel an unconscious need to create, as it were, a new picture, a new edition of ourselves to present to the fresh person who claims our interest; for them, we in a strange sense wish to, and do, start life anew.

BRIDGES Robert 1844-1930
1541 *The Growth of Love*
Beauty sat with me all the summer day,
Awaiting the sure triumph of her eye;
Nor mark'd I till we parted, how, hard by,
Love in her train stood ready for his prey.

1542 *'London Snow'*
All night it fell, and when full inches seven
It lay in the depth of its uncompacted lightness,
The clouds blew off from a high and frosty heaven;

And all woke earlier for the unaccustomed brightness
Of the winter dawning, the strange unheavenly glare.

BRIDGMAN Percy Williams 1882-1961
1543
There is no adequate defence, except stupidity, against the impact of a new idea.

BRIGHT John 1811-1889
1544
I am for 'Peace, retrenchment, and reform'.

1545
England is the mother of Parliaments.

1546
The knowledge of the ancient languages is mainly a luxury.

1547 *(during the American Civil War)*
My opinion is that the Northern States will manage somehow to muddle through.

BRINKLEY David
1548
This is the first convention of the space age - where a candidate can promise the moon and mean it.

BRITTEN Benjamin 1913-1970
1549
I am an arrogant and impatient listener, but in the case of a few composers, a very few, when I hear a work I do not like, I am convinced that it is my own fault. Verdi is one of those composers.

BROCKWAY George
1550
Labour is not a commodity, or a standard, or a means to an ulterior end, but an end in itself.

BRONOWSKI Jacob 1908-1974
1551
We are all afraid - for our confidence, for the future, for the world. That is the nature of the human imagination. Yet every man, every civilization, has gone forward because of its engagement with what it has set itself to do. The personal commitment and the emotional commitment working together as one, has made the Ascent of Man.

1552
We are all shot through with enough motives to make a massacre, any day of the week that we want to give them their head.

1553 *The Ascent of Man*
The world can only be grasped by action, not by contemplation.

1554 *The Ascent of Man*
The essence of science: ask an impertinent question, and you are on the way to a pertinent answer.

BRONTÉ Charlotte 1816-1855
1555 *Jane Eyre*
Reader, I married him.

1556 *Shirley*
Of late years an abundant shower of curates has fallen upon the North of England.

1557 *Shirley*
Be a governess! Better be a slave at once!

BRONTÉ Emily 1818-1848
1558 *'Remembrance'*
Cold in the earth - and fifteen wild Decembers,
From those brown hills, have melted into spring.

1559 *'Remembrance'*
But when the days of golden dreams had perished,
And even Despair was powerless to destroy,
Then did I learn how existence could be cherished,
Strengthened, and fed without the aid of joy.

1560 *Wuthering Heights*
My love for Heathcliff resembles the eternal rocks beneath - a source of little visible delight, but necessary.

BROOKE Rupert 1887-1915
1561 *'The Chilterns'*
And I shall find some girl perhaps,
And a better one than you,
With eyes as wise, but kindlier,
And lips as soft, but true.
And I dare say she will do.

1562 *'The Dead'*
Blow out, you bugles, over the rich Dead!
There's none of these so lonely and poor of old,
But, dying, has made us rarer gifts than gold.
These laid the world away; poured out the red
Sweet wine of youth; gave up the years to be
Of work and joy, and that unhoped serene,
That men call age; and those that would have been,
Their sons, they gave, their immortality.

1563 *'The Dead'*
Honour has come back, as a king, to earth,
And paid his subjects with a royal wage;
And Nobleness walks in our ways again;
And we have come into our heritage.

1564 *'Heaven'*
Fish say, they have their stream and pond;
But is there anything beyond?

1565 *'The Hill'*
And when we die
All's over that is ours; and life burns on
Through other lovers, other lips.

1566 *'The Life Beyond'*
I thought when love for you died, I should die.
It's dead. Alone, mostly strangely, I live on.

1567 *'The Old Vicarage, Grantchester'*
Unkempt about those hedges blows
An English unofficial rose.

1568 *'The Old Vicarage, Grantchester'*
Curates, long dust, will come and go
On lissom, clerical, printless toe;
And oft between the boughs is seen
The sly shade of a Rural Dean.

1569 *'The Old Vicarage, Grantchester'*
God! I will pack, and take a train,
And get me to England once again!
For England's the one land, I know,
Where men with Splendid Hearts may go.

1570 *'The Old Vicarage, Grantchester'*
For Cambridge people rarely smile,
Being urban, squat, and packed with guile.

1571 *'The Old Vicarage, Grantchester'*
Stands the Church clock at ten to three
And is there honey still for tea?

1572 *'Peace'*
Now, God be thanked Who has matched
us with His hour,
And caught our youth, and wakened us
from sleeping,
With hand made sure, clear eye, and
sharpened power,
To turn, as swimmers into cleanness
leaping.

1573 *'Peace'*
Naught broken save this body, lost but
breath;
Nothing to shake the laughing heart's long
peace there
But only agony, and that has ending;
And the worst friend and enemy is but
Death.

1574 *'The Soldier'*
If I should die, think only this of me:
That there's some corner of a foreign field
That is for ever England. There shall be
In that rich earth a richer dust concealed;
A dust whom England bore, shaped, made
aware,
Gave, once, her flowers to love, her ways
to roam,
A body of England's, breathing English air,
Washed by the rivers, blest by suns of
home.

BROOKNER Anita 1938-
1575 *Hotel du Lac*
Good women always think it is their fault
when someone else is being offensive. Bad
women never take the blame for anything.

BROOKS Mel 1926-
1576
Look at Jewish history. Unrelieved
lamenting would be intolerable. So, for
every ten Jews beating their breasts, God
designated one to be crazy and amuse the
breast-beaters. By the time I was five I
knew I was that one.

1577
Humour is just another defence against the
universe.

1578
Every human being has hundreds of
separate people living under his skin. The
talent of a writer is his ability to give them
their separate names, identities,
personalities and have them relate to other
characters living with him.

BROOKS Thomas 1608-1680
1579
No good deed ever goes unpunished.

BROOKS Van Wyck 1886-1963
1580
Nothing is so soothing to our self-esteem
as to find our bad traits in our forebears. It
seems to absolve us.

BROUGHAM Lord 1778-1868
1581 *(attributed)*
Education makes a people easy to lead, but
difficult to drive; easy to govern, but
impossible to enslave.

BROUN Heywood 1888-1939
1582
Men build bridges and throw railroads
across deserts, and yet they contend
successfully that the job of sewing on a
button is beyond them. Accordingly, they
don't have to sew buttons.

1583
Sports do not build character. They reveal
it.

BROWN Arthur
1584
Music is only sound expressing certain
patterns, so to what extent is that sound
architecture and to what extent theatre?

BROWN Bob
1585
Behind every successful man there's a lot
of unsuccessful years.

BROWN H. Rap 1943-
1586
I say violence is necessary. It is as
American as cherry pie.

BROWN Jerry 1938-
1587
Prisons don't rehabilitate, they don't
punish, they don't protect, so what the hell

do they do?

1588
The government is becoming the family of last resort.

BROWN John Mason 1900-
1589
To many people dramatic criticism must seem like an attempt to tattoo soap bubbles.

1590
It is in the hard rockpile labour of seeking to win, hold, or deserve a reader's interest that the pleasant agony of writing comes in.

BROWN Lew 1893-1958
1591
Life is just a bowl of cherries.

BROWN Thomas 1663-1704
1592
I do not love thee, Doctor Fell,
The reason why I cannot tell;
But this alone I know full well,
I do not love thee, Doctor Fell.

1593 *Letters from the Dead to the Living*
A little before you made a leap into the dark.

BROWNE Cecil 1932-
1594 *(reply to verse by William Norman Ewer)*
But not so odd
As those who choose
A Jewish God,
But spurn the Jews.

BROWNE Sir Thomas 1605-1682
1595
The vices we scoff at in others, laugh at us within ourselves.

1596 *The Garden of Cyrus*
The quincunx of heaven runs low, and 'tis time to close the five ports of knowledge.

1597 *Hydriotaphia*
Men have lost their reason in nothing so much as their religion, wherein stones and clouts make martyrs.

1598 *Hydriotaphia*
The long habit of living indisposeth us for dying.

1599 *Hydriotaphia*
Generations pass while some trees stand, and old families last not three oaks.

1600 *Hydriotaphia*
Man is a noble animal, splendid in ashes, and pompous in the grave.

1601 *Religio Medici*
Who can speak of eternity without a solecism, or think thereof without an ecstasy? Time we may comprehend, 'tis but five days elder than ourselves.

1602 *Religio Medici*
I have often admired the mystical way of Pythagoras, and the secret magic of numbers.

1603 *Religio Medici*
All things are artificial, for nature is the art of God.

1604 *Religio Medici*
Obstinacy in a bad cause, is but constancy in a good.

1605 *Religio Medici*
Persecution is a bad and indirect way to plant religion.

1606 *Religio Medici*
All places, all airs make unto me one country; I am in England, everywhere, and under any meridian.

1607 *Religio Medici*
This trivial and vulgar way of coition; it is the foolishest act a wise man commits in all his life, nor is there any thing that will more deject his cooled imagination, when he shall consider what an odd and unworthy piece of folly he hath committed.

1608 *Religio Medici*
We all labour against our own cure, for death is the cure of all diseases.

1609 *Religio Medici*
For the world, I count it not an inn, but an hospital, and a place, not to live, but to die in.

1610 *Religio Medici*
There is surely a piece of divinity in us, something that was before the elements,

and owes no homage unto the sun.

1611 *Religio Medici*
We term sleep a death, and yet it is waking
that kills us, and destroys those spirits
which are the house of life.

BROWNE Sir William 1692-1774
1612 *Literary Anecdotes Reply to Trapp's
epigram*
The King to Oxford sent a troop of horse,
For Tories own no argument but force:
With equal skill to Cambridge books he
sent,
For Whigs admit no force but argument.

BROWNING Elizabeth Barrett 1806-1861
1613
Light tomorrow with today!

1614 *Aurora Leigh*
The works of women are symbolical.
We sew, sew, prick our fingers, dull our
sight,
Producing what? A pair of slippers, sir,
To put on when you're weary.

1615 *Aurora Leigh*
Since when was genius found respectable?

1616 *Aurora Leigh*
The devil's most devilish when
respectable.

1617 *'To George Sand - A Desire'*
Thou large-brained woman and large-
hearted man.

1618 *'Grief'*
I tell you, hopeless grief is passionless.

1619 *Sonnets from the Portuguese*
I love thee with the breath,
Smiles, tears, of all my life! - and if God
choose,
I shall but love thee better after death.

1620 *Sonnets from the Portuguese*
How do I love thee? Let me count the
ways.

1621 *Sonnets from the Portuguese*
If thou must love me, let it be for naught
Except for love's sake only.

BROWNING Robert 1812-1889
1622
When pain ends, gain ends too.

1623
Fit for the sunshine, so, it followed him
A happy-tempered bringer of the best
Out of the worst.

1624
Less is more.

1625
Who hears music, feels his solitude
peopled at once.

1626
Your children are not dead. They are just
waiting until the world deserves them.

1627 *Aristophanes' Apology*
But, thanks to wine-lees and democracy,
We've still our stage where truth calls
spade a spade!

1628 *'In a Balcony'*
A man can have but one life and one
death,
One heaven, one hell.

1629 *'In a Balcony'*
I count life just a stuff
To try the soul's strength on, educe the
man.

1630 *'Bishop Blougram's Apology'*
All we have gained then by our unbelief
Is a life of doubt diversified by faith,
For one of faith diversified by doubt:
We called the chess-board white - we call it
black.

1631 *'Bishop Blougram's Apology'*
No, when the fight begins within himself,
A man's worth something.

1632 *'Bishop Blougram's Apology'*
He said true things, but called them by
wrong names.

1633 *'A Blot in the 'Scutcheon'*
I was so young, I loved him so, I had
No mother, God forgot me, and I fell.

1634 *'Christmas-Eve'*
In the natural fog of the good man's mind.

1635 *'Confessions'*
What is he buzzing in my ears?
'Now that I come to die,
Do I view the world as a vale of tears?'
Ah, reverend sir, not I!

1636 *'Confessions'*
We loved, sir - used to meet:
How sad and bad and mad it was -
But then, how it was sweet!

1637 *'Cristina'*
She should never have looked at me,
If she meant I should not love her!

1638 *'A Death in the Desert'*
Stung by the splendour of a sudden
thought.

1639 *'A Death in the Desert'*
... Progress, man's distinctive mark alone,
Not God's, and not the beasts': God is,
they are,
Man partly is and wholly hopes to be.

1640 *A Death in the Desert*
Such ever was love's way; to rise, it stoops.

1641 *'Easter-Day'*
'Tis well averred,
A scientific faith's absurd.

1642 *'Fifine at the Fair'*
So absolutely good is truth, truth never
hurts
The teller.

1643 *'By the Fireside'*
How well I know what I mean to do
When the long dark autumn-evenings
come.

1644 *'By the Fireside'*
Oh, the little more, and how much it is!
And the little less, and what worlds away!

1645 *'By the Fireside'*
If two lives join, there is oft a scar,
They are one and one, with a shadowy
third;
One near one is too far.

1646 *'Home-Thoughts, from Abroad'*
Oh, to be in England
Now that April's there.

1647 *'Home-Thoughts, from the Sea'*
Nobly, nobly Cape Saint Vincent to the
North-west died away:
Sunset ran, one glorious blood-red, reeking
into Cadiz Bay.

1648 *'How they brought the Good News from
Ghent to Aix'*
I sprang to the stirrup, and Joris, and he;
I galloped, Dirk galloped, we galloped all
three.

1649 *The Inn Album*
Ignorance is not innocence but sin.

1650 *La Saisiaz [prologue]*
Good, to forgive;
Best, to forget!
Living, we fret;
Dying, we live.

1651 *'My Last Duchess'*
She had
A heart - how shall I say? - too soon made
glad,
Too easily impressed: she liked whate'er
She looked on, and her looks went
everywhere.

1652 *'The Last Ride Together'*
Who knows but the world may end
tonight?

1653 *'The Lost Leader'*
Never glad confident morning again!

1654 *Luria*
Oppression makes the wise man mad.

1655 *'Never the Time and the Place'*
Never the time and the place
And the loved one all together.

1656 *'Old Pictures in Florence'*
Works done least rapidly, Art most
cherishes.

1657 *'The Patriot'*
It was roses, roses, all the way.

1658 *'The Patriot'*
The air broke into a mist with bells.

1659 *'Pictor Ignotus'*
Ah, thought which saddens while it
soothes!

1660 *'The Pied Piper of Hamelin'*
Rats!
They fought the dogs and killed the cats,
And bit the babies in the cradles,
And ate the cheeses out of the vats,
And licked the soup from the cooks' own
ladles,
Slit open the kegs of salted sprats,
Made nests inside men's Sunday hats,
And even spoiled the women's chats
By drowning their speaking
With shrieking and squeaking
In fifty different sharps and flats.

1661 *Pippa Passes*
The year's at the spring
And day's at the morn;
Morning's at seven;
The hill-side's dew-pearled;
The lark's on the wing;
The snail's on the thorn:
God's in his heaven -
All's right with the world!

1662 *'Rabbi Ben Ezra'*
Grow old along with me!
The best is yet to be.

1663 *'Rabbi Ben Ezra'*
Fancies that broke through language and
escaped.

1664 *The Ring and the Book*
Youth means love,
Vows can't change nature, priests are only
men.

1665 *The Ring and the Book*
Faultless to a fault.

1666 *The Ring and the Book*
There's a new tribunal now
higher than God's - the educated man's!

1667 *'Saul'*
'Tis not what man Does which exalts him,
but what man Would do!

1668 *Sordello*
Any nose
May ravage with impunity a rose.

1669 *'Any Wife to any Husband'*
Why need the other women know so
much?

BRUCE Lenny 1925-1966
1670
The whole motivation for any performer is
'Look at me, Ma.'

1671
The role of a comedian is to make the
audience laugh, at a minimum of once
every fifteen seconds.

BRUMMELL Beau 1778-1840
1672 *(of the Prince of Wales)*
Who's your fat friend?

1673 *Reminiscences of a Literary Life*
[Brummell] used to say that, whether it
was summer or winter, he always liked to
have the morning well-aired before he got
up.

BRUYERE Jean de la 1645-1696
1674
As long as men are liable to die and are
desirous to live, a physician will be made
fun of, but he will be well paid.

1675
A man must have very eminent qualities to
hold his own without being polite.

1676
It is a great misfortune neither to have
enough wit to talk well nor enough
judgement to be silent.

1677
A man often runs the risk of throwing
away a witticism if he admits that it is his
own.

1678 *Les Caractères ou les moeurs de ce siècle*
The onset and the waning of love make
themselves felt in the uneasiness
experienced at being alone together.

1679 *Les Caractères ou les moeurs de ce siècle*
The people have little intelligence, the
great no heart ... if I had to choose I should
have no hesitation: I would be of the
people.

1680 *Les Caractères ou les moeurs de ce siècle*
Man has but three events in his life: to be
born, to live, and to die. He is not
conscious of his birth, he suffers at his
death and he forgets to live.

1681 *Les Caractères ou les moeurs de ce siècle*
Between good sense and good taste there
is the same difference as between cause
and effect.

1682 *Les Caractères ou les moeurs de ce siècle*
Everything has been said, and we are more
than seven thousand years of human
thought too late.

1683 *Les Caractères ou les moeurs de ce siècle*
Making a book is a craft, as is making a
clock; it takes more than wit to become an
author.

BRYAN Willian Jennings 1860-1925
1684
The humblest citizen of all the land, when
clad in the armour of a righteous cause, is
stronger than all the hosts of error.

BUCHAN John 1875-1940
1685
An atheist is a man who has no invisible
means of support.

1686
'What would you call the highest
happiness?' Wratislaw was asked. 'The
sense of competence,' was the answer,
given without hesitation.

1687
We can pay our debt to the past by putting
the future in debt to ourselves.

1688
He disliked emotion, not because he felt
lightly, but because he felt deeply.

1689
The true definition of a snob is one who
craves for what separates men rather than
for what unites them.

1690 *Mr. Standfast*
Its a great life if you don't weaken.

BUCHANAN James 1791-1868
1691 *(to Abraham Lincoln)*
If you are as happy, my dear sir, on
entering this house as I am in leaving it
and returning home, you are the happiest
man in the country.

BUCHANAN Robert 1841-1901
1692 *'White Rose and Red'*
She just wore
Enough for modesty - no more.

BUCHMAN Frank 1878-1961
1693 *Remaking the World*
Suppose everybody cared enough,
everybody shared enough, wouldn't
everybody have enough? There is enough
in the world for everyone's need, but not
enough for everyone's greed.

BÜCHNER Georg 1813-1837
1694
Man is an abyss, and I turn giddy when I
look down into it.

BUCHWALD Art
1695
Television has a real problem. They have
no page two.

BUCK Pearl 1892-1973
1696
It is not healthy when a nation lives within
a nation, as coloured Americans are living
inside America. A nation cannot live
confident of its tomorrow if its refugees are
among its own citizens.

1697 *The Good Earth*
It is better to be first with an ugly woman
than the hundredth with a beauty.

BUCKLEY Jr. William F. 1925-
1698
A Conservative is a fellow who is standing
athwart history yelling 'Stop!'

BUCKOLL H. J. 1803-1871
1699 *Psalms and Hymns for Use of Rugby
School Chapel*
Lord, dismiss us with Thy blessing,
Thanks for mercies past received.
Pardon all, their faults confessing;
Time that's lost may all retrieve.

BUCKROSE J.E.
1700
Happiness comes more from loving than
being loved; and often when our affection
seems wounded it is only our vanity
bleeding. To love, and to be hurt often,
and to love again - this is the brave and
happy life.

BUFFON Comte de 1707-1788
1701
Never think that God's delays are God's denials. Hold on; hold fast; hold out. Patience is genius.

BULLER Arthur 1874-1944
1702 *'Relativity'*
There was a young lady named Bright,
Whose speed was far faster than light;
She set out one day
In a relative way
And returned on the previous night.

BULLOCK Lord
1703
Democracy is not about giving speeches; it is about making committees work.

BULMER-THOMAS Ivor 1905-
1704 *(of Harold Wilson)*
If he ever went to school without any boots it was because he was too big for them.

BÜLOW Prince Bernhard von 1849-1929
1705
We also demand our own place in the sun.

BULWER-LYTTON Edward 1803-1873
1706
Laws die, books never.

1707
Master books, but do not let them master you. Read to live, not live to read.

1708
In life it is difficult to say who do you the most mischief, enemies with the worst intentions, or friends with the best.

1709
A good cigar is as great a comfort to a man as a good cry is to a woman.

1710
A good heart is better than all the heads in the world.

1711
Genius does what it must, and talent does what it can.

1712
Life would be tolerably agreeable if it were not for its amusements.

1713 *The Parisians*
Revolutions are not made with rosewater.

1714 *Richelieu*
Beneath the rule of men entirely great,
The pen is mightier than the sword.

1715 *Richelieu*
In the lexicon of youth, which fate reserves
For a bright manhood, there is no such word
As - *fail*.

1716 *(of Tennyson)*
Out-babying Wordsworth and out-glittering Keats.

1717 *What will he do with it?*
There is no man so friendless but what he can find a friend sincere enough to tell him disagreeable truths.

BUNN Alfred 'Poet' c.1796-1860
1718 *The Bohemian Girl*
I dreamed that I dwelt in marble halls.

BUÑUEL Luis 1900-1983
1719
Thanks to God, I am still an atheist.

BUNYAN John 1628-1888
1720 *The Pilgrim's Progress*
As I walked through the wilderness of this world.

1721 *The Pilgrim's Progress*
The name of the slough was Despond.

1722 *The Pilgrim's Progress*
It is an hard matter for a man to go down into the valley of Humiliation ... and to catch no slip by the way.

1723 *The Pilgrim's Progress*
Hanging is too good for him, said Mr Cruelty.

1724 *The Pilgrim's Progress*
Sleep is sweet to the labouring man.

1725 *The Pilgrim's Progress*
Then I saw that there was a way to Hell, even from the gates of Heaven.

1726 *The Pilgrim's Progress*
So I awoke, and behold it was a dream.

1727 *The Pilgrim's Progress*
One leak will sink a ship, and one sin will destroy a sinner.

1728 *The Pilgrim's Progress*
A man there was, tho' some did count him mad,
The more he cast away, the more he had.

1729 *The Pilgrim's Progress*
Mercy ... laboured much for the poor ... an ornament to her profession.

1730 *The Pilgrim's Progress*
Who would true valour see,
Let him come hither;
One here will constant be,
Come wind, come weather.
There's no discouragement
Shall make him once relent
His first avowed intent
To be a pilgrim.

BURBANK Luther 1849-1926
1731
Heredity is nothing but stored environment.

BURCHFIELD Charles 1893-1967
1732
As an artist grows older, he has to fight disillusionment and learn to establish the same relation to nature as an adult as he had when a child.

BURGESS Anthony 1917-1993
1733
A clockwork orange.

1734
The downtrodden, who are the great creators of slang, hurl pithiness and colour at poverty and oppression.

BURGON John William 1813-1888
1735 *Petra*
Match me such marvel, save in Eastern clime -
A rose-red city - 'half as old as Time'!

BURKE Billie
1736
A woman past forty should make up her mind to be young - not her face.

1737
I am constantly amazed when I talk to young people to learn how much they know about sex and how little about soap.

BURKE Edmund 1729-1797
1738
The greater the power, the more dangerous the abuse.

1739
Your representative owes you, not his industry only, but his judgement; and he betrays, instead of serving you, if he sacrifices it to your opinion.

1740
The people are the masters.

1741
Bad laws are the worst sort of tyranny.

1742
The people never give up their liberties but under some delusion.

1743
Dangers by being despised grow great.

1744 *(attributed)*
It is necessary only for the good man to do nothing for evil to triumph.

1745
History is a pact between the dead, the living, and the yet unborn.

1746
The effect of liberty on individuals is that they may do what they please: we ought to see what it will please them to do, before we risk congratulations.

1747
By gnawing through a dyke, even a rat may drown a nation.

1748
A disposition to preserve, and an ability to improve, taken together, would be my standard of a statesman.

1749 *On American Taxation*
To tax and to please, no more than to love and to be wise, is not given to men.

1750 *On Conciliation with America*
The concessions of the weak are the concessions of fear.

1751 *On Conciliation with America*
The use of force alone is but temporary. It may subdue for a moment; but it does not remove the necessity of subduing again; and a nation is not governed, which is perpetually to be conquered.

1752 *On Conciliation with America*
Abstract liberty, like other mere abstractions, is not to be found.

1753 *On Conciliation with America*
I do not know the method of drawing up an indictment against an whole people.

1754 *On Conciliation with America*
Parties must ever exist in a free country.

1755 *Letter to a Member of the National Assembly*
Those who have been once intoxicated with power, and have derived any kind of emolument from it, even though for but one year, can never willingly abandon it.

1756 *Letter to a Member of the National Assembly*
Tyrants seldom want pretexts.

1757 *Letter to a Member of the National Assembly*
You can never plan the future by the past.

1758 *A Letter to a Noble Lord*
To innovate is not to reform.

1759 *Letter to the Sheriffs of Bristol*
Liberty too must be limited in order to be possessed.

1760 *Letter to the Sheriffs of Bristol*
Among a people generally corrupt, liberty cannot long exist.

1761 *Letter to William Smith*
Somebody has said, that a king may make a nobleman but he cannot make a gentleman.

1762 *Observations ... on the Present State of Nation*
There is, however, a limit at which forbearance ceases to be a virtue.

1763 *Reflections on the Revolution in France*
A state without the means of some change is without the means of its conservation.

1764 *Reflections on the Revolution in France*
Make the Revolution a parent of settlement, and not a nursery of future revolutions.

1765 *Reflections on the Revolution in France*
People will not look forward to posterity, who never look backward to their ancestors.

1766 *Reflections on the Revolution in France*
Those who attempt to level never equalize.

1767 *Reflections on the Revolution in France*
The age of chivalry is gone. That of sophisters, economists, and calculators, has succeeded; and the glory of Europe is extinguished for ever.

1768 *Reflections on the Revolution in France*
In the groves of their academy, at the end of every vista, you see nothing but the gallows.

1769 *Reflections on the Revolution in France*
Kings will be tyrants from policy when subjects are rebels from principle.

1770 *Reflections on the Revolution in France*
Man is by his constitution a religious animal; atheism is against not only our reason, but our instincts.

1771 *Reflections on the Revolution in France*
A perfect democracy is therefore the most shameless thing in the world.

1772 *Reflections on the Revolution in France*
Superstition is the religion of feeble minds.

1773 *Reflections on the Revolution in France*
Good order is the foundation of all good things.

1774 *On the Sublime and Beautiful*
No passion so effectually robs the mind of all its powers of acting and reasoning as fear.

1775 *On the Sublime and Beautiful*
Custom reconciles us to everything.

1776 Third Letter...on the Proposals for Peace
Well is it known that ambition can creep as well as soar.

1777 Thoughts on the Cause of the Present Discontents
To complain of the age we live in, to murmur at the present possessors of power, to lament the past, to conceive extravagant hopes of the future, are the common dispositions of the greatest part of mankind.

1778 Thoughts on the Cause of the Present Discontents
When bad men combine, the good must associate; else they will fall, one by one, an unpitied sacrifice in a contemptible struggle.

1779 Thoughts and Details on Scarcity
And having looked to government for bread, on the very first scarcity they will turn and bite the hand that fed them.

1780 A Tract on the Popery Laws
Laws, like houses, lean on one another.

1781 A Tract on the Popery Laws
In all forms of Government the people is the true legislator.

1782 Two Letters on the Proposals for Peace
All men that are ruined are ruined on the side of their natural propensities.

1783 (on the younger Pitt's maiden Speech)
Not merely a chip of the old 'block', but the old block itself.

BURNET Dana
1784
I'd rather have an inch of dog than miles of pedigree.

BURNETT Carol 1934-
1785
Comedy is tragedy - plus time.

BURNEY Fanny (Mme D'Arblay) 1752-1840
1786 Camilla
A little alarm now and then keeps life from stagnation.

1787 Camilla
It's a delightful thing to think of perfection; but it's vastly more amusing to talk of errors and absurdities.

1788 Camilla
No man is in love when he marries. He may have loved before; I have even heard he has sometimes loved after: but at the time never. There is something in the formalities of the matrimonial preparations that drive away all the little cupidons.

1789 Cecilia
Travelling is the ruin of all happiness! There's no looking at a building here after seeing Italy.

BURNHAM Daniel H. 1846-1912
1790
Make no little plans; they have no magic to stir men's blood ... Make big plans, aim high in hope and work.

BURNS George 1896-1996
1791
With the collapse of vaudeville new talent has no place to stink.

1792
I must be getting absent-minded. Whenever I complain that things aren't what they used to be, I always forget to include myself.

1793
Too bad that all the people who know how to run the country are busy driving taxicabs and cutting hair.

1794
Happiness? A good cigar, a good meal, and a good woman - or a bad woman; it depends on how much happiness you can handle.

BURNS John 1858-1943
1795
The Thames is liquid history.

BURNS Robert 1759-1796
1796
O Life! thou art a galling load,
Along a rough, a weary road,
To wretches such as I.

1797
Gie me a spark o' nature's fire,
That's a' the learning I desire.

1798
God knows, I'm no the thing I should be,
Nor am I even the thing I could be.

1799 *'Ae Fond Kiss'*
Ae fond kiss, and then we sever;
Ae fareweel, and then for ever!

1800 *'Ae Fond Kiss'*
Had we never lov'd sae kindly,
Had we never lov'd sae blindly,
Never met - or never parted,
We had ne'er been broken-hearted.

1801 *'For a'that and a'that'*
The rank is but the guinea's stamp,
The man's the gowd for a' that!

1802 *'Auld Lang Syne'*
Should auld acquaintance be forgot
And never brought to mind?

1803 *'Auld Lang Syne'*
We'll tak a cup o' kindness yet,
For auld lang syne.

1804 *'Auld Lang Syne'*
And there's a hand, my trusty fiere!
And gie's a hand o'thine!

1805 *'The Author's Earnest Cry and Prayer'*
Freedom and Whisky gan thegither!

1806 *'Bonnie Lesley'*
To see her is to love her,
And love but her for ever,
For Nature made her what she is,
And ne'er made anither!

1807 *'Comin thro' the rye'*
Gin a body meet a body
Comin thro' the rye,
Gin a body kiss a body
Need a body cry?

1808 *'Death and Dr Hornbook'*
I wasna fou, but just had plenty.

1809 *'The Deil's awa wi' th'Exciseman'*
There's threesome reels, there's foursome
reels,
There's hornpipes and strathspeys, man,
But the ae best dance e'er cam to the land

Was, the deil's awa wi' th'Exciseman.

1810 *'Epistle to a Young Friend'*
I waive the quantum o' the sin;
The hazard of concealing;
But och! it hardens a' within,
And petrifies the feeling!

1811 *'Epistle to a Young Friend'*
An atheist-laugh's a poor exchange
For Deity offended!

1812 *'Green Grow the Rashes'*
Green grow the rashes, O,
Green grow the rashes, O;
The sweetest hours that e're I spend,
Are spent among the lasses, O.

1813 *'My Heart's in the Highlands'*
My heart's in the Highlands, my heart is
not here;
My heart's in the Highlands a-chasing the
deer;
Chasing the wild deer, and following the
roe,
My heart's in the Highlands, wherever I
go.

1814 *'Hey for a Lass wi' a Tocher'*
O, gie me the lass that has acres o' charms,
O, gie me the lass wi' the weel-stockit
farms.

1815 *'The Jolly Beggars'*
Life is all a VARIORUM,
We regard not how it goes;
Let them cant about DECORUM,
Who have characters to lose.

1816 *'The Kirkudbright Grace'*
Some have meat and cannot eat,
Some cannot eat that want it:
But we have meat and we can eat,
Sae let the Lord be thankit.

1817 *'There was a Lass'*
A man may drink and no be drunk;
A man may fight and no be slain;
A man may kiss a bonnie lass,
And aye be welcome back again.

1818 *'To a Louse'*
O wad some Pow'r the giftie gie us
To see oursels as others see us!
It wad frae mony a blunder free us,
And foolish notion.

1819 *'Man was made to Mourn'*
Man's inhumanity to man
Makes countless thousands mourn!

1820 *'Man was made to Mourn'*
O Death! the poor man's dearest friend,
The kindest and the best!

1821 *'To a Mouse'*
Wee, sleekit, cow'rin, tim'rous beastie,
O what a panic's in thy breastie!
Thou need na start awa sae hasty,
Wi' bickering brattle!

1822 *'To a Mouse'*
The best laid schemes o'mice an' men
Gang aft a-gley.

1823 *'A Red Red Rose'*
O, my Luve's like a red, red rose
That's newly sprung in June;
O my Luve's like the melodie
That's sweetly play'd in tune.

1824 *'Robert Bruce's March to Bannockburn'*
Liberty's in every blow!
Let us do - or die!!!

1825 *(said shortly before his death)*
Don't let the awkward squad fire over me.

1826 *'Tam o' Shanter'*
Nae man can tether time or tide.

BURROUGHS John 1837-1921
1827
How beautifully the leaves grow old.
How full of light and colour are their last days.

BURROUGHS William 1914-
1828
Americans have a special horror of letting things happen their own way, without interference. They would like to jump down their stomachs, digest the food, and shovel the shit out.

BURROWS Sir Fred 1887-1973
1829 *(speech as last Governor of undivided Bengal)*
Unlike my predecessors I have devoted more of my life to shunting and hooting than to hunting and shooting.

BURTON Nat
1830 *'The White Cliffs of Dover'*
There'll be bluebirds over the white cliffs of Dover,
Tomorrow, just you wait and see.

BURTON Sir Richard 1821-1890
1831 *(note to his wife)*
Pay, pack, and follow at convenience.

BURTON Robert 1577-1640
1832
If the world will be gulled, let it be gulled.

1833
Set a beggar on horseback, and he will ride a gallop.

1834
Diogenes struck the father when the son swore.

1835 *The Anatomy of Melancholy*
All my joys to this are folly,
Naught so sweet as Melancholy.

1836 *The Anatomy of Melancholy*
A loose, plain, rude writer ... I call a spade a spade.

1837 *The Anatomy of Melancholy*
All poets are mad.

1838 *The Anatomy of Melancholy*
I may not here omit those two main plagues, and common dotages of human kind, wine and women, which have infatuated and besotted myriads of people.

1839 *The Anatomy of Melancholy*
From this it is clear how much the pen is worse than the sword.

1840 *The Anatomy of Melancholy*
One was never married, and that's his hell: another is, and that's his plague.

1841 *The Anatomy of Melancholy*
The gods are well pleased when they see great men contending with adversity.

1842 *The Anatomy of Melancholy*
What is a ship but a prison?

1843 *The Anatomy of Melancholy*
To enlarge or illustrate this power and effect of love is to set a candle in the sun.

1844 *The Anatomy of Melancholy*
England is a paradise for women, and hell for horses: Italy a paradise for horses, hell for women, as the diverb goes.

1845 *The Anatomy of Melancholy*
One religion is as true as another.

1846 *The Anatomy of Melancholy*
Be not solitary, be not idle.

BUSCH Wilhelm 1832-1908
1847
To become a father is not hard,
To be a father is, however.

BUSENBAUM Hermann 1600-1668
1848 *Medulla Theologiae Moralis*
The end justifies the means.

BUSH Barbara 1925-
1849
Good education is the essential foundation of a strong democracy.

BUSH Douglas 1896-1983
1850
The great humorist forgets himself in his delighted contemplation of other people.

BUSH George 1924-
1851 *(campaign pledge on taxation)*
Read my lips: no new taxes.

BUSSY-RABUTIN Comte de 1618-1693
1852
God is usually on the side of big squadrons and against little ones.

1853 *Histoire Amoureuse des Gaules: Maximes d'Amour*
Love comes from blindness,
Friendship from knowledge.

1854 *Histoire Amoureuse des Gaules: Maximes d'Amour*
Absence is to love what wind is to fire;
It extinguishes the small, it kindles the great.

BUSTON Charles
1855
To make pleasure pleasant, shorten.

BUTLER Nicholas Murray 1862-1947
1856 *(attributed)*
An expert is one who knows more and

more about less and less.

BUTLER Samuel 1835-1902
1857
Life is like playing a violin solo in public and learning the instrument as one goes on.

1858
The great pleasure of a dog is that you may make a fool of yourself with him and not only will he not scold you, but he will make a fool of himself too.

1859
The oldest books are still only just out to those who have not read them.

1860
Books should be tried by a judge and jury as though they were crimes.

1861
I can generally bear the separation, but I don't like the leave-taking.

1862
People in general are equally horrified at hearing the Christian religion doubted, and at seeing it practised.

1863
The test of a good critic is whether he knows when and how to believe on insufficient evidence.

1864
If life must not be taken too seriously - then so neither must death.

1865
Whatso'er we perpetrate
We do but row, we are steered by fate.

1866
It does not matter much what a man hates, provided he hates something.

1867
An apology for the Devil - it must be remembered that we have only heard one side of the case. God has written all the books.

1868
A hen is only an egg's way of making another egg.

1869
It has been said that though God cannot alter the past, historians can; it is perhaps because they can be useful to Him in this respect that He tolerates their existence.

1870
A lawyer's dream of heaven - every man reclaimed his property at the resurrection, and each tried to recover it from all his forefathers.

1871
We pay a person the compliment of acknowledging his superiority whenever we lie to him.

1872
I do not mind lying, but I hate inaccuracy.

1873
I reckon being ill is one of the greatest pleasures of life, provided one is not too ill and is not obliged to work till one is better.

1874
When you have told anyone you have left him a legacy, the only decent thing to do is to die at once.

1875
All philosophies, if you ride them home, are nonsense; but some are greater nonsense than others.

1876
Silence is not always tact, and it is tact that is golden, not silence.

1877
People care more about being thought to have good taste than about being thought either good, clever or amiable.

1878
To put one's trust in God is only a longer way of saying that one will chance it.

1879
It is the function of vice to keep virtue within reasonable grounds.

1880
A virtue to be serviceable must, like gold, be alloyed with some commoner but more durable metal.

1881
It is hard to come down the social ladder without tumbling off.

1882 *(attributed)*
Brigands demand your money or your life; women require both.

1883 *Further Extracts from Notebooks*
The three most important things a man has are, briefly, his private parts, his money, and his religious opinions.

1884 *Further Extracts from Notebooks*
Jesus! with all thy faults I love thee still.

1885 *Further Extracts from Notebooks*
Conscience is thoroughly well-bred and soon leaves off talking to those who do not wish to hear it.

1886 *Genuine Remains 'Miscellaneous Thoughts'*
All love at first, like generous wine,
Ferments and frets, until 'tis fine;
But when 'tis settled on the lee,
And from th'impurer matter free,
Becomes the richer still, the older,
And proves the pleasanter, the colder.

1887 *Hudibras*
He'd run in debt by disputation,
And pay with ratiocination.

1888 *Hudibras*
For all a rhetorician's rules
Teach nothing but to name his tools.

1889 *Hudibras*
He knew what's what, and that's as high
As metaphysic wit can fly.

1890 *Hudibras*
Compound for sins, they are inclined to,
By damning those they have no mind to.

1891 *Hudibras*
Great actions are not always true sons
Of great and mighty resolutions.

1892 *Hudibras*
She that with poetry is won,
Is but a desk to write upon.

1893 *Hudibras*
Love is a boy, by poets styled,
Then spare the rod, and spoil the child.

1894 *Hudibras*
Oaths are but words, and words but wind.

1895 *Hudibras*
What makes all doctrines plain and clear?
About two hundred pounds a year.
And that which was proved true before,
Prove false again? Two hundred more.

1896 *Hudibras*
He that complies against his will,
Is of his own opinion still.

1897 *Hudibras*
For Justice, though she's painted blind,
Is to the weaker side inclined.

1898 *Letters between Samuel Butler and Miss
E.M.Savage*
It was very good of God to let Carlyle and
Mrs Carlyle marry one another and so
make only two people miserable instead of
four.

1899 *Notebooks*
Life is one long process of getting tired.

1900 *Notebooks*
All progress is based upon a universal
innate desire on the part of every organism
to live beyond its income.

1901 *Notebooks*
The history of art is the history of revivals.

1902 *Notebooks*
Our ideas. They are for the most part like
bad sixpences and we spend our lives in
trying to pass them on one another.

1903 *Notebooks*
To live is like to love - all reason is against
it, and all healthy instinct for it.

1904 *The Way of All Flesh*
Adversity, if a man is set down to it by
degrees, is more supportable with
equanimity by most people than any great
prosperity arrived at in a single lifetime.

1905 *The Way of All Flesh*
All animals, except man, know that the
principal business of life is to enjoy it.

1906 *The Way of All Flesh*
The advantage of doing one's praising for
oneself is that one can lay it on so thick

and exactly in the right places.

1907 *The Way of All Flesh*
Young as he was, his instinct told him that
the best liar is he who makes the smallest
amount of lying go the longest way.

1908 *The Way of All Flesh*
'Tis better to have loved and lost than
never to have lost at all.

BUXTON Charles
1909
Pounds are the sons, not of pounds, but of
pence.

BYRNE Frankie
1910
Respect is love in plain clothes.

BYROM John 1692-1763
1911
Christians, awake! Salute the happy morn,
Whereon the Saviour of the world was
born.

1912
God bless the King, I mean the Faith's
Defender;
God bless - no harm in blessing - the
Pretender;
But who Pretender is, or who is King,
God bless us all - that's quite another
thing.

BYRON Lord 1788-1824
1913
Christians have burned each other, quite
persuaded
That all the apostles would have done as
they did.

1914
Though I love my country, I do not love
my countrymen.

1915
Admire, exult, despise, laugh, weep - for
here
There is such matter for all feelings: - Man!
Thou pendulum betwixt a smile and tear.

1916
The great art of life is sensation, to feel that
we exist, even in pain.

1917
Roll on, thou deep and dark blue ocean -
roll!
Ten thousand fleets sweep over thee in
vain;
Man marks the earth with ruin - his
control
Stops with the shore.

1918
If from Society we learn to live,
'Tis Solitude should teach us how to die;
It hath no flatterers.

1919 *'The Age of Bronze'*
For what were all these country patriots
born?
To hunt, and vote, and raise the price of
corn?

1920 *'So, we'll go no more a-roving'*
So, we'll go no more a-roving
So late into the night,
Though the heart be still as loving,
And the moon be still as bright.

1921 *Beppo*
Our cloudy climate, and our chilly women.

1922 *Beppo*
A pretty woman as was ever seen,
Fresh as the Angel o'er a new inn door.

1923 *The Bride of Abydos*
Where the virgins are soft as the roses they
twine,
And all, save the spirit of man, is divine.

1924 *Childe Harold's Pilgrimage*
Here all were noble, save Nobility.

1925 *Childe Harold's Pilgrimage*
On with the dance! let joy be unconfined;
No sleep till morn, when Youth and
Pleasure meet
To chase the glowing Hours with flying
feet.

1926 *Childe Harold's Pilgrimage*
He rushed into the field, and, foremost
fighting, fell.

1927 *Childe Harold's Pilgrimage*
Quiet to quick bosoms is a hell.

1928 *Childe Harold's Pilgrimage*
To fly from, need not be to hate, mankind.

1929 *Childe Harold's Pilgrimage*
I live not in myself, but I become
Portion of that around me; and to me,
High mountains are a feeling, but the hum
Of human cities torture.

1930 *Childe Harold's Pilgrimage*
Of its own beauty is the mind diseased.

1931 *Childe Harold's Pilgrimage*
Dark-heaving - boundless, endless, and
sublime -
The image of eternity.

1932 *'Churchill's Grave'*
The glory and the nothing of a name.

1933 *The Corsair*
Oh! too convincing - dangerously dear -
In woman's eye the unanswerable tear!

1934 *'The Curse of Minerva'(of Scotland)*
A land of meanness, sophistry, and mist.

1935 *'On This Day I Complete my Thirty-
Sixth Year'*
My days are in the yellow leaf;
The flowers and fruits of love are gone;
The worm, the canker, and the grief
Are mine alone!

1936 *'The Destruction of Sennacherib'*
The Assyrian came down like the wolf on
the fold,
And his cohorts were gleaming in purple
and gold;
And the sheen of their spears was like
stars on the sea,
When the blue wave rolls nightly on deep
Galilee.

1937 *'The Destruction of Sennacherib'*
For the Angel of Death spread his wings
on the blast,
And breathed in the face of the foe as he
passed.

1938 *'To Eliza'*
Still I can't contradict, what so oft has been
said,
'Though women are angels, yet wedlock's
the devil.'

1939 *English Bards and Scotch Reviewers*
A man must serve his time to every trade
Save censure - critics all are ready made.

Take hackneyed jokes from Miller, got by rote,
With just enough of learning to misquote.

1940 *English Bards and Scotch Reviewers*
Let simple Wordsworth chime his childish verse,
And brother Coleridge lull the babe at nurse.

1941 *English Bards and Scotch Reviewers*
And glory, like the phoenix midst her fires,
Exhales her odours, blazes, and expires.

1942 *English Bards and Scotch Reviewers*
Be warm but pure: be amorous but chaste.

1943 *(on the instantaneous success of Childe Harold)*
I awoke one morning and found myself famous.

1944 *Journal, 1813*
The more I see of men, the less I like them.
If I could but say so of women too, all would be well.

1945 *Don Juan*
And Coleridge, too, has lately taken wing,
But, like a hawk encumbered with his hood,
Explaining metaphysics to the nation -
I wish he would explain his explanation.

1946 *Don Juan*
Married, charming, chaste, and twenty-three.

1947 *Don Juan*
'Twas stange that one so young should thus concern
His brain about the action of the sky;
If you think 'twas philosphy that this did,
I can't help thinking puberty assisted.

1948 *Don Juan*
Sweet is revenge - especially to women.

1949 *Don Juan*
Pleasure's a sin, and sometimes sin's a pleasure.

1950 *Don Juan*
There's nought, no doubt, so much the spirit calms
As rum and true religion.

1951 *Don Juan*
And thus they form a group that's quite antique,
Half naked, loving, natural, and Greek.

1952 *Don Juan*
Alas! the love of women! It is known
To be a lovely and a fearful thing!

1953 *Don Juan*
In her first passion woman loves her lover,
In all the others all she loves is love.

1954 *Don Juan*
'Tis melancholy, and a fearful sign
Of human frailty, folly, also crime,
That love and marriage rarely can combine,
Although they both are born in the same clime;
Marriage from love, like vinegar from wine -
A sad, sour, sober beverage - by time
Is sharpened from its high celestial flavour,
Down to a very homely household savour.

1955 *Don Juan*
All tragedies are finished by a death,
All comedies are ended by a marriage;
The future states of both are left to faith.

1956 *Don Juan*
Dreading that climax of all human ills,
The inflammation of his weekly bills.

1957 *Don Juan*
But Shakespeare also says, 'tis very silly
'To gild refinèd gold, or paint the lily.'

1958 *Don Juan*
The mountains look on Marathon -
And Marathon looks on the sea;
And musing there an hour alone,
I dreamed that Greece might still be free.

1959 *Don Juan*
... That all-softening, overpowering knell,
The tocsin of the soul - the dinner bell.

1960 *Don Juan*
There is a tide in the affairs of women,
Which, taken at the flood, leads - God knows where.

1961 *Don Juan*
A lady of a 'certain age', which means
Certainly aged.

1962 *Don Juan*
Of all the horrid, hideous notes of woe,
Sadder than owl-songs or the midnight
blast,
Is that portentous phrase, 'I told you so.'

1963 *Don Juan*
'Tis strange - but true; for truth is always
strange;
Stranger than fiction.

1964 *Don Juan*
Let us have Wine and Women, Mirth and
Laughter
Sermons and soda-water the day after.

1965 *Don Juan*
Society is now one polished horde,
Formed of two mighty tribes,
The Bores and the Bored.

1966 *Don Juan*
What men call gallantry, and gods
adultery,
Is much more common where the climate's
sultry.

1967 *Don Juan*
A little still she strove, and much repented,
And whispering 'I will ne'er consent' -
consented.

1968 *Don Juan*
Man's love is of man's life a thing apart,
'Tis woman's whole existence.

1969 *Don Juan*
Merely innocent flirtation.
Not quite adultery, but adulteration.

1970 *Don Juan*
Now hatred is by far the longest pleasure;
Men love in haste, but they detest at
leisure.

1971 *Don Juan*
The English winter - ending in July,
To recommence in August.

1972 *(of Keats)*
Such writing is a sort of mental
masturbation - he is always f-gg-g his
imagination. I don't mean that he is

indecent but viciously soliciting his own
ideas into a state which is neither poetry
nor any thing else but a Bedlam vision
produced by raw pork and opium.

1973 *'L'Amitié est l'amour sans ailes'*
Friendship is Love without his wings!

1974 *Letter to Annabella Milbanke*
I by no means rank poetry high in the scale
of intelligence - this may look like
affectation - but it is my real opinion - it is
the lava of the imagination whose eruption
prevents an earthquake.

1975 *Letter to James Hogg*
Wordsworth - stupendous genius! damned
fool!

1976 *Letter to John Murray*
Pure invention is but the talent of a liar.

1977 *Letter to Lady Melbourne*
The seal is not yet fixed though the wax is
preparing for the impression.

1978 *Letter to Richard Hoppner*
The reading or non-reading a book - will
never keep down a single petticoat.

1979 *Letter to Thomas Moore*
What is hope? nothing but the paint on the
face of Existence; the least touch of truth
rubs it off, and then we see what a hollow-
cheeked harlot we have got hold of.

1980 *Letter to Thomas Moore*
Like other parties of the kind, it was first
silent, then talky, then argumentative, then
disputatious, then unintelligible, then
altogethery, then inarticulate, and then
drunk.

1981 *Manfred*
Sorrow is knowledge: they who know the
most
Must mourn the deepest o'er the fatal
truth,
The Tree of Knowledge is not that of Life.

1982 *Manfred*
Old man! 'tis not so difficult to die.

1983 *Marino Faliero*
You have deeply ventured;
But all must do so who would greatly win.

1984 *'So, we'll go no more a roving'*
Though the night was made for loving,
And the day returns too soon,
Yet we'll go no more a roving
By the light of the moon.

1985 *'Stanzas for Music'*
There's not a joy the world can give like
that it takes away.

1986 *The Two Foscari*
And when we think we lead, we are most
led.

1987 *The Vision of Judgement*
Of course his perspiration was but ichor,
Or some such other spiritual liquor.

1988 *The Vision of Judgement*
Yet still between his Darkness and his
Brightness
There passed a mutual glance of great
politeness.

1989 *The Vision of Judgement*
And when the tumult dwindled to a calm,
I left him practising the hundredth psalm.

1990 *'She Walks in Beauty'*
She walks in beauty, like the night
Of cloudless climes and starry skies;
And all that's best of dark and bright
Meet in her aspect and her eyes:
Thus mellowed to that tender light
Which heaven to gaudy day denies.

CABELL James Branch 1879-1958
1991 *Jurgen*
A man possesses nothing certainly save a
brief loan of his own body.

1992 *The Silver Stallion*
The optimist proclaims that we live in the
best of all possible worlds; and the
pessimist fears this is true.

CAESAR Irving 1895-
1993 *'Tea for Two'*
Picture you upon my knee,
Just tea for two and two for tea.

CAESAR Julius 100-44 BC
1994
Et tu, Brute?
You too, Brutus?

1995 *(at the crossing of the Rubicon)*
The die is cast.

1996 *(inscription)*
Veni, vidi, vici
I came, I saw, I conquered.

1997 *(oral tradition)*
Caesar's wife must be above suspicion.

CAHIER Charles
1998
Tout passe, tout casse, tout lasse
Everthing passes, everything perishes,
everything palls.

CAHN Peggy
1999
I believe that the sign of maturity is
accepting deferred gratification.

CAIN James M. 1892-1977
2000
The postman always rings twice.

CAINE Marti 1945-1995
2001 *(when told she had malignant limphoma)*
Does that mean I'm a lymphomaniac?

CAINE Michael 1933-
2002
The British Film Industry is alive and well
and living in Los Angeles.

2003 *in Alfie*
"My understanding of Women goes only
as far as the pleasure."

CAIRNS Sir Joseph 1920-1981
2004 *(on retiring as Lord Mayor of Belfast)*
The betrayal of Ulster, the cynical and
entirely undemocratic banishment of its
properly elected Parliament and a
relegation to the status of a fuzzy wuzzy
colony is, I hope, a last betrayal
contemplated by Downing Street because
it is the last that Ulster will countenance.

CAJAL Santiago Ramon y
2005
That which enters the mind through
reason can be corrected. That which is
admitted through faith, hardly ever.

CALISHER Hortense 1911-
2006
First publication is a pure, carnal leap into

that dark which one dreams is life.

CALLIMACHUS c.305-c.240 BC
2007
I loathe all things held in common.

2008
A great book is like great evil.

CALLWOOD June
2009
The central fact of North American history is that there were fifteen British Colonies before 1776. Thirteen rebelled and two did not.

CALVERLEY C.S. 1831-1884
2010 *'Contentment'*
Life is with such all beer and skittles;
They are not difficult to please
About their victuals.

CAMBRONNE Pierre, Baron de 1770-1842
2011 *(attributed, when called upon to surrender)*
The Guards die but do not surrender.

CAMDEN William 1551-1623
2012 *Remains concerning Britain 'Epitaphs'*
Betwixt the stirrup and the ground
Mercy I asked, mercy I found.

CAMERON Simon
2013
An honest politician is one who when he is bought will stay bought.

CAMPBELL Bushrod H.
2014
If I've learned anything in my seventy years it's that nothing's as good or as bad as it appears.

CAMPBELL Jane Montgomery 1817-1878
2015 *'We plough the fields, and scatter'*
We plough the fields, and scatter
The good seed on the land,
But it is fed and watered
By God's almighty hand;
He sends the snow in winter,
The warmth to swell the grain,
The breezes and the sunshine,
And soft refreshing rain.

CAMPBELL Patrick
2016
It seems to me that you can go sauntering along for a certain period, telling the English some interesting things about themselves, and then all at once it feels as if you had stepped on the prongs of a rake.

CAMPBELL Mrs Patrick 1865-1940
2017
It doesn't matter what you do in the bedroom as long as you don't do it in the street and frighten the horses.

2018 *(on her recent marriage)*
The deep, deep peace of the double-bed after the hurly-burly of the chaise-longue.

CAMPBELL Roy 1901-1957
2019
You praise the firm restraint with which they write -
I'm with you, there, of course:
They use the snaffle and the curb all right,
But where's the bloody horse?

CAMPBELL Thomas 1777-1844
2020 *(attributed)*
Now Barabbas was a publisher.

2021 *'Gertrude of Wyoming'*
Tomorrow let us do or die!

2022 *'The Jilted Nymph'*
Better be courted and jilted
Than never be courted at all.

CAMUS Albert 1913-1960
2023
Every artist preserves deep within him a single source from which, throughout his lifetime, he draws what he is and what he says and when the source dries up the work withers and crumbles.

2024
Beauty is unbearable, drives us to despair, offering us for a minute the glimpse of an eternity that we should like to stretch out over the whole of time.

2025
Charm is a way of getting the answer yes without having asked any clear question.

2026
As a remedy to life in society, I would suggest the big city. Nowadays it is the only desert within our reach.

2027
Without culture, and the relative freedom it presumes, society, even when perfect, is no more than a jungle. This is why every authentic creation is a gift to the future.

2028
Nothing is more despicable than respect based on fear.

2029
To be happy, we must not be too concerned with others.

2030
The innocent is the person who explains nothing.

2031
The slave begins by demanding justice and ends by wanting to wear a crown. He must dominate in his turn.

2032
If there is a sin against life, it consists perhaps not so much in despairing of life as in hoping for another, and in eluding the implacable grandeur of this life.

2033
He who despairs of the human condition is a coward, but he who has hope for it is a fool.

2034
A novel is never anything but a philosophy put into images.

2035
We always deceive ourselves twice about the people we love - first to their advantage, then to their disadvantage.

2036
An intense feeling carries with it its own universe, magnificent or wretched as the case may be.

2037
Politics, and the fate of mankind, are shaped by men without ideals and without greatness.

2038
To know oneself, one should assert oneself.

2039
We call first truths those we discover after all the others.

2040
I know myself too well to believe in pure virtue.

2041
There is dignity in work only when it is work freely accepted.

2042 *The Fall*
We seldom confide in those who are better than ourselves.

2043 *The Fall*
I'll tell you a great secret, my friend. Don't wait for the last judgement. It happens every day.

2044 *The Fall*
A single sentence will suffice for modern man: he fornicated and read the papers.

2045 *Notebooks*
An intellectual is someone whose mind watches itself.

2046 *The Rebel*
What is a rebel? A man who says no.

2047 *The Rebel*
All modern revolutions have ended in a reinforcement of the State.

CANNING George 1770-1827
2048
In matters of commerce the fault of the Dutch
Is offering too little and asking too much.
The French are with equal advantage content,
So we clap on Dutch bottoms just 20%.

2049
Give me the avowed, the erect, and manly foe,
Bold I can meet, perhaps may turn the blow;
But of all plagues, good Heaven, thy wrath can send,
Save, save, oh save me from the candid friend!

2050 *'The Oracle'*
Pitt is to Addington
As London is to Paddington.

CAPOTE Truman 1924-1984
2051
Venice is like eating an entire box of
chocolate liqueurs in one go.

2052
In California everyone goes to a therapist,
is a therapist, or is a therapist going to a
therapist.

2053 *(of Jack Kerouac)*
That's not writing, that's typing.

CAPP Al 1907-1979
2054 *(on abstract art)*
A product of the untalented, sold by the
unprincipled to the utterly bewildered.

CAPRA Frank 1897-1991
2055
A hunch is creativity trying to tell you
something.

2056
Automatic simply means that you can't
repair it yourself.

CAPRIATI Jennifer
2057
I don't care about being No. 1, but I'm
ready and willing to give battle, and that's
what sport is all about.

CARDES Liane
2058
Continuous effort - not strength or
intelligence - is the key to unlocking our
potential.

CARDOZO Benjamin N. 1870-1938
2059
There is an accuracy that defeats itself by
the overemphasis of details. I often say
that one must permit oneself, and quite
advisedly and deliberately, a certain
margin of misstatement.

CAREW Thomas c.1595-1640
2060 *'Inscription on Tomb of Lady Mary
Wentworth'*
Good to the poor, to kindred dear,
To servants kind, to friendship clear,

To nothing but herself severe.

2061 *'Mediocrity in Love Rejected'*
Give me more love or more disdain;
The torrid or the frozen zone.
Bring equal ease unto my pain,
The temperate affords me none;
Either extreme of love or hate,
Is sweeter than a calm estate.

2062 *A Pastoral Dialogue*
Love's flames will shine in every tear.

2063 *'A Song'*
Ask me no more where Jove bestows.
When June is past, the fading rose;

**CAREY George (Archbishop of
Canterbury)** 1935-
2064
I am not in the business of alloting sins.

CAREY Henry c.1687-1743
2065 *'Sally in our Alley'*
Of all the girls that are so smart
There's none like pretty Sally,
She is the darling of my heart,
And she lives in our alley.

CARLYLE Jane 1801-1866
2066 *Letter to Thomas Carlyle*
I am not at all the sort of person you and I
took me for.

CARLYLE Thomas 1795-1881
2067
A good book is the purest essence of a
human soul.

2068
If Jesus Christ were to come to-day, people
would not even crucify him. They would
ask him to dinner, and hear what he had to
say, and make fun of it.

2069
There is endless merit in a man's knowing
when to have done.

2070
The true university of these days is a
collection of books.

2071
The courage we desire and prize is not the
courage to die decently, but to live
manfully.

2072
What an enormous magnifier is tradition!
How a thing grows in the human memory
and in the human imagination, when love,
worship, and all that lies in the human
heart, is there to encourage it.

2073
The crash of the whole solar and stellar
systems could only kill you once.

2074
In the long run every government is the
exact symbol of its people, with their
wisdom and unwisdom.

2075
No sadder proof can be given by a man of
his own littleness, than disbelief in great
men.

2076
Nine-tenths of the miseries and vices of
mankind proceed from idleness.

2077
The tragedy of life is not so much what
men suffer, but rather what they miss.

2078
When the oak is felled the whole forest
echoes with its fall, but a hundred acorns
are sown in silence by an unnoticed
breeze.

2079
Burke said there were three Estates in
Parliament; but in the reporters' gallery
yonder, there sat a fourth Estate more
important than them all.

2080
All reform except a moral one will prove
unavailing.

2081
God Almighty never created a man half as
wise as he looks.

2082
He that can work is a born king of
something.

2083 *Critical and Miscellaneous Essays*
History is the essence of innumerable
biographies.

2084 *Critical and Miscellaneous Essays*
A well-written Life is almost as rare as a
well-spent one.

2085 *Critical and Miscellaneous Essays*
Under all speech that is good for anything
there lies a silence that is better. Silence is
deep as Eternity; speech is shallow as
Time.

2086 *Critical and Miscellaneous Essays*
The three great elements of modern
civilization, Gunpowder, Printing, and the
Protestant Religion.

2087 *Critical and Miscellaneous Essays*
A poet without love were a physical and
metaphysical impossibility.

2088 *History of the French Revolution*
A whiff of grapeshot.

2089 *History of French Revolution (of
Robespierre)*
The seagreen Incorruptible.

2090 *History of the French Revolution*
France was long a despotism tempered by
epigrams.

2091 *Past and Present*
Captains of industry.

2092 *On political economy, Latter-Day
Pamphlets*
The Dismal Science.

CARMAN Bliss 1861-1929
2093
Whether it be to failure or success, the first
need of being is endurance - to endure
with gladness if we can, with fortitude in
any event.

2094
Indifference may not wreck a man's life at
any one turn, but it will destroy him with
a kind of dryrot in the long run.

2095
The greatest joy in nature is the absence of
man.

2096
There is a passion for perfection which you
will rarely see fully developed; but you
may note this fact, that in successful lives

it is never wholly lacking.

CARNEGIE Dale 1888-1955
2097
How to win friends and influence people.

CARR E.H. 1892-1982
2098
Change is certain, progress is not.

CARREL Alexis 1873-1944
2099
A few observations and much reasoning
lead to error; many observations and a
little reasoning to truth.

CARROLL Lewis 1832-1898
2100 *Alice's Adventures in Wonderland*
'What is the use of a book' thought Alice,
'without pictures or conversations?'

2101 *Alice's Adventures in Wonderland*
'Curiouser and curiouser!' cried Alice.

2102 *Alice's Adventures in Wonderland*
How cheerfully he seems to grin,
How neatly spreads his claws,
And welcomes little fishes in
With gently smiling jaws!

2103 *Alice's Adventures in Wonderland*
'You are old, Father William,' the young
man said,
'And your hair has become very white;
And yet you incessantly stand on your
head -
Do you think, at your age, it is right?'

2104 *Alice's Adventures in Wonderland*
Speak roughly to your little boy,
And beat him when he sneezes;
He only does it to annoy,
Because he knows it teases.

2105 *Alice's Adventures in Wonderland*
Everything's got a moral, if you can only
find it.

2106 *Alice's Adventures in Wonderland*
'Will you walk a little faster?' said a
whiting to a snail,
'There's a porpoise close behind us, and
he's treading on my tail.'

2107 *Alice's Adventures in Wonderland*
Will you, won't you, will you, won't you,
will you join the dance?

2108 *Alice's Adventures in Wonderland*
'Where shall I begin, please your Majesty?'
he asked.
'Begin at the beginning,' the King said,
gravely, 'and go on till you come to the
end: then stop.'

2109 *Alice's Adventures in Wonderland*
'Twas brillig, and the slithy toves
Did gyre and gimble in the wabe;
All mimsy were the borogoves,
And the mome raths outgrabe.'
'Beware the Jabberwock, my son!
The jaws that bite, the claws that catch!'

2110 *Through the Looking-Glass*
'The time has come,' the Walrus said,
'To talk of many things:
Of shoes - and ships - and sealing wax -
Of cabbages - and kings -
And why the sea is boiling hot -
And whether pigs have wings.'

2111 *Through the Looking-Glass*
But answer came there none -

2112 *Through the Looking-Glass*
The rule is, jam tomorrow and jam
yesterday - but never jam today.

2113 *Through the Looking-Glass*
It's as large as life and twice as natural!

2114 *Through the Looking-Glass*
'The horror of that moment,' the King
went on, 'I shall never, never forget!' 'You
will, though,' the Queen said, 'if you don't
make a memorandum of it.'

2115 *Through the Looking-Glass*
Now here, you see, it takes all the running
you can do to keep in the same place. If
you want to get somewhere else, you must
run at least twice as fast as that!

2116 *Through the Looking-Glass*
What I tell you three times is true.

2117 *Through the Looking-Glass*
It's one of the most serious things that can
possibly happen to one in a battle - to get
one's head cut off.

2118 *Through the Looking-Glass*
Take care of the sense and the sounds will
take of themselves.

CARRUTH William Herbert 1859-1924
2119 *'Each In His Own Tongue'*
Some call it evolution,
And others call it God.

CARRUTHERS Charles Edwin
2120
In judging others, folks will work overtime
for no pay.

CARSON Jack
2121
A fan club is a group of people who tell an
actor he is not alone in the way he feels
about himself.

CARSON Lord 1854-1935
2122
My only great qualification for being put
at the head of the Navy is that I am very
much at sea.

CARSON Marco
2123
And by my grave you'd pray to have me
back
So I could see how well you look in black.

CARSON Rachael 1907-1964
2124
If a child is to keep alive his inborn sense
of wonder without any such gift from the
fairies, he needs the companionship of at
least one adult who can share it,
rediscovering with him the joy, excitement
and mystery of the world we live in.

2125
For the first time in the history of the
world, every human being is now
subjected to contact with dangerous
chemicals, from the moment of conception
until death.

2126
For the sense of smell, almost more than
any other, has the power to recall
memories and it is a pity that we use it so
little.

CARTER Boake
2127
In time of war the first casualty is truth.

CARTER Dyson
2128
I feel age like an icicle down my back.

CARTER Hodding
2129
There are only two lasting bequests we can
hope to give our children. One of these is
roots, the other, wings.

CARTER Jimmy 1924-
2130
I've looked on a lot of women with lust.
I've committed adultery in my heart many
times. This is something God recognizes I
will do - and I have done it - and God
forgives me for it.

CARTLAND Barbara 1901-
2131
A historical romance is the only kind of
book where chastity really counts.

CARY Joyce 1888-1957
2132
A man of eighty has outlived probably
three new schools of painting, two of
architecture and poetry, and a hundred in
dress.

2133
My novels point out that the world
consists entirely of exceptions.

2134 *The Horse's Mouth*
Sara could commit adultery at one end and
weep for her sins at the other, and enjoy
both operations at once.

CASSAVETES John
2135
No matter how old you get, if you can
keep the desire to be creative, you're
keeping the man-child alive.

CASSON Herbert
2136
Net - the biggest word in the language of
business.

CASSON Hugh 1910-
2137
The British love permanence more than
they love beauty.

CASTRO Fidel 1926-
2138
I am not a great fan of capitalism. But I am a realist.

2139 *(on battledress)*
Practical, simple, cheap and does not go out of fashion.

2140 *(title of pamphlet)*
History will absolve me.

CATLIN Wynn
2141
Diplomacy, the art of saying 'nice doggie' till you can find a rock.

CATO The Elder 234-149 BC
2142
After I am dead, I would rather have men ask why Cato has no monument than why he had one.

CATULLUS c.84-c.54 BC
2143 *Carmina*
For there is nothing sillier than a silly laugh.

2144 *Carmina*
But what a woman says to her lusting lover it is best to write in wind and swift-flowing water.

2145 *Carmina*
Give up wanting to deserve any thanks from anyone, or thinking that anybody can be grateful.

CÉLINE Louis-Ferdinand 1894-1961
2146
If you aren't rich, you should always look useful.

2147
History doesn't pass the dishes again.

CENTLIVRE Susannah c.1667-1723
2148
'Tis my opinion every man cheats in his way, and he is only honest who is not discovered.

CERVANTES Miguel de 1547-1616
2149
Every one is as God made him and oftentimes a good deal worse.

2150
Valour lies just halfway between rashness and cowardice.

2151
The guts carry the feet, not the feet the guts.

2152
You must not think, sir, to catch old birds with chaff.

2153
Man appoints, and God disappoints.

2154
God bears with the wicked, but not forever.

2155 *Don Quixote*
Let them eat the lie and swallow it with their bread. Whether the two were lovers' or no, they'll have accounted to God for it by now. I have my own fish to fry.

CHAGALL Marc 1889-1985
2156
The fingers must be educated, the thumb is born knowing.

2157
All colours are the friends of their neighbours and the lovers of their opposites.

2158
All our interior world is reality - and that perhaps more so than our apparent world.

2159
In our lives there is a simple colour, as on an artist's palette, which provides the meaning of life and art. It is the colour of love.

CHAMFORT Sebastien c.1741-1794
2160
Society is composed of two great classes: those who have more dinners than appetite, and those who have more appetite than dinners.

CHANDLER Raymond 1888-1959
2161
A good title is the title of a successful book.

2162
At least half the mystery novels published violate the law that the solution, once revealed, must seem to be inevitable.

2163 *Farewell My Lovely*
She gave me a smile I could feel in my hip pocket.

2164 *The Long Good-Bye*
Alcohol is like love: the first kiss is magic, the second is intimate, the third is routine. After that you just take the girl's clothes off.

CHANEL Coco 1883-1971
2165
There is time for work. And time for love. That leaves no other time.

2166
Jump out the window if you are the object of passion. Flee it if you feel it. Passion goes, boredom remains.

2167 *(on being asked where one should wear perfume)*
Wherever one wants to be kissed.

CHANNING William Ellery 1780-1842
2168
It is a greater work to educate a child, in the true and larger sense of the word, than to rule a state.

2169
Most joyful let the Poet be,
It is through him that all men see.

CHAPIN E.H.
2170
At the bottom of a good deal of the bravery that appears in the world there lurks a miserable cowardice. Men will face powder and steel because they cannot face public opinion.

CHAPMAN John Jay 1774-1845
2171
Every generation is a secret society and has incommunicable enthusiasms, tastes, and interests which are a mystery both to its predecessors and to posterity.

CHAR René 1907-
2172
In action, be primitive; in foresight, a strategist.

2173
For an inheritance to be really great, the hand of the defunct must not be seen.

2174
That which comes into the world to disturb nothing deserves neither respect nor patience.

CHARCOT Jean-Martin
2175
Symptoms, then, are in reality nothing but the cry from suffering organs.

CHARLEMAGNE 742-814
2176
To have another language is to possess a second soul.

2177
How awful incompatibility is, and how dreadfully destructive it can be for the players in this extraordinary drama. It has all the ingredients of a Greek tragedy. I never thought it would end up like this. How could I have got it all so wrong?

CHARLES, Prince of Wales 1948-
2178
Do you seriously expect me to be the first Prince of Wales in history not to have a mistress?

2179 *Letter to a friend*
We've had such a lovely Christmas, the two of us. It has been extraordinarily happy and cosy being able to share it together. Next year will be even nicer with a small one to join us as well.

CHASE Alexander
2180
The peak of tolerance is most readily achieved by those who are not burdened with convictions.

2181
The banalities of a great man pass for wit.

2182
Memory is the thing you forget with.

CHASE Edna Woolman
2183
Fashion can be bought. Style one must possess.

CHAUCER Geoffrey c.1343-1400
2184 *The Canterbury Tales*
He was a verray, parfit gentil knyght.

2185 *The Canterbury Tales*
And gladly wolde he lerne and gladly teche.

2186 *The Canterbury Tales*
Wel loved he garleek, oynons, and eek lekes,
And for to drynken strong wyn, reed as blood.

2187 *The Canterbury Tales*
Trouthe is the hyeste thyng that man may kepe.

2188 *The Canterbury Tales*
And therefore, at the kynges court, my brother,
Ech man for hymself, ther is noon oother.

2189 *The Canterbury Tales*
Kepe wel they tonge, and thenk upon the crowe.

2190 *The Canterbury Tales*
Derk was the nyght as pich, or as the cole,
And at the wyndow out she putte hir hole,
And Absolon, hym fil no bet be wers,
But with his mouth he kiste hir naked ers.

2191 *The Canterbury Tales*
'By God,' quod he, 'for pleynly, at a word,
Thy drasty rymyng is nat worth a toord!'

2192 *The Canterbury Tales*
'My lige lady, generally,' quod he,
'Wommen desiren to have sovereynetee
As wel over hir housbond as hir love.'

2193 *The Canterbury Tales*
That he is gentil that dooth gentil dedis.

2194 *The Romaunt of the Rose*
Thou shalt make castels thanne in Spayne
And dreme of joye, all but in vayne.

2195 *Tale of Melibee*
What is bettre than wisedoom? Womman.
And what is bettre than a good womman?

Nothyng.

2196 *Troilus and Criseyde*
It is nought good a slepyng hound to wake.

CHAUSSÉE Nivelle de la 1692-1754
2197 *La Gouvernante*
When everyone is wrong, everyone is right.

CHAVEZ Cesar 1927-1993
2198
Is some cases non-violence requires more militancy than violence.

CHAYEFSKY Paddy 1923-1981
2199
Television is not the truth. Television is a god-damned amusement park. Television is a circus, a carnival, a travelling troupe of acrobats, storytellers, dancers, singers, jugglers, sideshow freaks, lion tamers and football players. We're in the boredom-killing business.

CHAZAI
2200
A woman knows how to keep quiet when she is in the right, whereas a man, when he is in the right, will keep on talking.

CHEKHOV Anton 1860-1904
2201
Any idiot can face a crisis - it's this day-to-day living that wears you out.

2202
Medicine is my lawful wife. Literature is my mistress.

2203
A man and a woman marry because both of them don't know what to do with themselves.

2204 *Letter to Alexander Chekhov*
Brevity is the sister of talent.

2205 *The Seagull*
Women can't forgive failure.

2206 *Uncle Vanya*
Man has been endowed with reason, with the power to create, so that he can add to what he's been given. But up to now he hasn't been a creator, only a destroyer.

Forests keep disappearing, rivers dry up, wild life's become extinct, the climate's ruined and the land grows poorer and uglier every day.

2207 *Uncle Vanya*
A woman can become a man's friend only in the following stages - first an acquaintance, next a mistress, and only then a friend.

2208 *Uncle Vanya*
When a woman isn't beautiful, people always say, 'You have lovely eyes, you have lovely hair.'

CHENEY Dick 1941-
2209
It is easy to take liberty for granted, when you have never had it taken from you.

CHENNAULT Anna
2210
Equal opportunity is good, but special privilege even better.

CHEPIK Nikolai 1966-1985
2211 *(from his diary)*
Believing that a girl will wait is just like jumping with a parachute packed by someone else.

CHER 1946-
2212
The trouble with some women is they get all excited about nothing - and then they marry him!

PROVERBS and SAYINGS
2213
Enthusiasm is the greatest asset in the world. It beats money and power and influence.

CHESTERFIELD Lord 1694-1773
2214
Patience is a most necessary quality for business; many a man would rather you heard his story than grant his request.

2215
Without some dissimulation no business can be carried on at all.

2216
When a man is once in fashion, all he does is right.

2217
If you would convince others, seem open to conviction yourself.

2218 *Letters to his Son*
An injury is much sooner forgotten than an insult.

2219 *Letters to his son*
Women are much more like each other than men: they have, in truth, but two passions - vanity and love; these are their universal characteristics.

CHESTERTON G.K. 1874-1936
2220
Democracy means government by the uneducated, while aristocracy means government by the badly educated.

2221
There is nothing the matter with Americans except their ideals. The real American is all right; it is the ideal American who is all wrong.

2222
Men always talk about the most important things to perfect strangers.

2223
The paradox of courage is that a man must be a little careless of his life even in order to keep it.

2224
Tradition means giving votes to the most obscure of all classes - our ancestors. It is the democracy of the dead. Tradition refuses to submit to the small and arrogant oligarchy of those who merely happen to be walking around.

2225
We make our friends; we make our enemies; but God makes our next-door neighbour.

2226
The word 'good' has many meanings. For example, if a man were to shoot his grandmother at a range of five hundred

yards, I should call him a good shot, but not *necessarily* a good man.

2227
I am not absent-minded. It is the presence of mind that makes me unaware of everything else.

2228
Merely having an open mind is nothing. The object of opening the mind, as of opening the mouth, is to shut it again on something solid.

2229
Large organization is loose organization. Nay, it would be almost as true to say that organization is always disorganization.

2230
Psychoanalysis is confession without absolution.

2231
Angels fly because they take themselves lightly.

2232
Facts as facts do not always create a spirit of reality, because reality is a spirit.

2233
One may understand the cosmos, but never the ego; the self is more distant than any star.

2234
Silence is the unbearable repartee.

2235
The classes that wash most are those that work least.

2236
A man must love a thing very much if he not only practises it without any hope of fame and money, but even practises it without any hope of doing it well.

2237 *The Ballad of the White Horse*
I tell you naught for your comfort,
Yea, naught for your desire,
Save that the sky grows darker yet
And the sea rises higher.

2238 *The Defendant*
There is a road from the eye to the heart that does not go through the intellect.

2239 *The Defendant 'A Defence of Penny Dreadfuls'*
Literature is a luxury; fiction is a necessity.

2240 *'English Graves'*
They died to save their country and they only saved the world.

2241 *The Flying Inn*
The rich are the scum of the earth in every country.

2242 *Heretics*
Bigotry may be roughly defined as the anger of men who have no opinions.

2243 *'A Hymn'*
From all that terror teaches,
From lies of tongue and pen,
From all the easy speeches
That comfort cruel men,
From sale and profanation
Of honour and the sword,
From sleep and from damnation,
Deliver us, good Lord!

2244 *'Lepanto'*
Strong gongs groaning as the guns boom far,
Don John of Austria is going to the war.

2245 *The Man who was Thursday*
Thieves respect property. They merely wish the property to become their property that they may more perfectly respect it.

2246 *Orthodoxy*
All conservatism is based upon the idea that if you leave things alone you leave them as they are. But you do not. If you leave a thing alone you leave it to a torrent of change.

2247 *'The Rolling English Road'*
Before the Roman came to Rye or out to Severn strode,
The rolling English drunkard made the rolling English road.
A reeling road, a rolling road, that rambles round the shire,
And after him the parson ran, the sexton and the squire;

A merry road, a mazy road, and such as
we did tread
The night we went to Birmingham by way
of Beachy Head.

2248 *'The Secret People'*
Smile at us, pay us, pass us; but do not
quite forget.
For we are the people of England, that
never have spoken yet.

2249 *What's Wrong with the World*
The Christian ideal has not been tried and
found wanting. It has been found difficult;
and left untried.

2250 *What's Wrong with the World*
The prime truth of woman, the universal
mother ... that if a thing is worth doing, it
is worth doing badly.

CHEVALIER Maurice 1888-1972
2251
Old age is not so bad when you consider
the alternatives.

2252 *(attributed)*
Many a man has fallen in love with a girl
in a light so dim he would not have chosen
a suit by it.

2253
The crime of loving is forgetting.

CHIAROMENTE Nicola
2254
It is only through fiction and the
dimension of the imaginary that we can
learn something real about individual
experience. Any other approach is bound
to be general and abstract.

CHILDERS Erskine 1870-1922
2255
The riddle of the sands.

2256
Come closer, boys. It will be easier for
you.

CHILDS Richard S.
2257
A reformer is one who sets forth cheerfully
towards sure defeat.

CHING Cyrus
2258
I learned long ago never to wrestle with a
pig. You get dirty, and besides, the pig
likes it.

CHISHOLM Shirley
2259
Of my two 'handicaps', being female put
many more obstacles in my path than
being black.

CHOPIN Frédéric 1810-1849
2260
Every difficulty slurred over will be a
ghost to disturb your repose later on.

CHRISTIE Dame Agatha 1890-1976
2261 *An Autobiography*
War settles nothing ... to win a war is as
disastrous as to lose one!

2262 *At Bertram's Hotel*
I learned ... that one can never go back,
that one should not ever try to go back -
that the essence of life is going forward.
Life is really a One Way Street.

2263 *(of her own marriage)*
An archaeologist is the best husband any
woman can have. The older she gets, the
more interested he is in her.

2264 *The Mysterious Affair at Styles*
He [Hercule Poirot] tapped his forehead.
'These little grey cells. It is "up to them".'

CHRISTINA Queen of Sweden
2265
I love men, not because they are men, but
because they are not women.

CHURCH Richard Thomas 1893-1972
2266 *Be Frugal*
Be frugal in the gift of love,
Lest you should kindle in return
Love like your own, that may survive
Long after yours has ceased to burn.

CHURCHILL Charles 1731-1764
2267 *The Conference*
The only difference, after all their rout,
Is, that the one is in, the other out.

2268 *An Epistle to William Hogarth*
The danger chiefly lies in acting well;
No crime's so great as daring to excel.

2269 *The Ghost*
Just to the windward of the law.

2270 *The Ghost*
A joke's a very serious thing.

2271 *Night*
Keep up appearances; there lies the test;
The world wil give thee credit for the rest.

2272 *The Rosciad*
So much they talked, so very little said.

2273 *The Rosciad*
The two extremes appear like man and
wife,
Coupled together for the sake of strife.

CHURCHILL Lord Randolph 1849-1894
2274
Whenever by an unfortunate occurrence of
circumstances an opposition is compelled
to support the government, the support
should be given with a kick and not a
caress and should be withdrawn at the
first available moment.

2275
Ulster will fight; Ulster will be right.

2276 *(of Gladstone)*
An old man in a hurry.

CHURCHILL Sir Winston 1874-1965
2277
I am easily satisfied with the very best.

2278
We shape our buildings; thereafter they
shape us.

2279
Courage is rightly esteemed the first of
human qualities because it is the quality
which guarantees all others.

2280
It has been said that Democracy is the
worst form of government except all those
other forms that have been tried from time
to time.

2281
The English never draw a line without
blurring it.

2282
Where does the family start? It starts with
a young man falling in love with a girl - no
superior alternative has yet been found.

2283
It is a mistake to look too far ahead. Only
one link in the chain of destiny can be
handled at a time.

2284
When I am abroad, I always make it a rule
never to criticize or attack the government
of my own country. I make up for lost
time when I come home.

2285
We are all worms, but I do believe that I
am a glow-worm.

2286
Dictators ride to and fro on tigers from
which they dare not dismount. And the
tigers are getting hungry.

2287
An appeaser is one who feeds a crocodile -
hoping it will eat him last.

2288
The whole history of the world is summed
up in the fact that, when nations are
strong, they are not always just, and when
they wish to be just, they are no longer
strong.

2289
I have never accepted what many people
have kindly said, namely that I have
inspired the nation. It was the nation and
the race dwelling all around the globe that
had the lion heart. I had the luck to be
called upon to give the roar.

2290
Without a measureless and perpetual
uncertainty, the drama of human life
would be destroyed.

2291
Out of intense complexities intense
simplicities emerge.

2292
I cannot pretend to feel impartial about
colours. I rejoice with the brilliant ones
and am genuinely sorry for the poor
browns.

2293
Politics is more dangerous than war, for in
war you are only killed once.

2294
He has all of the virtues I dislike and none
of the vices I admire.

2295
Say what you have to say and the first
time you come to a sentence with a
grammatical ending - sit down.

2296
If you have an important point to make,
don't try to be subtle or clever. Use a pile-
driver. Hit the point once. Then come
back and hit it again. Then hit it a third
time - a tremendous whack!

2297
It is no use saying 'we are doing our best'.
You have got to succeed in doing what is
necessary.

2298
Never give in, never give in, never, never,
never, never - in nothing great or small,
large or petty - never give in except to
convictions of honour and good sense.

2299
War is mainly a catalogue of blunders.

2300
No one can guarantee success in war, but
only deserve it.

2301
In war, as in life, it is often necessary, when
some cherished scheme has failed, to take
up the best alternative open, and if so, it is
folly not to work for it with all your might.

2302
A fanatic is one who can't change his mind
and won't change the subject.

2303
So they [the Government] go on in strange
paradox, decided only to be undecided,

resolved to be irresolute, adamant for drift,
solid for fluidity, all-powerful to be
impotent.

2304
I cannot forecast to you the action of
Russia. It is a riddle wrapped in a mystery
inside an enigma.

2305
I have nothing to offer but blood, toil, tears
and sweat.

2306
What is our aim? ... Victory, victory at all
costs, victory in spite of all terror; victory,
however long and hard the road may be;
for without victory, there is no survival.

2307
We shall not flag or fail. We shall go on to
the end. We shall fight in France, we shall
fight on the seas and oceans, we shall fight
with growing confidence and growing
strength in the air, we shall defend our
island, whatever the cost may be. We shall
fight on the beaches, we shall fight on the
landing grounds, we shall fight in the
fields and in the streets, we shall fight in
the hills; we shall never surrender.

2308
Let us therefore brace ourselves to our
duty, and so bear ourselves that, if the
British Commonwealth and its Empire
lasts for a thousand years, men will still
say, 'This was their finest hour.'

2309
Never in the field of human conflict was so
much owed by so many to so few.

2310
Give us the tools and we will finish the
job.

2311
When I warned them [the French
Government] that Britain would fight on
alone whatever they did, their generals
told their Prime Minister and his divided
Cabinet, 'In three weeks England will have
her neck wrung like a chicken.' Some
chicken! Some neck!

2312
National compulsory insurance for all classes for all purposes from the cradle to the grave.

2313
The empires of the future are the empires of the mind.

2314
From Stettin in the Baltic to Trieste in the Adriatic and iron curtain has descended across the Continent.

2315
Now this is not the end. It is not even the beginning of the end. But it is, perhaps, the end of the beginning.

2316
To jaw-jaw is always better than to war-war.

2317
This is the sort of English up with which I will not put.

2318 *(of Clement Attlee)*
A sheep in sheep's clothing.

2319 *My Darling Clementine*
My most brilliant achievement was my ability to be able to persuade my wife to marry me.

2320 *The Second World War*
All I wanted was compliance with my wishes after reasonable discussion.

CIANO Count Galeazzo 1903-1944
2321 *Diary*
Victory has a hundred fathers, but defeat is an orphan.

CIARDI John 1916-
2322
A savage is simply a human organism that has not received enough news from the human race.

2323
Gentility is what is left over from rich ancestors after the money is gone.

2324
Modern art is what happens when painters stop looking at girls and persuade

themselves they have a better idea.

2325
Every parent is at some time the father of the unreturned prodigal, with nothing to do but keep his house open to hope.

2326
Boys are the cash of war. Whoever said: we're not free spenders - doesn't know our like.

2327
A university is what a college becomes when the faculty loses interest in students.

CIBBER Colley 1671-1757
2328 *The Double Gallant*
Oh! how many torments lie in the small circle of a wedding-ring!

2329 *Richard III*
Perish the thought!

CICERO Marcus Tullius 106-43 BC
2330
It has seemed to be more necessary to have regard to the weight of words rather than to their number.

2331
Old age is by nature rather talkative.

2332
Old age, especially an honoured old age, has so great authority, that this is of more value than all the pleasures of youth.

2333
Certain signs precede certain events.

2334
I never admired another's fortune so much that I became dissatisfied with my own.

2335
Hatred is settled anger.

2336
I am not ashamed to confess that I am ignorant of what I do not know.

2337
When you have no basis for an argument, abuse the plaintiff.

2338
We are in bondage to the law in order that we may be free.

2339
There is something pleasurable in calm remembrance of a past sorrow.

2340
The authority of those who profess to teach is often a positive hindrance to those who desire to learn.

2341
For it is commonly said: accomplished labours are pleasant.

2342 *In Catilinam Speech*
Oh, the times! Oh, the manners!

2343 *De Divinatione*
There is nothing so absurd but some philosopher has said it.

2344 *In Verrem Speech 5*
I am a Roman citizen.

CIORAN E.M.
2345
Democracy is a festival of mediocrity.

2346
No one can keep his griefs in their prime; they use themselves up.

CLAPHAM Lady Elizabeth 1911-1994
2347
I never drink gin. It makes me, by turns, bellicose, lachrymose and comatose.

CLARE John 1793-1864
2348 *(attributed)*
Language has not the power to speak what love indites:
The soul lies buried in the ink that writes.

2349 *'Child Harold'*
My life hath been one chain of contradictions,
Madhouses, prisons, whore-shops.

2350 *'Child Harold'*
They took me from my wife, and to save trouble
I wed again, and made the error double.

2351 *'Child Harold'*
Pale death, the grand physician, cures all pain;
The dead rest well who lived for joys in vain.

2352 *'Child Harold'*
Hopeless hope hopes on and meets no end,
Wastes without springs and homes without a friend.

2353 *'First Love'*
I never saw so sweet a face
As that I stood before.
My heart has left its dwelling place
And can return no more.

2354 *'To Mary'*
I sleep with thee, and wake with thee,
And yet thou are not there.

2355 *'The present is the funeral of the past'*
The present is the funeral of the past,
And man the living sepulchre of life.

CLARENDON Edward, Earl of 1609-1674
2356 *The History of the Rebellion (of Hampden)*
Without question, when he first drew the sword, he threw away the scabbard.

2357 *The History of the Rebellion (of Falkland)*
So enamoured on peace that he would have been glad the King should have bought it at any price.

2358 *The History of the Rebellion (of Cromwell)*
He will be looked upon by posterity as a brave bad man.

CLARK Jane
2359
All girlfriends are like bluebottles. Some are just a bit harder to swat.

CLARK Joe 1939-
2360
One of the luxuries of a politican's life is that you see yourself as others see you.

CLARK Kenneth 1903-1983
2361
We can destroy ourselves by cynicism and disillusion just as effectively as by bombs.

2362
True perfection is achieved only by those who are prepared to destroy it. It is a by-product of greatness.

2363 *Civilisation*
Medieval marriages were entirely a matter of property, and, as everyone knows, marriage without love means love without marriage.

CLARK Ramsay 1927-
2364
Turbulence is life force. It is opportunity. Let's love turbulence and use it for change.

CLARKE Arthur C. 1917-
2365
Any sufficiently advanced technology is indistinguishable from magic.

CLARKE John d. 1658
2366 *Paraemiologia Anglo-Latina 'Diligentia'*
He that would thrive
Must rise at five;
He that hath thriven
May lie till seven.

CLAUDIAN 4th Century AD
2367
The vices of monarchs can never remain hidden.

CLAUSEWITZ Karl von 1780-1831
2368 *Vom Kriege*
War is nothing but a continuation of politics with the admixture of other means.

CLAY Henry 1777-1852
2369
Statistics are no substitute for judgement.

2370 *(to Senator Preston of South Carolina)*
I had rather be right than be President.

CLEAVER Eldridge 1935-
2371
Too much agreement kills a chat.

CLEMENCEAU Georges 1841-1929
2372 *(attributed)*
War is too serious a matter to entrust to military men.

2373
It is easier to make war than to make peace.

2374
All the great pleasures in life are silent.

2375
All that I know I learned after I was thirty.

2376
There is no passion like that of a functionary for his function.

2377
War is a series of catastrophes which result in victory.

CLEVELAND John 1613-1658
2378 *'Epitaph on the Earl of Strafford'*
Here lies wise and valiant dust,
Huddled up, 'twixt fit and just:
Strafford, who was hurried hence
'Twixt treason and convenience.
He spent his time here in a mist,
A Papist, yet a Calvinist ...
Riddles lie here, or in a word,
Here lies blood; and let it lie
Speechless still, and never cry.

CLIFT Montgomery 1920-1966
2379
I have enough money to get by. I'm not independently wealthy, just independently lazy, I suppose.

CLINTON Bill 1946-
2380
There is nothing wrong with America that cannot be cured by what is right in America.

CLIVE Lord 1725-1774
2381 *(when his pistol twice failed to fire)*
I feel that I am reserved for some end or other.

CLOUGH Arthur Hugh 1819-1861
2382 *The Bothie of Tober-na-Vuolich*
Grace is given of God, but knowledge is bought in the market.

2383 *Dipsychus*
And almost everyone when age,
Disease, or sorrows strike him,
Inclines to think there is a God,
Or something very like Him.

2384 *'The Latest Decalogue'*
Thou shalt not kill; but need'st not strive
Officiously to keep alive.

2385 *'The Latest Decalogue'*
Do not adultery commit;
Advantage rarely comes of it.

2386 *'The Latest Decalogue'*
Thou shalt not steal; an empty feat,
When it's so lucrative to cheat.

2387 *'The Latest Decalogue'*
Thou shalt not covet; but tradition
Approves all forms of competition.

2388 *'Say not the struggle naught availeth'*
In front the sun climbs slow, how slowly,
But westward, look, the land is bright.

COBAIN Curt 1967-1994
2389 *(suicide note)*
The worst crime is faking it.

COBB Irvin S.
2390
If a woman likes another woman, she's
cordial. If she doesn't like her, she's very
cordial.

COBBETT William 1762-1835
2391
From a very early age, I had imbibed the
opinion, that it was every man's duty to do
all that lay in his power to leave his
country as good as he had found it.

COCKER Joe
2392
England to me was always the 3 o'clock
break - that endless gap between lunch
and the pub opening again.

COCTEAU Jean 1889-1963
2393
The greatest masterpiece in literature is
only a dictionary out of order.

2394
Style is a simple way of saying
complicated things.

2395
Art produces ugly things which frequently
become beautiful with time. Fashion, on
the other hand, produces beautiful things
which always become ugly with time.

2396
The joy of the young is to disobey - but the
trouble is that there are no longer any
orders.

2397 *Journal d'un inconnu*
Poetry is a religion with no hope.

2398 *Le Coq et l'Arlequin*
The essential in daring is to know how far
one can go too far.

2399 *Opium*
Life is a horizontal fall.

2400 *Opium*
Victor Hugo was a madman who thought
he was Victor Hugo.

COFFIN Harold
2401
A consumer is a shopper who is sore about
something.

COFFIN Rev. William Sloane 1924-
2402
I'm not ok - you're not ok, and that's ok.

2403
The world is too dangerous for anything
but truth, and too small for anything but
love.

COKE Sir Edward 1552-1634
2404
Corporations cannot commit treason, nor
be outlawed, nor excommunicated, for
they have no souls.

2405 *Institutes of Laws of England*
How long soever it hath continued, if it be
against reason, it is of no force in law.

2406 *Institutes of Laws of England*
For a man's house is his castle.

COLBERT Jean Baptiste 1619-1683
2407
The art of taxation consists in so plucking
the goose as to get the most feathers with
the least hissing.

COLBY Frank Moore
2408
Many people lose their tempers merely
from seeing you keep yours.

COLEMAN John S.

2409
The point to remember is that what the government gives, it must first take away.

COLERIDGE Samuel Taylor 1772-1834

2410
Advice is like snow; the softer it falls, the longer it dwells upon, and the deeper it sinks into, the mind.

2411
To most men, experience is like the stern lights of a ship, which illumine only the track it has passed.

2412
Only the wise possess ideas; the greater part of mankind are possessed by them.

2413
As long as there are readers to be delighted with calumny, there will be found reviewers to calumniate.

2414
What is an epigram? A dwarfish whole, Its body brevity, and wit its soul.

2415
So lonely 'twas that God himself Scarce seemed there to be.

2416 *'Epitaph on an Infant'*
Ere sin could blight or sorrow fade, Death came with friendly care: The opening bud to Heaven conveyed And bade it blossom there.

2417 *'Kubla Khan'*
In Xanadu did Kubla Khan A stately pleasure-dome decree: Where Alph, the sacred river, ran Through caverns measureless to man Down to a sunless sea. So twice five miles of fertile ground With walls and towers were girdled round.

2418 *'Kubla Khan'*
It was a miracle of rare device, A sunny pleasure-dome with caves of ice.

2419 *'Kubla Khan'*
And 'mid this tumult Kubla heard from far Ancestral voices prophesying war!

2420 *'The Rime of the Ancient Mariner'*
'God save thee, ancient Mariner! From the fiends that plague thee thus! - Why look'st thou so?' - With my cross-bow I shot the Albatross.

2421 *'The Rime of the Ancient Mariner'*
Water, water, everywhere, And all the boards did shrink; Water, water, everywhere, Nor any drop to drink. The very deep did rot: O Christ! That ever this should be! Yes, slimy things did crawl with legs Upon the slimy sea.

2422 *'The Rime of the Ancient Mariner'*
The Sun's rim dips; the stars rush out; At one stride comes the dark.

2423 *'The Rime of the Ancient Mariner'*
Like one, that on a lonesome road Doth walk in fear and dread, And having once turned round walks on, And turns no more his head; Because he knows, a frightful fiend Doth close behind him tread.

2424 *'The Rime of the Ancient Mariner'*
No voice; but oh! the silence sank Like music on my heart.

2425 *'The Rime of the Ancient Mariner'*
He prayeth well, who loveth well Both man and bird and beast. He prayeth best, who loveth best All things both great and small.

2426 *'The Rime of the Ancient Mariner'*
He went like one that hath been stunned, And is of sense forlorn: A sadder and a wiser man, He rose the morrow morn.

2427 *Seven Lectures on Shakespeare and Milton*
Reviewers are usually people who would have been poets, historians, biographers, &c., if they could; they have tried their talents at one or at the other, and have failed; therefore they turn critics.

2428 *Table Talk*
You abuse snuff! Perhaps it is the final cause of the human nose.

2429 *Table Talk*
Prose = words in their best order; - poetry
= the best words in the best order.

2430 *Table Talk*
The man's desire is for the woman; but the woman's desire is rarely other than for the desire of the man.

2431 *Table Talk*
In politics, what begins in fear usually ends in folly.

2432 *'Work without Hope'*
Work without hope draws nectar in a sieve,
And hope without an object cannot live.

COLES D.L.
2433
The age of strong belief is over, the good is no longer always very good.

COLETTE (Sidonie-Gabrielle) 1873-1954
2434
It takes time for the absent to assume their true shape in our thoughts. After death they take on a firmer outline and then cease to change.

2435
The woman who thinks she is intelligent demands equal rights with men. A woman who is intelligent does not.

2436 *Claudine and Annie*
When she raises her eyelids it's as though she were taking off all her clothes.

COLLIE G. Norman
2437
To make certain that crime does not pay, the government should take it over and try to run it.

COLLINGBOURNE William d.1484
2438 *The Concordance of Chronicles*
The Cat, the Rat, and Lovell our dog
Rule all England under a hog.

COLLINGWOOD Admiral Lord 1748-1810
2439 *(before the Battle of Trafalgar)*
Now, gentlemen, let us do something today which the world may talk of hereafter.

COLLINS John Churton 1848-1908
2440
To ask advice is in nine cases out of ten to tout for flattery.

2441
The world, like an accomplished hostess, pays most attention to those whom it will soonest forget.

COLLINS Mortimer 1827-1876
2442 *The Unknown Quantity*
A man is as old as he's feeling.
A woman as old as she looks.

COLLINS William 1721-1759
2443 *'Ode Written in the Year 1746'*
How sleep the brave, who sink to rest,
By all their country's wishes blest!

2444 *'The Passions, an Ode for Music'*
Love of peace, and lonely musing,
In hollow murmurs died away.

2445 *'Verses addressed to Sir Thomas Hanmer'*
Too nicely Jonson knew the critic's part,
Nature in him was almost lost in Art.

COLMAN The Younger, George 1762-1836
2446 *The Heir at Law*
Oh, London is a fine town,
A very famous city,
Where all the streets are paved with gold,
And all the maidens pretty.

COLTON Charles Caleb c.1780-1832
2447
Ennui has made more gamblers than avarice, more drunkards than thirst, and perhaps as many suicides as despair.

2448
Body and mind, like man and wife, do not always agree to die together.

2449
Never join with your friend when he abuses his horse or his wife unless the one is to be sold, and the other to be buried.

2450
We owe almost all our knowledge not to those who have agreed, but to those who have differed.

2451
If you cannot inspire a woman with love of you, fill her above the brim with love of herself; all that runs over will be yours.

2452
I have found by experience that they who have spent all their lives in cities, improve their talents but impair their virtues; and strengthen their minds but weaken their morals.

2453
Applause is the spur of noble minds, the end and aim of weak ones.

2454
We hate some persons because we do not know them; and will not know them because we hate them.

2455
There is a paradox in pride: it makes some men ridiculous, but prevents others from becoming so.

2456
Men will wrangle for religion, write for it, fight for it, die for it, anything but live for it.

2457
To dare to live alone is the rarest courage; since there are many who had rather meet their bitterest enemy in the field, than their own hearts in their closet.

2458 *Lacon*
When you have nothing to say, say nothing.

2459 *Lacon*
Examinations are formidable even to the best prepared, for the greatest fool may ask more than the wisest man can answer.

2460 *Lacon*
If you would be known, and not know, vegetate in a village; if you would know, and not be known, live in a city.

2461 *Lacon*
Friendship often ends in love; but love in friendship - never.

COMDEN Betty and GREEN Adolph
1919- and 1915-
2462 *'New York, New York'*
New York, New York, a helluva town,
The Bronx is up but the Battery's down,
And people ride in a hole in the ground:
New York, New York, It's a helluva town.

2463 *'The Party's Over'*
The party's over, it's time to call it a day.

COMFORT Alex 1920-
2464
Two weeks is about the ideal length of time to retire.

2465
The telephone is the most important single technological resource of later life.

2466
Sex ought to be a wholly satisfying link between two affectionate people from which they emerge unanxious, rewarded, and ready for more.

COMMONER Barry
2467
The first law of ecology is that everything is related to everything else.

COMPTON-BURNETT Dame Ivy 1884-1969
2468
Real life seems to have no plots.

2469
There is probably nothing like living together for blinding people to each other.

2470
There is more difference within the sexes than between them.

2471 *A Family and a Fortune*
Well, of course, people are only human ... But it really does not seem much for them to be.

2472 *A Family and a Fortune*
People don't resent having nothing nearly as much as too little.

2473 *The Mighty and their Fall*
There are different kinds of wrong. The people sinned against are not always the best.

2474 *Orion*
My point is that it [wickedness] is not punished, and that is why it is natural to be guilty of it. When it is likely to be punished, most of us avoid it.

CONANT James Bryant 1898-1978
2475
Democracy is a small hard core of common agreement, surrounded by a rich variety of individual differences.

2476
Each honest calling, each walk of life, has its own elite, its own aristocracy based on excellence of performance.

2477
Behold the turtle. He makes progress only when he sticks his neck out.

CONE Fairfax
2478
Advertising is what you do when you can't go to see somebody. That's all it is.

CONFUCIUS 551-479 BC
2479
Music produces a kind of pleasure which human nature cannot do without.

CONGREVE William 1670-1729
2480 *The Double Dealer*
There is nothing more unbecoming a man of quality than to laugh; Jesu, 'tis such a vulgar expression of the passion!

2481 *The Double Dealer*
She lays it on with a trowel.

2482 *The Double Dealer*
See how love and murder will out.

2483 *'Hymn to Harmony'*
Music alone with sudden charms can bind
The wand'ring sense, and calm the troubled mind.

2484 *Love for Love*
He that first cries out stop thief, is often he that has stolen the treasure.

2485 *Love for Love*
Women are like tricks by slight of hand,
Which, to admire, we should not understand.

2486 *The Mourning Bride*
Music has charms to soothe a savage breast.

2487 *The Mourning Bride*
Heaven has no rage, like love to hatred turned,
Nor Hell a fury, like a woman scorned.

2488 *The Way of the World*
These articles subscribed, if I continue to endure you a little longer, I may by degrees dwindle into a wife.

2489 *The Way of the World*
Courtship to marriage, as a very witty prologue to a very dull Play.

CONNELL James M. 1852-1929
2490 *'The Red Flag'*
The people's flag is deepest red;
It shrouded oft our martyred dead,
And ere their limbs grew stiff and cold,
Their heart's blood dyed its every fold.
Then raise the scarlet standard high!
Within its shade we'll live or die.
Tho' cowards flinch and traitors sneer,
We'll keep the red flag flying here.

CONNOLLY Cyril 1903-1974
2491
It is closing time in the gardens of the West and from now on an artist will be judged only by the resonance of his solitude or the quality of his despair.

2492
It is only in the country that we can get to know a person or a book.

2493
All charming people have something to conceal, usually their total dependence on the appreciation of others.

2494
The one way to get thin is to re-establish a purpose in life.

2495
Hate is the consequence of fear; we fear something before we hate it; a child who fears noises becomes a man who hates noise.

2496
Most people do not believe in anything very much and our greatest poetry is given to us by those that do.

2497
The man who is master of his passions is Reason's slave.

2498
We are all serving a life sentence in the dungeon of self.

2499
Better to write for yourself and have no public, than to write for the public and have no self.

2500 *Enemies of Promise*
Whom the gods wish to destroy they first call promising.

2501 *Enemies of Promise*
There is no more sombre enemy of good art than the pram in the hall.

2502 *The Unquiet Grave*
Life is a maze in which we take the wrong turning before we have learnt to walk.

2503 *The Unquiet Grave*
Imprisoned in every fat man a thin one is wildly signalling to be let out.

2504 *The Unquiet Grave*
There is no fury like an ex-wife searching for a new lover.

CONNOR Ralph 1860-1937
2505
I would often be a coward, but for the shame of it.

2506
Love, you know, seeks to make happy rather than to be happy.

CONRAD Joseph 1857-1924
2507
Action is consolatory. It is the enemy of thought and the friend of flattering illusions.

2508
History repeats itself, but the special call of an art which has passed away is never reproduced. It is utterly gone out of the world as the song of a destroyed wild bird.

2509
The last thing a woman will consent to discover in a man whom she loves, or on whom she simply depends, is want of courage.

2510
How does one kill fear, I wonder? How do you shoot a spectre through the heart, slash off its spectral head, take it by the spectral throat?

2511
As in political, so in literary action, a man wins friends for himself mostly by the passion of his prejudices.

2512
Caricature: putting the face of a joke upon the body of a truth.

2513
Who knows what true loneliness is - not the conventional word but the naked terror? To the lonely themselves it wears a mask. The most miserable outcast hugs some memory or some illusion.

2514
To have his path made clear for him is the aspiration of every human being in our beclouded and tempestuous existence.

2515
The sea - the truth must be confessed - has no generosity. No display of manly qualities - courage, hardihood, endurance, faithfulness - has ever been known to touch its irresponsible consciousness of power.

2516 *The Arrow of Gold*
In plucking the fruit of memory one runs the risk of spoiling its bloom.

2517 *Heart of Darkness*
The conquest of the earth, which mostly means the taking it away from those who have a different complexion or slightly flatter noses than ourselves, is not a pretty thing when you look into it.

2518 *Heart of Darkness*
We live, as we dream - alone.

CONSTABLE John 1776-1837
2519
I never saw an ugly thing in my life.

CONSTANT Benjamin 1767-1834
2520
Art for art's sake, ... perverts art.

COOK Dan
2521
The opera ain't over 'til the fat lady sings.

COOK Joe
2522
Of all my wife's relations I like myself the best.

COOLIDGE Calvin 1872-1933
2523
The chief business of the American people is business.

2524
The presidency does not yield to definition. Like the glory of a morning sunrise, it can be experienced - it can not be told.

2525
I think the American public wants a solemn ass as a president, and I think I'll go along with them.

2526
I have noticed that nothing I never said ever did me any harm.

2527
If you don't say anything, you won't be called on to repeat it.

2528
When more and more people are thrown out of work, unemployment results.

COOLIDGE Susan 1845-1905
2529 *What Katy Did*
Blessings brighten as they take their flight.

COOPER Alice 1948-
2530
We've been so bombarded with sex that sex isn't sexy any more. Romance is much sexier now. I think that in the 1990's, we're going to start seeing people dating again.

COPLAND Aaron 1900-1990
2531
If a literary man puts together two words about music, one of them will be wrong.

CORELLI Marie 1855-1924
2532
I never married because I have three pets at home that answer the same purpose as a husband. I have a dog that growls every morning, a parrot that swears all afternoon, and a cat that comes home late at night.

CORNEILLE Pierre 1606-1684
2533
Violence is just, where kindness is vain.

2534 *Le Cid*
When there is no peril in the fight, there is no glory in the triumph.

CORNFORD Frances 1886-1960
2535 *All Soul's Night*
My love came back to me
Under the November tree
Shelterless and dim.
He put his hand upon my shoulder,
He did not think me strange or older,
Nor I, him.

2536 *'Youth' (of Rupert Brooke)*
A young Apollo, golden-haired,
Stands dreaming on the verge of strife,
Magnificently unprepared
For the long littleness of life.

CORNFORD Francis M. 1874-1943
2537 *Microcosmographia Academica*
University printing presses exist, and are subsidised by the Government for the purpose of producing books which no one can read; and they are true to their high calling.

2538 *Microcosmographia Academica*
The Principle of Unripe Time is that people should not do at the present moment what they think right at that moment, because the moment at which they think it right has not yet arrived.

COROT Jean Baptiste 1796-1875
2539
I hope with all my heart there will be painting in heaven.

CORT David
2540
Sex is the great amateur art.

CORY William 1823-1892
2541 *'Heraclitus' (translation of Callimachus)*
I wept as I remembered how often you and
I
Had tired the sun with talking and sent
him down the sky.

COSBY Bill 1937-
2542
Human beings are the only creatures on
earth that allow their children to come
back home.

COSSMAN Joseph E.
2543
Obstacles are things a person sees when he
takes his eyes off his goal.

2544
Middle age is when your broad mind and
narrow waist begin to change places.

2545
The best way to remember your wife's
birthday is to forget it once.

COTGRAVE Randle
2546
Eat bread at pleasure, drink wine by
measure.

COTY René 1882-1962
2547
It's taken me all my life to understand that
it is not necessary to understand
everything.

COURTELINE Georges
2548
A woman never sees what we do for her,
she only sees what we don't do.

COURTENAY Walter R.
2549
God gave man work, not to burden him,
but to bless him, and useful work,
willingly, cheerfully, effectively done, has
always been the finest expression of the
human spirit.

COUSINS Norman 1915-1990
2550
The most costly disease is not cancer or
coronaries. The most costly disease is
boredom - costly for both individual and
society.

2551
The human body experiences a powerful
gravitational pull in the direction of hope.
That is why the patient's hopes are the
physician's secret weapon. They are the
hidden ingredients in any prescription.

2552
The eternal quest of the individual human
being is to shatter his loneliness.

2553
The possibility of war increases in direct
proportion to the effectiveness of the
instruments of war.

COUTELI
2554
We are dying of accuracy.

COWARD Noël 1899-1973
2555
As one gets older, one discovers
everything is going to be exactly the same
with different hats on.

2556
My body has certainly wandered a good
deal, but I have an uneasy suspicion that
my mind has not wandered enough.

2557
Good heavens, television is something you
appear on, you don't watch.

2558
Work is more fun than fun.

2559
I've sometimes thought of marrying - and
then I've thought again.

2560 *'Don't Let's Be Beastly to the Germans'*
Don't let's be beastly to the Germans
When our Victory is ultimately won.

2561 *'If Love Were All'*
I believe that since my life began
The most I've had is just
A talent to amuse.

2562 *'Mad about the Boy'*
Mad about the boy,
It's pretty funny but I'm mad about the
boy.
He has a gay appeal
That makes me feel
There may be something sad about the
boy.

2563 *'Mad Dogs and Englishmen'*
Mad dogs and Englishmen
Go out in the midday sun.

2564 *Private Lives*
Very flat, Norfolk.

2565 *Private Lives*
Extraordinary how potent cheap music is.

2566 *(of Randolph Churchill)*
Dear Randolph, utterly unspoiled by
failure!

2567 *(attributed - of the retreat from Dunkirk)*
The noise, my dear! And the people!

2568 *'Mrs Worthington'*
Don't put your daughter on the stage, Mrs
Worthington.

COWLEY Abraham 1618-1667
2569
Hope! of all ills that men endure
The only cheap and universal cure.

2570
Enjoy the present hour,
Be thankful for the past,
And neither fear nor wish
Th' approaches of the last.

2571 *'To Dr Scarborough'*
Life is an incurable disease.

2572 *'The Wish'*
The crowd, and buzz, and murmurings
Of this great hive, the city.

COWLEY Hannah 1743-1809
2573 *Who's the Dupe?*
But what is woman? - only one of Nature's
agreeable blunders.

COWLEY Malcolm 1898-1989
2574
They tell you that you'll lose your mind
when you grow older. What they don't tell

you is that you won't miss it very much.

2575 *(of old age)*
It is the fear of being as dependent as a
young child, while not being loved as a
child is loved, but merely being kept alive
against one's will.

COWPER William 1731-1800
2576
I am monarch of all I survey.

2577
He that has seen both sides of fifty has
lived to little purpose if he has no other
views of the world than he had when he
was much younger.

2578
A fool must now and then be right by
chance.

2579
Existence is a strange bargain. Life owes
us little; we owe it everything. The only
true happiness comes from squandering
ourselves for a purpose.

2580
Happiness depends, as Nature shows,
Less on exterior things than most suppose.

2581
Absence of occupation is not rest,
A mind quite vacant is a mind distress'd.

2582
How much a dunce that has been sent to
roam
Excels a dunce that has been kept at home!

2583 *'Conversation' (on tobacco)*
Pernicious weed! whose scent the fair
annoys.

2584 *'Hope'*
Men deal with life, as children with their
play,
Who first misuse, then cast their toys
away.

2585 *'Hope'*
And differing judgements serve but to
declare
That truth lies somewhere, if we knew but
where.

2586 'John Gilpin'
John Gilpin was a citizen
Of credit and renown,
A train-band captain eke was he
Of famous London Town.

2587 'Light Shining out of Darkness'
God moves in a mysterious way
His wonders to perform;
He plants his footsteps in the sea
And rides upon the storm.

2588 'The Progress of Error'
Remorse, the fatal egg by pleasure laid.

2589 'Table Talk'
Freedom has a thousand charms to show,
That slaves, howe'er contented, never
know.

2590 'Table Talk' (of Perjury)
To turn a penny in the way of trade.

2591 The Task
But war's a game, which, were their
subjects wise,
Kings would not play at.

2592 The Task
Knowledge is proud that he has learned so
much;
Wisdom is humble that he knows no more.

2593 The Task (of hunting)
Detested sport,
That owes its pleasures to another's pain.

2594 The Task 'The Sofa'
Thus first necessity invented stools,
Convenience next suggested elbow-chairs,
And luxury the accomplished sofa last.

2595 The Task 'The Sofa'
God made the country, and man made the
town.

2596 The Task 'The Timepiece'
There is a pleasure in poetic pains
Which only poets know.

2597 The Task 'The Timepiece'
Variety's the very spice of life,
That gives it all its flavour.

2598 'Tirocinium'
The parson knows enough who knows a
duke.

2599 'Truth'
He has no hope that never had a fear.

2600 'Walking with God'
Oh! for a closer walk with God.

CRABBE George 1754-1832
2601 'The Library'
Fashion, though Folly's child, and guide of
fools,
Rules e'en the wisest, and in learning
rules.

2602 Tales of the Hall
Secrets with girls, like loaded guns with
boys,
Are never valued till they make a noise.

2603 The Village
I grant indeed that fields and flocks have
charms,
For him that gazes or for him that farms.

CRAIG Cal
2604
Trouble is, kids feel they have to shock
their elders and each generation grows up
into something harder to shock.

CRANE Stephen 1871-1900
2605
Tradition, thou art for suckling children
Thou are the enlivening milk for babes,
But no meat for men is in thee.

CREIGHTON Bishop
2606
Never laugh feebly at what you know is
wrong.

CREWS Harry
2607
Survival is triumph enough.

CRICHTON Michael
2608
Abuse of power is not a male monopoly.

CRIPPS Agnes
2609
Educate a man and you educate an
individual - educate a woman and you
educate a family.

CRISP Quentin
2610
The young always have the same problem

- how to rebel and conform at the same time. They have now solved this by defying their parents and copying one another.

CRITCHLEY Julian 1930-
2611
The only safe pleasure for a parliamentarian is a bag of boiled sweets.

CROMWELL Oliver 1599-1658
2612
Mr Lely, I desire you would use all your skill to paint my picture truly like me, and not flatter me at all; but remark all these roughnesses, pimples, warts, and everything as you see me; otherwise I will never pay a farthing for it.

2613 *(addressing the Rump Parliament)*
You have sat too long here for any good you have been doing. Depart, I say, and let us have done with you. In the name of God, go!

2614 *(addressing the Rump Parliament)*
Take away that fool's bauble, the mace.

2615 *(of the execution of Charles I)*
Cruel necessity.

2616 *(last words)*
My design is to make what haste I can to be gone.

2617 *Letter to General Assembly of Kirk of Scotland*
I beseech you, in the bowels of Christ, think it possible you may be mistaken.

2618 *(to Parliament)*
You have accounted yourselves happy on being environed with a great ditch from all the world besides.

CRONKITE Walter 1916-
2619
Justice was born outside the home and a long way from it; and it has never been adopted there.

CROSBY Bing 1904-1977
2620
I think popular music in this country is one of the few things in the twentieth century that have made giant strides in reverse.

CROSSMAN R.H.S. 1907-1974
2621
The main task of a free society is to civilize the struggle for power. Slavery of the acquiescent majority to the ruthless few is the hereditary state of mankind; freedom, a rarely-acquired characteristic.

CUDLIPP Hugh 1913-
2622 *(of William Randolph Hearst)*
Truth for him was a moving target; he never aimed for the bull and rarely pierced the outer ring.

CULBERTSON Ely 1891-1955
2623
Politics. The diplomatic name for the law of the jungle.

CUMMING R.D.
2624
A good book has no ending.

CUMMINGS E. E. 1894-1962
2625
all ignorance toboggans into know
and trudges up to ignorance again.

2626
unlove's the heavenless hell and homeless
home ... lovers alone wear sunlight.

2627
a politician is an arse upon which
everyone has sat except a man.

2628
to be nobody but yourself - in a world
which is doing its best, night and day, to
make you everybody else - means to fight
the hardest battle which any human being
can fight, and never stop fighting.

2629
Be of love (a little) more careful than of
anything.

2630 *Collected Poems*
a pretty girl who naked is
is worth a million statues.

2631 *'since feeling is first'*
who pays any attention
to the syntax of things
will never wholly kiss you.

CUMMINGS William Thomas
2632
There are no atheists in the foxholes.

CUNNINGHAM James Vincent 1911-1985
2633 *Epigrams*
I married in my youth a wife.
She was my own, my very first.
She gave the best years of her life.
I hope nobody gets the worst.

CUPPY Will
2634
Henry VIII had so many wives because his dynastic sense was very strong whenever he saw a maid of honour.

2635
Etiquette means behaving yourself a little better than is absolutely essential.

CURIE Marie 1867-1934
2636
Nothing in life is to be feared. It is only to be understood.

CURTIS Tony
2637
I wouldn't be caught dead marrying a woman old enough to be my wife.

CUSHMAN Charlotte 1816-1876
2638
Goethe said there would be little left of him if you were to discard what he owed to others.

DAACON George
2639
If absolute power corrupts absolutely, where does that leave God?

DACRE Henry
2640 *Daisy Bell*
Daisy, Daisy, give me your answer do!
I'm half crazy, all for the love of you!
It won't be a stylish marriage,
I can't afford a carriage,
But you'll look sweet upon the seat
Of a bicycle made for two!

DALI Salvador 1904-1989
2641
I do not paint a portrait to look like the subject, rather does the person grow to look like his portrait.

2642
It is good taste, and good taste alone, that possesses the power to sterilize and is always the first handicap to any creative functioning.

DANGERFIELD Rodney 1921-
2643
I am at the age where food has taken the place of sex in my life. In fact, I've just had a mirror put over my kitchen table.

DANTE Alighieri 1265-1321
2644
The hottest places in hell are reserved for those who, in time of great moral crisis, maintain their neutrality.

DARROW Clarence 1857-1938
2645
There is no such thing as justice - in or out of court.

2646
I do not pretend to know what many ignorant men are sure of.

2647
The first half of our lives is ruined by our parents and the second half by our children.

2648
True patriotism hates injustice in its own land more than anywhere else.

DARWIN Charles 1809-1882
2649
The mystery of the beginning of all things is insoluble by us; and I for one must be content to remain agnostic.

2650
As for a future life, every man must judge for himself between conflicting vague possibilities.

DARWIN Sir Francis 1848-1925
2651
In science the credit goes to the man who convinces the world, not to the man to whom the idea first occurs.

D'AUREVILLY Barbey
2652
Next to the wound, what women makes
best is the bandage.

D'AVENANT Charles 1656-1714
2653 *Circe*
Custom, that unwritten law,
By which the people keep even kings in
awe.

D'AVENANT Sir William 1606-1668
2654
Had laws not been, we never had been
blam'd;
For not to know we sinn'd is innocence.

DAVIDSON John 1857-1909
2655 *'War Song'*
And blood in torrents pour
In vain - always in vain,
For war breeds war again.

DAVIDSON Sara
2656
The ability to laugh at life is right at the
top, with love and communication, in the
hierarchy of our needs. Humour has much
to do with pain; it exaggerates the
anxieties and absurdities we feel, so that
we gain distance and through laughter,
relief.

DAVIES Paul
2657
It may be bizarre, but in my opinion,
science offers a sure path to God and
religion.

DAVIES Robertson 1913-
2658
Female beauty is an important minor
sacrament ... I am not at all sure that
neglect of it does not constitute a sin of
some kind.

2659
Whether you are really right or not doesn't
matter; it's the belief that counts.

2660
The critic is the duenna in the passionate
affair between playwrights, actors and
audiences - a figure dreaded, and
occasionally comic, but never welcome,
never loved.

2661
The world is full of people whose notion of
a satisfactory future is, in fact, a return to
the idealized past.

2662
If a man wants to be of the greatest
possible value to his fellow-creatures, let
him begin the long, solitary task of
perfecting himself.

2663
The love of truth lies at the root of much
humour.

2664
As a general thing, people marry most
happily with their own kind. The trouble
lies in the fact that people usually marry at
an age when they do not really know what
their own kind is.

2665
The eye sees only what the mind is
prepared to comprehend.

2666
The most original thing a writer can do is
write like himself. It is also his most
difficult task.

DAVIES Sir John 1569-1626
2667 *'Nosce Teipsum'*
Skill comes so slow, and life so fast doth
fly,
We learn so little and forget so much.

2668 *'Orchestra, or a Poem of Dancing'*
This wondrous miracle did Love devise,
For dancing is love's proper exercise.

2669 *'Orchestra, or a Poem of Dancing'*
Kind nature first doth cause all things to
love;
Love makes them dance, and in just order
move.

DAVIES W.H. 1871-1940
2670 *'April's Charms'*
And hear the pleasant cuckoo, loud and
long -
The simple bird that thinks two notes a
song.

2671 *'Leisure'*
What is this life if, full of care,
We have no time to stand and stare.

2672 *Sweet Stay-at-Home*
I love thee for a heart that's kind -
Not for the knowledge in thy mind.

DAVIS Bette 1908-1989
2673
The person who wants to make it has to
sweat. There are no short cuts. And
you've got to have the guts to be hated.

2674
The real actor - like any real artist - has a
direct line to the collective heart.

2675 *in All About Eve*
"Fasten your seatbelts. It's going to be a
bumpy night."

2676 *in The Cabin in the Cotton*
"I'd luv to kiss ya, but I just washed my
hair."

DAVIS Jr. Sammy 1925-1990
2677 *Yes I Can*
Being a star has made it possible for me to
get insulted in places where the average
negro could never hope to go and get
insulted.

DAVIS William T.
2678
Only a few human beings should grow to
the square mile; they are commonly
planted too close.

DAVY Sir Humphrey 1778-1829
2679
The most important of my discoveries
have been suggested to me by my failures.

DAWKINS Richard 1941-
2680 *The Blind Watchmaker*
[Natural selection] has no vision, no
foresight, no sight at all. If it can be said to
play the role of watchmaker in nature, it is
the blind watchmaker.

2681 *The Blind Watchmaker*
The essence of life is statistical
improbability on a colossal scale.

2682 *The Selfish Gene*
They are in you and in me; they created us,
body and mind; and their preservation is
the ultimate rationale for our existence ...
they go by the name of genes, and we are
their survival machines.

DAWSON of Penn, Lord 1864-1945
2683 *(on eve of King George V's death)*
The King's life is moving peacefully
towards its close.

DAY Clarence 1874-1935
2684
Father expected a good deal of God. He
didn't actually accuse God of inefficiency,
but when he pi ..yed his tone was loud and
angry, like that of a dissatisfied guest in a
carelessly managed hotel.

DAY-LEWIS Cecil 1904-1972
2685
There's a kind of release
And a kind of torment in every goodbye
for every man.

2686 *'Hornpipe'*
Now the peak of summer's past, the sky is
overcast
And the love we swore would last for an
age seems deceit.

2687 *'Where are the War Poets?'*
It is the logic of our times,
No subject for immortal verse -
That we who lived by honest dreams
Defend the bad against the worse.

DAY-LEWIS Tamasin
2688
I haven't yet been able to find a happy
adulterer.

DEARMER Percy 1867-1936
2689
Jesu, good above all other,
Gentle Child of gentle Mother,
In a stable born our Brother,
Give us grace to persevere.

DE BEAUVOIR Simone 1908-1986
2690
The role of a retired person is no longer to
possess one.

DE BELLOY 1725-1775
2691 *Le Siège de Calais*
The more foreigners I saw, the more I loved my homeland.

DE BONO Edward 1933-
2692
The solid wealth of insurance companies and the success of those who organize gambling are some indication of the profits to be derived from the efficient use of chance.

2693
Think sideways!

2694
Removing the faults in a stage-coach may produce a perfect stage-coach, but it is unlikely to produce the first motor car.

2695
Many highly intelligent people are poor thinkers. Many people of average intelligence are skilled thinkers. The power of a car is separate from the way the car is driven.

2696 *The Use of Lateral Thinking [foreword]*
Some people are aware of another sort of thinking which ... leads to those simple ideas that are obvious only after they have been thought of ... the term 'lateral thinking' has been coined to describe this other sort of thinking; 'vertical thinking' is used to denote the conventional logical process.

DEBS Eugene Victor 1855-1926
2697 *(at his trial for sedition)*
When great changes occur in history, when great principles are involved, as a rule the majority are wrong.

DECATUR Stephen 1779-1820
2698 *(toast)*
Our country! In her intercourse with foreign nations, may she always be in the right; but our country, right or wrong.

DEDDOES Dick
2699
Horses and jockeys mature earlier than people - which is why horses are admitted to race tracks at the age of two, and jockeys before they are old enough to shave.

DEFOE Daniel 1660-1731
2700
Middle age is youth without its levity,
And age without decay.

2701
It is better to have a lion at the head of an army of sheep, than a sheep at the head of an army of lions.

2702 *'Character of the late Dr S. Annesley'*
The best of men cannot suspend their fate:
The good die early, and the bad die late.

2703 *The Complete English Tradesman*
Pleasure is a thief to business.

2704 *An Essay Upon Projects*
The soul is placed in the body like a rough diamond, and must be polished, or the lustre of it will never appear.

2705 *The Farther Adventures of Robinson Crusoe*
In trouble to be troubled
Is to have your trouble doubled.

2706 *The History of the Kentish Petition*
Nature has left this tincture in the blood,
That all men would be tyrants if they could.

2707 *A Hymn to the Pillory*
Actions receive their tincture from the times,
And as they change are virtues made or crimes.

2708 *Moll Flanders*
Vice came in always at the door of necessity, not at the door of inclination.

2709 *Robinson Crusoe*
My man Friday.

2710 *The Serious Reflections of Robinson Crusoe*
Necessity makes an honest man a knave.

2711 *The True-Born Englishman*
Fools out of favour grudge at knaves in place.

2712 *The True-Born Englishman*
Wherever God erects a house of prayer,
The Devil always builds a chapel there;

And 'twill be found, upon examination,
The latter has the largest congregation.

2713 *The True-Born Englishman*
In their religion they are so uneven,
That each one goes his own by-way to
heaven.

2714 *The True-Born Englishman*
From this amphibious ill-born mob began
That vain, ill-natured thing, an
Englishman.

2715 *The True-Born Englishman*
When kings the sword of justice first lay
down,
They are no kings, though they possess the
crown.
Titles are shadows, crowns are empty
things,
The good of subjects is the end of kings.

2716 *(of writing)*
Voyages in a paper boat.

DEGAS Edgar 1834-1917
2717
Art is vice. You don't marry it legitimately,
you rape it.

2718 *Degas, by himself*
There are some women who should barely
be spoken to; they should be caressed.

DE GAULLE Charles 1890-1970
2719
France has lost a battle. But France has not
lost the war!

2720
Authority doesn't work without prestige,
or prestige without distance.

2721
What we think about death only matters
for what death makes us think about life.

2722
How can you govern a country which has
246 varieties of cheese?

2723
Since a politician never believes what he
says, he is quite surprised to be taken at
his word.

2724
Greatness is a road leading towards the
unknown.

2725
A true leader always keeps an element of
surprise up his sleeve, which others cannot
grasp but which keeps his public excited
and breathless.

2726
Every man of action has a strong dose of
egotism, pride, hardness and cunning. But
all those things will be forgiven him,
indeed, they will be regarded as high
qualities, if he can make them the means to
achieve great ends.

2727
It will not be any European statesman who
will unite Europe: Europe will be united
by the Chinese.

2728
In order to become the master, the
politician poses as the servant.

2729
It so happens that the world is undergoing
a transformation to which no change that
has yet occurred can be compared, either
in scope or in rapidity.

2730
Diplomats are useful only in fair weather.
As soon as it rains, they drown in every
drop.

2731 *(of Napoleon)*
Before such a prodigious career, judgement
is torn between blame and admiration.

2732 *(to the people of Strasbourg)*
Yes, it is Europe, from the Atlantic to the
Urals, it is Europe, it is the whole of
Europe, that will decide the fate of the
world.

2733 *(replying to Clement Attlee)*
Politics are too serious a matter to be left to
the politicians.

DEKKER Thomas 1570-1641
2734 *Patient Grissill*
Golden slumbers kiss your eyes,
Smiles awake you when you rise.

DE KLERK F.W. 1936-
2735 *(of Nelson Mandela)*
A man of destiny knows that beyond the
hill lies another and another. The journey
is never complete.

DE LA MARE Walter 1873-1956
2736 *Autumn*
Sad winds where your voice was;
Tears, tears where my heart was;
And ever with me,
Child, ever with me,
Silence where hope was.

DELANEY Shelagh 1939-
2737 *A Taste of Honey*
Women never have young minds. They
are born three thousand years old.

DELANO Anthony
2738
She was not a woman likely to settle for
equality when sex gave her an advantage.

DELILLE Jacques 1738-1813
2739
Chance makes our parents, but choice
makes our friends.

DELORIA Jr. Vine
2740
When asked by an anthropologist what the
Indians called America before the white
man came, and Indian said simply 'Ours'.

DELORS Jacques 1925-
2741
Socialism is liberty, solidarity,
responsibility.

DEMOSTHENES 384-322 BC
2742
It is not possible to found a lasting power
upon injustice.

DEMPSEY Jack 1895-1983
2743 *(on losing World Heavyweight title)*
Honey, I just forgot to duck.

DENHAM Sir John 1615-1669
2744 *'Of Prudence'*
Youth, what man's age is like to be doth
show;
We may our ends by our beginnings know.

2745 *'To Richard Fanshaw'*
Such is our pride, our folly, or our fate,
That few, but such as cannot write,
translate.

DE NIRO Robert 1943-
2746 *in The King of Comedy*
"Better to be king for a night than a
schmuck for a lifetime."

DEPEW Chauncey 1834-1928
2747
It's pleasant to hear these nice words while
I'm still alive. I'd rather have the taffy
than the epitaphy.

DE QUINCEY Thomas 1785-1859
2748 *Confessions of an English Opium Eater*
... a duller spectacle this earth of ours has
not to show than a rainy Sunday in
London.

2749 *Confessions of an English Opium Eater*
Thou hast the keys of Paradise, oh just,
subtle, and mighty opium!

2750 *'On Murder Considered as One of the
Fine Arts'*
If once a man indulges himself in murder,
very soon he comes to think little of
robbing; and from robbing he comes next
to drinkine and sabbath-breaking, and
from that to incivility and procrastination.

DERBY Lord 1799-1869
2751
The duty of an Opposition [is] very simple
... to oppose everything, and propose
nothing.

DESCARTES René 1596-1650
2752 *Discourse on Method*
Common sense is the best distributed
commodity in the world, for every man is
convinced that he is well supplied with it.

2753 *Discourse on Method*
I think, therefore I am.

DESTOUCHES Philippe Néricault 1680-
1754
2754 *L'Obstacle imprévu*
The absent are always in the wrong.

DE VOTO Bernard 1897-1955
2755
The proper union of gin and vermouth is a great and sudden glory; it is one of the happiest marriages on earth, and one of the shortest lived.

DE VRIES Peter 1910-1993
2756
Who of us is mature enough for offspring before the offspring themselves arrive? The value of marriage is not that adults produce children but that children produce adults.

2757
If there's anything I hate it's the word humorist - I feel like countering with the word seriousist.

2758
The universe is like a safe to which there is a combination, but the combination is locked up in the safe.

2759
Celibacy is the worst form of self-abuse.

2760 *The Mackerel Plaza*
It is the final proof of God's omnipotence that he need not exist in order to save us.

DEWAR Lord 1864-1930
2761
[There are] only two classes of pedestrians in these days of reckless motor traffic - the quick, and the dead.

DEWAR Sir James 1842-1923
2762 *(attributed)*
Minds are like parachutes. They only function when they are open.

DEWEL Duane
2763
Any married man should forget his mistakes - no use two people remembering the same thing.

DEWEY John 1859-1952
2764
We only think when we are confronted with a problem.

DEWEY Thomas E. 1902-1971
2765
No man should be in public office who can't make more money in private life.

DEWING Thomas W.
2766
Why, if you're not in New York you are camping out.

DIANE Comtesse (Marie de Beausacq)
2767
Of all feats of skill, the most difficult is that of being honest.

2768
Wealth makes everything easy - honesty most of all.

2769
The power of habit and the charm of novelty are the two adverse forces which explain the follies of mankind.

DIAZ Porfirio 1830-1915
2770 *(attributed)*
Poor Mexico, so far from God and so close to the United States.

DIBDIN Charles 1745-1814
2771 *'The Lass that Loves a Sailor'*
But the standing toast that pleased the most
Was - The wind that blows, the ship that goes,
And the lass that loves a sailor!

DIBDIN Thomas 1771-1841
2772 *'The Snug Little Island'*
Oh! what a snug little Island,
A right little, tight little Island!

DICKENS Charles 1812-1870
2773
I have known a vast quantity of nonsense talked about bad men not looking you in the face. Don't trust that conventional idea. Dishonesty will stare honesty out of countenance, any day in the week, if there is anything to be got by it.

2774
If there were no bad people, there would be no good lawyers.

2775
Secret, and self-contained, and solitary as an oyster.

2776 *Barnaby Rudge*
These are strings ... in the human heart that had better not be wibrated.

2777 *Bleak House*
This is a London particular ... A fog, miss.

2778 *Bleak House*
The one great principle of the English law is, to make business for itself.

2779 *The Chimes 'The Second Quarter'*
O let us love our occupations,
Bless the squire and his relations,
Live upon our daily rations,
And always know our proper stations.

2780 *A Christmas Carol*
'Bah,' said Scrooge. 'Humbug!'

2781 *David Copperfield*
Barkis is willin'.

2782 *Great Expectations*
It is a most miserable thing to feel ashamed of home.

2783 *Hard Times*
Now, what I want is, Facts ... Facts alone are wanted in life.

2784 *Pickwick Papers*
Never sign a walentine with your own name.

DICKEY James 1923-
2785
Flight is the only true sensation that men have achieved in modern history.

DICKINSON Angie
2786
I dress for women - and I undress for men.

DICKINSON Emily 1830-1886
2787
Anger as soon as fed is dead -
'Tis starving makes it fat.

2788
Dying is a wild night and a new road.

2789
Fame is a bee
It has a song -
It has a sting -
Ah, too, it has a wing.

2790
For each ecstatic instant
We must an anguish pay
In keen and quivering ratio
To the ecstasy.

2791
The pedigree of honey
Does not concern the bee;
A clover, anytime, to him
Is aristocracy.

2792
Where thou art, that, is Home.

2793
'Hope' is the thing with feathers
That perches in the soul -
And sings the tune without words
And never stops - at all.

2794 *'The Bustle in a House'*
The Bustle in a House
The Morning after Death
Is solemnest of industries
Enacted upon Earth

The Sweeping up the Heart
And putting Love away
We shall not want to use again
Until Eternity.

2795 *'Elysium is as far as to'*
What fortitude the Soul contains,
That it can so endure
The accent of a coming Foot -
The opening of a Door.

2796 *'After great pain, a formal feeling comes'*
This is the Hour of Lead -
Remembered, if outlived,
As Freezing persons, recollect the Snow -
First - Chill - then Stupor - then the letting go.

2797 *'My life closed twice before its close'*
Parting is all we know of heaven,
And all we need of hell.

2798 *'They shut me up in prose'*
They shut me up in prose -
As when a little girl
They put me in the closet -
Because they liked me 'still'.

2799 *'Because I could not stop for Death'*
Because I could not stop for Death -
He kindly stopped for me -
The Carriage held but just Ourselves -
And Immortality.

2800 *'Success is counted sweetest'*
Success is counted sweetest
By those who ne'er succeed.
To comprehend a nectar
Requires sorest need.

DICKINSON Goldsworthy Lowes 1862-1932
2801 *The Greek View of Life*
Dissatisfaction with the world in which we live and determination to realise one that shall be better, are the prevailing characteristics of the modern spirit.

DICKINSON John 1732-1808
2802 *'The Liberty Song'*
Then join hand in hand, brave Americans all,
By uniting we stand, by dividing we fall.

2803 *Reasons for taking up arms against England*
Our cause is just, our union is perfect.

DICKMAN Franklin J.
2804
The glittering generalities of the speaker have left an impression more delightful than permanent.

DICKSON Paul 1939-
2805
Rowe's Rule: the odds are five to six that the light at the end of the tunnel is the headlight of an oncoming train.

DIDEROT Denis 1713-1784
2806 *Paradoxe sur le comédien*
It has been said that love robs those who have it of their wit, and gives it to those who have none.

DIDION Joan 1934-
2807
There is one last thing to remember: writers are always selling somebody out.

DIEFENBAKER John G. 1895-1979
2808
That one never asks a question unless he knows the answer is basic to parliamentary questioning.

2809
A question which can be answered without prejudice to the government is not a fit question to ask.

DIEM Ngo Dinh
2810 *(on becoming President of Vietnam)*
Follow me, if I advance; kill me if I retreat; revenge me if I die!

DIETRICH Marlene 1901-1991
2811 *(attributed)*
Most women set out to try to change a man - and when they have changed him, they do not like him.

2812
The average man is more interested in a woman who is interested in him than he is in a woman - any woman - with beautiful legs.

2813
How do you know when love is gone? If you said that you would be there at seven and get there by nine, and he or she has not called the police - it's gone.

DILLARD Annie
2814
I read about an Eskimo hunter who asked the local missionary priest, 'If I did not know abo' God and sin, would I go to hell?' 'No,' said the priest, 'not if you did not know.' 'Then why,' asked the Eskimo earnestly, 'did you tell me?'

2815
In literary history, generation follows generation in a rage.

DILLER Phyllis 1917-
2816 *Phyllis Diller's Housekeeping Hints*
Never go to bed mad. Stay up and fight.

DILLON Wentworth c.1633-1685
2817 *Art of Poetry*
But words once spoke can never be
recalled.

2818 *Essay on Translated Verse*
Choose an author as you choose a friend.

2819 *Essay on Translated Verse*
The multitude is always in the wrong.

DIMNET Ernest 1866-1954
2820
Too often we forget that genius ... depends
upon the data within its reach, that
Archimedes could not have devised
Edison's inventions.

2821 *What We Live By*
Architecture, of all the arts, is the one
which acts the most slowly, but the most
surely, on the soul.

DIOGENES c.400-c.325 BC
2822
Calumny is only the noise of madmen.

2823 *Plutarch Parallel Lives 'Alexander'*
Alexander ... asked him if he lacked
anything. 'Yes,' said he, 'that I do: that
you stand out of my sun a little.'

DIONYSIUS of Halicarnassus 30-7 BC
2824 *Ars Rhetorica*
History is philosophy learned from
examples.

DIRKSEN Everett 1896-1969
2825
The U.S. Senate - an old scow which
doesn't move very fast, but never sinks.

2826
Three Laws of Politics:
1. Get elected.
2. Get re-elected
3. Don't get mad, get even.

DISRAELI Benjamin 1804-1881
2827
The Continent will [not] suffer England to
be the workshop of the world.

2828
Thus you have a starving population, an
absentee aristocracy, and an alien Church,
and in addition the weakest executive in

the world. That is the Irish Question.

2829
The right hon. Gentleman caught the
Whigs bathing, and walked away with
their clothes.

2830
Protection is not a principle, but an
expedient.

2831
A Conservative Government is an
organized hypocrisy.

2832
He has to learn that petulance is not
sarcasm, and that insolence is not
invective.

2833
England does not love coalitions.

2834
Colonies do not cease to be colonies
because they are independent.

2835
You are not going, I hope, to leave the
destinies of the British Empire to prigs and
pedants.

2836
Man, my Lord, is a being born to believe.

2837
Party is organized opinion.

2838
Is man an ape or an angel? Now I am on
the side of the angels.

2839
Assassination has never changed the
history of the world.

2840
We have legalized confiscation,
consecrated sacrilege, and condoned high
treason.

2841
Increased means and increased leisure are
the two civilizers of man.

2842
A University should be a place of light, of
liberty, and of learning.

2843
An author who speaks about his own books is almost as bad as a mother who talks about her own children.

2844
Upon the education of the people of this country the fate of this country depends.

2845
I will not go down to posterity talking bad grammar.

2846 (attributed)
Damn your principles! Stick to your party.

2847
Protection is not only dead, but damned.

2848
Pray remember, Mr. Dean, no dogma, no Dean.

2849
Never complain and never explain.

2850 (attributed)
There are three kinds of lies: lies, damned lies and statistics.

2851
Anybody amuses me for once. A new acquaintance is like a new book. I prefer it, even if bad, to a classic.

2852
The magic of first love is our ignorance that it can ever end.

2853
No man is regular in his attendance at the House of Commons until he is married.

2854
Departure should be sudden.

2855
Great services are not cancelled by one act or by one single error.

2856
Predominant opinions are generally the opinions of the generation that is vanishing.

2857
My idea of an agreeable person is a person who agrees with me.

2858
Yes, I am a Jew, and when the ancestors of the right honourable gentlemen were brutal savages in an unknown land, mine were priests in the Temple of Solomon.

2859
An insular country, subject to fogs and with a powerful middle class, requires grave statesmen.

2860 (advice to a young man)
Talk as much as possible to women They ask so many questions.

2861 (on becoming Prime Minister)
I have climbed to the top of the greasy pole.

2862 Coningsby
No Government can be long secure without a formidable Opposition.

2863 Coningsby
Youth is a blunder; Manhood a struggle; Old Age a regret.

2864 Coningsby
It seems to me a barren thing this Conservatism - an unhappy cross-breed, the mule of politics that engenders nothing.

2865 Contarini Fleming
Read no history: nothing but biography, for that is life without theory.

2866 (on death bed, declining a visit from the Queen)
'No, it is better not, she would only ask me to take a message to Albert.'

2867 (on his elevation to the House of Lords)
I am dead; dead, but in the Elysian fields.

2868 Endymion
His Christianity was muscular.

2869 Endymion
Said Waldershare, 'Sensible men are all of the same religion.' ' And pray what is that?' ... 'Sensible men never tell.'

2870 (of Gladstone)
A sophistical rhetorician, inebriated with the exuberance of his own verbosity.

2871 *Henrietta Temple*
Time is the great physician.

2872 *Letter to Lord Malmesbury*
These wretched colonies will all be independent, too, in a few years, and are a millstone round our necks.

2873 *Lothair*
Every day when he looked into the glass, and gave the last touch to his consummate toilette, he offered his grateful thanks to Providence that his family was not unworthy of him.

2874 *Lothair*
A Protestant, if he wants aid or advice on any matter can only go to his solicitor.

2875 *Lothair*
London: a nation, not a city.

2876 *Lothair*
When a man fell into his anecdotage it was a sign for him to retire from the world.

2877 *Lothair*
You know who the critics are? The men who have failed in literature and art.

2878 *Lothair*
Every woman should marry - and no man.

2879 *(Maiden speech)*
Though I sit down now, the time will come when you will hear me.

2880 *(to Matthew Arnold)*
Everyone likes flattery; and when you come to Royalty you should lay it on with a trowel.

2881 *(on return from Congress of Berlin)*
[We] have brought you back peace - but a peace I hope with honour.

2882 *Sybil*
To do nothing and get something, formed a boy's ideal of a manly career.

2883 *Sybil*
I was told that the Priviledged and the People formed Two Nations.

2884 *(of the Treasury Bench)*
You behold a range of exhausted volcanoes.

2885 *Vivian Grey*
Experience is the child of Thought, and Thought is the child of Action. We cannot learn men from books.

D'ISRAELI Isaac 1766-1848
2886 *The Literary Character*
There is an art of reading, as well as an art of thinking, and an art of writing.

DIX William Chatterton 1837-1898
2887
As with gladness men of old
Did the guiding star behold,
As with joy they hailed its light,
Leading onward, beaming bright,
So, most gracious Lord, may we
Evermore be led to thee.

DOBIE J. Frank
2888
Luck is being ready for the chance.

2889
The only way a man can get civilized is to become a contemporary of himself.

DOBSON Henry Austin 1840-1921
2890 *'Fame is a Food'*
Fame is a food that dead men eat, -
I have no stomach for such meat.

2891 *'The Paradox of Time'*
Time goes, you say? Ah no!
Alas, Time stays, we go.

DOCTOROW E.L. 1931-
2892
History needs to be rewritten or it becomes mythology and then it can be used destructively.

DODD Ken 1931-
2893
Freud's theory was that when a joke opens a window ... you get a marvellous feeling of relief and elation. The trouble with Freud is that he never had to play the old Glasgow Empire on a Saturday night after Rangers and Celtic had both lost.

DONATUS Aelius c.300-399
2894
Confound those who have said our remarks before us.

DONLEAVY J.P. 1926-
2895 *The Ginger Man*
When you don't have any money, the
problem is food. When you have money,
it's sex. When you have both it's health.

DONNE John 1572-1631
2896
Love, all love of other sights controls.
And makes one little room an everywhere.

2897
I observe the physician with the same
diligence as the disease.

2898
The difference between the reason of man
and the instinct of the beast is this, that the
beast does but know, but the man knows
that he knows.

2899
Be thine own palace, or the world's thy
jail.

2900 *'Air and Angels'*
Just such disparity
As is 'twixt air and angels' purity,
'Twixt women's love, and men's will ever
be.

2901 *'The Anagram'*
Love built on beauty, soon as beauty, dies.

2902 *An Anatomy of the World: The First
Anniversary*
She, she is dead; she's dead; when thou
know'st this,
Thou know'st how dry a cinder this world
is.

2903 *'The Anniversary'*
Only our love hath no decay;
This, no tomorrow hath, nor yesterday,
Running it never runs from us away,
But truly keeps his first, last, everlasting
day.

2904 *'The Autumnal'*
No spring, nor summer beauty hath such
grace,
As I have seen in one autumnal face.

2905 *'The Bait'*
Come live with me, and be my love,
And we will some new pleasures prove

Of golden sands, and crystal brooks,
With silken lines, and silver hooks.

2906 *'Going to Bed'*
Full nakedness! All joys are due to thee,
As souls unbodied, bodies uncloth'd must
be.

2907 *'Break of Day'*
The day breaks not, it is my heart.

2908 *'The Canonization'*
For God's sake hold your tongue and let
me love.

2909 *Death's Duel*
We have a winding sheet in our mother's
womb, which grows with us from our
conception, and we come into the world,
wound up in that winding sheet, for we
come to seek a grave.

2910 *Devotions upon Emergent Occasions*
But I do nothing upon my self, and yet I
am mine own Executioner.

2911 *Devotions upon Emergent Occasions*
No man is an Island, entire of itself; every
man is a piece of the Continent, a part of
the main; if a clod be washed away by the
sea, Europe is the less.

2912 *Devotions upon Emergent Occasions*
Any man's death diminishes me, because I
am involved in mankind; and therefore
never send to know for whom the bell
tolls; it tolls for thee.

2913 *'The Good Morrow'*
I wonder by my troth, what thou, and I
Did, till we loved, were we not weaned till
then?
But sucked on country pleasures,
childishly?
Or snorted we in the seven sleepers den?

2914 *'To Sir Henry Wotton'*
More than kisses, letters mingle souls.

2915 *Holy Sonnets*
Death be not proud, though some have
called thee
Mighty and dreadful, for thou art not so.

2916 *Holy Sonnets*
One short sleep past, we wake eternally,
And death shall be no more; Death thou

shalt die.

2917 *Holy Sonnets*
Take me to you, imprison me, for I
Except you enthral me, never shall be free,
Nor ever chaste, except you ravish me.

2918 *Holy Sonnets*
What if this present were the world's last
night?

2919 *'A Lecture in the Shadow'*
Love is a growing or full constant light;
And his first minute, after noon, is night.

2920 *'Love's Deity'*
I long to talk with some old lover's ghost,
Who died before the god of Love was
born.

2921 *'To His Mistress Going to Bed'*
Licence my roving hands, and let them go,
Behind, before, above, between, below.
O my America, my new found land,
My kingdom, safeliest when with one man
manned.

2922 *'The Progress of the Soul'*
Nature's great masterpiece, an elephant,
The only harmless great thing.

2923 *Sermons*
[Death] comes equally to us all, and makes
us all equal when it comes.

2924 *Sermons*
So certainly is there nothing, nothing in
spiritual things, perfect in this world.

2925 *'Song'*
Go, and catch a falling star,
Get with child a mandrake root,
Tell me, where all past years are,
Or who cleft the Devil's foot.

2926 *'The Sun Rising'*
Love, all alike, no season knows, nor clime,
Nor hours, days, months, which are the
rags of time.

2927 *'The Triple Fool'*
I am two fools, I know,
For loving, and for saying so
In whining poetry.

2928 *(to his wife on being dismissed from service)*
John Donne, Anne Donne, Un-done.

DOREN Carl Van 1885-1950
2929
The race of man, while sheep in credulity,
are wolves for conformity.

DOREN Mark Van 1894-1972
2930
Wit is the only wall
Between us and the dark.

DORMAN-SMITH Sir Reginald 1899-1977
2931
Let 'Dig for Victory' be the motto of every
one with a garden and of every able-
bodied man and woman capable of
digging an allotment in their spare time.

DOSTOEVSKY Fedor 1821-1881
2932
Beauty will save the world.

2933
It seems, in fact, as though the second half
of a man's life is made up of nothing but
the habits he has accumulated during the
first half.

2934
What is hell? I maintain that it is the
suffering of being unable to love.

2935
Who doesn't desire his father's death?

2936 *The Brothers Karamazov*
If you were to destroy in mankind the
belief in immortality, not only love but
every living force maintaining the life of
the world would at once be dried up.

2937 *The Brothers Karamazov*
The awful thing is that beauty is
mysterious as well as terrible. God and
devil are fighting there, and the battlefield
is the heart of man.

2938 *The Brothers Karamazov*
Men reject the prophets and slay them, but
they love their martyrs and honour those
whom they have slain.

2939 *Crime and Punishment*
All people seem to be divided into
'ordinary' and 'extraordinary'. The
ordinary people must lead a life of strict
obedience and have no right to transgress
the law because ... they are ordinary.
Whereas the extraordinary people have the
right to commit any crime they like and
transgress the law in any way just because
they happen to be extraordinary.

2940 *Crime and Punishment*
Power is given only to him who dares to
stoop and take it ... one must have the
courage to dare.

2941 *House of the Dead*
To crush, to annihilate a man utterly, to
inflict on him the most terrible punishment
so that the most ferocious murderer would
shudder at it beforehand, one need only
give him work of an absolutely, completely
useless and irrational character.

DOUGLAS Keith 1920-1944
2942 *'Simplify me when I'm Dead'*
Remember me when I am dead
And simplify me when I'm dead.

2943 *'Vergissmeinnicht, 1943'*
But she would weep to see today
how on his skin the swart flies move;
the dust upon the paper eye
and the burst stomach like a cave.
For here the lover and killer are mingled
who had one body and one heart.
And death, who had the soldier singled
has done the lover mortal hurt.

DOUGLAS Lord Alfred 1870-1945
2944 *'Two Loves'*
I am the Love that dare not speak its name.

DOUGLAS Norman 1868-1952
2945
A man can believe in a considerable deal of
rubbish, and yet go about his daily work in
a rational and cheerful manner.

2946
Justice is too good for some people, and
not good enough for the rest.

2947
It takes a wise man to handle a lie. A fool
had better remain honest.

2948 *Almanac*
To find a friend one must close one eye.
To keep him - two.

2949 *South Wind*
Many a man who thinks to found a home
discovers that he has merely opened a
tavern for his friends.

DOWNES Donald
2950
Fear can be headier than whisky, once man
has acquired a taste for it.

DOWSON Ernest 1867-1900
2951 *'Non Sum Qualis Eram'*
I have forgot much, Cynara! gone with the
wind,
Flung roses, roses, riotously, with the
throng,
Dancing, to put thy pale, lost lilies out of
mind;
But I was desolate and sick of an old
passion,
Yea, all the time, because the dance was
long:
I have been faithful to thee, Cynara! in my
fashion.

2952 *'Vitae Summa Brevis'*
They are not long, the days of wine and
roses:
Out of a misty dream
Our path emerges for a while, then closes
Within a dream.

DOYLE Sir Arthur Conan 1859-1930
2953 *The Adventures of Sherlock Holmes*
Singularity is almost invariably a clue.

2954 *The Adventures of Sherlock Holmes*
It is my belief, Watson, founded upon my
experience, that the lowest and vilest alleys
in London do not present a more dreadful
record of sin than does the smiling and
beautiful countryside.

2955 *The Adventures of Sherlock Holmes*
A man should keep his little brain attic
stocked with all the furniture that he is
likely to use, and the rest he can put away
in the lumber room of his library, where he
can get it if he wants it.

2956 *The Adventures of Sherlock Holmes*
It is quite a three-pipe problem, ...

2957 *The Adventures of Sherlock Holmes*
You see, but you do not observe.

2958 *His Last Bow 'The Dying Detective'*
Of all ruins that of a noble mind is the
most deplorable.

2959 *The Memoirs of Sherlock Holmes*
'Excellent,' I cried. 'Elementary,' said he.

2960 *The Memoirs of Sherlock Holmes*
'Ex-Professor Moriarty of mathematical
celebrity ... is the Napoleon of Crime,
Watson.'

2961 *A Study in Scarlet*
London, that great cesspool into which all
the loungers and idlers of the Empire are
irresistibly drained.

2962 *A Study in Scarlet*
It is a capital mistake to theorize before
you have all the evidence. It biases the
judgement.

2963 *A Study in Scarlet*
Where there is no imagination there is no
horror.

2964 *The Sign of Four*
You know my methods. Apply them.

2965 *The Sign of Four*
It is the unofficial force - the Baker Street
irregulars.

2966 *The Valley of Fear*
Mediocrity knows nothing higher than
itself, but talent instantly recognizes
genius.

DOYLE Sir Francis 1810-1888
2967 *'The Unobstrusive Christian'*
His creed no parson ever knew,
For this was still his 'simple plan',
To have with clergymen to do
As little as a Christian can.

DRABBLE Margaret 1939-
2968 *A Natural Curiosity*
England's not a bad country ... It's just a
mean, cold, ugly, divided, tired, clapped-
out, post-imperial, post-industrial slag-
heap covered in polystyrene hamburger
cartons.

2969 *A Summer Bird-Cage*
Perhaps the rare and simple pleasure of
being seen for what one is compensates for
the misery of being it.

DRAKE Sir Francis c.1540-1596
2970 *(attributed)*
There is plenty of time to win this game,
and to thrash the Spaniards too.

2971 *(dispatch to Sir Francis Walsingham)*
There must be a beginning of any great
matter, but the continuing unto the end
until it be thoroughly finished yields the
true glory.

2972 *(of the expedition to Cadiz)*
The singeing of the King of Spain's Beard.

DRAYTON Michael 1563-1631
2973 *The Barons' Wars*
Ill news hath wings, and with the wind
doth go,
Comfort's a cripple and comes ever slow.

2974 *The Barons' Wars*
Thus when we fondly flatter our desires,
Our best conceits do prove the greatest
liars.

2975 *To the Cambro-Britons*
Fair stood the wind for France.

2976 *Poly-Olbion*
That shire which we the Heart of England
well may call.

DREW Elizabeth
2977
The world is not run by thought, nor by
imagination, but by opinion.

DRUCKER Peter 1909-
2978
There is nothing so useless as doing
efficiently that which should not be done
at all.

2979
Whenever you see a successful business,
someone once made a courageous
decision.

2980
Profitability is the sovereign criterion of
the enterprise.

2981
Along this tree
From root to crown
Ideas flow up
And vetoes down.

2982
The really important things are said over
cocktails and are never done.

DRUMMOND Thomas 1797-1840
2983 *Letter to the Earl of Donoughmore*
Property has its duties as well as its rights.

DRYDEN John 1631-1700
2984
Fight on, my merry men all,
I'm a little wounded, but I am not slain;
I will lay me down for to bleed a while,
Then I'll rise and fight with you again.

2985
Every inch that is not fool is rogue.

2986
There is a pleasure sure,
In being mad, which none but madmen
know!

2987
Ill habits gather by unseen degrees,
As brooks make rivers, rivers run to seas.

2988 *Absalom and Achitophel*
In pious times, ere priestcraft did begin,
Before polygamy was made a sin.

2989 *Absalom and Achitophel*
Plots, true or false, are necessary things,
To raise up commonwealths and ruin
kings.

2990 *Absalom and Achitophel*
Why should he, with wealth and honour
blest,
Refuse his age the needful hours of rest?
Punish a body which he could not please;
Bankrupt of life, yet prodigal of ease?
And all to leave what with his toil he won
To that unfeathered two-legged thing, a
son.

2991 *Absalom and Achitophel*
In friendship false, implacable in hate:
Resolved to ruin or to rule the state.

2992 *Absalom and Achitophel*
All empire is no more than power in trust.

2993 *Absalom and Achitophel*
Better one suffer, than a nation grieve.

2994 *Absalom and Achitophel*
But far more numerous was the herd of
such
Who think too little and who talk too
much.

2995 *Absalom and Achitophel*
A man so various that he seemed to be
Not one, but all mankind's epitome.
Stiff in opinions, always in the wrong;
Was everything by starts, and nothing
long:
But, in the course of one revolving moon,
Was chemist, fiddler, statesman, and
buffoon.

2996 *Absalom and Achitophel*
In squandering wealth was his peculiar
art:
Nothing went unrewarded, but desert.
Beggared by fools, whom still he found too
late:
He had his jest, and they had his estate.

2997 *Absalom and Achitophel*
Youth, beauty, graceful action seldom fail:
But common interest always will prevail:
And pity never ceases to be shown
To him, who makes the people's wrongs
his own.

2998 *Absalom and Achitophel*
Never was patriot yet, but was a fool.

2999 *Absalom and Achitophel*
Beware the fury of a patient man.

3000 *Alexander's Feast*
None but the brave deserves the fair.

3001 *Alexander's Feast*
War, he sung, is toil and trouble;
Honour but an empty bubble.

3002 *All for Love*
Errors, like straws, upon the surface flow;
He who would search for pearls must dive
below.

3003 *Aureng-Zebe*
Death, in itself, is nothing; but we fear,
To be we know not what, we know not
where.

3004 *'The Character of a Good Parson'*
Refined himself to soul, to curb the sense
And made almost a sin of abstinence.

3005 *The Conquest of Granada*
I am as free as nature first made man,
Ere the base laws of servitude began,
When wild in woods the noble savage ran.

3006 *The Conquest of Granada*
Thou strong seducer, opportunity!

3007 *Cymon and Iphigenia*
He trudged along unknowing what he
sought,
And whistled as he went, for want of
thought.

3008 *Cymon and Iphigenia*
She hugged the offender, and forgave the
offence.

3009 *Epistle 'To my honoured kinsman John
Driden'*
The wise, for cure, on exercise depend;
God never made his work, for man to
mend.

3010 *An Essay of Dramatic Poesy (of
Shakespeare)*
He was the man who of all modern, and
perhaps ancient poets, had the largest and
most comprehensive soul ... he is always
great.

3011 *Heroic Stanzas (death of Oliver
Cromwell)*
For he was great, ere fortune made him so.

3012 *The Hind and the Panther*
For present joys are more to flesh and
blood
Than a dull prospect of a distant good.

3013 *The Hind and the Panther*
By education most have been misled;
So they believe, because they so were bred.
The priest continues what the nurse began,
And thus the child imposes on the man.

3014 *The Indian Emperor*
And love's the noblest frailty of the mind.

3015 *The Indian Emperor*
Repentance is the virtue of weak minds.

3016 *The Indian Emperor*
For all the happiness mankind can gain
Is not in pleasure, but in rest from pain.

3017 *King Arthur*
War is the trade of kings.

3018 *MacFleknoe*
All human things are subject to decay,
And, when fate summons, monarchs must
obey.

3019 *The Maiden Queen*
I am resolved to grow fat and look young
till forty, and then slip out of the world
with the first wrinkle and the reputation of
five-and-twenty.

3020 *Sir Martin Mar-All*
For secrets are edged tools,
And must be kept from children and from
fools.

3021 *The Medal*
We loathe our manna, and we long for
quails.

3022 *The Medal*
But treason is not owned when 'tis
descried;
Successful crimes alone are justified.

3023 *Mithridates*
For, Heaven be thanked, we live in such an
age,
When no man dies for love, but on the
stage.

3024 *Palamon and Arcite*
But love's a malady without a cure.

3025 *Palamon and Arcite*
Repentance is but want of power to sin.

3026 *Palamon and Arcite*
Since every man who lives is born to die,
And none can boast sincere felicity,
With equal mind, what happens, let us
bear,
Nor joy nor grieve too much for things
beyond our care.

3027 *'The Prologue at Oxford, 1680'*
But 'tis the talent of our English nation,
Still to be plotting some new reformation.

3028 *'Prologue to the University of Oxon'*
So poetry, which is in Oxford made
An art, in London only is a trade.

3029 *Religio Laici*
A man is to be cheated into passion, but to
be reasoned into truth.

3030 *The Secular Masque*
A very merry, dancing, drinking,
Laughing, quaffing, and unthinking time.

3031 *The Secular Masque*
Joy ruled the day, and Love the night.

3032 *A Song for St Cecilia's Day*
What passion cannot Music raise and
quell?

3033 *A Song for St Cecilia's Day*
The soft complaining flute.

3034 *A Song for St Cecilia's Day*
The trumpet shall be heard on high,
The dead shall live, the living die,
And Music shall untune the sky.

3035 *(translation of Horace: Odes)*
Happy the man, and happy he alone,
He, who can call to-day his own:
He who, secure within, can say,
To-morrow do thy worst, for I have lived
to-day.

3036 *(translation of Juvenal: Satires)*
Look round the habitable world! how few
Know their own good; or knowing it,
pursue.

3037 *(translation of Ovid: The Art of Love)*
To see and be seen, in heaps they run;
Some to undo, and some to be undone.

3038 *(translation of Virgil: Aeneid)*
Arms, and the man I sing ...

3039 *Tyrannic Love*
All delays are dangerous in war.

DU MAURIER Daphne 1907-
3040
Writers should be read - but neither seen
nor heard.

DUBCEK Alexander 1921-
3041
... we followed such a policy that socialism
would not lose its human face.

DUBUFFET Jean 1901-1985
3042
Unless one says goodbye to what one
loves, and unless one travels to completely
new territories, one can expect merely a
long wearing away of oneself.

DUCHAMP Marcel 1887-1968
3043
It's not what you see that is art, art is the
gap.

DUDEK Louis
3044
There are two kinds of people: those who
are always well and those who are always
sick. Most of the evils of the world come
from the first sort and most of the
achievements from the second.

3045
A critic at best is a waiter at the great table
of literature.

3046
What is forgiven is usually well-
remembered.

DUELL Charles H.
3047 *(US Office of Patents 1899)*
Everything that can be invented has been
invented.

DULLES John Foster 1888-1959
3048
You have to take chances for peace, just as
you must take chances in war.

3049
The world will never have lasting peace so
long as men reserve for war the finest
human qualities.

DUMAS Alexandre ('Pere') 1802-1870
3050
All human wisdom is summed up in two
words - wait and hope.

3051 *The Three Musketeers*
All for one, one for all.

DUMAS Alexandre ('Fils') 1824-1895
3052
Business? It's quite simple. It's other
people's money.

3053 *(attributed)*
It is only rarely that one can see in a little
boy the promise of a man, but one can
almost always see in a little girl the threat
of a woman.

DUMBRILLE Douglas
3054 *in The Lives of A Bengal Lancer*
"We have ways of making men talk."

DUNBAR Paul Lawrence 1872-1906
3055 *'Sympathy'*
I know why the caged bird sings!

DUNCAN Sara Jeannette
3056
If you have anything to tell me of
importance, for God's sake begin at the
end.

3057
Clothes and courage have much to do with
each other.

3058
Why is it that when people have no
capacity for private usefulness they should
be so anxious to serve the public?

3059
A human being isn't an orchid, he must
draw something from the soil he grows in.

3060
One loses so many laughs by not laughing
at oneself.

DUNLOP Ian 1925-
3061
The shock of the new: seven historic
exhibitions of modern art.

DUNNE Dominick
3062
Let me tell you something about silence:
The bullshit stops.

DUNNE Finley Peter 1867-1936
3063
Many a man that couldn't direct ye to th'
drug store on th' corner when he was
thirty will get a respectful hearin' when

age has further impaired his mind.

3064
I see gr-reat changes takin' place ivry day,
but no change at all ivry fifty years.

3065
You can lead a man up to the university,
but you can't make him think.

3066
No matter whether the Constitution
follows the flag or not, the Supreme Court
follows the election return.

3067
An appeal is when ye ask wan court to
show its contempt for another court.

3068
A man's idee in a card game is war - crool,
devastatin' and pitiless. A lady's idee iv it
is a combynation iv larceny, embezzlement
an' burglary.

3069
Comfort the afflicted and afflict the
comfortable.

3070
Whin a man gets to be my age, he ducks
political meetin's, an' reads th' papers an'
weighs th' ividence an' th' argymints - pro-
argymints an' con-argymints, an' makes up
his mind ca'mly, an' votes th' Dimmycratic
Ticket.

3071
Th' prisidincy is th' highest office in th' gift
iv th people. Th' vice-prisidincy is th' next
highest an' the lowest. It isn't a crime
exactly. Ye can't be sint to jail f'r it, but it's
a kind iv a disgrace.

3072
Vice goes a long way tow'rd makin' life
bearable. A little vice now an' thin is
relished by th' best iv men.

DUNNING John (Baron Ashburton)
1731-1783
3073
The infulence of the Crown has increased,
is increasing, and ought to be diminished.

DUNSANY Lord 1906-
3074
It is very seldom that the same man knows much of science, and about the things that were known before science came.

DURANT Will 1885-1981
3075
The individual succumbs, but he does not die if he has left something to mankind.

3076
So I should say that civilizations begin with religion and stoicism: they end with scepticism and unbelief, and the undisciplined pursuit of individual pleasure. A civilization is born stoic and dies epicurean.

3077
Most of us spend too much time on the last twenty-four hours and too little on the last six thousand years.

3078
One of the lessons of history is that nothing is often a good thing to do and always a clever thing to say.

3079
Our knowledge is a receding mirage in an expanding desert of ignorance.

3080
When liberty destroys order, the hunger for order will destroy liberty.

3081
Tired mothers find that spanking takes less time than reasoning and penetrates sooner to the seat of the memory.

3082 *(on his 90th Birthday)*
The love we have in our youth is superficial compared to the love that an old man has for his old wife.

DURANTY Edmond
3083
It takes immense genius to represent, simply and sincerely, what we see in front of us.

DUROCHER Leo 1906-1991
3084
Nice guys. Finish last.

DURRELL Lawrence 1912-1990
3085 *Justine*
There are only three things to be done with a woman. You can love her, you can suffer for her, or you can turn her into literature.

DÜRRENMATT Friedrich 1921-1990
3086
What was once thought can never be unthought.

DURY Ian 1942-
3087
Sex and drugs and rock and roll.

3088 *'What a Waste'*
I could be the catalyst that sparks the revolution.
I could be an inmate in a long term institution
I could lean to wild extremes I could do or die,
I could yawn and be withdrawn and watch them gallop by,
What a waste, what a waste, what a waste, what a waste.

DUVALL Robert
3089 *Apocalypse Now*
"I love the smell of napalm in the morning...it smells like victory."

DYER Sir Edward 1545-1607
3090 *The Lowest Trees*
Seas have their source, and so have shallow springs:
And love is love, in beggars and in kings ...
True hearts have ears and eyes, no tongues to speak:
They hear and see, and sigh, and then they break.

3091 *'In praise of a contented mind'*
Some have too much, yet still do crave;
I little have, and seek no more.
They are but poor, though much they have,
And I am rich with little store.
They poor, I rich; they beg, I give;
They lack, I leave; they pine, I live.

DYER John 1700-1758
3092 *Grongar Hill*
But transient is the smile of fate:
A little rule, a little sway,
A sunbeam in a winter's day,

Is all the proud and mighty have
Between the cradle and the grave.

DYLAN Bob 1941-
3093 *'All I Really Want To Do'*
I ain't lookin' to block you up,
Shock or knock or lock you up,
Analyze you, categorize you,
Finalize you or advertise you.

3094 *'It's Alright, Ma (I'm Only Bleeding)'*
Money doesn't talk, it swears.

3095 *'Blowin' in the wind'*
The answer is blowin' in the wind.

3096 *'A Hard Rain's A Gonna Fall'*
... it's a hard rain's a gonna fall.

3097 *'Mr Tambourine Man'*
Hey! Mr Tambourine man, play a song for
me.

EAGLETON Professor Terry 1943-
3098
Philosophy, Wittgenstein considered, could
say something, but nothing that was really
important.

EASTWOOD Clint 1930-
3099 *in Sudden Impact*
"Go ahead. Make my day."

EBAN Abba 1915-
3100
History teaches us that men and nations
behave wisely once they have exhausted
all other alternatives.

EDDINGTON Sir Arthur 1882-1944
3101 *(attributed)*
Science is an edged tool, with which men
play like children, and cut their own
fingers.

3102 *The Nature of the Physical World*
... if your theory is found to be against the
second law of thermodynamics I give you
no hope; there is nothing for it but to
collapse in deepest humiliation.

EDEN Sir Anthony 1897-1977
3103 *(on the Suez Crisis)*
We are in an armed conflict; that is the
phrase I have used. There has been no
declaration of war.

EDGEWORTH Maria 1768-1849
3104
Artifical manners vanish the moment the
natural passions are touched.

3105 *Leonora*
What a misfortune it is to be born a
woman! ... Why seek for knowledge,
which can prove only that our
wretchedness is irremediable?

EDISON Thomas Alva 1847-1931
3106
Genius is one per cent inspiration, ninety-
nine per cent perspiration.

3107
Everything comes to him who hustles
while he waits.

3108
I am long on ideas, but short on time. I
expect to live only about a hundred years.

3109
Results! Why, man, I have gotten a lot of
results. I know several thousand things
that won't work.

EDMESTON James 1791-1867
3110
Lead us, Heavenly Father, lead us
O'er the world's tempestuous sea;

EDMONDS John Maxwell 1875-1958
3111
When you go home, tell them of us and
say,
'For your tomorrows these gave their
today.'

EDWARD VIII (Duke of Windsor) 1894-
1972
3112
The thing that impresses me most about
America is the way parents obey their
children.

3113 *(after abdication)*
At long last I am able to say a few words
of my own ... you must believe me when I
tell you that I have found it impossible to
carry the heavy burden of responsibility
and to discharge my duties as King as I
would wish to do without the help and
support of the woman I love.

3114 *(speaking at derelict Iron and Steel Works)*
Something should be done to get them at work again.

EDWARDS Murray D.
3115
Men of genius are the worst possible models for men of talent.

EDWARDS Oliver 1711-1791
3116
I have tried too in my time to be a philospher; but, I don't know how, cheerfulness was always breaking in.

3117
For my part not, I consider supper as a turnpike through which one must pass, in order to get to bed.

EDWARDS Richard 1523-1566
3118 *The Paradise of Dainty Devices*
The falling out of faithful friends, renewing is of love.

EDWARDS Robert C.
3119
Whisky drowns some troubles and floats a lot more.

3120
Never exaggerate your faults; your friends will attend to that.

EDWARDS Tryon
3121
Thoroughly to teach another is the best way to learn for yourself.

EGERTON Sarah 1670-1723
3122 *'The Emulation'*
We will our rights in learning's world maintain;
Wit's empire now shall know a female reign.

EHRLICH Paul R. 1932-
3123
The first rule of intelligent tinkering is to save all the parts.

EICHMANN Adolf 1906-1962
3124
Repentance is for little children.

EINSTEIN Albert 1879-1955
3125
God is subtle but he is not malicious.

3126
If my theory of relativity is proven correct, Germany will claim me as a German and France will declare that I am a citizen of the world. Should my theory prove untrue, France will say that I am a German and Germany will declare that I am a Jew.

3127
The unleashed power of the atom has changed everything save our modes of thinking and we thus drift toward unparalleled catastrophe.

3128
If A is a success in life, then A equals x plus y plus z. Work is x; y is play; and z is keeping your mouth shut.

3129
Nationalism is an infantile sickness. It is the measles of the human race.

3130
I never think of the future. It comes soon enough.

3131
Reading after a certain (time) diverts the mind too much from its creative pursuits. Any man who reads too much and uses his own brain too little falls into lazy habits of thinking.

3132
The environment is everything that isn't me.

3133
I can't believe that God plays dice with the universe.

3134
A hundred times every day I remind myself that my inner and outer life depend on the labours of other men, living and dead, and that I must exert myself in order to give in the same measure as I have received.

3135
We should take care not to make the intellect our god; it has, of course, powerful muscles, but no personality.

3136
Science is the attempt to make the chaotic diversity of our sense-experience correspond to a logically uniform system of thought.

3137
No amount of experimentation can ever prove me right; a single experiment can prove me wrong.

3138
I think and think for months and years. Ninety-nine times, the conclusion is false. The hundredth time I am right.

3139
A successful man is he who receives a great deal from his fellow men, usually incomparably more than corresponds to his service to them. The value of a man, however, should be seen in what he gives and not in what he is able to receive.

3140
When you sit with a nice girl for two hours, you think it's only a minute. But when you sit on a hot stove for a minute, you think it's two hours. That's relativity.

3141
If you are out to describe the truth, leave elegance to the tailor.

3142
How do I work? I grope.

3143
All space is slightly curved.

3144 *(of Relativity)*
I simply ignored axiom.

3145 *Science, Philosophy and Religion*
Science without religion is lame, religion without science is blind.

EISELEY Loren
3146
I no longer cared about survival - I merely loved.

3147
From the solitude of the wood, (Man) has passed to the more dreadful solitude of the heart.

3148
When the human mind exists in the light of reason and no more than reason, we may say with absolute certainty that Man and all that made him will be in that instant gone.

EISENBERG Leon
3149
The university is the last remaining platform for national dissent.

EISENHOWER Dwight D. 1890-1969
3150
Every gun that is made, every warship launched, every rocket fired signifies, in the final sense, a theft from those who hunger and are not fed, those who are cold and are not clothed.

3151
You have broader considerations that might follow what you might call the 'falling domino' principle.

3152
I think that people want peace so much that one of these days governments had better get out of the way and let them have it.

3153
When you appeal to force, there's one thing you must never do - lose.

3154
An intellectual is a man who takes more words than necessary to tell more than he knows.

3155
What counts is not necessarily the size of the dog in the fight - it's the size of the fight in the dog.

ELGAR Sir Edward 1857-1934
3156
There is music in the air.

ELIOT Charles W. 1834-1926
3157
All business proceeds on beliefs, on judgements of probabilities, and not on certainties.

ELIOT George 1819-1880
3158
It's them that takes advantage that gets advantage i' this world.

3159
Animals are such agreeable friends - they ask no questions, they pass no criticisms.

3160
Necessity does the work of courage.

3161
What makes life dreary is want of motive.

3162
Men's men: be they gentle or simple, they're much of a muchness.

3163
There is nothing will kill a man so soon as having nobody to find fault with but himself.

3164
Speech may be barren; but it is ridiculous to suppose that silence is always brooding on a nestful of eggs.

3165
Blessed is the man who, having nothing to say, abstains from giving us wordy evidence of the fact.

3166
To be right in great and memorable moments is perhaps the thing we should most desire for ourselves.

3167
You must either give people what they are used to, or what they don't understand.

3168 *Adam Bede*
Deep, unspeakable suffering may well be called a baptism, a regeneration, the initiation into a new state.

3169 *Adam Bede*
We hand folks over to God's mercy, and show none ourselves.

3170 *Daniel Deronda*
Gossip is a sort of smoke that comes from the dirty tobacco-pipes of those who diffuse it: it proves nothing but the bad taste of the smoker.

3171 *Daniel Deronda*
A difference of taste in jokes is a great strain on the affections.

3172 *Daniel Deronda*
Friendships begin with liking or gratitude - roots that can be pulled up.

3173 *Felix Holt*
An election is coming. Universal peace is declared, and the foxes have a sincere interest in prolonging the lives of the poultry.

3174 *Felix Holt*
'Abroad', that large home of ruined reputations.

3175 *Middlemarch*
A woman dictates before marriage in order that she may have an appetite for submission afterwards.

3176 *Middlemarch*
Among all forms of mistake, prophecy is the most gratuitous.

3177 *Middlemarch*
Plain women he regarded as he did the other severe facts of life, to be faced with philosophy and investigated by science.

3178 *Middlemarch*
A woman, let her be as good as she may, has got to put up with the life her husband makes for her.

3179 *The Mill on the Floss*
Anger and jealousy can no more bear to lose sight of their objects than love.

3180 *The Mill on the Floss*
The dead level of provincial existence.

3181 *The Mill on the Floss*
The happiest women, like the happiest nations, have no history.

3182 *The Mill on the Floss*
I should like to know what is the proper function of women, if it is not to make

reasons for husbands to stay at home, and still stronger reasons for bachelors to go out.

3183 *Scenes of Clerical Life*
In every parting there is an image of death.

3184 *Scenes of Clerical Life*
Errors look so very ugly in persons of small means - one feels they are taking quite a liberty in going astray; whereas people of fortune may naturally indulge in a few delinquencies.

ELIOT T.S. 1888-1965
3185
A play should give you something to think about. When I see a play and understand it the first time, then I know it can't be much good.

3186
The young feel tired at the end of an action;
The old at the beginning.

3187
In the last few years everything I'd done up to sixty or so has seemed very childish.

3188
You have now learned to see
That cats are much like you and me
And other people whom we find
Possessed of various types of mind.

3189
What is actual is actual only for one time.
And only for one place.

3190
No one can become really educated without having pursued some study in which he took no interest. For it is part of education to interest ourselves in subjects for which we have no aptitude.

3191
It is in fact a part of the function of education to help us to escape, not from our own time - for we are bound by that - but from the intellectual and emotional limitations of our time.

3192
I will show you fear in a handful of dust.

3193
The historical sense involves a perception, not only of the pastness of the past, but of its presence.

3194
All cases are unique and very similar to others.

3195
Philosophy - the purple bullfinch in the lilac tree.

3196
When a great poet has lived certain things have been done once for all, and cannot be achieved again.

3197
No honest poet can ever feel quite sure of the permanent value of what he has written: he may have wasted his time and messed up his life for nothing.

3198
The poet's mind is ... a receptacle for seizing and storing up numberless feelings, phrases, images, which remain there until all the particles which can unite to form a new compound are present together.

3199
Poetry is a mug's game.

3200
Human kind cannot bear very much reality.

3201
The overwhelming pressure of mediocrity, sluggish and indomitable as a glacier, will mitigate the most violent, and depress the most exalted revolution.

3202
Half of the harm that is done in this world
Is due to people who want to feel important.
They don't mean to do harm - but the harm does not interest them.

3203
I suppose some editors are failed writers - but so are most writers.

3204
An editor should tell the author his
writing is better than it is. Not a lot better,
a little better.

3205 *Ash-Wednesday*
Teach us to care and not to care
Teach us to sit still.

3206 *The Cocktail Party*
What is hell?
Hell is oneself,
Hell is alone, the other figures in it
Merely projections. There is nothing to
escape from
And nothing to escape to. One is always
alone.

3207 *The Family Reunion*
Success is relative:
It is what we can make of the mess we
have made of things.

3208 *'The Hollow Men'*
We are the hollow men ...

3209 *'The Hollow Men'*
Between the idea
And the reality
Between the motion
And the act
Falls the Shadow.

3210 *'The Hollow Men'*
This is the way the world ends
Not with a bang but a whimper.

3211 *'Journey of the Magi'*
A cold coming we had of it,
Just the worst time of the year
For a journey, and such a long journey:
The ways deep and the weather sharp,
The very dead of winter.

3212 *'The Love Song of J. Alfred Prufrock'*
Let us go then, you and I,
When the evening is spread out against the
sky
Like a patient etherized upon a table.

3213 *'The Love Song of J. Alfred Prufrock'*
I have measured out my life with coffee
spoons.

3214 *Murder in the Cathedral*
Yet we have gone on living,
Living and partly living.

3215 *Murder in the Cathedral*
The last temptation is the greatest treason:
To do the right deed for the wrong reason.

3216 *Murder in the Cathedral*
Clean the air! clean the sky! wash the
wind! take the stone from stone, take the
skin from the arm, take the muscle from
bone, and wash them.

3217 *Old Possum's Book of Practical Cats*
Macavity, Macavity, there's no one like
Macavity,
There never was a Cat of such
deceitfulness and suavity.
He always has an alibi, and one or two to
spare:
At whatever time the deed took place -
MACAVITY WASN'T THERE!

3218 *'Preludes'*
The winter evening settles down
With smell of steaks in passageways.
Six o'clock.
The burnt-out ends of smoky days.

3219 *Four Quartets 'Burnt Norton'*
Footfalls echo in the memory
Down the passage which we did not take
Towards the door we never opened ...

3220 *Four Quartets 'East Coker'*
In my beginning is my end.

3221 *Four Quartets 'Little Gidding'*
What we call the beginning is often the
end
And to make an end is to make a
beginning.

3222 *Four Quartets 'Little Gidding'*
So, while the light fails
On a winter's afternoon, in a secluded
chapel
History is now and England.

3223 *The Rock*
Where is the wisdom we have lost in
knowledge?
Where is the knowledge we have lost in
information?

3224 *The Rock*
And the wind shall say: 'Here were decent godless people:
Their only monument the asphalt road
And a thousand lost golf balls.'

3225 *The Sacred Wood*
Immature poets imitate; mature poets steal.

3226 *Selected Essays*
We know too much and are convinced of too little.

3227 *Selected Essays*
Poets in our civilization, as it exists at present, must be difficult.

3228 *Sweeney Agonistes*
Birth, and copulation, and death.
That's all the facts when you come to brass tacks:

3229 *The Waste Land*
April is the cruellest month, breeding
Lilacs out of the dead land, mixing
Memory and desire, stirring
Dull roots with spring rain.
Winter kept us warm, covering
Earth in forgetful snow, feeding
A little life with dried tubers.

3230 *The Waste Land*
The typist home at teatime, clears her breakfast, lights
Her stove, and lays out food in tins.

3231 *The Waste Land*
When lovely woman stoops to folly and
Paces about her room again, alone,
She smoothes her hair with automatic hand,
And puts a record on the gramophone.

3232 *The Waste Land*
To me ... [The Waste Land] was only the relief of a personal and wholly insignificant grouse against life; it is just a piece of rhythmical grumbling.

3233 *'Whispers of Immortality'*
Webster was much possessed by death
And saw the skull beneath the skin;
And breastless creatures underground
Leaned backward with a lipless grin.

3234 *'Whispers of Immortality'*
Grishkin is nice: her Russian eye
Is underlined for emphasis;
Uncorseted, her friendly bust
Gives promise of pneumatic bliss.

ELIZABETH I Queen 1533-1603
3235
I will never be by violence constrained to do anything.

3236
I have had good experience and trial of this world. I know what it is to be a subject, what to be a Sovereign, what to have good neighbours, and sometimes meet evil-willers.

3237
The queen of Scots is this day leichter of a fair son, and I am but a barren stock.

3238 *(attributed)*
I would not open windows into men's souls.

3239 *(attributed)*
Anger makes dull men witty, but it keeps them poor.

3240 *(to the dying Countess of Nottingham)*
God may pardon you, but I never can.

3241 *(to Edward de Vere)*
My Lord, I had forgot the fart.

3242 *The Golden Speech*
Though God hath raised me high, yet this I count the glory of my crown: that I have reigned with your loves.

3243 *(to leaders of her Council)*
I will make you shorter by the head.

3244 *(of Mary Queen of Scots)*
The daughter of debate, that eke discord doth sow.

3245 *(to troops at Tilbury on approach of Armada)*
I know I have the body of a weak and feeble woman, but I have the heart and stomach of a king, and of a king of England too; and think foul scorn that Parma or Spain, or any prince of Europe, should dare to invade the borders of my realm.

3246 *(after Sir Walter Raleigh)*
If thy heart fails thee, climb not at all.

3247 *(to William Cecil on his death-bed)*
I do entreat heaven daily for your longer
life, else will my people and myself stand
in need of cordials too. My comfort hath
been in my people's happiness and their
happiness in thy discretion.

3248 *(to William Cecil, who suffered from
gout)*
My lord, we make use of you, not for your
bad legs, but for your good head.

ELIZABETH II Queen 1926-
3249 *(on her 25th Wedding Anniversary)*
I think everybody really will concede that
on this, of all days, I should begin my
speech with the words 'My husband and
I'.

ELIZABETH, The Queen Mother 1900-
3250 *Letter to Edith Sitwell (after death of
George VI)*
How small and selfish is sorrow. But it
bangs one about until one is senseless.

3251 *(to a London policeman)*
I'm glad we've been bombed. It makes me
feel I can look the East End in the face.

ELLERTON Alf
3252
Belgium put the kibosh on the Kaiser.

ELLERTON John 1826-1893
3253
The day Thou gavest, Lord, is ended,
The darkness falls at Thy behest.

ELLIOT Henry Rutherford
3254
It it's sanity you're after
There's no recipe like
Laughter.
Laugh it off.

ELLIOTT Ebenezer 1781-1849
3255 *'Epigram'*
What is a communist? One who hath
yearnings
For equal division of unequal earnings.

ELLIOTT Jr. John
3256
Big ideas are so hard to recognize, so
fragile, so easy to kill. Don't forget that, all
of you who don't have them.

ELLIS George 1753-1815
3257 *'The Twelve Months'*
Snowy, Flowy, Blowy,
Showery, Flowery, Bowery,
Hoppy, Croppy, Droppy,
Breezy, Sneezy, Freezy.

ELLIS Havelock 1859-1939
3258
The sun, moon and stars would have
disappeared long ago had they been
within the reach of predatory human
hands.

3259
Life is livable because we know that
wherever we go most of the people we
meet will be restrained in their actions
toward us by an almost instinctive
network of taboos.

3260
Imagination is a poor substitute for
experience.

3261
If men and women are to understand each
other, to enter into each other's nature
with mutual sympathy, and to become
capable of genuine comradeship, the
foundation must be laid in youth.

3262 *Impressions and Comments*
What we call 'progress' is the exchange of
one nuisance for another nuisance.

3263 *Little Essays of Love and Virtue*
All civilization has from time to time
become a thin crust over a volcano of
revolution.

ELSTOW Friar
3264 *(when threated with drowning by Henry
VIII)*
With thanks to God we know the way to
heaven, to be as ready by water as by land,
and therefore we care not which way we
go.

EMERSON Ralph Waldo 1803-1882
3265 *(attributed)*
If a man write a better book, preach a
better sermon, or make a better mouse-trap
than his neighbour, tho' he build his house
in the woods, the world will make a beaten
path to his door.

3266
The world is all gates, all opportunities,
strings of tension waiting to be struck.

3267
The reward of a thing well done, is to have
done it.

3268
It is time to be old,
To take in sail.

3269
A good indignation brings out all one's
powers.

3270
When we quarrel, how we wish we had
been blameless.

3271
Perpetual modernness is the measure of
merit in every work of art.

3272
Though we travel the world over to find
the beautiful, we must carry it with us or
we find it not.

3273
The beautiful rests on the foundations of
the necessary.

3274
We ascribe beauty to that which is simple;
which has no superfluous parts; which
exactly answers its ends.

3275
'Tis the good reader that makes the good
book.

3276
Character is that which can do without
success.

3277
What is the city in which we sit here, but
an aggregate of incongrous materials,

which have obeyed the will of some man?

3278
Cities force growth and make men
talkative and entertaining, but they make
them artificial.

3279
The end of the human race will be that it
will eventually die of civilization.

3280
An institution is the lengthening shadow
of one man.

3281
A great part of courage is the courage of
having done the thing before.

3282
The creation of a thousand forests is in one
acorn.

3283
A cynic can chill and dishearten with a
single word.

3284
The things taught in schools are not an
education but the means of an education.

3285
I find the Englishman to be him of all men
who stands firmest in his shoes.

3286
I have heard with admiring submission the
experience of the lady who declared that
the sense of being well-dressed gives a
feeling of inward tranquillity, which
religion is powerless to bestow.

3287
Whatever limits us we call Fate.

3288
To believe your own thought, to believe
that what is true for you in your private
heart is true for all men - that is genius.

3289
In every work of genius we recognize our
own rejected thoughts; they come back to
us with a certain alienated majesty.

3290
Accept the place the divine providence has
found for you, the society of your

contemporaries, the connection of events.

3291
I hate the giving of the hand unless the whole man accompanies it.

3292
The only gift is a portion of thyself.

3293
Take egotism out, and you would castrate the benefactor.

3294
Every hero becomes a bore at last.

3295
A hero is no braver than an ordinary man, but he is brave five minutes longer.

3296
All history is but the lengthened shadow of a great man.

3297
A man builds a fine house; and now he has a master, and a task for life; he is to furnish, watch, show it, and keep it in repair the rest of his life.

3298
Every man is an impossibility until he is born.

3299
Extremes meet, and there is no better example than the naughtiness of humility.

3300
The sky is the daily bread of the eyes.

3301
Every man is a borrower and a mimic; life is theatrical and literature a quotation.

3302
If you shoot at a king you must kill him.

3303
Life consists in what a man is thinking of all day.

3304
The whole of what we know is a system of compensations. Each suffering is rewarded; each sacrifice is made up; every debt is paid.

3305
It has come to be practically a sort of rule in literature that a man, having once shown himself capable of original writing, is entitled thenceforth to steal from the writings of others at discretion.

3306
A person seldom falls sick but the bystanders are animated with a faint hope that he will die.

3307
Men are what their mothers made them.

3308
Shall we judge a country by the majority, or by the minority? By the minority, surely.

3309
Nature is reckless of the individual. When she has points to carry, she carries them.

3310
The eyes indicate the antiquity of the soul.

3311
People only see what they are prepared to see.

3312
Can anything be so elegant as to have few wants, and to serve them one's self?

3313
The peace of the man who has foresworn the use of the bullet seems to me not quite peace, but a canting impotence.

3314
Good manners are made up of petty sacrifices.

3315
There is always a best way of doing everything, if it be only to boil an egg. Manners are the happy ways of doing things.

3316
There is a certain satisfaction in coming down to the lowest ground of politics, for then we get rid of cant and hypocrisy.

3317
Some natures are too good to be spoiled by praise.

3318
I hate quotations.

3319
The merit claimed for the Anglican Church is that, if you let it alone, it will let you alone.

3320
There is a crack in everything God has made.

3321
No sensible person ever made an apology.

3322
Outside, among your fellows, among strangers, you must preserve appearances, a hundred things you cannot do; but inside, the terrible freedom!

3323
Sanity is very rare; every man almost, and every woman, has a dash of madness.

3324
Self-command is the main elegance.

3325
Every man is a consumer and ought to be a producer.

3326
All the great speakers were bad speakers at first.

3327
Speak what you think today in words as hard as cannon balls, and tomorrow speak what tomorrow thinks in hard words again, though it contradict everything you said today.

3328
No man should travel until he has learned the language of the country he visits, otherwise he voluntarily makes himself a great baby - so helpless and ridiculous.

3329
God offers to every mind its choice between truth and repose. Take which you please; you can never have both.

3330
It is the privilege of any human work which is well done to invest the doer with a certain haughtiness. He can well afford not to conciliate, whose faithful work will answer for him.

3331
We are as much informed of a writer's genius by what he selects as by what he originates.

3332
It makes a great difference in the force of a sentence whether a man be behind it or no.

3333 *(of architecture)*
The flowering of geometry.

3334 *'Concord Hymn'*
By the rude bridge that arched the flood,
Their flag to April's breeze unfurled,
Here once the embattled farmers stood,
And fired the shot heard round the world.

3335 *The Conduct of Life*
Make yourself necessary to someone.

3336 *The Conduct of Life*
Art is a jealous mistress.

3337 *The Conduct of Life*
The louder he talked of his honour, the faster we counted our spoons.

3338 *Essays*
A friend is a person with whom I may be sincere.
Before him I may think aloud.

3339 *Essays*
The only reward of virtue is virtue; the only way to have a friend is to be one.

3340 *Essays*
There is properly no history; only biography.

3341 *Essays*
The faith that stands on authority is not faith.

3342 *Essays*
In skating over thin ice, our safety is in our speed.

3343 *Essays*
It is so bad, then, to be misunderstood?
Pythagoras was misunderstood, and
Socrates, and Jesus, and Luther, and
Copernicus, and Galileo, and Newton, and
every pure and wise spirit that ever took
flesh. To be great is to be misunderstood.

3344 *Essays*
To fill the hour - that is happiness.

3345 *Essays*
The years teach much which the days
never know.

3346 *Essays*
Men are conservatives when they are least
vigorous, or when they are most luxurious.
They are conservatives after dinner.

3347 *Essays*
All mankind love a lover.

3348 *Essays*
Every man is wanted, and no man is
wanted much.

3349 *Fortune of the Republic*
What is a weed? A plant whose virtues
have not been discovered.

3350 *Journal*
Old age brings along with its uglinesses
the comfort that you will soon be out of it.

3351 *Representative Men*
Is not marriage an open question, when it
is alleged, from the beginning of the
world, that such as are in the institution
wish to get out; and such as are out wish
to get in.

ENGELS Friedrich 1820-1895
3352 *Anti-Dühring*
The State is not 'abolished', it withers
away.

EN-LAI Chou
3353
China has no income tax, no unemployed
and not a single soldier outside its own
territory.

EPHELIA
3354 *Female Poems*
And yet I love this false, this worthless
man,

With all the passion that a woman can;
Dote on his imperfections, though I spy
Nothing to love; I love, and know not why.

EPICTETUS AD c.50-130
3355
Nothing great is created suddenly, any
more than a bunch of grapes or a fig. If
you tell me that you desire a fig, I answer
you that there must be time. Let it first
blossom, then bear fruit, then ripen.

3356
Practice yourself, for heaven's sake, in little
things; and thence proceed to greater.

3357
There is only one way to happiness and
that is to cease worrying about things
which are beyond the power of our will.

3358
All philosophy lies in two words, sustain
and abstain.

3359
Here is the beginning of philosophy: a
recognition of the conflicts between men, a
search for their cause, a condemnation of
mere opinion ... and the discovery of a
standard of judgement.

3360
Nature has given to men one tongue, but
two ears, that we may hear from others
twice as much as we speak.

3361
First learn the meaning of what you say,
and then speak.

3362
If you would be a reader, read; if a writer,
write.

EPICURUS c.310-270 BC
3363
The time when, most of all, you should
withdraw into yourself is when you are
forced to be in a crowd.

EPSTEIN Sir Jacob 1880-1959
3364 *(attributed)*
Why don't they stick to murder and leave
art to us?

EPSTEIN Joseph
3365
There is no word equivalent to 'cuckold' for women.

ERASMUS c.1469-1536
3366
He who shuns the millstone, shuns the meal.

3367 *Adages*
In the country of the blind the one-eyed man is king.

ERICKSEN Sir John Eric
3368 *(in 1873)*
The abdomen, the chest, and the brain will forever be shut from the intrusion of the wise and humane surgeon.

ERICKSON Arthur 1924-
3369
Life is rich, always changing, always challenging, and we architects have the task of transmitting into wood, concrete, glass and steel, of transforming human aspirations into habitable and meaningful space.

ERIKSON Erik
3370
Healthy children will not fear life if their elders have integrity enough not to fear death.

3371
Do not mistake a child for his symptom.

3372
Genius as such can neither be explained nor treated away; only, at times, its delay and inhibition and its perversion to destructive or self-destructive ends.

ERSKINE John 1879-1951
3373
Temperance is the control of all the functions of our bodies. The man who refuses liquor, goes in for apple pie and develops a paunch, is no ethical leader for me.

ERTZ Susan 1894-1985
3374
He talked with more claret than clarity.

ESAR Evan
3375
The quizzical expression of the monkey at the zoo comes from his wondering whether he is his brother's keeper, or his keeper's brother.

3376
Housework is what woman does that nobody notices unless she hasn't done it.

ESCHENBACH Marie Ebner von 1830-1916
3377 *Aphorism*
We don't believe in rheumatism and true love until after the first attack.

ESSLIN Martin
3378
The dignity of man lies in his ability to face reality in all its meaninglessness.

ESTIENNE Henri 1531-1598
3379 *Les Prémices*
If youth knew; if age was able.

EUCLID c.300 BC
3380 *Elementa*
A line is length without breadth.

EURIPIDES c.485-406 BC
3381
There's nothing like the sight of an old enemy down on his luck.

3382
What we look for does not come to pass. God finds a way for what none foresaw.

3383
We know the good, we apprehend it clearly. But we can't bring it to achievement.

3384
Happiness is brief
It will not stay.
God batters at its sails.

3385
The worst, the least curable hatred is that which has superseded deep love.

3386
Man's most valuable trait
Is a judicious sense of what not to believe.

3387
Men are men, they needs must err.

3388
Money is the wise man's religion.

3389
I hate the philosopher who is not wise for himself.

EUWER Anthony
3390
As a beauty I am not a star,
There are others more handsome by far,
But my face - I don't mind it
For I am behind it.
It's the people in front get the jar.

EVANS Edith 1888-1976
3391
I seem to have an awful lot of people inside me.

EVANS Very Rev Eric (Dean of St Pauls) 1928-
3392
Deaneries and crown canonries are the last bastions of the eccentric.

EVERETT David 1769-1813
3393 *'Lines Written for a School Declamation' (aged 7)*
Large streams from little fountains flow,
Tall oaks from little acorns grow.

EWART Gavin 1916-
3394 *Love Song*
But the heart line on my hand
foretold you;
in your army of lovers
I am a private soldier.

EWER William Norman 1885-1976
3395 *Week-End Book*
How odd
Of God
To choose
The Jews.

EYRE Ivan
3396
When I look at a painting it isn't only the painting that I see but the thing that I am. If there is more in the painting than I am, then I won't see it.

EYRE Richard 1943-
3397
Nobody warns you that when your parents die, you have to be an adult because you are no longer anybody's child.

FADIMAN Clifton
3398
When you read a classic you do not see in the book more than you did before. You see more in *you* than there was before.

3399
One's first book, kiss, home run is always the best.

3400
Cheese - milk's leap toward immortality.

3401
One newspaper a day ought to be enough for anyone who still prefers to retain a little mental balance.

3402
When you travel, remember that a foreign country is not designed to make you comfortable. It is designed to make its own people comfortable.

3403
There are two kinds of writers - the great ones who can give you truths, and the lesser ones, who can only give you themselves.

FAGUET Émile 1847-1916
3404 *(of Voltaire's philosophy)*
A chaos of clear ideas.

FARJEON Eleanor 1881-1965
3405
The events of childhood do not pass but repeat themselves like seasons of the year.

3406 *Children's Bells*
Morning has broken
Like the first morning,
Blackbird has spoken
Like the first bird.
Praise for the singing!
Praise for the morning!
Praise for them, springing
Fresh from the Lord!

FARMER Edward c.1809-1876
3407 *'The Collier's Dying Child'*
I have no pain, dear mother, now;
But oh! I am so dry:
Just moisten poor Jim's lips once more;
And, mother, do not cry!

FAROUK (ex-King) 1920-1965
3408
The whole world is in revolt. Soon there
will be only five Kings left - the King of
England, the King of Spades, the King of
Clubs, the King of Hearts and the King of
Diamonds.

FARQUHAR George 1678-1707
3409 *The Beaux' Stratagem*
There is no scandal like rags, nor any
crime so shameful as poverty.

3410 *The Beaux' Stratagem*
No woman can be a beauty without a
fortune.

3411 *The Inconstant*
Crimes, like virtues, are their own rewards.

3412 *The Recruiting Officer*
Hanging and marriage, you know, go by
Destiny.

FAULKNER William 1897-1962
3413
A man shouldn't fool with booze until he's
fifty; then he's a damn fool if he doesn't.

3414
Too much happens ... Man performs,
engenders so much more than he can or
should have to bear. That's how he finds
that he can bear anything.

3415
An artist is a creature driven by demons.
He doesn't know why they choose him
and he's usually too busy to wonder why.

3416
I believe that man will not merely endure:
he will prevail. He is immortal, not
because he alone among creatures has an
inexhaustible voice, but because he has a
soul, a spirit capable of compassion and
sacrifice and endurance.

3417
The Swiss are not a people so much as a
neat, clean, quite solvent business.

FAWCETT Chris
3418
A building is a string of events belonging
together.

FAWKES Guy 1570-1606
3419
A desperate disease requires a dangerous
remedy.

FEATHER William
3420
The philosophy behind much advertising
is based on the old observation that every
man is really two men - the man he is and
the man he wants to be.

3421
A man of fifty looks as old as Santa Claus
to a girl of twenty.

3422
If you're naturally kind, you attract a lot of
people you don't like.

3423
The petty economies of the rich are just as
amazing as the silly extravagances of the
poor.

3424
That they may have a little peace, even the
best dogs are compelled to snarl
occasionally.

FEMINA Jerry Della
3425
Advertising is the most fun you can have
with your clothes on.

FENTON James 1949-
3426 *German Requiem*
It is not what they built. It is what they
knocked down.
It is not the houses. It is the spaces
between the houses.
It is not the streets that exist. It is the
streets that no longer exist.

FERBER Edna 1887-1968
3427
Being an old maid is like death by

drowning, a really delightful sensation after you cease to struggle.

3428
Life cannot defeat a writer who is in love with writing - for life itself is a writer's love until death.

FERDINAND I Emperor 1503-1564
3429 *(motto)*
Let justice be done, though the world perish.

FERGUSON David
3430
Show me the man and I'll show you the law.

FERRE Nels F.S.
3431
A man who exieriences no genuine satisfaction in life does not want peace. People court war to escape meaninglessness and boredom, to be relieved of fear and frustration.

FICHTE Immanuel Hermann von
3432
If we cannot live so as to be happy, let us at least live so as to deserve it.

FICKE Arthur Davison
3433
A man must learn to forgive himself.

FIELDING Henry 1707-1754
3434
Thwackum was for doing justice, and leaving mercy to heaven.

3435
His designs were strictly honourable, as the phrase is: that is, to rob a lady of her fortune by way of marriage.

3436
It requires a penetrating eye to discern a fool through the disguise of gaiety and good breeding.

3437
There is no greater folly than to seek to correct the natural infirmities of those we love.

3438 *Amelia*
It hath been often said, that it is not death, but dying, which is terrible.

3439 *Joseph Andrews*
To whom nothing is given, of him can nothing be required.

3440 *Joseph Andrews*
Public schools are the nurseries of all vice and immorality.

3441 *Love in Several Masques*
Love and scandal are the best sweeteners of tea.

3442 *Don Quixote in England*
... a-hunting we will go.

3443 *Tom Jones*
That monstrous animal, a husband and wife.

3444 *Tom Jones*
What is commonly called love, namely the desire of satisfying a voracious appetite with a certain quantity of delicate white human flesh.

FIELDS Dorothy 1905-1974
3445 *'On the Sunny Side of the Street'*
Grab your coat, and get your hat,
Leave your worries on the doorstep,
Just direct your feet
To the sunny side of the street.

FIELDS W.C. 1880-1946
3446
Last week I went to Philadelphia, but it was closed.

3447
Never give a sucker an even break.

3448
Hell, I never vote for anybody. I always vote against.

3449
We frequently hear of people dying from too much drinking. That this happens is a matter of record. But the blame almost always is placed on whisky. Why this should be I never could understand. You can die from drinking too much of anything - coffee, water, milk, soft drinks and all such stuff as that. And so long as

the presence of death lurks with anyone who goes through the simple act of swallowing, I will make mine whisky.

3450
I always keep a supply of stimulant handy in case I see a snake - which I also keep handy.

3451
It was a woman who drove me to drink - and, you know, I never even thanked her.

3452
Women are like elephants. They are interesting to look at, but I wouldn't like to own one.

3453 *You Can't Cheat an Honest Man*
Some weasel took the cork out of my lunch.

3454 *(when caught reading the Bible)*
I'm looking for loop-holes.

3455 *in You're Telling Me*
"It's a funny old world - a man's lucky if he gets out of it alive."

FINLEY John
3456
Maturity is the capacity to endure uncertainty.

FIRBANK Ronald 1886-1926
3457 *The Flower Beneath the Foot*
I remember the average curate at home as something between a eunuch and a snigger.

3458 *Vainglory*
All millionaires love a baked apple.

3459 *Valmouth*
'I know of no joy,' she airily began, 'greater than a cool white dress after the sweetness of confession.'

FISCHER Louis
3460
Biography is history seen through the prism of a person.

FISHER H.A.L. 1856-1940
3461 *A History of Europe*
Purity of race does not exist. Europe is a continent of energetic mongrels.

FISHER Irving 1857-1947
3462 *(in 1929)*
Stocks have reached what looks like a permanently high plateau.

FISHER John Arbuthnot 1841-1920
3463
Never contradict
Never explain
Never apologize.

3464 *Memories*
The best scale for an experiment is 12 inches to a foot.

FISHER Martin H.
3465
The specialist is a man who fears the other subjects.

3466
The practice of medicine is a thinker's art, the practice of surgery a plumber's.

3467
Knowledge is a process of piling up facts; wisdom lies in their simplification.

FISHER Marve
3468 *'An Old-Fashioned Girl'*
I want an old-fashioned house
With an old-fashioned fence
And an old-fashioned millionaire.

FITZGERALD Edward 1809-1883
3469
Taste is the feminine of genius.

3470 *The Rubáiyát of Omar Khayyám*
Ah, take the cash in hand and waive the rest;
Oh, the brave music of a distant drum!

3471 *The Rubáiyát of Omar Khayyám*
Ah, make the most of what we yet may spend,
Before we too into the dust descend;
Dust into dust, and under dust, to lie,
Sans wine, sans song, sans singer, and - sans End!

3472 *The Rubáiyát of Omar Khayyám*
The moving finger writes; and, having writ,
Moves on: nor all thy piety nor wit
Shall lure it back to cancel half a line,

Nor all thy tears wash out a word of it.

3473 *The Rubáiyát of Omar Khayyám*
And that inverted bowl we call The Sky,
Whereunder crawling cooped we live and
die.

3474 *The Rubáiyát of Omar Khayyám*
Indeed the idols I have loved so long
Have done my credit in this world much
wrong:
Have drowned my glory in a shallow cup
And sold my reputation for a song.

FITZGERALD F. Scott 1896-1940
3475
The beautiful and damned.

3476
America is a willingness of the heart.

3477
No grand idea was ever born in a
conference, but a lot of foolish ideas have
died there.

3478
Grown up, and that is a terribly hard thing
to do. It is much easier to skip it and go
from one childhood to another.

3479 *All the Sad Young Men*
Let me tell you about the very rich. They
are different from you and me.

3480 *The Crack-Up*
Show me a hero and I will write you a
tragedy.

3481 *The Great Gatsby*
In his blue gardens, men and girls came
and went like moths among the
whisperings and the champagne and the
stars.

3482 *The Great Gatsby*
Her voice is full of money.

3483 *The Great Gatsby*
They were careless people, Tom and Daisy
- they smashed up things and creatures
and then retreated back into their money
or their vast carelessness, or whatever it
was that kept them together, and let other
people clean up the mess they had made.

3484 *'Handle with Care'*
In a real dark night of the soul it is always
three o'clock in the morning.

3485 *The Last Tycoon*
There are no second acts in American lives.

3486 *The Last Tycoon*
One girl can be pretty - but a dozen are
only a chorus.

FITZGERALD Zelda 1900-1948
3487
Nobody has ever measured, even poets,
how much a heart can hold.

FITZHENRY R.I.
3488
Uncertainty and mystery are energies of
life. Don't let them scare you unduly, for
they keep boredom at bay and spark
creativity.

3489
Soon after a hard decision something
inevitably occurs to cast doubt. Holding
steady against that doubt usually proves
that decision.

3490
The voice is a second signature.

3491
The adversary system is a kind of warfare
in mufti.

3492
Timing, degree and conviction are the
three wise men in this life.

3493
The Englishman loves to roll his tongue
around the word, 'extraordinary'. It so
pleases him that he is reluctant to finish
the sound which goes on into harmonics
and overtones. The American publisher is
likewise inclined.

FITZWATER Marlin
3494 *(on inexperience at the White House)*
A few more fat, old bald men wouldn't
hurt the place.

**FLANDERS Michael and SWANN
Donald** 1922-1975 and 1923-1994
3495
Have some madeira, M'dear.

FLATMAN Thomas 1637-1688
3496 *The Defiance*
There's an experienced rebel, Time,
And in his squadrons Poverty;
There's Age that brings along with him
A terrible artillery:
And if against all these thou keep'st thy
crown,
Th'usurper Death will make thee lay it
down.

FLAUBERT Gustave 1821-1880
3497
Be regular and orderly in your life like a
bourgeois, so that you may be violent and
original in your work.

3498 *(letter to Ernest Feydeau)*
Books are made not like children but like
pyramids ... and are just as useless! ...
Jackals piss at their foot and the bourgeois
climb up on them.

3499 *(letter to Louis Bouilhet)*
Things seem to be going at a dizzy rate.
We are dancing not on a volcano, but on
the rotten seat of a latrine.

FLECKER James Elroy 1884-1915
3500 *The Dying Patriot*
Noon strikes on England, noon on Oxford
town,
Beauty she was statue cold - there's blood
upon her gown.

3501 *The Golden Journey to Samarkand*
When the great markets by the sea shut
fast
All that calm Sunday that goes on and on:
When even lovers find their peace at last,
And earth is but a star, that once had
shone.

3502 *The Golden Journey to Samarkand*
For lust of knowing what should not be
known,
We take the Golden Road to Samarkand.

3503 *To a Poet a Thousand Years Hence*
O friend unseen, unborn, unknown,
Student of our sweet English tongue,
Read out my words at night, alone;
I was a poet, I was young.

FLEMING Alexander D. 1881-1955
3504
A good gulp of hot whisky at bedtime - it's
not very scientific, but it helps.

FLEMING Ian 1908-1964
3505 *Dr. No*
A medium Vodka dry Martini - with a slice
of lemon peel. Shaken and not stirred.

FLETCHER John 1579-1625
3506 *The Bloody Brother*
Best while you have it use your breath,
There is no drinking after death.

3507 *The Bloody Brother*
And he that will go to bed sober,
Falls with the leaf still in October.

3508 *The Island Princess*
Let's meet, and either do, or die.

3509 *The Knight of Malta*
Of all the paths lead to a woman's love
Pity's the straightest.

FLETCHER Phineas 1582-1650
3510 *Sicelides*
Love is like linen often changed, the
sweeter.

3511 *Sicelides*
The coward's weapon, poison.

FLORIAN Jean-Pierre Claris de 1755-
1794
3512 *Célestine*
Love's pleasure lasts but a moment; love's
sorrow lasts all through life.

FLORIO John c.1553-1625
3513 *Second Frutes*
England is the paradise of women, the
purgatory of men, and the hell of horses.

FOCH Ferdinand 1851-1929
3514
Airplanes are interesting toys but of no
military value.

3515 *(message sent during Battle of the
Marne)*
My centre is giving way, my right is
retreating, situation excellent, I am
attacking.

3516 *(at the signing of the Treaty of Versailles)*
This is not a peace treaty, it is an armistice
for twenty years.

FOLEY J. 1906-1970
3517
Old soldiers never die,
They simply fade away.

FONDA Henry 1905-1982
3518
The best actors do not let the wheels show.

FOOT Michael 1913-
3519
Think of it! A second Chamber selected by
the Whips. A seraglio of eunuchs.

3520 *(of Norman Tebbit)*
It is not necessary that every time he rises
he should give his famous imitation of a
semi-house-trained polecat.

FOOTE Samuel 1720-1777
3521 *(of a dull law lord)*
He is not only dull in himself, but the
cause of dullness in others.

3522 *Letter to the Lord Chamberlain*
Between the muse and the magistrate there
is a natural confederacy; what the last
cannot punish the first often corrects.

FOOTE Shelby
3523
Longevity conquers scandal every time.

FORBES Malcolm S. 1919-1990
3524
Ability will never catch up with the
demand for it.

FORD Gerald 1909-
3525
I've had a lot of experience with people
smarter than I am.

3526
When a man is asked to make a speech,
the first thing he has to decide is what to
say.

3527
If the Government is big enough to give
you everything you want, it is big enough
to take away everything you have.

FORD Henry 1863-1947
3528
It is not the employer who pays wages - he
only handles the money. It is the product
that pays wages.

3529
Capital punishment is as fundamentally
wrong as a cure for crime as charity is
wrong as a cure for poverty.

3530
Anyone who stops learning is old, whether
at twenty or eighty. Anyone who keeps
learning stays young. The greatest thing in
life is to keep your mind young.

3531
Before everything else, getting ready is the
secret of success.

3532
History is more or less bunk.

3533 *(on choice of colour for the Model T Ford)*
Any colour - so long as it's black.

FORD Lena Guilbert 1870-1916
3534 *Till the Boys Come Home!*
Keep the Home-fires burning,
While your hearts are yearning,
Though your lads are far away
They dream of Home.
There's a silver lining
Through the dark cloud shining;
Turn the dark cloud inside out,
Till the boys come Home.

FORGY Howell 1908-1983
3535 *(at Pearl Harbor)*
Praise the Lord and pass the ammunition.

FORSTER E.M. 1879-1970
3536
Chicago - a facade of skyscrapers facing a
lake and behind the facade every type of
dubiousness.

3537
In the creative state a man is taken out of
himself. He lets down as it were a bucket
into his subconscious, and draws up
something which is normally beyond his
reach. He mixes this thing with his normal
experiences and out of the mixture he
makes a work of art.

3538
An efficiency-regime cannot be run without a few heroes stuck about it to carry off the dullness - much as plums have to be put into a bad pudding to make it palatable.

3539
It is pleasant to be transferred from an office where one is afraid of a sergeant-major into an office where one can intimidate generals, and perhaps this is why history is so attractive to the more timid among us.

3540
Our life on earth is, and ought to be, material and carnal. But we have not yet learned to manage our materialism and carnality properly; they are still entangled with the desire for ownership.

3541
How can I know what I think till I see what I say?

3542 *Abinger Harvest*
(Public schoolboys) go forth into a world that is not entirely composed of public-school men or even of Anglo-Saxons.

3543 *Abinger Harvest*
It is not that the Englishman can't feel - it is that he is afraid to feel.

3544 *Howards End*
To trust people is a luxury in which only the wealthy can indulge; the poor cannot afford it.

3545 *Howards End*
Only connect! ... Only connect the prose and the passion, and both will be exalted, and human love will be seen at its height.

3546 *Howards End*
Death destroys a man: the idea of death saves him.

3547 *The Longest Journey*
There is much good luck in the world, but it is luck. We are none of us safe.

3548 *A Passage to India*
The so-called white races are really pinko-grey.

3549 *A Passage to India*
Where there is officialism every human relationship suffers.

3550 *Two cheers for Democracy 'What I Believe'*
If I had to choose between betraying my country and betraying my friend, I hope I should have the guts to betray my country.

3551 *Two cheers for Democracy 'What I Believe'*
So Two cheers for Democracy: one because it admits variety and two because it permits criticism.

FORSTER W.E. 1878-1969
3552
What is the use of lying when truth, well distributed, serves the same purpose?

FOSDICK Harry Emerson 1878-1969
3553
Watch what people are cynical about, and one can often discover what they lack.

3554
Democracy is based upon the conviction that there are extraordinary possibilities in ordinary people.

3555
God is not a cosmic bellboy for whom we can press a button to get things done.

3556
Liberty is always dangerous - but it is the safest thing we have.

3557
Nothing in human life, least of all in religion, is ever right until it is beautiful.

FOSDICK Raymond B. 1883-1969
3558
It is always the minorities that hold the key of progress; it is always through those who are unafraid to be different that advance comes to human society.

FOSTER Stephen Collins 1826-1864
3559 *'Jeanie with the Light Brown Hair'*
I dream of Jeanie with the light brown hair,
Floating, like a vapour, on the soft summer air.

3560 *'The Old Folks at Home'*
Way down upon the Swanee River,
Far, far, away,
There's where my heart is turning ever;
There's where the old folks stay.

FOWLER Gene
3561
Writing is easy: all you do is sit staring at
the blank sheet of paper until the drops of
blood form on your forehead.

FOWLES John Robert 1926-
3562
Men love war because it allows them to
look serious; because it is the only thing
that stops women laughing at them.

3563 *The Aristos*
Passion destroys passion; we want what
puts an end to wanting what we want.

FRANCE Anatole 1844-1924
3564
Never lend books - nobody ever returns
them; the only books I have in my library
are those which people have lent me.

3565
I do not know any reading more easy,
more fascinating, more delightful than a
catalogue.

3566
Chance is the pseudonym of God when he
did not want to sign.

3567
All changes, even the most longed for,
have their melancholy, for what we leave
behind us is a part of ourselves; we must
die to one life before we can enter into
another.

3568
The good critic is he who narrates the
adventures of his soul among
masterpieces.

3569
If fifty million people say a foolish thing, it
is still a foolish thing.

3570
The law, in its majestic equality, forbids the
rich as well as the poor to sleep under

bridges, to beg in the streets, and to steal
bread.

3571
It is human nature to think wisely and to
act in an absurd fashion.

3572
I prefer the errors of enthusiasm to the
indifference of wisdom.

FRANCIS Brendan
3573
The big difference between sex for money
and sex for free is that sex for money
usually costs a lot less.

FRANCIS of Sales, Saint 1567-1622
3574
Nothing is more like a wise man than a
fool who holds his tongue.

3575
Do not wish to be anything but what you
are, and try to be that perfectly.

3576
If someone below us does not treat us
politely, we don't like anything he does. If,
instead, we take a liking to someone, we
forgive him anything he does.

3577
Have patience with all things, but chiefly
have patience with yourself. Do not lose
courage in considering your own
imperfections, but instantly set about
remedying them - every day begin the task
anew.

3578
While I am busy with little things, I am not
required to do greater things.

FRANCIS Xavier, Saint 1506-1552
3579
Give me the children until they are seven
and anyone may have them afterwards.

FRANK Lawrence K.
3580
Don't quote me; that's what you heard, not
what I said.

FRANKENBERG Lloyd
3581
The apparent serenity of the past is an oil

spread by time.

FRANKFURTER Felix 1882-1965

3582
The Court's authority - possessed of neither the purse nor the sword - ultimately rests on substantial public confidence in its moral sanctions.

3583
Fragile as reason is and limited as law is as the institutionalized medium of reason, that's all we have standing between us and the tyranny of mere will and the cruelty of unbridled, undisciplined feeling.

3584
It is a fair summary of history to say that the safeguards of liberty have frequently been forged in cases involving not very nice people.

3585
It simply is not true that war never settles anything.

FRANKLIN Benjamin 1706-1790

3586
If you want a thing done, go - if not, send.

3587
A child thinks twenty shillings and twenty years can scarce ever be spent.

3588
If a man empties his purse into his head, no one can take it from him.

3589
The greatest monarch on the proudest throne is obliged to sit upon his own arse.

3590
There are three faithful friends: an old wife, and old dog, and ready money.

3591
Who is wise? He that learns from everyone.
Who is powerful? He that governs his passions.
Who is rich? He that is content.
Who is that? Nobody.

3592
There is a difference between imitating a good man and counterfeiting him.

3593
Were the offer made true, I would engage to run again, from beginning to end, the same career of life. All I would ask should be the privilege of an author, to correct, in a second edition, certain errors of the first.

3594
God heals, and the doctor takes the fees.

3595
Nothing is more fatal to health an an overcare of it.

3596
Praise to the undeserving is severe satire.

3597
Resistance to tyrants is obedience to God.

3598 *Advice to a Young Tradesman*
Remember that time is money.

3599 *(letter to Georgiana Shipley)*
Here Skugg
Lies snug
As a bug
In as rug.

3600 *(letter to Jean Baptiste Le Roy)*
In this world nothing can be said to be certain, except death and taxes.

3601 *(letter to Josiah Quincy)*
There never was a good war, or a bad peace.

3602 *Poor Richard's Almanac*
Necessity never made a good bargain.

3603 *Poor Richard's Almanac*
He that lives upon hope will die fasting.

3604 *Poor Richard's Almanac*
Where there's marriage without love, there will be love without marriage.

3605 *(at the Signing of Declaration of Independence)*
We must indeed all hang together, or, most assuredly, we shall all hang separately.

FRANKS Baron 1905-

3606
A secret in the Oxford sense: you may tell it to only one person at a time.

FRAYN Michael 1933-
3607
I feel bad that I don't feel worse.

FRAZER Sir James 1854-1941
3608 *The Golden Bough*
The awe and dread with which the
untutored savage contemplates his
mother-in-law are amongst the most
familiar facts of anthropology.

FREDERICK The Great 1712-1786
3609
I love an opposition that has convictions.

FREUD Anna 1895-1982
3610
Creative minds have always been known
to survive any kind of bad training.

FREUD Clement 1924-
3611
If you resolve to give up smoking,
drinking and loving, you don't actually
live longer; it just seems longer.

FREUD Martin 1895-1982
3612
I didn't know the full facts of life until I
was 17. My father [Sigmund Freud] never
talked about his work.

FREUD Sigmund 1856-1939
3613
Hatred of Judaism is at bottom hatred of
Christianity.

3614
Toward the person who has died we adopt
a special attitude: something like
admiration for someone who has
accomplished a very difficult task.

3615
From error to error one discovers the entire
truth.

3616
It is unavoidable that if we learn more
about a great man's life, we shall also hear
of occasions on which he has done no
better than we, and has in fact come nearer
to us as a human being.

3617
A hero is a man who stands up manfully
against his father and in the end
victoriously overcomes him.

3618
Being entirely honest with oneself is a
good exercise.

3619
Life as we find it is too hard for us; it
entails too much pain, too many
disappointments, impossible tasks. We
cannot do without palliative remedies.

3620
Man should not strive to eliminate his
complexes, but to get in accord with them;
they are legitimately what directs his
conduct in the world.

3621
A man who has been the indisputable
favourite of his mother keeps for life the
feeling of a conqueror.

3622
When a man is freed of religion, he has a
better chance to live a normal and
wholesome life.

3623
The only unnatural sexual behaviour is
none at all.

3624 *The Interpretation of Dreams*
The interpretation of dreams is the royal
road to a knowledge of the unconscious
activities of the mind.

3625 *(letter to Marie Bonaparte)*
The great question that has never been
answered and which I have not yet been
able to answer, despite my thirty years of
research into the feminine soul, is 'What
does a woman want?'

FRIEDENBERG Edgar Z.
3626
Part of the American dream is to live long
and die young.

3627
The 'teenager' seems to have replaced the
Communist as the appropriate target for
public controversy and foreboding.

FRIEDLANDER Rabbi Albert
3628
Every generation harvests the dragon seeds of hatred sown by the previous generation.

FRIEDMAN Milton 1912-
3629
What kind of society isn't structured on greed? The problem of social organization is how to set up an arrangement under which greed will do the least harm; capitalism is that kind of a system.

3630
Inflation is one form of taxation that can be imposed without legislation.

FRIEDRICH Otto
3631
Madness is part of all of us, all the time, and it comes and goes, waxes and wanes.

FRIENDLY Fred
3632
Today's reporter is forced to become an educator more concerned with explaining the news than with being first on the scene.

FRISCH Max 1911-1991
3633
Technology - the knack of so arranging the world that we don't have to experience it.

FROMM Erich 1900-1980
3634
Giving is the highest expression of potency.

3635
Only the person who has faith in himself is able to be faithful to others.

3636
The mother-child relationship is paradoxical and, in a sense, tragic. It requires the most intense love on the mother's side, yet this very love must help the child grow away from the mother and to become fully independent.

3637
I think if you ask people what their concept of heaven is, they would say, if they are honest, that it is a big department store, with new things every week - all the money to buy them, and maybe a little more than the neighbours.

3638
Integrity simply means a willingness not to violate one's identity.

3639 *The Art of Loving*
Love is the only sane and satisfactory answer to the problem of human existence.

FROST David 1939-
3640
Television is an invention that permits you to be entertained in your living room by people you wouldn't have in your home.

FROST Robert 1874-1963
3641
The only way round is through.

3642
Americans are like a rich father who wishes he knew how to give his son the hardships that made him rich.

3643
Belief is better than anything else, and it is best when rapt - above paying its respects to anybody's doubt whatsoever.

3644
There may be little or much beyond the grave,
But the strong are saying nothing until they see.

3645
Education is the ability to listen to almost anything without losing your temper or your self-confidence.

3646
There's nothing I'm afraid of like scared people.

3647
Happiness makes up in height for what it lacks in length.

3648
At bottom the world isn't a joke. We only joke about it to avoid an issue with someone, to let someone know that we know he's there with his questions; to disarm him by seeming to have heard and

done justice to his side of the standing argument.

3649
Humour is the most engaging cowardice. With it myself I have been able to hold some of my enemy in play far out of gunshot.

3650
An idea is a feat of association, and the height of it is a good metaphor.

3651
A jury consists of twelve persons chosen to decide who has the better lawyer.

3652
A successful lawsuit is the one worn by a policeman.

3653
In three words I can sum up everything I've learned about life. It goes on.

3654
You've got to love what's lovable, and hate what's hateable. It takes brains to see the difference.

3655
Don't ever take a fence down until you know why it was put up.

3656
You've got to be brave and you've got to be bold. Brave enough to take your chance on your own discrimination - what's right and what's wrong, what's good and what's bad.

3657
You don't have to deserve your mother's love. You have to deserve your father's. He's more particular.

3658
Poetry should be common in experience but uncommon in books.

3659
A poem begins with a lump in the throat; a homesickness or a lovesickness. It is a reaching-out toward expression; an effort to find fulfilment. A complete poem is one where an emotion has found its thought and the thought has found words.

3660
Writing free verse is like playing tennis with the net down.

3661
Poetry is a way of taking life by the throat.

3662
A Liberal is a man too broadminded to take his own side in a quarrel.

3663
Don't be agnostic - be something.

3664
To be social is to be forgiving.

3665
The best things and best people rise out of their separateness; I'm against a homogenized society because I want the cream to rise.

3666
All thought is a feat of association; having what's in front of you bring up something in your mind that you almost didn't know you knew.

3667 *'Cluster of Faith'*
Forgive, O Lord, my little jokes on Thee
And I'll forgive Thy great big one on me.

3668 *'The Death of the Hired Man'*
'Home is the place where, when you have to go there,
They have to take you in.'

3669 *'Fire and Ice'*
Some say the world will end in fire,
Some say in ice.
From what I've tasted of desire
I hold with those who favour fire.
But if it had to perish twice,
I think I know enough of hate
To say that for destruction ice
Is also great
And would suffice.

3670 *'The Hardship of Accounting'*
Never ask of money spent
Where the spender thinks it went.
Nobody was ever meant
To remember or invent
What he did with every cent.

3671 *'Mending Wall'*
'Good fences make good neighbours.'

3672 *'Precaution'*
I never dared be radical when young
For fear it would make me conservative
when old.

FROUDE James A. 1818-1894
3673
You cannot dream yourself into a
character; you must hammer and forge
yourself one.

FRY Christopher 1907-
3674
Who, apart
From ourselves, can see any difference
between
Our victories and our defeats?

3675
The dark is light enough.

FRYE Northrop 1912-1991
3676
The bible should be taught so early and so
thoroughly that it sinks straight to the
bottom of the mind where everything that
comes along can settle on it.

3677
The most technologically efficient machine
that man has ever invented is the book.

3678
Separatism is a very healthy movement
within culture. It's a disastrous movement
within politics and economics.

3679
We are being swallowed up by the popular
culture of the United States, but then the
Americans are being swallowed up by it
too. It's just as much a threat to American
culture as it is to ours.

3680
Historically, a Canadian is an American
who rejects the Revolution.

3681
The human landscape of the New World
shows a conquest of nature by an
intelligence that does not love it.

3682
We must reject that most dismal and
fatuous notion that education is a
preparation for life.

3683
The simplest questions are the hardest to
answer.

3684
War appeals to young men because it is
fundamentally auto-eroticism.

3685
There is only one way to degrade mankind
permanently and that is to destroy
language.

3686
Writing: I certainly do rewrite my central
myth in every book, and would never read
or trust any writer who did not also do so.

3687
Beauty and truth may be attributes of good
writing, but if the writer deliberately aims
at truth, he is likely to find that what he
has hit is the didactic.

FUCIK Julius
3688
To be a man will continue to demand a
heroic heart as long as mankind is not
quite human.

FULFORD Robert 1923-
3689
My generation of Canadians grew up
believing that, if we were very good or
very smart, or both, we would some day
graduate from Canada.

FULLER Buckminster 1895-1983
3690
Don't fight forces; use them.

3691
A house is a machine for living.

3692
Pollution is nothing but resources we're
not harvesting.

3693
Either war is obsolete or men are.

3694 *Operating Manual for Spaceship Earth*
Now there is one outstandingly important fact regarding Spaceship Earth, and that is that no instruction book came with it.

FULLER Margaret 1810-1850
3695
Would that ... a sense of the true aim of life might elevate the tone of politics and trade till public and private honour become identical.

FULLER Thomas 1608-1661
3696
Good is not good, where better is expected.

3697
The great end of life is not knowledge, but action.

3698
Old foxes want no tutors.

3699
Light, God's eldest daughter, is a principal beauty in a building.

3700
Cheat me in the price but not in the goods.

3701
We could be cowards, if we had courage enough.

3702
The number of malefactors authorizes not the crime.

3703
Today is yesterday's pupil.

3704
The scalded cat fears even cold water.

3705
The Devil himself is good when he is pleased.

3706
Even doubtful accusations leave a stain behind them.

3707
Great and good are seldom the same man.

3708
He that resolves to deal with none but honest men, must leave off dealing.

3709
He is idle that might be better employed.

3710
He that flings dirt at another dirtieth himself most.

3711
A fox should not be on the jury at a goose's trial.

3712
That which is bitter to endure may be sweet to remember.

3713
Seeing's believing, but feeling's the truth.

3714
He that has a great nose thinks everybody is speaking of it.

3715
Pride, perceiving humility honourable, often borrows her cloak.

3716
Pride had rather go out of the way than go behind.

3717
What a day may bring, a day may take away.

3718
If an ass goes travelling, he'll not come back a horse.

3719
Trust thyself only, and another shall not betray thee.

3720
Riches enlarge, rather than satisfy appetites.

3721
Don't let your will roar when your power only whispers.

GABIROL Solomon Ibn c.1020-1070
3722
The space in a needle's eye is sufficient for two friends, but the whole world is scarcely big enough to hold two enemies.

3723
What is the test of good manners? Being able to bear patiently with bad ones.

GABLE Clark 1901-1960
3724 *in Gone With the Wind*
"Frankly, my dear, I don't **give** a damn."

GABOR Zsa Zsa 1919-
3725
I never hated a man enough to give him his diamonds back.

3726
Macho does not prove mucho.

3727 *(attributed)*
Never despise what it says in the women's magazines. It may not be subtle, but neither are men.

3728
A man is incomplete until he has married. Then he's finished.

3729
Husbands are like fires. They go out when unattended.

3730
I always believe in the old adage. Leave them while you're looking good.

3731 *(asked which of the Gabor women was the oldest)*
'She'll never admit it, but I believe it is Mama.'

GABOURY Étienne
3732
Architecture is space structured to serve man and to move him.

GADDIS William 1922-
3733
What's an artist, but the dregs of his work - the human shambles that follows it around?

GAISFORD Thomas 1779-1855
3734 *Christmas Day Sermon*
Nor can I do better, in conclusion, than impress upon you the study of Greek literature, which not only elevates above the vulgar herd, but leads not infrequently to positions of considerable emolument.

GAITSKELL Hugh 1906-1963
3735 *(at Labour Party Conference)*
There are some of us ... who will fight and fight and fight again to save the Party we love.

GALBRAITH J.K. 1908-
3736
Few people at the beginning of the nineteenth century needed an adman to tell them what they wanted.

3737
Washington is a place where men praise courage and act on elaborate personal cost-benefit calculations.

3738
People of privilege will always risk their complete destruction rather than surrender any material part of their advantage.

3739
Meetings are indispensable when you don't want to do anything.

3740
In economics, the majority is always wrong.

3741
One of the greatest pieces of economic wisdom is to know what you do not know.

3742
In all modern depressions, recessions, or growth-correction, as variously they are called, we never miss the goods that are not produced. We miss only the opportunities for the labour - for the jobs - that are not provided.

3743
More die in the United States of too much food than of too little.

3744
No intelligence system can predict what a government will do if it doesn't know itself.

3745
Humour is richly rewarding to the person who employs it. It has some value in gaining and holding attention. But it has no persuasive value at all.

3746
The conspicuously wealthy turn up urging the character-building value of privation for the poor.

3747
Technology means the systematic application of scientific or other organized knowledge to practical tasks.

3748
The more underdeveloped the country, the more overdeveloped the women.

3749 *The Affluent Society*
It is a far, far better thing to have a firm anchor in nonsense than to put out on the troubled seas of thought.

3750 *The Affluent Society*
The greater the wealth, the thicker will be the dirt.

GALEN c AD 130-201
3751
Employment is nature's physician, and is essential to human happiness.

GALLANT Mavis 1922-
3752
There are a great many opinions in this world, and a good half of them are professed by people who have never been in trouble.

GALLICO Paul 1897-1976
3753
No one can be as calculatedly rude as the British, which amazes Americans, who do not understand studied insult and can only offer abuse as a substitute.

GALLUP George 1901-1984
3754
I could prove God statistically.

GALSWORTHY John 1867-1933
3755
The value of a sentiment is the amount of sacrifice you are prepared to make for it.

3756
One's eyes are what one is, one's mouth what one becomes.

3757
A man of action forced into a state of thought is unhappy until he can get out of it.

GANDHI Indira 1917-1984
3758
I suppose leadership at one time meant muscles; but today it means getting along with people.

GANDHI Mahatma 1869-1948
3759
I am not built for academic writings. Action is my domain.

3760
To a man with an empty stomach food is god.

3761
Monotony is the law of nature. Look at the monotonous manner in which the sun rises. The monotony of necessary occupations is exhilarating and life-giving.

3762
It is possible for a single individual to defy the whole might of an unjust empire to save his honour, his religion, his soul and lay the foundation for that empire's fall or its regeneration.

3763
I consider myself a Hindu, Christian, Moslem, Jew, Buddhist, and Confucian.

3764
There are limits to self-indulgence, none to self-restraint.

3765
Non-violence is the first article of my faith. It is also the last article of my creed.

3766 *Non-Violence in Peace and War*
What difference does it make to the dead, the orphans and the homeless, whether the mad destruction is wrought under the name of totalitarianism or the holy name of liberty or democracy?

3767 *Non-Violence in Peace and War*
The moment the slave resolves that he will no longer be a slave, his fetters fall. He frees himself and shows the way to others.

Freedom and slavery are mental states.

GARBETT Archbishop C. 1875-1955
3768
Any fool can criticize, and many of them do.

GARCIA Jerry d.1995
3769
Truth is something you stumble into when you think you're going some place else.

GARDNER Ed 1901-1963
3770 *Duffy's Tavern*
Opera is when a guy gets stabbed in the back and, instead of bleeding, he sings.

GARDNER Herbert
3771
Once you get people laughing, they're listening and you can tell them almost anything.

GARDNER Dr Howard
3772
It isn't necessary to be a bastard to be a genius, but a disregard for others does seem necessary.

GARDNER John W. 1912-
3773
Art gropes, it stalks like a hunter lost in the woods, listening to itself and to everything around it, unsure of itself, waiting to pounce.

3774
The ultimate goal of the educational system is to shift to the individual the burden of pursuing his education.

3775
History never looks like history when you are living through it. It always looks confusing and messy, and it always feels uncomfortable.

3776
If one defines the term 'dropout' to mean a person who has given up serious effort to meet his responsibilities, then every business office, government agency, golf club and university faculty would yield its quota.

GARIBALDI Giuseppe 1807-1882
3777
Bacchus has drowned more men than Neptune.

3778
I can offer you neither honours nor wages; I offer you hunger, thirst, forced marches, battles and death. Anyone who loves his country, follow me.

GARLAND Judy 1922-1969
3779
If I'm such a legend, then why am I so lonely? Let me tell you, legends are all very well if you've got somebody around who loves you.

GARNER John Nance 1868-1967
3780
The vice-presidency isn't worth a pitcher of warm piss.

GARRICK David 1717-1779
3781 *'Heart of Oak'*
Heart of oak are our ships,
Heart of oak are our men:
We always are ready;
Steady, boys, steady;
We'll fight and we'll conquer again and again.

GARRISON William Lloyd 1805-1879
3782 *The Liberator*
I am in earnest - I will not equivocate - I will not excuse - I will not retreat a single inch - and I will be heard!

3783 *Massachusetts Anti-Slavery Society Resolution*
The compact which exists between the North and the South is 'a covenant with death and an agreement with hell'.

GARY Romain 1914-1990
3784
Humour is an affirmation of dignity, a declaration of man's superiority to all that befalls him.

GASCOIGNE George c.1534-1577
3785 *'Gascoigne's Good Morrow'*
The carrion crow, that loathsome beast,
Which cries against the rain,
Both for her hue and for the rest,
The Devil resembleth plain:

And as with guns we kill the crow,
For spoiling our relief,
The Devil so must we overthrow,
With gunshot of belief.

GASKELL Elizabeth 1810-1865
3786 *Cranford*
A man ... is *so* in the way in the house!

3787 *Cranford*
I'll not listen to reason ... Reason always
means what someone else has got to say.

3788 *Sylvia's Lovers*
That kind of patriotism which consists in
hating all other nations.

GASSET José Ortega y 1883-1955
3789
What makes a nation great is not primarily
its great men, but the stature of its
innumerable mediocre ones.

3790
I am I plus my circumstances.

3791
All life is the struggle, the effort to be itself.
The difficulties which I meet with in order
to realize my existence are precisely what
awaken and mobilize my activities, my
capacities.

3792
Today violence is the rhetoric of the
period.

GATES Bill 1955-
3793 *(of computer memory - in 1981)*
640K ought to be enough for anybody.

GATEWOOD W. Boyd
3794
Very few people go to the doctor when
they have a cold, they go to the theatre
instead.

GAUGUIN Paul 1848-1903
3795
Art is either plagiarist or revolutionist.

GAVARNI Paul 1801-1866
3796
Les enfants terribles.
The little terrors.

GAY John 1685-1732
3797
Who friendship with a knave hath made,
Is judged a partner in the trade.

3798
We only part to meet again.

3799 *The Beggar's Opera*
How, like a moth, the simple maid
Still plays about the flame!

3800 *The Beggar's Opera*
Our Polly is a sad slut! nor heeds what we
have taught her.
I wonder any man alive will ever rear a
daughter!

3801 *The Beggar's Opera*
Do you think your mother and I should
have lived comfortably so long together, if
ever we had been married?

3802 *The Beggar's Opera*
The comfortable estate of widowhood, is
the only hope that keeps up a wife's
spirits.

3803 *The Beggar's Opera*
If with me you'd fondly stray.
Over the hills and far away.

3804 *The Beggar's Opera*
Fill ev'ry glass, for wine inspires us,
And fires us
With courage, love and joy.
Women and wine should life employ.
Is there ought else on earth desirous?

3805 *The Beggar's Opera*
I must have women. There is nothing
unbends the mind like them.

3806 *The Beggar's Opera*
To cheat a man is nothing; but the woman
must have fine parts indeed who cheats a
woman!

3807 *The Beggar's Opera*
I am ready, my dear Lucy, to give you
satisfaction - if you think there is any in
marriage?

3808 *The Beggar's Opera*
In one respect indeed, our employment
may be reckoned dishonest, because, like
great Statesmen, we encourage those who

betray their friends.

3809 *The Beggar's Opera*
How happy could I be with either,
Were t'other dear charmer away!

3810 *The Captives*
She who has never loved, has never lived.

3811 *Dione*
Behold the victim of Parthenia's pride!
He saw, he sighed, he loved, was scorned
and died.

3812 *Dione*
A woman's friendship ever ends in love.

3813 *'My Own Epitaph'*
Life is a jest; and all things show it.
I thought so once; but now I know it.

3814 *Fables 'The Dog and the Fox'*
I know you lawyers can, with ease,
Twist words and meanings as you please;
That language, by your skill made pliant,
Will bend to favour ev'ry client.

3815 *Fables (introduction)*
Whence is thy learning? Hath thy toil
O'er books consumed the midnight oil?

3816 *Fables 'The Man, the Cat, the Dog and
Fly'*
Studious of elegance and ease,
Myself alone I seek to please.

3817 *Fables 'The Mastiffs'*
Those who in quarrels interpose,
Must often wipe a bloody nose.

3818 *Fables 'The Shepherd's Dog and the Wolf'*
An open foe may prove a curse,
But a pretended friend is worse.

3819 *Fables 'The Squire and his Cur'*
That politician tops his part,
Who readily can lie with art.

3820 *Fables 'The Vulture, the Sparrow,...
Birds'*
Give me, kind heaven, a private station,
A mind serene for contemplation.

3821 *'A Letter to a Lady'*
Praising all alike, is praising none.

3822 *'Polly'*
Whether we can afford it or no, we must
have superfluities.

3823 *'Polly'*
No, sir, tho' I was born and bred in
England, I can dare to be poor, which is
the only thing now-a-days men are
ashamed of.

3824 *'Polly'*
An inconstant woman, tho' she has no
chance to be very happy, can never be very
unhappy.

3825 *'Sweet William's Farewell to Black-Eyed
Susan'*
All in the Downs the fleet was moored,
The streamers waving in the wind,
When black-eyed Susan came aboard.

3826 *'The Toilette'*
A miss for pleasure, and a wife for breed.

GAY Noel 1898-1954
3827 *'Leaning on a Lamp-Post'*
I'm leaning on a lamp-post at the corner of
the street,
In case a certain little lady comes by.

GAYLEN Willard
3828
Shame and guilt are noble emotions
essential in the maintenance of civilized
society, and vital for the development of
some of the most refined and elegant
qualities of human potential - generosity,
service, self-sacrifice, unselfishness and
duty.

GEAYE Henry
3829
Motives and purposes are in the brain and
heart of man. Consequences are in the
world of fact.

GEDDES Sir Auckland
3830
So many come to the sickroom thinking of
themselves as men of science fighting
disease and not as healers with a little
knowledge helping nature to get a sick
man well.

GEDDES Sir Eric 1875-1937
3831
The Germans, if this Government is
returned, are going to pay every penny;
they are going to be squeezed as a lemon is
squeezed - until the pips squeak.

GELMAN Daniel C.
3832
Where secrecy reigns, carelessness and
ignorance delight to hide - skill loves the
light.

GENEEN Harold 1910-
3833
I don't believe in just ordering people to
do things. You have to sort of grab an oar
and row with them.

GEORGE Chief Dan
3834
When the white man came, we had the
land and they had the bibles. Now they
have the land and we have the bibles.

GEORGE Daniel
3835 *The Perpetual Pessimist*
O Freedom, what liberties are taken in thy
name!

GEORGE Henry 1839-1897
3836
The state, it cannot too often be repeated,
does nothing, and can give nothing, which
it does not take from somebody.

3837
Man is the only animal whose desires
increase as they are fed; the only animal
that is never satisfied.

GEORGE I King 1660-1727
3838
I hate all Boets and Bainters.

GEORGE II King 1683-1760
3839
We are come for your good, for all your
goods.

3840 *(of General Wolfe)*
Mad, is he? Then I hope he will *bite* some
of my other generals.

GEORGE III King 1738-1820
3841
Born and educated in this country, I glory
in the name of Briton.

3842 *(to Fanny Burney)*
Was there ever such stuff as great part of
Shakespeare? Only one must not say so!
But what think you? - what? - Is there not
sad stuff? what? - what?

GEORGE IV King 1762-1830
3843 *(on first meeting his wife to be)*
Harris, I am not well; pray get me a glass
of brandy.

GEORGE V King 1865-1936
3844
I venture to allude to the impression which
seemed generally to prevail among their
brethren across the seas, that the Old
Country must wake up if she intends to
maintain her old position of pre-eminence
in her Colonial trade against foreign
competitors.

3845
I have many times asked myself whether
there can be more potent advocates of
peace upon earth through the years to
come than this massed multitude of silent
witnesses to the desolation of war.

3846 *(of his son)*
After I am dead, the boy will ruin himself
in twelve months.

3847
Bugger Bognor.

3848 *(to Anthony Eden)*
I said to your predecessor: 'You know
what they're all saying, no more coals to
Newcastle, no more Hoares to Paris.' The
fellow didn't even laugh.

3849 *(to his private secretary on the morning
he died)*
How's the Empire?

GEORGE VI King 1895-1952
3850
Abroad is bloody.

3851 *(to Queen Mary)*
Personally I feel happier now that we have no allies to be polite to and to pamper.

GEORGE W.L. 1882-1926
3852
The true America is the Middle West, and Columbus discovered nothing at all except another Europe.

GERSHWIN Ira 1896-1983
3853 *Damsel in Distress*
A foggy day in London Town
Had me low and had me down.
I viewed the morning with alarm,
The British Museum had lost its charm.
How long, I wondered, could this thing last?
But the age of miracles hadn't passed,
For, suddenly, I saw you there
And through foggy London town the sun was shining everywhere.

3854 *Damsel in Distress*
Holding hands at midnight
'Neath a starry sky,
Nice work if you can get it,
And you can get it if you try.

3855 *Shall We Dance?*
The way you wear your hat,
The way you sip your tea,
The mem'ry of all that -
No, no! They can't take that away from me!

3856 *Funny Face*
You've made my life so glamorous,
You can't blame me for feeling amorous.

3857 *Girl Crazy*
Embrace me, my sweet embraceable you!
Embrace me, you irreplaceable you!
Just one look at you, my heart grew tipsy in me;
You and you alone bring out the gypsy in me!

3858 *The Goldwyn Follies*
In time the Rockies may crumble,
Gibraltar may tumble,
They're only made of clay,
But our love is here to stay.

GETTY Paul 1892-1976
3859
Going to work for a large company is like getting on a train. Are you going sixty miles an hour or is the train going sixty miles an hour and you're just sitting still?

3860
I have no complex about wealth. I have worked hard for my money, producing things people need. I believe that the able industrial leader who creates wealth and employment is more worthy of historical notice than politicians or soldiers.

GIACOSA Giuseppe and ILLICA Luigi
1847-1906 and 1857-1919
3861 *La Bohème*
Che gelida manina.
Your tiny hand is frozen.

GIBBON Edward 1737-1794
3862
The winds and waves are always on the side of the ablest navigators.

3863
Many a sober Christian would rather admit that a wafer is God than that God is a cruel and capricious tyrant.

3864
I was never less alone than when by myself.

3865 *The Decline and Fall of the Roman Empire*
The various modes of worship, which prevailed in the Roman world, were all considered by the people as equally true; by the philosopher, as equally false; and by the magistrate, as equally useful. And thus toleration produced not only mutual indulgence, but even religious concord.

3866 *The Decline and Fall of the Roman Empire*
The principles of a free constitution are irrecoverably lost, when the legislative power is nominated by the executive.

3867 *The Decline and Fall of the Roman Empire*
History ... is, indeed, little more than the register of the crimes, follies, and misfortunes of mankind.

3868 *The Decline and Fall of the Roman Empire*
In every age and country, the wiser, or at least the stronger, of the two sexes, has usurped the powers of the state, and confined the other to the cares and pleasures of domestic life.

3869 *The Decline and Fall of the Roman Empire*
Corruption, the most infallible symptom of constitutional liberty.

3870 *The Decline and Fall of the Roman Empire*
In every deed of mischief he had a heart to resolve, a head to contrive, and a hand to execute.

3871 *The Decline and Fall of the Roman Empire*
Our sympathy is cold to the relation of distant misery.

3872 *The Decline and Fall of the Roman Empire*
Persuasion is the resource of the feeble; and the feeble can seldom persuade.

3873 *The Decline and Fall of the Roman Empire*
All that is human must retrograde if it does not advance.

3874 *Memoirs of My Life*
The satirist may laugh, the philosopher may preach, but Reason herself will respect the prejudices and habits which have been consecrated by the experience of mankind.

3875 *Memoirs of My Life*
To the University of Oxford I acknowledge no obligation; and she will as cheerfully renounce me for a son, as I am willing to disclaim her for a mother. I spent fourteen months at Magdalen College: they proved the fourteen months the most idle and unprofitable of my whole life.

3876 *Memoirs of My Life*
Dr - well remembered that he had a salary to receive, and only forgot that he had a duty to perform.

3877 *Memoirs of My Life*
It was here that I suspended my religious inquiries (aged 17).

3878 *Memoirs of My Life*
I saw and loved.

3879 *Memoirs of My Life*
I sighed as a lover, I obeyed as a son.

3880 *Memoirs of My Life*
Crowds without company, and dissipation without pleasure.

3881 *Memoirs of My Life*
My English text is chaste, and all licentious passages are left in the obscurity of a learned language.

3882 *Memoirs of My Life*
The abbreviation of time, and the failure of hope, will always tinge with a browner shade the evening of life.

3883 *Memoirs of My Life (of his own army service)*
The captain of the Hampshire grenadiers ... has not been useless to the historian of the Roman empire.

3884 *Memoirs of My Life (of the dons at Oxford)*
Their dull and deep potations excused the brisk intemperance of youth.

GIBBON John Murray
3885
I always suspect an artist who is successful before he is dead.

GIBBONS Orlando 1583-1625
3886
The silver swan, who, living had no note, When death approached unlocked her silent throat.

GIBBONS Stella 1902-1989
3887 *Cold Comfort Farm*
Every year, in the fulness o' summer, when the sukebind hangs heavy from the wains ... 'tes the same. And when the spring comes her hour is upon her again. 'Tes the hand of Nature and we women cannot escape it.

3888 *Cold Comfort Farm*
Something nasty in the woodshed.

3889 *Cold Comfort Farm*
By god, D.H. Lawrence was right when he
had said there must be a dumb, dark, dull,
bitter belly-tension between a man and a
woman, and how else could this be
achieved save in the long monotony of
marriage?

GIBLIN II Frank J
3890
Be yourself. Who else is better qualified?

GIBRAN Kahlil 1883-1931
3891
The significance of a man is not what he
attains but rather in what he longs to
attain.

3892
No man can reveal to you aught but that
which already lies half asleep in the
dawning of your knowledge.

3893 *The New Frontier*
Are you a politician who says to himself: 'I
will use my country for my own benefit'?
... Or are you a devoted patriot, who
whispers in the ear of his inner self: 'I love
to serve my country as a faithful servant.'?

3894 *The Prophet 'On Children'*
Your children are not your children.
They are the sons and daughters of Life's
longing for itself.
They came through you but not from you
And though they are with you yet they
belong not to you.
You may give them your love but not your
thoughts,
For they have their own thoughts.
You may house their bodies but not their
souls,
For their souls dwell in the house of
tomorrow, which you cannot visit, not
even in your dreams.
You may strive to be like them, but seek
not to make them like you,
For life goes not backward nor tarries with
yesterday.
You are the bows from which your
children as living arrows are sent forth.

3895 *The Prophet 'On Marriage'*
But let there be spaces in your
togetherness.

And let the winds of the heavens dance
between you.

3896 *The Prophet 'On Work'*
Work is love made visible. And if you
cannot work with love but only with
distaste, it is better that you should leave
your work and sit at the gate of the temple
and take alms of those who work with joy.

3897 *Sand and Foam*
An exaggeration is a truth that has lost its
temper.

GIBSON Wilfrid 1878-1962
3898 *All Being Well*
I read your letter through and through,
And dreamt of all we'd say and do,
Till in my heart the thought of you
Rang like a bell.

3899 *'Lament'*
But we, how shall we turn to little things
And listen to the birds and winds and
streams
Made holy by their dreams,
Nor feel the heart-break in the heart of
things?

GIDE André 1869-1951
3900
A work of art is an exaggeration.

3901
One doesn't discover new lands without
consenting to lose sight of the shore for a
very long time.

3902
The world will be saved by one or two
people.

3903
Our judgements about things vary
according to the time left us to live - that
we think is left us to live.

3904
If one could recover the uncompromising
spirit of one's youth, one's greatest
indignation would be for what one has
become.

3905 *Journal*
The great secret of Stendhal, his great
shrewdness, consisted in writing *at once* ...

thought charged with emotion.

3906 *Les Caves du Vatican*
I believe ... that profit is not always what motivates man; that there are disinterested actions ... By *disinterested* I mean: gratuitous. And that evil acts, what people call evil, can be as gratuitous as good acts.

3907 *Les Faux Monnayeurs*
The whole effect of Christianity was to transfer the drama onto the moral plane.

GIESE W.
3908
Contemporary literature can be classified under three headings: the neurotic, the erotic and the tommy-rotic.

GIFFORD Frank
3909
Pro football is like nuclear warfare. There are no winners, only survivors.

GILBERT Sir Humphrey c.1537-1583
3910 *Third and Last Volume of the Voyages ...*
We are as near to heaven by sea as by land!

GILBERT W.S. 1836-1911
3911
See how the Fates their gifts allot.
For A is happy - B is not.
Yet B is worthy, I dare say,
Of more prosperity than A.

3912
Darwinian Man, though well-behaved,
At best is only a monkey shaved!

3913
As innocent as a new-laid egg.

3914
And whether you're an honest man, or whether you're a thief,
Depends on whose solicitor has given me my brief.

3915
You've no idea what a poor opinion I have of myself - and how little I deserve it.

3916 *The Gondoliers*
That celebrated,
Cultivated,
Underrated
Nobleman,

The Duke of Plaza Toro!

3917 *The Gondoliers*
Of that there is no manner of doubt -
No probable, possible shadow of doubt -
No possible doubt whatever.

3918 *The Gondoliers*
All shall equal be,
The Earl, the Marquis, and the Dook,
The Groom, the Butler, and the Cook,
The Aristocrat who banks with Coutts,
The Aristocrat who cleans the boots.

3919 *The Gondoliers*
But the privilege and pleasure
That we treasure beyond measure
Is to run on little errands for the Ministers of State.

3920 *The Gondoliers*
Take a pair of sparkling eyes,
Hidden, ever and anon,
In a merciful eclipse.

3921 *The Gondoliers*
Ambassadors cropped up like hay,
Prime Ministers and such as they
Grew like asparagus in May,
And dukes were three a penny.

3922 *The Gondoliers*
When every one is somebodee,
Then no one's anybody.

3923 *HMS Pinafore*
I'm called Little Buttercup - dear Little Buttercup,
Though I could never tell why.

3924 *HMS Pinafore*
What, never?
No, never!
What, *never*?
Hardly ever!

3925 *HMS Pinafore*
Though 'Bother it' I may
Occasionally say,
I never use a big, big D -

3926 *HMS Pinafore*
And so do his sisters, and his cousins and his aunts!
His sisters and his cousins,
Whom he reckons up by dozens,

And his aunts!

3927 *HMS Pinafore*
When I was a lad I served a term
As office boy to an Attorney's firm.
I cleaned the windows and I swept the floor,
And I polished up the handle of the big front door.
I polished up that handle so carefullee
That now I am the Ruler of the Queen's Navee!

3928 *HMS Pinafore*
I always voted at my party's call,
And I never thought of thinking for myself at all.

3929 *HMS Pinafore*
Stick close to your desks and never go to sea,
And you all may be Rulers of the Queen's Navee!

3930 *HMS Pinafore*
Things are seldom what they seem,
Skim milk masquerades as cream.

3931 *HMS Pinafore*
He is an Englishman!
For he himself has said it,
And it's greatly to his credit,
That he is an Englishman!

3932 *HMS Pinafore*
For he might have been a Roosian,
A French, or Turk, or Proosian,
Or perhaps Ital-ian!
But in spite of all temptations
To belong to other nations,
He remains an Englishman!

3933 *HMS Pinafore*
The other, upper crust,
A regular patrician.

3934 *Iolanthe*
Bow, bow, ye lower middle classes!
Bow, bow, ye tradesmen, bow, ye masses.

3935 *Iolanthe*
The Law is the true embodiment
Of everything that's excellent.
It has no kind of fault or flaw,
And I, my Lords, embody the Law.

3936 *Iolanthe*
Spurn not the nobly born
With love affected,
Nor treat with virtuous scorn
The well-connected.

3937 *Iolanthe*
Hearts just as pure and fair
May beat in Belgrave Square
As in the lowly air
Of Seven Dials.

3938 *Iolanthe*
I often think it's comical
How Nature always does contrive
That every boy and every gal,
That's born into the world alive,
Is either a little Liberal,
Or else a little Conservative!

3939 *Iolanthe*
When in that House MPs divide,
If they've a brain and cerebellum too,
They have to leave that brain outside,
And vote just as their leaders tell 'em to.

3940 *Iolanthe*
The prospect of a lot
Of dull MPs in close proximity,
All thinking for themselves is what
No man can face with equanimity.

3941 *Iolanthe*
The House of Peers, throughout the war,
Did nothing in particular,
And did it very well.

3942 *Iolanthe*
When you're lying awake with a dismal headache, and repose is taboo'd by anxiety,
I conceive you may use any language you choose to indulge in, without impropriety.

3943 *Iolanthe*
For you dream you are crossing the Channel, and tossing about in a steamer from Harwich -
Which is something between a large bathing machine and a very small second class carriage.

3944 *Iolanthe*
And bound on that journey you find your attorney (who started that morning from Devon);
He's a bit undersized, and you don't feel

surprised when he tells you he's only eleven.

3945 *Iolanthe*
In your shirt and your socks (the black silk with gold clocks), crossing Salisbury Plain on a bicycle.

3946 *Iolanthe*
The shares are a penny, and ever so many are taken by Rothschild and Baring,
And just as a few are allotted to you, you awake with a shudder despairing.

3947 *The Mikado*
A wandering minstrel I -
A thing of shreds and patches,
Of ballads, songs and snatches,
And dreamy lullaby!

3948 *The Mikado*
I can trace my ancestry back to a protoplasmal primordial atomic globule. Consequently, my family pride is something in-conceivable. I can't help it. I was born sneering.

3949 *The Mikado*
As some day it may happen that a victim must be found,
I've got a little list - I've got a little list
Of society offenders who might well be under ground
And who never would be missed - who never would be missed!

3950 *The Mikado*
The idiot who praises, with enthusiastic tone,
All centuries but this, and every country but his own.

3951 *The Mikado*
Three little maids from school are we,
Pert as a schoolgirl well can be,
Filled to the brim with girlish glee.

3952 *The Mikado*
Life is a joke that's just begun.

3953 *The Mikado*
Three little maids who, all unwary,

Come from a ladies' seminary.

3954 *The Mikado*
Modified rapture!

3955 *The Mikado*
Awaiting the sensation of a short, sharp shock,
From a cheap and chippy chopper on a big black block.

3956 *The Mikado*
Here's a how-de-doo!

3957 *The Mikado*
Here's a state of things!

3958 *The Mikado*
Matrimonial devotion
Doesn't seem to suit her notion.

3959 *The Mikado*
My object all sublime
I shall achieve in time -
To let the punishment fit the crime -
The punishment fit the crime.

3960 *The Mikado*
The music-hall singer attends a series
Of masses and fugues and 'ops'
By Bach, interwoven
With Spohr and Beethoven,
At classical Monday Pops.

3961 *The Mikado*
The billiard sharp whom any one catches,
His doom's extremely hard -
He's made to dwell -
In a dungeon cell
On a spot that's always barred.
And there he plays extravagant matches
In fitless finger-stalls
On a cloth untrue
With a twisted cue
And elliptical billiard balls.

3962 *The Mikado*
I have a left shoulder-blade that is a miracle of loveliness. People come miles to see it. My right elbow has a fascination that few can resist.

3963 *The Mikado*
Something lingering, with boiling oil in it, I fancy.

3964 *The Mikado*
Merely corroborative detail, intended to give artistic verisimiltude to an otherwise bald and unconvincing narrative.

3965 *The Mikado*
The flowers that bloom in the spring,
Tra la,
Have nothing to do with the case.

3966 *The Mikado*
I've got to take under my wing,
Tra la,
A most unattractive old thing,
Tra la,
With a caricature of a face.

3967 *The Mikado*
'Is it weakness of intellect, birdie?' I cried,
'Or a rather tough worm in your little
inside?'
With a shake of his poor little head he
replied,
'Oh, Willow, titwillow, titwillow!'

3968 *The Mikado*
He sobbed and he sighed, and a gurgle he
gave,
Then he plunged himself into the billowy
wave,
And an echo arose from the suicide's grave
'Oh willow, titwillow, titwillow!'

3969 *The Mikado*
There's a fascination frantic
In a ruin that's romantic;
Do you think you are sufficiently decayed?

3970 *Patience*
If you're anxious for to shine in the high
aesthetic line as a man of culture rare.

3971 *Patience*
You must lie upon the daisies and
discourse in novel phrases of your
complicated state of mind,
The meaning doesn't matter if it's only idle
chatter of a transcendental kind.

3972 *Patience*
Then a sentimental passion of a vegetable
fashion must excite your languid spleen,
An attachment à la Plato for a bashful
young potato, or a not too French French
bean!
Though the Philistines may jostle, you will
rank as an apostle in the high aesthetic
band,
If you walk down Piccadilly with a poppy
or a lily in your medieval hand.

3973 *Patience*
While this magnetic,
Peripatetic
Lover, he lived to learn,
By no endeavour
Can magnet ever
Attract a Silver Churn!

3974 *Patience*
'High diddle diddle'
Will rank as an idyll,
If I pronounce it chaste!

3975 *Patience*
Francesca di Rimini, miminy, piminy,
Je-ne-sais-quoi young man!

3976 *Patience*
A greenery-yallery, Grosvenor Gallery,
Foot-in-the-grave young man!

3977 *The Pirates of Penzance*
It is, it is a glorious thing
To be a Pirate King.

3978 *The Pirates of Penzance*
The question is, had he not been
A thing of beauty,
Would she be swayed by quite as keen
A sense of duty?

3979 *The Pirates of Penzance*
I'm very good at integral and differential
calculus,
I know the scientific names of beings
animalculous;
In short, in matters vegetable, animal, and
mineral,
I am the very model of a modern Major-
General.

3980 *The Pirates of Penzance*
About binomial theorem I'm teeming with
a lot of news,
With many cheerful facts about the square
on the hypotenuse.

3981 *The Pirates of Penzance*
When constabulary duty's to be done,
A policeman's lot is not a happy one.

3982 *The Pirates of Penzance*
They are no members of the common
throng;
They are all noblemen who have gone
wrong!

3983 *The Pirates of Penzance*
No Englishman unmoved that statement hears,
Because, with all our faults, we love our House of Peers.

3984 *Princess Ida*
To everybody's prejudice I know a thing or two;
I can tell a woman's age in half a minute - and I do!

3985 *Princess Ida*
Man is Nature's sole mistake!

3986 *Ruddigore*
You must stir it and stump it,
And blow your own trumpet,
Or trust me, you haven't a chance.

3987 *Ruddigore*
He combines the manners of a Marquis with the morals of a Methodist.

3988 *Ruddigore*
If a man can't forge his own will, whose will can he forge?

3989 *Ruddigore*
Some word that teems with hidden meaning - like Basingstoke.

3990 *Ruddigore*
This particularly rapid, unintelligible patter
Isn't generally heard, and if it is it doesn't matter.

3991 *The Sorcerer*
I was a pale young curate then.

3992 *Trial by Jury*
So I fell in love with a rich attorney's Elderly ugly daughter.

3993 *Trial by Jury*
She may very well pass for forty-three
In the dusk with a light behind her!

3994 *The Yeoman of the Guard*
It's a song of a merryman, moping mum,
Whose soul was sad, and whose glance was glum,
Who sipped no sup, and who craved no crumb,
As he sighed for the love of a ladye.

3995 *The Yeoman of the Guard*
'Tis ever thus with simple folk - an accepted wit has but to say 'Pass the mustard', and they roar their ribs out!

GILDER George
3996
Poverty is less a matter of income than of prospects. While the incomes of the poor have steadily risen through Great Society largesse, their prospects have plummeted as families have broken into dependent fragments.

GILL Eric 1882-1940
3997 *Art-nonsense and Other Essays*
That state is a state of slavery in which a man does what he likes to do in his spare time and in his working time that which is required of him.

GILMAN Charlotte Perkins 1860-1935
3998
The people people work with best are often very queer.

GINSBERG Allen 1926-
3999 *'Graffiti'*
What if someone gave a war & Nobody came?
Life would ring the bells of Ecstasy and Forever be Itself again.

4000 *Howl*
I saw the best minds of my generation destroyed by madness, starving hysterical naked,
dragging themselves through the negro streets at dawn looking for an angry fix,
angelheaded hipsters burning for the ancient heavenly connection to the starry dynamo in the machinery of the night.

4001 *'A Supermarket in California'*
What peaches and what penumbras! Whole families shopping at night! Aisles full of husbands! Wives in the avocados, babies in the tomatoes! - and you, Garcia Lorca what were you doing down by the watermelons?

GINSBERG Louis
4002
Life is ever
Since man was born,

Licking honey
From a thorn.

GIORDANO Bruno
4003
With luck on your side you can do without brains.

GIRAUDOUX Jean 1882-1944
4004 *La Guerre de Troie n'aura pas lieu*
As soon as war is declared it will be impossible to hold the poets back. Rhyme is still the most effective drum.

4005 *La Guerre de Troie n'aura pas lieu*
All of us here know there's no better way of exercising the imagination than the study of law. No poet ever interpreted nature as freely as a lawyer interprets the truth.

GISSING George 1857-1903
4006
This is one of the bitter curses of poverty: it leaves no right to be generous.

GLADSTONE W.E. 1809-1898
4007
This is the negation of God erected into a system of Government.

4008
Finance is, as it were, the stomach of the country, from which all the other organs take their tone.

4009
You cannot fight against the future. Time is on our side.

4010
My mission is to pacify Ireland.

4011
Swimming for his life, a man does not see much of the country through which the river winds.

4012
We have been borne down in a torrent of gin and beer.

4013
Let the Turks now carry away their abuses in the only possible manner, namely by carrying off themselves ... one and all, bag and baggage, shall I hope clear out from the province they have desolated and profaned.

4014
Our first site in Egypt, be it by larceny or be it by emption, will be the almost certain egg of a North African Empire, that will grow and grow until another Victoria and another Albert, titles of the Lake-sources of the White Nile, come within our borders; and till we finally join hands across the Equator with Natal and Cape Town, to say nothing of the Transvaal and the Orange River on the south, or of Abyssinia or Zanzibar to be swallowed by way of *viaticum* on our journey.

4015
The resources of civilization against its enemies are not yet exhausted.

4016
Ideal perfection is not the true basis of English legislation. We look at the attainable; we look at the practical; and we have too much English sense to be drawn away by those sanguine delineations of what might possibly be attained in Utopia, from a path which promises to enable us to effect great good for the people of England.

4017
I would tell them of my own intention to keep my counsel ... and I will venture to recommend them, as an old parliamentary hand, to do the same.

4018
This, if I understand it, is one of those golden moments of our history, one of those opportunities which may come and may go, but which rarely returns.

4019
I will venture to say, that upon the one great class of subjects, the largest and the most weighty of them all, where leading and determining considerations that ought to lead to a conclusion are truth, justice, and humanity - upon these, gentlemen, all the world over, I will back the masses against the classes.

4020
We are bound to lose Ireland in consequence of years of cruelty, stupidity and misgovernment and I would rather lose her as a friend than as a foe.

4021 *(of the Irish Land League)*
It is perfectly true that these gentlemen wish to march through rapine to disintegration and dismemberment of the Empire, and, I am sorry to say, even to the placing of different parts of the Empire in direct hostility one with the other.

4022 *(on public speaking)*
I absorb the vapour and return it as a flood.

4023 *(on relations with Queen Victoria)*
What that Sicilian mule was to me, I have been to the Queen.

GLASS Montague
4024
She was an aging singer who had to take every note above 'A' with her eyebrows.

GLEASON Jackie
4025
Thin people are beautiful but fat people are adorable.

GLENN Jr. John H. 1921-
4026
People are afraid of the future, of the unknown. If a man faces up to it, and takes the dare of the future, he can have some control over his destiny. That's an exciting idea to me, better than waiting with everybody else to see what's going to happen.

GLINKA Mikhail 1804-1857
4027
A nation creates music - the composer only arranges it.

GODARD Jean-Luc 1930-
4028
'Movies should have a beginning, a middle and an end,' harrumphed French film maker Georges Franju ... 'Certainly,' replied Jean-Luc Godard. 'But not necessarily in that order.'

4029 *Le Petit Soldat*
Photography is truth. The cinema is truth 24 times per second.

GODLEY A.D. 1856-1925
4030
What is this that roareth thus?
Can it be a Motor Bus?
Yes, the smell and hideous hum
Indicat Motorem Bum!...
How shall wretches live like us
Cincti Bis Motoribus?
Domine, defende nos
Contra hos Motores Bos!

4031 *'The Megalopsychiad'*
Great and good is the typical Don, and of evil and wrong the foe,
Good, and great, I'm a Don myself, and therefore I ought to know.

GODOLPHIN Sidney 1610-1643
4032 *'Song'*
Or love me less, or love me more
And play not with my liberty;
Either take all, or all restore,
Bind me at least, or set me free.

GODWIN William 1756-1836
4033 *An Enquiry...*
Perfectibility is one of the most unequivocal characteristics of the human species.

4034 *An Enquiry...*
Love of our country is another of those specious illusions, which have been invented by impostors in order to render the multitude the blind instruments of their crooked designs.

4035 *An Enquiry... (of the penal laws)*
What ... can be more shameless than for society to make an example of those whom she has goaded to the breach or order, instead of amending her own institutions which, by straining order into tyranny, produce the mischief?

4036 *An Enquiry... (of war)*
It is a most mistaken way of teaching men to feel they are brothers, by imbuing their mind with perpetual hatred.

GOEBBELS Joseph 1897-1945
4037
We can manage without butter but not, for
example, without guns. If we are attacked
we can only defend ourselves with guns
not with butter.

GOERING Hermann 1893-1946
4038
We have no butter ... but I ask you - would
you rather have butter or guns? ...
preparedness makes us powerful. Butter
merely makes us fat.

4039 *(instructions to Heydrich)*
I herewith commission you to carry out all
preparations with regard to ... a *total
solution* of the Jewish question in those
territories of Europe which are under
German influence.

GOETHE Johann von 1749-1832
4040
For a man to achieve all that is demanded
of him he must regard himself as greater
than he is.

4041
So, lively brisk old fellow, don't let age get
you down. White hairs or not, you can
still be a lover.

4042
I call architecture 'petrified music'.

4043
Art is called art because it is not nature.

4044
Ordinary people know little of the time
and effort it takes to learn to read. I have
been eighty years at it, and have not
reached my goal.

4045
A man can stand almost anything except a
succession of ordinary days.

4046
Talents are best nurtured in solitude:
character is best formed in the stormy
billows of the world.

4047
Character, in great and little things, means
carrying through what you feel able to do.

4048
If children grew up according to early
indications, we should have nothing but
geniuses.

4049
Unlike grownups, children have little need
to deceive themselves.

4050
We are never deceived; we deceive
ourselves.

4051
From desire I plunge to its fulfilment,
where I long once more for desire.

4052
It is better to be deceived by one's friends
than to deceive them.

4053
We can always redeem the man who
aspires and strives.

4054
It is said that no man is a hero to his valet.
That is because a hero can be recognized
only by a hero.

4055
We accept every person in the world as
that for which he gives himself out only he
must give himself out for something. We
can put up with the unpleasant more
easily than we can endure the insignificant.

4056
If you treat men the way they are you
never improve them. If you treat them the
way you want them to be, you do.

4057
There is nothing more frightening than
ignorance in action.

4058
When an idea is wanting, a word can
always be found to take its place.

4059
And here, poor fool, with all my lore,
I stand no wiser than before.

4060
He alone deserves liberty and life who
daily must win them anew.

4061
If a man thinks about his physical or moral state, he usually discovers that he is ill.

4062
The right man is the one that seizes the moment.

4063
A clever man commits no minor blunders.

4064
Mozart is the human incarnation of the divine force of creation.

4065
Every day look at a beautiful picture, read a beautiful poem, listen to some beautiful music, and if possible, say some reasonable thing.

4066
There is not a single outward mark of courtesy that does not have a deep moral basis.

4067
Daring ideas are like chessmen moved forward. They may be beaten, but they may start a winning game.

4068
There is no crime of which I do not deem myself capable.

4069
Let him who believes in immortality enjoy his happiness in silence without giving himself airs about it.

4070
Who does not know another language, does not know his own.

4071
Everyone believes in his youth that the world really began with him, and that all merely exists for his sake.

4072
For the rest of it, the last and greatest art is to limit and isolate oneself.

4073
I do not know myself, and God forbid that I should.

4074
Mastery often passes for egotism.

4075 *Der Gross-Cophta*
You must be master and win, or serve and lose, grieve or triumph, be the anvil or the hammer.

4076 *(attributed dying words)*
Mehr Licht!
More light!

4077 *Faust*
Man will err while yet he strives.

4078 *Faust*
Two souls dwell, alas! in my breast.

4079 *Faust*
I am the spirit that always denies.

4080 *Faust*
Deny yourself! You must deny yourself! That is the song that never ends.

4081 *Faust*
All theory, dear friend, is grey, but the golden tree of actual life springs ever green.

4082 *Faust*
My peace is gone,
My heart is heavy.

4083 *Faust*
The deed is all, the glory nothing.

4084 *Faust*
Eternal Woman draws us upward.

4085 *Italienische Reise*
Since it is a joy to have the benefit of what is good, it is a greater one to experience what is better, and in art the best is good enough.

4086 *Maximen und Reflexionen*
Superstition is the poetry of life.

4087 *Meher Baba*
Friendships are precious
Hugging friendships are very precious
On-going hugging friendships are the most precious of all.

4088 *Torquato Tasso*
Talent develops in quiet places, character in the full current of human life.

4089 *Wilhelm Meisters Lehrjahre*
Who never ate his bread in sorrow,
Who never spent the darksome hours
Weeping and watching for the morrow
He knows ye not, ye heavenly powers.

4090 *Wilhelm Meisters Lehrjahre*
Know you the land where the lemon-trees
bloom? In the dark foliage the gold
oranges glow; a soft wind hovers from the
sky, the myrtle is still and the laurel stands
tall - do you know it well? There, there, I
would go, O my beloved, with thee!

GOFFIN Harold
4091
Behind every successful man you'll find a
woman who has nothing to wear.

GOGOL Nikolai 1809-1852
4092
Don't blame the mirror if your face is
faulty.

4093 *Dead Souls*
As you pass from the tender years of
youth into harsh and embittered manhood,
make sure you take with you on your
journey all the human emotions! Don't
leave them on the road, for you will not
pick them up afterwards!

4094 *Dead Souls*
I am destined by the mysterious powers to
walk hand in hand with my strange
heroes, viewing life in all its immensity as
it rushes past me, viewing it through
laughter seen by the world and tears
unseen and unknown by it.

4095 *Dead Souls*
[Are not] you too, Russia, speeding along
like a spirited *troika* that nothing can
overtake? ... Everything on earth is flying
past, and looking askance, other nations
and states draw aside and make way.

GOLAS Thaddeus
4096
When you first learn to love hell, you will
be in heaven.

GOLDBERG Justice Arthur 1908-1990
4097
I am surprised nothing has been made of
the fact that astronaut Neil Armstrong

carried no sidearms when he landed on
the moon.

4098
If Columbus had had an advisory
committee he would probably still be at
the dock.

GOLDBERG Isaac 1887-1938
4099 *The Reflex*
Diplomacy is to do and say
The nastiest thing in the nicest way.

GOLDEN Harry 1896-1976
4100
A tablecloth restaurant is still one of the
great rewards of civilization.

GOLDMAN Albert
4101
The Jews have always been students, and
their greatest study is themselves.

GOLDMAN Emma 1869-1940
4102 *Anarchism and Other Essays*
Anarchism, then, really, stands for the
liberation of the human mind from the
dominion of religion; the liberation of the
human body from the dominion of
property; liberation from the shackles and
restraints of government.

GOLDSMITH Sir James 1933-
4103
Tolerance is a tremendous virtue, but the
immediate neighbours of tolerance are
apathy and weakness.

GOLDSMITH Oliver 1730-1774
4104
Conscience is a coward, and those faults it
has not strength enough to prevent, it
seldom has justice enough to accuse.

4105
Philosophy is a good horse in the stable,
but an errant jade on a journey.

4106
A modest woman, dressed out in all her
finery, is the most tremendous object of the
whole creation.

4107
There is no arguing with Johnson; for
when his pistol misses fire, he knocks you

down with the butt end of it.

4108
As I take my shoes from the shoemaker, and my coat from the tailor, so I take my religion from the priest.

4109 *The Bee no. 3*
The true use of speech is not so much to express our wants as to conceal them.

4110 *The Deserted Village*
Sweet Auburn, loveliest village of the plain,
Where health and plenty cheered the labouring swain.

4111 *The Deserted Village*
Ill fares the land, to hast'ning ills a prey,
Where wealth accumulates, and men decay;
Princes and lords may flourish, or may fade;
A breath can make them, as a breath has made;
But a bold peasantry, their country's pride,
When once destroyed, can never be supplied.

4112 *The Deserted Village*
How happy he who crowns in shades like these,
A youth of labour with an age of ease.

4113 *The Deserted Village*
The watchdog's voice that bayed the whisp'ring wind,
And the loud laugh that spoke the vacant mind.

4114 *The Deserted Village*
A man he was to all the country dear,
And passing rich with forty pounds a year;
Remote from towns he ran his godly race,
Nor e'er had changed nor wished to change his place.

4115 *The Deserted Village*
He chid their wand'rings, but relieved their pain.

4116 *The Deserted Village*
Truth from his lips prevailed with double sway,
And fools, who came to scoff, remained to pray.

4117 *The Deserted Village*
A man severe he was, and stern to view;
I knew him well, and every truant knew;
Well had the boding tremblers learned to trace
The day's disasters in his morning face;
Full well they laughed with counterfeited glee,
At all his jokes, for many a joke had he.

4118 *The Deserted Village*
The village all declared how much he knew;
'Twas certain he could write and cypher too.

4119 *The Deserted Village*
In arguing too, the parson owned his skill,
For e'en though vanquished, he could argue still;
While words of learned length, and thund'ring sound
Amazed the gazing rustics ranged around,
And still they gazed, and still the wonder grew,
That one small head could carry all he knew.

4120 *The Deserted Village*
The whitewashed wall, the nicely sanded floor,
The varnished clock that clicked behind the door;
The chest contrived a double debt to pay,
A bed at night, a chest of drawers by day.

4121 *The Deserted Village*
In all the silent manliness of grief.

4122 *The Deserted Village*
Thou source of all my bliss, and all my woe,
That found'st me poor at first, and keep'st me so.

4123 *'Edwin and Angelina, or the Hermit'*
Man wants but little here below,
Nor wants that little long.

4124 *'Elegy on the Death of a Mad Dog'*
The naked every day he clad,
When he put on his clothes.

4125 *'Elegy on the Death of a Mad Dog'*
The dog, to gain some private ends,
Went mad and bit the man.

4126 *'Elegy on the Death of a Mad Dog'*
The man recovered of the bite,
The dog it was that died.

4127 *'Elegy on Mrs. Mary Blaize'*
The doctor found, when she was dead,
Her last disorder mortal.

4128 *The Good-Natured Man*
This same philosophy is a good horse in
the stable, but an arrant jade on a journey.

4129 *The Good-Natured Man*
We must touch his weaknesses with a
delicate hand. There are some faults so
nearly allied to excellence, that we can
scarce weed out the fault without
eradicating the virtue.

4130 *The Good-Natured Man*
All his faults are such that one loves him
still the better for them.

4131 *The Good-Natured Man*
Friendship is a disinterested commerce
between equals; love, an abject intercourse
between tyrants and slaves.

4132 *The Good-Natured Man*
Silence is become his mother tongue.

4133 *The Good-Natured Man*
You, that are going to be married, think
things can never be done too fast; but we,
that are old, and know what we are about,
must elope methodically, madam.

4134 *'Logicians Refuted'*
Brutes never meet in bloody fray,
Nor cut each other's throats, for pay.

4135 *Retaliation*
Our Garrick's a salad; for in him we see
Oil, vinegar, sugar, and saltness agree.

4136 *Retaliation*
Here lies David Garrick, describe me, who
can,
An abridgement of all that was pleasant in
man.

4137 *Retaliation (of Edmund Burke)*
Who, too deep for his hearers, still went on
refining,
And thought of convincing, while they
thought of dining;
Though equal to all things, for all things

unfit,
Too nice for a statesman, too proud for a
wit.

4138 *Retaliation (of Garrick)*
On the stage he was natural, simple,
affecting;
'Twas only that when he was off he was
acting.

4139 *Retaliation (of Reynolds)*
When they talked of their Raphaels,
Correggios, and stuff,
He shifted his trumpet, and only took
snuff.

4140 *She Stoops to Conquer*
Is it one of my well-looking days, child?
Am I in face to-day?

4141 *She Stoops to Conquer*
The very pink of perfection.

4142 *She Stoops to Conquer*
I'll be with you in the squeezing of a
lemon.

4143 *She Stoops to Conquer*
It's a damned long, dark, boggy, dirty,
dangerous way.

4144 *She Stoops to Conquer*
This is Liberty-Hall, gentlemen.

4145 *She Stoops to Conquer*
The first blow is half the battle.

4146 *She Stoops to Conquer*
Was there ever such a cross-grained brute?

4147 *She Stoops to Conquer 'Song'*
Let schoolmasters puzzle their brain,
With grammar, and nonsense, and
learning,
Good liquor, I stoutly maintain,
Gives genius a better discerning.

4148 *The Traveller*
Where'er I roam, whatever realms to see,
My heart untravelled fondly turns to thee;
Still to my brother turns with ceaseless
pain,
And drags at each remove a lengthening
chain.

4149 *The Traveller*
Such is the patriot's boast, where'er we roam,
His first, best country ever is, at home.

4150 *The Traveller*
Pride in their port, defiance in their eye,
I see the lords of human kind pass by.

4151 *The Traveller*
Laws grind the poor, and rich men rule the law.

4152 *The Traveller*
How small, of all that human hearts endure,
That part which laws or kings can cause or cure!

4153 *The Vicar of Wakefield*
I was ever of opinion, that the honest man who married and brought up a large family, did more service than he who continued single and only talked of population.

4154 *The Vicar of Wakefield*
I ... chose my wife, as she did her wedding gown, not for a fine glossy surface, but such qualities as would wear well.

4155 *The Vicar of Wakefield*
All our adventures were by the fire-side, and all our migrations from the blue bed to the brown.

4156 *The Vicar of Wakefield*
The virtue which requires to be ever guarded is scarce worth the sentinel.

4157 *The Vicar of Wakefield*
It seemed to me pretty plain, that they had more of love than matrimony in them.

4158 *The Vicar of Wakefield*
When lovely woman stoops to folly
And finds too late that men betray,
What charm can soothe her melancholy,
What art can wash her guilt away?

GOLDWATER Barry 1909-
4159
A government that is big enough to give you all you want is big enough to take it all away.

4160
We shall return to proven ways - not because they are old, but because they are true.

4161 *(accepting the presidential nomination)*
I would remind you that extremism in the defence of liberty is no vice! And let me remind you also that moderation in the pursuit of justice is no virtue!

GOLDWYN Sam 1882-1974
4162
I read part of it all the way through.

4163
Chaplin is no businessman - all he knows is that he can't take anything less.

4164
From success you get a lot of things, but not that great inside thing that love brings you.

4165
If Roosevelt were alive he'd turn in his grave.

4166
I'm exhausted from not talking.

4167
Why should people pay good money to go out and see bad films when they can stay at home and see bad television for nothing?

4168
A verbal contract isn't worth the paper it is written on.

4169
That's the way with these directors, they're always biting the hand that lays the golden egg.

4170
Pictures are for entertainment, messages should be delivered by Western Union.

4171
Any man who goes to a psychiatrist should have his head examined.

4172 *(on resigning from Motion Picture Producers)*
Gentlemen, include me out.

GOMBRICH Ernst 1909-
4173
There is no such thing as art. There are only artists.

GOMPERS Samuel 1850-1924
4174
The worst crime against working people is a company which fails to operate at a profit.

GONCHAROV Ivan 1812-1891
4175
It is a trick among the dishonest to offer sacrifices that are not needed, or not possible, to avoid making those that are required.

4176 *Obolomov*
All his anxiety resolved itself into a sigh and dissolved into apathy and drowsiness.

4177 *Obolomov*
The trouble is that no devastating or redeeming fires have ever burnt in my life ... My life began by flickering out.

4178 *Obolomov*
You lost your ability for doing things in childhood, in Oblomovka ... It all began with your inability to put on your socks and ended by your inability to live.

GONDOLA Paul
4179
Every minute starts an hour.

GOODMAN Al
4180
The perfect computer has been developed. You just feed in your problems, and they never come out again.

GOODMAN Paul
4181
Few great men could pass Personnel.

4182
Enjoyment is not a goal, it is a feeling that accompanies important ongoing activity.

4183
The family is the American fascism.

4184
I have learned to have very modest goals for society and myself; things like clean air,

green grass, children with bright eyes, not being pushed around, useful work that suits one's abilities, plain tasty food, and occasional satisfying nookie.

GOODMAN Roy M.
4185
Remember that happiness is a way of travel - not a destination.

GOODRICH Rt. Rev. Philip 1929-
4186 *(opening conference on future of marriage)*
If you will excuse me using this expression, the attitude today is too often one of find it, fuck it, and forget it.

GORDON Adam Lindsay 1833-1870
4187 *Ye Wearie Wayfarer 'Fytte 8'*
Life is mostly froth and bubble,
Two things stand like stone,
Kindness in another's trouble,
Courage in your own.

GORDON Mack 1904-1959
4188 *'Chattanooga Choo-choo'*
Pardon me boy is that the Chattanooga Choo-choo,
Track twenty nine,
Boy you can gimme a shine.
I can afford to board a Chattanooga Choo-choo,
I've got my fare and just a trifle to spare.
You leave the Pennsylvania station 'bout a quarter to four,
Read a magazine and then you're in Baltimore,
Dinner in the diner nothing could be finer
Than to have your ham'n eggs in Carolina.

GORDON Ruth
4189
To be somebody you must last.

GORKY Maxim 1868-1936
4190
To an old man any place that's warm is homeland.

4191
Every new time will give its law.

GORMAN Teresa 1931-
4192
The Prime Minister has got the Parliamentary Party by the goolies.

GORRELL Stuart 1902-1963
4193 *'Georgia on my Mind'*
Georgia, Georgia, no peace I find,
Just an old sweet song keeps Georgia on
my mind.

GOULBURN Edward Meyrick 1818-1897
4194 *(sermon at Rugby School)*
Let the scintillations of your wit be like the
coruscations of summer lightning, lambent
but innocuous.

GOULD Bruce
4195
In England I would rather be a man, a
horse, a dog or a woman, in that order. In
America I think the order would be
reversed.

GOULD Gerald 1885-1936
4196 *Monogamy*
And you were very much in love with me,
And half I lured it on, and half I fled it,
Till honour turned its foolish face on mine
Taking for allies music and good wine -
And told me what I ought to say: I said it.

GOURMONT Rémy de 1858-1915
4197
It is fairly obvious that those who are in
favour of the death penalty have more
affinity with assassins than those who are
not.

4198
Very simple ideas lie within the reach only
of complex minds.

4199
Of all sexual aberrations, perhaps the most
peculiar is chastity.

GOWANS Alan
4200
By the laws of probability, North America
ought to speak French, not English, today.

GOWER John c.1330-1408
4201 *Confessio Amantis*
It hath and schal ben evermor
That love is maister wher he wile.

GOWERS Sir Ernest 1880-1966
4202
We are all esquires now, and we are none
of us gentlemen any more.

4203 *Plain Words*
It is not easy nowadays to remember
anything so contrary to all appearances as
that officials are the servants of the public;
and the official must try not to foster the
illusion that it is the other way round.

GOWRIE Lord 1939-
4204
Quality of life is an industry.

**GOYA (Francisco Joseé de Goya y
Lucientes)** 1746-1828
4205 *Los Caprichos*
The dream of reason produces monsters.

GRACIAN Baltasar 1601-1658
4206
Do not show your wounded finger, for
everything will knock up against it.

4207
A wise man gets more use from his
enemies than a fool from his friends.

4208
Even knowledge has to be in fashion and
where it is not it is wise to affect ignorance.

4209
Wise men appreciate all men, for they see
the good in each and know how hard it is
to make anything good.

4210
At twenty a man is a peacock, at thirty a
lion, at forty a camel, at fifty a serpent, at
sixty a dog, at seventy an ape, at eighty,
nothing at all.

4211
'No' and 'Yes' are words quickly said, but
they need a great amount of thought
before you utter them.

4212
Time and I against any two.

4213
The wise have a solid sense of silence and
the ability to keep a storehouse of secrets.
Their capacity and character are respected.

4214
A beautiful woman should break her
mirror early.

4215
Words are feminine; deeds are masculine.

GRAHAM Billy 1918-
4216
Everybody has a little bit of Watergate in him.

GRAHAM Clementina Stirling 1782-1877
4217 *Mystifications*
The best way to get the better of temptation is just to yield to it.

GRAHAM D.M. 1911-
4218 *(motion for debate at Oxford Union)*
That this House will in no circumstances fight for its King and Country.

GRAHAM Harry 1874-1936
4219 *More Ruthless Rhymes for Heartless Homes*
Weep not for little Léonie
Abducted by a French Marquis!
Though loss of honour was a wrench
Just think how it's improved her French.

4220 *Ruthless Rhymes for Heartless Homes*
O'er the rugged mountain's brow
Clara threw the twins she nursed,
And remarked, 'I wonder now
Which will reach the bottom first?'

4221 *Ruthless Rhymes for Heartless Homes*
Aunt Jane observed, the second time
She tumbled off a bus,
'The step is short from the Sublime
To the Ridiculous.'

4222 *Ruthless Rhymes for Heartless Homes*
'There's been an accident,' they said,
'Your servant's cut in half; he's dead!'
'Indeed!' said Mr Jones, 'and please,
Send me the half that's got my keys.'

4223 *Ruthless Rhymes for Heartless Homes*
Billy, in one of his nice new sashes,
Fell in the fire and was burnt to ashes;
Now, although the room grows chilly,
I haven't the heart to poke poor Billy.

GRAHAM James 1612-1650
4224 *'My Dear and Only Love'*
He either fears his fate too much,
Or his deserts are small,
That puts it not unto the touch
To win or lose it all.

GRAHAM Martha 1893-1991
4225
No artist is ahead of his time. He is his time. It is just that others are behind the time.

4226
The body never lies.

GRAHAME Kenneth 1859-1932
4227
The strongest human instinct is to impart information, the second strongest is to resist it.

4228
The clever men at Oxford
Know all there is to be knowed -
But they none of them know as half as much
As intelligent Mr. Toad.

4229 *The Golden Age*
Monkeys ... very sensibly refrain from speech, lest they should be set to earn their livings.

4230 *The Wind in the Willows*
There is *nothing* - absolutely nothing - half so much worth doing as simply messing about in boats.

GRANT Ulysses S. 1822-1885
4231
No terms except unconditional and immediate surrender can be accepted.

4232 *(inaugural address)*
I know no method to secure the repeal of bad or obnoxious laws so effective as their stringent execution.

GRASS Günter 1927-
4233
The job of a citizen is to keep his mouth open.

GRAVCHEV General Pavel
4234
The Armed forces are the only well-organised and reliable force in society.

GRAVES John Woodcock 1795-1886
4235 *'John Peel'*
D'ye ken John Peel with his coat so grey?
D'ye ken John Peel at the break of the day?

D'ye ken John Peel when he's far far away
With his hounds and his horn in the
morning?

GRAVES Robert 1895-1985
4236
I don't really feel my poems are mine at
all. I didn't create them out of nothing. I
owe them to my relations with other
people.

4237
There's no money in poetry, but then
there's no poetry in money either.

4238
Goodbye to all that.

4239 *'To Evoke Posterity'*
To evoke posterity
Is to weep on your own grave,
Ventriloquizing for the unborn.

4240 *Hedges Freaked With Snow*
No argument, no anger, no remorse,
No dividing of blame.
There was poison in the cup - why should
we ask
From whose hand it came?

4241 *Occupation: Writer*
In love as in sport, the amateur status must
be strictly maintained.

4242 *'The Persian Version'*
Truth-loving Persians do not dwell upon
The trivial skirmish fought near Marathon.

GRAVINA Gian Vinvenzo
4243
A bore is a man who deprives you of
solitude without providing you with
company.

GRAY G.L.
4244
The television commercial is the most
efficient power-packed capsule of
education that appears anywhere on TV.

GRAY John Chipman 1839-1915
4245 *Restraints on the Alienation of Property*
Dirt is only matter out of place.

GRAY Lord d.1612
4246 *(attributed)*
A dead woman bites not.

GRAY Thomas 1716-1771
4247
Where ignorance is bliss
'Tis folly to be wise.

4248 *Elegy Written in a Country Churchyard*
The curfew tolls the knell of parting day,
The lowing herd wind slowly o'er the lea,
The ploughman homeward plods his
weary way,
And leaves the world to darkness and to
me.
Now fades the glimmering landscape on
the sight,
And all the air a solemn stillness holds,
Save where the beetle wheels his droning
flight,
And drowsy tinklings lull the distant folds.

4249 *Elegy Written in a Country Churchyard*
Let not ambition mock their useful toil,
Their homely joys, and destiny obscure;
Nor grandeur hear with a disdainful smile,
The short and simple annals of the poor.
The boast of heraldry, the pomp of pow'r,
And all that beauty, all that wealth e'er
gave,
Awaits alike th' inevitable hour,
The paths of glory lead but to the grave.

4250 *Elegy Written in a Country Churchyard*
Can storied urn or animated bust
Back to its mansion call the fleeting breath?
Can honour's voice provoke the silent
dust,
Or flatt'ry soothe the dull cold ear of
death?

4251 *Elegy Written in a Country Churchyard*
Full many a gem of purest ray serene,
The dark unfathomed caves of ocean bear:
Full many a flower is born to blush
unseen,
And waste its sweetness on the desert air.

4252 *Elegy Written in a Country Churchyard*
Far from the madding crowd's ignoble
strife,
Their sober wishes never learned to stray;
Along the cool sequestered vale of life
They kept the noiseless tenor of their way.

4253 *Elegy Written in a Country Churchyard*
Here rests his head upon the lap of Earth
A youth to fortune and to fame unknown.

Fair Science frowned not on his humble
birth,
And Melancholy marked him for her own.

4254 *'Ode on the Death of a Favourite Cat'*
Not all that tempts your wand'ring eyes
And heedless hearts, is lawful prize;
Nor all, that glisters, gold.

4255 *Ode on a Distant Prospect of Eton
College*
Alas, regardless of their doom,
The little victims play!
No sense have they of ills to come,
Nor care beyond to-day.

4256 *'Sketch of his own Character'*
Too poor for a bribe, and too proud to
importune,
He had not the method of making a
fortune.

GREELEY Horace 1811-1872
4257
The darkest hour of any man's life is when
he sits down to plan how to get money
without earning it.

4258 *Hints toward Reforms*
Go West, young man, and grow up with
the country.

GREEN Benny 1927-
4259
A jazz musician is a juggler who uses
harmonies instead of oranges.

GREEN Matthew 1696-1737
4260 *The Grotto*
They politics like ours profess,
The greater prey upon the less.

GREEN Russell
4261
Heaven is the place where the donkey
finally catches up with his carrot: hell is
the eternity while he waits for it.

4262
A wife encourages her husband's egoism
in order to exercise her own.

GREENAWAY Peter
4263
Ultimately the best way to understand a
highly charged situation is to take a step

back.

GREENBERG Clement
4264
All profoundly original art looks ugly at
first.

GREENBURG Martin
4265
The terror of art lies in the representation
of the hidden reality with its shattering
effect.

GREENE Graham 1904-1991
4266
Hatred seems to operate on the same
glands as love; it even produces the same
actions. If we had not been taught how to
interpret the story of the Passion, would
we have been able to say from their actions
alone whether it was the jealous Judas or
the cowardly Peter who loved Christ?

4267
At the end of what is called the 'sexual life'
the only love which has lasted is the love
which has everything, every
disappointment, every failure and every
betrayal, which has accepted even the sad
fact that in the end there is no desire so
deep as the simple desire for
companionship.

4268
Fame is a powerful aphrodisiac.

4269 *The Comedians*
Communists have committed great crimes,
but at least they have not stood aside, like
an established society, and been
indifferent. I would rather have blood on
my hands than water, like Pilate.

4270 *The Heart of the Matter*
Nothing was ever lost by delay.

4271 *The Heart of the Matter*
Against the beautiful and the clever and
the successful, one can wage a pitiless war,
but not against the unattractive.

4272 *The Power and the Glory*
There is always one moment in childhood
when the door opens and lets the future in.

4273 *The Quiet American*
If only it were possible to love without injury - fidelity isn't enough ... The hurt is in the act of possession: we are too small in mind and body to posses another person without pride or to be possessed without humiliation.

GREENE Robert c.1560-1592
4274 *Perimedes*
'Men, when they lust, can many fancies feign.'

4275 *'The Shepherd's Wife's Song'*
Ah! what is love! It is a pretty thing,
As sweet unto a shepherd as a king,
And sweeter too;
For kings have cares that wait upon a crown,
And cares can make the sweetest love to frown.
Ah then, ah then,
If country loves such sweet desires do gain,
What lady would not love a shepherd swain?

GREER Germaine 1939-
4276
Most women still need a room of their own and the only way to find it may be outside their own home.

4277
I didn't fight to get women out from behind the vacuum cleaner to get them onto the board of Hoover.

4278
Women must learn to lighten up if we are to survive.

4279 *The Female Eunuch*
You can now see the Female Eunuch the world over.

4280 *The Female Eunuch*
Love, love, love - all the wretched cant of it, masking egotism, lust, masochism, fantasy under a mythology of sentimental postures.

GREGG Alan
4281
A thousand goodbyes come after death - the first six months of bereavement.

4282
A good education should leave much to be desired.

4283
The human race has had long experience and a find tradition in surviving adversity. But we now face a task for which we have little experience, the task of surviving prosperity.

GRELLET Stephen 1773-1855
4284 *(attributed)*
I expect to pass through this world but once; any good thing therefore that I can do, or any kindness that I can show to any fellow-creature, let me do it now; let me not defer or neglect it, for I shall not pass this way again.

GREY Sir Edward 1862-1933
4285 *25 Years*
The lamps are going out all over Europe; we shall not see them lit again in our lifetime.

GREY John
4286
And what's a butterfly? At best,
He's but a caterpillar, drest.

GRICE Glenn le
4287
Florida: God's waiting room.

GROPIUS Walter 1883-1969
4288
Society needs a good image of itself. That is the job of the architect.

4289
How can we expect our students to become bold and fearless in thought and action if we encase them in sentimental shrines feigning a culture which has long since disappeared?

GROSSMITH George and Weedon 1847-1912 and 1854-1919
4290 *The Diary of a Nobody*
What's the good of a home if you are never in it?

4291 *The Diary of a Nobody*
I left the room with silent dignity, but caught my foot in the mat.

4292 *The Diary of a Nobody*
I am a poor man, but I would gladly give ten shillings to find out who sent me the insulting Christmas card I received this morning.

GROTIUS Hugo 1583-1645
4293
Not to know certain things is a great part of wisdom.

GROVE Phillip B.
4294
A dictionary should be descriptive, not prescriptive.

GUEDALLA Philip 1889-1944
4295
The Lord Chief Justice of England recently said that the greater part of his judicial time was spent investigating collisions between propelled vehicles, each on its own side of the road, each sounding its horn and each stationary.

4296
I had always assumed that cliché was a suburb of Paris, until I discovered it to be a street in Oxford.

4297 *Mr Churchill*
... the little ships of England brought the Army home.

4298 *Masters and Men*
Any stigma, as the old saying is, will serve to beat a dogma.

4299 *Supers and Supermen*
The cheerful clatter of Sir James Barrie's cans as he went round with the milk of human kindness.

4300 *Supers and Supermen*
History repeats itself. Historians repeat each other.

GUÉRARD Albert
4301
Chivalry is the most delicate form of contempt.

GUINNESS Sir Alec 1914-
4302
Acting is happy agony.

GUITERMAN Arthur
4303
The porcupine, whom one must handle gloved,
May be respected, but is never loved.

4304
Amoebas at the start were not complex;
They tore themselves apart and started sex.

GUITRY Sacha 1885-1957
4305
You can pretend to be serious, but you can't pretend to be witty.

4306
The little I know, I owe to my ignorance.

4307
An ideal wife is one who remains faithful to you but tries to be just as if she weren't.

4308
Honest women are inconsolable for the mistakes they haven't made.

4309
Even the most respectable woman has a complete set of clothes in her wardrobe ready for a possible abduction.

4310 *(attributed remark to his fifth wife)*
The others were only my wives. But you, my dear, will be my widow.

GULBENKIAN Nubar 1896-1972
4311
The best number for a dinner party is two - myself and a dam' good head waiter.

GUNN Thom 1929-
4312 *Carnal Knowledge*
You know I know you know I know you know.

GUNTHER John 1901-1970
4313
All happiness depends on a leisurely breakfast.

4314
The first essence of journalism is to know what you want to know; the second, is to find out who will tell you.

GUTHRIE Woody 1912-1967
4315
Now as through this world I ramble,
I see lots of funny men,
Some rob you with a six gun
Some with a fountain pen.

GWYN Nell 1650-1687
4316 *(during the Popish Terror)*
Pray, good people, be civil. I am the
Protestant whore.

HABERMAN Jr. Philip W.
4317
A gourmet is just a glutton with brains.

HABGOOD John (Archbishop of York)
1927-
4318
The desire to be spoonfed, to have our
problems solved for us by someone else, to
be given the short, snappy answer, has
sunk deep into our culture.

4319 *(of teenage marriage)*
I think under 21 is almost always
disastrous.

HAGGARD Sir Henry Rider 1856-1925
4320 *She*
She who must be obeyed.

HAGUE Sir Douglas 1926-
4321
Our state schools were established to
produce clerks and book-keepers.

HAIG Earl 1861-1928
4322 *(of the 17th Earl of Derby)*
A very weak-minded fellow I am afraid,
and, like the feather pillow, bears the
marks of the last person who has sat on
him!

4323 *(order to British troops)*
Every position must be held to the last
man: there must be no retirement. With
our backs to the wall, and believing in the
justice of our cause, each one of us must
fight on to the end.

HAIGH Kenneth
4324
You need three things in the theatre - the
play, the actors and the audience, and each
must give something.

HAILSHAM Lord (Quintin Hogg) 1907-
4325 *The Case of Conservatism*
Conservatives do not believe that the
political struggle is the most important
thing in life ... The simplest of them prefer
fox-hunting - the wisest religion.

HALDANE J.B.S. 1892-1964
4326
I have never yet met a healthy person who
worries very much about his health, or a
really good person who worries much
about his own soul.

4327 *Possible Worlds and Other Essays*
Now, my own suspicion is that the
universe is not only queerer than we
suppose, but queerer than we *can* suppose
... I suspect that there are more things in
heaven and earth than are dreamed of, or
can be dreamed of, in any philosophy.

HALDEMAN H.R. 1929-
4328 *(of the Watergate affair)*
Once the toothpaste is out of the tube, it is
awfully hard to get it back in.

HALE Harlan
4329 *(of Care International in Rwanda)*
We've got 3 categories of refugees: the
living dead, the dying dead and the dead
dead.

HALE Nathan 1755-1776
4330 *(prior to his execution for spying)*
I only regret that I have but one life to lose
for my country.

HALIBURTON Thomas Chandler 1796-
1865
4331
I have learnt a good deal from my own
talk.

HALIFAX Lord George 1633-1695
4332
He that leaveth nothing to Chance will do
few things ill, but he will do very few
things.

4333
Anger raiseth invention, but it overheateth
the oven.

4334
A busy fool is fitter to be shut up than a downright madman.

4335
Men are not hanged for stealing horses, but that horses may not be stolen.

4336
Weak men are apt to be cruel because they stick at nothing that may repair the ill effect of their mistakes.

4337
Nothing has an uglier look to us than Reason, when it is not of our side.

HALL Joseph 1574-1656
4338 *Works*
Perfection is the child of Time.

HALL Radclyffe 1883-1943
4339 *The Well of Loneliness*
You're neither unnatural, nor abominable, nor mad; you're as much a part of what people call nature as anyone else; only you're unexplained as yet.

HALLA Sven
4340
The good should be grateful to the bad - for providing the world with a basis for comparison.

HALM Friedrich 1806-1871
4341
Two souls with but a single thought,
Two hearts that beat as one.

HALSER Professor A.H.
4342
The project as understood by feminists is making women more like men, but it ought to be making men more like women.

HALSEY Margaret 1910-
4343
Some persons talk simply because they think sound is more manageable than silence.

4344
Whatever the rest of the world thinks of the English gentleman, the English lady regards him apprehensively as something between God and a goat and equally

formidable on both scores.

4345 *With Malice Toward Some*
The English never smash in a face. They merely refrain from asking it to dinner.

HAMAKER L.S.
4346
Always remember that the soundest way to progress in any organization is to help the man ahead of you to get promoted.

HAMILTON Alex 1936-
4347
Those who stand for nothing fall for anything.

HAMILTON Alexander 1757-1804
4348
Power over a man's subsistence amounts to a power over his will.

HAMILTON Eleanor
4349
A compliment is a gift, not to be thrown away carelessly unless you want to hurt the giver.

HAMILTON Robert B.
4350
Man is a reasoning, rather than a reasonable animal.

HAMMARSKJÖLD Dag 1905-1961
4351
Never look down to test the ground before taking your next step; only he who keeps his eye fixed on the far horizon will find his right road.

4352
God does not die on the day when we cease to believe in a personal deity, but we die on the day when our lives cease to be illuminated by the steady radiance, renewed daily, of a wonder, the source of which is beyond all reason.

4353
Life only demands from the strength you possess. Only one feat is possible - not to have run away.

4354
Time goes by: reputation increases, ability declines.

4355
A task becomes a duty from the moment you suspect it to be an essential part of that integrity which alone entitles a man to assume responsibility.

HAMMERSTEIN II Oscar 1895-1960
4356
Do you love me because I'm beautiful, or am I beautiful because you love me?

4357 *Lady Be Good*
The last time I saw Paris
Her heart was warm and gay.

4358 *Showboat*
Ol' man river, dat ol' man river,
He must know sumpin', but don't say nothin',
He jus' keeps rollin',
He jus' keeps rollin' along.

4359 *South Pacific*
You've got to be taught to be afraid
Of people whose eyes are oddly made,
Of people whose skin is a different shade.
You've got to be carefully taught.

You've got to be taught before it's too late,
Before you are six or seven or eight,
To hate all the people your relatives hate.
You've got to be carefully taught.

HAMPTON Christopher 1946-
4360 *Savages*
A definition of capitalism ... the process whereby American girls turn into American women.

HAND Learned 1872-1961
4361
We accept the verdict of the past until the need for change cries out loudly enough to force upon us a choice between the comforts of further inertia and the irksomeness of action.

4362
The art of publicity is a black art.

4363
The aim of law is the maximum gratification of the nervous system of man.

4364
The spirit of liberty is the spirit which is not too sure that it is right.

4365
We shall succeed only so far as we continue that most distasteful of all activity, the intolerable labour of thought.

4366 *(of Samuel Goldwyn)*
A self-made man may prefer a self-made name.

HANDS Terry 1941-
4367
It is said that Hamlet is the first modern man - so obviously he must be insane.

HANNIBAL 247-182 BC
4368
We will either find a way, or make one.

HANRAHAN Brian 1949-
4369
I counted them all out and I counted them all back.

HARBACH Otto 1873-1963
4370
Smoke gets in your eyes.

4371 *The Wizard of Oz*
Somewhere over the rainbow.

HARBURG E.Y. 1898-1981
4372
The World would be a safer place,
If someone had a plan,
Before exploring Outer Space,
To find the Inner man.

4373
Brother can you spare a dime?

HARDING Warren G. 1865-1923
4374
My God, this is a hell of a job. I have no trouble with my enemies. I can take care of my enemies all right. But my damn friends, my goddamn friends. They're the ones that keep me walking the floor nights.

HARDWICKE Sir Cedric 1893-1964
4375
I regard England as my wife and America as my mistress.

HARDY Oliver 1892-1957
4376 *in The Laurel and Hardy Murder Case*
"Here's another fine mess you've gotten

me into."

HARDY Thomas 1840-1928
4377
Aspects are within us, and who seems most kingly is king.

4378
Measurement of life should be proportioned rather to the intensity of the experience than to its actual length.

4379
Love lives on propinquity, but dies on contact.

4380
That man's silence is wonderful to listen to.

4381
The business of the poet and novelist is to show the sorriness underlying the grandest things, and the grandeur underlying the sorriest things.

4382 *'On the Departure Platform'*
We kissed at the barrier; and passing through
She left me, and moment by moment got
Smaller and smaller, until to my view
She was but a spot.

4383 *The Dynasts*
War makes rattling good history; but Peace is poor reading.

4384 *The Hand of Ethelberta*
A lover without indiscretion is no lover at all.

4385 *'The Man he Killed'*
Yes; quaint and curious war is!
You shoot a fellow down
You'd treat if met where any bar is,
Or help to half-a-crown.

4386 *Tess of the D'Urbervilles - preface*
A novel is an impression, not an argument.

HARE Julius and HARE Augustus 1795-1855 and 1792-1834
4387
The greatest truths are the simplest, and so are the greatest men.

4388 *Guesses at Truth*
Half the failures in life arise from pulling in one's horse as he is leaping.

HARINGTON Sir John 1561-1612
4389
Books give not wisdom where none was before.
But where some is, there reading makes it more.

4390 *Epigrams*
Treason doth never prosper, what's the reason?
For if it prosper, none dare call it treason.

HARKNESS Richard
4391
What is a committee? A group of the unwilling, picked from the unfit, to do the unnecessary.

HARLECH Lord (David Ormsby Gore) 1918-1985
4392
It would indeed be a tragedy if the history of the human race proved to be nothing more than the story of an ape playing with a box of matches on a petrol dump.

4393
Britain will be honoured by historians more for the way she disposed of an empire than for the way in which she acquired it.

HARLOW Jean 1911-1937
4394 *in Hell's Angels*
"Excuse me while I slip into something more comfortable."

HARRIS Harwell Hamilton
4395
The house does not frame the view: it projects the beholder into it.

HARRIS Janet
4396
At its most basic root, the death or disintegration of one's parents is a harsh reminder of one's own mortality.

HARRIS Joel Chandler 1848-1908
4397
You k'n hide de fier, but what you guine do wid de smoke?

HARRIS Lawren
4398
A picture can become for us a highway between a particular thing and a universal feeling.

HARRIS Sydney J.
4399
The true test of independent judgement is being able to dislike someone who admires us.

4400
The two words 'information' and 'communication' are often used interchangeably, but they signify quite different things. Information is giving out; communication is getting through.

HART Josephine
4401
Poetry contains almost all you need to know about life.

HART Lorenz 1895-1943
4402 *Babes in Arms*
That's why the lady is a tramp.

4403 *'Mountain Greenery'*
Just two crazy people together.

HARTE Bret 1836-1902
4404
One big vice in a man is apt to keep out a great many smaller ones.

HARTLEY L.P. 1895-1972
4405 *The Go-Between*
The past is a foreign country: they do things differently there.

HASKINS Henry S.
4406
If a man hears much that a woman says, she is not beautiful.

4407
Disappointments should be cremated, not embalmed.

HASKINS Minnie Louise 1875-1957
4408 *Desert 'God Knows'*
And I said to the man who stood at the gate of the year: 'Give me a light that I may tread safely into the unknown.'
And he replied:

'Go out into the darkness and put your hand into the Hand of God. That shall be to you better than light and safer than a known way.'

HASTINGS Lewis
4409
The fact is that the possession of a highly social conscience about large-scale issues is no guarantee whatever of reasonable conduct in private relations.

HAVENS Leston L.
4410
The slow compromise, or even surrender, of our fondest hopes is a regular feature of normal human life.

HAVOC June
4411
You are all you will ever have for certain.

HAWKER R.S. 1803-1875
4412 *'The Song of the Western Men'*
And have they fixed the where and when?
And shall Trelawny die?
Here's twenty thousand Cornish men
Will know the reason why!

HAWKING Stephen 1942-
4413
The behaviour of the universe on a very large scale seems to be simple and not chaotic.

4414 *A Brief History of Time*
Each equation ... in the book would halve the sales.

4415 *A Brief History of Time*
If we find the answer to that [why it is that we and the universe exist], it would be the ultimate triumph of human reason - for then we would know the mind of God.

HAWTHORNE Nathaniel 1804-1864
4416
Selfishness is one of the qualities apt to inspire love.

4417
The world owes all its onward impulses to men ill at ease. The happy man inevitably confines himself within ancient limits.

HAY Ian 1876-1952
4418 *The Housemaster*
What do you mean, funny? Funnny-peculiar or funny ha-ha?

HAY John 1838-1905
4419
The best-loved man or maid in the town would perish with anguish could they hear all that their friends say in the course of a day.

HAYAKAWA S.I.
4420
We should keep the Panama Canal. After all we stole it fair and square.

4421
In the age of television, image becomes more important than substance.

HAYDON A. Eustace
4422
Fortunately for serious minds, a bias recognized is a bias sterilized.

HAYEK Friedrich 1899-1992
4423
Competition means decentralized planning by many separate persons.

HAYES J. Milton 1884-1940
4424 *The Green Eye of the Yellow God*
There's a one-eyed yellow idol to the north of Khatmandu,
There's a little marble cross below the town,
There's a broken-hearted woman tends the grave of Mad Carew,
And the Yellow God forever gazes down.

HAYS Brooks
4425
Back of every achievement is a proud wife and a surprised mother-in-law.

HAZLITT William 1778-1830
4426
Actors are the only honest hypocrites.

4427
Grace is the absence of everything that indicates pain or difficulty, hesitation or incongruity.

4428
Persons who undertake to pry into, or cleanse out all the filth of a common sewer, either cannot have very nice noses, or will soon lose them.

4429
There is nothing good to be had in the country, or, if there be, they will not let you have it.

4430
Wit is the salt of conversation, not the food.

4431
Without the aid of prejudice and custom, I should not be able to find my way across the room.

4432
Man is a make-believe animal - he is never so truly himself as when he is acting a part.

4433
Man is the only animal that laughs and weeps; for he is the only animal that is struck by the difference between what things are and what they might have been.

4434
We are not hypocrites in our sleep.

4435
Calumny requires no proof. The throwing out of malicious imputations against any character leaves a stain which no after-refutation can wipe out. To create an unfavourable impression, it is not necessary that cetain things should be true, but that they have been said.

4436
All that men really understand is confined to a very small compass; to their daily affairs and experience; to what they have an opportunity to know; and motives to study or practise. The rest is affectation and imposture.

4437
Indolence is a delightful but distressing state. We must be doing something to be happy.

4438
Those who are fond of setting things to rights have no great objection to setting them wrong.

4439
Landscape painting is the obvious resource of misanthropy.

4440
Prejudice is the child of ignorance.

4441
The truly proud man is satisfied with his own good opinion, and does not seek to make converts to it.

4442
It is essential to the triumph of reform that it shall never succeed.

4443
If we wish to know the force of human genius, we should read Shakespeare. If we wish to see the insignificance of human learning, we may study his commentators.

4444
Learning is the knowledge of that which none but the learned know.

4445
The most silent people are generally those who think most highly of themselves.

4446
If a person has no delicacy, he has you in his power.

4447
One truth discovered, one pang of regret at not being able to express it, is better than all the fluency and flippancy in the world.

4448 *The Round Table*
The art of pleasing consists in being pleased.

4449 *Sketches and Essays*
But of all footmen the lowest class is *literary footmen*.

4450 *Sketches and Essays*
A nickname is the heaviest stone that the devil can throw at a man.

4451 *The Spirit of the Age*
Mr Wordsworth's genius is a pure emanation of the Spirit of the Age. Had he lived in any other period of the world, he would never have been heard of.

4452 *Table Talk*
You will hear more good things on the outside of a stagecoach from London to Oxford than if you were to pass a twelvemonth with the undergraduates, or heads of colleges, of that famous university.

HAZZARD Shirley 1931-
4453 *The Transit of Venus*
The tragedy is not that love doesn't last. The tragedy is the love that lasts.

HEALEY Denis 1917-
4454
NATO is now a biological monstrosity - an organ without a function.

4455 *(on being criticized by Sir Geoffrey Howe)*
Like being savaged by a dead sheep.

HEARST William Randolph 1863-1951
4456
Don't be afraid to make a mistake, your readers might like it.

HEATH Edward 1916-
4457 *(on the Lonrho affair)*
The unpleasant and unacceptable face of capitalism.

HECHT Ben 1893-1964
4458 *Think, February 1963*
A man nearly always loves for other reasons than he thinks. A lover is apt to be as full of secrets from himself as is the object of his love from him.

HEGEL G.W.F. 1770-1831
4459 *Lectures on the Philosphy of World History*
Only in the state does man have a rational existence ... Man owes his entire existence to the state, and has his being within it alone. Whatever worth and spiritual reality he possesses are his solely by virtue of the state.

HEIN Piet
4460
If no thought
your mind does visit
make your speech
not too explicit.

HEINE Heinrich 1797-1856
4461
The Romans would never have had time to
conquer the world if they had been obliged
to learn Latin first of all.

4462
When the heroes go off the stage, the
clowns come on.

4463
It must require an inordinate share of
vanity and presumption after enjoying so
much that is good and beautiful on earth,
to ask the Lord for immortality in addition
to it all.

4464
Woman is at once apple and serpent.

4465
On wings of song.

4466 *Almansor*
Wherever books will be burned, men also,
in the end, are burned.

4467 *(as he died)*
God will pardon me. It's his business.

HELLER Joseph 1923-
4468
Frankly I'd like to see the government get
out of war altogether and leave the whole
field to private industry.

4469 *Catch-22*
Some men are born mediocre, some men
achieve mediocrity, and some men have
mediocrity thrust upon them. With Major
Major it had been all three.

4470 *Something Happened*
The company has a policy about getting
laid. It's okay ... Talking about getting
laid is even more okay than doing it, but
doing it is okay too, although talking about
getting laid with your own wife is never
okay.

HELLMAN Lillian 1907-1984
4471
If you are willing to take the punishment,
you're halfway through the battle. That
the issues may be trivial, the battle ugly, is
another point.

4472
Cynicism is an unpleasant way of saying
the truth.

4473
They're fancy talkers about themselves,
writers. If I had to give young writers
advice, I would say don't listen to writers
talking about writing or themselves.

4474 *Toys in the Attic*
People change and forget to tell each other.

HELPS Sir Arthur 1813-1875
4475
Men of much depth of mind can bear a
great deal of counsel; for it does not easily
deface their own character, nor render
their purposes indistinct.

4476
Reading is sometimes an ingenious device
for avoiding thought.

4477
If you would understand your own age,
read the works of fiction produced in it.
People in disguise speak freely.

HELVETIUS Claude-Adrien 1715-1771
4478
To limit the press is to insult a nation; to
prohibit reading of certain books is to
declare the inhabitants to be either fools or
slaves.

HEMANS Felicia 1793-1835
4479 *'Casabianca'*
The boy stood on the burning deck
Whence all but he had fled;
The flame that lit the battle's wreck
Shone round him o'er the dead.

4480 *'The Homes of England'*
The stately homes of England,
How beautiful they stand!

HEMINGWAY Ernest 1899-1961
4481
You lose it if you talk about it.

4482
Nobody knows what's in him until he tries to pull it out. If there's nothing, or very little, the shock can kill a man.

4483
If you are lucky enough to have lived in Paris as a young man, then wherever you go for the rest of your life, it stays with you, for Paris is a movable feast.

4484
The writer must write what he has to say, not speak it.

4485
The most essential gift for a good writer is a built-in, shockproof shit detector. This is the writer's radar and all great writers have had it.

4486
His (the writer's) standard of fidelity to the truth should be so high that his invention, out of his experience, should produce a truer account than anything factual can be.

4487 *For Whom the Bell Tolls*
But did thee feel the earth move?

HENDERSON Nelson
4488
The true meaning of life is to plant trees, under whose shade you do not expect to sit.

HENDREN L.L.
4489
Fathers send their sons to college either because they went to college, or because they didn't.

HENDRIX Jimi 1942-1970
4490 *'Purple Haze'*
Purple haze is in my brain
Lately things don't seem the same.

HENLEY W.E. 1849-1903
4491
Bland as a Jesuit, sober as a hymn.

4492 *'Invictus. In Memoriam R.T.H.B.'*
In the fell clutch of circumstance,
I have not winced nor cried aloud:
Under the bludgeonings of chance
My head is bloody, but unbowed.

4493 *'Invictus. In Memoriam R.T.H.B.'*
It matters not how strait the gate,
How charged with punishments the scroll,
I am the master of my fate:
I am the captain of my soul.

HENRI IV (King of Navarre) 1553-1610
4494 *(attributed)*
Paris is well worth a mass.

4495 *(of James I of England, attributed)*
The wisest fool in Christendom.

HENRICH Tommy
4496
Catching a fly ball is a pleasure, but knowing what to do with it is a business.

HENRY II King 1133-1189
4497 *(of Thomas Becket)*
Will no one rid me of this turbulent priest?

HENRY O. 1862-1910
4498 *Gentle Grafter 'Octopus Marooned'*
It was beautiful and simple as all truly great swindles are.

4499 *(last words)*
Turn up the lights; I don't want to go home in the dark.

4500 *Memoirs of a Yellow Dog*
If men knew how women pass the time when they are alone, they'd never marry.

HENRY Patrick 1736-1799
4501
For my part, whatever anguish of spirit it may cost, I am willing to know the whole truth - to know the worst and provide for it.

4502
I know not what course others may take; but as for me, give me liberty, or give me death!

HENRY Will
4503
What is research, but a blind date with knowledge?

HENRY William (Duke of Gloucester)
1743-1805
4504
Another damned, thick, square book!
Always scribble, scribble, scribble! Eh! Mr.
Gibbon?

HEPBURN Katharine 1909-
4505
If you give audiences a chance they'll do
half your acting for you.

4506
Only the really plain people know about
love - the very fascinating ones try so hard
to create an impression that they soon
exhaust their talents.

4507
If you're given a choice between money
and sex appeal, take the money. As you
get older, the money will become your sex
appeal.

4508 *in The African Queen*
"Nature, Mr Allnutt, is what we are put
into this world to rise above."

HERACLITUS c.544-483 BC
4509
All things flow, nothing abides.

HERBERT A.P. 1890-1971
4510
A highbrow is the kind of person who
looks at a sausage and thinks of Picasso.

4511
A dull speaker, like a plain woman, is
credited with all the virtues, for we
charitably suppose that a surface so
unattractive must be compensated by
interior blessings.

4512 *'The Farmer'*
The Farmer will never be happy again;
He carries his heart in his boots;
For either the rain is destroying his grain
Or the drought is destroying his roots.

4513 *'The President of the Board of Trade'*
This high official, all allow,
Is grossly overpaid;
There wasn't any Board, and now
There isn't any Trade.

4514 *Tough at the Top*
Nothing is wasted, nothing is in vain:
The seas roll over but the rocks remain.

4515 *Uncommon Law*
The critical period in matrimony is
breakfast-time.

4516 *Uncommon Law*
The Common Law of England has been
laboriously built about a mythical figure -
the figure of 'The Reasonable Man'.

HERBERT George 1593-1633
4517
The chicken is the country's, but the city
eats it.

4518
Deceive not thy physician, confessor, nor
lawyer.

4519
Drink not the third glass - which thou
can'st not tame when once it is within thee.

4520
A great ship asks deep water.

4521
Hope is the poor man's bread.

4522
You must lose a fly to catch a trout.

4523
One sword keeps another in the sheath.

4524
Let all the world in ev'ry corner sing
My God and King.

4525
Teach me, my God and King,
In all things Thee to see,
And what I do in any thing
To do it as for Thee.

4526
A man that looks on glass,
On it may stay his eye;
Or if he pleaseth, through it pass,
And then the heaven espy.

4527
He that makes a good war makes a good
peace.

4528 *'The 23rd Psalm'*
The God of love my Shepherd is,
And He that doth me feed:
While He is mine, and I am His,
What can I want or need?

4529 *'Affliction (1)'*
Ah, my dear God! though I am clean forgot,
Let me not love Thee, if I love Thee not.

HERBERT Jack
4530
A comedian is a fellow who finds other comedians too humorous to mention.

HERFORD Oliver
4531
Actresses will happen in the best regulated families.

4532
Only the young die good.

HERODOTUS c.485-425 BC
4533
Very few things happen at the right time, and the rest do not happen at all; the conscientious historian will correct these defects.

4534
This is the worst pain a man can suffer: to have insight into much and power over nothing.

4535
In peace, sons bury their fathers; in war, fathers bury their sons.

HEROLD Don
4536
Babies are such a nice way to start people.

4537
A humorist is a man who feels bad but who feels good about it.

4538
There's one thing about baldness - it's neat.

HEROLD J. Christopher
4539
Those who mistake their good luck for their merit are inevitably bound for disaster.

HERRICK Robert 1591-1674
4540
If a little labour, little are our gains.
Man's fortunes are according to his pains.

4541
Fain would I kiss my Julia's dainty leg,
Which is as white and hairless as an egg.

4542 *'Upon Julia's Clothes'*
Whenas in silks my Julia goes,
Then, then (methinks) how sweetly flows
That liquefaction of her clothes.
Next, when I cast mine eyes and see
That brave vibration each way free;
O how that glittering taketh me!

4543 *'An Ode for him' [Ben Jonson]*
And yet each verse of thine
Out-did the meat, out-did the frolic wine.

4544 *'To the Virgins, to Make Much of Time'*
Gather ye rosebuds while ye may,
Old Time is still a-flying;
And this same flower that smiles to-day,
To-morrow will be dying.

4545 *'To the Virgins, to Make Much of Time'*
Then be not coy, but use your time;
And while ye may, go marry:
For having lost but once your prime,
You may for ever tarry.

HERSCHENSOHN Bruce
4546
Boredom turns a man to sex, a woman to shopping, and it drives newscasters berserk.

HERSEY John 1914-1993
4547
Journalism allows it's readers to witness history. Fiction gives its readers an opportunity to live it.

HERSHEY Lenore
4548
Do give books - religious or otherwise - for Christmas. They're never fattening, seldom sinful, and permanently personal.

HERZOG Roman 1934-
4549
One cannot cancel out Hitler through Beethoven.

HESBURGH Rev. Theodore
4550
The most important thing a father can do for his children is to love their mother.

HESCHEL Abraham J.
4551
Our concern is not how to worship in the catacombs but how to remain human in the skyscrapers.

4552
Self-respect is the root of discipline: the sense of dignity grows with the ability to say no to oneself.

HESIOD fl.8th Century BC
4553
No gossip ever dies away entirely, if many people voice it: it, too, is a kind of divinity.

4554
The Gods rank work above virtues.

HESS Stephen
4555 *(of John Major)*
The other European leaders actually **ARE** old: he just acts old.

HESSE Hermann 1877-1962
4556
If you hate a person, you hate something in him that is part of yourself. What isn't part of ourselves doesn't disturb us.

4557
Every man is more than just himself; he also represents the unique, the very special and always significant and remarkable point at which the world's phenomena intersect, only once in this way, and never again.

4558
Those who are too lazy and comfortable to think for themselves and be their own judges obey the laws. Others sense their own laws within them.

4559
There is no reality except the one contained within us. That is why so many people live such an unreal life. They take the images outside them for reality and never allow the world within to assert itself.

HEWART Gordon 1870-1943
4560 *(Rex v Sussex Justices)*
A long line of cases shows that it is not merely of some importance, but is of fundamental importance that justice should not only be done, but should manifestly and undoubtedly be seen to be done.

HEWES Henry
4561
To be reborn is a constantly recurring human need.

HEYWARD Du Bose 1885-1940
4562 *Porgy and Bess 'Summertime'*
Summer time an' the livin' is easy,
Fish are jumpin' an' the cotton is high.
Oh, yo' daddy's rich, and yo' ma' is good-lookin',
So hush, little baby, don't yo' cry.

HEYWOOD John c.1497-1580
4563
The more haste, the less speed.

HICKS Sir John 1904-1989
4564 *Econometrica 'The Theory of Monopoly'*
The best of all monopoly profits is a quiet life.

HILL Rowland 1744-1833
4565
He did not see any reason why the devil should have all the good tunes.

HILLARY Sir Edmund 1919-
4566 *(on conquering Mount Everest)*
Well, we knocked the bastard off!

HILLEBRAND Fred 1893-
4567
Home James, and don't spare the horses.

HILLINGDON Lady 1857-1940
4568 *The Rise and Fall of the British Nanny*
I am happy now that Charles calls on my bedchamber less frequently than of old. As it is, I now endure but two calls a week and when I hear his steps outside my door I lie down on my bed, close my eyes, open my legs, and think of England.

HILLMAN Sidney 1887-1946
4569
Politics is the science of how who gets

what, when and why.

HILTON James 1900-1954
4570 Goodbye, Mr Chips
Nothing really wrong with him - only
anno domini, but that's the most fatal
complaint of all, in the end.

HIMMEL Sam
4571
A dictatorship is a country where they
have taken the politics out of politics.

HINCKS Clarence H.
4572
Nothing succeeds like one's own successor.

HINES James
4573
A gentle Quaker, hearing a strange noise in
his house one night, got up and discovered
a burglar busily at work. He went and got
his gun, came back and stood quietly in
the doorway. 'Friend' he said, 'I would do
thee no harm for the world, but thou
standest where I am about to shoot.'

HIPPOCRATES c.460-377 BC
4574
Wherever a doctor cannot do good, he
must be kept from doing harm.

HISLOP Ian 1960-
4575
What satirist ever toppled the
government? Swift managed to get one
small tax changed in his whole career.

HITCHCOCK Alfred 1899-1980
4576
Drama is life with the dull bits cut out.

4577
The only way to get rid of my fears is to
make films about them.

4578
Television has brought back murder into
the home - where it belongs.

HITCHCOCK R.D.
4579
In a truly heroic life there is no
peradventure. It is always doing or dying.

HITLER Adolf 1889-1945
4580
Belief is harder to shake than knowledge.

4581
With regard to the problem of the Sudeten
Germans, my patience is now at an end!

4582
Is Paris burning?

4583 *(of massacre of Roehm and associates)*
The night of the long knives.

4584 *Mein Kampf*
The broad mass of a nation ... will more
easily fall victim to a big lie than to a small
one.

HO Tao
4585
Good architecture is like a piece of
beautifully composed music crystallized in
space that elevates our spirits beyond the
limitation of time.

HOBBES Thomas 1588-1679
4586
If I had read as much as other men, I
should have known no more than they.

4587
Understanding is nothing else than
conception caused by speech.

4588
Words are wise men's counters, they do
but reckon by them; but they are the
money of fools.

4589 *(last words)*
I am about to take my last voyage, a great
leap in the dark.

4590 *Leviathan*
No arts; no letters; no society; and which is
worst of all, continual fear and danger of
violent death; and the life of man, solitary,
poor, nasty, brutish, and short.

4591 *Leviathan*
Force, and fraud, are in war the two
cardinal virtues.

4592 *Leviathan*
The papacy is not other than the ghost of
the deceased Roman Empire, sitting

crowned upon the grave thereof.

4593 *Leviathan*
The praise of ancient authors proceeds not from the reverence of the dead, but from the competition, and mutual envy of the living.

HOCHHUTH Rolf 1931-
4594
Men may be linked in friendship. Nations are linked only by interests.

HOCKNEY David 1937-
4595
Life doesn't have clear edges.

4596
The thing with high-tech is that you always end up using scissors.

HODGSON Ralph 1871-1962
4597
Did anyone ever have a boring dream?

4598 *'Bells of Heaven'*
'Twould ring the bells of Heaven
The wildest peal for years,
If Parson lost his senses
And people came to theirs,
And he and they together
Knelt down with angry prayers
For tamed and shabby tigers
And dancing dogs and bears,
And wretched, blind, pit ponies,
And little hunted hares.

HOFFA Jimmy c.1913-1975
4599
I may have faults but being wrong ain't one of them.

HOFFENSTEIN Samuel
4600
Breathes there a man with hide so tough
Who says two sexes aren't enough?

HOFFER Eric 1902-1983
4601
The end comes when we no longer talk with ourselves. It is the end of genuine thinking and the beginning of the final loneliness.

4602
When people are bored, it is primarily with their own selves.

4603
Every new adjustment is a crisis in self-esteem.

4604
It is a perplexing and unpleasant truth that when men already have 'something worth fighting for', they do not feel like fighting.

4605
You can discover what your enemy fears most by observing the means he uses to frighten you.

4606
Fear comes from uncertainty. When we are absolutely certain, whether of our worth or worthlessness, we are almost impervious to fear. Thus a feeling of utter unworthiness can be a source of courage.

4607
Passionate hatred can give meaning and purpose to an empty life.

4608
It is always safe to assume that people are more subtle and less sensitive than they seem.

4609
There can be no real freedom without the freedom to fail.

4610
There is a radicalism in all getting, and a conservatism in all keeping. Lovemaking is radical, while marriage is conservative.

4611
When people are free to do as they please, they usually imitate each other.
Originality is deliberate and forced, and partakes of the nature of a protest.

4612
It is the malady of our age that the young are so busy teaching us that they have no time left to learn.

4613
People in a hurry cannot think, cannot grow, nor can they decay. They are

preserved in a state of perpetual puerility.

4614
Rudeness is the weak man's imitation of strength.

4615
The poor on the borderline of starvation live purposeful lives. To be engaged in a desperate struggle for food and shelter is to be wholly free from a sense of futility.

4616
Power corrupts the few, while weakness corrupts the many.

4617
Our credulity is greatest concerning the things we know least about. And since we know least about ourselves, we are ready to believe all that is said about us. Hence the mysterious power of both flattery and calumny.

HOFFMAN August Heinrich 1798-1874
4618
Deutschland über alles
Germany above all.

HOFFMANN Heinrich 1809-1894
4619 *Struwwelpeter*
Look at little Johnny there,
Little Johnny Head-In-Air!

HOGG James 1770-1835
4620 *'O'er the Water to Charlie'*
We'll o'er the water, we'll o'er the sea,
We'll o'er the water to Charlie;
Come weel, come wo, we'll gather and go,
And live or die wi' Charlie.

HÖLDERLIN Friedrich 1770-1843
4621
I am mortal, born to love and to suffer.

HOLLAND Agnieszka
4622
In Hollywood they don't feel guilt.

HOLLAND Henry Scott 1847-1918
4623
Death is nothing at all; it does not count. I have only slipped away into the next room.

HOLLAND James
4624
The Middle East is a region where oil is thicker than blood.

HOLLAND J.G. 1819-1881
4625
There is no royal road to anything. One thing at a time, and all things in succession. That which grows slowly endures.

4626
God gives every bird its food, but he does not throw it into the nest.

HOLLWEG Theobald von Bethmann 1856-1921
4627
Just for a word 'neutrality' - a word which in wartime has so often been disregarded - just for a scrap of paper, Great Britain is going to make war on a kindred nation who desires nothing better than to be friends with her.

HOLMAN Libby
4628
I suppose you've heard all those wicked stories about me. Well, I've lived my life as it came and I've done bloody marvels with a bad hand.

HOLMES John Andrew
4629
It is well to remember that the entire population of the universe, with one trifling exception, is composed of others.

HOLMES John Hughes
4630
The universe is not hostile, nor yet is it friendly. It is simply indifferent.

HOLMES Oliver Wendell 1809-1894
4631
The young man knows the rules but the old man knows the exceptions.

4632
The axis of the earth sticks out visibly through the centre of each and every town or city.

4633
The great thing in this world is not so much where we stand, as in what direction we are moving.

4634
Nature, when she invented, manufactured and patented her authors, contrived to make critics out of the chips that were left.

4635
After sixty years the stern sentence of the burial service seems to have a meaning that one did not notice in former years. There begins to be something personal about it.

4636
He (Turgenev) had the air of his own statue erected by national subscription.

4637
Heredity is an omnibus in which all our ancestors ride, and every now and then one of them puts his head out and embarrasses us.

4638
A man is a kind of inverted thermometer, the bulb uppermost, and the column of self-valuation is all the time going up and down.

4639
Man's mind stretched to a new idea never goes back to its original dimensions.

4640
A weak mind does not accumulate force enough to hurt itself; stupidity often saves a man from going mad.

4641
Husband and wife come to look alike at last.

4642
A general flavour of mild decay,
But nothing local, as one may say.

4643
So long as the body is affected through the mind, no audacious device, even of the most manifestly dishonest character, can fail of producing occasional good to those who yield to it an implicit or even a partial faith.

4644
A man must get a thing before he can forget it.

4645
When you write in prose you say what you mean. When you write in rhyme you say what you must.

4646
Men are idolaters, and want something to look at and kiss and hug, or throw themselves down before; they always did, they always will, and if you don't make it of wood, you must make it of words.

4647
Apology is only egotism wrong side out.

4648
Apology - a desperate habit, and one that is rarely cured.

4649
Every real thought on every real subject knocks the wind out of somebody or other.

4650
Don't be consistent, but be simply true.

4651
Rough work, iconoclasm, but the only way to get at the truth.

4652
Nature is in earnest when she makes a woman.

4653
When the style is fully formed, if it has a sweet undersong, we call it beautiful, and the writer may do what he likes in words or syntax.

4654
It is the province of knowledge to speak and it is the privilege of wisdom to listen.

4655
Sweet is the scene where genial friendship plays
The pleasing game of interchanging praise.

4656 *The Autocrat of the Breakfast Table*
Man has his will - but woman has her way.

4657 *(of Samuel Francis Smith)*
Fate tried to conceal him by naming him Smith.

HOLMES Oliver Wendell Jr. 1841-1935
4658
Every calling is great when greatly pursued.

4659
The advice of the elders to young men is very apt to be as unreal as a list of the hundred best books.

4660
To be seventy years young is sometimes far more cheerful and hopeful than to be forty years old.

4661
A man over ninety is a great comfort to all his elderly neighbours: he is a picket-guard at the extreme outpost: and the young folks of sixty and seventy feel that the enemy must get by him before he can come near their camp.

4662
A person is always startled when he hears himself seriously called an old man for the first time.

4663
The trombone age (moving the page back and forth).

4664
Longevity is having a chronic disease and taking care of it.

4665
If you think that I am going to bother myself again before I die about social improvement, or read any of those stinking upward and onwarders - you err - I mean to have some good out of being old.

4666
Historic continuity with the past is not a duty, it is only a necessity.

4667
A sense of wrongdoing is an enhancement of pleasure.

4668
The life of the law has not been logic, it has been experience.

4669
Fame usually comes to those who are thinking about something else.

4670
This is a court of law, young man, not a court of justice.

4671
The reward of a general is not a bigger tent - but command.

4672
Life is action and passion; therefore, it is required of a man that he should share the passion and action of the time, at peril of being judged not to have lived.

4673
I am on the side of the unregenerate who affirm the worth of life as an end in itself, as against the saints who deny it.

4674
Life is painting a picture, not doing a sum.

4675
The mind of a bigot is like the pupil of the eye; the more light you pour upon it, the more it will contract.

HOLT John
4676
People should be free to find or make for themselves the kinds of educational experiences they want their children to have.

HOLYDAY Barten
4677
A man may as well open an oyster without a knife, as a lawyer's mouth without a fee.

HOME Lord (Sir Alec Douglas-Home) 1903-1995
4678
There are two problems in my life. The political ones are insoluble and the economic ones are incomprehensible.

HOMER fl.8th Century BC
4679
A decent boldness ever meets with friends.

4680
All strangers and beggars are from Zeus, and a gift, though small, is precious.

4681
Achilles absent, was Achilles still.

4682
A councillor ought not to sleep the whole night through - a man to whom the populace is entrusted, and who has many responsibilities.

4683
Men grow tired of sleep, love, singing and dancing sooner than of war.

4684 *The Iliad*
It lies in the lap of the gods.

HOMOLKA Oscar
4685
To really enjoy the better things in life, one must first have experienced the things they are better than.

HONEGGER Arthur 1892-1955
4686
The first requirement for a composer is to be dead.

HOOD Hugh
4687
Nothing ever tasted any better than a cold beer on a beautiful afternoon with nothing to look forward to but more of the same.

HOOD Thomas 1799-1845
4688 *Faithless Nelly Gray*
The love that loves a scarlet coat
Should be more uniform.

4689 *'Faithless Sally Brown'*
His death, which happened in his berth,
At forty-odd befell:
They went and told the sexton, and
The sexton tolled the bell.

4690 *'A Reflection'*
When Eve upon the first of Men
The apple pressed with specious cant,
Oh! what a thousand pities then
That Adam was not Adamant!

4691 *'I Remember'*
I remember, I remember,
The house where I was born,

The little window where the sun
Came peeping in at morn.

4692 *Up the Rhine*
Holland ... lies so low they're only saved by being dammed.

4693 *'The Song of the Shirt'*
O! men with sisters dear,
O! men with mothers and wives!
It is not linen you're wearing out,
But human creatures' lives!

4694 *'The Song of the Shirt'*
Oh! God! that bread should be so dear,
And flesh and blood so cheap!

HOOKER Richard c.1554-1600
4695 *Of the Laws of Ecclesiastical Polity*
He that goeth about to persuade a multitude, that they are not so well governed as they ought to be, shall never want attentive and favourable hearers.

HOOPER Ellen Sturgis 1816-1841
4696 *'Beauty and Duty'*
I slept, and dreamed that life was beauty;
I woke, and found that life was duty.

HOOVER Herbert 1874-1964
4697
Once upon a time my political opponents honored me as possessing the fabulous intellectual and economic power by which I created a worldwide depression all by myself.

HOPE Anthony 1863-1933
4698 *The Dolly Dialogues*
Economy is going without something you do want in case you should, some day, want something you probably won't want.

4699 *The Dolly Dialogues*
Bourgeois ... is an epithet which the riff-raff apply to what is respectable, and the aristocracy to what is decent.

HOPE Bob 1903-
4700
People who throw kisses are hopelessly lazy.

4701
The good news is that Jesus is coming back. The bad news is that he's really

pissed off.

4702
If you watch a game, it's fun. If you play it, it's recreation. If you work at it, it's golf.

4703 *(attributed)*
A bank is a place that will lend you money if you can prove that you don't need it.

4704
If you haven't any charity in your heart, you have the worst kind of heart trouble.

HOPKINS Anthony 1937-
4705 *in The Silence of the Lambs*
"I have to go now, Clarice, I'm having an old friend for dinner."

HOPKINS Gerard Manley 1844-1889
4706
To lift up the hands in prayer gives God glory, but a man with a dungfork in his hand, a woman with a slop-pail, give him glory too.

4707 *'Duns Scotus's Oxford'*
Towery city and branchy between towers;
Cuckoo-echoing, bell-swarmèd, lark-charmèd, rook-racked, river-rounded.

4708 *'Inversnaid'*
What would the world be, once bereft
Of wet and wildness? Let them be left,
O let them be left, wildness and wet;
Long live the weeds and the wilderness yet.

HOPKINS Harry 1890-1946
4709
Hunger is not debatable.

HOPPER Edward 1882-1967
4710
If you could say it in words there would be no reason to paint.

HORACE 65-8 BC
4711
He has half the deed done who has made a beginning.

4712
Acquittal of the guilty damns the judge.

4713
Dismiss the old horse in good time, lest he fail in the lists and the spectators laugh.

4714
The changing year's progressive plan
Proclaims mortality to man.

4715
Sport begets tumultuous strife and wrath, and wrath begets fierce quarrels and war to the death.

4716 *Ars Poetica*
It is hard to utter common notions in an individual way.

4717 *Ars Poetica*
Not gods, nor men, nor even booksellers have put up with poets being second-rate.

4718 *Epistles*
If possible honestly, if not, somehow, make money.

4719 *Epistles*
We are just statistics, born to consume resources.

4720 *Epistles*
Anger is a short madness.

4721 *Epistles*
Believe each day that has dawned is your last. Some hour to which you have not been looking forward will prove lovely.

4722 *Epistles*
And once sent out a word takes wing beyond recall.

4723 *Epistles*
No verse can give pleasure for long, nor last, that is written by drinkers of water.

4724 *Odes*
Never despair.

4725 *Odes*
Drop the question what tomorrow may bring, and count as profit every day that Fate allows you.

4726 *Odes*
When the going gets rough, remember to keep calm.

4727 *Odes*
Dulce et decorum est pro patria mori.
Sweet and honourable it is to die for one's country.

4728 *Odes*
Force, unaided by judgement, collapses through its own weight.

4729 *Odes*
Mix a little foolishness with your prudence: it's good to be silly at the right moment.

HORDER Lord Thomas 1910-
4730
It is the duty of a doctor to prolong life and it is not his duty to prolong the act of dying.

HORNER Marina
4731
What is important is to keep learning, to enjoy challenge, and to tolerate ambiguity. In the end there are no certain answers.

HORNEY Karen 1885-1952
4732
Fortunately, analysis is not the only way to resolve inner conflicts. Life itself remains a very effective therapist.

HOUSMAN A.E. 1859-1936
4733
Malt does more than Milton can
To justify God's ways to man.

4734
I, a stranger and afraid
In a world I never made.

4735
Nature, not content with denying him the ability to think, has endowed him with the ability to write.

4736 *Last Poems*
These, in the day when heaven was falling,
The hour when earth's foundations fled,
Followed their mercenary calling
And took their wages and are dead.

Their shoulders held the sky suspended;
They stood, and earth's foundations stay;
What God abandoned, these defended,
And saved the sum of things for pay.

4737 *More Poems*
Life, to be sure, is nothing much to lose;
But young men think it is, and we were young.

4738 *A Shropshire Lad*
Loveliest of trees, the cherry now
Is hung with bloom along the bough,
And stands about the woodland ride
Wearing white for Eastertide.

4739 *A Shropshire Lad*
And since to look at things in bloom
Fifty springs are little room,
About the woodlands I will go
To see the cherry hung with snow.

4740 *A Shropshire Lad*
When I was one-and-twenty
I heard a wise man say,
'Give crowns and pounds and guineas
But not your heart away;
Give pearls away and rubies,
But keep your fancy free.'
But I was one-and-twenty,
No use to talk to me.

HOWARD Elizabeth Jane 1923-
4741
Sex is like petrol. It's a galvaniser, a wonderful fuel for starting a relationship.

HOWARD Philip 1933-
4742
Most history is a record of the triumphs, disasters and follies of top people. The black hole in it is the way of life of mute, inglorious men and women who made no nuisance of themselves in the world.

HOWE Edgar Watson
4743
About all some men accomplish in life is to send a son to Harvard.

4744
A good scare is worth more to a man than good advice.

4745
A modest man is usually admired - if people ever hear of him.

4746
If you go to church, and like the singing better than the preaching, that's not

orthodox.

4747
Farmers worry only during the growing season, but town people worry all the time.

4748
If a friend is in trouble, don't annoy him by asking if there is anything you can do. Think up something appropriate and do it.

4749
What people say behind your back is your standing in the community.

4750
Even if a farmer intends to loaf, he gets up in time to get an early start.

4751
Abuse a man unjustly, and you will make friends for him.

4752
A man should be taller, older, heavier, uglier and hoarser than his wife.

4753
When people hear good music, it makes them homesick for something they never had, and never will have.

HOWE Irving
4754 *(of Thomas Hardy)*
He claimed his modest share of the general foolishness of the human race.

HOWE Joseph 1804-1873
4755
Poetry was the maiden I loved, but politics was the harridan I married.

HOWE Julia Ward 1819-1910
4756 *'Battle Hymn of the Republic'*
Mine eyes have seen the glory of the coming of the Lord:
He is trampling out the vintage where the grapes of wrath are stored;
He hath loosed the fateful lightning of his terrible swift sword:
His truth is marching on.

HOWELL James
4757
He that hath the name to be an early riser may sleep till noon.

HOWELLS William Dean 1837-1920
4758
Does it afflict you to find your books wearing out? I mean literally ... the mortality of all inanimate things is terrible to me, but that of books most of all.

4759
Some people can stay longer in an hour than others can in a week.

HOWITT Mary 1799-1888
4760 *'The Spider and the Fly'*
'Will you walk into my parlour?' said a spider to a fly:
''Tis the prettiest little parlour that ever you did spy.'

HOYLE Sir Fred 1915-
4761
Space isn't remote at all. It's only an hour's drive away if your car could go straight upwards.

HSIEH Tehyi
4762
If ignorance is indeed bliss, it is a very low grade of the article.

HUBBARD Elbert 1859-1915
4763
God will not look you over for medals, degrees or diplomas, but for scars.

4764
To escape criticism - do nothing, say nothing, be nothing.

4765
Every man is a damn fool for at least five minutes every day; wisdom consists in not exceeding the limit.

4766
Polygamy: an endeavour to get more out of life than there is in it.

4767
The man who is anybody and who does anything is surely going to be criticized, vilified, and misunderstood. This is part of the penalty for greatness, and every man understands, too, that it is no proof of greatness.

4768
A pessimist is one who has been compelled to live with an optimist.

4769
Pessimism is only the name that men of weak nerves give to wisdom.

4770
Mystic: a person who is puzzled before the obvious, but who understands the non-existent.

4771
Victory - a matter of staying power.

4772
We work to become, not to acquire.

4773 *The Motto Book*
Never explain - your friends do not need it and your enemies will not believe you anyway.

4774 *Philistine*
Life is just one damned thing after another.

4775 *The Roycroft Dictionary*
An editor - a person employed on a newspaper, whose business it is to separate the wheat from the chaff, and to see that the chaff is printed.

HUBBARD Kin 1868-1930
4776
It's pretty hard to be efficient without being obnoxious.

4777
The only way to entertain some folks is to listen to them.

4778
A friend that ain't in need is a friend indeed.

4779
Gossip is vice enjoyed vicariously - the sweet, subtle satisfaction without the risk.

4780
The fellow that owns his own home is always just coming out of a hardware store.

4781
Some folks can look so busy doing nothin' that they seem indispensable.

4782
I haven't heard of anybody who wants to stop living on account of the cost.

4783
Kindness goes a long way lots o' times when it ought t' stay at home.

4784
An optimist is a fellow who believes what's going to be will be postponed.

4785
The world gets better every day - then worse again in the evening.

4786
Some fellows pay a compliment like they expected a receipt.

4787
Folks that blurt out just what they think wouldn't be so bad if they thought.

4788
I don't know of anything better than a woman if you want to spend money where it will show.

HUBBARD L. Ron 1911-1986
4789
If you really want to make a million ... the quickest way is to start your own religion.

HUDSON William Henry 1841-1922
4790
You cannot fly like an eagle with the wings of a wren.

HUGHES Charles Evans 1862-1948
4791
We are under a Constitution, but the Constitution is what the judges say it is.

HUGHES J.B.
4792
If Moses had been a committee, the Israelites would still be in Egypt.

HUGHES Langston 1902-1967
4793 *'Children's Rhymes'*
Lies written down
For white folks
Ain't for us a-tall:
Liberty and Justice-
Huh!- *For All?*

4794 *'I,Too'*
I, too, sing America.
I am the darker brother.

HUGHES Richard 1900-1976
4795
All that non-fiction can do is answer
questions. It's fiction's business to ask
them.

HUGHES Rupert
4796
Her face was her chaperone.

HUGHES Thomas 1822-1896
4797 *Tom Brown's Schooldays*
It's more than a game. It's an institution.

HUGO Victor 1802-1885
4798
Forty is the old age of youth; fifty is the
youth of old age.

4799
If you would civilize a man, begin with his
grandmother.

4800
There are fathers who do not love their
children; there is no grandfather who does
not adore his grandson.

4801
No army can withstand the strength of an
idea whose time has come.

4802
The supreme happiness of life is the
conviction that we are loved.

4803
Sorrow is a fruit; God does not allow it to
grow on a branch that is too weak to bear
it.

4804
Everything bows to success, even
grammar.

4805
Those who live are those who fight.

4806
A stand can be made against invasion by
an army; no stand can be made against
invasion by an idea.

HULBERT Harold S.
4807
Children need love, especially when they
do not deserve it.

HULBERT James
4808
A company is judged by the president it
keeps.

HULL Josephine
4809
Playing Shakespeare is very tiring. You
never get to sit down, unless you're a king.

HUME Cardinal Basil 1923-
4810
Just as we are not in the numbers game, so
we are not in the power game.

4811 *(on homophobia and Catholicsm)*
To love one another, whether of the same
sex or of a different sex, is to have entered
the area of richest human experience.

HUME David 1711-1776
4812
Be a philosopher but, amid all your
philosophy be still a man.

4813 *Essays, Moral, Political, and Literary*
In all ages of the world, priests have been
enemies of liberty.

4814 *Essays, Moral, Political, and Literary*
The heart of man is made to reconcile the
most glaring contradictions.

4815 *A Treatise upon Human Nature*
Poets ... though liars by profession, always
endeavour to give an air of truth to their
fictions.

HUME John 1937-
4816
Every party in Ireland was founded on the
gun.

HUMPHREY Hubert 1911-1978
4817
The impersonal hand of government can
never replace the helping hand of a
neighbour.

4818
The right to be heard does not
automatically include the right to be taken

seriously.

4819
I've never thought my speeches were too long; I've rather enjoyed them.

HUNGERFORD Margaret Wolfe 1855-1897
4820 *Molly Bawn*
Beauty is altogether in the eye of the beholder.

HUNT Leigh 1784-1859
4821
If you are ever at a loss to support a flagging   conversation, introduce the subject of eating.

4822 *The Examiner 1808*
Never lay yourself open to what is called conviction: you might as well open your waist-coat to receive a knock-down blow.

4823 *Song of Fairies Robbing an Orchard*
Stolen kisses are always sweeter,
Stolen kisses much completer,
Stolen looks are nice in chapels,
Stolen, stolen, be your apples.

4824 *'The Story of Rimini' (1816)*
The two divinest things this world has got,
A lovely woman in a rural spot!

HUNTINGTON Collis P. 1821-1900
4825
Whatever is not nailed down is mine. Whatever I can pry loose is not nailed down.

HUPFELD Herman 1894-1951
4826 *'As Time Goes By'*
You must remember this, a kiss is still a kiss,
A sigh is just a sigh;
The fundamental things apply,
As time goes by.

HURD Douglas 1930-
4827
Summits are odd creatures.

4828
No substitute has been found for the energy which wells up through the nation state.

4829
Reality is always ahead of theory.

4830 *(to cheers)*
This is the last speech, on the last debate on the Maastricht treaty.

4831 *(in Gaza)*
A military occupation is a denial of human rights.

HUROK Sol 1888-1974
4832
When people don't want to come, nothing will stop them.

HUSSEIN 3addam 1937-
4833
The mother of battles.

HUTCHENS John K.
4834
A writer and nothing else: a man alone in a room with the English language, trying to get human feelings right.

HUTCHINSON Bruce
4835
Our sons, who so easily recognize our errors, and rightly denounce them, will have to confess their own, later on, and they may be as bad as ours, perhaps worse.

HUTCHINSON Sir Robert
4836
Vegetarianism is harmless enough, though it is apt to fill a man with wind and self-righteousness.

HUXLEY Aldous 1894-1963
4837
The advertisement is one of the most interesting and difficult of modern literary forms.

4838
An old codger, rampant, and still learning.

4839
To his dog, every man is Napoleon; hence the constant popularity of dogs.

4840
Children are remarkable for their intelligence and ardour, for their curiosity, their intolerance of shams, the clarity and

ruthlessness of their vision.

4841
A belief in hell and the knowledge that every ambition is doomed to frustration at the hands of a skeleton have never prevented the majority of human beings from behaving as though death were no more than an unfounded rumour, and survival a thing not beyond the bounds of possibility.

4842
Speed provides the one genuinely modern pleasure.

4843
Experience is not what happens to a man. It is what a man does with what happens to him.

4844
Experience teaches only the teachable.

4845
Every ceiling, when reached, becomes a floor, upon which one walks as a matter of course and prescriptive right.

4846
Nonsense is an assertion of man's spiritual freedom in spite of all the oppressions of circumstance.

4847
The natural rhythm of human life is routine punctuated by orgies.

4848
At any given moment, life is completely senseless. But viewed over a period, it seems to reveal itself as an organism existing in time, having a purpose, tending in a certain direction.

4849
The essay is a literary device for saying almost everything about almost anything.

4850
What we think and feel and are is to a great extent determined by the state of our ductless glands and our viscera.

4851
After silence, that which comes nearest to expressing the inexpressible is music.

4852
One of the great attractions of patriotism - it fulfills our worst wishes. In the person of our nation we are able, vicariously, to bully and cheat. Bully and cheat, what's more, with a feeling that we are profoundly virtuous.

4853
Every gain made by individuals or society is almost instantly taken for granted.

4854
There's only one corner of the universe you can be certain of improving and that's your own self.

4855
The greatest triumphs of propaganda have been accomplished, not by doing something, but by refraining from doing. Great is truth, but still greater, from a practical point of view, is silence about truth.

4856
That we are not much sicker and much madder than we are is due exclusively to that most blessed and blessing of all natural graces, sleep.

4857
There is no substitute for talent. Industry and all the virtues are of no avail.

4858
The traveller's eye view of men and women is not satisfying. A man might spend his life in trains and restaurants and know nothing of humanity at the end. To know, one must be an actor as well as a spectator.

4859
Why should human females become sterile in their forties, while female crocodiles continue to lay eggs into their third century?

4860
They intoxicate themselves with work so they won't see how they really are.

4861
Writers write to influence their readers, their preachers, their auditors, but always,

at bottom, to be more themselves.

4862 *Antic Hay*
There are few who would not rather be
taken in adultery than in provincialism.

4863 *Beyond the Mexique Bay*
Official dignity tends to increase in inverse
ratio to the importance of the country in
which the office is held.

4864 *Chrome Yellow*
The proper study of mankind is books.

4865 *Do What you Will*
Too much consistency is as bad for the
mind as it is for the body. Consistency is
contrary to nature, contrary to life. The
only completely consistent people are the
dead.

4866 *Eyeless in Gaza*
Chastity - the most unnatural of all the
sexual perversions.

4867 *Heaven and Hell*
'Bed,' as the Italian proverb succinctly puts
it, 'is the poor man's opera.'

4868 *Limbo*
I can sympathize with people's pains, but
not with their pleasures. There is
something curiously boring about
somebody else's happiness.

4869 *Ends and Means*
The end cannot justify the means, for the
simple and obvious reason that the means
employed determine the nature of the ends
produced.

4870 *'Fifth Philosopher's Song'*
A million million Spermatozoa,
All of them alive:
Out of their cataclysm but one poor Noah
Dare hope to survive.
And among that billion minus one
Might have chanced to be
Shakespeare, another Newton, a new
Donne -
But the One was me.

4871 *'Ninth Philosopher's Song'*
Beauty for some provides escape,
Who gain a happiness in eyeing
The gorgeous buttocks of the ape

Or Autumn sunsets exquisitely dying.

4872 *Point Counter Point*
Several excuses are always less convincing
than one.

HUXLEY Sir Julian 1887-1975
4873 *Religion without Revelation*
Operationally, God is beginning to
resemble not a ruler but the last fading
smile of a cosmic Cheshire cat.

HUXLEY Thomas 1825-1895
4874
The great end of life is not knowledge, but
action.

4875
Perhaps the most valuable result of all
education is the ability to make yourself
do the thing you have to do, when it ought
to be done, whether you like it or not; it is
the first lesson that ought to be learned,
and however early a man's training begins,
it is probably the last lesson that he learns
thoroughly.

4876
Sit down before fact as a little child, be
prepared to give up every preconceived
notion, follow humbly wherever and to
whatever abyss nature leads, or you shall
learn nothing.

4877
Every great advance in natural knowledge
has involved the absolute rejection of
authority.

4878
If some great power would agree to make
me always think what is true and do what
is right, on condition of being some sort of
clock and wound up every morning before
I got out of bed, I should close instantly
with the offer.

4879
The great tragedy of Science: the slaying of
a beautiful hypothesis by an ugly fact.

4880
Tolerably early in life I discovered that one
of the unpardonable sins, in the eyes of
most people, is for a man to go about
unlabelled. The world regards such a

person as the police do an unmuzzled dog.

4881
I am too much of a sceptic to deny the possibility of anything.

4882 *Collected Essays*
If a little knowledge is dangerous, where is the man who has so much as to be out of danger?

4883 *Science and Culture and Other Essays*
Irrationally held truths may be more harmful than reasoned errors.

HUXTABLE Ada Louise
4884
Washington is an endless series of mock palaces clearly built for clerks.

IBARRURI Dolores ('La Pasionaria')
1895-1989
4885
It is better to die on your feet than to live on your knees.

IBSEN Henrik 1828-1906
4886
One should never put on one's best trousers to go out to battle for freedom and truth.

4887
A minority may be right, and a majority is always wrong.

4888
The sea possesses a power over one's moods that has the effect of a will. The sea can hypnotize. Nature in general can do so.

ILES Francis 1893-1970
4889 *Malice Aforethought*
Murder is a serious business.

INGALLS Brian
4890
Grass is the forgiveness of nature - her constant benediction. Forests decay, harvests perish, flowers vanish, but grass is immortal.

INGE Charles 1868-1957
4891 *'On Monsieur Coué'*
This very remarkable man
Commends a most practical plan:

You can do what you want
If you don't think you can't,
So don't think you can't think you can.

INGE William R. 1860-1954
4892
Anxiety is the interest paid on trouble before it is due.

4893
What is originality? Undetected plagiarism.

4894
Public opinion: a vulgar, impertinent, anonymous tyrant who deliberately makes life unpleasant for any one of us who is not content to be the average man.

4895
There are two kinds of fools: one says, 'This is old, therefore it is good'; the other says, 'This is new, therefore it is better.'

4896
Let none of us delude himself by supposing that honesty is always the best policy. It is not.

4897
Literature flourishes best when it is half a trade and half an art.

4898
The whole of nature is a conjugation of the verb to eat, in the active and passive.

4899
Religion is a way of walking, not a way of talking.

4900
Of all tyrannies a country can suffer, the worst is the tyranny of the majority.

4901
Middle-aged people are often happier than the young: but it by no means follows that they ought to be...

4902
Because most of the saints were poor, it does not follow that most of the poor are saints.

4903
Christianity is good news; not good
advice.

4904
A man usually does his best work just
before he is found out.

4905 *End of an Age*
The enemies of Freedom do not argue;
they shout and they shoot.

4906 *End of an Age*
The effect of boredom on a large scale in
history is underestimated. It is a main
cause of revolutions, and would soon
bring to an end all the static Utopias and
the farmyard civilization of the Fabians.

4907 *Idea of Progress*
To become a popular religion, it is only
necessary for a superstition to enslave a
philosophy.

4908 *Outspoken Essays*
It takes in reality only one to make a
quarrel. It is useless for the sheep to pass
resolutions in favour of vegetarianism,
while the wolf remains of a different
opinion.

4909 *Outspoken Essays*
The nations which have put mankind and
posterity most in their debt have been
small states - Israel, Athens, Florence,
Elizabethan England.

INGELOW Jean 1820-1897
4910
I have lived to thank God that all my
prayers have not been answered.

INGERSOLL Robert G. 1833-1899
4911
In the republic of mediocrity, genius is
dangerous.

4912
An honest God is the noblest work of man.

4913
My creed is that:
Happiness is the only good.
The place to be happy is here.
The time to be happy is now.
The way to be happy is to make others so.

4914
I suppose it can be truthfully said that
hope is the only universal liar who never
loses his reputation for veracity.

4915
By physical liberty I mean the right to do
anything which does not interfere with the
happiness of another. By intellectual
liberty I mean the right to think wrong.

4916
With soap baptism is a good thing.

4917 *Some Reasons Why*
In nature there are neither rewards nor
punishments - there are consequences.

IONESCO Eugene 1912-1994
4918
Theatre is simply what cannot be
expressed by any other means; a
complexity of words, movements, gestures
that convey a vision of the world
inexpressible in any other way.

4919
You can only predict things after they've
happened.

IRVING John
4920
The object of war is to survive it.

IRVING Washington 1783-1859
4921
I am always at a loss to know how much
to believe of my own stories.

4922 *The Sketch Book*
A tart temper never mellows with age, and
a sharp tongue is the only edged tool that
grows keener with constant use.

ISHERWOOD Christopher 1904-1986
4923 *'The Common Cormorant'*
The common cormorant (or shag)
Lays eggs inside a paper bag,
You follow the idea, no doubt?
It's to keep the lightning out.
But what these unobservant birds
Have never thought of, is that herds
Of wandering bears might come with buns
And steal the bags to hold the crumbs.

ITAMINI Juzo
4924
If you imagine life as a book, the last page should be the best, not the blackest.

JACKSON Andrew 1767-1845
4925
Take time to deliberate; but when the time for action arrives, stop thinking and go in.

4926
One man with courage makes a majority.

4927
There goes a man made by the Lord Almighty and not by his tailor.

JACKSON George
4928
Patience has its limits. Take it too far, and it's cowardice.

4929
Only one-fourth of the sorrow in each man's life is caused by outside uncontrollable elements, the rest is self-imposed by failing to analyze and act with calmness.

JACKSON Holbrook 1874-1948
4930 *Platitudes in the Making*
As soon as an idea is accepted it is time to reject it.

JACKSON Jesse 1941-
4931
The Bible is nothing but a succession of civil rights struggles by the Jewish people against the oppressors.

4932
Your children need your presence more than your presents.

JACKSON Robert H. 1892-1954
4933
Men are more often bribed by their loyalties and ambitions than by money.

JACKSON Thomas (Stonewall) 1824-1863
4934
I like liquor - its taste and its effects - and that is just the reason why I never drink it.

JACOB Fred
4935
A good husband should always bore his wife.

JACOBS Jane
4936
In small settlements everyone knows your affairs. In the big city, everyone does not - only those you choose to tell will know about you. This is one of the attributes of cities that is precious to most city people.

JAFFREY Saeed
4937 *in My Beautiful Launderette*
"Take my advice, there's money in muck."

JAMES Baroness 1920-
4938 *(of English teaching)*
We cannot aspire to a classless society ... if some children are disadvantaged the moment they open their mouths.

JAMES Cyril 1901-1989
4939
A free man is as jealous of his responsibilities as he is of his liberties.

JAMES Edmund Storer
4940
The interests of childhood and youth are the interests of mankind.

JAMES Henry 1843-1916
4941
Deep experience is never peaceful.

4942
The real offence, as she ultimately perceived, was her having a mind of her own at all. Her mind was to be his - attached to his own like a small garden plot to a deer park.

4943 *'The Given Case'*
Women never dine alone. When they dine alone they don't dine.

4944 *Hawthorne*
It takes a great deal of history to produce a little literature.

4945 *Hawthorne*
He was imperfect, unfinished, inartistic; he was worse than provincial - he was parochial.

JAMES I King (JAMES VI of Scotland)
1566-1625
4946 *A Counterblast to Tobacco*
A branch of the sin of drunkenness, which is the root of all sins.

4947 *A Counterblast to Tobacco*
A custom loathsome to the eye, hateful to the nose, harmful to the brain, dangerous to the lungs, and in the black, stinking fume thereof, nearest resembling the horrible Stygian smoke of the pit that is bottomless.

4948 *(recorded by Archdeacon Plume)*
Dr Donne's verses are like the peace of God; they pass all understanding.

JAMES William 1842-1910
4949
Be willing to have it so; acceptance of what has happened is the first step to overcoming the consequences of any misfortune.

4950
Genius, in truth, means little more than the faculty of perceiving in an unhabitual way.

4951
As Charles Lamb says, there is nothing so nice as doing good by stealth and being found out by accident, so I now say it is even nicer to make heroic decisions and to be prevented by 'circumstances beyond your control' from ever trying to execute them.

4952
An unlearned carpenter of my acquaintance once said in my hearing: 'There is very little difference between one man and another, but what there is is *very important.*'

4953
The great use of life is to spend it for something that will outlast it.

4954
Lives based on having are less free than lives based either on doing or on being.

4955
So far war has been the only force that can discipline a whole community, and until an equivalent discipline is organized, I believe that war must have its way.

4956
The art of being wise is the art of knowing what to overlook.

4957
Footnotes, the little dogs yapping at the heels of the text.

4958
Man, biologically considered, and whatever else he may be into the bargain, is simply the most formidable of all the beasts of prey, and, indeed, the only one that preys systematically on its own species.

4959 *The Principles of Psychology*
The art of being wise is the art of knowing what to overlook.

4960 *The Varieties of Religious Experience*
There is no worse lie than a truth misunderstood by those who hear it.

JARRELL Randall 1914-1965
4961
More and more people think of the critic as an indispensable middle man between writer and reader, and would no more read a book alone, if they could help it, than have a baby alone.

4962
The dark, uneasy world of family life - where the greatest can fail and the humblest succeed.

4963
Ezra Pound - idiosyncrasy on a monument.

4964
The novel is a prose narrative of some length that has something wrong with it.

4965
A good poet is someone who manages, in a lifetime of standing out in thunderstorms, to be struck by lightning five or six times.

4966 *Pictures from an Institution*
To Americans, English manners are far more frightening than none at all.

JAY Douglas 1907-
4967 *(slogan for North Battersea by-election)*
Fair shares for all, is Labour's call.

JEANS Sir James 1877-1946
4968 *The Mysterious Universe*
Life exists in the universe only because the carbon atom possesses certain exceptional properties.

JEANS Ronald d.1973
4969
Actor-manager - one to whom the part is greater than the whole.

JEFFERIES Richard
4970
When I look in the glass I see that every line in my face means pessimism, but in spite of my face - that is my experience - I remain an optimist.

JEFFERSON Thomas 1743-1826
4971
No government ought to be without censors; and where the press is free, no one ever will.

4972
The mobs of great cities add just so much to the support of pure government as sores do to the strength of the human body.

4973
Every man wishes to pursue his occupation and to enjoy the fruits of his labours and the produce of his property in peace and safety, and with the least possible expense. When these things are accomplished, all the objects for which government ought to be established are answered.

4974
That government is best which governs the least, because its people discipline themselves.

4975
Whenever a man has cast a longing eye on office, a rottenness begins in his conduct.

4976
I hold it, that a little rebellion now and then is a good thing, and as necessary in the political world as storms in the physical.

4977
Walking is the best possible exercise. Habituate yourself to walk very far.

4978
Taste cannot be controlled by law.

4979
The man who fears no truths has nothing to fear from lies.

4980 *American Declaration of Independence*
We hold these truths to be sacred and undeniable; that all men are created equal and independent, that from that equal creation they derive rights inherent and inalienable, among which are the preservation of life, and liberty, and the pursuit of happiness.

JEFFREY Peter
4981 *If...*
"Education in Britain is a nubile Cinderella, sparsely clad and often interfered with."

JENKINS Dr David (Bishop of Durham) 1925-
4982
There is no doubting my belief in God, but the Church has driven me close to it.

4983
God is the surprise of the universe, not its answer.

JENKS Earlene Larson
4984
Have the courage to act instead of react.

JEROME Jerome K. 1859-1927
4985
Idleness, like kisses, to be sweet must be stolen.

4986
It is easy enough to say that poverty is no crime. No, if it were men wouldn't be ashamed of it. It's a blunder, though, and is punished as such.

4987 *They and I*
I want a house that has got over all its troubles; I don't want to spend the rest of my life bringing up a young and

inexperienced house.

4988 *Idle Thoughts of an Idle Fellow*
It is impossible to enjoy idling thoroughly unless one has plenty of work to do.

4989 *Idle Thoughts of an Idle Fellow*
Love is like the measles; we all have to go through it.

JEROME St. c.340-420
4990
You censure this with difficulty because you have allowed it to become customary.

JERROLD Douglas 1803-1857
4991
A Conservative is a man who will not look at the new moon, out of respect for that ancient institution, the old one.

4992
The ugliest of trades have their moments of pleasure. Now, if I was a grave digger, or even a hangman, there are some people I could work for with a great deal of enjoyment.

4993
Love the sea? I dote upon it - from the beach.

4994
Australia is so kind that, just tickle her with a hoe, and she laughs with a harvest.

4995 *The Life and Remains of Douglas Jerrold*
If an earthquake were to engulf England to-morrow, the English would manage to meet and dine somewhere among the rubbish, just to celebrate the event.

4996 *The Wit and Opinions of Douglas Jerrold*
The best thing I know between France and England is - the sea.

4997 *The Wit and Opinions of Douglas Jerrold*
Love's like the measles - all the worse when it comes late in life.

JIPCHO Ben
4998
Running for money doesn't make you run fast. It makes you run first.

JOACHIM Lord 1831-1907
4999
I have the courage of my opinions, but I have not the temerity to give a political blank cheque to Lord Salisbury.

JOAD C.E.M. 1891-1953
5000
My life is spent in a perpetual alternation between two rhythms, the rhythm of attracting people for fear I may be lonely, and the rhythm of trying to get rid of them because I know that I am bored.

JOBS Steve 1955-
5001 *(of attempts to get interest in the Apple PC)*
We went to Atari and said "We've got this amazing thing..." They said "No". Then we went to Hewlett-Packard; they said, "We don't need you. You haven't got through college yet."

JOHN PAUL II Pope 1920-
5002
In contrast with its original vocation of peace, the family is sadly seen to be the scene of tension and oppression.

5003
To be perfect as a woman does not mean to be like a man.

5004
Religion and peace go together, to wage war in the name of religion is a contradiction.

JOHN XXIII Pope 1881-1963
5005
See everything: overlook a great deal: correct a little.

5006
Italians come to ruin most generally in three ways - women, gambling and farming. My family chose the slowest one.

JOHNSON Gerald
5007
Heroes are created by popular demand, sometimes out of the scantiest materials ... such as the apple that William Tell never shot, the ride that Paul Revere never finished, the flag that Barbara Frietchie never waved.

JOHNSON Lionel 1867-1902
5008 *'The Precept of Silence'*
I know you: solitary griefs,
Desolate passions, aching hours.

JOHNSON Lyndon B. 1908-1973
5009
Doing what's right isn't the problem. It's knowing what's right.

5010
There is but one way for a president to deal with the Congress, and that is continuously, incessantly, and without interruption. If it's really going to work, the relationship between the president and the Congress has got to be almost incestuous.

5011
Only two things are necessary to keep one's wife happy. One is to let her think she is having her own way, and the other, to let her have it.

5012
While you're saving your face you're losing your ass. Never trust a man whose eyes are too close to his nose. I never trust a man unless I've got his pecker in my pocket. Better inside the tent pissing out than outside the tent pissing in.

5013
I am a free man, an American, a United States Senator, and a Democrat, in that order.

5014
We hope that the world will not narrow into a neighbourhood before it has broadened into a brotherhood.

5015
We are not about to send American boys 9 or 10,000 miles away from home to do what Asian boys ought to be doing for themselves.

5016
I don't want loyalty. I want *loyalty*. I want him to kiss my ass in Macy's window at high noon and tell me it smells like roses.

5017 *(of Gerald Ford)*
So dumb he can't fart and chew gum at the same time.

JOHNSON Paul 1928-
5018
Tories, in short, are atrophied Englishmen, lacking certain moral and intellectual reflexes. They are recognizable, homely - even, on occasions, endearing - but liable to turn very nasty at short notice.

JOHNSON Samuel 1709-1784
5019
(Adversity is) the state in which a man most easily becomes acquainted with himself, being especially free from admirers then.

5020
Promise, large promise, is the soul of an advertisement.

5021
Dictionaries are like watches. The worst is better than none at all and even the best cannot be expected to run quite true.

5022
No member of a society has a right to teach any doctrine contrary to what society holds to be true.

5023
Shame arises from the fear of man; conscience from the fear of God.

5024
That is the happiest conversation where there is no competition, no vanity, but a calm quiet interchange of sentiments.

5025
John Wesley's conversation is good, but he is never at leisure. He is always obliged to go at a certain hour. This is very disagreeable to a man who loves to fold his legs and have his talk out as I do.

5026
Every man who attacks my belief diminishes in some degree my confidence in it, and therefore makes me uneasy, and I am angry with him who makes me uneasy.

5027
Courage is a quality so necessary for maintaining virtue that it is always respected, even when it is associated with vice.

5028
The chains of habit are too weak to be felt until they are too strong to be broken.

5029
When a man knows he is to be hanged in a fortnight, it concentrates his mind wonderfully.

5030
Moderation is commonly firm, and firmness is commonly successful.

5031
Abstinence is as easy for me as temperance would be difficult.

5032
One of the disadvantages of wine is that it makes a man mistake words for thoughts.

5033
A man is in general better pleased when he has a good dinner upon his table, than when his wife talks Greek.

5034
None but a fool worries about things he cannot influence.

5035
The true genius is a mind of large general powers, accidentaly determined to some particular direction.

5036
I have found men more kind than I expected, and less just.

5037
Is not a patron one who looks with unconcern on a man struggling for life in the water, and, when he has reached ground, encumbers him with help?

5038
A man should be careful never to tell tales of himself to his own disadvantage. People may be amused at the time, but they will be remembered, and brought out against him upon some subsequent occasion.

5039
Hope is itself a species of happiness, and, perhaps, the chief happiness which this world affords.

5040
No man is a hypocrite in his pleasures.

5041
Almost all absurdity of conduct arises from the imitation of those whom we cannot resemble.

5042
A fly, Sir, may sting a stately horse and make him wince; but one is but an insect, and the other a horse still.

5043
Knowledge is of two kinds; we know a subject ourselves, or we know where we can find information upon it.

5044
A man must carry knowledge with him, if he would bring home knowledge.

5045
Man is not weak - knowledge is more than equivalent to force. The master of mechanics laughs at strength.

5046
It is the just doom of laziness and a gluttony to be inactive without ease, and drowsy without tranquillity.

5047
I deny the lawfulness of telling a lie to a sick man for fear of alarming him; you have no business with consequences, you are to tell the truth.

5048
The joy of life is variety; the tenderest love requires to be renewed by intervals of absence.

5049
Life is a progress from want to want, not from enjoyment to enjoyment.

5050
Nothing flatters a man as much as the happiness of his wife; he is always proud

of himself as the source of it.

5051
It is unjust to claim the privileges of age and retain the playthings of childhood.

5052
The true art of memory is the art of attention.

5053
As the faculty of writing has chiefly been a masculine endowment, the reproach of making the world miserable has always been thrown upon the women.

5054
Had I learned to fiddle, I should have done nothing else.

5055
Questioning is not the mode of conversation among gentlemen.

5056
Pride is seldom delicate: it will please itself with very mean advantages.

5057
Oats: A grain which in England is generally given to horses, but in Scotland supports the people.

5058
Don't think of retiring from the world until the world will be sorry that you retire.

5059
Being in a ship is being in a jail, with the chance of being drowned.

5060
Self-confidence is the first requisite to great undertakings.

5061
I live in the crowds of jollity, not so much to enjoy company as to shun myself.

5062
Silence propagates itself, and the longer talk has been suspended, the more difficult it is to find anything to say.

5063
The poor and the busy have no leisure for sentimental sorrow.

5064
While grief is fresh, every attempt to divert it only irritates.

5065
It is better to suffer wrong than to do it, and happier to be sometimes cheated than not to trust.

5066
Among the calamities of wars may be justly numbered the diminution of the love of truth by the falsehoods which interest dictates and credulity encourages.

5067
It is better to live rich than to die rich.

5068
Men know that women are an overmatch for them, and therefore they choose the weakest or the most ignorant. If they did not think so, they never could be afraid of women knowing as much as themselves.

5069
Read over your compositions, and when you meet a passage which you think is particularly fine, strike it out.

5070
The best part of every author is in general to be found in his book, I assure you.

5071
When an author is yet living, we estimate his powers by his worst performance; and when he is dead, we rate them by his best.

5072
The man who is asked by an author what he thinks of his work is put to the torture and is not obliged to speak the truth.

5073
What is written without effort is in general read without pleasure.

5074
Your manuscript is both good and original; but the parts that are good are not original, and the parts that are original are not good.

5075
Much may be made of a Scotchman if he be caught young.

5076
Every man has, some time in his life, an ambition to be a wag.

5077
Love is the wisdom of the fool and the folly of the wise.

5078
Of music Dr Johnson used to say that it was the only sensual pleasure without vice.

5079
I dogmatise and am contradicted, and in this conflict of opinions and sentiments I find delight.

5080
Corneille is to Shakespeare ... as a clipped hedge is to a forest.

5081
If the man who turnips cries,
Cry not when his father dies,
'Tis a proof that he had rather
Have a turnip than his father.

5082
'I would advise no man to marry, who is not likely to propagate understanding.'

5083
It is very strange, and very melancholy, that the paucity of human pleasures should persuade us ever to call hunting one of them.

5084
Was there ever yet anything written by mere man that was wished longer by its readers, excepting *Don Quixote, Robinson Crusoe,* and the *Pilgrim's Progress*?

5085
Never be afraid to think yourself fit for anything for which your friends think you fit.

5086 *Boswell - Life*
A man may write at any time, if he will set himself doggedly to it.

5087 *Boswell - Life*
If a man does not make new acquaintance as he advances through life, he will soon find himself left alone. A man, Sir, should keep his friendship in constant repair.

5088 *Boswell - Life*
Norway, too, has noble wild prospects; and Lapland is remarkable for prodigious noble wild prospects. But, Sir, let me tell you, the noblest prospect which a Scotchman ever sees, is the high road that leads him to England.

5089 *Boswell - Life*
A woman's preaching is like a dog's walking on his hinder legs. It is not done well; but you are surprised to find it done at all.

5090 *Boswell - Life*
Happiness consists in the multiplicity of agreeable consciousness.

5091 *Boswell - Life*
Every man has a lurking wish to appear considerable in his native place.

5092 *Boswell - Life*
All intellectual improvement arises from leisure.

5093 *Boswell - Life*
Patriotism is the last refuge of a scoundrel.

5094 *Boswell - Life*
There is now less flogging in our great schools than formerly, but then less is learned there; so that what the boys get at one end they lose at the other.

5095 *Boswell - Life*
There is nothing which has yet been contrived by man, by which so much happiness is produced as by a good tavern or inn.

5096 *Boswell - Life*
Marriages would in general be as happy, and often more so, if they were all made by the Lord Chancellor, upon a due consideration of characters and circumstances, without the parties having any choice in the matter.

5097 *Boswell - Life*
We would all be idle if we could.

5098 *Boswell - Life*
No man but a blockhead ever wrote, except for money.

5099 *Boswell - Life*
It is better that some should be unhappy than that none should be happy, which would be the case in a general state of equality.

5100 *Boswell - Life*
A man who has not been in Italy, is always conscious of an inferiority, from his not having seen what it is expected a man should see.

5101 *Boswell - Life*
When a man is tired of London, he is tired of life; for there is in London all that life can afford.

5102 *Boswell - Life*
All argument is against it [ghosts]; but all belief is for it.

5103 *Boswell - Life*
Every man thinks meanly of himself for not having been a soldier, or not having been at sea.

5104 *Boswell - Life*
A mere antiquarian is a rugged being.

5105 *Boswell - Life*
Were it not for imagination, Sir, a man would be as happy in the arms of a chambermaid as of a Duchess.

5106 *Boswell - Life*
Claret is the liquor for boys; port, for men; but he who aspires to be a hero (smiling) must drink brandy.

5107 *Boswell - Life*
A man who exposes himself when he is intoxicated, has not the art of getting drunk.

5108 *Boswell - Life*
Every man has a right to utter what he thinks truth, and every other man has a right to knock him down for it. Martyrdom is the test.

5109 *Boswell - Life*
A Frenchman must be always talking, whether he knows anything of the matter or not; an Englishman is content to say nothing, when he has nothing to say.

5110 *Boswell - Life*
Depend upon it, said he, that if a man talks of his misfortunes there is something in them that is not disagreeable to him; for where there is nothing but pure misery, there never is any recourse to the mention of it.

5111 *Boswell - Life*
Now, Sir, there are people whom one should like very well to drop, but would not wish to be dropped by.

5112 *Boswell - Life*
This merriment of parsons is mighty offensive.

5113 *Boswell - Life*
Classical quotation is the *parole* of literary men all over the world.

5114 *Boswell - Life*
Sir, I have two very cogent reasons for not printing any list of subscribers; one, that I have lost all the names; the other, that I have spent all the money.

5115 *Boswell - Life*
Always, Sir, set a high value on spontaneous kindness. He whose inclination prompts him to cultivate your friendship of his own accord, will love you more than one whom you have been at pains to attach to you.

5116 *Boswell - Life*
A wise Tory and a wise Whig, I believe, will agree. Their principles are the same, though their modes of thinking are different.

5117 *Boswell - Life*
How few of his friends' houses would a man choose to be at when he is sick.

5118 *Boswell - Life*
If a young or middle-aged man, when leaving a company, does not recollect where he laid his hat, it is nothing; but if the same inattention is discovered in an old man, people will shrug up their shoulders, and say, 'His memory is going'.

5119 *Boswell - Life*
My dear friend, clear your *mind* of cant ... You may *talk* in this manner; it is a mode

of talking in Society: but don't *think* foolishly.

5120 *Boswell - Life*
As I know more of mankind I expect less of them, and am ready now to call a man *a good man*, upon easier terms than I was formerly.

5121 *Boswell - Life*
Sir, I have found you an argument; but I am not obliged to find you an understanding.

5122 *Boswell - Life*
Who can run the race with Death?

5123 *Boswell - Life*
Sir, I look upon every day to be lost, in which I do not make a new acquaintance.

5124 *Boswell - Life*
An odd thought stikes me: we shall receive no letters in the grave.

5125 *Boswell - Life (on biography writing)*
The dogs don't know how to write trifles with dignity.

5126 *Boswell - Life (on the death of Mr Levett)*
Officious, innocent, sincere,
Of every friendless name the friend.
Yet still he fills affection's eye,
Obscurely wise, and coarsely kind.

5127 *Boswell - Life (on the death of Mr Levett)*
Then, with no throbs of fiery pain,
No cold gradations of decay,
Death broke at once the vital chain,
And freed his soul the nearest way.

5128 *Boswell - Life (of Mr Dudley Long)*
Mr Long's character is very *short*. It is nothing. He fills a chair.

5129 *Boswell - Life (on the Giant's Causeway)*
Worth seeing, yes; but not worth going to see.

5130 *Boswell - Life (on his illness)*
I will be conquered; I will not capitulate.

5131 *Boswell - Life (of Jeremiah Markland)*
I hate a fellow whom pride, or cowardice, or laziness drives into a corner, and who does nothing when he is there but sit and *growl*; let him come out as I do, and *bark*.

5132 *Boswell - Life (letter to Boswell)*
Remember that all tricks are either knavish or childish.

5133 *Boswell - Life (letter to Boswell)*
If you are idle, be not solitary; if you are solitary, be not idle.

5134 *Boswell - Life (letter to Boswell)*
Resolve not to be poor; whatever you have, spend less. Poverty is a great enemy to human happiness; it certainly destroys liberty, and it makes some virtues impracticable, and others extremely difficult.

5135 *Boswell - Life (of a man who remarried)*
A triumph of hope over experience.

5136 *Boswell - Life (on the merits of two minor poets)*
Sir, there is no settling the point of precedency between a louse and a flea.

5137 *Boswell - Life (of Milton's sonnets)*
Milton, Madam, was a genius that could cut a Colossus from a rock; but could not carve heads upon cherry-stones.

5138 *Boswell - Life (of Oliver Goldsmith)*
No man was more foolish when he had not a pen in his hand, or more wise when he had.

5139 *Boswell - Life (of Ossian)*
A man might write such stuff for ever, if he would *abandon* his mind to it.

5140 *Boswell - Life (parodying Henry Brooke)*
It might as well be said 'Who drives fat oxen should himself be fat.'

5141 *Boswell - Life (on roast mutton served at an inn)*
It is as bad as bad can be; it is ill-fed, ill-killed, ill-kept, and ill-drest.

5142 *Boswell - Life (of Thomas Gray's Odes)*
They are forced plants, raised in a hot-bed; and they are poor plants; they are but cucumbers after all.

5143 *Diary and Letters of Madame D'Arblay*
Before you flatter a man so grossly to his face, you should consider whether or not your flattery is worth his having.

5144 *A Dictionary of the English Language*
Every quotation contributes something to
the stability or enlargement of the
language.

5145 *A Dictionary of the English Language*
Dull. To make dictionaries is dull work.

5146 *A Dictionary of the English Language*
Lexicographer. A writer of dictionaries, a
harmless drudge.

5147 *A Dictionary of the English Language*
Network. Anything reticulated or
decussated at equal distances, with
interstices between the intersections.

5148 *A Free Enquiry*
The only end of writing is to enable the
readers better to enjoy life, or better to
endure it.

5149 *The Idler*
When two Englishmen meet, their first talk
is of the weather.

5150 *The Idler*
Nothing is more hopeless than a scheme of
merriment.

5151 *(attributed, in Instructions to Young*
Sportsmen)
Fly fishing may be a very pleasant
amusement; but angling or float fishing I
can only compare to a stick and a string,
with a worm at one end and a fool at the
other.

5152 *Lives of the English Poets*
A man, doubtful of his dinner, or
trembling at a creditor, is not much
disposed to abstracted meditation, or
remote enquiries.

5153 *London*
Of all the griefs that harrass the distressed,
Sure the most bitter is a scornful jest;
Fate never wounds more deep the
gen'rous heart,
Than when a blockhead's insult points the
dart.

5154 *The Rambler*
No place affords a more striking conviction
of the vanity of human hopes, than a
public library.

5155 *Rasselas*
Human life is everywhere a state in which
much is to be endured, and little to be
enjoyed.

5156 *Rasselas*
Marriage has many pains, but celibacy has
no pleasures.

5157 *(shortly before he died)*
Iam moriturus.
I who am about to die.

JOHNSON Vera
5158
There's such a thing as moderation, even
in telling the truth.

JOHNSTON Eric
5159
The dinosaur's eloquent lesson is that if
some bigness is good, an overabundance
of bigness is not necessarily better.

JOHNSTON Jennifer 1930-
5160
We are constantly at risk from the people
we love most. They are, after all, the only
people who can do us serious damage.

5161
People who haven't created a present for
themselves, as the Irish haven't, cannot
create a future, so the past assumes a great
importance.

5162
Perhaps I take the state of innocence very
seriously because it is a state of magic.
The loss of that state is what turns us into
adults.

JOLSON Al 1886-1950
5163 *in The Jazz Singer (first words spoken on*
screen)
"Wait a minute, wait a minute. You ain't
heard nuttin' yet."

JONES Clinton 1848-1936
5164
I never been in no situation where havin'
money made it any worse.

JONES Franklin P.
5165
Bargain: something you can't use at a price you can't resist.

5166
An extravagance is anything you buy that is of no earthly use to your wife.

5167
Experience enables you to recognize a mistake when you make it again.

5168
Most people like hard work, particularly when they're paying for it.

JONES Henry Arthur and HERMAN Henry 1851-1929 and 1832-1894
5169 *The Silver King*
O God! Put back Thy universe and give me yesterday.

JONES Le Roi
5170
The landscape should belong to the people who see it all the time.

JONES Paul 1747-1792
5171 *(as his ship was sinking)*
I have not yet begun to fight.

JONES Spike
5172
When the audience knows you know better, it's satire, but when they think you can't do any better, it's corn.

JONES Sir William 1746-1794
5173
Power should always be distrusted, in whatever hands it is placed.

5174 *(lines substituted in 'Six hours in sleep')*
Seven hours to law, to soothing slumber seven,
Ten to the world allot, and *all* to Heaven.

JONG Erica 1942-
5175
Everyone has a talent. What is rare is the courage to follow the talent to the dark places where it leads.

5176 *Fear of Flying*
The zipless fuck is absolutely pure. It is free of ulterior motives. There is no power

game. The man is not 'taking' and the woman is not 'giving' ... The zipless fuck is the purest thing there is. And it is rarer than the unicorn.

5177 *Fear of Flying*
Bigamy is having one husband too many. Monogamy is the same.

5178 *Fear of Flying*
Jealousy is all the fun you think they had.

JONSON Ben c.1573-1637
5179
Underneath this stone doth lie
As much beauty as could die.

5180
Memory, of all the powers of the mind, is the most delicate and frail.

5181
All men are Philosophers, to their inches.

5182
Donne, for not keeping of accent, deserved hanging ... Shakespeare wanted art.

5183 *The Alchemist*
Fortune, that favours fools.

5184 *The Alchemist*
The children of perdition are oft-times Made instruments even of the greatest works.

5185 *The Alchemist*
If I have outstripped
An old man's gravity, or stict canon, think What a young wife and a good brain may do:
Stretch age's truth sometimes, and crack it too.

5186 *Bartholomew Fair*
The lungs of the tobacconist are rotted, the liver spotted, the brain smoked like the backside of the pig-woman's booth here, and the whole body within, black as her pan you saw e'en now without.

5187 *Bartholomew Fair*
Neither do thou lust after that tawney weed tobacco.

5188 *Bartholomew Fair (of Ursula, the pig woman)*
The very womb and bed of enormity.

5189 *Catiline his Conspiracy*
PEOPLE: The Voice of Cato is the voice of Rome.
CATO: The voice of Rome is the consent of heaven!

5190 *Catiline his Conspiracy*
Where it concerns himself,
Who's angry at a slander makes it true.

5191 *'A Celebration of Charis'*
And it is not always face,
Clothes, or fortune gives the grace,
Or the feature, or the youth;
But the language, and the truth,
With the ardour and the passion,
Gives the lover weight and fashion.

5192 *'To Celia'*
Drink to me only with thine eyes
And I will pledge with mine;
Or leave a kiss but in the cup,
And I'll not look for wine.

5193 *Cynthia's Revels*
Slow, slow, fresh fount, keep time with my salt tears:
Yet, slower, yet; O faintly, gentle springs.

5194 *Cynthia's Revels*
Queen and huntress, chaste and fair,
Now the sun is laid to sleep,
Seated in thy silver chair,
State in wonted manner keep:
Hesperus entreats thy light,
Goddess, excellently bright.

5195 *The Entertainment at Althrope*
This is Mab, the Mistress-Fairy
That doth nightly rob the dairy.

5196 *Epicene*
Give me a look, give me a face,
That makes simplicity a grace;
Robes loosely flowing, hair as free:
Such sweet neglect more taketh me,
Than all the adulteries of art;
They strike mine eyes, but not my heart.

5197 *'Eupheme'*
The voice so sweet, the words so fair,
As some soft chime had stroked the air;

And though the sound were parted thence,
Still left an echo in the sense.

5198 *'To ... Sir Lucius Carey and Sir H. Morison'*
In small proportions we just beauty see,
And in short measures life may perfect be.

5199 *Every Man in His Humour*
I do honour the very flea of his dog.

5200 *Every Man out of His Humour*
My strict hand
Was made to seize on vice, and with a gripe
Squeeze out the humour of such spongy souls,
As lick up every idle vanity.

5201 *Every Man out of His Humour*
Blind Fortune still
Bestows her gifts on such as cannot use them.

5202 *'To the Memory of...William Shakespeare'*
He was not of an age, but for all time!

5203 *'To the Memory of... William Shakespeare'*
Thou hadst small Latin, and less Greek.

5204 *'To Penshurst'*
The blushing apricot and woolly peach
Hang on thy walls, that every child may reach.

5205 *The Poetaster*
Ramp up my genius, be not retrograde;
But boldly nominate a spade a spade.

5206 *The Poetaster*
Detraction is but baseness' varlet;
And apes are apes, though clothed in scarlet.

5207 *'On the Portrait of Shakespeare'*
Reader, look
Not on his picture, but his book.

5208 *Sejanus*
Tell proud Jove,
Between his power and thine there is no odds:
'Twas only fear first in the world made gods.

5209 *Timber, or Discoveries made upon Men and Matter*
The players have often mentioned it as an honour to Shakespeare that in his writing, whatsoever he penned, he never blotted out a line. My answer hath been 'Would he had blotted a thousand'.

5210 *Timber, or Discoveries made upon Men and Matter*
The fear of every man that heard him was, lest he should make an end.

5211 *Timber, or Discoveries made upon Men and Matter*
Talking and eloquence are not the same: to speak, and to speak well, are two things.

5212 *Volpone*
I glory
More in the cunning purchase of my wealth
Than in the glad possession.

5213 *Volpone*
Give 'em words;
Pour oil into their ears, and send them hence.

5214 *Volpone*
What a rare punishment
Is avarice to itself!

5215 *Volpone*
Whilst others have been at the balloo, I have been at my book, and am now past the craggy paths of study, and come to the flowery plains of honour and reputation.

5216 *Volpone*
Calumnies are answered best with silence.

5217 *Volpone*
Almost
All the wise world is little else in nature
But parasites or sub-parasites.

5218 *Volpone*
Suns, that set, may rise again;
But if once we lose this light,
'Tis with us perpetual night.

5219 *Volpone*
Our drink shall be prepared gold and amber;
Which we will take, until my roof whirl around
With the *vertigo*: and my dwarf shall dance.

5220 *Volpone*
Come, my Celia, let us prove,
While we can, the sports of love.

5221 *Volpone*
Honour! tut, a breath,
There's no such thing in nature; a mere term
Invented to awe fools.

5222 *Volpone*
You have a gift, sir, (thank your education),
Will never let you want, while there are men,
And malice, to breed causes.

5223 *Volpone*
Mischiefs feed
Like beasts, till they be fat, and then they bleed.

5224 *'To William Shakespeare'*
Soul of the Age!
The applause, delight, the wonder of our stage!

5225 *'That Women are but Men's Shadows'*
Follow a shadow, it still flies you;
Seem to fly it, it will pursue:
So court a mistress, she denies you;
Let her alone, she will court you.
Say, are not women truly then
Styled but the shadows of us men?

JOPLIN Janis 1943-1970
5226
On stage I make love to twenty-five thousand people; then I go home alone.

5227 *(when Eisenhower's death replaced her in Newsweek)*
Fourteen heart attacks and he had to die in my week. In MY week.

JORDAN David Starr
5228
The world stands aside to let anyone pass who knows where he is going.

JORDAN Thomas c.1612-1685
5229 *'How the War began'*
They plucked communion tables down

And broke our painted glasses;
They threw our altars to the ground
And tumbled down the crosses.
They set up Cromwell and his heir -
The Lord and Lady Claypole -
Because they hated Common Prayer,
The organ and the maypole.

JORTIN John 1698-1770
5230 *(adopted by Lord Nelson as his motto)*
Let him who has won it bear the palm.

JOSEPH Sir Keith 1918-1994
5231
Problems reproduce themselves from
generation to generation ... I refer to this as
a 'cycle of deprivation'.

5232 *(of national euphoria on the outcome of
World War 2)*
We [the Conservative Party] found it hard
to avoid the feeling that somehow the lean
and tight-lipped mufflered men in the
1930s dole queue were at least partly our
fault.

JOUBERT Joseph 1754-1824
5233
Drawing is speaking to the eye; talking is
painting to the ear.

5234
Children have more need of models than
of critics.

5235
Education should be gentle and stern, not
cold and lax.

5236
When my friends lack an eye, I look at
them in profile.

5237
Ambition is pitiless. Any merit that it
cannot use it finds despicable.

5238
Be charitable and indulgent to every one
but thyself.

5239
Imagination is the eye of the soul.

5240
Never cut what you can untie.

5241
To teach is to learn twice.

5242
Words, like eyeglasses, blur everything
that they do not make clear.

JOVANOVICH William
5243
Reading, like prayer, remains one of our
few private acts.

5244
Some words are like the old Roman
galleys; large-scaled and ponderous. They
sit low in the water even when their cargo
is light.

JOWETT Benjamin 1817-1893
5245
One man is as good as another until he has
written a book.

5246
Nowhere probably is there more true
feeling, and nowhere worse taste, than in a
churchyard.

5247
The lie in the soul is a true lie.

5248
We have sought truth, and sometimes
perhaps found it. But have we had any
fun?

5249
No married clergyman should refuse a
bishopric.

5250
Men get lazy, and substitute quantity of
work for quality.

5251
`Research' is a mere excuse for idleness.

5252
No one who has a great deal of energy will
long be popular in Oxford.

5253
There is a great deal of hard lying in the
world: especially among people whose
characters are above suspicion.

5254
Never explain: never apologize: never repeat the mistake.

5255
Don't expect too much: and don't attempt too little.

JOYCE James 1882-1941
5256
[on being asked by an admirer whether he might kiss the hand that wrote *Ulysses*]
No, it did lots of other things too.

5257 *Dubliners*
His soul swooned slowly as he heard the snow falling faintly through the universe and faintly falling, like the descent of their last end, upon all the living and the dead.

5258 *Finnegans Wake*
That ideal reader suffering from an ideal insomnia.

5259 *Finnegans Wake*
The flushpots of Euston and the hanging garments of Marylebone.

5260 *Finnegans Wake*
Tell me, tell me, tell me, elm! Night night! Telmetale of stem or stone. Beside the rivering waters of hitherandthithering waters of. Night!

5261 *Finnegans Wake*
All moanday, tearsday, wailsday, thumpsday, frightday, shatterday till the fear of the Law.

5262 *Finnegans Wake*
Three quarks for Muster Mark!

5263 *Finnegans Wake*
The Gracehoper was always jigging ajog, hoppy on akkant of his joyicity.

5264 *Finnegans Wake*
If I seen him bearing down on me now under whitespread wings like he'd come from Arkangels, I sink I'd die down over his feet, humbly dumbly, only to washup.

5265 *'The Holy Office'*
My little love in light attire
Knows the soft flame that is desire.

5266 *A Portrait of the Artist as a Young Man*
When the soul of a man is born in this country, there are nets flung at it to hold it back from flight. You talk to me of nationality, language, religion. I shall try to fly by those nets.

5267 *A Portrait of the Artist as a Young Man*
Ireland is the old sow that eats her farrow.

5268 *A Portrait of the Artist as a Young Man*
Pity is the feeling which arrests the mind in the presence of whatsoever is grave and constant in human sufferings and unites it with the human sufferer. Terror is the feeling which arrests the mind in the presence of whatsoever is grave and constant in human sufferings and unites it with the secret cause.

5269 *A Portrait of the Artist as a Young Man*
The artist, like the God of the creation, remains within or behind or beyond or above his handiwork, invisible, refined out of existence, indifferent, paring his fingernails.

5270 *A Portrait of the Artist as a Young Man*
I will not serve that in which I no longer believe whether it call itself my home, my fatherland or my church: and I will try to express myself in some mode of life or art as freely as I can and as wholly as I can, using for my defence the only arms I allow myself to use, silence, exile, and cunning.

5271 *A Portrait of the Artist as a Young Man*
Welcome, O life! I go to encounter for the millionth time the reality of experience and to forge in the smithy of my soul the uncreated conscience of my race ... Old father, old artificer, stand me now and ever in good stead.

5272 *'Sleep now, O sleep now'*
My kiss will give peace now
And quiet to your heart -
Sleep on in peace now,
O you unquiet heart!

5273 *Ulysses*
The snotgreen sea. The scrotumtightening sea.

5274 *Ulysses*
It is a symbol of Irish art. The cracked
lookingglass of a servant.

5275 *Ulysses*
When I makes tea I makes tea. And when
I makes water I makes water ... *Begob,
ma'am,* says Mrs Cahill, *God send you don't
make them in the one pot.*

5276 *Ulysses*
I fear those big words, Stephen said, which
make us so unhappy.

5277 *Ulysses*
History, Stephen said, is a nightmare from
which I am trying to awake.

5278 *Ulysses*
Lawn Tennyson, gentleman poet.

5279 *Ulysses*
He ... saw the dark tangled curls of his
bush floating, floating hair of the stream
around the limp father of thousands, a
languid floating flower.

5280 *Ulysses*
Come forth, Lazarus! And he came fifth
and lost the job.

5281 *Ulysses*
Plenty to see and hear and feel yet. Feel
live warm beings near you. They aren't
going to get me this innings. Warm beds;
warm full blooded life.

5282 *Ulysses*
A man of genius makes no mistakes. His
errors are volitional and are the portals of
discovery.

5283 *Ulysses*
But it's no use, says he. Force, hatred,
history, all that. That's not life for men and
women, insult and hatred. And everybody
knows that it's the very opposite of that
that is really life.

5284 *Ulysses*
Greater love than this, he said, no man
hath that a man lay down his wife for his
friend. Go thou and do likewise. Thus, or
words to that effect, saith Zarathustra,
sometime regius professor of French letters
to the university of Oxtail.

5285 *Ulysses*
The heaventree of stars hung with humid
nightblue fruit.

5286 *Ulysses*
He kissed me under the Moorish wall and
I thought well as well him as another and
then I asked him with my eyes to ask
again yes and then he asked me would I
yes to say yes my mountain flower and
first I put my arms around him yes and
drew him down to me so he could feel my
breasts all perfume yes and his heart was
going like mad and yes I said yes I will
Yes.

JOYCE Peggy
5287
It takes all the fun out of a bracelet if you
have to buy it yourself.

JUDD Walter H.
5288
People often say that, in a democracy,
decisions are made by a majority of the
people. Of course, that is not true.
Decisions are made by a majority of those
who make themselves heard and who vote
- a very different thing.

JUDGE Jack and WILLIAMS Harry 1878-
1938 and 1874-1924
5289 *'It's a Long Way to Tipperary'*
It's a long way to Tipperary,
It's a long way to go;
It's a long way to Tipperary,
To the sweetest girl I know!
Goodbye, Piccadilly,
Farewell, Leicester Square,
It's a long, long way to Tipperary,
But my heart's right there!

JULIAN of Norwich 1343-after 1416
5290 *Revelations of Divine Love*
Sin is behovely, but all shall be well and all
shall be well and all manner of thing shall
be well.

5291 *Revelations of Divine Love*
Wouldest thou wit thy Lord's meaning in
this thing? Wit it well: Love was his
meaning. Who shewed it thee? Love.
What shewed He thee? Love. Wherefore
shewed it He? for Love ... Thus was I
learned that Love is our Lord's meaning.

JUNG Carl 1875-1961
5292
Nothing has a stronger influence psychologically on their environment, and especially on their children, than the unlived lives of the parents.

5293
Seldom, or perhaps never, does a marriage develop into an individual relationship smoothly and without crises; there is no coming to consciousness without pain.

5294
Great talents are the most lovely and often the most dangerous fruits on the tree of humanity. They hang upon the most slender twigs that are easily snapped off.

5295
A man who has not passed through the inferno of his passions has never overcome them.

5296
As far as we can discern, the sole purpose of human existence is to kindle a light in the darkness of mere being.

5297
Every form of addiction is bad, no matter whether the narcotic be alcohol or morphine or idealism.

5298
If there is anything that we wish to change in the child, we should first examine it and see whether it is not something that could better be changed in ourselves.

5299
Where love rules, there is no will to power, and where power predominates, there love is lacking. The one is the shadow of the other.

JUNIUS
5300
If individuals have no virtues, their vices may be of use to us.

5301
The right of election is the very essence of the constitution.

5302 *The Letters of Junius*
The liberty of the press is the *Palladium* of all the civil, political, and religious rights of an Englishman.

5303 *Public Advertiser*
There is a holy mistaken zeal in politics as well as in religion. By persuading others, we convince ourselves.

5304 *Public Advertiser*
However distinguished by rank or property, in the rights of freedom we are all equal.

5305 *Public Advertiser*
The injustice done to an individual is sometimes of service to the public.

JUSTINIAN AD 483-565
5306 *Institutes*
Justice is the constant and perpetual wish to render to every one his due.

JUVENAL AD c.60-c.130
5307
Luxury is more deadly than any foe.

5308
Honesty's praised, then left to freeze.

5309 *Satires*
No one ever suddenly became depraved.

5310 *Satires*
The misfortunes of poverty carry with them nothing harder to bear than that it makes men ridiculous.

5311 *Satires*
They do not easily rise out of obscurity whose talents obstruct at home.

5312 *Satires*
Everything in Rome has its price.

5313 *Satires*
A rare bird on this earth, like nothing so much as a black swan.

5314 *Satires*
Panem et circenses.
Bread and the big match.
[usually misquoted as 'bread and circuses']

5315 *Satires*
Orandum est ut sit mens sana in corpore sano.

You should pray to have a sound mind in a sound body.

5316 *Satires*
No guilty man is acquitted if judged by himself.

5317 *Satires*
Revenge is always the pleasure of a paltry, feeble, tiny mind.

5318 *Satires (on Hannibal)*
Death alone reveals how small are men's poor bodies.

KAEL Pauline 1919-
5319
One of the surest signs of the Philistine is his reverence for the superior tastes of those who put him down.

KAFKA Franz 1883-1924
5320
One must not cheat anybody, not even the world of one's triumph.

5321 *The Trial*
You may object that it is not a trial at all; you are quite right, for it is only a trial if I recognize it as such.

5322 *The Trial*
It's often better to be in chains than to be free.

KAHN Gus and EGAN Raymond 1886-1941 and 1890-1952
5323 *'Ain't We Got Fun'*
There's nothing surer,
The rich get rich and the poor get children.
In the meantime, in between time,
Ain't we got fun.

KAISER Henry J. 1882-1967
5324
Trouble is only opportunity in work clothes.

5325
When your work speaks for itself, don't interrupt.

KAN Alphonse
5326
Every man has three characters - that which he exhibits, that which he has, and that which he thinks he has.

KANE Marie Elizabeth
5327 *(when thirteen years old)*
I feel when people say 'bigger and better' they should say 'bigger and badder'.

KANIN Garson
5328
Whenever I'm asked what college I attended, I'm tempted to reply, 'Thornton Wilder'.

5329
In a professional once engaged, the performance of the job comes first.

5330
Amateurs hope. Professionals work.

KANT Immanuel 1724-1804
5331
Every man is to be respected as an absolute end in himself: and it is a crime against the dignity that belongs to him as a human being, to use him as a mere means for some external purpose.

5332
The desire of a man for a woman is not directed at her because she is a human being, but because she is a woman. That she is a human being is of no concern to him.

5333
Out of the crooked timber of humanity no straight thing can ever be made.

5334 *Critique of Practical Reason*
Two things fill the mind with ever new and increasing wonder and awe, the more often and the more seriously reflection concentrates upon them: the starry heaven above me and the moral law within me.

5335 *Foundation of the Metaphysics of Morals*
Nothing in the world - indeed nothing even beyond the world - can possibly be conceived which could be called good without qualification except a *good will*.

5336 *Foundation of the Metaphysics of Ethics*
Happiness is not an ideal of reason but of imagination.

KAPP K. William
5337
Had there been a computer a hundred years ago, it would probably have predicted that by now there would be so many horse-drawn vehicles it would be impossible to clear up all the manure.

KAPPEL Frederick
5338
The Bell system is like a damn big dragon. You kick it in the tail, and two years later, it feels it in its head.

KARR Alphonse 1808-1890
5339
If we are to abolish the death penalty, let the murderers take the first step.

5340
Plus ça change, plus c'est la même chose.
The more things change, the more they are the same.

KASLUCK Lady
5341
The worst thing about work in the house or home is that whatever you do is destroyed, laid waste or eaten within twenty-four hours.

KASSAK Lajos
5342
The father of every good work is discontent, and its mother is diligence.

KAUFMAN George S. 1889-1961
5343
I like terra firma - the more firma, the less terra.

5344
Satire is what closes Saturday night.

KAUFMAN Gerald 1930-
5345 *(on the Labour Party's New Hope for Britain)*
The longest suicide note in history.

KAUFMAN Paul and ANTHONY Mike
5346
Poetry in motion.

KAUFMANN Christoph 1753-1795
5347 *(of a period of literary ferment)*
Storm and stress.

KAUFMANN Walter
5348
Faith means intense, usually confident, belief that is not based on evidence sufficient to command assent from every reasonable person.

KAVANAGH Patrick 1905-1967
5349 *'The Great Hunger'*
Clay is the word and clay is the flesh
Where the potato-gatherers like mechanized scarecrows move
Along the side-fall of the hill - Maguire and his men.

5350 *'The Great Hunger'*
That was how his life happened.
No mad hooves galloping in the sky,
But the weak, washy way of true tragedy -
A sick horse nosing around the meadow for a clean place to die.

5351 *'Inniskeen Road: July Evening'*
I hate what every poet hates in spite
Of all the solemn talk of contemplation.
Oh, Alexander Selkirk knew the plight
Of being king and government and nation.
A road, a mile of kingdom, I am king
Of banks and stones and every blooming thing.

KAZAN Elia 1909-
5352
You've got to keep fighting - you've got to risk your life every six months to stay alive.

KAZANTZAKIS Nikos 1883-1957
5353
Every perfect traveller always creates the country where he travels.

KEATE Stuart
5354
Canada reminds me of vichyssoise - it's cold, half-French and difficult to stir.

KEATS John 1795-1821
5355
A proverb is no proverb to you till life has illustrated it.

5356
In disease Medical Men guess: if they cannot ascertain a disease, they call it nervous.

5357 'Addressed to [Haydon]'
... Other spirits there are standing apart
Upon the forehead of the age to come.

5358 'To Autumn'
Season of mists and mellow fruitfulness,
Close bosom-friend of the maturing sun;
Conspiring with him how to load and bless
With fruit the vines that round the thatch-eaves run.

5359 'To Autumn'
Then in a wailful choir the small gnats mourn
Among the river sallows, borne aloft
Or sinking as the light wind lives or dies.

5360 'To Autumn'
The red-breast whistles from a garden-croft;
And gathering swallows twitter in the skies.

5361 'Bards of Passion and of Mirth'
Where the nightingale doth sing
Not a senseless, trancèd thing,
But diving melodious truth.

5362 'Bright star, would I were steadfast as thou art'
Still, still to hear her tender-taken breath,
And so live ever - or else swoon to death.

5363 'In drear nighted December'
In drear nighted December
Too happy, happy tree
Thy branches ne'er remember
Their green felicity.

5364 Endymion
A thing of beauty is a joy for ever:
Its loveliness increases; it will never
Pass into nothingness; but still will keep
A bower quiet for us, and a sleep
Full of sweet dreams, and health, and quiet breathing.

5365 Endymion
Here is wine,
Alive with sparkles.

5366 Endymion
Their smiles,
Wan as primroses gathered at midnight

By chilly fingered spring.

5367 Endymion (preface)
The imagination of a boy is healthy, and the mature imagination of a man is healthy; but there is a space of life between, in which the soul is in a ferment, the character undecided, the way of life uncertain, the ambition thick-sighted: thence proceeds mawkishness.

5368 (epitaph for himself)
Here lies one whose name was writ in water.

5369 'The Eve of St Agnes'
St Agnes' Eve - Ah, bitter chill it was!
The owl, for all his feathers, was a-cold;
The hare limped trembling through the frozen grass,
And silent was the flock in woolly fold.

5370 'The Eve of St Agnes'
The silver, snarling trumpets 'gan to chide.

5371 'The Eve of St Agnes'
And soft adorings from their loves receive
Upon the honey'd middle of the night.

5372 'The Eve of St Agnes'
The music, yearning like a God in pain.

5373 'The Eve of St Agnes'
A poor, weak, palsy-stricken, churchyard thing.

5374 'The Eve of St Agnes'
Out went the taper as she hurried in;
Its little smoke, in pallid moonshine, died.

5375 'The Eve of St Agnes'
By degrees
Her rich attire creeps rustling to her knees.

5376 'The Eve of St Agnes'
Trembling in her soft and chilly nest.

5377 'The Eve of St Agnes'
As though a rose should shut, and be a bud again.

5378 'The Eve of St Agnes'
He played an ancient ditty, long since mute,
In Provence called, 'La belle dame sans mercy.'

5379 'The Eve of St Agnes'
And the long carpets rose along the gusty floor.

5380 'The Eve of St Agnes'
And they are gone: aye, ages long ago
These lovers fled away into the storm.

5381 'The Fall of Hyperion'
Fanatics have their dreams, wherewith they weave
A paradise for a sect.

5382 'The Fall of Hyperion'
The poet and the dreamer are distinct,
Diverse, sheet opposite, antipodes.
The one pours out a balm upon the world,
The other vexes it.

5383 'Fancy'
Ever let the fancy roam,
Pleasure never is at home.

5384 'Fancy'
Where's the face
One would meet in every place?

5385 'On First Looking into Chapman's Homer'
Much have I travelled in the realms of gold,
And many goodly states and kingdoms seen.

5386 'On First Looking into Chapman's Homer'
Then felt I like some watcher of the skies
When a new planet swims into his ken;
Or like stout Cortez when with eagle eyes
He stared at the Pacific - and all his men
Looked at each other with a wild surmise -
Silent, upon a peak in Darien.

5387 'To George Felton Mayhew'
Sweet are the pleasures that to verse belong,
And doubly sweet a brotherhood in song.

5388 'To Homer'
Aye on the shores of darkness there is light,
And precipices show untrodden green,
There is a budding morrow in midnight,
There is a triple sight in blindness keen.

5389 'The Human Seasons'
Four seasons fill the measure of the year;
There are four seasons in the mind of man.

5390 'Hyperion: A Fragment'
That large utterance of the early gods!

5391 'Hyperion: A Fragment'
O aching time! O moments big as years!

5392 'Hyperion: A Fragment'
As when, upon a trancèd summer-night,
Those green-robed senators of mighty woods,
Tall oaks, branch-charmèd by the earnest stars,
Dream, and so dream all night without a stir.

5393 'Hyperion: A Fragment'
Sometimes eagle's wings,
Unseen before by gods or wondering men,
Darkened the place.

5394 'Hyperion: A Fragment'
And still they were the same bright, patient stars.

5395 'Hyperion: A Fragment'
Knowledge enormous makes a god of me.

5396 'Isabella; or, The Pot of Basil'
Why were they proud? again we ask aloud,
Why in the name of Glory were they proud?

5397 'Isabella; or, The Pot of Basil'
And she forgot the stars, the moon, and sun,
And she forgot the blue above the trees,
And she forgot the dells where waters run,
And she forgot the chilly autumn breeze;
She had no knowledge when the day was done,
And the new morn she saw not; but in peace
Hung over her sweet Basil evermore,
And moistened it with tears unto the core.

5398 'Isabella; or, The Pot of Basil'
'For cruel 'tis,' said she,
'To steal my Basil-pot away from me'

5399 *'To J.H. Reynolds, Esq.'*
It is a flaw
In happiness, to see beyond our bourn -
It forces us in summer skies to mourn:
It spoils the singing of the nightingale.

5400 *'La belle dame sans merci'*
Oh, what can ail thee knight at arms
Alone and palely loitering?
The sedge has withered from the lake
And no birds sing!

5401 *'La belle dame sans merci'*
I see a lily on thy brow
With anguish moist and fever dew,
And on thy cheeks a fading rose
Fast withereth too.

5402 *'La belle dame sans merci'*
I met a lady in the meads
Full beautiful, a faery's child
Her hair was long, her foot was light
And her eyes were wild.

5403 *'La belle dame sans merci'*
She looked at me as she did love
And made sweet moan.

5404 *'La belle dame sans merci'*
I set her on my pacing steed
And nothing else saw all day long
For sidelong would she bend and sing
A faery's song.

5405 *'La belle dame sans merci'*
... La belle dame sans merci
Thee hath in thrall.

5406 *'La belle dame sans merci'*
I saw their starved lips in the gloam
With horrid warning gapèd wide
And I awoke and found me here
On the cold hill's side.

5407 *'Lamia'*
Philosophy will clip an Angel's wings,
Conquer all mysteries by rule and line,
Empty the haunted air, the gnomed mine -
Unweave a rainbow.

5408 *'Lamia'*
She was a gordian shape of dazzling hue,
Vermillion-spotted, golden, green, and
blue;
Striped like a zebra, freckled like a pard,
Eyed like a peacock, and all crimson

barred.

5409 *'Lamia'*
Love in a hut, with water and a crust,
Is - Love, forgive us! - cinders, ashes, dust;
Love in a palace is perhaps at last
More grievous torment than a hermit's
fast.

5410 *'Lamia'*
That purple-linèd palace of sweet sin.

5411 *'Lamia'*
In pale contented sort of discontent.

5412 *'To Leigh Hunt, Esq.'*
Glory and loveliness have passed away.

5413 *Letter to Benjamin Bailey*
A long poem is a test of invention which I
take to be the polar star of poetry, as fancy
is the sails, and imagination the rudder.

5414 *Letter to Benjamin Bailey*
I am certain of nothing but the holiness of
the heart's affections and the truth of
imagination - what the imagination seizes
as beauty must be truth - whether it
existed before or not.

5415 *Letter to Benjamin Bailey*
I have never yet been able to perceive how
anything can be known for truth by
consecutive reasoning - and yet it must be.

5416 *Letter to Benjamin Bailey*
O for a life of sensations rather than of
thoughts!

5417 *Letter to Benjamin Bailey*
Scenery is fine - but human nature is finer.

5418 *Letter to Benjamin Bailey*
I am in a temper that if I were under water
I would scarcely kick to come to the top.

5419 *Letter to Fanny Brawne*
I have met with women whom I really
think would like to be married to a poem
and to be given away by a novel.

5420 *Letter to Fanny Brawne*
I wish you could invent some means to
make me at all happy without you. Every
hour I am more and more concentrated in
you; every thing else tastes like chaff in my
mouth.

5421 *Letter to George and Georgiana Keats*
The roaring of the wind is my wife and the stars through the window pane are my children.

5422 *Letter to George and Georgiana Keats*
A man's life of any worth is a continual allegory.

5423 *Letter to George and Georgiana Keats*
All clean and comfortable I sit down to write.

5424 *Letter to George and Georgiana Keats*
The only means of strengthening one's intellect is to make up one's mind about nothing - to let the mind be a thoroughfare for all thoughts. Not a select party.

5425 *Letter to George and Thomas Keats*
The excellence of every art is its intensity, capable of making all disagreeables evaporate, from their being in close relationship with beauty and truth.

5426 *Letter to George and Thomas Keats*
There is nothing stable in the world - uproar's your only music.

5427 *Letter to J.H. Reynolds*
A man should have the fine point of his soul taken off to become fit for this world.

5428 *Letter to J.H. Reynolds*
Poetry should be great and unobtrusive, a thing which enters into one's soul, and does not startle it or amaze it with itself, but with its subject.

5429 *Letter to J.H. Reynolds*
It is impossible to live in a country which is continually under hatches ... Rain! Rain! Rain!

5430 *Letter to J.H. Reynolds*
There is an awful warmth about my heart like a load of immortality.

5431 *Letter to John Taylor*
Poetry should surprise by a fine excess, and not by singularity - it should strike the reader as a wording of his own highest thoughts, and appear almost a remembrance.

5432 *Letter to John Taylor*
If poetry comes not as naturally as the leaves to a tree it had better not come at all.

5433 *Letter to B. R. Haydon*
It is true that in the height of enthusiasm I have been cheated into some fine passages but that is nothing.

5434 *'Lines on the Mermaid Tavern'*
Souls of poets dead and gone,
What Elysium have ye known
Happy field or mossy cavern
Choicer than the Mermaid Tavern?

5435 *'Ode on a Grecian Urn'*
Thou still unravished bride of quietness,
Thou foster-child of silence and slow time.

5436 *'Ode on a Grecian Urn'*
Heard melodies are sweet, but those unheard
Are sweeter; therefore, ye soft pipes, play on;
Not to the sensual ear, but, more endeared,
Pipe to the spirit ditties of no tone.

5437 *'Ode on a Grecian Urn'*
For ever piping songs for ever new.

5438 *'Ode on a Grecian Urn'*
For ever warm and still to be enjoyed,
For ever panting, and for ever young;
All breathing human passion far above,
That leaves a heart high-sorrowful and cloyed,
A burning forehead, and a parching tongue.

5439 *'Ode on a Grecian Urn'*
O Attic shape! Fair attitude!

5440 *'Ode on a Grecian Urn'*
'Beauty is truth, truth beauty,' - that is all
Ye know on earth, and all ye need to know.

5441 *'Ode on Melancholy'*
No, no, go not to Lethe, neither twist
Wolf's-bane, tight-rooted, for its poisonous wine.

5442 *'Ode on Melancholy'*
Nor let the beetle, nor the death-moth be
Your mournful Psyche.

5443 *'Ode on Melancholy'*
But when the melancholy fit shall fall
Sudden from heaven like a weeping cloud,
That fosters the droop-headed flowers all,
And hides the green hill in an April
shroud;
Then glut thy sorrow on a morning rose.

5444 *'Ode on Melancholy'*
She dwells with Beauty - Beauty that must
die;
And Joy, whose hand is ever at his lips
Bidding adieu; and aching Pleasure nigh,
Turning to poison while the bee-mouth
sips.

5445 *'Ode to a Nightingale'*
Fade far away, dissolve, and quite forget
What thou among the leaves hast never
known,
The weariness, the fever, and the fret
Here, where men sit and hear each other
groan;
Where palsy shakes a few, sad, last grey
hairs,
Where youth grows pale, and spectre-thin,
and dies;
Where but to think is to be full of sorrow
And leaden-eyed despairs.

5446 *'Ode to a Nightingale'*
Away! away! for I will fly to thee,
Not charioted by Bacchus and his pards,
But on the viewless wings of Poesy,
Though the dull brain perplexes and
retards:
Already with thee! tender is the night.

5447 *'Ode to a Nightingale'*
I cannot see what flowers are at my feet,
Nor what soft incense hangs upon the
boughs.

5448 *'Ode to a Nightingale'*
Now more than ever seems it rich to die,
To cease upon the midnight with no pain.

5449 *'Ode to a Nightingale'*
Thou wast not born for death, immortal
bird!
No hungry generations tread thee down;
The voice I hear this passing night was
heard
In ancient days by emperor and clown:

5450 *'Ode to a Nightingale'*
Was it a vision, or a waking dream?
Fled is that music: do I wake or sleep?

5451 *'Ode to Psyche'*
Nor virgin-choir to make delicious moan
Upon the midnight hours.

5452 *'Ode to Psyche'*
A bright torch, and a casement ope at
night,
To let the warm Love in!

5453 *'On Seeing the Elgin Marbles'*
Mortality
Weighs heavily on me like unwilling sleep.

5454 *'Shed no tear - O shed no tear'*
Dry your eyes - O dry your eyes
For I was taught in Paradise
To ease my breast of melodies.

5455 *'Sleep and Poetry'*
Stop and consider! life is but a day;
A fragile dew-drop on its perilous way
From a tree's summit;

5456 *'Sleep and Poetry'*
O for ten years, that I may overwhelm
Myself in poesy; so I may do the deed
That my own soul has to itself decreed.

5457 *'Sleep and Poetry'*
They swayed about upon a rocking horse,
And thought it Pegasus.

5458 *'Sleep and Poetry'*
And they shall be accounted poet kings
Who simply tell the most heart-easing
things.

5459 *'O Solitude! if I must with thee dwell'*
Yet the sweet converse of an innocent
mind,
Whose words are images of thoughts
refined,
Is my soul's pleasure; and it sure must be
Almost the highest bliss of human-kind,
When to thy haunts two kindred spirits
flee.

5460 *'Sonnet to Sleep'*
O soft embalmer of the still midnight,
Shutting, with careful fingers and benign
Our gloom-pleased eyes.

5461 *'Sonnet to Sleep'*
Turn the key deftly in the oilèd wards,
And seal the hushèd casket of my soul.

5462 *'I stood tip-toe upon a little hill'*
And then there crept
A little noiseless noise among the leaves,
Born of the very sigh that silence heaves.

5463 *'I stood tip-toe upon a little hill'*
Here are sweet peas, on tip-toe for a flight.

5464 *'When I have fears that I may cease to be'*
When I behold, upon the night's starred
face
Huge cloudy symbols of a high romance.

5465 *'To one who has been long in city pent'*
To one who has been long in city pent,
'Tis very sweet to look into the fair
And open face of heaven.

5466 *'Woman! when I behold thee flippant, vain'*
Woman! when I behold thee flippant, vain,
Inconstant, childish, proud, and full of
fancies.

KEBLE John 1792-1866
5467
If the Church of England were to fail, it
would be found in my parish.

5468 *The Christian Year 'Blessed are the pure...'*
Blessed are the pure in heart,
For they shall see our God,
The secret of the Lord is theirs,
Their soul is Christ's abode.

5469 *The Christian Year 'Morning'*
The trivial round, the common task,
Would furnish all we ought to ask;
Room to deny ourselves; a road
To bring us, daily, nearer God.

5470 *The Christian Year 'Septuagesima'*
There is a book, who runs may read,
Which heavenly truth imparts,
And all the lore its scholars need,
Pure eyes and Christian hearts.

5471 *'Holy Matrimony'*
The voice that breathed o'er Eden,
That earliest wedding-day,
The primal marriage blessing,

It hath not passed away.

KELLER Helen 1880-1968
5472
When one door of happiness closes,
another opens; but often we look so long at
the closed door that we do not see the one
which has been opened for us.

5473
Many persons have a wrong idea of what
constitutes true happiness. It is not
attained through self-gratification but
through fidelity to a worthy purpose.

5474
Science may have found a cure for most
evils: but it has found no remedy for the
worst of them all - the apathy of human
beings.

5475
It is not possible for civilization to flow
backward while there is youth in the
world. Youth may be headstrong, but it
will advance its allotted length.

KELLY Bishop Francis
5476
Convictions are the mainsprings of action,
the driving powers of life. What a man
lives are his convictions.

KELLY Hugh 1739-1777
5477 *False Delicacy*
Your people of refined sentiments are the
most troublesome creatures in the world to
deal with.

5478 *Memoirs of a Magdalen*
Of all the stages in a woman's life, none is
so dangerous as the period between her
acknowledgement of a passion for a man,
and the day set apart for her nuptials.

KELLY Vesta M.
5479
Snowflakes are one of nature's most fragile
things, but just look what they can do
when they stick together.

KELLY Walt 1913-1973
5480
We have met the enemy, and he is us.

KELLY William M. 1811-1888
5481
Man is a slow, sloppy and brilliant thinker;
the machine is fast, accurate and stupid.

KELVIN Lord 1824-1907
5482
Heavier-than-air flying machines are
impossible.

KEMPIS Thomas à 1379-1471
5483
Man proposes; God disposes.

5484
Intelligence must follow faith, never
precede it, and never destroy it.

5485 *De Imitatione Christi*
Seek not to know who said this or that, but
take note of what has been said.

5486 *De Imitatione Christi*
It is much safer to be in a subordinate
position than in authority.

5487 *De Imitatione Christi*
Today the man is here; tomorrow he is
gone. And when he is 'out of sight',
quickly also is he out of mind.

5488 *De Imitatione Christi*
We are sometimes stirred by emotion and
take it for zeal.

5489 *De Imitatione Christi*
If you bear the cross gladly, it will bear
you.

KEMPTON Murray
5490
America ... an economic system prouder of
the distribution of its products than of the
products themselves.

5491
To say that an idea is fashionable is to say,
I think, that it has been adulterated to a
point where it is hardly an idea at all.

KEMPTON Sally
5492
Women are the true maintenance class.
Society is built upon their acquiescence
and upon their small and necessary
labours.

5493
It is hard to fight an enemy who has
outposts in your head.

KEN Thomas 1637-1711
5494 *'Evening Hymn'*
All praise to thee, my God, this night,
For all the blessings of the light;
Keep me, O keep me, King of Kings,
Beneath thy own almighty wings.

5495 *'Evening Hymn'*
Teach me to live, that I may dread
The grave as little as my bed.

5496 *'Morning Hymn'*
Redeem thy mis-spent time that's past,
And live this day as if thy last.

KENDALL Paul Murray
5497
On the trail of another man, the biographer
must put up with finding himself at every
turn: any biography uneasily shelters an
autobiography within it.

KENEALLY Thomas 1935-
5498 *(talking of his book, Schindlers Ark)*
The Holocaust is a Gentile problem not a
Jewish one.

KENNEDY Florynce
5499
If men could get pregnant, abortion would
be a sacrament.

KENNEDY John F. 1917-1963
5500
There are risks and costs to a program of
action. But they are far less than the long-
range risks and costs of comfortable
inaction.

5501
Everything changes but change itself.

5502
We will neglect our cities to our peril, for
in neglecting them we neglect the nation.

5503
The courage of life is often a less dramatic
spectacle that the courage of a final
moment; but it is no less a magnificent
mixture of triumph and tragedy. A man
does what he must - in spite of personal

consequences, in spite of obstacles and dangers and pressures - and that is the basis of all morality.

5504
Once you say you're going to settle for second, that's what happens to you in life, I find.

5505
When we got into office, the thing that surprised me most was to find that things were just as bad as we'd been saying they were.

5506
The Family of Man is more than three billion strong. It lives in more than one hundred nations. Most of its members are not white. Most of them are not Christians. Most of them know nothing about free enterprise, or due process of law, or the Australian ballot.

5507
All free men, wherever they may live, are citizens of Berlin. And therefore, as a free man, I take pride in the words 'Ich bin ein Berliner'.

5508
Too often we ... enjoy the comfort of opinion without the discomfort of thought.

5509
If we are strong, our strength will speak for itself. If we are weak, words will be no help.

5510
Those who make peaceful revolution impossible will make violent revolution inevitable.

5511
The complacent, the self-indulgent, the soft societies are about to be swept away with the debris of history.

5512
War will exist until that distant day when the conscientious objector enjoys the same reputation and prestige that the warrior does today.

5513
Anyone who is honestly seeking a job and can't find it, deserves the attention of the United States government, and the people.

5514
When power leads man toward arrogance, poetry reminds him of his limitations. When power narrows the areas of man's concern, poetry reminds him of the richness and diversity of his existence. When power corrupts, poetry cleanses. For art establishes the basic human truths which must serve as the touchstone of our judgement.

5515
In free society art is not a weapon ... Artists are not engineers of the soul.

5516 *(accepting the Democratic nomination)*
We stand today on the edge of a new frontier ... But the New Frontier of which I speak is not a set of promises - it is a set of challenges. It sums up not what I intend to offer the American people, but what I intend to ask of them.

5517 *(after appointing his brother Attorney General)*
I don't see what's wrong with giving Bobby a little experience before he starts to practise law.

5518 *(asked how he became a war hero)*
It was involuntary. They sank my boat.

5519 *(inaugural address)*
Let the word go forth from this time and place, to friend and foe alike, that the torch has been passed to a new generation of Americans - born in this century, tempered by war, disciplined by a hard and bitter peace, proud of our ancient heritage - and unwilling to witness or permit the slow undoing of those human rights to which this nation has always been committed, and to which we are committed today at home and around the world.

5520 *(Inaugural address)*
Let every nation know, whether it wishes us well or ill, that we shall pay any price, bear any burden, meet any hardship, support any friend, oppose any foe to

assure the survival and the success of liberty.

5521 *(Inaugural address)*
If a free society cannot help the many who are poor, it cannot save the few who are rich.

5522 *(Inaugural address)*
Let us never negotiate out of fear. But let us never fear to negotiate.

5523 *(Inaugural address)*
All this will not be finished in the first 100 days. Nor will it be finished in the first 1,000 days, nor in the life of this Administration, nor even perhaps in our lifetime on this planet. But let us begin.

5524 *(Inaugural address)*
Now the trumpet summons us again - not as a call to bear arms, though arms we need - not as a call to battle, though embattled we are - but a call to bear the burden of a long twilight struggle, year in and year out, 'rejoicing in hope, patient in tribulation' - a struggle against the common enemies of man: tyranny, poverty, disease and war itself.

5525 *(Inaugural address)*
And so, my fellow Americans: ask not what your country can do for you - ask what you can do for your country.

5526 *(on proposed Civil Rights Bill)*
No one has been barred on account of his race from fighting or dying for America - there are no 'white' or 'coloured' signs on the foxholes or graveyards of battle.

5527 *(to United Nations General Assembly)*
Mankind must put an end to war or war will put an end to mankind.

KENNEDY Joseph P. 1888-1969
5528
When the going gets tough, the tough get going.

5529 *(telegraphed message to J F Kennedy)*
Don't buy a single vote more than necessary. I'll be damned if I'm going to pay for a landslide.

KENNEDY Robert F. 1925-1968
5530
Only those who dare to fail greatly can ever achieve greatly.

5531
Don't get mad, get even.

5532
Moral courage is a more rare commodity than bravery in battle or great intelligence.

5533
One fifth of the people are against everything all the time.

KEPES Gyorgy
5534
The really great visual experience today is to fly over a huge city and look down into the night. It's like a tremendous jubilant Christmas tree. You just feel life is worth living - when you come down you may have some doubts.

KEROUAC Jack 1922-1969
5535
The beat generation.

KERR Clark 1911-
5536 *(whilst President, University of California)*
I find the three major administrative problems on a campus are sex for the students, athletics for the alumni and parking for the faculty.

KERR Jean 1923-
5537
The thing about having a baby is that thereafter you have it.

5538 *Mary, Mary*
Being divorced is like being hit by a truck - if you survive, you start looking very carefully to the left and right.

KETTERING Charles F. 1876-1958
5539
My interest is in the future because I am going to spend the rest of my life there.

5540
It is easy to build a philosophy. It doesn't have to run.

KEY Ellen 1849-1926
5541 *The Morality of Women and Other Essays*
Love is moral even without legal marriage, but marriage is immoral without love.

KEY Francis Scott 1779-1843
5542 'The Star-Spangled Banner'
'Tis the star-spangled banner; O long may it wave
O'er the land of the free, and the home of the brave.

KEYES Jr. Ken
5543
A loving person lives in a loving world. A hostile person lives in a hostile world: everyone you meet is your mirror.

KEYNES John Maynard 1883-1946
5544
I work for a Government I despise for ends I think criminal.

5545 *The Economic Consequences of the Peace*
Like Odysseus, the President [Woodrow Wilson] looked wiser when he was seated.

5546 *The Economic Consequences of the Peace*
Lenin was right. There is no subtler, no surer means of overturning the existing basis of society than to debauch the currency. The process engages all the hidden forces of economic law on the side of destruction, and does it in a manner which not one man in a million is able to diagnose.

5547 *The End of Laissez-Faire*
I do not know which makes a man more conservative - to know nothing but the present, or nothing but the past.

5548 *The End of Laissez-Faire*
The important thing for Government is not to do things which individuals are doing already, and to do them a little better or a little worse; but to do those things which at present are not done at all.

5549 *Essays in Biography 'Mr Lloyd George'*
This extraordinary figure of our time, this syren, this goat-footed bard, this half-human visitor to our age from the hag-ridden magic and enchanted woods of Celtic antiquity.

5550 *General Theory*
We take it as a fundamental psychological rule of any modern community that, when its real income is increased, it will not increase its consumption by an equal *absolute* amount.

5551 *General Theory*
If the Treasury were to fill old bottles with banknotes, bury them at suitable depths in disused coalmines which are then filled up to the surface with town rubbish, and leave it to private enterprise on well-tried principles of *laissez-faire* to dig the notes up again (the right to do so being obtained, of course, by tendering for leases of the note-bearing territory) there need be no more unemployment and, with the help of the repercussions, the real income of the community, and its capital wealth also, would probably become a good deal greater than it actually is.

5552 *General Theory*
Practical men, who believe themselves to be quite exempt from any intellectual influences, are usually the slaves of some defunct economist. Madmen in authority, who hear voices in the air, are distilling their frenzy from some academic scribbler of a few years back.

5553 *(of his poor results in the Civil Service exams)*
I evidently knew more about economics than my examiners.

5554 *A Tract on Monetary Reform*
In the long run we are all dead.

KEYNES John Neville 1852-1949
5555 *The Scope and Method of Political Economy*
A *positive science* may be defined as a body of systematized knowledge concerning what is; a *normative* or *regular science* a body of systematized knowledge relating to criteria of what ought to be, and concerned therefore with the ideal as distinguished from the actual.

KEYSERLING Hermann 1880-1946
5556
The greatest American superstition is belief in facts.

KHRUSHCHEV Nikita 1894-1971

5557

I don't like the life here in New York.
There is no greenery. It would make a
stone sick.

5558

You do not know, you cannot know, the
difficulty of life of a politician. It means
every minute of the day or night, every
ounce of your energy. There is no rest, no
relaxation. Enjoyment? A politician does
not know the meaning of the word.

5559

Politicians are the same all over. They
promise to build a bridge even when there
is no river.

5560

If we should promise people nothing
better than only revolution, they would
scratch their heads and say, 'Isn't it better
to have good goulash?'

5561

If anyone believes that our smiles involve
abandonment of the teaching of Marx,
Engels and Lenin he deceives himself.
Those who wait for that must wait until a
shrimp learns to whistle.

5562

About the capitalist States, it doesn't
depend on you whether or not we exist. If
you don't like us, don't accept our
invitations and don't invite us to come to
see you. Whether you like it or not,
history is on our side. We will bury you.

5563

Anyone who believes that the worker can
be lulled by fine revolutionary phrases is
mistaken ... If no concern is shown for the
growth of material and spiritual riches, the
people will listen today, they will listen
tomorrow, and then they may say: 'Why
do you promise us everything for the
future? You are talking, so to speak, about
life beyond the grave. The priest has
already told us about this.'

5564

If one cannot catch the bird of paradise,
better take a wet hen.

5565

If you start throwing hedgehogs under me,
I shall throw a couple of porcupines under
you.

KIERAN John

5566

I am a part of all I have read.

KIERKEGAARD Sören 1813-1855

5567

Anxiety is the dizziness of freedom.

5568

Most people believe that the Christian
commandments are intentionally a little
too severe - like setting a clock half an
hour ahead to make sure of not being late
in the morning.

5569

Wherever there is a crowd there is untruth.

5570

The sadness in legitimate humour consists
in the fact that honestly, and without
deceit, it reflects in a purely human way
upon what it is to be a child.

5571

People hardly ever make use of the
freedom they have, for example, freedom
of thought; instead they demand freedom
of speech as a compensation.

5572

Life can only be understood backwards;
but it must be lived forwards.

5573

What our age lacks is not reflection but
passion.

KILMER Joyce 1886-1918

5574

Things have a terrible permanence when
people die.

5575 *'Trees'*

I think that I shall never see
A poem lovely as a tree.

5576 *'Trees'*

Poems are made by fools like me,
But only God can make a tree.

KILMUIR Lord (Sir David Maxwell Fyfe)
1900-1967
5577
Loyalty is the Tory's secret weapon.

KILVERT Francis 1840-1879
5578 *Diary*
Of all noxious animals, too, the most
noxious is a tourist. And of all tourists the
most vulgar, ill-bred, offensive and
loathsome is the British tourist.

5579 *Diary*
The Vicar of St Ives says the smell of fish
there is sometimes so terrific as to stop the
church clock.

5580 *Diary*
It is a fine thing to be out on the hills
alone. A man can hardly be a beast or a
fool alone on a great mountain.

KING Benjamin Franklin 1857-1894
5581 *'The Pessimist'*
Nothing to do but work,
Nothing to eat but food,
Nothing to wear but clothes
To keep one from going nude.
Nothing to breathe but air,
Quick as a flash 't is gone;
Nowhere to fall but off,
Nowhere to stand but on.
5582 *'The Pessimist'*
Nowhere to go but out,
Nowhere to come but back.

KING Henry 1592-1669
5583 *'An Exequy'*
My last Good night! Thou wilt not wake
Till I thy fate shall overtake:
Till age, or grief, or sickness must
Marry my body to that dust
It so much loves.

5584 *'The Surrender'*
We that did nothing study but the way
To love each other, ...
Must learn the hateful art, how to forget.

KING Martin Luther 1929-1968
5585
The ultimate measure of a man is not
where he stands in moments of comfort
and convenience, but where he stands at
times of challenge and controversy.

5586
Human Salvation lies in the hands of the
creatively maladjusted.

5587
Don't hate, it's too big a burden to bear.

5588
Non-violence is a powerful and just
weapon. It is a weapon unique in history,
which cuts without wounding and enobles
the man who wields it. It is a sword that
heals.

5589
I want to be the white man's brother, not
his brother-in-law.

5590
Injustice anywhere is a threat to justice
everywhere.

5591
The Negro's great stumbling block in the
stride toward freedom is not the White
Citizens Councillor or the Ku Klux
Klanner but the white moderate who is
more devoted to order than to justice; who
prefers a negative peace which is the
absence of tension to a positive peace
which is the presence of justice.

5592
I submit to you that if a man hasn't
discovered something he will die for, he
isn't fit to live.

5593
I have a dream that one day on the red
hills of Georgia the sons of former slaves
and the sons of former slave owners will
be able to sit down together at the table of
brotherhood ...
I have a dream that my four little children
will one day live in a nation where they
will not be judged by the colour of their
skin but by the content of their character.

5594
We must learn to live together as brothers
or perish together as fools.

5595 *(day before assassination)*
I just want to do God's will. And he's
allowed me to go up to the mountain.
And I've looked over, and I've seen the

promised land ... So I'm happy tonight.
I'm not worried about anything. I'm not
fearing any man.

5596 *Strength to Love*
The means by which we live have
outdistanced the ends for which we live.
Our scientific power has outrun our
spiritual power. We have guided missiles
and misguided men.

5597 *Where Do We Go From Here?*
A riot is at bottom the language of the
unheard.

KING Stoddard 1889-1933
5598 *'There's a Long, Long Trail'*
There's a long, long trail awinding
Into the land of my dreams.

KING William Lyon Mackenzie 1874-
1950
5599
Not necessarily conscription, but
conscription if necessary.

5600
Government in the last analysis is
organized opinion. Where there is little or
no public opinion, there is likely to be bad
government, which sooner or later
becomes autocratic government.

5601
I really believe my greatest service is in the
many unwise steps I prevent.

5602
The promises of yesterday are the taxes of
today.

KINGSLEY Charles 1819-1875
5603
We act as though comfort and luxury were
the chief requirements of life, when all that
we need to make us really happy is
something to be enthusiastic about.

5604
He was one of those men who possess
almost every gift, except the gift of the
power to use them.

5605
Truth, for its own sake, had never been a
virtue with the Roman clergy.

5606 *'Airly Beacon'*
Airly Beacon, Airly Beacon;
Oh the pleasant sight to see
Shires and towns from Airly Beacon,
While my love climbed up to me!

5607 *'A Farewell'*
Be good, sweet maid, and let who will be
clever;
Do noble things, not dream them, all day
long:
And so make life, death, and that vast for-
ever
One grand, sweet song.

5608 *Health and Education*
To be discontented with the divine
discontent, and to be ashamed with the
noble shame, is the very germ and first
upgrowth of all virtue.

5609 *'The Invitation. To Tom Hughes'*
What we can we will be,
Honest Englishmen.
Do the work that's nearest,
Though it's dull at whiles,
Helping, when we meet them,
Lame dogs over stiles.

5610 *Letters to the Chartists*
We have used the Bible as if it was a
constable's handbook - an opium-dose for
keeping beasts of burden patient while
they are being overloaded.

5611 *'Ode to the North-East Wind'*
'Tis the hard grey weather
Breeds hard English men.

5612 *'Ode to the North-East Wind'*
Come; and strong within us
Stir the Vikings' blood;
Bracing brain and sinew;
Blow, thou wind of God!

5613 *'The Sands of Dee'*
'O Mary, go and call the cattle home,
And call the cattle home,
And call the cattle home,
Across the sands of Dee.'
The western wind was wild and dank with
foam,
And all alone went she.

5614 *'The Three Fishers'*
Three fishers went sailing away to the west,
Away to the west as the sun went down;
Each thought on the woman who loved him the best,
And the children stood watching them out of the town.

5615 *'The Three Fishers'*
For men must work, and women must weep,
And there's little to earn, and many to keep,
Though the harbour bar be moaning.

5616 *The Water Babies*
As thorough an Englishman as ever coveted his neighbour's goods.

5617 *The Water Babies 'Young and Old'*
When all the world is young, lad,
And all the trees are green;
And every goose a swan, lad,
And every lass a queen;
Then hey for boot and horse, lad,
And round the world away:
Young blood must have its course, lad,
And every dog his day.

5618 *Westward Ho!*
Eustace is a man no longer; he is become a thing, a tool, a Jesuit.

KINGSMILL Hugh 1889-1949
5619
Society is based on the assumption that everyone is alike and no one is alive.

5620 *(on friends)*
God's apology for relations.

5621 *'Two Poems, after A.E. Housman'*
What still alive at twenty-two,
A clean upstanding chap like you?
Sure, if your throat 'tis hard to slit,
Slit your girl's and swing for it.

Like enough, you won't be glad,
When they come to hang you, lad:
But bacon's not the only thing
That's cured by hanging from a string.

KINNOCK Neil 1942-
5622
I will regret to my dying day that I failed to lead you to the victory you deserved.

5623 *(on Tory re-election)*
I warn you not to be ordinary, I warn you not to be young, I warn you not to fall ill, and I warn you not to grow old.

KIPLING Rudyard 1865-1936
5624
There was a small boy of Quebec
Who was buried in snow to the neck:
When they said 'Are you friz?'
He replied 'Yes, I is -
But we don't call this cold in Quebec!'

5625
Nations have passed away and left no traces,
And history gives the naked cause of it -
One single simple reason in all cases;
They fell because their peoples were not fit.

5626
All the people like us are We,
And everyone else is They.

5627
The man who would be king.

5628 *'The Absent-Minded Beggar'*
When you've shouted 'Rule Britannia',
when you've sung 'God save the Queen' -
When you've finished killing Kruger with your mouth.

5629 *For All We Have and Are*
There is but one task for all -
For each one life to give.
What stands if freedom fall?
Who dies if England live?

5630 *'The Anvil'*
England's on the anvil - hear the hammers ring -
Clanging from the Severn to the Tyne!
Never was a blacksmith like our Norman King -
England's being hammered, hammered, hammered into line!

5631 *'The Ballad of East and West'*
Oh, East is East, and West is West, and never the twain shall meet,
Till Earth and Sky stand presently at God's great Judgement Seat;
But there is neither East nor West, Border, nor Breed, nor Birth,

When two strong men stand face to face,
tho' they come from the ends of earth!

5632 *'The Ballad of the King's Jest'*
And the talk slid north, and the talk slid
south,
With the sliding puffs from the hookah-
mouth.
Four things greater than all things are,
Women and Horses and Power and War.

5633 *Barrack-Room Ballads*
There be triple ways to take, of the eagle or
the snake,
Or the way of a man with a maid;
But the sweetest way to me is a ship's
upon the sea
In the heel of the North-East Trade.

5634 *The Betrothed*
And a woman is only a woman but a good
cigar is a Smoke.

5635 *'Boots'*
Foot - foot - foot - foot - sloggin' over
Africa -
(Boots - boots - boots - boots - movin' up
and down again!)

5636 *'Common Form'*
If any question why we died,
Tell them, because our fathers lied.

5637 *'The Conundrum of the Workshops'*
We know that the tail must wag the dog,
for the horse is drawn by the cart;
But the Devil whoops, as he whooped of
old: 'It's clever, but is it Art?'

5638 *'Danny Deever'*
For they're hangin' Danny Deever, you can
hear the Dead March play,
The regiment's in 'ollow square - they're
hanging him to-day;
They've taken of his buttons off an' cut his
stripes away,
An' they're hangin' Danny Deever in the
mornin'.

5639 *'The 'Eathen'*
The 'eathen in 'is blindness bows down to
wood an' stone;
'E don't obey no orders unless they is 'is
own;

5640 *'The 'Eathen'*
The 'eathen in 'is blindness must end
where 'e began.
But the backbone of the Army is the non-
commissioned man!

5641 *'The English Flag'*
Winds of the World, give answer! They
are whimpering to and fro -
And what should they know of England
who only England know?

5642 *'The Female of the Species'*
The female of the species is more deadly
than the male.

5643 *'Fuzzy-Wuzzy'*
So 'ere's *to* you, Fuzzy-Wuzzy, at your
'ome in the Soudan;
You're a pore benighted 'eathen but a first-
class fightin' man;
An' 'ere's *to* you, Fuzzy-Wuzzy, with your
'ayrick 'ead of 'air -
You big black boundin' beggar - for you
broke a British square!

5644 *'Gentlemen-Rankers'*
We're poor little lambs who've lost our
way,
Baa! Baa! Baa!
We're little black sheep who've gone
astray,
Baa-aa-aa!
Gentlemen-rankers out on the spree,
Damned from here to Eternity,
God ha' mercy on such as we,
Baa! Yah! Bah!

5645 *'The Glory of the Garden'*
Our England is a garden, and such gardens
are not made
By singing:- 'Oh, how beautiful!' and
sitting in the shade,
While better men than we go out and start
their working lives
At grubbing weeds from gravel paths with
broken dinner-knives.

5646 *'The Gods of the Copybook Headings'*
As it will be in the future, it was at the
birth of Man -
There are only four things certain since
Social Progress began:-
That the Dog returns to his Vomit and the
Sow returns to her Mire,

And the burnt Fool's bandaged finger goes
wabbling back to the Fire.

5647 *'Gunga Din'*
The uniform 'e wore
Was nothin' much before,
An' rather less than 'arf o' that be'ind.

5648 *'Gunga Din'*
Though I've belted you and flayed you,
By the livin' Gawd that made you,
You're a better man than I am, Gunga Din!

5649 *'The Islanders'*
Then ye returned to your trinkets; then ye
contented your souls
With the flannelled fools at the wicket or
the muddied oafs at the goals.

5650 *The Jungle Book 'Road Song of the
BandarLog'*
Brother, thy tail hangs down behind!

5651 *Just So Stories 'The Cat that Walked ...'*
He walked by himself, and all places were
alike to him.

5652 *Just So Stories 'The Cat that Walked ...'*
And he went back through the Wet Wild
Woods, waving his wild tail and walking
by his wild lone. But he never told
anybody.

5653 *Just So Stories 'The Elephant's Child'*
Then the Elephant's Child put his head
down close to the Crocodile's musky,
tusky mouth, and the Crocodile caught
him by his little nose ... 'Led go! You are
hurtig be!'

5654 *Just So Stories 'The Elephant's Child'*
I keep six honest serving-men
(They taught me all I knew);
Their names are What and Why and When
And How and Where and Who.

5655 *Just So Stories 'How the Camel got his
Hump'*
The cure for this ill is not to sit still,
Or frowst with a book by the fire;
But to take a large hoe and a shovel also,
And dig till you gently perspire.

5656 *Just So Stories 'How the Whale ...'*
And the small 'Stute Fish said in a small
'stute

voice, 'Noble and generous Cetacean, have
you ever tasted Man?' 'No,' said the
Whale. 'What is it like?' 'Nice,' said the
small 'Stute Fish. 'Nice but nubbly.'

5657 *Just So Stories 'How the Whale ...'*
He had his Mummy's leave to paddle, or
else he would never have done it, because
he was a man of infinite-resource-and-
sagacity.

5658 *Kim*
The mad all are in God's keeping.

5659 *'The Ladies'*
I've taken my fun where I've found it,
An' now I must pay for my fun,
For the more you 'ave known o' the others
The less will you settle to one.

5660 *'The Ladies'*
When you get to a man in the case,
They're like as a row of pins -
For the Colonel's Lady an' Judy O'Grady
Are sisters under their skins!

5661 *'Our Lady of the Snows'*
A Nation spoke to a Nation,
A Throne sent word to a Throne:
'Daughter am I in my mother's house,
But mistress in my own.
The gates are mine to open,
As the gates are mine to close,
And I abide by my Mother's House.'
Said our Lady of the Snows.

5662 *'The Last Chantey'*
And Ye take mine honour from me if Ye
take away the sea!

5663 *'The Liner She's a Lady'*
The Liner she's a lady, an' she never looks
nor 'eeds -
The Man-o'-War's 'er 'usband, an' 'e gives
'er all she needs;
But, oh, the little cargo boats that sail the
wet seas roun',
They're just the same as you an' me a-
plyin' up and down!

5664 *'Mandalay'*
On the road to Mandalay,
Where the flyin'-fishes play,
An' the dawn comes up like thunder outer
China 'crost the Bay!

5665 'Mandalay'
An' I seed her first a-smokin' of a whackin'
white cheroot,
An' a-wastin' Christian kisses on an
'eathen idol's foot.

5666 'Mandalay'
Ship me somewheres east of Suez, where
the best is like the worst,
Where there aren't no Ten Commandments
an' a man can raise a thirst.

5667 (of Max Aitken's political standpoint)
Power without responsibility: the
prerogative of the harlot throughout the
ages.

5668 The Naulahka
And the end of the fight is a tombstone
white, with the name of the late deceased,
And the epitaph drear: 'A fool lies here
who tried to hustle the East'.

5669 'In the Neolithic Age'
There are nine and sixty ways of
constructing tribal lays,
And - every - single - one - of - them - is -
right!

5670 'Pagett, MP'
The toad beneath the harrow knows
Exactly where each tooth-point goes;
The butterfly upon the road
Preaches contentment to that toad.

5671 'In Partibus'
But I consort with long-haired things
In velvet collar-rolls,
Who talk about the Aims of Art,
And 'theories' and 'goals',
And moo and coo with women-folk
About their blessed souls.

5672 Plain Tales from the Hills
Every one is more or less mad on one
point.

5673 Plain Tales from the Hills
Take my word for it, the silliest woman can
manage a clever man; but it takes a very
clever woman to manage a fool.

5674 'The Power of the Dog'
There is sorrow enough in the natural way
From men and women to fill our day;
But when we are certain of sorrow in store,

Why do we always arrange for more?
Brothers and Sisters, I bid you beware
Of giving your heart to a dog to tear.

5675 Puck of Pook's Hill 'Harp Song...'
What is a woman that you forsake her,
And the hearth-fire and the home-acre,
To go with the old grey Widow-maker?

5676 Puck of Pook's Hill 'A Smuggler's Song'
Five and twenty ponies,
Trotting through the dark-
Brandy for the parson,
'Baccy for the Clerk;
Laces for a lady, letters for a spy,
Watch the wall, my darling, while the
Gentlemen go by!

5677 Puck of Pook's Hill 'A Tree Song'
Of all the trees that grow so fair,
Old England to adorn,
Greater are none beneath the Sun,
Than Oak, and Ash, and Thorn.

5678 'Recessional'
The tumult and the shouting dies -
The captains and the kings depart -
Still stands Thine ancient Sacrifice,
An humble and a contrite heart.
Lord God of Hosts, be with us yet,
Lest we forget - lest we forget!

5679 'Recessional'
Far-called our navies melt away -
On dune and headland sinks the fire -
Lo, all our pomp of yesterday
Is one with Nineveh, and Tyre!

5680 'Recessional'
If, drunk with sight of power, we loose
Wild tongues that have not Thee in awe -
Such boasting as the Gentiles use,
Or lesser breeds without the Law.

5681 Rewards and Fairies 'If -'
If you can keep your head when all about
you
Are losing theirs and blaming it on you;

5682 Rewards and Fairies 'If -'
If you can trust yourself when all men
doubt you,
But make allowance for their doubting too;
If you can wait and not be tired by
waiting,
Or being lied about, don't deal in lies,

Or being hated, don't give way to hating,
And yet don't look too good, nor talk too
wise;

5683 *Rewards and Fairies 'If -'*
If you can dream - and not make dreams
your master;
If you can think - and not make thoughts
your aim,
If you can meet with triumph and disaster
And treat those two imposters just the
same ...

5684 *Rewards and Fairies 'If -'*
If you can talk with crowds and keep your
virtue,
Or walk with Kings - nor lose the common
touch,
If neither foes nor loving friends can hurt
you,
If all men count with you, but none too
much;

5685 *Rewards and Fairies 'If -'*
If you can fill the unforgiving minute
With sixty seconds' worth of distance run,
Yours is the Earth and everything that's in
it,
And - which is more - you'll be a Man, my
son!

5686 *Rewards and Fairies 'The Thousandth
Man'*
One man in a thousand, Solomon says,
Will stick more close than a brother.

5687 *Rewards and Fairies 'The Way
through...'*
They shut the road through the woods
Seventy years ago.
Weather and rain have undone it again,
And now you would never know
There was once a road through the woods.

5688 *The Second Jungle Book 'Law of the
Jungle'*
Now this is the Law of the Jungle - as old
and as true as the sky;
And the Wolf that shall keep it may
prosper, but the Wolf that shall break it
must die.

5689 *'The Song of the Dead'*
We have fed our sea for a thousand years
And she calls us, still unfed,

Though there's never a wave of all her
waves
But marks our English dead:

5690 *'The Song of the Dead'*
We have strawed our best to the weed's
unrest
To the shark and sheering gull.
If blood be the price of admiralty,
Lord God, we ha' paid in full!

5691 *The Story of the Gadsbys*
Down to Gehenna or up to the Throne,
He travels the fastest who travels alone.

5692 *The Story of the Gadsbys 'Poor Dear
Mamma'*
Being kissed by a man who *didn't* wax his
moustache was - like eating an egg
without salt.

5693 *'Tomlinson'*
For the sin ye do by two and two ye must
pay for one by one!

5694 *'Tommy'*
For it's Tommy this, an' Tommy that, an'
'Chuck him out, the brute!'
But it's 'Saviour of 'is country' when the
guns begin to shoot.

5695 *Traffics and Discoveries 'Mrs Bathurst'*
'Tisn't beauty, so to speak, nor good talk
necessarily. It's just It. Some women'll
stay in a man's memory if they once
walked down a street.

5696 *'The Vampire'*
A fool there was and he made his prayer
(Even as you and I!)
To a rag and a bone and a hank of hair
(We called her the woman who did not
care)
But the fool he called her his lady fair -
(Even as you and I!)

5697 *'What Dane-geld means'*
It is always a temptation to a rich and lazy
nation,
To puff and look important and to say:-
'Though we know we should defeat you,
we have not the time to meet you,
We will therefore pay you cash to go away.

5698 *'When Earth's Last Picture is Painted'*
And only the Master shall praise us, and
only the Master shall blame;
And no one shall work for money, and no
one shall work for fame,
But each for the joy of the working, and
each, in his separate star,
Shall draw the Thing as he sees It for the
God of Things as They are!

5699 *'The White Man's Burden'*
Take up the White Man's burden -
Send forth the best ye breed -
Go, bind your sons to exile
To serve your captives' need.

5700 *'The Young British Soldier'*
When you're wounded and left on
Afghanistan's plains
And the women come out to cut up what
remains
Just roll on your rifle and blow out your
brains
An' go to your Gawd like a soldier.

KISSINGER Henry 1923-
5701
Now when I bore people at a party, they
think it's their fault.

5702
The illegal we do immediately. The
unconstitutional takes a little longer.

5703
The history of things that didn't happen
has never been written.

5704
Intelligence is not all that important in the
exercise of power and is often, in point of
fact, useless. Just as a leader doesn't need
intelligence, a man in my job doesn't need
too much of it either.

5705
Power is the ultimate aphrodisiac.

5706
We are the President's men.

KITCHENER Lord 1850-1916
5707 *(to the Prince of Wales during First
World War)*
I don't mind your being killed, but I object
to your being taken prisoner.

5708 *(to soldiers of British Expeditionary
Force)*
You are ordered abroad as a soldier of the
King to help our French comrades against
the invasion of a common enemy ... In this
new experience you may find temptations
both in wine and women. You must
entirely resist both temptations, and, while
treating all women with perfect courtesy,
you should avoid any intimacy. Do your
duty bravely. Fear God. Honour the king.

KLEE Paul 1879-1940
5709
The more horrifying this world becomes,
the more art becomes abstract.

5710
Art does not reproduce the visible; rather,
it makes visible.

KLOPSTOCK Friedrich 1724-1803
5711 *(of a passage in one of his poems)*
God and I both knew what it meant once;
now God alone knows.

KNIGHT Charles and LYLE Kenneth
5712 *'Here we are! Here we are again!!'*
When there's trouble brewing,
When there's something doing,
Are we downhearted?
No! Let 'em all come!

KNIGHT Frank H. 1885-1973
5713 *Risk, Uncertainty and Profit*
Costs merely register competing
attractions.

KNOWLES Mary 1733-1807
5714 *(of Samuel Johnson)*
He gets at the substance of a book directly;
he tears out the heart of it.

KNOX John c.1505-1572
5715
As the world is wearie of me so am I of it.

5716
A man with God is always in the majority.

5717
The First Blast of the Trumpet Against the
Monstrous Regiment of Women.

KNOX Ronald 1888-1957

5718
O God, for as much as without Thee
We are not enabled to doubt Thee,
Help us all by Thy grace
To convince the whole race
It knows nothing whatever about Thee.

5719
There once was a man who said, 'God
Must think it exceedingly odd
If he finds that this tree
Continues to be
When there's no one about in the Quad.'

5720
It's not the taste of water I object to. It's the after-effects.

5721
The room smelt of not having been smoked in.

5722 *'Absolute and Abitofhell'*
When suave politeness, tempering bigot zeal,
Corrected *I believe to One does feel.*

5723 *(advertisement placed in a newspaper)*
Evangelical vicar, in want of a portable, second-hand font, would dispose, for the same, of a portrait, in frame, of the Bishop, elect, of Vermont.

5724 *(definition of a baby, attributed)*
A loud noise at one end and no sense of responsibility at the other.

5725 *'Magister Reformator'*
Hail him like Etonians, without a single word,
Absolutely silent and indefinitely bored.

5726 *'After the party'*
The tumult and the shouting dies,
The captains and the kings depart,
And we are left with large supplies
Of cold blancmange and rhubarb tart.

5727 *(on being asked to perform a baptism in English)*
The baby doesn't understand English and the Devil knows Latin.

5728 *A Spiritual Aeneid*
After all, what was a paradox but a statement of the obvious so as to make it sound untrue?

KNOX Vicesimus 1752-1821
5729 *Essays Moral and Literary*
That learning belongs not to the female character, and that the female mind is not capable of a degree of improvement equal to that of the other sex, are narrow and unphilosophical prejudices.

5730 *In A Vindication of the Rights of Women*
Can anything be more absurd than keeping women in a state of ignorance, and yet so vehemently to insist on their resisting temptation?

KOCH Kenneth
5731
One trouble with a kind of falsely therapeutic and always reassuring attitude that it is easy to fall into with old people, is the tendency to be satisfied with too little.

KOCH William
5732
Frontal attack never works, sneak attack is always the best.

KOEHLER Ted
5733 *'Stormy Weather'*
Stormy weather,
Since my man and I ain't together.

KOESTLER Arthur 1905-1983
5734
Nothing is more sad than the death of an illusion.

5735
Wars are not fought for territory, but for words. Man's deadliest weapon is language. He is susceptible to being hypnotized by slogans as he is to infectious diseases. And where there is an epidemic, the group-mind takes over.

5736
A writer's ambition should be ... to trade a hundred contemporary readers for ten readers in ten years' time and for one reader in a hundred years.

5737
The more original a discovery, the more obvious it seems afterwards.

5738 *Darkness at Noon*
One may not regard the world as a sort of metaphysical brothel for emotions.

5739 *Darkness at Noon*
The definition of the individual was: a multitude of one million divided by one million.

5740 *The Ghost in the Machine*
Behaviourism is indeed a kind of flat-earth view of the mind ... it has substituted for the erstwhile anthropomorphic view of the rat, a ratomorphic view of man.

5741 *The Ghost in the Machine*
God seems to have left the receiver off the hook, and time is running out.

KOHL Helmut 1930-
5742
We all need Europe, but Germans need it most of all.

The KORAN
5743
That which God writes on thy forehead, thou wilt come to it.

5744
Give God time.

5745
He deserves paradise who makes his companions laugh.

KORZYBSKI Alfred 1879-1950
5746
There are two ways to slide easily through life; to believe everything or doubt everything. Both ways save us from thinking.

KOSINSKI Jerzy 1933-1991
5747
You don't die in the United States, you underachieve.

KRAUS Karl
5748
Stupidity is an elemental force for which no earthquake is a match.

5749
He who gladly does without the praise of the crowd will not miss the opportunity of becoming his own fan.

5750
A writer is someone who can make a riddle out of an answer.

KRISHNAMURTI Jiddu 1895-1986
5751
Discipline does not mean suppression and control, nor is it adjustment to a pattern or ideology. It means a mind that sees 'what is' and learns from 'what was'.

5752
Truth is a pathless land, and you cannot approach it by any path whatsoever, by any religion, by any sect.

5753
Religion is the frozen thought of men out of which they build temples.

KRISTOFFERSON Kris 1936-
5754 *'Me and Bobby McGee'*
Freedom's just another word for nothin' left to lose,
Nothin' ain't worth nothin', but it's free.

KRISTOL Irving
5755
Even if we can't be happy, we must always be cheerful.

KRONENBERGER Louis
5756
Individualism is rather like innocence; there must be something unconscious about it.

KRONSBERG Jeremy Joe
5757
Every which way but loose.

KRUSE Scott M.
5758
As a matter of biology, if something bites you it is probably female.

KRUTCH Joseph Wood 1893-1970
5759
True tragedy may be defined as a dramatic work in which the outward failure of the principal personage is compensated for by

the dignity and greatness of his character.

5760
Cats seem to go on the principle that it never does any harm to ask for what you want.

5761
It is from the artist that society gains its loftier images of itself.

5762
Civilizations die from philosophical calm, irony, and the sense of fair play quite as surely as they die of debauchery.

5763
A humanist is anyone who rejects the attempt to describe or account for man wholly on the basis of physics, chemistry or animal behaviour.

5764
When a man wantonly destroys a work of man we call him a vandal; when a man destroys one of the works of God, we call him a sportsman.

5765
Though many have tried, no one has ever yet explained away the decisive fact that science, which can do so much, cannot decide what it ought to do.

5766 *The Twelve Seasons 'February'*
The most serious charge which can be brought against New England is not Puritanism but February.

KRYLOV Ivan
5767
The weak against the strong,
Is always in the wrong.

KUBRICK Stanley 1928-
5768
The great nations have always acted like gangsters, and the small nations like prostitutes.

KUMAR Satish 1937-
5769 *'Prayer for Peace'*
Lead me from death to life, from falsehood to truth.
Lead me from despair to hope, from fear to trust.
Lead me from hate to love, from war to peace.
Let peace fill our heart, our world, our universe.

KUNDERA Milan 1929-
5770
The unbearable lightness of being.

KUPCINET Irv
5771
Air pollution is turning Mother Nature prematurely gray.

KUSMENKO Mika
5772
Female empowerment is such vague terminology that I doubt it exists in any language but English.

KYD Thomas 1558-1594
5773 *The Spanish Tragedy*
Oh eyes, no eyes, but fountains fraught with tears;
Oh life, no life, but lively form of death;
Oh world, no world, but mass of public wrongs.

5774 *The Spanish Tragedy*
Thus must we toil in other men's extremes,
That know not how to remedy our own.

5775 *The Spanish Tragedy*
I am never better than when I am mad. Then methinks I am a brave fellow; then I do wonders. But reason abuseth me, and there's the torment, there's the hell.

5776 *The Spanish Tragedy*
For what's a play without a woman in it?

LA BRUYERE Jean de 1645-1696
5777 *Les Caractères, 'De la société et la conversation'*
There are some who speak one moment before they think.

5778 *Les Caractères, 'De l'homme'*
The majority of men devote the greater part of their lives to making their remaining years unhappy.

5779 *Les Caractères, 'De quelques usages'*
The punishment of a criminal is an example to the rabble; but every decent man is concerned if an innocent person is

condemned.

5780 *Les Caractères, 'Des femmes'*
Women run to extremes; they are either
better or worse than men.

5781 *Les Caractères, 'Des ouvrages de l'esprit'*
The pleasure of criticizing robs us of the
pleasure of being moved by some very fine
things.

5782 *Les Caractères, 'Du coeur'*
Liberality lies less in giving liberally than
in the timeliness of the gift.

5783 *Les Caractères, 'Du coeur'*
One must laugh before one is happy, or
one may die without ever laughing at all.

LA FONTAINE Jean de 1621-1695
5784
One returns to the place one came from.

5785
Everyone has his faults which he
continually repeats; neither fear nor shame
can cure them.

5786
By the work one knows the workman.

5787 *Fables 'Démocrite et les Abdéritains'*
He knows the universe and does not know
himself.

5788 *Fables 'L'Alouette et ... Maître d'un
Champ'*
Rely only on yourself; it is a common
proverb.

5789 *Fables 'La Mort et le Bûcheron'*
Rather suffer than die is man's motto.

5790 *Fables 'La Mort et le Mourant'*
Death never takes the wise man by
surprise; he is always ready to go.

5791 *Fables 'L'Ane et le Chien'*
People must help one another; it is nature's
law.

5792 *Fables 'Le Chartier Embourbé'*
Aide-toi, le ciel t'aidera.
Help yourself, and heaven will help you.

5793 *Fables 'Le Chêne et le Roseau'*
I bend and I break not.

5794 *Fables 'Le Coq et le Renard'*
It is doubly pleasing to trick the trickster.

5795 *Fables 'Le Corbeau et le Renard'*
Be advised that all flatterers live at the
expense of those who listen to them.

5796 *Fables 'Le Lion et le Rat'*
Patience and passage of time do more than
strength and fury.

5797 *Fables 'Le Loup et l'Agneau'*
The reason of the strongest is always the
best.

5798 *Fables 'Le Meunier, son Fils et l'Ane'*
The greatest ass of the three is not the one
you would think.

5799 *Fables 'Le Milan et le Rossignol'*
A hungry stomach has no ears.

5800 *Fables 'L'Enfant et le Maître d'École'*
My friend, get me out of danger. You can
make your speech afterwards.

5801 *Fables 'Le Rat de Ville et le Rat des
Champs'*
But someone disturbed the feast.

5802 *Fables 'Le Renard et le Bouc'*
This fellow did not see further than his
own nose.

5803 *Fables 'Le Renard et le Bouc'*
In all matters one must consider the end.

5804 *Fables 'L'Ours et les deux Compagnons'*
Never sell the bear's skin before one has
killed the beast.

5805 *Fables 'Parole de Socrate'*
Everyone calls himself a friend, but only a
fool relies on it; nothing is commoner than
the name, nothing rarer than the thing.

LA MANCE Thomas
5806
Life is what happens to us while we are
making other plans.

LA ROCHE Jaquelin
5807
If I advance, follow me! If I retreat, kill
me! If I die, avenge me!

LA ROCHEFOUCAULD François Duc de
1613-1680

5808
We promise according to our hopes, and perform according to our fears.

5809
Few people know how to be old.

5810
Quarrels would not last long if the fault was only on one side.

5811
We often forgive those who bore us, but can't forgive those whom we bore.

5812
Moderation is an ostentatious proof of our strength of character.

5813
He who lives without folly is not as wise as he thinks.

5814
It is not enough to succeed, a friend must fail.

5815
Before we set our hearts too much upon anything, let us examine how happy they are, who already possess it.

5816
No man deserves to be praised for his goodness unless he has the strength of character to be wicked. All other goodness is generally nothing but indolence or impotence of will.

5817
Generosity is the vanity of giving.

5818
There are bad people who would be less dangerous if they were quite devoid of goodness.

5819
Hope, deceitful as it is, serves at least to lead us to the end of life along an agreeable road.

5820
Of all our faults, the one that we excuse most easily is idleness.

5821
We are lazier in our minds than in our bodies.

5822
If we resist our passions, it is more due to their weakness than to our strength.

5823
Weak people cannot be sincere.

5824
When our vices leave us, we flatter ourselves with the credit of having left them.

5825
There are few chaste women who are not tired of their trade.

5826
We are oftener treacherous through weakness than through calculation.

5827
What is perfectly true is perfectly witty.

5828 *Maxims*
Absence diminishes little passions and increases great ones just as the wind blows out a candle and fans a fire.

5829 *Maxims*
We are all strong enough to bear the misfortunes of others.

5830 *Maxims*
There are good marriages, but no delightful ones.

5831 *Maxims*
Hypocrisy is a tribute which vice pays to virtue.

5832 *Maxims*
The height of cleverness is to be able to conceal it.

5833 *Maxims*
There is scarcely a single man sufficiently aware to know all the evil he does.

5834 *Maxims*
In most of mankind gratitude is merely a secret hope for greater favours.

5835 *Maxims*
The accent of one's birthplace lingers in
the mind and in the heart as it does in
one's speech.

5836 *Maxims*
We need greater virtues to bear good
fortune than bad.

5837 *Maxims*
If we had no faults we should not take so
much pleasure in noticing them in others.

5838 *Maxims*
If one judges love by the majority of its
effects, it is more like hatred than like
friendship.

5839 *Maxims*
Love of justice in most men is no more
than the fear of suffering injustice.

5840 *Maxims*
It is more shameful to distrust one's
friends than to be deceived by them.

5841 *Maxims*
Everyone complains of his memory, but no
one complains of his judgement.

5842 *Maxims*
The intellect is always fooled by the heart.

5843 *Maxims*
One gives nothing so freely as advice.

5844 *Maxims*
One had rather malign oneself than not
speak of oneself at all.

5845 *Maxims*
To refuse praise reveals a desire to be
praised twice over.

5846 *Maxims*
Flattery is false coin that is only current
thanks to our vanity.

5847 *Maxims*
We only confess our little faults to
persuade people that we have no large
ones.

5848 *Maxims*
We seldom attribute common sense except
to those who agree with us.

5849 *Maxims*
One can find women who have never had
a love affair, but it is rare to find a woman
who has had only one.

5850 *Maxims*
There are very few people who are not
ashamed of having been in love when they
no longer love each other.

5851 *Réflexions ou Maximes Morales*
In the misfortune of our best friends, we
always find something which is not
displeasing to us.

5852 *Sentences et Maximes de Morale*
One is never as unhappy as one thinks, nor
as happy as one hopes.

LACKINGTON James 1746-1815
5853 *Memoirs*
At last, by singing and repeating
enthusiastic amorous hymns, and
ignorantly applying particular texts of
scripture, I got my imagination to the
proper pitch, and thus was I born again in
an instant.

LACTANTIUS c.240-320
5854
Nobody is poor unless he stand in need of
justice.

LAFORGUE Jules 1860-1887
5855
Ah! que la vie est quotidienne.
Oh, what a day-to-day business life is.

LAING R.D. 1927-1989
5856
When family relations are no longer
harmonious, we have filial children and
devoted parents.

5857
The psychiatrist must become a fellow
traveller with his patient.

5858 *The Politics of Experience*
The brotherhood of man is evoked by
particular men according to their
circumstances ... In the name of our
freedom and our brotherhood we are
prepared to blow up the other half of
mankind and to be blown up in turn.

5859 *The Politics of Experience*
Madness need not be all breakdown. It may also be break-through.

5860 *(of schizophrenia)*
The divided self.

5861 *Self and Others*
True guilt is guilt at the obligation one owes to oneself to be oneself. False guilt is guilt felt at not being what other people feel one ought to be or assume that one is.

LAMARTINE Alphonse de 1790-1869
5862
Limited in his nature, infinite in his desires, man is a fallen god who remembers heaven.

5863
If one had but a single glance to give the world, one should gaze on Istanbul.

5864 *Le Lac*
O time, suspend your flight, and you, happy hours, stay your feet! Let us savour the swift delights of our life's loveliest days!

5865 *'L'Isolement'*
Sometimes, when one person is missing, the whole world seems depopulated.

LAMB A.J. 1870-1928
5866
She's a bird in gilded cage.

LAMB Lady Caroline 1785-1828
5867 *(on first meeting Lord Byron)*
Mad, bad, and dangerous to know.

LAMB Charles 1775-1834
5868
We do not go (to the theatre) like our ancestors, to escape from the pressure of reality, so much as to confirm our experience of it.

5869
Here cometh April again, and as far as I can see the world hath more fools in it than ever.

5870
New Year's Day is every man's birthday.

5871
To be sick is to enjoy monarchal prerogatives.

5872
The only true time which a man can properly call his own, is that which he has all to himself; the rest, though in some sense he may be said to live it, is other people's time, not his.

5873
If dirt were trumps, what hands you would hold!

5874 *(on the death of his mother)*
I have something more to do than feel.

5875 *Essays of Elia 'A Bachelor's Complaint'*
I know that a sweet child is the sweetest thing in nature ... but the prettier the kind of a thing is, the more desirable it is that it should be pretty of its kind.

5876 *Essays of Elia 'Mrs Battle's Opinions'*
She unbent her mind afterwards - over a book.

5877 *Essays of Elia 'Mrs Battle's Opinions on Whist'*
They do not play at cards, but only play at playing at them.

5878 *Essays of Elia 'Mrs Battle's Opinions on Whist'*
Man is a gaming animal. He must always be trying to get the better in something or other.

5879 *Essays of Elia 'A Chapter on Ears'*
Sentimentally I am disposed to harmony. But organically I am incapable of a tune.

5880 *Essays of Elia 'A Dissertation upon Roast Pig'*
Presents, I often say, endear Absents.

5881 *Essays of Elia 'Dream Children'*
We are nothing; less than nothing, and dreams. We are only what might have been, and must wait upon the tedious shores of Lethe millions of ages before we have existence, and a name.

5882 *Essays of Elia 'Imperfect Sympathies'*
I am, in plainer words, a bundle of prejudices - made up of likings and dis-

likings.

5883 *Essays of Elia 'Imperfect Sympathies'*
I have been trying all my life to like
Scotchmen, and am obliged to desist from
the experiment of despair.

5884 *Essays of Elia 'The Old and the New
Schoolmaster'*
Boys are capital fellows in their own way,
among their mates; but they are unwholesome companions for grown people.

5885 *Essays of Elia 'Oxford in the Vacation'*
A votary of the desk - a notched and cropt
scrivener - one that sucks his substance, as
certain sick people are said to do, through
a quill.

5886 *Essays of Elia 'Quakers' Meeting'*
The uncommunicating muteness of fishes.

5887 *Essays of Elia 'The Two Races of Men'*
The human species, according to the best
theory I can form of it, is composed of two
distinct races, *the men who borrow*, and *the
men who lend*.

5888 *Essays of Elia 'The Two Races of Men'*
Your *borrowers of books* - those mutilators of
collections, spoilers of the symmetry of
shelves, and creators of odd volumes.

5889 *Essays of Elia 'Valentine's Day'*
Not many sounds in life, and I include all
urban and all rural sounds, exceed in
interest a knock at the door.

5890 *Essays of Elia 'Witches, and Other...'*
Credulity is the man's weakness, but the
child's strength.

5891 *'A Farewell to Tobacco'*
For thy sake, Tobacco, I
Would do any thing but die.

5892 *'Hester'*
Gone before
To that unknown and silent shore.

5893 *'On an Infant Dying as soon as Born'*
Riddle of destiny, who can show
What thy short visit meant, or know
What thy errand here below?

5894 *'The Jovial Crew'*
What a lass that were to go a-gipsying
through the world with.

5895 *Last Essays of Elia 'The Convalescent'*
How sickness enlarges the dimensions of a
man's self to himself.

5896 *Last Essays of Elia 'Detached Thoughts'*
Books think for me.

5897 *Last Essays of Elia 'Detached Thoughts'*
Things in books' clothing.

5898 *Last Essays of Elia 'Detached Thoughts'*
Newspapers always excite curiosity. No
one ever lays one down without a feeling
of disappointment.

5899 *Last Essays of Elia 'Poor Relations'*
A poor relation - is the most irrelevant
thing in nature.

5900 *Last Essays of Elia 'Popular Fallacies'*
[A pun] is a pistol let off at the ear; not a
feather to tickle the intellect.

5901 *Letter to B.W. Proctor*
When my sonnet was rejected, I exclaimed,
'Damn the age; I will write for Antiquity!'

5902 *Letter to Dorothy Wordsworth*
How I like to be liked, and what I do to be
liked!

5903 *Letter to Southey*
Anything awful makes me laugh. I mis-
behaved once at a funeral.

5904 *Letter to S.T. Coleridge*
Cultivate simplicity, Coleridge.

5905 *Letter to Thomas Manning*
The man must have a rare recipe for
melancholy, who can be dull in Fleet
Street.

5906 *Letter to Thomas Manning*
Nothing puzzles me more than time and
space; and yet nothing troubles me less, as
I never think about them.

5907 *Letter to Thomas Manning*
This very night I am going to leave off
tobacco! Surely there must be some other
world in which this unconquerable
purpose shall be realized.

5908 *Letter to Wordsworth (of Coleridge)*
An Archangel a little damaged.

5909 *'The Old Familiar Faces'*
I have had playmates, I have had
companions,
In my days of childhood, in my youthful
school-days,
All, all are gone, the old familiar faces.

5910 *'Parental Recollections'*
A child's a plaything for an hour.

5911 *'Table Talk by the late Elia'*
The greatest pleasure I know, is to do a
good action by stealth, and to have it
found out by accident.

5912 *(written in a copy of Coeleb's In Search of
a Wife)*
If ever I marry a wife,
I'll marry a landlord's daughter,
For then I may sit in the bar,
And drink cold brandy and water.

LAMBERT Constant 1905-1951
5913
The average English critic is a don *manqué*,
hopelessly parochial when not
exaggeratedly teutonophile, over whose
desk must surely hang the motto
(presumably in Gothic lettering) 'Above all
no enthusiasm'.

5914 *Music Ho!*
The whole trouble with a folk song is that
once you have played it through there is
nothing much you can do except play it
over again and play it rather louder.

LAMBTON John George 1792-1840
5915
£40,000 a year a moderate income - such a
one as a man *might jog on with.*

LAMMING George 1927-
5916
In the castle of my skin.

LAMONT Norman 1942-
5917
We give the impression of being in office
but not in power.

5918
Politics is like surfing. You are bound to
fall off from time to time.

LAMPEDUSA Prince Giuseppe di 1896-
1957
5919 *The Leopard*
If we want things to stay as they are,
things will have to change.

LAMPTON William James 1859-1917
5920 *June Weddings*
Same old slippers,
Same old rice,
Same old glimpse of
Paradise.

LANCE Bert 1931-
5921 *Nation's Business*
If it ain't broke, don't fix it.

LANDERS Ann 1918-
5922
Trouble is the common denominator of
living. It is the great equalizer.

5923
Class is an aura of confidence that is being
sure without being cocky. Class has
nothing to do with money. Class never
runs scared. It is self-discipline and self-
knowledge. It's the sure-footedness that
comes with having proved you can meet
life.

5924
Television has proved that people will look
at anything rather than each other.

5925
If you want your children to listen, try
talking softly - to someone else.

5926
We wouldn't worry so much about what
people thought of us if we knew how
seldom they did.

LANDON Letitia Elizabeth (L.E.L.) 1802-
1838
5927 *Apple Blossoms*
As beautiful as woman's blush,
As evanescent too.

5928 *'The Poor'*
Few, save the poor, feel for the poor.

LANDOR Walter Savage 1775-1864

5929
A man's vanity tells him what is honour; a man's conscience what is justice.

5930
Great men too often have greater faults than little men can find room for.

5931
Literature is the effort of man to indemnify himself for the wrongs of his condition.

5932
An ingenuous mind feels in unmerited praise the bitterest reproof.

5933 *'Death stands above me'*
Death stands above me, whispering low
I know not what into my ear;
Of his strange language all I know
Is, there is not a word of fear.

5934 *Deceive Me Once Again*
You smiled, you spoke, and I believed,
By every word and smile deceived.
Another man would hope no more;
Nor hope I what I hoped before:
But let not this last wish be vain:
Deceive, deceive me once again!

5935 *'Dying Speech of an Old Philosopher'*
I strove with none; for none was worth my strife;
Nature I loved, and, next to Nature, Art.

5936 *Epigram in The Atlas*
George the First was always reckoned
Vile, but viler George the Second;
And what mortal ever heard
Any good of George the Third?
When from earth the Fourth descended
God be praised the Georges ended!

5937 *'To Ianthe'*
'Tis verse that gives
Immortal youth to mortal maids.

5938 *Imaginary Conversations 'Aesop and Rhodope'*
There are no fields of amaranth on this side of the grave.

5939 *Imaginary Conversations*
Prose on certain occasions can bear a great deal of poetry: on the other hand, poetry sinks and swoons under a moderate weight of prose.

5940 *Imaginary Conversations 'Pollio and Calvus'*
States, like men, have their growth, their manhood, their decrepitude, their decay.

5941 *Imaginary Conversations*
Clear writers, like clear fountains, do not seem so deep as they are; the turbid look the most profound.

5942 *Imaginary Conversations*
Fleas know not whether they are upon the body of a giant or upon one of ordinary size.

5943 *'Ireland never was contented'*
Ireland never was contented ...
Say you so? You are demented.
Ireland was contented when
All could use the sword and pen.

5944 *'To Robert Browning'*
There is delight in singing, tho' none hear
Beside the singer.

5945 *'Rose Aylmer'*
Ah, what avails the sceptred race!
Ah, what the form divine!

5946 *'To Wordsworth: Those Who Have Laid the Harp ...'*
Thee gentle Spenser fondly led;
But me he mostly sent to bed.

LANE George Martin 1823-1897
5947 *One Fish-Ball*
The waiter roars it through the hall:
'We don't give bread with one fish-ball!'

LANG Andrew 1844-1912
5948
He uses statistics as a drunken man uses lamp-posts - for support rather than illumination.

5949 *'Almae Matres'*
St Andrews by the Northern sea,
A haunted town it is to me!

5950 *'Brahma'*
If the wild bowler thinks he bowls,
Or if the batsman thinks he's bowled,
They know not, poor misguided souls,
They too shall perish unconsoled.

I am the batsman and the bat,
I am the bowler and the ball,
The umpire, the pavilion cat,
The roller, pitch and stumps, and all.

5951 *'The Odyssey'*
They hear like ocean on a western beach
The surge and thunder of the Odyssey.

LANG Julia 1921-
5952 *on Listen with Mother*
"Are you sitting comfortably? Then I'll
begin."

LANGBRIDGE Frederick 1849-1923
5953 *Cluster of Quiet Thoughts*
Two men look out through the same bars:
One sees the mud, and one the stars.

LANGER Susanne 1895-1985
5954 *Mind*
Art is the objectification of feeling, and the
subjectification of nature.

LANGLAND William c.1330-1400
5955 *The Vision of Piers Plowman*
In a somer seson, whan softe was the
sonne.

5956 *The Vision of Piers Plowman*
A faire feeld ful of folk fond I ther bitwene
Of alle manere of men, the meene and the
riche,
Werchynge and wandrynge as the world
asketh.

5957 *The Vision of Piers Plowman*
A gloton of wordes.

5958 *The Vision of Piers Plowman*
Whan alle tresors arn tried, Truthe is the
beste.

5959 *The Vision of Piers Plowman*
Brewesters and baksters, bochiers and
cokes -
For thise are men on this molde that moost
harm wercheth
To the povere peple.

5960 *The Vision of Piers Plowman*
For if hevene be on this erthe, and ese to
any soule,
It is in cloistre or in scole.

5961 *The Vision of Piers Plowman*
Suffraunce is a soverayn vertue, and a
swift vengeaunce.
Who suffreth moore than God?

5962 *The Vision of Piers Plowman*
Grammer, the ground of al.

5963 *The Vision of Piers Plowman*
Innocence is next God, and nyght and day
it crieth
'Vengeaunce! Vengeaunce! Forgyve be it
nevere
That shente us and shedde oure blood!

5964 *The Vision of Piers Plowman*
'After sharpest shoures,' quath Pees 'most
shene is the sonne;
Is no weder warmer than after watry
cloudes.'

5965 *The Vision of Piers Plowman*
Forthi be noght abassed to bide and to be
nedy,
Since he that wroghte al the world was
wilfulliche nedy.

LANGTON Stephen c.1150-1228
5966 *The 'Golden Sequence' for Whit Sunday*
Come, Holy Spirit, and send out from
heaven the beam of your light.

LAO-TSU c.604-531 BC
5967
The reality of the building does not consist
in the roof and walls, but in the space
within to be lived in.

5968
To lead the people, walk behind them.

5969
As for the best leaders, the people do not
notice their existence. The next best, the
people honour and praise. The next, the
people fear, and the next the people hate.
When the best leader's work is done, the
people say, 'we did it ourselves!'

5970 *Tao-Tê-Ching*
Heaven and Earth are not ruthful;
To them the Ten Thousand Things are but
as straw dogs.

5971 *Tao-Tê-Ching*
The Way is like an empty vessel that yet
may be drawn from.

LAPHAM Lewis H.
5972
The supply of government exceeds the
demand.

LARDNER Ring 1885-1933
5973
They gave each other a smile with a future
in it.

5974
How can you write if you can't cry?

5975 *The Young Immigrunts*
Are you lost daddy I arsked tenderly.
Shut up he explained.

LARKIN Philip 1922-1985
5976 *'Annus Mirabilis'*
Sexual intercourse began
In nineteen sixty-three
(Which was rather late for me) -
Between the end of the *Chatterley* ban
And the Beatles' first LP.

5977 *'An Arundel Tomb'*
Time has transfigured them into
Untruth. The stone fidelity
They hardly meant has come to be
Their final blazon, and to prove
Our almost-instinct almost true:
What will survive of us is love.

5978 *'Church Going'*
Hatless, I take off
My cycle-clips in awkward reverence.

5979 *'Church Going'*
A serious house on serious earth it is,
In whose blent air all our compulsions
meet,
Are recognised, and robed as destinies.

5980 *'Days'*
What are days for?
Days are where we live.
They come, they wake us
Time and time over.
They are to be happy in:
Where can we live but days?

5981 *'Dockery & Son'*
Life is first boredom, then fear.
Whether or not we use it, it goes,
And leaves what something hidden from
us chose,
And age, and then the only end of age.

5982 *'High Windows'*
Rather than words comes the thought of
high windows:
The sun-comprehending glass,
And beyond it, the deep blue air, that
shows
Nothing, and is nowhere, and is endless.

5983 *'Homage to a Government'*
Next year we shall be living in a country
That brought its soldiers home for lack of
money.
The statues will be standing in the same
Tree-muffled squares, and look nearly the
same.
Our children will not know it's a different
country.
All we can hope to leave them now is
money.

5984 *'MCMXIV'*
Never such innocence,
Never before or since,
As changed itself to past
Without a word - the men
Leaving the gardens tidy,
The thousands of marriages
Lasting a little while longer:
Never such innocence again.

5985 *(novel formula)*
A beginning, a muddle, and an end.

5986 *'The Old Fools'*
Perhaps being old is having lighted rooms
Inside your head, and people in them,
acting.
People you know, yet can't quite name.

5987 *'Study of Reading Habits'*
Don't read too much now: the dude
Who lets the girl down before
The hero arrives, the chap
Who's yellow and keeps the store,
Seem far too familiar. Get stewed:
Books are a load of crap.

5988 *'I Remember, I Remember'*
Nothing, like something, happens
anywhere.

5989 *Required Writing*
Deprivation is for me what daffodils were
for Wordsworth.

5990 *'Toads'*
Why should I let the toad *work*
Squat on my life?
Can't I use my wit as a pitchfork
And drive the brute off?

Six days of the week it soils
With its sickening poison -
Just for paying a few bills!
That's out of proportion.

5991 *'Toads Revisited'*
Give me your arm, old toad;
Help me down Cemetery Road.

5992 *'This Be The Verse'*
They fuck you up, your mum and dad.
They may not mean to, but they do.
They fill you with the faults they had
And add some extra, just for you.

5993 *'This Be The Verse'*
Man hands on misery to man.
It deepens like a coastal shelf.
Get out as early as you can,
And don't have any kids yourself.

5994 *'The Whitsun Weddings'*
I thought of London spread out in the sun,
Its postal districts packed like squares of
wheat.

LATHAM Peter
5995
Common sense is in medicine the master
workman.

LATIMER Hugh c.1485-1555
5996 *(prior to being burned for heresy)*
Be of good comfort Master Ridley, and
play the man. We shall this day light such
a candle by God's grace in England, as (I
trust) shall never be put out.

5997 *The Second Sermon preached ...*
The drop of rain maketh a hole in the
stone, not by violence, but by oft falling.

LAUDER Sir Harry 1870-1950
5998
The future is not a gift - it is an
achievement.

5999
If y'can say
It's a braw brecht moonlecht necht,
Yer a' recht, ye ken.

6000
O! it's nice to get up in the mornin',
But it's nicer to stay in bed.

6001 *'The End of the Road'*
Keep right on to the end of the road,
Keep right on to the end.
Tho' the way be long, let your heart be
strong,
Keep right on round the bend.
Tho' you're tired and weary,
Still journey on
Till you come to your happy abode,
Where all you love you've been dreaming
of
Will be there at the end of the road.

6002 *'I Love a Lassie'*
I love a lassie, a bonnie, bonnie lassie,
She's as pure as the lily in the dell.
She's as sweet as the heather, the bonnie
bloomin' heather -
Mary, ma Scotch Bluebell.

6003 *'Roamin' in the Gloamin''*
Roamin' in the gloamin',
On the bonnie banks o' Clyde.
Roamin' in the gloamin'
Wae my lassie by my side.

LAURENCE Margaret
6004
Follow your heart, and you perish.

LAURENCE William L. 1888-1977
6005 *(of first atomic explosion)*
At first it was a giant column that soon
took the shape of a supramundane
mushroom.

LAURIER Rt. Hon. Sir Wilfrid 1841-1919
6006
The Englishman respects your opinions,
but he never thinks of your feelings.

LAVATER Johann Kaspar
6007
He who, when called upon to speak a disagreeable truth, tells it boldly and has done, is both bolder and milder than he who nibbles in a low voice and never ceases nibbling.

LAVER James 1899-1975
6008
Clothes are nothing less than the furniture of the mind made visible.

6009 *Taste and Fashion*
The same costume will be
Indecent ... 10 years before its time
Shameless ... 5 years before its time
Outré (daring) 1 year before its time
Smart
Dowdy ... 1 year after its time
Hideous ... 10 years after its time
Ridiculous ... 20 years after its time
Amusing ... 30 years after its time
Quaint ... 50 years after its time
Charming ... 70 years after its time
Romantic ... 100 years after its time
Beautiful ... 150 years after its time

LAW Andrew Bonar 1858-1923
6010
If I am a great man, then a good many of the great men of history are frauds.

6011
There is no such thing as inevitable war. If war comes it will be from failure of human wisdom.

LAW Vernon
6012
Experience is the worst teacher; it gives the test before presenting the lesson.

LAW William
6013
Be intent upon the perfection of the present day.

LAWRENCE D.H. 1885-1930
6014
Art-speech is the only truth. An artist is usually a damned liar but his art, if it be art, will tell you the truth of his day. And that is all that matters. Away with eternal truth. The truth lives from day to day, and the marvellous Plato of yesterday is chiefly bosh today.

6015
Life is ours to be spent, not to be saved.

6016
Never trust the artist. Trust the tale. The proper function of a critic is to save the tale from the artist who created it.

6017 *'Don'ts'*
Don't be sucked in by the su superior,
don't swallow the culture bait,
don't drink, don't drink and get beerier and beerier,
do learn to discriminate.

6018 *Dull London*
The English people on the whole are surely the *nicest* people in the world, and everyone makes everything so easy for everybody else, that there is almost nothing to resist at all.

6019 *Etruscan Places 'Cerveteri'*
To the Puritan all things are impure, as somebody says.

6020 *Now It's Happened*
Too much of the humble Willy wet-leg
And the holy can't-help-it touch.

6021 *'How Beastly the Bourgeois Is'*
How beastly the bourgeois is
Especially the male of the species.

6022 *Lady Chatterley's Lover*
Ours is essentially a tragic age, so we refuse to take it tragically.

6023 *Lady Chatterley's Lover*
And here lies the vast importance of the novel, properly handled. It can inform and lead into new places the flow of our sympathetic consciousness and it can lead our sympathy away in recoil from things gone dead.

6024 *Lady Chatterley's Lover*
John Thomas says good-night to Lady Jane, a little droopingly, but with a hopeful heart.

6025 *'Leave Sex Alone'*
... While we think of it, and talk of it
Let us leave it alone, physically, keep

apart.
For while we have sex in the mind, we truly have none in the body.

6026 *Letter to A.W. McLeod*
Tragedy ought really to be a great kick at misery.

6027 *Letter to Edward Garnett*
Curse the blasted, jelly-boned swines, the slimy, the belly-wriggling invertebrates, the miserable sodding rotters, the flaming sods, the snivelling, dribbling, dithering, palsied, pulse-less lot that make up England today. They've got white of egg in their veins, and their spunk is that watery it's a marvel they can breed. They *can* nothing but frog-spawn - the gibberers! God, how I hate them!

6028 *Letter to J. Middleton Murry*
The dead don't die. They look on and help.

6029 *Letter to J. Middleton Murry*
I want to go south, where there is no autumn, where the cold doesn't crouch over one like a snow-leopard waiting to pounce. The heart of the North is dead, and the fingers of cold are corpse fingers.

6030 *Letter to Lady Cynthia Asquith*
I like to write when I feel spiteful; it's like having a good sneeze.

6031 *'Mountain Lion'*
Men! The only animal in the world to fear!

6032 *Phoenix*
The English ... are paralysed by fear. That is what thwarts and distorts the Anglo-Saxon existence ... Nothing could be more lovely and fearless than Chaucer. But already Shakespeare is morbid with fear, fear of consequences. That is the strange phenomenon of the English Renaissance: this mystic terror of the consequences, the consequences of action.

6033 *Phoenix*
If you try to nail anything down in the novel, either it kills the novel, or the novel gets up and walks away with the nail.

6034 *Phoenix*
Morality in the novel is the trembling instability of the balance. When the novelist puts his thumb in the scale, to pull down the balance to his own predilection, that is immorality.

6035 *Phoenix*
Pornography is the attempt to insult sex, to do dirt on it.

6036 *Phoenix*
In life ... no new thing has ever arisen, or can arise, save out of the impulse of the male upon the female, the female upon the male. The interaction of the male and female spirit begot the wheel, the plough, and the first utterance that was made on the face of the earth.

6037 *Phoenix*
The novel is the one bright book of life.

6038 *'Piano'*
So now it is vain for the singer to burst into clamour
With the great black piano appassionato. The glamour
Of childish days is upon me, my manhood is cast
Down in the flood of remembrance, I weep like a child for the past.

6039 *'Self-Pity'*
I never saw a wild thing
Sorry for itself.

6040 *'Snake'*
A snake came to my water-trough
On a hot, hot day, and I in pyjamas for the heat,
To drink there.

6041 *'Snake'*
And so, I missed my chance with one of the lords
Of life.
And I have something to expiate:
A pettiness.

6042 *'Song of a Man who has Come Through'*
Not I, not I, but the wind that blows through me!
A fine wind is blowing the new direction of Time.

6043 *'When I Read Shakespeare'*
When I read Shakespeare I am struck with
wonder
That such trivial people should muse and
thunder
In such lovely language.

6044 *The White Peacock*
Be a good animal, true to your instincts.

6045 *Women in Love*
Don't you find it a beautiful clean thought,
a world empty of people, just
uninterrupted grass, and a hare sitting up?

LAWRENCE T.E. 1888-1935
6046 *The Mint*
Many men would take the death-sentence
without a whimper to escape the life-
sentence which fate carries in her other
hand.

6047 *The Mint*
The trumpets came out brazenly with the
last post. We all swallowed our spittle,
chokingly, while our eyes smarted against
our wills. A man hates to be moved to
folly by a noise.

6048 *The Seven Pillars of Wisdom*
I loved you, so I drew these tides of men
into my hands and wrote my will across
the sky in stars
To earn you freedom, the seven pillared
worthy house, that your eyes might be
shining for me
When we came.

LAWRENSON Helen
6049
Whatever else can be said about sex, it
cannot be called a dignified performance.

6050
You have to go back to the Children's
Crusade in 1212 AD to find as unfortunate
and fatuous an attempt at manipulated
hysteria as the Women's Liberation
Movement.

LAWSON Sonia 1934-
6051
You're not meant to understand - They're
bloody works of art.

LAZARUS Arnold and FAY Alan
6052
We firmly believe that therapy is education
rather than healing; that it is growth rather
than treatment.

LAZARUS Emma 1849-1887
6053 *'The New Colossus' (inscribed on Statue
of Liberty)*
Give me your tired, your poor,
Your huddled masses yearning to breathe
free,
The wretched refuse of your teeming
shore,
Send these, the homeless, tempest-tossed,
to me:
I lift my lamp beside the golden door.

LE CARRÉ John 1931-
6054
He has the gift of quiet.

6055
The spy who came in from the cold.

6056 *A Perfect Spy*
Love is whatever you can still betray ...
Betrayal can only happen if you love.

LE CORBUSIER 1887-1965
6057
The materials of city planning are sky,
space, trees, steel and cement in that order
and in that hierarchy.

6058
Genius is personal, decided by fate, but it
expresses itself by means of system. There
is no work of art without system.

6059
A house is a machine for living in.

6060
This frightful word [function] was born
under other skies than those I have loved -
those where the sun reigns supreme.

LE GALLIENNE Richard 1866-1947
6061 *'The Cry of the Little Peoples'*
The cry of the Little People goes up to God
in vain,
For the world is given over to the cruel
sons of Cain.

6062 *Song*
She's somewhere in the sunlight strong,
Her tears are in the falling rain,
She calls me in the wind's soft song,
And with the flowers she comes again.

LEACH Sir Edmund 1910-1989
6063 *(Reith Lectures)*
Far from being the basis of the good
society, the family, with its narrow privacy
and tawdry secrets, is the source of all our
discontents.

LEACH Jim
6064
Patriotism is when you risk your life not
when you risk your wallet.

LEACH Reggie
6065
Success is not the result of spontaneous
combustion. You must set yourself on fire.

LEACOCK Stephen 1869-1944
6066
When actors begin to think, it is time for a
change. They are not fitted for it.

6067
Advertising may be described as the
science of arresting the human intelligence
long enough to get money from it.

6068
The sorrows and disasters of Europe
always brought fortune to America.

6069
The Lord said 'let there be wheat' and
Saskatchewan was born.

6070
I'm a great believer in luck. I find the
harder I work, the more I have of it.

6071
The British are terribly lazy about fighting.
They like to get it over and done with and
then set up a game of cricket.

6072
The best definition of humour I know is:
humour may be defined as the kindly
contemplation of the incongruities of life,
and the artistic expression thereof. I think
this is the best I know because I wrote it

myself.

6073
You encourage a comic man too much, and
he gets silly.

6074
Any man will admit if need be that his
sight is not good, or that he cannot swim
or shoots badly with a rifle, but to touch
upon his sense of humour is to give him
mortal affront.

6075
Life, we learn too late, is in the living, in
the tissue of every day and hour.

6076
The classics are only primitive literature.
They belong to the same class as primitive
machinery and primitive music and
primitive medicine.

6077
Many a man in love with a dimple makes
the mistake of marrying the whole girl.

6078
A half truth, like half a brick, is always
more forcible as an argument than a whole
one. It carries better.

6079
Writing is no trouble: you just jot down
ideas as they occur to you. The jotting is
simplicity itself - it is the occurring which
is difficult.

6080 *Here are my Lectures*
I am what is called a *professor emeritus* from
the Latin *e*, 'out', and *meritus*, 'so he ought
to be'.

6081 *Literary Lapses 'Boarding-House
Geometry'*
The landlady of a boarding-house is a
parallelogram - that is, an oblong figure,
which cannot be described, but which is
equal to anything.

6082 *Literary Lapses 'A Manual of Education'*
Electricity is of two kinds, positive and
negative. The difference is, I presume, that
one comes a little more expensive, but is
more durable; the other is a cheaper thing,
but the moths get into it.

6083 Literary Lapses 'Reflections on Riding'
There are no handles to a horse, but the
1910 model has a string to each side of its
face for turning its head when there is
anything you want it to see.

*6084 Nonsense Novels 'Gertrude the
Governess'*
He flung himself from the room, flung
himself upon his horse and rode madly off
in all directions.

6085 My Remarkable Uncle
A sportsman is a man who, every now
and then, simply has to get out and kill
something. Not that he's cruel. He
wouldn't hurt a fly. It's not big enough.

LEAPOR Mary 1722-1746
6086 'An Essay on Woman'
Woman, a pleasing but a short-lived
flower,
Too soft for business and too weak for
power:
A wife in bondage, or neglected maid:
Despised, if ugly; if she's fair, betrayed.

6087 'Mira to Octavia'
In spite of all romantic poets sing,
This gold, my dearest, is an useful thing.

LEAR Edward 1812-1888
6088 A Book of Nonsense
There was an Old Man with a beard,
Who said, 'It is just as I feared! -

Two Owls and a Hen,
Four Larks and a Wren,
Have all built their nests in my beard!'

6089 Book of Nonsense
There was an Old Man in a tree,
Who was horribly bored by a bee;
When they said, 'Does it buzz?'
He replied, 'Yes, it does!
It's a regular brute of a bee!'

6090 'The Courtship of the Yonghy-Bonghy-Bó
On the coast of Coromandel
Where the early pumpkins blow,
In the middle of the woods,
Lived the Yonghy-Bonghy-Bó.
Two old chairs, and half a candle;
One old jug without a handle,
These were all his worldly goods.

6091 'The Dong with a Luminous Nose'
'The Dong! - the Dong!
The wandering Dong through the forest
goes!
The Dong! - the Dong!
The Dong with a Luminous Nose!'

6092 'The Jumblies'
Far and few, far and few,
Are the lands were the Jumblies live;
Their heads are green, and their hands are
blue,
And they went to sea in a Sieve.

6093 'The Jumblies'
They called aloud 'Our Sieve ain't big,
But we don't care a button! We don't care
a fig!'

6094 Nonsense Songs (preface)
'How pleasant to know Mr Lear!'
Who has written such volumes of stuff!
Some think him ill-tempered and queer,
But a few think him pleasant enough.

6095 Nonsense Songs (preface)
He has many friends, laymen and clerical.
Old Foss is the name of his cat:
His body is perfectly spherical,
He weareth a runcible hat.

6096 'The Owl and the Pussy-Cat'
The Owl and the Pussy-Cat went to sea
In a beautiful pea-green boat.
They took some honey, and plenty of
money,
Wrapped up in a five-pound note.
The Owl looked up to the Stars above
And sang to a small guitar,
'Oh lovely Pussy! O Pussy, my love,
What a beautiful Pussy you are.'

6097 'The Owl and the Pussy-Cat'
'Dear Pig, are you willing to sell for one
shilling
Your ring?' Said the Piggy, 'I will.'

6098 'The Owl and the Pussy-Cat'
They dined on mince, and slices of quince,
Which they ate with a runcible spoon;
And hand in hand, on the edge of the
sand,
They danced by the light of the moon.

6099 *'The Pobble Who Has No Toes'*
The Pobble who has no toes
Had once as many as we;
When they said, 'Some day you may lose
them all';
He replied, 'Fish fiddle de-dee!'

6100 *'The Pobble Who Has No Toes'*
When boats or ships came near him
He tinkledy-binkledy-winkled a bell.

6101 *'The Quangle-Wangle's Hat'*
'But the longer I live on this Crumpetty
Tree
The plainer than ever it seems to me
That very few people come this way
And that life on the whole is far from gay!'
Said the Quangle-Wangle Quee.

6102 *'The Two Old Bachelors'*
And what can we expect if we haven't any
dinner,
But to lose our teeth and eyelashes and
keep on growing thinner.

LEARY Timothy 1920-
6103
If you take the game of life seriously, if you
take your nervous system seriously, if you
take your sense organs seriously, if you
take the energy process seriously, you
must turn on, tune in and drop out.

LEAVIS F.R. 1895-1978
6104
The common pursuit.

6105 *The Great Tradition*
The few really great - the major novelists ...
are significant in terms of the human
awareness they promote; awareness of the
possibilities of life.

6106 *New Bearings in English Poetry*
The Sitwells belong to the history of
publicity rather than of poetry.

LEAVITT Robert Keith
6107
People don't ask for facts in making up
their minds. They would rather have one
good, soul-satisfying emotion than a dozen
facts.

LEBOWITZ Fran 1946-
6108
Ask your child what he wants for dinner
only if he is buying.

6109 *Metropolitan Life*
There is no such thing as inner peace.
There is only nervousness or death.

6110 *Metropolitan Life*
Life is something to do when you can't
sleep.

LEC Stanislaw 1909-1966
6111
I give you bitter pills in sugar coating. The
pills are harmless: the poison is in the
sugar.

6112
In a war of ideas it is people who get
killed.

6113 *Unkempt Thoughts*
Is it progress if a cannibal uses knife and
fork?

LEDRU-ROLLIN Alexandre
6114
I've got to follow them - I am their leader.

LEE Gypsy Rose 1914-1970
6115 *(attributed)*
God is love, but get it in writing.

LEE Harper 1926-
6116 *To Kill a Mockingbird*
Shoot all the bluejays you want, if you can
hit 'em, but remember it's a sin to kill a
mockingbird.

LEE Henry ('Light-Horse Harry') 1756-
1818
6117 *(funeral Oration for George Washington)*
A citizen, first in war, first in peace, and
first in the hearts of his countrymen.

LEE Laurie 1914-
6118
The urge to write is also the fear of death -
the need to leave messages saying 'I was
here, I saw it too.'

6119 *Cider with Rosie*
I was set down from the carrier's cart at
the age of three; and there with a sense of
bewilderment and terror my life in the

village began.

6120 *'Day of these Days'*
Such a morning it is when love
leans through geranium windows
and calls with a cockerel's tongue.
When red-haired girls scamper like roses
over the rain-green grass,
and the sun drips honey.

LEE Nathaniel c.1653-1692
6121 *Oedipus (with John Dryden)*
When the sun sets, shadows, that showed
at noon
But small, appear most long and terrible.

6122 *The Rival Queens*
He speaks the kindest words, and looks
such things,
Vows with so much passion, swears with
so much grace.
That 'tis a kind of heaven to be deluded by
him.

6123 *The Rival Queens*
'Tis beauty calls and glory leads the way.

6124 *The Rival Queens*
When Greeks joined Greeks, then was the
tug of war!

6125 *The Rival Queens*
Philip fought men, but Alexander women.

6126 *Theodosius*
Man, false man, smiling, destructive man.

LEE Robert E. 1807-1870
6127
The devil's name is Dullness.

6128
We have fought this fight as long, and as
well as we know how. We have been
defeated. For us, as a Christian people,
there is now but one course to pursue. We
must accept the situation.

6129 *(after the battle of Fredericksburg,
attributed)*
It is well that war is so terrible. We should
grow too fond of it.

6130 *(last words)*
Let the tent be struck.

LEES-MILNE James
6131
Seven years is about the limit for passion.

LEHMAN Ernest 1920-
6132
Sweet smell of success.

LEHRER Tom 1928-
6133
It is a sobering thought, that when Mozart
was my age, he had been dead for two
years.

6134 *'We Will All Go Together When We Go'*
Life is like a sewer. What you get out of it
depends on what you put into it.

6135 *'Lobachevski'*
Plagiarize! Let no one else's work evade
your eyes,
Remember why the good Lord made your
eyes.

LEIBNIZ Gottfried Wilhelm 1646-1716
6136
Two things are identical if one can be
substituted for the other without affecting
the truth.

6137 *Letter to S. Clarke*
We should like Nature to go no further; we
should like it to be finite, like our mind;
but this is to ignore the greatness and
majesty of the Author of things.

6138 *Letter on a General Principle ... Laws of
Nature*
It is God who is the ultimate reason of
things, and the knowledge of God is no
less the beginning of science than his
essence and will are the beginning of
beings.

6139 *Letter to Magnus Wedderkopf*
God wills the things which he understands
to be the best and most harmonious and
selects them, as it were, from an infinite
number of all possibilities.

6140 *The Monadology*
It is the knowledge of necessary and
eternal truths which distinguishes us from
mere animals, and gives us *Reason* and the
sciences, raising us to knowledge of
ourselves and of God. It is this in us

which we call the rational soul or *Mind*.

6141 *Studies in Physics and the Nature of Body*
There is nothing without a reason.

LEIGH Fred W. d.1924
6142 *'Waiting at the Church'*
Here's the very note,
This is what he wrote -
'Can't get away to marry you today,
My wife won't let me!'

6143 *'Waiting At The Church'*
There was I, waiting at the church,
Waiting at the church, waiting at the church,
When I found he'd left me in the lurch,
Lor' how it did upset me!...

6144 *'Why Am I Always the Bridesmaid?'*
Why am I always the bridesmaid,
Never the blushing bride?

LEIGH H.S. 1837-1883
6145
If you wish to grow thinner, diminish your dinner.

6146 *'An Allegory, written in Deep Dejection'*
That loathsome centipede, Remorse,
Invaded with a stealthy tread
My nasal organ.

6147 *Carols of Cockayne*
The rapturous, wild, and ineffable pleasure
Of drinking at somebody else's expense.

6148 *'Only Seven'*
I wondered hugely what she meant,
And said, 'I'm bad at riddles;
But I know where little girls are sent
For telling taradiddles.'

6149 *'The Twins'*
In form and feature, face and limb,
I grew so like my brother
That folks got taking me for him
And each for one another.

6150 *'The Twins'*
For one of us was born a twin
And not a soul knew which.

LEIGH Vivien 1913-1967
6151 *in A Streetcar Named Desire*
"I don't want realism - I want magic."

LEMAY Curtis E. 1906-1990
6152 *(of the North Vietnamese)*
They've got to draw in their horns and stop their aggression, or we're going to bomb them back into the Stone Age.

LEMM Leesa
6153 *(testifying before an industrial tribunal)*
Two slow dances do not constitute a love affair.

LENCLOS Ninon de 1620-1705
6154 *(attributed)*
Old age is woman's hell.

LENIN 1870-1924
6155
Communism is Soviet power plus the electrification of the whole country.

6156
Imperialism is the monopoly stage of capitalism.

6157
Liberty is precious - so precious that it must be rationed.

6158 *(of George Bernard Shaw)*
A good man fallen among Fabians.

6159 *State and Revolution*
Democracy is *not* identical with majority rule. Democracy is a *State* which recognizes the subjection of the minority to the majority, that is, an organization for the systematic use of *force* by one class against the other, by one part of the population against another.

6160 *State and Revolution*
While the State exists, there can be no freedom. When there is freedom there will be no State.

LENNON John 1940-1980
6161 *(of The Beatles in 1966)*
We're more popular than Jesus now; I don't know which will go first - rock'n'roll or Christianity.

6162 *'Imagine'*
Imagine there's no heaven,
It's easy if you try,
No hell below us,
Above us only sky,

Imagine all the people
Living for today.

6163 *(at Royal Variety Performance)*
Will those in the cheap seats clap their
hands? All the rest of you, just rattle your
jewellery.

LENNON John and McCARTNEY Paul
1940-1980 and 1942-
6164
All we are saying is
Give peace a chance.

6165 *'Can't Buy Me Love'*
I don't care too much for money,
For money can't buy me love.

6166 *'A Day in the Life'*
I heard the news today, oh boy.
Four thousand holes in Blackburn
Lancashire.
And though the holes were rather small,
They had to count them all.
Now they know how many holes it takes
to fill the Albert Hall.
I'd love to turn you on.

6167 *'Eleanor Rigby'*
Eleanor Rigby picks up the rice in the
church where a wedding has been
Lives in a dream.
Waits at the window, wearing the face that
she keeps in a jar by the door,
Who is it for?
All the lonely people, where do they all
come from?

6168 *'A Hard Day's Night'*
It's been a hard day's night,
And I've been working like a dog.

6169 *'With a Little Help From My Friends'*
Oh I get by with a little help from my
friends,
Mm, I get high with a little help from my
friends.

6170 *'I am the Walrus'*
I am he
As you are me
And we are all together.

6171 *'When I'm Sixty-Four'*
Will you still need me, will you still feed
me,

When I'm sixty four?

LENO Dan 1860-1904
6172 *Dan Leno Hys Booke*
Ah! What is man? Wherefore does he
why? Whence did he whence? Whither is
he withering?

LENT Edwin
6173
Cats are living adornments.

LENTHALL William 1591-1662
6174 *(to Charles I)*
I have neither eye to see, nor tongue to
speak here, but as the house is pleased to
direct me.

LEONARDO DA VINCI 1452-1519
6175
Just as courage imperils life, fear protects
it.

6176
The common sense is that which judges
the things given to it by other senses.

6177
A good painter is to paint two main things,
namely men and the working of man's
mind.

6178
Life well spent is long.

6179
Iron rusts from disuse; stagnant water
loses it purity and in cold weather
becomes frozen; even so does inaction sap
the vigour of the mind.

6180
Human subtlety ... will never devise an
invention more beautiful, more simple or
more direct than does Nature, because in
her inventions nothing is lacking, and
nothing is superfluous.

6181
Every man at three years old is half his
height.

6182
The poet ranks far below the painter in the
representation of visible things, and far
below the musician in that of invisible
things.

6183 *Notebooks*
While I thought that I was learning how to live, I have been learning how to die.

LERMONTOV Mikhail 1814-1841
6184 *A Hero of our Time*
Happy people are ignoramuses and glory is nothing else but success, and to achieve it one only has to be cunning.

6185 *A Hero of our Time*
The love of savages isn't much better than the love of noble ladies; ignorance and simple-heartedness can be as tiresome as coquetry.

6186 *A Hero of our Time*
Of two close friends, one is always the slave of the other.

6187 *A Hero of our Time*
I am like a man yawning at a ball; the only reason he does not go home to bed is that his carriage has not arrived yet.

6188 *A Hero of our Time*
I have always been the essential character of the fifth act.

6189 *'I'm lonely and sad'*
What is passion? That sickness so sweet, either early or late,
Will vanish at reason's protesting;
And life, if you ever, attentive and cool, contemplate,
Is but empty and meaningless jesting.

LERNER Alan Jay 1918-1986
6190 *'Camelot'*
Don't let it be forgot,
That once there was a spot -
For one brief shining moment
That was known as Camelot.

6191 *My Fair Lady 'You Did It'*
Oozing charm from every pore,
He oiled his way around the floor.

6192 *My Fair Lady 'A Hymn to Him'*
Why can't a woman be more like a man?
Men are so honest, so thoroughly square;
Eternally noble, historically fair;
Who, when you win, will always give your back a pat.
Why can't a woman be like that?

6193 *My Fair Lady 'I've Grown Accustomed to her Face'*
I've grown accustomed to the trace
Of something in the air;
Accustomed to her face.

6194 *My Fair Lady 'The Rain in Spain'*
The rain in Spain stays mainly in the plain.

6195 *My Fair Lady 'The Rain in Spain'*
In Hertford, Hereford, and Hampshire,
Hurricanes hardly happen.

6196 *Gigi 'I Remember it Well'*
We met at nine.
We met at eight.
I was on time.
No, you were late.
Ah yes! I remember it well.

LERNER Max
6197
What is dangerous about tranquillizers is that whatever peace of mind they bring is packaged peace of mind. Where you buy a pill and buy peace with it, you get conditioned to cheap solutions instead of deep ones.

6198
I have a simple principle for the conduct of life - never to resist an adequate temptation.

LESAGE Alain René 1668-1747
6199 *Crispin rival de son maître*
Justice is such a fine thing that we cannot pay too dearly for it.

6200 *Le Diable boîteux*
They made peace between us; we embraced, and we have been mortal enemies ever since.

LESPINASSE Julie de
6201
The logic of the heart is absurd.

LESSING Doris 1919-
6202
Growing up is after all only the understanding that one's unique and incredible experience is what everyone shares.

6203
Think wrongly, if you please, but in all cases think for yourself.

6204
Women are the cowards they are because they have been semi-slaves for so long. The number of women prepared to stand up for what they really think, feel, experience, with a man they are in love with is still very small.

6205 *The Grass is Singing*
When old settlers say 'One has to understand the country,' what they mean is, 'You have to get used to our ideas about the native.'

6206 *The Habit of Loving*
Pleasure resorts are like film stars and royalty ... embarrassed by the figures they cut in the fantasies of people who have never met them.

6207 *Particularly Cats*
What is charm then? The free giving of a grace, the spending of something given by nature in her role of spendthrift ... something extra, superfluous, unnecessary, essentially a power thrown away.

LESSING G.E. 1729-1781
6208 *Eine Duplik*
If God were to hold out enclosed in His right hand all Truth, and in His left hand just the active search for Truth, though with the condition that I should always err therein, and He should say to me: Choose! I should humbly take His left hand and say: Father! Give me this one; absolute Truth belongs to Thee alone.

6209 *Emilia Galotti*
A man who does not lose his reason over certain things has none to lose.

6210 *'Lied aus dem Spanischen'*
Yesterday I loved, today I suffer, tomorrow I die: but I still think fondly, today and tomorrow, of yesterday.

6211 *Minna von Barnhelm*
One single grateful thought raised to heaven is the most perfect prayer.

LESTER Richard 1932-
6212
Film-making has become a kind of hysterical pregnancy.

L'ESTRANGE Sir Roger 1616-1704
6213 *Aesop's Fables*
It is with our passions as it is with fire and water, they are good servants, but bad masters.

6214 *Aesop's Fables*
Though this may be play to you, 'tis death to us.

LETTE Kathy
6215
As a breastfeeding mother you are basically just meals on heels.

LETTS Winifred Mary 1882-1972
6216 *'The Spires of Oxford'*
I saw the spires of Oxford
As I was passing by,
The grey spires of Oxford
Against a pearl-grey sky;
My heart was with the Oxford men
Who went abroad to die.

LEVANT Oscar 1906-1972
6217
There is a thin line between genius and insanity. I have erased this line.

6218
Epigram: a wisecrack that has played Carnegie Hall.

LEVENSTEIN Ros
6219 *(advertising slogan)*
I'm only here for the beer.

LEVERSON Ada 1865-1936
6220 *Letters to the Sphinx (of Oscar Wilde)*
He seemed at ease and to have the look of the last gentleman in Europe.

6221 *Tenterhooks*
You don't know a woman until you have had a letter from her.

6222 *The Twelfth Hour*
'No hurry, no hurry,' said Sir James, with that air of self-denial that conveys the urgent necessity of intense speed.

LEVIN Bernard 1928-
6223 *(of Mao Tse-tung)*
Whom the mad would destroy, they first make gods.

6224 *The Pendulum Years*
Paul Getty ... had always been vastly, immeasurably wealthy, and yet went about looking like a man who cannot quite remember whether he remembered to turn the gas off before leaving home.

6225 *The Pendulum Years*
In every age of transition men are never so firmly bound to one way of life as when they are about to abandon it, so that fanaticism and intolerance reach their most intense forms just before tolerance and mutual acceptance come to be the natural order of things.

6226 *The Pendulum Years (of Macmillan and Wilson)*
Between them, then, Walrus and Carpenter, they divided up the Sixties.

6227 *The Pendulum Years (of Macmillan)*
The Stag at Bay with the mentality of a fox at large.

LEVINE Ellen
6228
Sexual revolution has allowed us an equal opportunity to ogle.

LEVINSON Sam
6229
Insanity is hereditary - you can get it from your children.

LÉVIS Duc de 1764-1830
6230 *Maximes et Réflexions*
Noblesse oblige.
Nobility has its obligations.

6231 *Maximes et Réflexions*
Gouverner, c'est choisir.
To govern is to choose.

LÉVI-STRAUSS Claude 1908-1990
6232 *La Pensée sauvage*
Language is a form of human reason, and has its reasons which are unknown to man.

LEWES G.H. 1817-1878
6233 *The Physiology of Common Life*
Murder, like talent, seems occasionally to run in families.

6234 *Ranthorpe*
The pen, in our age, weighs heavier in the social scale than the sword of a Norman Baron.

6235 *The Spanish Drama*
Many a genius has been slow of growth. Oaks that flourish for a thousand years do not spring up into beauty like a reed.

LEWIN Kurt
6236
A successful individual typically sets his next goal somewhat but not too much above his last achievement. In this way he steadily raises his level of aspiration.

LEWIS Alun 1915-1944
6237 *Goodbye*
So we must say Goodbye, my darling,
And go, as lovers go, for ever;
Tonight remains, to pack and fix on labels
And make an end of lying down together.

LEWIS C.S. 1898-1963
6238
I believe in Christianity as I believe that the sun has risen. Not only because I see it, but because I see everything by it.

6239
Unsatisfied desire is in itself more desirable than any other satisfaction.

6240
The safest road to Hell is the gradual one - the gentle slope, soft underfoot, without sudden turnings, without milestones, without signposts.

6241
A woman means by unselfishness chiefly taking trouble for others; a man means not giving trouble to others. Thus each sex regards the other as basically selfish.

6242
Courage is not simply *one* of the virtues but the form of every virtue at the testing point.

6243 *The Screwtape Letters*
We have trained them [men] to think of the
Future as a promised land which favoured
heroes attain - not as something which
everyone reaches at the rate of sixty
minutes an hour, whatever he does,
whoever he is.

6244 *The Screwtape Letters*
She's the sort of woman who lives for
others - you can always tell the others by
their hunted expression.

6245 *'Unreal Estates'*
I'd sooner live among people who don't
cheat at cards than among people who are
earnest about not cheating at cards.

LEWIS Esther c.1747-1789
6246 *'A Mirror for Detractors'*
Are simple women only fit
To dress, to darn, to flower, or knit,
To mind the distaff, or the spit?
Why are the needle and the pen
Thought incompatible by men?

LEWIS Sir George Cornewall 1806-1863
6247
Life would be tolerable but for its
amusements.

LEWIS Joe E.
6248
You only live once - but if you work it
right, once is enough.

LEWIS John Spedan 1885-1963
6249 *(motto of the John Lewis Partnership)*
Never knowingly undersold.

LEWIS Sinclair 1885-1951
6250
It can't happen here.

6251 *The American Fear of Literature*
Our American professors like their
literature clear and cold and pure and very
dead.

6252 *Babbitt*
His motor car was poetry and tragedy,
love and heroism. The office was his
pirate ship but the car his perilous
excursion ashore.

6253 *Babbitt*
In other countries, art and literature are left
to a lot of shabby bums living in attics and
feeding on booze and spaghetti, but in
America the successful writer or picture-
painter is indistinguishable from any other
decent business man.

6254 *Babbitt*
She did her work with the thoroughness of
a mind which reveres detail and never
quite understands them.

LEWIS Stephen
6255 *(to Morton Shulman)*
How do you make a million?
You start with $900,000.

LEWIS Wyndham 1882-1957
6256
Art is the expression of an enormous
preference.

6257
People are so overwhelmed with the
prestige of their instruments that they
consider their personal judgement of
hardly any account.

6258 *The Apes of God*
Those prosperous mountebanks who
alternately imitate and mock at and
traduce those figures they at once admire
and hate.

LEWISOHN Lewis L.
6259
His shortcoming is his long staying.

LEY Robert 1890-1945
6260 *(German Labour Front slogan from 1933)*
Kraft durch Freude.
Strength through joy.

LEYBOURNE George d.1884
6261 *'The Flying Trapese'*
He'd fly through the air with the greatest
of ease,
A daring young man on the flying trapeze.

LIBERACE Wladziu Valentino 1919-1987
6262 *Autobiography*
When the reviews are bad I tell my staff
that they can join me as I cry all the way to
the bank.

LICHTENBERG G.C. 1742-1799
6263
A book is a mirror: if an ass peers into it, you can't expect an apostle to look out.

6264
Barbaric accuracy - whimpering humility.

6265
Never undertake anything for which you wouldn't have the courage to ask the blessings of heaven.

6266
Most men of education are more superstitious than they admit - nay, than they think.

6267
Everyone is a genius at least once a year; a real genius has his original ideas closer together.

6268
Sometimes men come by the name of genius in the same way that certain insects come by the name of centipede - not because they have a hundred feet, but because most people can't count above fourteen.

6269
One can live in this world on soothsaying but not on truth saying.

LICHTENBERG Joseph
6270
If moderation is a fault, then indifference is a crime.

LIDDON H.P. 1829-1890
6271
What we do upon some great occasion will probably depend on what we already are: and what we are will be the result of previous years of self-discipline.

LIEBLING A.J.
6272
Freedom of the press is guaranteed only to those who own one.

6273
I can write better than anyone who can write faster, and I can write faster than anyone who can write better.

LILIENTHAL David
6274 *1899-1981*
Big business is basic to the very life of this country; and yet many - perhaps most - Americans have a deep-seated fear and an emotional repugnance to it. Here is monumental contradiction.

LILLIE Beatrice 1894-1989
6275 *(to a waiter who had spilled soup down her neck)*
Never darken my Dior again!

LILLO George 1693-1739
6276 *The Fatal Curiosity*
There's sure no passion in the human soul, But finds its food in music.

LINCOLN Abraham 1809-1865
6277
I'm a slow walker, but I never walk back.

6278
What kills a skunk is the publicity it gives itself.

6279
He has a right to criticize, who has a heart to help.

6280
As I would not be a slave, so I would not be a master. This expresses my idea of democracy.

6281
With high hope for the future, no prediction is ventured.

6282
Every man is said to have his peculiar ambition.

6283
We trust, sir, that God is on our side. It is more important to know that we are on God's side.

6284
Any people anywhere, being inclined and having the power, have the right to rise up and shake off the existing government and form a new one. This is a most valuable and sacred right - a right which we hope and believe is to liberate the world.

6285
Must a government of necessity be too
strong for the liberties of its people or too
weak to maintain its own existence?

6286
We hold the power and bear the
responsibility.

6287
The legitimate object of government is to
do for a community of people, whatever
they need to have done, but cannot do at
all, or cannot so well do for themselves, in
their separate and individual capacities.

6288
The dogmas of the quiet past are
inadequate to the stormy present. As our
case is new, so we must think anew and
act anew. We must disenthrall ourselves,
and then we shall save our country.

6289
Marriage is neither heaven nor hell; it is
simply purgatory.

6290
Every man over forty is responsible for his
face.

6291
I have been driven many times to my
knees by the overwhelming conviction that
I had nowhere else to go. My own
wisdom, and that of all about me seemed
insufficent for the day.

6292
Honest statemanship is the wise
employment of individual meannesses for
the public good.

6293
Seriously, I do not think I am fit for the
presidency.

6294
I feel like the man who was tarred and
feathered and ridden out of town on a rail.
To the man who asked how he liked it he
said: 'If it wasn't for the honour of the
thing, I'd rather walk.'

6295
I desire to so conduct the affairs of this
administration that if, at the end ... I have
lost every friend on earth, I shall have one
friend left, and that friend shall be down
inside me.

6296
When you have got an elephant by the
hind leg, and he is trying to run away, it is
best to let him run.

6297
A woman is the only thing I am afraid of
that I know will not hurt me.

6298
To give victory to the right, not bloody
bullets, but peaceful ballots only, are
necessary.

6299
'A house divided against itself cannot
stand.' I believe this government cannot
endure permanently, half slave and half
free.

6300
What is conservatism? Is it not adherence
to the old and tried, against the new and
untried?

6301
Let us have faith that right makes might,
and in that faith, let us, to the end, dare to
do our duty as we understand it.

6302
I take the official oath to-day with no
mental reservations, and with no purpose
to construe the Constitution or laws by any
hypercritical rules.

6303
This country, with its institutions, belongs
to the people who inhabit it. Whenever
they shall grow weary of the existing
government, they can exercise their
constitutional right of amending it, or their
revolutionary right to dismember or
overthrow it.

6304
Fellow citizens, we cannot escape history
... The fiery trial through which we pass
will light us down in honour or dishonour

to the last generation.

6305
In giving freedom to the slave, we assure freedom to the free - honourable alike in what we give and what we preserve. We shall nobly save, or meanly lose, the last, best hope of earth.

6306
Fondly do we hope, fervently do we pray, that this mighty scourge of war may speedily pass away.

6307
With malice toward none; with charity for all; with firmness in the right, as God gives us to see the right, let us strive on to finish the work we are in.

6308
Our fathers brought forth upon this continent a new nation, conceived in liberty, and dedicated to the proposition that all men are created equal.

6309
We here highly resolve that the dead shall not have died in vain, that this nation, under God, shall have a new birth of freedom; and that government of the people, by the people, and for the people, shall not perish from the earth.

6310 *(attributed)*
You may fool all the people some of the time; you can even fool some of the people all the time; but you can't fool all of the people all the time.

6311 *(attributed)*
The Lord prefers common-looking people. That is why he makes so many of them.

6312 *(judgement of a book)*
People who like this sort of thing will find this the sort of thing they like.

6313 *Letter to A.G. Hodges*
I claim not to have controlled events, but confess plainly that events have controlled me.

6314 *Letter to Horace Greeley*
I have here stated my purpose according to my views of official duty and I intend no

modification of my oft-expressed personal wish that all men everywhere could be free.

6315 *(reply to National Union League)*
It is not best to swap horses when crossing streams.

LINDBERGH Anne Morrow 1906-
6316
A simple enough pleasure, surely, to have breakfast alone with one's husband, but how seldom married people in the midst of life achieve it.

6317
The fundamental magic of flying is a miracle that has nothing to do with any of its practical purposes - purposes of speed, accessibility and convenience - and will not change as they change.

6318
Woman's normal occupations in general run counter to creative life, or contemplative life, or saintly life.

LINDNER R.M. 1914-1956
6319
Rebel without a cause.

LINDSAY Vachel 1879-1931
6320 *'The Congo'*
Then I saw the Congo, creeping through the black,
Cutting through the forest with a golden track.

6321 *'The Congo'*
Mumbo-Jumbo is dead in the jungle.

6322 *'General William Booth Enters into Heaven' (1913)*
Booth died blind and still by faith he trod,
Eyes still dazzled by the ways of God.

LINDSEY Ben
6323
I demand for the unmarried mother, as a sacred channel of life, the same reverence and respect as for the married mother; for Maternity is a cosmic thing and once it has come to pass, our conventions must not be permitted to blaspheme it.

6324
I do beseech you to direct your efforts more to preparing youth for the path and less to preparing the path for the youth.

LINKLATER Eric 1899-1974
6325 *Juan in America*
'The people [in America] are all too clean. They spend all their time changing their shirts and washing themselves. You can't feel fierce and revolutionary in a bathroom.

LINKLETTER Art 1912-
6326 *A Child's Garden of Misinformation*
The four stages of man are infancy, childhood, adolescence and obsolescence.

LINLEY George 1798-1865
6327 *'God Bless the Prince of Wales'*
Among our ancient mountains,
And from our lovely vales,
Oh, let the prayer re-echo:
'God bless the Prince of Wales!'

LIPPMANN Walter 1899-1974
6328
While the right to talk may be the beginning of freedom, the necessity of listening is what makes the right important.

6329
In a democracy, the opposition is not only tolerated as constitutional, but must be maintained because it is indispensable.

6330
Life is an irreversible process and for that reason its future can never be a repetition of the past.

6331
A man has honour if he holds himself to an ideal of conduct though it is inconvenient, unprofitable or dangerous to do so.

6332
The final test of a leader is that he leaves behind in other men the conviction and the will to carry on.

6333
The first principle of a civilized state is that the power is legitimate only when it is under contract.

6334
Many a time I have wanted to stop talking and find out what I really believed.

LIPSIUS Justus 1547-1606
6335
He who does not desire or fear the uncertain day or capricious fate, is equal to the gods above and loftier than mortals.

LITTLER William 1908-
6336
The cheap, no matter how charming, how immediate, does not wear so well. It has a way of telling its whole story the first time through.

LITTLEWOOD Joan and CHILTON Charles 1914-1991 and 1914-
6337
Oh what a lovely war.

LITVINOV Maxim 1876-1951
6338 *Note to the Allies*
Peace is indivisible.

LIVY (Titus Livius) 59 BC-AD 17
6339
A gentleman is mindful no less of the freedom of others than of his own dignity.

6340 *(battle cry)*
Vae victis.
Down with the defeated!

6341 *(of Hannibal's ambush of the Romans)*
Pugna magna victi sumus.
We were defeated in a great battle.

LLEWELLYN Karl
6342
Law ... begins when someone takes to doing something someone else does not like.

LLEWELLYN Richard 1907-1983
6343
How green was my valley.

LLOYD C.F.
6344
God made me on a morning when he had nothing else to do.

LLOYD GEORGE David 1863-1945

6345
Don't be afraid to take a big step if one is indicated. You can't cross a chasm in two small jumps.

6346
Whenever the Germans found the Canadian Corps coming into the line, they prepared for the worst.

6347
A fully-equipped duke costs as much to keep up as two Dreadnoughts; and dukes are just as great a terror and they last longer.

6348
The great peaks of honour we had forgotten - Duty, Patriotism, and - clad in glittering white - the great pinnacle of Sacrifice, pointing like a rugged finger to Heaven.

6349
What is our task? To make Britain a fit country for heroes to live in.

6350
[Clemenceau] knows that the finest eloquence is that which gets things done and the worst is that which delays them.

6351
A politician was a person with whose politics you did not agree. When you did agree, he was a statesman.

6352
Negotiating with de Valera ... is like trying to pick up mercury with a fork.

6353
The world is becoming like a lunatic asylum run by lunatics.

6354 *(of Ramsay MacDonald)*
Sufficient conscience to bother him, but not sufficient to keep him straight.

6355 *(of World War I)*
At eleven o'clock this morning came to an end the cruellest and most terrible war that has ever scourged mankind. I hope we may say that thus, this fateful morning, came to an end all wars.

LLOYD Marie 1870-1922

6356
A little of what you fancy does you good.

6357
I'm one of the ruins that Cromwell knocked about a bit.

LLOYD Robert 1733-1764
6358 *'The Hare and the Tortoise'*
Slow and steady wins the race.

6359 *'The Law-Student'*
Turn parson, Colman, that's the way to thrive;
Your parsons are the happiest men alive.

6360 *'The Law-Student' (of Lord Mansfield)*
Alone from Jargon born to rescue Law,
From precedent, grave hum, and formal saw!
To strip chicanery of its vain pretence,
And marry Common Law to Common Sense!

6361 *'Shakespeare'*
True Genius, like Armida's wand,
Can raise the spring from barren land.
While all the art of Imitation,
Is pilf'ring from the first creation.

LOCKE John 1632-1704
6362
The thoughts that come often unsought, and, as it were, drop into the mind, are commonly the most valuable of any we have.

6363 *An Essay concerning Human Understanding*
New opinions are always suspected, and usually opposed, without any other reason but because they are not already common.

6364 *An Essay concerning Human Understanding*
The commonwealth of learning is not at this time without master-builders, whose mighty designs, in advancing the sciences, will leave lasting monuments to the admiration of posterity ... 'tis ambition enough to be employed as an under-labourer in clearing ground a little, and removing some of the rubbish that lies in the way of knowledge.

6365 *An Essay concerning Human Understanding*
General propositions are seldom mentioned in the huts of Indians: much less are they to be found in the thoughts of children.

6366 *An Essay concerning Human Understanding*
Nature never makes excellent things for mean or no uses.

6367 *An Essay concerning Human Understanding*
No man's knowledge here can go beyond his experience.

6368 *An Essay concerning Human Understanding*
It is one thing to show a man that he is in error, and another to put him in possession of truth.

6369 *An Essay concerning Human Understanding*
Reason is natural revelation, whereby the eternal Father of light, and fountain of all knowledge communicates to mankind that portion of truth which he has laid within the reach of their natural faculties.

6370 *An Essay concerning Human Understanding*
Crooked things may be as stiff and unflexible as straight: and men may be as positive in error as in truth.

6371 *An Essay concerning Human Understanding*
All men are liable to error; and most men are, in many points, by passion or interest, under temptation to it.

6372 *Second Treatise of Civil Government*
[That] ill deserves the name of confinement which hedges us in only from bogs and precipices. So that, however it may be mistaken, the end of law is, not to abolish or restrain, but to preserve and enlarge freedom.

6373 *Second Treatise of Civil Government*
Man ... hath by nature a power ... to preserve his property - that is, his life, liberty, and estate - against the injuries and attempts of other men.

6374 *Second Treatise of Civil Government*
Man being ... by nature all free, equal, and independent, no one can be put out of this estate, and subjected to the political power of another, without his own consent.

6375 *Second Treatise of Civil Government*
The only way by which any one divests himself of his natural liberty and puts on the bonds of civil society is by agreeing with other men to join and unite into a community.

6376 *Second Treatise of Civil Government*
This power to act according to discretion for the public good, without the prescription of the law, and sometimes even against it, is that which is called prerogative.

6377 *Some Thoughts Concerning Education*
The rod, which is the only instrument of government that tutors generally know, or ever think of, is the most unfit of any to be used in education.

6378 *Some Thoughts Concerning Education*
You would think him a very foolish fellow, that should not value a virtuous, or a wise man, infinitely before a great scholar.

LOCKER-LAMPSON Frederick 1821-1895
6379 *'The Jester's Plea'*
The world's as ugly, ay, as sin,
And almost as delightful.

6380 *'The Jester's Plea'*
And many are afraid of God -
And more of Mrs Grundy.

6381 *'The Jester's Plea'*
Some men are good for righting wrongs,
And some for writing verses.

LOCKHART John Gibson 1794-1854
6382 *Epitaph for Patrick ('Peter'), Lord Robertson*
Here lies that peerless paper peer Lord Peter,
Who broke the laws of God and man and metre.

LODGE David 1935-
6383 *The British Museum is Falling Down*
Literature is mostly about having sex and

not much about having children. Life is the other way round.

6384 *Changing Places*
Four times, under our educational rules, the human pack is shuffled and cut - at eleven-plus, sixteen-plus, eighteen-plus and twenty-plus - and happy is he who comes top of the deck on each occasion, but especially the last. This is called Finals, the very name of which implies that nothing of importance can happen after it.

6385 *Small World*
I gave up screwing around a long time ago. I came to the conclusion that sex is a sublimation of the work instinct.

6386 *Small World*
Another law of academic life: *it is impossible to be excessive in flattery of one's peers.*

LODGE George Cabot 1873-1909
6387
When you are accustomed to anything, you are estranged from it.

LODGE Jr. Henry Cabot 1850-1924
6388
This organization (United Nations) is created to prevent you from going to hell. It isn't created to take you to heaven.

LODGE Thomas 1558-1625
6389 *'Love in my bosom like a bee'*
Love in my bosom like a bee
Doth suck his sweet.

6390 *'Love guards the roses of thy lips'*
Love guards the roses of thy lips
And flies about them like a bee;
If I approach he forward skips,
And if I kiss he stingeth me.

6391 *'Margarite of America'*
Devils are not so black as they are painted.

LOESSER Frank 1910-1969
6392 *'Boys in the Back Room'*
See what the boys in the back room will have
And tell them I'm having the same.

6393 *'The King's New Clothes'*
Isn't it grand! Isn't it fine! Look at the cut, the style, the line!
The suit of clothes is altogether, but altogether it's altogether
The most remarkable suit of clothes that I have ever seen.

LOEVINGER Lee
6394
Television is the literature of the illiterate, the culture of the low-brow, the wealth of the poor, the privilege of the underprivileged, the exclusive club of the excluded masses.

6395
Television is a gold goose that lays scrambled eggs; and it is futile and probably fatal to beat it for not laying caviar.

LOGAN John 1748-1788
6396 *To the Cuckoo (attributed)*
Thou hast no sorrow in thy song,
No winter in thy year.

LOGAU Friedrich von 1604-1655
6397 *(translated by Longfellow)*
Though the mills of God grind slowly, yet they grind exceeding small;
Though with patience He stands waiting, with exactness grinds He all.

LOGUE Christopher 1926-
6398 *Christopher Logues ABC 'M'*
Said Marx: 'Don't be snobbish, we seek to abolish
The 3rd Class, not the 1st.'

LOLLABRIGIDA Gina
6399
The light is better than a plastic surgeon.

LOMBARDI Vince 1913-1970
6400
Winning isn't everything. It is the only thing.

6401
Fatigue makes cowards of us all.

6402
If you aren't fired with enthusiasm, you'll be fired with enthusiasm.

LOMBROSO Cesare 1836-1909
6403 *The Man of Genius*
The ignorant man always adores what he
cannot understand.

LONERGAN Bernard 1904-1985
6404
In philosophy an individual is becoming
himself.

LONG Huey 1893-1935
6405
Bible's the greatest book ever written. But
I sure don't need anybody I can buy for six
bits and a chew of tobacco to explain it to
me. When I need preachers I buy 'em
cheap.

6406 *(attributed)*
The time has come for all good men to rise
above principle.

6407 *(to journalists on his political
personality)*
Oh hell, say that I am *sui generis* and let it
go at that.

LONGFELLOW Henry Wadsworth 1807-
1882
6408
We judge ourselves by what we feel
capable of doing, while others judge us by
what we have already done.

6409
Each morning sees some task begun,
Each evening sees it close.
Something attempted, something done,
Has earned a night's repose.

6410
All things must change to something new,
to something strange.

6411
To say the least, a town life makes one
more tolerant and liberal in one's
judgement of others.

6412
If we could read the secret history of our
enemies, we should find in each man's life,
sorrow and suffering enough to disarm all
hostility.

6413
In this world, a man must either be anvil
or hammer.

6414 *'The Arrow and the Song'*
I shot an arrow into the air,
It fell to earth, I knew not where.

6415 *'The Arrow and the Song'*
And the song, from beginning to end,
I found again in the heart of a friend.

6416 *'The Bridge'*
I stood on the bridge at midnight,
As the clocks were striking the hour.

6417 *'The Building of the Ship'*
Thou, too, sail on, O Ship of State!
Sail on, O Union, strong and great!
Humanity with all its fears,
With all the hopes of future years,
Is hanging breathless on thy fate!

6418 *'Children'*
Ye are better than all the ballads
That ever were sung or said;
For ye are living poems,
And all the rest are dead.

6419 *'The Children's Hour'*
Between the dark and the daylight,
When the night is beginning to lower,
Comes a pause in the day's occupations,
That is known as the Children's Hour.

6420 *(composed for his second daughter)*
There was a little girl
Who had a little curl
Right in the middle of her forehead,
When she was good
She was very, very good,
But when she was bad she was horrid.

6421 *'The Day is Done'*
The cares that infest the day
Shall fold their tents, like the Arabs,
And as silently steal away.

6422 *'The Day is Done'*
The bards sublime,
Whose distant footsteps echo
Through the corridors of Time.

6423 *'Elegiac Verse'*
If you would hit the mark, you must aim a
little above it;

Every arrow that flies feels the attraction of earth.

6424 *Evangeline*
This is the forest primeval.

6425 *Evangeline*
Sorrow and silence are strong, and patient endurance is godlike.

6426 *Evangeline, 'Prelude'*
Silently one by one, in the infinite meadows of heaven
Blossomed the lovely stars, the forget-me-nots of the angels.

6427 *'Excelsior'*
The shades of night were falling fast,
As through an Alpine village passed
A youth, who bore, 'mid snow and ice,
A banner with the strange device,
Excelsior!

6428 *'Excelsior'*
'Try not the Pass!' the old man said;
'Dark lowers the tempest overhead.'

6429 *'Excelsior'*
A traveller, by the faithful hound,
Half-buried in the snow was found.

6430 *'Giotto's Tower'*
Giotto's tower,
The lily of Florence blossoming in stone.

6431 *'God's-Acre'*
I like that ancient Saxon phrase, which calls
The burial-ground God's-Acre!

6432 *Hiawatha's Childhood 'The Song of Hiawatha'*
By the shore of Gitche Gumee,
By the shining Big-Sea-Water,
Stood the wigwam of Nokomis.

6433 *'Holidays'*
The holiest of all holidays are those
Kept by ourselves in silence and apart;
The secret anniversaries of the heart.

6434 *'The Ladder of Saint Augustine'*
The heights by great men reached and kept
Were not attained by sudden flight,
But they, while their companions slept,
Were toiling upward in the night.

6435 *'My Lost Youth'*
'A boy's will is the wind's will
And the thoughts of youth are long, long thoughts.'

6436 *'Maidenhood'*
Standing, with reluctant feet,
Where the brook and river meet,
Womanhood and childhood fleet!

6437 *'Michael Angelo'*
The men that women marry,
And why they marry them, will always be
A marvel and a mystery to the world.

6438 *'Nuremberg'(on Albrecht Dürer)*
Emigravit is the inscription on the
tombstone where he lies;
Dead he is not, but departed - for the artist never dies.

6439 *'The Poets'*
Not in the clamour of the crowded street,
Not in the shouts and plaudits of the throng,
But in ourselves, are triumph and defeat.

6440 *'A Psalm of Life'*
Tell me not, in mournful numbers,
Life is but an empty dream!
For the soul is dead that slumbers,
And things are not what they seem.
Life is real! Life is earnest!
And the grave is not its goal;
Dust thou art, to dust returnest,
Was not spoken of the soul.

6441 *'A Psalm of Life'*
Art is long, and Time is fleeting,
And our hearts, though stout and brave,
Still, like muffled drums, are beating
Funeral marches to the grave.

6442 *'A Psalm of Life'*
Trust no Future, howe'er pleasant!
Let the dead Past bury its dead!
Act - act in the living Present!
Heart within, and God o'erhead!

6443 *'A Psalm of Life'*
Lives of great men all remind us
We can make our lives sublime,
And, departing, leave behind us
Footprints on the sands of time.

6444 *'A Psalm of Life'*
Let us, then, be up and doing,
With a heart for any fate;
Still achieving, still pursuing,
Learn to labour and to wait.

6445 *'A Psalm of Life'*
There is no flock, however watched and
tended,
But one dead lamb is there!
There is no fireside, howsoe'er defended,
But has one vacant chair!

6446 *'The Reaper and the Flowers'*
There is a Reaper whose name is Death,
And, with his sickle keen,
He reaps the bearded grain at a breath,
And the flowers that grow between.

6447 *'Santa Filomena' (on Florence
Nightingale)*
A Lady with a Lamp shall stand
In the great history of the land,
A noble type of good,
Heroic womanhood.

6448 *'The Secret of the Sea'*
'Wouldst thou' - so the helmsman
answered,
'Learn the secret of the sea?
Only those who brave its dangers
Comprehend its mystery!'

6449 *'The Slave's Dream'*
The forests, with their myriad tongues,
Shouted of liberty;
And the Blast of the Desert cried aloud,
With a voice so wild and free,
That he started in his sleep and smiled
At their tempestuous glee.

6450 *'The Song of Hiawatha'*
From the waterfall he named her,
Minnehaha, Laughing Water.

6451 *Tales of a Wayside Inn 'Elizabeth'*
Ships that pass in the night, and speak
each other in passing;
Only a signal shown and a distant voice in
the darkness;
So on the ocean of life we pass and speak
one another,
Only a look and a voice; then darkness
again and a silence.

6452 *Tales of A Wayside Inn 'The Student's
Tale'*
Our ingress into the world
Was naked and bare;
Our progress through the world
Is trouble and care.

6453 *'The Village Blacksmith'*
Under a spreading chestnut tree
The village smithy stands;
The smith, a mighty man is he,
With large and sinewy hands;
And the muscles of his brawny arms
Are strong as iron bands.

6454 *'The Wreck of the Hesperus'*
But the father answered never a word,
A frozen corpse was he.

LONGWORTH Alice Roosevelt
6455
My speciality is detached malevolence.

6456 *(attributed)*
If you can't say something good about
someone, sit right here by me.

6457
I have a simple philosophy. Fill what's
empty. Empty what's full. And scratch
where it itches.

LOON Hendrick Willem van 1882-1944
6458
The history of the world is the record of a
man in quest of his daily bread and butter.

LOOS Anita 1893-1981
6459
I'm furious about Women's Liberationists.
They keep getting up on soapboxes and
proclaiming that women are brighter than
men. That's true, but it should be kept
very quiet or it ruins the whole racket.

6460 *Gentlemen Prefer Blondes*
This gentleman said a girl with brains
ought to do something with them besides
think.

6461 *Gentlemen Prefer Blondes*
She always believed in the old addage,
'Leave them while you're looking good.'

6462 *Gentlemen Prefer Blondes*
Fun is fun but no girl wants to laugh all of
the time.

6463 *Gentlemen Prefer Blondes*
Kissing your hand may make you feel
very, very good but a diamond and safire
bracelet lasts for ever.

LORD Peter
6464
Nobody does nothing for nobody for
naught.

LORENZ Konrad 1903-1989
6465
I believe I've found the missing link
between animal and civilized man. It is
us.

6466 *On Agression*
It is a good morning exercise for a research
scientist to discard a pet hypothesis every
day before breakfast. It keeps him young.

LOUIS Joe 1914-1981
6467
I don't like money actually, but it quiets
my nerves.

LOUIS XIV King 1638-1715
6468
L'État c'est moi.
I am the State.

6469
J'ai failli attendre.
I was nearly kept waiting.

6470
Every time I create an appointment, I
create a hundred malcontents and one
ingrate.

6471 *(attributed)*
Ah, if I were not king, I should lose my
temper.

6472
First feelings are always the most natural.

6473 *(on accession of his grandson to Spanish throne)*
The Pyrenees are no more.

LOUIS XVIII King 1755-1824
6474 *(attributed)*
Punctuality is the politeness of kings.

LOVELACE Richard 1618-1658
6475 *'To Althea, From Prison'*
When I lie tangled in her hair,
And fettered to her eye;
The Gods, that wanton in the air
Know no such liberty.

6476 *'To Althea, From Prison'*
When thirsty grief in wine we steep,
When healths and draughts go free,
Fishes, that tipple in the deep,
Know no such liberty.

6477 *'To Althea, From Prison'*
Stone walls do not a prison make,
Nor iron bars a cage;
Minds innocent and quiet take
That for an hermitage;
If I have freedom in my love,
And in my soul am free;
Angels alone, that soar above,
Enjoy such liberty.

6478 *'The Ant'*
Forbear, thou great good husband, little
ant.

6479 *'Gratiana Dancing and Singing'*
And when she ceased, we sighing saw
The floor lay paved with broken hearts.

6480 *'To Lucasta, Going Beyond the Seas'*
If to be absent were to be
Away from thee;
Or that when I am gone,
You or I were alone;
Then my Lucasta might I crave
Pity from blust'ring wind, or swallowing
wave.

6481 *'To Lucasta, Going to the Wars'*
True; a new mistress now I chase,
The first foe in the field;
And with a stronger faith embrace
A sword, a horse, a shield.

Yet this inconstancy is such,
As you too shall adore;
I could not love thee, Dear, so much,
Loved I not honour more.

6482 *'The Scrutiny'*
Lady, it is already morn,
And 'twas last night I swore to thee
That fond impossibility.

LOVELL Sir Bernard 1913-
6483
Youth is vivid rather than happy.

LOVELL Maria 1803-1877
6484 *'Ingomar the Barbarian'*
Two souls with but a single thought,
Two hearts that beat as one.

LOVEMAN Robert 1864-1923
6485 *April Rain*
It is not raining rain to me,
It's raining violets.

LOVER Samuel 1797-1868
6486 *Handy Andy*
When once the itch of literature comes
over a man, nothing can cure it but the
scratching of a pen.

LOW Sir David 1891-1963
6487
I have never met anyone who wasn't
against war. Even Hitler and Mussolini
were, according to themselves.

LOWE Robert (Viscount Sherbrooke)
1811-1892
6488
The Chancellor of the Exchequer is a man
whose duties make him more or less of a
taxing machine. He is intrusted with a
certain amount of misery which it is his
duty to distribute as fairly as he can.

6489 *(on the passing of the Reform Bill)*
I believe it will be absolutely necessary
that you should prevail on our future
masters to learn their letters.

LOWELL A.L. 1856-1943
6490 *(while President of Harvard)*
The freshmen bring a little knowledge in
and the seniors take none out, so it
accumulates through the years.

LOWELL Amy 1874-1925
6491 *'Patterns'*
And the softness of my body will be
guarded by embrace
By each button, hook, and lace.

For the man who should loose me is dead,
Fighting with the Duke in Flanders,
In a pattern called a war.
Christ! What are patterns for?

6492 *'Sheppy'*
I [Death] was astonished to see him in
Baghdad, for
I had an appointment with him tonight in
Samarra.

6493 *'Sword Blades and Poppy Seed'*
All books are either dreams or swords,
You can cut, or you can drug, with words.

LOWELL James Russell 1819-1891
6494
What a sense of security in an old book
which time has criticized for us!

6495
In creating, the only hard thing's to begin;
A grass-blade's no easier to make than an
oak.

6496
Nature fits all her children with something
to do,
He who would write and can't write, can
surely review.

6497
Talent is that which is in a man's power;
genius is that in whose power a man is.

6498
God'll send the bill to you.

6499
The pressure of public opinion is like the
pressure of the atmosphere; you can't see it
- but all the same, it is sixteen pounds to
the square inch.

6500
The foolish and the dead alone never
change their opinions.

6501
Ah, men do not know how much strength
is in poise,
That he goes the farthest who goes far
enough.

6502
A ginooine statesman should be on his
guard, if he must hev beliefs, not to b'lieve

'em too hard.

6503
Take a winter as you find him and he turns out to be a thoroughly honest fellow with no nonsense in him: and tolerating none in you, which is a great comfort in the long run.

6504
May is a pious fraud of the almanac
A ghastly parody of real Spring
Shaped out of snow and breathed with eastern wind.

6505
Whatever you may be sure of, be sure of this - that you are dreadfully like other people.

6506
Solitude is as needful to the imagination as society is wholesome for the character.

6507 *Among My Books 'Shakespeare Once More'*
A wise scepticism is the first attribute of a good critic.

6508 *The Biglow Papers*
An' you've gut to git up airly
Ef you want to take in God.

6509 *The Biglow Papers*
It ain't by princerples nor men
My preudunt course is steadied, -
I scent wich pays the best, an' then
Go into it baldheaded.

6510 *The Biglow Papers*
We've a war, an' a debt, an' a flag; an' ef this
Ain't to be inderpendunt, why, wut on airth is?

6511 *The Biglow Papers*
He's been true to *one* party - an' thet is himself.

6512 *The Biglow Papers*
But libbaty's a kind o'thing
That don't agree with niggers.

6513 *The Biglow Papers*
An' in convartin' public trusts
To very privit uses.

6514 *The Biglow Papers*
I *don't* believe in princerple,
But oh, I *du* in interest.

6515 *The Biglow Papers*
God makes sech nights, all white and still,
Fur'z you can look or listen.

6516 *The Biglow Papers*
All kin' o' smily round the lips,
An' teary round the lashes.

6517 *The Biglow Papers*
My gran'ther's rule was safer 'n 't is to crow:
Don't never prophesy - onless ye know.

6518 *'On the Capture of Fugitive Slaves'*
Before Man made us citizens, great Nature made us men.

6519 *Democracy and other Addresses 'Democracy'*
There is no good in arguing with the inevitable. The only argument available with an east wind is to put on your overcoat.

6520 *Democracy and other Addresses 'Democracy'*
The misfortunes hardest to bear are those which never come.

6521 *'A Fable for Critics'*
There comes Poe with his raven like Barnaby Rudge,
Three-fifths of him genius, and two-fifths sheer fudge.

6522 *'A Glance Behind the Curtain'*
No man is born into the world, whose work
Is not born with him; there is always work,
And tools to work withal, for those who will:
And blessèd are the horny hands of toil!

6523 *'The Present Crisis'*
Once to every man and nation comes the moment to decide,
In the strife of Truth with Falsehood, for the good or evil side.

6524 *'The Present Crisis'*
Truth forever on the scaffold, Wrong forever on the throne, -

Yet that scaffold sways the future, and,
behind the dim unknown,
Standeth God within the shadow, keeping
watch above his own.

6525 *'The Present Crisis'*
New occasions teach new duties: Time
makes ancient good uncouth;
They must upward still, and onward, who
would keep abreast of Truth.

LOWELL Robert 1917-1977
6526 *'Since 1939'*
We feel the machine slipping from our
hands
As if someone else were steering;
If we see light at the end of the tunnel,
It's the light of the oncoming train.

6527 *'Our Afterlife I'*
After fifty
the clock can't stop,
each saving breath
takes something.

6528 *'The Day'*
It's amazing
the day is still here
like lightning on an open field,
terra firma and transient
swimming on variation,
fresh as when man first broke
like the crocus all over the earth.

6529 *'During Fever'*
Terrible that old life of decency
without unseemly intimacy
or quarrels, when the unemancipated
woman
still had her Freudian papa and maids!

6530 *'Memories of West Street and Lepke'*
These are the tranquillized *Fifties*,
and I am forty. Ought I to regret my seed-
time?

6531 *'Middle Age'*
At forty-five,
What next, what next?
At every corner,
I meet my Father,
my age, still alive.

6532 *'We Took Our Paradise'*
Folly comes from something -
the present, yes,

we are in it,
it's the infection
of things gone.

6533 *'The Quaker Graveyard in Nantucket'*
The Lord survives the rainbow of His will.

6534 *'Skunk Hour'*
My mind's not right.
A car radio bleats,
'Love, O careless Love ...' I hear
my ill-spirit sob in each blood cell,
as if my hand were at its throat ...
I myself am hell,
nobody's here.

6535 *'Tenth Muse'*
But I suppose even God was born
too late to trust the old religion -
all those settings out
that never left the ground,
beginning in wisdom, dying in doubt.

6536 *'For the Union Dead'*
The aquarium is gone. Everywhere,
giant finned cars nose forward like fish;
a savage servility
slides by on grease.

6537 *'For the Union Dead'*
Their monument sticks like a fishbone
in the city's throat.

6538 *'Waking Early Sunday Morning'*
Pity the planet, all joy gone
from this sweet volcanic cone;
peace to our children when they fall
in small war on the heels of small war -
until the end of time
to police the earth, a ghost
orbiting forever lost
in our monotonous sublime.

LOWER Arthur R.M.
6539
All zeal runs down. What replaces it?
Intellectualism.

LOWNDES William 1652-1724
6540
Take care of the pence, and the pounds
will take care of themselves.

LOWRY Malcolm 1909-1957
6541
Fear ringed by doubt is my eternal moon.

301

6542
I like prefaces. I read them. Sometimes I do not read any further.

6543 *Under the Volcano*
How alike are the groans of love to those of the dying.

LOYOLA St Ignatius 1491-1556
6544 *'Prayer for Generosity'*
Teach us, good Lord, to serve Thee as
Thou deservest:
To give and not to count the cost;
To fight and not to heed the wounds;
To toil and not to seek for rest;
To labour and not to ask for any reward
Save that of knowing that we do Thy will.

LUBBOCK John
6545
A poor woman from Manchester, on being taken to the seaside, is said to have expressed her delight on seeing for the first time something of which there was enough for everybody.

LUCAN 39-65 AD
6546 *Pharsalia*
Thinking nothing done while anything remained to be done.

6547 *Pharsalia*
Jupiter is whatever you see, whichever way you move.

6548 *Pharsalia*
The victorious cause pleased the Gods, but the conquered one pleased Cato.

6549 *Pharsalia*
Caesar lives after his battles, but his fortune has perished.

6550 *Pharsalia (of Pompey)*
There stands the ghost of a great name.

LUCAS Charles L.
6551
Civilization is just a slow process of learning to be kind.

LUCAS E.V. 1868-1938
6552
One of the most adventurous things left is to go to bed, for no one can lay a hand on our dreams.

LUCAS George 1944-
6553 *Star Wars*
Man your ships, and may the force be with you.

LUCE Clare Booth 1903-1987
6554
Censorship, like charity, should begin at home; but unlike charity, it should end there.

6555
Technological man can't believe in anything that can't be measured, taped, or put into a computer.

LUCIUS Cary 1610-1643
6556 *Discourses of Infallibility*
When it is not necessary to change, it is necessary not to change.

LUCKMAN Charles
6557
Success is that old A B C - ability, breaks and courage.

LUCRETIUS 99-55 BC
6558
Sweet is it, when on the high seas the winds are lashing the waters, to gaze from the land on another's struggles.

6559 *De Rerum Natura*
So much wrong could religion induce.

6560 *De Rerum Natura*
Nothing can be created out of nothing.

6561 *De Rerum Natura*
Some races increase, others are reduced, and in a short while the generations of living creatures are changed and like runners relay the torch of life.

6562 *De Rerum Natura*
Death therefore is nothing to us nor does it concern us a scrap, seeing that the nature of the spirit we possess is something mortal.

6563 *De Rerum Natura*
And life is given to none freehold, but it is leasehold for all.

6564 *De Rerum Natura*
From the midst of the fountain of delights rises something bitter that chokes them all

amongst the flowers.

6565 *De Rerum Natura*
What is food to one man is bitter poison to others.

LUMLEY Joanna
6566
What sustains the human spirit is gorgeousness.

LUND Robert S.
6567
Every man of genius is considerably helped by being dead.

LUTHER Martin 1483-1546
6568
I never work better than when I am inspired by anger; for when I am angry, I can write, pray, and preach well, for then my whole temperament is quickened, my understanding sharpened, and all mundane vexations and temptations depart.

6569
Christian life consists of faith and charity.

6570 *(attributed)*
Who loves not women, wine and song,
Remains a fool his whole life long.

6571
Every thing that is done in the world is done by hope.

6572
The fewer the words, the better the prayer.

6573
I am more afraid of my own heart than of the Pope and all his cardinals. I have within me the great Pope, Self.

6574
Peace if possible, but truth at any rate.

6575
If I had heard that as many devils would set on me in Worms as there are tiles on the roofs, I should none the less have ridden there.

6576 *Colloquia Mensalia*
For, where God built a church, there the devil would also build a chapel ... In such

sort is the devil always God's ape.

6577 *(attributed, at the Diet of Worms)*
Hier stehe ich. Ich kann nicht anders. Gott helfe mir. Amen.
Here stand I. I can do no other. God help me. Amen.

6578 *'Eine feste Burg ist unser Gott'*
A safe stronghold our God is still,
A trusty shield and weapon.

6579 *Large Catechism*
The confidence and faith of the heart alone make both God and an idol.

6580 *Large Catechism 'The First Commandment'*
Whatever your heart clings to and confides in, that is really your God.

6581 *Letter to Melanchthon*
Be a sinner and sin strongly, but more strongly have faith and rejoice in Christ.

6582 *Tischreden oder Colloquia*
So our Lord God commonly gives riches to those gross asses to whom He vouchsafes nothing else.

LUTOSLAWSKI Witold 1913-
6583
Our role is to offer a message from an ideal world.

LUXEMBURG Rosa 1871-1919
6584 *Die Russische Revolution*
Freedom is always and exclusively freedom for the one who thinks differently.

LYDGATE John c.1370-c.1451
6585 *The Fall of Princes*
Sithe he off Inglissh in makyng was the beste,
Preie onto God to yiue his soule good reste.

6586 *The Fall of Princes*
Comparisouns doon offte gret greuaunce.

6587 *The Fall of Princes (of Chaucer)*
Sithe off oure language he was the lodesterre.

6588 *Secrets of Old Philosophers*
Woord is but wynd; leff woord and tak the dede.

6589 *The Story of Thebes*
Love is mor than gold or gret richesse.

LYLY John c.1554-1606
6590
It is a blind goose that cometh to the fox's
sermon.

6591
Where the mind is past hope, the heart is
past shame.

6592
If all the earth were paper white
And all the sea were ink
'Twere not enough for me to write
As my poor heart doth think.

6593 *Campaspe*
Cupid and my Campaspe played
At cards for kisses, Cupid paid.

6594 *Campaspe*
What bird so sings, yet so does wail?
O 'tis the ravished nightingale.
Jug, jug, jug, jug, tereu, she cries,
And still her woes at midnight rise.

6595 *Euphues*
It seems to me (said she) that you are in
some brown study.

6596 *The Maydes Metamorphosis*
Night hath a thousand eyes.

LYND Robert 1879-1949
6597
One of the greatest joys known to man is
to take a flight into ignorance in search of
knowledge.

6598
There is nothing in which the birds differ
more from man than the way in which
they can build and yet leave a landscape as
it was before.

6599
It may be the games are silly. But, then, so
are human beings.

6600
It is in games that many men discover
their paradise.

LYNES Russell
6601
Cynicism - the intellectual cripple's
substitute for intelligence.

6602
The true snob never rests; there is always a
higher goal to attain, and there are, by the
same token, always more and more people
to look down upon.

LYONS Lord
6603
If you're given champagne at lunch, there's
a catch somewhere.

LYSANDER d.395 BC
6604
Deceive boys with toys, but men with
oaths.

LYTE Henry Francis 1793-1847
6605 *'Abide with Me'*
Abide with me: fast falls the eventide;
The darkness deepens; Lord, with me
abide:
When other helpers fail, and comforts flee,
Help of the helpless, O abide with me.
Swift to its close ebbs out life's little day;
Earth's joys grow dim, its glories pass
away;
Change and decay in all around I see;
O Thou, who changest not, abide with me.

6606 *'Praise, my soul, the King of heaven'*
Father-like, he tends and spares us;
Well our feeble frame he knows ...
Praise him! Praise him!
Widely as his mercy flows.

LYTTELTON George 1709-1773
6607 *'Advice to a Lady'*
Seek to be good, but aim not to be great;
A woman's noblest station is retreat.

McALPINE Lord 1942-
6608
The party needs a good scrub with a hard
brush.

McARTHUR Alexander and LONG H.
Kingley
6609 *'Advice to a Lady'*
Battles and sex are the only free diversions
in slum life. Couple them with drink,
which costs money, and you have the three

principal outlets for that escape complex which is for ever working in the tenement dweller's subconscious mind.

MacARTHUR Douglas 1880-1964
6610
In war, indeed, there can be no substitute for victory.

McARTHUR Peter
6611
A satirist is a man who discovers unpleasant things about himself and then says them about other people.

MacCAIG Norman 1910-
6612 *Sounds of the Day*
When the door
Scraped shut, it was the end
Of all the sounds there are.
You left me
Beside the quietest fire in the world.

McCARTHY Eugene 1916-
6613
He's like a football coach who's smart enough to win the game, and dumb enough to think it's important.

6614
The Senate is the last primitive society in the world. We still worship the elders of the tribe and honour the territorial imperative.

McCARTHY Joseph 19087-1957
6615
McCarthyism is Americanism with its sleeves rolled.

McCARTHY Mary 1912-1989
6616
Bureaucracy, the rule of no one, has become the modern form of despotism.

6617
Liberty, as it is conceived by current opinion, has nothing inherent about it; it is a sort of gift or trust bestowed on the individual by the state pending good behaviour.

6618 *On the Contrary*
The immense popularity of American movies abroad demonstrates that Europe is the unfinished negative of which America is the proof.

6619 *On the Contrary*
If someone tells you he is going to make a 'realistic decision', you immediately understand that he has resolved to do something bad.

6620 *On the Contrary*
In violence, we forget who we are.

6621 *On the Contrary*
There are no new truths, but only truths that have not been recognized by those who have perceived them without noticing.

6622 *(of Lillian Hellmann)*
Every word she writes is a lie, including 'and' and 'the'.

McCLENAHAN John L.
6623
It requires a great deal of faith for a man to be cured by his own placebos.

McCLUNG Nellie 1873-1951
6624
Chivalry is a poor substitute for justice, if one cannot have both. Chivalry is something like the icing on cake, sweet, but not nourishing.

6625
Never retract, never explain, never apologize - get the thing done and let them howl.

6626
By nice women ... you probably mean selfish women who have no more thought for the underpriviledged, overworked women than a pussycat in a sunny window for the starving kitten in the street. Now in that sense I am not a nice woman, for I do care.

6627
The economic dependence of women is perhaps the greatest injustice that has been done to us, and has worked the greatest injury to the race.

6628
Women who set a low value on themselves make life hard for all women.

6629 *(to a heckler about women being elected)*
This proves what a purifying effect women would have on politics.

McCLURE Robert 1807-1873
6630
A = r + p (or Adventure equals risk plus purpose)

McCORD David 1897-
6631 *'Remainders' (epitaph for a waiter)*
By and by
God caught his eye.

McCORMICK Anne O'Hare d.1954
6632
Today the real test of power is not capacity to make war but capacity to prevent it.

McCRAE John 1872-1918
6633 *'In Flanders Fields'*
In Flanders fields the poppies blow
Between the crosses, row on row.

6634 *'In Flanders Fields'*
To you from failing hands we throw
The torch; be yours to hold it high.
If ye break faith with us who die
We shall not sleep, though poppies grow.

MacDIARMID Hugh 1892-1978
6635 *A Drunk Man Looks at the Thistle*
I'll ha'e nae hauf-way hoose, but aye be whaur
Extremes meet - it's the only way I ken
To dodge the curst conceit o' bein' richt
That damns the vast majority o' men.

6636 *A Drunk Man Looks at the Thistle*
He's no a man ava',
And lacks a proper pride,
Gin less than a' the world
Can ser' him for a bride!

6637 *The International Brigade*
It is very rarely that a man loves
And when he does it is nearly always fatal.

MacDONALD George 1824-1905
6638
It is not by driving away our brother that we can be alone with God.

6639
To be trusted is a greater compliment than to be loved.

6640 *David Elginbrod*
Here lie I, Martin Elginbrodde:
Hae mercy o' my soul, Lord God;
As I wad do, were I Lord God,
And ye were Martin Elginbrodde.

6641 *'That Holy Thing'*
They all were looking for a king
To slay their foes, and lift them high;
Thou cam'st, a little baby thing,
That made a woman cry.

6642 *At the Back of the North Wind*
Where did you come from, baby dear?
Out of the everywhere into here.

MacDONALD Sir John A. 1815-1891
6643
Confederation is only yet in the gristle, and it will require five years more before it hardens into bone.

6644
When Fortune empties her chamberpot on your head, smile and say 'We are going to have a summer shower'.

6645
A new Member requires the experience of his first session in the House to teach him how to hang up his overcoat and take his seat in a manner befitting a gentleman.

6646
Macdonald's Law: Never write a letter if you can help it, and never destroy one.

MacDONALD Ramsay 1866-1937
6647
We hear war called murder. It is not: it is suicide.

6648 *(after forming the National Government)*
Tomorrow every Duchess in London will be wanting to kiss me!

MacDONALD Ross 1888-1964
6649
The walls of books around him, dense with the past, formed a kind of insulation against the present world and its disasters.

McEWAN Ian 1948-
6650 *The Child in Time*
Shakespeare would have grasped wave functions, Donne would have understood

complementarity and relative time. They would have been excited. What richness! They would have plundered this new science for their imagery. And they would have educated their audiences too. But you 'arts' people, you're not only ignorant of these magnificent things, you're rather proud of knowing nothing.

McFEE William 1881-1966
6651
One must choose between Obscurity with Efficiency, and Fame with its inevitable collateral of Bluff.

6652
The world belongs to the enthusiast who keeps cool.

McGEACHY J.B.
6653
We sing about the North, but live as far south as possible.

McGINLEY Phyllis 1905-
6654
Not reading poetry amounts to a national pastime here.

6655
Nothing fails like success; nothing is so defeated as yesterday's triumphant cause.

McGOUGH Roger 1937-
6656 'Comeclose and Sleepnow'
You will put on a dress of guilt
and shoes with broken high ideals.

6657 'Let Me Die a Youngman's Death'
Let me die a youngman's death
Not a clean & in-between-
The-sheets, holy-water death,
Not a famous-last-words
Peaceful out-of-breath death.

6658 'A lot of Water has Flown under your Bridge'
i remember how
when we lay together for the first time
the room smiled,
said 'excuse me',
and tiptoed away.

McGREGOR Douglas 1906-1964
6659
Man is a wanting animal - as soon as one

of his needs is satisfied, another appears in its place. This process is unending. It continues from birth to death.

McGREGOR Jimmy
6660 'Football Crazy'
Oh, he's football crazy, he's football mad
And the football it has robbed him o' the wee bit sense he had.

MacGREGOR Sir Ian 1912-
6661 (during the coal-miners' strike)
People are now discovering the price of insubordination and insurrection. And boy, are we going to make it stick!

McHUGH Vincent
6662
Self-expression is for babies and seals, where it can be charming. A writer's business is to affect the reader.

MacINNES Colm
6663
At rare moments in history, by a series of accidents never to be repeated, arise flower societies in which the cult of happiness is paramount, hedonistic, mindless, intent upon the glorious physical instant.

McINTYRE Leslie M.
6664
Nobody objects to a woman being a good writer or sculptor or geneticist if at the same time she manages to be a good wife, good mother, good looking, good tempered, well groomed and unaggressive.

MACKAY Charles 1814-1889
6665
There is no such thing as death,
In nature, nothing dies:
From each sad moment of decay
Some forms of life arise.

McKAY Claude 1890-1948
6666 'If We Must Die'
If we must die, let it not be like hogs
Hunted and penned in an inglorious spot,
While round us bark the mad and hungry dogs,
Making their mock at our accursed lot.

MACKENZIE Sir Compton 1883-1972
6667 The Adventures of Sylvia Scarlett
Prostitution. Selling one's body to keep

one's soul: this is the meaning of the sins that were forgiven to the woman because she loved much: one might say of most marriages that they were selling one's soul to keep one's body.

6668 *Literature in My Time*
Women do not find it difficult nowadays to behave like men, but they often find it extremely difficult to behave like gentlemen.

6669 *Vestal Fire*
You are offered a piece of bread and butter that feels like a damp handkerchief and sometimes, when cucumber is added to it, like a wet one.

MACKENZIE William Lyon 1795-1861
6670
He is ... like many other geniuses, a greater friend to the bottle, than the bottle is to him.

MACKINTOSH Sir James 1765-1832
6671 *The Causes of the Revolution*
Disciplined inaction.

6672 *Dissertation on the Progress of Ethical Philosophy*
Men are never so good or so bad as their opinions.

6673 *Vindiciae Gallicae*
The Commons, faithful to their system, remained in a wise and masterly inactivity.

MACLAINE Shirley 1934-
6674
When you look back ... on your love affairs ... what you really find out is that the only person you really go to bed with is yourself.

MACLAREN Alexander 1826-1910
6675 *Expositions of Holy Scripture: Acts of the Apostles*
'The Church is an anvil which has worn out many hammers', and the story of the first collision is, in essentials, the story of all.

McLAUGHLIN Mignon
6676
It's important to our friends to believe that we are unreservedly frank with them, and important to friendship that we are not.

6677
We'd all like a reputation for generosity and we'd all like to buy it cheap.

6678
No one has ever loved anyone the way everyone wants to be loved.

6679
Every society honours its live conformists and its dead troublemakers.

6680
Our strength is often composed of the weakness that we're damned if we are going to show.

McLEAN Don 1945-
6681 *'American Pie' (on death of Buddy Holly)*
I can't remember if I cried
When I read about his widowed bride.
Something touched me deep inside
The day the music died.

MacLEISH Archibald 1892-1982
6682
Around, around the sun we go:
The moon goes round the earth.
We do not die of death:
We die of vertigo.

6683
We have no choice but to be guilty,
God is unthinkable if we are innocent.

6684
The perversion of the mind is only possible when those who should be heard in its defence are silent.

6685 *'Ars Poetica'*
A Poem should be palpable and mute
As a globed fruit
Dumb
As old medallions to the thumb
Silent as the sleeve-worn stone
Of casement ledges where the moss has grown -
A poem should be wordless
As the flight of birds.

6686 *'Ars Poetica'*
A poem should not mean
But be.

MACLENNAN Hugh 1907-1990

6687
An artist has to take life as he finds it. Life by itself is formless wherever it is. Art must give it form.

6688
The farmer's way of saving money: to be owed by someone he trusted.

6689
A novel must be exceptionally good to live as long as the average cat.

McLEOD Fiona 1855-1905
6690 *'The Lonely Hunter'*
My heart is a lonely hunter that hunts on a lonely hill.

McLUHAN Marshall 1911-1980
6691
Ads are the cave art of the twentieth century.

6692
Art at its most significant is a Distant Early Warning System that can always be relied on to tell the old culture what is beginning to happen to it.

6693
A successful book cannot afford to be more than ten per cent new.

6694
Our sense of identity is our sense of density.

6695
One matter Englishmen don't think in the least funny is their happy consciousness of possessing a deep sense of humour.

6696
Money is the poor people's credit card.

6697
Good taste is the first refuge of the non-creative. It is the last ditch stand of the artist.

6698
Violence is the quest for identity. When identity disappears with technological innovation, violence is the natural recourse.

6699
Publication is a self-invasion of privacy.

6700 *The Gutenberg Galaxy*
The new electronic interdependence recreates the world in the image of a global village.

6701 *Understanding Media*
The medium is the message.

6702 *Understanding Media*
The name of a man is a numbing blow from which he never recovers.

6703 *Understanding Media*
The car has become an article of dress without which we feel uncertain, unclad and incomplete in the urban compound.

MACMAHON Comte de 1808-1893
6704 *(at taking of Malakoff fortress, Crimean War)*
J'y suis, j'y reste.
Here I am, and here I stay.

MACMILLAN Sir Harold 1894-1986
6705
You will find the Americans much as the Greeks found the Romans: great, big, vulgar, bustling peole more vigorous than we are and also more idle, with more unspoiled virtues but also more corrupt.

6706
It was a storm in a tea cup, but in politics we sail in paper boats.

6707
I have never found, in a long experience of politics, that criticism is ever inhibited by ignorance.

6708
Let us be frank about it: most of our people have never had it so good.

6709
I thought the best thing to do was to settle up these little local difficulties [resignation of the Chancellor of the Exchequer and others], and then turn to the wider vision of the Commonwealth.

6710
There are three bodies no sensible man directly challenges: the Roman Catholic

Church, the Brigade of Guards and the National Union of Mineworkers.

6711 *(of Aneurin Bevan)*
He enjoys prophesying the imminent fall of the capitalist system and is prepared to play a part, any part, in its burial, except that of mute.

6712 *(at Cape Town)*
The wind of change is blowing through this continent, and, whether we like it or not, this growth of [African] national consciousness is a political fact.

6713 *(on the life of a Foreign Secretary)*
Forever poised between a cliché and an indiscretion.

6714 *(on privatization)*
First of all the Georgian silver goes, and then all that nice furniture that used to be in the saloon. Then the Canalettos go.

6715 *(on the Profumo affair)*
I was determined that no British government should be brought down by the action of two tarts.

McNABB Vincent
6716
There are no short cuts to Heaven, only the ordinary way of ordinary things.

McNALLY Leonard 1752-1820
6717 *The Lass of Richmond Hill*
On Richmond Hill there lives a lass,
More sweet than May day morn,
Whose charms all other maids surpass,
A rose without a thorn.

MacNEICE Louis 1907-1963
6718 *Autumn Journal*
Better authentic mammon than a bogus god.

6719 *'Bagpipe Music'*
It's no go the merrygoround, it's no go the rickshaw,
All we want is a limousine and a ticket for the peepshow.

6720 *'Bagpipe Music'*
It's no go the Government grants, it's no go the elections,
Sit on your arse for fifty years and hang your hat on a pension.

6721 *'Bagpipe Music'*
It's no go my honey love, it's no go my poppet;
Work your hands from day to day, the winds will blow the profit.
The glass is falling hour by hour, the glass will fall for ever,
But if you break the bloody glass you won't hold up the weather.

6722 *'The British Museum Reading Room'*
And under the totem poles - the ancient terror -
Between the enormous fluted Ionic columns
There seeps from heavily jowled or hawk-like foreign faces
The guttural sorrow of the refugees.

6723 *'Débâcle'*
Crumbling between the fingers, under the feet,
Crumbling behind the eyes,
Their world gives way and dies
And something twangs and breaks at the end of the street.

6724 *'Les Sylphides'*
So they were married - to be the more together -
And found they were never again so much together,
Divided by the morning tea,
By the evening paper,
By children and tradesmen's bills.

6725 *'Meeting Point'*
Time was away and somewhere else,
There were two glasses and two chairs
And two people with the one pulse
(Somebody stopped the moving stairs):
Time was away and somewhere else.

6726 *'Snow'*
World is crazier and more of it than we think,
Incorrigibly plural. I peel and portion
A tangerine and spit the pips and feel
The drunkenness of things being various.

6727 *'Sunday Morning'*
Down the road someone is practising scales,

The notes like little fishes vanish with a
wink of tails,
Man's heart expands to tinker with his car
For this is Sunday morning, Fate's great
bazaar.

6728 *'Sunlight on the Garden'*
The sunlight on the garden
Hardens and grows cold,
We cannot cage the minute
Within its net of gold,
When all is told
We cannot beg for pardon.

6729 *'Thalassa'*
By a high star our course is set,
Our end is Life. Put out to sea.

MacPHAIL Agnes 1890-1954
6730
Do not rely completely on any other
human being, however dear. We meet all
life's greatest tests alone.

McPHEE John
6731
Behind every tennis player there is another
tennis player.

McWILLIAM Candia
6732
With the birth of each child you lose two
novels.

MACAULAY Baron (Thomas Babington)
1800-1859
6733
It seems that the creative faculty and the
critical faculty cannot exist together in
their highest perfection.

6734
An intellectual is someone whose mind
watches itself.

6735
The English Bible, a book which, if
everything else in our language should
perish, would alone suffice to show the
whole extent of its beauty and power.

6736
Knowledge advances by steps, and not by
leaps.

6737 *'The Armada'*
The rugged miners poured to war from
mendip's sunless caves.

6738 *'The Battle of Naseby'*
Obadiah Bind-their-kings-in-chains-and-
their-nobles-with-links-of-iron.

6739 *'The Battle of Naseby'*
Oh, wherefore come ye forth in triumph
from the north,
With your hands, and your feet, and your
raiment all red?
And wherefore doth your rout send forth a
joyous shout?
And whence be the grapes of the wine-
press which ye tread?

6740 *Biographical Essays 'Frederic the Great'*
In order that he might rob a neighbour
whom he had promised to defend, black
men fought on the coast of Coromandel,
and red men scalped each other by the
Great Lakes of North America.

6741 *'Essay on Athenian Orators'*
The object of oratory alone is not truth, but
persuasion.

6742 *Essays ... 'Gladstone on Church and
State'*
The rising hope of those stern and
unbending Tories.

6743 *Essays ... 'Hallam'*
The business of everybody is the business
of nobody.

6744 *Essays ... 'Hallam'*
The gallery in which the reporters sit has
become a fourth estate of the realm.

6745 *Essays ... 'Horace Walpole'*
The conformation of his mind was such
that whatever was little seemed to him
great, and whatever was great seemed to
him little.

6746 *Essays ... 'Sir James Mackintosh'*
The highest intellects, like the tops of
mountains, are the first to catch and to
reflect the dawn.

6747 *Essays ... 'Sir James Mackintosh'*
The history of England is emphatically the
history of progress.

6748 *Essays ... 'John Hampden'*
He knew that the essence of war is violence, and that moderation in war is imbecility.

6749 *Essays ... 'Lord Bacon'*
An acre in Middlesex is better than a principality in Utopia.

6750 *Essays ... 'Lord Clive'*
Every schoolboy knows who imprisoned Montezuma, and who strangled Atahualpa.

6751 *Essays ... 'Machiavelli'*
Out of his surname they have coined an epithet for a knave, and out of his Christian name a synonym for the Devil.

6752 *Essays ... 'Milton'*
As civilization advances, poetry almost necessarily declines.

6753 *Essays ... 'Milton'*
If men are to wait for liberty till they become wise and good in slavery, they may indeed wait for ever.

6754 *Essays ... 'Milton' (about Puritans)*
Nobles by the right of an earlier creation, and priests by the imposition of a mightier hand.

6755 *Essays ... 'Moore's - Life of Lord Byron'*
We know no spectacle so ridiculous as the British public in one of its periodical fits of morality.

6756 *Essays ... 'Moore's - Life of Lord Byron'*
From the poetry of Lord Byron they drew a system of ethics, compounded of misanthropy and voluptuousness, a system in which the two great commandments were, to hate your neighbour, and to love your neighbour's wife.

6757 *Essays ... (of Richard Steele)*
A rake among scholars, and a scholar among rakes.

6758 *Essays ... 'Samuel Johnson'*
The gigantic body, the huge massy face, seamed with the scars of disease, the brown coat, the black worsted stockings, the grey wig with the scorched foretop, the dirty hands, the nails bitten and pared to the quick.

6759 *Essays ... 'Samuel Johnson' (of writers)*
They knew luxury; they knew beggary; but they never knew comfort.

6760 *Essays ... 'Southey's Colloquies'*
We have heard it said that five per cent is the natural interest of money.

6761 *Essays ... 'Von Ranke'*
She [the Roman Catholic Church] may still exist in undiminished vigour when some traveller from New Zealand shall, in the midst of a vast solitude, take his stand on a broken arch of London Bridge to sketch the ruins of St Paul's.

6762 *Essays ... 'Von Ranke'*
She [the Church of Rome] thoroughly understands what no other church has ever understood, how to deal with enthusiasts.

6763 *Essays ... 'Warren Hastings'*
The Chief Justice was rich, quiet, and infamous.

6764 *Essays ... 'Warren Hastings'*
That temple of silence and reconciliation [Westminster Abbey] where the enmities of twenty generations lie buried.

6765 *Essays ... 'The War of Succession in Spain'*
The reluctant obedience of distant provinces generally costs more than it [the territory] is worth.

6766 *History of England*
I shall cheerfully bear the reproach of having descended below the dignity of history.

6767 *History of England*
Thus our democracy was, from an early period, the most aristocratic, and our aristocracy the most democratic in the world.

6768 *History of England*
The Puritan hated bear-baiting, not because it gave pain to the bear, but because it gave pleasure to the spectators.

6769 *History of England*
There were gentlemen and there were
seamen in the navy of Charles the Second.
But the seamen were not gentlemen; and
the gentlemen were not seamen.

6770 *'A Jacobite's Epitaph'*
To my true king I offered free from stain
Courage and faith; vain faith, and courage
vain.

6771 *'A Jacobite's Epitaph'*
By those white cliffs I never more must
see,
By that dear language which I spake like
thee,
Forget all feuds, and shed one English tear
O'er English dust. A broken heart lies
here.

6772 *(of John Dryden)*
His imagination resembled the wings of an
ostrich. It enabled him to run, though not
to soar.

6773 *Lays of Ancient Rome*
Let no man stop to plunder,
But slay, and slay, and slay;
The Gods who live for ever
Are on our side to-day.

6774 *Lays of Ancient Rome 'Horatius'*
The out spake brave Horatius,
The Captain of the Gate:
'To every man upon this earth
Death cometh soon or late.
And how can man die better
Than facing fearful odds,
For the ashes of his fathers,
And the temples of his Gods?'

6775 *Lays of Ancient Rome 'Horatius'*
Now who will stand on either hand,
And keep the bridge with me?

6776 *Lays of Ancient Rome 'Horatius'*
Then none was for a party;
Then all were for the state;
The the great man helped the poor,
And the poor man loved the great:
Then lands were fairly portioned;
The spoils were fairly sold:
The Romans were like brothers
In the brave days of old.

6777 *Lays of Ancient Rome 'Horatius'*
Was none who would be foremost
To lead such dire attack;
But those behind cried 'Forward!'
And those before cried 'Back!'

6778 *Lays of Ancient Rome 'Horatius'*
Oh, Tiber! father Tiber
To whom the Romans pray,
A Roman's life, a Roman's arms,
Take thou in charge this day!

6779 *Lays of Ancient Rome 'Horatius'*
And even the ranks of Tuscany
Could scarce forbear to cheer.

6780 *Lays of Ancient Rome 'Horatius'*
With weeping and with laughter
Still is the story told,
How well Horatius kept the bridge
In the brave days of old.

6781 *Literary Essays 'Milton'*
Perhaps no person can be a poet, or can
even enjoy poetry, without a certain
unsoundness of mind.

MACAULAY Dame Rose 1889-1958
6782
Women have one great advantage over
men. It is commonly thought that if they
marry they have done enough, and need
career no further. If a man marries, on the
other hand, public opinion is all against
him if he takes this view.

6783
It was a book to kill time for those who
like it better dead.

6784 *Crewe Train*
Gentlemen know that fresh *air* should be
kept in its proper place - out of doors - and
that, God having given us indoors and
out-of-doors, we should not attempt to do
away with this distinction.

6785 *Poetry Review*
Poem me no poems.

6786 *The Towers of Trebizond*
'Take my camel, dear,' said my aunt Dot,
as she climbed down from this animal on
her return from High Mass.

MACHIAVELLI Niccolo 1469-1527
6787
Men are always wicked at bottom unless they are made good by some compulsion.

6788
Where the willingness is great, the difficulties cannot be great.

6789
Men hesitate less to injure a man who makes himself loved than to injure one who makes himself feared, for their love is held by a chain of obligation which, because of men's wickedness, is broken on every occasion for the sake of selfish profit; but their fear is secured by a dread of punishment.

6790 *'Advice to Raffaello Girolami'*
And if, to be sure, sometimes you need to conceal a fact with words, do it in such a way that it does not become known, or, if it does become known, that you have a ready and quick defence.

6791 *(during the coal-miners' strike)*
Benefits should be granted little by little, so that they may be better enjoyed.

6792 *Discourse - Livy*
It is necessary for him who lays out a state and arranges laws for it to presuppose that all men are evil and that they are always going to act according to the wickedness of their spirits whenever they have free scope.

6793 *The Prince*
Men should be either treated generously or destroyed, because they take revenge for slight injuries - for heavy ones they cannot.

6794 *The Prince*
It is much safer for a prince to be feared than loved, if he is to fail in one of the two.

6795 *The Prince*
Let no one oppose this belief of mine with that well-worn proverb: 'He who builds on the people builds on mud'.

6796 *The Prince*
So long as the great majority of men are not deprived of either property or honour, they are satisfied.

6797 *The Prince*
There is no other way for securing yourself against flatteries except that men understand that they do not offend you by telling you the truth; but when everybody can tell you the truth, you fail to get respect.

MACHLOWITZ Marilyn
6798
Workaholics are energized rather than enervated by their work - their energy paradoxically expands as it is expended.

6799
Because it is less structured than work, leisure time leaves workaholics at a loss for what to do. Workaholics practically climb the wall when they can't work.

MACHLUP Fritz 1902-1983
6800
Let us remember the unfortunate econometrician who, in one of the major functions of his system, had to use a proxy for risk and a dummy for sex.

MADAN Geoffrey 1895-1947
6801
King George, passing slowly in a closed car, looking like a big, rather worn *penny* in the window.

6802
The great tragedy of the classical languages is to have been born twins.

6803
Peers: a kind of eye-shade or smoked glass, to protect us from the full glare of Royalty.

6804
Conservative ideal of freedom and progress: everyone to have an unfettered opportunity of remaining exactly where they are.

6805
Attractive Etonians who go straight onto the Stock Exchange missing University on their fathers' advice: the raw material of the great bores.

6806
To say you should treat a duke as an ordinary man is like telling you to read the Bible like an ordinary book.

6807
A marquis is a sort of four-move chess problem.

6808
The cat which isn't let out of the bag often becomes a skeleton in the cupboard.

6809
I love drink, so long as it isn't in moderation.

6810 *Livre sans nom: Twelve Reflections*
The dust of exploded beliefs may make a fine sunset.

MADARIAGA Salvador de 1886-1978
6811 *Morning Without Noon*
Since, in the main, it is not armaments that cause wars but wars (or the fears thereof) that cause armaments, it follows that every nation will at every moment strive to keep its armament in an efficient state as required by its fear, otherwise styled security.

MADDEN Samuel 1686-1765
6812 *Boulter's Monument*
Words are men's daughters, but God's sons are things.

MADISON James 1751-1836
6813 *The Federalist*
Liberty is to faction what air is to fire, an ailment without which it instantly expires. But it could not be less folly to abolish liberty, which is essential to political life, because it nourishes faction than it would be to wish the annihilation of air, which is essential to animal life, because it imparts to fire its destructive agency.

MADONNA 1959-
6814
The definition of S & M is letting someone hurt you that you know would never hurt you.

MAETERLINCK Maurice 1862-1949
6815
What man is there that does not

laboriously, though all unconsciously, himself fashion the sorrow that is to be the pivot of his life.

MAGARY James
6816
Computers can figure out all kinds of problems, except the things in the world that just don't add up.

MAGEE William Connor 1821-1891
6817 *(on the Intoxicating Liquor Bill)*
It would be better that England should be free than that England should be compulsorily sober.

MAGNA CARTA 1215
6818 *Clause 1*
That the English Church shall be free.

6819 *Clause 39*
No free man shall be taken or imprisoned or dispossessed, or outlawed or exiled, or in any way destroyed, nor will we go upon him, nor will we send against him except by the lawful judgement of his peers or by the law of the land.

6820 *Clause 40*
To no man will we sell, or deny, or delay, right or justice.

MAHAN Alfred Thayer 1840-1914
6821
Force is never more operative than when it is known to exist but is not brandished.

MAHBUBANI Kishore
6822
To have good Government you often need less, not more, democracy.

MAHLER Gustav 1860-1911
6823 *(on seeing Niagara Falls)*
Fortissimo at last!

MAHON Derek 1941-
6824 *Antarctica (title poem)*
'I am just going outside and may be some time.'
The others nod, pretending not to know.
At the heart of the ridiculous, the sublime.

MAILER Norman 1923-
6825
With the pride of the artist, you must blow

against the walls of every power that exists, the small trumpet of your defiance.

6826
The private terror of the liberal spirit is invariably suicide, not murder.

6827
I think it's bad to talk about one's present work, for it spoils something at the root of the creative act. It discharges the tension.

6828
The highest prize in a world of men is the most beautiful woman available on your arm and living there in her heart loyal to you.

6829 *Cannibals and Christians*
Sentimentality is the emotional promiscuity of those who have no sentiment.

6830 *A Fire on the Moon*
The horror of the Twentieth Century was the size of each event, and the paucity of its reverberation.

6831 *Marilyn*
Marilyn who was every man's love affair with America, Marilyn Monroe who was blonde and beautiful and had a sweet little rinky-dink of a voice and all the cleanliness of all the clean American backyards.

6832 *The Presidential Papers*
Ultimately a hero is a man who would argue with the Gods, and so awakens devils to contest his vision.

6833 *Voices of Dissent*
Hip is the sophistication of the wise primitive in a giant jungle.

MAINE Sir Henry 1822-1888
6834 *Ancient Law*
The movement of the progressive societies has hitherto been a movement *from Status to Contract.*

6835 *Village Communities*
Except the blind forces of Nature, nothing moves in this world which is not Greek in its origin.

MAISTRE Josephe de 1753-1821
6836 *Lettres et Opuscules Inédits*
Every country has the government it deserves.

MAJOR John 1943-
6837
I am fit, I am well, I am here - I am staying.

6838
Society needs to condemn a little more and understand a little less.

6839
Good order brings good learning.

6840
I am more a European in my head than in my heart.

6841
My trade has never been in adjectives.

6842
I am a coalition government on my own.

MALAMUD Bernard 1914-1986
6843 *Dublin's Lives*
The past exudes legend: one can't make pure clay of time's mud. There is no life that can be recaptured wholly; as it was. Which is to say that all biography is ultimately fiction.

MALCOLM Janet
6844
If you scratch a great photograph, you find two things: a painting and a photograph.

MALHERBE François de 1555-1628
6845 *(on his death bed, to a priest)*
Stop, Sir, stop - go away: I cannot bear your style.

MALLARMÉ Stéphane 1842-1898
6846
Prélude à l'après-midi d'un faune.
Prelude to the afternoon of a fawn.

6847
A throw of the dice will never eliminate chance.

6848 *'Brise Marin'*
The flesh, alas, is wearied; and I have read all the books there are.

6849 *Plusieurs Sonnets*
That virgin, vital, fine day: today.

MALLET (or MALLOCH) David c.1705-1765
6850 *'Imitation of Horace'*
O grant me, Heaven, a middle state,
Neither too humble nor too great;
More than enough, for nature's ends,
With something left to treat my friends.

MALLORY George Leigh 1886-1924
6851 *(on being asked why he wanted to climb Everest)*
Because it's there.

MALONE Dudley Field
6852
I have never in my life learned anything from any man who agreed with me.

MALONEY Martin
6853
If anything is poisoning our lives and weakening our society, it is reality - and not the fabrication of television writers and producers.

MALORY Sir Thomas d.1471
6854 *Le Morte D'Arthur*
Whoso pulleth out this sword of this stone and anvil is rightwise King born of all England.

6855 *Le Morte D'Arthur*
God defend me, said Dinadan, for the joy of love is too short, and the sorrow thereof, and what cometh thereof, dureth over long.

6856 *Le Morte D'Arthur*
Through this man and me hath all this war been wrought, and the death of the most noblest knights of the world; for through our love that we have loved together is my most noble lord slain.

6857 *Le Morte D'Arthur*
This beast went to the well and drank, and the noise was in the beast's belly like unto the questing of thirty couple hounds, but all the while the beast drank there was no noise in the beast's belly.

6858 *Le Morte D'Arthur*
So they rode till they came to a lake that was a fair water and broad. And in the midst Arthur was ware of an arm clothed in white samite, that held a fair sword in that hand.

6859 *Le Morte D'Arthur*
The month of May was come, when every lusty heart beginneth to blossom, and to bring forth fruit.

6860 *Le Morte D'Arthur*
For love that time was not as love is nowadays.

6861 *Le Morte D'Arthur*
And much more am I sorrier for my good knights' loss than for the loss of my fair queen; for queens I might have enough, but such a fellowship of good knights shall never be together in no company.

6862 *Le Morte D'Arthur*
For as well as I have loved thee heretofore, mine heart will not serve now to see thee; for through thee and me is the flower of kings and knights destroyed.

MALRAUX André 1901-1976
6863
All art is a revolt against man's fate.

6864
Man is a dog's ideal of what God should be.

6865
The mind supplies the idea of a nation, but what gives this idea its sentimental force is a community of dreams.

6866
La Condition humaine.
The human condition.

6867 *Les Noyers d'Altenburg*
Man knows that the world is not made on a human scale; and he wishes that it were.

6868 *L'Espoir*
There are not fifty ways of fighting, there's only one, and that's to win. Neither revolution nor war consists in doing what one pleases.

6869 *Les Voix du silence*
Art is a revolt against fate.

MALTHUS Thomas Robert 1766-1834
6870 *Essay on the Principle of Population*
Population, when unchecked, increases in a geometrical ratio. Subsistence only increases in an arithmetical ratio.

6871 *Essay on the Principle of Population*
The perpetual struggle for room and food.

MAMET David 1947-
6872
Writing is not a political tool. Drama never changed anybody's mind.

MANCROFT Lord 1957-
6873 *Bees in Some Bonnets*
Cricket - a game which the English, not being a spiritual people, have invented in order to give themselves some conception of eternity.

MANDALE W.R.
6874 *'Pop Goes the Weasel'*
Up and down the City Road,
In and out the Eagle,
That's the way the money goes -
Pop goes the weasel!

MANDELA Winnie 1934-
6875
With that stick of matches, with our necklace, we shall liberate this country.

MANDELSTAM Osip 1892-1938
6876 *'The Age'(translated by C.M. Bowra)*
The age is rocking the wave
with human grief
to a golden beat, and an adder
is breathing in time with it in the grass.

The buds will go on swelling,
the rush of green will explode,
but your spine has been shattered,
my splendid derelict, my age.
Cruel and feeble, you'll look back
with the smile of a half-wit:
an animal that could run once,
staring at its own tracks.

6877 *Selected Poems (translated by D. McDuff)*
Perhaps my whisper was already born before my lips.

6878 *'Tristia'(translated by C.M. Bowra)*
I've studied all the lore of separation
From grievances bare-headed in the night.

6879 *'Tristia'(translated by C.M. Bowra)*
Only in war our fate has consummation,
And divination too will perish them.

MANET Edouard 1832-1883
6880
The country has charms only for those not obliged to stay there.

MANION Clarence C.
6881
The average man that I encounter all over the country regards government as a sort of great milk cow, with its head in the clouds eating air, and growing a full teat for everybody on earth.

MANLEY Mrs 1663-1724
6882 *The Lost Lover*
No time like the present.

MANN Horace 1796-1859
6883
Character is what God and the angels know of us; reputation is what men and women think of us.

6884
We put things in order - God does the rest. Lay an iron bar east and west, it is not magnetized. Lay it north and south and it is.

6885 *'Lost, Two Golden Hours'*
Lost, yesterday, somewhere between Sunrise and Sunset, two golden hours, each set with sixty diamond minutes. No reward is offered, for they are gone forever.

MANN Thomas 1875-1955
6886
Habituation is a falling asleep or fatiguing of the sense of time; which explains why young years pass slowly, while later life flings itself faster and faster upon its course.

6887
He who loves the more is the inferior and must suffer.

6888
A human being who is first of all an invalid is all body; therein lies his inhumanity and his debasement.

6889
Opinions cannot survive if one has no chance to fight for them.

6890
Human reason needs only to will more strongly than fate, and she *is* fate.

6891
Time cools, time clarifies; no mood can be maintained quite unaltered through the course of hours.

6892
Speech is civilization itself. The word, even the most contradictory word, preserves contact - it is silence which isolates.

6893 *The Confessions of Felix Krull*
Our capacity for disgust, let me observe, is in proportion of our desires; that is in proportion to the intensity of our attachment to the things of this world.

6894 *The Magic Mountain*
Time has no divisions to mark its passage, there is never a thunderstorm or blare of trumpets to announce the beginning of a new month or year. Even when a new century begins it is only we mortals who ring bells and fire off pistols.

6895 *The Magic Mountain*
Waiting we say is long. We might just as well - or more accurately - say it is short, since it consumes whole spaces of time without our living them or making any use of them as such.

6896 *The Magic Mountain*
We come out of the dark and go into the dark again, and in between lie the experiences of our life. But the beginning and end, birth and death, we do not experience; they have no subjective character, they fall entirely in the category of objective events, and that's that.

6897 *The Magic Mountain*
A man's dying is more the survivors' affair than his own.

MANNERS Lord John 1818-1906
6898 *England's Trust*
Let wealth and commerce, laws and learning die,
But leave us still our old nobility!

MANNES Marya
6899
The sign of an intelligent people is their ability to control emotions by the application of reason.

6900
To lead means to direct and to exact, and no man dares do either - he might be unpopular. What authority we are given now is a trinity: the grin, the generality, and God (the Word).

MANSFIELD Katherine 1888-1923
6901
Make it a rule of life never to regret and never look back. Regret is an appalling waste of energy; you can't build on it; it's good only for wallowing in.

6902 *Journal*
E.M. Forster never gets any further than warming the teapot. He's a rare fine hand at that. Feel this teapot. Is it not beautifully warm? Yes, but there ain't going to be no tea.

6903 *Journal*
Whenever I prepare for a journey I prepare as though for death. Should I never return, all is in order.

6904 *Letter to John Middleton Murray*
I hate the sort of licence that English people give themselves ... to spread over and flop and roll about. I feel as fastidious as though I wrote with acid.

MAO TSE-TUNG 1893-1976
6905
The guerilla must live amongst the people as the fish lives in the water.

6906
Politics is war without bloodshed while war is politics with bloodshed.

6907
Every Communist must grasp the truth, 'Political power grows out of the barrel of a gun'.

6908
The atom bomb is a paper tiger which the United States reactionaries use to scare people. It looks terrible, but in fact it isn't ... All reactionaries are paper tigers.

6909
Letting a hundred flowers blossom and a hundred schools of thought contend is the policy for promoting progress in the arts and the sciences and a flourishing socialist culture in our land.

MARCEAU Marcel 1923-
6910
Dance is in the air ... Mime is on the floor.

MARCY William Learned 1786-1857
6911
The politicians of New York ... see nothing wrong in the rule, that to the victor belong the spoils of the enemy.

MARGOLYES Miriam 1941-
6912
Life, if you're fat, is a minefield - you have to pick your way, otherwise you blow up.

MARIE of Rumania, Queen
6913
Fashion exists for women with no taste, etiquette for people with no breeding.

MARIE Queen of Rumania
6914
When a man loves his children with an excess of passion, be sure that he is not happy.

6915
A woman's virtue ought indeed to be great: since it often has to suffice for two.

6916
Between husband and wife a shadow of courtship should always subsist.

MARIE-ANTOINETTE Queen 1755-1793
6917 *(on being told that her people had no bread)*
Qu'ils mangent de la brioche.

Let them eat cake.

MARKEL Lester
6918
What you see is news, what you know is background, what you feel is opinion.

MARKHAM Edwin 1852-1940
6919 *'The Man with the Hoe'*
Bowed by the weight of centuries he leans
Upon his hoe and gazes on the ground,
The emptiness of ages in his face,
And on his back the burden of the world.
Who made him dead to rapture and despair,
A thing that grieves not and that never hopes,
Stolid and stunned, a brother to the ox?

MARKS Johnny 1909-1985
6920 *'Rudolph, the Red-Nosed Reindeer'*
Rudolph, the Red-Nosed Reindeer
Had a very shiny nose,
And if you ever saw it,
You would even say it glows.

MARLEY Bob 1945-1981
6921 *'I Shot the Sheriff'*
I shot the sheriff
But I swear it was in self-defence
I shot the sheriff
And they say it is a capital offence.

6922 *'Get up, Stand up'*
Get up, stand up
Stand up for your rights
Get up, stand up
Never give up the fight.

MARLOWE Christopher 1564-1593
6923 *Doctor Faustus*
Sweet Analytics, 'tis thou hast ravished me.

6924 *Doctor Faustus*
I'll have them fly to India for gold,
Ransack the ocean for orient pearl.

6925 *Doctor Faustus*
Hell hath no limits nor is circumscribed
In one self place, where we are is Hell,
And to be short, when all the world dissolves,
And every creature shall be purified,
All places shall be hell that are not heaven.

6926 *Doctor Faustus*
Was this the face that launched a thousand ships,
And burnt the topless towers of Ilium?
Sweet Helen, make me immortal with a kiss!
Her lips suck forth my soul: see, where it flies!
Come Helen, come give me my soul again.
Here will I dwell, for heaven be in these lips,
And all is dross that is not Helena.

6927 *Doctor Faustus*
Now hast thou but one bare hour to live,
And then thou must be damned perpetually.
Stand still, you ever-moving spheres of heaven,
That time may cease, and midnight never come.
Fair nature's eye, rise, rise again and make
Perpetual day; or let this hour be but
A year, a month, a week, a natural day
That Faustus may repent and save his soul.

6928 *Doctor Faustus*
O lente lente currite noctis equi.
The stars move still, time runs, the clock will strike,
The devil will come, and Faustus must be damned.
O I'll leap up to my God: who pulls me down?
See, see, where Christ's blood streams in the firmament.
One drop would save my soul, half a drop, ah my Christ.

6929 *Doctor Faustus*
You stars that reigned at my nativity,
Whose influence hath allotted death and hell,
Now draw up Faustus like a foggy mist ...

6930 *Doctor Faustus*
O soul, be changed into little water drops,
And fall into the ocean, ne'er be found:
My God, my God, look not so fierce on me.

6931 *Doctor Faustus*
Oh, thou art fairer than the evening air
Clad in the beauty of a thousand stars.

6932 *Doctor Faustus*
Ugly hell, gape not! come not, Lucifer!
I'll burn my books!

6933 *Doctor Faustus*
Cut is the branch that might have grown full straight,
And burnèd is Apollo's laurel-bough,
That sometime grew within this learnèd man.

6934 *Edward II*
My men, like satyrs grazing on the lawns,
Shall with their goat feet dance an antic hay.

6935 *Edward II*
Stand still you watches of the element;
All times and seasons, rest you at a stay,
That Edward may be still fair England's king.

6936 *Hero and Leander*
Who ever loved that loved not at first sight?

6937 *Hero and Leander*
And as she wept, her tears to pearl he turned,
And wound them on his arm, and for her mourned.

6938 *Hero and Leander*
Like untun'd golden strings all women are
Which long time lie untouch'd, will harshly jar.

6939 *The Jew of Malta*
I count religion but a childish toy,
And hold there is no sin byt ignorance.

6940 *The Jew of Malta*
Thus methinks should men of judgement frame
Their means of traffic from the vulgar trade,
And, as their wealth increaseth, so enclose
Infinite riches in a little room.

6941 *The Jew of Malta*
As for myself, I walk abroad o'nights
And kill sick people groaning under walls:
Sometimes I go about and poison wells.

6942 *The Jew of Malta*
BARNARDINE: Thou hast committed-
BARABAS: Fornication? But that was in another
ountry: and besides, the wench is dead.

6943 *The Massacre at Paris*
That like I best, that flies beyond my reach.

6944 *The Passionate Shepherd to his Love*
And I will make thee beds of roses
And a thousand fragrant posies.

6945 *Tamburlaine the Great*
From jigging veins of rhyming mother-wits,
And such conceits as clownage keeps in pay,
We'll lead you to the stately tents of war.

6946 *Tamburlaine the Great*
Our swords shall play the orators for us.

6947 *Tamburlaine the Great*
Accurst be he that first invented war.

6948 *Tamburlaine the Great*
Is it not passing fair to be a king,
And ride in triumph through Persepolis?

6949 *Tamburlaine the Great*
Nature that framed us of four elements,
Warring within our breasts for regiment,
Doth teach us all to have aspiring minds.

6950 *Tamburlaine the Great*
Virtue is the fount whence honour springs.

6951 *Tamburlaine the Great*
Ah fair Zenocrate, divine Zenocrate,
Fair is too foul an epithet for thee.

6952 *Tamburlaine the Great*
Now walk the angels on the walls of heaven,
As sentinels to warn th'immortal souls,
To entertain divine Zenocrate.

6953 *Tamburlaine the Great*
Yet let me kiss my Lord before I die,
And let me die with kissing of my Lord.

6954 *Tamburlaine the Great*
More childish valorous than manly wise.

6955 *Tamburlaine the Great*
Holla, ye pampered jades of Asia!
What, can ye draw but twenty miles a day?

MARQUEZ Gabriel Garcia 1928-
6956
While a person does not give up on sex, sex does not give up on the person.

MARQUIS Don 1878-1937
6957
Pity the meek for they shall inherit the earth.

6958
Ours is a world where people don't know what they want and are willing to go through hell to get it.

6959
Happiness is the interval between periods of unhappiness.

6960
Happiness comes fleetingly now and then,
To those who have learned to do without it
And to them only.

6961
The successful people are the ones who think up things for the rest of the world to keep busy at.

6962
Writing a book of poetry is like dropping a rose petal down the Grand Canyon and waiting for the echo.

6963
The art of newspaper paragraphing is to stroke a platitude until it purrs like an epigram.

6964 *archy does his part*
boss there is always
a comforting thought
in time of trouble when
it is not our trouble.

6965 *archy and mehitabel*
procrastination is the
art of keeping
up with yesterday.

6966 *archy and mehitabel*
an optimist is a guy
that has never had
much experience.

6967 *archy and mehitabel*
but wotthehell wotthehell
oh i should worry and fret
death and I will coquette
there s a dance in the old dame yet
toujours gai toujours gai.

6968 *archys life of mehitabel*
honesty is a good
thing but
it is not profitable to
its possessor
unless it is
kept under control.

6969 *archys life of mehitabel*
did you ever
notice that when
a politician
does get an idea
he usually
gets it all wrong.

6970 *archys life of mehitabel*
now and then
there is a person born
who is so unlucky
that he runs into accidents
which started to happen
to somebody else.

MARRIOT John 1780-1825
6971 *'Thou, whose eternal Word'*
Thou, whose eternal Word
Chaos and darkness heard,
And took their flight,
Hear us, we humbly pray,
And, where the Gospel-day
Sheds not its glorious ray,
Let there be light!

MARRYAT Captain Frederick 1792-1848
6972 *Japhet, in Search of a Father*
There's no getting blood out of a turnip.

6973 *The King's Own*
As savage as a bear with a sore head.

6974 *Mr Midshipman Easy*
All zeal ... all zeal, Mr Easy.

6975 *Mr Midshipman Easy (of an illegitimate baby)*
If you please, ma'am, it was a very little one.

6976 *Settlers in Canada*
Every man paddle his own canoe.

MARSHALL Herbert
6977
There's nothing an economist should fear so much as applause.

MARSHALL John 1755-1835
6978
The power to tax involves the power to destroy.

MARSHALOV Boris
6979
Congress is so strange. A man gets up to speak and says nothing. Nobody listens, then everybody disagrees.

MARSTON John 1576-1634
6980 *Satire VII*
'A man, a man!' 'Peace, Cynic, yon is one:
A complete soul of all perfection.'
'What, mean'st thou him that walks all open-breasted,
Drawn through the ear, with ribands, plumy-crested;
He that doth snort in fat-fed luxury,
And gapes for some grinding monopoly;
He that in effeminate invention,
In beastly source of all pollution,
In riot, lust, and fleshly seeming sweetness,
Sleeps sound, secure, under the shade of greatness?

6981 *The Scourge of Villainy*
Foul canker of fair virtuous action,
Vile blaster of the freshest blooms on earth,
Envy's abhorrèd child, Detraction ...

6982 *The Scourge of Villainy*
My mind disdains the dungy muddy scum
Of abject thoughts and Envy's raging hate.

MARTIAL AD c.40-c.104
6983
Lawyers are men who hire out their words and anger.

6984 *Epigrammata*
Believe me, wise men don't say 'I shall live to do that', tomorrow's life's too late; live today.

6985 *Epigrammata*
I don't love you Sabidius, and I can't tell
you why;
All I can tell you is this, that I don't love
you.

6986 *Epigrammata*
They praise those works, but read these.

6987 *Epigrammata*
Life's not just being alive, but being well.

6988 *Epigrammata*
Difficult or easy, pleasant or bitter, you are
the same you: I cannot live with you - or
without you.

6989 *Epigrammata*
Rus in urbe.
Country in the town.

MARTIN Dean 1917-1995
6990
Marriage is not a word but a sentence.

MARTINDELL Jackson
6991
Capital is past savings accumulated for
future production.

MARTINEAU Harriet 1802-1876
6992 *Society in America*
Anyone must see at a glance that if men
and women marry those whom they do
not love, they must love those whom they
do not marry.

MARTINEZ Jacinto Benaventey
6993
When one admires an artist it is important
not to know him personally.

MARTIN-WIELAND Christoph
6994
An illusion which makes me happy is
worth a verity which drags me to the
ground.

MARVELL Andrew 1621-1678
6995 *'Upon Appleton House'*
What luckless apple did we taste,
To make us mortal, and thee waste?

6996 *'Upon Appleton House'*
Unhappy birds! what does it boot
To build below the grass's root,
When lowness is unsafe as height,

And chance o'ertakes, what 'scapeth spite?

6997 *'Upon Appleton House'*
'Tis not what once it was, the world,
But a rude heap together hurled.

6998 *'Upon Appleton House'*
But now the salmon-fishers moist
Their leathern boats begin to hoist;
And, like Antipodes in shoes,
Have shod their heads in their canoes.

6999 *'Bermudas'*
Where the remote Burmudas ride
In the ocean's bosom unespied.

7000 *'Bermudas'*
He hangs in shades the orange bright,
Like golden lamps in a green night.

7001 *'Bermudas'*
And makes the hollow seas, that roar,
Proclaim the ambergris on shore.
He cast (of which we rather boast)
The gospel's pearl upon our coast.

7002 *'To His Coy Mistress'*
Had we but world enough, and time,
This coyness, lady, were no crime.

7003 *'To His Coy Mistress'*
I would
Love you ten years before the flood:
And you should, if you please, refuse
Till the conversion of the Jews
My vegetable love should grow
Vaster than empires, and more slow.

7004 *'To His Coy Mistress'*
But at my back I always hear
Time's wingèd chariot hurrying near:
And yonder all before us lie
Deserts of vast eternity.
Thy beauty shall no more be found;
Nor, in thy marble vault, shall sound
My echoing song; then worms shall try
That long preserved virginity:
And your quaint honour turn to dust;
And into ashes all my lust.
The grave's a fine and private place,
But none, I think, do there embrace.

7005 *'To His Coy Mistress'*
Let us roll all our strength, and all
Our sweetness, up into one ball:
And tear our pleasures with rough strife,

Thorough the iron gates of life.
Thus, though we cannot make our sun
Stand still, yet we will make him run.

7006 'The Definition of Love'
My love is of a birth as rare
As 'tis for object strange and high:
It was begotten by Despair
Upon Impossibility.

Magnanimous Despair alone
Could show me so divine a thing,
Where feeble Hope could ne'er have flown
But vainly flapped its tinsel wing.

7007 'The Definition of Love'
As lines (so loves) oblique may well
Themselves in every angle greet:
But ours so truly parallel,
Though infinite, can never meet.

Therefore the love which us doth bind,
But Fate so enviously debars,
Is the conjunction of the mind,
And opposition of the stars.

7008 'The First Anniversary of the
Government...'
Choosing each stone, and poising every
weight,
Trying the measures of the breadth and
height;
Here pulling down, and there erecting
new,
Founding a firm state by proportions true.

7009 'The Garden'
How vainly men themselves amaze
To win the palm, the oak, or bays,
And their uncessant labours see
Crowned from some single herb or tree.

7010 'The Garden'
Fair Quiet, have I found thee here,
And Innocence, thy sister dear!

7011 'The Garden'
Society is all but rude,
To this delicious solitude.

7012 'The Garden'
Stumbling on melons, as I pass,
Ensnared with flowers, I fall on grass.

7013 'The Garden'
Meanwhile the mind, from pleasure less,
Withdraws into its happiness.

7014 'The Garden'
Annihilating all that's made
To a green thought in a green shade.

7015 'The Garden'
Here at the fountain's sliding foot,
Or at some fruit-tree's mossy root,
Casting the body's vest aside,
My soul into the boughs does glide.

7016 'The Garden'
Such was the happy garden-state,
While man there walked without a mate.

7017 'The Garden'
But 'twas beyond a mortal's share
To wander solitary there:
Two paradises 'twere in one
To live in paradise alone.

7018 'An Horatian Ode upon Cromwell's
Return from Ireland'
He nothing common did or mean
Upon that memorable scene:
But with his keener eye
The axe's edge did try.

7019 'An Horatian Ode upon Cromwell's
Return...'
And now the Irish are ashamed
To see themselves in one year tamed:
So much one man can do,
That does both act and know.

7020 'The Mower to the Glow-worms'
Ye country comets, that portend
No war, nor prince's funeral,
Shining unto no higher end
Than to presage the grass's fall.

7021 'The Nymph Complaining for the Death
of her Fawn'
I have a garden of my own
But so with roses overgrown,
And lilies, that you would it guess
To be a little wilderness.

7022 'The Nymph Complaining for the Death
of her Fawn'
Had it lived long, it would have been
Lilies without, roses within.

7023 'The Statue in Stocks-Market' (of Charles
II)
For though the whole world cannot show
such another,

Yet we'd better by far have him than his brother.

MARVELL Holt
7024 *'These Foolish Things Remind Me of You'*
A cigarette that bears a lipstick's traces
An airline ticket to romantic places;
And still my heart has wings
These foolish things
Remind me of you.

MARX Chico 1891-1961
7025 *(when discovered by his wife with a chorus girl)*
I wasn't kissing her, I was just whispering in her mouth.

MARX Groucho 1895-1977
7026
There is one way to find out if a man is honest - ask him. If he says 'yes,' you know he is crooked.

7027
One of the best hearing aids a man can have is an attentive wife.

7028
I never forget a face, but in your case I'll make an exception.

7029 *(attributed)*
A man is only as old as the woman he feels.

7030 *in The Coconuts*
"Your eyes shine like the pants of my blue serge suit."

7031 *in A Day at the Races*
"Either he's dead, or my watch has stopped."

7032 *in A Day at the Races*
"I've never been so insulted in my life..."
" Well, it's early yet."

7033 *in Duck Soup*
"Remember, you're fighting for this woman's honour ... which is probably more than she ever did."

7034 *in Duck Soup*
"If you can't leave in a taxi you can leave in a huff. If that's too soon, you can leave in a minute and a huff."

7035 *Groucho and Me*
Please accept my resignation. I don't want to belong to any club that will accept me as a member.

7036 *in A Night in Casablanca*
"Send two dozen roses to Room 424 and put 'Emily, I love you' on the back of the bill."

MARX Karl 1818-1883
7037
The more of himself man attributes to God, the less he has left in himself.

7038
What I did that was new was to prove ... that the class struggle necessarily leads to the dictatorship of the proletariat.

7039 *A Contribution... Hegel's Philosophy of Right*
Religion ... is the opium of the people.

7040 *A Contribution ... of Political Economy*
Mankind always sets itself only such problems as it can solve; since, looking at the matter more closely, it will always be found that the task itself arises only when the material conditions for its solution already exist or are at least in the process of formation.

7041 *A Contribution ... of Political Economy*
It is not the consciousness of men that determines their being, but, on the contrary, their social being that determines their consciousness.

7042 *Critique of the Gotha Programme*
From each according to his abilities, to each according to his needs.

7043 *The Eighteenth Brumaire of Louis Bonaparte*
Hegel says somewhere that all great events and personalities in world history reappear in one fashion or another. He forgot to add: the first time as tragedy, the second as farce.

7044 *Theses on Feuerbach*
The philosophers have only interpreted the world in various ways; the point is to change it.

MARX Karl and ENGELS Friedrich 1818-1883 and 1820-1895
7045 *The Communist Manifesto*
A spectre is haunting Europe - the spectre of Communism.

7046 *The Communist Manifesto*
The history of all hitherto existing society is the history of class struggles.

7047 *The Communist Manifesto*
In place of the old bourgeois society, with its classes and class antagonists, we shall have an association, in which the free development of each is the free development of all.

7048 *The Communist Manifesto*
The proletarians have nothing to lose but their chains. They have a world to win. WORKING MEN OF ALL COUNTRIES, UNITE!

MARY I, Queen (Mary Tudor) 1516-1558
7049
When I am dead and opened, you shall find 'Calais' lying in my heart.

MARY Queen 1867-1953
7050 *Letter to the Duke of Windsor*
I do not think you have ever realised the shock, which the attitude you took up caused your family and the whole nation. It seemed inconceivable to those who had made such sacrifices during the war that you, as their King, refused a lesser sacrifice.

MARY Princess
7051
Go in in front of Royalty: but never pass in front of them.

MARY Queen 1867-1953
7052 *(after abdication of her son, King Edward VIII)*
All *this* thrown away for *that*.

MARY Queen of Scots 1542-1587
7053 *(motto)*
En ma fin git mon commencement.
In my end is my beginning.

MASARYK Jan 1886-1948
7054
Dictators are rulers who always look good until the last ten minutes.

MASEFIELD John 1878-1967
7055
An art in which the artist by means of rhythm and great sincerity can convey to others the sentiment which he feels about life.

7056
Once in a century a man may be ruined or made insufferable by praise. But surely once a minute something generous dies for want of it.

7057 *Captain Stratton's Fancy*
Oh some are fond of Spanish wine, and some are fond of French.

7058 *'Cargoes'*
Quinquireme of Nineveh from distant Ophir
Rowing home to haven in sunny Palestine,
With a cargo of ivory,
And apes and peacocks,
Sandalwood, cedarwood, and sweet white wine.

7059 *'Cargoes'*
Dirty British coaster with a salt-caked smoke stack,
Butting through the Channel in the mad March days,
With a cargo of Tyne coal,
Road-rails, pig lead,
Firewood, ironware, and cheap tin trays.

7060 *'C.L.M.'*
In the dark womb where I began
My mother's life made me a man.
Through all the months of human birth
Her beauty fed my common earth.
I cannot see, nor breathe, nor stir,
But through the death of some of her.

7061 *'The Everlasting Mercy'*
The corn that makes the holy bread
By which the soul of man is fed,
The holy bread, the food unpriced,
Thy everlasting mercy, Christ.

7062 *Laugh and Be Merry*
Laugh and be merry, remember, better the world with a song.
Better the world with a blow in the teeth of a wrong.

7063 *Pompey The Great*
Death opens unknown doors. It is most
grand to die.

7064 *Roadways*
One road leads to London,
One road runs to Wales,
My road leads me seawards
To the white dipping sails.

7065 *'Sea Fever'*
I must go down to the sea again, to the
lonely sea and the sky,
And all I ask is a tall ship and a star to
steer her by,
And the wheel's kick and the wind's song
and the white sail's shaking,
And a grey mist on the sea's face and a
grey dawn breaking.

7066 *'Sea Fever'*
I must go down to the sea again, for the
call of the running tide
Is a wild call and a clear call that may not
be denied.

7067 *'Sea Fever'*
I must go down to the sea again, to the
vagrant gypsy life,
To the gull's way and the whale's way
where the wind's like a whetted knife;
And all I ask is a merry yarn from a
laughing fellow-rover,
And quiet sleep and a sweet dream when
the long trick's over.

MASLOW Abraham 1908-1970
7068
I can feel guilty about the past,
apprehensive about the future, but only in
the present can I act. The ability to be in
the present moment is a major component
of mental wellness.

MASON Donald 1913-
7069 *(radio message)*
Sighted sub, sank same.

MASSE Marcel 1936-
7070
The more the world is specialized the more
it will be run by generalists.

MASSEY Anna 1937-
7071
Optimism is like a spiritual magnet.

MASSINGER Philip 1583-1640
7072
Immature poets imitate: mature poets
steal.

7073 *The Bashful Lover*
Ambition, in a private man a vice,
Is in a prince the virtue.

7074 *The Bondman*
He that would govern others, first should
be
The master of himself.

7075 *The City Madam*
Pray enter
You are learned Europeans and we worse
Than ignorant Americans.

7076 *The Duke of Milan*
Now speak,
Or be for ever silent.

7077 *The Great Duke of Florence*
I am driven
Into a desperate strait and cannot steer
A middle course.

7078 *A New Way to Pay Old Debts*
The devil turned precisian!

7079 *The Parliament of Love*
Oh that thou hadst like others been all
words,
And no performance.

7080 *A Very Woman*
Death hath a thousand doors to let out life:
I shall find one.

MASSON Tom
7081
Hamlet is the tragedy of tackling a family
problem too soon after college.

7082
'Be yourself!' is about the worst advice you
can give to some people.

7083
You can always get someone to love you -
even if you have to do it yourself.

MATHEW Father
7084
Horse-sense is something a horse has that
prevents him betting on people.

MATHEW Sir James 1830-1908
7085
In England, justice is open to all - like the
Ritz Hotel.

MATHEWS Shailer 1863-1941
7086
An epigram is a half-truth so stated as to
irritate the person who believes the other
half.

MATISSE Henri 1869-1954
7087
A work should contain its total meaning
within itself and should impress it on the
spectator before he even knows the subject.

7088
There is nothing more difficult for a truly
creative painter than to paint a rose,
because before he can do so he has first to
forget all the roses that were ever painted.

MATTHEWS Brander 1852-1929
7089
A highbrow is a person educated beyond
his intelligence.

MATTHEWS W.
7090
Unless a man has trained himself for his
chance, the chance will only make him
ridiculous.

7091
In the world a man lives in his own age; in
solitude in all ages.

MAUDSLEY Henry 1771-1831
7092
The sorrow which has no vent in tears may
make other organs weep.

MAUGHAM W. Somerset 1874-1965
7093
Beauty is an ecstasy; it is as simple as
hunger. There is really nothing to be said
about it.

7094
Something wonderful and strange that the
artist fashions out of the chaos of the
world in the torment of his soul.

7095
I have not been afraid of excess: excess on
occasion is exhilarating. It prevents
moderation from acquiring the deadening
effect of a habit.

7096
Dinner, a time when ... one should eat
wisely but not too well, and talk well but
not too wisely.

7097
It is dangerous to let the public behind the
scenes. They are easily disillusioned and
then they are angry with you, for it was
the illusion they loved.

7098
Imagination grows by exercise, and
contrary to common belief, is more
powerful in the mature than in the young.

7099
American women expect to find in their
husbands a perfection that English women
only hope to find in their butlers.

7100
A Unitarian very earnestly disbelieves
what everyone else believes.

7101 *(attributed)*
The love that lasts longest is the love that
is never returned.

7102 *Our Betters*
The degree of a nation's civilization is
marked by its disregard for the necessities
of existence.

7103 *The Bread-Winner*
You know, of course, that the Tasmanians,
who never committed adultery, are now
extinct.

7104 *Cakes and Ale*
Hypocrisy is the most difficult and nerve-
racking vice that any man can pursue; it
needs an unceasing vigilance and a rare
detachment of spirit. It cannot, like
adultery or gluttony, be practised at spare
moments; it is a whole-time job.

7105 *Cakes and Ale*
From the earliest times the old have
rubbed it into the young that they are

wiser than they, and before the young had discovered what nonsense this was they were old too, and it profited them to carry on the imposture.

7106 *Cakes and Ale*
Poor Henry [James], he's spending eternity wandering round and round a stately park and the fence is just too high for him to peep over and they're having tea just too far away for him to hear what the countess is saying.

7107 *The Circle*
You can't learn too soon that the most useful thing about a principle is that it can always be sacrificed to expediency.

7108 *The Circle*
A woman will always sacrifice herself if you give her the opportunity. It is her favourite form of self-indulgence.

7109 *The Circle*
When married people don't get on they can separate, but if they're not married it's impossible. It's a tie that only death can sever.

7110 *Of Human Bondage*
Like all weak men he laid an exaggerated stress on not changing one's mind.

7111 *Of Human Bondage*
People ask you for criticism, but they only want praise.

7112 *Of Human Bondage*
Money is like a sixth sense without which you cannot make a complete use of the other five.

7113 *The Moon and Sixpence*
Impropriety is the soul of wit.

7114 *The Moon and Sixpence*
It is not true that suffering ennobles the character; happiness does that sometimes, but suffering, for the most part, makes men petty and vindictive.

7115 *The Moon and Sixpence*
A woman can forgive a man for the harm he does her, but she can never forgive him for the sacrifices he makes on her account.

7116 *The Moon and Sixpence*
Because women can do nothing except love, they've given it a ridiculous importance.

7117 *The Summing Up*
I would sooner read a time-table or a catalogue than nothing at all ... They are much more entertaining than half the novels that are written.

7118 *A Writer's Notebook*
Few misfortunes can befall a boy which bring worse consequences than to have a really affectionate mother.

7119 *A Writer's Notebook*
Music-hall songs provide the dull with wit, just as proverbs provide them with wisdom.

7120 *A Writer's Notebook*
Men have an extraordinarily erroneous opinion of their position in nature; and the error is ineradicable.

7121 *A Writer's Notebook*
Sentimentality is only sentiment that rubs you up the wrong way.

MAULDIN Bill 1921-
7122 *(cartoon caption)*
I feel like a fugitive from th' law of averages.

MAUPASSANT Guy de 1850-1893
7123
Get black on white.

MAURIAC François 1885-1970
7124
Human love is often but the encounter of two weaknesses.

7125
No love, no friendship can cross the path of our destiny without leaving some mark on it forever.

MAUROIS André 1885-1967
7126
Growing old is no more than a bad habit which a busy man has no time to form.

7127
Business is a combination of war and sport.

7128
If you create an act, you create a habit. If you create a habit, you create a character. If you create a character, you create a destiny.

7129
In literature as in love we are astounded by what is chosen by others.

7130
Men fear silence as they fear solitude, because both give them a glimpse of the terror of life's nothingness.

7131
The effectiveness of work increases according to geometric progression if there are no interruptions.

7132
Style is the hallmark of a temperament stamped upon the material at hand.

MAXTON James 1885-1946
7133 *(opposing disaffiliation of SILP from Labour)*
All I say is, if you cannot ride two horses you have no right in the circus.

MAXWELL William
7134
Happiness is the light on the water. The water is cold and dark and deep.

MAY Rollo
7135
Anxiety is essential to the human condition. The confrontation with anxiety can relieve us from boredom, sharpen the sensitivity and assure the presence of tension that is necessary to preserve human existence.

7136
Anxiety is the experience of Being affirming itself against non-Being.

7137
Hate is not the opposite of love; apathy is.

7138
Depression is the inability to construct a future.

7139
I think Dostoevsky was right, that every human being must have a point at which he stands against the culture, where he says, this is me and the damned world can go to hell.

MAYAKOVSKY Vladimir 1893-1930
7140 *'The Cloud in Trousers'*
If you wish -
... I'll be irreproachably tender;
not a man, but - a cloud in trousers!

7141 *'Conversation with Inspector of Taxes ....'*
In our language rhyme is a barrel. A barrel of dynamite. The line is a fuse. The line smoulders to the end and explodes; and the town is blown sky-high in a stanza.

7142 *'Conversation with Inspector of Taxes....'*
Our duty is to blare like brazen-throated horns in the fog of philistinism and in seething storms. The poet is always indebted to the universe, paying interest and fines on sorrow.

7143 *'Homewards'*
I want to be understood by my country, and if I am not - never mind, I will pass over my native land sideways, as a slanted rain passes.

7144 *'Letter ... to Comrade Kostorov on Nature of Love'*
To us love says humming that the heart's stalled motor has begun working again.

7145 *'Our March' (translated by C.M. Bowra)*
Tramp squares with rebellious treading!
Up heads! As proud peaks be seen!
In the second flood we are spreading
Every city on earth will be clean.

7146 *'At the Top of my Voice' (translated by C.M. Bowra)*
Deploying in a parade
the armies of my pages,
I pass in review
the front of my lines.
Verses stand
lead-heavily,
ready for death
and for immortal fame.

7147 *(from unfinished poem, and in suicide letter)*
The love boat has crashed against the everyday. You and I, we are quits, and there is no point in listing mutual pains, sorrows, and hurts.

MAYHEW Jonathan 1720-1766
7148 *A Discourse ... to the Higher Powers*
Rulers have no authority from God to do mischief.

7149 *A Discourse ... to the Higher Powers*
As soon as the prince sets himself up above the law, he loses the king in the tyrant; he does to all intents and purpose unking himself ... And in such cases, has no more right to be obeyed, than any inferior officer who acts beyond his commission.

MEAD Margaret 1901-1978
7150
No matter how many communes anybody invents, the family always creeps back.

7151
In almost any society, I think, the quality of the non-conformists is like to be just as good as, and no better than that of the conformists.

7152
Each suburban housewife spends her time presiding over a power plant sufficient to have staffed the palace of a Roman emperor with a hundred slaves.

7153 *Sex and Temperament in Three Primitive Societies*
The knowledge that the personalities of the two sexes are socially produced is congenial to every programme that looks forward towards a planned order of society. It is a two-edged sword.

MEAD Shepherd 1914-
7154
How to succeed in business without really trying.

MEANY George 1894-1980
7155
Anybody who has any doubt about the ingenuity or the resourcefulness of a plumber never got a bill from one.

MEARNS Hughes 1875-1965
7156 *The Psycho-ed*
As I was walking up the stair
I met a man who wasn't there.
He wasn't there again today.
I wish, I wish he'd stay away.

MEDICI Cosimo de 1389-1464
7157
We read that we ought to forgive our enemies; but we do not read that we ought to forgive our friends.

MEIR Golda 1898-1978
7158
Don't be so humble. You're not that great.

7159
We Jews have a secret weapon in our struggle with the Arabs - we have no place to go.

7160
Whether women are better than men I cannot say - but I can say they are certainly no worse.

7161
Can we today measure devotion to husband and children by our indifference to everything else?

MELBOURNE William Lamb 2nd Lord 1779-1848
7162
While I cannot be regarded as a pillar, I must be regarded as a buttress of the church, because I support if from outside.

7163 *(attributed)*
Now, is it to lower the price of corn, or isn't it? It is not much matter which we say, but mind, we must all say *the same*.

7164
God help the Minister that meddles with art!

7165 *(of the Catholic Emancipation Act)*
What all the wise men promised has not happened, and what all the d-d fools said would happen has come to pass.

7166 *(on being dismissed by William IV)*
I have always thought complaints of ill-usage contemptible, whether from a

seduced disappointed girl or a turned-out Prime Minister.

7167 *(on hearing an evangelical sermon)*
Things have come to a pretty pass when religion is allowed to invade the sphere of private life.

7168 *(replying to a politician)*
What I want is men who will support me when I am in the wrong.

MELLON Andrew 1855-1937
7169
Gentlemen prefer bonds.

MELVILLE Herman 1819-1891
7170
From without, no wonderful effect is wrought within ourselves, unless some interior, responding wonder meets it.

7171 *Hawthorne and His Mosses*
That Calvinistic sense of innate depravity and original sin from whose visitations, in some shape or other, no deeply thinking mind is always and wholly free.

7172 *Hawthorne and His Mosses*
Genius, all over the world, stands hand in hand, and one shock of recognition runs the whole circle round.

7173 *Moby Dick*
But when a man's religion becomes really frantic; when it is a positive torment to him; and, in fine, makes this earth of ours an uncomfortable inn to lodge in; then I think it high time to take that individual aside and argue the point with him.

7174 *Moby Dick*
A whaleship was my Yale College and my Harvard.

7175 *Moby Dick*
Aye, toil as we may, we all sleep at last on the field. Sleep? Aye, and rust amid greenness; as last year's scythes flung down, and left in the half-cut swaths.

7176 *Moby Dick*
Towards thee I roll, thou all-destroying but unconquering whale ... from hell's heart I stab at thee.

7177 *Moby Dick*
Better sleep with a sober cannibal than a drunken Christian.

MENANDER 342-c.292 BC
7178 *Dis Exapaton*
Whom the gods love dies young.

7179 *The Lady of Andros in Menander*
We live, not as we wish to, but as we can.

MENCIUS 372-289 BC
7180
There is no greater delight than to be conscious of sincerity on self-examination.

MENCKEN H.L. 1880-1956
7181
Nobody ever went broke underestimating the taste of the American public.

7182
Nothing can come out of an artist that is not in the man.

7183
The basic fact about human existence is not that it is a tragedy, but that it is a bore.

7184
Conscience is a mother-in-law whose visit never ends.

7185
Penetrating so many secrets, we cease to believe in the unknowable. But there it sits nevertheless, calmly licking its chops.

7186
A cynic is a man who, when he smells flowers, looks around for a coffin.

7187
What men value in the world is not rights, but privileges.

7188
A celebrity is one who is known to many persons he is glad he doesn't know.

7189
God is a comedian whose audience is afraid to laugh.

7190
Under democracy, one party always devotes its chief energies to trying to prove that the other party is unfit to rule - and

both commonly succeed, and are right.

7191
Injustice is relatively easy to bear; what stings is justice.

7192
A judge is a law student who marks his own examination papers.

7193
No matter how happily a woman may be married, it always pleases her to discover that there is a nice man who wishes she were not.

7194
If, after I depart this vale, you ever remember me and have thought to please my ghost, forgive some sinner and wink your eye at some homely girl.

7195
Men have a much better time of it than women. For one thing, they marry later. For another thing, they die earlier.

7196
The double standard of morality will survive in this world so long as the woman whose husband has been lured away is favoured with the sympathetic tears of other women, and a man whose wife has made off is laughed at by other men.

7197
Opera in English is, in the main, just about as sensible as baseball in Italian.

7198
One may no more live in the world without picking up the moral prejudices of the world than one will be able to go to hell without perspiring.

7199
I hate all sports as rabidly as a person who likes sports hates common sense.

7200
Time is a great legalizer, even in the fields of morals.

7201
Women have simple tastes. They get pleasure out of the conversation of children in arms and men in love.

7202
He [Calvin Coolidge] slept more than any other President, whether by day or by night. Nero fiddled, but Coolidge only snored.

7203
The saddest life is that of a political aspirant under democracy. His failure is ignominious and his success is disgraceful.

7204
I've made it a rule never to drink by daylight and never to refuse a drink after dark.

7205 *Chrestomathy*
Love is the delusion that one woman differs from another.

7206 *Chrestomathy*
Puritanism. The haunting fear that someone, somewhere, may be happy.

7207 *A Little Book in C major*
Democracy is the theory that the common people know what they want, and deserve to get it good and hard.

7208 *A Little Book in C major*
Conscience: the inner voice which warns us that someone may be looking.

7209 *Notebooks*
It is now quite lawful for a Catholic woman to avoid pregnancy by a resort to mathematics, though she is still forbidden to resort to physics and chemistry.

7210 *Prejudices*
Women hate revolutions and revolutionists. They like men who are docile, and well regarded at the bank, and never late at meals.

MENDES-FRANCE Pierre 1907-1982
7211
To govern is to choose.

MENNINGER Karl
7212
Neurotic means he is not as sensible as I am, and psychotic means he's even worse than my brother-in-law.

7213
What's done to children, they will do to society.

7214
Listening is a magnetic and strange thing, a creative force. The friends who listen to us are the ones we move toward, and we want to sit in their radius. When we are listened to, it creates us, makes us unfold and expand.

MENNINGER William 1899-1966
7215
What the world needs is some 'do-give-a-damn' pills.

7216
Mental health problems do not affect three or four out of every five persons, but one out of one.

MERCER David 1928-1980
7217
A suitable case for treatment.

MERCER Johnny 1909-1976
7218
That old black magic.

7219 *'Ac-cent-tchu-ate the Positive'*
You've got to ac-cent-tchu-ate the positive
Elim-my-nate the negative
Latch on to the affirmative
Don't mess with Mister In-between.

7220 *'One For My Baby'*
We're drinking my friend,
To the end of a brief episode,
Make it one for my baby
And one more for the road.

7221 *'Jeepers Creepers'*
Jeepers Creepers - where'd you get those peepers?
Jeepers Creepers - where'd get those eyes?

MEREDITH George 1828-1909
7222
Caricature is rough truth.

7223
Published memoirs indicate the end of a man's activity, and that he acknowledges the end.

7224
Cultivated men and women who do not skim the cream of life, and are attached to the duties, yet escape the harsher blows, make acute and balanced observers.

7225
The well of true wit is truth itself.

7226
The lark ascending.

7227 *Beauchamp's Career*
Thoughts of heroes were as good as warming-pans.

7228 *One of Our Conquerors*
None of your dam punctilio.

7229 *Diana of the Crossways*
A witty woman is a treasure; a witty beauty is a power.

7230 *Diana of the Crossways*
'Tis Ireland gives England her soldiers, her generals too.

7231 *Diana of the Crossways*
There is nothing the body suffers the soul may not profit by.

7232 *Diana of the Crossways*
As we to the brutes, poets are to us.

7233 *The Egoist*
A Phoebus Apollo turned fasting friar.

7234 *The Egoist*
A dainty rogue in porcelain.

7235 *The Egoist*
Cynicism is intellectual dandyism without the coxcomb's feathers.

7236 *The Egoist*
In ... the Book of Egoism it is written:
Possession without obligation to the object possessed approaches felicity.

7237 *'Love in the Valley'*
She whom I love is hard to catch and conquer,
Hard, but O the glory of the winning were she won!

7238 *'Lucifer in Starlight'*
On a starred night Prince Lucifer uprose.
Tired of his dark dominion swung the

fiend ...

7239 *'Lucifer in Starlight'*
Around the ancient track marched, rank on rank,
The army of unalterable law.

7240 *Modern Love*
'I play for Seasons; not Eternities!'
Says Nature.

7241 *Modern Love*
In tragic life, God wot,
No villain need be! Passions spin the plot:
We are betrayed by what is false within.

7242 *Modern Love*
Ah, what a dusty answer gets the soul
When hot for certainties in this our life!

7243 *Modern Love*
Not till the fire is dying in the grate,
Look we for any kinship with the stars.

7244 *Modern Love*
And if I drink oblivion of a day,
So shorten I the stature of my soul.

7245 *Modern Love*
That rarest gift
To Beauty, Common Sense.

7246 *The Ordeal of Richard Feverel*
I expect that Woman will be the last thing civilized by Man.

7247 *The Ordeal of Richard Feverel*
In action Wisdom goes by majorities.

7248 *The Ordeal of Richard Feverel*
Who rises from prayer a better man, his prayer is answered.

7249 *The Ordeal of Richard Feverel*
Kissing don't last: cookery do!

7250 *The Ordeal of Richard Feverel*
Speech is the small change of silence.

7251 *Vittoria*
Much benevolence of the passive order may be traced to a disinclination to inflict pain upon oneself.

MEREDITH Owen 1831-1891
7252 *'Last Words of a Sensitive Second-Rate Poet'*
Genius does what it must, and Talent does what it can.

7253 *Lucile*
We may live without poetry, music and art;
We may live without conscience, and live without heart;
We may live without friends; we may live without books;
But civilized man cannot live without cooks.
He may live without books, - what is knowledge but grieving?
He may live without hope, - what is hope but deceiving?
He may live without love, - what is passion but pining?
But where is the man that can live without dining?

MERRILL James 1926-
7254 *'Museum Piece'*
The good grey guardians of art
Patrol the halls on spongy shoes,
Impartially protective, though
Perhaps suspicious of Toulouse.
Here dozes one against the wall,
Disposed upon a funeral chair.
A Degas dancer pirouettes
Upon the parting of his hair.

7255 *'The Thousand and Second Night'*
Free me, I pray, to go in search of joys
Unembroidered by your high, soft voice,
Along that stony path the senses pave.

MERRITT Dixon Lanier 1879-1972
7256
Oh, a wondrous bird is the pelican!
His beak holds more than his belican.
He takes in his beak
Food enough for a week.
But I'll be darned if I know how the helican.

MERTON Thomas 1915-1968
7257
The truth that many people never understand, until it is too late, is that the more you try to avoid suffering the more you suffer because smaller and more insignificant things begin to torture you in proportion to your fear of being hurt.

7258
Violence is essentially wordless, and it can begin only where thought and rational communication have broken down.

METTERNICH Prince 1773-1859
7259
Error has never approached my spirit.

7260 *Concessionen und Nichtconcessionen*
The greatest gift of any stateman rests not in knowing what concessions to make, but recognizing when to make them.

7261 *Letter to Count Bombelles*
Der Kaiser ist Alles, Wien ist nichts!

The Emperor is everything, Vienna is nothing.

7262 *Mein Politisches Testament*
The word 'freedom' means for me not a point of departure but a genuine point of arrival. The point of departure is defined by the word 'order'. Freedom cannot exist without the concept of order.

7263 *(to Pulmerston)*
Italy is a geographical expression.

MEYER Alan H.
7264
The best ad is a good product.

MEYER Sir Anthony 1920-
7265 *(speaking against the Falklands War)*
I question the right of that great Moloch, national sovereignty, to burn its children to save its pride.

MICHAELS Leonard
7266
Reasons are whores.

MICHELANGELO 1474-1564
7267
It is well with me only when I have a chisel in my hand.

7268
Beauty is the purgation of superfluities.

MICHELET Jules 1798-1874
7269
Women are perfectly well aware that the more they seem to obey the more they rule.

MICHENER Wendy
7270
The British are just as keen to make money as the Americans, but they prefer hypocrisy to a blatantly commercial attitude.

MIDDLETON Thomas c.1580-1627
7271
Anything for a quiet life.

7272 *Blurt, Master-Constable*
I never heard
Of any true affection, but 'twas nipt
With care.

7273 *The Changeling*
Beneath the stars, upon yon meteor
Ever hung my fate, 'mongst things corruptible.

7274 *The Changeling (with William Rowley)*
I could not get the ring without the finger.

7275 *The Changeling (with William Rowley)*
Y'are the deed's creature.

7276 *The Revenger's Tragedy*
Does the silk-worm expend her yellow labours
For thee? for thee does she undo herself?

7277 *The Witch*
There's no hate lost between us.

7278 *The Witch*
Though I be poor, I'm honest.

7279 *No Wit, No Help, Like a Woman's*
By many a happy accident.

MIKES George 1912-1987
7280 *How to be an Alien*
On the Continent people have good food; in England people have good table manners.

7281 *How to be an Alien*
Continental people have sex life; the English have hot-water bottles.

7282 *How to be an Alien*
An Englishman, even if he is alone, forms an orderly queue of one.

MILES Sarah
7283
Isn't it amazing that there's no copyright

on your own life?

MILL John Stuart 1806-1873
7284
We can never be sure that the opinion we are endeavouring to stifle is a false opinion; and if we were sure, stifling it would be an evil still.

7285
His eminence was due to the flatness of the surrounding landscape.

7286
Unquestionably, it is possible to do without happiness; it is done involuntarily by nineteen-twentieths of mankind.

7287 *Auguste Comte and Positivism*
As often as a study is cultivated by narrow minds, they will draw from it narrow conclusions.

7288 *Autobiography*
Ask yourself whether you are happy, and you cease to be so.

7289 *Autobiography*
No great improvements in the lot of mankind are possible, until a great change takes place in the fundamental constitution of their modes of thought.

7290 *Considerations on Representative Government*
The Conservatives ... being by the law of their existence the stupidest party.

7291 *Dissertations and Discussions*
When society requires to be rebuilt, there is no use in attempting to rebuild it on the old plan.

7292 *Dissertations and Discussions*
If we may be excused the antithesis, we should say that eloquence is *heard*, poetry is *overheard*.

7293 *Dissertations and Discussions*
Detention by the State of the unearned increment of rent.

7294 *Letter to Alexander Bain*
The most important thing women have to do is to stir up the zeal of women themselves.

7295 *On Liberty*
The sole end for which mankind are warranted, individually or collectively, in interfering with the liberty of action of any of their number, is self-protection.

7296 *On Liberty*
The only purpose for which power can be rightfully exercised over any member of a civilized community, against his will, is to prevent harm to others. His own good, either physical or moral, is not a sufficient warrant.

7297 *On Liberty*
If all mankind minus one were of one opinion, and only one person were of the contrary opinion, mankind would be no more justified in silencing that one person, than he, if he had the power, would be justified in silencing mankind.

7298 *On Liberty*
A party of order or stability, and a party of progress or reform, are both necessary elements of a healthy state of political life.

7299 *On Liberty*
The liberty of the individual must be thus far limited; he must not make himself a nuisance to other people.

7300 *On Liberty*
Liberty consists in doing what one desires.

7301 *On Liberty*
A State which dwarfs its men, in order that they may be more docile instruments in its hands even for beneficial purposes, will find that with small men no great thing can really be accomplished.

7302 *On Liberty*
He who knows only his own side of the case knows little of that.

7303 *On Liberty*
All good things which exist are the fruits of originality.

7304 *On Liberty*
The worth of a State, in the long run, is the worth of the individuals composing it.

7305 *Speech on Perfectibility*
The great majority of those who speak of
perfectibility as a dream, do so because
they feel that it is one which would afford
them no pleasure if it were realized.

7306 *The Subjection of Women*
The principle which regulates the existing
social relations between the two sexes - the
legal subordination of one sex to the other
- is wrong in itself, and now one of the
chief hindrances to human improvement.

7307 *The Subjection of Women*
What is now called the nature of women is
an eminently artificial thing - the result of
forced repression in some directions,
unnatural stimulation in others.

7308 *The Subjection of Women*
No slave is a slave to the same lengths,
and in so full a sense of the word, as a wife
is.

7309 *The Subjection of Women*
If married life were all that it might be
expected to be, looking to the laws alone,
society would be a hell upon earth.

7310 *The Subjection of Women*
The true virtue of human beings is fitness
to live together as equals; claiming nothing
for themselves but what they as freely
concede to everyone else; regarding
command of any kind as an exceptional
necessity, and in all cases a temporary one.

MILLAY Edna St Vincent 1892-1950
7311
Strange how few
After all's said and done, the things that
are
Of moment.

7312
With him for a sire, and her for a dam
What should I be, but just what I am?

7313
It is not true that life is one damn thing
after another - it's one damn thing over
and over.

7314
Where you used to be, there is a hole in the
world, which I find myself constantly

walking around in the daytime, and falling
into at night. I miss you like hell.

7315
April,
Comes like an idiot, babbling, and
strewing flowers.

7316
A person who publishes a book appears
willfully in public with his pants down.

7317 *'Childhood is the Kingdom where Nobody
dies'*
Childhood is not from birth to a certain
age and at a certain age
The child is grown, and puts away childish
things.
Childhood is the kindgom where nobody
dies.
Nobody that matters, that is.

7318 *'Dirge Without Music'*
Down, down, down into the darkness of
the grave
Gently they go, the beautiful, the tender,
the kind;
Quietly they go, the intelligent, the witty,
the brave.
I know. But I do not approve. And I am
not resigned.

7319 *A Few Figs From Thistles 'First Fig'*
My candle burns at both ends;
It will not last the night;
But ah, my foes, and oh, my friends -
It gives a lovely light.

7320 *A Few Figs From Thistles 'Second Fig'*
Safe upon solid rock the ugly houses
stand:
Come and see my shining palace built
upon the sand!

7321 *The Harp-Weaver and Other Poems*
I only know that summer sang in me
A little while, that in me sings no more.

7322 *'Passer Mortuus Est'*
After all, my erstwhile dear,
My no longer cherished,
Need we say it was not love,
Now that love is perished?

7323 *'Thursday'*
And if I loved you Wednesday,
Well what is that to you?
I do not love you Thursday -
So much is true.

MILLE Agnes de 1905-1993
7324
Living is a form of not being sure, not
knowing what next or how. The moment
you know how, you begin to die a little.
The artist never entirely knows. We guess.
We may be wrong, but we take leap after
leap in the dark.

MILLE James de
7325
Horror is a feeling that cannot last long;
human nature is incapable of supporting
it.

MILLER Arthur 1915-
7326
The task of the real intellectual consists of
analyzing illusions in order to discover
their causes.

7327
A good newspaper is a nation talking to
itself.

7328
If there weren't any anti-semitism, I
wouldn't think of myself as Jewish.

7329 *The Crucible*
All organization is and must be grounded
on the idea of exclusion and prohibition
just as two objects cannot occupy the same
space.

7330 *Death of a Salesman*
The world is an oyster, but you don't crack
it open on a mattress.

7331 *Death of a Salesman 'Requiem'*
A salesman is got to dream, boy. It comes
with the territory.

7332 *(describing Eastern Europe)*
A theatre where no-one is allowed to walk
out and everyone is forced to applause.

7333 *After the Fall*
A suicide kills two people, Maggie, that's
what it's for!

7334 *The Price*
The car, the furniture, the wife, the
children - everything has to be disposable.
Because you see the main thing today is -
shopping.

7335 *'Shadows of the Gods'*
The structure of a play is always the story
of how the birds came home to roost.

7336 *A View from the Bridge*
This is Red Hook, not Sicily ... This is the
gullet of New York swallowing the
tonnage of the world.

MILLER Jr. Frank
7337
The day you write to please everyone you
no longer are in journalism. You are in
show business.

MILLER H.T. 1873-1948
7338
Give us men to match our mountains,
Give us men to match our plains:
Men with empires in their purpose
And new eras in their brains.

MILLER Harlan
7339
Often the difference between a successful
marriage and a mediocre one consists of
leaving about three or four things a day
unsaid.

MILLER Henry 1891-1980
7340
The study of crime begins with the
knowledge of oneself.

7341
Destiny is what you are supposed to do in
life. Fate is what kicks you in the ass to
make you do it.

7342
Life, as it is called, is for most of us one
long postponement.

7343
The one thing we can never get enough of
is love. And the one thing we never give
enough of is love.

7344
I struggled in the beginning. I said I was
going to write the truth, so help me God.
And I thought I was. I found I couldn't.
Nobody can write the absolute truth.

7345 *Big Sur and the Oranges of Hieronymus
Bosch*
Sex is one of the nine reasons for
reincarnation ... The other eight are
unimportant.

7346 *Tropic of Cancer*
Even before the music begins there is that
bored look on people's faces. A polite
form of self-imposed torture, the concert.

7347 *Tropic of Cancer*
Every man with a bellyful of the classics is
an enemy to the human race.

MILLER Joaquin 1839-1913
7348
The biggest dog has been a pup.

MILLER Jonathan 1934-
7349 *Beyond the Fringe*
In fact, I'm not really a *Jew*. Just Jew-*ish*.
Not the whole hog, you know.

MILLER Max 1895-1963
7350 *The Max Miller Blue Book*
There was a little girl who had a little curl,
Right in the middle of her forehead;
When she was good she was very very
good,
And when she was bad she was very very
popular.

MILLER Olin
7351
One of the best things people could do for
their decendants would be to sharply limit
the number of them.

MILLER William 1810-1872
7352 *'Willie Winkie'*
Wee Willie Winkie rins through the town,
Up stairs and down stairs in his nicht-
gown,
Tirling at the window, crying at the lock,
Are the weans in their bed, for it's now ten
o'clock?

MILLIGAN Spike 1918-
7353 *The Goon Show 'Only in the mating
season'*
'Do you come here often?'

7354 *The Last Goon Show of All*
Contraceptives should be used on every
conceivable occasion.

7355 *Puckoon*
Money couldn't buy friends but you got a
better class of enemy.

MILLS Hugh
7356
Nothing unites the English like war.
Nothing divides them like Picasso.

MILLSTEIN Gilbert
7357
He speaks English with the flawless
imperfection of a New Yorker.

MILMAN Henry Hart 1791-1868
7358 *The Belvedere Apollo*
And the cold marble leapt to life a god.

7359 *'Ride on! ride on in majesty!'*
Ride on! ride on in majesty!
The wingèd squadrons of the sky
Look down with sad and wond'ring eyes
To see the approaching sacrifice.

7360 *'Ride On! ride on in majesty!'*
Ride on! ride on in majesty!
In lowly pomp ride on to die.

MILNE A.A. 1882-1956
7361
One of the advantages of being disorderly
is that one is constantly making exciting
discoveries.

7362 *The House at Pooh Corner*
The more he looked inside the more Piglet
wasn't there.

7363 *The House at Pooh Corner*
'I don't *want* him,' said Rabbit. 'But it's
always useful to know where a friend-and-
relation *is*, whether you want him or
whether you don't.

7364 *The House at Pooh Corner*
He respects Owl, because you can't help
respecting anybody who can spell
TUESDAY, even if he doesn't spell it right;

but spelling isn't everything. There are days when spelling Tuesday simply doesn't count.

7365 *The House at Pooh Corner*
Pooh began to feel a little more comfortable, because when you are a Bear of Very Little Brain, and you Think of Things, you find sometimes that a Thing which seemed very Thingish inside you is quite different when it gets out into the open and has other people looking at it.

7366 *When We Were Very Young 'Buckingham Palace'*
They're changing guard at Buckingham Palace -
Christopher Robin went down with Alice.
Alice is marrying one of the guard.
'A soldier's life is terrible hard,'
Says Alice.

7367 *When We Were Very Young 'Disobedience'*
James James
Morrison Morrison
Weatherby George Dupree
Took great
Care of his Mother,
Though he was only three.
James James
Said to his Mother,
'Mother,' he said, said he;
'You must never go down to the end of the town, if you don't go down with me.'

7368 *When We Were Very Young 'The Dormouse ...'*
There once was a Dormouse who lived in a bed
Of delphiniums (blue) and geraniums (red),
And all the day long he'd a wonderful view
Of geraniums (red) and delphiniums (blue)

7369 *When We Were Very Young 'King's Breakfast'*
The King asked
The Queen, and
The Queen asked
The Dairymaid:
'Could we have some butter for
The Royal slice of bread?'

7370 *When We Were Very Young 'Rice Pudding'*
What is the matter with Mary Jane?
She's perfectly well and she hasn't a pain,
And it's lovely rice pudding for dinner again!
What *is* the matter with Mary Jane.

7371 *When We Were Very Young 'Vespers'*
Hush! Hush! Whisper who dares!
Christopher Robin is saying his prayers.

7372 *Winnie-the-Pooh*
Isn't it funny
How a bear likes honey?
Buzz! Buzz! Buzz!
I wonder why he does?

7373 *Winnie-the-Pooh*
How sweet to be a Cloud
Floating in the Blue!
It makes him very proud
To be a little cloud.

7374 *Winnie-the-Pooh*
Time for a little something.

7375 *Winnie-the-Pooh*
My spelling is Wobbly. It's good spelling but it Wobbles, and the letters get in the wrong places.

7376 *Winnie-the-Pooh*
Owl hasn't exactly got Brain, but he Knows Things.

7377 *Winnie-the-Pooh*
I am a Bear of Very Little Brain and long words Bother me.

7378 *Winnie-the-Pooh*
I have decided to catch a Heffalump.

7379 *Winnie-the-Pooh*
'Pathetic,' he said. 'That's what it is. Pathetic.'

MILNER Alfred 1854-1925
7380
If we believe a thing to be bad, and if we have a right to prevent it, it is our duty to try to prevent it and to damn the consequences.

MILTON John 1608-1674
7381
Where no hope is left, is left no fear.

7382
Reason is also choice.

7383 *An Apology for Smectymnuus*
He who would not be frustrate of his hope
to write well hereafter in laudable things,
ought himself to be a true poem.

7384 *An Apology for Smectymnuus*
His words ... like so many nimble and airy
servitors trip about him at command.

7385 *'Arcades'*
Such sweet compulsion doth in music lie.

7386 *Areopagitica*
For this is not the liberty which we can
hope, that no grievance ever should arise
in the Commonwealth, that let no man in
this world expect; but when complaints are
freely heard, deeply considered, and
speedily reformed, then is the utmost
bound of civil liberty attained that wise
men look for.

7387 *Areopagitica*
Books are not absolutely dead things, but
do contain a potency of life in them to be
as active as that soul was whose progeny
they are; nay they do preserve as in a vial
the purest efficacy and extraction of that
living intellect that bred them.

7388 *Areopagitica*
As good almost kill a man as kill a good
book: who kills a man kills a reasonable
creature, God's image; but he who
destroys a good book, kills reason itself,
kills the image of God, as it were in the
eye.

7389 *Areopagitica*
A good book is the precious life-blood of a
master spirit, embalmed and treasured up
on purpose to a life beyond life.

7390 *Areopagitica*
It was from out the rind of one apple
tasted that the knowledge of good and evil
as two twins cleaving together leaped forth
into the world. And perhaps this is that
doom that Adam fell into of knowing good
and evil, that is to say, of knowing good by
evil.

7391 *Areopagitica*
Assuredly we bring not innocence into the
world, we bring impurity much rather:
that which purifies us is trial, and trial is
by what is contrary.

7392 *Areopagitica*
If we think to regulate printing, thereby to
rectify manners, we must regulate all
recreations and pastimes, all that is
delightful to man.

7393 *Areopagitica*
And who shall silence all the airs and
madrigals, that whisper softness in
chambers?

7394 *Areopagitica*
To be still searching what we know not, by
what we know, still closing up truth to
truth as we find it (for all her body is
homogeneal and proportional), this is the
golden rule in theology as well as in
arithmetic, and makes up the best
harmony in a church.

7395 *Areopagitica*
Where there is much desire to learn, there
of necessity will be much arguing, much
writing, many opinions; for opinion in
good men is but knowledge in the making.

7396 *Areopagitica*
Methinks I see in my mind a noble and
puissant nation rousing herself like a
strong man after sleep, and shaking her
invincible locks. Methinks I see her as an
eagle mewing her mighty youth, and
kindling her undazzled eyes at the full
midday beam.

7397 *Areopagitica*
Give me the liberty to know, to utter, and
to argue freely according to conscience,
above all liberties.

7398 *Areopagitica*
Though all the winds of doctrine were let
loose to play upon the earth, so Truth be in
the field, we do injuriously by licensing
and prohibiting to misdoubt her strength.
Let her and Falsehood grapple; who ever
knew Truth put to the worse, in a free and
open encounter?

7399 *Areopagitica (of London)*
Behold now this vast city; a city of refuge,
the mansion-house of liberty, encompassed
and surrounded with his protection.

7400 *Comus*
Before the starry threshold of Jove's Court
My mansion is.

7401 *Comus*
Above the smoke and stir of this dim spot,
Which men call earth.

7402 *Comus*
Yet some there be that by due steps aspire
To lay their just hands on that golden key
That opes the palace of eternity.

7403 *Comus*
That like to rich and various gems inlay
The unadornèd bosom of the deep.

7404 *Comus*
An old and haughty nation proud in arms.

7405 *Comus*
And the gilded car of day
His glowing axle doth allay
In the steep Atlantic stream.

7406 *Comus*
What hath night to do with sleep?

7407 *Comus*
Come, knit hands, and beat the ground,
In a light fantastic round.

7408 *Comus*
O thievish Night
Why shouldst thou, but for some felonious
end,
In thy dark lantern thus close up the stars,
That Nature hung in heaven, and filled
their lamps
With everlasting oil, to give due light
To the misled and lonely traveller?

7409 *Comus*
Was I deceived, or did a sable cloud
Turn forth her silver lining on the night?

7410 *Comus*
Sweet Echo, sweetest nymph that liv'st
unseen
Within thy airy shell
By slow meander's margent green,
And in the violet-embroidered vale.

7411 *Comus*
Can any mortal mixture of earth's mould
Breathe such divine enchanting
ravishment?

7412 *Comus*
Such sober certainty of waking bliss
I never heard till now.

7413 *Comus*
With thy long levelled rule of streaming
light.

7414 *Comus*
Virtue could see to do what Virtue would
By her own radiant light, though sun and
moon
Were in the flat sea sunk ...

7415 *Comus*
But he that hides a dark soul, and foul
thoughts
Benighted walks under the midday sun;
Himself is his own dungeon.

7416 *Comus*
Yet where an equal poise of hope and fear
Does arbitrate the event, my nature is
That I incline to hope, rather than fear,
And gladly banish squint suspicion.

7417 *Comus*
'Tis chastity, my brother, chastity:
She that has that, is clad in complete steel.

7418 *Comus*
How charming is divine philosophy!
Not harsh and crabbèd, as dull fools
suppose,
But musical as is Apollo's lute,
And a perpetual feast of nectared sweets,
Where no crude surfeit reigns.

7419 *Comus*
And filled the air with barbarous
dissonance.

7420 *Comus*
I was all ear,
And took in strains that might create a
soul
Under the ribs of death.

7421 *Comus*
Against the threats
Of malice or of sorcery, or that power

Which erring men call chance, this I hold
firm,
Virtue may be assailed, but never hurt,
Surprised by unjust force, but not
enthralled.

7422 *Comus*
O foolishness of men! that lend their ears
To those budge doctors of the Stoic fur,
And fetch their precepts from the Cynic
tub,
Praising the lean and sallow Abstinence.

7423 *Comus*
Beauty is Nature's coin, must not be
hoarded,
But must be current, and the good thereof
Consists in mutual and partaken bliss.

7424 *Comus*
Obtruding false rules pranked in reason's
garb.

7425 *Comus*
Sabrina fair,
Listen where thou art sitting
Under the glassy, cool, translucent wave,
In twisted braids of lilies knitting
The loose train of thy amber-dropping
hair.

7426 *Comus*
Thus I set my printless feet
O'er the cowslip's velvet head,
That bends not as I tread.

7427 *Comus*
Love Virtue, she alone is free,
She can teach ye how to climb
Higher than the sphery chime;
Or, if Virtue feeble were,
Heaven itself would stoop to her.

7428 *'On the Death of a Fair Infant Dying of a
Cough'*
O fairest flower no sooner blown but
blasted,
Soft silken primrose fading timelessly.

7429 *The Doctrine and Discipline of Divorce*
Let not England forget her precedence of
teaching nations how to live.

7430 *Of Education*
I call therefore a complete and generous
education that which fits a man to perform

justly, skilfully and magnanimously all the
offices both private and public of peace
and war.

7431 *Of Education*
Ornate rhetoric taught out of the rule of
Plato ... To which poetry would be made
subsequent, or indeed rather precedent, as
being less subtle and fine, but more
simple, sensuous and passionate.

7432 *Of Education 'Their Exercise'*
In those vernal seasons of the year, when
the air is calm and pleasant, it were an
injury and sullenness against nature not to
go out, and see her riches, and partake in
her rejoicing with heaven and earth.

7433 *'Let us with a gladsome mind'*
Let us with a gladsome mind
Praise the Lord, for he is kind,
For his mercies ay endure,
Ever faithful, ever sure.

7434 *'Il Penseroso'*
Hence, vain deluding joys,
The brood of folly without father bred.

7435 *'Il Penseroso'*
As thick and numberless
As the gay motes that people the
sunbeams.

7436 *'Il Penseroso'*
Hail, divinest Melancholy,
Whose saintly visage is too bright
To hit the sense of human sight;
And therefore to our weaker view,
O'erlaid with black staid wisdom's hue.

7437 *'Il Penseroso'*
Come, pensive nun, devout and pure,
Sober, steadfast, and demure.

7438 *'Il Penseroso'*
And join with thee calm Peace, and Quiet,
Spare Fast, that oft with gods doth diet.

7439 *'Il Penseroso'*
And add to these retirèd Leisure,
That in trim gardens takes his pleasure.

7440 *'Il Penseroso'*
Sweet bird that shunn'st the noise of folly,
Most musical, most melancholy!

7441 *'Il Penseroso'*
And missing thee, I walk unseen
On the dry smooth-shaven green,
To behold the wandering moon,
Riding near her highest noon,
Like one that had been led astray
Through the heaven's wide pathless way;
And oft, as if her head she bowed,
Stooping through a fleecy cloud.

7442 *'Il Penseroso'*
Oft on a plat of rising ground,
I hear the far-off curfew sound
Over some wide-watered shore,
Swinging slow with sullen roar.

7443 *'Il Penseroso'*
Where glowing embers through the room
Teach light to counterfeit a gloom,
Far from all resort of mirth,
Save the cricket on the hearth.

7444 *'Il Penseroso'*
Or bid the soul of Orpheus sing
Such notes as warbled to the string,
Drew iron tears down Pluto's cheeck.

7445 *'Il Penseroso'*
Where more is meant than meets the ear.

7446 *'Il Penseroso'*
Hide me from day's garish eye,
While the bee with honied thigh,
That at her flowery work doth sing,
And the waters murmuring
And such consort as they keep,
Entice the dewy-feathered Sleep.

7447 *'Il Penseroso'*
But let my due feet never fail
To walk the studious cloister's pale.

7448 *'Il Penseroso'*
And love the high embowèd roof,
With antique pillars' massy proof,
And storied windows richly dight,
Casting a dim religious light.
There let the pealing organ blow
To the full-voiced quire below,
In service high, and anthems clear,
As may with sweetness, through mine ear,
Dissolve me into ecstasies,
And bring all heaven before mine eyes.

7449 *'Il Penseroso'*
Till old experience do attain
To something like prophetic strain.

7450 *The Judgement of Martin Bucer*
I owe no light or leading received from
any man in the discovery of this truth.

7451 *'L'Allegro'*
Hence, loathèd Melancholy,
Of Cerberus, and blackest Midnight born,
In Stygian cave forlorn
'Mongst horrid shapes, and shrieks, and
sights unholy.

7452 *'L'Allegro'*
Haste thee nymph, and bring with thee
Jest and youthful jollity,
Quips and cranks, and wanton wiles,
Nods, and becks, and wreathèd smiles.

7453 *'L'Allegro'*
Sport that wrinkled Care derides,
And Laughter holding both his sides.
Come, and trip it as ye go
On the light fantastic toe,
And in thy right hand lead with thee,
The mountain nymph, sweet Liberty.

7454 *'L'Allegro'*
Mirth, admit me of thy crew
To live with her, and live with thee,
In unreprovèd pleasures free.

7455 *'L'Allegro'*
While the cock with lively din
Scatters the rear of darkness thin,
And to the stack, or the barn door,
Stoutly struts his dames before.

7456 *'L'Allegro'*
Right against the eastern gate,
Where the great sun begins his state.

7457 *'L'Allegro'*
While the ploughman near at hand,
Whistles o'er the furrowed land,
And the milkmaid singeth blithe,
And the mower whets his scythe,
And every shepherd tells his tale
Under the hawthorn in the dale.

7458 *'L'Allegro'*
Meadows trim with daisies pied,
Shallow brooks, and rivers wide,
Towers, and battlements it sees

Bosomed high in tufted trees,
Where perhaps some beauty lies,
The cynosure of neighbouring eyes.

7459 'L'Allegro'
Of herbs, and other country messes,
Which the neat-handed Phyllis dresses.

7460 'L'Allegro'
And the jocund rebecks sound
To many a youth, and many a maid,
Dancing in the chequered shade;
And young and old come forth to play
On a sunshine holiday.

7461 'L'Allegro'
Then to the spicy nut-brown ale.

7462 'L'Allegro'
Towered cities please us then,
And the busy hum of men.

7463 'L'Allegro'
With store of ladies, whose bright eyes
Rain influence, and judge the prize
Of wit or arms.

7464 'L'Allegro'
Then to the well-trod stage anon,
If Jonson's learnèd sock be on,
Or sweetest Shakespeare fancy's child,
Warble his native wood-notes wild.

7465 'L'Allegro'
And ever against eating cares,
Lap me in soft Lydian airs,
Married to immortal verse
Such as the meeting soul may pierce
In notes, with many a winding bout
Of linkèd sweetness long drawn out.

7466 'L'Allegro'
Such strains as would have won the ear
Of Pluto, to have quite set free
His half-regained Eurydice.

7467 'L'Allegro' (of Mirth, one of three Graces)
So buxom, blithe, and debonair.

7468 'To the Lord General Cromwell'
... Peace hath her victories
No less renowned than war.

7469 'On Lord General Fairfax ... Siege of
Colchester'
For what can war, but endless war still
breed?

7470 'Lycidas'
Hence with denial vain, and coy excuse.

7471 'Lycidas'
For we were nursed upon the self-same
hill.

7472 'Lycidas'
But O the heavy change, now thou art
gone,
Now thou art gone, and never must
return!

7473 'Lycidas'
The woods, and desert caves,
With wild thyme and the gadding vine
o'ergrown.

7474 'Lycidas'
Where were ye nymphs, when the
remorseless deep
Closed o'er the head of your loved
Lycidas?

7475 'Lycidas'
Alas! What boots it with uncessant care
To tend the homely slighted shepherd's
trade,
And strictly meditate the thankless muse;
Were it not better done as others use,
To sport with Amaryllis in the shade,
Or with the tangles of Neaera's hair?

7476 'Lycidas'
Fame is the spur that the clear spirit doth
raise
(That last infirmity of noble mind)
To scorn delights, and live laborious days;
But the fair guerdon when we hope to
find,
And think to burst out into sudden blaze,
Comes the blind Fury with th'abhorrèd
shears,
And slits the thin-spun life.

7477 'Lycidas'
Fame is no plant that grows on mortal soil.

7478 'Lycidas'
It was that fatal and perfidious bark
Built in th' eclipse, and rigged with curses
dark,
That sunk so low that sacred head of thine.

7479 *'Lycidas'*
Last came, and last did go,
The pilot of the Galilean lake,
Two massy keys he bore of metals twain
(The golden opes, the iron shuts amain).

7480 *'Lycidas'*
Return, Alpheus, the dread voice is past
That shrunk thy streams; return Sicillian
muse.

7481 *'Lycidas'*
Bring the rathe primrose that forsaken
dies,
The tufted crow-toe, and pale jessamine,
The white pink, and the pansy freaked
with jet,
The glowing violet,
The musk-rose, and the well-attired
woodbine,
The cowslips wan that hang the pensive
head,
And every flower that sad embroidery
wears:
Bid amaranthus all his beauty shed,
And daffodillies fill their cups with tears,
To strew the laureate hearse where Lycid
lies.

7482 *'Lycidas'*
For Lycidas your sorrow is not dead,
Sunk though he be beneath the watery
floor;
So sinks the day-star in the ocean bed,
And yet anon repairs his drooping head,
And tricks his beams, and with new
spangled ore,
Flames in the forehead of the morning sky:
So Lycidas sunk low, but mounted high,
Through the dear might of Him that
walked the waves.

7483 *'Lycidas'*
At last he rose, and twitched his mantle
blue:
Tomorrow to fresh woods, and pastures
new.

7484 *'On the Morning of Christ's Nativity'*
This is the month, and this the happy
morn
Wherein the son of heaven's eternal king,
Of wedded maid, and virgin mother born,
Our great redemption from above did

bring;
For so the holy sages once did sing,
That he our deadly forfeit should release,
And with his father work us a perpetual
peace.

7485 *'On the Morning of Christ's Nativity'*
The star-led wizards haste with odours
sweet.

7486 *'On the Morning of Christ's Nativity'*
It was the winter wild,
While the heaven-born-child
All meanly wrapped in the rude manger
lies;
Nature in awe to him
Had doffed her gaudy trim,
With her great master so to sympathize.

7487 *'On the Morning of Christ's Nativity'*
No war, or battle's sound
Was heard the world around,
The idle spear and shield were high up
hung.

7488 *'On the Morning of Christ's Nativity'*
The stars with deep amaze
Stand fixed in steadfast gaze,
Bending one way their precious influence,
And will not take their flight
For all the morning light,
Or Lucifer that often warned them thence;
But in their glimmering orbs did glow,
Until their Lord himself bespake, and bid
them go.

7489 *'On the Morning of Christ's Nativity'*
Perhaps their loves, or else their sheep,
Was all that did their silly thoughts so
busy keep.

7490 *'On the Morning of Christ's Nativity'*
The helmèd cherubim
And sworded seraphim
Are seen in glittering ranks with wings
displayed.

7491 *'On the Morning of Christ's Nativity'*
Ring out, ye crystal spheres,
Once bless our human ears
(If ye have power to touch our senses so),
And let your silver chime
Move in melodious time;
And let the base of heaven's deep organ
blow,

And with your ninefold harmony
Make up full consort to the angelic
symphony.

7492 'On the Morning of Christ's Nativity'
For if such holy song
Enwrap our fancy long,
Time will run back, and fetch the age of
gold,
And speckled vanity
Will sicken soon and die.

7493 'On the Morning of Christ's Nativity'
And hell itself will pass away,
And leave her dolorous mansions to the
peering day.

7494 'On the Morning of Christ's Nativity'
Swinges the scaly horror of his folded tail.

7495 'On the Morning of Christ's Nativity'
The oracles are dumb,
No voice or hideous hum
Runs through the archèd roof in words
deceiving.
Apollo from his shrine
Can no more divine,
With hollow shriek the steep of Delphos
leaving.

7496 'On the Morning of Christ's Nativity'
So when the sun in bed,
Curtained with cloudy red,
Pillows his chin upon an orient wave.

7497 'On the Morning of Christ's Nativity'
But see the virgin blest,
Hath laid her babe to rest.
Time is our tedious song should here have
ending.

7498 'On the New Forcers of Conscience ...'
New *Presbyter* is but old *Priest* writ larger.

7499 *Paradise Lost*
Of man's first disobedience, and the fruit
Of that forbidden tree, whose mortal taste
Brought death into the world, and all our
woe,
With loss of Eden.

7500 *Paradise Lost*
Things unattempted yet in prose or rhyme.

7501 *Paradise Lost*
What in me is dark
Illumine, what is low raise and support;
That to the height of this great argument
I may assert eternal providence,
And justify the ways of God to men.

7502 *Paradise Lost*
The infernal serpent; he it was, whose
guile
Stirred up with envy and revenge,
deceived
The mother of mankind.

7503 *Paradise Lost*
Him the almighty power
Hurled headlong flaming from the ethereal
sky
With hideous ruin and combustion down
To bottomless perdition, there to dwell
In adamantine chains and penal fire,
Who durst defy the omnipotent to arms.

7504 *Paradise Lost*
A dungeon horrible, on all sides round
As one great furnace flamed, yet from
those flames
No light, but rather darkness visible
Served only to discover sights of woe,
Regions of sorrow, doleful shades, where
peace
And rest can never dwell, hope never
comes
That comes to all.

7505 *Paradise Lost*
... But O how fallen! how changed
From him, who in the happy realms of
light
Clothed with transcendent brightness didst
outshine
Myriads though bright.

7506 *Paradise Lost*
United thoughts and counsels, equal hope
And hazard in the glorious enterprise.

7507 *Paradise Lost*
Yet not for those,
Nor what the potent victor in his rage
Can else inflict, do I repent or change,
Though changed in outward lustre; that
fixed mind
And high disdain, from sense of injured
merit.

7508 *Paradise Lost*
... What though the field be lost?
All is not lost; the unconquerable will,
And study of revenge, immortal hate,
And courage never to submit or yield:
And what is else not to be overcome?

7509 *Paradise Lost*
Vaunting aloud, but racked with deep
despair.

7510 *Paradise Lost*
Fallen cherub, to be weak is miserable,
Doing or suffering: but of this be sure,
To do aught good never will be our task,
But ever to do ill our sole delight.

7511 *Paradise Lost*
And out of good still to find means of evil.

7512 *Paradise Lost*
What reinforcement we may gain from
hope;
If not, what resolution from despair.

7513 *Paradise Lost*
The will
And high permission of all-ruling heaven
Left him at large to his own dark designs,
That with reiterated crimes he might
Heap on himself damnation.

7514 *Paradise Lost*
Is this the region, this the soil, the clime,
Said then the lost archangel, this the seat
That we must change for heaven, this
mournful gloom
For that celestial light?

7515 *Paradise Lost*
Farewell, happy fields
Where joy for ever dwells: hail horrors,
hail
Infernal world, and thou profoundest hell
Receive thy new possessor: one who
brings
A mind not to be changed by place or time.
The mind is its own place, and in itself
Can make a heaven of hell, a hell of
heaven.

7516 *Paradise Lost*
To reign is worth ambition though in hell:
Better to reign in hell, than serve in
heaven.

7517 *Paradise Lost*
His spear, to equal which the tallest pine
Hewn on Norwegian hills, to be the mast
Of some great admiral, were but a wand
He walked with to support uneasy steps
Over the burning marl.

7518 *Paradise Lost*
Thick as autumnal leaves that strew the
brooks
In Vallombrosa, where the Etrurian shades
High overarched imbower.

7519 *Paradise Lost*
First Moloch, horrid king besmeared with
blood
Of human sacrifice, and parents' tears.

7520 *Paradise Lost*
But in what shape they choose,
Dilated or condensed, bright or obscure,
Can execute their aery purposes.

7521 *Paradise Lost*
Astarte, queen of heaven, with crescent
horns.

7522 *Paradise Lost*
And when night
Darkens the streets, then wander forth the
sons
Of Belial, flown with insolence and wine.

7523 *Paradise Lost*
The imperial ensign, which full high
advanced
Shone like a meteor streaming to the wind.

7524 *Paradise Lost*
Sonorous metal blowing martial sounds:
At which the universal host upsent
A shout that tore hell's concave, and
beyond
Frighted the reign of Chaos and old Night.

7525 *Paradise Lost*
Anon they move
In perfect phalanx to the Dorian mode
Of flutes and soft recorders.

7526 *Paradise Lost*
What resounds
In fable or romance of Uther's son
Begirt with British and Armoric knights;
And all who since, baptized or infidel,
Jousted in Aspramont or Montalban,

Damasco, or Marocco, or Trebisond,
Or whom Biserta sent from Afric shore
When Charlemain with all his peerage fell
By Fontarabia.

7527 *Paradise Lost*
... As when the sun new risen
Looks through the horizontal misty air
Shorn of his beams, or from behind the moon
In dim eclipse disastrous twilight sheds
On half the nations, and with fear of change
Perplexes monarchs.

7528 *Paradise Lost*
Who overcomes
By force, hath overcome but half his foe.

7529 *Paradise Lost*
Mammon led them on,
Mammon, the least erected spirit that fell
From heaven, for even in heaven his looks and thoughts
Were always downward bent, admiring more
The riches of heaven's pavement, trodden gold,
Than aught divine or holy else enjoyed
In vision beatific.

7530 *Paradise Lost*
Let none admire
That riches grow in hell; that soil may best
Deserve the precious bane.

7531 *Paradise Lost*
Anon out of the earth a fabric huge
Rose like an exhalation.

7532 *Paradise Lost*
From morn
To noon he fell, from noon to dewy eve,
A summer's day; and with the setting sun
Dropped from the zenith like a falling star.

7533 *Paradise Lost*
Nor aught availed him now
To have built in heaven high towers; nor did he scape
By all his engines, but was headlong sent
With his industrious crew to build in hell.

7534 *Paradise Lost*
... Pandemonium, the high capital
Of Satan and his peers.

7535 *Paradise Lost*
High on a throne of royal state, which far
Outshone the wealth of Ormuz and of Ind,
Or where the gorgeous East with richest hand
Showers on her kings barbaric pearl and gold,
Satan exalted sat, by merit raised
To that bad eminence; and from despair
Thus high uplifted beyond hope.

7536 *Paradise Lost*
... The strongest and the fiercest spirit
That fought in heaven; now fiercer by despair:
His trust was with the eternal to be deemed
Equal in strength, and rather than be less
Cared not to be at all.

7537 *Paradise Lost*
My sentence is for open war: of wiles
More unexpert, I boast not.

7538 *Paradise Lost*
For who would lose,
Though full of pain, this intellectual being,
Those thoughts that wander through eternity,
To perish rather, swallowed up and lost
In the wide womb of uncreated night,
Devoid of sense and motion?

7539 *Paradise Lost*
There to converse with everlasting groans,
Unrespited, unpitied, unreprieved,
Ages of hopeless end.

7540 *Paradise Lost*
Thus Belial with words clothed in reason's garb
Counselled ignoble ease, and peaceful sloth,
Not peace.

7541 *Paradise Lost*
Our torments also may in length of time
Become our elements.

7542 *Paradise Lost*
With grave
Aspect he rose, and in his rising seemed
A pillar of state; deep on his front engraven
Deliberation sat and public care;

And princely counsel in his face yet shone,
Majestic though in ruin.

7543 *Paradise Lost*
To sit in darkness here
Hatching vain empires.

7544 *Paradise Lost*
... Who shall tempt with wandering feet
The dark unbottomed infinite abyss
And through the palpable obscure find out
His uncouth way.

7545 *Paradise Lost*
Long is the way
And hard, that out of hell leads up to light.

7546 *Paradise Lost*
O shame to men! Devil with devil damned
Firm concord holds, men only disagree
Of creatures rational.

7547 *Paradise Lost*
The parching air
Burns frore, and cold performs the effect of
fire.

7548 *Paradise Lost*
Feel by turns the bitter change
Of fierce extremes, extremes by change
more fierce.

7549 *Paradise Lost*
O'er many a frozen, many a fiery alp,
Rocks, caves, lakes, fens, bogs, dens, and
shades of death,
A universe of death, which God by curse
Created evil, for evil only good,
Where all life dies, death lives, and nature
breeds,
Perverse, all monstrous, all prodigious
things,
Abominable, inutterable, and worse
Than fables yet have feigned, or fear
conceived,
Gorgons and Hydras, and Chimeras dire.

7550 *Paradise Lost*
The other shape,
If shape it might be called that shape had
none
Distinguishable in member, joint, or limb,
Or substance might be called that shadow
seemed,
For each seemed either; black it stood as
night,

Fierce as ten Furies, terrible as hell,
And shook a dreadful dart; what seemed
his head
The likeness of a kingly crown had on.

7551 *Paradise Lost*
Whence and what art thou, execrable
shape?

7552 *Paradise Lost*
Incensed with indignation Satan stood
Unterrified, and like a comet burned
That fires the length of Ophiuchus huge
In the Artic sky, and from his horrid hair
Shakes pestilence and war.

7553 *Paradise Lost*
... Their fatal hands
No second stroke intend.

7554 *Paradise Lost*
I fled, and cried out Death!
Hell trembled at the hideous name, and
sighed
From all her caves, and back resounded
Death.

7555 *Paradise Lost*
On a sudden open fly
With impetuous recoil and jarring sound
The infernal doors, and on their hinges
grate
Harsh thunder.

7556 *Paradise Lost*
Chaos umpire sits,
And by decision more embroils the fray
By which he reigns; next him high arbiter
Chance governs all.

7557 *Paradise Lost*
Sable-vested Night, eldest of things.

7558 *Paradise Lost*
With ruin upon ruin, rout on rout,
Confusion worse confounded.

7559 *Paradise Lost*
Hail, holy Light, offspring of heaven first-
born,
Or of the eternal co-eternal beam
May I express thee unblamed? since God is
light,
And never but in unapproachèd light
Dwelt from eternity, dwelt then in thee,
Bright effluence of bright essence increate.

Or hear'st thou rather pure ethereal
stream,
Whose fountain who shall tell?

7560 *Paradise Lost*
Die he or justice must.

7561 *Paradise Lost*
Dark with excessive bright.

7562 *Paradise Lost*
So on this windy sea of land, the fiend
Walked up and down alone bent on his
prey.

7563 *Paradise Lost*
Into a limbo large and broad, since called
The Paradise of Fools, to few unknown.

7564 *Paradise Lost*
For neither man nor angel can discern
Hypocrisy, the only evil that walks
Invisible, except to God alone.

7565 *Paradise Lost*
At whose sight all the stars
Hide their diminished heads.

7566 *Paradise Lost*
Warring in heaven against heaven's
matchless king.

7567 *Paradise Lost*
A grateful mind
By owing owes not, but still pays, at once
Indebted and discharged.

7568 *Paradise Lost*
Me miserable! which way shall I fly
Infinite wrath, and infinite despair?
Which way I fly is hell; myself am hell;
And in the lowest deep a lower deep
Still threatening to devour me opens wide,
To which the hell I suffer seems a heaven.

7569 *Paradise Lost*
So farewell hope, and with hope farewell
fear,
Farewell remorse! All good to me is lost;
Evil, be thou my good.

7570 *Paradise Lost*
So clomb this first grand thief into God's
fold:
So since into his church lewd hirelings
climb.
Thence up he flew, and on the tree of life,

The middle tree and highest there that
grew,
Sat like a cormorant.

7571 *Paradise Lost*
Groves whose rich trees wept odorous
gums and balm,
Others whose fruit burnished with golden
rind
Hung amiable, Hesperian fables true,
If true, here only.

7572 *Paradise Lost*
Flowers of all hue, and without thorn the
rose.

7573 *Paradise Lost*
Not that fair field
Of Enna, where Proserpine gathering
flowers
Herself a fairer flower by gloomy Dis
Was gathered, which cost Ceres all that
pain.

7574 *Paradise Lost*
For contemplation he and valour formed,
For softness she and sweet attractive grace,
He for God only, she for God in him:
His fair large front and eye sublime
declared
Absolute rule.

7575 *Paradise Lost*
And by her yielded, by him best received,
Yielded with coy submission, modest
pride,
And sweet reluctant amorous delay.

7576 *Paradise Lost*
Adam, the goodliest man of men since
born
His sons, the fairest of her daughters Eve.

7577 *Paradise Lost*
The unwieldy elephant
To make them mirth used all his might,
and wreathed
His lithe proboscis.

7578 *Paradise Lost*
These two
Emparadised in one another's arms
The happier Eden, shall enjoy their fill
Of bliss on bliss.

7579 *Paradise Lost*
Now came still evening on, and twilight
grey
Had in her sober livery all things clad;
Silence accompanied, for beast and bird,
They to their grassy couch, these to their
nests
Were slunk, all but the wakeful
nightingale;
She all night long her amorous descant
sung;
Silence was pleased: now glowed the
firmament
With living sapphires: Hesperus that led
The starry host, rode brightest, till the
moon
Rising in clouded majesty, at length
Apparent queen unveiled her peerless
light,
And o'er the dark her silver mantle threw.

7580 *Paradise Lost*
God is thy law, thou mine: to know no
more
Is woman's happiest knowledge and her
praise.
With thee conversing I forget all time.

7581 *Paradise Lost*
Sweet the coming on
Of grateful evening mild, then silent night
With this her solemn bird and this fair
moon,
And these the gems of heaven, her starry
train.

7582 *Paradise Lost*
Millions of spiritual creatures walk the
earth
Unseen, both when we wake, and when
we sleep.

7583 *Paradise Lost*
Hail, wedded love, mysterious law, true
source
Of human offspring, sole propriety
In Paradise of all things common else.

7584 *Paradise Lost*
Sleep on
Blest pair; and O yet happiest if ye seek
No happier state, and know to know no
more.

7585 *Paradise Lost*
Him there they found
Squat like a toad, close at the ear of Eve.

7586 *Paradise Lost*
But wherefore thou alone? Wherefore with
thee
Came not all hell broke loose?

7587 *Paradise Lost*
Then when I am thy captive talk of chains,
Proud limitary cherub.

7588 *Paradise Lost*
His sleep
Was airy light from pure digestion bred.

7589 *Paradise Lost*
My fairest, my espoused, my latest found,
Heaven's last best gift, my ever new
delight.

7590 *Paradise Lost*
Best image of myself and dearer half.

7591 *Paradise Lost*
On earth join all ye creatures to extol
Him first, him last, him midst, and without
end.

7592 *Paradise Lost*
So saying, with dispatchful looks in haste
She turns, on hospitable thoughts intent.

7593 *Paradise Lost*
Nor jealousy
Was understood, the injured lover's hell.

7594 *Paradise Lost*
Freely we serve,
Because we freely love, as in our will
To love or not; in this we stand or fall.

7595 *Paradise Lost*
What if earth
Be but the shadow of heaven, and things
therein
Each to other like, more than on earth is
thought?

7596 *Paradise Lost*
Hear all ye angels, progeny of light,
Thrones, dominations, princedoms,
virtues, powers.

7597 *Paradise Lost*
All seemed well pleased, all seemed, but
were not all.

7598 *Paradise Lost*
Satan, so call him now, his former name
Is heard no more in heaven.

7599 *Paradise Lost*
Servant of God, well done, well hast thou
fought
The better fight, who single has
maintained
Against revolted multitudes the cause
Of truth, in word mightier than they in
arms.

7600 *Paradise Lost*
Standing on earth, not rapt above the pole,
More safe I sing with mortal voice,
unchanged
To hoarse or mute, though fall'n on evil
days,
On evil days though fallen, and evil
tongues.

7601 *Paradise Lost*
Necessity and chance
Approach not me, and what I will is fate.

7602 *Paradise Lost*
There Leviathan
Hugest of living creatures, on the deep
Stretched like a promontory sleeps or
swims,
And seems a moving land, and at his gills
Draws in, and at his trunk spouts out a
sea.

7603 *Paradise Lost*
The planets in their stations listening
stood,
While the bright pomp ascended jubilant.
Open, ye everlasting gates, they sung,
Open, ye heavens, your living doors; let in
The great creator from his work returned
Magnificent, his six days' work, a world.

7604 *Paradise Lost*
He his fabric of the heavens
Hath left to their disputes, perhaps to
move
His laughter at their quaint opinions wide
Hereafter, when they come to model
heaven

And calculate the stars, how they will
wield
The mighty frame, how build, unbuild,
contrive
To save appearances, how gird the sphere
With centric and eccentric scribbled o'er,
Cycle and epicycle, orb in orb.

7605 *Paradise Lost*
Heaven is for thee too high
To know what passes there; be lowly wise:
Think only what concerns thee and thy
being.

7606 *Paradise Lost*
Tell me, how may I know him, how adore,
From whom I have that thus I move and
live,
And feel that I am happier than I know?

7607 *Paradise Lost*
In solitude
What happiness? who can enjoy alone,
Or all enjoying, what contentment find?

7608 *Paradise Lost*
So absolute she seems
And in herself complete, so well to know
Her own, that what she wills to do or say
Seems wisest, virtuousest, discreetest, best.

7609 *Paradise Lost*
Oft-times nothing profits more
Than self esteem, grounded on just and
right
Well managed.

7610 *Paradise Lost*
The serpent subtlest beast of all the field.

7611 *Paradise Lost*
For solitude sometimes is best society,
And short retirement urges sweet return.

7612 *Paradise Lost*
As one who long in populous city pent,
Where houses thick and sewers annoy the
air,
Forth issuing on a summer's morn to
breathe
Among the pleasant villages and farms
Adjoined, from each thing met conceives
delight.

7613 *Paradise Lost*
She fair, divinely fair, fit love for gods.

7614 *Paradise Lost*
God so commanded, and left that
command
Sole daughter of his voice; the rest, we live
Law to our selves, our reason is our law.

7615 *Paradise Lost*
Her rash hand in evil hour
Forth reaching to the fruit, she plucked,
she ate:
Earth felt the wound, and Nature from her
seat
Sighing through all her works gave signs
of woe
That all was lost.

7616 *Paradise Lost*
O fairest of creation, last and best
Of all God's works, creature in whom
excelled
Whatever can to sight or thought be
formed,
Holy, divine, good, amiable or sweet!

7617 *Paradise Lost*
For with thee
Certain my resolution is to die;
How can I live without thee, how forgo
Thy sweet converse and love so dearly
joined,
To live again in these wild woods forlorn?

7618 *Paradise Lost*
Flesh of flesh,
Bone of my bone thou art, and from thy
state
Mine never shall be parted, bliss or woe.

7619 *Paradise Lost*
What thou art is mine;
Our state cannot be severed, we are one,
One flesh; to lose thee were to lose my self.

7620 *Paradise Lost*
... Yet I shall temper so
Justice with mercy.

7621 *Paradise Lost*
He hears
On all sides, from innumerable tongues
A dismal universal hiss, the sound
Of public scorn.

7622 *Paradise Lost*
O why did God,
Creator wise, that peopled highest heaven

With spirits masculine, create at last
This novelty on earth, this fair defect
Of nature?

7623 *Paradise Lost*
Demoniac frenzy, moping melancholy
And moon-struck madness.

7624 *Paradise Lost*
Henceforth I fly not death, nor would
prolong
Life much, bent rather how I may be quit
Fairest and easiest of this cumbrous
charge,
Which I must keep till my appointed day
Of rendering up, and patiently attend
My dissolution.

7625 *Paradise Lost*
Nor love thy life, nor hate; but what thou
liv'st
Live well, how long or short permit to
heaven.

7626 *Paradise Lost*
... The evening star,
Love's harbinger.

7627 *Paradise Lost*
For now I see
Peace to corrupt no less than war to waste.

7628 *Paradise Lost*
Light out of darkness! full of doubt I stand,
Whether I should repent me now of sin
By me done and occasioned, or rejoice
Much more, that much more good thereof
shall spring.

7629 *Paradise Lost*
Only add
Deeds to thy knowledge answerable, add
faith,
Add virtue, patience, temperance, add
love,
By name to come called Charity, the soul
Of all the rest: then wilt thou not be loath
To leave this Paradise, but shalt possess
A paradise within thee, happier far.

7630 *Paradise Lost*
In me is no delay; with thee to go,
Is to stay here; without thee here to stay,
Is to go hence unwilling; thou to me
Art all things under heaven, all places
thou,

Who for my wilful crime art banished
hence.

7631 *Paradise Lost*
They looking back, all the eastern side
beheld
Of Paradise, so late their happy seat,
Waved over by that flaming brand, the
gate
With dreadful faces thronged and fiery
arms.
Some natural tears they dropped, but
wiped them soon;
The world was all before them, where to
choose
Their place of rest, and Providence their
guide:
They hand in hand, with wandering steps
and slow,
Through Eden took their solitary way.

7632 *Paradise Lost (the Pygmies)*
... That small infantry
Warred on by cranes.

7633 *Paradise Lost 'The Verse'*
Rhyme being no necessary adjunct or true
ornament of poem or good verse, in longer
works especially, but the invention of a
barbarous age, to set off wretched matter
and lame metre.

7634 *Paradise Lost 'The Verse'*
The troublesome and modern bondage of
rhyming.

7635 *Paradise Regained*
Skilled to retire, and in retiring draw
Hearts after them tangled in amorous nets.

7636 *Paradise Regained*
Of whom to be dispraised were no small
praise.

7637 *Paradise Regained*
But on occasion's forelock watchful wait.

7638 *Paradise Regained*
... The childhood shows the man,
As morning shows the day. Be famous
then
By wisdom; as thy empire must extend,
So let extend thy mind o'er all the world.

7639 *Paradise Regained*
Athens, the eye of Greece, mother of arts
And eloquence, native to famous wits
Or hospitable, in her sweet recess,
City or suburban, studious walks and
shades;
See there the olive grove of Acadame,
Plato's retirement, where the Attic bird
Trills her thick-warbled notes the summer
long.

7640 *Paradise Regained*
The first and wisest of them all professed
To know this only, that he nothing knew.

7641 *Paradise Regained*
Who reads
Incessantly, and to his reading brings not
A spirit and judgement equal or superior
(And what he brings, what needs he
elsewhere seek?)
Uncertain and unsettled still remains,
Deep-versed in books and shallow in
himself.

7642 *Paradise Regained (of the prophets)*
In them is plainest taught, and easiest
learnt,
What makes a nation happy, and keeps it
so.

7643 *Paradise Regained (of Saul)*
He who seeking asses found a kingdom.

7644 *'The Passion'*
But headlong joy is ever on the wing.

7645 *The Reason of Church Government*
This manner of writing [prose] wherein
knowing myself inferior to myself ... I have
the use, as I may account it, but of my left
hand.

7646 *The Reason of Church Government*
By labour and intent study (which I take to
be my portion in this life) joined with the
strong propensity of nature, I might
perhaps leave something so written to
aftertimes, as they should not willingly let
it die.

7647 *The Reason of Church Government*
The land had once enfranchised herself
from this impertinent yoke of prelaty,
under whose inquisitorious and tyrannical
duncery no free and splendid wit can

flourish.

7648 *The Reason of Church Government*
Beholding the bright countenance of truth
in the quiet and still air of delightful
studies.

7649 *Samson Agonistes*
Ask for this great deliverer now, and find
him
Eyeless in Gaza at the mill with slaves.

7650 *Samson Agonistes*
O dark, dark, dark, amid the blaze of
noon,
Irrecoverably dark, total eclipse
Without all hope of day!

7651 *Samson Agonistes*
The sun to me is dark
And silent as the moon,
When she deserts the night
Hid in her vacant interlunar cave.

7652 *Samson Agonistes*
To live a life half dead, a living death.

7653 *Samson Agonistes*
Ran on embattled armies clad in iron,
And, weaponless himself,
Made arms ridiculous.

7654 *Samson Agonistes*
Wisest men

Have erred, and by bad women been
deceived;
And shall again, pretend they ne'er so
wise.

7655 *Samson Agonistes*
Just are the ways of God,
And justifiable to men;
Unless there be who think not God at all.

7656 *Samson Agonistes*
... Of such doctrine never was there school,
But the heart of the fool,
And no man therein doctor but himself.

7657 *Samson Agonistes*
But what availed this temperance, not
complete
Against another object more enticing?
What boots it at one gate to make defence,
And at another to let in the foe?

7658 *Samson Agonistes*
That grounded maxim
So rife and celebrated in the mouths
Of wisest men; that to the public good
Private respects must yield.

7659 *Samson Agonistes*
Yet beauty, though injurious, hath strange
power,
After offence returning, to regain
Love once possessed.

7660 *Samson Agonistes*
Love-quarrels oft in pleasing concord end.

7661 *Samson Agonistes*
Lords are lordliest in their wine.

7662 *Samson Agonistes*
For evil news rides post, while good news
baits.

7663 *Samson Agonistes*
And as an evening dragon came,
Assailant on the perchèd roosts,
And nests in order ranged
Of tame villatic fowl.

7664 *Samson Agonistes*
Like that self-begotten bird
In the Arabian woods embossed,
That no second knows nor third,
And lay erewhile a holocaust.

7665 *Samson Agonistes*
And though her body die, her fame
survives,
A secular bird ages of lives.

7666 *Samson Agonistes*
Samson hath quit himself
Like Samson, and heroically hath finished
A life heroic.

7667 *Samson Agonistes*
Nothing is here for tears, nothing to wail
Or knock the breast, no weakness, no
contempt,
Dispraise, or blame, nothing but well and
fair,
And what may quiet us in a death so
noble.

7668 *Samson Agonistes*
All is best, though we oft doubt,
What the unsearchable dispose

Of highest wisdom brings about,
And ever best found in the close.

7669 *Samson Agonistes*
His servants he, with new acquist
Of true experience from this great event
With peace and consolation hath
dismissed,
And calm of mind, all passion spent.

7670 *(of his school, Christ College)*
'A stony-hearted step-mother.'

7671 *'On Shakespeare'*
What needs my Shakespeare for his
honoured bones,
The labour of an age in pilèd stones,
Or that his hallowed relics should be hid
Under a star-ypointing pyramid?

7672 *'At a Solemn Music'*
Blest pair of Sirens, pledges of heaven's
joy,
Sphere-born harmonious sisters, Voice, and
Verse.

7673 *'At a Solemn Music'*
Where the bright seraphim in burning row
Their loud uplifted angel trumpets blow.

7674 *Sonnet 12 'I did but prompt the age'*
I did but prompt the age to quit their clogs
By the known rules of ancient liberty,
When straight a barbarous noise environs
me
Of owls and cuckoos, asses, apes, and
dogs.

7675 *Sonnet 12 'I did but prompt the age'*
Licence they mean when they cry liberty;
For who loves that, must first be wise and
good.

7676 *Sonnet 16 'When I consider how my light
is spent'*
When I consider how my light is spent,
E're half my days, in this dark world and
wide,
And that one talent which is death to hide
Lodged with me useless ...
Doth God exact day-labour, light denied,
I fondly ask; but patience to prevent
That murmur, soon replies, God doth not
need
Either man's work or his own gifts, who
best

Bear his mild yoke, they serve him best,
his state
Is kingly. Thousands at his bidding speed
And post o'er land and ocean without rest:
They also serve who only stand and wait.

7677 *Sonnet 18 'Cyriack, whose grandsire ..'*
Today deep thoughts resolve with me to
drench
In mirth, that after no repenting draws.

7678 *Sonnet 19 'Methought I saw my late
espousèd saint'*
Methought I saw my late espousèd saint
Brought to me like Alcestis from the grave.

7679 *Sonnet 19 'Methought I saw my late
espousèd saint'*
But oh as to embrace me she inclined
I waked, she fled, and day brought back
my night.

7680 *Sonnet 7 'How soon hath time'*
How soon hath time the subtle thief of
youth,
Stol'n on his wing my three and twentieth
year!

7681 *The Tenure of Kings and Magistrates*
None can love freedom heartily, but good
men; the rest love not freedom, but licence.

7682 *The Tenure of Kings and Magistrates*
No man who knows aught, can be so
stupid to deny that all men naturally were
born free.

7683 *The...Way to Establish a Free
Commonwealth*
What I have spoken, is the language of
that which is not called amiss *The good old
Cause.*

7684 *'On Time'*
Fly envious Time, till thou run out thy
race,
Call on the lazy leaden-stepping hours.

7685 *'On the University Carrier'*
Showed him his room where he must
lodge that night,
Pulled off his boots, and took away the
light:
If any ask for him, it shall be said,
Hobson has supped, and's newly gone to
bed.

MILVERTON Lord 1930-
7686
The ideal committee is one with me as chairman, and two other members in bed with flu.

MIRABEAU Comte de 1749-1791
7687 *(attributed)*
La guerre est l'industrie nationale de la Prusse.
War is the national industry of Prussia.

MIRO Joán 1893-1983
7688
The painting rises from the brushstrokes as a poem rises from the words. The meaning comes later.

MISTINGUETT 1874-1956
7689
A kiss can be a comma, a question mark, or an exclamation point. That's basic spelling that every woman ought to know.

MITCHELL Adrian 1932-
7690 *Poems*
Most people ignore most poetry
because
most poetry ignores most people.

MITCHELL Joni 1945-
7691 *'Both Sides Now'*
I've looked at life from both sides now,
From win and lose and still somehow
It's life's illusions I recall;
I really don't know life at all.

7692 *'Woodstock'*
We are stardust,
We are golden,
And we got to get ourselves
Back to the garden.

7693 *'Big Yellow Taxi'*
They paved paradise
And put up a parking lot,
With a pink hotel,
A boutique, and a swinging hot spot.

MITCHELL Langdon
7694
Marriage is three parts love and seven parts forgiveness of sins.

MITCHELL Margaret 1900-1949
7695 *Gone with the Wind*
Death and taxes and childbirth! There's never any convenient time for any of them.

7696 *Gone with the Wind*
I wish I could care what you do or where you go but I can't ... My dear, I don't give a damn.

7697 *Gone with the Wind*
After all, tomorrow is another day.

MITCHELL S. Weir 1829-1914
7698
The arctic loneliness of age.

MITFORD Mary Russell 1787-1855
7699 *(of Jane Austen)*
Perpendicular, precise and taciturn.

MITFORD Nancy 1904-1973
7700 *Love in a Cold Climate*
'Always be civil to the girls, you never know who they may marry' is an aphorism which has saved many an English spinster from being treated like an Indian widow.

7701 *Noblesse Oblige*
An aristocracy in a republic is like a chicken whose head has been cut off: it may run about in a lively way, but in fact it is dead.

7702 *The Pursuit of Love*
Wooing, so tiring.

7703 *The Pursuit of Love*
Frogs ... are slightly better than Huns or Wops, but abroad is unutterably bloody and foreigners are fiends.

MITTERAND President François 1916-
7704
Nothing is won forever in human affairs, but everything is always possible.

7705 *(to his adviser)*
You, Attali, are a mere chapter. I am the entire volume.

MIZNER Wilson 1876-1933
7706
A fellow who is always declaring he's no fool usually has his suspicions.

7707
The cuckoo who is on to himself is halfway out of the clock.

7708
I've had several years in Hollywood and I
still think the movie heroes are in the
audience.

7709
Be nice to people on your way up because
you'll meet 'em on your way down.

7710
If you steal from one author, it's
plagiarism; if you steal from many, it's
research.

7711 *(of Hollywood)*
A trip through a sewer in a glass-bottomed
boat.

MOLIÉRE 1622-1673
7712
Long is the road from conception to
completion.

7713
The more we love our friends, the less we
flatter them; it is by excusing nothing that
pure love shows itself.

7714
A doctor wastes no time with patients; and
if you have to die, he will put the business
through quicker than anybody else.

7715
You never see the old austerity
That was the essence of civility;
Young people hereabouts, unbridled, now
Just want.

7716
It is permitted me to take good fortune
where I find it.

7717 *Don Juan*
He who lives without tobacco is not
worthy to live.

7718 *La Critique de l'école des femmes*
It's an odd job, making decent people
laugh.

7719 *La Critique de l'école des femmes*
I shouldn't be surprised if the greatest rule
of all weren't to give pleasure.

7720 *Le Dépit amoureux*
One dies only once, and it's for such a long
time!

7721 *Les Femmes savantes*
It's good food and not fine words that
keeps me alive.

7722 *Les Femmes savantes*
Rags and tatters, if you like: I am fond of
my rags and tatters.

7723 *Les Femmes savantes*
A knowledgeable fool is a greater fool than
an ignorant fool.

7724 *Les Femmes savantes*
Reading and marriage don't go well
together.

7725 *Les Précieuses Ridicules*
People of quality know everything without
ever having been taught anything.

7726 *The Misanthrope*
What's needed in this world is an
accommodating sort of virtue.

7727 *The Misanthrope*
Of all human follies there's none could be
greater
Than trying to render our fellow-men
better.

7728 *The Misanthrope*
One should look long and carefully at
oneself before one considers judging
others.

7729 *The Miser*
Always present your front to the world.

7730 *The Miser*
One should eat to live, and not live to eat.

7731 *Monsieur de Pourceaugnac*
Here [in Paris] they hang a man first, and
try him afterwards.

7732 *The Sicilian*
Assassination is the quickest way.

7733 *Tartuffe*
I am not the less human for being devout.

7734 *Tartuffe*
God it is true, does some delights
condemn,

But 'tis not hard to come to terms with
Him.

7735 *Tartuffe*
It is public scandal that constitutes offence,
and to sin in secret is not to sin at all.

7736 *Tartuffe*
Man, I can assure you, is a nasty creature.

7737 *The Would-be Gentleman*
All that is not prose is verse; and all that is
not verse is prose.

7738 *The Would-be Gentleman*
Ah, it's a lovely thing, to know a thing or
two.

MOLLINEUX Mary 1651-1695
7739 *'Solitude'*
How sweet is harmless solitude!
What can its joys control?
Tumults and noise may not intrude,
To interrupt the soul.

MOLTKE Helmuth Von 1800-1891
7740 *Letter to Dr. J.K. Bluntschli*
Everlasting peace is a dream, and not even
a pleasant one; and war is a necessary part
of God's arrangement of the world ...
Without war the world would deteriorate
into materialism.

MONDALE Walter 1928-
7741
There will be no veterans of World War III.

MONKHOUSE William Cosmo 1840-
1901
7742 *Nonsense Rhymes*
There once was an old man of Lyme
Who married three wives at a time,
When asked 'Why a third?'
He replied, 'One's absurd!
And bigamy, Sir, is a crime!'

MONMOUTH Duke of 1649-1685
7743 *(to his executioner)*
Do not hack me as you did my Lord
Russell.

MONRO Harold 1879-1932
7744 *Milk for the Cat*
When the tea is brought at five o'clock,
And all the neat curtains are drawn with
care,

The little black cat with bright green eys
Is suddenly purring there.

7745 *Milk for the Cat*
The white saucer like some full moon
descends
At last from the clouds of the table above.

MONROE Marilyn 1926-1962
7746 *in Gentlemen Prefer Blondes*
"I always say a kiss on the hand might feel
very good, but a diamond tiara lasts
forever."

MONSELL John Samuel Bewley 1811-
1875
7747 *'Fight the good fight with all thy might'*
Fight the good fight with all thy might,
Christ is thy strength and Christ thy right;
Lay hold on life, and it shall be
Thy joy and crown eternally.

7748 *'O worship the Lord in the beauty of
holiness'*
O worship the Lord in the beauty of
holiness,
Bow down before him, his glory proclaim;
With gold of obedience and incense of
lowliness,
Kneel and adore him: the Lord is his name.

MONTAGU Ashley 1905-
7749
In Victorian times the purpose of life was
to develop a personality once and for all
and then stand on it.

7750
Today, while the titular head of the family
may still be the father, everyone knows
that he is little more than chairman, at
most, of the entertainment committee.

MONTAGU Lady Mary Wortley 1689-
1762
7751
I give myself, sometimes, admirable
advice, but I am incapable of taking it.

7752 *(attributed)*
This world consists of men, women, and
Herveys.

7753
People wish their enemies dead - but I do
not; I say give them the gout, give them

the stone!

7754 *'Answered, for Lord William Hamilton'*
But the fruit that can fall without shaking,
Indeed is too mellow for me.

7755 *To the Imitator of the First Satire of
Horace*
Satire should, like a polished razor keen,
Wound with a touch that's scarcely felt or
seen.

7756 *Letter to daughter Mary, Countess of
Bute*
Civility costs nothing and buys everything.

7757 *Letter to husband, Edward Wortley
Montagu*
General notions are generally wrong.

7758 *The Plain Dealer*
Let this great maxim be my virtue's guide:
In part she is to blame, who has been tried,
He comes too near, that comes to be
denied.

7759 *Six Town Eclogues 'The Lover'*
And we meet with champagne and a
chicken at last.

7760 *Six Town Eclogues 'The Lover'*
As Ovid has sweetly in parable told,
We harden like trees, and like rivers grow
cold.

7761 *Summary of Lord Lyttelton's Advice*
Be plain in dress, and sober in your diet;
In short, my deary! kiss me, and be quiet.

7762 *'Verses on Self-Murder'*
In chains and darkness, wherefore should I
stay,
And mourn in prison, while I keep the
key?

MONTAGUE C.E. 1867-1928
7763 *Disenchantment*
War hath no fury like a non-combatant.

7764 *Fiery Particles*
I was born below par to th' extent of two
whiskies.

MONTAIGNE Michel de 1533-1592
7765
There is no passion so much transports the
sincerity of judgement as doth anger.

7766
The Ancient Mariner said to Neptune
during a great storm, 'O God, you will
save me if you wish, but I am going to go
on holding my tiller straight.'

7767
All the fame I look for in life is to have
lived it quietly.

7768
If you press me to say why I loved him, I
can say no more than it was because he
was he, and I was I.

7769
There is no man so good, who, were he to
submit all his thoughts and actions to the
laws, would not deserve hanging ten times
in his life.

7770
Once conform, once do what others do
because they do it, and a kind of lethargy
steals over all the finer senses of the soul.

7771
Whatever is enforced by command is more
imputed to him who exacts than to him
who performs.

7772
No doctor takes pleasure in the health
even of his friends.

7773
It is commonly seen by experience that
excellent memories do often accompany
weak judgements.

7774
The beauty of stature is the only beauty of
men.

7775
No man is so exquisitely honest or upright
in living but that ten times in his life he
might not lawfully be hanged.

7776
There never were two opinions alike in all
the world, no more than two hours or two
grains: the most universal quality is
diversity.

7777
There is no course of life so weak and sottish as that which is managed by order, method and discipline.

7778
Philosophy is doubt.

7779
I have never seen a greater monster or miracle in the world than myself.

7780
I speak the truth, not so much as I would, but as much as I dare; and I dare a little more, as I grow older.

7781
When I religiously confess myself to myself, I find that the best virtue I have has in it some tincture of vice.

7782
A wise man sees as much as he ought, not as much as he can.

7783
The word is half his that speaks, and half his that hears it.

7784
I quote others in order to better express my own self.

7785 *Essays*
One should be ever booted and spurred and ready to depart.

7786 *Essays*
To make judgements about great and lofty things, a soul of the same stature is needed; otherwise we ascribe to them that vice which is our own.

7787 *Essays*
The ceaseless labour of your life is to build the house of death.

7788 *Essays*
The value of life lies not in the length of days but in the use you make of them; he has lived for a long time who has little lived. Whether you have lived enough depends not on the number of your years but on your will.

7789 *Essays*
It should be noted that children at play are not playing about; their games should be seen as their most serious-minded activity.

7790 *Essays*
There is scarcely any less bother in the running of a family than in that of an entire state. And domestic business is no less importunate for being less important.

7791 *Essays*
The greatest thing in the world is to know how to be oneself.

7792 *Essays*
Fame and tranquility can never be bedfellows.

7793 *Essays*
Living is my job and my art.

7794 *Essays*
Virtue shuns ease as a companion ... It demands a rough and thorny path.

7795 *Essays*
Our religion is made so as to wipe out vices; it covers them up, nourishes them, incites them.

7796 *Essays*
When I play with my cat, who knows whether she isn't amusing herself with me more than I am with her?

7797 *Essays*
Unless a man feels he has a good enough memory, he should never venture to lie.

7798 *Essays*
A woman who goes to bed with a man ought to lay aside her modesty with her skirt, and put it on again with her petticoat.

7799 *Essays*
A little of everything and nothing thoroughly.

7800 *Essays*
Life is a dream; when we sleep we are awake, and when awake we sleep.

7801 *Essays*
Que sais-je?
What do I know?

7802 *Essays*
It [marriage] is like a cage; one sees the birds outside desperate to get in, and those inside equally desperate to get out.

7803 *Essays*
The world is but a school of inquiry.

7804 *Essays*
Poverty of goods is easily cured; poverty of soul, impossible.

7805 *Essays*
It might well be said of me that here I have merely made up a bunch of other men's flowers, and provided nothing of my own but the string to bind them.

7806 *Essays*
A man who fears suffering is already suffering from what he fears.

MONTALE Eugenio 1896-1981
7807 *'Felicità raggiunta'*
Happiness, for you we walk on a knife edge. To the eyes you are a flickering light, to the feet, thin ice that cracks; and so may no one touch you who loves you.

MONTALVO Juan 1832-1889
7808
Old age is an island surrounded by death.

7809
There is nothing harder than the softness of indifference.

MONTESQUIEU Charles Baron de 1689-1755
7810
Republics are brought to their ends by luxury; monarchies by poverty.

7811
An empire founded by war has to maintain itself by war.

7812 *L'Esprit de lois, XI*
Liberty is the right to do everything which the laws allow.

7813 *Lettres Persanes*
Men should be bewailed at their birth, and not at their death.

7814 *Lettres Persanes*
There is a very good saying that if triangles invented a god, they would make him three-sided.

7815 *Pensées diverses 'Portrait de Montesquieu'*
I suffer from the disease of writing books and being ashamed of them when they are finished.

7816 *Pensées et fragments inédits*
Great lords have their pleasures, but the people have fun.

MONTGOMERY Lucy Maud 1874-1942
7817
Worrying helps you some. It seems as if you are doing something when you're worrying.

MONTGOMERY Robert 1807-1855
7818 *Luther: a Poem 'Man's Need and God's Supply'*
The solitary monk who shook the world.

7819 *The Omnipresence of the Deity*
And thou, vast ocean! on whose awful face Time's iron feet can print no ruin-trace.

MONTHERLANT Henri de 1896-1972
7820
Great ideas are not charitable.

MONTROND Casimir Comte de 1768-1843
7821 *(attributed)*
Have no truck with first impulses for they are always generous ones.

7822 *(attributed)*
If something pleasant happens to you, don't forget to tell it to your friends, to make them feel bad.

MONTROSE Percy
7823 *'Clementine'*
In a cavern, in a canyon,
Excavating for a mine,
Dwelt a miner, Forty-niner,
And his daughter, Clementine.
Oh, my darling, oh my darling, oh my darling Clementine!
Thou art lost and gone for ever, dreadful sorry, Clementine.

7824 *'Clementine'*
Light she was and like a fairy,
And her shoes were number nine;
Herring boxes without topses,
Sandals were for Clementine.

7825 *'Clementine'*
But I kissed her little sister,
And forgot my Clementine.

MOODIE Susanna 1803-1885
7826
When things come to the worst, they
generally mend.

MOODY D.L. 1837-1899
7827
If I take care of my character, my
reputation will take care of itself.

MOORE Brian 1921-
7828
We also serve who only punctuate.

MOORE Clement C. 1779-1863
7829 *'A Visit from St Nicholas'*
'Twas the night before Christmas, when all
through the house
Not a creature was stirring, not even a
mouse;
The stockings were hung by the chimney
with care,
In hopes that St Nicholas soon would be
there.

MOORE Edward 1712-1757
7830 *The Foundling*
This is adding insult to injuries.

7831 *The Foundling*
I am rich beyond the dreams of avarice.

MOORE George 1852-1933
7832
A literary movement consists of five or six
people who live in the same town and hate
each other cordially.

7833
Ireland is a fatal disease; fatal to
Englishmen and doubly fatal to Irishmen.

7834
No place in England where everyone can
go is considered respectable.

7835 *The Bending of the Bough*
All reformers are bachelors.

7836 *The Brook Kerith*
A man travels the world in search of what
he needs and returns home to find it.

7837 *Hail and Farewell: Ave*
Art must be parochial in the beginning to
become cosmopolitan in the end.

7838 *Impressions and Opinions 'Balzac'*
The lot of critics is to be remembered by
what they failed to understand.

MOORE Henry 1831-1895
7839
Now I really make the little idea from clay,
and I hold it in my hand. I can turn it,
look at it from underneath, see if from one
view, hold it against the sky, imagine it any
size I like, and really be in control, almost
like God creating something.

MOORE Marianne 1887-1972
7840
Beauty is everlasting
And dust is for a time.

7841
I'm troubled. I'm dissatisfied. I'm Irish.

7842
Poetry is all nouns and verbs.

7843 *'Poetry'*
I, too, dislike it: there are things that are
important beyond all this fiddle.
Reading it, however, with a perfect
contempt for it, one discovers in it, after
all, a place for the genuine.

7844 *'Poetry'*
Nor till the poets among us can be
'literalists of
the imagination' - above
insolence and triviality and can present
for inspection, imaginary gardens with real
toads in them, shall we have
it.

7845 *'Silence'*
My father used to say,
'Superior people never make long visits,
have to be shown Longfellow's grave
or the glass flowers at Harvard'.

7846 *'Silence'*
Nor was he insincere in saying, 'Make my
house your inn'.
Inns are not residences.

MOORE Mavor
7847
Vice is as much a part of human nature as
folly, and pornography may be as
necessary to vent vice as satire is to vent
folly.

MOORE Sparkle
7848
The Strip Club is another form of safe sex.

MOORE Sturge 1870-1944
7849 *'The Gazelles'*
Then, cleaving the grass, gazelles appear
(The gentler dolphins of kindlier waves)
With sensitive heads alert of ear;
Frail crowds that a delicate hearing saves.

MOORE Thomas 1779-1852
7850 *'Believe me, if all those endearing young
charms'*
Believe me, if all those endearing young
charms,
Which I gaze on so fondly today,
Were to change by tomorrow, and fleet in
my arms,
Like fairy gifts fading away!
Thou wouldst still be adored as this
moment thou art.

7851 *'Believe me, if all those endearing young
charms'*
No, the heart that has truly loved never
forgets,
But as truly loves on to the close,
As the sun-flower turns on her god, when
he sets,
The same look which she turned when he
rose.

7852 *'Farewell! - but whenever'*
You may break, you may shatter the vase,
if you will,
But the scent of the roses will hang round
it still.

7853 *The Fudge Family in Paris*
Who can help loving the land that has
taught us
Six hundred and eighty-five ways to dress

eggs?

7854 *The Fudge Family in Paris*
I may, without vanity, hint -
Though an angel should write, still 'tis
devils must print.

7855 *'The harp that once through Tara's halls'*
The harp that once through Tara's halls
The soul of music shed,
Now hangs as mute on Tara's walls
As if that soul were fled.
So sleeps the pride of former days,
So glory's thrill is o'er;
And hearts, that once beat high for praise,
Now feel that pulse no more.

7856 *Lalla Rookh 'The Fire-Worshippers'*
Like Dead Sea fruits, that tempt the eye,
But turn to ashes on the lips!

7857 *'Love's Young Dream'*
No, there's nothing half so sweet in life
As love's young dream.

7858 *'The Minstrel Boy'*
The Minstrel Boy to the war is gone,
In the ranks of death you'll find him;
His father's sword he has girded on,
And his wild harp slung behind him.

7859 *'Oft in the Stilly Night'*
Oft, in the stilly night,
Ere Slumber's chain has bound me,
Fond Memory brings the light
Of other days around me.

7860 *'Oh! blame not the bard'*
Oh! blame not the bard, if he fly to the
bowers,
Where Pleasure lies, carelessly smiling at
Fame.

7861 *'Oh! breathe not his name'*
Oh! breathe not his name, let it sleep in the
shade,
Where cold and unhonoured his relics are
laid.

7862 *'Rich and rare were the gems she wore'*
Rich and rare were the gems she wore,
And a bright gold ring on her wand she
bore.

7863 *'The time I've lost in wooing'*
My only books
Were woman's looks,
And folly's all they've taught me.

7864 *"Tis the last rose of summer'*
'Tis the last rose of summer
Left blooming alone;
All her lovely companions
Are faded and gone.

7865 *'The young May moon'*
Then awake! the heavens look bright, my dear;
'Tis never too late for delight, my dear;
And the best of all ways
To lengthen our days
Is to steal a few hours from the night, my dear!

MORDAUNT Thomas Osbert 1730-1809
7866
Sound, sound the clarion, fill the fife,
Throughout the sensual world proclaim,
One crowded hour of glorious life
Is worth an age without a name.

MORDDEN Ethan
7867
For most singers the first half of the career involves extending one's repertoire, the second half trimming it.

MORE Hannah 1745-1833
7868
In grief we know the worst of what we feel,
But who can tell the end of what we fear?

7869
Imagination frames events unknown,
In wild, fantastic shapes of hideous ruin,
And what it fears, creates.

7870
Going to the opera, like getting drunk, is a sin that carries its own punishment with it and that a very severe one.

7871 *'An Address to the Meeting in Spa Fields'*
For you'll ne'er mend your fortunes, nor help the just cause,
By breaking of windows, or breaking of laws.

7872 *Christian Morals*
Man cannot be safely trusted with a life of leisure.

7873 *Essays ... for Young Ladies 'On Dissipation'*
The prevailing manners of an age depend more than we are aware, or are willing to allow, on the conduct of the women; this is one of the principal hinges on which the great machine of human society turns.

7874 *Florio*
Small habits, well pursued betimes,
May reach the dignity of crimes.

7875 *Florio*
He liked those literary cooks
Who skim the cream of others' books;
And ruin half an author's graces
By plucking bon-mots from their places.

7876 *Moses in the Bulrushes*
Did not God
Sometimes withhold in mercy what we ask,
We should be ruined at our own request.

MORE Sir Thomas 1478-1535
7877
We may not look at our pleasure to go to heaven in feather-beds; it is not the way.

7878
Is not this house [the Tower of London] as nigh heaven as my own?

7879 *(to his executioner)*
Pluck up thy spirits, man, and be not afraid to do thine office; my neck is very short; take heed therefore thou strike not awry, for saving of thine honesty.

7880 *(to his executioner, pulling his beard aside)*
This hath not offended the king.

7881 *(to a friend who had versified a mediocre book)*
Yea, marry, now it is somewhat, for now it is rhyme; before, it was neither rhyme nor reason.

7882 *(on mounting the scaffold)*
I pray you, master Lieutenant, see me safe up, and my coming down let me shift for

my self.

7883 *Utopia*
Your sheep, that were wont to be so meek
and tame, and so small eaters, now, as I
hear say, be become so great devourers,
and so wild, that they eat up and swallow
down the very men themselves.

MORELL Thomas 1703-1784
7884 *Judas Maccabeus*
See the conquering hero comes!
Sound the trumpets, beat the drums!

MORGAN Arthur E. 1886-1956
7885
Lack of something to feel important about
is almost the greatest tragedy a man may
have.

MORGAN Augustus de 1806-1871
7886 *A Budget of Paradoxes*
Great fleas have little fleas upon their
backs to bite 'em,
And little fleas have lesser fleas, and so *ad
infinitum.*

MORGAN Charles Langbridge 1894-1958
7887 *(attributed)*
There is no surprise more magical than the
surprise of being loved: It is God's finger
on man's shoulder.

MORGAN J.P. 1837-1913
7888
Well, I don't know as I want a lawyer to
tell me what I cannot do. I hire him to tell
me how to do what I want to do.

MORGAN Robin 1941-
7889
Sisterhood is powerful.

MORGENSTERN Christian
7890
Home is not where you live but where
they understand you.

7891
Humour is the contemplation of the finite
from the point of view of the infinite.

7892
To me, the term 'middle-class' connotes a
safe, comfortable, middle-of-the-road
policy. Above all, our language is 'middle-

class' in the middle of our road. To drive it
to one side or the other or even off the
road, is the noblest task of the future.

MORLEY Christopher 1890-1957
7893
New York, the nation's thyroid gland.

7894
A town that has no ceiling price,
A town of double-talk;
A town so big men name her twice,
Like so; 'N'Yawk, N'Yawk.'

7895
We've had bad luck with our kids - they've
all grown up.

7896
All cities are mad: but the madness is
gallant. All cities are beautiful: but the
beauty is grim.

7897
The enemies of the future are always the
very nicest people.

7898
There are three ingredients in the good life;
learning, earning and yearning.

7899
Any man worth his salt has by the time he
is forty-five accumulated a crown of
thorns, and the problem is to learn to wear
it over one ear.

7900
No man is lonely while eating spaghetti - it
requires so much attention.

7901
We are only cave men who have lost their
cave.

7902
The courage of the poet is to keep ajar the
door that leads into madness.

7903
My theology, briefly,
Is that the universe
Was dictated
But not signed.

7904
There is only one success - to be able to spend your life in your own way.

7905
It is unfair to blame man too fiercely for being pugnacious; he learned the habit from nature.

7906 *Thunder on the Left*
Life is a foreign language: all men mispronounce it.

MORLEY Lord John 1838-1923
7907
Politics is a field where action is one long second best and where the choice constantly lies between two blunders.

7908
It makes all the difference in the world whether we put truth in the first place, or in the second place.

7909
He who hates vice hates men.

7910 *On Compromise*
You have not converted a man because you have silenced him.

7911 *Critical Miscellanies*
The golden Gospel of Silence is effectively compressed in thirty fine volumes.

MORLEY Robert 1908-1992
7912
We are articulate, but we are not particularly conversational. An Englishman won't talk for the sake of talking. He doesn't mind silence. But after the silence, he sometimes says something.

MORNAY Suzanne
7913
In extreme youth, in our most humiliating sorrow, we think we are alone. When we are older we find that others have suffered too.

MORPHY Countess
7914 *English Recipes*
The tragedy of English cooking is that 'plain' cooking cannot be entrusted to 'plain' cooks.

MORRIS Charles 1745-1838
7915 *The Contrast*
If one must have a villa in summer to dwell,
Oh give me the sweet shady side of Pall Mall!

7916 *'Country and Town'*
But a house is much more to my mind than a tree,
And for groves, O! a good grove of chimneys for me.

MORRIS Desmond 1928-
7917
Life is like a very short visit to a toyshop between birth and death.

7918 *The Human Zoo*
The city is not a concrete jungle, it is a human zoo.

7919 *The Naked Ape*
There are one hundred and ninety-three living species of monkeys and apes. One hundred and ninety-two of them are covered with hair. The exception is a naked ape self-named *Homo sapiens*.

MORRIS George Pope 1802-1864
7920 *'Woodman, Spare That Tree'*
Woodman, spare that tree!
Touch not a single bough!
In youth it sheltered me,
And I'll protect it now.

MORRIS James
7921
He was one of those men whose constitutional inability to make small talk forfeits all one's sympathy, and makes one think that social grace is sometimes a moral duty.

MORRIS Robert T.
7922
I hate funerals, and would not attend my own if it could be avoided, but it is well for every man to stop once in a while to think of what sort of a collection of mourners he is training for his final event.

MORRIS William 1834-1896
7923 *Chants for Socialists 'March of the Workers'*
What is this, the sound and rumour?

What is this that all men hear,
Like the wind in hollow valleys when the
storm is drawing near,
Like the rolling on of ocean in the eventide
of fear?
'Tis the people marching on.

7924 *A Dream of John Ball*
Fellowship is heaven, and lack of
fellowship is hell: fellowship is life, and
lack of fellowship is death: and the deeds
that ye do upon the earth, it is for
fellowship's sake that ye do them.

7925 *The Earthly Paradise*
Forget six counties overhung with smoke,
Forget the snorting steam and piston
stroke,
Forget the spreading of the hideous town;
Think rather of the pack-horse on the
down,
And dream of London, small and white
and clean,
The clear Thames bordered by its gardens
green.

7926 *The Earthly Paradise 'An Apology'*
The idle singer of an empty day.

7927 *The Earthly Paradise 'An Apology'*
Dreamer of dreams, born out of my due
time,
Why should I strive to set the crooked
straight?
Let it suffice me that my murmuring
rhyme
Beats with light wing against the ivory
gate,
Telling a tale not too importunate.

7928 *'The Haystack in the Floods'*
Had she come all the way for this,
To part at last without a kiss?

7929 *Hopes and Fears for Art*
Have nothing in your houses that you do
not know to be useful, or believe to be
beautiful.

7930 *News from Nowhere*
The reward of labour is life.

MORRISON Edmund
7931
Like stones, words are laborious and
unforgiving, and the fitting of them

together, like the fitting of stones, demands
great patience and strength of purpose and
particular skill.

MORRISON Jim 1943-1971
7932 *'Five to One'*
Five to one, baby, one in five,
No one here gets out alive ...
They got the guns but we got the numbers
Gonna win, yeah, we're taking over.

7933 *'Light My Fire'*
C'mon, baby, light my fire.

MORRISON Toni 1931-
7934
We die. That may be the meaning of our
lives. But we do language. That may be
the measure of our lives.

MORROW Dwight 1873-1931
7935
As I get older ... I become more convinced
that good government is not a substitute
for self-government.

7936
We judge ourselves by our motives and
others by their actions.

7937 *Letter to his son*
The world is divided into people who do
things and people who get the credit. Try,
if you can, to belong to the first class.
There's far less competition.

MORTIMER John 1923-
7938
The virtue of much literature is that it is
dangerous and may do you extreme harm.

7939
[Irritable judges] suffer from a bad case of
premature adjudication.

7940 *(attributed, of himself)*
Champagne socialist.

7941
Being successful in England is a dangerous
occupation.

7942 *Clinging to the Wreckage*
The law seems like a sort of maze through
which a client must be led to safety, a
collection of reefs, rocks, and underwater
hazards through which he or she must be

piloted.

7943 *Paradise Postponed*
They do you a decent death on the hunting-field.

7944 *A Voyage Round My Father*
At school I never minded the lessons. I just resented having to work terribly hard at playing.

7945 *A Voyage Round My Father*
No brilliance is needed in the law. Nothing but common sense, and relatively clean finger nails.

MORTON Rogers 1914-1979
7946 *(after losing primaries as Ford's campaign manager)*
I'm not going to rearrange the furniture on the deck of the Titanic.

MOSES Grandma 1860-1961
7947
I paint from the top down. First the sky, then the mountains, then the hills, then the houses, then the cattle, and then the people.

MOSES Ludwig van
7948
Government is the only institution that can take a valuable commodity like paper, and make it worthless by applying ink.

MOSES Robert 1888-1981
7949
Once you sink that first stake, they'll never make you pull it up.

MOSLEY Sir Oswald 1896-1980
7950
I am not, and never have been, a man of the right. My position was on the left and is now in the centre of politics.

MOSTEL Zero 1915-1977
7951
I wanted to say something about the universe. There's God, angels, plants ... and horseshit.

MOTHERWELL Robert 1915-1991
7952
Abstract art is uniquely modern. It is a fundamentally romantic response to

modern life - rebellious, individualistic, unconventional, sensitive, irritable.

MOTION Andrew 1952-
7953 *'Leaving Belfast'*
Each sudden gust of light explains itself as flames, but neither they, nor even

bombs redoubled on the hills tonight can quite include me in their fear. What does remains invisible, is lost in curt societies whose deaths become

revenge by morning, and whose homes are nothing more than all they pity most.

MOTLEY John Lothrop 1814-1877
7954
Give us the luxuries of life, and we will dispense with its necessities.

7955 *(of William of Orange)*
As long as he lived, he was the guiding-star of a whole brave nation, and when he died the little children cried in the streets.

MOULTON Lord 1844-1921
7956
Tyranny is yielding to the lust of governing.

MOUNTBATTEN Louis, Earl 1900-1979
7957
The nuclear arms race has no military purpose. Wars cannot be fought with nuclear weapons. Their existence only adds to our perils.

MOZART Wolfgang Amadeus 1756-1791
7958
I write as a sow piddles.

MUGABE Robert 1924-
7959
Cricket civilizes people and creates good gentlemen. I want everyone to play cricket in Zimbabwe; I want ours to be a nation of gentlemen.

MUGGERIDGE Malcolm 1903-1990
7960
When you reach your sixties, you have to decide whether you're going to be a sot or an ascetic. In other words if you want to go on working after you're sixty, some degree of asceticism is inevitable.

7961
Few men of action have been able to make a graceful exit at the appropriate time.

7962
Good taste and humour are a contradiction in terms, like a chaste whore.

7963
An orgy looks particularly alluring seen through the mists of righteous indignation.

7964 *The Infernal Grove*
To succeed pre-eminently in English public life it is necessary to conform either to the popular image of a bookie or of a clergyman; Churchill being a perfect example of the former, Halifax of the latter.

7965 *Tread Softly*
The orgasm has replaced the Cross as the focus of longing and the image of fulfilment.

7966 *Tread Softly (of Sir Anthony Eden)*
He was not only a bore; he bored for England.

MUIR Edwin 1887-1959
7967 *Journeys and Places 'Hölderlin's Journey'*
And without fear the lawless roads
Ran wrong through all the land.

MULLER Herbert J.
7968
Few have heard of Fra Luca Parioli, the inventor of double entry bookkeeping, but he has probably had more influence on human life than has Dante or Michelangelo.

MUMFORD Ethel Watts
7969
O wad some power the giftie gie us to see some people before they see us.

MUMFORD Lewis 1895-1990
7970
Our national flower is the concrete cloverleaf.

7971
One of the functions of intelligence is to take account of the dangers that come from trusting solely to the intelligence.

7972 *The Brown Decades*
Every generation revolts against its fathers and makes friends with its grandfathers.

MUNTHE Axel 1857-1949
7973
Christ - an anarchist who succeeded.

7974
A man can stand a lot as long as he can stand himself. He can live without hope, without friends, without books, even without music, as long as he can listen to his own thoughts.

MURDOCH Dame Iris 1919-
7975
We live in a fantasy world, a world of illusion. The great task in life is to find reality.

7976 *The Bell*
Dora Greenfield left her husband because she was afraid of him. She decided six months later to return to him for the same reason.

7977 *Nuns and Soldiers*
Only in our virtues are we original, because virtue is difficult ... Vices are general, virtues are particular.

7978 *'The Sublime and the Beautiful Revisited'*
Freedom is not choosing; that is merely the move that we make when all is already lost. Freedom is knowing and understanding and respecting things quite other than ourselves.

7979 *'The Sublime and the Good'*
Love is the extremely difficult realisation that something other than oneself is real.

MURRAY Jim
7980 *(on the death of Casey Stengel)*
Well, God is certainly getting an earful tonight.

MURRAY Lord William 1705-1793
7981 *(advice to newly appointed colonial governor)*
Consider what you think justice requires, and decide accordingly. But never give your reasons; for your judgement will probably be right, but your reasons will certainly be wrong.

MURROW Edward R. 1908-1965
7982
Everyone is a prisoner of his own experiences. No one can eliminate prejudices - just recognize them.

7983
He [Winston Churchill] mobilized the English language and sent it into battle to steady his fellow countrymen and hearten those Europeans upon whom the long dark night of tyranny had descended.

7984 *(of the Vietnam War)*
Anyone who isn't confused doesn't really understand the situation.

MURRY John Middleton 1889-1957
7985
There is nothing more dangerous to the formation of a prose style than the endeavour to make it poetic.

MUSSELMAN M.M.
7986
One of the best things about marriage is that it gets young people to bed at a decent hour.

MUSSET Alfred de 1810-1857
7987 *La Coupe et les lèvres*
I hate like death the situation of the plagiarist; the glass I drink from is not large, but at least it is my own.

7988 *'L'Espoir en Dieu'*
I can't help it, the idea of the infinite torments me.

7989 *Lorenzaccio*
Great artists have no country.

7990 *Rollo*
I have come too late into a world too old.

MUSSOLINI Benito 1883-1945
7991
If I advance, follow me! If I retreat, cut me down! If I die, avenge me!

7992
You know what I think about violence. For me it is profoundly moral - more moral than compromises and transactions.

7993 *(to a station-master)*
We must leave exactly on time ... From now on everything must function to perfection.

MUSSORGSKY Modeste Petrovich 1839-1881
7994
Art is not an end in itself, but a means of addressing humanity.

MUSTE A.J. 1885-1967
7995
There is no way to peace. Peace is the way.

NABOKOV Vladimir 1899-1977
7996
Genius is an African who dreams up snow.

7997
No one can any longer write in the fat style of Strauss. That was killed by Stravinsky. He stripped the body of much of its clothes. Music is the craft of building structures with sound and that is what Stravinsky represents.

7998 *Pale Fire*
Life is a great surprise. I do not see why death should not be an even greater one.

7999 *Speak, Memory*
The cradle rocks above an abyss, and common sense tells us that our existence is but a brief crack of light between two eternities of darkness.

8000 *Strong Opinions*
I think like a genius, I write like a distinguished author, and I speak like a child.

8001 *Strong Opinions*
A work of art has no importance whatever to society. It is only important to the individual, and only the individual reader is important to me.

NADER Ralph 1934-
8002
Unsafe at any speed.

NAIPAUL V.S. 1932-
8003
One always writes comedy at the moment of deepest hysteria.

NAIRN Ian 1930-
8004
If what is called development is allowed to multiply at the present rate, then by the end of the century Great Britain will consist of isolated oases of preserved monuments in a desert of wire, concrete roads, cosy plots and bungalows ... Upon this new Britain the *Review* bestows a name in the hope that it will stick - SUBTOPIA.

NAITO Fern
8005
When you've got them by their wallets, their hearts and minds will follow.

NAMATH Joe 1943-
8006
When you win, nothing hurts.

NANSEN Fridtjof 1861-1930
8007
Never stop because you are afraid - you are never so likely to be wrong. Never keep a line of retreat: it is a wretched invention. The difficult is what takes a little time; the impossible is what takes a little longer.

NAPOLÉON I (Bonaparte) 1769-1821
8008
In war, three-quarters turns on personal character and relations; the balance of manpower and materials counts only for the remaining quarter.

8009 *(attributed)*
An army marches on its stomach.

8010
L'Angleterre est une nation de boutiquiers.
England is a nation of shopkeepers.

8011
Soldiers, consider that from the summit of these pyramids, forty centuries look down upon you.

8012
Le courage de l'improviste.
Spontaneous courage.

8013 *(on the introduction of the metric system)*
Nothing is more contrary to the organization of the mind, of the memory,

and of the imagination ... The new system of weights and measures will be a stumbling block and the source of difficulties for several generations ... It's just tormenting the people with trivia!!!

8014 *Letter to Consul Cambacérès (of the Channel)*
It is a mere ditch, and will be crossed as soon as someone has the courage to attempt it.

8015 *Letter to Empress Josephine (justifying divorce)*
I still love you, but ...

8016 *Letter to J. Finckenstein*
It is easier to put up with unpleasantness from a man of one's own way of thinking than from one who takes an entirely different point of view.

8017 *Letter to the King of Holland*
A prince who gets a reputation for good nature in the first year of his reign, is laughed at in the second.

8018 *(attributed, but probably apocryphal)*
Not tonight, Josephine.

8019 *(reply to Spanish king)*
The bullet that is to kill me has not yet been moulded.

8020 *(after the retreat from Moscow)*
There is only one step from the sublime to the ridiculous.

8021 *(when asked how to deal with the Pope)*
As though he had 200,000 men.

NASH Ogden 1902-1971
8022
Middle age: when you're sitting at home on Saturday night and the telephone rings and you hope it isn't for you.

8023
Senescence begins
And middle age ends,
The day your descendants
Outnumber your friends.

8024
Another good thing about gossip is that it is within everybody's reach,
And it is much more interesting than any

other form of speech.

8025
Poets aren't very useful,
Because they aren't consumeful or very
produceful.

8026
Progress might have been all right once,
but it's gone on too long.

8027
Parsely
is gharsley.

8028
In the world of mules there are no rules.

8029
Purity is obscurity.

8030
Ask Daddy, He Won't Know.

8031 *The Canary*
The song of canaries
Never varies,
And when they're moulting
They're pretty revolting.

8032 *'The Cow'*
The cow is of the bovine ilk;
One end is moo, the other, milk.

8033 *England Expects*
Children aren't happy with nothing to
ignore,
And that's what parents were created for.

8034 *'Family Court'*
One would be in less danger
From the wiles of the stranger
If one's own kin and kith
Were more fun to be with.

8035 *'Lather as You Go'*
Beneath this slab
John Brown is stowed.
He watched the ads,
And not the road.

8036 *'Lines on Facing Forty'*
I have a bone to pick with Fate.
Come here and tell me, girlie,
Do you think my mind is maturing late,
Or simply rotted early?

8037 *'The Perfect Husband'*
He tells you when you've got on too much
lipstick,
And helps you with your girdle when
your hips stick.

8038 *'Plea for Less Malice Toward None'*
Any kiddie in school can love like a fool,
But hating, my boy, is an art.

8039 *'Reflections on Ice-breaking'*
Candy
Is dandy
But liquor
Is quicker.

8040 *'Samson Agonistes'*
I test my bath before I sit,
And I'm always moved to wonderment
That what chills the finger not a bit
Is so frigid upon the fundament.

8041 *'Song of the Open Road'*
I think that I shall never see
A billboard lovely as a tree.
Perhaps, unless the billboards fall,
I'll never see a tree at all.

8042 *'What's the Use?'*
Sure, deck your lower limbs in pants;
Yours are the limbs, my sweeting.
You look divine as you advance -
Have you seen yourself retreating?

NASHE Thomas 1567-1601
8043 *Summer's Last Will and Testament*
Beauty is but a flower
Which wrinkles will devour;
Brightness falls from the air;
Dust hath closed Helen's eye.
I am sick, I must die.
Lord have mercy on us.

8044 *Summer's Last Will and Testament*
From winter, plague and pestilence, good
lord, deliver us!

NATHAN George Jean 1882-1958
8045
Opening night is the night before the play
is ready to open.

8046
I drink to make other people interesting.

8047
Love demands infinitely less than
friendship.

NAVRATILOVA Martina 1956-
8048
The moment of victory is much too short
to live for that and nothing else.

NAYLOR James Ball 1860-1945
8049 *'King David and King Solomon'*
King David and King Solomon
Led merry, merry lives,
With many, many lady friends,
And many, many wives;
But when old age crept over them -
With many, many qualms! -
King Solomon wrote the Proverbs
And King David wrote the Psalms.

NEALE John Mason 1818-1866
8050
Good King Wenceslas looked out,
On the Feast of Stephen;
When the snow lay round about,
Deep and crisp and even.

8051
In his master's steps he trod,
Where the snow lay dinted.

8052
Jesusalem the golden,
With milk and honey blest,
Beneath thy contemplation
Sink heart and voice opprest.

NEEDHAM Richard J.
8053
People who are brutally honest get more
satisfaction out of the brutality than out of
the honesty.

8054
Love is a fever which marriage puts to bed
and cures.

8055
People are like birds - from a distance,
beautiful: from close up, those sharp beaks,
those beady little eyes.

8056
Power is a drug on which the politicians
are hooked. They buy it from the voters,
using the voters' own money.

8057
God punishes us mildly by ignoring our
prayers and severely by answering them.

8058
When a man tells me he's run out of steam
in the sex department, I'll tell him, 'Count
your blessings; you've escaped from the
clutches of a cruel tyrant. Enjoy!'

NEHRU Jawaharlal 1889-1964
8059
Democracy is good. I say this because
other systems are worse.

8060 *'Basic Approach'*
Democracy and socialism are means to an
end, not the end itself.

8061 *'Basic Approach'*
Normally speaking, it may be said that the
forces of a capitalist society, if left
unchecked, tend to make the rich richer
and the poor poorer and thus increase the
gap between them.

8062 *(following Gandhi's assassination)*
The light has gone out of our lives and
there is darkness everywhere.

NELLIST Dave 1952-
8063
The quickest way to become a left winger
in the Labour Party today is to stand still
for six months.

NELSON Horatio Lord 1758-1805
8064
In case signals can neither be seen nor
perfectly understood, no captain can do
very wrong if he places his ship alongside
the enemy.

8065
Something must be left to chance; nothing
is sure in a sea fight beyond all others.

8066
Close with a Frenchman, but out-
manoeuvre a   Russian.

8067
You must consider every man your enemy
who speaks ill of your king: and ... you
must hate a Frenchman as you hate the
devil.

8068 *(before the battle of the Nile)*
Before this time to-morrow I shall have
gained a peerage, or Westminster Abbey.

8069 *(at the battle of Trafalgar)*
England expects that every man will do his
duty.

8070 *(at the battle of Trafalgar)*
This is too warm work, Hardy, to last long.

8071 *(at the battle of Trafalgar)*
Thank God, I have done my duty.

8072 *(at the battle of Trafalgar)*
Kiss me, Hardy.

8073 *(putting telescope to his blind eye)*
I have a right to be blind sometimes ... I
really do not see the signal!

8074 *(when asked to cover the stars on his
uniform)*
In honour I gained them, and in honour I
will die with them.

NELSON John Kirk
8075
More and more these days I find myself
pondering on how to reconcile my net
income with my gross habits.

NERO AD 37-68
8076
What an artist dies with me!

NERVAL Gérard de 1808-1855
8077 *Les Chimères 'El Desdichado'*
I am the darkly shaded, the bereaved, the
inconsolate, the prince of Aquitaine, with
the blasted tower. My only *star* is dead,
and my star-strewn lute carries on it the
black *sun* of *melancholy*.

8078 *Les Chimères 'Le Christ aux Oliviers'*
God is dead! Heaven is empty - Weep,
children, you no longer have a father.

NEURATH Otto 1882-1945
8079 *Logical Positivism 'Protocal Sentences'*
We are like sailors who must rebuild their
ship on the open sea, never able to
dismantle it in dry-dock and to reconstruct
it there out of the best materials.

NEVILL Dorothy d.1913
8080
The real art of conversation is not only to
say the right thing in the right place but to
leave unsaid the wrong thing at the
tempting moment.

NEWBOLT Sir Henry 1862-1938
8081 *'Clifton Chapel'*
To set the cause above renown,
To love the game beyond the prize,
To honour, while you strike him down,
The foe that comes with fearless eyes.

8082 *'Drake's Drum'*
'Take my drum to England, hang et by the
shore,
Strike et when your powder's runnin' low;
If the Dons sight Devon, I'll quit the port
o' Heaven,
An' drum them up the Channel as we
drummed them long ago.'

8083 *'Drake's Drum'*
Drake he's in his hammock till the great
Armadas come.
(Capten, art tha sleepin' there below?)

8084 *'Drake's Drum'*
Call him on the deep sea, call him up the
Sound,
Call him when ye sail to meet the foe;
Where the old trade's plyin' an' the old
flag flyin'
They shall find him ware an' wakin', as
they found him long ago!

8085 *'He Fell Among Thieves'*
'Ye have robbed,' said he, 'ye have
slaughtered and made an end,
Take your ill-got plunder, and bury the
dead.'

8086 *'The Fighting Téméraire'*
Now the sunset breezes shiver,
And she's fading down the river,
But in England's song for ever
She's the Fighting Téméraire.

8087 *'Vitaï Lampada'*
There's a breathless hush in the Close to-
night -
Ten to make and the match to win -
A bumping pitch and a blinding light,
An hour to play and the last man in.

And it's not for the sake of a ribboned
coat,
Or the selfish hope of a season's fame,
But his Captain's hand on his shoulder
smote -
'Play up! play up! and play the game'.

8088 *'Vitaï Lampada'*
The river of death has brimmed its banks
And England's far and honour a name,
But the voice of a schoolboy rallies the
ranks.
'Play up! play up! and play the game!'

NEWLEY Anthony and BRICUSSE Leslie
1931- and 1931-
8089
Stop the world, I want to get off.

NEWLOVE John
8090
If you know nothing, be pleased to know
nothing.

NEWMAN Andrea
8091
Toothache doesn't stop hurting because
someone else has cancer.

NEWMAN Ernest 1868-1959
8092
The good composer is slowly discovered,
the bad composer is slowly found out.

NEWMAN John Henry, Cardinal 1801-
1890
8093
Let us act on what we have, since we have
not what we wish.

8094
We should ever conduct ourselves towards
our enemy as if he were one day to be our
friend.

8095
Growth is the only evidence of life.

8096
Reason is God's gift, but so are the
passions. Reason is as guilty as passion.

8097 *Apologia pro Vita Sua*
It is very difficult to get up resentment
towards persons whom one has never
seen.

8098 *Apologia pro Vita Sua*
There is such a thing as legitimate warfare:
war has its laws; there are things which
may fairly be done, and things which may
not be done ... He has attempted (as I may
call it) to *poison the wells*.

8099 *Apologia pro Vita Sua*
I will vanquish, not my Accuser, but my
judges.

8100 *Apologia pro Vita Sua*
Two and two only supreme and
luminously self-evident beings, myself and
my Creator.

8101 *Apologia pro Vita Sua*
Ten thousand difficulties do not make one
doubt.

8102 *Apologia pro Vita Sua*
The all-corroding, all-dissolving scepticism
of the intellect in religious enquiries.

8103 *The Dream of Gerontius*
Praise to the Holiest in the height,
And in the depth be praise;
In all his words most wonderful,
Most sure in all His ways.

8104 *'Faith and Reason, ...'*
When men understand what each other
mean, they see, for the most part, that
controversy is either superfluous or
hopeless.

8105 *The Idea of a University*
It is almost a definition of a gentleman to
say that he is one who never inflicts pain.

8106 *'Lead, kindly Light'*
Lead, kindly Light, amid the encircling
gloom,
Lead thou me on;
The night is dark, and I am far from home.

8107 *'Lead, kindly Light'*
I loved the garish day, and spite of fears,
Pride ruled my will: remember not past
years.

8108 *Letter to Mrs William Froude*
We can believe what we choose. We are
answerable for what we choose to believe.

8109 *Sermons Bearing on Subjects of the Day*
May He support us all the day long, till the
shades lengthen, and the evening comes,
and the busy world is hushed, and the
fever of life is over, and our work is done!
Then in His mercy may he give us a safe
lodging, and a holy rest, and peace at the
last.

8110 *'The Usurpations of Reason'*
It is as absurd to argue men, as to torture
them, into believing.

NEWMAN Paul 1925-
8111 *in Butch Cassidy and the Sundance Kid*
"He'll feel a lot better once we've robbed a
couple of banks."

NEWMAN Peter
8112
Power tends to connect; absolute power
connects absolutely.

NEWTON A. Edward
8113
The formula for complete happiness is to
be very busy with the unimportant.

NEWTON Sir Isaac 1642-1727
8114
I don't know what I may seem to the
world, but as to myself, I seem to have
been only like a boy playing on the sea-
shore and diverting myself in now and
then finding a smoother pebble or a
prettier shell than ordinary, whilst the
great ocean of truth lay all undiscovered
before me.

8115 *(to a dog who destroyed some of his work)*
O Diamond! Diamond! thou little knowest
the mischief done!

8116 *Letter to Edmond Halley*
Philosophy is such an impertinently
litigious lady that a man has as good be
engaged in law suits as have to do with
her.

8117 *Letter to Robert Hooke*
If I have seen further it is by standing on
the shoulders of giants.

8118 *Opticks*
Whence is it that Nature does nothing in
vain: and whence arises all that order and

beauty which we see in the world? ... does
it not appear from phenomena that there is
a Being incorporeal, living, intelligent,
omnipresent, who in infinite space, as it
were in his Sensory, sees the things
themselves intimately, and thoroughly
perceives them, and comprehends them
wholly.

8119 *Opticks*
The changing of bodies into light, and light
into bodies, is very comfortable to the
course of Nature, which seems delighted
with transmutations.

8120 *Principia Mathematica*
Every body continues in its state of rest, or
of uniform motion in a right line, unless it
is compelled to change that state by forces
impressed upon it.

8121 *Principia Mathematica*
The alteration of motion is ever
proportional to the motive force
impressed; and is made in the direction of
the right line in which that force is
impressed.

8122 *Principia Mathematica*
To every action there is always opposed an
equal reaction: or the mutual actions of
two bodies upon each other are always
equal, and directed to contrary parts.

8123 *Principia Mathematica*
Hypotheses non fingo.
I do not feign hypotheses.

NEWTON John 1725-1807
8124 *'Amazing grace'*
Amazing grace! how sweet the sound
That saved a wretch like me!
I once was lost, but now am found,
Was blind, but now I see.

8125 *'How sweet the name of Jesus sounds'*
How sweet the name of Jesus sounds
In a believer's ear!
It soothes his sorrows, heals his wounds,
And drives away his fear.

NICHOLAS I 1796-1855
8126
Turkey is a dying man. We may
endeavour to keep him alive, but we shall
not succeed. He will, he must die.

8127 *(attributed)*
Russia has two generals in whom she can confide - Generals Janvier [January] and Février [February].

NICHOLSON Jack 1937-
8128
You only lie to two people; your girlfriend and the police. Everyone else you tell the truth to.

NICIAS c.470-413 BC
8129
For a city consists in men, and not in walls nor in ships empty of men.

NICOLLE Charles 1866-1936
8130
Chance favours only those who know how to court her.

NICOLSON Sir Harold 1886-1968
8131
The worst thing, I fear, about being no longer young, is that one is no longer young.

8132
To be a good diarist, one must have a little snouty, sneaky mind.

8133 *(anticipating the aftermath of World War 2)*
We shall have to walk and live a Woolworth life hereafter.

8134 *Diaries and Letters*
I am haunted by mental decay such as I saw creeping over Ramsay MacDonald. A gradual dimming of the lights.

8135 *(of King George V)*
For seventeen years he did nothing at all but kill animals and stick in stamps.

8136 *Public Faces*
Ponderous and uncertain is that relation between pressure and resistance which constitutes the balance of power. The arch of peace is morticed by no iron tendons ... One night a handful of dust will patter from the vaulting: the bats will squeak and wheel in sudden panic: nor can the fragile fingers of man then stay the rush and rumble of destruction.

NIEBUHR Reinhold 1892-1971
8137
O God, give us serenity to accept what cannot be changed; courage to change what should be changed, and wisdom to distinguish the one from the other.

8138
The mastery of nature is vainly believed to be an adequate substitute for self-mastery.

8139
The sad duty of politics is to establish justice in a sinful world.

8140 *Children of Light and Children of Darkness*
Man's capacity for justice makes democracy possible, but man's inclination to injustice makes democracy necessary.

NIEMÖLLER Martin 1892-1984
8141
When Hitler attacked the Jews I was not a Jew, therefore, I was not concerned. And when Hitler attacked the Catholics, I was not a Catholic, and therefore, I was not concerned. And when Hitler attacked the unions and the industrialists, I was not a member of the unions and I was not concerned. Then, Hitler attacked me and the Protestant church - and there was nobody left to be concerned.

NIETZSCHE Friedrich 1844-1900
8142
What does not destroy me, makes me strong.

8143
In architecture the pride of man, his triumph over gravitation, his will to power, assume a visible form. Architecture is a sort of oratory of power by means of forms.

8144
Speaking generally, punishment hardens and numbs, it produces concentration, it sharpens the consciousness of alienation, it strengthens the power of resistance.

8145
Insanity in individuals is rare - but in groups, parties, nations, and epochs, it is the rule.

8146
When a hundred men stand together, each of them loses his mind and gets another one.

8147
The most unendurable thing, to be sure, the really terrible thing, would be a life without habits, a life which continually required improvisation.

8148
Our destiny rules over us, even when we are not yet aware of it; it is the future that makes laws for our today.

8149
The abdomen is the reason why man does not easily take himself for a god.

8150
Should not the giver be thankful that the receiver received? Is not giving a need? Is not receiving, mercy?

8151
To do great things is difficult, but to command great things is more difficult.

8152
It is not the strength, but the duration, of great sentiments that makes great men.

8153
Of what is great, one must either be silent, or speak with greatness - that means cynically and with innocence.

8154
The historian looks backward. In the end he also believes backward.

8155
The more you let yourself go, the less others let you go.

8156
A joke is an epigram on the death of a feeling.

8157
Not to he who is offensive to us are we most unfair, but to he who does not concern us at all.

8158
The lie is a condition of life.

8159
I understand by 'freedom of spirit' something quite definite - the unconditional will to say No, where it is dangerous to say No.

8160
He who has a why to live can bear with almost anyhow.

8161
The lonely one offers his hand too quickly to whomever he encounters.

8162
The advantage of a bad memory is that one enjoys several times the same good thing for the first time.

8163
A woman may very well form a friendship with a man, but for this to endure, it must be assisted by a little physical antipathy.

8164
Without music, life would be a mistake.

8165
When one has not had a good father, one must create one.

8166
There are no facts, only interpretations.

8167
One is healthy when one can laugh at the earnestness and zeal with which one has been hypnotized by any single detail of one's life.

8168
Never to talk of oneself is a form of hypocrisy.

8169
Sleeping is no mean art. For its sake one must stay awake all day.

8170
Profundity of thought belongs to youth, clarity of thought to old age.

8171
Ascetic: one who makes a necessity of virtue.

8172
When thou goest to woman, take thy whip.

8173
Has a woman who knew that she was well dressed ever caught a cold?

8174
A politician divides mankind into two classes: tools and enemies.

8175 *The Antichrist*
Woman was God's second blunder.

8176 *The Antichrist*
When a man is in love he endures more than at other times; he submits to everything.

8177 *Die fröhliche Wissenschaft*
God is dead: but considering the state the species Man is in, there will perhaps be caves, for ages yet, in which his shadow will be shown.

8178 *Die fröhliche Wissenschaft*
Morality is the herd-instinct in the individual.

8179 *Die fröhliche Wissenschaft*
The Christian resolution to find the world ugly and bad has made the world ugly and bad.

8180 *Die fröhliche Wissenschaft*
Believe me! The secret of reaping the greatest fruitfulness and the greatest enjoyment from life is *to live dangerously!*

8181 *Ecce Homo*
As an artist, a man has no home in Europe save in Paris.

8182 *Ecce Homo*
My time has not yet come either; some are born posthumously.

8183 *Jenseits von Gut und Böse*
He who fights with monsters might take care lest he thereby become a monster. And if you gaze for long into an abyss, the abyss gazes also into you.

8184 *Jenseits von Gut und Böse*
The thought of suicide is a great source of comfort: with it a calm passage is to be

made across many a bad night.

8185 *Jenseits von Gut und Böse*
Herren-Moral und Sklaven-Moral.
Master-morality and slave-morality.

8186 *Jenseits von Gut und Böse*
Is not life a hundred times too short for us to bore ourselves?

8187 *Menschliches, Allzumenschliches*
Wit is the epitaph of an emotion.

8188 *Thus spoke Zarathustra*
I teach you the superman. Man is something to be surpassed.

NIGHTINGALE Earl
8189
Success is the progressive realization of a worthy ideal.

NIGHTINGALE Florence 1820-1910
8190
The very first requirement in a hospital is that it should do the sick no harm.

8191 *Notes on Nursing*
No *man*, not even a doctor, ever gives any other definition of what a nurse should be than this - 'devoted and obedient'. This definition would do just as well for a porter. It might even do for a horse. It would not do for a policeman.

8192 *(on the Order of Merit being brought to her home)*
Too kind, too kind.

NIN Anaïs 1903-1977
8193
A war regarded as inevitable or even probable, and therefore much prepared for, has a very good chance of eventually being fought.

8194
It is the function of art to renew our perception. What we are familiar with we cease to see. The writer shakes up the familiar scene, and as if by magic, we see a new meaning in it.

NIXON Richard 1913-1944
8195
I let the American people down, and I have to carry that burden for the rest of

my life. My political life is over. I will never again have an opportunity to serve in any official position. Maybe I can give a little advice from time to time.

8196
Those who hate you don't win unless you hate them - and then you destroy yourself.

8197
The people's right to change what does not work is one of the greatest principles of our system of government.

8198
You know very well that whether you are on page one or page thirty depends on whether they fear you. It is just as simple as that.

8199
The great silent majority.

8200
I welcome this kind of examination because people have got to know whether or not their President is a crook. Well, I'm not a crook.

8201
When the President does it, that means that it is not illegal.

8202
I brought myself down. I gave them a sword. And they stuck it in.

8203 *(farewell address)*
This country needs good farmers, good businessmen, good plumbers, good carpenters.

8204 *(on Watergate)*
There can be no whitewash at the White House.

NIZER Louis 1902-
8205
In cross-examination, as in fishing, nothing is more ungainly than a fisherman pulled into the water by his catch.

NOCHLIN Linda
8206
Safe taste is bad taste.

NOEL Thomas 1799-1861
8207 *'The Pauper's Drive'*
Rattle his bones over the stones;
He's only a pauper, whom nobody owns!

NOLTE Dorothy Law
8208
If a child lives with approval, he learns to live with himself.

NORDEN Dennis
8209 *(dictum on television scripts)*
We don't want it good - we want it Tuesday.

NORFOLK Charles Howard, Duke of 1746-1815
8210
If a man is to go to the devil, he may as well go thither from the House of Lords as from any other place on earth.

NORRIS Kathleen 1880-
8211
Just the knowledge that a good book is awaiting one at the end of a long day makes that day happier.

8212
There is no solitude in the world like that of the big city.

8213
Marriage; a job. Happiness or unhappiness has nothing to do with it.

NORTH Christopher 1785-1854
8214
His majesty's dominions, on which the sun ever sets.

8215
Laws were made to be broken.

8216
Insultin the sun, and quarrellin wi' the equawtor.

8217
Animosities are mortal, but the Humanities live for ever.

8218
Such accidents will happen in the best-regulated families.

8219
I cannot sit still, James, and hear you abuse the shopocracy.

NORTHCLIFFE Lord 1865-1922
8220
The power of the press is very great, but not so great as the power of suppress.

8221
When I want a peerage, I shall buy it like an honest man.

NORTON Caroline 1808-1877
8222 *'Not Lost but Gone Before'*
For death and life, in ceaseless strife,
Beat wild on this world's shore,
And all our calm is in that balm -
Not lost but gone before.

NORWORTH Jack 1879-1959
8223 *'Shine On, Harvest Moon'*
Oh, shine on, shine on, harvest moon
Up in the sky.
I ain't had no lovin'
Since April, January, June, or July.

NOVALIS 1772-1801
8224
Character is perfectly educated will.

8225
Not only England, but every Englishman is an island.

8226 *Heinrich von Ofterdingen*
I often feel, and ever more deeply I realise, that fate and character are the same conception.

8227 *(of Spinoza, attributed)*
A God-intoxicated man.

NYE Bill
8228 *Autobiography*
I have been told that Wagner's music is better than it sounds.

NYE Edgar Wilson
8229
There must be at least 500 million rats in the United States; of course, I am speaking only from memory.

OATES Captain Lawrence 1880-1912
8230 *(last words)*
I am just going outside and may be some time.

O'BRIEN Edna 1936-
8231
August is a wicked month.

O'BRIEN Flann 1911-1966
8232 *The Hard Life*
It is not that I half knew my mother. I knew half of her: the lower half - her lap, legs, feet, her hands and wrists as she bent forward.

8233 *At Swim-Two-Birds*
The conclusion of your syllogism, I said lightly, is fallacious, being based upon licensed premises.

8234 *At Swim-Two-Birds*
A pint of plain is your only man.

O'CASEY Sean 1880-1964
8235
You cannot put a rope around the neck of an idea: you cannot put an idea up against a barrack-square wall and riddle it with bullets: you cannot confine it in the strongest prison cell that your slaves could ever build.

8236 *Juno and the Paycock*
The whole worl's in a state o' chassis!

8237 *Juno and the Paycock*
The Polis as Polis, in this city, is Null an' Void!

8238 *(of P.G. Wodehouse)*
English literature's performing flea.

8239 *The Plough and the Stars*
There's no reason to bring religion into it. I think we ought to have as great a regard for religion as we can, so as to keep it out of as many things as possible.

8240 *The Plough and the Stars*
It's my rule never to lose me temper till it would be dethrimental to keep it.

OCHS Adolph S. 1858-1935
8241 *(motto of the New York Times)*
All the news that's fit to print.

O'CONNELL Daniel 1775-1847
8242
The Englishman has all the qualities of a

poker except its occasional warmth.

8243
Whatever little we have gained, we have
gained by agitation, while we have
uniformly lost by moderation.

8244
Peel's smile: like the silver plate on a
coffin.

O'CONNOR Frank 1903-1966
8245
No man is as anti-feminist as a really
feminine woman.

ODETS Clifford 1906-1963
8246
Sex - the poor man's polo.

O'DONNELL Emmett
8247
Retirement: statutory senility.

O'FAOLAIN Sean 1900-
8248
An Irish queer: a fellow who prefers
women to drink.

8249
Celibacy bestows on a man the qualified
freedom of a besieged city where one
sometimes has to eat rats.

8250
Love lives in sealed bottles of regret.

OGBURN Jr. Charleton
8251
Happiness to a dog is what lies on the
other side of a door.

OGILVY David 1911-
8252 *(advice to advertising copywriters)*
The consumer is not a moron; she's your
wife.

OGILVY James 1664-1730
8253 *(as he signed the Act of Union)*
Now there's ane end of ane old song.

O'HARA Frank 1926-1966
8254
It is easy to be beautiful; it is difficult to
appear so.

O'HARA John 1905-1970
8255 *The Portable F. Scott Fitzgerald*
An artist is his own fault.

O'HARA Neal
8256
We forget that money gives its value - that
someone exchanged work for it.

O'HARA Theodore 1820-1867
8257 *'The Bivouac of the Dead'*
Sons of the dark and bloody ground.

O'KEEFE Patrick 1872-1934
8258 *(slogan for the Society of American
Florists)*
Say it with flowers.

O'KEEFFE John 1747-1833
8259 *The Agreeable Surprise*
Amo, amas, I love a lass,
As a cedar tall and slender;
Sweet cowslip's grace
Is her nom'native case,
And she's of the feminine gender.

8260 *The Irish Mimic*
Fat, fair and forty were all the toasts of the
young men.

OLDMAN Gary
8261 *in Prick Up Your Ears*
"I'm from the gutter and don't you forget
it, because I won't."

OLIVER Frederick Scott 1864-1934
8262 *The Endless Adventure*
A wise politician will never grudge a
genuflexion or a rapture if it is expected of
him by prevalent opinion.

OLIVIER Sir Laurence 1907-1989
8263
Shakespeare - the nearest thing in
incarnation to the eye of God.

8264
Acting is a masochistic form of
exhibitionism. It is not quite the
occupation of an adult.

8265 *(appealing on behalf of the Rose Theatre
remains)*
Can a muse of fire exist under a ceiling of
commerce?

8266 *(introduction to his screen adaptation of Hamlet)*
The tragedy of a man who could not make up his mind.

8267 *(after a performance as 'Othello')*
I know it was wonderful, but I don't know how I did it.

8268 *in Rebecca*
"I'm asking you to marry me, you little fool"

OLSEN Ken 1926-
8269 *(whilst President of Digital Equipment Corp 1977)*
There is no reason why anyone would want to have a computer in their home.

O'MALLEY Austin
8270
The best blood will sometimes get into a fool or a mosquito.

8271
A hole is nothing at all, but you can break your neck in it.

ONASSIS Aristotle 1906-1975
8272
The secret of business is to know something that nobody else knows.

ONASSIS Jacqueline 1929-1994
8273 *The Fitzgeralds and the Kennedys*
It was a very spasmodic courtship, conducted mainly at long distance with a great clanking of coins in dozens of phone booths.

O'NEAL Ryan
8274 *in Love Story*
"Love means never having to say you're sorry."

O'NEIL Max
8275
Flirtation - attention without intention.

O'NEILL Eugene 1888-1953
8276
Man's loneliness is but his fear of life.

8277
The child was diseased at birth - stricken with an hereditary ill that only the most vital men are able to shake off. I mean poverty - the most deadly and prevalent of all diseases.

8278
The iceman cometh.

8279
A long day's journey into night.

8280 *Marco Millions*
Life is perhaps most wisely regarded as a bad dream between two awakenings, and every day is a life in miniature.

8281 *Mourning becomes Electra*
The sea hates a coward!

ONO Yoko 1933-
8282
Woman is the nigger of the world.

OPIE John 1761-1807
8283 *(asked with what he mixed his colours)*
I mix them with my brains, sir.

OPPENHEIMER J. Robert 1904-1967
8284 *(of Albert Einstein)*
Any man whose errors take ten years to correct, is quite a man.

8285 *Open Mind*
In some sort of crude sense which no vulgarity, no humour, no overstatement can quite extinguish, the physicists have known sin; and this is a knowledge which they cannot lose.

ORBACH Susie 1946-
8286
Fat is a feminist issue.

ORCZY Baroness 1865-1947
8287 *The Scarlet Pimpernel*
We seek him here, we seek him there,
Those Frenchies seek him everywhere.
Is he in heaven? - Is he in hell?
That demmed, elusive Pimpernel?

O'REILLY J.B. 1844-1890
8288 *In Bohemia*
The organized charity, scrimped and iced,
In the name of a cautious, statistical Christ.

ORTEGA y GASSET José 1883-1955
8289 *La Rebelión de las Masas*
Civilization is nothing more than the effort to reduce the use of force to the last resort.

8290 *Meditaciones del Quijote*
I am I plus my surroundings, and if I do
not preserve the latter I do not preserve
myself.

ORTON Joe 1933-1967
8291 *Entertaining Mr Sloane*
I'd the upbringing a nun would envy ...
Until I was fifteen I was more familiar with
Africa than my own body.

8292 *Entertaining Mr. Sloane*
Even if he thee worshipped with his body,
his mind would be elsewhere.

8293 *Loot*
Every luxury was lavished on you -
atheism, breast-feeding, circumcision.

8294 *Loot*
Policemen, like red squirrels, must be
protected.

8295 *Loot*
Reading isn't an occupation we encourage
among police officers. We try to keep the
paper work down to a minimum.

8296 *What the Butler Saw*
You were born with your legs apart.
They'll send you to the grave in a Y-
shaped coffin.

ORTON William A.
8297
If you keep your mind sufficiently open,
people will throw a lot of rubbish into it.

ORWELL George 1903-1950
8298
Most people get a fair amount of fun out of
their lives, but on balance life is suffering
and only the very sound or the very
foolish imagine otherwise.

8299
In our age there is no such thing as
'keeping out of politics'. All issues are
political issues.

8300
Liberal - a power worshipper without
power.

8301
International sport is war without
shooting.

8302
No doubt alcohol, tobacco, and so forth,
are things that a saint must avoid, but
sainthood is also a thing that human
beings must avoid.

8303
The great enemy of clear language is
insincerity. When there is a gap between
one's real and one's declared aims, one
turns as if it were instinctively to long
words and exhausted idioms, like a
cuttlefish squirting out ink.

8304
Whatever is funny is subversive, every
joke is ultimately a custard pie ... A dirty
joke is a sort of mental rebellion.

8305
Keep the aspidistra flying.

8306 *(attributed)*
Advertising is the rattling of a stick inside
a swill bucket.

8307 *Animal Farm*
Man is the only creature that consumes
without producing.

8308 *Animal Farm*
Four legs good, two legs bad.

8309 *Animal Farm*
All animals are equal but some animals are
more equal than others.

8310 *Collected Essays*
Good prose is like a window-pane.

8311 *Coming up For Air*
I'm fat, but I'm thin inside. Has it ever
struck you that there's a thin man inside
every fat man, just as they say there's a
statue inside every block of stone?

8312 *(last words in his notebook)*
At 50, everyone has the face he deserves.

8313 *The Lion and the Unicorn*
Probably the battle of Waterloo *was* won on
the playing-fields of Eton, but the opening
battles of all subsequent wars have been
lost there.

8314 *Nineteen Eighty-Four*
BIG BROTHER IS WATCHING YOU.

8315 *Nineteen Eighty-Four*
War is peace. Freedom is slavery.
Ignorance is strength.

8316 *Nineteen Eighty-Four*
Doublethink means the power of holding
two contradictory beliefs in one's mind
simultaneously, and accepting both of
them.

8317 *Nineteen Eighty-Four*
Power is not a means, it is an end. One
does not establish a dictatorship in order
to safeguard a revolution; one makes the
revolution in order to establish the
dictatorship.

8318 *Nineteen Eighty-Four*
If you want a picture of the future, imagine
a boot stamping on a human face - for
ever.

8319 *Polemic, May*
The quickest way of ending a war is to lose
it.

8320 *The Road to Wigan Pier*
A person of bourgeois origin goes through
life with some expectation of getting what
he wants, within reasonable limits. Hence
the fact that in times of stress 'educated'
people tend to come to the front.

8321 *The Road to Wigan Pier*
In a Lancashire cotton-town you could
probably go for months on end without
once hearing an 'educated' accent, whereas
there can hardly be a town in the South of
England where you could throw a brick
without hitting the niece of a bishop.

8322 *The Road to Wigan Pier*
The typical Socialist is ... a prim little man
with a white-collar job, usually a secret
teetotaller and often with vegetarian
leanings, with a history of Nonconformity
behind him, and, above all, with a social
position which he has no intention of
forfeiting.

8323 *The Road to Wigan Pier*
To the ordinary working man, the sort you
would meet in any pub on Saturday night,
Socialism does not mean much more than
better wages and shorter hours and
nobody bossing you about.

8324 *The Road to Wigan Pier*
The high-water mark, so to speak, of
Socialist literature is W.H. Auden, a sort of
gutless Kipling.

8325 *The Road to Wigan Pier*
We of the sinking middle class ... may sink
without further struggles into the working
class where we belong, and probably when
we get there it will not be so dreadful as
we feared, for, after all, we have nothing to
lose but our aitches.

8326 *Shooting an Elephant*
Serious sport has nothing to do with fair
play. It is bound up with hatred, jealousy,
boastfulness, and disregard of all the rules.

8327 *Shooting an Elephant*
In our time, political speech and writing
are largely the defence of the indefensible.

8328 *Shooting an Elephant*
Political language ... is designed to make
lies sound truthful and murder
respectable, and to give an appearance of
solidity to pure wind.

8329 *Shooting an Elephant*
Saints should always be judged guilty
until they are proved innocent.

OSBORN Robert
8330
America once had the clarity of a pioneer
axe.

OSBORNE John 1929-
8331
Monarchy is the gold filling in the mouth
of decay.

8332 *The Entertainer*
Don't clap too hard - it's a very old
building.

8333 *The Entertainer*
Thank God we're normal,
Yes, this is our finest shower!

8334 *The Entertainer*
But I have a go, lady, don't I? I'ave a go. I
do.

8335 *Look Back in Anger*
His knowledge of life and ordinary human
beings is so hazy, he really deserves some

sort of decoration for it - a medal inscribed 'For Vaguery in the Field'.

8336 *Look Back in Anger*
Slamming their doors, stamping their high heels, banging their irons and saucepans - the eternal flaming racket of the female.

8337 *Look Back in Anger*
I don't think one 'comes down' from Jimmy's university. According to him, it's not even red brick, but white tile.

8338 *Look Back in Anger*
They spend their time mostly looking forward to the past.

8339 *Look Back in Anger*
There aren't any good, brave causes left. If the big bang does come, and we all get killed off, it won't be in aid of the old-fashioned, grand design. It'll just be for the Brave New Nothing-very-much-thank-you. About as pointless and inglorious as stepping in front of a bus.

8340 *Time Present*
She's like the old line about justice - not only must be done, but must be seen to be done.

O'SHAUGHNESSY Arthur 1844-1881
8341 *'Ode'*
We are the music makers,
We are the dreamers of dreams ...
We are the movers and shakers
Of the world for ever, it seems.

8342 *'Ode'*
For each age is a dream that is dying,
Or one that is coming to birth.

OSLER Sir William 1849-1919
8343
The Scots are the backbone of Canada. They are all right in their three vital parts - head, heart and haggis.

8344
It is strange how the memory of a man may float to posterity on what he would have himself regarded as the most trifling of his works.

8345
It is much more important to know what sort of a patient has a disease than what sort of a disease a patient has.

8346
The desire to take medicine is perhaps the greatest feature which distinguishes man from animals.

8347
One of the first duties of the physician is to educate the masses not to take medicine.

8348
In science the credit goes to the man who convinces the world, not to the man to whom the idea first occurs.

8349
Look wise, say nothing, and grunt. Speech was given to conceal thought.

8350 *Aphorisms from his Bedside Teachings*
That man can interrogate as well as observe nature, was a lesson slowly learned in his evolution.

8351 *Aphorisms from his Bedside Teachings*
One finger in the throat and one in the rectum makes a good diagnostician.

8352 *Science and Immortality*
The natural man has only two primal passions, to get and beget.

OTIS James 1725-1783
8353 *(Watchword of the American Revolution)*
Taxation without representation is tyranny.

O'TOOLE Peter 1932-
8354
Relationships get more difficult as you get older. The idea now of beginning to go through all that again is unsupportable, so I don't bother.

OTWAY Thomas 1652-1685
8355 *Venice Preserved*
No praying, it spoils business.

OUIDA 1839-1908
8356
The longest absence is less perilous to love than the terrible trials of incessant proximity.

OVERBURY Thomas 1581-1613
8357
The man who has not anything to boast of but his illustrious ancestors is like a potato - the only good belonging to him is underground.

OVERSTREET Bonaro
8358
Psychiatrists today ... see the irrational hostility that people everywhere vent upon one another as chiefly projected self-hate.

OVERSTREET Harry A. 1876-1970
8359
The immature mind hops from one thing to another; the mature mind seeks to follow through.

8360
Newspapers have developed what might be called a vested interest in catastrophe. If they can spot a fight, they play up that fight. If they can uncover a tragedy, they will headline that tragedy.

OVID 43 BC-AD c.17
8361
Judgement of beauty can err, what with the wine and the dark.

8362
Chance is always powerful. Let your hook be always cast. In the pool where you least expect it, will be a fish.

8363
If you want to be loved, be lovable.

8364
In an easy cause any man may be eloquent.

8365
A woman is always buying something.

8366
Whether they give or refuse, women are glad to have been asked.

8367 *Ars Amatoria*
It is convenient that there be gods, and, as it is convenient, let us believe that there are.

8368 *Ars Amatoria*
Perhaps my name too will be linked with theirs.

8369 *Epistulae Ex Ponto*
Though the strength is lacking, yet the willingness is commendable.

8370 *Epistulae Ex Ponto*
Dripping water hollows out a stone, a ring is worn away by use.

8371 *Metamorphoses*
You will go most safely by the middle way.

8372 *Metamorphoses*
Plenty has made me poor.

8373 *Metamorphoses*
I see the better things, and approve; I follow the worse.

8374 *Metamorphoses*
Time the devourer of everything.

8375 *Remedia Amoris*
You who seek an end of love, love will yield to business: be busy, and you will be safe.

OWEN David 1938-
8376
Very few wars are brought to an end tidily.

OWEN John c.1563-1622
8377 *Epigrams*
God and the doctor we alike adore
But only when in danger, not before;
The danger o'er, both are alike requited,
God is forgotten, and the Doctor slighted.

OWEN Robert 1771-1858
8378 *(to W. Allen)*
All the world is queer save thee and me, and even thou art a little queer.

OWEN Wilfred 1893-1918
8379
My subject is War, and the pity of War. The Poetry is in the pity.

8380
All a poet can do today is warn.

8381 *'Anthem for Doomed Youth'*
What passing-bells for these who die as cattle?
Only the monstrous anger of the guns.

Only the stuttering rifles' rapid rattle
Can patter out their hasty orisons.
No mockeries now for them; no prayers
nor bells,
Nor any voice of mourning save the choirs
The shrill, demented choirs of wailing
shells;
And bugles calling for them from sad
shires.

8382 *'Anthem for Doomed Youth'*
The pallor of girls' brows shall be their
pall;
Their flowers the tenderness of patient
minds,
And each slow dusk a drawing-down of
blinds.

8383 *'Futility'*
Move him into the sun -
Gently its touch awoke him once,
At home, whispering of fields half-sown.

8384 *'Greater Lover'*
Red lips are not so red
As the stained stones kissed by the English
dead.

8385 *'Strange Meeting'*
'Strange friend,' I said, 'here is no cause to
mourn.'
'None,' said that other, 'save the undone
years,
The hopelessness. Whatever hope is
yours,
Was my life also.'

OXENSTIERNA Count 1583-1654
8386 *Letter to his son*
Dost thou not know, my son, with how
little wisdom the world is governed?

OZ Amos 1939-
8387
The death of a parent makes you ready for
the call 'Next please'.

PACAUD George W.
8388
Why inflict pain on oneself, when so many
others are ready to save us the trouble?

PACHET Pierre
8389
Louis Pasteur's theory of germs is
ridiculous fiction.

PACINO Al 1940-
8390 *in The Godfather*
"My father made him an offer he couldn't
refuse."

PACKARD Vance 1914-
8391 *(study of the advertising industry)*
The hidden persuaders.

PADEREWSKI Ignacy Jan 1860-1941
8392
Before I was a genius I was a drudge.

PAGE Irvine H.
8393
I came, I saw, I concurred.

PAGE Shebly
8394
The number of agency people required to
shoot a commercial on location is in direct
proportion to the mean temperature of the
location.

PAGE William Tyler 1868-1942
8395 *American's Creed*
A government of the people, by the
people, for the people, whose just powers
are derived from the consent of the
governed.

8396 *American's Creed*
A perfect Union, one and inseparable,
established upon those principles of
freedom, equality, justice, and humanity
for which American patriots sacrificed
their lives and fortunes.

PAGNOL Marcel 1895-1974
8397 *Marius*
Honour is like a match, you can only use it
once.

8398 *Topaze*
It's better to choose the culprits than to
seek them out.

PAIGE Satchel 1906-1982
8399
Never let your head hang down. Never
give up and sit down and grieve. Find
another way. And don't pray when it rains
if you don't pray when the sun shines.

8400
Never look behind you. Something may
be gaining on you.

8401
If your stomach disputes you, lie down
and pacify it with cool thoughts.

8402
(Airplanes) may kill you, but they ain't
likely to hurt you.

PAINE Thomas 1737-1809
8403
Those who expect to reap the blessings of
freedom must, like men, undergo the
fatigue of supporting it.

8404 *The Age of Reason*
Infidelity does not consist in believing, or
in disbelieving, it consists in professing to
believe what one does not believe.

8405 *The Age of Reason*
Any system of religion that has any thing
in it that shocks the mind of a child cannot
be a true system.

8406 *The Age of Reason*
The sublime and the ridiculous are often
so nearly related, that it is difficult to class
them separately. One step above the
sublime, makes the ridiculous; and one
step above the ridiculous, makes the
sublime again.

8407 *Common Sense*
Government, even in its best state, is but a
necessary evil; in its worst state, an
intolerable one.

8408 *The Crisis*
These are the times that try men's souls.
The summer soldier and the sunshine
patriot will, in this crisis, shrink from the
service of their country.

8409 *(of Edmund Burke)*
As he rose like a rocket, he fell like the
stick.

8410 *Letter ... on the Invasion of England*
The religion of humanity.

8411 *The Rights of Man*
Lay then the axe to the root, and teach
governments humanity. It is their

sanguinary punishments which corrupt
mankind.

8412 *The Rights of Man*
Titles are but nicknames, and every
nickname is a title.

8413 *The Rights of Man*
When, in countries that are called civilized,
we see age going to the workhouse and
youth to the gallows, something must be
wrong in the system of government.

8414 *The Rights of Man*
My country is the world, and my religion
is to do good.

PALAFOX José de 1780-1847
8415 *(at the siege of Saragossa)*
Guerra a cuchillo.
War by the knife.

PALEY Grace
8416
All that is really necessary for survival of
the fittest, it seems, is an interest in life,
good, bad or peculiar.

PALEY William 1743-1805
8417 *Principles of Moral and Political
Philosophy*
Who can refute a sneer?

PALMA Brian de
8418
No Art has a shorter life than Political Art.

PALMER Lilli
8419
I sweat. If anything comes easy to me, I
mistrust it.

PALMER Samuel 1805-1881
8420
A picture has been said to be something
between a thing and a thought.

PALMERSTON Lord 1784-1865
8421
We have no eternal allies and we have no
perpetual enemies. Our interests are
eternal and perpetual, and those interests
it is our duty to follow.

8422
What is merit? The opinion one man
entertains of another.

8423
The function of a government is to calm, rather than to excite agitation.

8424 *(of Foreign Office handwriting)*
Iron railings leaning out of the perpendicular.

8425 *(last words)*
Die, my dear Doctor, that's the last thing I shall do!

8426 *(of a projected Palmerston-Disraeli coalition)*
You may call it combination, you may call it the accidental and fortuitous concurrence of atoms.

8427 *(attributed, when asked whether English has a word for sensibilité)*
Yes we have. Humbug.

PANCHATANTRA
8428
A great man does not lose his self-possession when he is afflicted; the ocean is not made muddy by the falling in of its banks.

8429
One should seek for the salutary in the unpleasant: if it is there, it is after all nectar. One should seek for the deceitful in the pleasant: if it is there it is after all poison.

PANKHURST Dame Christabel 1880-1958
8430 *Unshackled*
Never lose your temper with the Press or the public is a major rule of political life.

8431 *Votes for Women*
We are here to claim our right as women, not only to be free, but to fight for freedom. That it is our right as well as our duty.

PARISH Mitchell
8432 *'Deep Purple'*
When the deep purple falls over sleepy garden walls,
And the stars begin to flicker in the sky,
Thru' the mist of a memory you wander back to me,
Breathing my name with a sigh.

PARKER Charlie 1920-1955
8433
Music is your own experience, your thoughts, your wisdom. If you don't live it it won't come out of your horn.

PARKER Dorothy 1893-1967
8434
They sicken of the calm that know the storm.

8435
Where, unwilling, dies the rose,
Buds the new, another year.

8436
It cost me never a stab nor squirm
To tread by chance upon a worm.
'Aha, my little dear' I say,
'Your clan will pay me back one day.'

8437
He and I had an office so tiny that an inch smaller and it would have been adultery.

8438
Where's the man could ease the heart
Like a satin gown?

8439
I shall stay the way I am
Because I do not give a damn.

8440
There's a hell of a distance between wisecracking and wit. Wit has truth in it; wisecracking is simply callisthenics with words.

8441 *(attributed)*
If all the girls attending the Yale Prom were laid end to end, I wouldn't be at all surprised.

8442 *'Ballade of a Great Weariness'*
Scratch a lover, and find a foe.

8443 *'Comment'*
Oh, life is a glorious cycle of song,
A medley of extemporanea;
And love is a thing that can never go wrong;
And I am Marie of Roumania.

8444 *'Inventory'*
Four be the things I'd been better without:
Love, curiosity, freckles, and doubt.

8445 *(of Katherine Hepburn)*
She ran the whole gamut of the emotions
from A to B.

8446 *'Here Lies'*
And I'll stay off Verlaine too; he was
always chasing Rimbauds.

8447 *'Here Lies'*
Sorrow is tranquillity remembered in
emotion.

8448 *'News Item'*
Men seldom make passes
At girls who wear glasses.

8449 *'Résumé'*
Poisons pain you;
Rivers are damp;
Acid stains you;
And drugs cause cramp.
Guns aren't lawful;
Nooses give;
Gas smells awful;
You might as well live.

8450 *(suggested epitaph for herself)*
Excuse My Dust.

8451 *'Unfortunate Coincidence'*
By the time you say you're his,
Shivering and sighing
And he vows his passion is
Infinite, undying -
Lady, make a note of this:
One of you is lying.

PARKER Martin 1600-1656
8452 *'The Valiant Sailors'*
You gentlemen of England
Who live at home at ease,
How little do you think
On the dangers of the seas.

PARKER Ross and CHARLES Hugh
1914-1974 and 1907-
8453 *'There'll always be an England'*
There'll always be an England
While there's a country lane,
Wherever there's a cottage small
Beside a field of grain.

PARKINSON Northcote 1909-1993
8454
Expansion means complexity and
complexity decay.

8455 *The Law and the Profits*
Expenditure rises to meet income.

8456 *Parkinson's Law*
Work expands so as to fill the time
available for its completion.

8457 *Parkinson's Law*
Time spent on any item of the agenda will
be in inverse proportion to the sum
involved.

8458 *Parkinson's Law*
The man who is denied the opportunity of
taking decisions of importance begins to
regard as important the decisions he is
allowed to take.

8459 *Parkinson's Law*
Men enter local politics solely as a result of
being unhappily married.

PARNELL Charles Stewart 1846-1891
8460
No man has a right to fix the boundary of
the march of a nation; no man has a right
to say to his country - thus far shalt thou
go and no further.

PARNELL Thomas 1679-1718
8461
Let time that makes you homely, make you
sage.

PARR Samuel 1747-1825
8462 *(of Dr Johnson)*
Now that the old lion is dead, every ass
thinks he may kick at him.

PARRIS Matthew 1949-
8463
Being an MP feeds your vanity and starves
your self respect.

PARTRIDGE Marianne
8464
As a woman, to be competitive is to be
passive.

PASCAL Blaise 1623-1662
8465
No animal admires another animal.

8466
The majority is the best way, because it is
visible, and has strength to make itself
obeyed. Yet it is the opinion of the least

able.

8467
If a soldier or labourer complains of the hardship of his lot, set him to do nothing.

8468
Two things control man's nature: instinct and experience.

8469
The last advance of reason is to recognize that it is surpassed by innumerable things; it is feeble if it cannot realize that.

8470
All our reasoning ends in surrender to feeling.

8471
Our own interests are still an exquisite means for dazzling our eyes agreeably.

8472
Let is not be said that I have said nothing new. The arrangement of the material is new.

8473 *Pensées*
The last thing one knows in constructing a work is what to put first.

8474 *Pensées*
When we see a natural style, we are quite surprised and delighted, for we expected to see an author and we find a man.

8475 *Pensées*
How vain painting is, exciting admiration by its resemblance to things of which we do not admire the originals.

8476 *Pensées*
Had Cleopatra's nose been shorter, the whole face of the world would have changed.

8477 *Pensées*
The eternal silence of these infinite spaces [the heavens] terrifies me.

8478 *Pensées*
On mourra seul.
We shall die alone.

8479 *Pensées*
The heart has its reasons which reason knows nothing of.

8480 *Pensées*
Man is only a reed, the weakest thing in nature; but he is a thinking reed.

8481 *Pensées*
Continual eloquence is tedious.

8482 *Pensées*
The *self* is hateful.

8483 *Pensées*
Comfort yourself, you would not seek me if you had not found me.

8484 *Pensées*
Not to care for philosophy is to be a true philosopher.

8485 *Pensées*
The more intelligence one has the more people one finds original. Commonplace people see no difference between men.

8486 *The Provincial Letters*
I have made this [letter] longer than usual, only because I have not had the time to make it shorter.

PASQUA Charles 1927-
8487
Fear of the policeman is the beginning of wisdom.

PASTERNAK Boris 1890-1960
8488
In every generation there has to be some fool who will speak the truth as he sees it.

8489 *Doctor Zhivago*
Man is born to live, not to prepare for life.

8490 *Doctor Zhivago*
Most people experience love, without noticing that there is anything remarkable about it.

8491 *Doctor Zhivago*
I don't like people who have never fallen or stumbled. Their virtue is lifeless and it isn't of much value. Life hasn't revealed its beauty to them.

8492 *Doctor Zhivago*
Art always serves beauty, and beauty is the joy of possessing form, and form is the key to organic life since no living thing can exist without it.

8493 *Doctor Zhivago*
Yet the order of the acts is planned
And the end of the way inescapable.
I am alone; all drowns in the Pharisees'
hyprocrisy.
To live your life is not as simple as to cross
a field.

8494 *Doctor Zhivago*
Love is not weakness. It is strong. Only
the sacrament of marriage can contain it.

8495 *'My Sister Life'*
My sister life's in flood today, she's broken
her waves over us all in the spring rain.

8496 *'When It Clears Up'*
World, nature, Universe's Essence,
With secret trembling, to the end,
I will thy long and moving service
In tears of happiness attend.

8497 *'When I Grow Weary'*
In time to come, I tell them, we'll be equal
to any living now. If cripples, then
no matter; we shall just have been run over
by 'New Man' in the wagon of his 'Plan'.

8498 *(to the woman who inspired 'Lara' in Dr. Zhivago)*
Let me lock your beauty
In the dark tower of a poem.

PASTEUR Louis 1822-1895
8499
Let me tell you the secret that has led me
to my goal. My strength lies solely in my
tenacity.

8500
Blessed is he who carries within himself a
god and an ideal and who obeys it - an
ideal of art, of science, or gospel virtues.
Therein lie the springs of great thoughts
and great actions.

8501
In the field of observation, chance favours
the prepared mind.

8502
There are no such things as applied
sciences, only applications of science.

PATER Walter 1839-1894
8503
All art constantly aspires towards the
condition of music.

8504 *(of the Mona Lisa)*
She is older than the rocks among which
she sits; like the vampire, she has been
dead many times, and learned the secrets
of the grave.

8505 *Studies in the History of the Renaissance*
To burn always with this hard, gemlike
flame, to maintain this ecstasy, is success in
life.

PATERSON 'Banjo' 1864-1941
8506 *'Waltzing Matilda'*
Once a jolly swagman camped by a
billabong,
Under the shade of a coolibah tree;
And he sang as he watched and waited till
his 'Billy' boiled:
'You'll come a waltzing, Matilda, with me.'

PATMORE Coventry 1823-1896
8507 *The Angel in the House*
We love, Fool, for the good we do,
Not that which unto us is done!

8508 *The Angel in the House*
'I saw you take his kiss!' ''Tis true.'
'O modesty!' ''Twas strictly kept:
He thought me asleep; at least, I knew
He thought I thought he thought I slept.'

8509 *The Angel in the House*
A woman is a foreign land,
Of which, though there he settle young,
A man will ne'er quite understand
The customs, politics and tongue.

8510 *'Olympus'*
Some dish more sharply spiced than this
Milk-soup men call domestic bliss.

8511 *The Victories of Love*
He that but once too nearly hears
The music of forfended spheres
Is thenceforth lonely, and for all
His days as one who treads the Wall
Of China, and, on this hand, sees
Cities and their civilities
And, on the other, lions.

PATTON George S. 1885-1945
8512
Courage is fear holding on a minute
longer.

8513
Never tell people how to do things. Tell
them what to do and they will surprise
you with their ingenuity.

PAUL Elliot 1891-1958
8514
Patience makes a woman beautiful in
middle age.

PAUL Leslie 1905-1985
8515
Angry young man.

PAUL Saint AD 3-68
8516
Faith is the substance of things hoped for,
the evidence of things not seen.

PAVESE Cesare
8517
Every luxury must be paid for, and
everything is a luxury, starting with being
in the world.

8518
Whatever people may say, the fastidious
formal manner of the upper classes is
preferable to the slovenly easygoing
behaviour of the common middle class. In
moments of crisis, the former know how to
act, the latter become uncouth brutes.

PAYN James 1830-1898
8519
I had never had a piece of toast
Particularly long and wide,
But fell upon the sanded floor,
And always on the buttered side.

PAYNE J.H. 1791-1852
8520 *Clari, or, The Maid of Milan 'Home,
Sweet Home'*
Mid pleasures and palaces though we may
roam,
Be it ever so humble, there's no place like
home.

PAZ Octavio 1914-
8521
Solitude is the profoundest fact of the
human condition. Man is the only being
who knows he is alone.

8522
Our democratic capitalist society has
converted Eros into an employee of
Mammon.

PEACOCK Thomas Love 1785-1866
8523 *Gryll Grange*
A Sympathizer would seem to imply a
certain degree of benevolent feeling.
Nothing of the kind. It signifies a ready-
made accomplice in any species of political
villainy.

8524 *'Love and Age'*
But though first love's impassioned
blindness
Has passed away in colder light,
I still have thought of you with kindness,
And shall do, till our last good-night.

8525 *Melincourt*
Marriage may often be a stormy lake, but
celibacy is almost always a muddy
horsepond.

8526 *'The Misfortunes of Elphin'*
Not drunk is he who from the floor
Can rise alone and still drink more;
But drunk is he, who prostrate lies,
Without the power to drink or rise.

8527 *'The Misfortunes of Elphin'*
The mountain sheep are sweeter,
But the valley sheep are fatter;
We therefore deemed it meeter
To carry off the latter.

8528 *Nightmare Abbey*
Laughter is pleasant, but the exertion is too
much for me.

8529 *Nightmare Abbey*
He was sent, as usual, to a public school,
where a little learning was painfully
beaten into him, and from thence to the
university, where it was carefully taken out
of him.

PEARSON Hesketh 1887-1964
8530 *Common Misquotations*
Misquotation is, in fact, the pride and
privilege of the learned. A widely-read
man never quotes accurately, for the rather

obvious reason that he has read too widely.

8531 *The Pilgrim Daughters*
There is no stronger craving in the world
than that of the rich for titles, except
perhaps that of the titled for riches.

PEARSON Lester 1897-1972
8532
The strongest pressure in the world can be
friendly pressure.

8533 *(defining attitude toward U.S.)*
The situation is one something like living
with your wife. Sometimes it is difficult
and even irritating to live with her, but it is
always impossible to live without her.

PEARSON Maryon
8534
Behind every great man there is a
surprised woman.

PEEL Paul
8535
It is no rest to be idle.

PEEL Robert 1788-1850
8536
Public opinion is a compound of folly,
weakness, prejudice, wrong feeling, right
feeling, obstinacy, and newspaper
paragraphs.

PEELE George c.1556-1596
8537 *The Hunting of Cupid*
What thing is love for (well I wot) love is a
thing.
It is a prick, it is a sting,
It is a pretty, pretty thing;
It is a fire, it is a coal
Whose flame creeps in at every hole.

8538 *The Old Wive's Tale*
When as the rye reach to the chin,
And chopcherry, chopcherry ripe within,
Strawberries swimming in the cream,
And schoolboys playing in the stream,
Then O, then O, then O, my true love said,
Till that time come again,
She could not live a maid.

8539 *Polyhymnia*
Goddess, allow this aged man his right,
To be your beadsman now that was your
knight.

PÉGUY Charles 1873-1914
8540
When a man dies, he does not just die of
the disease he has: he dies of his whole
life.

8541
It has never been given to a man to attain
at once his happiness and his salvation.

8542
One must always tell what one sees.
Above all, which is more difficult, one
must always see what one sees.

8543
Short of genius, a rich man cannot imagine
poverty.

8544 *Basic Verities*
He who does not bellow the truth when he
knows the truth makes himself the
accomplice of liars and forgers.

8545 *Basic Verities*
Tyranny is always better organised than
freedom.

8546 *Basic Verities*
The sinner is at the heart of Christianity ...
No one is as competent as the sinner in
matters of Christianity. No one, except a
saint.

PEI Mario 1901-1978
8547
Good architecture lets nature in.

PEMBROKE Henry Herbert, 2nd Earl of
c.1534-1601
8548
A parliament can do any thing but make a
man a woman, and a woman a man.

PEMBROKE Henry Herbert, 10th Earl of
1734-1794
8549
Dr Johnson's sayings would not appear so
extraordinary, were it not for his bow-wow
way.

PENDENYS Arthur 1865-1946
8550
A good meal makes a man feel more
charitable toward the whole world than
any sermon.

PENN William 1644-1718
8551
Avoid popularity; it has many snares, and no real benefit.

8552 *No Cross, No Crown*
No pain, no palm; no thorns, no throne; no gall, no glory; no cross, no crown.

8553 *Some Fruits of Solitude*
It is a reproach to religion and government to suffer so much poverty and excess.

8554 *Some Fruits of Solitude*
Men are generally more careful of the breed of their horses and dogs than of their children.

PENROSE Roger 1931-
8555 *The Emperor's New Mind*
Consciousness ... is the phenomenon whereby the universe's very existence is made known.

PEPYS Samuel 1633-1703
8556 *Diary*
Strange the difference of men's talk!

8557 *Diary*
And so to bed.

8558 *Diary*
I went out to Charing Cross, to see Major-general Harrison hanged, drawn, and quartered; which was done there, he looking as cheerful as any man could do in that condition.

8559 *Diary*
A good honest and painful sermon.

8560 *Diary*
If ever I was foxed it was now.

8561 *Diary*
But methought it lessened my esteem of a king, that he should not be able to command the rain.

8562 *Diary*
I see it is impossible for the King to have things done as cheap as other men.

8563 *Diary*
But Lord! to see the absurd nature of Englishmen, that cannot forbear laughing and jeering at everything that looks strange.

8564 *Diary*
My wife, who, poor wretch, is troubled with her lonely life.

8565 *Diary*
A woman sober, and no high flyer, as he calls it.

8566 *Diary*
Most of their discourse was about hunting, in a dialect I understand very little.

8567 *Diary*
While we were talking came by several poor creatures carried by, by constables, for being at a conventicle ... I would to God they would either conform, or be more wise, and not be catched!

8568 *Diary*
Strange to see how a good dinner and feasting reconciles everybody.

8569 *Diary*
Strange to say what delight we married people have to see these poor fools decoyed into our condition.

8570 *Diary*
Music and women I cannot but give way to, whatever my business is.

8571 *Diary*
But it is pretty to see what money will do.

8572 *Diary*
Home, and, being washing-day, dined upon cold meat.

8573 *Diary (ad fin)*
And so I betake myself to that course, which is almost as much as to see myself go into my grave - for which, and all the discomforts that will accompany my being blind, the good God prepare me!

8574 *Diary (of Nell Gwynne)*
Pretty witty Nell.

PERCIVAL Lloyd
8575
The physically fit can enjoy their vices.

PERELMAN S.J. 1904-1979
8576
There is such a thing as too much couth.

8577
Crazy like a fox.

8578 *Quotations for Speakers and Writers*
Love is not the dying moan of a distant
violin - it's the triumphant twang of a
bedspring.

PERES Shimon 1923-
8579
A leader who rides to war is always
having applause; a leader who rides to
peace is always being criticized.

8580
Peace is made with yesterday's enemies.
What is the alternative?

8581
The peace process is like a wedding night
in a minefield.

PERICLES c.495-429 BC
8582
We do not imitate, but are a model to
others.

8583
For famous men have the whole earth as
their memorial.

8584 *(funeral oration)*
Our love of what is beautiful does not lead
to extravagance; our love of the things of
the mind does not make us soft.

PERKINS Anthony 1932-1992
8585 *in Psycho*
"A boy's best friend is his mother."

PERKINS Maxwell 1884-1947
8586
Every good thing that comes is
accompanied by trouble.

8587
I believe the writer ... should always be the
final judge. I have always held to that
position and have sometimes seen books
hurt thereby, but at least as often helped.
The book belongs to the author.

8588
You have to throw yourself away when
you write.

8589 *(advice to Marcia Davenport)*
Just get it down on paper, and then we'll
see what to do with it.

PERLMAN Itzhak 1945-
8590
Ask many of us who are disabled what we
would like in life and you would be
surprised how few would say, 'Not to be
disabled'. We accept our limitations.

PERRONET Edward 1726-1792
8591 *'All hail the power of Jesus' Name'*
All hail the power of Jesus' Name;
Let Angels prostrate fall;
Bring forth the royal diadem
To crown Him Lord of all.

PERRY Jimmy
8592 *'Who do you think you are kidding,
Mister Hitler'*
Who do you think you are kidding, Mister
Hitler?
If you think we're on the run?
We are the boys who will stop your little
game
We are the boys who will make you think
again.

PERSE St. John 1887-1975
8593
The only menace is inertia.

PERSIUS AD 34-62
8594 *Satires*
And don't consult anyone's opinions but
your own.

8595 *Satires*
Let them recognize virtue and rot for
having lost it.

8596 *Satires*
Confront disease at its onset.

8597 *Satires*
Live with yourself: get to know how
poorly furnished you are.

PERSONS Ted
8598
Things ain't what they used to be.

PÉTAIN Henri Philippe 1856-1951
8599
To write one's memoirs is to speak ill of

everybody except oneself.

PETER Irene
8600
Ignorance is no excuse, it's the real thing.

PETER Laurence 1910-1990
8601
If we lacked imagination enough to foresee something better, life would indeed be a tragedy.

8602
When I want your opinion I'll give it to you.

8603
Psychiatry enables us to correct our faults by confessing our parents' shortcomings.

8604
Early to bed, early to rise, work like hell, and advertise.

8605
The cave-dweller's wife complained that he hadn't dragged her anywhere in months.

8606
Work is accomplished by those employees who have not yet reached their level of incompetence.

8607 *The Peter Principle*
In a hierarchy every employee tends to rise to his level of incompetence.

PETRONIUS d. AD 65
8608
Delight of lust is gross and brief
And weariness treads on desire.

8609 *Satyricon*
He's gone to join the majority [the dead].

8610 *Satyricon*
Horace's careful felicity.

PETROWSKY Christina
8611
Autumn is the bite of a harvest apple.

PETTITO Anthony J.
8612
The best way to bring up some children is short.

PFIZER Beryl
8613
All the movies used to be 'colossal'. Now they're all 'frank'. I think I liked 'colossal' better.

8614
A little public scandal is good once in a while - takes the tension out of the news.

8615
I wonder what language truck drivers are using, now that everyone is using theirs?

PHAEDRUS fl.c.AD 8
8616
Everyone ought to bear patiently the results of his own conduct.

PHELPS Edward John 1822-1900
8617
The man who makes no mistakes does not usually make anything.

PHELPS William Lyon
8618
This is the final test of a gentleman: his respect for those who can be of no possible service to him.

8619
The belief that youth is the happiest time of life is founded upon a fallacy. The happiest person is the person who thinks the most interesting thoughts, and we grow happier as we grow older.

PHILBY Kim 1912-1988
8620
To betray, you must first belong.

PHILIP 'Jack' 1840-1900
8621 *(at the battle of Santiago)*
Don't cheer, men; those poor devils are dying.

PHILIP Prince, Duke of Edinburgh 1921-
8622
When a man opens the car door for his wife, it's either a new car or a new wife.

PHILIPS Ambrose c.1675-1749
8623 *The First Pastoral*
The flowers anew, returning seasons bring;
But beauty faded has no second spring.

8624 *'A Winter-Piece'*
There solid billows of enormous size,
Alps of green ice, in wild disorder rise.

PHILLIPS H.I. 1887-1965
8625
Oratory: the art of making deep noises
from the chest sound like important
messages from the brain.

PHILLIPS Morgan 1902-1963
8626
The Labour Party owes more to
Methodism than to Marxism.

PHILLIPS Stephen 1864-1915
8627 *Ulysses*
Behold me now
A man not old, but mellow, like good
wine.
Not over-jealous, yet an eager husband.

PHILLIPS Wendell 1811-1884
8628
What is defeat? Nothing but education,
nothing but the first step toward
something better.

8629
One on God's side is a majority.

8630
Law is nothing unless close behind it
stands a warm, living public opinion.

8631
Governments exist to protect the rights of
minorities. The loved and the rich need no
protection - they have many friends and
few enemies.

8632
Politics is but the common pulse beat.

8633
Every step of progress the world has made
has been from scaffold to scaffold, and
from stake to stake.

8634
We live under a government of men and
morning newspapers.

8635
Every man meets his Waterloo at last.

PIAZZOLLA Aslor
8636
Good music is everything that swings.
Mozart also swings.

PICASSO Pablo 1881-1973
8637
Art washes away from the soul the dust of
everyday life.

8638
Every child is an artist. The problem is
how to remain an artist once he grows up.

8639
I paint objects as I think them, not as I see
them.

8640
I do not seek. I find.

8641
Everyone wants to understand painting.
Why don't they try to understand the
singing of birds? People love the night, a
flower, everything that surrounds them
without trying to understand them. But
painting - that they *must* understand.

8642
Painting is a blind man's profession. He
paints not what he sees, but what he feels,
what he tells himself about what he has
seen.

8643
Painting is just another way of keeping a
diary.

8644
Photographers, along with dentists, are the
two professions never satisfied with what
they do. Every dentist would like to be a
doctor and inside every photographer is a
painter trying to get out.

8645
Taste is the enemy of creativeness.

8646
It takes a long time to become young.

8647
We all know that Art is not truth. Art is a
lie that makes us realize truth.

8648
God is really only another artist. He invented the giraffe, the elephant, and the cat. He has no real style. He just goes on trying other things.

8649
Every positive value has its price in negative terms ... The genius of Einstein leads to Hiroshima.

PIERCE Lorne
8650
A publisher is somebody looking for someone who has something to say.

PINDAR 518-438 BC
8651
Learn what you are, and be such.

8652 *Olympian Odes*
Water is best. But gold shines like fire blazing in the night, supreme of lordly wealth.

8653 *Pythian Odes*
My soul, do not seek immortal life, but exhaust the realm of the possible.

PINDAR Peter 1738-1819
8654 *Expostulatory Odes*
Care to our coffin adds a nail no doubt;
And ev're grin, so merry, draws one out.

8655 *(to the Royal Academicians)*
What rage for fame attends both great and small!
Better be damned than mentioned not at all!

PINERO Sir Arthur Wing 1855-1934
8656
How many 'coming men' has one known? Where on earth do they all go to?

8657
I believe the future is only the past again, entered through another gate.

8658 *Second Mrs Tanqueray*
From forty to fifty a man is at heart either a stoic or a satyr.

8659 *Second Mrs Tanqueray*
I love fruit, when it is expensive.

PINOCHET Augusto 1915-
8660
There have never been dictatorships here. I am a democrat.

PINTER Harold 1930-
8661
One way of looking at speech is to say it is a constant stratagem to cover nakedness.

8662 *The Caretaker*
Them bastards at the monastery let me down again.

8663 *The Homecoming*
Apart from the known and the unknown, what else is there?

8664 *(on being asked what his plays were about)*
The weasel under the cocktail cabinet.

PIRANDELLO Luigi 1867-1936
8665
You too must not count overmuch on your reality as you feel it today, since, like that of yesterday, it may prove an illusion for you tomorrow.

PIRSIG Robert M. 1928-
8666 *Zen and the Art of Motorcycle Maintenance*
That's the classical mind at work, runs fine inside but looks dingy on the surface.

PITT William (The Elder) 1708-1778
8667
The atrocious crime of being a young man ... I shall neither attempt to palliate nor deny.

8668
The poorest man may in his cottage bid defiance to all the forces of the Crown. It may be frail - its roof may shake - the wind may blow through it - the storm may enter - the rain may enter - but the King of England cannot enter!

8669
Confidence is a plant of slow growth in an aged bosom: youth is the season of credulity.

8670
Unlimited power is apt to corrupt the minds of those who possess it.

8671
There is something behind the throne greater than the King himself.

8672
We have a Calvinistic creed, a Popish liturgy, and an Arminian clergy.

8673
You cannot conquer America.

8674
I invoke the genius of the Constitution!

8675
The parks are the lungs of London.

8676 *(attributed)*
Our watchword is security.

PITT William (The Younger) 1759-1806
8677
Necessity is the plea for every infringement of human freedom: it is the argument of tyrants; it is the creed of slaves.

8678 *(on hearing of Napleon's victory at Austerlitz)*
Roll up that map; it will not be wanted these ten years.

8679 *(replying to a toast, as saviour of his country)*
England has saved herself by her exertions, and will, as I trust, save Europe by her example.

PITTER Ruth 1897-1992
8680 *But for Lust*
But for lust we could be friends,
On each other's necks could weep:
In each other's arms could sleep
In the calm the cradle lends.

PIUS VII Pope 1742-1823
8681 *(attempting to reach an agreement with Napoleon)*
We are prepared to go to the gates of Hell - but no further.

PLANCK Max 1858-1947
8682 *A Scientific Autobiography*
A new scientific truth does not triumph by convincing its opponents and making them see the light, but rather because its opponents eventually die, and a new generation grows up that is familiar with it.

PLATH Sylvia 1932-1963
8683
For me, poetry is an evasion of the real job of writing prose.

8684 *'The Applicant'*
A living doll, everywhere you look.
It can sew, it can cook,
It can talk, talk, talk.
It works, there is nothing wrong with it.
You have a hole, it's a poultice.
You have an eye, it's an image.
My boy, it's your last resort.
Will you marry it, marry it, marry it.

8685 *'Apprehensions'*
Is there no way out of the mind?

8686 *'Daddy'*
I have always been scared of *you*,
With your Luftwaffe, your gobbledygoo.
And your neat moustache
And your Aryan eye, bright blue.
Panzer-man, panzer-man, O You -

8687 *'Daddy'*
Every woman adores a Fascist,
The boot in the face, the brute
Brute heart of a brute like you.

8688 *'Lady Lazarus'*
Dying,
Is an art, like everything else.

8689 *'Morning Song'*
Love set you going like a fat gold watch.
The midwife slapped your footsoles, and your bald cry
Took its place among the elements.

8690 *'Widow'*
Widow. The word consumes itself.

PLATO 429-347 BC
8691
The spiritual eyesight improves as the physical eyesight declines.

8692
Everything that deceives may be said to enchant.

8693
Boys should abstain from all use of wine until their eighteenth year, for it is wrong to add fire to fire.

8694
The most effective kind of education is that a child should play amongst lovely things.

8695
All learning has an emotional base.

8696
There are three classes of men - lovers of wisdom, lovers of honour, lovers of gain.

8697
When the mind is thinking, it is talking to itself.

8698
I have hardly ever known a mathematician who was capable of reasoning.

8699 *Apology*
Socrates is guilty of corrupting the minds of the young, and of believing in deities of his own invention instead of the gods recognized by the State.

8700 *Euthyphro 10*
Is that which is holy loved by the gods because it is holy, or is it holy because it is loved by the gods?

8701 *The Republic*
The blame is his who chooses: God is blameless.

8702 *Republic*
I wonder if we could contrive ... some magnificent myth that would in itself carry conviction to our whole community.

8703 *Republic*
There will be no end to the troubles of states, or indeed, my dear Glaucon, of humanity itself, till philosophers become kings in this world, or till those we now call kings and rulers really and truly become philosophers.

8704 *Republic*
Democracy passes into despotism.

PLAUTUS c.250-184 BC
8705
The bell never rings of itself; unless someone handles or moves it, it is dumb.

8706
Always bring money along with your complaints.

8707
It is customary these days to ignore what should be done in favour of what pleases us.

8708 *Asinaria*
A man is a wolf rather than a man to another man, when he hasn't yet found out what he's like.

8709 *Bacchides*
He whom the gods favour dies young.

8710 *Persa*
A sentence is enough for a sensible man.

PLAYER Gary 1935-
8711
The harder you work, the luckier you get.

PLINY (The Elder) AD 23-79
8712
The brain is the citadel of sense perception.

8713 *Natural History*
Harmless thunderbolts.

8714 *Natural History*
Africa always brings [us] something new.

8715 *Natural History*
Addito salis grano.
With the addition of a grain of salt.

8716 *Natural History*
In vino veritas.
Truth comes out in wine.

8717 *Natural History*
Sal Atticum.
Attic salt.

8718 *Natural History*
Nulla dies sine linea.
Not a day without a line.

PLINY (The Younger) AD 62-c.114
8719
Prosperity tries the fortunate; adversity the great.

PLOMER William 1903-1973
8720 *'The Boer War'*
Out of that bungled, unwise war
An alp of unforgiveness grew.

8721 *'Father and Son: 1939'*
With first-rate sherry flowing into second-rate whores,
And third-rate conversation without one single pause:
Just like a young couple
Between the wars.

8722 *'Mews Flat Mona'*
On a sofa upholstered in panther skin
Mona did researches in original sin.

8723 *'Playboy of the Demi-World: 1938'*
A rose-red sissy half as old as time.

PLOMIN Professor Robert
8724 *(on how to have gifted children)*
Marry an intelligent person.

PLOTINUS 205-270
8725 *Enneads III*
And here we have, incidentally, lighted upon the cause of the Circuit of the All; it is a movement which seeks perpetuity by way of futurity.

PLUNKETT Joseph 1887-1916
8726 *I see His Blood*
I see His blood upon the rose
And in the stars the glory of His eyes.

PLUTARCH AD c.46-c.120
8727
Character is long-standing habit.

8728
It is a hard matter, my fellow citizens, to argue with the belly, since it has no ears.

8729
Those who aim at great deeds must also suffer greatly.

8730
It is indeed a desirable thing to be well descended, but the glory belongs to our ancestors.

8731
Rest is the sweet sauce of labour.

8732 *Parallel Lives 'Lysander'*
He who cheats with an oath acknowledges that he is afraid of his enemy, but that he thinks little of God.

POCOCK R.
8733
The land too poor for any other crop, is best for raising men.

POE Edgar Allan 1809-1849
8734
Man's real life is happy, chiefly because he is ever expecting that it soon will be so.

8735 *'Annabel Lee'*
This maiden she lived with no other thought
Than to love and be loved by me.

8736 *'Annabel Lee'*
I was a child and she was a child,
In this kingdom by the sea;
But we loved with a love which was more than love -
I and my Annabel Lee.

8737 *'For Annie'*
The fever called 'Living'
Is conquered at last.

8738 *'The Bells'*
Keeping time, time, time,
In a sort of Runic rhyme,
To the tintinnabulation that so musically wells
From the bells, bells, bells, bells.

8739 *'A Dream within a Dream'*
All that we see or seem
Is but a dream within a dream.

8740 *'To Helen'*
Helen, thy beauty is to me
Like those Nicean barks of yore, ...
...Thy Naiad airs have brought me home,
To the glory that was Greece
And the grandeur that was Rome.

8741 *'The Raven'*
Once upon a midnight dreary, while I pondered, weak and weary,
Over many a quaint and curious volume of

forgotten lore,
White I nodded, nearly napping, suddenly there came a tapping,
As of someone gently rapping, rapping at my chamber door.

8742 *'The Raven'*
Take thy beak from out my heart, and take thy form from off my door!
Quoth the Raven, 'Nevermore'.

POGREBIN Letty Cottin
8743
No labourer in the world is expected to work for room, board, and love - except the housewife.

8744
Boys don't make passes at female smart-asses.

POINCARÉ Henri 1854-1912
8745 *Science and Hypothesis*
Science is built up of facts, as a house is built of stones; but an accumulation of facts is no more a science than a heap of stones is a house.

POITIERS Diane de 1499-1566
8746
We only make a dupe of the friend whose advice we ask, for we never tell him all; and it is usually what we have left unsaid that decides our conduct.

POLLARD J.G.
8747
Executive ability is deciding quickly and getting somebody else to do the work.

POLLOCK Channing
8748
A critic is a legless man who teaches running.

8749
Marriage is a great institution, and no family should be without it.

POLLOCK Frances
8750
I have learned little from the years that fly; but I have wrung the colour from the years.

POMERANTZ Hart
8751
To some lawyers, all facts are created equal.

POMFRET John 1667-1702
8752 *'Reason'*
We live and learn, but not the wiser grow.

POMPADOUR Madame de 1721-1764
8753
Après nous le déluge.
After us the deluge.

POMPIDOU Georges 1911-1974
8754
A statesman is a politician who places himself at the service of the nation. A politician is a statesman who places the nation at his service.

POPE Alexander 1688-1744
8755
I never knew any man in my life who could not bear another's misfortunes perfectly like a Christian.

8756
Be not the first by whom the new are tried
Nor yet the last to lay the old aside.

8757
Know then thyself, presume not God to scan:
The proper study of mankind is man.

8758
Alive, ridiculous, and dead forgot?

8759
The hungry judges soon the sentence sign,
And wretches hang that jurymen may dine.

8760
A perfect judge will read each word of wit with the same spirit that its author writ.

8761
Sickness is a sort of early old age; it teaches us a diffidence in our earthly state.

8762
Light quirks of music, broken and uneven,
Make the soul dance upon a jig of heaven.

8763
A man of business may talk of philosophy;
a man who has none may practise it.

8764
Party-spirit ... which at best is but the
madness of many for the gain of a few.

8765 *The Dunciad*
Poetic Justice, with her lifted scale,
Where, in nice balance, truth with gold she
weighs,
And solid pudding against empty praise.

8766 *The Dunciad*
While pensive poets painful vigils keep,
Sleepless themselves, to give their readers
sleep.

8767 *The Dunciad*
Gentle Dullness ever loves a joke.

8768 *The Dunciad*
A brain of feathers, and a heart of lead.

8769 *The Dunciad*
How little, mark! that portion of the ball,
Where, faint at best, the beams of science
fall.

8770 *The Dunciad*
All crowd, who foremost shall be damned
to Fame.

8771 *The Dunciad*
A wit with dunces, and a dunce with wits.

8772 *The Dunciad*
Whate'er the talents, or howe'er designed,
We hang one jingling padlock on the mind.

8773 *The Dunciad*
The Right Divine of Kings to govern
wrong.

8774 *The Dunciad*
For thee explain a thing till all men doubt
it,
And write about it, Goddess, and about it.

8775 *The Dunciad*
With the same cement, ever sure to bind,
We bring to one dead level ev'ry mind.
Then take him to develop, if you can,
And hew the block off, and get out the
man.

8776 *The Dunciad*
She marked thee there,
Stretched on the rack of a too easy chair,
And heard thy everlasting yawn confess
The pains and penalties of idleness.

8777 *The Dunciad*
Religion blushing veils her sacred fires,
And unawares Morality expires.

8778 *The Dunciad*
Lo! thy dread empire, Chaos! is restored;
Light dies before thy uncreating word:
Thy hand, great Anarch! lets the curtain
fall;
And universal darkness buries all.

8779 *The Dunciad*
Vital spark of heav'nly flame!
Quit, oh quit this mortal frame:
Trembling, hoping, ling'ring, flying,
Oh the pain, the bliss of dying!

8780 *'The Dying Christian to his Soul'*
I mount! I fly!
O grave! where is thy victory?
O death! where is thy sting?

8781 *'Elegy to the Memory of an Unfortunate
Lady'*
Is it, in heav'n, a crime to love too well?

8782 *'Elegy to the Memory of an Unfortunate
Lady'*
Is there no bright reversion in the sky,
For those who greatly think, or bravely
die?

8783 *'Elegy to the Memory of an Unfortunate
Lady'*
Ambition first sprung from your blest
abodes;
The glorious fault of angels and of gods.

8784 *'Elegy to the Memory of an Unfortunate
Lady'*
A heap of dust alone remains of thee;
'Tis all thou art, and all the proud shall be!

8785 *Eloisa to Abelard*
Oh happy state! when souls each other
draw,
When love is liberty, and nature, law:
All then is full, possessing, and possessed,
No craving void left aching in the breast.

8786 *Eloisa to Abelard*
How happy is the blameless Vestal's lot!
The world forgetting, by the world forgot.

8787 *Eloisa to Abelard*
One thought of thee puts all the pomp to
flight,
Priests, tapers, temples, swim before my
sight.

8788 *Eloisa to Abelard*
See my lips tremble, and my eye-balls roll,
Suck my last breath, and catch my flying
soul!

8789 *'Epigram: You beat your pate'*
You beat your pate, and fancy wit will
come:
Knock as you please, there's nobody at
home.

8790 *'Epigram from the French'*
Sir, I admit your gen'ral rule
That every poet is a fool:
But you yourself may serve to show it,
That every fool is not a poet.

8791 *'An Epistle to Dr Arbuthnot'*
Shut, shut the door, good John! fatigued I
said,
Tie up the knocker, say I'm sick, I'm dead,
The dog-star rages!

8792 *'An Epistle to Dr Arbuthnot'*
You think this cruel? take it for a rule,
No creature smarts so little as a fool.

8793 *'An Epistle to Dr Arbuthnot'*
Destroy his fib, or sophistry; in vain,
The creature's at his dirty work again.

8794 *'An Epistle to Dr Arbuthnot'*
As yet a child, nor yet a fool to fame,
I lisped in numbers, for the numbers came.

8795 *'An Epistle to Dr Arbuthnot'*
To help me through this long disease, my
life.

8796 *'An Epistle to Dr Arbuthnot'*
And he, whose fustian's so sublimely bad,
It is not poetry, but prose run mad.

8797 *'An Epistle to Dr Arbuthnot'*
Who breaks a butterfly upon a wheel?

8798 *'An Epistle to Dr Arbuthnot'*
Yet let me flap this bug with gilded wings,
This painted child of dirt that stinks and
stings.

8799 *'An Epistle to Dr Arbuthnot'*
Eternal smiles his emptiness betray,
As shallow streams run dimpling all the
way.

8800 *'An Epistle to Dr Arbuthnot'*
And he himself one vile antithesis.

8801 *'An Epistle to Dr Arbuthnot'*
A cherub's face, a reptile all the rest.

8802 *'Epistle to Dr Arbuthnot'*
Curst be the verse, how well soe'er it flow,
That tends to make one worthy man my
foe.

8803 *'An Epistle to Dr Arbuthnot'* (*of his own
father*)
Unlearn'd, he knew no schoolman's subtle
art,
No language, but the language of the
heart.

8804 *Epistles to Several Persons 'To a Lady'*
Chaste to her husband, frank to all beside,
A teeming mistress, but a barren bride.

8805 *Epistles to Several Persons 'To a Lady'*
Virtue she finds too painful an endeavour,
Content to dwell in decencies for ever.

8806 *Epistles to Several Persons 'To a Lady'*
Still round and round the ghosts of Beauty
glide,
And haunt the places where their honour
died.
See how the world its veterans rewards!
A youth of frolics, and old age of cards.

8807 *Epistles to Several Persons 'To a Lady'*
And mistress of herself, though china fall.

8808 *Epistles to Several Persons 'To a Lady'*
Woman's at best a contradiction still.

8809 *Epistles to Several Persons 'To Lord
Bathurst'*
Who shall decide, when doctors disagree.

8810 *Epistles to Several Persons 'To Lord
Bathurst'*
But thousands die, without or this or that,

Die, and endow a college, or a cat.

8811 *Epistles to Several Persons 'To Lord Bathurst'*
The ruling passion, be it what it will,
The ruling passion conquers reason still.

8812 *Epistles to Several Persons 'To Lord Cobham'*
'Tis education forms the common mind,
Just as the twig is bent, the tree's inclined.

8813 *'Epitaph: On Mr Gay in Westminster Abbey'*
Of manners gentle, of affections mild;
In wit, a man; simplicity, a child;
With native humour temp'ring virtuous rage,
Formed to delight at once and lash the age.

8814 *'Epitaph: Intended for Sir Isaac Newton'*
Nature, and Nature's laws lay hid in night.
God said, *Let Newton be!* and all was light.

8815 *An Essay on Criticism*
A little learning is a dangerous thing;
Drink deep, or taste not the Pierian spring:
There shallow draughts intoxicate the brain,
And drinking largely sobers us again.

8816 *An Essay on Criticism*
Whoever thinks a faultless piece to see,
Thinks what ne'er was, nor is, nor e'er shall be.

8817 *An Essay on Criticism*
Poets like painters, thus unskilled to trace
The naked nature and the living grace,
With gold and jewels cover ev'ry part,
And hide with ornaments their want of art.
True wit is Nature to advantage dressed,
What oft was thought, but ne'er so well expressed.

8818 *An Essay on Criticism*
Expression is the dress of thought.

8819 *An Essay on Criticism*
As some to church repair,
Not for the doctrine, but the music there.

8820 *An Essay on Criticism*
True ease in writing comes from art, not chance,
As those move easiest who have learned to dance.
'Tis not enough no harshness gives offence,
The sound must seem an echo to the sense.

8821 *An Essay on Criticism*
Yet let not each gay turn thy rapture move,
For fools admire, but men of sense approve.

8822 *An Essay on Criticism*
Some praise at morning what they blame at night;
But always think the last opinion right.

8823 *An Essay on Criticism*
To err is human; to forgive, divine.

8824 *An Essay on Criticism*
All seems infected that th'infected spy,
As all looks yellow to the jaundiced eye.

8825 *An Essay on Criticism*
Men must be taught as if you taught them not,
And things unknown proposed as things forgot.

8826 *An Essay on Criticism*
The bookful blockhead, ignorantly read,
With loads of learned lumber in his head.

8827 *An Essay on Criticism*
For fools rush in where angels fear to tread.

8828 *An Essay on Criticism*
True wit is nature to advantage dressed,
What oft was thought but ne'er so well expressed.

8829 *An Essay on Criticism*
While expletives their feeble aid do join,
And ten low words oft creep in one dull line.

8830 *An Essay on Man*
Awake, my St John! leave all meaner things
To low ambition, and the pride of kings.
Let us (since Life can little more supply
Than just to look about us and to die)
Expatiate free o'er all this scene of man;
A mighty maze! but not without a plan.

8831 *An Essay on Man*
Eye Nature's walks, shoot Folly as it flies,
And catch the Manners living as they rise.

Laugh where we must, be candid where we can;
But vindicate the ways of God to man.

8832 *An Essay on Man*
Observe how system into system runs,
What other planets circle other suns.

8833 *An Essay on Man*
Who sees with equal eye, as God of all,
A hero perish, or a sparrow fall,
Atoms or systems into ruin hurled,
And now a bubble burst, and now a world.

8834 *An Essay on Man*
Pride still is aiming at the blest abodes,
Men would be angels, angels would be gods.

8835 *An Essay on Man*
Why has not man a microscopic eye?
For this plain reason, man is not a fly.

8836 *An Essay on Man*
The spider's touch, how exquisitely fine!
Feels at each thread, and lives along the line.

8837 *An Essay on Man*
All are but parts of one stupendous whole,
Whose body, Nature is, and God the soul.

8838 *An Essay on Man*
All nature is but art, unknown to thee;
All chance, direction, which thou canst not see;
All discord, harmony, not understood;
All partial evil, universal good:
And, spite of Pride, in erring Reason's spite,
One truth is clear, 'Whatever IS, IS RIGHT'.

8839 *An Essay on Man*
Created half to rise, and half to fall;
Great lord of all things, yet a prey to all;
Sole judge of truth, in endless error hurled;
The glory, jest, and riddle of the world!

8840 *An Essay on Man*
Go, teach Eternal Wisdom how to rule -
Then drop into thyself, and be a fool!

8841 *An Essay on Man*
Fixed like a plant on his peculiar spot,
To draw nutrition, propagate, and rot.

8842 *An Essay on Man*
Vice is a monster of so frightful mien,
As, to be hated, needs but to be seen;
Yet seen too oft, familiar with her face,
We first endure, then pity, then embrace.

8843 *An Essay on Man*
The learn'd is happy nature to explore,
The fool is happy that he knows no more.

8844 *An Essay on Man*
Behold the child, by Nature's kindly law
Pleased with a rattle, tickled with a straw.

8845 *An Essay on Man*
Scarfs, garters, gold, amuse his riper stage;
And beads and pray'r-books are the toys of age:
Pleased with this bauble still, as that before;
Till tired he sleeps, and life's poor play is o'er!

8846 *An Essay on Man*
For forms of government let fools contest;
Whate'er is best administered is best.

8847 *An Essay on Man*
Thus God and nature linked the gen'ral frame,
And bade self-love and social be the same.

8848 *An Essay on Man*
Oh Happiness! our being's end and aim!
Good, pleasure, ease, content! whate'er thy name:
That something still which prompts th'eternal sigh,
For which we bear to live, or dare to die.

8849 *An Essay on Man*
A wit's a feather, and a chief a rod;
An honest man's the noblest work of God.

8850 *An Essay on Man*
Slave to no sect, who takes no private road,
But looks thro' Nature, up to Nature's God.

8851 *An Essay on Man*
All our knowledge is, ourselves to know.

8852 *An Essay on Man*
Hope springs eternal in the human breast
Man never is, but always to be blest.

8853 *To George, Lord Lyttelton*
Here am I, dying of a hundred good
symptoms.

8854 *Imitations of Horace*
Our Gen'rals now, retired to their estates,
Hang their old trophies o'er the garden
gates,
In life's cool ev'ning satiate of applause.

8855 *Imitations of Horace*
Not to go back, is somewhat to advance,
And men must walk at least before they
dance.

8856 *Imitations of Horace*
Get place and wealth, if possible, with
grace;
If not, by any means get wealth and place.

8857 *Imitations of Horace*
Not to admire, is all the art I know,
To make men happy, and to keep them so.

8858 *Imitations of Horace*
The worst of madmen is a saint run mad.

8859 *Imitations of Horace*
Shakespeare (whom you and ev'ry play-
house bill
Style the divine, the matchless, what you
will)
For gain, not glory, winged his roving
flight,
And grew immortal in his own despite.

8860 *Imitations of Horace*
The people's voice is odd,
It is, and it is not, the voice of God.

8861 *Imitations of Horace*
But those who cannot write, and those
who can,
All rhyme, and scrawl, and scribble, to a
man.

8862 *Imitations of Horace*
There still remains, to mortify a wit,
The many-headed monster of the pit.

8863 *Imitations of Horace*
Ask you what provocation I have had?
The strong antipathy of good to bad.

8864 *Imitations of Horace*
Yes, I am proud; I must be proud to see
Men not afraid of God, afraid of me.

8865 *Martinus Scriblerus ...*
Ye gods! annihilate but space and time,
And make two lovers happy.

8866 *Miscellanies*
To endeavour to work upon the vulgar
with fine sense, is like attempting to hew
blocks with a razor.

8867 *Miscellanies*
A man should never be ashamed to own
he has been in the wrong, which is but
saying, in other words, that he is wiser today than he was yesterday.

8868 *Miscellanies*
It is with narrow-souled people as with
narrow-necked bottles: the less they have
in them, the more noise they make in
pouring it out.

8869 *Moral Essays*
Woman's at best a contradiction still.

8870 *'Ode on Solitude' (written when aged
about 12)*
Happy the man, whose wish and care
A few paternal acres bound,
Content to breathe his native air,
In his own ground.

8871 *'Ode on Solitude' (written when aged
about 12)*
Thus let me live, unseen, unknown;
Thus unlamented let me die;
Steal from the world, and not a stone
Tell where I lie.

8872 *The Rape of the Lock*
What dire offence from am'rous causes
springs,
What mighty contests rise from trivial
things.

8873 *The Rape of the Lock*
If to her share some female errors fall,
Look on her face, and you'll forget 'em all.

8874 *The Rape of the Lock*
Fair tresses man's imperial race insnare,
And beauty draws us with a single hair.

8875 *The Rape of the Lock*
Coffee, (which makes the politician wise,
And see thro' all things with his half-shut
eyes).

8876 *The Rape of the Lock*
Not louder shrieks to pitying heav'n are
cast,
When husbands or when lapdogs breathe
their last.

8877 *The Rape of the Lock*
Beauties in vain their pretty eyes may roll;
Charms strike the sight, but merit wins the
soul.

8878 *'The Universal Prayer'*
Teach me to feel another's woe;
To hide the fault I see;
That mercy I to others show,
That mercy show to me.

POPPER Sir Karl 1902-1994
8879 *The Open Society and its Enemies*
We may become the makers of our fate
when we have ceased to pose as its
prophets.

8880 *The Open Society and its Enemies*
We must plan for freedom, and not only
for security, if for no other reason than that
only freedom can make security secure.

8881 *The Open Society and its Enemies*
There is no history of mankind, there are
only many histories of all kinds of aspects
of human life. And one of these is the
history of political power. This is elevated
into the history of the world.

8882 *'The Philosophy of Science'*
Science must begin with myths, and with
the criticism of myths.

8883 *The Poverty of Historicism*
Piecemeal social engineering resembles
physical engineering in regarding the *ends*
as beyond the province of technology.

PORCHIA Antonio
8884
One lives in the hope of becoming a
memory.

PORTER Cole 1891-1964
8885
Miss Otis regrets (she's unable to lunch
today).

8886
My heart belongs to Daddy.

8887 *'Anything Goes'*
In olden days a glimpse of stocking
Was looked on as something shocking
Now, heaven knows,
Anything goes.

8888 *'Begin the Beguine'*
When they begin the Beguine
It brings back the sound of music so
tender,
It brings back a night of tropical splendour,
It brings back a memory ever green.

8889 *'Well, Did You Evah?*
Have you heard it's in the stars,
Next July we collide with Mars?
Well, did your evah! What a swell party
this is.

8890 *'Just One of Those Things'*
So goodbye dear, and Amen,
Here's hoping we meet now and then,
It was great fun,
But it was just one of those things.

8891 *'I Get a Kick Out of You'*
I get no kick from champagne,
Mere alcohol doesn't thrill me at all,
So tell my why should it be true
That I get a kick out of you?

8892 *'Let's Do It'*
Birds do it, bees do it,
Even educated fleas do it.
Let's do it, let's fall in love.

8893 *'Night and Day'*
Night and day, you are the one,
Only you beneath the moon and under the
sun.

8894 *'Every Time We Say Goodbye'*
When you're near there's such an air of
spring about it;
I can hear a lark somewhere begin to sing
about it;
There's no love song finer,
But how strange the change from major to

minor
Every time we say goodbye.

8895 *'You're the Top'*
You're the top! You're the Coliseum,
You're the top! You're the Louvre Museum,
You're a melody
From a symphony by Strauss,
You're a Bendel bonnet,
A Shakespeare sonnet,
You're Mickey Mouse!

PORTEUS Beilby 1731-1808
8896 *Death*
... One murder made a villain,
Millions a hero.

8897 *Death*
War its thousands slays, Peace its ten thousands.

8898 *Death*
Teach him how to live,
And, oh! still harder lesson! how to die.

PORTILLO Michael 1953-
8899
Conservatives are not xenophobic - we are patriotic.

POST Emily 1872-1960
8900
The attributes of a great lady may still be found in the rule of the four S's: Sincerity, Simplicity, Sympathy, and Serenity.

POTTER Beatrix 1866-1943
8901 *The Tailor of Gloucester*
I am worn to a ravelling ... I am undone and worn to a thread-paper, for I have NO MORE TWIST.

8902 *The Tale of the Flopsy Bunnies*
It is said that the effect of eating too much lettuce is 'soporific'.

8903 *The Tale of Peter Rabbit*
Don't go into Mr McGregor's garden: your father had an accident there, he was put into a pie by Mrs McGregor.

POTTER Dennis 1935-1994
8904
Religion has always been the wound, not the bandage.

POTTER Henry Codman 1835-1908
8905 *Bishop Potter's Address*
We have exchanged the Washingtonian dignity for the Jeffersonian simplicity, which was, in truth, only another name for the Jacksonian vulgarity.

POTTER Stephen 1900-1969
8906
The theory and practice of gamesmanship or the art of winning games without actually cheating.

8907 *Lifemanship*
How to be one up - how to make the other man feel that something has gone wrong, however slightly.

8908 *Lifemanship*
Each of us can, by ploy or gambit, most naturally gain the advantage.

8909 *One-Upmanship (on wine-tasting)*
A good general rule is to state that the bouquet is better than the taste, and vice versa.

POTTIER Eugene 1816-1887
8910 *'L'Internationale'*
C'est la lutte finale
Groupons-nous, et, demain,
L'Internationale
Sera le genre humain.
This is the final conflict: let us form up and, tomorrow, the International will encompass the human race.

POUND Ezra 1885-1972
8911
Properly we should read for power. Man reading should be man intensely alive. The book should be a ball of light in one's hand.

8912
No man understands a deep book until he has seen and lived at least part of its contents.

8913 *The ABC of Reading*
Any general statement is like a cheque drawn on a bank. Its value depends on what is there to meet it.

8914 *The ABC of Reading*
Literature is news that STAYS news.

8915 *The ABC of Reading*
Real education must ultimately be limited
to one who INSISTS on knowing, the rest
is mere sheep-herding.

8916 *'Ancient Music'*
Winter is icummen in,
Lhude sing Goddamm,
Raineth drop and staineth slop,
And how the wind doth ramm!
Sing: Goddamm.

8917 *'Cino'*
Bah! I have sung women in three cities,
But it is all the same;
And I will sing of the sun.

8918 *Draft of XXX Cantos*
Hang it all, Robert Browning,
There can be but the one 'Sordello'.

8919 *Draft of XXX Cantos*
In the gloom, the gold gathers the light
against it.

8920 *Draft of XXX Cantos*
And even I can remember
A day when the historians left blanks in
their writings,
I mean for things they didn't know.

8921 *'The Garden'*
And she is dying piece-meal
of a sort of emotional anaemia.

And round about there is a rabble
of the filthy, sturdy, unkillable infants of
the very poor.

8922 *'Mr Housman's Message'*
O woe, woe,
People are born and die,
We also shall be dead pretty soon
Therefore let us act as if we were dead
already.

8923 *How to Read*
Great literature is simply language charged
with meaning to the utmost possible
degree.

8924 *Hugh Selwyn Mauberley*
For three years, out of key with his time,
He strove to resuscitate the dead art
Of poetry; to maintain 'the sublime'
In the old sense. Wrong from the start -

8925 *Hugh Selwyn Mauberley*
The age demanded an image
Of its accelerated grimace,
Something for the modern stage,
Not, at any rate, an Attic grace;
Not, not certainly, the obscure reveries
Of the inward gaze;
Better mendacities
Than the classics in paraphrase!

8926 *Hugh Selwyn Mauberley*
Died some, pro patria,
non 'dulce' non 'et decor' ...
walked eye-deep in hell
believing in old men's lies, the unbelieving
came home, home to a lie.

8927 *Hugh Selwyn Mauberley*
hysterias, trench confessions,
laughter out of dead bellies.

8928 *Literary Essays*
Artists are the antennae of the race, but the
bullet-headed many will never learn to
trust their great artists.

8929 *'In a Station of the Metro'*
The apparition of these faces in the crowd;
Petals on a wet, black bough.

8930 *'Villanelle; the psychological hour'*
I had over-prepared the event,
that much was ominous.
With middle-ageing care
I had laid out just the right books.
I had almost turned down the pages.

POUND Roscoe 1870-1964
8931
The law must be stable and yet is must not
stand still.

POWELL Anthony 1905-
8932
One hears about life all the time from
different people with very different
narrative gifts.

8933
Books do furnish a room.

8934
A dance to the music of time.

8935 *The Acceptance World*
He fell in love with himself at first sight
and it is a passion to which he has always
remained faithful.

8936 *The Acceptance World*
Dinner at the Huntercombes' possessed
only two dramatic features - the wine was
a farce and the food a tragedy.

8937 *A Question of Upbringing*
He's so wet you could shoot snipe off him.

8938 *Temporary Kings*
Growing old is like being increasingly
penalised for a crime you haven't
committed.

POWELL Enoch 1912-
8939
History is littered with the wars which
everybody knew would never happen.

8940
As I look ahead, I am filled with
foreboding. Like the Roman, I seem to see
'the River Tiber foaming with much
blood'.

8941
A plumber who has Latin is a better
plumber than one who does not.

POWELL Sir John 1645-1713
8942 *Lord Raymond's Reports*
Let us consider the reason of the case. For
nothing is law that is not reason.

POWELL Laurence Clark
8943
Writing is a solitary occupation. Family,
friends and society are the natural enemies
of a writer. He must be alone,
uninterrupted and slightly savage if he is
to sustain and complete an undertaking.

POWER John O'Connor 1846-
8944 *(of the Liberal Unionists)*
The mules of politics: without pride of
ancestry, or hope of posterity.

PRAED W.M. 1802-1839
8945 *The Chant of the Brazen Head*
I think that nought is worth a thought,
And I'm a fool for thinking.

8946 *Goodnight to the Season*
The ice of her Ladyship's manners,
The ice of his Lordship's champagne.

8947 *'The Talented Man'*
Of science and logic he chatters
As fine and as fast as he can;
Though I am no judge of such matters,
I'm sure he's a talented man.

PRESTON Keith 1884-1927
8948 *'The Liberators'*
Of all the literary scenes
Saddest this sight to me:
The graves of little magazines
Who died to make verse free.

PRÉVERT Jacques 1900-1977
8949 *Les Enfants du Paradis*
Love is so simple.

8950 *'Pater Noster'*
Our Father which art in heaven
Stay there
And we will stay on earth
Which is sometimes so pretty.

PRIESTLEY J.B. 1894-1984
8951
I sometimes wish they would swagger
more now, buy bigger overcoats and
wilder hats, and retain those traces of
make-up that put them outside
respectability and keep them rogues and
vagabonds, which is what, at heart - bless
'em - they are.

8952
One of the delights known to age, and
beyond the grasp of youth, is that of 'not
going'.

8953
Any fool can be fussy and rid himself of
energy all over the place, but a man has to
have something in him before he can settle
down to do nothing.

8954
God can stand being told by Professor
Ayer and Marganita Laski that He
doesn't exist.

8955 *Good Companions*
To say that these men paid their shillings
to watch twenty-two hirelings kick a ball is

merely to say that a violin is wood and catgut, that *Hamlet* is so much paper and ink. For a shilling the Bruddersford United AFC offered you Conflict and Art.

8956 *Saturn Over the Water*
I can't help feeling wary when I hear anything said about the masses. First you take their faces from 'em by calling 'em the masses and then you accuse 'em of not having any faces.

PRIESTLEY Joseph 1733-1804
8957 *An Essay on the First Principles of Government*
Every man, when he comes to be sensible of his natural rights, and to feel his own importance, will consider himself as fully equal to any other person whatever.

PRIOR Matthew 1664-1721
8958
He's half absolv'd
Who has confess'd.

8959
Similies are like songs of love:
They much describe, they nothing prove.

8960 *'A Better Answer'*
I court others in verse: but I love thee in prose:
And they have my whimsies, but thou hast my heart.

8961 *'To a Child of Quality of Five Years Old'*
For, as our different ages move,
'Tis so ordained (would Fate but mend it!)
That I shall be past making love,
When she begins to comprehend it.

8962 *'An English Padlock'*
Be to her virtues very kind;
Be to her faults a little blind;
Let all her ways be unconfined;
And clap your padlock - on her mind.

8963 *'Epitaph'*
Nobles and heralds, by your leave,
Here lies what once was Matthew Prior,
The son of Adam and of Eve,
Can Stuart or Nassau go higher?

8964 *'To the Hon. Charles Montague'*
From ignorance our comfort flows,
The only wretched are the wise.

8965 *'Jinny the Just'*
For the idiom of words very little she heeded,
Provided the matter she drove at succeeded,
She took and gave languages just as she needed.

8966 *'Paolo Purganti and his Wife'*
The doctor understood the call;
But had not always wherewithal.

8967 *'Upon this Passage in Scaligerana'*
They never taste who always drink;
They always talk, who never think.

8968 *'The Remedy Worse than the Disease'*
Cured yesterday of my disease,
I died last night of my physician.

8969 *'Solomon'*
What is a King? - a man condemned to bear
The public burden of the nation's care.

8970 *'A True Maid'*
No, no; for my virginity,
When I lose that, say Rose, I'll die:
Behind the elms last night, cried Dick,
Rose, were you not extremely sick?

PRITCHETT V.S. 1900-
8971
The word for New York is activity.

8972
A natural New Yorker is a native of the present tense.

8973
Those mausoleums of inactive masculinity are places for men who prefer armchairs to women.

8974
Queen Victoria - a mixture of national landlady and actress.

8975
The mark of genius is an incessant activity of mind. Genius is a spiritual greed.

8976
The State, that cawing rookery of committees and subcommittees.

8977 *The Living Novel*
The principle of procrastinated rape is said to be the ruling one in all the great best-sellers.

PROCTER Adelaide Ann 1825-1864
8978 *'A Lost Chord'*
Seated one day at the organ,
I was weary and ill at ease,
And my fingers wandered idly
Over the noisy keys.

8979 *'A Lost Chord'*
But I struck one chord of music,
Like the sound of a great Amen.

PROCTER J.J.
8980
There are things of deadly earnest that can only be safely mentioned under cover of a joke.

PROPERTIUS c.50-16 BC
8981
Give the historians something to write about.

8982 *Elegies*
Even if strength fail, boldness at least will deserve praise: in great endeavours even to have had the will is enough.

PROTAGORAS 490-421 BC
8983
[That] man is the measure of all things.

PROUDHON Pierre-Jospeh 1809-1865
8984 *Qu'est-ce que la propriété?*
La propriété c'est le vol.
Property is theft.

PROUST Marcel 1871-1922
8985
Until I saw Chardin's painting, I never realized how much beauty lay around me in my parents' house, in the half-cleared table, in the corner of a tablecloth left awry, in the knife beside the empty oyster shell.

8986
There are perhaps no days of our childhood we lived so fully as those we believe we left without having lived them: those we spent with a favourite book.

8987
The one thing more difficult than following a regimen is not imposing it on others.

8988
At the heart of our friendly or purely social relations, there lurks a hostility momentarily cured but recurring in fits and starts.

8989
Let us leave pretty women to men without imagination.

8990
That which we remember of our conduct is ignored by our closest neighbour; but that which we have forgotten having said, or even what we never said, will cause laughter even into the next world.

8991
A la recherche du temps perdu.
In search of lost time.

8992
There can be no peace of mind in love, since the advantage one has secured is never anything but a fresh starting-point for further desires.

8993 *Cities of the Plain*
'Anyhow,' Mme de Cambremer went on, 'I have a horror of sunsets, they're so romantic, so operatic.'

8994 *Guermantes Way*
Everything we think of as great has come to us from neurotics. It is they and they alone who found religions and create great works of art. The world will never realise how much it owes to them and what they have suffered in order to bestow their gifts on it.

8995 *Guermantes Way*
There is nothing like desire for preventing the things one says from bearing any resemblance to what one has in one's mind.

8996 *A l'ombre des jeunes filles en fleurs*
One becomes moral as soon as one is unhappy.

8997 *Swann's Way*
For a long time I used to go to bed early.

8998 *Swann's Way*
To think that I've wasted years of my life, that I've longed to die, that I've experienced my greatest love for a woman who didn't appeal to me, who wasn't even my type.

8999 *Time Regained*
One of those telegrams of which M. de Guermantes had wittily fixed the formula: 'Cannot come, lie follows'.

9000 *Time Regained*
The true paradises are the paradises that we have lost.

9001 *Time Regained*
For if unhappiness develops the forces of the mind, happiness alone is salutary to the body.

PROVERBS and SAYINGS
9002
Trouble will rain on those who are already wet.

9003
Fire tries gold, misfortune men.

9004
A great city, a great solitude.

9005
Hunger is the best sauce.

9006
That which is escaped now is pain to come.

9007
Nature, time and patience are the three great physicians.

9008
The tongue ever turns to the aching tooth.

9009
What was hard to endure is sweet to recall.

9010
All would live long, but none would be old.

9011
An indecent mind is a perpetual feast.

9012 *African*
Indecision is like a stepchild: if he doesn't wash his hands, he is called dirty; if he does, he is wasting the water.

9013 *African*
When elephants fight it is the grass that suffers.

9014 *American Indian*
Listen or thy tongue will keep thee deaf.

9015 *American Indian*
Never criticize a man until you've walked a mile in his moccasins.

9016 *Arab*
Throw a lucky man into the sea, and he will come up with a fish in his mouth.

9017 *Arab*
The enemy of my enemy is my friend.

9018 *Arab*
God sells knowledge for labour - honour for risk.

9019 *Arab*
After dinner, rest a while, after supper walk a mile.

9020 *Arab*
The sinning is the best part of repentance.

9021 *Arab*
It is a good thing to speak the truth: but it is a better thing to know the truth and to talk about date stones.

9022 *Asidic*
For the unlearned, old age is winter; for the learned, it is the season of the harvest.

9023 *Australian Aboriginal*
Hypocrite - mouth one way, belly 'nother way.

9024 *Australian Aboriginal*
Those who lose dreaming are lost.

9025 *Belgian*
Experience is the comb that Nature gives us when we are bald.

9026 *Bosnian*
Who lies for you, will lie against you.

9027 *Canadian Indian*
Love Canada or give it back.

9028 *Chinese*
A book is like a garden carried in the pocket.

9029 *Chinese*
Make happy those who are near, and those who are far will come.

9030 *Chinese*
If heaven made him, earth can find some use for him.

9031 *Chinese*
People in the West are always getting ready to live.

9032 *Chinese*
Married couples who love each other tell each other a thousand things without talking.

9033 *Chinese*
The palest ink is better than the best memory.

9034 *Chinese*
One dog barks at something, the rest bark at him.

9035 *Chinese*
With time and patience the mulberry leaf becomes a silk gown.

9036 *Chinese*
When you have only two pennies left in the world, buy a loaf of bread with one, and a lily with the other.

9037 *Chinese*
I hear and I forget. I see and I remember. I do and I understand.

9038 *Chinese*
To be uncertain is to be uncomfortable, but to be certain is to be ridiculous.

9039 *Chinese*
If you don't want anyone to know it, don't do it.

9040 *Colombian*
He who must die must die in the dark, even though he sells candles.

9041 *Congolese*
The teeth are smiling, but is the heart?

9042 *Cree Indian*
There is no chance for old fools.

9043 *Czechoslovakian*
When you buy, use your eyes and your mind, not your ears.

9044 *Danish*
Lawyers and painters can soon change white to black.

9045 *Dutch*
He who is outside his door already has a hard part of his journey behind him.

9046 *Dutch*
God does not pay weekly, but he pays at the end.

9047 *Dutch*
A handful of patience is worth more than a bushel of brains.

9048 *Dutch*
God made the ocean, but the Dutch made Holland.

9049 *English*
Everyone must row with the oars he has.

9050 *English*
The absent are always wrong.

9051 *English*
The shortest answer is doing.

9052 *English*
A Scotch mist may wet an Englishman to the skin.

9053 *English*
Danger and delight grow on one stalk.

9054 *English*
Affectation is a greater enemy to the face than smallpox.

9055 *English*
We are usually the best men when in the worst health.

9056 *English*
There's none so blind as those who won't see.

9057 *English*
When a proud man hears another praised, he feels himself injured.

9058 *English*
As old as the itch.

9059 *English*
A man of words and not of deeds,
Is like a garden full of weeds.

9060 *English*
One of these days is none of these days.

9061 *English*
Don't fall before you're pushed.

9062 *English*
There is but an hour a day between a good
housewife and a bad one.

9063 *Ethiopian*
When spider webs unite, they can tie up a
lion.

9064 *French*
He who can lick can bite.

9065 *French*
The price spoils the pleasure.

9066 *French*
Tout passe, tout lasse, tout casse.
Everything passes; everything wears out;
everything breaks.

9067 *French*
The worst is not always certain but it's
very likely.

9068 *French*
A good meal ought to begin with hunger.

9069 *French*
There is no such thing as a pretty good
omelette.

9070 *French*
Only great men may have great faults.

9071 *French*
There's a pinch of the madman in every
great man.

9072 *French*
With enough 'ifs' we could put Paris into a
bottle.

9073 *French*
There is one who kisses, and the other who
offers a cheek.

9074 *French*
Gratitude is the heart's memory.

9075 *French*
To want to forget something is to think of
it.

9076 *French*
A father is a banker provided by nature.

9077 *French*
Nothing is so burdensome as a secret.

9078 *French*
L'amour est aveugle; l'amitié ferme les yeux
Love is blind; friendship closes its eyes.

9079 *German*
It's the whole, not the detail, that matters.

9080 *German*
God gives the nuts, but he does not crack
them.

9081 *German*
Old birds are hard to pluck.

9082 *German*
Whose bread I eat, his song I sing.

9083 *German*
Good things are not done in a hurry.

9084 *German*
When the fox preaches, look to your geese.

9085 *German*
Invalids live longest.

9086 *German*
The eyes believe themselves; the ears
believe other people.

9087 *German*
Who takes the child by the hand takes the
mother by the heart.

9088 *German*
Better silent than stupid.

9089 *German*
Truth has a handsome countenance but
torn garments.

9090 *Greek*
Whatever is good to know is difficult to
learn.

9091 *Greek*
It is easier to talk than to hold one's tongue.

9092 *Hindu*
An arch never sleeps.

9093 *Hindu*
If you ask the hungry man how much is two and two, he replies four loaves.

9094 *Hindu*
Dictators ride to and fro upon tigers from which they dare not dismount.

9095 *Hindu*
Fatigue is the best pillow.

9096 *Hindu*
There is nothing noble about being superior to some other man. The true nobility is in being superior to your previous self.

9097 *Hottentot*
Good is when I steal other people's wives and cattle; bad is when they steal mine.

9098 *Irish*
Better be quarrelling than lonesome.

9099 *Irish*
Every invalid is a physician.

9100 *Irish*
Money swore an oath that nobody who did not love it should ever have it.

9101 *Irish*
A dimple in the chin; a devil within.

9102 *Irish*
Trust me, but look to thyself.

9103 *Irish*
Seeing's believing - but feeling is God's own truth.

9104 *Italian*
He that jokes confesses.

9105 *Italian*
Below the navel there is neither religion nor truth.

9106 *Italian*
Since the house is on fire let us warm ourselves.

9107 *Italian*
Summer is the mother of the poor.

9108 *Italian*
If it is not true, it is a happy invention.

9109 *Japanese*
The go-between wears out a thousand sandals.

9110 *Japanese*
The crow that mimics a cormorant gets drowned.

9111 *Japanese*
The nail that sticks out is hammered down.

9112 *Japanese*
Fall seven times, stand up eight.

9113 *Jewish*
What you don't see with your eyes, don't invent with your tongue.

9114 *Jewish*
Worries go down better with soup than without.

9115 *Jewish*
Make sure to send a lazy man for the Angel of Death.

9116 *Jewish*
The innkeeper loves the drunkard, but not for a son-in-law.

9117 *Jewish*
The poor schlemiel is a man who falls on his back and breaks his nose.

9118 *Jewish*
Good men need no recommendation and bad men it wouldn't help.

9119 *Jewish*
The hardest work is to go idle.

9120 *Jewish*
Truth is the safest lie.

9121 *Jewish*
A half-truth is a whole lie.

9122 *Jewish*
You can't force anyone to love you or to lend you money.

9123 *Jewish*
With money in your pocket, you are wise,
and you are handsome, and you sing well
too.

9124 *Jewish*
If the rich could hire other people to die
for them, the poor would make a
wonderful living.

9125 *Jewish*
God could not be everywhere and
therefore he made mothers.

9126 *Jewish*
Pride is the mask of one's own faults.

9127 *Jewish*
'For example' is not proof.

9128 *Jewish*
Do not make yourself so big. You are not
so small.

9129 *Jewish*
Sleep faster, we need the pillows.

9130 *Jewish*
A wise man hears one word and
understands two.

9131 *Korean*
Where there are no tigers, a wildcat is very
self-important.

9132 *Lancashire*
Shake a bridle over a Yorkshireman's
grave, and he'll rise and steal a horse.

9133 *Latin*
By learning you will teach; by teaching
you will learn.

9134 *Latin*
Fortune is fickle and soon asks back what
he has given.

9135 *Latin*
God will be present, whether asked or not.

9136 *Latin*
To spur a willing horse.

9137 *Latin*
Vox populi, vox dei.
The voice of the people is the voice of God.

9138 *Latin*
Sweet is war to those who have never
experienced it.

9139 *Latin*
Deliberate often - decide once.

9140 *Latin*
Nature abhors a vacuum.

9141 *Latvian*
A smiling face is half the meal.

9142 *Malay*
Don't think there are no crocodiles because
the water is calm.

9143 *Malay*
Though a tree grow ever so high, the
falling leaves return to the root.

9144 *Maltese*
Time gives good advice.

9145 *Medieval*
Habit is second nature.

9146 *Medieval*
You cannot argue with someone who
denies the first principles.

9147 *Medieval*
Ignorance excuses from sin.

9148 *Medieval*
It is better to be than not to be.

9149 *Medieval*
Nature gives to each what is appropriate.

9150 *Medieval*
Nature always desires what is better.

9151 *Medieval*
A good man and a good citizen are not the
same thing.

9152 *Medieval*
All men naturally desire to know.

9153 *Medieval*
There should be no enmity among seekers
after the truth.

9154 *Medieval*
Parents love their children more than
children love their parents.

9155 *Medieval*
The touchstone of knowledge is the ability
to teach.

9156 *Medieval*
Silence is a women's finest ornament.

9157 *Medieval*
Time is the measure of movement.

9158 *Moroccan*
None but a mule deserves his family.

9159 *Nigerian*
When the mouse laughs at the cat there's a
hole nearby.

9160 *Norwegian*
Many become brave when brought to bay.

9161 *(old bookseller)*
It fell dead from the Press.

9162 *Persian*
If fortune turns against you, even jelly
breaks your tooth.

9163 *Persian*
When its time has come, the prey goes to
the hunter.

9164 *Persian*
He who wants a rose must respect the
thorn.

9165 *Persian*
The man who speaks the truth is always at
ease.

9166 *Polish*
Even were a cook to cook a fly, he would
keep the breast for himself.

9167 *Polish*
Fish, to taste right, must swim three times -
in water, in butter and in wine.

9168 *Polish*
The greater love is a mother's; then comes
a dog's; then a sweetheart's.

9169 *Portuguese*
Visits always give pleasure - if not the
arrival, the departure.

9170 *Post-classical*
Post coitum omne animal triste.
After coition every animal is sad.

9171 *Rabbinical*
Don't limit a child to your own learning,
for he was born in another time.

9172 *Rhodesian*
A bull does not enjoy fame in two herds.

9173 *Russian*
Don't buy the house; buy the
neighbourhood.

9174 *Russian*
If you were born lucky, even your rooster
will lay eggs.

9175 *Russian*
No matter how much you feed a wolf, he
will always return to the forest.

9176 *Russian*
Believe not your own brother - believe,
instead, your own blind eye.

9177 *Russian*
Gossip needs no carriage.

9178 *Russian*
If the thunder is not loud, the peasant
forgets to cross himself.

9179 *Russian*
The rich would have to eat money, but
luckily the poor provide food.

9180 *Scottish*
The Devil's boots don't creak.

9181 *Scottish*
What may be done at any time will be
done at no time.

9182 *Siberian*
June's too soon, July's too late - for
summer.

9183 *Sioux*
A people without history is like wind on
the buffalo grass.

9184 *Spanish*
From a fallen tree, all making kindling.

9185 *Spanish*
You can't have more bugs than a
blanketful.

9186 *Spanish*
Don't offer me advice, give me money.

9187 *Spanish*
Drink nothing without seeing it; sign nothing without reading it.

9188 *Spanish*
Whoever gossips to you will gossip of you.

9189 *Spanish*
No revenge is more honourable than the one not taken.

9190 *Spanish*
How beautiful it is to do nothing, and then rest afterward.

9191 *Spanish*
Laws, like the spider's web, catch the fly and let the hawk go free.

9192 *Spanish*
Tomorrow is often the busiest day of the year.

9193 *Spanish*
Woe to the house where the hen crows and the rooster keeps still.

9194 *Spanish*
An ounce of mother is worth a pound of clergy.

9195 *Spanish*
If I die, I forgive you: if I recover, we shall see.

9196 *Spanish*
When three people call you an ass, put on a bridle.

9197 *Spanish*
Speaking without thinking is shooting without taking aim.

9198 *Swedish*
The afternoon knows what the morning never suspected.

9199 *Swedish*
When a blind man carries the lame man, both go forward.

9200 *Turkish*
If you speak the truth you have a foot in the stirrup.

9201 *Yiddish*
The world is more exacting that God himself.

9202 *Yiddish*
If you can't bite, don't show your teeth.

9203 *Zen*
A beautiful woman who is pleasing to men is good only for frightening fish when she falls into the water.

PUBLILIUS Syrus 1st century BC
9204 *Sententiae*
A beautiful face is a mute recommendation.

9205 *Sententiae*
He gives the poor man twice as much good who gives quickly.

9206 *Sententiae*
The judge is condemned when the guilty party is acquitted.

9207 *Sententiae*
Necessity gives the law without itself acknowledging one.

PUCCINI Giacomo 1858-1924
9208
Art is a kind of illness.

PULTENEY William 1684-1764
9209 *'The Honest Jury'*
For Sir Ph-p well knows
That innuendos
Will serve him no longer in verse or in prose,
Since twelve honest men have decided the cause,
And were judges of fact, tho' not judges of laws.

PUNCH 1841-1992
9210
Advice to persons about to marry - 'Don't'.

9211
You pays your money and you takes your choice.

9212
The Half-Way House to Rome, Oxford.

9213
What is better than presence of mind in a railway accident? Absence of body.

9214
Never do today what you can put off till
tomorrow.

9215
What is Matter? - Never mind.
What is Mind? - No matter.

9216
It ain't the 'unting as 'urts 'im, it's the
'ammer, 'ammer, 'ammer along the 'ard
'igh road.

9217
Nothink for nothink 'ere, and precious
little for sixpence.

9218
It appears the Americans have taken
umbrage.
The deuce they have!
Whereabouts is that?

9219
Go directly - see what she's doing, and tell
her she mustn't.

9220
There was an old owl lived in an oak
The more he heard, the less he spoke;
The less he spoke, the more he heard
O, if men were all like that wise bird!

9221
It's worse than wicked, my dear, it's
vulgar.

9222
I never read books - I *write* them.

9223
I am not hungry; but thank goodness, I am
greedy.

9224
What sort of a doctor is he?
Oh well, I don't know very much about his
ability; but he's got a very good bedside
manner!

9225
I used your soap two years ago; since then
I have used no other.

9226
Nearly all our best men are dead! Carlyle,
Tennyson, Browning, George Eliot! - I'm

not feeling very well myself.

9227
Botticelli isn't a wine, you Juggins!
Botticelli's a *cheese*!

9228
I'm afraid you've got a bad egg, Mr Jones.
Oh no, my Lord, I assure you! Parts of it
are excellent!

9229
Look here, Steward, if this is coffee, I want
tea; but if this is tea, then I wish for coffee.

9230
Sometimes I sits and thinks, and then
again I just sits.

PURSUIT Dan
9231
All children wear the sign: 'I want to be
important NOW'. Many of our juvenile
delinquency problems arise because
nobody reads the sign.

PUSHKIN Alexander 1799-1837
9232
Please, never despise the translator. He's
the mailman of human civilization.

9233 *Eugene Onegin*
From early youth his dedication
Was to a single occupation ...
The science of the tender passion.

9234 *Eugene Onegin*
A man of sense, I am conceding,
Can pay attention to his nails;
Why should one quarrel with good
breeding?
With some folk, custom's rule prevails.

9235 *Eugene Onegin*
A woman's love for us increases
The less we love her, sooth to say -
She stoops, she falls, her struggling ceases;
Caught fast, she cannot get away.

9236 *Eugene Onegin*
The sky breathed autumn, sombre,
shrouded;
Shorter and shorter grew the days;
Sad murmurs filled the woodland ways
As the dark coverts were denuded;

9237 *Eugene Onegin*
Moscow: those syllables can start
A tumult in the Russian heart.

9238 *'The Poet'*
No sooner does the divine word touch his
keen hearing than the poet's soul starts
like an eagle that has been roused.

9239 *'Remembrances'*
When trade and traffic and all the noise of
town
Is dimmed, and on the streets and squares
The filmy curtain of the night sinks down
With sleep, the recompense of cares,
To me the darkness brings not sleep nor
rest.

9240 *'It's Time'*
It's time, my dear, it's time! The heart
demands its quittance -
As day flies after day and each bears off its
pittance
Withdrawn from living's store and
meanwhile you and I
Draw up our plans to live ... And then,
why then, we'll die.

PUTNAM Israel 1718-1790
9241 *(at Bunker Hill)*
Men, you are all marksmen - don't one of
you fire until you see the white of their
eyes.

PUTNAM VI
9242
The entire sum of existence is the magic of
being needed by just one person.

PUZO Mario 1920-
9243 *The Godfather*
I'll make him an offer he can't refuse.

9244 *The Godfather*
A lawyer with his briefcase can steal more
than a hundred men with guns.

PYM Barbara 1913-1980
9245 *Jane and Prudence*
It is better taste somehow that a man
should be unfaithful to his wife away from
home.

9246 *Less than Angels*
She experienced all the cosiness and
irritation which can come from living with

thoroughly nice people with whom one
has nothing in common.

QUARLES Francis 1592-1644
9247 *Divine Fancies*
Our God and soldiers we alike adore
Ev'n at the brink of danger; not before:
After deliverance, both alike requited,
Our God's forgotten, and our soldiers
slighted.

9248 *Emblems*
I wish thee as much pleasure in the
reading, as I had in the writing.

9249 *Emblems*
My soul, sit thou a patient looker-on;
Judge not the play before the play is done:
Her plot hath many changes; every day
Speaks a new scene; the last act crowns the
play.

9250 *Emblems*
We spend our midday sweat, our midnight
oil;
We tire the night in thought, the day in
toil.

9251 *Emblems*
Be wisely worldly, be not worldly wise.

9252 *Emblems*
Man is Heaven's masterpiece.

9253 *Emblems*
Thou art my way; I wander, if thou fly;
Thou art my light; if hid, how blind am I!
Thou art my life; if thou withdraw, I die.

9254 *Hieroglyphics of the Life of Man*
He that begins to live, begins to die.

9255 *The Shepherd's Oracles*
We'll cry both arts and learning down,
And hey! then up go we!

QUENEAU Raymond 1903-1976
9256
Learning to learn is to know how to
navigate in a forest of facts, ideas and
theories, a proliferation of constantly
changing items of knowledge. Learning to
learn is to know what to ignore but at the
same time not rejecting innovation and
research.

9257
Man's usual routine is to work and to dream and work and dream.

QUENNELL Peter 1905-
9258 *The Sign of the Fish*
An elderly fallen angel travelling incognito.

QUILLER-COUCH Sir Arthur (Q) 1863-1944
9259
The best is the best, though a hundred judges have declared it so.

9260 *'Lady Jane. Sapphics'*
Simple this tale! - but delicately perfumed
As the sweet roadside honeysuckle. That's why,
Difficult though its metre was to tackle,
I'm glad I wrote it.

QUINAULT Philippe 1635-1688
9261
It is not wise to be wiser than is necessary.

QUINCY Josiah 1772-1864
9262 *Abridgement of Debates of Congress*
As it will be the right of all, so it will be the duty of some, definitely to prepare for a separation, amicably if they can, violently if they must.

QUINE W.V.O. 1908-
9263 *Quiddities*
It is the tension between the scientist's laws and his own attempted breaches of them that powers the engines of science and makes it forge ahead.

9264 *Theories and Things*
Students of the heavens are separable into astronomers and astrologers as readily as are the minor domestic ruminants into sheep and goats, but the separation of philosophers into sages and cranks seems to be more sensitive to frames of reference.

QUINTILIAN AD 42-118
9265
A liar should have a good memory.

9266
The obscurity of a writer is generally in proportion to his incapacity.

RABELAIS François c.1494-c.1553
9267
There are more old drunkards than old physicians.

9268
I never sleep in comfort save when I am hearing a sermon or praying to God.

9269 *Gargantua*
The appetite grows by eating.

9270 *Gargantua*
I drink for the thirst to come.

9271 *(attributed last words)*
I am going to seek a great perhaps ... Bring down the curtain, the farce is played out.

RACINE Jean 1639-1699
9272
A single word often betrays a great design.

9273 *Andromaque*
I have loved him too much not to feel any hatred for him.

9274 *Andromaque*
I loved you when you were inconsistent. What should I have done if you had been faithful.

9275 *Athalie*
It was during the horror of a deep night.

9276 *Athalie*
She wavers, she hesitates. In a word, she is a woman.

9277 *Les Plaideurs*
Honour, without money, is just a disease.

9278 *Phèdre*
Crime, like virtue, has its degrees.

RADDALL Thomas H.
9279
Don't brood on what's past, but never forget it either.

RADFORD Arthur William 1896-1973
9280
A decision is the action an executive must take when he has information so incomplete that the answer does not suggest itself.

RADNER Gilda
9281
I can always be distracted by love, but eventually I get horny for my creativity.

RAE Bob
9282
Forgiving is all; forgetting is another thing.

RAE John 1931-
9283 *The Custard Boys*
War is, after all, the universal perversion ... war stories, the pornography of war.

RAINBOROWE Thomas d.1648
9284 *(army debates at Putney)*
The poorest he that is in England hath a life to live as the greatest he.

RAINE Craig 1944-
9285
Reality is prodigal, but fiction must be laconic.

RAINE Kathleen 1908-
9286
The work of the artist is to heal the soul.

RAKOFF Aman Vivian
9287
Communication is and should be hell fire and sparks as well as sweetness and light.

RALEGH Sir Walter 1552-1618
9288
Hatreds are the cinders of affection.

9289
Tell zeal it wants devotion;
Tell love it is but lust;
Tell time it metes but motion;
Tell flesh it is but dust;
And wish them not reply,
For thou must give the lie.

9290
It is not truth, but opinion that can travel the world without a passport.

9291 *'Conceit begotten by the Eyes'*
Desire, nor reason hath, nor rest,
And blind doth seldom choose the best.

9292 *(on feeling the edge of the axe at his execution)*
'Tis a sharp remedy, but a sure one for all ills.

9293 *The History of the World*
[History] hath triumphed over time, which besides it, nothing but eternity hath triumphed over.

9294 *The History of the World*
Whosoever, in writing a modern history, shall follow truth too near the heels, it may happily strike out his teeth.

9295 *The History of the World*
O eloquent, just, and mighty Death! ... thou hast drawn together all the far-stretched greatness, all the pride, cruelty, and ambition of man, and covered it all over with these two narrow words, *Hic jacet* [Here lies].

9296 *'As You came From the Holy Land'*
Love is a durable fire,
In the mind ever burning:
Never sick, never old, never dead,
From itself never turning.

9297 *'On the Life of Man'*
We die in earnest, that's no jest.

9298 *Line written on a window-pane*
Fain would I climb, yet fear I to fall.

9299 *'The Passionate Man's Pilgrimage'*
Give me my scallop-shell of quiet,
My staff of faith to walk upon,
My scrip of joy, immortal diet,
My bottle of salvation,
My gown of glory, hope's true gage,
And thus I'll take my pilgrimage.

9300 *(returning to prison from his trial)*
The world itself is but a large prison, out of which some are daily led to execution.

9301 *'Sir Walter Ralegh to the Queen'*
Our passions are most like to floods and streams;
The shallow murmur, but the deep are dumb.

RALEIGH Sir Walter Alexander 1861-1922
9302 *'Stans Puer ad Mensam'*
Eat slowly: only men in rags
And gluttons old in sin
Mistake themselves for carpet bags
And tumble victuals in.

9303 *'Wishes of an Elderly Man'*
I wish I loved the Human Race;
I wish I loved its silly face;
I wish I liked the way it walks;
I wish I liked the way it talks;
And when I'm introduced to one
I wish I thought *What Jolly Fun!*

RAND Ayn 1905-1982
9304
The skyline of New York is a monument of
a splendour that no pyramids or palaces
will ever equal or approach.

9305
Upper classes are a nation's past; the
middle-class is its future.

9306
What is a demanding pleasure? A pleasure
that demands the use of one's mind; not in
the sense of problem solving, but in the
sense of exercising discrimination,
judgement, awareness.

9307
To demand 'sense' is the hallmark of
nonsense. Nature does not make sense.
Nothing makes sense.

RANDALL Clarence
9308
Every man who has lived his life to the full
should, by the time his senior years are
reached, have established a reserve
inventory of unfinished thinking.

RANDALL Stanley J.
9309
The closest to perfection a person ever
comes is when he fills out a job application
form.

RANKIN Ruth
9310
The government is concerned about the
population explosion, and the population
is concerned about the government
explosion.

RANSOM John Crowe 1888-1974
9311 *'Here Lies a Lady'*
Here lies a lady of beauty and high degree.
Of chills and fever she died, of fever and
chills,
The delight of her husband, her aunts, an
infant of three,
And of medicos marvelling sweetly on her
ills.

9312 *'Winter Remembered'*
Two evils, monstrous either one apart,
Possessed me, and were long and loath at
going:
A cry of Absence, Absence, in the heart,
And in the wood the furious winter
blowing.

RAPHAEL Frederic 1931-
9313
Truth may be stranger than fiction, but
fiction is truer.

9314 *Darling*
Your idea of fidelity is not having more
than one man in bed at the same time.

9315 *The Glittering Prizes, 'A Sex Life'*
I come from suburbia ... and I don't ever
want to go back. It's the one place in the
world that's further away from anywhere
else.

RAPSON Ralph
9316
Develop an infallible technique and then
place yourself at the mercy of inspiration.

RATH Dorothy H.
9317
I have come back again to where I belong;
not an enchanted place, but the walls are
strong.

RATNER Herbert
9318
The doctor, if he forgets he is only the
assistant to nature and zealously takes
over the stage, may so add to what nature
is already doing well that he actually
throws the patient into shock by the vigour
he adds to nature's forces.

RATTIGAN Terence 1911-1977
9319 *In Praise of Love*
Do you know what 'le vice Anglais' - the
English vice - really is? ... It's our refusal
to admit our emotions. We think they
demean us, I suppose.

431

9320 *Separate Tables*
You can be in the Horseguards and still be common, dear.

RAVERAT Gwen 1885-1957
9321 *Period Piece*
Ladies were ladies in those days; they did not do things themselves.

RAY John 1628-1705
9322
The honester the man, the worse luck.

9323
Many without punishment, none without sin.

RAYBURN Sam 1882-1961
9324
Any jackass can kick down a barn, but it takes a good carpenter to build one.

RAYMOND F.J.
9325
Next to being shot at and missed, nothing is quite as satisfying as an income tax refund.

READ Sir Herbert 1893-1968
9326 *International Surrealist Exhibition Catalogue*
Do not judge this movement kindly. It is not just another amusing stunt. It is defiant - the desperate act of men too profoundly convinced of the rottenness of our civilization to want to save a shred of its respectability.

9327 *The Meaning of Art*
Art is ... pattern informed by sensibility.

READE Charles 1814-1884
9328
Not a day passes over the earth, but men and women of no note do great deeds, speak great words and suffer noble sorrows.

9329 *(attributed)*
Sow an act, and you reap a habit. Sow a habit and you reap a character. Sow a character, and you reap a destiny.

9330 *The Cloister and the Hearth*
Courage, mon ami, le diable est mort!
Take courage, my friend, the devil is dead!

REAGAN Ronald 1911-
9331
Abortion is advocated only by persons who have themselves been born.

9332
Politics is supposed to be the second oldest profession. I have come to realize that it bears a very close resemblance to the first.

9333
You can tell a lot about a fellow's character by his way of eating jellybeans.

9334
Middle age is when you're faced with two temptations and you choose the one that will get you home by nine o'clock.

9335 *(after assassination attempt)*
Nothing in life is so exhilarating as to be shot at without result.

9336 *(of Col. Gadaffi of Libya)*
This mad dog of the Middle East.

9337 *(following hijack of a US plane)*
We are especially not going to tolerate these attacks from outlaw states run by the strangest collection of misfits, Looney Tunes, and squalid criminals since the advent of the Third Reich.

REED Henry 1914-1986
9338 *Not a Drum was Heard:...*
In a civil war, a general must know ... exactly when to move over to the other side.

9339 *Emily Butler*
I think it may justly be said that English women in general are very common diatonic little numbers.

9340 *A Very Great Man Indeed*
Modest? My word no ... He was an all-the-lights-on man.

9341 *A Very Great Man Indeed*
I have known her pass the whole evening without mentioning a single book, or *in fact anything unpleasant*, at all.

9342 *Private Life of Hilda Tablet*
And the sooner the tea's out of the way, the sooner we can get out the gin, eh?

REED John 1887-1920
9343
Ten days that shook the world.

REED Rex
9344
In Hollywood, if you don't have
happiness, you send out for it.

REEVE Christopher
9345 *in Superman*
"I never drink when I fly."

REGER Max 1873-1916
9346
I am sitting in the smallest room in my
house. I have your review in front of me.
Soon it will be behind me.

REGNARD Jean François
9347
We love without reason, and without
reason we hate.

REICHMANN Paul
9348
You build on cost and you borrow on
value.

REID Kate
9349
Acting is not being emotional, but being
able to express emotion.

REIK Theodor 1888-1969
9350
In our civilization, men are afraid that they
will not be men enough and women are
afraid that they might be considered only
women.

9351
Even the wisest men make fools of
themselves about women, and even the
most foolish women are wise about men.

9352
Work and love - these are the basics.
Without them there is neurosis.

REINHARDT Adina
9353
Art disease is caused by a hardening of the
categories.

REINHARDT Gottfried
9354
Money is good for bribing yourself
through the inconveniences of life.

REMARQUE Erich Maria 1898-1970
9355
Im Westen nichts Neues.
All Quiet on the Western Front.

RENAN Ernest 1823-1892
9356
Man makes holy what he believes, as he
makes beautiful what he loves.

9357
A nation is a body of people who have
done great things together.

RENARD Jules 1864-1910
9358
I am afraid I shall not find Him, but I shall
still look for Him. If He exists, He may be
appreciative of my efforts.

9359
A cold in the head causes less suffering
than an idea.

9360
Failure is not our only punishment for
laziness: there is also the success of others.

9361
I have a remarkable memory; I forget
everything. It is wonderfully convenient.
It is as though the world were constantly
renewing itself for me.

9362
Les bourgeois, ce sont les autres.
The bourgeois are other people.

RENDALL Montague John 1862-1950
9363 *(motto of the BBC)*
Nation shall speak peace unto nation.

RENOIR Jean 1894-1979
9364 *My Life and My Films*
Is it possible to succeed without any act of
betrayal?

RENOIR Pierre Auguste 1841-1919
9365
A painter who has the feel of breasts and
buttocks is saved.

9366 *(attributed)*
I paint with my prick.

9367 *(of the men of the French Commune)*
They were madmen; but they had in them
that little flame which is not to be snuffed
out.

REPPLIER Agnes 1858-1950
9368
A man who listens because he has nothing
to say can hardly be a source of
inspiration. The only listening that counts
is that of the talker who alternately absorbs
and expresses ideas.

9369
It is not easy to find happiness in
ourselves, and it is not possible to find it
elsewhere.

9370
It has been wisely said that we cannot
really love anybody at whom we never
laugh.

REYNOLD Gillian
9371
Art is life rearranged until it makes sense.

REYNOLDS Sir Joshua 1723-1792
9372 *Discourses on Art*
If you have great talents, industry will
improve them: if you have but moderate
abilities, industry will supply their
deficiency.

9373 *Discourses on Art*
A mere copier of nature can never produce
anything great.

9374 *Discourses on Art*
Could we teach taste or genius by rules,
they would be no longer taste and genius.

9375 *Discourses on Art*
The value and rank of every art is in
proportion to the mental labour employed
in it, or the mental pleasure produced by
it.

REYNOLDS Malvina 1900-1978
9376 *'Little Boxes'*
Little boxes on the hillside ...
And they're all made out of ticky-tacky
And they all look just the same.

RHODES Cecil 1853-1902
9377
Ask any man what nationality he would
prefer to be, and ninety-nine out of a
hundred will tell you that they would
prefer to be Englishmen.

9378 *(on the day of his death)*
So little done, so much to do.

RHYS Jean 1894-1979
9379 *The Left Bank 'Illusion'*
The perpetual hunger to be beautiful and
that thirst to be loved which is the real
curse of Eve.

9380 *The Left Bank 'In the Rue de l'Arrivée'*
Only the hopeless are starkly sincere and ...
only the unhappy can either give or take
sympathy.

9381 *(describing herself)*
A doormat in a world of boots.

9382 *Good Morning, Midnight*
Some must cry so that others may be able
to laugh the more heartily.

9383 *Voyage in the Dark*
The feeling of Sunday is the same
everywhere, heavy, melancholy, standing
still. Like when they say 'As it was in the
beginning, is now, and ever shall be, world
without end'.

RICE Grantland 1880-1954
9384 *'Alumnus Football'*
For when the One Great Scorer comes to
mark against your name,
He writes - not that you won or lost - but
how you played the Game.

9385 *'The Two Sides of War'*
All wars are planned by old men
In council rooms apart.

RICE Tim 1944-
9386 *Jesus Christ Superstar 'Herod's Song'*
Prove to me that you're no fool,
Walk across my swimming pool.

RICHARDS Rebecca
9387
Oh, to be only half as wonderful as my
child thought I was when he was small,
and only half as stupid as my teenager

now thinks I am.

RICHARDSON Justin
9388
If only I hadn't had sisters
How much more romantic I'd be
But my sisters were such little blisters
That all women are sisters to me.

RICHARDSON Samuel 1689-1761
9389 *Clarissa*
It is more difficult to catch a bird than a lady.

9390 *Clarissa*
Mine is the most plotting heart in the world.

9391 *History of Sir Charles Grandison*
A feeling heart is a blessing that no one, who has it, would be without; and it is a moral security of innocence.

RICHLER Mordecai 1931-
9392
Listen your Lordship, I'm a respecter of institutions. Even in Paris, I remained a Canadian. I puffed hashish, but I didn't inhale.

9393
There are ten commandments, right? Well, it's like an exam. You get eight out of ten, you're just about top of the class.

9394
Wherever I travel, I'm too late. The orgy has moved elsewhere.

9395
I work every day - or at least I force myself into office or room. I may get nothing done, but you don't earn bonuses without putting in time. Nothing may come for three months, but you don't earn the fourth without it.

9396
Fundamentally, all writing is about the same thing; it's about dying, about the brief flicker of time we have here, and the frustrations that it creates.

RICHTER Hans 1843-1916
9397 *(attributed)*
Up with your damned nonsense will I put

twice, or perhaps once, but sometimes always, by God, never.

RICHTER Jean Paul 1763-1825
9398
What makes old age so sad is not that our joys but our hopes cease.

9399
A variety of nothing is superior to a monotony of something.

9400
No one is more profoundly sad than he who laughs too much.

9401
Man's feelings are always purest and most glowing in the hour of meeting and of farewell.

9402
It is simpler and easier to flatter men than to praise them.

9403
There is a certain noble pride, through which merits shine brighter than through modesty.

9404
Sleep, riches and health to be truly enjoyed must be interrupted.

9405
Providence has given to the French the empire of the land, to the English that of the sea, and to the Germans that of - the air!

RICKENBACKER Eddie 1890-1973
9406
Courage is doing what you're afraid to do. There can be no courage unless you're scared.

RIDDING George 1828-1904
9407
I feel a feeling which I feel you all feel.

RIDER Mike
9408
Designers and freelance artists and editors can set their hourly rates by dividing their annual income needs by 1000.

RIIS Sharon
9409
Basically, I'm interested in friendship, sex and death.

RILKE Rainer Maria 1875-1926
9410
The gnarled fidelity of an old habit.

9411
Fame is the sum of the misunderstanding that gathers about a new name.

9412
Nothing in the world can one imagine beforehand, not the least thing. Everything is made up of so many unique particulars that cannot be foreseen.

9413
Do continue to believe that with your feeling and your work you are taking part in the greatest; the more strongly you cultivate in yourself this belief, the more will reality and the world go forth from it.

9414
Love consists in this, that two solitudes protect and touch and greet each other.

9415
Oh longing for places that were not
Cherished enough in that fleeting hour
How I long to make good from afar
The forgotten gesture, the additional act.

9416 *Letter to Paula Modersohn-Becker*
I hold this to be the highest task for a bond between two people: that each protects the solitude of the other.

RIMBAUD Arthur 1854-1891
9417 *'Ma Bohème'*
I was walking along, hands in holey pockets; my overcoat also was entering the realms of the ideal.

9418 *'Le Bâteau ivre'*
Sweeter than the flesh of tart apples to children, the green water penetrates my wooden hull.

9419 *'Le Bâteau ivre'*
I have bathed in the Poem of the Sea, steeped in stars, and milky, devouring the green azures.

9420 *'Le Bâteau ivre'*
I pine for Europe of the ancient parapets!

9421 *'Voyelles'*
A black, E white, I red, U green, O blue: vowels, some day I will tell of the births that may be yours.

RINEY Hal 1932-
9422 *(slogan for Ronald Reagan's election campaign)*
It's morning again in America.

RITZ César 1850-1918
9423
Le client n'a jamais tort.
The customer is never wrong.

RIVAROL Antoine de 1753-1801
9424
What is not clear is not French.

ROADE W. Winwood
9425
Men prefer to believe that they are degenerated angels, rather than elevated apes.

ROBBINS Leonard H.
9426
How a minority,
Reaching majority,
Seizing authority,
Hates a minority!

ROBBINS Lord 1898-1984
9427 *Essay on the Nature ... of Economic Science*
Economics is the science which studies human behaviour as a relationship between ends and scarce means which have alternative uses.

ROBESPIERRE Maximilien 1758-1794
9428
Wickedness is the root of despotism as virtue is the essence of the Republic.

9429 *Déclaration des droits de l'homme*
Any law which violates the inalienable rights of man is essentially unjust and tyrannical; it is not a law at all.

9430 *Lettres à ses commettans*
The general will rules in society as the private will governs each separate

individual.

ROBIN Leo 1900-
9431 *Gentlemen Prefer Blondes 'Diamonds...'*
A kiss on the hand may be quite
continental,
But diamonds are a girl's best friend ...

9432 *Gentlemen Prefer Blondes 'Diamonds...'*
Men grow cold as girls grow old
And we all lose our charms in the end.
But square cut or pear shape,
These rocks won't lose their shape,
Diamonds are a girl's best friend.

9433 *(with Ralph Rainger)*
Thanks for the memory.

ROBINSON Edwin Arlington 1869-1935
9434 *'John Brown'*
I shall have more to say when I am dead.

9435 *Literature in the Making*
The world is not a 'prison house', but a
kind of kindergarten, where millions of
bewildered infants are trying to spell God
with the wrong blocks.

ROBINSON James Harvey 1863-1935
9436
We find it hard to believe that other
people's thoughts are as silly as our own,
but they probably are.

ROCHE Arthur Somers
9437
Anxiety is a thin stream of fear trickling
through the mind. If encouraged, it cuts a
channel into which all other thoughts are
drained.

ROCHE Sir Boyle 1743-1807
9438 *(attributed)*
Mr Speaker, I smell a rat; I see him forming
in the air and darkening the sky; but I'll
nip him in the bud.

ROCHE John P.
9439
In politics, a straight line is the shortest
distance to disaster.

ROCHESTER John Wilmot, Earl of 1647-
1680
9440 *'Against Constancy'*
Tell me no more of constancy,

that frivolous pretence,
Of cold age, narrow jealousy,
disease and want of sense.

9441 *'The King's Epitaph' (Charles II)*
Here lies a great and mighty king
Whose promise none relies on;
He never said a foolish thing,
Nor ever did a wise one.

9442 *'A Letter from Artemisia in the Town to
Chloe...'*
Love ...
That cordial drop heaven in our cup has
thrown
To make the nauseous draught of life go
down.

9443 *'Upon Nothing'*
Nothing, thou elder brother even to shade
Thou hadst a being ere the world was
made,
And, well fixed, art alone of ending not
afraid.

9444 *'A Ramble in St James' Park'*
... Natural freedoms are but just:
There's something generous in mere lust.

9445 *'A Satire against Mankind'*
Reason, an *ignis fatuus* of the mind,
Which leaves the light of nature, sense,
behind.

9446 *'A Satire against Mankind'*
For all men would be cowards if they
durst.

9447 *'Song'*
Love a woman? You're an ass!
'Tis a most insipid passion
To choose out for your happiness
The silliest part of God's creation.

ROCKEFELLER 2nd John D. 1874-1960
9448
I was born into it and there was nothing I
could do about it. It was there, like air or
food, or any other element. The only
question with wealth is what you do with
it.

ROCKEFELLER 3rd John D. 1906-1978
9449
Everyone likes to think that he has done
reasonably well in life, so that it comes as a

shock to find our children believing differently. The temptation is to tune them out; it takes much more courage to listen.

ROCKEFELLER John D. 1839-1937
9450
Good management consists of showing average people how to do the work of superior people.

9451
The ability to deal with people is as purchasable a commodity as sugar or coffee. And I pay more for that ability than for any other under the sun.

ROCKEFELLER Nelson 1908-1979
9452
It is essential that we enable young people to see themselves as participants in one of the most exciting eras in history, and to have a sense of purpose in relation to it.

ROCKNE Knute 1888-1931
9453
Show me a good and gracious loser, and I'll show you a failure.

RODDENBERRY Gene 1921-1991
9454 *Star Trek*
These are the voyages of the starship *Enterprise*. Its five-year mission ... to boldly go where no man has gone before.

9455 *Star Trek*
Beam us up, Mr Scott.
(usually quoted as "Beam me up, Scotty")

RODGERS Richard 1902-1979
9456 *No Strings 'The Sweetest Sounds'*
The sweetest sounds I'll ever hear
Are still inside my head.
The kindest words I'll ever know
Are waiting to be said.

RODIN Auguste 1840-1917
9457
One must work, nothing but work, and one must have patience.

9458
I invent nothing. I rediscover.

ROETHKE Theodore 1908-1963
9459
I learn by going where I have to go.

9460
Deep in their roots,
All flowers keep the light.

9461 *'The Adamant'*
Truth never is undone;
Its shafts remain.

9462 *'Dolour'*
I have known the inexorable sadness of pencils,
Neat in their boxes, dolour of pad and paper-weight,
All the misery of manilla folders and mucilage,
Desolation in immaculate public places.

9463 *'The Exorcism'*
In a dark wood I saw -
I saw my several selves
Come running from the leaves,
Lewd, tiny, careless lives
That scuttled under stones,
Or broke, but would not go.

9464 *'Open House'*
My secrets cry aloud.
I have no need for tongue.
My heart keeps open house,
My doors are widely flung.
An epic of the eyes
My love with no disguise.

ROGERS Ginger 1911-1995
9465
When two people love each other, they don't look at each other, they look in the same direction.

ROGERS Samuel 1763-1855
9466 *(attributed)*
A man who attempts to read all the new productions must do as the fleas do - skip.

9467 *'To -, 1814'*
There's such a charm in melancholy,
I would not, if I could, be gay.

9468 *'Human Life'*
Think nothing done while aught remains to do.

9469 *'Human Life'*
Then, never less alone than when alone,
Those whom he loved so long and sees no more,

Loved and still loves - not dead - but gone before,
He gathers round him.

9470 *Jacqueline*
To know her was to love her.

9471 *Table Talk*
Sheridan was listened to with such attention that you might have heard a pin drop.

9472 *Table Talk*
It doesn't much signify whom one marries, for one is sure to find next morning that it was someone else.

ROGERS Thorold 1823-1890
9473
See, ladling butter from alternate tubs
Stubbs butters Freeman, Freeman butters Stubbs.

ROGERS Will 1879-1935
9474
A holding company is the people you give your money to while you're being searched.

9475
Invest in inflation. It's the only thing going up.

9476
Don't gamble; take all your savings and buy some good stock and hold it till it goes up, then sell it. If it don't go up, don't buy it.

9477
The schools ain't what they used to be and never was.

9478
Be thankful we're not getting all the government we're paying for.

9479
Being a hero is about the shortest-lived profession on earth.

9480
This thing of being a hero, about the main thing to it is to know when to die.

9481
We are all here for a spell, get all the good laughs you can.

9482
Everybody is ignorant, only on different subjects.

9483
It isn't what we don't know that gives us trouble, it's what we know that ain't so.

9484
A difference of opinion is what makes horse racing and missionaries.

9485
I'm not a member of any organized party, I'm a Democrat.

9486
More men have been elected between Sundown and Sun-up than ever were elected between Sun-up and Sundown.

9487
If you ever injected truth into politics you would have no politics.

9488
Politics has got so expensive that it takes lots of money to even get beat with.

9489
One revolution is like one cocktail, it just gets you organized for the next.

9490
The income tax has made more liars out of the American people than golf has. Even when you make a tax form out on the level, you don't know when it's through, if you are a crook or a martyr.

9491
When you put down the good things you ought to have done, and leave out the bad things you did do - well, that's memoirs.

9492
Well, all I know is what I read in the papers.

9493
You can't say civilization don't advance, however, for in every war they kill you in a new way.

9494
Half our life is spent trying to find
something to do with the time we have
rushed through life trying to save.

9495 *Autobiography*
There is only one thing that can kill the
movies, and that is education.

9496 *The Illiterate Digest*
The more you read and observe about this
Politics thing, you got to admit that each
party is worse than the other.

9497 *The Illiterate Digest*
Everthing is funny as long as it is
happening to Somebody Else.

9498 *Weekly Articles*
Communism is like prohibition, it's a good
idea but it won't work.

ROGOW Arnold A.
9499
Ultimately politics in a democracy reflects
values much more than it shapes them.

ROHE Mies Van der 1886-1969
9500
Architecture begins when you place two
bricks *carefully* together.

ROLAND Madame 1754-1793
9501
O liberty! O liberty! what crimes are
committed in thy name!

ROLFE Frederick William ('Baron Corvo')
1860-1913
9502 *Hadrian VII*
That cold, white, candent voice which was
more caustic than silver nitrate and more
thrilling than a scream.

9503 *Hadrian VII*
Pray for the repose of His soul. He was so
tired.

ROLLIN Charles 1661-1741
9504
The highest and most lofty trees have the
most reason to dread the thunder.

RONSARD Pierre de 1524-1585
9505 *Odes, à Cassandre (translated by Andrew
Lang)*
See, Mignonne, hath not the rose

That this morning did unclose
Her purple mantle to the light,
Lost, before the day be dead,
The glory of her raiment red,
Her colour, bright as yours is bright?

ROONEY Mickey
9506
You always pass failure on the way to
success.

ROOSEVELT Eleanor 1884-1962
9507
What one has to do usually can be done.

9508
Life has got to be lived - that's all there is
to it. At seventy, I would say the
advantage is that you take life more
calmly. You know that 'this, too, shall
pass!'

9509
Character building begins in our infancy,
and continues until death.

9510
When you cease to make a contribution
you begin to die.

9511
I think somehow we learn who we really
are and then live with that decision.

9512
No one can make you feel inferior without
your consent.

ROOSEVELT Franklin D. 1882-1945
9513
If I were starting life over again, I am
inclined to think that I would go into the
advertising business in preference to
almost any other. The general raising of
standards of modern civilization among all
groups of people during the past half-
century would have been impossible
without that spreading of the knowledge
of higher standards by means of
advertising.

9514
I think we consider too much the good
luck of the early bird, and not enough the
bad luck of the early worm.

9515
So let me assert my firm belief that the only thing we have to fear is fear itself - nameless, unreasoning, unjustified terror which paralyzes needed efforts to convert retreat into advance.

9516
It is common sense to take a method and try it. If it fails, admit it frankly and try another, but above all, try something.

9517
I have no expectation of making a hit every time I come to bat.

9518
These unhappy times call for the building of plans that ... build from the bottom up and not from the top down, that put their faith once more in the forgotten man at the bottom of the economic pyramid.

9519
I have said this before, but I shall say it again and again and again: Your boys are not going to be sent into any foreign wars.

9520
We look forward to a world founded upon four essential human freedoms. The first is freedom of speech and expression - everywhere in the world. The second is freedom of every person to worship God in his own way - everywhere in the world. The third is freedom from want ... everywhere in the world. The fourth is freedom from fear ... anywhere in the world.

9521
Books can not be killed by fire. People die, but books never die. No man and no force can abolish memory.

9522 *(accepting Presidential nomination)*
I pledge you, I pledge myself, to a new deal for the American people. Let us all here assembled constitute ourselves prophets of a new order of competence and courage. This is a call to arms.

9523 *'Fireside Chat'*
We have the men - the skill - the wealth - and above all, the will ... We must be the great arsenal of democracy.

9524 *(inaugural address)*
The only thing we have to fear is fear itself.

9525 *(inaugural address)*
In the field of world policy I would dedicate this Nation to the policy of the good neighbour.

9526 *(second inaugural address)*
I see one-third of a nation ill-housed, ill-clad, ill-nourished.

ROOSEVELT Theodore 1858-1919
9527
Do what you can, with what you have, where you are.

9528
No man is above the law and no man is below it: nor do we ask any man's permission when we ask him to obey it.

9529
Nine-tenths of wisdom consists in being wise in time.

9530
I am only an average man, but, by George, I work harder at it than the average man.

9531
I wish to preach, not the doctrine of ignoble ease, but the doctrine of the strenuous life.

9532
A man who is good enough to shed his blood for the country is good enough to be given a square deal afterwards. More than that no man is entitled to, and less than that no man shall have.

9533
The men with the muck-rakes are often indispensable to the well-being of society; but only if they know when to stop raking the muck.

9534
There is no room in this country for hyphenated Americanism.

9535
The most successful politician is he who says what everybody is thinking most often and in the loudest voice.

9536 *Autobiography*
Foolish fanatics ... the men who form the
lunatic fringe in all reform movements.

ROREM Ned 1923-
9537 *The Paris Diary of Ned Rorem*
Quarrels in France strengthen a love affair.
In America they end it.

ROSCOMMON Earl of 1637-1685
9538 *Essay on Translated Verse*
Choose an author as you choose a friend.

9539 *Essay on Translated Verse*
Immodest words admit of no defence,
For want of decency is want of sense.

9540 *Essay on Translated Verse*
The multitude is always in the wrong.

ROSE Billy 1899-1966
9541
Never invest your money in anything that
eats or needs repairing.

ROSEBERY Lord 1847-1929
9542
It is beginning to be hinted that we are a
nation of amateurs.

9543
The Empire is a Commonwealth of
Nations.

9544 *(on remaining outside Liberal Party
leadership)*
I must plough my furrow alone.

**ROSENBERG Ethel and ROSENBERG
Julius** 1916-1953 and 1918-1953
9545 *(letter from Julius before their execution)*
We are the first victims of American
Fascism.

ROSENBERG John D.
9546
New York is notoriously inhospitable to
the past, disowning it whenever it can.

ROSENBERG Leo
9547
First you forget names, then you forget
faces, then you forget to pull your zipper
up, then you forget to pull your zipper
down.

ROSS Alan S.C. 1907-1980
9548
U and Non-U, An Essay in Sociological
Linguistics.

ROSSELLINI Roberto 1906-1977
9549
Noble acts and momentous events happen
in the same way and produce the same
impression as the ordinary facts.

ROSSETTI Christina 1830-1894
9550 *'A Birthday'*
Because the birthday of my life
Is come, my love is come to me.

9551 *'Mid-Winter'*
In the bleak mid-winter
Frosty wind made moan,
Earth stood hard as iron,
Water like a stone.

9552 *'Oh roses for the flush of youth'*
Oh roses for the flush of youth,
And laurel for the perfect prime;
But pluck an ivy branch for me
Grown old before my time.

9553 *'Remember'*
Remember me when I am gone away,
Gone far away into the silent land.
Better by far you should forget and smile
Than you should remember and be sad.

9554 *'Rest'*
O Earth, lie heavily upon her eyes;
Seal her sweet eyes weary of watching,
Earth.

9555 *'Rest'*
Silence more musical than any song.

9556 *'When I am dead'*
When I am dead, my dearest,
Sing no sad songs for me.

ROSSETTI Dante Gabriel 1828-1882
9557
Conception, my boy, fundamental
brainwork, is what makes the difference in
all art.

9558
The worst moment for the atheist is when
he is really thankful, and has nobody to
thank.

9559 *'The Blessed Damozel'*
The blessed damozel leaned out
From the gold bar of Heaven;
Her eyes were deeper than the depth
Of waters stilled at even;
She had three lilies in her hand,
And the stars in her hair were seven.

9560 *'The Blessed Damozel'*
Her hair that lay along her back
Was yellow like ripe corn.

9561 *'The Blessed Damozel'*
As low as where this earth
Spins like a fretful midge.

9562 *'The Blessed Damozel'*
And the souls mounting up to God
Went by her like thin flames.

9563 *The House of Life*
A sonnet is a moment's monument -
Memorial from the Soul's eternity
To one dead deathless hour.

9564 *The House of Life 'Body's Beauty'*
And round his heart one strangling golden hair.

9565 *The House of Life 'Lost Days'*
I do not see them here; but after death
God knows I know the faces I shall see,
Each one a murdered self, with low last breath.

9566 *The House of Life 'Silent Noon'*
'Tis visible silence, still as the hour-glass.

9567 *The House of Life 'Silent Noon'*
Oh! clasp we to our hearts, for deathless dower,
This close-companioned inarticulate hour
When twofold silence was the song of love.

9568 *The House of Life 'A Superscription'*
Look in my face; my name is Might-have-been;
I am also called No-more, Too-late, Farewell.

9569 *The House of Life 'A Superscription'*
Sleepless with cold commemorative eyes.

9570 *'Soothsay'*
Unto the man of yearning thought
And aspiration, to do nought

Is in itself almost an act.

9571 *'Sudden Light'*
I have been here before,
But when or how I cannot tell:
I know the grass beyond the door,
The sweet keen smell,
The sighing sound, the lights around the shore.

ROSSINI Gioacchino 1792-1868
9572
One cannot judge 'Lohengrin' from a first hearing, and I certainly do not intend to hear it a second time.

9573
How wonderful opera would be if there were no singers.

9574
Wagner has lovely moments but awful quarters of an hour.

9575
Give me a laundry-list and I'll set it to music.

ROSSITER Clinton
9576
The final greatness of the presidency lies in the truth that it is not just an office of incredible power but a breeding ground of indestructible myth.

ROSTAND Edmond 1868-1918
9577 *Cyrano de Bergerac*
A large nose is in fact the sign of an affable man, good, courteous, witty, liberal, courageous, such as I am.

9578 *La Princesse Lointaine*
The dream, alone, is of interest. What is life, without a dream?

ROSTAND Jean 1894-1977
9579
My pessimism goes to the point of suspecting the sincerity of the pessimists.

9580 *Le Mariage*
A married couple are well suited when both partners usually feel the need for a quarrel at the same time.

9581 *Pensées d'un biologiste*
Kill a man, and you are an assassin. Kill
millions of men, and you are a conqueror.
Kill everyone, and you are a god.

ROSTEN Leo 1908-
9582 *(of W.C. Fields)*
Any man who hates dogs and babies can't
be all bad.

ROTH Philip 1933-
9583 *Portnoy's Complaint*
A Jewish man with parents alive is a
fifteen-year-old boy, and will remain a
fifteen-year-old boy until *they die!*

9584 *Portnoy's Complaint*
Doctor, my doctor, what do you say, LET'S
PUT THE ID BACK IN YID!

ROTHSCHILD Baron 1840-1915
9585
It isn't enough for you to love money - it's
also necessary that money should love
you.

ROTSTEIN Abraham
9586
Every dogma has its day.

9587
Power is the recognition of necessity.

ROTTEN Johnny
9588
Love is two minutes and fifty seconds of
squelching.

ROUAULT Georges 1871-1958
9589
For me, painting is a way to forget life. It
is a cry in the night, a strangled laugh.

ROUGET DE LISLE Claude-Joseph 1760-
1836
9590 *'La Marseillaise'*
Come, children of our country, the day of
glory has arrived ... To arms, citizens! Form
your battalions!

ROUPELL Charles
9591 *(attributed)*
To play billiards well is a sign of an ill-
spent youth.

ROUSSEAU Jean-Jacques 1712-1778
9592
I hate books; they teach us only to talk
about what we do not know.

9593
Happiness: a good bank account, a good
cook and a good digestion.

9594
Whoever blushes is already guilty; true
innocence is ashamed of nothing.

9595
Little privations are easily endured when
the heart is better treated than the body.

9596
Man was born free, and everywhere he is
in shackles.

9597
Everything is good when it leaves the
Creator's hands; everything degenerates in
the hands of man.

ROUTH Martin Joseph 1755-1854
9598 *(attributed)*
You will find it a very good practice
always to verify your references, sir!

ROUX Joseph
9599
Science is for those who learn; poetry for
those who know.

ROWAN Carl T. 1925-
9600
A minority group has 'arrived' only when
it has the right to produce some fools and
scoundrels without the entire group
paying for it.

ROWE Nicholas 1674-1718
9601
The joys of meeting pay the pangs of
absence;
Else who could bear it?

9602 *The Fair Penitent*
Is this that haughty, gallant, gay Lothario?

9603 *The Fair Penitent*
Like Helen, in the night when Troy was
sacked.

9604 *The Fair Penitent*
Death is the privilege of human nature,
And life without it were not worth our
taking.

ROWLAND Helen 1875-1950
9605
Failing to be there when a man wants her
is a woman's greatest sin, except to be
there when he doesn't want her.

9606 *A Guide to Men*
A husband is what is left of a lover, after
the nerve has been extracted.

9607 *A Guide to Men*
Somehow a bachelor never quite gets over
the idea that he is a thing of beauty and a
boy forever.

9608 *A Guide to Men*
The follies which a man regrets most in his
life, are those which he didn't commit
when he had the opportunity.

9609 *Reflections of a Bachelor Girl*
When you see what some girls marry, you
realize how much they must hate to work
for a living.

9610 *The Rubaiyat of a Bachelor*
Never trust a husband too far, nor a
bachelor too near.

9611 *The Wit of Women*
Before marriage, a man will lie awake
thinking about something you said; after
marriage, he'll fall asleep before you finish
saying it.

ROWLAND Richard c.1881-1947
9612 *(of the take-over of United Artists)*
The lunatics have taken charge of the
asylum.

ROXBOROUGH Henry
9613
Sport is one area where no participant is
worried about another's race, religion or
wealth: and where the only concern is
'Have you come to play?'

ROY Gabrielle 1909-
9614
The life of a writer is tragic: the more we
advance, the farther there is to go and the
more there is to say, the less time there is
to say it.

ROYCE Josiah 1855-1916
9615
Unless you can find some sort of loyalty,
you cannot find unity and peace in your
active living.

9616
Thinking is like loving and dying - each of
us must do it for himself.

ROYDEN Maude 1876-1956
9617
The Church should go forward along the
path of progress and be no longer satisfied
only to represent the Conservative Party at
prayer.

ROYDE-SMITH Naomi c.1875-1964
9618 *Weekend Book*
I know two things about the horse
And one of them is rather coarse.

RUBENS Paul Alfred 1875-1917
9619 *'Your King and Country Want You'*
Oh! we don't want to lose you but we
think you ought to go
For your King and your Country both
need you so.

RUBENS Peter Paul 1577-1640
9620
Sir, when their backsides look good
enough to slap, there's nothing more to do.

RUBIN Theodore Isaac
9621
Compassion for myself is the most
powerful healer of them all.

RUBINSTEIN Artur 1888-1982
9622
When I was young, I used to have
successes with women because I was
young. Now I have successes with women
because I am old. Middle age was the
hardest part.

9623
I am tired before the concert, not
afterward.

9624
Of course there is no formula for success except, perhaps, an unconditional acceptance of life and what it brings.

RUBINSTEIN Helena 1871-1965
9625
There are no ugly women, only lazy ones.

RUNES Dagobert
9626
Happy the man who gains sagacity in youth, but thrice happy he who retains the fervour of youth in age.

9627
If tomorrow were never to come, it would not be worth living today.

9628
Work is man's most natural form of relaxation.

RUNYON Damon 1884-1946
9629
Much as he is opposed to lawbreaking, he is not bigoted about it.

9630
The race is not always to the swift nor the battle to the strong - but that's the way to bet.

9631
Guys and dolls.

9632 *'A Very Honourable Guy'*
Always try to rub up against money, for if you rub up against money long enough, some of it may rub off on you.

9633 *'The Idyll of Miss Sarah Brown'*
At such an hour the sinners are still in bed resting up from their sinning of the night before, so they will be in good shape for more sinning a little later on.

9634 *'A Nice Price'*
I long ago came to the conclusion that all life is 6 to 5 against.

RUSK Dean 1909-
9635
One of the best ways to persuade others is with your ears.

9636
One third of the people of the world are asleep at any given moment. The other two thirds are awake and probably stirring up trouble somewhere.

9637 *(of the Cuban missile crisis)*
We're eyeball to eyeball, and I think the other fellow just blinked.

RUSKIN John 1819-1900
9638
The beauty of the animal form is in exact proportion to the amount of moral and intellectual virtue expressed by it.

9639
If a book is worth reading, it is worth buying.

9640
There is hardly anything in the world that some man can't make a little worse and sell a little cheaper, and the people who consider price only are this man's lawful prey.

9641
To make your children capable of honesty is the beginning of education.

9642
When love and skill work together expect a masterpiece.

9643
No one can do me any good by loving me; I have more love than I need, or could do any good with; but people do me good by making me love them - which isn't easy.

9644
The purest and most thoughtful minds are those which love colour the most.

9645 *(attributed)*
A single villa can mar a landscape, and dethrone a dynasty of hills.

9646 *Unto this Last*
Soldiers of the ploughshare as well as soldiers of the sword.

9647 *Unto this Last*
Government and co-operation are in all things the laws of life; anarchy and competition the laws of death.

9648 *Unto this Last*
There is no wealth but life.

9649 *Lectures on Architecture and Painting*
No person who is not a great sculptor or painter can be an architect. If he is not a sculptor or painter, he can only be a *builder*.

9650 *Modern Painters*
All violent feelings ... produce in us a falseness in all our impressions of external things, which I would generally characterize as the 'Pathetic Fallacy'.

9651 *Modern Painters*
Mountains are the beginning and the end of all natural scenery.

9652 *Sesame and Lilies*
All books are divisible into two classes, the books of the hour, and the books of all time.

9653 *Sesame and Lilies*
Be sure that you go to the author to get at his meaning, not to find yours.

9654 *Sesame and Lilies*
Which of us ... is to do the hard and dirty work for the rest - and for what pay? Who is to do the pleasant and clean work, and for what pay?

9655 *Sesame and Lilies*
We call ourselves a rich nation, and we are filthy and foolish enough to thumb each other's books out of circulating libraries!

9656 *Seven Lamps of Architecture*
When we build, let us think that we build for ever.

9657 *Stones of Venice*
Remember that the most beautiful things in the world are the most useless; peacocks and lilies for instance.

9658 *Time and Tide*
Your honesty is *not* to be based either on religion or policy. Both your religion and policy must be based on *it*.

9659 *The Two Paths*
Fine art is that in which the hand, the head, and the heart of man go together.

9660 *The Two Paths*
Not only is there but one way of *doing* things rightly, but there is only one way of *seeing* them, and that is, seeing the whole of them.

9661 *On Whistler's Nocturne in Black and Gold*
I have seen, and heard, much of Cockney impudence before now; but never expected to hear a coxcomb ask two hundred guineas for flinging a pot of paint in the public's face.

RUSSELL Bertrand 1872-1970
9662
Anything you're good at contributes to happiness.

9663
The more we realize our minuteness and our impotence in the face of cosmic forces, the more astonishing becomes what human beings have achieved.

9664
It is only in marriage with the world that our ideals can bear fruit; divorced from it they remain barren.

9665
The most savage controversies are those about matters as to which there is no good evidence either way.

9666
'Change' is scientific, 'progress' is ethical; change is indubitable, whereas progress is a matter of controversy.

9667
Every man is encompassed by a cloud of comforting convictions, which move with him like flies on a summer day.

9668
The reformative effect of punishment is a belief that dies hard, chiefly, I think, because it is so satisfying to our sadistic impulses.

9669
The average man's opinions are much less foolish than they would be if he thought for himself.

9670
Cynicism such as one finds very frequently among the most highly educated young men and women of the West, results from the combination of comfort and powerlessness.

9671
Many people would die sooner than think; in fact, they do.

9672
Drunkenness is temporary suicide: the happiness that it brings is merely negative, a momentary cessation of unhappiness.

9673
If we were all given by magic the power to read each other's thoughts, I suppose the first effect would be to dissolve all friendships.

9674
One must care about a world one will not see.

9675
To be without some of the things you want is an indispensable part of happiness.

9676
There is much pleasure to be gained from useless knowledge.

9677
In all affairs, love, religion, politics or business, it's a healthy idea, now and then, to hang a question mark on things you have long taken for granted.

9678
The good life, as I conceive it, is a happy life. I do not mean that if you are good you will be happy - I mean that if you are happy you will be good.

9679
There was never any reason to believe in any innate superiority of the male, except his superior muscle.

9680
It is preoccupation with possession, more than anything else, that prevents men from living freely and nobly.

9681
The fundamental defect of fathers is that they want their children to be a credit to them.

9682
Science is what you know, philosophy is what you don't know.

9683
To teach how to live with uncertainty, and yet without being paralyzed by hesitation, is perhaps the chief thing that philosophy in our age can still do for those who study it.

9684
I do not believe that any peacock envies another peacock his tail, because every peacock is persuaded that his own tail is the finest in the world. The consequence of this is that peacocks are peaceable birds.

9685
What men want is not knowledge, but certainty.

9686
Simpson succeeded in proving that there was no harm in giving anaesthetics to men, because God put Adam into a deep sleep when He extracted his rib. But male ecclesiastics remained unconvinced as regards the sufferings of women, at any rate in childbirth.

9687 *(of Sir Anthony Eden)*
Not a gentleman; dresses too well.

9688 *Autobiography*
Three passions, simple but overwhelmingly strong, have governed my life: the longing for love, the search for knowledge and unbearable pity for the suffering of mankind.

9689 *The Conquest of Happiness*
To be able to use leisure intelligently will be the last product of an intelligent civilization.

9690 *The Conquest of Happiness*
Men who are unhappy, like men who sleep badly, are always proud of the fact.

9691 *The Conquest of Happiness*
Boredom is ... a vital problem for the moralist, since half the sins of mankind are caused by the fear of it.

9692 *The Conquest of Happiness*
One of the symptoms of approaching nervous breakdown is the belief that one's work is terribly important, and that to take a holiday would bring all kinds of disaster.

9693 *The Conquest of Happiness*
One should as a rule respect public opinion in so far as is necessary to avoid starvation and to keep out of prison, but anything that goes beyond this is voluntary submission to an unnecessary tyranny.

9694 *The Conquest of Happiness*
A sense of duty is useful in work, but offensive in personal relations. People wish to be liked, not to be endured with patient resignation.

9695 *The Conquest of Happiness*
Of all forms of caution, caution in love is perhaps the most fatal to true happiness.

9696 *Marriage and Morals*
To fear love is to fear life, and those who fear life are already three parts dead.

9697 *Mysticism and Logic*
The law of causality, I believe, ... is a relic of a bygone age, surviving, like the monarchy, only because it is erroneously supposed to do no harm.

9698 *Mysticism and Logic*
Brief and Powerless is Man's life; on him and all his race the slow, sure doom falls pitiless and dark.

9699 *Sceptical Essays*
We have two kinds of morality side by side: one which we preach but do not practice, and the other which we practice but seldom preach.

9700 *Sceptical Essays*
It is obvious that 'obscenity' is not a term capable of exact legal definition; in the practice of the Courts, it means 'anything that shocks the magistrate'.

9701 *The Scientific Outlook*
When I come to die I shall not feel I have lived in vain. I have seen the earth run red at evening, the dew sparkling in the morning, and the snow shining under a frosty sun.

RUSSELL Dora 1894-1986
9702 *Hypatia*
We want better reasons for having children than not knowing how to prevent them.

RUSSELL Foster Meharny
9703
Every story has three sides to it - yours, mine and the facts.

RUSSELL George W. 1867-1935
9704
Our hearts were drunk with a beauty Our eyes could never see.

RUSSELL Lord John 1792-1878
9705
If peace cannot be maintained with honour, it is no longer peace.

9706
Among the defects of the Bill, which were numerous, one provision was conspicuous by its presence and another by its absence.

9707 *(attributed)*
A proverb is one man's wit and all men's wisdom.

9708 *(on defeat of the second Reform Bill)*
It is impossible that the whisper of a faction should prevail against the voice of a nation.

RUSSELL Sir William Howard 1820-1907
9709 *(of the Russians charging the British at Crimea)*
They dashed on towards that thin red line tipped with steel.

RUTHERFORD Lord 1871-1937
9710 *(attributed)*
All science is either physics or stamp collecting.

9711 *(attributed)*
We haven't got the money, so we've got to think!

9712 *(in 1937)*
The energy produced by the breaking down of the atom is a very poor kind of thing. Anyone who expects a source of power from the transformation of these atoms is talking moonshine.

RUTHERFORD Mark 1831-1913
9713
Most of us have no real loves and no real hatreds. Blessed is love, less blessed is hatred, but thrice accursed is that indifference which is neither one nor the other.

RYAN Joe
9714
A committee of one gets things done.

RYLE Gilbert 1900-1976
9715 *The Concept of Mind*
Philosophy is the replacement of category-habits by category-disciplines.

9716 *The Concept of Mind*
The dogma of the Ghost in the Machine.

SAADI c.1184-c.1292
9717
Whoever has his foe at his mercy, and does not kill him, is his own enemy.

SACKLER Howard 1929-
9718 *Good-bye Fidel*
Affairs, like revolutions, should only have beginnings.

SACKS Dr. Oliver
9719
People can be consumed by creativity as they are by tuberculosis.

SACKVILLE-WEST Vita 1892-1962
9720 *The King's Daughter*
The greater cats with golden eyes
Stare out between the bars.
Deserts are there, and different skies,
And night with different stars.

9721 *The Land 'Winter'*
The country habit has me by the heart,
For he's bewitched for ever who has seen,
Not with his eyes but with his vision, Spring
Flow down the woods and stipple leaves with sun.

SAGAN Carl 1934-
9722
It is of interest to note that while some dolphins are reported to have learned English - up to fifty words used in correct context - no human being has been reported to have learned dolphinese.

9723
Who are we? We find that we live on an insignificant planet of a humdrum star lost in a galaxy tucked away in some forgotten corner of a universe in which there are far more galaxies than people.

SAGAN Françoise 1935-1994
9724
I like men to behave like men. I like them strong and childish.

9725
Every little girl knows about love. It is only her capacity to suffer because of it that increases.

9726 *La Chamade*
To jealousy, nothing is more frightful than laughter.

SAID Edward
9727
The intellectual should be a disrupter or a dissenter - a nay sayer.

ST LAURENT Yves 1936-
9728
Fashions fade - style is eternal.

SAINT-EXUPÉRY Antoine de 1900-1944
9729
To be a man is to feel that one's own stone contributes to building the edifice of the world.

9730
A chief is a man who assumes responsibility. He says, 'I was beaten', he does not say 'My men were beaten'.

9731
A single event can awaken within us a stranger totally unknown to us. To live is to be slowly born.

9732
What saves a man is to take a step. Then another step. It is always the same step, but you have to take it.

9733
The field of consciousness is tiny. It accepts only one problem at a time. Get into a fist fight, put your mind on the strategy of the fight, and you will not feel the other fellow's punches.

9734
Night, when words fade and things come alive, when the destructive analysis of day is done, and all that is truly important becomes whole and sound again. When man reassembles his fragmentary self and grows with the calm of a tree.

9735 *Le Petit Prince*
Grown-ups never understand anything for themselves, and it is tiresome for children to be always and forever explaining things to them.

9736 *Le Petit Prince*
It is only with the heart that one can see rightly; what is essential is invisible to the eye.

9737 *Wind, Sand and Stars*
Experience shows us that love does not consist in gazing at each other but in looking together in the same direction.

SAKI (Hector Hugh Monro) 1870-1916
9738
The clock struck eleven with the respectful unobtrusiveness of one whose mission in life is to be ignored.

9739
Hating anything in the way of ill-natured gossip ourselves, we are always grateful to those who do it for us and do it well.

9740
Oysters are more beautiful than any religion ... there's nothing in Christianity or Buddhism that quite matches the sympathetic unselfishness of an oyster.

9741 *Chronicles of Clovis*
The people of Crete unfortunately make more history than they can consume

locally.

9742 *Chronicles of Clovis*
All decent people live beyond their incomes nowadays, and those who aren't respectable live beyond other peoples'.

9743 *Reginald*
The cook was a good cook, as cooks go; and as good cooks go, she went.

9744 *Reginald*
I always say beauty is only sin deep.

9745 *Reginald in Russia*
Good gracious, you've got to educate him first. You can't expect a boy to be vicious till he's been to a good school.

9746 *Reginald in Russia*
Addresses are given to us to conceal our whereabouts.

9747 *The Square Egg*
A little inaccuracy sometimes saves tons of explanation.

9748 *Toys of Peace and Other Papers*
Children with Hyacinth's temperament don't know better as they grow older; they merely know more.

9749 *The Unbearable Bassington*
We all know that Prime Ministers are wedded to the truth, but like other married couples they sometimes live apart.

SALINGER J.D. 1919-
9750
A confessional passage has probably never been written that didn't stink a little bit of the writer's pride in having given up his pride.

9751 *The Catcher in the Rye*
Sex is something I really don't understand too hot. You never know *where* the hell you are. I keep making up these sex rules for myself, and then I break them right away.

SALISBURY Lord 1830-1903
9752
We are part of the community of Europe and we must do our duty as such.

9753
Horny-handed sons of toil.

9754 *(comparing his role with that of Gladstone)*
I rank myself no higher in the scheme of things than a policeman - whose utility would disappear if there were no criminals.

9755 *(of the Daily Mail)*
By office boys for office boys.

9756 *(of Iain Macleod, Colonial Secretary)*
Too clever by half.

9757 *Letter to Lord Lytton*
English policy is to float lazily downstream, occasionally putting out a diplomatic boathook to avoid collisions.

9758 *Letter to Lord Lytton*
No lesson seems to be so deeply inculcated by the experience of life as that you never should trust experts. If you believe the doctors, nothing is wholesome: if you believe the theologians, nothing is innocent: if you believe the soldiers, nothing is safe.

SALLUST 86-34 BC
9759 *Catiline*
Coveting other men's property, and squandering his own.

9760 *Catiline*
To like and dislike the same things, that is indeed true friendship.

SALMON Andrew
9761
There is only one truth, steadfast, healing, salutary, and that is the absurd.

SALVANDY Comte de 1795-1856
9762 *(just before the revolution)*
We are dancing on a volcano.

SAMPSON Anthony 1926-
9763 *Anatomy of Britain*
Members [of civil service orders] rise from CMG (known sometimes in Whitehall as 'Call Me God') to the KCMG ('Kindly Call Me God') to - for a select few governors and super-ambassadors - the GCMG ('God Calls Me God').

SAMUEL Lord 1870-1963
9764
Equality of opportunity is an equal opportunity to prove unequal talents.

9765 *A Book of Quotations*
A library is thought in cold storage.

9766 *Book of Quotations*
It takes two to make a marriage a success and only one to make it a failure.

9767 *Romanes Lecture*
Without doubt the greatest injury of all was done by basing morals on myth. For, sooner or later, myth is recognized for what it is, and disappears. Then morality loses the foundation on which it has been built.

SAMUELSON Paul A. 1915-
9768 *Economics*
The consumer, so it is said, is the king ... each is a voter who uses his money as votes to get the things done that he wants done.

SAND George 1804-1876
9769
Work is not man's punishment. It is his reward and his strength, his glory and his pleasure.

SANDBURG Carl 1878-1967
9770
Hope is an echo, hope ties itself yonder, yonder.

9771
Poetry is the journal of a sea animal living on land, wanting to fly in the air.

9772
One of the greatest necessities in America is to discover creative solitude.

9773
Sometime they'll give a war and nobody will come.

9774
Slang is a language that rolls up its sleeves, spits on its hands and goes to work.

9775 *'Chicago'*
Stormy, husky, brawling,
City of the Big Shoulders.

9776 *'Cool Tombs'*
When Abraham Lincoln was shovelled
into the tombs,
he forgot the copperheads and the
assassin...
In the dust, in the cool tombs.

9777 *'Fog'*
The fog comes
on little cat feet.
It sits looking
over harbour and city
on silent haunches
and then moves on.

9778 *'Grass'*
Pile the bodies high at Austerlitz and
Waterloo.
Shovel them under and let me work -
I am the grass; I cover all.

9779 *Incidentals*
I am an idealist. I don't know where I'm
going but I'm on the way.

9780 *'Poetry Considered'*
Poetry is the opening and closing of a
door, leaving those who look through to
guess about what is seen during a
moment.

9781 *'Prairie'*
I tell you the past is a bucket of ashes.

SANDERS Henry 'Red'
9782
Sure, winning isn't everything. It's the
only thing.

SANGER Margaret 1883-1966
9783
No woman can call herself free who does
not own and control her body. No woman
can call herself free until she can choose
consciously whether she will or will not be
a mother.

SANTAYANA George 1863-1952
9784
Before you contradict an old man, my fair
friend, you should endeavour to
understand him.

9785
An artist may visit a museum but only a
pedant can live there.

9786
Art is a delayed echo.

9787
Since barbarism has its pleasures it
naturally has its apologists.

9788
Habit is stronger than reason.

9789
There is nothing to which men, while they
have food and drink, cannot reconcile
themselves.

9790
Nothing you can lose by dying is half so
precious as the readiness to die, which is
man's charter of nobility.

9791
A child educated only at school is an
uneducated child.

9792
Friendship is almost always the union of a
part of one mind with a part of another;
people are friends in spots.

9793
Real unselfishness consists in sharing the
interests of others.

9794
Government is the political representative
of a natural equilibrium, of custom, or
inertia; it is by no means a representative
of reason.

9795
Knowledge of what is possible is the
beginning of happiness.

9796
I believe in the possibility of happiness, if
one cultivates intuition and outlives the
grosser passions, including optimism.

9797
Happiness is the only sanction of life;
where happiness fails, existence remains a
mad and lamentable experiment.

9798
It would hardly be possible to exaggerate
man's wretchedness if it were not so easy
to overestimate his sensibility.

9799
Man is as full of potentiality as he is of impotence.

9800
For an idea ever to be fashionable is ominous, since it must afterwards be always old-fashioned.

9801
Every real object must cease to be what it seemed and none could ever be what the whole soul desired.

9802
Intelligence is quickness in seeing things as they are.

9803
By nature's kindly disposition, most questions which it is beyond man's power to answer do not occur to him at all.

9804
Popular poets are the parish priests of the Muse, retailing her ancient divinations to a long since converted public.

9805
Each religion, by the help of more or less myth which it takes more or less seriously, proposes some method of fortifying the human soul and enabling it to make its peace with destiny.

9806
My atheism, like that of Spinoza, is true piety towards the universe and denies only gods fashioned by men in their own image, to be servants of their human interest.

9807
Work and love - these are the basics; waking life is a dream controlled.

9808
If a man really knew himself he would utterly despise the ignorant notions others might form on a subject in which he had such matchless opportunities for observation.

9809
The truth is cruel, but it can be loved, and it makes free those who have loved it.

9810
Almost every wise saying has an opposite one, no less wise, to balance it.

9811 *Introduction to the Ethics of Spinoza*
The Bible is literature, not dogma.

9812 *The Life of Reason*
Fanaticism consists in redoubling your effort when you have forgotten your aim.

9813 *The Life of Reason*
Those who cannot remember the past are condemned to repeat it.

9814 *The Life of Reason*
It takes patience to appreciate domestic bliss; volatile spirits prefer unhappiness.

9815 *The Life of Reason*
An artist is a dreamer consenting to dream of the actual world.

9816 *Soliloquies in England*
There is no cure for birth and death save to enjoy the interval.

9817 *Soliloquies in England, 'The British Character'*
England is the paradise of individuality, eccentricity, heresy, anomalies, hobbies, and humours.

9818 *The Unknowable*
It is a great advantage for a system of philosophy to be substantially true.

SAPHIR Moritz G.
9819
Love makes of the wisest man a fool, and of the most foolish woman, a sage.

9820
The mirror is the conscience of women; they never do a thing without first consulting it.

SAPHIR Morty
9821
Man's attitude toward great qualities in others is often the same as toward high mountains - he admires them but he prefers to walk around them.

SAPIRSTEIN Milton R.
9822
Our unconsciousness is like a vast

subterranean factory with intricate machinery that is never idle, where work goes on day and night from the time we are born until the moment of our death.

SARAH 1st Duchess of Marlborough 1660-1744
9823
The Duke returned from the wars today and did pleasure me in his top-boots.

9824 *(refusing marriage offer from Duke of Somerset)*
If I were young and handsome as I was, instead of old and faded as I am, and you could lay the empire of the world at my feet, you should never share the heart and hand that once belonged to John, Duke of Marlborough.

SARGENT John Singer 1856-1925
9825
A portrait is a painting with something wrong with the mouth.

9826
Every time I paint a portrait I lose a friend.

SARONY Leslie 1897-1985
9827
Ain't it grand to be blooming well dead?

SAROYAN William 1908-1981
9828
Every man in the world is better than someone else. And not as good as some oneelse.

9829
The greatest happiness you can have is knowing that you do not necessarily require happiness.

SARRAUTE Nathalie 1902-
9830
Radio and television ... have succeeded in lifting the manufacture of banality out of the sphere of handicraft and placed it in that of a major industry.

SARTRE Jean-Paul 1905-1980
9831
Once freedom lights its beacon in a man's heart, the gods are powerless against him.

9832
Once you hear the details of victory, it is heard to distinguish it from a defeat.

9833
The writer is committed when he plunges to the very depths of himself with the intent to disclose, not his individuality, but his person in the complex society that conditions and supports him.

9834 *Words*
Like all dreamers, I mistook disenchantment for truth.

9835 *Words*
I confused things with their names: that is belief.

9836 *Words*
There is no good father, that's the rule. Don't lay the blame on men but on the bond of paternity, which is rotten. To beget children, nothing better; to *have* them, what iniquity!

9837 *Words*
The poor don't know that their function in life is to exercise our generosity.

9838 *Words*
She believed in nothing; only her scepticism kept her from being an atheist.

9839 *The Flies*
Human life begins on the far side of despair.

9840 *Huis Clos*
Hell is other people.

9841 *Lucifer and the Lord*
When the rich wage war it's the poor who die.

9842 *Being and Nothingness*
Existence precedes and rules essence.

9843 *Being and Nothingness*
I am condemned to be free.

9844 *Being and Nothingness*
Man is a useless passion.

9845 *(refusing the Nobel Prize in Stockholm)*
A writer must refuse, ..., to allow himself to be transformed into an institution.

SASSOON Siegfried 1886-1967

9846 *'Dreamers'*
Soldiers are citizens of death's grey land,
Drawing no dividend from time's
tomorrows.

9847 *'Everyone Sang'*
Everyone suddenly burst out singing;
And I was filled with such delight
As prisoned birds must find in freedom.

9848 *'Everyone Sang'*
The song was wordless; the singing will
never be done.

9849 *'The General'*
But he did for them both by his plan of
attack.

9850 *'Does it Matter?'*
Does it matter? - losing your sight? ...
There's such splendid work for the blind;
And people will always be kind,
As you sit on the terrace remembering
And turning your face to the light.

SASSOON Vidal

9851
Hair is another name for sex.

SAVILE George 1633-1695

9852 *Political, Moral, and Miscellaneous
Thoughts and Reflections*
Anger is never without an argument, but
seldom with a good one.

9853 *Political, Moral, and Miscellaneous
Thoughts and Reflections*
Malice is of a low stature, but it hath very
long arms.

9854 *Political, Moral, and Miscellaneous
Thoughts and Reflections*
When the people contend for their liberty,
they seldom get anything by their victory
but new masters.

9855 *Political, Moral, and Miscellaneous
Thoughts and Reflections*
Men are not hanged for stealing horses,
but that horses may not be stolen.

SAY Jean Baptiste

9856
It is the aim of good government to
stimulate production, of bad government

to encourage consumption.

SAYERS Dorothy L. 1893-1957

9857 *Creed or Chaos?*
A society in which consumption has to be
artificially stimulated in order to keep
production going is a society founded on
trash and waste, and such a society is a
house built upon sand.

9858 *That's Why I Never Read Modern Novels*
As I grow older and older,
And totter towards the tomb,
I find that I care less and less
Whom goes to bed with whom.

SCALPONE Al

9859 *(motto for Roman Catholic Family
Rosary Crusade)*
The family that prays together stays
together.

SCANLON Hugh 1913-

9860
Of course liberty is not licence. Liberty in
my view is conforming to majority
opinion.

SCARGILL Arthur 1938-

9861 *(evidence to House of Commons Select
Committee)*
Parliament itself would not exist in its
present form had people not defied the
law.

SCHARPING Rudolf 1947-

9862
Remembrance is the secret of
reconciliation.

SCHAUBLE Wolfgang 1942-

9863
The soul of Germany is Europe, it is not
the D. Mark.

SCHELLING Friedrich von 1775-1854

9864 *Philosophie der Kunst*
Architecture in general is frozen music.

SCHERER Paul 1933-

9865
Love is a spendthrift, leaves its arithmetic
at home, is always 'in the red'.

SCHICK Béla 1877-1967

9866

It is very difficult to slow down. The
practice of medicine is like the heart
muscle's contraction - it's all or none.

SCHIFF Leonard

9867

Electric clocks reveal to you
Precisely when your fuses blew.

SCHILLER Friedrich von 1759-1805

9868

The world is ruled only by consideration
of advantages.

9869

The will of man is his happiness.

9870

The world's history is constant, like the
laws of nature, and simple, like the souls
of men. The same conditions continually
produce the same results.

9871

I am better than my reputation.

9872 *Don Carlos*

The sun does not set in my dominions.

9873 *'An Die Freude'*

All men become brothers under your
tender wing.

9874 *Die Jungfrau von Orleans*

With stupidity the gods themselves
struggle in vain.

9875 *'Resignation'*

The world's history is the world's
judgement.

SCHLAGGENBERG Kajetan von

9876

Maturity consists of no longer being taken
in by oneself.

SCHLESINGER Jr. Arthur 1917-

9877

What we need is a rebirth of satire, of
dissent, of irreverence, of an
uncompromising insistance that phoniness
is phony and platitudes are platitudinous.

9878

Almost all important questions are
important precisely because they are not
susceptible to quantitative answer.

SCHNABEL Artur 1882-1951

9879

The notes I handle no better than many
pianists. But the pauses between the notes
- ah, that is where the art resides!

9880 *My Life and Music*

I know two kinds of audiences only - one
coughing, and one not coughing.

9881 *(of Mozart's sonatas)*

Too easy for children, and too difficult for
artists.

SCHNITZLER Arthur 1862-1931

9882

Martyrdom has always been a proof of the
intensity, never of the correctness of a
belief.

SCHOPENHAUER Arthur 1788-1860

9883

Not to go to the theatre is like making
one's toilet without a mirror.

9884

We should comport ourselves with the
masterpieces of art as with exalted
personages - stand quietly before them and
wait till they speak to us.

9885

Any book which is at all important should
be re-read immediately.

9886

The fly ought to be used as the symbol of
impertinence and audacity; for whilst all
other animals shun man more than
anything else, and run away even before
he comes near them, the fly lights upon his
very nose.

9887

If you want to know your true opinion of
someone, watch the effect produced in you
by the first sight of a letter from him.

9888

Hatred comes from the heart; contempt
from the head; and neither feeling is quite

within our control.

9889
Fame is something which must be won; honour is something which must not be lost.

9890
Money is human happiness in the abstract.

9891
A man never feels the want of what it never occurs to him to ask for.

9892
(Politeness is) a tacit agreement that people's miserable defects, whether moral or intellectual, shall on either side be ignored and not be made the subject of reproach.

9893
Pride is the direct appreciation of oneself.

9894
Reason deserves to be called a prophet; for in showing up the consequence and effect of our actions in the present, does it not tell us what the future will be?

9895
Necessity is the constant scourge of the lower classes, ennui of the higher ones.

9896
Every truth passes through three stages before it is recognized. In the first it is ridiculed, in the second it is opposed, in the third it is regarded as self-evident.

9897
The will is the strong blind man who carries on his shoulders the lame man who can see.

9898
Obstinacy is the result of the will forcing itself into the place of the intellect.

9899
In early youth, as we contemplate our coming life, we are like children in a theatre before the curtain is raised, sitting there in high spirits and eagerly waiting for the play to begin.

9900
Intellect is invisible to the man who has none.

9901
Every parting gives a foretaste of death; every coming together again a foretaste of the resurrection.

9902
The fundamental fault of the female character is that is has no sense of justice.

SCHUDSON Michael
9903
Buy me and you will overcome the anxieties I have just reminded you of.

SCHULLER Robert
9904
Someone once said to me, 'Reverend Schuller, I hope you live to see all your dreams fulfilled'. I replied, 'I hope not, because if I live and all my dreams are fulfilled, I'm dead'. It's unfulfilled dreams that keep you alive.

SCHULZ Charles M. 1922-
9905
My life has no purpose, no direction, no aim, no meaning, and yet I'm happy. I can't figure it out. What am I doing right?

9906
I've developed a new philosophy - I only dread one day at a time.

9907
Jogging is very beneficial. It's good for your legs and your feet. It's also very good for the ground. It makes it feel needed.

SCHURZ Carl 1829-1906
9908
My country, right or wrong; if right, to be kept right; and if wrong, to be set right!

SCHWEITZER Albert 1875-1965
9909
One thing I know: the only ones among you who will be really happy are those who will have sought and found how to serve.

9910
Happiness? That's nothng more than health and a poor memory.

9911
Man can hardly even recognize the devils of his own creation.

9912
As we acquire more knowledge, things do not become more comprehensible, but more mysterious.

9913
A man does not have to be an angel in order to be a saint.

9914
A great secret of success is to go through life as a man who never gets used up.

9915
Thought is the strongest thing we have. Work done by true and profound thought - that is a real force.

SCIPIO Africanus 236-184 BC
9916
Never less idle than when unoccupied, nor less alone than when without company.

SCOTT C.P. 1846-1932
9917
Television? The word is half Latin and half Greek. No good can come of it.

9918
Comment is free, but facts are sacred.

SCOTT F.R.
9919
An arena
large as Europe
Silent
waiting the contest.

9920
The world is my country,
The human race is my race.
The spirit of man is my god,
The future of man is my heaven.

SCOTT Howard
9921
A criminal is a person with predatory instincts who has not sufficient capital to form a corporation.

SCOTT Robert 1868-1912
9922 *(last journal entry)*
For God's sake look after our people.

9923 *(last letter to his wife)*
Make the boy interested in natural history if you can; it is better than games.

9924 *'Message to the Public'*
Had we lived, I should have had a tale to tell of the hardihood, endurance, and courage of my companions which would have stirred the heart of every Englishman. These rough notes and our dead bodies must tell the tale.

9925 *(of the South Pole)*
Great God! this is an awful place.

SCOTT Sir Walter 1771-1832
9926
One hour of life, crowded to the full with glorious action, and filled with noble risks, is worth whole years of those mean observances of paltry decorum.

9927 *The Antiquary*
It's no fish ye're buying - it's men's lives.

9928 *The Bride of Lammermoor*
Vacant heart and hand, and eye -
Easy live and quiet die.

9929 *The Bride of Lammermoor*
I live by twa trades ... fiddle, sir, and spade; filling the world, and emptying of it.

9930 *The Heart of Midlothian*
The hour is come, but not the man.

9931 *The Lady of the Lake*
His ready speech flowed fair and free,
In phrase of gentlest courtesy;
Yet seemed that tone, and gesture bland,
Less used to sue than to command.

9932 *The Lady of the Lake*
He is gone on the mountain,
He is lost to the forest,
Like a summer-dried fountain,
When our need was the sorest.

9933 *The Lady of the Lake*
Hail to the chief who in triumph advances!

9934 *The Lady of the Lake*
And the stern joy which warriors feel
In foemen worthy of their steel.

9935 *The Lay of the Last Minstrel*
If thou would'st view fair Melrose aright,
Go visit it by the pale moonlight.

9936 *The Lay of the Last Minstrel*
They waste their toil
For the vain tribute of a smile.

9937 *The Lay of the Last Minstrel*
The unpremeditated lay.

9938 *The Lay of the Last Minstrel*
Love rules the court, the camp, the grove,
And men below, and saints above;
For love is heaven, and heaven is love.

9939 *The Lay of the Last Minstrel*
True love's the gift which God has given
To man alone beneath the heaven.

9940 *The Lay of the Last Minstrel*
Breathes there the man, with soul so dead,
Who never to himself hath said,
This is my own, my native land!

9941 *The Lay of the Last Minstrel*
The wretch, concentred all in self,
Living, shall forfeit fair renown,
And, doubly dying, shall go down
To the vile dust, from whence he sprung,
Unwept, unhonoured, and unsung.

9942 *Letter to J.G. Lockhart, 1830*
All men who have turned out worth
anything have had the chief hand in their
own education.

9943 *The Lord of the Isles*
O! many a shaft, at random sent,
Finds mark the archer little meant!
And many a word, at random spoken,
May soothe or wound a heart that's
broken.

9944 *Marmion*
Had'st thou but lived, though stripped of
power,
A watchman on the lonely tower.

9945 *Marmion*
And come he slow, or come he fast,
It is but Death who comes at last.

9946 *Marmion*
O what a tangled web we weave,
When first we practise to deceive!

9947 *Marmion*
O Woman! in our hours of ease,
Uncertain, coy, and hard to please,
And variable as the shade
By the light quivering aspen made;
When pain and anguish wring the brow,
A ministering angel thou!

9948 *Redgauntlet*
The ae half of the warld thinks the tither
daft.

9949 *Rob Roy*
But with the morning cool repentance
came.

9950 *Rob Roy*
There's a gude time coming.

9951 *The Talisman*
Rouse the lion from his lair.

SCOTT William 1745-1836
9952
A dinner lubricates business.

9953 *(attributed opinion, while Advocate-*
General)
A precedent embalms a principle.

SCOTT-MAXWELL Florida
9954
No matter how old a mother is, she
watches her middle-aged children for signs
of improvement.

SEDLEY Sir Charles c.1639-1701
9955 *'Love still has something'*
Love still has something of the sea
From whence his mother rose.

9956 *'Phyllis Knotting'*
Phyllis, without frown or smile,
Sat and knotted all the while.

9957 *'Song'*
Phyllis is my only joy,
Faithless as the winds or seas;
Sometimes coming, sometimes coy,
Yet she never fails to please.

9958 *'Song'*
She deceiving,
I believing;
What need lovers wish for more?

SEEGER Alan 1888-1916
9959 *'I Have a Rendezvous with Death'*
I have a rendezvous with Death
At some disputed barricade.

SEEGER Pete 1919-
9960
Where have all the flowers gone?

SEELEY Sir John 1834-1895
9961
History is past politics; and politics present
history.

9962 *The Expansion of England*
We [the English] seem, as it were, to have
conquered and peopled half the world in a
fit of absence of mind.

SEGAL Erich 1937-
9963 *Love Story*
Love means never having to say you're
sorry.

SÉGUR Sophie Rostopchine
9964
God keeps the wicked to give them time to
repent.

SELDEN John 1584-1654
9965 *Table Talk 'Friends'*
Old friends are best. King James used to
call for his old shoes; they were easiest for
his feet.

9966 *Table Talk 'Humility'*
'Tis not the drinking that is to be blamed,
but the excess.

9967 *Table Talk 'Of a King'*
A king is a thing men have made for their
own sakes, for quietness' sake. Just as in a
family one man is appointed to buy the
meat.

9968 *Table Talk 'Law'*
Ignorance of the law excuses no man; not
that all men know the law, but because 'tis
an excuse every man will plead, and no
man can tell how to confute him.

9969 *Table Talk 'Libels'*
Take a straw and throw it up into the air,
you shall see by that which way the wind
is.

9970 *Table Talk 'Marriage'*
Marriage is nothing but a civil contract.

9971 *Table Talk 'Parson'*
There never was a merry world since the
fairies left off dancing, and the Parson left
conjuring.

9972 *Table Talk 'Pleasure'*
Pleasure is nothing else but the
intermission of pain.

9973 *Table Talk 'Preaching'*
Preachers say, Do as I say, not as I do.

SELDON Arthur 1584-1654
9974 *Capitalism*
Government of the busy by the bossy for
the bully.

SELLAR W.C. and YEATMAN R.J. 1898-
1951 and 1898-1968
9975 *1066 and All That*
The Roman Conquest was, however, a
Good Thing, since the Britons were only
natives at the time.

9976 *1066 and All That*
The Cavaliers (Wrong but Wromatic) and
the Roundheads (Right but Repulsive).

9977 *1066 and All That*
The National Debt is a very Good Thing
and it would be dangerous to pay it off, for
fear of Political Economy.

9978 *1066 and All That*
Napoleon's armies always used to march
on their stomachs shouting: 'Vive
l'Intérieur!'

9979 *1066 and All That 'Compulsory Preface'*
History is not what you thought. *It is what
you can remember.*

9980 *And Now All This*
For every person who wants to teach there
are approximately thirty who don't want
to learn - much.

SENDAK Maurice 1928-
9981
William Blake really is important, my cornerstone. Nobody ever told me before he did that childhood was such a damned serious business.

SENECA c.4 BC-AD 65
9982
Night brings our troubles to the light rather than banishes them.

9983
No untroubled day has ever dawned for me.

9984
When I think over what I have said, I envy dumb people.

9985
Constant exposure to dangers will breed contempt for them.

9986
Drunkenness is nothing but voluntary madness.

9987
Fate rules the affairs of mankind with no recognizable order.

9988
A great step toward independence is a good-humoured stomach.

9989
The foremost art of kings is the power to endure hatred.

9990
Whom they have injured, they also hate.

9991
It is often better not to see an insult, than to avenge it.

9992
Injustice never rules forever.

9993
A good mind possesses a kingdom: a great fortune is a great slavery.

9994
There is nothing so bitter, that a patient mind cannot find some solace for it.

9995
Failure changes for the better, success for the worse.

9996
Time discovered truth.

9997
Vices can be learnt, even without a teacher.

9998
All cruelty springs from weakness.

9999
Love of bustle is not industry.

10000
Even while they teach, men learn.

10001
Eternal law has arranged nothing better than this, that it has given us one way in to life, but many ways out.

10002
Anyone can stop a man's life, but no one his death.

SENN J.P.
10003
Let us respect gray hairs, especially our own.

SERVICE Robert 1874-1958
10004
The happy man is he who knows his limitations, yet bows to no false gods.

10005
It isn't the mountain ahead that wears you out - it's the grain of sand in your shoe.

10006 *'The Cremation of Sam McGee'*
A promise made is a debt unpaid, and the trail has its own stern code.

10007 *'It is Later Thank You Think'*
Ah! the clock is always slow;
It is later than you think.

10008 *'The Law of the Yukon'*
This is the law of the Yukon, that only the Strong shall thrive;
That surely the Weak shall perish, and only the Fit survive.

10009 *'Michael'*
When we, the Workers, all demand: 'What
are WE fighting for?' ...
Then, then we'll end that stupid crime,
that devil's madness - War.

SETH Vikram
10010
Boredom provides a stronger inclination to
write than anything.

SÉVIGNÉ Mme de 1626-1692
10011 *(attributed)*
The more I see of men, the more I admire
dogs.

SEWARD William 1801-1872
10012
I know, and all the world knows, that
revolutions never go backward.

SEXTON Anne 1928-1974
10013 *'Old'*
In a dream you are never eighty.

SEYMOUR Horatio
10014
After listening to thousands of pleas for
pardon to offenders, I can hardly recall a
case where I did not feel that I might have
fallen as my fellow man had done, if I had
been subjected to the same demoralizing
influences and pressed by the same
temptations.

SHADWELL Thomas 1642-1692
10015 *Psyche*
Words may be false and full of art,
Sighs are the natural language of the heart.

10016 *A True Widow*
And wit's the noblest frailty of the mind.

10017 *A True Widow*
The haste of a fool is the slowest thing in
the world.

10018 *A True Widow*
Every man loves what he is good at.

SHAFFER Ivan
10019
A man isn't a man until he has to meet a
payroll.

SHAFFER Peter 1926-
10020 *Equus*
All my wife has ever taken from the
Mediterranean - from that whole vast
intuitive culture - are four bottles of
Chianti to make into lamps.

10021 *Equus*
The Ordinary made beautiful; ... the
Average made lethal.

SHAKESPEARE William 1564-1616
10022 *As You Like It*
When I was at home, I was in a better
place; but travellers must be content.

10023 *As You Like It*
Sir, you have wrestled well, and
overthrown
More than your enemies.

10024 *As You Like It*
O, how full of briers is this working-day
world!

10025 *As You Like It*
Sweet are the uses of adversity,
Which like the toad, ugly and venomous,
Wears yet a precious jewel in his head;
And this our life, exempt from public
haunt,
Finds tongues in trees, books in the
running brooks,
Sermons in stones, and good in everything.

10026 *As You Like It*
If thou remember'st not the slightest folly
That ever love did make thee run into
Thou has not loved.

10027 *As You Like It*
Under the greenwood tree
Who loves to lie with me.

10028 *As You Like It*
Who doth ambition shun
And loves to live i' the sun,
Seeking the food he eats,
And pleased with what he gets.

10029 *As You Like It*
And so, from hour to hour, we ripe and
ripe,
And then from hour to hour, we rot and
rot:
And thereby hangs a tale.

10030 *As You Like It*
All the world's a stage,
And all the men and women merely
players:
They have their exits and their entrances;
And one man in his time plays many parts,
His acts being seven ages.

10031 *As You Like It*
Last scene of all,
That ends this strange eventful history,
Is second childishness, and mere oblivion,
Sans teeth, sans eyes, sans taste, sans
everything.

10032 *As You Like It*
Blow, blow, thou winter wind,
Thou art not so unkind
As man's ingratitude.

10033 *As You Like It*
Most friendship is feigning, most loving
mere folly.

10034 *As You Like It*
He that wants money, means, and content
is without three good friends.

10035 *As You Like It*
Do you not know I am a woman? when I
think, I must speak.

10036 *As You Like It*
I do desire we may be better strangers.

10037 *As You Like It*
I pray you, do not fall in love with me,
For I am falser than vows made in wine.

10038 *As You Like It*
Men have died from time to time, and
worms have eaten them, but not for love.

10039 *As You Like It*
Men are April when they woo, December
when they wed: maids are May when they
are maids, but the sky changes when they
are wives.

10040 *As You Like It*
Your 'if' is the only peace-maker; much
virtue in 'if'.

10041 *Much Ado About Nothing*
How much better is it to weep at joy than
to joy at weeping.

10042 *Much Ado About Nothing*
Speak low, if you speak love.

10043 *Much Ado About Nothing*
Friendship is constant in all other things
Save in the office and affairs of love.

10044 *Much Ado About Nothing*
Sigh no more, ladies, sigh no more,
Men were deceivers ever;
One foot in sea, and one on shore,
To one thing constant never.

10045 *Much Ado About Nothing*
Doth not the appetite alter? A man loves
the meat in his youth that he cannot
endure in his age.

10046 *Much Ado About Nothing*
When I said I would die a bachelor, I did
not think I should live till I were married.

10047 *Much Ado About Nothing*
Everyone can master a grief but he that has
it.

10048 *Much Ado About Nothing*
To be a well-favoured man is the gift of
fortune; but to write and read comes by
nature.

10049 *Much Ado About Nothing*
I thank God, I am as honest as any man
living, that is an old man and no honester
than I.

10050 *Much Ado About Nothing*
Comparisons are odorous.

10051 *Much Ado About Nothing*
There was never yet philosopher
That could endure the toothache patiently.

10052 *All's Well that Ends Well*
It were all one
That I should love a bright particular star
And think to wed it, he is so above me.

10053 *All's Well that Ends Well*
The hind that would be mated with the
lion
Must die of love.

10054 *All's Well that Ends Well*
Our remedies oft in ourselves do lie
Which we ascribed to heaven.

10055 *All's Well that Ends Well*
A young man married is a man that's
marred.

10056 *All's Well that Ends Well*
The web of our life is of a mingled yarn,
good and ill together.

10057 *Antony and Cleopatra*
The stroke of death is as a lover's pinch,
Which hurts and is desired.

10058 *Antony and Cleopatra*
The triple pillar of the world transformed
Into a strumpet's fool.

10059 *Antony and Cleopatra*
There's beggary in the love that can be
reckoned.

10060 *Antony and Cleopatra*
Let Rome in Tiber melt, and the wide arch
Of the ranged empire fall. Here is my
space.

10061 *Antony and Cleopatra*
O excellent! I love long life better than figs.

10062 *Antony and Cleopatra*
A Roman thought hath struck him.

10063 *Antony and Cleopatra*
Indeed the tears live in an onion that
should water this sorrow.

10064 *Antony and Cleopatra*
In time we hate that which we often fear.

10065 *Antony and Cleopatra*
Eternity was in our lips and eyes,
Bliss in our brows bent.

10066 *Antony and Cleopatra*
The demi-Atlas of this earth, the arm
And burgonet of men. He's speaking now,
Or murmuring, 'Where's my serpent of old
Nile?'

10067 *Antony and Cleopatra*
My salad days,
When I was green in judgment, cold in
blood,
To say as I said then!

10068 *Antony and Cleopatra*
The barge she sat in, like a burnished
throne,
Burned on the water; the poop was beaten

gold,
Purple the sails, and so perfumed, that
The winds were love-sick with them.

10069 *Antony and Cleopatra*
The city cast
Her people out upon her, and Antony,
Enthroned i' the market-place, did sit
alone,
Whistling to the air; which, but for
vacancy,
Had gone to gaze on Cleopatra too
And made a gap in nature.

10070 *Antony and Cleopatra*
Age cannot wither her, nor custom stale
Her infinite variety; other women cloy
The appetites they feed, but she makes
hungry
Where most she satisfied.

10071 *Antony and Cleopatra*
Give me some music - music, moody food
Of us that trade in love.

10072 *Antony and Cleopatra*
I will praise any man that will praise me.

10073 *Antony and Cleopatra*
Against the blown rose may they stop their
nose,
That kneeled unto the buds.

10074 *Antony and Cleopatra*
Let's have one other gaudy night: ...
Let's mock the midnight bell.

10075 *Antony and Cleopatra*
To business that we love we rise betime,
And go to 't with delight.

10076 *Antony and Cleopatra*
Unarm, Eros; the long day's task is done,
And we must sleep.

10077 *Antony and Cleopatra*
I am dying, Egypt, dying; only
I here importune death awhile, until
Of many thousand kisses the poor last
I lay upon thy lips.

10078 *Antony and Cleopatra*
The crown o' the earth doth melt. My
lord!
O! withered is the garland of the war,
The soldier's pole is fall'n; young boys and

girls
Are level now with men; the odds is gone,
And there is nothing left remarkable
Beneath the visiting moon.

10079 *Antony and Cleopatra*
A rarer spirit never
Did steer humanity; but you, gods, will give us
Some faults to make us men.

10080 *Antony and Cleopatra*
The bright day is done,
And we are for the dark.

10081 *Antony and Cleopatra*
My resolution's placed, and I have nothing
Of woman in me; now from head to foot
I am marble-constant, now the fleeting moon
No planet is of mine.

10082 *Antony and Cleopatra*
Give me my robe, put on my crown; I have
Immortal longings in me.

10083 *Antony and Cleopatra*
Dost thou not see my baby at my breast,
That sucks the nurse asleep?

10084 *Antony and Cleopatra*
No grave upon the earth shall clip in it
A pair so famous.

10085 *The Comedy of Errors*
I to the world am like a drop of water
That in the ocean seeks another drop,
Who, falling there to find his fellow forth,
Unseen, inquisitive, confounds himself.

10086 *Coriolanus*
Action is eloquence.

10087 *Coriolanus*
Custom calls me to 't:
What custom wills, in all things should we do't,
The dust on antique time would lie unswept,
And mountainous error be too highly heaped
For truth to o'erpeer.

10088 *Coriolanus*
What is the city but the people?

10089 *Coriolanus*
Like a dull actor now,
I have forgot my part, and I am out,
Even to a full disgrace.

10090 *Cymbeline*
Fortune brings in some boats that are not steered.

10091 *Cymbeline*
Weariness
Can snore upon the flint, when resty sloth
Finds the down pillow hard.

10092 *Cymbeline*
How hard it is to hide the sparks of nature!

10093 *Cymbeline*
Fear no more the heat o' the sun,
Nor the furious winter's rages;
Thou thy wordly task hast done,
Home art gone and ta'en thy wages:
Golden lads and girls all must,
As chimney-sweepers, come to dust.

10094 *Cymbeline*
Every good servant does not all commands.

10095 *Cymbeline*
He that sleeps feels not the toothache.

10096 *Hamlet*
The undiscovered country from whose bourn no traveller returns.

10097 *Hamlet*
God has given you one face, and you make yourselves another.

10098 *Hamlet*
A politician ... one that would circumvent God.

10099 *Hamlet*
For some must watch, while some must sleep; thus runs the world away.

10100 *Hamlet*
A little more than kin, and less than kind.

10101 *Hamlet*
But I have that within which passeth show;
These but the trappings and the suits of woe.

10102 *Hamlet*
O! that this too too solid flesh would melt,
Thaw, and resolve itself into a dew;
Or that the Everlasting had not fixed
His canon 'gainst self-slaughter! O God! O
God!
How weary, stale, flat, and unprofitable
Seem to me all the uses of this world.

10103 *Hamlet*
Frailty, thy name is woman!

10104 *Hamlet*
It is not, nor it cannot come to good;
But break, my heart, for I must hold my
tongue.

10105 *Hamlet*
He was a man, take him for all in all,
I shall not look upon his like again.

10106 *Hamlet*
Foul deeds will rise,
Though all the earth o'erwhelm them, to
men's eyes.

10107 *Hamlet*
Do not, as some ungracious pastors do,
Show me the steep and thorny way to
heaven,
Whiles, like a puffed and reckless libertine,
Himself the primrose path of dalliance
treads,
And recks not his own rede.

10108 *Hamlet*
Give every man thine ear, but few thy
voice;
Take each man's censure, but reserve thy
judgement.
Costly thy habit as thy purse can buy,
But not expressed in fancy; rich, not
gaudy;
For the apparel oft proclaims the man ...
Neither a borrower, nor a lender be;
For loan oft loses both itself and friend,
And borrowing dulls the edge of
husbandry,
This above all: to thine own self be true,
And it must follow, as the night the day,
Thou canst not then be false to any man.

10109 *Hamlet*
But to my mind - though I am native here,
And to the manner born - it is a custom

More honoured in the breach than the
observance.

10110 *Hamlet*
Something is rotten in the state of
Denmark.

10111 *Hamlet*
Murder most foul, as in the best it is;
But this most foul, strange, and unnatural.

10112 *Hamlet*
These are but wild and whirling words,
my lord.

10113 *Hamlet*
There are more things in heaven and earth,
Horatio,
Than are dreamt of in your philosophy.

10114 *Hamlet*
The time is out of joint; O cursèd spite,
That ever I was born to set it right!

10115 *Hamlet*
Brevity is the soul of wit.

10116 *Hamlet*
Doubt thou the stars are fire;
Doubt that the sun doth move;
Doubt truth to be a liar;
But never doubt I love.

10117 *Hamlet*
Ay, sir; to be honest, as this world goes, is
to be one man picked out of ten thousand.

10118 *Hamlet*
Though this be madness, yet there is
method in't.

10119 *Hamlet*
There is nothing either good or bad, but
thinking makes it so.

10120 *Hamlet*
What a piece of work is a man! How noble
in reason! how infinite in faculty! in form,
in moving, how express and admirable! in
action how like an angel! in apprehension
how like a god! the beauty of the world!
the paragon of animals! And yet, to me,
what is this quintessence of dust? man
delights not me; no, nor woman neither,
though, by your smiling, you seem to say
so.

10121 *Hamlet*
I am but mad north-north-west; when the
wind is southerly, I know a hawk from a
handsaw.

10122 *Hamlet*
Use every man after his desert, and who
should 'scape whipping?

10123 *Hamlet*
The play's the thing
Wherein I'll catch the conscience of the
king.

10124 *Hamlet*
To be, or not to be: that is the question:
Whether 'tis nobler in the mind to suffer
The slings and arrows of outrageous
fortune,
Or to take arms against a sea of troubles,
And by opposing end them?

10125 *Hamlet*
To sleep: perchance to dream: ay, there's
the rub;
For in that sleep of death what dreams
may come
When we have shuffled off this mortal coil,
Must give us pause.

10126 *Hamlet*
Thus conscience doth make cowards of us
all;
And thus the native hue of resolution
Is sicklied o'er with the pale cast of
thought.

10127 *Hamlet*
Get thee to a nunnery: why wouldst thou
be a breeder of sinners?

10128 *Hamlet*
Suit the action to the word, the word to the
action.

10129 *Hamlet*
The lady doth protest too much, methinks.

10130 *Hamlet*
Let me be cruel, not unnatural;
I will speak daggers to her, but use none.

10131 *Hamlet*
My words fly up, my thoughts remain
below:
Words without thoughts never to heaven
go.

10132 *Hamlet*
A king of shreds and patches.

10133 *Hamlet*
I must be cruel only to be kind.

10134 *Hamlet*
Diseases desperate grown,
By desperate appliances are relieved,
Or not at all.

10135 *Hamlet*
We go to gain a little patch of ground,
That hath in it no profit but the name.

10136 *Hamlet*
How all occasions do inform against me,
And spur my dull revenge! What is a
man,
If his chief good and market of his time
Be but to sleep and feed? a beast, no more.

10137 *Hamlet*
Some craven scruple
Of thinking too precisely on the event.

10138 *Hamlet*
When sorrows come, they come not single
spies,
But in battalions.

10139 *Hamlet*
There's such divinity doth hedge a king,
That treason can but peep to what it
would.

10140 *Hamlet*
There's rosemary, that's for remembrance;
pray, love, remember: and there is pansies,
that's for thoughts.

10141 *Hamlet*
Too much of water hast thou, poor
Ophelia,
And therefore I forbid my tears; but yet
It is our trick, nature her custom holds,
Let shame say what it will.

10142 *Hamlet*
Alas, poor Yorick. I knew him, Horatio; a
fellow of infinite jest, of most excellent
fancy.

10143 *Hamlet*
There's a divinity that shapes our ends,
Rough-hew them how we will.

10144 *Hamlet*
If thou didst ever hold me in thy heart,
Absent thee from felicity awhile,
And in this harsh world draw thy breath
in pain,
To tell my story.

10145 *Hamlet*
The rest is silence.

10146 *Henry IV, Part 1*
Thou hast the most unsavoury similies.

10147 *Henry IV, Part 1*
If all the year were playing holidays,
To sport would be as tedious as to work;
But when they seldom come, they wished
to come.

10148 *Henry IV, Part 1*
Go hang thyself in thine own heir-
apparent garters!

10149 *Henry IV, Part 1*
Falstaff sweats to death
And lards the lean earth as he walks along.

10150 *Henry IV, Part 1*
Out of this nettle, danger, we pluck this
flower, safety.

10151 *Henry IV, Part 1*
If sack and sugar be a fault, God help the
wicked!

10152 *Henry IV, Part 1*
For my part, I may speak it to my shame,
I have a truant been to chivalry.

10153 *Henry IV, Part 1*
Honour pricks me on. Yea, but how if
honour prick me off when I come on? how
then? Can honour set-to a leg? No. Or an
arm? No. Or take away the grief of a
wound? No. Honour hath no skill in
surgery, then? No. What is honour? A
word. What is that word, honour? Air.

10154 *Henry IV, Part 1*
O gentlemen! the time of life is short;
To spend that shortness basely were too
long.

10155 *Henry IV, Part 2*
I am as poor as Job, my lord, but not so
patient.

10156 *Henry IV, Part 2*
It was always yet the trick of our English
nation, if they have a good thing, to make
it too common.

10157 *Henry IV, Part 2*
Doth it not show vilely in me to desire
small beer?

10158 *Henry IV, Part 2*
Let the end try the man.

10159 *Henry IV, Part 2*
He was indeed the glass
Wherein the noble youth did dress
themselves.

10160 *Henry IV, Part 2*
Is it not strange that desire should so many
years outlive performance?

10161 *Henry IV, Part 2*
Uneasy lies the head that wears the crown.

10162 *Henry IV, Part 2*
There is a history in all men's lives,
Figuring the nature of the times deceased,
The which observed, a man my prophesy,
With a near aim, of the main chance of
things
As yet not come to life, which in their
seeds
And weak beginnings lie intreasurèd.

10163 *Henry IV, Part 2*
We have heard the chimes at midnight.

10164 *Henry IV, Part 2*
I care not; a man can die but once; we owe
God a death.

10165 *Henry IV, Part 2*
Thy wish was father, Harry, to that
thought.

10166 *Henry IV, Part 2*
Commit
The oldest sins the newest kind of ways.

10167 *Henry V*
O! for a Muse of fire, that would ascend
The brightest heaven of invention;
A kingdom for a stage, princes to act

And monarchs to behold the swelling scene.

10168 *Henry V*
I dare not fight; but I will wink and hold out mine iron.

10169 *Henry V*
Once more unto the breach, dear friends, once more;
Or close the wall up with our English dead!
In peace there's nothing so becomes a man
As modest stillness and humility:
But when the blast of war blows in our ears,
Then imitate the action of the tiger;
Stiffen the sinews, summon up the blood,
Disguise fair nature with hard-favoured rage;
Then lend the eye a terrible aspect.

10170 *Henry V*
I see you stand like greyhounds in the slips,
Straining upon the start. The game's afoot:
Follow your spirit; and, upon this charge
Cry 'God for Harry! England and Saint George!'

10171 *Henry V*
Would I were in an alehouse in London! I would give all my fame for a pot of ale, and safety.

10172 *Henry V*
Men of few words are the best men.

10173 *Henry V*
A little touch of Harry in the night.

10174 *Henry V*
I think the king is but a man, as I am: the violet smells to him as it doth to me.

10175 *Henry V*
Every subject's duty is the king's; but every subject's soul is his own.

10176 *Henry V*
Old men forget: yet all shall be forgot,
But he'll remember with advantages
What feats he did that day.

10177 *Henry V*
And gentlemen in England, now a-bed
Shall think themsleves accursed they were not here,
And hold their manhoods cheap whiles any speaks
That fought with us upon Saint Crispin's day.

10178 *Henry VI, Part 1*
Unbidden guests
Are often welcomest when they are gone.

10179 *Henry VI, Part 2*
Could I come near your beauty with my nails
I'd set my ten commandments in your face.

10180 *Henry VI, Part 2*
What stronger breastplate than a heart untainted!
Thrice is he armèd that hath his quarrel just,
And he but naked, though locked up in steel,
Whose conscience with injustice is corrupted.

10181 *Henry VI, Part 3*
Suspicion always haunts the guilty mind;
The thief doth fear each bush an officer.

10182 *Henry VIII*
Heat not a furnace for your foe so hot
That it do singe yourself.

10183 *Henry VIII*
I would not be a queen
For all the world.

10184 *Henry VIII*
A peace above all earthly dignities,
A still and quiet conscience.

10185 *Henry VIII*
Had I but served my God with half the zeal
I served my king, he would not in mine age
Have left me naked to mine enemies.

10186 *Henry VIII*
Men's evil manners live in brass; their virtues
We write in water.

10187 *Henry VIII*
Some come to take their ease
And sleep an act or two.

10188 *Julius Caesar*
Men at some time are masters of their
fates:
The fault, dear Brutus, is not in our stars,
But in ourselves, that we are underlings.

10189 *Julius Caesar*
Why, man, he doth bestride the narrow
world
Like a Colossus; and we petty men
Walk under his huge legs, and peep about
To find ourselves dishonourable graves.
Men at some time are masters of their
fates:
The fault, dear Brutus, is not in our stars,
But in ourselves, that we are underlings.

10190 *Julius Caesar*
Let me have men about me that are fat;
Sleek-headed men and such as sleep
o'nights;
Yond' Cassius has a lean and hungry look;
He thinks too much: such men are
dangerous.

10191 *Julius Caesar*
Those that understood him smiled at one
another and shook their heads; but, for
mine own part, it was Greek to me.

10192 *Julius Caesar*
Nor stony tower, nor walls of beaten brass,
Nor airless dungeon, nor strong links of
iron,
Can be retentive to the strength of spirit;
But life, being weary of these worldly bars,
Never lacks power to dismiss itself.

10193 *Julius Caesar*
Let's carve him as a dish fit for the gods,
Not hew him as a carcass fit for hounds.

10194 *Julius Caesar*
Cowards die many times before their
deaths;
The valiant never taste of death but once.

10195 *Julius Caesar*
Et tu, Brute? Then fall, Caesar!

10196 *Julius Caesar*
That we shall die, we know; 'tis but the
time
And drawing days out, that men stand
upon.

10197 *Julius Caesar*
He that cuts off twenty years of life
Cuts off so many years of fearing death.

10198 *Julius Caesar*
O mighty Caesar! dost thou lie so low?
Are all thy conquests, glories, triumphs,
spoils,
Shrunk to this little measure?

10199 *Julius Caesar*
O! pardon me, thou bleeding piece of
earth,
That I am meek and gentle with these
butchers;
Thou art the ruins of the noblest man
That ever livèd in the tide of times.

10200 *Julius Caesar*
Cry, 'Havoc!' and let slip the dogs of war.

10201 *Julius Caesar*
Passion, I see, is catching.

10202 *Julius Caesar*
Not that I loved Caesar less, but that I
loved Rome more.

10203 *Julius Caesar*
Friends, Romans, countrymen, lend me
your ears;
I come to bury Caesar, not to praise him.
The evil that men do lives after them,
The good is oft interrèd with their bones;
So let it be with Caesar.

10204 *Julius Caesar*
He was my friend, faithful and just to me:
But Brutus says he was ambitious;
And Brutus is an honourable man.

10205 *Julius Caesar*
Ambition should be made of sterner stuff.

10206 *Julius Caesar*
You are not wood, you are not stones, but
men;
And, being men, hearing the will of
Caesar,
It will inflame you, it will make you mad.

10207 *Julius Caesar*
If you have tears, prepare to shed them
now.

10208 *Julius Caesar*
This was the most unkindest cut of all;
For when the noble Caesar saw him stab,
Ingratitude, more strong than traitors'
arms,
Quite vanquished him: then burst his
mighty heart.

10209 *Julius Caesar*
For I have neither wit, nor words, nor
worth,
Action, nor utterance, nor power of
speech,
To stir men's blood; I only speak right on;
I tell you that which you yourselves do
know.

10210 *Julius Caesar*
I had rather be a dog, and bay the moon,
Than such a Roman.

10211 *Julius Caesar*
Do not presume too much upon my love;
I may do that I shall be sorry for.

10212 *Julius Caesar*
A friend should bear his friend's
infirmities,
But Brutus makes mine greater than they
are.

10213 *Julius Caesar*
There is a tide in the affairs of men,
Which, taken at the flood, leads on to
fortune;
Omitted, all the voyage of their life
Is bound in shallows and in miseries.

10214 *Julius Caesar*
The deep of night is crept upon our talk,
And nature must obey necessity.

10215 *King John*
Well, whiles I am a beggar, I will rail,
And say there is no sin, but to be rich;
And, being rich, my virtue then shall be,
To say there is no vice, but beggary.

10216 *King John*
Old Time the clock-setter.

10217 *King John*
Bell, book, and candle shall not drive me
back,
When gold and silver becks me to come
on.

10218 *King John*
Life is as tedious as a twice-told tale,
Vexing the dull ear of a drowsy man.

10219 *King John*
To gild refinèd gold, to paint the lily,
To throw a perfume on the violet,
To smooth the ice, or add another hue
Unto the rainbow, or with taper light
To seek the beauteous eye of heaven to
garnish,
Is wasteful and ridiculous excess.

10220 *King John*
How oft the sight of means to do ill deeds
Make ill deeds done!

10221 *King John*
Heaven take my soul, and England keep
my bones!

10222 *King John*
I beg cold comfort; and you are so strait
And so ingrateful, you deny me that.

10223 *King Lear*
Mend your speech a little,
Lest it may mar your fortunes.

10224 *King Lear*
Nothing will come of nothing: speak again.

10225 *King Lear*
Come not between the dragon and his
wrath.

10226 *King Lear*
Love is not love
When it is mingled with regards that stand
Aloof from the entire point.

10227 *King Lear*
This is the excellent foppery of the world,
that, when we are sick in fortune - often
the surfeit of our own behaviour - we
make guilty of our own disasters the sun,
the moon, and the stars.

10228 *King Lear*
Have more than thou showest,
Speak less than thou knowest,

Lend less than thou owest.

10229 *King Lear*
Ingratitude, thou marble-hearted fiend,
More hideous, when thou show'st thee in a child,
Than the sea-monster.

10230 *King Lear*
How sharper than a serpent's tooth it is
To have a thankless child!

10231 *King Lear*
O! let me not be mad, not mad, sweet heaven;
Keep me in temper; I would not be mad!

10232 *King Lear*
Thou whoreson zed! thou unnecessary letter!

10233 *King Lear*
Down, thou climbing sorrow!
Thy element's below.

10234 *King Lear*
O reason not the need! Our basest beggars
Are in the poorest thing superfluous.
Allow not nature more than nature needs,
Man's life is cheap as beast's.

10235 *King Lear*
Blow, winds, and crack your cheeks! rage! blow!
You cataracts and hurricanoes, spout
Till you have drenched our steeples, drowned the cocks!

10236 *King Lear*
There was never yet fair woman but she made mouths in a glass.

10237 *King Lear*
The art of our necessities is strange,
That can make vile things precious.

10238 *King Lear*
O! that way madness lies; let me shun that.

10239 *King Lear*
I have no way, and therefore want no eyes;
I stumbled when I saw.

10240 *King Lear*
The worst is not,
So long as we can say, 'This is the worst.'

10241 *King Lear*
As flies to wanton boys, are we to the gods;
They kill us for their sport.

10242 *King Lear*
Every inch a king.

10243 *King Lear*
The wren goes to't, and the small gilded fly
Does lecher in my sight.
Let copulation thrive.

10244 *King Lear*
Get thee glass eyes;
And, like a scurvy politician, seem
To see the things thou dost not.

10245 *King Lear*
When we are born we cry that we are come
To this great stage of fools.

10246 *King Lear*
Men must endure
Their going hence, even as their coming hither:
Ripeness is all.

10247 *King Lear*
The gods are just, and of our pleasant vices
Make instruments to plague us.

10248 *King Lear*
The wheel is come full circle.

10249 *Love's Labour's Lost*
At Christmas I no more desire a rose
Than wish a snow in May's new-fangled mirth;
But like of each thing that in season grows.

10250 *Love's Labour's Lost*
He hath not fed of the dainties that are bred in a book; he hath not eat paper, as it were; he hath not drunk ink.

10251 *Love's Labour's Lost*
He draweth out the thread of his verbosity finer than the staple of his argument.

10252 *Love's Labour's Lost*
A jest's prosperity lies in the ear
Of him that hears it, never in the tongue
Of him that makes it.

10253 *Macbeth*
FIRST WITCH: When shall we three meet
again
In thunder, lightning, or in rain?
SECOND WITCH: When the hurly-burly's
done,
When the battle's lost and won.

10254 *Macbeth*
So foul and fair a day I have not seen.

10255 *Macbeth*
Were such things here as we do speak
about?
Or have we eaten on the insane root
That takes the reason prisoner?

10256 *Macbeth*
This supernatural soliciting
Cannot be ill, cannot be good.

10257 *Macbeth*
Come what come may,
Time and the hour runs through the
roughest day.

10258 *Macbeth*
Nothing in his life
Became him like the leaving it: he died
As one that had been studied in his death
To throw away the dearest thing he owed
As 'twere a careless trifle.

10259 *Macbeth*
Yet I do fear thy nature;
It is too full o' the milk of human kindness
To catch the nearest way.

10260 *Macbeth*
The raven himself is hoarse
That croaks the fatal entrance of Duncan
Under my battlements.

10261 *Macbeth*
If it were done when 'tis done, then 'twere
well
It were done quickly.

10262 *Macbeth*
I have no spur
To prick the sides of my intent, but only
Vaulting ambition, which o'erleaps itself,
And falls on the other.

10263 *Macbeth*
I dare do all that may become a man;
Who dares do more is none.

10264 *Macbeth*
False face must hide what the false heart
doth know.

10265 *Macbeth*
Is this a dagger which I see before me,
The handle toward my hand?

10266 *Macbeth*
The attempt and not the deed,
Confounds us.

10267 *Macbeth*
Methought I heard a voice cry, 'Sleep no
more!
Macbeth does murder sleep.'

10268 *Macbeth*
The sleeping and the dead
Are but as pictures; 'tis the eye of
childhood
That fears a painted devil.

10269 *Macbeth*
A little water clears us of this deed.

10270 *Macbeth*
The wine of life is drawn, and the mere
lees
Is left this vault to brag of.

10271 *Macbeth*
Come, seeling night,
Scarf up the tender eye of pitiful day,
And with thy bloody and invisible hand,
Cancel and tear to pieces that great bond
Which keeps me pale!

10272 *Macbeth*
... Now I am cabined, cribbed, confined,
bound in
To saucy doubts and fears.

10273 *Macbeth*
Stand not upon the order of your going.

10274 *Macbeth*
I am in blood
Stepped in so far that, should I wade no
more,
Returning were as tedious as go o'er.

10275 *Macbeth*
Double, double toil and trouble;
Fire burn and cauldron bubble.

10276 *Macbeth*
Eye of newt, and toe of frog,
Wool of bat, and tongue of dog,
Adder's fork, and blind-worm's sting,
Lizard's leg, and howlet's wing,
For a charm of powerful trouble,
Like a hell-broth boil and bubble.

10277 *Macbeth*
By the pricking of my thumbs,
Something wicked this way comes.

10278 *Macbeth*
Be bloody, bold, and resolute; laugh to
scorn
The power of man, for none of woman
born
Shall harm Macbeth.

10279 *Macbeth*
When our actions do not,
Our fears do make us traitors.

10280 *Macbeth*
Out, damned spot! out, I say!

10281 *Macbeth*
Yet who would have thought the old man
to have had so much blood in him?

10282 *Macbeth*
Here's the smell of the blood still: all the
perfumes of Arabia will not sweeten this
little hand.

10283 *Macbeth*
What's done cannot be undone.

10284 *Macbeth*
Foul whisperings are abroad. Unnatural
deeds
Do breed unnatural troubles; infected
minds
To their deaf pillows will discharge their
secrets.

10285 *Macbeth*
I have lived long enough: my way of life
Is fall'n into the sear, the yellow leaf;
And that which should accompany old
age,
As honour, love, obedience, troops of
friends,
I must not look to have.

10286 *Macbeth*
I have supped full with horrors;
Direness, familiar to my slaughterous
thoughts,
Cannot once start me.

10287 *Macbeth*
To-morrow, and to-morrow, and to-
morrow,
Creeps in this petty pace from day to day,
To the last syllable of recorded time;
And all our yesterdays have lighted fools
The way to dusty death. Out, out, brief
candle!
Life's but a walking shadow, a poor player,
That struts and frets his hour upon the
stage
And then is heard no more; it is a tale
Told by an idiot, full of sound and fury,
Signifying nothing.

10288 *Macbeth*
I 'gin to be aweary of the sun,
And wish the estate o' the world were now
undone.

10289 *Measure for Measure*
We must not make a scarecrow of the law,
Setting it up to fear the birds of prey,
And let it keep one shape, till custom make
it
Their perch and not their terror.

10290 *Measure for Measure*
Man, proud man,
Drest in a little brief authority,
Most ignorant of what he's most assured,
His glassy essence, like an angry ape,
Plays such fantastic tricks before high
heaven,
As make the angels weep.

10291 *Measure for Measure*
That in the captain's but a choleric word,
Which in the soldier is flat blasphemy.

10292 *Measure for Measure*
Is this her fault or mine?
The tempter or the tempted, who sins
most?

10293 *Measure for Measure*
The miserable have no other medicine
But only hope:
I have hope to live and am prepared to die.

10294 *Measure for Measure*
Thou hast nor youth nor age;
But, as it were, an after-dinner's sleep,
Dreaming on both.

10295 *Measure for Measure*
Ay, but to die, and go we know not where;
To lie in cold obstruction and to rot.

10296 *Measure for Measure*
The hand that hath made you fair hath
made you good.

10297 *Measure for Measure*
I am a kind of burr; I shall stick.

10298 *Measure for Measure*
Haste still pays haste, and leisure answers
leisure;
Like doth quit like, and Measure still for
Measure.

10299 *Measure for Measure*
They say best men are moulded out of
faults,
And, for the most, become much more the
better
For being a little bad.

10300 *The Merchant of Venice*
God made him, and therefore let him pass
for a man.

10301 *The Merchant of Venice*
They are as sick that surfeit with too much,
as they that starve with nothing. It is no
mean happiness, therefore, to be seated in
the mean.

10302 *The Merchant of Venice*
If to do were as easy as to know what were
good to do, chapels had been churches,
and poor men's cottages princes' palaces.

10303 *The Merchant of Venice*
There is not one among them but I dote on
his very absence.

10304 *The Merchant of Venice*
How like a fawning publican he looks!

10305 *The Merchant of Venice*
The devil can cite Scripture for his
purpose.
An evil soul, producing holy witness,
Is like a villain with a smiling cheek,
A goodly apple rotten at the heart.

10306 *The Merchant of Venice*
You call me misbeliever, cut-throat dog,
And spit upon my Jewish gabardine,
And all for use of that which is mine own.

10307 *The Merchant of Venice*
It is a wise father that knows his own
child.

10308 *The Merchant of Venice*
Truth will come to light; murder cannot be
hid long.

10309 *The Merchant of Venice*
Love is blind, and lovers cannot see
The pretty follies that themselves commit.

10310 *The Merchant of Venice*
My daughter! O my ducats! O my
daughter!
Fled with a Christian! O my Christian
ducats!
Justice! the law! my ducats, and my
daughter!

10311 *The Merchant of Venice*
I will not choose what many men desire,
Because I will not jump with common
spirits
And rank me with the barbarous
multitude.

10312 *The Merchant of Venice*
Let him look to his bond.

10313 *The Merchant of Venice*
Hath not a Jew eyes? hath not a Jew hands,
organs, dimensions, senses, affections,
passions? fed with the same food, hurt
with the same weapons, subject to the
same diseases, healed by the same means,
warmed and cooled by the same winter
and summer, as a Christian is? If you
prick us, do we not bleed? if you tickle us,
do we not laugh? if you poison us, do we
not die? and if you wrong us, shall we not
revenge? If we are like you in the rest, we
will resemble you in that.

10314 *The Merchant of Venice*
Tell me, where is fancy bred,
Or in the heart, or in the head?
How begot, how nourishèd ...?

It is engendered in the eyes,
With gazing fed; and fancy dies
In the cradle where it lies.

10315 *The Merchant of Venice*
There is no vice so simple but assumes
Some mark of virtue on his outward parts.

10316 *The Merchant of Venice*
The quality of mercy is not strained,
It droppeth as the gentle rain from heaven
Upon the place beneath: it is twice blessed;
It blesseth him that gives and him that
takes.

10317 *The Merchant of Venice*
A Daniel come to judgement! yea, a
Daniel!

10318 *The Merchant of Venice*
How sweet the moonlight sleeps upon this
bank!
Here will we sit, and let the sounds of
music
Creep in our ears.

10319 *The Merchant of Venice*
I am never merry when I hear sweet
music.

10320 *The Merchant of Venice*
The man that hath no music in himself,
Nor is not moved with concord of sweet
sounds,
Is fit for treasons, stratagems, and spoils.

10321 *The Merchant of Venice*
How far that little candle throws his
beams!
So shines a good deed in a naughty world.

10322 *The Merchant of Venice*
This night methinks is but the daylight
sick.

10323 *The Merchant of Venice*
A light wife doth make a heavy husband.

10324 *The Merry Wives of Windsor*
Why, then the world's mine oyster,
Which I with sword will open.

10325 *The Merry Wives of Windsor*
O, what a world of vile ill-favoured faults
Looks handsome in three hundred pounds
a year!

10326 *The Merry Wives of Windsor*
There is divinity in odd numbers, either in
nativity, chance or death.

10327 *A Midsummer Night's Dream*
For aught that ever I could read,
Could ever hear by tale or history,
The course of true love never did run
smooth.

10328 *A Midsummer Night's Dream*
Love looks not with the eyes, but with the
mind,
And therefore is winged Cupid painted
blind.

10329 *A Midsummer Night's Dream*
I must go seek some dew-drops here,
And hang a pearl in every cowslip's ear.

10330 *A Midsummer Night's Dream*
Ill met by moonlight, proud Titania.

10331 *A Midsummer Night's Dream*
I know a bank whereon the wild thyme
blows,
Where oxlips and the nodding violet
grows
Quite over-canopied with luscious
woodbine.

10332 *A Midsummer Night's Dream*
A lion among ladies, is a most dreadful
thing; for there is not a more fearful wild-
fowl than your lion living.

10333 *A Midsummer Night's Dream*
What angel wakes me from my flowery
bed?

10334 *A Midsummer Night's Dream*
Lord, what fools these mortals be!

10335 *A Midsummer Night's Dream*
The lunatic, the lover, and the poet,
Are of imagination all compact.

10336 *A Midsummer Night's Dream*
And, as imagination bodies forth
The forms of things unknown, the poet's
pen
Turns them to shapes, and gives to airy

nothing
A local habitation and a name.

10337 *A Midsummer Night's Dream*
If we shadows have offended,
Think but this, and all is mended,
That you have but slumbered here
While these visions did appear.

10338 *Othello*
Reputation is an idle and most false
imposition; oft got without merit, and lost
without deserving.

10339 *Othello*
There are many events in the womb of
time which will be delivered.

10340 *Othello*
Do not put me to't,
For I am nothing if not critical.

10341 *Othello*
To suckle fools and chronicle small beer.

10342 *Othello*
'Tis pride that pulls the country down.

10343 *Othello*
O! I have lost my reputation. I have lost
the immortal part of myself, and what
remains is bestial.

10344 *Othello*
Who steals my purse steals trash; 'tis
something, nothing;
'Twas mine, 'tis his, and has been slave to
thousands;
But he that filches from me my good name
Robs me of that which not enriches him,
And makes me poor indeed.

10345 *Othello*
O! beware, my lord, of jealousy;
It is the green-eyed monster which doth
mock
The meat it feeds on.

10346 *Othello*
O curse of marriage!
That we can call these delicate creatures
ours,
And not their appetites. I had rather be a
toad,
And live upon the vapour of a dungeon,
Than keep a corner in the thing I love

For others' uses.

10347 *Othello*
Trifles light as air
Are to the jealous confirmations strong
As proofs of holy writ.

10348 *Othello*
Farewell the neighing steed and the shrill
trump,
The spirit-stirring drum, the ear-piercing
fife,
The royal banner, and all quality,
Pride, pomp, and circumstance of glorious
war!

10349 *Othello*
Unkindness may do much;
And his unkindness may defeat my life,
But never taint my love.

10350 *Othello*
Let husbands know
Their wives have sense like them. They
see, and smell,
And have their palates both for sweet and
sour,
As husbands have.

10351 *Othello*
Put out the light, and then put out the
light:
If I quench thee, thou flaming minister,
I can again thy former light restore,
Should I repent me; but once put out thy
light,
Thou cunning'st pattern of excelling
nature,
I know not where is that Promethean heat
That can thy light relume.

10352 *Othello*
Speak of me as I am; nothing extenuate,
Nor set down aught in malice: then, must
you speak
Of one that loved not wisely but too well;
Of one not easily jealous, but being
wrought,
Perplexed in the extreme; of one whose
hand,
Like the base Indian, threw a pearl away
Richer than all his tribe.

10353 *Pericles*
Few love to hear the sins they love to act.

10354 *Pericles*
O you gods!
Why do you make us love your goodly gifts,
And snatch them straight away?

10355 *Pericles*
This world to me is but a ceaseless storm
Whirring me from my friends.

10356 *Richard II*
The purest treasure mortal times afford
Is spotless reputation; that away,
Men are but gilded loam or painted clay.

10357 *Richard II*
Take honour from me, and my life is done.

10358 *Richard II*
Things sweet to taste prove in digestion sour.

10359 *Richard II*
Teach thy necessity to reason thus;
There is no virtue like necessity.

10360 *Richard II*
This royal throne of kings, this sceptered isle,
This earth of majesty, this seat of Mars,
This other Eden, demi-paradise,
This fortress built by Nature for herself
Against infection and the hand of war,
This happy breed of men, this little world,
This precious stone set in the silver sea,
Which serves it in the office of a wall,
Or as a moat defensive to a house,
Against the envy of less happier lands,
This blessèd plot, this earth, this realm, this England,
This nurse, this teeming womb of royal kings,
Feared by their breed and famous by their birth.

10361 *Richard II*
Grace me no grace, nor uncle me no uncle.

10362 *Richard II*
Not all the water in the rough rude sea
Can wash the balm from an anointed king;
The breath of worldly men cannot depose
The deputy elected by the Lord.

10363 *Richard II*
The worst is death, and death will have his day.

10364 *Richard II*
For God's sake, let us sit upon the ground
And tell sad stories of the death of kings:
How some have been deposed; some slain in war;
Some haunted by the ghosts they have deposed;
Some poisoned by their wives; some sleeping killed;
All murdered: for within the hollow crown
That rounds the mortal temples of a king
Keeps Death his court.

10365 *Richard II*
The purple testament of bleeding war.

10366 *Richard II*
What must the king do now? Must he submit?
The king shall do it; must he be deposed?
The king shall be contented: must he lose
The name of king? o' God's name, let it go.

10367 *Richard II*
You may my glories and my state depose,
But not my griefs; still am I king of those.

10368 *Richard II*
How sour sweet music is,
When time is broke, and no proportion kept!
So is it in the music of men's lives.

10369 *Richard II*
I wasted time, and now doth time waste me.

10370 *Richard II*
Mount, mount, my soul! thy seat is up on high;
Whilst my gross flesh sinks downwards, here to die.

10371 *Richard III*
Now is the winter of our discontent
Made glorious summer by this sun of York.

10372 *Richard III*
Sent before my time
Into this breathing world, scarce half made up.

10373 *Richard III*
And therefore, since I cannot prove a lover,
To entertain these fair well-spoken days,
I am determinèd to prove a villain,
And hate the idle pleasures of these days.

10374 *Richard III*
No beast so fierce but knows some touch
of pity.

10375 *Richard III*
Lord, Lord! methought what pain it was to
drown:
What dreadful noise of water in mine ears!
What sights of ugly death within mine
eyes!

10376 *Richard III*
Woe to the land that's governed by a child!

10377 *Richard III*
So wise so young, they say, do never live
long.

10378 *Richard III*
I am not in the giving vein to-day.

10379 *Richard III*
Conscience is but a word that cowards use,
Devised at first to keep the strong in awe.

10380 *Richard III*
A horse! a horse! my kingdom for a horse!

10381 *Romeo and Juliet*
Adversity's sweet milk, philosophy.

10382 *Romeo and Juliet*
From forth the fatal loins of these two foes
A pair of star-crossed lovers take their life.

10383 *Romeo and Juliet*
You and I are past our dancing days.

10384 *Romeo and Juliet*
O! she doth teach the torches to burn
bright.
It seems she hangs upon the cheek of night
Like a rich jewel in an Ethiop's ear;
Beauty too rich for use, for earth too dear.

10385 *Romeo and Juliet*
My only love sprung from my only hate!
Too early seen unknown, and known too
late!

10386 *Romeo and Juliet*
He jests at scars, that never felt a wound.
But, soft! what light through yonder
window breaks?
It is the east, and Juliet is the sun.

10387 *Romeo and Juliet*
O Romeo, Romeo! wherefore art thou
Romeo?

10388 *Romeo and Juliet*
What's in a name? that which we call a
rose
By any other name would smell as sweet.

10389 *Romeo and Juliet*
What love can do that dares love attempt.

10390 *Romeo and Juliet*
O! swear not by the moon, the inconstant
moon,
That monthly changes in her circled orb,
Lest that thy love prove likewise variable.

10391 *Romeo and Juliet*
My bounty is as boundless as the sea,
My love as deep; the more I give to thee,
The more I have, for both are infinite.

10392 *Romeo and Juliet*
Good-night, good-night! parting is such
sweet sorrow
That I shall say good-night till it be
morrow.

10393 *Romeo and Juliet*
A plague o' both your houses!

10394 *Romeo and Juliet*
Thank me no thankings, nor proud me no
prouds.

10395 *Romeo and Juliet*
Death lies on her like an untimely frost
Upon the sweetest flower of all the field.

10396 *The Taming of the Shrew*
There's a small choice in rotten apples.

10397 *The Taming of the Shrew*
Nothing comes amiss, so money comes
withal.

10398 *The Taming of the Shrew*
O! this learning, what a thing it is.

10399 *The Taming of the Shrew*
I am ashamed that women are so simple
To offer war where they should kneel for
peace.

10400 *The Tempest*
Full fathom five thy father lies;
Of his bones are coral made:
Those are pearls that were his eyes:
Nothing of him that doth fade,
But doth suffer a sea-change
Into something rich and strange.

10101 *The Tempest*
Misery acquaints a man with strange
bedfellows.

10402 *The Tempest*
He that dies pays all debts.

10403 *The Tempest*
We are such stuff
As dreams are made on, and our little life
Is rounded with a sleep.

10404 *The Tempest*
But this rough magic
I here abjure ...
...   I'll break my staff,
Bury it certain fathoms in the earth,
And, deeper than did ever plummet
sound,
I'll drown my book.

10405 *The Tempest*
How beauteous mankind is! O brave new
world,
That has such people in't.

10406 *Timon of Athens*
Every man has his fault, and honesty is
his.

10407 *Timon of Athens*
'Tis not enough to help the feeble up,
But to support him after.

10408 *Timon of Athens*
I wonder men dare trust themselves with
men.

10409 *Timon of Athens*
Like madness is the glory of this life.

10410 *Timon of Athens*
Men shut their doors against a setting sun.

10411 *Timon of Athens*
Nothing emboldens sin so much as mercy.

10412 *Troilus and Cressida*
Modest doubt is call'd
The beacon of the wise.

10413 *Troilus and Cressida*
Women are angels, wooing:
Things won are done; joy's soul lies in the
doing;
That she beloved knows nought that
knows not this:
Men prize the thing ungained more than it
is.

10414 *Troilus and Cressida*
O! when degree is shaked,
Which is the ladder to all high designs,
The enterprise is sick.

10415 *Troilus and Cressida*
To be wise, and love,
Exceeds man's might.

10416 *Troilus and Cressida*
Time hath, my lord, a wallet at his back,
Wherein he puts alms for oblivion,
A great-sized monster of ingratitudes.

10417 *Troilus and Cressida*
Perseverance, dear my lord,
Keeps honour bright: to have done, is to
hang
Quite out of fashion, like a rusty mail
In monumental mockery.

10418 *Troilus and Cressida*
One touch of nature makes the whole
world kin.

10419 *Troilus and Cressida*
The end crowns all,
And that old common arbitrator, Time,
Will one day end it.

10420 *Troilus and Cressida*
Lechery, lechery; still, wars and lechery:
nothing else holds fashion.

10421 *Troilus and Cressida*
Hector is dead; there is no more to say.

10422 *Twelfth Night*
If music be the food of love, play on;
Give me excess of it, that, surfeiting,
The appetite may sicken, and so die.

10423 *Twelfth Night*
Is it a world to hide virtues in?

10424 *Twelfth Night*
Many a good hanging prevents a bad
marriage.

10425 *Twelfth Night*
Not to be a-bed after midnight is to be up
betimes.

10426 *Twelfth Night*
What is love? 'tis not hereafter;
Present mirth hath present laughter;
What's to come is still unsure:
In delay there lies no plenty;
Then come kiss me, sweet and twenty,
Youth's a stuff will not endure.

10427 *Twelfth Night*
Dost thou think, because thou art virtuous,
there shall be no more cakes and ale?

10428 *Twelfth Night*
My purpose is, indeed, a horse of that
colour.

10429 *Twelfth Night*
Let thy love be younger than thyself,
Or thy affection cannot hold the bent.

10430 *Twelfth Night*
She never told her love,
But let concealment, like a worm i' the
bud,
Feed on her damask cheek: she pined in
thought;
And with a green and yellow melancholy,
She sat like patience on a monument,
Smiling at grief.

10431 *Twelfth Night*
Some men are born great, some achieve
greatness, and some have greatness thrust
upon them.

10432 *Twelfth Night*
Love sought is good, but giv'n unsought is
better.

10433 *Twelfth Night*
Go, hang yourselves all! you are idle
shallow things: I am not of your element.

10434 *Twelfth Night*
If this were played upon a stage now, I
could condemn it as an improbable fiction.

10435 *Twelfth Night*
Still you keep o' the windy side of the law.

10436 *Twelfth Night*
I hate ingratitude more in a man
Than lying, vainness, babbling
drunkenness,
Or any taint of vice whose strong
corruption
Inhabits our frail blood.

10437 *The Two Gentlemen of Verona*
Home-keeping youth have ever homely
wits.

10438 *The Two Gentlemen of Verona*
He was more than over shoes in love.

10439 *The Two Gentlemen of Verona*
I have no other but a woman's reason:
I think him so, because I think him so.

10440 *The Two Gentlemen of Verona*
O heaven! were man
But constant, he were perfect.

10441 *The Winter's Tale*
It is a heretic that makes the fire,
Not she which burns in 't.

10442 *The Winter's Tale*
I am a feather for each wind that blows.

10443 *The Winter's Tale*
What's gone and what's past help
Should be past grief.

10444 *The Winter's Tale*
A snapper-up of unconsidered trifles.

10445 *The Winter's Tale*
She is
The queen of curds and cream.

10446 *The Winter's Tale*
This dream of mine,
Being now awake, I'll queen it no inch
further,
But milk my ewes and weep.

10447 *The Winter's Tale*
Though I am not naturally honest, I am so
sometimes by chance.

10448 *The Winter's Tale (stage direction)*
Exit, pursued by a bear.

10449 *The Passionate Pilgrim (attribution doubtful)*
Crabbed age and youth cannot live together:
Youth is full of pleasance, age is full of care.

10450 *The Passionate Pilgrim (attribution doubtful)*
Age, I do abhor thee, youth, I do adore thee.

10451 *The Rape of Lucrece*
Beauty itself doth of itself persuade
The eyes of men without an orator.

10452 *The Rape of Lucrece*
Who buys a minute's mirth to wail a week?
Or sells eternity to get a toy?
For one sweet grape who will the vine destroy?

10453 *The Rape of Lucrece*
Time's glory is to calm contending kings,
To unmask falsehood, and bring truth to light.

10454 *Sonnet 2*
When forty winters shall besiege thy brow,
And dig deep trenches in thy beauty's field.

10455 *Sonnet 3*
Thou art thy mother's glass, and she in thee
Calls back the lovely April of her prime.

10456 *Sonnet 8*
Music to hear, why hear'st thou music sadly?
Sweets with sweets war not, joy delights in joy:
Why lov'st thou that which thou receiv'st not gladly,
Or else receiv'st with pleasure thine annoy?
If the true concord of well-tunèd sounds,
By unions married, do offend thine ear,
They do but sweetly chide thee.

10457 *Sonnet 12*
When lofty trees I see barren of leaves,
Which erst from heat did canopy the herd,
And summer's green all girded up in sheaves,

Borne on the bier with white and bristly beard.

10458 *Sonnet 17*
If I could write the beauty of your eyes
And in fresh numbers number all your graces,
The age to come would say, 'This poet lies.'

10459 *Sonnet 18*
Shall I compare thee to a summer's day?
Thou art more lovely and more temperate:
Rough winds do shake the darling buds of May,
And summer's lease hath all too short a date.

10460 *Sonnet 29*
When in disgrace with fortune and men's eyes
I all alone beweep my outcast state,
And trouble deaf heaven with my bootless cries,
And look upon myself and curse my fate.

10461 *Sonnet 29*
Haply I think on thee - and then my state,
Like to the lark at break of day arising
From sullen earth, sings hymns at heaven's gate;
For thy sweet love remembered such wealth brings
That then I scorn to change my state with kings.

10462 *Sonnet 30*
When to the sessions of sweet silent thought
I summon up remembrance of things past,
I sigh the lack of many a thing I sought,
And with old woes new wail my dear times' waste.

10463 *Sonnet 55*
Not marble, nor the gilded monuments
Of princes, shall outlive this powerful rhyme;
But you shall shine more bright in these contents
Than unswept stone, besmeared with sluttish time.

10464 *Sonnet 57*
So true a fool is love that in your will,
Though you do anything, he thinks no ill.

10465 *Sonnet 60*
Like as the waves make towards the
pebbled shore,
So do our minutes hasten to their end.

10466 *Sonnet 64*
When I have seen the hungry ocean gain
Advantage on the kingdom of the shore.

10467 *Sonnet 73*
That time of year thou mayst in me behold
When yellow leaves, or none, or few, do
hang
Upon those boughs which shake against
the cold.

10468 *Sonnet 87*
Farewell! thou art too dear for my
possessing,
And like enough thou know'st thy
estimate:
The charter of thy worth gives thee
releasing;
My bonds in thee are all determinate.

10469 *Sonnet 87*
Thus have I had thee, as a dream doth
flatter,
In sleep a king, but, waking, no such
matter.

10470 *Sonnet 94*
For sweetest things turn sourest by their
deeds;
Lilies that fester smell far worse than
weeds.

10471 *Sonnet 97*
How like a winter hath my absence been
From thee, the pleasure of the fleeting
year!
What freezings have I felt, what dark days
seen!
What old December's bareness
everywhere!

10472 *Sonnet 106*
When in the chronicle of wasted time
I see descriptions of the fairest wights.

10473 *Sonnet 106*
For we, which now behold these present
days,
Have eyes to wonder, but lack tongues to
praise.

10474 *Sonnet 116*
Let me not to the marriage of true minds
Admit impediments. Love is not love
Which alters when it alteration finds,
Or bends with the remover to remove:
O, no! it is an ever-fixèd mark,
That looks on tempests and is never
shaken.

10475 *Sonnet 116*
Love alters not with his brief hours and
weeks,
But bears it out even to the edge of doom.
If this be error, and upon me proved,
I never writ, nor no man ever loved.

10476 *Sonnet 129*
The expense of spirit in a waste of shame
Is lust in action; and till action, lust
Is perjured, murderous, bloody, full of
blame,
Savage, extreme, rude, cruel, not to trust;
Enjoyed no sooner but despisèd straight.

10477 *Sonnet 130*
And yet, by heaven, I think my love as rare
As any she belied with false compare.

10478 *Sonnet 138*
When my love swears that she is made of
truth,
I do believe her, though I know she lies.

10479 *Sonnet 144*
Two loves I have of comfort and despair,
Which like two spirits do suggest me still:
The better angel is a man right fair,
The worser spirit a woman, coloured ill.

10480 *Venus and Adonis*
Love is a spirit all compact of fire,
Not gross to sink, but light, and will
aspire.

10481 *Venus and Adonis*
Love comforteth like sunshine after rain.

10482 *(epitaph on his tomb, probably self-
composed)*
Good friend, for Jesu's sake forbear

To dig the dust enclosed here.
Blest be the man that spares these stones,
And curst be he that moves my bones.

SHAMGAR Judge Meir
10483
The complete truth is not the prerogative
of the human judge.

SHANKLY Bill 1914-1981
10484
Some people think football is a matter of
life and death ... I can assure them it is
much more serious than that.

SHARPE Tom 1928-
10485 *Indecent Exposure*
The South African police would leave no
stone unturned to see that nothing
disturbed the even terror of their lives.

SHAW George Bernard 1856-1950
10486
My opportunities were still there; nay, they
multiplied tenfold; but the strength and
youth to cope with them began to fail, and
to need eking out with the shifty cunning
of experience.

10487
The test of a man or woman's breeding is
how they behave in a quarrel.

10488
All professions are a conspiracy against the
country.

10489
She had lost the art of conversation, but
not, unfortunately, the power of speech.

10490
I often quote myself. It adds spice to my
conversation.

10491
Everything happens to everybody sooner
or later if there is time enough.

10492
Men are wise in proportion, not to their
experience, but to their capacity for
experience.

10493
Fashions, after all, are only induced
epidemics.

10494
What is life but a series of inspired follies?
The difficulty is to find them to do.

10495
Beware of the man whose God is in the
skies.

10496
My only policy is to profess evil and do
good.

10497
The art of government is the organization
of idolatry.

10498
Hatred is the coward's revenge for being
intimidated.

10499
A perpetual holiday is a good working
definition of hell.

10500
The savage bows down to idols of wood
and stone, the civilized man to idols of
flesh and blood.

10501
Do not do unto others as you would that
they should do unto you. Their tastes may
not be the same.

10502
I was taught when I was young that if
people would only love one another, all
would be well with the world. This
seemed simple and very nice; but I found
when I tried to put it in practice not only
that other people were seldom lovable, but
that I was not very lovable myself.

10503
Love is a gross exaggeration of the
difference between one person and
everybody else.

10504
You don't learn to hold your own by
standing on guard, but by attacking, and
getting well hammered yourself.

10505
Morality is not respectability.

10506
The best brought-up children are those who have seen their parents as they are. Hypocrisy is not the parents' first duty.

10507
The philosopher is Nature's pilot - and there you have our difference; to be in hell is to drift: to be in heaven is to steer.

10508
Modern poverty is not the poverty that was blest in the Sermon on the Mount.

10509
A great devotee of the gospel of getting on.

10510
Reformers have the idea that change can be achieved by brute sanity.

10511
Religion is a great force - the only real motive force in the world; but you must get a man through his own religion, not through yours.

10512
Christianity might be a good thing if anyone ever tried it.

10513
I believe in the discipline of silence and could talk for hours about it.

10514
The secret of being miserable is to have leisure to bother about whether you are happy or not. The cure for it is occupation.

10515
I work as my father drank.

10516
When I was a young man I observed that nine out of ten things I did were failures. I didn't want to be a failure, so I did ten times more work.

10517
Never believe anything a writer tells you about himself. A man comes to believe in the end the lies he tells himself about himself.

10518
My method is to take the utmost trouble to find the right thing to say, and then to say it with the utmost levity.

10519
Silence is the most perfect expression of scorn.

10520
[Dancing is] a perpendicular expression of a horizontal desire.

10521 *(attributed)*
England and America are two countries divided by a common language.

10522 *Annajanska*
All great truths begin as blasphemies.

10523 *The Apple Cart*
One man that has a mind and knows it can always beat ten men who haven't and don't.

10524 *The Apple Cart*
I never resist temptation, because I have found that things that are bad for me do not tempt me.

10525 *Arms and the Man*
You're not a man, you're a machine.

10526 *Caesar and Cleopatra*
When a stupid man is doing something he is ashamed of, he always declares that it is his duty.

10527 *Candida*
We have no more right to consume happiness without producing it than to consume wealth without producing it.

10528 *Candida*
It is easy - terribly easy - to shake a man's faith in himself. To take advantage of that to break a man's spirit is devil's work.

10529 *Candida*
I'm only a beer teetotaller, not a champagne teetotaller.

10530 *The Devil's Disciple*
The worst sin towards our fellow creatures is not to hate them, but to be indifferent to them: that's the essence of inhumanity.

10531 *The Devil's Disciple*
Martyrdom ... the only way in which a man can become famous without ability.

10532 *The Devil's Disciple*
I never expect a soldier to think.

10533 *The Devil's Disciple*
SWINDON: What will history say?
BURGOYNE: History, sir, will tell lies as usual.

10534 *The Devil's Disciple*
The British soldier can stand up to anything except the British War Office.

10535 *The Doctor's Dilemma*
All professions are conspiracies against the laity.

10536 *Everybody's Political What's What?*
A government which robs Peter to pay Paul can always depend on the support of Paul.

10537 *Fanny's First Play*
It's all that the young can do for the old, to shock them and keep them up to date.

10538 *Getting Married*
What God hath joined together no man ever shall put asunder: God will take care of that.

10539 *Getting Married 'The Right to Motherhood'*
The one point on which all women are in furious secret rebellion against the existing law is the saddling of the right to a child with the obligation to become the servant of a man.

10540 *John Bull's Other Island*
An Irishman's heart is nothing but his imagination.

10541 *John Bull's Other Island*
What really flatters a man is that you think him worth flattering.

10542 *John Bull's Other Island*
There are only two qualities in the world: efficiency and inefficiency, and only two sorts of people: the efficient and the inefficient.

10543 *Major Barbara*
I am a Millionaire. That is my religion.

10544 *Major Barbara*
Wot prawce Selvytion nah?

10545 *Major Barbara*
Alcohol is a very necessary article ... It enables Parliament to do things at eleven at night that no sane person would do at eleven in the morning.

10546 *Major Barbara*
He knows nothing; and he thinks he knows everything. That points clearly to a political career.

10547 *Major Barbara*
Nothing is ever done in this world until men are prepared to kill one another if it is not done.

10548 *Man and Superman*
But a lifetime of happiness! No man alive could bear it: it would be hell on earth.

10549 *Man and Superman*
An Englishman thinks he is moral when he is only uncomfortable.

10550 *Man and Superman*
When the military man approaches, the world locks up its spoons and packs off its womankind.

10551 *Man and Superman*
What is virtue but the Trade Unionism of the married?

10552 *Man and Superman*
It is a woman's business to get married as soon as possible, and a man's to keep unmarried as long as he can.

10553 *Man and Superman*
There are two tragedies in life. One is to lose your heart's desire. The other is to gain it.

10554 *Man and Superman 'Maxims: Democracy'*
Democracy substitutes election by the incompetent many for appointment by the corrupt few.

10555 *Man and Superman 'Maxims: Education'*
He who can, does. He who cannot, teaches.

10556 *Man and Superman 'Maxims: How to Beat Children'*
If you strike a child take care that you strike it in anger, even at the risk of maiming it for life. A blow in cold blood neither can nor should be forgiven.

10557 *Man and Superman 'Maxims: Liberty and Equality'*
Liberty means responsibility. That is why most men dread it.

10558 *Man and Superman 'Maxims: Marriage'*
Marriage is popular because it combines the maximum of temptation with the maximum of opportunity.

10559 *Man and Superman 'Maxims: Reason'*
The reasonable man adapts himself to the world: the unreasonable one persists in trying to adapt the world to himself. Therefore all progress depends on the unreasonable man.

10560 *Man and Superman 'Maxims: Stray Sayings'*
Every man over forty is a scoundrel.

10561 *Man and Superman 'Maxims: Stray Sayings'*
Youth, which is forgiven everything, forgives itself nothing: age, which forgives itself everything, is forgiven nothing.

10562 *Man and Superman 'Maxims: Stray Sayings'*
Take care to get what you like or you will be forced to like what you get.

10563 *Man and Superman 'The Revolutionist's Handbook'*
Revolutions have never lightened the burden of tyranny: they have only shifted it to another shoulder.

10564 *Back to Methuselah*
I enjoy convalescence. It is the part that makes illness worthwhile.

10565 *Misalliance*
Anarchism is a game at which the police can beat you.

10566 *O'Flaherty V.C.*
You'll never have a quiet world till you knock the patriotism out of the human race.

10567 *The Philanderer*
The fickleness of the woman I love is only equalled by the infernal constancy of the women who love me.

10568 *Plays Pleasant and Unpleasant*
There is only one religion, though there are a hundred versions of it.

10569 *Pygmalion*
PICKERING: Have you no morals, man?
DOOLITTLE: Can't afford them, Governor.

10570 *Saint Joan*
If ever I utter an oath again may my soul be blasted to eternal damnation!

10571 *Saint Joan*
How can what an Englishman believes be heresy? It is a contradiction in terms.

10572 *The Showing-Up of Blanco Posnet*
Assassination is the extreme form of censorship.

10573 *(of William Morris)*
You can lose a man like that by your own death, but not by his.

SHAW Henry Wheeler (Josh Billings)
1818-1885
10574 *Josh Billings, his Sayings*
Thrice is he armed that hath his quarrel just,
But four times he who gets his blow in fust.

10575 *Proverb*
It is better to know nothing than to know what ain't so.

SHAWN Ted 1891-1972
10576
Dance is the only art of which we ourselves are the stuff of which it is made.

SHAY R.E.
10577
Depend on the rabbit's foot if you will, but remember it didn't work for the rabbit!

SHEEHY Gail
10578
When men reach their sixties and retire, they go to pieces. Women just go right on cooking.

SHEEN Fulton 1895-1979
10579
An atheist is a man who has no invisible means of support.

SHELDON William H.
10580
Happiness is essentially a state of going somewhere, wholeheartedly, one-directionally, without regret or reservation.

SHELLEY Mary 1797-1851
10581
Nothing contributes so much to tranquilize the mind as a steady purpose - a point on which the soul may fix its intellectual eye.

10582 *Frankenstein*
You seek for knowledge and wisdom as I once did; and I ardently hope that the gratification of your wishes may not be a serpent to sting you, as mine has been.

10583 *(of her son's education)*
Teach him to think for himself? Oh, my God, teach him rather to think like other people.

SHELLEY Percy Bysshe 1792-1822
10584
Reason respects the differences, and imagination the similitudes of things.

10585 *Adonais*
To that high Capital, where kingly Death Keeps his pale court in beauty and decay, He came.

10586 *Adonais*
She faded, like a cloud which had outwept its rain.

10587 *Adonais*
Winter is come and gone,
But grief returns with the revolving year.

10588 *Adonais*
From the great morning of the world when first
God dawned on Chaos.

10589 *Adonais*
Dust to the dust! but the pure spirit shall flow
Back to the burning fountain whence it came,
A portion of the Eternal.

10590 *Adonais*
He hath awakened from the dream of life -
'Tis we, who lost in stormy visions, keep
With phantoms an unprofitable strife,
And in mad trance, strike with our spirit's knife
Invulnerable nothings.

10591 *Adonais*
From the contagion of the world's slow stain
He is secure, and now can never mourn
A heart grown cold, a head grown grey in vain.

10592 *Adonais*
He is a portion of the loveliness
Which once he made more lovely.

10593 *Adonais*
Life, like a dome of many-coloured glass,
Stains the white radiance of Eternity,
Until Death tramples it to fragments.

10594 *'The Cloud'*
I am the daughter of Earth and Water,
And the nursling of the Sky;
I pass through the pores of the ocean and shores;
I change, but I cannot die.

10595 *'The Cloud'*
I silently laugh at my own cenotaph,
And out of the caverns of rain,
Like a child from the womb, like a ghost from the tomb,
I arise and unbuild it again.

10596 *Declaration of Rights*
Titles are tinsel, power a corrupter, glory a bubble, and excessive wealth a libel on its possessor.

10597 *Defence of Poetry*
Poetry is the record of the best and
happiest moments of the happiest and best
minds.

10598 *'Epipsychidion'*
I never was attached to that great sect,
Whose doctrine is that each one should
select
Out of the crowd a mistress or a friend,
And all the rest, though fair and wise,
commend
To cold oblivion.

10599 *'An Exhortation'*
Chameleons feed on light and air:
Poets' food is love and fame.

10600 *'Good Night'*
Good-night? ah! no; the hour is ill
Which severs those it should unite;
Let us remain together still,
Then it will be *good* night.

10601 *Hellas*
The world's great age begins anew,
The golden years return,
The earth doth like a snake renew
Her winter weeds outworn;
Heaven smiles, and faiths and empires
gleam,
Like wrecks of a dissolving dream.

10602 *Hellas*
The world is weary of the past,
Oh, might it die or rest at last!

10603 *'Letter to Maria Gisborne'*
Have you not heard
When a man marries, dies or turns
Hindoo,
His best friends hear no more of him?

10604 *'Letter to Maria Gisborne'(of Thomas
Love Peacock)*
His fine wit
Makes such a wound, the knife is lost in it.

10605 *'Lines: When the lamp'*
When the lamp is shattered
The light in the dust lies dead -
When the cloud is scattered
The rainbow's glory is shed.
When the lute is broken,
Sweet tones are remembered not;
When the lips have spoken,

Loved accents are soon forgot.

10606 *'Lines written amongst the Euganean
Hills'(Venice)*
Sun-girt city, thou hast been
Ocean's child, and then his queen;
Now is come a darker day,
And thou soon must be his prey.

10607 *'The Mask of Anarchy'*
I met Murder on the way -
He had a mask like Castlereagh.

10608 *'Mutability'*
Nought may endure but Mutability.

10609 *'Ode to the West Wind'*
O wild West Wind, thou breath of
Autumn's being,
Thou, from whose unseen presence the
leaves dead
Are driven, like ghosts from an enchanter
fleeing,
Yellow, and black, and pale, and hectic red,
Pestilence-striken multitudes.

10610 *'Ode to the West Wind'*
Oh, lift me as a wave, a leaf, a cloud!
I fall upon the thorns of life! I bleed!

10611 *'Ode to the West Wind'*
Make me thy lyre, even as the forest is:
What if my leaves are falling like its own!

10612 *'Ode to the West Wind'*
Scatter, as from an unextinguished hearth
Ashes and sparks, my words among
mankind!
Be through my lips to unawakened earth
The trumpet of a prophecy! O, Wind,
If Winter comes, can Spring be far behind?

10613 *'Ozymandias'*
I met a traveller from an antique land
Who said: Two vast and trunkless legs of
stone
Stand in the desert.

10614 *'Ozymandias'*
'My name is Ozymandias, king of kings;
Look on my works, ye Mighty, and
despair!'

10615 *'Peter Bell the Third'*
Hell is a city much like London -
A populous and smoky city.

10616 *'Prometheus Unbound'*
It doth repent me; words are quick and
vain;
Grief for awhile is blind, and so was mine.

10617 *'Prometheus Unbound'*
The dust of creeds outworn.

10618 *'Prometheus Unbound'*
On a poet's lips I slept
Dreaming like a love-adept
In the sound his breathing kept.

10619 *'Prometheus Unbound'*
He gave man speech, and speech created
thought,
Which is the measure of the universe.

10620 *'Prometheus Unbound'*
A traveller from the cradle to the grave
Through the dim night of this immortal
day.

10621 *'Prometheus Unbound'*
Familiar acts are beautiful through love.

10622 *'The Revolt of Islam'*
With hue like that when some great
painter dips
His pencil in the gloom of earthquake and
eclipse.

10623 *'To a Skylark'*
Hail to thee, blithe Spirit!
Bird thou never wert,
That from Heaven, or near it,
Pourest thy full heart
In profuse strains of unpremeditated art.

10624 *'To a Skylark'*
And singing still dost soar, and soaring
ever singest.

10625 *'To a Skylark'*
Like an unbodied joy whose race is just
begun.

10626 *'To a Skylark'*
We look before and after,
And pine for what is not:
Our sincerest laughter
With some pain is fraught;
Our sweetest songs are those that tell of
saddest thought.

10627 *'To a Skylark'*
Teach me half the gladness
That thy brain must know,
Such harmonious madness
From my lips would flow
The world should listen then - as I am
listening now.

10628 *'Song to the Men of England'*
Men of England, wherefore plough
For the lords who lay ye low?

10629 *'Song to the Men of England'*
The seed ye sow, another reaps;
The wealth ye find, another keeps;
The robes ye weave, another wears;
The arms ye forge, another bears.

10630 *'Sonnet'*
Lift not the painted veil which those who
live
Call Life.

10631 *'Sonnet: England in 1819'*
An old, mad, blind, despised, and dying
king.

SHENSTONE William 1714-1763
10632 *Works in Verse and Prose*
Laws are generally found to be nets of
such a texture, as the little creep through,
the great break through, and the middle-
sized are alone entangled in.

10633 *'Written at an Inn at Henley'*
Whoe'er has travelled life's dull round,
Where'er his stages may have been,
May sigh to think he still has found
The warmest welcome, at an inn.

SHERIDAN Philip Henry 1831-1888
10634 *(attributed)*
The only good Indian is a dead Indian.

SHERIDAN Richard Brinsley 1751-1816
10635
Our memories are independent of our
wills. It is not so easy to forget.

10636
The Right Honourable gentleman is
indebted to his memory for his jests and to
his imagination for his facts.

10637 *'Clio's Protest'*
You write with ease, to show your
breeding,
But easy writing's vile hard reading.

10638 *The Critic*
If it is abuse - why one is always sure to
hear of it from one damned goodnatured
friend or another!

10639 *The Critic*
I wish sir, you would practise this without
me. I can't stay dying here all night.

10640 *The Critic*
An oyster may be crossed in love!

10641 *The Duenna*
I was struck all of a heap.

10642 *The Duenna*
Conscience has no more to do with
gallantry than it has with politics.

10643 *The Rivals*
Illiterate him, I say, quite from your
memory.

10644 *The Rivals*
'Tis safest in matrimony to begin with a
little aversion.

10645 *The Rivals*
He is the very pineapple of politeness!

10646 *The Rivals*
An aspersion upon my parts of speech!
was ever such a brute! Sure, if I reprehend
anything in this world, it is the use of my
oracular tongue, and a nice derangement
of epitaphs!

10647 *The School for Scandal*
You had no taste when you married me.

10648 *The School for Scandal*
Here is the whole set! a character dead at
every word.

10649 *The School for Scandal*
An unforgiving eye, and a damned
disinheriting countenance!

SHERMAN William 1820-1891
10650
There is many a boy here to-day who looks
on war as all glory, but, boys, it is all hell.

10651 *(defining courage)*
A perfect sensibility of the measure of
danger, and a mental willingness to endure
it.

SHINN Florence Scovel
10652
Intuition is a spiritual faculty and does not
explain, but simply points the way.

SHINWELL Emanuel 1884-1986
10653
We know that the organised workers of the
country are our friends. As for the rest,
they don't matter a tinker's cuss.

SHIPLEY Sir Arthur 1861-1927
10654 *Life 'Ere you were Queen of Sheba'*
When we were a soft amoeba, in ages past
and gone,
Ere you were Queen of Sheba, or I King
Solomon,
Alone and undivided, we lived a life of
sloth,
Whatever you did, I did; one dinner
served for both.
Anon came separation, by fission and
divorce,
A lonely pseudopodium I wandered on
my course.

SHIRLEY James 1596-1666
10655 *The Contention of Ajax and Ulysses*
There is no armour against fate;
Death lays his icy hand on kings.

10656 *The Contention of Ajax and Ulysses*
Only the actions of the just
Smell sweet, and blossom in their dust.

10657 *The Wedding*
How little room
Do we take up in death, that, living know
No bounds?

SHORE Dinah
10658
Trouble is a part of your life, and if you
don't share it, you don't give the person
who loves you a chance to love you
enough.

SHRINER Herb
10659
Our doctor would never really operate
unless it was necessary. He was just that

way. If he didn't need the money, he wouldn't lay a hand on you.

SHULTZ George P. 1920-
10660
Nothing ever gets settled in this town (Washington). It's not like running a company or even a university. It's a seething debating society, in which the debate never stops; in which people never give up, including me, and that's the atmosphere in which you administer.

SHUTE Evan
10661
Change must be measured from a known base line.

SICKERT Walter 1860-1942
10662 *'The Language of Art'*
Nothing knits man to man, ... like the frequent passage from hand to hand of cash.

SIDNEY Algernon 1622-1683
10663 *Discourses concerning Government*
Liars ought to have good memories.

10664 *Discourses concerning Government*
Men lived like fishes; the great ones devoured the small.

10665 *Discourses concerning Government*
'Tis not necessary to light a candle to the sun.

SIDNEY Sir Philip 1554-1586
10666 *Arcadia*
Who shoots at the mid-day sun, though he be sure he shall never hit the mark; yet as sure he is he shall shoot higher than who aims but at a bush.

10667 *Arcadia*
My true love hath my heart and I have his,
By just exchange one for the other giv'n;
I hold his dear, and mine he cannot miss,
There never was a better bargain driv'n.

10668 *Astrophel and Stella*
They love indeed who quake to say they love.

10669 *Astrophel and Stella, Sonnet 1*
'Fool,' said my Muse to me, 'look in thy heart and write.'

10670 *Certain Sonnets*
Leave me, O Love which reachest but to dust,
And thou, my mind, aspire to higher things;
Grow rich in that which never taketh rust;
Whatever fades, but fading pleasure brings.

10671 *The Defence of Poetry*
Comedy is an imitation of the common errors of our life

SIEYES Emmanuel Joseph 1748-1836
10672 *(attributed, voting for the death of Louis XVI)*
La mort, sans phrases.
Death, without rhetoric.

10673 *(asked what he had done during the French Revolution)*
J'ai vécu.
I survived.

SIFTON Clifford Sir 1861-1929
10674
I think a stalwart peasant in a sheepskin coat, born on the soil, whose forefathers have been farmers for ten generations, with a stout wife and a half-dozen chickens, is good quality.

SIGISMUND Emperor 1361-1437
10675 *(to prelate who had criticized his Latin)*
I am the Roman Emperor, and am above grammar.

SIGNORET Simone 1921-1985
10676
Pains do not hold a marriage together. It is threads, hundreds of tiny threads which sew people together through the years. That's what makes a marriage last - more than passion or even sex.

SIGOURNEY Lydia 1791-1865
10677
The strength of a nation, especially of a republican nation, is in the intelligent and well-ordered homes of the people.

10678
Whatever you would have your children become, strive to exhibit in your own lives and conversation.

SILLITOE Alan 1928-
10679
The loneliness of the long-distance runner.

SILLS Beverly 1929-
10680
You may be disappointed if you fail, but you are doomed if you don't try.

SIMENON Georges 1903-1989
10681
Writing is not a profession but a vocation of unhappiness.

SIMON Paul 1942-
10682 *'Bridge over Troubled Water'*
Like a bridge over troubled water
I will lay me down.

10683 *'Mrs Robinson' The Graduate*
And here's to you, Mrs Robinson
Jesus loves you more than you will know.

10684 *'Sound of Silence'*
People talking without speaking
People hearing without listening ...
'Fools,' said I, 'You do not know
Silence like a cancer grows.'

SIMONIDES c.556-486 BC
10685 *(attributed)*
Go, tell the Spartans, thou who passest by,
That here obedient to their laws we lie.

10686 *In Plutarch*
Painting is silent poetry, poetry is eloquent painting.

SIMONSON Lee 1888-1967
10687
An artist has been defined as a neurotic who continually cures himself with his art.

10688
Any event, once it has occurred, can be made to appear inevitable by a competent historian.

SIMPSON N.F. 1919-
10689 *A Resounding Tinkle*
A problem left to itself dries up or goes rotten. But fertilize a problem with a solution - you'll hatch out dozens.

SIMPSON O.J. 1947-
10690
Fear of losing is what makes competitors

so great. Show me a gracious loser and I'll show you a perennial loser.

SIMPSON Wallis 1896-1986
10691
I don't remember any love affairs. One must keep love affairs quiet.

10692 *Letter to Edward VIII*
I look a hundred and weigh 110 - you won't love me when you see the wreck that England has made of me.

SIMS Sylvia
10693
You can have your face lifted but there comes a time when you are still going to be offered the Nurse, not Juliet.

SINCLAIR Gordon John
10694 *in Gregory's Girl*
"It doesn't look nice. If women were meant to play football they'd have their tits somewhere else."

SINGER Isaac Bashevis 1904-1991
10695
The waste basket is a writer's best friend.

10696
Writing has power, but its power has no vector. Writers can stir the mind, but they can't direct it. Time changes things, God changes things, the dictators change things, but writers can't change anything.

10697
A good writer is basically a story-teller, not a scholar or a redeemer of mankind.

SISSON C.H. 1914-
10698 *In The London Zoo*
Here lies a civil servant. He was civil
To everyone, and servant to the devil.

SITWELL Dame Edith 1887-1964
10699
A great many people now reading and writing would be better employed in keeping rabbits.

10700
I have often wished I had time to cultivate modesty ... But I am too busy thinking about myself.

10701 *Façade 'Aubade'*
Jane, Jane,
Tall as a crane,
The morning light creaks down again.

10702 *Façade 'Dark Song'*
The fire was furry as a bear.

10703 *Façade 'Lullaby for Jumbo'*
Jumbo asleep!
Grey leaves thick-furred
As his ears, keep
Conversation blurred.

10704 *'Still Falls the Rain'*
Still falls the Rain -
Dark as the world of man, black as our loss
Blind as the nineteen hundred and forty
nails
Upon the Cross.

10705 *'The Sleeping Beauty'*
Forget-me-nots, whose eyes of childish
blue,
Gold-starred like heaven, speak of love
still true.

SITWELL Sir Osbert 1892-1969
10706
The artist, like the idiot, or clown, sits on
the edge of the world, and a push may
send him over it.

10707 *'On the Coast of Coromandel'*
On the coast of Coromandel
Dance they to the tunes of Handel.

10708 *At the House of Mrs Kinfoot*
The British Bourgeoise
Is not born,
And does not die,
But, if it is ill,
It has a frightened look in its eyes.

10709 *'Milordo Inglese'*
In reality, killing time
Is only the name for another of the
multifarious ways
By which Time kills us.

SKELTON John c.1460-1529
10710 *The Bouge of Court*
The sovereign'st thing that any man may
have
Is little to say, and much to hear and see.

10711 *The Garland of Laurel' To Mistress
Margaret Hussey'*
With solace and gladness,
Much mirth and no madness,
All good and no badness;
So joyously,
So maidenly,
So womanly,
Her demeaning.

10712 *Magnificence*
I blunder, I bluster, I blow, and I blother,
I make on the one day, and I mar on the
other.
Busy, busy, and ever busy,
I dance up and down till I am dizzy.

SKELTON Robin
10713
I have no history but the length of my
bones.

SKINNER B.F. 1904-1990
10714
Education is what survives when what has
been learnt has been forgotten.

10715 *Contingencies of Reinforcement*
The real question is not whether machines
think but whether men do.

SKINNER Cornelia Otis 1901-1979
10716
Women keep a special corner of their
hearts for sins they have never committed.

SMART Christopher 1722-1771
10717 *Hymns and Spiritual Songs 'The
Nativity ...'*
God all-bounteous, all-creative,
Whom no ills from good dissuade,
Is incarnate, and a native
Of the very world he made.

10718 *Jubilate Agno*
For in my nature I quested for beauty, but
God, God hath sent me to sea for pearls.

10719 *Jubilate Agno*
For sincerity is a jewel which is pure and
transparent, eternal and inestimable.

10720 *Jubilate Agno*
For Charity is cold in the multitude of
possessions, and the rich are covetous of
their crumbs.

10721 *Jubilate Agno*
I will consider my Cat Jeoffrey.
For he is the servant of the Living God
duly and daily serving him.

10722 *A Song to David*
Strong is the lion - like a coal
His eye-ball - like a bastion's mole
His chest against his foes:

10723 *A Song to David*
Glorious the northern lights astream;
Glorious the song, when God's the theme;
Glorious the thunder's roar.

SMILES Samuel 1812-1904
10724 *Duty*
We each day dig our graves with our teeth.

10725 *Self-Help*
The spirit of self-help is the root of all
genuine growth in the individual.

10726 *Self-Help*
The shortest way to do many things is to
do only one thing at once.

10727 *Self-Help*
Cheerfulness gives elasticity to the spirit.
Spectres fly before it.

10728 *Self-Help*
We often discover what *will* do, by finding
out what will not do; and probably he who
never made a mistake never made a
discovery.

10729 *Thrift*
A place for everything, and everything in
its place.

SMITH Adam 1723-1790
10730
Man, an animal that makes bargains.

10731 *Theory of Moral Sentiments*
Though our brother is on the rack, as long
as we ourselves are at ease, our senses will
never inform us of what he suffers.

10732 *Wealth of Nations*
It is not from the benevolence of the
butcher, the brewer, or the baker, that we
expect our dinner, but from their regard to
their own interest. We address ourselves
not to their humanity but their self love.

10733 *Wealth of Nations*
People of the same trade seldom meet
together, even for merriment and
diversion, but the conversation ends in a
conspiracy against the public, or in some
contrivance to raise prices.

10734 *Wealth of Nations*
Consumption is the sole end and purpose
of production; and the interest of the
producer ought to be attended to only so
far as it may be necessary for promoting
that of the consumer.

10735 *Wealth of Nations*
There is no art which one government
sooner learns of another than that of
draining money from the pockets of the
people.

SMITH Alexander 1830-1867
10736
If you wish to preserve your secret, wrap it
up in frankness.

SMITH A.W. 1937-
10737
Where there is one Englishman there is a
garden. Where there are two Englishmen
there will be a club. But this does not
mean any falling off in the number of
gardens. There will be three. The club
will have one too.

SMITH Charles Merrill
10738
The cocktail party - a device for paying off
obligations to people you don't want to
invite to dinner.

SMITH Sir Cyril 1928-
10739 *(of the House of Commons)*
The longest running farce in the West End.

SMITH Dodie 1896-1990
10740 *Dear Octopus*
The family - that dear octopus from whose
tentacles we never quite escape.

SMITH Edgar 1857-1938
10741 *'Heaven Will Protect the Working-Girl'*
You may tempt the upper classes
With your villainous demi-tasses,
But; Heaven will protect a working-girl!

496

SMITH F.E. 1872-1930
10742
The world continues to offer glittering prizes to those who have stout hearts and sharp swords.

10743 *Contemporary Personalities*
We have the highest authority for believing that the meek shall inherit the earth; though I have never found any particular corroboration of this aphorism in the records of Somerset House.

10744 *Law, Life and Letters*
Nature has no cure for this sort of madness [Bolshevism], though I have known a legacy from a rich relative work wonders.

SMITH Goldwin 1823-1910
10745
The father of confederation is deadlock.

SMITH Hannah Whitall
10746
The true secret of giving advice is, after you have honestly given it, to be perfectly indifferent whether it is taken or not and never persist in trying to set people right.

SMITH Horace 1779-1849
10747
Inconsistency is the only thing in which men are consistent.

SMITH Ian 1919-
10748
I don't believe in black majority rule in Rhodesia - not in a thousand years.

SMITH James and Horace 1775-1839 and 1779-1849
10749 *Rejected Addresses 'Cui Bono?'*
Sated with home, of wife, of children tired.
The restless soul is driven abroad to roam;
Sated abroad, all seen and all admired,
The restless soul is driven to ramble home.

10750 *Rejected Addresses, 'Loyal Effusion'*
Who makes the quartern loaf and Luddites rise?
Who fills the butchers' shops with large blue flies?

10751 *Rejected Addresses, 'Loyal Effusion'*
God bless the Army, bless their coats of scarlet,

God bless the Navy, bless the Princess Charlotte.

SMITH John 1938-1995
10752 *(of John Major)*
I sometimes think that when the Prime Minister tries to select a weapon it is the boomerang he finds most effective.

SMITH Logan Pearsall 1865-1946
10753
I cannot forgive my friends for dying: I do not find these vanishing acts of theirs at all amusing.

10754
We need new friends. Some of us are cannibals who have eaten their old friends up; others must have ever-renewed audiences before whom to re-enact an ideal version of their lives.

10755
Don't tell your friends their social faults; they will cure the fault and never forgive you.

10756
Charming people live up to the very edge of their charm, and behave as outrageously as the world will let them.

10757
How it infuriates a bigot, when he is forced to drag out his dark convictions!

10758
Self-respecting people do not care to peep at their reflections in unexpected mirrors, or to see themselves as others see them.

10759
There are few sorrows, however poignant, in which a good income is of no avail.

10760
How can they say my life isn't a success? Have I not for more than sixty years got enough to eat and escaped being eaten?

10761
Every author, however modest, keeps a most outrageous vanity chained like a madman in the padded cell of his breast.

10762
Don't laugh at a youth for his affectations;
he's only trying on one face after another
till he finds his own.

10763 *Afterthoughts*
There are two things to aim at in life: first,
to get what you want; and, after that, to
enjoy it. Only the wisest of mankind
achieve the second.

10764 *Afterthoughts 'Age and Death'*
There is more felicity on the far side of
baldness than young men can possibly
imagine.

10765 *Afterthoughts 'Age and Death'*
The denunciation of the young is a
necessary part of the hygiene of older
people, and greatly assists the circulation
of their blood.

10766 *Afterthoughts 'All Trivia'*
What I like in a good author is not what he
says, but what he whispers.

10767 *Afterthoughts 'Art and Letters'*
The test of a vocation is the love of the
drudgery it involves.

10768 *Afterthoughts 'Art and Letters'*
A best-seller is the gilded tomb of a
mediocre talent.

10769 *Afterthoughts 'Life and Human Nature'*
An improper mind is a perpetual feast.

10770 *Afterthoughts 'Myself'*
People say that life is the thing, but I prefer
reading.

10771 *Afterthoughts 'Other People'*
Those who set out to serve both God and
Mammon soon discover that there is no
God.

10772 *Afterthoughts 'Other People'*
Most people sell their souls, and live with
a good conscience on the proceeds.

10773 *Afterthoughts 'In the World'*
To suppose, as we all suppose, that we
could be rich and not behave as the rich
behave, is like supposing that we could
drink all day and keep absolutely sober.

SMITH Maggie 1934-
10774 *in The Prime of Miss Jean Brodie*
"Give me a girl at an impressionable age
and she is mine for life."

SMITH Minnie
10775
I am as my Creator made me, and since He
is satisfied, so am I.

SMITH Ray
10776
The Americans believe they answered all
first questions in 1776: since then they've
just been hammering out the practical
details.

SMITH Samuel Francis 1808-1895
10777 *'America'*
My country, 'tis of thee,
Sweet land of liberty,
Of thee I sing.

SMITH Stevie 1902-1971
10778
A good time was had by all.

10779
If there wasn't death, I think you couldn't
go on.

10780 *'This Englishwoman'*
This Englishwoman is so refined
She has no bosom and no behind.

10781 *'The Galloping Cat'*
Oh I am a cat that likes to
Gallop about doing good.

10782 *Novel on Yellow Paper*
If you cannot have your dear husband for
a comfort and a delight, for a breadwinner
and a crosspatch, for a sofa, chair or a hot-
water bottle, one can use him as a Cross to
be Borne.

10783 *'The Past'*
People who are always praising the past
And especially the times of faith as best
Ought to go and live in the Middle Ages
And be burnt at the stake as witches and
sages.

10784 *'Not Waving but Drowning'*
Oh, no no no, it was too cold always
(Still the dead one lay moaning)

I was much too far out all my life
And not waving but drowning.

SMITH Sydney 1771-1845

10785
He has returned from Italy a greater bore
than ever; he bores on architecture,
painting, statuary and music.

10786
You never say a word of yourself, dear
Lady Grey. You have that dreadful sin of
anti-egotism.

10787
Great men hallow a whole people, and lift
up all who live in their time.

10788
Oh, don't tell me of facts - I never believe
in facts; you know Canning said nothing
was so fallacious as facts, except figures.

10789
It is always considered a piece of
impertinence in England if a man of less
than two or three thousand a year has any
opinions at all upon important subjects.

10790
Politeness is good nature regulated by
good sense.

10791
Among the smaller duties in life, I hardly
know any one more important than that of
not praising when praise is not due.

10792
Never try to reason the prejudice out of a
man. It was not reasoned into him, and
cannot be reasoned out.

10793
It requires a surgical operation to get a joke
well into a Scotch understanding.

10794
No furniture so charming as books.

10795
How can a bishop marry? How can he
flirt? The most he can say is, 'I will see
you in the vestry after service.'

10796
As the French say, there are three sexes -
men, women, and clergymen.

10797
My definition of marriage ... it resembles a
pair of shears, so joined that they cannot
be separated; often moving in opposite
directions, yet always punishing anyone
who comes between them.

10798
I never read a book before reviewing it; it
prejudices a man so.

10799
What a pity it is that we have no
amusements in England but vice and
religion!

10800
Death must be distinguished from dying,
with which it is often confused.

10801
What two ideas are more inseparable than
Beer and Britannia?

10802
I am just going to pray for you at St Paul's,
but with no very lively hope of success.

10803
Poverty is no disgrace to a man, but it is
confoundedly inconvenient.

10804
Heat, ma'am! It was so dreadful here that
I found there was nothing left for it but to
take off my flesh and sit in my bones.

10805
What you don't know would make a great
book.

10806 *Letter to Miss G. Harcourt*
I have no relish for the country; it is a kind
of healthy grave.

10807 *Letters of Peter Plymley*
The moment the very name of Ireland is
mentioned, the English seem to bid adieu
to common feeling, common prudence,
and common sense, and to act with the
barbarity of tyrants, and the fatuity of
idiots.

10808 *(of Macaulay)*
He not only overflowed with learning, but
stood in the slop.

10809 *(of Macauley)*
He has occasional flashes of silence, that
make his conversation perfectly delightful.

10810 *'Receipt for a Salad'*
Let onion atoms lurk within the bowl,
And, scarce-suspected, animate the whole.

10811 *'Receipt for a Salad'*
Serenely full, the epicure would say,
Fate cannot harm me, I have dined to-day.

10812 *Sketches of Moral Philosophy*
I never could find any man who could
think for two minutes together.

10813 *(of Whewell)*
Science is his forte, and omniscience his
foible.

SMITH Walter Chalmers 1824-1908
10814 *'Immortal, invisible, God only wise'*
We blossom and flourish as leaves on the
tree,
And wither and perish; but naught
changeth thee.

SMITH Willie ('The Lion') 1897-
10815
Romance without finance is no good.

SMOLLETT Tobias 1721-1771
10816 *The Adventures of Sir Launcelot
Greaves*
I think for my part one half of the nation is
mad - and the other not very sound.

10817 *Humphry Clinker*
I am pent up in frowzy lodgings, where
there is not room enough to swing a cat.

SMYTH Harley S.
10818 *(medical maxim)*
When you hear hoofbeats, think of horses
before zebras.

SNOW C.P. 1905-1980
10819 *Homecomings*
The official world, the corridors of power.

SNOWDEN Philip 1864-1937
10820 *(on Labour Party's election programme)*
This is not Socialism. It is Bolshevism run
mad.

SOCRATES 469-399 BC
10821
I know nothing except the fact of my
ignorance.

10822 *(looking at multitude of wares exposed
for sale)*
How many things I can do without!

10823 *In Plato - Apology*
Virtue does not come from money, but
from virtue comes money and all other
good things to man, both to the individual
and to the state.

10824 *In Plato - Crito*
It is never right to do wrong or to requite
wrong with wrong; or when we suffer evil
to defend ourselves by doing evil in
return.

10825 *In Plato - Phaedo*
It is perfectly certain that the soul is
immortal and imperishable, and our souls
will actually exist in another world.

10826 *Plutarch, De Exilio*
I am a citizen, not of Athens or Greece, but
of the world.

10827 *Plutarch, Moralia, 'How a Young Man
Ought to ...'*
Bad men live to eat and drink, whereas
good men eat and drink in order to live.

SOLON c.640-c.556 BC
10828
If all our misfortunes were laid in one
common heap, whence everyone must take
an equal portion, most people would be
content to take their own and depart.

10829
I grow old ever learning many things.

10830
Call no man happy before he dies, he is at
best but fortunate.

SOLZHENITSYN Aleksandr 1918-
10831
If one is forever cautious, can one remain a
human being?

10832
For a country to have a great writer is to have another government.

10833
One can build the Empire State Building, discipline the Prussian army, make a state hierarchy mightier than God, yet fail to overcome the unaccountable superiority of certain human beings.

10834
If only there were evil people somewhere, insidiously committing evil deeds, and it were necessary only to separate them from the rest of us and destroy them. But the line dividing good and evil cuts through the heart of every human being. And who is willing to destroy a piece of his own heart?

10835
Talent is always conscious of its own abundance, and does not object to sharing.

10836
No one can bar the road to truth, and to advance its cause I'm ready to accept even death.

10837
All revolutions unleash the most elemental barbarism.

10838 *One Day in the Life of Ivan Denisovich*
Work was like a stick. It had two ends. When you worked for the knowing you gave them quality; when you worked for a fool you simply gave him eye-wash.

10839 *One Day in the Life of Ivan Denisovich*
The thoughts of a prisoner - they're not free either. They keep returning to the same things.

10840 *The First Circle*
When you've robbed a man of *everything* he's no longer in your power - he's free again.

SOMERVILLE William 1675-1742
10841 *The Chase*
The chase, the sport of kings;
Image of war, without its guilt.

10842 *The Chase*
Hail, happy Britain! highly favoured isle,
And Heaven's peculiar care!

SOMOZA Anastasio 1925-1980
10843 *(replying to an accusation of ballot-rigging)*
You won the elections, but I won the count.

SONDHEIM Stephen 1930-
10844 *Gypsy*
Everything's coming up roses.

10845 *A Little Night Music 'Every Day a Little ..'*
Ev'ry day a little death
On the lips and in the eyes,
In the murmurs, in the pauses,
In the gestures, in the sighs.
Ev'ry day a little dies.

10846 *A Little Night Music 'Send in the Clowns'*
Isn't it rich?
Are we a pair?
Me here at last on the ground, you in mid-air ...
Isn't it bliss?
Don't you approve?
One who keeps tearing around, one who can't move ...
Where are the clowns?
Send in the clowns.

10847 *West Side Story*
I like to be in America!
O.K. by me in America!
Ev'rything free in America
For a small fee in America!

SONTAG Susan 1933-
10848
What is most beautiful in virile men is something feminine; what is most beautiful in feminine women is something masculine.

10849
Instead of just recording reality, photographs have become the norm for the way things appear to us, thereby changing the very idea of reality and of realism.

10850
The camera makes everyone a tourist in other people's reality, and eventually in one's own.

10851
Life is not about significant details, illuminated in a flash, fixed forever. Photographs are.

10852
Interpretation is the revenge of the intellect upon art.

10853
Illness is the night-side of life, a more onerous citizenship. Everyone who is born holds dual citizenship, in the kingdom of the well and in the kingdom of the sick.

10854
What pornography is really about, ultimately, isn't sex but death.

SOPER Baron 1903-
10855 *(on the quality of debate in the House of Lords)*
It is, I think, good evidence of life after death.

SOPHOCLES c.496-406
10856
The keenest sorrow is to recognize ourselves as the sole cause of all our adversities.

10857
It is terrible to speak well and be wrong.

10858
Time is a kindly god.

10859
Most gladly indeed am I rid of it all [sex], as though I had escaped from a mad and savage master.

10860 *Ajax*
Enemies' gifts are no gifts and do no good.

10861 *Antigone*
There are many wonderful things, and nothing is more wonderful than man.

SORLEY Charles Hamilton 1895-1915
10862 *'To Poets'*
We have a dumb spirit within:

The exceeding bitter agony
But not the exceeding bitter cry.

SOULE John L.B. 1815-1891
10863
Go West, young man, go West!

SOUTH Robert 1634-1716
10864 *Twelve Sermons* ...
An Aristotle was but the rubbish of an Adam, and Athens but the rudiments of Paradise.

SOUTHERNE Thomas 1660-1746
10865 *Sir Anthony Love*
Love is but discovery:
When that is made, the pleasure's done.

10866 *The Loyal Brother*
When we're worn,
Hacked hewn with constant service, thrown aside
To rust in peace, or rot in hospitals.

SOUTHEY Robert 1774-1843
10867
It has been more wittily than charitably said that hell is paved with good intentions. They have their place in heaven also.

10868
What will not woman, gentle woman dare
When strong affection stirs her spirit up?

10869 *'The Battle of Blenheim'*
'And everybody praise the Duke,
Who this great fight did win.'
'But what good came of it at last?'
Quoth little Peterkin.
'Why that I cannot tell,' said he,
'But 'twas a famous victory.'

10870 *'The Battle of Blenheim'*
He came to ask what he had found,
That was so large, and smooth, and round.

10871 *'The Battle of Blenheim'*
But what they fought each other for,
I could not well make out.

10872 *Colloquies on the Progress ... of Society*
The arts babblative and scribblative.

10873 *Colloquies on the Progress ... of Society*
The march of intellect.

10874 *The Curse of Kehama*
Thou hast been called, O Sleep! the friend of Woe,
But 'tis the happy who have called thee so.

10875 *The Curse of Kehama (motto)*
Curses are like young chickens, they always come home to roost.

10876 *'The Devil's Walk' (written with Coleridge)*
From his brimstone bed, at break of day
A walking the Devil is gone,
To look at his little snug farm of the World,
And see how his stock went on.

10877 *The Doctor*
Your true lover of literature is never fastidious.

10878 *The Doctor*
Beware of those who are homeless by choice.

10879 *The Doctor*
Live as long as you may, the first twenty years are the longest half of your life.

10880 *'The Lay of the Laureate'*
My name is Death: the last best friend am I.

10881 *Madoc*
Blue, darkly, deeply, beautifully blue.

10882 *Madoc*
We wage no war with women nor with priests.

10883 *'The March to Moscow'*
And last of all an Admiral came,
A terrible man with a terrible name -
A name which you all know by sight very well,
But which no one can speak, and no one can spell.

10884 *'The Old Man's Comforts'*
In the days of my youth I remembered my God!
And He hath not forgotten my age.

SOUTHWELL Robert c.1561-1595
10885 *'Content and Rich'*
To rise by other's fall
I deem a losing gain;
All states with others' ruins built

To ruin run amain.

10886 *'Loss in Delays'*
Good is best when soonest wrought,
Lingered labours come to naught.

10887 *'Times go by Turns'*
Times go by turns, and chances change by course,
From foul to fair, from better hap to worse.

SPARK Muriel 1918-
10888
It is impossible to repent of love. The sin of love does not exist.

10889 *The Comforters*
The one certain way for a woman to hold a man is to leave him for religion.

10890 *The Prime of Miss Jean Brodie*
I am putting old heads on your young shoulders ... all my pupils are the crème de la crème.

10891 *The Prime of Miss Jean Brodie*
Give me a girl at an impressionable age, and she is mine for life.

10892 *The Prime of Miss Jean Brodie*
One's prime is elusive. You little girls, when you grow up, must be on the alert to recognize your prime at whatever time of your life it may occur.

10893 *The Prime of Miss Jean Brodie*
To me education is a leading out of what is already there in the pupil's soul. To Miss Mackay it is a putting in of something that is not there, and that is not what I call education, I call it intrusion.

10894 *The Wit of Women*
Do you think it pleases a man when he looks into a woman's eyes and sees a reflection of the British Museum Reading Room?

SPARROW John 1906-1992
10895
That indefatigable and unsavoury engine of pollution, the dog.

10896 *Epitaph for Maurice Bowra*
Without you, Heaven would be too dull to bear,
And Hell would not be Hell if you are

there.

SPENCER Herbert 1820-1903
10897
It was remarked to me ... that to play
billiards was the sign of an ill-spent youth.

10898 *Definitions*
Time: That which man is always trying to
kill, but which ends in killing him.

10899 *Education*
Science is organized knowledge.

10900 *Education*
People are beginning to see that the first
requisite to success in life is to be a good
animal.

10901 *Essays 'The Americans'*
The Republican form of Government is the
highest form of government; but because
of this it requires the highest type of
human nature - a type nowhere at present
existing.

10902 *Essays 'Prison Ethics'*
Absolute morality is the regulation of
conduct in such a way that pain shall not
be inflicted.

10903 *First Principles*
Evolution ... is - a change from an
indefinite, incoherent homogeneity, to a
definite coherent heterogeneity.

10904 *Principles of Biology*
This survival of the fittest implies
multiplication of the fittest.

10905 *Principles of Ethics*
How often misused words generate
misleading thoughts.

10906 *Social Statics*
Progress, therefore, is not an accident, but
a necessity ... It is a part of nature.

10907 *Social Statics*
Education has for its object the formation
of character.

10908 *Social Statics*
Opinion is ultimately determined by the
feelings, and not by the intellect.

SPENCER Countess Raine 1929-
10909 *The Spencers on Spas*
Alas, for our towns and cities. Monstrous
carbuncles of concrete have erupted in
gentle Georgian Squares.

SPENDER Sir Stephen 1909-1995
10910
Born of the sun they travelled a short
while towards the sun
And left the vivid air signed with their
honour.

10911
Never being, but always at the edge of
Being.

10912
I must have love enough to run a factory
on,
Or give a city power, or drive a train.

10913 *'The Express'*
After the first powerful plain manifesto
The black statement of pistons, without
more fuss
But gliding like a queen, she leaves the
station.

10914 *'My parents kept me from children who
were rough'*
My parents kept me from children who
were rough
And who threw words like stones and
who wore torn clothes.

10915 *'What I expected, was'*
What I had not foreseen
Was the gradual day
Weakening the will
Leaking the brightness away.

10916 *'Who live under the shadow of a war'*
Who live under the shadow of a war,
What can I do that matters?

SPENGLER Oswald 1880-1936
10917
The secret of all victory lies in the
organization of the non-obvious.

SPENSER Edmund c.1552-1599
10918 *Amoretti*
The merry cuckoo, messenger of Spring,
His trumpet shrill hath thrice already
sounded.

10919 *Amoretti*
So let us love, dear Love, like as we ought,
- Love is the lesson which the Lord us
taught.

10920 *'Epithalamion'*
Ah! when will this long weary day have
end,
And lend me leave to come unto my love?

10921 *The Faerie Queen*
A gentle knight was pricking on the plain.

10922 *The Faerie Queen*
Her angel's face
As the great eye of heaven shinèd bright,
And made a sunshine in the shady place.

10923 *The Faerie Queen*
Still as he fled, his eye was backward cast,
As if his fear still followed him behind.

10924 *The Faerie Queen*
That darksome cave they enter, there they
find
That cursèd man, low sitting on the
ground,
Musing full sadly in his sullen mind.

10925 *The Faerie Queen*
Sleep after toil, port after stormy seas,
Ease after war, death after life does greatly
please.

10926 *The Faerie Queen*
So double was his pains, so double be his
praise.

10927 *The Faerie Queen*
Upon her eyelids many Graces sate,
Under the shadow of her even brows.

10928 *The Faerie Queen*
And all for love, and nothing for reward.

10929 *The Faerie Queen*
Gather therefore the rose, whilst yet is
prime,
For soon comes age, that will her pride
deflower.

10930 *The Faerie Queen*
And painful pleasure turns to pleasing
pain.

10931 *The Faerie Queen*
The gentle mind by gentle deeds is known.
For a man by nothing is so well bewrayed,
As by his manners.

10932 *The Shepherd's Calendar 'July'*
And he that strives to touch the stars,
Oft stumbles at a straw.

10933 *The Shepherd's Calendar 'Letter to
Gabriel Harvey'*
So now they have made our English
tongue a gallimaufry or hodgepodge of all
other speeches.

10934 *The Shepherd's Calendar 'March.
Willy's Emblem'*
To be wise and eke to love,
Is granted scarce to God above.

SPETTIGUE Doug
10935
Husbands don't really count ... in the
miracle of birth.

SPINOZA Baruch 1632-1677
10936
Will and intellect are one and the same
thing.

10937
Peace is not an absence of war, it is a
virtue, a state of mind, a disposition for
benevolence, confidence, justice.

10938 *Ethics*
By *God* I mean a being absolutely infinite -
that is, a substance consisting in infinite
attributes, of which each expresses eternal
and infinite essentiality.

10939 *Ethics*
Man is a social animal.

10940 *Ethics*
We feel and know that we are eternal.

10941 *Tractatus Politicus*
I have striven not to laugh at human
actions, not to weep at them, nor to hate
them, but to understand them.

SPOCK Dr. Benjamin 1903-
10942
There are only two things a child will
share willingly - communicable diseases
and his mother's age.

10943 *(of Vietnamese War)*
To win in Vietnam, we will have to exterminate a nation.

SPOONER Rev. W.A. 1844-1930
10944
You will find as you grow older that the weight of rages will press harder and harder upon the employer.

10945 *(attributed)*
I remember your name perfectly, but I just can't think of your face.

10946 *(attributed)*
Let us drink to the queer old Dean.

10947 *(attributed)*
Sir, you have tasted two whole worms; you have hissed all my mystery lectures and been caught fighting a liar in the quad; you will leave Oxford by the next town drain.

10948 *(announcing the hymn in New College Chapel)*
Kinquering Congs their titles take.

SPRING Dick 1950-
10949
The real Ireland is walking in spirit behind the coffins of your sons.

SPRING-RICE Sir Cecil 1859-1918
10950 *(of American politics)*
Dullness, occasionally relieved by rascality.

10951 *The Masque of Balliol*
I am the Dean of Christ Church, Sir:
There's my wife; look well at her.
She's the Broad and I'm the High;
We are the University.

10952 *'I Vow to Thee, My Country'*
I vow to thee, my country - all earthly things above -
Entire and whole and perfect, the service of my love.

10953 *'I Vow to Thee, My Country'*
Here ways are ways of gentleness and all her paths are Peace.

SPRINGSTEEN Bruce 1949-
10954 *'Born to Run'*
We gotta get out while we're young,
'Cause tramps like us, baby, we were born to run.

10955 *'Born in the USA'*
Born down in a dead man's town
The first kick I took was when I hit the ground.

10956 *'The River'*
Is a dream a lie if it don't come true,
Or is it something worse?

SPURGEON Charles Haddon 1834-1992
10957
Learn to say 'No'; it will be of more use to you than to be able to read Latin.

SQUIRE Sir J.C. 1884-1958
10958 *'Ballade of Soporific Absorption'*
But I'm not so think as you drunk I am.

10959 *'In continuation of Pope on Newton'*
It did not last: the Devil howling 'Ho!
Let Einstein be!' restored the status quo.

STACKMAN Elvin
10960
Science cannot stop while ethics catches up
- and nobody should expect scientists to do all the thinking for the country.

STALIN Joseph 1879-1953
10961
Writers are the engineers of human souls.

10962
The rich experience of history teaches that up to now not a single class has vountarily made way for another class.

10963 *Foundations of Leninism*
The State is an instrument in the hands of the ruling class, used to break the resistance of the adversaries of that class.

10964 *(when asked to encourage Catholicism in Russia)*
The Pope! How many divisions has *he* got?

STANFIELD Robert
10965
He is a pragmatist. He is not right wing, nor left wing nor any wing.

STANISLAW II King 1764-1795
10966
To believe with certainty we must begin

with doubting.

STANLEY Sir Henry Morton 1841-1904
10967
Dr Livingstone, I presume?

STANTON Edwin McMasters 1814-1869
10968 *(of Abraham Lincoln, following his assassination)*
Now he belongs to the ages.

STANTON Elizabeth Cady 1815-1902
10969
Social science affirms that a woman's place in society marks the level of civilization.

10970 *Letter to Susan B. Anthony*
Woman's degradation is a man's idea of his sexual rights. Our religion, laws, customs, are all founded on the belief that woman was made for man.

STARK Freya 1893-1993
10971
Absence is one of the most useful ingredients of family life, and to do it rightly is an art like any other.

STARK John 1728-1822
10972
We beat them to-day or Molly Stark's a widow.

STARR Roger
10973
Money is the most egalitarian force in society. It confers power on whoever holds it.

STAÉL Mme de 1766-1817
10974
One must choose in life between boredom and suffering.

10975
Wit consists in knowing the resemblance of things which differ and the difference of things which are alike.

10976 *Corinne*
To be totally understanding makes one very indulgent.

10977 *Delphine*
A man can brave opinion, a woman must submit to it.

10978 *(attributed, asked what she talked of with lover)*
Speech happens not to be his language.

STAÉL Talleyrand
10979 *(of Mme. de Staël)*
She is such a good friend that she would throw all her acquaintances into the water for the pleasure of fishing them out.

STEAD Christina 1902-1983
10980 *House of All Nations*
A self-made man is one who believes in luck and sends his son to Oxford.

STEELE Sir Richard 1672-1729
10981
When one has no design but to speak plain truth, he may say a great deal in a very narrow compass.

10982
The insupportable labour of doing nothing.

10983
A woman seldom writes her mind but in her postscript.

10984
There are so few who can grow old with a good grace.

10985
Reading is to the mind what exercise is to the body.

10986 *(of Lady E. Hastings)*
To love her is a liberal education.

10987 *The Lover*
Women dissemble their Passions better than Men, but Men subdue their Passions better than Women.

10988 *(of The Tatler)*
It is to be noted that when any part of this paper appears dull there is a design in it.

STEFFENS Lincoln 1866-1936
10989 *(following a visit to the Soviet Union in 1919)*
I have seen the future; and it works.

STEICHEN Edward 1879-1973
10990
Photography records the gamut of feelings

written on the human face; the beauty of the earth and skies that man has inherited; and the wealth and confusion man has created. It is a major force in explaining man to man.

STEIN Gertrude 1874-1946
10991
The central theme of the novel is that they were glad to see each other.

10992
When you get there, there isn't any there there.

10993
You have to learn to do everything, even to die.

10994
One of the laws of paleontology is that an animal which must protect itself with thick armour is degenerate. It is usually a sign that the species is on the road to extinction.

10995
Everybody gets so much common information all day long that they lose their common sense.

10996
I understand you undertake to overthrow my undertaking.

10997
Money is always there but the pockets change; it is not in the same pockets after a change, and that is all there is to say about money.

10998
I write for myself and strangers. The strangers, dear Readers, are an afterthought.

10999 *Autobiography of Alice B. Toklas*
Remarks are not literature.

11000 *The Geographical History of America*
In the United States there is more space where nobody is than where anybody is. That is what makes America what it is.

11001 *Sacred Emily*
Rose is a rose is a rose, is a rose.

11002 *Four Saints in Three Acts*
Pigeons on the grass alas.

11003 *(of the young who served in the First World War)*
You are all a lost generation.

STEINBECK John 1902-1968
11004 *The Grapes of Wrath*
Man, unlike any other thing organic or inorganic in the universe, grows beyond his work, walks up the stairs of his concepts, emerges ahead of his accomplishments.

STEINBERG Saul
11005
The life of the creative man is led, directed and controlled by boredom. Avoiding boredom is one of our most important purposes.

11006
Doodling is the brooding of the hand.

STEINEM Gloria 1934-
11007
The first problem for all of us, men and women, is not to learn, but to unlearn.

11008
A woman without a man is like a fish without a bicycle.

11009
We are becoming the men we wanted to marry.

11010
Outrageous acts and everyday rebellions.

STEKEL Wilhelm
11011
Anxiety is fear of one's self.

STENDHAL 1783-1842
11012
One can acquire everything in solitude except character.

11013
The first qualification for a historian is to have no ability to invent.

11014
If you want to be witty, work on your character and say what you think on every

occasion.

11015 *Le Rouge et le noir*
A novel is a mirror which passes over a
highway. Sometimes it reflects to your
eyes the blue of the skies, at others the
churned-up mud of the road.

STENGEL Casey 1889-1975
11016
Going to bed with a woman never hurt a
ball player. It's staying up all night
looking for them that does you in.

STEPHEN J.K. 1859-1892
11017 *'To R.K.'*
Will there never come a season
Which shall rid us from the curse
Of a prose which knows no reason
And an unmelodious verse ...

11018 *'To R.K.'*
When the Rudyards cease from kipling
And the Haggards ride no more.

11019 *'A Sonnet' (parodying Wordsworth)*
.. an old half-witted sheep
Which bleats articulate monotony,
And indicates that two and one are three.

STEPHEN Leslie 1832-1904
11020
Every man who says frankly and fully
what he thinks is doing a public service.

STEPHEN Sir James Fitzjames 1829-1894
11021 *Liberty, Equality and Fraternity*
The way in which the man of genius rules
is by persuading an efficient minority to
coerce an indifferent and self-indulgent
majority.

STEPHENS James 1882-1950
11022
Originality does not consist in saying what
no one has ever said before, but in saying
exactly what you think yourself.

11023 *The Crock of Gold*
Finality is death. Perfection is finality.
Nothing is perfect. There are lumps in it.

11024 *'The Snare'*
I hear a sudden cry of pain!
There is a rabbit in a snare.

STERN Gil
11025
Man is a complex being: he makes deserts
bloom and lakes die.

STERNE Laurence 1713-1768
11026
God tempers the wind to the shorn lamb.

11027
A man cannot dress, without his ideas get
clothed at the same time.

11028
Philosophy has a fine saying for
everything - for Death it has an entire set.

11029 *A Sentimental Journey*
They order, said I, this matter better in
France.

11030 *A Sentimental Journey*
As an Englishman does not travel to see
Englishmen, I retired to my room.

11031 *A Sentimental Journey*
If ever I do a mean action, it must be in
some interval betwixt one passion and
another.

11032 *A Sentimental Journey*
There are worse occupations in this world
than feeling a woman's pulse.

11033 *Sermons*
This sad vicissitude of things.

11034 *Tristram Shandy*
I wish either my father or my mother, or
indeed both of them, as they were in duty
both equally bound to it, had minded what
they were about when they begot me.

11035 *Tristram Shandy*
As we jog on, either laugh with me, or at
me, or in short do anything - only keep
your temper.

11036 *Tristram Shandy*
'Tis known by the name of perseverance in
a good cause - and of obstinacy in a bad
one.

11037 *Tristram Shandy*
Digressions, incontestably, are the
sunshine; they are the life, the soul of
reading; take them out of this book for

instance, you might as well take the book along with them.

11038 *Tristram Shandy*
Writing, when properly managed (as you may be sure I think mine is) is but a different name for conversation.

11039 *Tristram Shandy*
Whenever a man talks loudly against religion, always suspect that it is not his reason, but his passions which have got the better of his creed.

11040 *Tristram Shandy*
'Our armies swore terribly in Flanders,' cried my uncle Toby, 'but nothing to this.'

11041 *Tristram Shandy*
Of all the cants which are canted in this canting world, though the cant of hypocrites may be the worst, the cant of criticism is the most tormenting!

11042 *Tristram Shandy*
There is a North-west passage to the intellectual World.

11043 *Tristram Shandy*
My brother Toby, quoth she, is going to be married to Mrs Wadman.
Then he will never, quoth my father, lie *diagonally* in his bed again as long as he lives.

11044 *Tristram Shandy*
A man should know something of his own country too, before he goes abroad.

11045 *Tristram Shandy*
And who are you? said he. Don't puzzle me, said I.

11046 *Tristram Shandy*
'-d!' said my mother, 'what is all this story about?'
'A Cock and a Bull', said Yorick.

11047 *Tristram Shandy*
The nonsense of the old women (of both sexes).

STEUBEN Baron von 1730-1794
11048
You say to your soldier, 'Do this' and he does it. But I am obliged to say to the American, 'This is why you ought to do

this' and then he does it.

STEVENS Brooks
11049
Our whole economy is based on planned obsolescence ... we make good products, we induce people to buy them, and then the next year we deliberately introduce something that will make these products old-fashioned, out of date, obsolete.

STEVENS Wallace 1879-1955
11050
Frogs Eat Butterflies. Snakes Eat Frogs. Hogs Eat Snakes. Men Eat Hogs.

11051 *'Adagia'*
The poet is the priest of the invisible.

11052 *'Bantams in Pine Woods'*
Chieftain Iffucan of Azcan in caftan
Of tan with henna hackles, halt!

11053 *'Disillusionment of Ten O'Clock'*
Only, here and there, an old sailor,
Drunk and asleep in his boots,
Catches tigers
In red weather.

11054 *'The Emperor of Ice-Cream'*
Let be be finale of seem.
The only emperor is the emperor of ice-cream.

11055 *'A High-Toned old Christian Woman'*
Poetry is the supreme fiction, madame.

11056 *'The Man with the Blue Guitar'*
They said, 'You have a blue guitar,
You do not play things as they are.'
The man replied, 'Things as they are
Are changed upon the blue guitar.'

11057 *'Of Mere Being'*
The palm at the end of the mind,
Beyond the last thought, rises ...
A gold-feathered bird
Sings in the palm.

11058 *The Noble Rider and the Sound of Words*
What makes the poet the potent figure that he is, or was, or ought to be, is that he creates the world to which we turn incessantly and without knowing it and that he gives to life the supreme fictions

without which we are unable to conceive of it.

11059 *Notes Toward a Supreme Fiction*
They will get it straight one day at the Sorbonne.
We shall return at twilight from the lecture
Pleased that the irrational is rational.

11060 *'An Ordinary Evening in New Haven'*
We keep coming back and coming back
To the real: to the hotel instead of the hymns
That fall upon it out of the wind.

11061 *'Thirteen Ways of Looking at a Blackbird'*
I do not know which to prefer,
The beauty of inflections
Or the beauty of innuendos,
The blackbird whistling
Or just after.

STEVENSON Adlai 1900-1965
11062
Some people approach every problem with an open mouth.

11063
Laws are never as effective as habits.

11064
My definition of a free society is a society where it is safe to be unpopular.

11065
A hungry man is not a free man.

11066
It is said that a wise man who stands firm is a statesman, and a foolish man who stands firm is a catastrophe.

11067
Every age needs men who will redeem the time by living with a vision of things that are to be.

11068
It is not the years in your life but the life in your years that counts.

11069
It is often easier to fight for principles than to live up to them.

11070
Patriotism is not short, frenzied outbursts of emotion, but the tranquil and steady dedication of a lifetime.

11071
I have said what I meant and meant what I said. I have not done as well as I should like to have done, but I have done my best, frankly and forthrightly; no man can do more, and you are entitled to no less.

11072
I'm not an old, experienced hand at politics. But I am now seasoned enough to have learned that the hardest thing about any political campaign is how to win without proving that your are unworthy of winning.

11073
In America, any boy may become president, and I suppose it's just one of the risks he takes.

11074
What a man knows at fifty that he did not know at twenty is for the most part incommunicable.

11075
I suppose flattery hurts no one, that is, if you don't inhale.

11076
If they [the Republicans] will stop telling lies about the Democrats, we will stop telling the truth about them.

11077
Let's talk sense to the American people. Let's tell them the truth, that there are no gains without pains.

11078
There is no evil in the atom; only in men's souls.

11079
A funny thing happened to me on the way to the White House.

11080
We hear the Secretary of State [John Foster Dulles] boasting of his brinkmanship - the art of bringing us to the edge of the abyss.

11081 *(on learning of Eleanor Roosevelt's death)*
She would rather light a candle than curse the darkness, and her glow has warmed the world.

STEVENSON Anne 1933-
11082 *'Green Mountain, Black Mountain'*
Blackbirds are the cellos of the deep farms.

STEVENSON Robert Louis 1850-1894
11083
Is there anything in life so disenchanting as attainment?

11084
Absences are a good influence in love and keep it bright and delicate.

11085
By the time a man gets well into his seventies his continued existence is a mere miracle.

11086
For God's sake give me the young man who has brains enough to make a fool of himself.

11087
Extreme busyness, whether at school, or college, kirk or market, is a symptom of deficient vitality; and a faculty for idleness implies a catholic appetite and a strong sense of personal identity.

11088
Marriage is one long conversation checkered by disputes.

11089
If your morals make you dreary, depend on it they are wrong.

11090
For my part, I travel not to go anywhere, but to go. I travel for travel's sake. The great affair is to move.

11091
The Saints are the Sinners who keep on trying.

11092
If a man loves the labour of his trade, apart from any question of success or fame, the gods have called him.

11093
There is but one art, to omit.

11094
Keep busy at something. A busy person never has time to be unhappy.

11095 *Across the Plains 'Beggars'*
Everyone lives by selling something.

11096 *Across the Plains 'A Christmas Sermon'*
A mortified appetite is never a wise companion.

11097 *Ballads 'Christmas at Sea'*
But all that I could think of, in the darkness and the cold,
Was that I was leaving home and my folks were growing old.

11098 *A Child's Garden of Verses 'Bed in Summer'*
In winter I get up at night
And dress by yellow candle-light.
In summer, quite the other way -
I have to go to bed by day.

11099 *A Child's Garden of Verses 'Happy Thought'*
The world is so full of a number of things,
I'm sure we should all be as happy as kings.

11100 *A Child's Garden of Verses 'Looking Forward'*
When I am grown to man's estate
I shall be very proud and great,
And tell the other girls and boys
Not to meddle with my toys.

11101 *A Child's Garden of Verses 'System'*
The child that is not clean and neat,
With lots of toys and things to eat,
He is a naughty child, I'm sure -
Or else his dear papa is poor.

11102 *A Child's Garden of Verses 'Whole Duty ...'*
A child should always say what's true,
And speak when he is spoken to,
And behave mannerly at table:
At least as far as he is able.

11103 *Familiar Studies of Men and Books*
Politics is perhaps the only profession for which no preparation is thought necessary.

11104 *Kidnapped*
I've a grand memory for forgetting, David.

11105 *Letter to Sidney Colvin*
I believe in an ultimate decency of things.

11106 *New Arabian Nights 'The Rajah's Diamond'*
I regard you with an indifference closely bordering on aversion.

11107 *New Arabian Nights 'The Suicide Club'*
The devil, depend upon it, can sometimes do a very gentlemanly thing.

11108 *Songs of Travel 'The Vagabond'*
Wealth I seek not, hope nor love,
Nor a friend to know me;
All I seek, the heaven above
And the road below me.

11109 *Treasure Island*
Fifteen men on the dead man's chest
Yo-ho-ho, and a bottle of rum!
Drink and the devil had done for the rest -
Yo-ho-ho, and a bottle of rum!

11110 *Treasure Island*
Tip me the black spot.

11111 *Treasure Island*
Many's the long night I've dreamed of cheese - toasted, mostly.

11112 *Virginibus Puerisque*
In marriage, a man becomes slack and selfish, and undergoes a fatty degeneration of his moral being.

11113 *Virginibus Puerisque*
Marriage is like life in this - that it is a field of battle, and not a bed of roses.

11114 *Virginibus Puerisque*
To marry is to domesticate the Recording Angel. Once you are married, there is nothing left for you, not even suicide, but to be good.

11115 *Virginibus Puerisque*
The cruellest lies are often told in silence.

11116 *Virginibus Puerisque 'Aes Triplex'*
Even if the doctor does not give you a year, even if he hesitates about a month, make one brave push and see what can be accomplished in a week.

11117 *Virginibus Puerisque 'An Apology for Idlers'*
There is no duty we so much underrate as the duty of being happy.

11118 *Virginibus Puerisque 'An Apology for Idlers'*
He sows hurry and reaps indigestion.

11119 *Virginibus Puerisque 'Crabbed Age and Youth'*
Old and young, we are all on our last cruise.

11120 *Virginibus Puerisque 'El Dorado'*
To travel hopefully is a better thing than to arrive, and the true success is to labour.

11121 *The Wrong Box (with Lloyd Osborne)*
What hangs people ... is the unfortunate circumstance of guilt.

11122 *The Wrong Box (with Lloyd Osborne)*
Nothing like a little judicious levity.

STILL John
11123
The memories of men are too frail a thread to hang history from.

STING
11124
Cocaine is God's way of telling you you've got too much money.

STINNETT Caskie 1911-
11125
The trouble with being a hypochondriac these days is that antibiotics have cured all the good diseases.

11126 *Out of the Red*
A diplomat ... is a person who can tell you to go to hell in such a way that you actually look forward to the trip.

STIPE Michael
11127
I believe in the theory that anyone can get laid, it's just a matter of lowering your standards!

STOCKDALE Edmund
11128
Money isn't everything - but it's a long way ahead of what comes next.

STODDARD Elizabeth Drew 1823-1902
11129 *Two Men*
A woman despises a man for loving her,
unless she returns his love.

STODDARD R.H.
11130
We love in others what we lack ourselves,
and would be everything but what we are.

STONE I.F. 1907-1989
11131
If you live long enough the venerability
factor creeps in; you get accused of things
you never did and praised for virtues you
never had.

11132
Every government is run by liars and
nothing they say should be believed.

11133
Every emancipation has in it the seeds of a
new slavery, and every truth easily
becomes a lie.

STONE Professor Lawrence
11134 *(of the ingredients of marriage)*
Affection was a late 18th century
development.

STONE Samuel John 1839-1900
11135 *Lyra Fidelium 'The Church's one
foundation'*
The Church's one foundation
Is Jesus Christ, her Lord;
She is his new creation
By water and the word.

STOPES Marie 1880-1958
11136 *Married Love*
An impersonal and scientific knowledge of
the structure of our bodies is the surest
safeguard against prurient curiosity and
lascivious gloating.

STOPPARD Tom 1937-
11137
Age is a high price to pay for maturity.

11138
It's better to be quotable than to be honest.

11139
Everything has to be taken on trust; truth
is only that which is taken to be true. It's

the currency of living. There may be
nothing behind it, but it doesn't make any
difference so long as it is honoured.

11140
You could say you'd seen the future after
visiting America. I don't think you could
add: 'and it works'.

11141 *Jumpers*
It's not the voting that's democracy, it's the
counting.

11142 *Lord Malquist and Mr Moon*
The House of Lords, an illusion to which I
have never been able to subscribe -
responsibility without power, the
prerogative of the eunuch throughout the
ages.

11143 *Night and Day*
The media. It sounds like a convention of
spiritualists.

11144 *Night and Day*
I'm with you on the free press. It's the
newspapers I can't stand.

11145 *Night and Day*
Comment is free but facts are on expenses.

11146 *Rosencrantz and Guildenstern are Dead*
You're familiar with the tragedies of
antiquity, are you? The great homicidal
classics?

11147 *Rosencrantz and Guildenstern are Dead*
All your life you live so close to truth, it
becomes a permanent blur in the corner of
your eye, and when something nudges it
into outline it is like being ambushed by a
grotesque.

11148 *Rosencrantz and Guildenstern are Dead*
Eternity's a terrible thought. I mean,
where's it all going to end?

11149 *Rosencrantz and Guildenstern are Dead*
The bad end unhappily, the good
unluckily. That is what tragedy means.

11150 *Rosencrantz and Guildenstern are Dead*
Life is a gamble at terrible odds - if it was a
bet, you wouldn't take it.

11151 *Rosencrantz and Guildenstern are Dead*
Death is not anything ... death is not ... It's
the absence of presence, nothing more ...
the endless time of never coming back ... a
gap you can't see, and when the wind
blows through it, it makes no sound.

11152 *Travesties*
War is capitalism with the gloves off and
many who go to war know it but they go
to war because they don't want to be a
hero.

STOREY Wilbur F.
11153
It is a newspaper's duty to print the news
and raise hell.

STORR Anthony 1920-
11154
That man is an aggressive creature will
hardly be disputed. With the exception of
certain rodents, no other vertebrate
habitually destroys members of its own
species.

STORY William Wetmore 1819-1895
11155
Of every noble work the silent part is best,
Of all expression that cannot be expressed.

STOWE Harriet Beecher 1811-1896
11156 *Uncle Tom's Cabin*
'Never was born!' persisted Topsy ... 'never
had no father, nor mother, nor nothin'. I
was raised by a speculator, with lots of
others.'

11157 *Uncle Tom's Cabin*
I s'pect I growed. Don't think nobody
never made me.

STRACHEY Lionel
11158
A brilliant epigram is a solemn platitude
gone to a masquerade ball.

STRACHEY Lytton 1880-1932
11159
Happiness is the perpetual possession of
being well deceived.

11160
Discretion is not the better part of
biography.

11161 *(on his deathbed)*
If this is dying, then I don't think much of
it.

11162 *Eminent Victorians*
Ignorance is the first requisite of the
historian - ignorance, which simplifies and
clarifies, which selects and omits, with a
placid perfection unattainable by the
highest art.

11163 *Eminent Victorians 'Cardinal Manning'*
The time was out of joint, and he was only
too delighted to have been born to set it
right.

11164 *Eminent Victorians 'Florence
Nightingale'*
Her conception of God was certainly not
orthodox. She felt towards Him as she
might have felt towards a glorified
sanitary engineer; and in some of her
speculations she seems hardly to
distinguish between the Deity and the
Drains.

11165 *Pope*
The verses, when they were written,
resembled nothing so much as spoonfuls
of boiling oil, ladled out by a fiendish
monkey at an upstairs window upon such
passers-by whom the wretch had a grudge
against.

STRAVINSKY Igor 1882-1971
11166
Old age is a time of humiliations, the most
disagreeable of which, for me, is that I
cannot work long at sustained high
pressure with no leaks in concentration.

11167
Childhood - a period of waiting for the
moment when I could send everyone and
everything connected with it to hell.

11168
Conformism is so hot on the heels of the
mass-produced avant garde that the 'ins'
and the 'outs' change places with the
speed of mach 3.

11169
I know that the twelve notes in each octave
and the varieties of rhythm offer me
oppotunities that all of human genius will

never exhaust.

11170
Music is given to us specifically to make order of things, to move from an anarchic, individualistic state to a regulated, perfectly concious one, which alone insures vitality and durability.

11171
Conductors' careers are made for the most part with 'romantic' music. 'Classic' music eliminates the conductor; we do not remember him in it.

11172 *(attributed)*
Academism results when the reasons for the rule change, but not the rule.

STREETER Edward
11173
Travel is ninety per cent anticipation and ten per cent recollection.

STRINDBERG Johan August 1849-1912
11174
Growing old - it's not nice, but it's interesting.

STRINGER Arthur 1922-
11175
Society, my dear, is like salt water, good to swim in but hard to swallow.

STRUNSKY Simeon 1879-1948
11176
To renew ties with the past need not always be daydreaming; it may be tapping old sources of strength for new tasks.

11177
If you want to understand democracy, spend less time in the library with Plato, and more time in the buses with people.

11178
Famous remarks are very seldom quoted correctly.

11179
Once a man would spend a week patiently waiting if he missed a stage coach, but now he rages if he misses the first section of a revolving door.

STUBBS John Heath 1918-
11180
Its always good to remember that people find it easier to name 10 artists from any century than 10 politicians.

STUDDERT KENNEDY G.A. 1883-1929
11181
It is much easier to do and die than it is to reason why.

11182 *Peace Rhymes of a Padre 'Indifference'*
When Jesus came to Birmingham they simply passed Him by,
They never hurt a hair of Him, they only let Him die.

11183 *More Rough Rhymes of a Padre 'Waste'*
Waste of Blood, and waste of Tears,
Waste of youth's most precious years,
Waste of ways the saints have trod,
Waste of Glory, waste of God,
War!

SUCKLING Sir John 1609-1642
11184 *Aglaura 'Song'*
If of herself she will not love,
Nothing can make her:
The devil take her!

11185 *'A Ballad upon a Wedding'*
Her feet beneath her petticoat,
Like little mice, stole in and out,
As if they feared the light.

11186 *'Against Fruition'*
Women enjoyed (whatsoe'er before they've been)
Are like romances read, or sights once seen: ...
'Tis expectation makes a blessing dear;
It were not heaven, if we knew what it were.

11187 *'Love's Offence'*
Love is the fart
Of every heart:
It pains a man when 'tis kept close,
And others doth offend, when 'tis let loose.

SUETONIUS c.70-c.140
11188 *Augustus*
Festina lente.
Hasten slowly.

11189 *Augustus*
He so improved the city that he justly
boasted he had found it brick and left it
marble.

11190 *Claudius*
Ave, Imperator, morituri te salutant
Hail, Emperor, those about to die salute
you.

SULLIVAN Henry Stack
11191
When the satisfaction or the security of
another person becomes as significant to
one as one's own satisfaction or security,
then the state of love exists.

SULLIVAN Louis Henri 1856-1924
11192 *The Tall Office Building Artistically
Considered*
Form follows function.

SULLY Maximilen de Béthune, Duc de
1559-1641
11193 *(attributed)*
The English take their pleasures sadly after
the fashion of their country.

11194 *Mémoires*
Tilling and grazing are the two breasts by
which France is fed.

SULZBERGER Arthur Hays 1891-1968
11195 *(on journalism)*
We tell the public which way the cat is
jumping. The public will take care of the
cat.

SUMMERSKILL Edith 1901-1980
11196
The housewife is the Cinderella of the
affluent state ... She is wholly dependent
on the whim of an individual to give her
money for the essentials of life.

SUMNER William Graham 1840-1874
11197
The forgotten man. He is the clean, quiet,
virtuous domestic citizen who pays his
debts and his taxes and is never heard of
outside his little circle.... He works, he
votes, generally he prays, but his chief
business in life is to pay.

SURTEES R.S. 1805-1864
11198 *The Analysis of the Hunting Field*
More people are flattered into virtue than
bullied out of vice.

11199 *Mr Facey Romford's Hounds*
Better be killed than frightened to death.

11200 *Mr Facey Romford's Hounds*
Life would be very pleasant if it were not
for its enjoyments.

11201 *Mr Facey Romford's Hounds*
Everyone knows that the real business of a
ball is either to look out for a wife, to look
after a wife, or to look after somebody
else's wife

11202 *Handley Cross*
'Unting is all that's worth living for ... it's
the sport of kings, the image of war
without its guilt, and only five-and-twenty
per cent of its danger.

11203 *Handley Cross*
I'll fill hup the chinks wi' cheese.

11204 *Handley Cross*
It ar'n't that I loves the fox less, but that I
loves the 'ound more.

11205 *Hillingdon Hall*
Three things I never lends - my 'oss, my
wife, and my name.

11206 *Jorrocks's Jaunts and Jollities*
Champagne certainly gives one werry
gentlemanly ideas, but for a continuance, I
don't know but I should prefer mild hale.

11207 *Ask Mamma*
The only infallible rule we know is, that
the man who is always talking about being
a gentleman never is one.

11208 *Mr Sponge's Sporting Tour*
The young ladies entered the drawing-
room in the full fervour of sisterly
animosity.

11209 *Mr Sponge's Sporting Tour*
He was a gentleman who was generally
spoken of as having nothing a-year, paid
quarterly.

11210 *Mr Sponge's Sporting Tour*
There is no secret so close as that between a rider and his horse.

SUSSER Dr. Laurence
11211
Workaholics commit slow suicide by refusing to allow the child inside them to play.

SUTHERLAND Graham 1903-1980
11212
I don't think anyone is free - one creates one's own prison.

SUTTON David 1944-
11213 *'Geomancies'*
Sorrow in all lands, and grievous omens.
Great anger in the dragon of the hills,
And silent now the earth's green oracles
That will not speak again of innocence.

SWAFFER Hannen 1879-1962
11214
Freedom of the press in Britain means freedom to print such of the proprietor's prejudices as the advertisers don't object to.

SWANSON Gloria 1897-1983
11215 *(of her passport photo)*
If I look like this, I need the trip.

11216 *in Sunset Boulevard*
"I am big. It is the pictures got small."

SWEET Ben
11217
The greatest success is successful self-acceptance.

SWIFT Jonathan 1667-1745
11218
When the world has once begun to use us ill, it afterwards continues the same treatment with less scruple or ceremony, as men do to a whore.

11219
Dignity, high station, or great riches are in some sort necessary to old men, in order to keep the younger at a distance, who are otherwise too apt to insult them upon the score of their age.

11220
When men grow virtuous in their old age, they only make a sacrifice to God of the devil's leavings.

11221
No wise man ever wished to be younger.

11222
He was a bold man that first ate an oyster.

11223
When a true genius appears in the world you may know him by this sign, that the dunces are all in confederacy against him.

11224
What some invent, the rest enlarge.

11225
May you live all the days of your life.

11226
'Tis an old maxim in the schools,
That flattery's the food of fools;
Yet now and then your men of wit
Will condescend to take a bit.

11227
Usually speaking, the worst-bred person in company is a young traveller just returned from abroad.

11228
Most sorts of diversion in men, children and other animals, are in imitation of fighting.

11229
I shall be like that tree, I shall die at the top.

11230 *The Battle of the Books*
Satire is a sort of glass, wherein beholders do generally discover everybody's face but their own.

11231 *The Battle of the Books*
Instead of dirt and poison we have rather chosen to fill our hives with honey and wax; thus furnishing mankind with the two noblest of things, which are sweetness and light.

11232 *A Critical Essay upon the Faculties of the Mind*
Laws are like cobwebs, which may catch

small flies, but let wasps and hornets break through.

11233 *A Critical Essay upon the Faculties of the Mind*
There is nothing in this world constant, but inconstancy.

11234 *On the Death of Dr Swift*
Some great misfortune to portend,
No enemy can match a friend.

11235 'To Mr Delany'
Hated by fools, and fools to hate,
Be that my motto and my fate.

11236 *The Drapier's Letters*
I have heard of a man who had a mind to sell his house, and therefore carried a piece of brick in his pocket, which he shewed as a pattern to encourage purchasers.

11237 (epitaph)
Where fierce indignation can no longer tear his heart.

11238 *Gulliver's Travels 'A Voyage to Brobdingnag'*
I cannot but conclude the bulk of your natives to be the most pernicious race of little odious vermin that nature ever suffered to crawl upon the surface of the earth.

11239 *Gulliver's Travels 'A Voyage to Houyhnhnms'*
I told him ... that we ate when we were not hungry, and drank without the provocation of thirst.

11240 *Gulliver's Travels 'Voyage to Lilliput'*
Big-endians and small-endians.

11241 'The Journal'
How haughtily he lifts his nose,
To tell what every schoolboy knows.

11242 *Journal of a Modern Lady*
Convey a libel in a frown,
And wink a reputation down.

11243 *Journal to Stella*
We were to do more business after dinner; but after dinner is after dinner - an old saying and a true, 'much drinking, little thinking'.

11244 *Journal to Stella*
We are so fond of one another, because our ailments are the same.

11245 *Journal to Stella*
I love good creditable acquaintance; I love to be the worst of the company.

11246 *Letter to Bolingbroke*
Not die here in a rage, like a poisoned rat in a hole.

11247 *Letter to Miss Vanhomrigh*
If Heaven had looked upon riches to be a valuable thing, it would not have given them to such a scoundrel.

11248 *Letter to Pope*
Principally I hate and detest that animal called man; although I heartily love John, Peter, Thomas, and so forth.

11249 *Letter to a Young Gentleman ....Holy Orders*
Proper words in proper places, make the true definition of a style.

11250 'Ode to Sir W. Temple'
Philosophy! the lumber of the schools.

11251 'A Pastoral Dialogue between Richmond Lodge ...'
Walls have tongues, and hedges ears.

11252 'On Poetry'
As learned commentators view
In Homer more than Homer knew.

11253 'On Poetry'
Hobbes clearly proves, that every creature Lives in a state of war by nature.

11254 'On Poetry'
So, naturalists observe, a flea
Hath smaller fleas that on him prey;
And these have smaller fleas to bite 'em,
And so proceed *ad infinitum*.
Thus every poet, in his kind,
Is bit by him that comes behind.

11255 *Polite Conversation*
Faith, that's as well said, as if I had said it myself.

11256 *Polite Conversation*
Promises and pie-crust are made to be broken.

11257 *Polite Conversation*
Bachelor's fare; bread and cheese, and
kisses.

11258 *Polite Conversation*
'Tis happy for him, that his father was
before him.

11259 *Polite Conversation*
Why, everyone one as they like; as the
good woman said when she kissed her
cow.

11260 *A Tale of a Tub*
Last week I saw a woman flayed, and you
will hardly believe, how much it altered
her person for the worse.

11261 *Thoughts on Various Subjects*
We have just enough religion to make us
hate, but not enough to make us love one
another.

11262 *Thoughts on Various Subjects*
Few are qualified to shine in company; but
it is in most men's power to be agreeable.

11263 *Thoughts on Various Subjects*
Every man desires to live long; but no man
would be old.

11264 *'Verses on the Death of Dr Swift'*
The rest will give a shrug, and cry,
'I'm sorry - but we all must die!'

11265 *'Verses on the Death of Dr Swift'*
Yet malice never was his aim;
He lashed the vice, but spared the name;
No individual could resent,
Where thousands equally were meant.

SWINBURNE Algernon Charles 1837-
1909
11266 *'Anactoria'*
Superflux of pain.

11267 *'Atalanta in Calydon'*
Maiden, and mistress of the months and
stars
Now folded in the flowerless fields of
heaven.

11268 *'Atalanta in Calydon'*
And in green underwood and cover
Blossom by blossom the spring begins.

11269 *'Atalanta in Calydon'*
Before the beginning of years
There came to the making of man
Time with a gift of tears,
Grief with a glass that ran.

11270 *'Atalanta in Calydon'*
Strength without hands to smite,
Love that endures for a breath;
Night, the shadow of light,
And Life, the shadow of death.

11271 *'Atalanta in Calydon'*
For words divide and rend;
But silence is most noble till the end.

11272 *'Atalanta in Calydon'*
He weaves, and is clothed with derision;
Sows, and he shall not reap;
His life is a watch or a vision
Between a sleep and a sleep.

11273 *'Ballad of François Villon'*
Villon, our sad bad glad mad brother's
name.

11274 *'Dolores'*
Change in a trice
The lilies and languors of virtue
For the raptures and roses of vice.

11275 *'Dolores'*
O splendid and sterile Dolores,
Our Lady of Pain.

11276 *'Dolores'*
Ah beautiful passionate body
That never has ached with a heart!

11277 *'Dolores'*
And love is more cruel than lust.
Time turns the old days to derision
Our loves into corpses or wives.

11278 *'Erotion'*
I shall remember while the light lives yet
And in the night time I shall not forget.

11279 *'A Forsaken Garden'*
In a coign of the cliff between lowland and
highland,
At the sea-down's edge between
windward and lee,
Walled round with rocks as an inland
island,
The ghost of a garden fronts the sea.

11280 *'A Forsaken Garden'*
As a god self-slain on his own strange
altar,
Death lies dead.

11281 *'The Garden of Proserpine'*
Pale, beyond porch and portal,
Crowned with calm leaves, she stands
Who gathers all things mortal
With cold immortal hands.

11282 *The Heptalogia 'The Higher Pantheism
...'*
Fiddle, we know, is diddle: and diddle, we
take it, is dee.

11283 *'Hymn of Man'*
But God, if a God there be, is the substance
of men which is man.

11284 *'Hymn to Proserpine'*
Thou hast conquered, O pale Galilean; the
world has grown grey from thy breath;
We have drunken of things Lethean, and
fed on the fullness of death.

11285 *'An Interlude'*
And the best and the worst of this is
That neither is most to blame,
If you have forgotten my kisses
And I have forgotten your name.

11286 *'Itylus'*
Till life forget and death remember,
Till thou remember and I forget.

11287 *'The Triumph of Time'*
I will go back to the great sweet mother,
Mother and lover of men, the sea.
I will go down to her, I and no other,
Close with her, kiss her and mix her with
me.

SWINNERTON Frank 1884-1982
11288
The wisest man I have ever known once
said to me: 'Nine out of every ten people
improve on acquaintance,' and I have
found his words true.

SWOPE Herbert Bayard
11289
I cannot give you the formula for success,
but I can give you the formula for failure,
which is - try to please everybody.

SYMONDS John Addington 1840-1893
11290
These things shall be! A loftier race
Than e'er the world hath known shall rise,
With flame of freedom in their souls,
And light of knowledge in their eyes.

SYMONS Arthur 1865-1945
11291
An invitation is the sincerest form of
flattery.

11292 *Memory*
As a perfume doth remain
In the folds where it hath lain,
So the thought of you, remaining
Deeply folded in my brain,
Will not leave me: all things leave me:
You remain.

SYNGE John Millington 1871-1909
11293
Before verse can be human again it must
learn to be brutal.

11294 *The Aran Islands*
We do be afraid of the sea, and we do only
be drownded now and again.

11295 *The Aran Islands*
'A translation is no translation,' he said,
'unless it will give you the music of a
poem along with the words of it.'

11296 *The Playboy of the Western World*
Oh my grief, I've lost him surely. I've lost
the only Playboy of the Western World.

SYRUS Publilius 1st Century BC
11297
Everything is worth what its purchaser
will pay for it.

11298
There are some remedies worse than the
disease.

SZASZ Thomas 1920-
11299
If you talk to God, you are praying; if God
talks to you, you have schizophrenia.

11300 *The Second Sin*
Traditionally, sex has been a very private,
secretive activity. Herein perhaps lies its
powerful force for uniting people in a

strong bond. As we make sex less secretive, we may rob it of its power to hold men and women together.

11301 *The Second Sin 'Childhood'*
A child becomes an adult when he realizes that he has a right not only to be right but also to be wrong.

11302 *The Second Sin 'Education'*
A teacher should have maximal authority and minimal power.

11303 *The Second Sin 'Emotions'*
Happiness is an imaginary condition, formerly often attributed by the living to the dead, now usually attributed by adults to children, and by children to adults.

11304 *The Second Sin 'Personal Conduct'*
The stupid neither forgive nor forget; the naïve forgive and forget; the wise forgive but do not forget.

11305 *The Second Sin 'Science and Scientism'*
Formerly, when religion was strong and science weak, men mistook magic for medicine; now, when science is strong and religion weak, men mistake medicine for magic.

11306 *The Second Sin 'Sex'*
Masturbation: the primary sexual activity of mankind. In the nineteenth century, it was a disease; in the twentieth, it's a cure.

11307 *The Second Sin 'Social Relations'*
Two wrongs don't make a right, but they make a good excuse.

SZELL George 1897-1970
11308
Conductors must give unmistakable and suggestive signals to the orchestra, not choreography to the audience.

SZENT-GYÖRGYI Albert von 1893-1986
11309
Discovery consists of seeing what everybody has seen and thinking what nobody has thought.

TACITUS AD c.56-c.117
11310
Greater things are believed of those who are absent.

11311
Candour and generosity, unless tempered by due moderation, lead to ruin.

11312
Things forbidden have a secret charm.

11313 *Agricola*
They make a wilderness and call it peace.

11314 *Agricola*
It is part of human nature to hate the man you have hurt.

11315 *Annals*
With neither anger nor partiality.

11316 *Annals (of Petronius)*
The arbiter of taste.

11317 *Histories*
These times having the rare good fortune that you may think what you like and say what you think.

11318 *Histories*
The gods are on the side of the stronger.

TAFT William Howard 1857-1930
11319
Some men are graduated from college cum laude, some are graduated summa cum laude, and some are graduated mirabile dictu.

TAGORE Sir Rabindranath 1861-1941
11320
He only may chastise who loves.

11321
The mountain remains unmoved at seeming defeat by the mist.

11322
Men are cruel, but man is kind.

11323
The soil, in return for her service, keeps the tree tied to her; the sky asks nothing and leaves it free.

11324 *Fireflies*
Bigotry tries to keep truth safe in its hand
With a grip that kills it.

TAINE Hippolyte 1828-1893
11325
There are four varieties in society; the

lovers, the ambitious, observers, and fools.
The fools are the happiest.

TALBOT Nellie
11326
Jesus wants me for a sunbeam.

TALLENTYRE S.G.
11327
The crowning blessing of life - to be born
with a bias to some pursuit.

TALLEYRAND Charles Maurice de 1754-
1838
11328
The art of putting the right men in the
right places is first in the science of
government; but that of finding places for
the discontented is the most difficult.

11329
The art of statemanship is to foresee the
inevitable and to expedite its occurrence.

11330
Above all, gentlemen, not the slightest
zeal.

11331 *(announcing Napoleon's defeat at
Borodino)*
This is the beginning of the end.

The TALMUD
11332
The burden is equal to the horse's strength.

11333
Would that life were like the shadow cast
by a wall or a tree, but it is like the shadow
of a bird in flight.

11334
The sun will set without thy assistance.

11335
Three things are good in little measure and
evil in large: yeast, salt and hesitation.

11336
The deeper the sorrow the less tongue it
hath.

11337
It is not upon thee to finish the work;
neither art thou free to abstain from it.

TANFIELD Elizabeth Lady c.1565-1628
11338 *(epitaph for her husband)*
Love made me poet,
And this I writ;
My heart did do it,
And not my wit.

TARKINGTON Booth 1869-1946
11339 *(attributed)*
An ideal wife is any woman who has an
ideal husband.

11340 *Penrod*
There are two things that will be believed
of any man whatsoever, and one of them is
that he has taken to drink.

TARSHIS Jerome
11341
The history of medicine is a story of
amazing foolishness and amazing
intelligence.

TATE Nahum 1652-1715
11342 *Dido and Aeneas 'Dido's Lament'*
When I am laid in earth my wrongs create
No trouble in thy breast.
Remember me, but ah! forget my fate.

11343 *'While Shepherds Watched'*
While shepherds watched their flocks by
night,
All seated on the ground,
The angel of the Lord came down,
And glory shone around.

TAWNEY R.H. 1880-1962
11344
Clever men are impressed in their
differences from their fellows. Wise men
are conscious of their resemblance to them.

11345
If a man has important work, and enough
leisure and income to enable him to do it
properly, he is in possession of as much
happiness as is good for any of the
children of Adam.

11346 *The Acquisitive Society*
The characteristic virtue of Englishmen is
power of sustained practical activity and
their characteristic vice a reluctance to test
the quality of that activity by reference to
principles.

11347 *The Acquisitive Society*
Militarism ... is fetish worship. It is the
prostration of men's souls and the
laceration of their bodies to appease an
idol.

11348 *(declining the offer of a peerage)*
What harm have I ever done to the Labour
Party?

11349 *Religion and the Rise of Capitalism*
A reasonable estimate of economic
organisation must allow for the fact that,
unless industry is to be paralysed by
recurrent revolts on the part of outraged
human nature, it must satisfy criteria
which are not purely economic.

TAYLOR A.J.P. 1906-1990
11350
History is not another name for the past, as
many people imply. It is the name for
stories about the past.

11351 *English History 1914-45*
History gets thicker as it approaches recent
times.

11352 *'Mistaken Lessons from the Past'*
Like most of those who study history, he
[Napoleon III] learned from the mistakes
of the past how to make new ones.

11353 *The Origins of the Second World War*
Human blunders usually do more to shape
history than human wickedness.

11354 *Politicians, Socialism and Historians*
If men are to respect each other for what
they are, they must cease to respect each
other for what they own.

11355 *Rumours of Wars*
Crimea: The War That Would Not Boil.

TAYLOR Ann and TAYLOR Jane 1782-
1866 and 1783-1824
11356 *Hymns for Infant Minds 'A Child's
Hymn of Praise'*
I thank the goodness and the grace
Which on my birth have smiled,
And made me, in these Christian days,
A happy English child.

11357 *Original Poems for Infant Minds 'My
Mother'*
Who ran to help me when I fell,
And would some pretty story tell,
Or kiss the place to make it well?
My Mother.

11358 *Rhymes for the Nursery 'The Star'*
Twinkle, twinkle, little star,
How I wonder what you are!
Up above the world so high,
Like a diamond in the sky!

11359 *Rhymes for the Nursery 'The Way to be
Happy'*
How pleasant it is, at the end of the day,
No follies to have to repent;
But reflect on the past, and be able to say,
That my time has been properly spent.

TAYLOR Bayard 1825-1878
11360
The loving are the daring.

11361 *'Bedouin Song'*
Till the sun grows cold,
And the stars are old,
And the leaves of the Judgement Book
unfold.

TAYLOR Bert Leston 1866-1921
11362
A bore is a man who, when you ask him
how he is, tells you.

TAYLOR Elizabeth 1932-
11363 *in Cat on a Hot Tin Roof*
"I'm not living with you. We occupy the
same cage, that's all."

11364 *(on her first brief marriage at 19)*
I have a woman's body and a child's
emotions.

TAYLOR Henry
11365
The world knows nothing of its greatest
men.

11366
Shy and unready men are great betrayers
of secrets; for there are few wants more
urgent for the moment than the want of
something to say.

TAYLOR Bishop Jeremy 1613-1667
11367 *Ductor Dubitantium 'When in Rome, do as the Romans do'*
If you are at Rome, live in the Roman style; if you are elsewhere, live as they live elsewhere.

11368 *The Real Prescence ...*
This thing ... that can be understood and not expressed, may take a neuter gender; and every schoolboy knows it.

11369 *The Rule and Exercise of Holy Dying*
As our life is very short, so it is very miserable, and therefore it is well it is short.

11370 *The Rule and Exercise of Holy Dying*
Desperate by too quick a sense of a constant infelicity.

11371 *Sermons 'The Marriage Ring'*
The union of hands and hearts.

11372 *Sermons 'Married Love'*
He that loves not his wife and children, feeds a lioness at home and broods a nest of sorrows.

TAYLOR Joe
11373
It takes time to save time.

TAYLOR W.M.
11374
Temptation rarely comes in working hours. It is in their leisure time that men are made or marred.

TEALE Edwin Way
11375
In nature, there is less death and destruction than death and transmutation.

TEASDALE Sara 1884-1933
11376
Beauty, more than bitterness
Makes the heart break.

TEBBIT Norman 1931-
11377
I grew up in the Thirties with our unemployed father. He did not riot, he got on his bike and looked for work.

11378
It is a mistake to judge people by their friends. Judge them by their enemies. I am very proud of my enemies.

TEMPLE William 1881-1944
11379
Learning passes for wisdom among those who want both.

11380
It is a mistake to suppose that God is only, or even chiefly, concerned with religion.

11381 *(attributed)*
Personally, I have always looked on cricket as organized loafing.

11382 *In The Life of the Church and the Order of Society*
Human status ought not to depend upon the changing demands of the economic process.

TENNYSON Alfred Lord 1809-1892
11383
He makes no friend who never made a foe.

11384
I am a part of all that I have met.

11385
The happiness of a man in this life does not consist in the absence but in the mastery of his passions.

11386
Self-reverence, self-knowledge, self-control - these three alone lead to sovereign power.

11387
Sleep - kinsman thou to death and trance and madness.

11388 *'The Ancient Sage'*
For nothing worthy proving can be proven,
Nor yet disproven: wherefore thou be wise,
Cleave ever to the sunnier side of doubt.

11389 *'Break, Break, Break'*
But O for the touch of a vanished hand,
And the sound of a voice that is still!

11390 *'The Brook'*
I come from haunts of coot and hern,
I make a sudden sally
And sparkle out among the fern,
To bicker down a valley.

11391 *'The Brook'*
For men may come and men may go,
But I go on for ever.

11392 *'The Charge of the Light Brigade'*
Half a league, half a league,
Half a league onward,
All in the valley of Death
Rode the six hundred.

11393 *'The Charge of the Light Brigade'*
'Forward, the Light Brigade!'
Was there a man dismayed?
Not though the soldier knew
Some one had blundered:
Their's not to make reply,
Their's not to reason why,
Their's but to do and die:
Into the valley of Death
Rode the six hundred.
Cannon to right of them,
Cannon to left of them,
Cannon in front of them
Volleyed and thundered.

11394 *'The Charge of the Light Brigade'*
Into the jaws of Death,
Into the mouth of Hell.

11395 *(of Churton Collins)*
A louse in the locks of literature.

11396 *'Crossing the Bar'*
Twilight and evening bell,
And after that the dark!
And may there be no sadness of farewell,
When I embark.

11397 *'The Eagle'*
The wrinkled sea beneath him crawls;
He watches from his mountain walls,
And like a thunderbolt he falls.

11398 *'Far-Far-Away'*
The mellow lin-lan-lone of evening bells.

11399 *'Fatima'*
O Love, O fire! once he drew
With one long kiss my whole soul through
My lips, as sunlight drinketh dew.

11400 *'Sir Galahad'*
My strength is as the strength of ten,
Because my heart is pure.

11401 *'The Gardener's Daughter'*
More black than ashbuds in the front of
March.

11402 *'The Gardener's Daughter'*
News from the humming city comes to it
In sound of funeral or of marriage bells.

11403 *'The Gardener's Daughter'*
Half light, half shade,
She stood, a sight to make an old man
young.

11404 *'Godiva'*
Then she rode forth, clothed on with
chastity.

11405 *'The Golden Year'*
Ah! when shall all men's good
Be each man's rule, and universal peace
Lie like a shaft of light across the land?

11406 *'The Golden Year'*
Through all the circle of the golden year.

11407 *'The Grandmother'*
That a lie which is all a lie may be met and
fought with outright,
But a lie which is part a truth is a harder
matter to fight.

11408 *'Hands all Round'*
Pray God our greatness may not fail
Through craven fears of being great.

11409 *'The Higher Pantheism'*
Closer is He than breathing, and nearer
than hands and feet.

11410 Idylls of the King *'The Coming of
Arthur'*
Man's word is God in man.

11411 Idylls of the King *'The Coming of
Arthur'*
Rain, rain, and sun! a rainbow in the sky!
A young man will be wiser by and by;
An old man's wit may wander ere he die.

11412 Idylls of the King *'The Coming of
Arthur'*
From the great deep to the great deep he
goes.

11413 *Idylls of the King 'The Coming of Arthur'*
Blow trumpet, for the world is white with May.

11414 *Idylls of the King - Dedication*
Wearing the white flower of a blameless life,
Before a thousand peering littlenesses.

11415 *Idylls of the King 'Gareth and Lynette'*
Live pure, speak true, right wrong, follow the King -
Else, wherefore born?

11416 *Idylls of the King 'The Holy Grail'*
For good ye are and bad, and like to coins,
Some true, some light, but every one of you
Stamped with the image of the King.

11417 *Idylls of the King 'Lancelot and Elaine'*
He is all fault who hath no fault at all:
For who loves me must have a touch of earth.

11418 *Idylls of the King 'Lancelot and Elaine'*
I know not if I know what true love is,
But if I know, then, if I love not him,
I know there is none other I can love.

11419 *Idylls of the King 'Lancelot and Elaine'*
His honour rooted in dishonour stood,
And faith unfaithful kept him falsely true.

11420 *Idylls of the King 'Lancelot and Elaine'*
He makes no friend who never made a foe.

11421 *Idylls of the King 'The Last Tournament'*
The dirty nurse, Experience, in her kind
Hath fouled me.

11422 *Idylls of the King 'The Marriage of Geraint'*
Our hoard is little, but our hearts are great.

11423 *Idylls of the King 'The Marriage of Geraint'*
For man is man and master of his fate.

11424 *Idylls of the King 'Merlin and Vivien'*
It is the little rift within the lute,
That by and by will make the music mute,
And ever widening slowly silence all.

11425 *Idylls of the King 'Merlin and Vivien'*
And trust me not at all or all in all.

11426 *Idylls of the King 'Merlin and Vivien'*
Man dreams of fame while woman wakes to love.

11427 *Idylls of the King 'Merlin and Vivien'*
Where blind and naked Ignorance
Delivers brawling judgements, unashamed,
On all things all day long.

11428 *Idylls of the King 'The Passing of Arthur'*
I found Him in the shining of the stars,
I marked Him in the flowering of His fields,
But in His ways with men I find Him not.

11429 *Idylls of the King 'The Passing of Arthur'*
Authority forgets a dying king.

11430 *Idylls of the King 'The Passing of Arthur'*
And the days darken round me, and the years,
Among new men, strange faces, other minds.

11431 *Idylls of the King 'The Passing of Arthur'*
The old order changeth, yielding place to new,
And God fulfils himself in many ways,
Lest one good custom should corrupt the world.

11432 *Idylls of the King 'The Passing of Arthur'*
If thou shouldst never see my face again,
Pray for my soul. More things are wrought by prayer
Than this world dreams of.

11433 *'Lady Clara Vere de Vere'*
'Tis only noble to be good.
Kind hearts are more than coronets,
And simple faith than Norman blood.

11434 *'Lady Clara Vere de Vere'*
A simple maiden in her flower
Is worth a hundred coats of arms.

11435 'The Lady of Shalott'
Willows whiten, aspens quiver,
Little breezes dusk and shiver.

11436 'The Lady of Shalott'
Or when the moon was overhead,
Came two young lovers lately wed;
'I am half sick of shadows,' said
The Lady of Shalott.

11437 'The Lady of Shalott'
A bow-shot from her bower-eaves,
He rode between the barley-sheaves,
The sun came dazzling through the leaves,
And flamed upon the brazen greaves
Of bold Sir Lancelot.

11438 'The Lady of Shalott'
She left the web, she left the loom,
She made three paces through the room,
She saw the water-lily bloom,
She saw the helmet and the plume,
She looked down to Camelot.
Out flew the Web and floated wide;
The mirror cracked from side to side;
'The curse is come upon me,' cried
The Lady of Shalott.

11439 'Locksley Hall'
In the spring a young man's fancy lightly
turns to thoughts of love.

11440 'Locksley Hall'
And our spirits rushed together at the
touching of the lips.

11441 'Locksley Hall'
He will hold thee, when his passion shall
have spent its novel force,
Something better than his dog, a little
dearer than his horse.

11442 'Locksley Hall'
This is truth the poet sings,
That a sorrow's crown of sorrow is
remembering happier things.

11443 'Locksley Hall'
Like a dog, he hunts in dreams.

11444 'Locksley Hall'
But the jingling of the guinea helps the
hurt that Honour feels.

11445 'Locksley Hall'
Till the war-drum throbbed no longer, and
the battle-flags were furled
In the Parliament of man, the Federation of
the world.

11446 'Locksley Hall'
Science moves, but slowly slowly, creeping
on from point to point.

11447 'Locksley Hall'
Yet I doubt not through the ages one
increasing purpose runs,
And the thoughts of men are widened
with the process of the suns.

11448 'Locksley Hall'
Knowledge comes, but wisdom lingers.

11449 'Locksley Hall'
I will take some savage woman, she shall
rear my dusky race.

11450 'Locksley Hall'
I the heir of all the ages, in the foremost
files of time.

11451 'Locksley Hall'
Forward, forward let us range,
Let the great world spin for ever down the
ringing grooves of change.

11452 'Locksley Hall'
Better fifty years of Europe than a cycle of
Cathay.

11453 'The Lotos-Eaters'
All things are taken from us, and become
Portions and parcels of the dreadful Past.

11454 'The Lotos-Eaters' Choric Song
Live and lie reclined
On the hills like Gods together, careless of
mankind.

11455 'Mariana'
Her tears fell with the dews at even;
Her tears fell ere the dews were dried.

11456 'Maud'
Faultily faultless, icily regular, splendidly
null,
Dead perfection, no more.

11457 'Maud'
One still strong man in a blatant land,
Whatever they call him, what care I,

Aristocrat, democrat, autocrat - one
Who can rule and dare not lie.

11458 'Maud'
Gorgonised me from head to foot
With a stony British stare.

11459 'Maud'
Come into the garden, Maud,
For the black bat, night, has flown,
Come into the garden, Maud,
I am here at the gate alone;
And the woodbine spices are wafted
abroad,
And the musk of the rose is blown.

For a breeze of morning moves,
And the planet of Love is on high,
Beginning to faint in the light that she
loves
On a bed of daffodil sky.

11460 'Maud'
Queen rose of the rosebud garden of girls.

11461 'Maud'
O that 'twere possible
After long grief and pain
To find the arms of my true love
Round me once again!

11462 'Maud'
I embrace the purpose of God, and the
doom assigned.

11463 In Memoriam
Dark house, by which once more I stand
Here in the long unlovely street.

11464 In Memoriam
I hold it true, whate'er befall;
I feel it when I sorrow most;
'Tis better to have loved and lost
Than never to have loved at all.

11465 In Memoriam
Nature, red in tooth and claw.

11466 In Memoriam
But I was born to other things.

11467 In Memoriam
There rolls the deep where grew the tree.

11468 In Memoriam A.H.H.
Thou madest man, he knows not why,
He thinks he was not made to die.

11469 In Memoriam A.H.H.
Our little systems have their day;
They have their day and cease to be:
They are but broken lights of thee,
And thou, O Lord, art more than they.

11470 In Memoriam A.H.H.
I held it truth, with him who sings
To one clear harp in divers tones,
That men may rise on stepping-stones
Of their dead selves to higher things.

11471 In Memoriam A.H.H.
For words, like Nature, half reveal
And half conceal the Soul within.

11472 In Memoriam A.H.H.
The last red leaf is whirled away,
The rooks are blown about the skies.

11473 In Memoriam A.H.H.
The Shadow cloaked from head to foot,
Who keeps the keys of all the creeds.

11474 In Memoriam A.H.H.
And Thought leapt out to wed with
Thought
Ere Thought could wed itself with Speech.

11475 In Memoriam A.H.H.
I envy not in any moods
The captive void of noble rage,
The linnet born within the cage,
That never knew the summer woods.

11476 In Memoriam A.H.H.
Her eyes are homes of silent prayer.

11477 In Memoriam A.H.H.
Be near me when my light is low,
When the blood creeps, and the nerves
prick
And tingle; and the heart is sick,
And all the wheels of Being are slow.

11478 In Memoriam A.H.H.
Time, a maniac scattering dust,
And Life, a Fury slinging flame.

11479 In Memoriam A.H.H.
Oh yet we trust that somehow good
Will be the final goal of ill.

11480 In Memoriam A.H.H.
But what am I?
An infant crying in the night:
An infant crying for the light:

And with no language but a cry.

11481 *In Memoriam A.H.H.*
The great world's altar-stairs
That slope through darkness up to God.

11482 *In Memoriam A.H.H.*
Peace; come away: we do him wrong
To sing so wildly: let us go.

11483 *In Memoriam A.H.H.*
O Sorrow, wilt thou live with me
No casual mistress, but a wife.

11484 *In Memoriam A.H.H.*
Who breaks his birth's invidious bar,
And graps the skirts of happy chance,
And breasts the blows of circumstance,
And grapples with his evil star.

11485 *In Memoriam A.H.H.*
So many worlds, so much to do,
So little done, such things to be.

11486 *In Memoriam A.H.H.*
And round thee with the breeze of song
To stir a little dust of praise.

11487 *In Memoriam A.H.H.*
God's finger touched him, and he slept.

11488 *In Memoriam A.H.H.*
Fresh from brawling courts
And dusty purlieus of the law.

11489 *In Memoriam A.H.H.*
You tell me, doubt is Devil-born.

11490 *In Memoriam A.H.H.*
There lives more faith in honest doubt,
Believe me, than in half the creeds.

11491 *In Memoriam A.H.H.*
Their meetings made December June,
Their every parting was to die.

11492 *In Memoriam A.H.H.*
He seems so near and yet so far.

11493 *In Memoriam A.H.H.*
Ring out the old, ring in the new,
Ring, happy bells, across the snow:
The year is going, let him go;
Ring out the false, ring in the true.

11494 *In Memoriam A.H.H.*
One God, one law, one element,
And one far-off divine event,

To which the whole creation moves.

11495 *In Memoriam A.H.H. (of Nature)*
So careful of the type she seems,
So careless of the single life.

11496 *'Merlin and The Gleam'*
After it, follow it,
Follow The Gleam.

11497 *'Northern Farmer. New Style'*
'Doänt thou marry for munny, but goä
wheer munny is!'

11498 *'Ode on the Death of the Duke of
Wellington'*
The last great Englishman is low.

11499 *'Ode on the Death of the Duke of
Wellington'*
O good grey head which all men knew!

11500 *'Ode on the Death of the Duke of
Wellington'*
Who never sold the truth to serve the hour,
Nor paltered with Eternal God for power.

11501 *'Ode on the Death of the Duke of
Wellington'*
This is England's greatest son,
He that gained a hundred fights,
Nor ever lost an English gun.

11502 *'Ode on the Death of the Duke of
Wellington'*
In that world-earthquake, Waterloo!

11503 *'The Princess'*
And blessings on the falling out
That all the more endears,
When we fall out with those we love
And kiss again with tears!

11504 *'The Princess'*
Quoted odes, and jewels five-words-long,
That on the stretched forefinger of all Time
Sparkle for ever.

11505 *'The Princess'*
Sweet and low, sweet and low,
Wind of the western sea.

11506 *'The Princess'*
Our echoes roll from soul to soul,
And grow for ever and for ever.

11507 *'The Princess'*
Tears from the depth of some divine
despair.

11508 *'The Princess'*
Man is the hunter; woman is his game:
The sleek and shining creatures of the
chase,
We hunt them for the beauty of their skins;
They love us for it, and we ride them
down.

11509 *'The Princess'*
The woman is so hard
Upon the woman.

11510 *'The Princess'*
Now slides the silent meteor on, and
leaves
A shining furrow, as thy thoughts in me.

11511 *'The Princess'*
The moan of doves in immemorial elms,
And murmuring of innumerable bees.

11512 *'The Princess'*
No little lily-handed baronet he,
A great broad-shouldered genial
Englishman.

11513 *'The Princess'*
O tell her, brief is life but love is long.

11514 *'The Princess'*
Ask me no more: thy fate and mine are
sealed:
I strove against the stream and all in vain:
Let the great river take me to the main:
No more, dear love, for at a touch I yield;
Ask me no more.

11515 *'The Princess'*
The woman's cause is man's: they rise or
sink
Together.

11516 *'To the Revd F.D. Maurice'*
You'll have no scandal while you dine,
But honest talk and wholsome wine.

11517 *'The Revenge'*
I should count myself the coward if I left
them, my Lord Howard,
To these Inquisition dogs and the
devildoms of Spain.

11518 *'The Revenge'*
And they blest him in their pain, that they
were not left to Spain,
To the thumbscrew and the stake, for the
glory of the Lord.

11519 *'The Revenge'*
I have fought for Queen and Faith like a
valiant man and true;
I have only done my duty as a man is
bound to do.

11520 *'Tithonus'*
Here at the quiet limit of the world,
A white-haired shadow roaming like a
dream
The ever-silent spaces of the East.

11521 *'The Two Voices'*
No life that breathes with human breath
Has ever truly longed for death.

11522 *'Ulysses'*
How dull it is to pause, to make an end,
To rust unburnished, not to shine in use!
As though to breathe were life.

11523 *'Ulysses'*
This grey spirit yearning in desire
To follow knowledge like a sinking star,
Beyond the utmost bound of human
thought.

11524 *'Ulysses'*
The long day wanes: the slow moon
climbs: the deep
Moans round with many voices.

11525 *'To Virgil'*
Wielder of the stateliest measure
ever moulded by the lips of man.

11526 *'The Vision of Sin'*
Every moment dies a man,
Every moment one is born.

11527 *'Will Waterproof's Lyrical Monologue'*
Or that eternal want of pence,
Which vexes public men.

11528 *'Come not, when I am dead'*
Come not, when I am dead,
To drop thy foolish tears upon my grave,
To trample round my fallen head,
And vex the unhappy dust thou wouldst
not save.

TERENCE c.190-159 BC
11529
Of my friends I am the only one I have left.

11530
My closest relation is myself.

11531
I know the nature of women;
When you want to, they don't want to;
And when you don't want to, they desire
exceedingly.

11532 *Andria*
Hence those tears.

11533 *Andria*
Lovers' rows make love whole.

11534 *Eunuchus - prologue*
Nothing has yet been said that's not been
said before.

11535 *Heauton Timorumenos*
I am a man, I count nothing human foreign
to me.

11536 *Phormio*
Fortune favours the bold.

11537 *Phormio*
There are as many opinions as there are
people: each has his own correct way.
[each a law unto himself]

TERESA Mother 1910-
11538
Loneliness and the feeling of being
unwanted is the most terrible poverty.

11539
One filled with joy preaches without
preaching.

TERTULLIAN c.160-c.220
11540 *Apologeticus*
See how these Christians love one another.

11541 *Apologeticus*
The blood of the martyrs is the seed of the
Church.

TESSIER Josephine
11542
Anything that comes easy, comes wrong.

TESSIMOND A.S.J. 1902-1962
11543 *'Cats'*
Cats, no less liquid than their shadows,
Offer no angles to the wind.
They slip, diminished, neat, through
loopholes
Less than themselves.

THACKERAY William Makepeace 1811-
1863
11544
Charlotte, having seen his body borne
before her on a shutter, like a well
conducted person, went on cutting bread
and butter.

11545
Mother is the name of God in the lips and
hearts of children.

11546
The world is a looking glass and gives
back to every man the reflection of his own
face.

11547 *Henry Esmond*
'Tis strange what a man may do, and a
woman yet think him an angel.

11548 *The History of Henry Esmond*
We love being in love, that's the truth on't.

11549 *The Newcomes*
What money is better bestowed than that
of a schoolboy's tip?

11550 *Pendennis*
Yes, I am a fatal man, Madame Fribsbi. To
inspire hopeless passion is my destiny.

11551 *Pendennis*
Remember, it is as easy to marry a rich
woman as a poor woman.

11552 *Pendennis*
For a slashing article, sir, there's nobody
like the Capting.

11553 *Pendennis*
The *Pall Mall Gazette* is written by
gentlemen for gentlemen.

11554 *The Rose and the Ring*
Business first; pleasure afterwards.

11555 *Vanity Fair*
A woman with fair opportunities and without a positive hump, may marry whom she likes.

11556 *Vanity Fair*
Whenever he met a great man he grovelled before him, and my-lorded him as only a free-born Briton can do.

11557 *Vanity Fair*
If a man's character is to be abused, say what you will, there's nobody like a relation to do the business.

11558 *Vanity Fair*
Them's my sentiments!

11559 *Vanity Fair*
Nothing like blood, sir, in hosses, dawgs, and men.

11560 *Vanity Fair*
I think I could be a good woman if I had five thousand a year.

11561 *Vanity Fair*
Some cynical Frenchman has said that there are two parties to a love transaction; the one who loves and the other who condescends to be so treated.

THATCHER Margaret 1925-
11562
The lady's not for turning.

11563
We must try to find ways to starve the terrorist and the hijacker of the oxygen of publicity on which they depend.

11564
No one would remember the Good Samaritan if he'd only had good intentions. He had money as well.

11565
There is no such thing as Society. There are individual men and women, and there are families.

11566
We have become a grandmother.

11567
The Act of Concensus is the negation of leadership.

11568
Women are much better at saying no than men.

11569 *(of Falklands campaign)*
It is exciting to have a real crisis on your hands, when you have spent half your political life dealing with humdrum issues like the environment.

THEOCRITUS c.310-c.250 BC
11570
Man will ever stand in need of man.

THIRY Paul
11571
Buildings should be good neighbours.

THOMAS Brandon 1856-1914
11572 *Charley's Aunt*
I'm Charley's aunt from Brazil - where the nuts come from.

THOMAS Dylan 1914-1953
11573
My education was the liberty I had to read indiscriminately and all the time, with my eyes hanging out.

11574
The function of posterity is to look after itself.

11575
Hands have not tears to flow.

11576 *'And death shall have no dominion'*
Though they go mad they shall be sane,
Though they sink through the sea they shall rise again;
Though lovers be lost love shall not;
And death shall have no dominion.

11577 *(defining an alcoholic)*
A man you don't like who drinks as much as you do.

11578 *'Do Not Go Gentle into that Good Night'*
Do not go gentle into that good night,
Old age should burn and rave at close of day;
Rage, rage against the dying of the light.

11579 *'Fern Hill'*
Oh as I was young and easy in the mercy of his means,

Time held me green and dying
Though I sang in my chains like the sea.

11580 *'The force that through the green fuse ...'*
The force that through the green fuse
drives the flower
Drives my green age.

11581 *'The force that through the green fuse ...'*
And I am dumb to tell the lover's tomb
How at my sheet goes the same crooked
worm.

11582 *'Shall Gods be said to Thump the Clouds?'*
Shall gods be said to thump the clouds
When clouds are cursed by thunder?

11583 *'The hand that signed the paper felled ...'*
The hand that signed the treaty bred a
fever,
And famine grew, and locusts came;
Great is the hand that holds dominion over
Man by a scribbled name.

11584 *'Light breaks where no sun shines'*
Light breaks where no sun shines;
Where no sea runs, the waters of the heart
Push in their tides.

11585 *Under Milk Wood*
To begin at the beginning: It is spring,
moonless night in the small town, starless
and bible-black.

11586 *Under Milk Wood*
Chasing the naughty couples down the
grassgreen gooseberried double bed of the
wood.

11587 *Under Milk Wood*
Before you let the sun in, mind it wipes its
shoes.

11588 *Under Milk Wood*
Oh, isn't life a terrible thing, thank God?

11589 *Under Milk Wood*
The boys are dreaming wicked or of the
bucking ranches of the night and the
jollyrodgered sea.

11590 *Under Milk Wood*
Sleeping as quiet as death, side by
wrinkled side, toothless, salt and brown,
like two old kippers in a box.

11591 *Under Milk Wood*
Straightfaced in his cunning sleep he pulls
the legs of his dreams.

11592 *Under Milk Wood*
Nothing grows in our garden, only
washing. And babies.

11593 *Under Milk Wood*
It is always opening time in the Sailors
Arms.

11594 *Under Milk Wood*
Seventeen and never been sweet in the
grass ho ho.

11595 *Under Milk Wood*
Gomer Owen who kissed her once by the
pig-sty when she wasn't looking and never
kissed her again although she was looking
all the time.

11596 *Quite Early One Morning*
There is only one position for an artist
anywhere: and that is, upright.

11597 *'A Refusal to Mourn the Death...'*
Deep with the first dead lies London's
daughter,
Robed in the long friends,
The grains beyond age, the dark veins of
her mother,
Secret by the unmourning water
Of the riding Thames.
After the first death, there is no other.

11598 *(of Wales)*
The land of my fathers. My fathers can
have it.

THOMAS Edith M. 1854-1925
11599
What mighty battles have I seen and heard
waged between the trees and the west
wind - an Iliad fought in the fields of air.

THOMAS Edward 1878-1917
11600 *'Adlestrop'*
Yes; I remember Adlestrop -
The name, because one afternoon
Of heat the express-train drew up there
Unwontedly. It was late June.

11601 *'Out In The Dark'*
How weak and little is the light,
All the universe of sight,

Love and delight,
Before the might,
If you love it not, of night.

11602 *'Early one morning in May I set out'*
The past is the only dead thing that smells
sweet.

11603 *'Lights Out'*
I have come to the borders of sleep,
The unfathomable deep
Forest where all must lose
Their way.

11604 *'The Trumpet'*
Open your eyes to the air
That has washed the eyes of the stars
Through all the dewy night:
Up with the light,
To the old wards:
Arise, arise.

11605 *'The Unknown'*
I have not seen,
I have no news of her;
I can tell only
She is not here, but there
She might have been.

THOMAS Elizabeth 1675-1731
11606 *'A New Litany, ... invitation to a
wedding'*
From marrying in haste, and repenting at
leisure;
Not liking the person, yet liking his
treasure:
Libera nos.

THOMAS Irene
11607
Protestant women may take the pill.
Roman Catholic women must keep taking
The Tablet.

THOMAS Lewis
11608
Cats - a standing rebuke to behavioural
scientist ... least human of all creatures.

11609
Most things get better by themselves.
Most things, in fact, are better by morning.

THOMAS R.S. 1913-
11610 *'They'*
There is no love

For such, only a willed
gentleness.

11611 *'In a Country Church'*
The dry whisper of unseen wings,
Bats not angels, in the high roof.

11612 *'Pietà'*
In the darkness ... the sound of a man
Breathing, testing his faith
On emptiness, nailing his questions
One by one to an untenanted cross.

11613 *'Welsh Landscape'*
Worrying the carcase of an old song.

THOMAS Terry 1911-1990
11614 *in I'm All Right Jack*
"We've got men here who can break into a
muck sweat merely by standing still."

THOMPSON E.P.
11615
For two decades the state has been taking
liberties, and these liberties were once
ours.

THOMPSON Francis 1859-1907
11616 *'Daisy'*
Nothing begins, and nothing ends,
That is not paid with moan;
For we are born in other's pain,
And perish in our own.

11617 *'The Hound of Heaven'*
I fled Him, down the nights and down the
days;
I fled Him, down the arches of the years;
I fled Him, down the labyrinthine ways
Of my own mind; and in the mist of tears
I hid from Him, and under running
laughter.

11618 *'The Hound of Heaven'*
All things betray thee, who betrayest Me.

11619 *'The Hound of Heaven'*
I said to Dawn: Be sudden - to Eve:
Be soon.

11620 *'The Hound of Heaven'*
To all swift things for swiftness did I sue;
Clung to the whistling mane of every
wind.

11621 *'A Judgement in Heaven'*
There is no expeditious road
To pack and label men for God,
And save them by the barrel-load.
Some may perchance, with strange surprise,
Have blundered into Paradise.

11622 *'The Kingdom of God'*
O world invisible, we view thee,
O world intangible, we touch thee,
O world unknowable, we know thee,
Inapprehensible, we clutch thee!

11623 *'The Kingdom of God'*
The angels keep their ancient places -
Turn but a stone, and start a wing!
'Tis ye, 'tis your estrangèd faces,
That miss the many-splendoured thing.

11624 *'The Kingdom of God'*
Shall shine the traffic of Jacob's ladder
Pitched betwixt Heaven and Charing Cross.

11625 *'To a Snowflake'*
What heart could have thought you?
Past our devisal
(O filigree petal!)
Fashioned so purely,
Fragilely, surely,
From what Paradisal
Imagineless metal,
Too costly for cost?

11626 *'To a Snowflake'*
Insculped and embossed,
With His hammer of wind,
And His graver of frost.

THOMPSON Kent
11627
If you're on the merry-go-round, you have to go round.

THOMPSON William Hepworth 1810-1886
11628 *(of Sir Richard Jebb)*
What time he can spare from the adornment of his person he devotes to the neglect of his duties.

THOMSON James 1700-1748
11629 *Alfred: a Masque*
When Britain first, at heaven's command,
Arose from out the azure main,

This was the charter of the land,
And guardian angels sung this strain:
'Rule, Britannia, rule the waves;
Britons never will be slaves.'

11630 *The Castle of Indolence*
A little round, fat, oily man of God.

11631 *'Epitaph on Solomon Mendez'*
Here lies a man who never lived,
Yet still from death was flying;
Who, if not sick, was never well;
And died - for fear of dying!

11632 *The Seasons 'Spring'*
Delightful task! to rear the tender thought,
To teach the young idea how to shoot.

11633 *The Seasons 'Spring'*
An elegant sufficiency, content,
Retirement, rural quiet, friendship, books.

11634 *The Seasons 'Summer'*
O'er heaven and earth, far as the ranging eye
Can sweep, a dazzling deluge reigns; and all
From pole to pole is undistinguished blaze.

11635 *The Seasons 'Summer'*
Ships, dim-discovered, dropping from the clouds.

11636 *The Seasons 'Summer'*
Sighed and looked unutterable things.

11637 *The Seasons 'Winter'*
Welcome, kindred glooms!
Congenial horrors, hail!

11638 *The Seasons 'Winter'*
Studious let me sit,
And hold high converse with the mighty dead.

THOMSON James 1834-1882
11639 *'The City of Dreadful Night'*
The City is of Night; perchance of Death,
But certainly of Night.

11640 *'The City of Dreadful Night'*
The chambers of the mansion of my heart,
In every one whereof thine image dwells,
Are black with grief eternal for thy sake.

11641 *'The City of Dreadful Night'*
I find no hint throughout the universe
Of good or ill, of blessing or of curse;
I find alone Necessity Supreme.

11642 *'Sunday at Hampstead'*
As we rush, as we rush in the train,
The trees and the houses go wheeling
back,
But the starry heavens above that plain
Come flying on our track.

11643 *'Sunday up the River'*
Give a man a horse he can ride,
Give a man a boat he can sail.

**THOMSON Roy (Baron Thomson of
Fleet) 1894-1976**
11644
Socialism has been preached for so long
the British people no longer have any
sense of personal responsibility.

11645
I'm frank, brutally frank. And even when
I'm not frank, I look frank.

11646
If people knew what they had to do to be
successful, most people wouldn't.

11647 *(on the profitability of commercial TV in
Britain)*
Like having your own licence to print
money.

THOREAU Henry David 1817-1862
11648
He is the best sailor who can steer within
fewest points of the wind, and exact a
motive power out of the greatest obstacles.

11649
The frontiers are not east or west, north or
south, but wherever a man fronts a fact.

11650
What recommends commerce to me is its
enterprise and bravery. It does not clasp
its hands and pray to Jupiter.

11651
I think that there is nothing, not even
crime, more opposed to poetry, to
philosophy, ay, to life itself than this
incessant business.

11652
That man is richest whose pleasures are
the cheapest.

11653
Most of the luxuries, and many of the so-
called comforts, of life are not only not
indispensable, but positive hindrances to
the elevation of mankind.

11654
How often we find ourselves turning our
backs on our actual friends, that we may
go and meet their ideal cousins.

11655
If I knew ... that a man was coming to my
house with the conscious design of doing
me good, I should run for my life.

11656
Through our own recovered innocence we
discern the innocence of our neighbours.

11657
To know that we know what we know, and
that we do not know what we do not
know, that is true knowledge.

11658
'Tis healthy to be sick sometimes.

11659
What is morality but immemorial custom?
Conscience is the chief of conservatives.

11660
You cannot receive a shock unless you
have an electric affinity for that which
shocks you.

11661
Do not be too moral. You may cheat
yourself out of much life. So aim above
morality. Be not simply good; be good for
something.

11662
The bluebird carries the sky on his back.

11663
The eye is the jewel of the body.

11664
Colour, which is the poet's wealth, is so
expensive that most take to mere outline
sketches and become men of science.

11665
Politics is the gizzard of society, full of gut and gravel.

11666
I never found the companion that was so companionable as solitude.

11667
If one advances confidently in the direction of his dreams, and endeavours to live the life which he has imagined, he will meet with a success unexpected in common hours.

11668
I have travelled a good deal in Concord.

11669
I think that we may safely trust a good deal more than we do.

11670
Between whom there is hearty truth, there is love.

11671
It takes two to speak the truth - one to speak, and another to hear.

11672
It is characteristic of wisdom not to do desperate things.

11673
Beware all enterprises that require new clothes.

11674
How vain it is to sit down to write when you have not stood up to live.

11675
We like that a sentence should read as if its author, had he held a plough instead of a pen, could have drawn a furrow deep and straight to the end.

11676
As for style of writing, if one has anything to say, it drops from him simply and directly, as a stone falls to the ground.

11677
The youth gets together this material to build a bridge to the moon, or perchance, a palace or temple on earth, and at length,

the middle-aged man concludes to build a woodshed with them.

11678
Some circumstantial evidence is very strong, as when you find a trout in the milk.

11679 *Walden 'Conclusion'*
If a man does not keep pace with his companions, perhaps it is because he hears a different drummer. Let him step to the music which he hears, however measured or far away.

11680 *Walden 'Conclusion'*
The government of the world I live in was not framed, like that of Britain, in after-dinner conversations over the wine.

11681 *Walden 'Economy'*
As if you could kill time without injuring eternity.

11682 *Walden 'Economy'*
The mass of men lead lives of quiet desperation.

11683 *Walden 'Economy'*
As for Doing-good, that is one of the professions which are full.

11684 *Walden 'Sounds'*
The three-o'clock in the morning courage, which Bonaparte thought was the rarest.

11685 *Walden 'Where I Lived, and What I Lived For'*
Our life is frittered away by detail ... Simplify, simplify.

11686 *Walden 'Where I Lived, and What I Lived For'*
Time is but the stream I go a-fishing in.

THOREAU Marshall
11687
A man is rich in proportion to the things he can afford to let alone.

THORPE Jeremy 1929-
11688 *(on Macmillan sacking seven of his Cabinet)*
Greater love hath no man than this, that he lay down his friends for his life.

THURBER James 1894-1961
11689
It's a naive domestic burgundy without any breeding, but I think you'll be amused by its presumption.

11690
Humour is emotional chaos remembered in tranquillity.

11691
A lady of forty-seven who has been married twenty-seven years and has six children knows what love really is and once described it for me like this: 'Love is what you've been through with somebody.'

11692
Though statisticians in our time
Have never kept the score
Man wants a great deal here below
And Woman even more.

11693
Man is flying too fast for a world that is round. Soon he will catch up with himself in a great rear-end collision and Man will never know that what hit him from behind was Man.

11694
The difference between our decadence and the Russians' is that while theirs is brutal, ours is apathetic.

11695
We all have flaws, and mine is being wicked.

11696
Woman's place is in the wrong.

11697
The war between men and women.

11698
Well, if I called the wrong number, why did you answer the phone?

11699 *'The Bear Who Let It Alone'*
You might as well fall flat on your face as lean over too far backward.

11700 *My Life and Hard Times*
Her own mother lived the latter years of her life in the horrible suspicion that

electricity was dripping invisibly all over the house.

THURLOW Edward 1731-1806
11701
When I forget my sovereign, may God forget me!

11702
As guardian of His majesty's conscience.

11703 *(attributed)*
Did you ever expect a corporation to have a conscience, when it has no soul to be damned, and no body to be kicked.

TIBBET Paul W.
11704 *(of atomic bomb explosion)*
A mushroom of boiling dust up to 20,000 feet.

TICHNOR Don
11705
To convert an hourly wage to an approximate yearly salary, double the wage and change the decimal to a comma.

TICKELL Thomas 1686-1740
11706
Boredom is rage spread thin.

11707 *Colin and Lucy*
I hear a voice you cannot hear,
Which says I must not stay;
I see a hand you cannot see,
Which beckons me away.

11708 *'To the Earl of Warwick. On the Death of Mr Addison'*
There taught us how to live; and (oh! too high
The price for knowledge) taught us how to die.

TILLICH Paul 1886-1965
11709
Language has created the word 'loneliness' to express the pain of being alone, and the word 'solitude' to express the glory of being alone.

11710
The passion for truth is silenced by answers which have the weight of undisputed authority.

11711
The joy about our work is spoiled when we perform it not because of what we produce but because of the pleasure with which it can provide us, or the pain against which it can protect us.

11712 *(attributed)*
The first duty of love is to listen.

11713 *The Courage To Be*
Neurosis is the way of avoiding non-being by avoiding being.

11714 *Dynamics of Faith*
Faith is the state of being ultimately concerned.

TILLOTSON John 1630-1694
11715 *Sermon 93*
If God were not a necessary Being of himself, He might almost seem to be made for the use and benefit of mankind.

TITUS AD 39-81
11716 *(on having done nothing to help anybody all day)*
Friends, I have lost a day.

TOCQUEVILLE Alexis de 1805-1859
11717
In politics a community of hatred is almost always the foundation of friendships.

11718 *De la Démocratie en Amérique*
Of all nations, those submit to civilization with the most difficulty which habitually live by the chase.

11719 *De la Démocratie en Amérique*
What is understood by republican government in the United States is the slow and quiet action of society upon itself.

11720 *De la Démocratie en Amérique*
The Russians and the Americans ... Their starting point is different, and their courses are not the same; yet each of them seems to be marked out by the will of Heaven to sway the destinies of half the globe.

11721 *L'Ancien régime*
Despots themselves do not deny that freedom is excellent; only they desire it for themselves alone, and they maintain that everyone else is altogether unworthy of it.

11722 *L'Ancien régime*
History is a gallery of pictures in which there are few originals and many copies.

11723 *L'Ancien régime*
He who desires in liberty anything other than itself is born to be a servant.

TOFFLER Alvin 1928-
11724
Still round the corner there may wait,
A new road, or a secret gate.

11725
Parenthood remains the greatest single preserve of the amateur.

11726 *Future Shock*
'Future shock' ... the shattering stress and disorientation that we induce in individuals by subjecting them to too much change in too short a time.

TOLKIEN J.R.R. 1892-1973
11727 *The Fellowship of the Ring*
One Ring to rule them all, One Ring to find them
One Ring to bring them all and in the darkness bind them.

11728 *The Hobbit*
Never laugh at live dragons.

TOLSTOY Leo 1828-1910
11729
Art is a human activity, consisting in this, that one man consciously, by means of external signs, hands on to others feelings he has worked through, and other people are infected by these feelings and also experience them.

11730
All art has this characteristic - it unites people.

11731
It is amazing how complete is the delusion that beauty is goodness.

11732
Government is an association of men who do violence to the rest of us.

11733
Music is the shorthand of emotion.

11734
Work is the inevitable condition of human life, the true source of human welfare.

11735 *Anna Karenina*
All happy families resemble one another, but each unhappy family is unhappy in its own way.

11736 *Anna Karenina*
There are no conditions of life to which a man cannot get accustomed, especially if he sees them accepted by everyone about him.

11737 *Anna Karenina*
The candle by which she had been reading the book ... flared up with a brighter light, illuminating for her everything that before had been enshrouded in darkness, flickered, grew dim, and went out for ever.

11738 *Memoirs of a Madman*
I am always with myself, and it is I who am my tormentor.

11739 *War and Peace*
In historical events great men - so-called - are but labels serving to give a name to the event, and like labels they have the least possible connexion with the event itself.

11740 *War and Peace*
Pure and complete sorrow is as impossible as pure and complete joy.

11741 *War and Peace*
The most powerful weapon of ignorance - the diffusion of printed material.

11742 *What Then Must We Do?*
I sit on a man's back, choking him and making him carry me, and yet assure myself and others that I am very sorry for him and wish to ease his lot by all possible means - except by getting off his back.

TOMALIN Claire 1933-
11743
Everybody is vulnerable through love of their children. Hostages to fortune.

TOMLIN Lily
11744
We're all in this together - by ourselves.

TOMLINSON H.M. 1873-1958
11745
I do not love the sea. The look of it is disquieting. There is something in the very sound of it that stirs the premonition felt while we listen to noble music; we become inexplicably troubled.

TOPLADY Augustus Montague 1740-1778
11746 *'Rock of Ages, cleft for me'*
Rock of Ages, cleft for me,
Let me hide myself in Thee.

TOSCANINI Arturo 1867-1957
11747
When I was very young, I kissed my first woman, and smoked my first cigarette on the same day. Believe me, never since have I wasted any more time on tobacco.

TOUSSENEL A.
11748 *L'Esprit des bêtes*
The more one gets to know of men, the more one values dogs.

TOWNSHEND Pete 1945-
11749
The critical moment for you as a teenager is when you realise you're on your own.

11750 *'My Generation'*
Hope I die before I get old.

TOYNBEE Arnold 1889-1975
11751
We have been God-like in our planned breeding of our domestic plants and animals, but rabbit-like in our unplanned breeding of ourselves.

11752
We are in the first age since the dawn of civilization in which people have dared to think it practicable to make the benefits of civilization available to the whole human race.

11753
To be able to fill leisure intelligently is the last product of civilization.

11754
Civilization is a movement - not a condition; a voyage - not a harbour.

11755
The history of almost every civilization furnishes examples of geographical expansion coinciding with deterioration in quality.

TRAHERNE Thomas c.1637-1674
11756 *Centuries of Meditations 'First Century'*
An empty book is like an infant's soul, in which anything may be written. It is capable of all things, but containeth nothing.

11757 *Centuries of Meditations 'First Century'*
You never enjoy the world aright, till the sea itself floweth in your veins, till you are clothed with the heavens, and crowned with the stars: and perceive yourself to be the sole heir of the whole world.

11758 *Centuries of Meditations 'Third Century'*
The green trees when I saw them first ... transported and ravished me, their sweetness and unusual beauty made my heart to leap and almost mad with ecstasy, they were such strange and wonderful things.

11759 *'Wonder'*
I within did flow
With seas of life, like wine.
I nothing in this world did know,
But 'twas divine!

TRAILL Henry Duff 1842-1900
11760 *'After Dilettante Concetti'*
Look in my face. My name is Used-to-was;
I am also called Played-out and Done-to-death,
And It-will-wash-no-more.

TRAPP Joseph 1679-1747
11761 *(of George I's donation of Library to Cambridge)*
The King, observing with judicious eyes
The state of both his universities,
To Oxford sent a troop of horse, and why?
That learned body wanted loyalty;
To Cambridge books, as very well discerning

How much that loyal body wanted learning.

TRAVIS Merle 1917-1983
11762 *'Sixteen Tons'*
Sixteen tons, what do you get?
Another day older and deeper in debt.
Say brother, don't you call me 'cause I can't go
I owe my soul to the company store.

TREE Sir Herbert Beerbohm 1852-1917
11763 *(to females assembled to play ladies-in-waiting)*
Ladies, just a little more virginity, if you don't mind.

11764 *(of Israel Zangwill)*
He is an old bore. Even the grave yawns for him.

11765 *(pressed by gramophone company for testimonial)*
Sirs, I have tested your machine. It adds a new terror to life and makes death a long-felt want.

TRENCH Herbert 1865-1923
11766
Come, let us make love deathless.

TRENT Lord 1889-1956
11767
As I learnt very early in my life in Whitehall, the acid test of any political question is: What is the alternative?

TREVELYAN G.M. 1876-1962
11768 *English Social History*
Disinterested intellectual curiosity is the life-blood of real civilization.

11769 *English Social History*
If the French noblesse had been capable of playing cricket with their peasants, their chateaux would never have been burnt.

11770 *English Social History*
It [education] has produced a vast population able to read but unable to distinguish what is worth reading.

TREVOR William 1928-
11771 *(of the troubles in Northern Ireland)*
A disease in the family that is never mentioned.

TRIBE Laurence H.
11772
An excess of law inescapably weakens the rule of law.

TRILLIN Calvin
11773 *(attributed)*
The shelf life of the modern hardback writer is somewhere between the milk and the yoghurt.

TRILLING Lionel 1905-1975
11774
It is now life and not art that requires the willing suspension of disbelief.

TRINDER Tommy 1909-1989
11775 *(of American troops in Britain during World War 2)*
Overpaid, overfed, oversexed, and over here.

TROLLOPE Anthony 1815-1882
11776
There is no villainy to which education cannot reconcile us.

11777 *Autobiography*
He must have known me had he seen me as he was wont to see me, for he was in the habit of flogging me constantly. Perhaps he did not recognize me by my face.

11778 *Autobiography*
Take away from English authors their copyrights, and you would very soon take away from England her authors.

11779 *Autobiography*
Three hours a day will produce as much as a man ought to write.

11780 *Ayala's Angel*
A man's mind will very generally refuse to make itself up until it be driven and compelled by emergency.

11781 *Barchester Towers*
... She well knew the great architectural secret of decorating her constructions, and never descended to construct a decoration.

11782 *The Bertrams*
Those who have courage to love should have courage to suffer.

11783 *Doctor Thorne*
There is no road to wealth so easy and respectable as that of matrimony.

11784 *Doctor Thorne*
Let no man boast himself that he has got through the perils of winter till at least the seventh of May.

11785 *Miss Mackenzie*
If you wish to get the sweetest fragrance from the herb at your feet, tread on it and bruise it.

11786 *Orley Farm*
It is because we put up with bad things that hotel-keepers continue to give them to us.

11787 *Orley Farm*
As for conceit, what man will do any good who is not conceited? Nobody holds a good opinion of a man who has a low opinion of himself.

11788 *Phineas Finn*
She knew how to allure by denying, and to make the gift rich by delaying it.

11789 *Phineas Redux*
What man thinks of changing himself so as to suit his wife? And yet men expect that women shall put on altogether new characters when they are married, and girls think that they can do so.

11790 *The Small House at Allington*
I doubt whether any girl would be satisfied with her lover's mind if she knew the whole of it.

11791 *The Warden*
The tenth Muse, who now governs the periodical press.

11792 *The Way We Live Now*
Love is like any other luxury. You have no right to it unless you can afford it.

TROLLOPE Joanna 1943-
11793
The middleclass is the backbone of England. In intellectual circles that's been absolutely unsayable.

TRONCHIN Théodore 1709-1781
11794
In medicine, sins of commission are mortal, sins of omission venial.

TROTSKY Leon 1879-1940
11795
Not believing in force is the same as not believing in gravitation.

11796 *Diary in Exile*
Old age is the most unexpected of all things that happen to a man.

11797 *History of the Russian Revolution*
Civilization has made the peasantry its pack animal. The bourgeoisie in the long run only changed the form of the pack.

11798 *History of the Russian Revolution*
You [the Mensheviks] are pitiful isolated individuals; you are bankrupts; your role is played out. Go where you belong from now on - into the dustbin of history!

11799 *What Next?*
Where force is necessary, there it must be applied boldly, decisively and completely. But one must know the limitations of force; one must know when to blend force with a manoeuvre, a blow with an agreement.

TROTTER Wilfred 1951-
11800
Disease often tells its secrets in a casual parenthesis.

TROUBRIDGE St Vincent 1895-1963
11801
There is an iron curtain across Europe.

TRUDEAU Pierre Elliott 1919-
11802
Living next to the United States is in some ways like sleeping with an elephant. No matter how friendly and even-tempered is the beast, one is affected by every twitch and grunt.

11803
Canada is not a country for the cold of heart or the cold of feet.

11804
The democracy which embodies and guarantees our freedom is not powerless, passive or blind, nor is it in retreat. It has no intention of giving way to the savage fantasies of its adversaries. It is not prepared to give advance blessing to its own destruction.

11805
The essential ingredient of politics is timing.

11806
In academic life you seek to state absolute truths; in politics you seek to accommodate truth to the facts around you.

11807
Power only tires those who don't exercise it.

TRUDELL Dennis
11808
Sloppy, raggedy-assed old life. I love it. I never want to die.

TRUMAN Harry S. 1884-1972
11809
Democracy is based on the conviction that man has the moral and intellectual capacity, as well as the inalienable right, to govern himself with reason and justice.

11810
The president is the representative of the whole nation and he's the only lobbyist that all the one hundred and sixty million people in this country have.

11811
Well, I wouldn't say that I was in the 'great' class, but I had a great time while I was trying to be great.

11812
Within the first few months I discovered that being a president is like riding a tiger. A man has to keep riding or be swallowed.

11813
Wherever you have an efficient government you have a dictatorship.

11814
I never give them [the public] hell. I just tell the truth, and they think it is hell.

11815
A politician is a man who understands government, and it takes a politician to run a government.
A statesman is a politician who's been dead 10 or 15 years.

11816
It's a recession when your neighbour loses his job; it's a depression when you lose yours.

11817 *(attributed)*
Always be sincere, even if you don't mean it.

11818 *Letter to his sister*
All the President is, is a glorified public relations man who spends his time flattering, kissing and kicking people to get them to do what they are supposed to do anyway.

TUCHMAN Barbara W. 1912-1989
11819
War is the unfolding of miscalculations.

11820 *August 1914*
Dead battles, like dead generals, hold the military mind in their dead grip and Germans, no less than other peoples, prepare for the last war.

11821 *August 1914*
No more distressing moment can ever face a British government than that which requires it to come to a hard, fast and specific decision.

11822 *August 1914*
For one August in its history Paris was French - and silent.

TUCKER Antony fl. 1653-1661
11823 *(attributed, whilst Master of St. John's College, Oxford)*
With their godliness they may deceive me, with their learning they cannot.

TUCKER Sophie 1884-1966
11824
From birth to 18 a girl needs good parents. From 18 to 35, she needs good looks. From 35 to 55, good personality. From 55 on, she needs good cash.

TUER A.W. 1838-1900
11825 *(title of Portuguese-English conversational guide)*
English as she is Spoke.

TUPPER Martin 1810-1889
11826 *Proverbial Philosophy 'Of Reading'*
A good book is the best of friends, the same to-day and for ever.

TURGENEV Ivan 1818-1823
11827 *Fathers and Sons*
Nature is not a temple, but a workshop, and man's the workman in it.

11828 *Fathers and Sons*
I share no one's ideas. I have my own.

11829 *Fathers and Sons*
Just try and set death aside. It sets you aside, and that's the end of it!

11830 *Fathers and Sons*
Whatever a man prays for, he prays for a miracle. Every prayer reduces itself to this: Great God, grant that twice two be not four.

TURNER Walter James Redfern 1889-1946
11831 *'Romance'*
When I was but thirteen or so
I went into a golden land,
Chimborazo, Cotopaxi
Took me by the hand.

TUSSER Thomas c.1524-1580
11832 *Five Hundred Points of Good Husbandry*
At Christmas play and make good cheer,
For Christmas comes but once a year.

11833 *Five Hundred Points of Good Husbandry*
Who goeth a-borrowing
Goeth a-sorrowing.
Few lend (but fools)
Their working tools.

11834 *Five Hundred Points of Good Husbandry*
In doing of either, let wit bear a stroke,
For buying or selling of pig in a poke.

11835 *Five Hundred Points of Good Husbandry*
Some respite to husbands the weather may send,
But housewives' affairs have never an end.

11836 *Five Hundred Points of Good Husbandry*
Seek home for rest,
For home is best.

TWAIN Mark 1835-1910
11837
Noise proves nothing. Often a hen who has merely laid an egg cackles as if she had laid an asteroid.

11838
Put all thine eggs in one basket and - watch that basket.

11839
Fewer things are harder to put up with than the annoyance of a good example.

11840
That kind of so-called housekeeping where they have six Bibles and no cork-screw.

11841
The man who does not read good books has no advantage over the man who can't read them.

11842
Fame is a vapour, popularity an accident; the only earthly certainty is oblivion.

11843
Everyone is a moon and has a dark side which he never shows to anybody.

11844
I was born modest; not all over, but in spots.

11845
Ethical man - a Christian holding four aces.

11846
There are those who would misteach us that to stick in a rut is consistency - and a virtue, and that to climb out of the rut is inconsistency - and a vice.

11847
Courage is resistance to fear, mastery of fear, not absence of fear.

11848
Tomorrow night I appear for the first time before a Boston audience - 4000 critics.

11849
The reports of my death are greatly exaggerated.

11850
The human race is a race of cowards; and I am not only marching in that procession but carrying a banner.

11851
Let us be thankful for the fools. But for them the rest of us could not succeed.

11852
We may not pay Satan reverence, for that would be indiscreet, but we can at least respect his talents.

11853
It is better to deserve honours and not have them than to have them and not deserve them.

11854
Life would be infinitely happier if we could only be born at the age of eighty and gradually approach eighteen.

11855
Biographies are but the clothes and buttons of the man - the biography of the man himself cannot be written.

11856
It isn't so astonishing, the number of things that I can remember, as the number of things I can remember that aren't so.

11857
In his private heart no man much respects himself.

11858
Make money and the whole world will conspire to call you a gentleman.

11859
Richard Wagner, a musician who wrote music which is better than it sounds.

11860
What a good thing Adam had - when he said a good thing, he knew nobody had said it before.

11861
Each man must for himself alone decide what is right and what is wrong, which course is patriotic and which isn't. You cannot shirk this and be a man.

11862
The Creator made Italy with designs by Michelangelo.

11863
I can live for two months on a good compliment.

11864
In prayer we call ourselves 'worms of the dust', but it is only on a sort of tacit understanding that the remark shall not be taken at par.

11865
In certain trying circumstances, urgent circumstances, desperate circumstances, profanity furnishes a relief denied even to prayer.

11866
We are chameleons, and our partialities and prejudices change places with an easy and blessed facility.

11867
Get your facts first, and then you can distort 'em as much as you please.

11868
When we remember that we are all mad, the mysteries disappear and life stands explained.

11869
The pause - that impressive silence, that eloquent silence, that geometrically progressive silence which often achieves a desired effect where no combination of words, howsoever felicitous, could accomplish it.

11870
Golf is a good walk spoiled.

11871
Travel is fatal to prejudice, bigotry and narrow-mindedness.

11872
There is no unhappiness like the misery of sighting land again after a cheerful, careless voyage.

11873
If you tell the truth you don't have to remember anything.

11874
I am opposed to millionaires, but it would be dangerous to offer me the position.

11875
I wish to become rich, so that I can instruct the people and glorify honest poverty a little, like those kind-hearted, fat, benevolent people do.

11876
We should be careful to get out of an experience only the wisdom that is in it - and stop there, lest we be like the cat that sits down on a hot stove-lid. She will never sit down on a hot stove-lid again - and that is well; but also she will never sit down on a cold one anymore.

11877
Wit is the sudden marriage of ideas which, before their union, were not perceived to have any relation.

11878
The difference between the right word and the almost right word is the difference between lightning and the lightning bug.

11879
In Paris they simply stared when I spoke to them in French; I never did succeed in making those idiots understand their own language.

11880
I conceive that the right way to write a story for boys is to write so that it will not only interest boys but strongly interest any man who has ever been a boy. That immensely enlarges the audience.

11881
When I was a boy of fourteen, my father was so ignorant I could hardly stand to have the old man around. But when I got to be twenty-one, I was astonished at how much the old man had learned in seven years.

11882
When I was younger, I could remember anything, whether it had happened or not.

11883
Consider well the proportion of things. It is better to be a young June bug, than an old bird of paradise.

11884 *The Adventures of Huckleberry Finn*
There was things which he stretched, but mainly he told the truth.

11885 *The Adventures of Huckleberry Finn*
'Pilgrim's Progress', about a man that left his family, it didn't say why ... The statement was interesting, but tough.

11886 *The Adventures of Huckleberry Finn*
All kings is mostly rapscallions.

11887 *The Adventures of Huckleberry Finn*
Hain't we got all the fools in town on our side? and ain't that a big enough majority in any town.

11888 *A Curious Dream 'Facts concerning...'*
Soap and education are not as sudden as a massacre, but they are more deadly in the long run.

11889 *A Curious Dream 'A Mysterious Visit'*
Barring that natural expression of villainy which we all have, the man looked honest enough.

11890 *Following the Equator*
Truth is the most valuable thing we have. Let us economize it.

11891 *Following the Equator*
It is by the goodness of God that in our country we have those three unspeakably precious things: freedom of speech, freedom of conscience, and the prudence never to practise either of them.

11892 *Following the Equator*
Man is the Only Animal that Blushes. Or needs to.

11893 *Following the Equator*
There are several good protections against temptations, but the surest is cowardice.

11894 *Following the Equator*
It takes your enemy and your friend, working together, to hurt you to the heart: the one to slander you and the other to get the news to you.

11895 *The Innocents Abroad*
They spell it Vinci and pronounce it Vinchy; foreigners always spell better than they pronounce.

11896 *Notebooks*
Familiarity breeds contempt - and children.

11897 *Notebooks*
Good breeding consists in concealing how much we think of ourselves and how little we think of the other person.

11898 *Pudd'nhead Wilson*
Cauliflower is nothing but cabbage with a college education.

11899 *Pudd'nhead Wilson*
When angry, count four; when very angry, swear.

11900 *Pudd'nhead Wilson*
As to the Adjective: when in doubt, strike it out.

TYNAN Kenneth 1927-1980
11901
The unique thing about Margaret Rutherford is that she can act with her chin alone. Among its many moods I especially cherish the chin commanding, the chin in doubt, and the chin at bay.

11902
A critic is a man who knows the way but can't drive the car.

11903
All of life is more or less what the French would call '*s'imposer*' - to be able to create one's own terms for what one does.

11904
A neurosis is a secret you don't know you're keeping.

11905
What, when drunk, one sees in other women, one sees in Garbo sober.

11906 *Curtains (of Noel Coward)*
Forty years ago he was Slightly in *Peter Pan*, and you might say that he has been wholly in *Peter Pan* ever since.

11907 *Tynan Right and Left*
Drama criticism ... [is] a self-knowing account of the way in which one's consciousness has been modified during an evening in the theatre.

TZU-SUN
11908
If you know the enemy and know yourself you need not fear the results of a hundred battles.

11909
The supreme excellence is not to win a hundred victories in a hundred battles. The supreme excellence is to subdue the armies of your enemies without even having to fight them.

UDALL Steward
11910
Gross National Product is our Holy Grail.

UDKOFF Bob
11911
Hate is such a luxurious emotion, it can only be spent on one we love.

UNDERHILL Frank
11912
A nation is a body of people who have done great things together in the past and hope to do great things together in the future.

UNRUH Jesse
11913
Money is the mother's milk of politics.

UPDIKE John 1932-
11914
The Englishman is under no constitutional obligation to believe that all men are created equal. The American agony is therefore scarcely intelligible, like a saint's self-flagellation viewed by an atheist.

11915
Every marriage tends to consist of an aristocrat and a peasant, of a teacher and a learner.

11916
Russia is the only country of the world you can be homesick for while you're still in it.

11917
The artist brings something into the world that didn't exist before, and ... he does it without destroying something else.

11918 *Assorted Prose 'Confessions of a Wild Bore'*
A healthy male adult bore consumes *each year* one and a half times his own weight in other people's patience.

11919 *Assorted Prose 'More Love ... Western World'*
The heart *prefers* to move against the grain of circumstance; perversity is the soul's very life.

11920 *Picked Up Pieces (of England)*
A soggy little island huffing and puffing to keep up with Western Europe.

11921 *Picked Up Pieces 'London Life'*
America is a land whose centre is nowhere; England one whose centre is everywhere.

11922 *Problems 'How to love America ...'*
America is a vast conspiracy to make you happy.

USTINOV Sir Peter 1921-
11923
By increasing the size of the keyhole, today's playwrights are in danger of doing away with the door.

11924
Comedy is simply a funny way of being serious.

11925
Parents are the bones on which children cut their teeth.

11926
Laughter would be bereaved if snobbery died.

11927
If Botticelli were alive today he'd be working for *Vogue*.

11928
Love is an act of endless forgiveness; a tender look that becomes a habit.

11929 *Dear Me*
Laughter ... the most civilized music in the world.

11930 *Dear Me*
I do not believe that friends are necessarily the people you like best, they are merely the people who got there first.

11931 *(on imitating Harold Macmillan - attributed)*
Talk as though you have a cathedral in your mouth.

11932 *Romanoff and Juliet*
At the age of four with paper hats and wooden swords we're all Generals. Only some of us never grow out of it.

11933 *Romanoff and Juliet*
This is a free country, madam. We have a right to share your privacy in a public place.

VADIM Roger 1928-
11934
Youth has become a class.

VALENTINE Alan
11935
Whenever science makes a discovery, the devil grabs it while the angels are debating the best way to use it.

VALERIUS MAXIMUS fl. AD c.15
11936 *Facta et Dicta Memorabilia*
I appeal from Philip drunk to Philip sober.

VALÉRY Paul 1871-1945
11937
An artist never really finishes his work, he merely abandons it.

11938
A businessman is a hybrid of a dancer and a calculator.

11939
Conscience reigns but it does not govern.

11940
History is the science of what never happens twice.

11941
If some great catastrophe is not announced every morning, we feel a certain void. 'Nothing in the paper today,' we sigh.

11942
Peace is a virtual, mute, sustained victory of potential powers against probable greeds.

11943
To penetrate one's being, one must go armed to the teeth.

11944 *Littérature*
A poem is never finished; it's always an accident that puts a stop to it - that is to say, gives it to the public.

11945 *Moralités*
Science means simply the aggregate of all the recipes that are always successful. The rest is literature.

11946 *Tel Quel 1 'Moralités'*
God created man and, finding him not sufficiently alone, gave him a companion to make him feel his solitude more keenly.

11947 *Tel Quel 2 'Rhumbs'*
Politics is the art of preventing people from taking part in affairs which properly concern them.

VAN GOGH Vincent 1853-1890
11948
One may have a blazing hearth in one's soul, and yet no one ever comes to sit by it.

11949
As a painter I shall never signify anything of importance. I feel it absolutely.

11950
I dream my painting, and then I paint my dream.

11951
It's as interesting and as difficult to say a thing well as to paint it. There is the art of lines and colours, but the art of words exists too, and will never be less important.

VAN HORNE William 1843-1915
11952
The biggest things are always the easiest to do because there is no competition.

VAN MILDERT Bishop
11953
Want of friends argues either want of humility or of courage, or both.

VANBRUGH Sir John 1664-1726
11954
The want of a thing is perplexing enough, but the possession of it is intolerable.

11955 *The Provoked Husband*
Much of a muchness.

11956 *The Relapse*
When once a woman has given you her heart, you can never get rid of the rest of her body.

11957 *The Relapse*
In matters of love men's eyes are always bigger than their bellies. They have violent appetites, 'tis true; but they have soon dined.

VAUGHAN Bill
11958
One trouble with growing older is that it gets progressively tougher to find a famous historical figure who didn't amount to much when he was your age.

11959
Occasionally we sigh for an earlier day when we could just look at the stars without worrying whether they were theirs or ours.

VAUGHAN Harry
11960
If you can't stand the heat, get out of the kitchen.

VAUGHAN Henry 1622-1695
11961
Caesar had perished from the world of men
Had not his sword been rescued by his pen.

11962 *Silex Scintillans 'They are all gone'*
They are all gone into the world of light,
And I alone sit lingering here;
Their very memory is fair and bright,
And my sad thoughts doth clear.

11963 *Silex Scintillans 'They are all gone'*
I see them walking in an air of glory,
Whose light doth trample on my days.

11964 *Silex Scintillans 'They are all gone'*
Dear, beauteous death! the jewel of the just,
Shining nowhere but in the dark.

11965 *Silex Scintillans 'Man'*
Man is the shuttle, to whose winding quest
And passage through these looms
God ordered motion, but ordained no rest.

11966 *Silex Scintillans 'Peace'*
My soul, there is a country
Far beyond the stars,
Where stands a wingèd sentry
All skilful in the wars;
There, above noise and danger,
Sweet Peace is crowned with smiles,
And One born in a manger
Commands the beauteous files.

11967 *Silex Scintillans 'The Retreat'*
Happy those early days, when I
Shined in my angel-infancy.
Before I understood this place
Appointed for my second race,
Or taught my soul to fancy aught
But a white, celestial thought.

11968 *Silex Scintillans 'The Retreat'*
And in those weaker glories spy
Some shadows of eternity.

11969 *Silex Scintillans 'The Retreat'*
But felt through all this fleshly dress
Bright shoots of everlastingness.

11970 *Silex Scintillans 'The World'*
I saw Eternity the other night,
Like a great ring of pure and endless light,

All calm, as it was bright.

11971 *Silex Scintillans 'The World'*
And round beneath it, Time in hours, days, years,
Driv'n by the spheres
Like a vast shadow moved; in which the world
And all her train were hurled.

VAUGHAN Sam
11972
The editorial job has become, unlike the ancient age when one judged what one read, a job of making judgements on outlines, ideas, reputations, previous books, scenarios, treatments, talk and promises.

VAUVENARGUES Marquis de 1715-1747
11973
To achieve great things, we must live as though we were never going to die.

11974
The most absurd and reckless aspirations have sometimes led to extraordinary success.

11975
The mind reaches great heights only by spurts.

11976
The lazy are always wanting to do something.

11977
All men are born truthful, and die liars.

11978
When we are sick our virtues and our vices are in abeyance.

11979
If virtue were its own reward, it would no longer be a human quality, but supernatural.

11980
Vice stirs up war; virtue fights.

VAUX Thomas 1510-1556
11981 *'The Aged Lover Renounceth Love'*
For age with stealing steps
Hath clawed me with his clutch,
And lusty life away she leaps,

As there had been none such.

VEBLEN Thorsten 1857-1929
11982
All business sagacity reduces itself in the last analysis to a judicious use of sabotage.

11983
Conservatism is the maintenance of conventions already in force.

11984
In order to stand well in the eyes of the community, it is necessary to come up to a certain, somewhat indefinite, conventional standard of wealth.

VEGETIUS AD 379-395
11985
Let him who desires peace, prepare for war.

VERGNIAUD Pierre 1753-1793
11986
There was reason to fear that the Revolution, like Saturn, might devour in turn each one of her children.

VERLAINE Paul 1844-1896
11987 *'Art poétique'*
All the rest is mere fine writing.

11988 *'Chanson d'Automne'*
The drawn-out sobs of autumn's violins wound my heart with a monotonous languor.

11989 *Romances sans paroles 'Ariettes oubliées'*
Tears are shed in my heart like the rain on the town.

VESPASIAN AD 9-79
11990 *(replying to objection to tax public lavatories)*
Money has no smell.

11991 *(when fatally ill)*
Woe is me, I think I am becoming a god.

VICTORIA Queen 1819-1901
11992
The important thing is not what they think of me, it is what I think of them.

11993 *(attributed)*
We are not amused.

11994 *(on the Boer War during 'Black Week')*
We are not interested in the possibilities of
defeat; they do not exist.

11995 *(of Gladstone)*
He speaks to me as if I was a public
meeting.

11996 *(on Gladstone's last appointment as
P.M.)*
The danger to the country, to Europe, to
her vast Empire, which is involved in
having all these great interests entrusted to
the shaking hand of an old, wild, and
incomprehensible man of 82, is very great!

11997 *(on being shown a chart of the line of
succession)*
I will be good.

11998 *(of St Paul's Cathedral)*
Dirty, dark, and undevotional.

VIDAL Gore 1925-
11999
A talent for drama is not a talent for
writing, but is an ability to articulate
human relationships.

12000
[Commercialism is] doing well that which
should not be done at all.

12001
I'm all for bringing back the birch, but only
between consenting adults.

12002
Whenever a friend succeeds, a little
something in me dies.

12003 *(of Ronald Regan)*
A triumph of the embalmer's art.

VIERA GALLO José Antonio 1943-
12004
Socialism can only arrive by bicycle.

VIGNY Alfred de 1797-1863
12005 *La Bouteille à la mer*
The true God, the mighty God, is the God
of ideas.

12006 *La Maison du Berger*
I love the majesty of human suffering.

12007 *La Mort du loup*
Only silence is great; all else is weakness.

12008 *Moïse*
Alas, Lord, I am powerful but alone. Let
me sleep the sleep of the earth.

12009 *Servitude et grandeur militaire*
An army is a nation within a nation; it is
one of the vices of our age.

VILLARS Marshall de 1653-1734
12010
God save me from my friends - I can
protect myself from my enemies.

VILLIERS George 1628-1687
12011 *The Dramatic Works*
The world is made up for the most part of
fools and knaves, both irreconcilable foes
to truth.

12012 *The Rehearsal*
Ay, now the plot thickens very much upon
us.

**VILLIERS DE L'ISLE-ADAM Philippe-
Auguste 1838-1889**
12013 *Axël*
Living? The servants will do that for us.

VILLON François 1431-c.1465
12014 *Le Grand Testament 'Ballade des dames
du temps jadis'*
But where are the snows of yesteryear?

12015 *Le Grand Testament 'Ballade pour prier
Nostre Dame'*
In this faith I wish to live and to die.

**VINCENT Field Marshall Sir Richard
1931-**
12016
The first principle of war is: For God's sake
decide what you're trying to achieve
before you go out and start doing it.

VIRGIL 70-19 BC
12017 *Aeneid*
Trust one who has tried.

12018 *Aeneid*
I sing of arms and the man.

12019 *Aeneid*
Why such great anger in those heavenly
minds?

12020 *Aeneid*
So massive was the effort to found the Roman nation.

12021 *Aeneid*
Odd figures swimming were glimpsed in the waste of waters.

12022 *Aeneid*
O you who have borne even heavier things, God will grant an end to these too.

12023 *Aeneid*
Maybe one day it will be cheering to remember even these things.

12024 *Aeneid*
No stranger to trouble myself I am learning to care for the unhappy.

12025 *Aeneid*
Do not trust the horse, Trojans. Whatever it is, I fear the Greeks even when they bring gifts.

12026 *Aeneid*
From the one crime recognize all as culprits.

12027 *Aeneid*
The only safe course for the defeated is to expect no safety.

12028 *Aeneid*
The gods thought otherwise.

12029 *Aeneid*
To what do you not drive human hearts, cursed craving for gold!

12030 *Aeneid*
Fickle and changeable always is woman.

12031 *Aeneid*
Rise up from my dead bones, avenger!

12032 *Aeneid*
They can because they think they can.

12033 *Aeneid*
I see wars, horrible wars, and the Tiber foaming with much blood.

12034 *Aeneid*
Darkling they went under the lonely night through the shadow and through the empty dwellings and unsubstantial realms of Hades.

12035 *Aeneid*
If I am unable to make the gods above relent, I shall move Hell.

12036 *Aeneid*
Blessings on your young courage, boy; that's the way to the stars.

12037 *Aeneid*
Fortune assists the bold.

12038 *Aeneid*
Trust one who has gone through it.

12039 *Eclogues no.2*
Don't bank too much on your complexion, lovely boy.

12040 *Eclogues no.3*
There's a snake hidden in the grass.

12041 *Eclogues no.8*
Now I know what Love is.

12042 *Eclogues no.8*
We can't all do everything.

12043 *Eclogues no.10*
Love conquers all things: let us too give in to Love.

12044 *Georgics no.2 (of Lucretius)*
Lucky is he who has been able to understand the causes of things.

12045 *Georgics no.3*
Irretrievable time is flying.

VOLNEY Constantin, Comte de 1757-1820
12046
The first book of the nation is the dictionary of its language.

VOLTAIRE 1694-1778
12047
I advise you to go on living solely to enrage those who are paying your annuities. It is the only pleasure I have left.

12048
Weakness on both sides is, as we know, the motto of all quarrels.

12049
Ask a toad what is beauty? ... a female with two great round eyes coming out of

her little head, a large flat mouth, a yellow belly and a brown back.

12050
I know I am among civilized men because they are fighting so savagely.

12051
Originality is nothing but judicious imitation.

12052
Fear succeeds crime - it is its punishment.

12053
England has forty-two religions and only two sauces.

12054
What a heavy burden is a name that has become too famous.

12055
It is hard to free fools from the chains they revere.

12056
If God made us in his image, we have certainly returned the compliment.

12057
The best government is a benevolent tyranny tempered by an occasional assassination.

12058
Whoever serves his country well has no need of ancestors.

12059
All the ancient histories, as one of our wits has said, are but fables that have been agreed upon.

12060
We never live, but we are always in the expectation of living.

12061
When it is a question of money, everybody is of the same religion.

12062
Men argue, nature acts.

12063
We offer up prayers to God only because we have made Him after our own image.

We treat Him like a Pasha, or a Sultan, who is capable of being exasperated and appeased.

12064
Doubt is not a pleasant condition, but certainty is.

12065
I never was ruined but twice - once when I lost a lawsuit, and once when I gained one.

12066
Never having been able to succeed in the world, he took his revenge by speaking ill of it.

12067
There are truths that are not for all men, nor for all times.

12068
Work banishes those three great evils, boredom, vice, and poverty.

12069 *(attributed)*
I disapprove of what you say, but I will defend to the death your right to say it.

12070 *Candide*
In this best of possible worlds ... all is for the best. [usually quoted 'All is for the best in the best of all possible worlds.']

12071 *Candide*
If we do not find anything pleasant, at least we shall find something new.

12072 *Candide*
In this country [England] it is thought well to kill an admiral from time to time to encourage the others.

12073 *Candide*
We must cultivate our garden.

12074 *Candide*
The best is the enemy of the good.

12075 *Dialogues 'Le Chapon et la poularde'*
[Men] use thought only to justify their injustices, and speech only to conceal their thoughts.

12076 *Discours en vers sur l'homme 'De la nature'*
The secret of being a bore ... is to tell everything.

12077 *Épîtres 'A l'Auteur du livre des trois ...'*
If God did not exist, it would be necessary
to invent him.

12078 *Essai sur l'histoire générale...*
This agglomeration which was called and
which still calls itself the Holy Roman
Empire was neither holy, nor Roman, nor
an empire.

12079 *Le Mondain*
The superfluous, a very necessary thing.

12080 *L'Enfant prodigue*
All styles are good except the tiresome
kind.

12081 *L'Ingénu*
Indeed, history is nothing more than a
tableau of crimes and misfortunes.

12082 *The Piccini Notebooks*
Governments need both shepherds and
butchers.

12083 *The Piccini Notebooks*
God is on the side not of the heavy
battalions, but of the best shots.

12084 *'Première Lettre sur Oedipe'*
We owe respect to the living; to the dead
we owe only truth.

12085 *Thoughts of a Philosopher*
Marriage is the only adventure open to the
cowardly.

12086 *(when asked to renounce the Devil, on
deathbed)*
This is no time for making new enemies.

VONNEGUT Kurt 1922-
12087
Educating a beautiful woman is like
pouring honey into a fine Swiss watch:
everything stops.

VORSE Mary Heaton
12088
(Writing) - the art of applying the seat of
the pants to the seat of the chair.

VOZNESENKSY Andrei 1933-
12089
The times spat at me. I spit back at the
times.

WAGNER Robert 1930-
12090
As a parent you just hang on for the ride.

WALDERGRAVE William 1946-
12091
Much of Government's activity is more
like poker than chess. You don't put all
your cards on the table.

WALKER Alice 1944-
12092 *'We Have a Beautiful Mother'*
We have a beautiful
mother
Her green lap
immense
Her brown embrace
eternal
Her blue body
everything
we know.

12093 *'Expect nothing'*
Expect nothing. Live frugally
on surprise.

12094 *'Did This Happen To Your Mother? ...'*
... Needs grow too fast;
they come up like weeds.
Through cracks in the conversation.
Through silences in the dark.
Through everything you thought was
concrete.

12095 *'The QPP'*
The quietly pacifist peaceful
always die
to make room for men
who shout. Who tell lies to
children, and crush the corners
off of old men's dreams.

WALKER James J.
12096
A reformer is a guy who rides through a
sewer in a glass-bottomed boat.

WALL Max 1908-1990
12097
Show business is like sex. When it's
wonderful, it's wonderful. But when it
isn't very good, it's still all right.

WALLACE Edgar 1875-1932
12098
What is a highbrow? He is a man who has

found something more interesting than women.

WALLACE George 1919-
12099 (*inaugural speech as Governor of Alabama*)
Segregation now, segregation tomorrow and segregation forever!

WALLACE Henry 1888-1965
12100
The century on which we are entering - the century which will come out of this war - can be and must be the century of the common man.

WALLACE Joe
12101
Ours is a sovereign nation
Bows to no foreign will
But whenever they cough in Washington
They spit on Parliament Hill.

WALLACE Lew 1827-1905
12102 *The Prince of India*
Beauty is altogether in the eye of the beholder.

WALLACE William Ross 1819-1881
12103 *'What rules the world'*
For the hand that rocks the cradle
Is the hand that rules the world.

WALLAS Graham 1858-1932
12104 *The Art of Thought*
The little girl had the making of a poet in her who, being told to be sure of her meaning before she spoke, said, 'How can I know what I think till I see what I say?'

WALLER Edmund 1606-1687
12105
Vexed sailors curse the rain
For which poor shepherds prayed in vain.

12106 *'Of English Verse'*
Poets that lasting marble seek
Must carve in Latin or in Greek.

12107 *'On a Girdle'*
That which her slender waist confined
Shall now my joyful temples bind;
No monarch but would give his crown
His arms might do what this has done.

12108 *'Of the Last Verses in the Book'*
Leaving the old, both worlds at once they view,
That stand upon the threshold of the new.

12109 *'Go, lovely rose!'*
Go, lovely rose!
Tell her, that wastes her time and me,
That now she knows,
When I resemble her to thee,
How sweet and fair she seems to be.

12110 *'Panegyric to My Lord Protector'*
Rome, though her eagle through the world had flown,
Could never make this island all her own.

12111 *'Of a War with Spain'*
Others may use the ocean as their road,
Only the English make it their abode.

12112 *'To My Young Lady Lucy Sidney'*
Why came I so untimely forth
Into a world which, wanting thee,
Could entertain us with no worth,
Or shadow of felicity?

WALLPORT Gordon
12113
A mark of maturity seems to be the range and extent of one's feeling of self-involvement in abstract ideals.

WALPOLE Horace 1717-1797
12114
I am in a moment of pretty wellness.

12115
Virtue knows to a farthing what it has lost by not having been vice.

12116 *Letter to Anne, Countess of Upper Ossory*
This world is a comedy to those that think, a tragedy to those that feel.

12117 *Letter to Anne, Countess of Upper Ossory*
Tell me, ye divines, which is the most virtuous man, he who begets twenty bastards, or he who sacrifices an hundred thousand lives?

12118 *Letter to Caroline, Countess of Ailesbury*
When people will not weed their own

minds, they are apt to be overrun with nettles.

12119 *Letter to Chrisopher Wren*
One of the greatest geniuses that ever existed, Shakespeare, undoubtedly wanted taste.

12120 *Letter to George Montagu*
Every drop of ink in my pen ran cold.

12121 *Letter to George Montagu*
The best sun we have is made of Newcastle coal.

12122 *Letter to George Selwyn*
It is charming to totter into vogue.

12123 *Letter to Hon. Henry Conway*
But, thank God! the Thames is between me and the Duchess of Queensberry.

12124 *Letter to Sir Horace Mann*
Our supreme governors, the mob.

12125 *Letter to Sir Horace Mann*
When will the world know that peace and propagation are the two most delightful things in it?

12126 *Letter to Revd. William Cole*
The way to ensure summer in England is to have it framed and glazed in a comfortable room.

12127 *Memoirs of the Reign of King George II*
Whoever knows the interior of affairs, must be sensible to how many more events the faults of statesmen give birth, than are produced by their good intentions.

WALPOLE Sir Hugh 1884-1941
12128 *Fortitude*
'Tisn't life that matters! 'Tis the courage you bring to it.

WALPOLE Sir Robert 1676-1745
12129
I always tell a young man not to use the word `always'.

12130
The balance of power.

12131 *(on the declaration of war with Spain)*
They now *ring* the bells, but they will soon *wring* their hands.

12132 *(of fellow parliamentarians)*
All those men have their price.

WALSH William 1663-1708
12133 'The Despairing Lover'
A lover forsaken
A new love may get,
But a neck when once broken
Can never be set.

12134 'Song: Of All the Torments'
In love alone we hate to find
Companions of our woe.

12135 'Song: Of All the Torments'
I can endure my own despair,
But not another's hope.

WALTERS Barbara
12136
I can get a better grasp of what is going on in the world from one good Washington dinner party than from all the background information NBC piles on my desk.

WALTERS Maryanne
12137
The point of therapy is to get unhooked, not to thrash around on how you got hooked.

WALTON Izaak 1593-1683
12138
Of this blest man, let his just praise be given,
Heaven was in him, before he was in Heaven.

12139 *The Compleat Angler*
Good company and good discourse are the very sinews of virtue.

12140 *The Compleat Angler*
An excellent angler, and now with God.

12141 *The Compleat Angler*
I love such mirth as does not make friends ashamed to look upon one another next morning.

12142 *The Compleat Angler*
No man can lose what he never had.

12143 *The Compleat Angler*
Use him as though you loved him.

12144 *The Compleat Angler*
The dish of meat is too good for any but anglers, or very honest men.

12145 *The Compleat Angler 'Epistle to the Reader'*
Angling may be said to be so like the mathematics, that it can never be fully learnt.

12146 *The Compleat Angler 'Epistle to the Reader'*
As no man is born an artist, so no man is born an angler.

WANAMAKER Zöe
12147
Laughter can be an aphrodisiac, yet it can also be a substitute for sex.

WARBURTON William 1698-1779
12148 *(to Lord Sandwich)*
Orthodoxy is my doxy; heterodoxy is another man's doxy.

WARD Artemus 1834-1867
12149
Why don't you show us a statesman who can rise up to the emergency, and cave in the emergency's head?

12150 *Artemus Ward His Book 'Fourth of July Oration'*
I'm not a politician and my other habits are good.

12151 *Artemus Ward His Book 'The Showman's Courtship'*
I wish thar was winders to my Sole, sed I, so that you could see some of my feelins.

12152 *Artemus Ward His Book 'A Visit to Brigham Young'*
I girdid up my Lions & fled the Seen.

12153 *Artemus Ward His Book 'Woman's Rights'*
The female woman is one of the greatest institooshuns of which this land can boste.

12154 *Artemus Ward in London*
It is a pity that Chawcer, who had geneyus, was so unedicated. He's the wuss speller I know of.

12155 *Artemus Ward in London*
Let us all be happy, and live within our means, even if we have to borrer the money to do it with.

12156 *Artemus Ward's Lecture*
Why is this thus? What is the reason of this thusness?

12157 *Artemus Ward's Lecture 'Brigham Young's...'*
He is dreadfully married. He's the most married man I ever saw in my life.

WARD Nathaniel 1578-1652
12158 *Epigram*
The world is full of care, much like unto a bubble;
Woman and care, and care and women, and women and care and trouble.

WARD Thomas 1577-1639
12159 *England's Reformation*
Where to elect there is but one,
'Tis Hobson's choice, - take that or none.

WARE Eugene Fitch 1841-1911
12160
Work brings its own relief;
He who most idle is
Has most of grief.

WARHOL Andy 1927-1987
12161
Some day each of us will be famous for fifteen minutes.

12162
The most exciting thing is *not* doing it. If you fall in love with someone and never do it, it's much more exciting.

WARNER Charles Dudley 1829-1900
12163
It is one of the beautiful compensations of this life that no one can sincerely try to help another without helping himself.

12164
There isn't a wife in the world who has not taken the exact measure of her husband, weighed him and settled him in her own mind, and knows him as well as if she had ordered him after designs and specifications of her own.

WARNER H.M.
12165 *(of talking pictures - in 1927)*
Who the hell wants to hear actors talk?

WARNER Susan 1819-1885
12166 *The Love of Jesus*
Jesus loves me - this I know,
For the Bible tells me so.

WARREN Earl 1891-1974
12167
I'm very pleased with each advancing
year. It stems back to when I was forty. I
was a bit upset about reaching that
milestone, but an older friend consoled
me. 'Don't complain about growing old -
many people don't have that privilege.'

12168
We are now at the point where we must
decide whether we are to honour the
concept of a plural society which gains
strength through diversity, or whether we
are to have bitter fragmentation that will
result in perpetual tension and strife.

12169
The sports page records people's
accomplishments, the front page usually
records nothing but man's failures.

WARREN Robert Penn 1905-1989
12170
For what is a poem but a hazardous
attempt at self-understanding: it is the
deepest part of autobiography.

WASHINGTON George 1732-1799
12171
Government is not reason, it is not
eloquence - it is force.

12172
My movement to the chair of government
will be accompanied by feelings not unlike
those of a culprit who is going to the place
of execution.

12173
To persevere in one's duty and be silent, is
the best answer to calumny.

12174
I shall never ask, never refuse, nor ever
resign an office.

12175
I beg leave to assure the Congress that no
pecuniary consideration could have
tempted me to accept this arduous
employment at the expense of my
domestic ease and happiness. I do not
wish to make any profit from it.

12176
Few men have virtue to withstand the
highest bidder.

12177
I can't tell a lie, Pa; you know I can't tell a
lie. I did cut it with my hatchet.

12178 *General Orders*
The time is now near at hand which must
probably determine whether Americans
are to be freemen or slaves.

12179 *General Orders*
The fate of unborn millions will now
depend, under God, on the courage and
conduct of this army. Our cruel and
unrelenting enemy leaves us only the
choice of brave resistance, or the most
abject submission. We have, therefore, to
resolve to conquer or die.

12180 *President's Address*
'Tis our true policy to steer clear of
permanent alliances, with any portion of
the foreign world.

12181 *President's Address*
Let me ... warn you in the most solemn
manner against the baneful effects of the
spirit of party.

WASHINGTON Ned 1901-1976
12182 *'My Foolish Heart'*
There's a line between love and fascination
That's hard to see on an evening such as
this,
For they both give the very same sensation
When you're lost in the magic of a kiss.

12183 *(song from the film Pinocchio)*
Hi diddle dee dee (an actor's life for me).

WATKYNS Richard
12184
When I was born I did lament and cry
And now each day doth shew the reason
why.

WATKYNS Rowland c.1616-1664
12185 *'Antipathy'*
I love him not, but show no reason can
Wherefore, but this, *I do not love* the man.

WATSON Arthur K. 1867-1947
12186
Show me a man with both feet on the
ground and I'll show you a man who can't
put his pants on.

WATSON Thomas
12187 *(whilst Chairman of IBM in 1943)*
I think there's a world market for maybe
five computers.

WATSON William c.1559-1603
12188 *A Decacordon of Ten Quodlibeticall
Questions*
Let justice be done though the heavens fall.

WATSON Sir William 1858-1936
12189 *April*
April, April
Laugh thy girlish laughter;
Then, the moment after,
Weep thy girlish tears!

12190 *A Study in Contrasts*
The staid, conservative,
Came-over-with-the Conqueror type of
mind.

WATTENBERG Ben
12191
Like most successful politicians Clinton
has a coalition in his brain.

WATTS Isaac 1674-1748
12192
Let me be dressed fine as I will,
Flies, worms, and flowers, exceed me still.

12193 *Divine Songs for Children 'Against
Evil'*
One sickly sheep infects the flock,
And poisons all the rest.

12194 *Divine Songs for Children 'Against
Idleness'*
How doth the little busy bee
Improve each shining hour,
And gather honey all the day
From every opening flower!

12195 *Divine Songs for Children 'Against
Idleness'*
For Satan finds some mischief still
For idle hands to do.

12196 *Divine Songs for Children 'Against
Quarrelling'*
Let dogs delight to bark and bite,
For God hath made them so.

12197 *Divine Songs for Children 'Love
between Brothers'*
Birds in their little nests agree
And 'tis a shameful sight,
When children of one family
Fall out, and chide, and fight.

12198 *Divine Songs for Children 'The
Sluggard'*
'Tis the voice of the sluggard; I heard him
complain,
'You have waked me too soon, I must
slumber again'.
As the door on its hinges, so he on his bed,
Turns his sides and his shoulders and his
heavy head.

12199 *Hymns and Spiritual Songs
'Crucifixion ...'*
When I survey the wondrous cross
On which the prince of glory died,
My richest gain I count but loss,
And pour contempt on all my pride.

12200 *The Psalms of David Imitated Psalm 90*
Our God, our help in ages past
Our hope for years to come,
Our shelter from the stormy blast,
And our eternal home.

WAUGH Evelyn 1903-1966
12201
Winston Churchill is always expecting
rabbits to come out of an empty hat.

12202
Perhaps host and guest is really the
happiest relation for father and son.

12203
Punctuality is the virtue of the bored.

12204
Manners are especially the need of the
plain. The pretty can get away with
anything.

12205 *Decline and Fall*
I haven't been to sleep for over a year.
That's why I go to bed early. One needs
more rest if one doesn't sleep.

12206 *Decline and Fall*
Very hard for a man with a wig to keep
order.

12207 *Decline and Fall*
That's the public-school system all over.
They may kick you out, but they never let
you down.

12208 *The Loved One*
You never find an Englishman among the
under-dogs - except in England, of course.

12209 *'An Open Letter'*
Impotence and sodomy are socially O.K.
but birth control is flagrantly middle-class.

12210 *Scoop*
News is what a chap who doesn't care
much about anything wants to read. And
it's only news until he's read it. After that
it's dead.

12211 *Scoop*
I will not stand for being called a woman
in my own house.

12212 *Scoop*
Other nations use 'force'; we Britons alone
use 'Might'.

12213 *Vile Bodies*
All this fuss about sleeping together. For
physical pleasure I'd sooner go to my
dentist any day.

12214 *(asked what he did for his college)*
I drink for it.

WAVELL Lord 1883-1950
12215 *(attributed)*
(Love) is like a cigar. If it goes out, you
can light it again but it never tastes quite
the same.

WAYNE John 1907-1979
12216
Tomorrow is the most important thing in
life. Comes in to us at midnight very
clean. It's perfect when it arrives and it
puts itself in our hands and hopes we've
learnt something from yesterday.

12217 *in She wore a Yellow Ribbon*
"Never apologise and never explain. It's a
sign of weakness."

WEATHERLY Frederick 1848-1929
12218 *'The Old Brigade'*
Where are the boys of the old Brigade,
Who fought with us side by side?

12219 *'Roses of Picardy'*
Roses are flowering in Picardy,
But there's never a rose like you.

WEBB Sidney (Baron Passfield) 1859-
1947
12220
The inevitability of gradualness cannot fail
to be appreciated.

12221
Marriage is the waste-paper basket of the
emotions.

WEBER Max 1864-1920
12222 *Archiv für Sozialwissenschaft..*
The protestant ethic and the spirit of
capitalism.

12223 *'Politik als Beruf'*
The State is a relation of men dominating
men, a relation supported by means of
legitimate (i.e. considered to be legitimate)
violence.

12224 *'Politik als Beruf'*
The experience of the irrationality of the
world has been the driving force of all
religious revolution.

WEBSTER Daniel 1782-1852
12225
The people's government, made for the
people, made by the people, and
answerable to the people.

12226
Liberty *and* Union, now and forever, one
and inseparable.

12227
I was born an American; I will live an
American; I shall die an American.

12228
The past, at least, is secure.

12229 *(on completion of Bunker Hill Monument)*
Thank God, I - I also - am an American!

12230 *(on joining overcrowded legal profession)*
There is always room at the top.

WEBSTER John c.1580-c.1625
12231 *The Devil's Law-Case*
Vain the ambition of kings,
Who seek by trophies and dead things,
To leave a living name behind,
And weave but nets to catch the wind.

12232 *The Duchess of Malfi*
Unequal nature, to place women's hearts
So far upon the left side.

12233 *The Duchess of Malfi*
Why should only I ...
Be cased up, like a holy relic? I have youth
And a little beauty.

12234 *The Duchess of Malfi*
Raised by that curious engine, your white hand.

12235 *The Duchess of Malfi*
Glories, like glow-worms, afar off shine bright,
But looked to near, have neither heat nor light.

12236 *The Duchess of Malfi*
I know death hath ten thousand several doors
For men to take their exits.

12237 *The Duchess of Malfi*
Cover her face, mine eyes dazzle: she died young.

12238 *The Duchess of Malfi*
Physicians are like kings - they brook no contradiction.

12239 *The Duchess of Malfi*
We are merely the stars' tennis-balls, struck and bandied
Which way please them.

12240 *The White Devil*
Fortune's a right whore:
If she give aught, she deals it in small parcels,
That she may take away all at one swoop.

12241 *The White Devil*
Only the deep sense of some deathless shame.

12242 *The White Devil*
Cowardly dogs bark loudest.

12243 *The White Devil*
But keep the wolf far thence that's foe to men,
For with his nails he'll dig them up again.

12244 *The White Devil*
There's nothing of so infinite vexation
As man's own thoughts.

12245 *The White Devil*
I have caught
An everlasting cold; I have lost my voice
Most irrecoverably.

WEBSTER Noah 1758-1843
12246
Power is always right, weakness always wrong. Power is always insolent and despotic.

WEDGWOOD Josiah 1730-1795
12247 *(legend on Wedgwood cameo)*
Am I not a man and a brother.

WEEKS Edward
12248
To live with fear and not be afraid is the final test of maturity.

WEIL Simone 1909-1943
12249
Those who serve a cause are not those who love that cause. They are those who love the life which has to be led in order to serve it - except in the case of the very purest, and they are rare.

12250
A hateful act is the transference to others of the degradation we bear in ourselves.

12251
The intelligent man who is proud of his intelligence is like the condemned man who is proud of his large cell.

12252
All sins are attempts to fill voids.

12253
What a country calls its vital economic interests are not the things which enable its citizens to live, but the things which enable it to make war.

WEINBERGER Harry
12254
The greatest right in the world is the right to be wrong.

WEINREICH Max
12255
A language is a dialect with its own army and navy.

WEISSMULLER Johnny 1904-1984
12256 *(summing up his role in Tarzan)*
Me Tarzan, you Jane.

WEITZ John
12257
When a woman dresses up for an occasion, the man should become the black velvet pillow for the jewel.

WEIZMANN Chaim 1874-1952
12258
Miracles sometimes occur, but one has to work terribly hard for them.

WELCH Raquel 1940-
12259
The mind can also be an erogenous zone.

WELDON Fay 1931-
12260
Hell is not other people, hell is no other people.

WELLES Orson 1915-1985
12261
Every actor in his heart believes everything bad that's printed about him.

12262
A film is never really good unless the camera is an eye in the head of a poet.

12263 *(of the RKO studios)*
The biggest electric train set any boy ever had!

12264 *in The Third Man*
"In Italy for thirty years under the Borgias they had warfare, terror, murder, bloodshed - they produced Michelangelo, Leonardo da Vinci and the Renaissance. In Switzerland they had brotherly love, five hundred years of democracy and peace and what did that produce ...? The cuckoo clock."

WELLINGTON Duke of 1769-1852
12265
Nothing except a battle lost can be half so melancholy as a battle won.

12266 *(attributed)*
The battle of Waterloo was won on the playing fields of Eton.

12267
I used to say of him [Napoleon] that his presence on the field made the difference of forty thousand men.

12268
Ours [our army] is composed of the scum of the earth - the mere scum of the earth.

12269
Possible? Is anything impossible? Read the newspapers.

12270 *(advice to a new MP)*
Don't quote Latin; say what you have to say, and then sit down.

12271 *The Croker Papers*
All the business of war, and indeed all the business of life, is to endeavour to find out what you don't know by what you do; that's what I called 'guessing what was at the other side of the hill'.

12272 *(replying to a blackmail threat - attributed)*
Publish and be damned.

12273 *(attributed, on reviewing his troops)*
I don't know what effect these men will have on the enemy, but by God, they frighten *me*.

12274 *(on seeing the first Reformed Parliament)*
I never saw so many shocking bad hats in my life.

12275 *(of steam locomotives)*
I see no reason to suppose that these machines will ever force themselves into general use.

WELLS Carolyn 1869-1942
12276
We should live and learn; but by the time we've learned, it's too late to live.

WELLS C.M. 1908-
12277
All port tastes the same after lunch.

WELLS H.G. 1866-1946
12278
Advertising is legalized lying.

12279
To be honest, one must be inconsistent.

12280
Crude classifications and false generalizations are the curse of organized life.

12281
I want to go ahead of Father Time with a scythe of my own.

12282
The shape of things to come.

12283
The war that will end war.

12284 *The History of Mr Polly*
I'll make a gory mess of you. I'll cut bits orf you.

12285 *Kipps*
'I'm a Norfan, both sides,' he would explain, with the air of one who had seen trouble.

12286 *Kipps*
'I was thinking jest what a Rum Go everything is.'

12287 *The Outline of History*
Human history becomes more and more a race between education and catastrophe.

12288 *Select Conversations with an Uncle*
Bah! the thing is not a nose at all, but a bit of primordial chaos clapped on to my face.

12289 *The Wife of Sir Isaac Harman*
Moral indignation is jealousy with a halo.

WELTY Eudora 1909-
12290
Children, like animals, use all their senses to discover the world. Then artists come along and discover it the same way all over again.

WENDELL Barrett 1855-1921
12291
Words and sentences are subjects of revision; paragraphs and whole compositions are subjects of prevision.

WESKER Arnold 1932-
12292 *Chips with Everything*
It said 'Chips with everything'. Chips with every damn thing. You breed babies and you eat chips with everything.

12293 *Roots*
Education ent only books and music - it's asking questions, all the time. There are millions of us, all over the country, and no one, not one of us, is asking questions, we're all taking the easiest way out.

WESLEY Charles 1707-1788
12294 *'And can it be'*
Amazing love! How can it be
That thou, my God, shouldst die for me?

12295 *'Gentle Jesus ...'*
Gentle Jesus, meek and mild,
Look upon a little child;
Pity my simplicity,
Suffer me to come to thee.

12296 *'Hymn for Christmas'*
Hail, the heaven-born Prince of Peace!
Hail, the Sun of Righteousness!

WESLEY John 1703-1791
12297
Passion and prejudice govern the world; only under the name of reason.

12298
Beware you be not swallowed up in books! An ounce of love is worth a pound of knowledge.

12299 *Journal*
I went to America to convert the Indians; but oh, who shall convert me?

12300 *Journal*
I look upon all the world as my parish.

12301 *Journal*
I have this day lived fourscore years ...
God grant that I may never live to be
useless!

12302 *Letter to Miss March*
Though I am always in haste, I am never
in a hurry.

12303 *Sermons on Several Occasions*
I design plain truth for plain people.

WESLEY Samuel 1662-1735
12304 *'An Epistle to a Friend concerning
Poetry'*
Style is the dress of thought; a modest
dress,
Neat, but not gaudy, will true critics
please.

WEST Jessamyn
12305
Fiction reveals truth that reality obscures.

12306
It is very easy to forgive others their
mistakes. It takes more gut and gumption
to forgive them for having witnessed your
own.

WEST Mae 1892-1980
12307
When choosing between two evils, I
always like to take the one I've never tried
before.

12308
Too much of a good thing can be
wonderful.

12309
I used to be snow-white ... but I drifted.

12310 *(attributed)*
When I'm good, I'm very good, but when
I'm bad, I'm better.

12311
I generally avoid temptation unless I can't
resist it.

12312 *in Belle of the Nineties*
"A man in the house is worth two in the
street."

12313 *in Every Day's a Holiday*
"I always say, keep a diary and some day
it'll keep you."

12314 *in I'm No Angel*
"It's not the men in my life that counts -
it's the life in my men."

12315 *in Klondike Annie*
"Give a man a free hand and he'll try to
put it all over you."

12316 *in My Little Chickadee*
"Is that a gun in your pocket, or are you
just glad to see me?"

12317 *The Wit and Wisdom of Mae West*
When women go wrong, men go right
after them.

12318 *in She Done Him Wrong*
"Why don't you come up sometime, and
see me?" [usually quoted: 'Why don't you
come up and see me sometime?']

WEST Rebecca 1892-1983
12319 *There is No Conversation*
It is queer how it is always one's virtues
and not one's vices that precipitate one
into disaster.

12320 *(of Michael Arlen)*
Every other inch a gentleman.

12321 *The Salt of the Earth*
The point is that nobody likes having salt
rubbed into their wounds, even if it is the
salt of the earth.

WEST-MEADS Zelda 1947-
12322
For most people, infidelity feels like the
ultimate betrayal. Very few people can
cope with the thought of their partner
making love to, touching, and having
candlelight dinners with somebody else.

WESTCOTT Brooke Foss 1825-1901
12323
Great occasions do not make heroes or
cowards; they simply unveil them to the
eyes of men. Silently and imperceptibly, as
we wake or sleep, we grow strong or
weak; and at last some crisis shows what
we have become.

12324
What we can do for another is the test of powers; what we can suffer is the test of love.

WESTCOTT Edward Noyes 1846-1898
12325
They say a reasonable amount o' fleas is good for a dog - it keeps him from broodin' over bein' a dog mebbe.

12326
The only man who can change his mind is the man who's got one.

12327
I reckon there's as much human nature in some folks as there is in others, if not more.

WESTON Edward 1996-1958
12328
Art is based on order. The world is full of 'sloppy Bohemians' and their work betrays them.

WESTON R.P. and LEE Bert 1878-1936 and 1880-1947
12329 *'Good-bye-ee!'*
Good-bye-ee! - Good-bye-ee!
Wipe the tear, baby dear, from your eye-ee.
Tho' it's hard to part, I know,
I'll be tickled to death to go.
Don't cry-ee - don't sigh-ee!
There's a silver lining in the sky-ee!
Bonsoir, old thing! cheerio! chin-chin!
Nahpoo! Toodle-oo! Good-bye-ee!

WHARTON Edith 1862-1937
12330
In any really good subject, one has only to probe deep enough to come to tears.

12331 *The Descent of Man 'The Other Two'*
If he paid for each day's comfort with the small change of his illusions, he grew daily to value the comfort more and set less store upon the coin.

12332 *Ethan Frome*
People struggled on for years with 'troubles', but they almost always succumbed to 'complications'.

12333 *Xingu and Other Stories 'Xingu'*
Mrs Ballinger is one of the ladies who pursue Culture in bands, as though it were dangerous to meet it alone.

WHATELY Richard 1787-1863
12334 *Apophthegms*
Preach not because you have to say something, but because you have something to say.

12335 *Apophthegms*
Happiness is no laughing matter.

12336 *Apophthegms*
It is a folly to expect men to do all that they may reasonably be expected to do.

12337 *Apophthegms*
Honesty is the best policy; but he who is governed by that maxim is not an honest man.

12338 *(of 'Authorized Version' of The Bible)*
Never forget that this is *not* the Bible. This, gentlemen, is only a *translation* of the Bible.

12339 *Introductory lectures on Political Economy*
It is not that pearls fetch a high price *because* men have dived for them; but on the contrary, men dive for them because they fetch a high price.

WHEWELL William 1794-1866
12340 *Elementary Treatise on Mechanics*
Hence no force however great can stretch a cord however fine into an horizontal line which is accurately straight: there will always be a bending downwards.

12341 *Philosophy of the Inductive Sciences*
Man is the interpreter of nature, science the right interpretation.

WHISTLER James McNeill 1834-1903
12342
Two and two continue to make four, in spite of the whine of the amateur for three, or the cry of the critic for five.

12343
Nature is usually wrong.

12344
To say to the painter that Nature is to be taken as she is, is to say to the player that

he may sit on the piano.

12345 *(in his case against Ruskin)*
[Replying to the question 'For two days'
labour, you ask two hundred guineas?']
No, I ask it for the knowledge of a lifetime.

12346 *The Gentle Art of Making Enemies*
I am not arguing with you - I am telling
you.

12347 *(to a lady reminded of his work by a
'haze')*
Yes madam, Nature is creeping up.

12348 *Mr Whistler's 'Ten O'Clock'*
Art is upon the Town!

WHITE E.B. 1899-1985
12349
Reading is the work of the alert mind, is
demanding, and under ideal conditions
produces finally a sort of ecstasy. This
gives the experience of reading a sublimity
and power unequalled by any other form
of communication.

12350
Commuters give the city its tidal
restlessness, natives give it solidity and
continuity, but the settlers give it passion.

12351
At present, I am a sojourner in the city
again, but here in the green warmth of a
city backyard, I see only the countenance
of spring in the country.

12352
His words leap across rivers and
mountains, but his thoughts are still only
six inches long.

12353
Democracy is the recurrent suspicion that
more than half of the people are right more
than half of the time.

12354
Humour plays close to the big, hot fire,
which is the truth, and the reader feels the
heat.

12355
Humour can be dissected, as a frog can,
but the thing dies in the process.

12356
I liked to sail alone. The sea was the same
as a girl to me - I did not want anyone else
along.

12357
The first day of spring was once the time
for taking the young virgins into the fields,
there in dalliance to set an example in
fertility for Nature to follow. Now we just
set the clock an hour ahead and change the
oil in the crankcase.

12358
If the world were merely seductive, that
would be easy. If it were merely
challenging, that would be no problem.
But I rise in the morning torn between a
desire to improve (or save) the world and
a desire to enjoy (or savour) the world.
This makes it hard to plan the day.

12359
Advice to young writers who want to get
ahead without any annoying delays: don't
write about Man, write about a man.

12360 *'The Commuter'*
Commuter - one who spends his life
In riding to and from his wife;
A man who shaves and takes a train,
And then rides back to shave again.

WHITE H. Kirke 1785-1806
12361 *'Oft in danger, oft in woe'*
Oft in danger, oft in woe,
Onward, Christians, onward go;
Bear the toil, maintain the strife,
Strengthened with the Bread of Life.

WHITE John
12362
There are three kinds of people in the
world: those who can't stand Picasso,
those who can't stand Raphael and those
who've never heard of either of them.

WHITE Patrick 1912-1990
12363 *The Tree of Man*
Conversation is imperative if gaps are to
be filled, and old age, it is the last gap but
one.

WHITE Paul Dudley 1886-1973
12364
A vigorous five-mile walk will do more

good for an unhappy but otherwise healthy adult than all the medicine and psychology in the world.

WHITE T.H. 1906-1964
12365
The once and future king.

12366 *Farewell Victoria*
The Victorians had not been anxious to go away for the weekend. The Edwardians, on the contrary, were nomadic.

12367 *The Sword in the Stone*
But I unfortunately was born at the wrong end of time, and I have to live *backwards* from in front.

WHITE Theodore
12368
Quality - in its classic Greek sense - how to live with grace and intelligence, with bravery and mercy.

12369
There is no excitement anywhere in the world, short of war, to match the excitement of the American presidential campaign.

WHITE William Allen 1868-1944
12370 *(when Roosevelt retired from Presidential campaign)*
All dressed up, with nowhere to go.

WHITE William Hale 1831-1913
12371
Blessed are they who heal us of self-despisings. Of all services which can be done to man, I know of none more precious.

WHITEFIELD George
12372
It is better to wear out than to rust out.

WHITEHEAD Alfred North 1861-1947
12373
From the moment of birth we are immersed in action, and can only fitfully guide it by taking thought.

12374
The total absence of humour in the Bible is one of the most singular things in all literature.

12375
A civilized society is one that exhibits the five qualities of truth, beauty, adventure, art and peace.

12376
Not a sentence or a word is independent of the circumstances under which it is uttered.

12377
The factor in human life provocative of a noble discontent is the gradual emergence of a sense of criticism, founded upon appreciation of beauty, and of intellectual distinction, and of duty.

12378
Education with inert ideas is not only useless; it is above all things harmful.

12379
The antithesis between a technical and a liberal education is fallacious. There can be no adequate technical education which is not liberal, and no liberal education which is not technical.

12380
Ideas won't keep: something must be done about them.

12381
Not ignorance, but ignorance of ignorance is the death of knowledge.

12382
The only justification in the use of force is to reduce the amount of force necessary to be used.

12383
The major advances in civilization are processes which all but wreck the societies in which they occur.

12384
The art of progress is to preserve order amid change, and to preserve change amid order.

12385
A science which hesitates to forget its founders is lost.

12386
Vigorous societies harbour a certain extravagance of objectives.

12387
A man really writes for an audience of about ten persons. Of course if others like it, that is clear gain. But if those ten are satisfied, he is content.

12388
The deepest definition of youth is life as yet untouched by tragedy.

12389 *Adventures of Ideas*
Life is an offensive, directed against the repetitious mechanism of the Universe.

12390 *Dialogues*
Intelligence is quickness to apprehend as distinct from ability, which is capacity to act wisely on the thing apprehended.

12391 *Dialogues*
What is morality in any given time or place? It is what the majority then and there happen to like, and immorality is what they dislike.

12392 *Dialogues*
Art is the imposing of a pattern on experience, and our aesthetic enjoyment is recognition of the pattern.

12393 *Introduction to Mathematics*
Civilization advances by extending the number of important operations which we can perform without thinking about them.

12394 *Process and Reality*
The safest general characterization of the European philosophical tradition is that it consists of a series of footnotes to Plato.

12395 *(of scientific revolution in 16th Century)*
Since a babe was born in a manger, it may be doubted whether so great a thing has happened with so little stir.

WHITEHORN Katharine 1926-
12396 *Roundabout 'The Office Party'*
Bringing down the mighty from their seats is an agreeable and necessary pastime, but no one supposes that the mighty, having struggled so hard to get seated, will enjoy the dethronement.

12397 *Shouts and Murmurs 'Hats'*
Hats divide generally into three classes: offensive hats, defensive hats, and shrapnel.

12398 *Sunday Best 'Decoding the West'*
I wouldn't say when you've seen one Western you've seen the lot; but when you've seen the lot you get the feeling you've seen one.

WHITMAN Walt 1819-1892
12399
The dirtiest book of all is the expurgated book.

12400
It is native personality, and that alone, that endows a man to stand before presidents or generals, or in any distinguished collection, with aplomb - and not culture, or any intellect whatever.

12401
There is that indescribable freshness and unconsciousness about an illiterate person that humbles and mocks the power of the noblest expressive genius.

12402
To have great poets there must be great audiences too.

12403
I am as bad as the worst, but, thank God, I am as good as the best.

12404
Do I contradict myself?
Very well, then I contradict myself,
I am large, I contain multitudes.

12405
Out of every fruition of success, no matter what, comes forth something to make a new effort necessary.

12406
I sing the body electric.

12407 *'Out of the cradle endlessly rocking'*
Out of the cradle endlessly rocking,
Out of the mocking-bird's throat, the musical shuttle ...
A reminiscence sing.

12408 *Leaves of Grass - preface*
The United States themselves are essentially the greatest poem.

12409 *'So Long!'*
Camerado, this is no book,
Who touches this touches a man.

12410 *'Song of the Broad Axe'*
Where the populace rise at once against the never-ending audacity of elected persons.

12411 *'Song of Myself'*
I celebrate myself, and sing myself.

12412 *'Song of Myself'*
Urge and urge and urge,
Always the procreant urge of the world.

12413 *'Song of Myself'*
I also say it is good to fall, battles are lost in the same spirit in which they are won.

12414 *'Song of Myself'*
I believe a leaf of grass is no less than the journey-work of the stars.

12415 *'Song of Myself'*
I think I could turn and live with animals, they are so placid and self-contained.

12416 *'Song of Myself'*
Behold, I do not give lectures or a little charity,
When I give I give myself.

12417 *'Song of Myself'*
I sound my barbaric yawp over the roofs of the world.

WHITTIER John Greenleaf 1807-1892
12418 *'Barbara Frietchie'*
'Shoot, if you must, this old grey head,
But spare your country's flag,' she said.

12419 *'The Brewing of Soma'*
Dear Lord and Father of mankind,
Forgive our foolish ways!

12420 *'Maud Muller'*
For of all sad words of tongue or pen,
The saddest are these: 'It might have been!'

12421 *'Memories'*
The Indian Summer of the heart!

12422 *'Worship'*
O brother man! fold to thy heart thy brother.

WHITTINGTON Robert c.1480-1530
12423 *(of Sir Thomas More)*
A man for all seasons.

WHITTON Charlotte 1896-1975
12424
Whatever women do they must do twice as well as men to be thought half as good. Luckily, this is not difficult.

WHUR Cornelius
12425 *'The Female Friend'*
While lasting joys the man attend
Who has a faithful female friend.

WHYTE Lancelot Law
12426
Thought is born of failure.

WHYTE-MELVILLE George John 1821-1878
12427 *'The Good Grey Mare'*
But I freely admit that the best of my fun I owe it to horse and hound.

WICKHAM Anna 1884-1947
12428 *'The Affinity'*
It is well within the order of things
That man should listen when his mate sings;
But the true male never yet walked
Who liked to listen when his mate talked.

WIENER Norbert 1894-1964
12429
The simple faith in progress is not a conviction belonging to strength, but one belonging to acquiescence and thence to weakness.

WIESEL Elie 1928-
12430
Not to transmit an experience is to betray it.

12431
The opposite of love is not hate, it's indifference.

WIGGAN A.E.
12432
Intelligence appears to be the thing that

enables a man to get along without
education. Education appears to be the
thing that enables a man to get along
without the use of his intelligence.

WIGGLESWORTH E.
12433
Man's happiness springs mainly from
moderate troubles, which afford the mind
a healthful stimulus, and are followed by a
reaction which produces a cheerful flow of
spirits.

WILBERFORCE Samuel 1805-1873
12434 *Impromptu verse (attributed)*
If I were a cassowary
On the plains of Timbuctoo,
I would eat a missionary,
Cassock, band, and hymn-book too.

12435 *(to T.H. Huxley)*
Was it through his grandfather or his
grandmother that he claimed his descent
from a monkey?

WILBUR Richard 1921-
12436 *'Advice to a Prophet'*
Spare us all word of the weapons, their
force and range,
The long numbers that rocket the mind;
Our slow, unreckoning hearts will be left
behind,
Unable to fear what is too strange.

12437 *'Epistemology'*
We milk the cow of the world, and as we
do
We whisper in her ear, 'You are not true'.

12438 *'Mind'*
Mind in its purest play is like some bat
That beats about in caverns all alone,
Contriving by a kind of senseless wit
Not to conclude against a wall of stone.

WILCOX Ella Wheeler 1855-1919
12439
And from the discontent of man
The world's best progress springs.

12440 *'Solitude'*
Laugh and the world laughs with you;
Weep, and you weep alone;
For the sad old earth must borrow its
mirth,
But has trouble enough of its own.

12441 *'The World's Need'*
So many gods, so many creeds,
So many paths that wind and wind,
While just the art of being kind
Is all the sad world needs.

WILDE Oscar 1854-1900
12442
The only thing to do with good advice is to
pass it on. It is never any use to oneself.

12443
The tragedy of old age is not that one is
old, but that one is young.

12444
Arguments are to be avoided - they are
always vulgar and often convincing.

12445
She is a peacock in everything but beauty.

12446
The only beautiful things are the things
that do not concern us.

12447
Anybody can be good in the country.
There are no temptations there.

12448
Consistency is the last refuge of the
unimaginative.

12449
If England treats her criminals the way she
has treated me, she doesn't deserve to
have any.

12450
When critics disagree, the artist is in
accord with himself.

12451
Fashion is that by which the fantastic
becomes for a moment universal.

12452
The public is wonderfully tolerant. It
forgives everything except genius.

12453
There is luxury in self-reproach. When we
blame ourselves we feel that no one else
has the right to blame us.

12454
I hope you have not been leading a double life, pretending to be wicked and being really good all the time. That would be hypocrisy.

12455
I played with an idea, and grew wilful; tossed it into the air and transformed it; let it escape and recaptured it; made it iridescent with fancy, and winged it with paradox.

12456
For he who lives more lives than one, More deaths than one must die.

12457
Men become old, but they never become good.

12458
To become the spectator of one's own life is to escape the suffering of life.

12459
Pessimist - one who, when he has the choice of two evils, chooses both.

12460
A sentimentalist is simply one who desires to have the luxury of an emotion without paying for it.

12461
It is only shallow people who do not judge by appearances. The true mystery of the world is the visible, not the invisible.

12462
A true gentleman is one who is never unintentionally rude.

12463
Only the shallow know themselves.

12464
It is a dangerous thing to reform anyone.

12465
It is not the prisoners who need reformation, it is the prisons.

12466
My great mistake, the fault for which I can't forgive myself, is that one day I ceased my obstinate pursuit of my own individuality.

12467
Nothing is so dangerous as being too modern; one is apt to grow old-fashioned quite suddenly.

12468
Success is a science. If you have the conditions, you get the result.

12469
Nothing that is worth knowing can be taught.

12470
The only way to get rid of a temptation is to yield to it. Resist it, and your soul grows sick with longing for the things it has forbidden to itself.

12471
Punctuality is the thief of time.

12472
As long as war is regarded as wicked, it will always have its fascination. When it is looked upon as vulgar, it will cease to be popular.

12473
I've put my genius into my life; I've only put my talent into my works.

12474
English conversationalists have a miraculous power of turning wine into water.

12475
I have nothing to declare except my genius.

12476
Work is the curse of the drinking classes.

12477 *The Ballad of Reading Gaol*
I never saw a man who looked
With such a wistful eye
Upon that little tent of blue
Which prisoners call the sky.

12478 *The Ballad of Reading Gaol*
Yet each man kills the thing he loves,
By each let this be heard,
Some do it with a bitter look,
Some with a flattering word.

The coward does it with a kiss,
The brave man with a sword!

12479 *The Ballad of Reading Gaol*
Something was dead in each of us,
And what was dead was Hope.

12480 *(of Bernard Shaw)*
He hasn't an enemy in the world, and
none of his friends like him.

12481 *An Ideal Husband*
Men can be analysed, women ... merely
adored.

12482 *An Ideal Husband*
Questions are never indiscreet. Answers
sometimes are.

12483 *An Ideal Husband*
To love oneself is the beginning of a
lifelong romance.

12484 *The Importance of Being Earnest*
Really, if the lower orders don't set us a
good example, what on earth is the use of
them?

12485 *The Importance of Being Earnest*
The truth is rarely pure, and never simple.

12486 *The Importance of Being Earnest*
To lose one parent, Mr Worthing, may be
regarded as a misfortune; to lose both
looks like carelessness.

12487 *The Importance of Being Earnest*
In married life three is company and two
none.

12488 *The Importance of Being Earnest*
All women become like their mothers.
That is their tragedy. No man does. That's
his.

12489 *The Importance of Being Earnest*
The good ended happily, and the bad
unhappily. That is what fiction means.

12490 *The Importance of Being Earnest*
None of us are perfect. I myself am
peculiarly susceptible to draughts.

12491 *The Importance of Being Earnest*
I never travel without my diary. One
should always have something sensational
to read in the train.

12492 *The Importance of Being Earnest*
This suspense is terrible. I hope it will last.

12493 *Impressions of America 'Leadville'*
Please do not shoot the pianist. He is
doing his best.

12494 *Intentions 'The Critic as Artist'*
Every great man nowadays has his
disciples, and it is always Judas who
writes the biography.

12495 *Intentions 'The Critic as Artist'*
The one duty we owe to history is to
rewrite it.

12496 *Intentions 'The Critic as Artist'*
A little sincerity is a dangerous thing, and
a great deal of it is absolutely fatal.

12497 *Lady Windermere's Fan*
I can resist everything except temptation.

12498 *Lady Windermere's Fan*
We are all in the gutter, but some of us are
looking at the stars.

12499 *Lady Windermere's Fan*
What is a cynic?
A man who knows the price of everything
and the value of nothing.

12500 *Lady Windermere's Fan*
Experience is the name every one gives to
their mistakes.

12501 *(to Mrs Leverson on his release from
prison)*
My dear, you're the only woman in the
world who'd have known the right hat to
wear on an occasion like this.

12502 *The Picture of Dorian Gray*
There is no such thing as a moral or an
immoral book. Books are well written, or
badly written.

12503 *The Picture of Dorian Gray*
There is only one thing in the world worse
than being talked about, and that is not
being talked about.

12504 *The Picture of Dorian Gray*
A man cannot be too careful in the choice
of his enemies.

12505 *The Picture of Dorian Gray*
A cigarette is the perfect type of a perfect pleasure. It is exquisite, and it leaves one unsatisfied. What more can one want?

12506 *Sebastian Melmoth*
A thing is not necessarily true because a man dies for it.

12507 *Sebastian Melmoth 'The Soul of Man ...'*
Democracy means simply the bludgeoning of the people by the people for the people.

12508 *(when told of huge fee for surgical operation)*
Ah, well, then, I suppose that I shall have to die beyond my means.

12509 *A Woman of No Importance*
The English country gentleman galloping after a fox - the unspeakable in full pursuit of the uneatable.

12510 *A Woman of No Importance*
One should never trust a woman who tells one her real age. A woman who would tell one that, would tell one anything.

12511 *A Woman of No Importance*
The Book of Life begins with a man and a woman in a garden.
It ends with Revelations.

12512 *A Woman of No Importance*
Children begin by loving their parents; after a time they judge them; rarely, if ever, do they forgive them.

12513 *A Woman of No Importance*
You should study the Peerage, Gerald ... It is the best thing in fiction the English have ever done.

12514 *A Woman of No Importance*
Twenty years of romance make a woman look like a ruin; but twenty years of marriage make her something like a public building.

WILDER Billy 1906-
12515
Hindsight is always twenty-twenty.

WILDER Thornton 1897-1975
12516
Many plays, certainly mine, are like blank cheques. The actors and directors put their own signatures on them.

12517
A play visibly represents pure existing.

12518
Pride, avarice and envy are in every home.

12519
For what human ill does not dawn seem to be an alleviation?

12520
Literature is the orchestration of platitudes.

12521
Nurse one vice in your bosom. Give it the attention it deserves and let your virtues spring up modestly around it. Then you'll have the miser who's no liar; and the drunkard who's the benefactor of a whole city.

12522
If a man has no vices, he's in great danger of making vices about his virtues, and there's a spectacle.

12523
The unecumbered stage encourages the truth operative in everyone. The less seen, the more heard. The eye is the enemy of the ear in real drama.

12524 *The Merchant of Yonkers*
Marriage is a bribe to make a housekeeper think she's a householder.

12525 *The Merchant of Yonkers*
The fights are the best part of married life. The rest is merely so-so.

WILHELM II ('Kaiser Bill') 1859-1941
12526
We have ... fought for our place in the sun and have won it.

WILL George
12527
World War II was the last government program that really worked.

WILLIAM The Silent 1533-1584
12528
One need not hope in order to undertake; nor succeed in order to persevere.

WILLIAM III (William of Orange) 1650-1702

12529
There is one way never to see it [my country] lost, and that is to die in the last ditch.

12530
Every bullet has its billet.

WILLIAMS Charles 1886-1945

12531
Hell is indefinite.

WILLIAMS Harry and JUDGE Jack 1874-1924 and 1878-1938

12532 *'It's a Long Way to Tipperary'*
Good-bye Piccadilly, Farewell Leicester Square;
It's a long, long way to Tipperary, but my heart's right there!

WILLIAMS Heathcote

12533
Reason is an emotion for the sexless.

WILLIAMS Isaac 1802-1865

12534 *'Be thou my Guardian and my Guide'*
Be thou my Guardian and my Guide,
And hear me when I call;
Let not my slippery footsteps slide,
And hold me lest I fall.

WILLIAMS Nigel

12535
This is the BBC - we are not making programmes for the glitterati or the literati of any kindy of arty.

WILLIAMS Tennessee 1911-1983

12536
A high station in life is earned by the gallantry with which appalling experiences are survived with grace.

12537
A vacuum is a hell of a lot better than some of the stuff that nature replaces it with.

12538
I can't stand a naked light bulb, any more than I can stand a rude remark or a vulgar action.

12539
I don't ask for your pity, but just your understanding - no, not even that - no. Just for your recognition of me in you, and the enemy, time, in us all.

12540
Make voyages. Attempt them. There's nothing else.

12541 *Camino Real*
We have to distrust each other. It's our only defence against betrayal.

12542 *Camino Real*
We're all of us guinea pigs in the laboratory of God. Humanity is just a work in progress.

12543 *Cat on a Hot Tin Roof*
What is the victory of a cat on a hot tin roof? - I wish I knew ... Just staying on it, I guess, as long as she can.

12544 *Cat on a Hot Tin Roof*
Mendacity is a system that we live in. Liquor is one way out an' death's the other.

12545 *The Glass Menagerie*
I didn't go to the moon, I went much further - for time is the longest distance between two places.

12546 *Orpheus Descending*
We're all of us sentenced to solitary confinement inside our own skins, for life!

12547 *A Streetcar named Desire*
I have always depended on the kindness of strangers.

WILLIAMS William Carlos 1883-1963

12548 *'To Ford Madox Ford in Heaven'*
Is it any better in heaven, my friend Ford,
Than you found it in Provence?

12549 *'Paterson'*
Minds like beds always made up,
(more stony than a shore)
unwilling or unable.

12550 *'Paterson'*
No woman is virtuous
who does not give herself to her lover
- forthwith.

WILLIAMSON Nicol

12551
If you can make a woman laugh you can do anything with her.

12552
Nothing means anything until you're doing it.

WILLKIE Wendell 1892-1944

12553 *An American Programme*
The constitution does not provide for first and second class citizens.

12554 *One World*
Freedom is an indivisible word. If we want to enjoy it, and fight for it, we must be prepared to extend it to everyone, whether they are rich or poor, whether they agree with us or not, no matter what their race or colour of their skin.

12555 *One World*
There exists in the world today a gigantic reservoir of good will toward us, the American people.

WILLS Garry

12556
Politicians make good company for a while just as children do - their self-enjoyment is contagious. But they soon exhaust their favourite subjects - themselves.

WILSON A.N. 1950-

12557
Twenty years ago the cleverest people did become dons, but not any more. The really clever people now want to be lawyers or journalists.

WILSON Earl

12558
Gossip is when you hear something you like about someone you don't.

WILSON Edmund 1895-1972

12559
I think with my right hand.

WILSON Ethel 1890-

12560
Dullness is a misdemeanour.

12561
The business of writing is one of the four or five most private things in the world.

WILSON Senator Gordon

12562 *(after meeting with IRA)*
They told me that history is on their side.

WILSON Sir Harold 1916-1995

12563
One man's wage rise is another man's price increase.

12564
In politics a week is a very long time.

12565
The office of president requires the constitution of an athlete, the patience of a mother, the endurance of an early Christian.

12566
All these financiers, all the little gnomes in Zurich and the other financial centres about whom we keep on hearing.

12567
This party is a moral crusade or it is nothing.

12568
From now the pound abroad is worth 14 per cent or so less in terms of other currencies. It does not mean, of course, that the pound here in Britain, in your pocket or purse or in your bank, has been devalued.

12569
The Monarchy is a labour-intensive industry.

WILSON Sandy 1924-

12570
It's never too late to have a fling
For autumn is just as nice as spring
And it's never too late to fall in love.

12571 *The Boyfriend*
We've got to have
We plot to have
For it's so dreary not to have
That certain thing called the Boy Friend.

12572 *The Boy Friend*
But it's nicer, much nicer in Nice.

WILSON Woodrow 1856-1924

12573
The men who act stand nearer to the mass of man than the men who write; and it is in their hands that new thought gets its translation into the crude language of deeds.

12574
The man who is swimming against the stream knows the strength of it.

12575
If you think about what you ought to do for other people, your character will take care of itself.

12576
You cannot be friends upon any other terms than upon the terms of equality.

12577
A friend of mine says that every man who takes office in Washington either grows or swells, and when I give a man an office, I watch him carefully to see whether he is swelling or growing.

12578
No man ever saw a government. I live in the midst of the Government of the United States, but I never saw the Government of the United States.

12579
A man's rootage is more important than his leafage.

12580
I not only use all the brains I have, but all I can borrow.

12581
When you come into the presence of a leader of men, you know that you have come into the presence of fire - that it is best not uncautiously to touch that man - that there is something that makes it dangerous to cross him.

12582
The world must be made safe for democracy. Its peace must be planted upon the tested foundations of political liberty.

12583
Nothing was ever done so systematically as nothing is being done now.

12584
I'm a vague, conjunctured personality, more made up of opinions and academic prepossessions than of human traits and red corpuscles.

12585
It is a fearful thing to lead this great peaceful people into war, into the most terrible and disastrous of all wars, civilization itself seeming to be in the balance. But the right is more precious than peace, and we shall fight for the things which we have always carried nearest our hearts - for democracy.

12586
The history of liberty is a history of the limitation of governmental power, not the increase of it.

12587
No nation is fit to sit in judgement upon any other nation.

12588
There is such a thing as a man being too proud to fight; there is such a thing as a nation being so right that it does not need to convince others by force that it is right.

12589
We have stood apart, studiously neutral.

12590
It must be a peace without victory ... Only a peace between equals can last.

12591
Armed neutrality is ineffectual enough at best.

12592
America is the only idealistic nation in the world.

12593
Once lead this people into war and they will forget there ever was such a thing as tolerance.

12594 (last words)
I am a broken machine. I am ready to go.

WINCHELL Walter 1897-1972
12595
Gossip is the art of saying nothing in a
way that leaves practically nothing unsaid.

WINCHILSEA Lady Anne Finch 1661-
1720
12596 *'Enquiry after Peace'*
Thirst of wealth no quiet knows,
But near the death-bed fiercer grows.

12597 *'Enquiry after Peace'*
Love (if such a thing there be)
Is all despair, or ecstasy.
Poetry's the feverish fit,
Th' o'erflowing of unbounded wit.

12598 *'The Spleen' (1701)*
We faint beneath the aromatic pain.

WINDHAM William 1750-1810
12599
Those entrusted with arms ... should be
persons of some substance and stake in the
country.

WINTHROP Robert Charles 1809-1894
12600
A Star for every State, and a State for every
Star.

WITHER George 1588-1667
12601 *A Collection of Emblems*
And when I mind with how much
greediness
We seek the present gain in everything,
Not caring (so our lust we may possess)
What damage to posterity we bring ...

12602 *A Description of Love 'I Loved a lass ...*
I loved a lass, a fair one,
As fair as e'er was seen;
She was indeed a rare one,
Another Sheba queen.

12603 *Sonnet*
Shall I, wasting in despair,
Die because a woman's fair?

12604 *Sonnet*
For, if she be not for me,
What care I how fair she be.

WITTGENSTEIN Ludwig 1889-1951
12605
The limits of my language mean the limits

of my world.

12606
Philosophy is a battle aginst the
bewitchment of our intelligence by means
of language.

12607
The philosopher's treatment of a question
is like the treatment of an illness.

12608
What is your aim in philosophy? - To show
the fly the way out of the fly-bottle.

12609
The world of the happy is quite different
from that of the unhappy.

WODEHOUSE P.G. 1881-1975
12610
Why don't you get a haircut; you look like
a chrysanthemum.

12611
The butler entered the room, a solemn
procession of one.

12612 *The Adventures of Sally*
When you marry, Sally, grab a chump. Tap
his forehead first, and if it rings solid,
don't hesitate. All the unhappy marriages
come from the husbands having brains.

12613 *The Code of the Woosters*
He spoke with a certain what-is-it in his
voice, and I could see that, if not actually
disgruntled, he was far from being
gruntled.

12614 *The Code of the Woosters*
Slice him where you like, a hellhound is
always a hellhound.

12615 *The Inimitable Jeeves*
It was my Uncle George who discovered
that alcohol was a food well in advance of
medical thought.

12616 *My Man Jeeves 'Rallying Round Old
George'*
What a queer thing Life is! So unlike
anything else, don't you know, if you see
what I mean.

12617 *The Man Upstairs*
It is a good rule in life never to apologize.
The right sort of people do not want
apologies, and the wrong sort take a mean
advantage of them.

WOLF Marcus
12618 *(at his trial)*
Your honour is not my honour.

WOLFE Charles 1791-1823
12619 'The Burial of Sir John Moore at
Corunna'
Not a drum was heard, not a funeral note,
As his corse to the rampart we hurried.

12620 'The Burial of Sir John Moore at
Corunna'
We buried him darkly at dead of night,
The sods with our bayonets turning.

12621 'The Burial of Sir John Moore at
Corunna'
We carved not a line, and we raised not a
stone -
But we left him alone with his glory.

WOLFE Humbert 1886-1940
12622 'Over the Fire'
You cannot hope
to bribe or twist,
thank God! the
British journalist.
But, seeing what
the man will do
unbribed, there's
no occasion to.

WOLFE Thomas 1900-1938
12623
That enfabled rock, that ship of life, that
swarming, million-footed, tower-masted,
sky-soaring citadel that bears the magic
name of the Island of Manhattan.

12624
This is the artist, then - life's hungry man,
the glutton of eternity, beauty's miser,
glory's slave.

12625
Loneliness is and always has been the
central and inevitable experience of every
man.

12626
The reason a writer writes a book is to
forget a book and the reason a reader reads
one is to remember it.

12627 *Look Homeward, Angel*
Most of the time we think we're sick, it's
all in the mind.

WOLFE Tom 1931-
12628
The bonfire of the vanities.

12629
Radical Chic ... is only radical in Style; in
its heart it is part of Society and its
tradition - Politics, like Rock, Pop, and
Camp, has its uses.

12630 *Mauve Gloves and Madmen 'The Me
Decade'*
We are now in the Me Decade - seeing the
upward roll of ... the third great religious
wave in American history ... and this one
has the mightiest, holiest roll of all, the
beat that goes ... *Me ... Me ... Me ... Me.*

WOLFENDEN John
12631
Schoolmasters and parents exist to be
grown out of.

WOLLSTONECRAFT Mary 1759-1797
12632 *A Vindication of the Rights of Woman*
A king is always a king - and a woman
always a woman: his authority and her sex
ever stand between them and rational
converse.

12633 *A Vindication of the Rights of Woman*
I do not wish them [women] to have
power over men; but over themselves.

12634 *A Vindication of the Rights of Woman*
Taught from infancy that beauty is
woman's sceptre, the mind shapes itself to
the body, and roaming round its gilt cage,
only seeks to adorn its prison.

12635 *A Vindication of the Rights of Woman*
A slavish bondage to parents cramps every
faculty of the mind.

WOLSEY Thomas c.1475-1530
12636
Father Abbot, I am come to lay my bones

amongst you.

12637
Had I but served God as diligently as I have served the King, he would not have given me over in my grey hairs.

WOMBAT R.T.
12638
The lazy man gets round the sun as quickly as the busy one.

WOOD James Mason
12639
Education today, more than ever before, must see clearly the dual objectives: education for living and educating for making a living.

WOOD Mrs Henry 1814-1887
12640 *East Lynne*
Dead! and ... never called me mother.

WOODCOCK George 1904-1979
12641
Pioneers did not produce original works of art, because they were creating original human environments; they did not imagine utopias because they were shaping them.

12642
It is not in life but in art that self-fulfillment is to be found.

WOODFORD Jack
12643
Few human beings are proof against the implied flattery of rapt attention.

WOODRUFF Julia Louise Matilda 1833-1909
12644
Out of the strain of the Doing
Into the peace of the Done.

WOODS Harry
12645 *'Side by Side'*
Oh we ain't got a barrel of money,
Maybe we're ragged and funny,
But we'll travel along
Singin' a song,
Side by side.

WOOLF Virginia 1882-1941
12646
A biography is considered complete if it merely accounts for six or seven selves, whereas a person may well have as many as a thousand.

12647
One of the signs of passing youth is the birth of a sense of fellowship with other human beings as we take our place among them.

12648
Money dignifies what is frivolous if unpaid for.

12649
The first duty of a lecturer - to hand you after an hour's discourse a nugget of pure truth to wrap up between the pages of your notebooks and keep on the mantelpiece for ever.

12650
Have you any notion how many books are written about women in the course of one year? Have you any notion how many are written by men? Are you aware that you are, perhaps, the most discussed animal in the universe?

12651
As for my next book, I am going to hold myself from writing it till I have it impending in me: grown heavy in my mind like a ripe pear, pendant, gravid, asking to be cut or it will fall.

12652 *The Common Reader 'Lady Dorothy Nevill'*
In one of those comfortably padded lunatic asylums which are known, euphemistically, as the stately homes of England.

12653 *The Common Reader 'The Modern Essay'*
We are nauseated by the sight of trivial personalities decomposing in the eternity of print.

12654 *The Common Reader 'Modern Fiction'*
Examine for a moment an ordinary mind on an ordinary day.

12655 *The Common Reader 'Modern Fiction'*
Life is not a series of gig lamps
symmetrically arranged; life is a luminous
halo, a semi-transparent envelope
surrounding us from the beginning of
consciousness to the end.

12656 *(of E.M. Forster)*
He is limp and damp and milder than the
breath of a cow.

12657 *Jacob's Room*
Each had his past shut in him like the
leaves of a book known to him by heart;
and his friends could only read the title.

12658 *To the Lighthouse*
So that is marriage, Lily thought, a man
and a woman looking at a girl throwing a
ball.

12659 *A Room of One's Own*
A woman must have money and a room of
her own if she is to write fiction.

12660 *A Room of One's Own*
Women have served all these centuries as
looking-glasses possessing the magic and
delicious power of reflecting the figure of a
man at twice its natural size.

12661 *A Room of One's Own*
Literature is strewn with the wreckage of
men who have minded beyond reason the
opinions of others.

12662 *A Room of One's Own*
Why are women ... so much more
interesting to men than men are to
women?

WOOLLCOTT Alexander 1887-1943
12663
The English have an extraordinary ability
for flying into a great calm.

12664
All the things I really like to do are either
immoral, illegal or fattening.

12665
A broker is a man who takes your fortune
and runs it into a shoestring.

12666
I must get out of these wet clothes and into
a dry Martini.

WOOTON Sir Henry 1568-1639
12667
Critics are like brushers of noblemen's
clothes.

12668
An ambassador is an honest man sent to
lie abroad for the good of his country.

12669 *'The Character of a Happy Life'*
Lord of himself, though not of lands,
And having nothing, yet hath all.

12670 *'Upon the Death of Sir Albertus
Moreton's Wife'*
He first deceased; she for a little tried
To live without him: liked it not, and died.

12671 *'On His Mistress, the Queen of
Bohemia'*
You meaner beauties of the night,
That poorly satisfy our eyes,
More by your number, than your light;
You common people of the skies,
What are you when the moon shall rise?

12672 *'Poem written in his youth'*
Untrue she was; yet I believed her eyes,
Instructed spies,
Till I was taught, that love was but a
school
To breed a fool.

12673 *'Upon the sudden restraint of Earl of
Somerset'*
No man marks the narrow space
'Twixt a prison and a smile.

WORDSWORTH Dorothy 1771-1855
12674 Journals 'Alfoxden Journal'
One only leaf upon the top of a tree - the
sole remaining leaf - danced round and
round like a rag blown by the wind.

WORDSWORTH Dame Elizabeth 1840-
1932
12675 *'Good and Clever'*
If all the good people were clever,
And all clever people were good,
The world would be nicer than ever
We thought that it possibly could.

WORDSWORTH William 1770-1850
12676
A man he seems of cheerful yesterdays
And confident tomorrows.

12677 'The Affliction of Margaret -'
My apprehensions come in crowds;
I dread the rustling of the grass:
The very shadows of the clouds
Have power to shake me as they pass.

12678 'The Borderers'
Action is transitory - a step, a blow,
The motion of a muscle - this way or that -
'Tis done, and in the after vacancy
We wonder at ourselves like men betrayed:
Suffering is permanent, obscure and dark,
And shares the nature of infinity.

12679 'To a Butterfly, I've Watched you now'
Sweet childish days, that were as long
As twenty days are now.

12680 'Composed upon Westminster Bridge'
Earth has not anything to show more fair:
Dull would he be of soul who could pass
by
A sight so touching in its majesty.

12681 'Composed upon Westminster Bridge'
Dear God! the very houses seem asleep;
And all that mighty heart is lying still!

12682 'To the Cuckoo'
Thrice welcome, darling of the spring!
Even yet thou art to me
No bird, but an invisible thing,
A voice, a mystery.

12683 'To the Daisy'
Oft on the dappled turf at ease
I sit, and play with similies,
Loose types of things through all degrees.

12684 'She dwelt among the untrodden ways'
She dwelt among the untrodden ways
Beside the springs of Dove,
A maid whom there were none to praise
And very few to love.

12685 'She dwelt among the untrodden ways'
But she is in her grave, and, ho,
The difference to me!

12686 'Elegiac Stanzas'(on picture of Peele
Castle)
The light that never was, on sea or land,
The consecration, and the Poet's dream.

12687 'The Excursion'
Oh! many are the Poets that are sown
By Nature; men endowed with highest
gifts,
The vision and the faculty divine;
Yet wanting the accomplishment of verse.

12688 'The Excursion'
The good die first,
And they whose hearts are dry as summer
dust
Burn to the socket.

12689 'The Excursion'
Society became my glittering bride,
And airy hopes my children.

12690 'The Excursion'
Strongest minds
Are often those of whom the noisy world
Hears least.

12691 'The Fountain'
The wiser mind
Mourns less for what age takes away
Than what it leaves behind.

12692 'The French Revolution, as it Appeared
...'
Bliss was it in that dawn to be alive,
But to be young was very heaven!

12693 'My heart leaps up when I behold'
My heart leaps up when I behold
A rainbow in the sky.

12694 'My heart leaps up when I behold'
The Child is father of the Man.

12695 'Laodamia'
The gods approve
The depth, and not the tumult, of the soul.

12696 Letter to Lady Beaumont
Every great and original writer, in
proportion as he is great and original,
must himself create the taste by which he
is to be relished.

12697 'Lines composed ... above Tintern
Abbey'
That best portion of a good man's life,
His little, nameless, unremembered, acts
Of kindness and of love.

12698 *'Lines composed ... above Tintern Abbey'*
That blessed mood
In which the burthen of the mystery,
In which the heavy and the weary weight
Of all this unintelligible world,
Is lightened.

12699 *'Lines composed ... above Tintern Abbey'*
I have learned
To look on nature, not as in the hour
Of thoughtless youth; but hearing oftentimes
The still, sad music of humanity.

12700 *'Lines composed ... above Tintern Abbey'*
And I have felt
A presence that disturbs me with the joy
Of elevated thoughts; a sense sublime
Of something far more deeply interfused,
Whose dwelling is the light of setting suns,
And the round ocean and the living air,
And the blue sky, and in the mind of man;
A motion and a spirit, that impels
All thinking things, all objects of all thoughts,
And rolls through all things.

12701 *'Lines composed ... above Tintern Abbey'*
All the mighty world
Of eye and ear, both what they half-create,
And what perceive.

12702 *'Lines composed ... above Tintern Abbey'*
Nature never did betray
The heart that loved her.

12703 *'Lines Written in Early Spring'*
And much it grieved my heart to think
What man has made of man.

12704 *Lyrical Ballads - Preface*
Poetry is the breath and finer spirit of all knowledge; it is the impassioned expression which is in the countenance of all science.

12705 *Lyrical Ballads - Preface*
Poetry is the spontaneous overflow of powerful feelings: it takes its origin from emotion recollected in tranquillity.

12706 *'Milton! thou shouldst be living ...'*
Milton! thou shouldst be living at this hour:
England hath need of thee.

12707 *National Independence and Liberty 'November 1806'*
Another year! - another deadly blow!
Another mighty empire overthrown!
And we are left, or shall be left, alone.

12708 *'Ode. Intimations of Immortality'*
The rainbow comes and goes,
And lovely is the rose,
The moon doth with delight
Look round her when the heavens are bare;
Waters on a starry night
Are beautiful and fair;
The sunshine is a glorious birth;
But yet I know, where'er I go,
That there hath passed away a glory from the earth.

12709 *'Ode. Intimations of Immortality'*
A timely utterance gave that thought relief,
And I again am strong.

12710 *'Ode. Intimations of Immortality'*
The winds come to me from the fields of sleep.

12711 *'Ode. Intimations of Immortality'*
Whither is fled the visionary gleam?
Where is it now, the glory and the dream?

12712 *'Ode. Intimations of Immortality'*
Our birth is but a sleep and a forgetting.

12713 *'Ode. Intimations of Immortality'*
And not in utter nakedness,
But trailing clouds of glory do we come
From God, who is our home.

12714 *'Ode. Intimations of Immortality'*
As if his whole vocation
Were endless imitation.

12715 *'Ode. Intimations of Immortality'*
Though nothing can bring back the hour
Of splendour in the grass, of glory in the flower;
We will grieve not, rather find
Strength in what remains behind ...
In the faith that looks through death,
In years that bring the philosophic mind.

12716 'Ode. Intimations of Immortality'
To me the meanest flower that blows can
give
Thoughts that do often lie too deep for
tears.

12717 Peter Bell
Some sipping punch, some sipping tea,
But as you by their faces see
All silent, and all damned?

12718 Peter Bell - prologue
There's something in a flying horse,
There's something in a huge balloon;
But through the clouds I'll never float
Until I have a little Boat,
Shaped like the crescent-moon.

12719 'She Was a Phantom of Delight'
She was a phantom of delight
When first she gleamed upon my sight;
A lovely apparition, sent
To be a moment's ornament.

12720 'She Was a Phantom of Delight'
And now I see with eye serene
The very pulse of the machine;
A being breathing thoughtful breath,
A traveller between life and death.

12721 'She Was a Phantom of Delight'
A perfect woman, nobly planned,
To warn, to comfort, and command.

12722 'A Poet's Epitaph'
One that would peep and botanize
Upon his mother's grave?

12723 'A Poet's Epitaph'
A reasoning, self-sufficing thing,
An intellectual All-in-all!

12724 'A Poet's Epitaph'
The harvest of a quiet eye
That broods and sleeps on his own heart.

12725 The Prelude
Made one long bathing of a summer's day.

12726 The Prelude
Dust as we are, the immortal spirit grows
Like harmony in music; there is a dark
Inscrutable workmanship that reconciles
Discordant elements, makes them cling
together
In one society.

12727 The Prelude
And I was taught to feel, perhaps too
much,
The self-sufficing power of Solitude.

12728 The Prelude
Science appears but what in truth she is,
Not as our glory and our absolute boast,
But as a succedaneum, and a prop
To our infirmity.

12729 The Prelude
We were brothers all
In honour, as in one community,
Scholars and gentlemen.

12730 The Prelude
Through the turnings intricate of verse,
Present themselves as objects recognised,
In flashes, and with glory not their own.

12731 'Resolution and Independence'
We poets in our youth begin in gladness;
But thereof comes in the end despondency
and madness.

12732 'The River Duddon'- 'After-Thought'
Still glides the Stream, and shall for ever
glide;
The Form remains, the Function never
dies.

12733 'The River Duddon'- 'After-Thought'
Enough, if something from our hands have
power
To live, and act, and serve the future hour.

12734 'Rob Roy's Grave'
The good old rule
Sufficeth them, the simple plan,
That they should take who have the
power,
And they should keep who can.

12735 'Scorn not the Sonnet'
Scorn not the Sonnet; Critic, you have
frowned,
Mindless of its just honours; with this key
Shakespeare unlocked his heart.

12736 'To Sleep'
A flock of sheep that leisurely pass by,
One after one; the sound of rain, and bees
Murmuring: the fall of rivers, winds and
seas,
Smooth fields, white sheets of water, and

pure sky;
I have thought of all by turns, and yet do lie
Sleepless!

12737 'To Sleep'
Blessed barrier between day and day.

12738 'To Sleep'
Suprised by joy - impatient as the wind
I turned to share the transport.

12739 'To Sleep'
The holy time is quiet as a nun
Breathless with adoration.

12740 'To Sleep'
The world is too much with us; late and soon,
Getting and spending, we lay waste our powers.

12741 'A slumber did my spirit seal'
A slumber did my spirit seal;
I had no human fears:
She seemed a thing that could not feel
The touch of earthly years.

No motion has she now, no force;
She neither hears nor sees;
Rolled round in earth's diurnal course,
With rocks, and stones, and trees.

12742 'The Tables Turned'
One impulse from a vernal wood
May teach you more of man,
Of moral evil and of good,
Than all the sages can.

12743 'The Tables Turned'
Our meddling intellect
Mis-shapes the beauteous forms of things:-
We murder to dissect.

12744 'Tis Said that some have Died'
'Tis said that some have died for love.

12745 'I travelled among unknown men'
I travelled among unknown men,
In lands beyond the sea;
Nor England! did I know till then
What love I bore to thee.

12746 'I wandered lonely as a cloud'
I wandered lonely as a cloud
That floats on high o'er vales and hills,

When all at once I saw a crowd,
A host, of golden daffodils.

12747 'I wandered lonely as a cloud'
And then my heart with pleasure fills,
And dances with the daffodils.

12748 'Written in March'
Like an army defeated
The snow hath retreated.

WORK H.C. 1832-1884
12749 'Grandfather's Clock'
But it stopped short - never to go again -
When the old man died.

12750 'Come Home, Father'
Father, dear father, come home with me now,
The clock in the steeple strikes one.

12751 'Wake Nicodemus'
There's a good time coming, it's almost here,
'Twas a long, long time on the way.

WRIGHT Frank Lloyd 1867-1959
12752
Pictures deface walls oftener than they decorate them.

12753
Early in life I had to choose between arrogance and hypocritical humility. I chose honest arrogance and have seen no occasion to change.

12754
No house should ever be on a hill, or on anything. It should be of the hill. Hill and house should live together, each the happier for the other.

12755
A doctor can bury his mistakes, but an architect can only advise his clients to plant vines.

12756
An idea is salvation by imagination.

12757
I hate intellectuals. They are from the top down. I am from the bottom up.

12758
Television is chewing gum for the eyes.

12759 *Autobiography*
The necessities were going by default to
save the luxuries until I hardly knew
which were necessities and which luxuries.

WRIGHT Ronald 1908-
12760
Societies that do not eat people are
fascinated by those that do.

WRIGHT Steven
12761
The older you get, the more you learn to
see what you've been taught to see. When
you're a kid, you see what's there.

WRIGLEY Jr. William 1861-1932
12762
When two men in business always agree,
one of them is unnecessary.

WROTH Lady Mary c.1586-c.1652
12763 *'Love, a child, is ever crying'*
Love, a child, is ever crying:
Please him and he straight is flying.
Give him, he the more is craving,
Never satisfied with having.

WUNDERLICH Paul
12764
I refuse to explain everything, because if
you know too much about yourself, you
become impotent. Better not to know
what it is that makes you tick.

WYATT Sir Thomas c.1503-1542
12765 *'Farewell, Love'*
Farewell, Love, and all thy laws forever.
Thy baited hooks shall tangle me no more.

12766 *'They flee from me'*
They flee from me, that sometime did me
seek
With naked foot, stalking in my chamber.

WYBROW Bob
12767
We have three sexes: men, women who are
housewives, and other women.

WYCHERLEY William c.1640-1716
12768 *The Country Wife*
A mistress should be like a little country
retreat near the town, not to dwell in
constantly, but only for a night and away.

12769 *The Country Wife*
Go to your business, I say, pleasure, whilst
I go to my pleasure, business.

12770 *The Country Wife*
Women and fortune are truest still to those
that trust 'em.

WYKEHAM William of 1324-1404
12771 *(motto)*
Manners maketh man.

WYLIE Philip 1902-
12772
If liberty has any meaning it means
freedom to improve.

WYLIE William T.
12773
Your can't automate in the arts. Since the
sixteenth century there has been no change
in the number of people necessary to
produce *Hamlet*.

X Malcolm 1925-1965
12774
Power never takes a back step - only in the
face of more power.

YATES Douglas
12775
No scientific theory achieves public
acceptance until it has been thoroughly
discredited.

YATES John. 1925-
12776
There is a lot to be said in the Decade of
Evangelism for believing more and more
in less and less.

YBARRA Thomas Russell 1880-
12777 *'The Christian'*
A Christian is a man who feels
Repentance on a Sunday
For what he did on Saturday
And is going to do on Monday.

YEAMES W.F. 1835-1918
12778 *(title of painting)*
And when did you last see your father?

YEATS William Butler 1865-1939
12779
Style, personality - deliberately adopted
and therefore a mask - is the only escape

from the hot-faced bargainers and money-changers.

12780
Education is not the filling of a pail, but the lighting of a fire.

12781
Life is a long preparation for something that never happens.

12782
Only that which does not teach, which does not cry out, which does not condescend, which does not explain, is irresistible.

12783
All empty souls tend to extreme opinion.

12784
Of our conflicts with others we make rhetoric; of our conflicts with ourselves we make poetry.

12785
A statesman is an easy man,
He tells his lies by rote;
A journalist makes up his lies
And takes you by the throat;
So stay at home and drink your beer
And let the neighbours vote.

12786
Be secret and exult,
Because of all things known
That is most difficult.

12787 *'All Things can Tempt Me'*
When I was young,
I had not given a penny for a song
Did not the poet sing it with such airs,
That one believed he had a sword upstairs.

12788 *'Among School Children'*
O body swayed to music, O brightening glance,
How can we know the dancer from the dance?

12789 *'Byzantium'*
A starlit or a moonlit dome distains
All that man is;
All mere complexities,
The fury and the mire of human veins.

12790 *'The Circus Animals' Desertion'*
Now that my ladder's gone
I must lie down where all ladders start
In the foul rag and bone shop of the heart.

12791 *'A Coat'*
For there's more enterprise
In walking naked.

12792 *'The Coming of Wisdom with Time'*
Though leaves are many, the root is one;
Through all the lying days of my youth
I swayed my leaves and flowers in the sun;
Now I may wither into the truth.

12793 *'The Countess Cathleen'*
The years like great black oxen tread the world,
And God the herdsman goads them on behind,
And I am broken by their passing feet.

12794 *A Drinking Song*
Wine comes in at the mouth
And love comes in at the eye;
That's all we shall know for truth
Before we grow old and die.

12795 *'Easter, 1916'*
I have met them at close of day
Coming with vivid faces
From counter or desk among grey
Eighteenth-century houses.
I have passed with a nod of the head
Or polite meaningless words.

12796 *'Easter, 1916'*
Changed, changed utterly:
A terrible beauty is born.

12797 *'Ego Dominus Tuus'*
The rhetorician would deceive his neighbours,
The sentimentalist himself; while art
Is but a vision of reality.

12798 *'An Irish Airman Foresees his Death'*
Nor law, nor duty bade me fight,
Nor public men, nor cheering crowds,
A lonely impulse of delight
Drove to this tumult in the clouds.

12799 *Letters on Poetry ... to Dorothy Wellesley*
Think like a wise man but express yourself like the common people.

12800 'In Memory of Eva Gore Booth and Con Markiewicz'
The innocent and the beautiful
Have no enemy but time.

12801 'The Municipal Gallery Re-visited'
Think where man's glory most begins and ends
And say my glory was I had such friends.

12802 'From Oedipus at Colonus'
The second best's a gay goodnight and quickly turn away.

12803 'The Pity of Love'
A pity beyond all telling,
Is hid in the heart of love.

12804 'Politics'
How can I, that girl standing there,
My attention fix
On Roman or on Russian
Or on Spanish politics?

12805 'Remorse for Intemperate Speech'
I carry from my mother's womb
A fanatic heart.

12806 'Down by the Salley Gardens'
Down by the salley gardens my love and I did meet;
She passed the salley gardens with little snow-white feet.
She bid me take love easy, as the leaves grow on the tree;
But I, being young and foolish, with her would not agree.

12807 'The Second Coming'
The best lack all conviction, while the worst
Are full of passionate intensity.

12808 'The Second Coming'
And what rough beast, its hour come round at last,
Slouches towards Bethlehem to be born?

12809 'No Second Troy'
Why, what could she have done being what she is?
Was there another Troy for her to burn?

12810 'The Secret Rose'
Far-off, most secret and inviolate Rose,
Enfold me in my hour of hours.

12811 'September, 1913'
Romantic Ireland's dead and gone,
It's with O'Leary in the grave.

12812 'Song of Wandering Aengus'
And pluck till time and times are done,
The silver apples of the moon,
The golden apples of the sun.

12813 'The Spur'
You think it horrible that lust and rage
Should dance attendance upon my old age;
They were not such a plague when I was young.

12814 'On being asked for a War Poem'
I think it better that at times like these
We poets keep our mouths shut.

12815 'When You Are Old'
When you are old and grey and full of sleep,
And nodding by the fire, take down this book
And slowly read and dream of the soft look
Your eyes had once, and of their shadows deep.

12816 'He Wishes for the Cloths of Heaven'
Tread softly because you tread on my dreams.

YEATS-BROWN Francis 1888-1944
12817
To me the charm of an encyclopedia is that it knows - and I needn't.

YELTSIN Boris 1931-
12818
It is Russia's mission to be first among equals.

12819
Today is the last day of the past.

YESENIN Sergei 1895-1925
12820 (before committing suicide)
In this life there's nothing new in dying,
But nor, of course, is living any newer.

12821 'Pleasure's for the Bad'
It's always the good feel rotten.
Pleasure's for those who are bad.

12822 *'I Have One Remaining Pastime'*
I indulged in obscenities and scandals
In order to burn more bright.

YEVTUSHENKO Yevgeny 1933-
12823
Time has a way of demonstrating ... the
most subborn are the most intelligent.

12824
A show of envy is an insult to oneself.

12825 *'No People are Uninteresting'*
No people are uninteresting.
Their fate is like the chronicle of planets.
Nothing in them is not particular,
and planet is dissimilar from planet.

YOGANANDA Paramahansa
12826
There is a magnet in your heart that will
attract true friends. That magnet is
unselfishness, thinking of others first ...
when you learn to live for others, they will
live for you.

12827
Learn to see God in all persons, of
whatever race or creed. You will know
what divine love is when you begin to feel
your oneness with every human being, not
before. In mutual service we forget the
little self and glimpse the one measureless
self, the spirit that unifies all men.

YOST Charles 1907-1981
12828
A leader may symbolize and express what
is best in his people, like Pericles, or what
is worst, like Hitler, but he cannot
successfully express what is only in his
heart and not in theirs.

12829
Romanticism is the expression of man's
urge to rise above reason and common
sense, just as rationalism is the expression
of his urge to rise above theology and
emotion.

YOUNG Arthur
12830
There is a great difference between a good
physician and a bad one; yet very little
between a good one and none at all.

YOUNG Edward 1683-1765
12831
Tomorrow is a satire on today,
And shows its weakness.

12832 *The Love of Fame*
Some for renown on scraps of learning
dote,
And think they grow immortal as they
quote.

12833 *The Love of Fame*
None think the great unhappy, but the
great.

12834 *The Love of Fame*
Be wise with speed;
A fool at forty is a fool indeed.

12835 *The Love of Fame*
With skill she vibrates her eternal tongue,
For ever most divinely in the wrong.

12836 *The Love of Fame*
One to destroy, is murder by the law;
And gibbets keep the lifted hand in awe;
To murder thousands, takes a specious
name,
'War's glorious art', and gives immortal
fame.

12837 *The Love of Fame*
How commentators each dark passage
shun,
And hold their farthing candle to the sun.

12838 *Night Thoughts 'Night 1'*
Tired Nature's sweet restorer, balmy sleep!

12839 *Night Thoughts 'Night 1'*
Be wise to-day; 'tis madness to defer.

12840 *Night Thoughts 'Night 1'*
Procrastination is the thief of time.

12841 *Night Thoughts 'Night 1'*
At thirty a man suspects himself a fool;
Knows it at forty, and reforms his plan;
At fifty chides his infamous delay,
Pushes his prudent purpose to resolve;
In all the magnanimity of thought
Resolves; and re-resolves; then dies the
same.

12842 *Night Thoughts 'Night 1'*
All men think all men mortal, but
themselves.

12843 *Night Thoughts 'Night 4'*
Man wants but little, nor that little long.

12844 *Night Thoughts 'Night 5'*
By night an atheist half believes in God.

12845 *The Revenge*
Life is the desert, life the solitude;
Death joins us to the great majority.

YOUNG G.W. 1846-1919
12846 *'The Lips That Touch Liquor'*
Though in silence, with blighted affection,
I pine,
Yet the lips that touch liquor must never
touch mine!

YOUNG Jock
12847
The person by far the most likely to kill
you is yourself.

YOUNG Michael 1915-
12848 *The Rise of the Meritocracy*
Today we frankly recognize that
democracy can be no more than aspiration,
and have rule not so much by the people
as by the cleverest people; not an
aristocracy of birth, not a plutocracy of
wealth, but a true meritocracy of talent.

YOUNG Owen D. 1874-1962
12849
I really believe that more harm is done by
old men who cling to their influence than
by young men who anticipate it.

YOURCENAR Marguerite 1903-1987
12850
He had come to that time in his life (it
varies from every man) when a human
being gives himself over to his demon or
to his genius, according to a mysterious
law which orders him either to destroy or
to surpass himself.

YUTANG Lin 1895-1976
12851
Sometimes it is more important to discover
what one cannot do, than what one can do.

12852
A solemn funeral is inconceivable to the
Chinese mind.

12853
All women's dresses are merely variations
on the eternal struggle between the
admitted desire to dress and the
unadmitted desire to undress.

ZAMYATIN Yevgeny 1884-1937
12854 *Essays 'I am Afraid'*
There can by no bronze literature, there
can only be a newspaper literature, which
is read today, and used for wrapping soap
tomorrow.

12855 *'Literature, Revolution and Entropy'*
Heretics are the only bitter remedy against
the entropy of human thought.

ZANGWILL Israel 1864-1926
12856
In how many lives does Love really play a
dominant part? The average taxpayer is
no more capable of a 'grand passion' than
of a grand opera.

12857 *Children of the Ghetto*
Scratch the Christian and you find the
pagan - spoiled.

12858 *The Melting Pot*
America is God's Crucible, the great
Melting-Pot where all the races of Europe
are melting and re-forming!

ZAPATA Emiliano 1879-1919
12859 *(of the maderistas)*
Many of them, so as to curry favour with
tyrants, for a fistful of coins, or through
bribery or corruption, are shedding the
blood of their brothers.

ZAPPA Frank 1940-
12860
Rock journalism is people who can't write
interviewing people who can't talk for
people who can't read.

ZILBOORG Gregory
12861
There is more than a mere suspicion that
the scientist who comes to ask
metaphysical questions and turns away
from metaphysical answers may be afraid
of those answers.

ZINGERS 'Smile'
12862
The first sign of maturity is the discovery that the volume knob also turns to the left.

The ZOHAR
12863
It is the way of a dog that if he is hit by a stone, he bites a fellow dog.

ZOLA Émile 1840-1902
12864
A work of art is a corner of creation seen through a temperament.

12865
If you ask me what I came to do in this world, I, an artist, will answer you: 'I am here to live out loud.'

12866 *La Bête humaine*
Don't go on looking at me like that, because you'll wear your eyes out.

12867 *(open letter on the Dreyfus affair)*
J'accuse.
I accuse.

ZUCKER Carl
12868
What children expect from grownups is not to be 'understood', but only to be loved, even though this love may be expressed clumsily or in sternness. Intimacy does not exist between generations - only trust.

KEYWORD INDEX

ACQUAINTANCE 1254, 1802, 2207, 2851, 5087, 5123, 11245, 11288
ACQUIRE 4772, 11012
ACQUITTAL 4712
ACQUITTED 5316, 9206
ACT 477, 3571, 3737, 6188, 7019, 8093, 8922, 9249, 9570, 10353, 12573
ACTING 868, 4138, 4302, 4432, 4505, 8264, 9349
ACTION 165, 1553, 2172, 2507, 2726, 3697, 3757, 3759, 4361, 4874, 5500, 7907, 7961, 8122, 9926, 10086, 10128, 11031, 12373, 12678
ACTIONS 1891, 2707, 7936, 8500, 9894, 10279, 10656, 10941
ACTIVITY 4182, 4365, 7223, 8971, 11346, 11729
ACTOR 441, 1518, 2121, 2674, 10089, 12183, 12261
ACTOR-MANAGER 4969
ACTORS 3518, 4324, 4426, 12165, 12516
ACTRESS 4531, 8974
ACTS 1074, 3485, 9549, 12697
ACTUAL 3189, 5555
AD 7264
AD INFINITUM 7886, 11254
ADAM 335, 387, 835, 1466, 1472, 4690, 7576, 11345, 11860
ADAPT 10559
ADDED 1171
ADDICTION 5297
ADDICTIVE 593
ADDITION 8715
ADDRESSES 9746
ADJECTIVE 358, 6841, 11900
ADJUDICATION 7939
ADJUSTMENT 4603
ADLESTROP 11600
ADMAN 3736
ADMINISTER 8846, 10660
ADMINISTRATION 5523, 6295
ADMINISTRATIVE 5536
ADMIRAL 10883
ADMIRATION 1484, 3614
ADMIRE 102, 1386, 1915, 2485, 6258, 8857
ADMIRED 823, 4745
ADMIRERS 5019
ADMIRES 6993, 8465, 9821
ADMIT 3731
ADOPTED 2619

ADORABLE 1450
ADORATION 12739
ADORE 4800, 6481, 7606, 7748, 8377, 9247, 10450
ADORED 7850, 12481
ADORINGS 5371
ADORNMENT 6173, 11628
ADS 6691, 8035
ADULT 235, 3397, 8264, 11301
ADULTERATED 5491
ADULTERER 2688
ADULTERIES 5196
ADULTERY 1966, 1969, 2130, 2134, 2385, 4862, 7103, 8437
ADULTS 2756, 5162, 11303, 12001
ADVANCE 173, 3558, 3873, 5807, 7991, 9493, 9515
ADVANCES 9933, 12383
ADVANTAGE 2035, 2385, 2738, 3158, 6782, 8162, 8908, 10466, 11841, 12617
ADVANTAGES 1464, 5056, 9868
ADVENTURE 113, 875, 6630, 12085
ADVENTURES 4155
ADVENTUROUS 6552
ADVERSARY 3491, 11804
ADVERSITY 709, 710, 711, 1277, 1841, 1904, 4283, 5019, 8719, 10025, 10381, 10856
ADVERTISE 8604
ADVERTISEMENT 4837, 5020
ADVERTISERS 11214
ADVERTISING 1436, 2478, 3420, 6067, 8306, 9513, 12278
ADVICE 71, 1278, 1287, 2410, 2440, 4744, 4903, 4937, 5843, 7082, 7751, 8195, 8746, 9144, 9186, 9210, 10746, 12359, 12442
ADVISE 1021
AESTHETIC 3970
AFFABLE 9577
AFFAIR 2660, 5849, 6153, 9537, 11090
AFFAIRS 708, 4936, 6674, 9677, 9718, 10043, 10691, 11947, 12127
AFFECT 6662, 7216
AFFECTATION 1974, 9054, 10762
AFFECTING 6136
AFFECTION 652, 1700, 5126, 7272, 9288, 10429, 10868, 11134, 12846
AFFECTIONATE 7118
AFFECTIONS 3171
AFFINITY 11660
AFFLICT 3069, 4758
AFFLICTED 8428

ANOMALIES	9817
ANOTHER	1134, 6149, 10097,
10629	
ANSWER	19, 1241, 1554, 2025,
2111, 2640, 2808, 3095, 3683, 4318, 4415, 4983,	
5750, 7242, 9051, 9280, 9803, 9878, 11698	
ANSWERABLE	8108, 12225
ANSWERED	4910, 6454, 7248
ANSWERING	8057
ANSWERS	577, 4731, 12482,
12861	
ANT	6478
ANTHROPOMORPHIC	5740
ANTI-EGOTISM	10786
ANTI-FEMINIST	8245
ANTI-SEMITISM	7328
ANTIBIOTICS	11125
ANTICIPATE	12849
ANTICIPATION	11173
ANTIPATHY	8163, 8863
ANTIPODES	6998
ANTIQUARIAN	5104
ANTIQUE	961, 7448, 10087
ANTIQUITIES	699
ANTIQUITY	3310, 5901
ANTITHESIS	8800, 12379
ANVIL	1385, 4075, 5630,
6413, 6675	
ANXIETY	3942, 4176, 4892,
5567, 7135, 7136, 9437, 9903, 11011	
ANXIOUS	3970
ANYBODY	3448, 3922, 4767,
11000, 12447	
ANYHOW	8160
ANYONE	10002
ANYTHING	1564, 3771, 4347,
7271, 8887, 9640, 12551	
ANYWHERE	1126, 1491, 5988
APART	8663, 9749, 12589
APATHETIC	11694
APATHY	4103, 5474
APE	2838, 4392, 6576
APES	5206, 7919, 9425
APHRODISIAC	1011, 4268, 12147
APLOMB	12400
APOLLO	130, 2536, 7418, 7495
APOLOGISTS	9787
APOLOGIZE	1255, 3463, 5254,
6625, 12217, 12617	
APOLOGY	3321, 4647, 4648, 5620
APOSTLE	3972
APOSTLES	515, 1913
APPAREL	10108

APPARENT	2158
APPARITION	8929, 12719
APPEAL	3067, 8998, 11936
APPEAR	187, 273, 906, 8254,
11848	
APPEARANCES	2271, 3322, 12461
APPEASER	2287
APPETITE	2160, 3444, 9269,
10045, 10422, 11087, 11096	
APPETITES	3720, 10070, 11957
APPLAUSE	2453, 5224, 6977,
7332, 8579, 8854	
APPLE	1204, 3458, 4690,
6995, 7390, 8611	
APPLES	4823, 9418, 10396,
12812	
APPLICATION	8502, 9309
APPLY	2964
APPOINTED	7624, 9967, 11967
APPOINTMENT	1364, 6470, 6492
APPOINTS	2153
APPRECIATION	9893
APPREHEND	12390
APPREHENSION	12677
APPREHENSIVE	7068
APPRENTICESHIP	848
APPROACH	942, 7601
APPROPRIATE	7961, 9149
APPROVAL	8208
APPROVE	8373, 8821
APRICOT	5204
APRIL	269, 1646, 3229, 3334,
5869, 7315, 10455, 12189	
APTITUDE	3190
AQUARIUM	6536
AQUITAINE	8077
ARABS	7159
ARBITER	11316
ARBITRATE	7416
ARBITRATOR	10419
ARCADIA	431
ARCH	9092
ARCH-ENEMY	448
ARCH-FLATTERER	737
ARCHAEOLOGIST	2263
ARCHANGEL	5908, 7514
ARCHANGELS	5264
ARCHER	9943
ARCHIMEDES	2820
ARCHITECT	4288, 9649, 12755
ARCHITECTS	3369
ARCHITECTURAL	11781

ARCHITECTURE   1514, 1584, 2821, 3732, 4042, 4585, 8143, 8547, 9500, 9864

ARCTIC   7698

ARDOUR   5191

ARDUA   392

ARENA   9919

ARGUE   910, 6832, 7173, 7397, 8110, 8728, 9146

ARGUING   4107, 4119, 7395, 12346

ARGUMENT   348, 1612, 2337, 3648, 4240, 4386, 5102, 5121, 6519, 9852, 10251, 12444

ARGUMENTS   3070

ARISE   11604

ARISTOCRACY   2220, 2791, 2828, 6767, 7701

ARISTOCRAT   3918, 11457, 11915

ARISTOCRATIC   516

ARISTOTLE   10864

ARITHMETIC   9865

ARITHMETICAL   6870

ARM   236, 554, 628, 6858, 9590

ARMADAS   8083

ARMAMENTS   6811

ARMCHAIRS   8973

ARMED   4234, 10180, 10574, 11943, 12591

ARMIES   309, 7653, 11040

ARMINIAN   8672

ARMISTICE   3516

ARMOUR   10655, 10994

ARMS   3038, 7599, 8680, 9522, 9853, 10629, 12018, 12599

ARMSTRONG   4097

ARMY   3394, 4297, 4801, 4806, 5640, 7239, 8009, 10751, 12009, 12255, 12748

AROMATIC   12598

AROSE   11629

AROUND   134, 6682

ARRANGEMENT   8472

ARRANGING   3633

ARRIVAL   7262

ARRIVE   11120

ARRIVED   2538, 9600

ARROGANCE   12753

ARROW   6414, 6423

ARROWS   1345, 3894

ARSE   2190, 2627, 3589, 6720

ARSENAL   9523

ART   197, 591, 800, 861, 893, 981, 1014, 1071, 1090, 1302, 1319, 1331, 1520, 1656, 2395, 2520, 2540, 2717, 2877, 3028, 3061, 3271, 3336, 3364, 3537, 3773, 3900, 4043, 4072, 4085, 4174, 4362, 4448, 4897, 5182, 5196, 5637, 5710, 6051, 6253, 6256, 6441, 6691, 6692, 6869, 6965, 7055, 7164, 7793, 7837, 7952, 7994, 8001, 8169, 8194, 8418, 8492, 8503, 8637, 8647, 8688, 8820, 8857, 9208, 9327, 9353, 9371, 9375, 9557, 9659, 9786, 10576, 10852, 10971, 11093, 11729, 11730, 12328, 12348, 12392, 12642, 12864

ART-SPEECH   6014

ARTHUR   6858

ARTICLES   2488

ARTICULATE   7912, 11999

ARTIFICER   5271

ARTIFICIAL   3278, 7307

ARTIST   565, 1504, 1732, 2023, 2491, 3415, 3733, 4225, 5269, 5761, 6438, 6687, 6697, 7094, 7182, 7324, 8076, 8181, 8255, 8638, 8648, 8928, 9286, 9785, 9815, 10687, 10706, 11596, 11917, 11937, 12146, 12450, 12624, 12865

ARTISTIC   3964

ARTISTS   810, 4174, 7989, 11180, 12290

ARTS   4590, 7639, 9255, 12773

ARYAN   8686

ASCENDING   7226

ASCENT   1551

ASCETIC   7960, 8171

ASCRIBED   10054

ASHAMED   2336, 2782, 3823, 4986, 5608, 5850, 7019, 7815, 8867, 10399, 10526, 12141

ASHBUDS   11401

ASHES   1413, 4223, 6774, 7856, 9781

ASHORE   6252

ASIA   6955

ASIAN   5015

ASIDE   5228, 8756, 11829

ASK   1173, 4795, 9891, 11514

ASKED   5072, 5286, 8366, 9135

ASLEEP   3892, 9611, 9636, 12681

ASPARAGUS   908, 3921

ASPECTS   4377, 8881

ASPERSION   10646

ASPIDISTRA   8305

ASPIRATION   2514, 6236, 12848

ASPIRATIONS   11974

ASPIRE   10480, 10670

ASS   2525, 3718, 5798, 8462, 9196

ASSASSIN   4197, 9581, 9776

AWAY	3803, 9245	BALDHEADED	6509
AWE	2653, 3608, 5221	BALDNESS	4538, 10764
AWEARY	10288	BALKANS	1304
AWFUL	9574, 9925	BALL	6187, 8769, 11201
AWKWARD	1825	BALLADS	3947, 6418
AWOKE	1726, 1943, 5406, 8383	BALLIOL	987
AXE	330, 7018, 8330, 8411	BALLOO	5215
AXIOM	3144	BALLOTS	6298
AXIS	4632	BALLS	878
AXLE	7405	BALM	5382, 10362
BABBLATIVE	10872	BALTIC	2314
BABE	7497	BALTIMORE	4188
BABES	2605	BANALITIES	2181
BABIES	1660, 4536, 9582,	BANALITY	1480, 9830
11592, 12292		BANDAGE	2652, 8904
BABY	323, 351, 873, 4961,	BANDIED	12239
5537, 5727, 6641, 6642, 7220, 7933, 10083		BANE	7530
BABYLON	1432	BANG	354, 3210
BACCHUS	3777, 5446	BANISH	7630, 9982
BACCY	5676	BANK	154, 4703, 6262, 8111,
BACH	3960	10331, 12039	
BACHELOR	434, 9607, 9610,	BANKRUPTCY	38
10046, 11257		BANNER	6427, 11850
BACHELORS	3182, 7835	BAPTISM	3168, 4916
BACK	960, 2123, 2262, 4369,	BAR	5615
4749, 5582, 6277, 6777, 8855, 9315, 11060, 11662,		BARABBAS	2020
11742		BARBARIANS	516
BACK ROOM	6392	BARBARISM	9787, 10837
BACKBONE	5640, 8343, 11793	BARBARITY	10807
BACKGROUND	6918	BARBAROUS	7419
BACKS	4323, 11654	BARD	7860
BACKSIDES	9620	BARDS	6422
BACKWARD	8154, 10012, 10923,	BARGAIN	3602, 5165, 10667
11699		BARGAINS	10730
BACKWARDS	5572, 12367	BARGE	10068
BACKYARD	12351	BARK	5131, 9034
BAD	15, 221, 420, 962,	BARKING	207
1058, 1506, 1778, 1902, 2014, 2702, 2774, 3326,		BARN	9324
3607, 4340, 5141, 5505, 5818, 6619, 7380, 8206,		BARNABY RUDGE	6521
9097, 9118, 9228, 9582, 10299, 10524, 10827, 11786,		BARREL	6907
12310, 12403, 12489		BARREL-LOAD	11621
BAD LUCK	7895	BARREN	3237, 6361, 9664
BADDER	5327	BARRICADE	9959, 9959
BADLY	2250	BARRIE	4299
BAG	4923, 6808	BARRIER	12737
BAGGAGE	4013	BASEBALL	242, 890, 7197
BAGHDAD	6492	BASHFULNESS	58
BAIT	6017	BASIC	4396
BAITS	7662	BASICS	9807
BAKER	2965	BASIL	5397
BALANCE	1227, 3401, 6034,	BASIL-POT	5398
8136, 8765, 9810, 12130			
BALD	781, 1446, 9025		

BASINGSTOKE	3989	BEATIFIC	7529
BASKET	11838	BEATING	6441
BASTARD	3772, 4566	BEATLES	5976
BASTARDS	8662, 12117	BEATS	2213
BASTION	3392	BEAUTEOUS	10405
BAT	9517, 12438	BEAUTIES	8877, 12671
BATH	8040	BEAUTIFUL	417, 444, 912, 2208,
BATHED	9419	2395, 2812, 3272, 3273, 3475, 3557, 4065, 4214,
BATHING	3943, 12725	4271, 4356, 4406, 4480, 4498, 4653, 5927, 6009,
BATHROOM	1373, 6325	6045, 6828, 7896, 7929, 8055, 8254, 8514, 8584,
BATS	760, 11611	9204, 9657, 10621, 10848, 12446, 12800
BATSMAN	5950	BEAUTIFULLY	10881
BATTALIONS	9590, 10138, 12083	BEAUTY	117, 289, 529, 683,
BATTLE	1209, 2057, 2117,	714, 1342, 1541, 1930, 1990, 2024, 2137, 2658, 2901,
2628, 2719, 4471, 4479, 4886, 5524, 5526, 6341,		2904, 2932, 2937, 3274, 3390, 3410, 3500, 3687,
7983, 9630, 10253, 11113, 12265		3699, 3978, 4696, 4820, 4871, 5179, 5364, 5440,
BATTLE-FLAGS	11445	5444, 5695, 6123, 6235, 6735, 6931, 7060, 7093,
BATTLEFIELD	2937	7268, 7423, 7458, 7659, 7774, 7840, 8043, 8361,
BATTLEMENTS	7458	8492, 8498, 8623, 8806, 8985, 9607, 9638, 9704,
BATTLES	4833, 6609, 8313,	9744, 10179, 10384, 10451, 10454, 10458, 10718,
11599, 11908		10990, 11376, 11731, 11758, 12049, 12102, 12233,
BAUBLE	8845	12445, 12634, 12796
BAY	9160	BEAVERBROOK	572
BAYED	4113	BECAUSE	424, 514, 6851, 7768
BAYONET	353, 12620	BECKONS	11707
BBC	12535	BECOMING	1503, 11009, 11991
BE	3575, 6686, 8651,	BED	103, 132, 177, 183,
10124		198, 304, 1018, 1039, 2816, 4120, 4867, 5946, 6000,
BE PREPARED	777	6187, 6674, 7352, 7685, 7798, 7986, 8557, 8997,
BEACH	4993	9314, 9858, 11016, 11098, 12198, 12549
BEACHES	2307	BEDCHAMBER	4568
BEACHY HEAD	2247	BEDFELLOWS	7792, 10401
BEACON	5606, 9831, 10412	BEDLAM	1972
BEADSMAN	8539	BEDROOM	2017
BEAK	7256, 8742	BEDSIDE	9224
BEAM	7527, 9455	BEDSPRING	8578
BEAR	1522, 3414, 5489,	BEE	136, 2789, 2791, 6089,
6845, 6973, 7365, 7377, 10448, 10548, 10702		6389, 6390, 7446, 12194
BEAR-BAITING	6768	BEER	2010, 4687, 6219,
BEARABLE	3072	10157, 10341, 10529, 10801
BEARD	2972, 6088, 10457	BEES	8892, 11511
BEARETH	746	BEETHOVEN	3960, 4549
BEARING	5264	BEETLE	5442
BEARS	4598, 4923	BEFELL	4689
BEAST	492, 5580, 6857, 7610,	BEFORE	321, 3074, 8222, 9571,
10136, 10374, 11802, 12808		10265, 11534
BEASTIE	316, 1821	BEG	6728
BEASTLY	2560	BEGAN	4071
BEASTS	5223	BEGET	8352, 9836, 11034,
BEAT	2104, 4341, 5535,	12117
7407, 10523, 10972		BEGGAR	1833, 5643, 10215
BEATEN	3265, 4067, 8529, 9730	BEGGARED	2996
		BEGGARS	3090, 10234
		BEGGARY	6759, 10059

BEGIN 3056, 5952, 6495, 6554, 11585

BEGINNING 292, 1141, 1146, 2108, 2315, 2649, 3220, 3221, 4028, 4711, 5985, 6138, 7053, 9383, 11269, 11331

BEGINNINGS 9718, 10162

BEGINS 8961, 9254, 11616

BEGUINE 8888

BEGUN 5171

BEHAVE 349, 6668, 9724, 10773, 11102

BEHAVING 2635

BEHAVIOUR 4413, 5763, 6617, 9427

BEHAVIOURISM 5740

BEHIND 1181, 3716, 3993, 5650, 5968, 6731, 8400, 9346, 10780

BEHOLD 3811, 5464, 10473

BEHOLDER 4820, 12102

BEING 7041, 7136, 7605, 8100, 10911, 11477

BELGRAVE 3937

BELIAL 7522

BELIEF 1394, 2433, 2659, 3643, 4580, 4982, 5026, 5102, 5348, 9515, 9835, 9882

BELIEFS 6502, 6810

BELIEVE 755, 874, 982, 1148, 2496, 2836, 2945, 3288, 3386, 3730, 4617, 4921, 5746, 6238, 7380, 8108, 8367, 9086, 9176, 9413, 9425, 9758, 10517, 10966, 11105

BELIEVED 72, 6334, 9838, 11132, 11310, 11340

BELIEVER 8125

BELIEVES 773, 7100, 9356, 12261, 12844

BELIEVING 8110, 8404, 8699, 9958, 11795, 12776

BELL 2912, 4689, 5338, 6100, 8705, 10074, 10217

BELLBOY 3555

BELLE 5405

BELLICOSE 2347

BELLIES 11957

BELLS 421, 4598, 8738, 11398, 11402

BELLY 6857, 8728, 9023

BELLY-TENSION 3889

BELLYFUL 7347

BELONG 3894, 5170, 8620, 9317, 11798

BELONGS 10968

BELOVED 1325, 4090, 10413

BELOW 548

BELOW PAR 7764

BELT 548

BELTED 5648

BENCH 307

BEND 5793, 12340

BENEFACTOR 3293, 12521

BENEFICIAL 9907

BENEFIT 3893, 4085, 8551, 11715

BENEFITS 6791, 11752

BENEVOLENCE 7251, 10732

BENEVOLENT 8523

BENT 7562, 8232

BEQUESTS 2129

BEREAVED 8077, 11926

BEREAVEMENT 4281

BERLINER 5507

BERMUDAS 6999

BESIEGED 8249

BESMEARED 7519, 10463

BEST 22, 403, 1662, 1820, 1990, 2277, 2297, 2425, 2633, 3315, 3399, 3665, 4924, 6585, 7668, 9055, 9259, 10172, 10299, 11071, 11836, 11836, 12070, 12074, 12083, 12493, 12802, 12807

BEST FRIEND 9431

BEST-LOVED 4419

BEST-SELLER 1437, 1440, 10768

BEST-SELLERS 8977

BESTIAL 10343

BESTOWS 2063

BESTRIDE 10189

BET 9630, 11150

BETHLEHEM 12808

BETIMES 10425

BETRAY 3719, 3808, 4158, 8620, 11618, 12430, 12702

BETRAYAL 2004, 6056, 9364, 12322, 12541

BETRAYED 816, 7241

BETRAYERS 11366

BETRAYING 3550

BETRAYS 1739, 9272

BETTER 666, 805, 940, 1243, 1561, 2042, 2195, 3204, 3265, 3696, 4785, 5548, 5648, 5780, 5878, 6273, 7023, 7062, 7160, 7248, 7516, 7727, 8111, 8373, 9148, 9748, 9828, 9871, 10299, 10479, 11464, 11568, 11609, 12310

BETTING 7084

BETWEEN 10797

BEWAILED 7813

BEWARE 94, 1174, 10495, 10878, 11673

BEWILDERED 588, 2054

BLIND MAN 9897

BLINDING 2469

BLINDLY 1800

BLINDNESS 5388, 5639

BLINDS 8382

BLINKED 9637

BLISS 3234, 4122, 5459, 7412, 7423, 7578, 8510, 9814, 10065, 10846, 12692

BLISTERS 9388

BLITHE 10623

BLOCK 1783, 3093, 3955

BLOCKHEAD 5098, 5153, 8826

BLOCKS 9435

BLONDE 6831

BLOOD 1224, 1303, 2186, 2305, 2490, 2655, 3561, 5690, 5963, 6928, 6972, 8270, 8726, 8940, 9532, 10274, 10281, 10282, 11477, 11541, 11559, 12859

BLOODSHED 6906

BLOODY 3817, 3850, 8257, 10271

BLOOM 877, 2516, 4739, 11025

BLOOMING 7864

BLOSSOM 2416, 6859, 10656, 10814, 11268

BLOTTED 5209

BLOW 3986, 5858, 6825, 6912, 10032, 10235, 10574, 11413

BLOWING 3095, 6042, 6712

BLOWS 245, 5828

BLUDGEONING 12507

BLUDGEONINGS 4492

BLUE 3481, 10705, 10881

BLUEBELL 6002

BLUEBIRD 1830, 11662

BLUEBOTTLES 2359

BLUEJAYS 6116

BLUNDER 1057, 1288, 1818, 8175, 10712

BLUNDERED 11393

BLUNDERS 1282, 2299, 2573, 4063, 7907, 11353

BLUR 11147

BLURRING 2281

BLUSHES 9594, 11892

BOARD 4513

BOAST 7537, 8357

BOASTING 5680

BOAT 2716, 11643, 12718

BOATHOOK 9757

BOATS 4230, 6100, 10090

BOBBY 5517

BODIES 251, 1073, 5821, 6710, 8119, 9778, 9924, 11136

BODY 924, 1413, 1434, 1807, 2414, 2448, 2551, 2556, 3245, 4226, 4643, 4972, 5315, 7231, 7665, 8120, 8291, 8292, 8837, 9001, 9595, 9783, 10985, 11544, 11703, 11956, 12406

BOGNOR 3847

BOGS 6372

BOGUS 6718

BOHEMIANS 12328

BOIL 3315, 11355

BOLD 3656, 11222, 11536, 12037

BOLDLY 6007, 9454

BOLDNESS 4679, 8982

BOLSHEVISM 10820

BOMB 6152, 6908

BOMBED 826, 3251

BOMBS 1104, 2361, 7953

BON-MOTS 7875

BONAPARTE 11684

BOND 410, 10312

BONDAGE 2338, 12635

BONDS 6375, 7169, 10468

BONE 1219, 1267, 6643, 7618, 8036

BONES 7671, 8207, 10221, 10400, 10482, 10713, 10804, 11925, 12636

BONFIRE 12628

BONNET 8895

BONNIE 6003

BONSOIR 12329

BONUSES 9395

BOOK 198, 1118, 1437, 1683, 2008, 2067, 2100, 2492, 2624, 2851, 3275, 4504, 4961, 5070, 5207, 5215, 5470, 5714, 5876, 6037, 6693, 6783, 7388, 7389, 8211, 8587, 8911, 8912, 8986, 9028, 9341, 9639, 9885, 10250, 10798, 10805, 11037, 11756, 11826, 12399, 12409, 12511, 12626, 12651, 12657, 12815

BOOK-KEEPERS 4321

BOOKIE 7964

BOOKKEEPING 7968

BOOKS 87, 597, 707, 717, 775, 862, 1706, 1707, 1859, 1860, 2070, 2537, 2843, 3498, 3564, 3658, 3815, 4389, 4466, 4478, 4548, 4659, 4758, 4864, 5888, 5896, 5987, 6493, 6649, 7387, 7641, 7815, 7863, 8930, 8933, 9521, 9592, 9652, 9655, 10794, 11841, 12298, 12502, 12650

BOOKSELLERS 4717

BOOKSHOPS 1029

BOOKSTORE 939

BOOMERANG 10752

BOOT 8318, 8687

BOOTED	7785
BOOTH	6322
BOOTS	1704, 3918, 4512, 5635, 7685, 9381
BOOZE	3413
BORE	3294, 4243, 4935, 5701, 5811, 7183, 7966, 8186, 10785, 11362, 11764, 11918, 12076
BORED	4602, 5000, 5725, 7346, 12203
BOREDOM	1457, 2166, 2550, 3488, 4546, 4906, 5981, 7135, 9691, 10010, 10974, 11005, 11706
BOREDOM-KILLING	2199
BORES	6805
BORING	189, 4597
BORN	123, 303, 556, 722, 1234, 1320, 1381, 1439, 1504, 1919, 2836, 3026, 3105, 3298, 3823, 3841, 4691, 5853, 6522, 6535, 7764, 8182, 8489, 9331, 9448, 9731, 9822, 10114, 10245, 10278, 10431, 10708, 10910, 10955, 11156, 11163, 11327, 11415, 11466, 11526, 11854, 12146, 12184, 12227, 12367, 12395, 12808
BORNE	4012, 12022
BORROW	1254, 5887, 9348, 12155, 12580
BORROWER	3301, 10108
BORROWING	11833
BOSOM	10780
BOSS	6964
BOSSING	8323
BOSSY	9974
BOSTON	279, 460, 1456, 11848
BOTHER	3925
BOTTICELLI	9227, 11927
BOTTLE	6670, 9072, 11109
BOTTLES	569, 8250, 8868
BOTTOM	4220, 12757
BOUGH	4738, 10467
BOUGHT	2013
BOUND	11519
BOUNDARY	8460
BOUNTY	10391
BOUQUET	8909
BOURGEOIS	3497, 3498, 4699, 6021, 7047, 8320, 9362
BOURGEOISE	10708
BOURGEOISIE	11797
BOW	1345, 3934
BOW-SHOT	11437
BOW-WOW	8549
BOWED	6919
BOWELS	2617

BOWLER	5950
BOXES	9376
BOY	296, 2562, 4188, 4479, 8114, 8585, 9583, 9607, 9923, 11073, 11880, 12263
BOY FRIEND	12571
BOYS	2326, 5884, 6392, 8592, 8693, 9519, 11589, 12218
BRACE	2308
BRACELET	5287
BRACES	1341
BRAIDS	7425
BRAIN	156, 544, 2955, 3131, 3368, 3939, 4490, 5185, 7376, 7377, 8625, 8712, 8768
BRAINS	549, 3654, 4003, 6460, 7338, 8283, 9047, 11086, 12580, 12612
BRAINWORK	9557
BRANCH	4803, 4946, 5363, 6933
BRANCHY	4707
BRANDISHED	6821
BRANDY	3843, 5106, 5676, 5912
BRASSIERE	861
BRAVE	1700, 2358, 2443, 3000, 3656, 5542, 5775, 8339, 9160, 10405
BRAVELY	5708
BRAVERY	2170, 5532, 11650, 12368
BRAW	5999
BRAWLING	1246
BRAZIL	11572
BREACH	10109, 10169
BREAD	311, 2546, 4521, 4694, 5314, 5947, 6458, 6669, 7061, 7369, 9036, 9082, 11257
BREADTH	3380
BREADWINNER	10782
BREAK	1042, 3090, 3447, 5793, 8271, 9751, 10104, 10528
BREAKDOWN	5859, 9692
BREAKFAST	693, 4313, 6316
BREAKFAST-TIME	4515
BREAKING	7871
BREAKS	644, 6723, 8797, 9066, 9117, 11484
BREAST	508, 4078, 8785, 9166, 10083, 10761
BREAST-BEATERS	1576
BREASTFEEDING	6215
BREASTPLATE	10180
BREASTS	5286, 9365, 11194
BREATH	3506, 4111, 4250, 5362, 6527, 8788, 9565, 12656

BREATHE 415, 5581, 7612, 7861, 8876, 11522

BREATHED 1937

BREATHES 9940, 11521

BREATHING 1574, 10618, 11409

BREATHLESS 12739

BREED 3826, 5699, 7469, 8554, 10360

BREEDING 3436, 6913, 9234, 10487, 10637, 11689, 11751, 11897

BREEZE 11486

BREEZES 11435

BREEZY 3257

BRETHREN 3844

BREVITY 2204, 10115

BREWERY 329

BRIBE 4933, 12524, 12622

BRIBERY 12859

BRIBING 9354

BRICK 6078, 8321, 9500, 11189, 11236

BRIDE 5435, 6144, 6636, 8804, 12689

BRIDESMAID 6144

BRIDGE 998, 1101, 5559, 6416, 6775, 6780, 10682, 11677

BRIDLE 9132, 9196

BRIEF 9698, 11513

BRIEFCASE 9244

BRIERS 10024

BRIGADE 12218

BRIGANDS 1882

BRIGHT 126, 1357, 1702, 2388, 7559, 9505

BRIGHTEN 2529

BRIGHTNESS 1542, 10915

BRILLIANCE 7945

BRILLIANT 555

BRILLIG 2109

BRIMSTONE 10876

BRING 3717

BRING BACK 8888

BRING UP 1289, 8612

BRINGER 1623

BRINGING 606

BRINKMANSHIP 11080

BRITAIN 9, 503, 2311, 4393, 6349, 10842

BRITANNIA 10801

BRITISH 569, 860, 1453, 2137, 2835, 3753, 3853, 5578, 6071, 6755, 7270, 10534, 11644

BRITON 3841

BRITONS 9975, 11629

BROADMINDED 3662

BROKE 998, 5643, 5921, 6382, 7181

BROKEN 1573, 3406, 5028, 8215, 11256, 12594, 12793

BROKEN-HEARTED 1800, 4424

BROKER 12665

BRONCHITIS 101

BRONX 2462

BROOD 9279, 12724

BROODING 3164, 11006

BROOK 6436, 7458

BROTHEL 1339, 5738

BROTHER 320, 999, 1413, 4148, 4373, 4794, 5686, 6149, 6638, 6919, 7023, 8314, 9176, 9443, 10731, 12247, 12422

BROTHER-IN-LAW 5589

BROTHERHOOD 391, 5014, 5593, 5858

BROTHERS 4036, 5594, 9873, 12729, 12859

BROUGHT 1192

BROW 9947, 10927

BROWN 6595, 11590

BRUISE 11785

BRUSH 6608

BRUSHERS 12667

BRUSHSTROKES 7688

BRUTAL 11293, 11694

BRUTALLY 8053, 11645

BRUTE 4146, 5694, 6089, 8687

BRUTES 4134, 7232, 8518

BRUTUS 1994, 10188, 10204

BUBBLE 1589, 3001, 8833, 10276, 12158

BUCK 354, 414

BUCKET 1227, 9781

BUCKINGHAM 7366

BUCKLE 700

BUD 2416, 5377

BUDDHISM 9740

BUDS 6876, 8435, 10073, 10459

BUFFOON 2995

BUG 8798

BUGLES 1562, 1562, 8381

BUGS 1025, 9185

BUILD 1582, 6598, 6996, 7787, 9348, 9518, 9656, 10833

BUILDER 9649

BUILDING 3418, 5967

BUILDINGS 2278, 11571

BUILDS 182, 1353, 3297, 6795

BUILT 673, 1248, 3426, 6088, 7533
BULB 12538
BULL 9172
BULLET 3313, 8019, 12530
BULLETS 6298, 8235
BULLIED 11198
BULLSHIT 3062
BULLY 4852, 9974
BULWARK 503, 1312
BUMP 316
BUMPY 2675
BUMS 6253
BUNCH 7805
BUNGLED 8720
BUNK 3532
BURDEN 1136, 3113, 3774, 5587, 6919, 8195, 8969, 11332, 12054
BUREAUCRACY 839, 6616
BURGLAR 4573
BURGLARY 3068
BURGLED 443
BURGUNDY 11689
BURIAL 4635
BURIAL-GROUND 6431
BURIED 545, 2449, 6764, 12620
BURKE 2079
BURN 351, 6932, 8505, 12688, 12809, 12822
BURNED 995, 4466
BURNING 1004, 4479, 4582, 5438, 7517, 9296
BURNISHED 10068
BURNS 10441
BURNT 4177, 10783
BURPS 863
BURR 10297
BURST 524
BURY 1027, 1176, 4535, 5551, 6442, 8085, 10203, 10404
BUS 4030, 8339
BUSES 11177
BUSIEST 9192
BUSINESS 21, 77, 647, 733, 782, 916, 1078, 2064, 2136, 2214, 2215, 2523, 2778, 2979, 3052, 3157, 3417, 4381, 4467, 4496, 6274, 6743, 7127, 7154, 8272, 8355, 8570, 8763, 9952, 10075, 10552, 11197, 11243, 11554, 11651, 11982, 12762, 12769
BUSINESSMAN 4163, 11938
BUSTLE 9999

BUSY 558, 3415, 3578, 4781, 6961, 7462, 7489, 8375, 9974, 10700, 10712, 11094, 12638
BUSYNESS 11087
BUT 949, 8015
BUTCHERS 10199, 10750, 12082
BUTLER 12611
BUTLERS 993, 7099
BUTT 4107
BUTTER 4037, 4038, 7369, 9167, 9473, 11544
BUTTERCUP 3923
BUTTERED 8519
BUTTERFLY 136, 4286, 8797
BUTTOCKS 4871, 9365
BUTTON 3555, 6093, 6491
BUTTONS 849, 1582, 5638
BUTTRESS 7162
BUXOM 7467
BUY 5287, 5529, 6405, 8221, 9043, 9903, 10452
BUYING 6108, 8365, 9639, 11834
BUYS 201
BUZZING 1635
BY-PRODUCT 2362
BYMATTER 718
BYRON 6756
BYSTANDERS 3306
CABBAGE 2110, 11898
CABINED 10272
CABINET 546, 791
CABOTS 1456
CADIZ BAY 1647
CAESAR 319, 371, 1187, 1448, 1997, 6549, 10198, 11961
CAFTAN 11052
CAGE 1324, 6728, 7802, 11363, 11475
CAGED 3055
CAIN 6061
CAJOLERY 1112
CAKE 552, 6917, 10427
CALAIS 7049
CALAMITIES 5066
CALCULATE 7604
CALCULATION 5826
CALCULATOR 11938
CALCULUS 3979
CALIFORNIA 2052
CALL 110, 526, 5524, 7066, 8084, 8966, 9763
CALLED 11698, 11760

CALLING 2476, 4658

CALLISTHENICS 8440

CALM 17, 2061, 2483, 4726, 8184, 8423, 8434, 9142, 9734, 12663

CALMLY 9508

CALORIES 1022

CALUMNY 2413, 2822, 4435, 5216, 12173

CALVINISTIC 7171, 8672

CAMBRIDGE 779, 1570, 11761

CAME 1996, 8393

CAMEL 206, 6786

CAMELOT 6190, 11438

CAMERA 565, 10850, 12262

CAMERADO 12409

CAMPASPE 6593

CAMPING 2766

CAMPUS 5536

CAN 9527, 10555, 12032

CAN'T 4891, 6142, 6250, 12042

CAN'T-HELP-IT 6020

CANADA 1468, 3689, 5354, 9027, 11803

CANADIAN 3680, 9392

CANALETTOS 6714

CANARY 8031

CANCEL 10271

CANCER 1, 8091, 10684

CANDID 8831

CANDLE 119, 1843, 5996, 7319, 10287, 10321, 10665, 11081, 11737, 12837

CANDLES 9040

CANDOUR 11311

CANDY 8039

CANKER 6981

CANNIBAL 6113, 7177

CANNIBALS 10754

CANNING 10788

CANNON 1405, 11393

CANOE 6976, 6998

CANOPY 10457

CANTS 11041

CAPABLE 174, 1403, 4068, 6408

CAPACITIES 3791

CAPITAL 2962, 6921, 6991, 7534, 9921, 10585

CAPITALISM 1493, 2138, 3629, 4360, 4457, 6156, 11152, 12222

CAPITALIST 5562, 6711, 8061, 8522

CAPITULATE 5130

CAPTAIN 2091, 3883, 4493, 8064, 8087, 10291, 11552

CAPTIVE 5699, 7587

CAR 2694, 2695, 6252, 6703, 7334, 7405, 8622

CARBORUNDUM 306

CARBUNCLE 10909

CARCASE 11613

CARD GAME 3068

CARDS 5877, 6593, 12091

CARE 788, 1317, 1353, 1693, 1877, 3026, 3205, 6540, 6626, 7367, 7696, 7827, 8484, 8654, 9674, 10164, 10538, 12024, 12158, 12575

CAREER 361, 2731, 2882, 3593, 6782, 11171

CAREFUL 2629, 8554, 11495, 12504

CAREFULLY 3927

CARELESS 2223, 3483, 11454, 11495

CARELESSNESS 12486

CARES 4275, 6421

CARESSED 2718

CARGO 5244, 5663, 7059

CARICATURE 2512, 3966, 7222

CARLYLE 1898

CARNEGIE 6218

CAROLINA 4188

CARPENTER 4952, 9324

CARPET 5379, 9302

CARRIAGE 2640, 2799, 3943, 6187, 9177

CARRION 3785

CARRY 400, 1473, 3272, 3309, 5044, 6078, 8527, 11742

CARS 884, 6536

CART 6119

CARVE 10193, 12106

CARVED 12621

CASE 623, 3965, 7217

CASH 3470, 10662, 11824

CASKET 5461

CASSOWARY 12434

CAST 1424, 1728, 1995, 7001

CASTLE 2406, 5916

CASTLES 2194

CASTRATE 3293

CASUALTY 2127

CAT 2532, 3217, 6689, 6808, 7744, 7796, 9159, 10721, 10781, 10817, 11195, 12543

CAT FEET 9777

CATACLYSM 4870

CATACOMBS 4551

CLAMOUR	6439
CLAN	8436
CLANGING	5630
CLAP	8332
CLARET	3374, 5106
CLARION	7866
CLARITY	8170, 8330
CLASS	1519, 4019, 5923, 6398, 7038, 7046, 8518, 10962, 11934
CLASSES	2160, 2312, 8174, 8696, 10741
CLASSIC	2851, 3398, 11171
CLASSICAL	3960, 5113, 8666
CLASSICS	6076, 7347, 8925, 11146
CLASSIFICATIONS	12280
CLASSLESS	4938
CLATTER	1012, 4299
CLAW	11465
CLAWED	11981
CLAWS	2102
CLAY	3858, 5349, 7839, 10356
CLEAN	3216, 6325, 6657, 7145
CLEANED	3927
CLEANLINESS	6831
CLEANNESS	1572
CLEANSED	1343
CLEAR	5242, 9424
CLEAVE	1220
CLEMENTINE	7823, 7824
CLEOPATRA	8476, 10069
CLERGY	5605, 9194
CLERGYMAN	5249, 7964
CLERGYMEN	2967, 10796
CLERICAL	1568
CLERKS	4321, 4884
CLEVER	549, 3078, 4063, 5607, 5673, 9756, 11344, 12675
CLEVEREST	290, 12557
CLEVERNESS	5832
CLICHÉ	4296
CLIENT	3814
CLIFF	1830
CLIFFS	6771
CLIMATE	1538, 1966
CLIMB	3246, 7427, 9298
CLIMBED	188, 2861
CLING	1032, 12726
CLINTON	12191
CLIVE	1055
CLOAK	3715

CLOCK	554, 1571, 4120, 5568, 5579, 6527, 7707, 9738, 10007, 12357, 12750
CLOCK-SETTER	10216
CLOCKS	6416, 9867
CLOCKWORK	1733
CLOGS	7674
CLOISTER	5960
CLOSE	178, 672, 4568
CLOSED	3446
CLOSER	1309, 2256, 2600, 6267, 11409
CLOSES	5472
CLOSET	2457, 2798
CLOSING	2491
CLOTH	838
CLOTHED	11027
CLOTHES	947, 2164, 2436, 2829, 3057, 3425, 4542, 6008, 6393, 11673, 11855, 12666
CLOTHING	97, 2318, 5897
CLOUD	5443, 7140, 7373, 7410, 10586, 10605, 12746
CLOUDS	1542, 7745, 11582, 12713, 12718
CLOUDY	1921, 7496
CLOVERLEAF	7970
CLOWNS	4462, 10846
CLUB	1287, 6394, 7035, 10737
CLUE	2953
CLUTCH	11622
CLUTCHING	527
CLUTTERED	199
COACH	6613, 11179
COAL	1119, 12121
COALITION	2833, 6842, 12191
COALMINES	5551
COARSE	9618
COASTER	7059
COAT	211, 4108
COBWEBS	11232
COCAINE	11124
COCK	919, 7455, 11046
COCKEREL	6120
COCKTAIL	8664, 9489, 10738
CODE	10006
CODFISH	1023
CODGER	4838
COERCE	11021
COFFEE	263, 8875, 9229
COFFIN	139, 946, 7186, 8244, 8296, 8654, 10949
COHORTS	1936

COIN 12331
COINS 8273, 11416
COITION 1607, 9170
COLD 678, 889, 1558, 3704, 5406, 6029, 6055, 7547, 7760, 8173, 9359, 10067, 10784, 11281, 11803, 12120, 12245
COLD BLOOD 10556
COLD STORAGE 9765
COLERIDGE 1940, 1945, 5904
COLISEUM 8895
COLLECTIONS 5888
COLLEGE 2327, 4489, 5001, 5328, 7081, 11319
COLLIDE 8889
COLLISION 11693
COLLISIONS 4295, 9757
COLONIAL 3844
COLONIES 2009, 2834, 2872
COLOSSAL 8613
COLOSSUS 5137, 10189
COLOUR 2, 2159, 3533, 5593, 8750, 9644, 11664, 12554
COLOURED 10479
COLOURS 2157, 2292
COLUMBUS 3852, 4098
COLUMN 4638
COMATOSE 2347
COMB 1446
COMBINATION 2758, 8426
COMBUSTION 6065
COME 1179, 3130, 3839, 4832, 5712, 6642, 7353, 7928, 9627, 9773, 12282, 12318
COMEDIAN 1671, 4530, 7189
COMEDY 1785, 1955, 8003, 10671, 11924, 12116
COMES 8278
COMET 7552
COMETS 7020
COMFORT 639, 1420, 1709, 2237, 2973, 3069, 5508, 5585, 5603, 6503, 6759, 8184, 8483, 10222
COMFORTABLE 3402, 4394, 5423
COMFORTING 6964
COMFORTS 710, 10481
COMIC 6073
COMICAL 3938
COMING 400, 8656, 9950, 12751
COMMAND 4671, 7310, 7384, 7771, 8151, 8561, 9931, 10094, 12721
COMMANDED 7614
COMMANDMENTS 5568, 5666, 9393, 10179

COMMEMORATIVE 9569
COMMENDABLE 8369
COMMENDATION 1257
COMMENT 9918, 11145
COMMENTATORS 4443, 12837
COMMERCE 1273, 2048, 8265, 11650
COMMERCIAL 4244, 8394
COMMISSION 4039, 7149
COMMIT 9608, 10166
COMMITMENT 1551
COMMITTED 6942, 9833
COMMITTEE 141, 206, 300, 4098, 4391, 4792, 7686, 7750, 9714
COMMITTEES 1703, 8976
COMMODITY 9451
COMMON 233, 595, 1125, 2007, 2997, 3982, 4716, 5684, 6360, 6363, 7018, 7207, 7583, 9320, 9339, 10156, 10807, 10995, 12100, 12671, 12799
COMMON SENSE 6176, 7999
COMMON-LOOKING 6311
COMMONER 5805
COMMONPLACE 8485
COMMONS 2853, 6673
COMMONWEALTH 2308, 6709, 7386, 9543
COMMUNES 7150
COMMUNICATION 436, 4400, 7258, 9287, 12349
COMMUNISM 6155, 7045, 9498
COMMUNIST 3255, 3627, 6907
COMMUNISTS 4269
COMMUNITY 1269, 4955, 6287, 7296, 9752, 12729
COMMUTER 12350, 12360
COMPACT 3783
COMPANION 999, 7794, 11666
COMPANIONS 739, 6434, 12134
COMPANIONSHIP 29, 1065, 4267
COMPANY 4243, 4470, 4808, 5061, 11245, 11262, 12139, 12487
COMPARE 10459, 10477
COMPARED 2729
COMPARISON 4340
COMPARISONS 6586, 10050
COMPASS 10981
COMPASSION 9621
COMPELLED 11780
COMPENSATIONS 3304, 12163
COMPETENCE 1686
COMPETITION 2387, 4423, 4593, 5024, 7937, 11952
COMPETITIVE 8464

COMPETITORS 10690
COMPLACENT 5511
COMPLAIN 1777, 2849
COMPLAINING 3033
COMPLAINT 4570
COMPLAINTS 7166, 7386, 8706
COMPLETE 7608
COMPLETION 7712, 8456
COMPLEX 4304, 11025
COMPLEXES 3620
COMPLEXION 579, 12039
COMPLEXITIES 2291, 12789
COMPLEXITY 8454
COMPLIANCE 2320
COMPLICATED 2394
COMPLICATIONS 12332
COMPLIES 1896
COMPLIMENT 1871, 4349, 4786, 11863, 12056
COMPOSED 4629
COMPOSER 4027, 4686, 8092
COMPOSERS 1549
COMPOUND 1890
COMPREHEND 2665, 8118
COMPREHENSIBLE 9912
COMPRESSED 7911
COMPROMISE 4410, 7992
COMPULSION 7385
COMPULSORILY 6817
COMPUTER 4180, 5337, 6555, 8269
COMPUTERS 364, 6816, 12187
COMRADESHIP 3261
CONCAVE 7524
CONCEAL 2493, 5832, 6790, 9746
CONCEALING 11897
CONCEALMENT 10430
CONCEDE 7310
CONCEIT 11787
CONCEITS 6945
CONCEIVABLE 7354
CONCEIVED 884
CONCENSUS 11567
CONCENTRATED 5420
CONCENTRATES 5029
CONCENTRATION 8144, 11166
CONCEPTION 2909, 4587, 7712, 8226, 9557, 11164
CONCEPTS 11004
CONCERN 513, 8157, 11947, 12446
CONCERNED 2029, 8141, 11714
CONCERT 7346, 9623

CONCESSIONS 1750, 7260
CONCILIATE 3330
CONCLUSION 1366, 7287, 9634
CONCORD 7660, 10320, 10456, 11668
CONCRETE 7970, 10909, 12094
CONCRETE JUNGLE 7918
CONCURRED 8393
CONCURRENCE 8426
CONDEMN 1298, 6838, 7734, 10434
CONDEMNED 5779, 9206, 9843, 12251
CONDESCEND 11226, 11561, 12782
CONDITION 2033, 5931, 6866, 8569
CONDITIONS 9870, 11736, 12468
CONDUCT 513, 6295, 6331, 7873, 8616, 8746, 8990, 10902
CONDUCTORS 936, 11171, 11308
CONFEDERACY 11223
CONFEDERATION 6643, 10745
CONFERENCE 756, 3477
CONFESS 4835, 5847, 7781, 8958, 9104
CONFESSING 8603
CONFESSION 285, 810, 2230, 3459, 8927
CONFESSIONAL 9750
CONFIDE 2042
CONFIDENCE 3582, 6579, 8669
CONFIDENTLY 11667
CONFIDES 6580
CONFINE 8235
CONFINEMENT 6372, 12546
CONFIRMATION 299, 10347
CONFLICT 2309, 3103, 5079, 8910, 8955
CONFLICTS 4732, 12784
CONFORM 7770, 7964, 8567
CONFORMATION 6745
CONFORMING 9860
CONFORMISM 11168
CONFORMISTS 6679, 7151
CONFOUND 2894, 10266
CONFRONT 8596
CONFUSED 7984, 9835, 10800
CONFUSING 3775
CONFUSION 688, 7558
CONGENIAL 7153
CONGO 6320
CONGRATULATIONS 1746
CONGREGATION 2712

4999, 5027, 5175, 5503, 5532, 6175, 6242, 6770, 7508, 7902, 8012, 8014, 8137, 8512, 9330, 9406, 9924, 11684, 11782, 11847, 11953, 12036, 12128, 12179

COURAGEOUS 9577

COURSE 4502, 6509, 6729, 7077, 8573, 10327, 11720

COURT 2188, 2645, 3066, 3582, 5225, 8130, 8960, 10585

COURTED 2022

COURTESY 4066, 5708, 9931

COURTS 9700, 11488

COURTSHIP 2489, 6916, 8273

COUSIN 3926

COUSINS 11654

COUTH 8576

COUTTS 3918

COVENANT 3783

COVER 12237

COVET 5616

COVETING 9759

COVETOUS 10720

COW 915, 6881, 8032, 11259, 12437

COWARD 2033, 2505, 3511, 4104, 8281, 10498, 11517

COWARDICE 2150, 2170, 3649, 4928, 11893

COWARDLY 12085, 12242

COWARDS 2490, 3701, 6204, 6401, 9446, 10126, 10194, 10379, 11850, 12323

COWSLIP 7426

COXCOMB 7235, 9661

COY 4545, 7470, 9957

COYNESS 7002

CRABBED 10449

CRACK 3320, 9080

CRADLE 946, 2312, 3092, 7999, 8680, 10314, 10620, 12103, 12407

CRAMPS 12635

CRANE 10701

CRASH 2073

CRAVED 3994

CRAVING 8531, 12029, 12763

CRAWL 11238

CRAZY 213, 405, 1576, 2640, 4403, 8577

CREAK 9180

CREAM 3665, 3930, 7224, 7875

CREATE 1540, 4236, 7128, 8165, 11903, 12696

CREATED 2081, 2682, 3355, 6388, 6560, 8839

CREATES 5353, 7869, 11058

CREATING 6495, 7839

CREATION 2027, 4064, 6361, 7616, 9447, 9911, 11135, 11494, 12864

CREATIVE 2135, 3537, 3610, 6733, 11005

CREATIVENESS 8645

CREATIVITY 2055, 3488, 9281, 9719

CREATOR 7603, 7622, 8100, 9597, 10775, 11862

CREATURE 7275, 7829, 8307, 8793, 11253

CREATURES 70, 126, 342, 2542, 4827, 7582, 7591, 8567

CREDIT 3931, 6696, 7937, 9681

CREDITORS 38

CREDULITY 4617, 5890, 8669

CREED 2967, 3765, 11039

CREEDS 10617, 11473, 11490

CREEP 10287

CREEPING 11446, 12347

CREMATED 4407

CREPT 5462

CRESCENT 7521

CRESCENT-MOON 12718

CRETE 9741

CRICKET 6071, 6873, 7443, 7959, 11381, 11769

CRIED 6681

CRIES 10460

CRIME 51, 2268, 2389, 2437, 2960, 3071, 3529, 3702, 3959, 4068, 4986, 7002, 7340, 8667, 8781, 8938, 9278, 10009, 11651, 12026, 12052

CRIMEA 11355

CRIMES 2707, 3022, 3411, 7513, 7874, 9501, 12081

CRIMINAL 5544, 9921

CRIMINALS 9754, 12449

CRIPPLES 8497

CRISIS 2644, 8408, 8518, 11569, 12323

CRISP 8050

CRITERIA 5555

CRITIC 1863, 2660, 3045, 3568, 4961, 5913, 6016, 6507, 8748, 11902, 12342, 12735

CRITICAL 6733, 10340, 11749

CRITICISM 520, 792, 1367, 1589, 3551, 4764, 6707, 7111, 8882, 11041, 11907, 12377

CRITICIZE 2284, 3768, 6279, 9015

CRITICIZED 4767, 6494, 8579

CRITICIZING 5781

CRITICS 967, 1939, 2427, 2877, 4634, 5234, 7838, 11848, 12304, 12450, 12667
CROAKS 10260
CROCODILE 2287, 5653
CROCODILES 766, 4859, 9142
CROCUS 6528
CROMWELL 929, 5229, 6357
CROOK 8200, 9490
CROOKED 1321, 4034, 5333, 6370, 7026
CROP 8733
CROSS 853, 5229, 5489, 7965, 10704, 10782, 11612, 12199, 12581
CROSS-BOW 2420
CROSS-GRAINED 4146
CROSSED 658, 8014
CROSSES 6633
CROSSING 6315
CROW 2189, 3785, 6517, 9110
CROWD 730, 866, 953, 2572, 3363, 5569, 5749, 8770, 12746
CROWDS 3880, 5061, 7849
CROWING 120
CROWN 537, 1115, 1237, 2031, 2715, 3073, 3242, 7899, 8552, 8591, 10078, 10082, 10161, 10364
CROWNED 7009
CROWNS 10419
CRUCIFIED 127
CRUCIFY 2068
CRUEL 2615, 4336, 5398, 8792, 9809, 10130, 10133, 11322
CRUELLEST 3229, 11115
CRUELTY 1328, 9998
CRUISE 11119
CRUMBLING 6723
CRUMBS 4923
CRUMPETTY 6101
CRUSADE 6050, 12567
CRUSH 2941, 12095
CRUSOE 5084
CRY 1709, 1807, 3407, 5081, 5974, 6061, 6262, 8689, 9255, 9382, 9589, 10170, 10245, 11024, 12184
CRYING 11480
CRYSTAL 1118
CUCKOLD 3365
CUCKOO 2670, 7707, 10918
CUCKOO CLOCK 12264
CUCKOO-ECHOING 4707
CUCUMBER 5142, 6669
CUE 3961
CULPRIT 12172

CULPRITS 8398, 12026
CULT 159, 6663
CULTIVATE 5115, 5904, 12073
CULTIVATED 3916, 7224
CULTURE 512, 515, 966, 2027, 3679, 3970, 4289, 4318, 6394, 6692, 7139, 12333, 12400
CUNNING 719, 5270, 6184
CUP 1189, 1803
CUPID 6593, 10328
CUPIDONS 1788
CUR 207
CURATE 3457, 3991
CURATES 1556, 1568
CURDS 10445
CURE 4, 991, 2569, 3024, 5655, 5785, 9816, 10514, 10744, 11306
CURED 2380, 4648, 5621, 6623, 7804, 8968
CURES 8054, 10687
CURFEW 4248, 7442
CURIOSITY 188, 4840, 5898, 11136, 11768
CURIOUSER 2101
CURL 6420, 7350
CURRENCY 11139, 12568
CURRENT 7423
CURSE 6027, 9379, 10460, 11017, 11438, 12476
CURSED 10482
CURSES 4006, 7478, 10875
CURTAIN 8778, 9271
CURTAINS 7744
CURVE 324
CURVED 3143
CURZON 386
CUSTARD PIE 8304
CUSTOM 1775, 2653, 4947, 9234, 10087, 10109, 11431, 11659
CUSTOMARY 4990, 8707
CUSTOMER 9423
CUT 5240, 6393, 10208, 12177, 12284
CUTS 10197
CUTTING 986
CUTTLEFISH 8303
CYCLE 5231, 7604
CYCLE-CLIPS 5978
CYNIC 1258, 3283, 7186, 7422, 12499
CYNICAL 968, 3553
CYNICALLY 8153

CYNICISM	2361, 4472, 6601, 7235, 9670
DADDY	343, 8030, 8886
DAFFODIL	11459
DAFFODILLS	7481
DAFFODILS	5989, 12746, 12747
DAFT	9948
DAGGER	10265
DAGGERS	10130
DAINTILY	1102, 1103
DAINTY	4541
DAIRY	5195
DAIRYMAID	7369
DAISIES	3971
DAISY	2640
DALLIANCE	10107
DAM	7312
DAMAGE	5160, 12601
DAMES	7455
DAMMED	4692
DAMN	308, 3724, 5901, 7313, 7696, 8439
DAMNATION	593, 1414, 7513
DAMNED	2847, 3475, 4143, 4774, 5644, 6927, 7546, 8655, 8770, 12272, 12717
DAMNING	1890
DAMNS	6635
DAMOZEL	9559
DANCE	1079, 1809, 1925, 2951, 6910, 6967, 8820, 8855, 8934, 10576, 10707, 12813
DANCED	6098
DANCER	11938, 12788
DANCES	6153, 12747
DANCING	1083, 2668, 7460, 9762, 10383
DANDYISM	7235
DANGER	39, 1417, 2268, 4882, 5800, 8034, 8377, 9053, 9247, 10150, 10651, 11202, 11996, 12361
DANGEROUS	111, 1738, 4143, 4882, 4947, 5478, 5818, 5867, 7938, 7941, 7985, 8815, 10190, 12333, 12464, 12467, 12496
DANGEROUSLY	8180
DANGERS	559, 1743, 6448, 7971, 8452, 9985
DANIEL	10317
DARE	7780, 10263, 10868
DARES	389, 2940, 10389
DARING	190, 2398, 11360
DARK	907, 1593, 2190, 2422, 2930, 3675, 4499, 4589, 5175, 6428, 6896, 7513, 7561, 7650, 9040, 10080, 10704, 11843, 11964

DARK-HEAVING	1931
DARKEN	5393, 6275
DARKER	4794
DARKEST	4257
DARKLING	12034
DARKNESS	119, 1175, 1988, 3253, 4408, 5296, 5388, 6605, 7504, 7628, 7999, 8062, 8778, 9239, 11612
DARKSOME	4089, 10924
DARLING	864, 2065, 7823, 10459
DARWINIAN	3912
DATE	1036
DATING	2530
DAUGHTER	2568, 3244, 3800, 5661, 7614, 10310, 10594
DAUGHTERS	496, 6812
DAVID	8049
DAWN	6746, 7065, 11619, 12519
DAWNED	9983, 10588
DAY	7, 1452, 2043, 2907, 3064, 3099, 3253, 3717, 4721, 4725, 6013, 6528, 6681, 7697, 8107, 8211, 8718, 9240, 9328, 9586, 9983, 10080, 10254, 10363, 10915, 11359, 11469, 11524, 12737
DAY-LABOUR	7676
DAY-TO-DAY	2201, 5855
DAYDREAMING	11176
DAYLIGHT	10322
DAYS	164, 1426, 1935, 2952, 3218, 3345, 5980, 7788, 7865, 11225, 11430, 12679
DAZZLE	12237
DAZZLING	8471, 11634
DE VALERA	6352
DEAD	208, 320, 419, 504, 824, 874, 990, 1006, 1055, 1176, 1566, 1626, 2761, 2867, 2902, 2942, 3034, 3846, 3885, 4127, 4246, 4329, 4479, 4686, 4865, 5554, 5689, 6028, 6133, 6251, 6418, 6438, 6442, 6491, 6500, 6567, 6783, 6942, 7031, 7049, 7701, 8078, 8177, 8384, 8922, 9161, 9226, 9434, 9556, 9696, 9827, 10421, 10634, 10784, 11528, 11597, 11602, 11638, 11815, 11820, 12084, 12210, 12479, 12640
DEADLOCK	10745
DEADLY	5642, 11888, 12707
DEAF	9014
DEAL	6762, 9532
DEALING	3708
DEAN	1568, 2848, 10946, 10951
DEANERIES	3392
DEAR	3724, 7696, 10468
DEARER	7590
DEAREST	10258

DEATH 3, 113, 177, 209, 305, 347, 421, 469, 720, 721, 723, 797, 921, 1104, 1132, 1133, 1142, 1144, 1412, 1420, 1573, 1608, 1619, 1820, 1864, 2125, 2351, 2434, 2721, 2794, 2799, 2912, 2915, 2916, 2923, 2935, 2943, 3003, 3183, 3228, 3233, 3370, 3438, 3449, 3496, 3546, 3600, 3886, 4197, 4250, 4281, 4396, 4502, 4623, 4689, 4715, 4841, 5122, 5127, 5318, 5339, 5362, 5773, 5790, 5933, 6109, 6214, 6562, 6659, 6665, 6682, 6774, 6856, 6903, 6929, 7060, 7063, 7080, 7499, 7549, 7554, 7624, 7652, 7667, 7695, 7787, 7808, 7813, 7858, 7943, 7998, 8088, 8387, 8780, 9295, 9409, 9509, 9604, 9647, 9822, 9846, 9901, 9945, 10002, 10057, 10125, 10194, 10197, 10363, 10364, 10375, 10395, 10573, 10585, 10593, 10655, 10657, 10672, 10779, 10800, 10836, 10845, 10854, 10880, 10925, 11023, 11028, 11151, 11199, 11280, 11375, 11387, 11392, 11394, 11521, 11576, 11631, 11639, 11765, 11829, 11849, 11964, 12236, 12544, 12845

DEATH-MOTH 5442

DEATH-SENTENCE 6046

DEATHBED 626, 12596

DEATHLESS 9563, 11766

DEATHS 7953, 12456

DEBASEMENT 6888

DEBATABLE 4709

DEBATE 3244, 4830, 10660

DEBAUCH 1462, 5546

DEBAUCHE 1260

DEBAUCHERY 5762

DEBONAIR 7467

DEBRIS 5511

DEBT 1687, 1887, 4120, 4909, 9977, 10006, 11762

DEBTOR 706

DEBTS 10402

DECADE 12630

DECADENCE 11694

DECAY 2903, 3018, 4642, 5940, 6665, 8134, 8331, 8454

DECAYED 3969

DECEASED 5668, 10162, 12670

DECEIT 1352, 2686

DECEITFUL 8429

DECEITFULNESS 3217

DECEIVE 2035, 4049, 4518, 6604, 9946, 11823, 12797

DECEIVED 889, 4050, 4052, 5840, 5934, 7502, 7654, 11159

DECEIVERS 1436, 10044

DECEIVES 8692

DECEIVING 9958

DECEMBER 871, 5363

DECEMBERS 1558

DECENCY 6529, 8805, 9539, 11105

DECENDANTS 7351

DECENT 4699, 6253, 7943, 9742

DECENTLY 2071

DECENTRALIZED 4423

DECIDE 5765, 6523, 8809, 9139, 12016

DECISION 2979, 3489, 8458, 9280, 9511, 11821

DECLARE 12475

DECLARING 7706

DECLINES 6752

DECLINING 764

DECOMPOSING 12653

DECORATE 12752

DECORATING 11781

DECORATION 8335

DECORUM 1815, 9926

DECREED 5456

DEDICATION 9233, 11070

DEE 5613, 11282

DEED 879, 1579, 3215, 4083, 4711, 5456, 6588, 7275, 9059, 10266, 10269, 10321

DEEDS 2193, 4215, 7629, 7924, 8729, 9328, 10106, 10220, 12573

DEEP 252, 2085, 4137, 5941, 11412, 11467, 11524, 12241

DEEP-VERSED 7641

DEER 1813

DEFACE 12752

DEFEAT 941, 2257, 2321, 3674, 5697, 6439, 8628, 9832, 10349, 11321, 11994

DEFEATED 365, 6128, 6340, 6341, 6655, 12027

DEFECT 1363, 7622, 9681

DEFECTS 9706, 9892

DEFENCE 396, 826, 827, 1312, 1543, 1577, 5270, 6790, 7657, 8327, 12541

DEFEND 823, 2307, 2687, 4037, 6740, 10824, 12069

DEFENDED 6445

DEFENDER 1912

DEFIANCE 396, 4150, 8668

DEFIANT 9326

DEFICIENCIES 479

DEFIED 747, 9861

DEFINITION 2524, 6814, 8191, 9700

DEFLOWER 10929

DEFORMITY 550

DEFUNCT 2173

DEFY 3762

DEFYING 2610

DEGAS	7254
DEGENERATE	9597, 10994
DEGENERATION	11112
DEGRADATION	10970, 12250
DEGRADE	3685
DEGREE	1458, 10414
DEGREES	5375, 9278
DEITY	1811, 4352, 11164
DELAY	404, 7630
DELAYING	11788
DELAYS	1701, 3039, 6350,
12359	
DELEGATE	1443
DELETED	428
DELIBERATE	4925, 9139
DELIBERATES	63
DELIBERATION	7542
DELICACY	4446
DELICATE	5056
DELIGHT	328, 626, 1320, 1334,
5079, 6545, 7180, 7589, 7612, 7865, 8813, 9311,	
9847, 10075, 12798	
DELIGHTFUL	5830, 6379, 7392,
12125	
DELIGHTS	5864, 6564, 7734,
10120	
DELINQUENCIES	3184
DELINQUENCY	9231
DELIVER	316, 1414, 2243, 8044
DELIVERANCE	9247
DELIVERED	10339
DELIVERER	7649
DELPHINIUMS	7368
DELPHOS	7495
DELUGE	8753
DELUSION	174, 1742, 7205, 11731
DEMAND	1294, 3524, 5007,
5972, 9306	
DEMEAN	9319
DEMEANING	10711
DEMI-ATLAS	10066
DEMOCRACY	494, 566, 574, 1516,
1627, 1703, 1771, 1849, 2220, 2280, 2345, 2475,	
3551, 3554, 5288, 6159, 6280, 6329, 6767, 6822,	
7190, 7207, 8059, 8060, 8140, 8704, 9499, 9523,	
10554, 11141, 11177, 11804, 11809, 12353, 12507,	
12582, 12585, 12848	
DEMOCRAT	5013, 8660, 9485
DEMOCRATIC	858, 3070
DEMOCRATS	11076
DEMOLISHED	1063
DEMON	12850
DEMONIAC	7623

DEMONS	3415
DENIAL	7470
DENIED	7758, 8458
DENIES	4079, 9146
DENMARK	10110
DENOUNCE	4835
DENSITY	6694
DENTIST	8644, 12213
DENUDED	9236
DENUNCIATION	10765
DENY	713, 4080, 5469, 10222
DENYING	11788
DEPART	1247, 2613, 5726, 7194
DEPARTED	6438
DEPARTMENT	3637
DEPARTURE	2854, 9169
DEPEND	10577, 11382
DEPENDED	12547
DEPENDENCE	816, 2493, 6627
DEPENDENT	2575, 11196
DEPLORABLE	2958
DEPLOYING	7146
DEPOPULATED	5865
DEPOSED	10366
DEPOSIT	154
DEPRAVED	5309
DEPRAVITY	7171
DEPRESS	3201
DEPRESSION	3742, 4697, 7138,
11816	
DEPRIVATION	5989
DEPRIVED	696, 6796
DERISION	11277
DESCANT	7579
DESCENDANTS	8023
DESCENDED	2314, 5936, 6766, 8730
DESCENDING	701
DESCENT	5257
DESCRIBE	5763, 8959
DESCRIPTIONS	10472
DESCRIPTIVE	4294
DESERT	2026, 6449, 8004,
10122, 10613	
DESERTS	604, 4224, 9720
DESERVE	2300, 3432, 3657,
3915, 4807, 7207, 11853	
DESERVES	1626, 6836, 8312
DESIGN	2616, 9272, 10981,
10988, 11655	
DESIGNERS	9408
DESIGNING	1054
DESIRABLE	5875

5157, 5179, 5227, 5444, 5448, 5574, 5592, 5688, 5783, 5789, 5891, 6183, 6657, 6666, 6898, 6953, 7063, 7178, 7195, 7324, 7560, 7617, 7714, 7934, 7991, 8043, 8074, 8126, 8381, 8425, 8478, 8782, 8810, 8898, 8970, 9040, 9124, 9195, 9253, 9254, 9297, 9480, 9510, 9583, 9671, 9701, 10053, 10164, 10196, 10295, 10370, 10594, 10993, 11025, 11181, 11182, 11190, 11229, 11246, 11264, 11393, 11468, 11708, 11750, 11808, 11973, 12227, 12294, 12456, 12508, 12603, 12794

DIED   127, 1381, 2240, 3614, 3811, 4126, 5374, 5636, 8926, 8968, 9311, 10038, 12237, 12670, 12744, 12749

DIES   445, 1311, 2901, 4379, 4553, 5629, 7317, 7720, 8076, 8540, 8709, 10402, 10845, 11526, 12002, 12355, 12506, 12841

DIET   7438, 7761

DIFFERED   2450

DIFFERENCE   970, 1681, 2267, 2470, 3332, 3674, 3766, 4433, 4952, 7908, 8485, 8556, 10503, 10975, 11878, 12267, 12685, 12830

DIFFERENCES   2475, 11344

DIFFERENT   406, 2555, 3479, 5983, 7365, 8016

DIFFERENTLY   224, 4405

DIFFERS   7205

DIFFICULT   1292, 2249, 3227, 6668, 6988, 8007, 8151, 8354, 8987, 9881, 12424, 12786

DIFFICULTIES   3791, 6709, 6788, 8101

DIFFICULTY   2260, 5558, 10494

DIG   2931, 5655, 10482, 10724, 12243

DIGEST   215, 3446

DIGESTED   707

DIGESTION   7588, 9593, 10358

DIGNIFIED   790, 6049

DIGNIFIES   12648

DIGNITY   12, 433, 482, 1399, 2041, 3378, 4291, 4863, 5125, 5331, 6339, 8905, 11219

DIGRESSIONS   11037

DIGS   1210

DILATED   7520

DIME   4373

DIMENSIONS   4639, 5895

DIMINISHED   537, 3073, 7565

DIMMED   9239

DIMMING   8134

DIMPLE   6077, 9101

DINE   322, 1054, 4943, 4995, 11516

DINED   1495, 10811

DINGY   8666

DINING   4137, 7253

DINNER   249, 1959, 2068, 4311, 4705, 5033, 6102, 6108, 6145, 7096, 8568, 8936, 9019, 9952, 10732, 10738, 11243

DINNER PARTY   12136

DINNER-KNIVES   5645

DINNERS   2160

DINOSAUR   5159

DIOGENES   1834

DIOR   6275

DIPLOMACY   2141, 4099

DIPLOMAT   275, 2730, 11126

DIPLOMATIC   8, 2623

DIRECTION   4848, 5035, 6084, 8121, 9465

DIRECTOR   4169

DIRECTS   3620

DIREFUL   646

DIRT   3710, 3750, 4245, 11231

DIRTIEST   12399

DIRTY   9012, 11998

DIRTY JOKE   8304

DIRTY WORK   8793

DISABLED   8590

DISADVANTAGE   2035, 5032, 5038

DISADVANTAGED   4938

DISAGREE   7546

DISAGREEABLE   5025, 5110

DISAGREEABLES   5425

DISAGREES   6979

DISAPPEAR   9754

DISAPPEARED   3258

DISAPPOINTED   994

DISAPPOINTING   888

DISAPPOINTMENT   4407, 5898

DISAPPOINTS   2153

DISAPPROVE   12069

DISARM   6412

DISASTER   4117, 4539, 9439, 9692, 12319, 12319

DISASTROUS   4319

DISBELIEF   2075, 11774

DISBELIEVES   7100

DISCHARGES   6827

DISCIPLES   12494

DISCIPLINE   886, 4552, 4955, 4974, 5751, 9715, 10513

DISCIPLINED   6671

DISCLOSE   9833

DISCOMFORTS   8573

DISCONTENT   530, 5411, 6063, 10371, 12377, 12439

DISCONTENTED	5608, 11328
DISCORD	62
DISCOURAGEMENT	1730
DISCOURSE	8566
DISCOVER	2039, 2509, 3901,
10728, 12290, 12851	
DISCOVERED	24, 8092
DISCOVERERS	702
DISCOVERIES	2679, 7361
DISCOVERY	3359, 7450, 10865,
11309, 11935	
DISCREDITED	12775
DISCRETION	3247, 6376, 11160
DISCRIMINATE	6017
DISCRIMINATION	323, 9306
DISCUSSED	12650
DISCUSSION	574, 2320
DISDAIN	7507
DISEASE	295, 367, 511, 751,
2550, 2897, 3419, 4664, 5356, 7815, 7833, 8345,	
8795, 9277, 11298, 11306, 11771, 11800	
DISEASED	8277
DISEASES	439, 1608, 5735,
10134, 10942, 11125	
DISENCHANTING	11083
DISENCHANTMENT	9834
DISGRACE	331, 3071, 10089,
10460, 10803	
DISGRUNTLED	12613
DISGUISE	787, 1522, 3436, 9464
DISGUST	6893
DISH	8510, 10193
DISHES	2147
DISHONEST	681, 3808, 4175
DISHONESTY	2773
DISILLUSIONMENT	1732
DISINCLINATION	7251
DISINHERITING	10649
DISINTERESTED	3906
DISLIKE	823, 4399, 7843
DISMAL	2092
DISMEMBERMENT	4021
DISMISS	4713
DISMISSED	7669
DISMOUNT	2286, 9094
DISOBEDIENCE	7499
DISOBEY	2396
DISORDER	8624
DISORDERLY	7361
DISORGANIZATION	2229
DISPARITY	2900
DISPATCH	65

DISPATCHFUL	7592
DISPLEASING	5851
DISPOSABLE	7334
DISPOSED	4393
DISPOSES	5483
DISPOSITION	1748, 1777
DISPOSSESSED	1472
DISPRAISE	7636, 7667
DISPUTES	11088
DISQUIETING	11745
DISREGARD	3772, 7102
DISRUPTER	9727
DISSATISFACTION	2801
DISSATISFIED	2334
DISSECTED	12355
DISSENT	3149
DISSENTER	9727
DISSIMULATION	2215
DISSIPATION	3880
DISSOLUTION	7624
DISSOLVE	9673
DISSOLVED	4176
DISSOLVES	6925
DISTANCE	1444, 8273, 12545
DISTINCTIVE	1639
DISTINGUISH	913, 11770
DISTINGUISHABLE	7550
DISTINGUISHED	70, 8000
DISTINGUISHES	6140, 8346
DISTORT	11867
DISTRACTED	9281
DISTRESS'D	2581
DISTRESSING	11821
DISTRIBUTE	6488
DISTRIBUTION	5490
DISTRUST	12541
DISTURB	1520, 2174
DISTURBED	5801
DITCH	2618, 8014, 12529
DITTY	5378
DIVE	12339
DIVERSION	6609, 11228
DIVERSITY	7776, 12168
DIVIDED	1161, 5739, 5860,
6226, 6724, 7937, 10521	
DIVIDEND	9846
DIVIDING	2802
DIVINATION	6879
DIVINATIONS	9804
DIVINE	68, 215, 3446, 5945,
7006, 7529, 8042, 8859, 11494, 11759, 12827	
DIVINE SERVICE	411

DIVINENESS 700

DIVINEST 4824

DIVINITY 1610, 4553, 10139, 10143, 10326

DIVISIONS 10964

DIVORCE 578

DIVORCED 5538, 9664

DIZZINESS 5567

DIZZY 3499, 10712

DO 836, 846, 1824, 2021, 2203, 3508, 4748, 5902, 8513, 8589, 9039, 9321, 9378, 9494, 9507, 9973, 10302, 11048, 11181, 11393, 12851

DOCK 4098

DOCTOR 5, 461, 1108, 3594, 3794, 4127, 4574, 7656, 7714, 7772, 8191, 8377, 8966, 9224, 9318, 9584, 10659, 11116, 12755

DOCTORS 8809

DOCTRINE 1895, 5022, 7398, 7656, 8819, 9531, 10598

DOG 938, 1452, 1858, 2532, 3155, 3590, 4125, 4126, 4839, 5199, 5617, 5646, 5674, 6864, 7348, 8251, 9034, 9168, 10210, 10895, 11441, 11443, 12325, 12863

DOG-STAR 8791

DOGGEDLY 5086

DOGMA 2848, 4298, 9586, 9716, 9811

DOGMAS 6288

DOGMATISE 5079

DOGS 2563, 6666, 7674, 9582, 10011, 10200, 11748, 12196, 12242

DOING 169, 785, 1017, 1524, 4579, 4954, 5009, 6444, 7817, 9219, 9660, 12000, 12162, 12552, 12644

DOING-GOOD 11683

DOINGS 1245

DOLE 5232

DOLEFUL 7504

DOLL 8684

DOLLAR 1279

DOLLS 9631

DOLORES 11275

DOLPHINESE 9722

DOLPHINS 7849

DOMESTIC 3868, 7790, 8510

DOMESTICATE 11114

DOMINANT 1264

DOMINATE 2031

DOMINATING 12223

DOMINION 4102, 7238, 11576, 11583

DOMINIONS 8214, 9872

DOMINO 3151

DON 4031

DONE 967, 1416, 2982, 3196, 3267, 3281, 3586, 4560, 6350, 6546, 6571, 8340, 8507, 9181, 9395, 9507, 9714, 10093, 10261, 10283, 10547, 12000, 12380, 12583, 12644, 12809

DONG 6091

DONKEY 4261

DONNE 2928, 4948, 5182, 6650

DONS 12557

DOODLING 11006

DOOM 4255, 7390, 9698, 10475, 11462

DOOMED 10680

DOOR 942, 2795, 3219, 3265, 4272, 5472, 6612, 8251, 8742, 8791, 9045, 9780, 11179, 11923

DOORMAT 9381

DOORS 7080, 7555, 9464, 10410, 12236

DORIAN 7525

DORMOUSE 7368

DOTAGES 1838

DOTE 10303

DOUBLE 10275, 10926, 12454

DOUBLE BED 2018, 11586

DOUBLED 2705

DOUBLETHINK 8316

DOUBT 989, 1630, 3489, 3643, 3917, 5682, 5718, 5746, 7628, 7668, 7778, 8101, 10116, 10412, 11388, 11489, 11490, 11900, 12064

DOUBTFUL 5152

DOUBTING 10966

DOUBTS 697, 5534, 10272

DOVER 827, 1830

DOVES 11511

DOWN 3655, 6340, 6602, 6715, 7318, 7709, 7882, 7947, 8399

DOWNFALL 1404

DOWNHEARTED 5712

DOWNING STREET 2004

DOWNS 3825

DOWNTRODDEN 1734

DOWNWARD 7529

DOXY 12148

DOZENS 3926

DOZES 7254

DRAGGED 8605

DRAGON 5338, 7663, 10225

DRAGONS 11728

DRAIN 10947

DRAINING 10735

DRAINS 11164

DRAKE 8083

DUST 1072, 1223, 1227, 1413, 1574, 3192, 3471, 4250, 5583, 6440, 6810, 7004, 7840, 8450, 8637, 8784, 9941, 10589, 10617, 11478, 11486, 11528, 11704, 12726

DUST-HEAP 1300

DUSTBIN 11798

DUTCH 2048, 9048

DUTIES 2983, 6525, 7224, 8347, 10791, 11628

DUTY 777, 2308, 2391, 3876, 3978, 4666, 4696, 4730, 6301, 6314, 6348, 7142, 7380, 7921, 8069, 8071, 8431, 9262, 9694, 9752, 10175, 10526, 11034, 11117, 11519, 12377

DWARF 5219

DWARFISH 2414

DWARFS 7301

DWELL 1246, 12768

DWELLING 2353, 12700

DWELT 7559, 12684

DWINDLE 2488

DYING 129, 1465, 1562, 1598, 1650, 2554, 2788, 3438, 3449, 4579, 4730, 6543, 6897, 8342, 8621, 8688, 8779, 8853, 8921, 9396, 9616, 9790, 9941, 10077, 10639, 10753, 10800, 11161, 11429, 11578, 12820

DYKE 1747

EACH 2188

EAGLE 125, 1486, 4790, 6874, 7396, 9238

EAR 587, 7420, 7445, 7466, 7585, 7899, 10108, 10252

EARFUL 7980

EARL 3918

EARLY 4750, 6508, 7032, 8604, 8997, 10385

EARN 1487, 4229, 5615, 9395

EARNEST 6245, 8980

EARNING 4257

EARS 1162, 3360, 5799, 8728, 9086, 9635, 10203, 10703, 11251

EARTH 114, 219, 342, 472, 582, 603, 1166, 1229, 1251, 1413, 1422, 2542, 3501, 3694, 4487, 4736, 5631, 5685, 6538, 7401, 7531, 7591, 7595, 8583, 8656, 8950, 9030, 9328, 9554, 9561, 9701, 10113, 10149, 11417, 12268, 12321, 12680, 12741

EARTHQUAKE 1974, 4995, 5748, 10622, 11502

EASE 2061, 6220, 6261, 9165, 9531, 10187, 10731, 10925, 11742

EASIER 2256

EASIEST 9965, 11952, 12293

EAST 5631

EAST END 3251

EASTERN 1735, 6504, 7456

EASTERTIDE 4738

EASY 6018, 8419, 9881, 9928, 10528, 11542

EAT 132, 215, 583, 1191, 1208, 1221, 1226, 1816, 2287, 3446, 4898, 6917, 7096, 7730, 7883, 9302, 12760

EATEN 5341, 10255

EATING 1039, 2051, 4821, 9269

EATS 9541

ECCENTRIC 3392

ECCENTRICITY 9817

ECHO 5197, 6962, 8820, 9770, 9786

ECHOES 11506

ECLIPSE 3920, 7478, 7527, 7650, 10622

ECOLOGY 2467

ECONOMETRICIAN 6800

ECONOMIC 4678, 5490, 5546, 9518, 11349, 11382, 12253

ECONOMICAL 502

ECONOMICS 144, 3740, 5553, 9427

ECONOMIES 3423

ECONOMIST 6977

ECONOMIZE 11890

ECONOMY 4698, 9977, 11049

ECSTASY 1601, 2790, 3999, 7093, 7448, 8505, 12349

ECSTATIC 2790

EDEN 5471, 7499, 7578, 7631, 10360

EDGE 4595, 10706, 10756, 10911, 11080

EDIFICE 9729

EDISON 2820

EDITOR 3204, 4775

EDITORIAL 11972

EDITORS 3203

EDUCATE 2168, 2609, 8347, 9745

EDUCATED 1666, 2156, 3190, 6650, 8320, 8321, 9670, 9791

EDUCATING 12087

EDUCATION 26, 454, 761, 891, 1261, 1388, 1464, 1581, 1849, 2844, 3013, 3191, 3284, 3645, 3682, 3774, 4244, 4282, 4875, 4981, 5235, 6266, 6377, 7430, 8628, 8694, 8812, 8915, 9495, 9641, 9942, 10714, 10893, 10907, 10986, 11573, 11776, 11888, 11898, 12287, 12293, 12378, 12379, 12432, 12639, 12780

EDUCATIONAL 4676, 6384

EDUCATOR 3632

EDWARD 6935

EDWARDIANS 12366

EFFECT 1262, 4265, 8902, 9887

ENVIRONMENT	1731, 3132, 11569
ENVIRONMENTS	12641
ENVY	962, 1199, 11475,
12824	
EPICURE	10811
EPICUREAN	3076
EPIDEMICS	10493
EPIGRAM	2414, 6218, 7086,
8156, 11158	
EPITAPH	1262, 5668
EPITAPHS	10646
EPITAPHY	2747
EPITHET	6951
EPITOME	2995
EQUAL	345, 433, 485, 487,
872, 2923, 3255, 3918, 4137, 4980, 5147, 5304, 6081,	
6308, 7416, 7536, 8122, 8309, 8497, 8751, 8833,	
8957, 11914	
EQUALITY	475, 2738, 5099, 9764,
12576	
EQUALIZE	1766
EQUALIZER	5922
EQUALLED	10567
EQUALS	727, 7310, 12590,
12818	
EQUATION	4414
EQUATOR	4014, 8216
EQUILIBRIUM	9794
EQUITY	1488
EQUIVOCATE	3782
ERASED	6217
ERECTING	7008
ERECTION	346
EROGENOUS	12259
EROS	8522, 10076
EROTIC	3908
ERR	3387, 8823
ERRAND	5893
ERRANDS	3919
ERRED	1415, 7654
ERROR	688, 2099, 2350, 2855,
3615, 6368, 6370, 6371, 7120, 7259, 10087, 10475	
ERRORS	242, 1253, 1347, 3002,
3184, 3593, 4835, 4883, 5282, 8284, 10671	
ERSTWHILE	7322
ESCAPE	3191, 6046, 6609,
12458, 12779	
ESCAPED	1230, 9006, 10760,
10859	
ESKIMO	2814
ESPOUSED	7589
ESPRIT	50
ESPY	4526

ESQUIRES	4202
ESSAY	4849, 9548
ESSE	46
ESSENCE	2681, 6138, 7559, 8496
ESSENTIAL	1299, 4355, 6188
ESSENTIALITY	10938
ESTATE	2079, 2996, 6374,
6744, 10288	
ESTEEM	7609, 8561
ESTIMATION	1291
ESTRANGED	6387
ET TU	10195
ETERNAL	315, 1413, 1560, 4084,
6541, 7559, 8421, 8852, 10001, 10570, 10589, 10719,	
10940, 12092, 12200	
ETERNALLY	2916, 7747
ETERNITIES	7999
ETERNITY	33, 632, 634, 636,
1323, 1601, 1931, 2024, 2794, 5644, 6873, 7004,	
9293, 9563, 10065, 10452, 11148, 11970	
ETHEREAL	7503, 7559
ETHERIZED	3212
ETHICAL	1507, 11845
ETHICS	6756, 10960
ETHIOPIAN	1228
ETIQUETTE	2635, 6913
ETON	243, 8313, 12266
ETONIANS	5725, 6805
ETRURIAN	7518
EUNUCH	3457, 4279, 11142
EUNUCHS	967, 3519
EUREKA	471
EUROPE	817, 2727, 2732, 3852,
4285, 6618, 8679, 9752, 9863, 9919, 11452, 11801,	
11920	
EUROPEAN	6840
EUROPEANS	7075, 7983
EUSTACE	5618
EVANESCENT	5927
EVANGELISM	12776
EVE	835, 4690, 7576, 7585,
11619	
EVEN	2826, 5531
EVENING	1483, 3212, 3218,
3882, 7579, 7581, 7626, 8854, 9341	
EVENT	8930, 9731, 10137,
10688, 11494, 11739	
EVENTS	83, 160, 1263, 1680,
2333, 3405, 3418, 6313, 6896, 7869, 9549, 10339	
EVER	3924, 9656, 11391
EVER-SILENT	11520
EVERLASTING	2903, 7539, 7603,
7840, 10102	

FAIR 579, 1040, 2730, 2975, 3000, 4967, 5465, 5956, 6192, 6951, 7613, 10296, 12602, 12604, 12680

FAIR PLAY 8326

FAIRER 6931

FAIREST 7616

FAIRIES 873, 9971

FAIRY 874, 5195, 7824, 7850

FAITH 167, 179, 1131, 1137, 1537, 1630, 1641, 2005, 3341, 3635, 3765, 4643, 5348, 5484, 6301, 6322, 6481, 6581, 6623, 6634, 6770, 7629, 8516, 9518, 10528, 10783, 11255, 11419, 11490, 11612, 11714, 12015, 12429, 12715

FAITH-HEALER 333

FAITHFUL 2951, 3635, 3893, 4307, 7433, 9274

FAITHLESS 600, 9957

FAKING 2389

FALKLANDS 1446

FALL 57, 1018, 1210, 1242, 1778, 3096, 5918, 6711, 7594, 9061, 9112, 9298, 10195, 10610, 10885, 11699, 12413

FALL OUT 11503

FALLACIOUS 8233

FALLACY 8619, 9650

FALLEN 1198, 1556, 7505, 7510, 8491

FALLING 3118, 3151, 7314

FALLS 9117, 10262, 11397

FALSE 765, 1174, 1895, 3138, 3865, 5861, 10108, 10264, 10338, 11493

FALSEHOOD 7398

FALSENESS 9650

FALSER 10037

FAME 213, 562, 746, 2789, 2890, 4268, 4669, 6651, 7146, 7476, 7477, 7665, 7767, 7792, 7860, 8655, 8770, 9172, 9411, 9889, 11842

FAMILIAR 5987, 10621

FAMILIARITY 11896

FAMILIES 4531, 8218, 11565, 11735

FAMILY 262, 1588, 2282, 2609, 4183, 4962, 5002, 5506, 5856, 7150, 7750, 7790, 8749, 9158, 9859, 10740, 10971, 11885

FAMINE 11583

FAMOUS 1020, 1201, 1943, 8583, 10084, 10531, 12054, 12161

FAN 5749

FAN CLUB 2121

FANATIC 2302, 12805

FANATICISM 6225, 9812

FANATICS 5381, 9536

FANCIES 1663, 4274, 5466

FANCY 4740, 5383, 5413, 6356, 10314, 11439

FANS 5828

FANTASIES 6206

FANTASTIC 7407, 12451

FANTASY 4280, 7975

FAR 2398, 2770, 3560, 4977, 9029, 11492

FARCE 7043, 9271, 10739

FAREWELL 1799, 7515, 7569, 9401, 10348, 10468, 12532

FARM 112, 10876

FARMER 4512, 4750, 6688

FARMERS 4747, 10674

FARMING 164

FARMS 1814, 2603

FARROW 5267

FART 3241, 5017, 11187

FARTHEST 6501

FARTHING 2612

FASCINATED 12760

FASCINATING 4506

FASCINATION 3962, 3969, 12472

FASCISM 1471, 4183, 9545

FASCIST 8687

FASHION 1058, 1400, 2139, 2183, 2216, 2395, 2601, 2951, 6913, 10417, 10420, 11193, 12451

FASHIONABLE 9800

FASHIONED 11625

FASHIONS 9728, 10493

FAST 4133, 4998

FASTER 1702, 6273, 6886

FASTIDIOUS 6904, 10877

FASTING 3603, 7233

FAT 178, 1672, 2503, 2521, 3494, 4025, 5140, 6912, 8260, 8286, 8311, 10190

FATAL 3595, 6395, 6637, 7478, 7553, 7833, 10382, 11550, 12496

FATE 1486, 1865, 2702, 2732, 2844, 3287, 4224, 4657, 4725, 5153, 5583, 6046, 6058, 6335, 6417, 6863, 6890, 7007, 7273, 7341, 7601, 8036, 8226, 8879, 9987, 10188, 10655, 11342, 11423, 11514, 12179, 12825

FATEFUL 6355

FATES 3911, 10189

FATHER 330, 432, 1153, 1847, 2325, 3612, 4550, 5081, 5279, 5342, 6454, 6531, 7750, 7845, 8078, 8165, 8950, 9076, 9836, 10165, 10307, 10400, 10515, 10745, 11034, 11258, 11377, 11881, 12202, 12419, 12694, 12750, 12778

FATHER-LIKE 6606

FATHERS 1201, 4489, 4800, 6308, 6774, 6805, 9681, 11598

FIFTY 2577, 4798, 6527, 11452

FIG 1013, 6093, 10061

FIGHT 407, 919, 1346, 1446, 1631, 1817, 2307, 2311, 2816, 2984, 3155, 3690, 3735, 4009, 4218, 4323, 4805, 5171, 5493, 6544, 6889, 6922, 7599, 7747, 9733, 10168, 10869, 11069, 11909, 12197, 12798

FIGHTING 1271, 1277, 2628, 4604, 5352, 5643, 6071, 6868, 7033, 10009, 10947, 11228, 12050

FIGHTS 313, 8183, 12525

FIGURE 59

FIGURES 358, 10788

FILCHES 10344

FILIGREE 11625

FILL 3344, 5685, 6457, 8456, 11203

FILLED 3951

FILLING 8331, 9929

FILM 2002, 12262

FILM-MAKING 6212

FILMS 4167, 4577

FILTHY 9655

FINAL 619, 5977

FINALE 11054

FINALITY 11023

FINALS 6384

FINANCE 4008, 10815

FINANCIAL 153, 12566

FINANCIERS 12566

FINCHLEY 1006

FIND 1173, 2105, 2688, 2948, 4368, 5043, 8640, 9358, 10812, 11428, 11727

FINDS 528

FINE 1452, 6849, 8666

FINERY 4106

FINEST 2308, 9684

FINGER 401, 7274, 7887, 8351

FINGERNAILS 7945

FINGERS 2156, 3101, 6029, 8978

FINISH 932, 2310, 3084, 11337

FINISHED 3728, 5523, 7815

FINITE 6137, 7891

FIRE 399, 523, 995, 1345, 1797, 1825, 3669, 4223, 4397, 6065, 6813, 7243, 7933, 8265, 8537, 8693, 9003, 9106, 9241, 9296, 9521, 10441, 10480, 10702, 12780

FIRED 6402

FIRES 3729, 4177

FIRM 472, 11066

FIRMNESS 5030

FIRST 772, 1149, 1185, 1697, 3399, 4145, 4998, 6936, 7908, 8473, 8756, 8935, 11930

FIRST-RATE 8721

FIRSTBORN 7559

FISH 1119, 1564, 2155, 6536, 6905, 8362, 9016, 9167, 9927, 11008

FISH-BALL 5947

FISH-KNIVES 1102

FISHBONE 6537

FISHERMAN 8205

FISHERS 5614

FISHES 5886, 6476, 6727, 10664

FISHING 10979

FIT 5085, 5427, 5625, 6293, 6837, 7430, 8575, 9962, 10008

FITTEST 8416, 10904

FIVE 7932

FIVE-CENT 23

FIVE-POUND 6096

FIX 4000, 5921

FIXED 4412, 10851

FLAG 2490, 3334, 12418

FLAME 8505, 8537, 8779, 9367, 11478

FLAMES 7482, 7953, 9562

FLANDERS 6491, 6633, 11040

FLAT 2564

FLATTER 2612, 5143, 5824, 7713, 9402, 10469

FLATTERED 11198

FLATTERERS 1918, 5795

FLATTERIES 6797

FLATTERING 11818

FLATTERS 5050, 10541

FLATTERY 2440, 2880, 4617, 5846, 6386, 11075, 11226, 11291, 12643

FLAUBERT 883

FLAVOUR 2597, 4642

FLAW 466, 5399, 11695

FLAYED 11260

FLEA 5136, 5199, 8238, 11254

FLEAS 5942, 7886, 8892, 9466, 12325

FLED 5380, 10923, 11617, 12152

FLEE 226, 2166, 12766

FLEET 6436

FLEET STREET 5905

FLEETING 9415, 10471

FLEETINGLY 6960

FLESH	460, 895, 1219, 1220,
3444, 4694, 6848, 7618, 10102, 10370, 10804	
FLEW	1371
FLICKERED	11737
FLICKERING	4177, 7807
FLIES	6943, 9667, 10241,
10750, 12192	
FLIGHT	2529, 2785, 5266,
6434, 6597, 6971	
FLING	12570
FLINGING	9661
FLINGS	3710
FLINT	1445
FLIPPANT	5466
FLIRT	10795
FLIRTATION	1969, 8275
FLOAT	9757
FLOATING	3559, 5279, 7373
FLOATS	3119
FLOCK	953, 6445
FLOCKS	11343
FLOGGING	5094, 11777
FLOOD	1960, 4022, 7003,
7145, 10213	
FLOODED	1021
FLOOR	4845, 5379, 6479, 8519
FLOP	780
FLORIDA	4287
FLOURISHING	6909
FLOW	4509, 11759
FLOWER	612, 4544, 5279, 6663,
6862, 7428, 7573, 7970, 8043, 10395, 11414, 12194,	
12716	
FLOWERING	3333
FLOWERLESS	11267
FLOWERS	613, 945, 1935, 3965,
5447, 6062, 6446, 6564, 6909, 7012, 7186, 7315,	
7572, 7805, 8258, 8623, 9460, 9960	
FLOWERY	5215, 7446, 10333
FLOWING	1217
FLU	7686
FLUENCY	4447
FLUNG	6084
FLUSHPOTS	5259
FLUTE	3033, 7525
FLY	255, 261, 760, 1928,
4522, 4760, 5042, 5151, 5266, 5446, 5534, 6085,	
6261, 7568, 7684, 8835, 9166, 9345, 9771, 9886	
FLY-BOTTLE	12608
FLYING	4095, 5482, 6317,
8305, 11693, 12045, 12663, 12718	
FLYING-FISH	5664
FOCUS	7965

FOE	1050, 1356, 2049,
3818, 4031, 5307, 6481, 7528, 7657, 8081, 8084,	
8442, 8802, 9717, 10182, 11383, 11420	
FOEMEN	9934
FOES	10382, 10722, 12011
FOG	1634, 2777, 2859, 9777
FOGGY	434, 3853, 6929
FOLD	12422
FOLK	499, 879, 5914
FOLKS	3560, 11097, 12327
FOLLIES	1280, 2769, 7727,
9608, 10309, 10494	
FOLLOW	110, 633, 1478, 1831,
2810, 3778, 4876, 4902, 6114, 8005, 8359, 8373,	
11415, 11496	
FOLLOWED	1415
FOLLOWERS	563
FOLLOWING	372
FOLLY	1268, 1338, 1607,
2301, 2431, 3231, 3437, 4247, 5077, 5813, 6047,	
6532, 7434, 7847, 7863, 8536, 8831, 10026, 12336	
FOND	6129, 7722, 11244
FONDER	325, 905
FONT	5723
FOOD	1534, 2643, 2895,
3230, 3743, 3760, 6565, 6871, 7280, 7721, 8936,	
9179, 9789, 10071, 10422, 10599, 12615	
FOOL	232, 337, 457, 570,
1259, 1282, 1337, 1338, 1386, 1858, 1975, 2033,	
2459, 2578, 2947, 2985, 2998, 3413, 3574, 3768,	
4059, 4207, 4334, 4495, 4765, 5034, 5151, 5646,	
5668, 5673, 5696, 6310, 6570, 7656, 7706, 7723,	
8268, 8270, 8488, 8790, 8792, 8794, 8840, 8843,	
8945, 8953, 9386, 9819, 10017, 10464, 10669, 11086,	
12672, 12834, 12841	
FOOLISH	290, 1236, 1261, 3569,
5138, 6378, 6500, 7024, 9351, 9441, 9669, 11066,	
12806	
FOOLISHEST	1607
FOOLISHNESS	4729, 4754, 7422,
11341	
FOOLS	294, 705, 2711, 2927,
3020, 4116, 4588, 4895, 5183, 5576, 5594, 5869,	
7165, 7418, 7563, 8569, 8821, 8827, 9042, 10334,	
11226, 11235, 11325, 11851, 11887, 12011, 12055	
FOOT	903, 3464, 5635, 10577
FOOTBALL	1368, 3909, 6660,
10484, 10694	
FOOTMEN	4449
FOOTPRINTS	6443
FOOTSOLES	8689
FOOTSTEPS	894, 2587, 6422
FOPPERY	10227
FORBEARANCE	1762
FORBID	3570, 4073

FORBIDDEN   7499, 11312, 12470

FORCE   1751, 2405, 3153, 4234, 4591, 4728, 5283, 6159, 6553, 6821, 7214, 8121, 8289, 9122, 9915, 10511, 10973, 11300, 11580, 11795, 11799, 12171, 12212, 12340, 12382, 12588

FORCED   5142, 10562

FORCES   1396, 8120, 9318

FORCIBLE   6078

FOREBEARS   1580

FOREBODING   8940

FOREHEAD   5357, 5743, 6420, 7350

FOREIGN   224, 1120, 1574, 4405, 6722, 8509, 11535, 12180

FOREIGNERS   2691, 7703, 11895

FORELOCK   7637

FOREMOST   6777

FOREPLAY   1035

FORESAW   3382

FORESEE   8601

FORESEEN   9412, 10915

FORESIGHT   2172

FOREST   5080, 6091, 6320, 6424, 9175

FORESTS   1357, 3282, 6449

FOREVER   2154, 6885, 7746, 9992, 12099

FORFEIT   7484, 9941

FORFEITING   8322

FORGAVE   3008

FORGE   3584, 3673, 3988, 9263, 10629

FORGERS   8544

FORGET   514, 535, 558, 937, 1650, 1792, 2114, 2182, 2441, 2545, 4186, 4474, 4644, 5584, 5678, 6620, 7028, 7580, 7925, 8261, 8873, 9075, 9279, 9361, 9547, 9553, 10176, 10635, 11278, 11286, 11304, 11701, 12385, 12626

FORGET-ME-NOTS   10705

FORGETS   7851

FORGETTING   2253, 9282, 11104, 12712

FORGIVE   1159, 1291, 1650, 2205, 3433, 3576, 3667, 5811, 7115, 7157, 7194, 8823, 9195, 10755, 11304, 12306, 12419, 12512

FORGIVEN   3046, 10556

FORGIVENESS   1351, 4890, 7694, 11928

FORGIVES   2130, 10561

FORGIVING   3664, 9282

FORGOT   2743, 2951, 4529, 5397, 7825, 8758, 8825

FORGOTTEN   452, 597, 8990, 9415, 9518, 9812, 10714, 11285

FORK   6352

FORLORN   2426, 7617

FORM   6149, 6687, 8143, 8492, 11192, 12732

FORMALITIES   1788

FORMATION   10907

FORMED   638

FORMIDABLE   4344, 4958

FORMULA   8113, 8999, 9624, 11289

FORNICATED   2044

FORNICATION   6942

FORSAKE   1424

FORSEE   116

FORSTER   6902

FORTH   3542, 5280

FORTISSIMO   6823

FORTITUDE   682, 2093

FORTRESS   10360

FORTUNATE   10830

FORTUNE   661, 728, 729, 1377, 2334, 3011, 3184, 3410, 4253, 4256, 5183, 5836, 6068, 6549, 6644, 7716, 9134, 9162, 9993, 10048, 10090, 10227, 11317, 11536, 12037, 12240, 12665

FORTUNES   7871, 10223

FORTY   442, 1477, 1736, 3019, 4660, 4798, 6530, 8260, 8658, 10560, 12167

FORTY-FIVE   6531, 7899

FORTY-NINER   7823

FORTY-THREE   3993

FORTY-TWO   19

FORWARD   2262, 6777, 8338, 9199, 11126, 11393, 11451

FORWARDS   5572

FOSS   6095

FOSTER-CHILD   5435

FOUGHT   1660, 6128, 7536, 8193, 10177, 10871, 11407, 11519, 12218, 12526

FOUL   10111, 10254

FOULED   11421

FOUND   4904, 5248, 6707, 8092, 8124, 8483, 8708, 10633, 10870, 12020

FOUNDATION   45, 1052, 1773, 1849, 3273, 9767, 11135

FOUNDERS   12385

FOUNDING   1535

FOUNT   5193, 6950

FOUNTAIN   6369, 6564, 7015, 7559, 10589

FOUR   43, 8308, 8444, 11932

FOURSCORE   12301

FOWL   7663

FOX   6227, 6590, 8577, 9084, 11204, 12509

FOX-HUNTING 4325

FOXED 8560

FOXES 3698

FOXHOLES 2632

FRAGILE 3256, 5455, 5479, 8136

FRAGMENTATION 12168

FRAGMENTS 3996

FRAGRANCE 11785

FRAIL 5180, 11123

FRAILTY 3014, 10016, 10103

FRAME 8847

FRAMED 11680, 12126

FRANCE 2090, 2719, 2975, 4996, 11029, 11194

FRANK 6676, 6708, 8613, 11645

FRANKLY 11020

FRANKNESS 10736

FRAUDS 6010

FRECKLES 8444

FRED 320

FREE 13, 100, 177, 355, 433, 447, 633, 841, 848, 1015, 1049, 1123, 1150, 1754, 2338, 2917, 3005, 3573, 4032, 4611, 4676, 4939, 4971, 5013, 5322, 5507, 5521, 5542, 5754, 6299, 6314, 6374, 6449, 6817, 6818, 6819, 7047, 7171, 7255, 7466, 7682, 9191, 9596, 9783, 9843, 9918, 10839, 10840, 10847, 11064, 11065, 11212, 11323, 11933, 12055

FREE PRESS 11144

FREE-BORN 11556

FREE-WILL 1109

FREED 3622

FREEDOM 391, 822, 886, 1398, 1496, 1805, 2589, 2621, 3322, 3767, 3835, 4609, 4846, 5304, 5567, 5571, 5591, 5629, 5754, 5858, 6048, 6160, 6272, 6305, 6309, 6328, 6339, 6372, 6584, 6804, 7262, 7262, 7681, 7978, 8159, 8315, 8396, 8403, 8431, 8545, 8677, 8880, 9831, 9847, 11214, 11290, 11721, 11804, 11891, 12554, 12772

FREEDOMS 9444, 9520

FREEHOLD 6563

FREELY 1178, 5843, 7594, 9680

FREEMASONRY 963

FREEMEN 12178

FREEZE 5308

FREEZING 2796, 10471

FRENCH 250, 307, 752, 1307, 1497, 2048, 4200, 4219, 7057, 9405, 9424, 10796, 11769, 11879

FRENCHIES 8287

FRENCHMAN 5109, 8066, 8067, 11561

FRENZY 5552, 7623

FRESH 6528, 7483

FRESH AIR 538

FRESHMEN 6490

FRESHNESS 12401

FRETFUL 9561

FREUD 2893

FREUDIAN 6529

FRIDAY 2709

FRIEND 30, 34, 1003, 1196, 1356, 1672, 1820, 2049, 2207, 2352, 2449, 2507, 2818, 3338, 3339, 3503, 3550, 3818, 4020, 4573, 4705, 4748, 4778, 5126, 5805, 6295, 7363, 8094, 8385, 8585, 9017, 9432, 9538, 9826, 10204, 10212, 10880, 10979, 11234, 11383, 11420, 12002

FRIENDLESS 1717

FRIENDLY 8532

FRIENDS 298, 481, 1154, 1708, 2157, 2225, 2511, 2739, 3120, 3159, 3590, 3722, 4052, 4374, 4419, 4627, 4679, 4751, 4773, 5117, 5236, 5851, 6095, 6169, 6186, 6676, 7157, 7355, 7713, 7822, 8023, 8680, 9965, 10034, 10203, 10285, 10355, 10603, 10653, 10754, 10755, 11378, 11529, 11654, 11688, 11716, 11826, 11930, 11953, 12010, 12141, 12480, 12576, 12801, 12826

FRIENDSHIP 34, 647, 727, 1853, 1973, 2461, 2991, 3797, 3812, 4131, 4655, 5087, 5115, 5838, 6676, 8047, 8163, 9078, 9409, 9760, 9792, 10033, 10043

FRIENDSHIPS 3172, 4087, 9673, 11717

FRIGHTEN 1450, 1479, 2017, 4605, 12273

FRIGHTENED 10708, 11199

FRIGHTENING 4057, 4966, 9203

FRIGHTFUL 6060, 9726

FRIGID 8040

FRINGE 9536

FRIVOLOUS 9440, 12648

FRIZ 5624

FROG-SPAWN 6027

FROGS 7703, 11050

FRONT 162, 3083, 7051, 7729, 12169, 12367

FRONTIER 5516

FRONTIERS 827, 11649

FROST 10395, 11626

FROSTY 9551

FROWN 4253, 11242

FROWZY 10817

FROZEN 3861, 5369, 7549, 9864

FRUGAL 2266

FRUIT 2516, 4803, 6859, 7571, 7615, 7754, 8659, 9664

FRUITFULNESS 5358

FRUITS	5294, 7856	GALAXY	9723
FRUSTRATE	7383	GALILEAN	7479
FRUSTRATION	3431, 4841, 9396	GALILEE	1936
FUCK	1035, 4186, 5176, 5992	GALLANT	568
FUDGE	6521	GALLANTRY	1966, 10642, 12536
FUEL	4741	GALLERY	3976, 6744
FUGITIVE	7122	GALLEYS	5244
FULFILLED	9904	GALLING	1796
FULFILMENT	3659, 4051, 7965	GALLOP	1833, 10781
FULL	1206, 1808, 2671,	GALLOPED	1648
10811, 11099		GALLOPING	5350
FULLY-EQUIPPED	6347	GALLOWS	1768, 8413
FUN	149, 1322, 2068, 2558,	GAMBLE	9476, 11150
3425, 5178, 5248, 5323, 5659, 6462, 7816, 8034,		GAMBLERS	2447
8298, 8890, 12427		GAMBLING	2692
FUNCTION	2762, 8194, 9837,	GAME	916, 1075, 1095, 2970,
11192, 12732		4797, 8081, 8087, 8592, 9384, 11508	
FUNCTIONARY	2376	GAMES	1092, 1107, 6599,
FUNCTIONS	6800	6600, 7789, 9923	
FUNDAMENT	8040	GAMESMANSHIP	8906
FUNERAL	5903, 6441, 7020,	GAMING	5878
12619, 12852		GAMUT	8445
FUNERALS	7922	GANGSTERS	5768
FUNNY	3455, 4418, 6695,	GAP	2392, 3043, 11151,
7372, 8304, 9497, 11079, 12645		12363	
FURNACE	7504, 10182	GARBO	11905
FURNACES	1463	GARCIA LORCA	4001
FURNISH	5469, 8933	GARDEN	732, 1472, 4942, 5645,
FURNISHED	8597	7021, 7692, 9028, 10737, 11279, 11459, 11460,	
FURNISHING	11231	12073, 12511	
FURNITURE	2955, 6008, 6714,	GARDEN-STATE	7016
7946, 10794		GARDENS	12806
FURROW	9544, 11510, 11675	GARLAND	10078
FURROWED	7457	GARLIC	214, 2186
FURRY	10702	GARRICK	4135, 4136
FURTHER	297, 5802, 8681, 9315	GAS	6224, 8449
FURY	2487, 2504, 2999, 7476	GATE	4408, 7657, 8657
FUSE	7141, 9867	GATES	7005, 8681
FUSS	1373	GATHER	4544, 4620, 10929
FUSTIAN	8796	GATHERED	599, 1183
FUTILITY	4615	GAUDY	10074
FUTURE	7, 364, 628, 1687,	GAY	2562, 8821, 9467
1955, 2313, 2650, 2661, 3130, 4026, 4272, 5161,		GAZA	7649
5539, 5646, 5973, 5998, 6330, 8148, 8318, 8657,		GAZELLES	7849
9305, 9894, 10989, 11140, 11726, 11912, 12365,		GAZING	9737
12733		GEESE	9084
FUTURITY	8725	GEM	4251
FUZZY WUZZY	2004, 5643	GEMS	7403, 7862
GAIN	1164, 1622, 4853,	GENDER	8259
8764, 8859, 10135, 10553, 10885		GENEALOGIST	223
GAINED	8243, 11501, 12065	GENERAL	9338, 12275
GAINING	8400	GENERALISTS	7070
GAINS	715, 4540, 11077		

GENERALLY	7757
GENERALS	7230, 8127, 8854,
11820, 11932	
GENERATION	89, 320, 956, 2171,
2815, 3628, 3689, 5231, 5535, 6304, 7972, 8488,	
8682, 11003	
GENERATIONS	1212, 1599, 5449,
6561, 6764	
GENEROSITY	2515, 3828, 5817,
6677, 9837, 11311	
GENEROUS	4006, 7056, 7821
GENES	2682
GENESIS	269
GENIUS	17, 169, 217, 570, 852,
897, 1066, 1321, 1615, 1711, 1975, 2820, 2966, 3083,	
3106, 3115, 3288, 3289, 3372, 3469, 3772, 4147,	
4443, 4911, 4950, 5035, 5205, 5282, 6058, 6217,	
6235, 6267, 6268, 6361, 6497, 6521, 6567, 7172,	
7252, 7996, 8000, 8392, 8543, 8674, 8975, 9374,	
11021, 11169, 11223, 12401, 12452, 12473, 12475,	
12850	
GENIUSES	581, 4048, 6670, 12119
GENTEEL	1462
GENTILE	5498
GENTILES	5680
GENTILITY	1329, 2323
GENTLE	2184, 2193, 2689,
3162, 5235, 6240, 8813, 10868, 10931, 11578, 12295	
GENTLEMAN	140, 271, 349, 568,
797, 829, 835, 846, 1761, 4344, 6220, 6339, 6645,	
8105, 8618, 9687, 10636, 11207, 11209, 11858,	
12320, 12462, 12509	
GENTLEMANLY	533, 11107, 11206
GENTLEMEN	4021, 4172, 4202,
5055, 5676, 6668, 6769, 7169, 7959, 8452, 10177,	
11330, 11553, 12729	
GENTLENESS	11610
GENUINE	7843
GEOGRAPHICAL	7263
GEOGRAPHY	1056
GEOMETRICAL	6870
GEOMETRY	3333
GEORGE	1057, 5936
GEORGIA	4193
GEORGIAN	6714, 10909
GERANIUMS	7368
GERMAN	1306, 4039
GERMANS	2560, 3831, 4581,
5742, 6346, 9405, 11820	
GERMANY	4618, 9863
GERMINATES	168
GERMS	439, 8389
GESTURE	1392

GET	1181, 4644, 6922,
10562, 10763	
GETTY	6224
GHARSLEY	8027
GHOST	2920, 4592, 6550,
9716, 10595	
GHOSTS	8806, 10609
GHOULIES	316
GIANT	1480, 5942, 6005
GIANTS	8117
GIBBETS	12836
GIBBON	4504
GIBRALTER	3858
GIDDY	1694
GIFT	80, 449, 1395, 2027,
3292, 3446, 4485, 4680, 5222, 5998, 6054, 6617,	
7245, 7260, 7589, 8096, 9939, 11269, 11788	
GIFTIE	1818, 7969
GIFTS	1562, 10354, 10860,
12025, 12687	
GIGANTIC	6758
GILD	1957, 10219
GILDED	5866, 10356
GIMBLE	2109
GIN	1379, 2347, 9342
GIOTTO	6430
GIRD	7604
GIRDED	12152
GIRDLE	8037
GIRL	289, 1106, 1561, 2211,
2630, 3421, 6420, 6460, 6462, 7350, 9725, 10774,	
10891, 11790, 12104, 12356, 12804	
GIRLFRIEND	2359, 8128
GIRLS	118, 420, 2065, 2324,
4360, 7700, 8441	
GIVE	380, 495, 614, 1178,
1231, 3527, 4159, 6053, 6544, 7343, 8366, 8602,	
9027, 12416	
GIVE IN	2298
GIVEN	822, 1173, 3439
GIVER	8150
GIVES	851, 2806, 3139, 5843,
9205	
GIVING	3634, 5782, 10378
GIZZARD	11665
GLACIER	3201
GLAD	1430, 1651, 1653
GLADNESS	10627, 12731
GLADSOME	7433
GLAMOROUS	3856
GLANCE	5863
GLANDS	4850

GLASS 1002, 4526, 6721, 10159, 11230, 11546

GLASS EYE 10244

GLASS-BOTTOMED 7711, 12096

GLASSES 8448

GLEAM 11496

GLEN 158

GLIDE 12732

GLIMMERING 7488

GLISTERING 1511

GLISTERS 4254

GLITTERATI 12535

GLITTERING 4542, 7490, 10742

GLOAMING 6003

GLOBAL 6700

GLOOM 225, 8919

GLOOMS 11637

GLORIA 357

GLORIES 10367, 11968

GLORIFIED 11818

GLORIOUS 3977, 7506, 10371, 10723

GLORY 190, 225, 339, 357, 698, 1122, 1212, 1767, 1932, 2534, 2971, 3841, 4083, 4706, 4756, 5412, 6123, 7237, 8730, 8839, 9299, 9590, 10409, 10453, 10596, 10596, 10650, 11183, 11343, 11518, 11963, 12235, 12621, 12708, 12708, 12711, 12713, 12728, 12730, 12801

GLOSSY 4154

GLOW 11081

GLOW-WORM 2285, 12235

GLOWS 6920

GLUTTON 4317, 5957

GLUTTONS 9302

GNARLED 9410

GNASHING 1175

GNATS 5359

GNAWING 1747

GNOMES 12566

GO 926, 2613, 3586, 6845, 7630, 8334, 11090, 11391

GO ON 10779

GO-BETWEEN 9109

GOADED 4035

GOAL 856, 2543, 3774, 4044, 6236, 6602

GOALS 4184, 5649

GOAT 983, 6934

GOD 104, 154, 155, 186, 218, 219, 253, 267, 269, 339, 463, 847, 851, 865, 871, 928, 938, 1081, 1129, 1146, 1158, 1184, 1187, 1203, 1276, 1423, 1429, 1435, 1456, 1633, 1719, 1852, 1867, 1869, 1912, 2081, 2119, 2154, 2383, 2415, 2639, 2657, 2684, 2712, 2814, 2937, 3125, 3169, 3240, 3242, 3320, 3555, 3566, 3594, 3760, 3863, 4287, 4344, 4352, 4415, 4528, 4736, 4763, 4873, 4983, 5395, 5469, 5595, 5711, 5716, 5743, 5744, 6115, 6208, 6283, 6322, 6344, 6508, 6535, 6577, 6580, 6631, 6638, 6683, 6855, 6864, 6884, 7189, 7388, 7574, 7622, 7655, 7734, 7814, 7951, 7980, 8057, 8149, 8177, 8263, 8377, 8500, 8648, 8701, 8732, 8847, 8849, 8954, 9048, 9125, 9137, 9247, 9581, 9686, 9763, 9964, 10097, 10185, 10300, 10495, 10538, 10717, 10718, 10771, 10833, 10938, 11283, 11299, 11380, 11410, 11431, 11481, 11487, 11545, 11715, 11946, 11965, 12005, 12022, 12063, 12077, 12083, 12140, 12196, 12827

GOD'S 8629

GOD'S-ACRE 6431

GOD-INTOXICATED 8227

GOD-LIKE 11751

GODDAMM 8916

GODDESS 5194, 8539

GODLINESS 11823

GODOT 926

GODS 1841, 4554, 4684, 4717, 5208, 5390, 6223, 6335, 6773, 6774, 7178, 7613, 8367, 8699, 8700, 8709, 9806, 9831, 9874, 10004, 10193, 10241, 10247, 11092, 11318, 11454, 12028, 12441, 12695

GOES 1501, 11412

GOETHE 2638

GOING 4726, 5228, 5528, 9459, 9779, 10246

GOLD 1117, 6087, 6589, 7862, 8652, 8765, 8919, 10217, 12029

GOLD-STARRED 10705

GOLDEN 1876, 2734, 4018, 4169, 7479, 7692, 10601, 11406, 11831

GOLF 24, 3224, 4702, 11870

GONE 2813, 5380, 5487, 5892, 5909, 6480, 7472, 8609, 9469, 9932, 10443, 11962

GONGS 2244

GOOD 220, 221, 369, 464, 627, 802, 1009, 1048, 1058, 1156, 1244, 1284, 1331, 1723, 1744, 1877, 2014, 2060, 2226, 2433, 2702, 2946, 3012, 3036, 3383, 3696, 3705, 3707, 3730, 3839, 4016, 4209, 4284, 4290, 4340, 4537, 4574, 5074, 5120, 5245, 5335, 6158, 6406, 6420, 6456, 6461, 6607, 6664, 6672, 6708, 6787, 7296, 7350, 7510, 7511, 7681, 7769, 8203, 8507, 8586, 9083, 9097, 9118, 9151, 9205, 9491, 9643, 9662, 9678, 9743, 9828, 9917, 9950, 10018, 10119, 10156, 10296, 10496, 10778, 10827, 10834, 10886, 10900, 11405, 11479, 11560, 11641, 11655, 11661, 11860, 11997, 12310, 12403, 12447, 12457, 12489, 12675, 12688, 12751, 12821

GOOD WILL 12555

GOOD WORKS	1167	GRACES	10458, 10927
GOOD-NIGHT	8524, 10392, 10600	GRACIOUS	1431, 10690
GOODBYE	956, 2685, 3042, 4238,	GRADUALNESS	12220
6237, 8890, 8894, 12329		GRADUATE	3689
GOODNATURED	10638	GRADUATED	11319
GOODNESS	1526, 5816, 5818,	GRAIL	11910
11731, 11891		GRAIN	1323
GOODNIGHT	12802	GRAMMAR	2845, 4804, 5962,
GOODS	481, 1434	10675	
GOOLIES	4192	GRAMMATICAL	2295
GOOSE	6395, 6590	GRAND	6393, 9827
GOOSEBERRIED	11586	GRAND CANYON	6962
GORDIAN	5408	GRANDEUR	4249, 4381, 8740
GORED	1461	GRANDFATHER	12435
GORGEOUSNESS	6566	GRANDFATHERS	7972
GORGONISED	11458	GRANDMOTHER	4799, 11566
GORGONS	7549	GRANDSON	4800
GORY	12284	GRANT	1417, 1493, 6850,
GOSPEL	7001, 7911, 10509	11830	
GOSSIP	3170, 4553, 4779,	GRANTED	2209, 4853, 9677
8024, 9177, 9739, 12558, 12595		GRAPE	10452
GOSSIPS	9188	GRAPES	4756, 6739
GOTTEN	4376	GRAPESHOT	2088
GOULASH	5560	GRAPPLES	11484
GOURMET	4317	GRASP	12136
GOUT	7753	GRASPING	94
GOVERN	994, 1581, 2722, 6231,	GRASS	415, 1104, 4890, 9013,
7074, 7211, 8773, 11809, 11939		9571, 9778, 11002, 12040, 12414	
GOVERNED	4695, 8386, 10376,	GRATEFUL	2145, 7567, 9739
12337		GRATIFICATION	539, 1999, 4363, 10582
GOVERNESS	1557	GRATITUDE	5834, 9074
GOVERNING	1401, 7956	GRATUITOUS	3176, 3906
GOVERNMENT	39, 42, 44, 784, 792,	GRAVE	421, 425, 1133, 2123,
943, 1122, 1588, 1779, 1781, 2074, 2274, 2280, 2284,		2312, 2909, 3092, 3644, 4165, 4249, 4592, 4992,	
2409, 2437, 2809, 2831, 2862, 3527, 3744, 4007,		5124, 5495, 5938, 6440, 7004, 7318, 7678, 8504,	
4159, 4468, 4575, 4817, 4971, 4972, 4973, 4974,		8573, 10084, 10620, 11528, 11764, 12685, 12722,	
5544, 5548, 5600, 6284, 6285, 6287, 6299, 6303,		12811	
6309, 6715, 6720, 6822, 6836, 6842, 6881, 7948,		GRAVES	8948, 10724
8197, 8395, 8407, 8413, 8423, 8553, 8634, 8846,		GRAVEYARDS	5526
9310, 9478, 9647, 9794, 9856, 9974, 10497, 10536,		GRAVITATION	11795
10735, 10832, 10901, 11132, 11328, 11680, 11732,		GRAVITY	54
11813, 11815, 11821, 12057, 12091, 12171, 12225,		GRAY	5771, 10003
12527, 12578		GRAZING	11194
GOVERNMENTAL	12586	GREASE	6536
GOVERNMENTS	45, 1067, 3152, 8411,	GREASY	2861
8631, 12082		GREAT	15, 133, 553, 1233,
GOVERNORS	12124	1348, 1690, 2425, 3010, 3011, 3343, 3403, 3707,	
GOVERNS	4974, 7556, 9430,	3789, 4181, 4658, 5930, 6010, 6443, 6607, 6745,	
11791		6776, 6915, 7158, 8151, 8153, 8199, 8534, 9070,	
GOWN	8438	11100, 11811, 12833	
GRACE	882, 1501, 2382, 2689,	GREAT MEN	10787
2904, 4427, 5191, 5196, 5718, 7921, 8124, 8856,		GREATER	4040, 7727, 11688
10361, 10984, 12536			
GRACEHOPER	5263		

GREATEST 137, 4387, 7791, 9284, 9413, 11365, 11501
GREATNESS 135, 544, 2037, 2724, 4767, 10431, 11408
GREECE 1958, 8740
GREED 1693, 3629, 8975, 11942
GREEDINESS 12601
GREEDY 9223
GREEK 1951, 2177, 3734, 5033, 5203, 6835, 9917, 10191, 12368
GREEKS 109, 1510, 6124, 12025
GREEN 127, 1344, 1812, 4081, 6343, 7014, 10067, 11580
GREEN-EYED 10345
GREENERY 3976, 5557
GREENSLEEVES 328
GREENWOOD 10027
GREIVANCE 6586
GREY 2264, 12637
GREYHOUNDS 10170
GRIEF 679, 721, 803, 1214, 1358, 1618, 1935, 4121, 5064, 6476, 6876, 7868, 10047, 10430, 10443, 10587, 10616, 11269, 11461, 11640, 12160
GRIEFS 731, 744, 2346, 5008, 5153, 10367
GRIEVANCE 6878, 7386
GRIEVE 332, 2993, 8399
GRIEVED 12703
GRIN 2102, 8654
GRIND 6397
GRIP 11324
GRISTLE 6643
GROAN 5445
GROANS 6543
GROOVES 11451
GROPE 3142
GROSS 8075, 11910
GROUCHO 416
GROUND 134, 1492, 5962, 6994, 7442, 8257, 9907, 10135, 10955, 12186
GROUP 141, 1951
GROUP-MIND 5735
GROUSE 3232
GROVE 7916
GROVELLED 11556
GROVES 1768
GROW 881, 922, 1662, 4258, 11506, 11932
GROWED 11157
GROWING 6202
GROWL 5131

GROWN 3478, 7895, 11100, 12631
GROWNUPS 4049, 9735
GROWS 3059, 11004, 11592, 12577
GROWS UP 8638
GROWTH 1, 3278, 5940, 6052, 8095, 10725
GRUBBING 5645
GRUDGE 231, 8262, 11165
GRUMBLING 3232
GRUNT 8349
GUARD 6502
GUARDED 4156
GUARDIAN 11702, 12534
GUARDIANS 7254
GUARDS 2011
GUERILLA 6905
GUESS 5356, 9780
GUESSING 12271
GUEST 2684
GUESTS 342, 958, 10178
GUIDE 363, 2601, 7758
GUIDELINES 1443
GUIDING-STAR 7955
GUILT 778, 1395, 4158, 4622, 5861, 10841, 11121, 11202
GUILTLESS 1286
GUILTY 1314, 2474, 5316, 6683, 7068, 8329, 9594, 10181, 10227
GUINEA 1801, 11444
GUINEA PIGS 12542
GUITAR 359, 11056
GULL 7067
GULLED 1832
GULLET 7336
GUM 12758
GUN 1001, 3150, 4816, 12316
GUNGA DIN 5648
GUNPOWDER 368, 2086
GUNS 4037, 4038, 5694, 7932, 9244
GUNSHOT 3649
GUT 11665, 12306
GUTLESS 8324
GUTS 2151, 2673
GUTTER 8261, 12498
GUYS 3084, 9631
GYPSY 3857
HABIT 4648, 7095, 7126, 8727, 9145, 9329, 9410, 9715, 9788, 11928
HABITATION 10336

HABITS 2933, 2987, 7874, 8075, 8147, 11063, 12150

HABITUATION 6886

HACK 7743

HACKLES 11052

HADES 12034

HAGGARDS 11018

HAGGIS 8343

HAIL 7515, 9933, 12296

HAIR 5402, 7919, 8874, 9560, 9564, 9851

HAIRCUT 12610

HAIRY 188

HALE 11206

HALF 1100, 2647, 2933, 4145, 8232, 9756, 11403, 12353

HALF-A-CROWN 4385

HALF-BROTHER 802

HALF-BURIED 6429

HALF-CREATE 12701

HALF-HUMAN 5549

HALF-MENTAL 1096

HALF-TRUTH 7086, 9121

HALF-WAY 6635, 9212

HALF-WIT 6876

HALF-WITTED 11019

HALLOW 10787

HALO 12655

HALVE 4414

HAMLET 878, 4367, 7081, 12773

HAMMER 6413, 9216, 11626

HAMMERED 5630, 9111, 10504

HAND 68, 1169, 1572, 1804, 3291, 3861, 3870, 4240, 4408, 4817, 6098, 8161, 9659, 10296, 10662, 11389, 11583, 12103, 12234, 12315, 12559

HANDBOOK 5610

HANDEL 10707

HANDICAP 2259, 2642

HANDICRAFT 9830

HANDIWORK 5269

HANDKERCHIEF 439, 6669

HANDLE 282, 1794, 10265

HANDLES 6083

HANDMAID 704

HANDS 728, 5173, 5873, 9597, 10313, 11371, 11409, 11575

HANDSHAKES 880

HANDSOME 3390, 9089, 10325

HANG 1276, 3605, 5204, 5621, 7731, 8918, 10148, 10433

HANGED 4335, 5029, 7775, 8558, 9855

HANGING 1723, 3412, 5259, 5638, 7769, 10424

HANGMAN 4992

HANGS 7000, 11121

HAPPEN 634, 1828, 4026, 4533, 5703, 6250, 7165

HAPPENED 4919, 11079, 11882, 12395

HAPPENS 4843, 7822

HAPPIER 3851, 4901, 7584, 7606, 8211, 11854

HAPPIEST 1279, 3181, 10597, 11325

HAPPINESS 44, 345, 648, 654, 808, 843, 869, 960, 1052, 1122, 1686, 1700, 1789, 1794, 2579, 2580, 3016, 3247, 3344, 3357, 3384, 3647, 3751, 4069, 4185, 4313, 4802, 4868, 4871, 4913, 5039, 5050, 5090, 5095, 5134, 5336, 5473, 6663, 6959, 6960, 7013, 7114, 7134, 7286, 7807, 8113, 8213, 8251, 8541, 8848, 9344, 9369, 9593, 9662, 9675, 9695, 9795, 9796, 9797, 9829, 9869, 9890, 9910, 10301, 10527, 10548, 10580, 11159, 11303, 11345, 11385, 12335, 12433

HAPPY 1138, 1691, 2029, 2506, 3035, 3432, 3809, 3824, 3911, 3981, 4112, 4437, 4512, 5011, 5099, 5105, 5420, 5755, 5815, 5852, 5980, 6914, 7206, 7288, 7484, 7505, 8734, 8785, 8843, 8857, 8870, 9029, 9678, 9905, 9909, 10004, 10830, 10874, 11117, 11258, 11356, 11922, 11967, 12155, 12609

HARBINGER 7626

HARD 1211, 1847, 1881, 3096, 4328, 5611, 6168, 6628, 11509

HARD-FACED 830

HARDEN 1810, 7760

HARDER 2604, 7809, 8711

HARDSHIP 395, 8467

HARDSHIPS 3642

HARDWARE 4780

HARDY 8072

HARE 594, 6045

HARK 524

HARLOT 1979, 5667

HARLOW 551

HARM 2526, 3202, 4574, 5959, 7115, 7296, 7938, 8190, 9697, 10278, 11348, 12849

HARMFUL 12378

HARMLESS 2922, 8713

HARMONIES 4259

HARMONIOUS 5856, 6139, 7672, 10627

HARMONY 117, 5879, 7394, 7491, 12726

HARP 7855, 7858, 11470

HARPIC	1033
HARPISTS	246
HARRIDAN	4755
HARRISON	8558
HARRY	10170, 10173
HARSHNESS	8820
HARVARD	4743, 7174, 7845
HARVEST	4994, 8611, 9022, 12724
HARVESTING	3692
HARVESTS	3628
HASHISH	9392
HASTE	624, 1249, 2616, 4563, 7592, 10017, 10298, 11606, 12302
HASTEN	1385, 11188
HAT	140, 12201, 12501
HATCH	10689
HATCHED	96
HATCHES	5429
HATCHING	7543
HATE	480, 735, 1156, 1239, 1928, 2454, 2495, 3291, 3318, 3654, 3838, 4359, 4556, 5351, 5587, 6027, 6756, 6982, 7137, 7199, 7210, 7277, 7832, 7987, 8067, 8196, 9347, 9990, 10064, 10530, 11248, 11261, 11314, 11911, 12431
HATED	3725, 8842, 11235
HATEFUL	4947, 8482, 12250
HATES	1866, 7909, 9426, 9582
HATING	1045, 3788, 8038, 9739
HATLESS	1099, 5978
HATRED	837, 1112, 1970, 2335, 3385, 3613, 3628, 4036, 4266, 4607, 5838, 8326, 9273, 9713, 9888, 9989, 10498, 11717
HATREDS	9288
HATS	1101, 12274, 12397
HAUGHTILY	11241
HAUGHTINESS	3330
HAUGHTY	1242, 7404, 9602
HAUNT	8806
HAUNTED	1070, 5949, 8134
HAUNTS	11390
HAVE	877, 1447, 4411, 8093, 9527, 10228, 12571
HAVING	4954, 12763
HAVOC	10200
HAWK	1945, 10121
HAZARD	189, 1810
HAZARDS	7942
HAZE	4490
HAZY	8335
HE	6170

HEAD	668, 1552, 2103, 2117, 3243, 3248, 3588, 4119, 4171, 4492, 5653, 5986, 6840, 7474, 9456, 10591, 11499
HEAD-IN-AIR	4619
HEADACHE	3942
HEADLAND	5679
HEADLINE	8360
HEADLONG	7533
HEADS	1499, 1710, 6092
HEADSTRONG	5475
HEAL	1155, 9286, 12371
HEALED	10313
HEALER	3830, 9621
HEALING	2, 604
HEALS	5588
HEALTH	22, 1370, 1416, 2895, 3595, 4110, 4326, 6476, 7772, 9910
HEALTHY	1517, 1696, 8167, 10806, 11658, 12364
HEAP	6997, 10641, 10828
HEAR	100, 620, 1162, 1885, 2879, 3360, 3616, 4419, 4452, 4745, 5944, 9037, 9572, 10638, 11671, 11707, 12534
HEARD	3580, 3782, 3990, 4451, 4818, 5210, 7272, 7598, 8889, 9220, 12362, 12523
HEARING	7027
HEARS	4406, 7783, 8511, 8932, 12690, 12741
HEART	172, 325, 508, 687, 859, 1027, 1083, 1244, 1252, 1287, 1474, 1573, 1651, 1679, 1710, 1813, 1920, 2072, 2238, 2353, 2539, 2674, 2736, 2776, 2794, 2907, 2976, 3147, 3288, 3394, 3487, 3560, 3781, 3870, 3898, 4082, 4357, 4704, 4740, 4814, 5196, 5227, 5272, 5286, 5438, 5674, 5714, 5842, 6004, 6201, 6415, 6444, 6579, 6580, 6592, 6690, 6771, 6862, 7024, 7049, 7656, 7851, 8438, 8479, 8768, 8886, 9041, 9240, 9390, 9391, 9464, 9564, 9595, 9659, 9736, 9824, 9831, 9866, 9943, 10015, 10104, 10144, 10180, 10208, 10264, 10314, 10540, 10591, 10667, 10669, 10834, 11187, 11276, 11338, 11376, 11400, 11584, 11625, 11640, 11803, 11857, 11919, 11956, 11988, 12421, 12681, 12693, 12702, 12747, 12790, 12805
HEART-BREAK	3899
HEART-EASING	5458
HEARTH	11948
HEARTH-FIRE	5675
HEARTS	1250, 1569, 3090, 3937, 4341, 5815, 6117, 6441, 6479, 6484, 7635, 7855, 8005, 9567, 9704, 10716, 11371, 11422, 11433, 12029, 12232, 12688
HEAT	10804, 11960, 12235
HEATHEN	5639, 5640

HEAVEN	67, 114, 870, 1083, 1182, 1188, 1323, 1596, 1628, 1725, 1990, 2487, 2713, 2797, 3264, 3637, 3910, 4096, 4261, 4327, 4736, 5174, 5189, 5334, 5465, 5792, 5862, 5960, 5966, 5970, 6122, 6162, 6211, 6388, 6716, 6925, 7427, 7448, 7486, 7513, 7514, 7515, 7529, 7566, 7595, 7598, 7605, 7625, 7630, 7877, 7878, 8078, 8082, 8781, 9030, 9920, 9938, 10107, 10131, 10507, 10623, 10741, 10867, 10896, 11108, 11247, 11267, 11634, 12138, 12548, 12692
HEAVENLY	4089, 12019
HEAVENS	7604, 12188
HEAVENTREE	5285
HEAVIER	6234
HEAVINESS	1236
HEAVY	715, 1250, 10323
HEDGE	5080
HEDGEHOGS	5565
HEDGES	11251
HEELS	6
HEFFALUMP	7378
HEIGHT	3647, 6181
HEIGHTS	1404, 6434, 11975
HEIR	11450, 11757
HEIR-APPARENT	10148
HELEN	6926, 8740, 9603
HELICOPTERS	1372
HELL	93, 222, 801, 870, 1088, 1354, 1725, 1840, 1844, 1927, 2644, 2797, 2814, 2934, 3206, 3513, 4096, 4261, 4841, 6154, 6162, 6240, 6388, 6407, 6534, 6925, 6958, 7139, 7198, 7493, 7515, 7533, 7545, 7554, 7568, 7586, 7593, 8681, 8926, 9840, 10499, 10507, 10548, 10615, 10650, 10867, 10896, 11126, 11153, 11167, 11394, 11814, 12035, 12260, 12531
HELL FIRE	9287
HELL-BROTH	10276
HELLHOUND	12614
HELP	95, 129, 360, 582, 1423, 5791, 5792, 6028, 6169, 6279, 6605, 7817, 8795, 11357, 12200
HELPING	5609, 12163
HELPLESS	1355, 3328
HEN	1868, 5564, 9193
HENRY VIII	2634
HERALDRY	4249
HERB	11785
HERBS	7459
HERD-INSTINCT	8178
HERDS	9172
HERDSMAN	12793
HERE	413, 414, 424, 974, 3957, 5487, 6219, 6704, 6837, 11631
HEREDITARY	8277

HEREDITY	1731, 4637
HERESIES	1537
HERESY	14, 10571
HERETIC	10441, 12855
HERITAGE	1563, 5519
HERMIT	5409
HERMITAGE	6477
HERO	3294, 3295, 3480, 3617, 4054, 5987, 6832, 7884, 8833, 8896, 9479, 9480, 11152
HEROES	3538, 4462, 5007, 6243, 6349, 7227, 7708, 12323
HEROIC	3688, 4579, 4951, 6447
HEROICALLY	7666
HERRING BOXES	7824
HERSELF	11184
HERTFORD	6195
HESITATES	9276
HESITATION	11335
HESPERIAN	7571
HESPERUS	5194, 7579
HETERODOXY	12148
HETEROGENEITY	10903
HEW	8866
HI	12183
HID	8814, 10308, 11617
HIDDEN	2367, 3920, 5981, 8391
HIDE	1035, 7415, 7446, 8878, 10092, 10423, 11746
HIDEOUS	7925
HIERARCHY	8607
HIGH	2537, 3462, 7605
HIGH FLYER	8565
HIGH HEELS	8336
HIGH MASS	6786
HIGH-MINDEDNESS	1512
HIGH-TECH	4596
HIGH-WATER	8324
HIGHBROW	4510, 7089, 12098
HIGHER	8963, 10666, 11470
HIGHEST	9504, 10901
HIGHLANDS	1813
HIGHLY	4445
HIGHWAY	4398
HILL	2735, 12754
HILLS	5580
HILLSIDE	1661, 9376
HIM	11428
HIMSELF	831, 1063, 5787, 6511, 7974, 8800, 9616
HIND	10053
HINDRANCE	2340

HINDRANCES	7306, 11653
HINDSIGHT	12515
HINDU	3763
HINGES	7555, 7873
HINTED	9542
HIP	2163, 6833
HIRE	1439, 6983, 7888
HIRELINGS	8955
HIROSHIMA	8649
HIS	8451
HISS	7621
HISSING	2407
HISTORIAN	3883, 4533, 8154, 10688, 11013, 11162
HISTORIANS	1869, 4393, 8920, 8981
HISTORICAL	3193, 11739, 11958
HISTORICALLY	3680
HISTORIES	757, 12059
HISTORY	12, 82, 340, 489, 596, 699, 863, 880, 1263, 1300, 1502, 1745, 1795, 1901, 2083, 2125, 2140, 2147, 2288, 2508, 2785, 2824, 2839, 2865, 2892, 3078, 3181, 3222, 3296, 3340, 3460, 3532, 3539, 3584, 3775, 3867, 4300, 4742, 4944, 5277, 5345, 5562, 5625, 5703, 6010, 6304, 6412, 6447, 6458, 6663, 6747, 6766, 7046, 8881, 8939, 9183, 9294, 9452, 9741, 9870, 9875, 9961, 9979, 10031, 10162, 10533, 10713, 10962, 11123, 11350, 11351, 11352, 11353, 11722, 11755, 11798, 11940, 12081, 12287, 12495, 12562
HIT	140, 1094, 9517, 12863
HITLER	4549, 6487, 8141, 8592, 12828
HIVE	2572, 11231
HOARD	11422
HOARDED	7423
HOARES	3848
HOBBES	11253
HOBBY	291
HOBSON	7685, 12159
HODGEPODGE	10933
HOE	4994, 6919
HOG	7349
HOGS	6666, 11050
HOLD	2908, 10889
HOLDING	3854, 9474
HOLE	1530, 5997, 7314, 8271, 9159
HOLEY	9417
HOLIDAY	7460, 9692, 10499
HOLIDAYS	6433, 10147
HOLINESS	5414, 7748
HOLLAND	4692
HOLLOW	3208, 10364
HOLLYWOOD	4622, 7708, 9344
HOLOCAUST	5498, 7664
HOLY	98, 1216, 7484, 7492, 7616, 8700, 9356, 12078
HOMAGE	1610
HOME	88, 249, 519, 531, 639, 1081, 1110, 1456, 2542, 2582, 2792, 2949, 3534, 3640, 3668, 4149, 4276, 4290, 4567, 4578, 4780, 4783, 5270, 7836, 7890, 8106, 8181, 8269, 8452, 8520, 8789, 8926, 9334, 10022, 11836, 12518, 12713, 12750
HOME-FIRES	3534
HOME-KEEPING	10437
HOMELAND	2691, 4190
HOMELESS	6053, 10878
HOMELY	1026, 1954, 5018, 8461, 10437
HOMER	484, 1062, 11252
HOMES	10677
HOMESICK	4753, 11916
HOMICIDAL	11146
HOMO SAPIENS	7919
HOMOGENEITY	10903
HOMOGENIZED	3665
HONEST	426, 539, 2148, 2710, 2767, 3618, 3708, 3914, 4308, 4912, 5609, 6192, 6503, 7026, 7278, 7775, 8559, 10049, 10117, 10447, 11138, 11516, 11889, 12144, 12279
HONESTER	9322
HONESTLY	4718
HONESTY	1024, 2768, 2773, 4896, 5308, 6968, 7879, 8053, 9641, 9658, 10406, 12337
HONEY	1217, 1571, 6120, 7372, 12087, 12194
HONEYSUCKLE	9260
HONOUR	226, 1190, 1563, 2243, 2881, 2938, 3001, 3337, 3695, 3762, 4196, 4219, 5221, 5662, 5708, 6294, 6331, 6348, 6481, 6614, 6950, 7033, 8074, 8081, 8397, 8806, 9018, 9277, 9705, 9889, 10153, 10285, 10357, 10417, 10910, 11419, 11444, 12618
HONOURABLE	3435, 4727, 6305, 9189, 10204
HONOURED	1212, 2332, 11139
HONOURS	482, 3778, 11853
HOOFBEATS	10818
HOOK	8362, 12765
HOOKAH-MOUTH	5632
HOOKED	12137
HOOVER	4277
HOPE	527, 556, 660, 693, 1402, 1423, 1979, 2325, 2432, 2551, 2569, 2599, 2793, 3603, 3802, 3882, 4521, 4914, 5039, 5135, 5819, 5834, 5934, 6281, 6305, 6306, 6571, 6591,

6742, 7006, 7381, 7383, 7416, 7504, 7650, 8385, 8852, 8884, 9770, 10293, 12135, 12200, 12479, 12528, 12528

HOPED — 1137

HOPEFUL — 6024

HOPEFULLY — 11120

HOPELESS — 2352, 5150, 7539, 9380

HOPELESSNESS — 8385

HOPES — 646, 4410, 6417, 9398

HOPPY — 3257, 5263

HORACE — 8610

HORATIUS — 6774, 6780

HORDE — 1965

HORIZON — 4351

HORIZONTAL — 580, 2399, 10520, 12340

HORN — 4235, 8433

HORNPIPES — 1809

HORNY — 9281

HORNY-HANDED — 9753

HORRIBLE — 12813

HORRID — 5406, 6420, 7451

HORRIFIED — 1862

HORRIFYING — 5709

HORROR — 2114, 2963, 6830, 7325, 7494, 9275

HORRORS — 10286, 11637

HORSE — 499, 972, 3718, 4105, 4128, 4388, 5042, 5350, 5457, 5637, 9132, 9136, 9618, 10380, 10428, 11210, 11332, 11643, 12025, 12427

HORSE-SENSE — 7084

HORSEBACK — 1833

HORSEGUARDS — 9320

HORSEPOND — 8525

HORSES — 2699, 4567, 5057, 9855, 10818, 11559

HORSESHIT — 7951

HOSPITABLE — 7592

HOSPITAL — 1609, 8190

HOST — 955, 7524, 12202

HOSTAGES — 738, 11743

HOSTILE — 5543

HOSTILITIES — 1484

HOSTILITY — 4021, 8358, 8988

HOSTS — 958

HOT SPOT — 7693

HOT-BED — 5142

HOT-WATER — 7281

HOTEL — 7693

HOTEL-KEEPERS — 11786

HOUND — 2196, 6429, 11204, 12427

HOUNDS — 4235, 10193

HOUR — 4179, 4759, 4761, 6243, 9062, 9567, 9633, 9652, 9930, 10029, 10257, 12810

HOUR-GLASS — 9566

HOURLY — 9408

HOURS — 673, 3077, 3140, 5008, 5864, 6885, 6891

HOUSE — 88, 1152, 1161, 1246, 1248, 1430, 2406, 3691, 3939, 3941, 4218, 4987, 5979, 6059, 6174, 6299, 6645, 7846, 7878, 7916, 8745, 8985, 9173, 9857, 11236, 11463, 12312, 12754

HOUSE OF LORDS — 11142

HOUSEHOLDER — 12524

HOUSEKEEPING — 11840

HOUSES — 1481, 3426, 7320, 7929, 10393, 12681

HOUSETOP — 1246

HOUSEWIFE — 1110, 7152, 8743, 9062, 11196

HOUSEWIVES — 11835, 12767

HOUSEWORK — 3376

HOUSTON — 125

HOW — 5654, 8267

HOW-DE-DOO — 3956

HOWL — 6625

HUE — 10622

HUFF — 7034

HUGGED — 3008

HUGGING — 4087

HULL — 9418

HUM — 4030

HUMAN — 433, 1578, 2322, 2471, 2542, 2678, 3041, 3200, 3258, 3571, 3616, 3688, 3873, 4152, 4283, 4392, 4561, 4859, 5332, 5417, 5887, 6180, 6599, 6866, 6867, 6888, 7135, 7436, 7733, 7918, 8302, 8823, 8852, 8910, 9604, 9663, 10831, 11293, 11314, 11535, 11608, 11979, 12789

HUMAN RACE — 9303, 10566

HUMANIST — 5763

HUMANITIES — 8217

HUMANITY — 84, 1038, 6417, 7994, 8410, 8703, 10079, 10732, 12542, 12699

HUMBLE — 133, 5678, 6850, 7158, 8520

HUMBLES — 12401

HUMBLEST — 1684

HUMBLY — 6208

HUMBUG — 2780, 8427

HUMDRUM — 11569

HUMILIATION — 591, 1722, 3102

HUMILIATIONS — 11166

HUMILITY — 1308, 3299, 3715, 6264, 11953, 12753

HUMORIST	1850, 2757, 4537
HUMOROUS	4530
HUMOUR	115, 799, 1577, 2656, 2663, 3649, 3745, 3784, 5570, 6072, 6074, 6695, 7891, 8813, 11690, 12354, 12355, 12374
HUMP	11555
HUNCH	2055
HUNDRED	10692
HUNDREDTH	1697
HUNGER	609, 1165, 1197, 3150, 4709, 9005, 9068, 9379
HUNGRY	9093, 9223, 10190, 11065, 12624
HUNS	7703
HUNTED	6244
HUNTER	594, 6690, 9163, 11508
HUNTING	1829, 5083, 8566, 9216, 11202
HUNTING-FIELD	7943
HUNTS	11443
HURL	1734
HURLED	6997
HURLY-BURLY	10253
HURRICANES	6195
HURRICANOES	10235
HURRY	112, 2276, 4613, 6222, 9083, 11118, 12302
HURT	719, 914, 1251, 1325, 3494, 4349, 4640, 5684, 6297, 6814, 7257, 8402, 10313, 11182, 11314, 11444, 11894
HURTING	8091
HURTS	8006
HUSBAND	237, 259, 1043, 2192, 3178, 3249, 3443, 4641, 4935, 5177, 6478, 6916, 7976, 8627, 9606, 9610, 10323, 10782, 11339, 12164
HUSBANDS	840, 3182, 8876, 10350, 10935, 11835
HUSH	4562, 7371, 8087
HUSTLES	3107
HYBRID	11938
HYGIENE	10765
HYMNS	5853, 10461, 11060
HYPHEN	791
HYPNOTIZE	4888
HYPNOTIZED	8167
HYPOCHONDRIA	4
HYPOCHONDRIAC	11125
HYPOCRISY	842, 2831, 3316, 5831, 7104, 7270, 7564, 8168, 10506, 12454
HYPOCRITE	5040, 9023
HYPOCRITES	4426, 4434, 11041
HYPOTENUSE	3980
HYPOTHESES	8123
HYPOTHESIS	4879, 6466
HYSTERIA	901, 6050, 8003, 8927
I	137, 3790, 11997
ICE	552, 3342, 3669, 7807, 8946
ICE-CREAM	11054
ICED	522, 8288
ICEMAN	8278
ICICLE	2128
ICING	6624
ICONOCLASM	4651
IDEA	86, 111, 229, 309, 563, 668, 1394, 1543, 2651, 3209, 3650, 4058, 4801, 4806, 5491, 6865, 6969, 7839, 8235, 8348, 9359, 9677, 9800, 12455, 12756
IDEAL	2882, 6583, 8189, 8500, 9417, 11339
IDEALISM	5297
IDEALIST	9779
IDEALISTIC	12592
IDEAS	474, 586, 1059, 1902, 2412, 2696, 2981, 3108, 3256, 3404, 3477, 4067, 4198, 7820, 9368, 10801, 11027, 11828, 11877, 12005, 12378, 12380
IDENTICAL	6136
IDENTITY	3638, 6694, 6698, 11087
IDEOLOGY	1, 5751
IDIOM	8965
IDIOSYNCRASY	4963
IDIOT	1264, 2201, 3950, 7315, 10287
IDIOTS	10807
IDLE	1846, 3709, 3875, 5097, 5133, 6705, 7926, 8535, 9119, 9916, 12160, 12195
IDLENESS	2076, 4985, 5251, 5820, 8776, 11087
IDLING	4988
IDOL	6579, 11347
IDOLATERS	4646
IDOLATRY	10497
IDOLS	1463, 3474, 10500
IDYLL	3974
IF	10040
IFS	9072
IGNORAMUS	1265, 6184
IGNORANCE	26, 1388, 1649, 2625, 2852, 3079, 4057, 4208, 4247, 4306, 4440, 4762, 5730, 6185, 6707, 6939, 8315, 8600, 8964, 9147, 9968, 10821, 11162, 11427, 11741, 12381
IGNORANT	1064, 1195, 1285, 2336, 2646, 6403, 6650, 7723, 9482, 10290, 11881
IGNORE	8033, 8707, 9256

IMPURE	6019	INDEED	4778
IMPURITY	7391	INDEFATIGABLE	10895
IN	2267	INDEFENSIBLE	8327
IN COMMON	9246	INDEFINITE	12531
IN LOVE	10438	INDEPENDENCE	9988
IN VAIN	11514	INDEPENDENT	2834, 2872, 3636,
INABILITY	4178, 7921	6510, 12376	
INACCURACY	1872, 9747	INDIA	6924
INACTION	5500, 6179, 6671	INDIAN	280, 2740, 10634,
INACTIVITY	6673	12421	
INAPPREHENSIBLE	11622	INDIANS	819, 6365, 12299
INCAPABLE	7325, 7751	INDICTMENT	1753
INCAPACITY	1336, 9266	INDIFFERENCE	2094, 6270, 7161,
INCARNATE	10717	7809, 9713, 11106, 12431	
INCARNATION	4064, 8263	INDIFFERENT	4630, 10530, 10746
INCENSE	5447	INDIGESTION	457, 11118
INCENSED	7552	INDIGNATION	3269, 3904, 7963,
INCEST	904	11237, 12289	
INCESTUOUS	5010	INDIGNITY	1000
INCH	1784, 2985, 10242,	INDISCREET	12482
12320		INDISCRETION	4384, 6713
INCHES	5181	INDISPENSABLE	3739, 4781, 6329,
INCISORS	798	9675, 11653	
INCITES	7795	INDISTINCT	4475
INCLUDE	4172	INDIVIDUAL	2609, 3762, 4716,
INCOGNITO	9258	5305, 5739, 6404, 8001, 8178, 9430, 10823, 11565	
INCOME	654, 5550, 8075, 8455,	INDIVIDUALISM	5756
10759, 11345		INDIVIDUALITY	9833, 12466
INCOME TAX	9325	INDIVIDUALLY	141
INCOMES	3996, 9742	INDIVIDUALS	5548, 7304, 8145
INCOMMUNICABLE	11074	INDIVISIBLE	6338
INCOMPATIBILITY	2177	INDOCTRINATION	812
INCOMPATIBLE	6246	INDOLENCE	4437, 5816
INCOMPETENCE	8606, 8607	INDOORS	6784
INCOMPETENT	854, 10554	INDUBITABLE	9666
INCOMPLETE	3728	INDUCE	11049
INCOMPLETENESS	84	INDULGENT	5238, 10976
INCOMPREHENSIBLE	4678	INDUSTRIAL	3860
INCONGRUITIES	6072	INDUSTRIOUS	7533
INCONSISTENCY	51, 10747	INDUSTRY	2091, 4204, 4857,
INCONSISTENT	9274, 12279	7687, 9372, 9830, 9999, 11349, 12569	
INCONSTANCY	977, 11233	INEFFECTUAL	12591
INCONSTANT	3824	INEFFICIENCY	2684
INCONVENIENCE	645	INEFFICIENT	10542
INCONVENIENT	1292, 10803	INELEGANCE	650
INCORRUPTIBLE	2089	INEQUALITY	487
INCREASED	2841	INERTIA	4361, 8593
INCREASES	9235	INESCAPABLE	8493
INCURABLE	2571	INEVITABILITY	12220
INDEBTED	7142, 7567, 10636	INEVITABLE	2162, 4249, 6519,
INDECENT	1972, 6009, 9011	10688, 11329	
INDECISION	9012	INEXPERIENCED	193
		INFAMOUS	6763

IRRESPONSIBLE	2515
IRRETRIEVABLE	663
IRREVERSIBLE	6330
IRRITATE	7086
IRRITATES	5064
IRRITATING	8533
ISLAND	1119, 2307, 2772, 2911, 7808, 8225, 11279, 11920, 12110
ISLE	905, 10360, 10842
ISLINGTON	1332
ISRAEL	1203, 4909
ISSUES	4409, 4471, 8299
ISTANBUL	5863
IT	9658
ITALIAN	1497, 7197
ITALIANS	5006
ITALY	1789, 1844, 5100, 7263, 10785, 11862, 12264
ITCH	671, 6486, 9058
ITCHES	264
IVORY	7058, 7927
IVY	74, 9552
JABBERWOCK	2109
JACKALS	3498
JACKASS	9324
JACKSONIAN	8905
JACOB	11624
JADE	4105, 4128
JAIL	2899, 5059
JAM	2112
JAMES	7367
JANE	10701, 12256
JAR	6938
JARGON	1059, 6360
JAUNDICED	8824
JAW-JAW	2316
JAWS	2102, 11394
JAZZ	4259
JE-NE-SAIS-QUOI	3975
JEALOUS	10347, 10352
JEALOUSY	1328, 3179, 5178, 7593, 9726, 10345, 12289
JEANIE	3559
JEEPERS	7221
JEFFERSONIAN	8905
JELLY	9162
JELLYBEANS	9333
JERUSALEM	1332, 1344, 1346
JESSAMINE	7481
JEST	483, 5153, 9297, 10142, 10252
JESTING	6189

JESTS	10386
JESU	2689
JESUIT	5618
JESUS	128, 1031, 1329, 4701, 6161, 8591, 10683, 11182, 11326, 12166
JEW	2858, 3126, 7349, 8141, 10313
JEWEL	10025, 10384, 10719, 11663, 11964, 12257
JEWELLERY	6163
JEWELS	11504
JEWISH	1576, 1594, 4039, 4931, 5498, 7328, 9583, 10306
JEWS	3395, 4101, 7159
JIG	8762
JIGGING	6945
JILTED	2022
JINGLING	11444
JOB	557, 1138, 2310, 4233, 4374, 5280, 5513, 7718, 7793, 10155
JOBS	1401, 3742
JOCKEYS	2699
JOG	5915, 11035
JOGGING	9907
JOHN	366
JOHN BROWN	425, 8035
JOHN PEEL	4235
JOHN THOMAS	6024
JOHNNY	4619
JOHNSON	4107, 5078, 8549
JOIN	1645, 2107, 7438
JOINED	1184, 1435, 10538
JOINT	1379, 10114, 11163
JOKE	2270, 2512, 3648, 3952, 8156, 8767, 8980, 10793
JOKES	3667, 4117, 9104
JOLLITY	7452
JOLLYRODGERED	11589
JONSON	2445, 7464
JOSEPHINE	8018
JOSS-STICKS	1512
JOSTLING	1348
JOTTING	6079
JOURNAL	1460, 9771
JOURNALISM	507, 4314, 4547, 7337
JOURNALIST	12622, 12785
JOURNALISTS	1301
JOURNEY	860, 1287, 2735, 3211, 3944, 4014, 6001, 6903, 8279, 9045
JOUSTED	7526
JOVE	2063, 5208, 7400

JOY 1157, 1559, 1985, 3031, 3459, 6260, 6855, 7644, 9934, 10041, 10625, 11539, 11740, 12738

JOYCE 1121

JOYS 731, 744, 1354, 1835, 3012, 6597, 7434, 7739, 9601, 12425

JUBILANT 7603

JUDAS 4266, 12494

JUDGE 231, 346, 1172, 3308, 4712, 6408, 7192, 7463, 7936, 8587, 8760, 8947, 9206, 9326, 9572, 10483, 11378, 12512

JUDGED 1172, 4672, 5593

JUDGEMENT 69, 212, 920, 1676, 2043, 2369, 2731, 2962, 4399, 4728, 5631, 5841, 6257, 6411, 6940, 7641, 7765, 7981, 8361, 9875, 10108, 10317, 12587

JUDGEMENT BOOK 11361

JUDGEMENTS 2585, 3903, 7773, 7786, 11427, 11972

JUDGES 4558, 4791, 6176, 7939, 8099, 8759, 9209, 9259

JUDGING 2120, 7728

JUDICIOUS 11122

JUG 6594

JULIET 10386, 10693

JUMBLIES 6092

JUMBO 10703

JUMP 2166, 10311

JUMPING 11195

JUMPS 664, 6345

JUNE 2063, 9182

JUNGLE 2027, 2623, 6321

JUPITER 6547, 11650

JURISDICTION 1410

JURY 3651, 3711

JURYMEN 8759

JUST 379, 1157, 1489, 2288, 5036, 7655, 10656

JUSTICE 261, 615, 748, 1041, 1085, 1897, 2619, 2645, 2715, 2946, 3429, 4104, 4295, 4560, 4670, 4793, 5306, 5590, 5591, 5839, 5854, 6199, 6624, 6763, 6820, 7085, 7191, 7560, 7620, 7981, 8139, 8140, 8340, 9902, 10310, 10937, 12188

JUSTIFIABLE 7655

JUSTIFICATION 12382

JUSTIFIED 7297

JUSTIFY 4733, 7501

KAISER 3252

KARL MARX 366

KEATS 1716

KEENER 4922

KEEP 247, 1016, 2408, 2948, 4420, 5494, 5681, 6001, 12313, 12380

KEEPING 5658, 8299

KEY 5461, 7402, 7762, 8492, 8924

KEYHOLE 11923

KEYS 4222, 7479, 8978, 11473

KHATMANDU 4424

KIBOSH 3252

KICK 1128, 2274, 5418, 8462, 8891, 10955, 12207

KICKED 72

KICKS 7341

KID 1380, 12761

KIDDIE 8038

KIDDIES 1102

KIDDING 8592

KIDS 2604, 5993, 7895

KILL 826, 2073, 2384, 2510, 2810, 3163, 3302, 6085, 6116, 6941, 7388, 8019, 8135, 8402, 9493, 9581, 9717, 10241, 10547, 10898, 11681, 12072, 12847

KILLED 365, 2293, 5707, 5804, 6112, 11199

KILLING 31, 5628, 10709, 10898

KILLS 1087, 6033, 12478

KIN 713, 8034, 10100, 10418

KIND 2060, 2664, 2672, 3422, 5036, 6551, 8192, 9850, 10100, 10133, 11322, 12441

KINDERGARTEN 9435

KINDEST 9456

KINDLE 523, 2266, 5296

KINDLES 1854

KINDLIER 1561

KINDLING 9184

KINDLY 9763, 10858

KINDNESS 1803, 2533, 4187, 4284, 4783, 5115, 8524, 10259, 12547

KING 268, 378, 1311, 1313, 1612, 1761, 2082, 2683, 2746, 3245, 4218, 4377, 5351, 5627, 6471, 6641, 6770, 6854, 6935, 6948, 7369, 7880, 8067, 8561, 8562, 8668, 8671, 8969, 9441, 9619, 9967, 10132, 10139, 10174, 10185, 10242, 10362, 10366, 10367, 10631, 11415, 11416, 11429, 11761, 12365, 12632, 12637

KING GEORGE 6801

KINGDOM 1158, 1165, 1171, 1182, 2921, 7643, 9993, 10380

KINGLY 7550

KINGS 1769, 2110, 2591, 2715, 2989, 3408, 4275, 8703, 8773, 9989, 10360, 10364, 11099, 11886

KINQUERING 10948

LEARNED 248, 278, 1392, 2014, 2375, 3328, 5094, 6852, 6960, 8750, 8843, 9722, 11072, 11252, 11881, 12276

LEARNER 11915

LEARNING 764, 1857, 2601, 2842, 3530, 3815, 4147, 4444, 4731, 4838, 5729, 6183, 6364, 6839, 7898, 8529, 8695, 8815, 9133, 9171, 9255, 9256, 10398, 10808, 10829, 11379, 11761, 11823, 12832

LEARNS 4875, 5751

LEARNT 2502, 4331, 7642, 9997, 12145

LEASEHOLD 6563

LEAST 727

LEATHERN 6998

LEAVE 332, 1200, 1220, 2246, 2990, 3567, 3730, 4093, 6461, 10670, 10920, 11292

LEAVE OUT 9491

LEAVE-TAKING 1861

LEAVES 5432, 9143, 9463, 10609, 10611, 12691, 12792

LEAVING 1691, 10258, 11097, 12108

LEAVINGS 11220

LECHER 10243

LECHERY 10420

LECTURE 11059

LECTURER 12649

LECTURES 12416

LED 1986, 5653

LEES 10270

LEFT 286, 372, 1169, 2638, 4382, 7037, 7976, 10965, 11529, 12232

LEFT HAND 7645

LEFT WINGER 8063

LEG 6296

LEGACY 1874, 10744

LEGAL 7306

LEGALIZED 2840

LEGEND 3779

LEGISLATION 3630, 4016

LEGISLATIVE 791, 3866

LEGISLATOR 1781

LEGISLATURE 789

LEGITIMATE 12223

LEGLESS 8748

LEGS 3248, 4568, 8296, 8308, 9907

LEICESTER 5289

LEISURE 1454, 5092, 6799, 7439, 7872, 9689, 10298, 10514, 11374, 11606, 11753

LEMON 4142

LEMON-TREES 4090

LEND 1254, 3564, 5887, 9122, 10203, 10228, 11205, 11833

LENGTH 3380, 3647

LENIN 5546, 5561

LENT 530

LEOPARD 1228

LESS 64, 453, 578, 1624, 1644, 1856, 5647, 8155, 8868

LESSER 3403

LESSON 4875, 6012, 8898, 9758, 10919

LESSONS 7944

LET 6971

LETHAL 438, 10021

LETHARGY 7770

LETHE 5441, 5881

LETTER 718, 741, 3898, 6221, 9887, 10232

LETTERS 606, 2914, 5124, 6489

LETTUCE 8902

LEVEL 1766, 3180

LEVIATHAN 7602

LEVITY 10518, 11122

LEXICOGRAPHER 5146

LEXICON 1715

LIAR 834, 995, 1976, 4914, 9265

LIARS 2974, 4815, 9490, 10663, 11132, 11977

LIBEL 11242

LIBERAL 3662, 3938, 8300, 10986, 12379

LIBERALITY 5782

LIBERATE 6284, 6875

LIBERATES 373

LIBERATION 4102

LIBERATIONISTS 6459

LIBERTIES 1742, 3835, 4939, 11615

LIBERTINE 10107

LIBERTY 39, 302, 345, 734, 982, 1085, 1746, 1752, 1759, 1760, 1824, 2209, 3080, 3556, 3584, 3766, 3869, 4032, 4060, 4364, 4502, 4793, 4813, 4915, 4980, 5302, 5520, 6157, 6308, 6375, 6449, 6475, 6476, 6477, 6512, 6617, 6753, 6813, 7295, 7299, 7300, 7386, 7386, 7397, 7453, 7674, 7675, 7812, 9501, 9854, 9860, 10557, 10777, 11723, 12226, 12582, 12586, 12772

LIBERTY-HALL 4144

LIBRARIES 9655

LIBRARY 673, 674, 1030, 2955, 5154, 9765, 11177

LICENCE 6904, 7675, 7681, 9860, 11647

LICENSED 8233

LICENTIOUS 3881

LICK 9064

LIE 281, 502, 763, 1069, 1871, 2155, 2366, 3819, 4584, 4960, 5047, 5179, 5247, 6622, 6640, 7797, 8128, 8158, 8647, 8999, 9120, 9121, 9289, 10027, 10956, 11407, 11457, 12177, 12668, 12790

LIED 5636, 5682

LIES 338, 484, 552, 1326, 1521, 2378, 2850, 4226, 4793, 4979, 5368, 8328, 8926, 8963, 9026, 9441, 10458, 10478, 10517, 10533, 11076, 11115, 12095, 12785

LIEUTENANT 7882

LIFE 19, 171, 301, 367, 406, 429, 448, 498, 564, 629, 635, 807, 856, 859, 862, 1068, 1151, 1153, 1154, 1199, 1218, 1412, 1565, 1591, 1628, 1680, 1712, 1796, 1815, 1857, 1864, 1899, 1905, 1916, 2032, 2262, 2290, 2349, 2399, 2468, 2502, 2547, 2561, 2571, 2671, 2721, 3259, 3303, 3370, 3428, 3540, 3619, 3653, 3813, 3894, 3952, 3999, 4002, 4081, 4187, 4330, 4353, 4378, 4483, 4576, 4590, 4595, 4672, 4673, 4674, 4737, 4766, 4774, 4847, 4848, 4924, 4953, 4968, 4987, 5048, 5049, 5101, 5155, 5283, 5350, 5422, 5455, 5504, 5539, 5572, 5629, 5746, 5806, 5855, 5981, 6015, 6036, 6075, 6101, 6110, 6119, 6134, 6175, 6178, 6225, 6247, 6318, 6383, 6440, 6563, 6570, 6665, 6687, 6729, 6896, 7060, 7283, 7313, 7342, 7358, 7389, 7476, 7624, 7625, 7652, 7691, 7777, 7800, 7866, 7898, 7904, 7906, 7917, 7930, 7954, 7998, 8095, 8109, 8147, 8158, 8164, 8167, 8180, 8186, 8276, 8280, 8416, 8418, 8443, 8491, 8495, 8540, 8601, 8734, 8795, 8932, 9253, 9308, 9371, 9442, 9494, 9494, 9508, 9550, 9578, 9604, 9614, 9624, 9634, 9647, 9648, 9678, 9696, 9698, 9807, 9839, 9899, 9905, 9914, 9926, 10001, 10002, 10025, 10056, 10061, 10154, 10192, 10218, 10234, 10258, 10357, 10403, 10409, 10494, 10590, 10593, 10630, 10671, 10760, 10763, 10770, 10774, 10851, 10855, 10900, 11068, 11150, 11200, 11225, 11270, 11272, 11333, 11369, 11385, 11414, 11478, 11521, 11588, 11661, 11685, 11734, 11774, 11808, 11854, 11868, 11903, 12128, 12271, 12314, 12314, 12458, 12616, 12642, 12655, 12697, 12781, 12845, 12850

LIFE-BLOOD 7389, 11768

LIFE-GIVING 3761

LIFE-JACKET 861

LIFELESS 8491

LIFETIME 541, 808, 2746, 5523, 10548, 11070, 12345

LIFT 10610, 10630, 10787

LIGHT 119, 180, 772, 1167, 1474, 1984, 2252, 2805, 2919, 3559, 3675, 3699, 4076, 4408, 4675, 5218, 5966, 6399, 6526, 7134, 7319, 7408, 7443, 7450, 7453, 7545, 7559, 7596, 7628, 7676, 7933, 7953, 7999, 8062, 8106, 8814,

8911, 8919, 9253, 9287, 9445, 9460, 10323, 10351, 10386, 10480, 10701, 11231, 11584, 11962, 11963, 11970, 12215, 12686

LIGHT BRIGADE 11393

LIGHTEN 4278

LIGHTLY 2231

LIGHTNESS 5770

LIGHTNING 544, 4194, 4923, 11878

LIGHTS 2411, 4499, 9340, 9571, 11469

LIKE 176, 595, 622, 667, 1944, 2383, 2811, 3422, 6312, 6342, 6505, 6943, 7210, 9760, 10562, 11259, 11930, 12480

LIKED 5902, 9694

LIKELY 9067

LIKING 651, 869, 899, 3576, 11606

LIKINGS 5882

LILAC 3195

LILIES 7021, 7022, 9559, 10470

LILY 1957, 5401, 6430, 9036, 10219

LILY-HANDED 11512

LIMBO 7563

LIMBS 8042

LIMIT 4072, 4765, 7351, 9171, 11520

LIMITATIONS 3191, 8590, 10004, 11799

LIMITED 7299

LIMITS 3287, 4417, 6925, 12605

LIMP 12656

LIN-LAN-LONE 11398

LINCOLN 1026, 9776

LINE 2281, 6217, 8718, 8836, 9709

LINEN 3510, 4693

LINER 5663

LINES 7007

LINGERING 3963

LINGUISTICS 9548

LINING 866

LINK 2283, 6465

LINKED 8368

LINNET 11475

LION 2289, 2701, 8462, 9951, 10053, 10332, 10722

LIONESS 11372

LIONS 8511

LIP 687

LIPS 1851, 6390, 6877, 6926, 11440, 11545, 12846

LIPSTICK 8037

LIQUID 11543

LIQUOR 4147, 4934, 8039, 12544, 12846

LIST 3949

LISTEN 3645, 3787, 3899, 4380, 4473, 4777, 5563, 5795, 9014, 9449, 10627, 11712, 12428

LISTENER 1549

LISTENING 811, 1518, 3771, 6328, 7214, 10014, 10684

LISTENS 6979, 9368

LIT 4285

LITERALISTS 7844

LITERARY 983, 2511, 2531, 2815, 4449, 4837, 4849, 5113, 7832, 8948

LITERATURE 234, 235, 507, 577, 1451, 2202, 2239, 2877, 3045, 3085, 3305, 3908, 4897, 4944, 5931, 6076, 6251, 6383, 6486, 7129, 7938, 8238, 8914, 8923, 9811, 10877, 10999, 11395, 11945, 12374, 12520, 12661, 12854

LITIGANT 1267

LITIGIOUS 8116

LITTLE 1460, 2472, 3091, 3226, 3899, 4123, 6356, 6745, 6975, 7302, 9378, 10710, 11335, 11485, 12843

LITTLENESS 2075

LITTLENESSES 11414

LIVE 313, 481, 692, 950, 1317, 1566, 1903, 1929, 2456, 2460, 2518, 3611, 3626, 3903, 4805, 4885, 5067, 5281, 5495, 5496, 5592, 5980, 6183, 6248, 6927, 6984, 6988, 7179, 7198, 7253, 7454, 7617, 7625, 7717, 7730, 8160, 8208, 8433, 8449, 8533, 8597, 8848, 8871, 9031, 9683, 9928, 10377, 10449, 10827, 10879, 11069, 11131, 11225, 11263, 11367, 11415, 11454, 11667, 11674, 11708, 11863, 11973, 12015, 12060, 12276, 12368, 12826, 12865

LIVED 518, 1381, 2351, 3035, 3801, 3810, 4628, 4910, 7022, 7767, 7788, 8912, 8986, 9508, 9701, 9924, 9944, 10285, 11631

LIVERY 7579

LIVES 440, 635, 2647, 4693, 4954, 5778, 6443, 8298, 9927, 10678, 10754, 11095, 11682, 12456

LIVING 166, 231, 504, 630, 1598, 1745, 2469, 3214, 4329, 4562, 4782, 5983, 6075, 6442, 7324, 7775, 7793, 8737, 9615, 10657, 11363, 11802, 12013, 12084, 12639, 12706, 12820

LIVINGSTONE 10967

LLAMA 983

LLOYD GEORGE 432

LOAFING 11381

LOAN 674, 1991

LOATHE 2007

LOAVES 9093

LOBBYIST 11810

LOCAL 4642

LOCATION 8394

LOCKS 7396

LODESTERRE 6587

LODGE 7685

LODGINGS 10817

LOGIC 2687, 4668, 6201

LOGICALLY 564, 3136

LOHENGRIN 9572

LOITERING 5400

LONDON 2446, 2586, 2777, 2875, 2954, 2961, 3853, 5101, 5994, 7064, 7925, 8675, 10615, 11597

LONDON BRIDGE 6761

LONE 5652

LONELINESS 2513, 2552, 4601, 7698, 8276, 10679, 11538, 11709, 12625

LONELY 1562, 1562, 2415, 3779, 5000, 6167, 6690, 7900, 8161, 8511, 12034

LONESOME 2423, 9098

LONG 260, 1527, 5128, 5289, 5554, 6121, 6178, 6259, 7413, 7545, 8026, 8070, 8279, 8646, 9010, 11513, 12564

LONG-DISTANCE 10679

LONGED 11521

LONGER 3295, 3611, 5702, 8486

LONGEST 7101, 9085, 10879

LONGEVITY 3523, 4664

LONGING 4975, 9415

LONGINGS 10082

LOOK 729, 2641, 3382, 3396, 3857, 4970, 5924, 5953, 6515, 7728, 9358, 9465, 10105, 10312, 11215, 11760, 12478

LOOK AFTER 9922, 11574

LOOKED 1637, 5386, 5403, 7362, 7691

LOOKER-ON 9249

LOOKIN-GLASS 5274

LOOKING 180, 565, 1380, 1488, 2773, 3454, 5538, 7208, 11016, 11595, 12658, 12866

LOOKING-GLASS 12660

LOOKS 1651, 2442, 4823, 7863, 10304, 11824

LOOMS 11965

LOOPHOLES 3454, 11543

LOOSE 4825, 5757

LORD 79, 126, 556, 558, 614, 1203, 1231, 1419, 1428, 1699, 2887, 3241, 3406, 4463, 5291, 6533, 6640, 6953, 7488, 7748, 8839, 12669

LORDLY 8652

LORDS 4150, 7661, 7816, 8210, 10628

LORDSHIP 872

LORDSHIPS 348

LORE 5470

LOS ANGELES 2002

LOSE 94, 143, 210, 412, 1164, 2261, 2408, 2574, 3153, 4481, 4737, 6099, 6102, 6209, 7538, 7619, 8319, 9024, 9619, 9826, 10553, 10573, 11603, 12142, 12486

LOSER 9453, 10690

LOSES 528, 635, 3060, 8146

LOSING 164, 1451, 5012, 5681

LOST 30, 970, 1908, 4270, 5114, 5123, 5975, 6295, 6885, 7277, 7508, 7615, 7823, 7901, 7978, 8124, 8222, 8313, 8991, 9000, 9889, 9932, 11003, 11296, 11464, 11501, 11716, 12065, 12265, 12413, 12529

LOT 3391

LOTHARIO 9602

LOUD 12865

LOUDER 5914

LOUDEST 9535, 12242

LOUSE 5136, 11395

LOVABLE 8363, 10502

LOVE 150, 175, 321, 408, 409, 422, 426, 441, 444, 448, 449, 450, 517, 556, 567, 576, 595, 599, 601, 609, 610, 612, 622, 658, 664, 708, 721, 778, 804, 864, 898, 913, 914, 963, 976, 977, 997, 1050, 1088, 1140, 1154, 1156, 1327, 1349, 1352, 1353, 1354, 1359, 1360, 1361, 1367, 1376, 1474, 1533, 1536, 1541, 1560, 1566, 1592, 1619, 1620, 1621, 1637, 1640, 1678, 1806, 1823, 1853, 1884, 1886, 1893, 1910, 1914, 1952, 1953, 1954, 1968, 1970, 2035, 2061, 2062, 2087, 2159, 2165, 2219, 2236, 2252, 2265, 2266, 2348, 2403, 2451, 2461, 2482, 2506, 2535, 2629, 2668, 2669, 2672, 2686, 2794, 2806, 2813, 2852, 2896, 2900, 2901, 2903, 2905, 2908, 2919, 2920, 2926, 2934, 2936, 2944, 3014, 3023, 3024, 3031, 3082, 3085, 3090, 3354, 3377, 3385, 3428, 3437, 3441, 3444, 3509, 3510, 3545, 3604, 3636, 3639, 3654, 3657, 3812, 3858, 3896, 3992, 3994, 4032, 4131, 4157, 4196, 4201, 4267, 4273, 4275, 4280, 4356, 4379, 4416, 4453, 4506, 4529, 4550, 4621, 4688, 4800, 4807, 4811, 4989, 4997, 5048, 5077, 5115, 5160, 5220, 5226, 5265, 5284, 5291, 5299, 5409, 5452, 5541, 5584, 5606, 5769, 5838, 5850, 6056, 6120, 6165, 6185, 6389, 6390, 6477, 6481, 6534, 6543, 6589, 6756, 6789, 6856, 6860, 6985, 6992, 7003, 7006, 7007, 7036, 7083, 7101, 7116, 7124, 7125, 7137, 7144, 7147, 7205, 7237, 7253, 7322, 7343, 7583, 7594,

7613, 7625, 7659, 7694, 7713, 7857, 7979, 8015, 8038, 8047, 8054, 8176, 8250, 8274, 8356, 8375, 8443, 8444, 8490, 8494, 8507, 8524, 8537, 8578, 8584, 8641, 8689, 8735, 8781, 8785, 8892, 8935, 8949, 8960, 8961, 8992, 9027, 9078, 9100, 9122, 9154, 9168, 9235, 9281, 9296, 9347, 9352, 9370, 9414, 9442, 9447, 9464, 9465, 9470, 9550, 9585, 9588, 9642, 9688, 9695, 9696, 9725, 9737, 9807, 9819, 9865, 9938, 9939, 9955, 9963, 10026, 10037, 10038, 10042, 10043, 10052, 10059, 10071, 10116, 10211, 10226, 10309, 10327, 10328, 10346, 10349, 10353, 10385, 10389, 10391, 10415, 10426, 10429, 10432, 10461, 10464, 10474, 10475, 10477, 10480, 10481, 10502, 10503, 10621, 10640, 10658, 10667, 10668, 10692, 10705, 10865, 10888, 10912, 10919, 10920, 10928, 10934, 10986, 11084, 11130, 11184, 11187, 11191, 11248, 11261, 11270, 11277, 11418, 11426, 11439, 11459, 11461, 11508, 11513, 11514, 11533, 11540, 11548, 11561, 11576, 11601, 11610, 11670, 11691, 11712, 11743, 11766, 11782, 11792, 11911, 11928, 12041, 12043, 12134, 12162, 12182, 12185, 12264, 12294, 12298, 12322, 12324, 12431, 12483, 12570, 12597, 12672, 12744, 12745, 12763, 12765, 12794, 12803, 12806, 12856

LOVE SONG 8894

LOVE-QUARRELS 7660

LOVE-SICK 10068

LOVED 518, 679, 987, 1325, 1381, 1636, 1655, 1700, 1788, 1800, 1908, 2575, 2913, 3146, 3810, 3878, 4303, 4802, 6048, 6667, 6678, 6794, 6862, 6936, 7323, 7768, 7887, 8363, 8700, 8736, 9273, 9274, 9303, 9469, 9809, 10202, 11464, 12143, 12602, 12868

LOVELIEST 4738

LOVELINESS 3962, 5364, 10592

LOVELL 2438

LOVELY 2208, 4721, 4824, 6337, 7738, 10592

LOVEMAKING 4610

LOVER 820, 1953, 2144, 2504, 3347, 3879, 3973, 4041, 4384, 5191, 7593, 8442, 9606, 10373, 10877, 11790, 12133, 12550

LOVERS 1565, 2155, 2157, 2626, 3501, 6237, 8696, 8865, 9958, 10382, 11436

LOVES 1009, 2425, 3779, 4130, 4458, 6570, 6637, 6887, 6914, 7675, 7807, 9356, 9713, 10018, 10479, 11320, 11372, 11417

LOVING 236, 660, 1984, 2253, 5543, 7853, 8223, 9616, 9643, 10033, 11129, 11360, 12512

LOW 4692, 4762

LOWBROW 1084

LOWELLS 1456

LOWER 7163, 12484

LOWLY 128

LOYAL 6828

LOYALTIES 519, 4933

MALEFACTORS	3702
MALEVOLENCE	6455
MALICE	1288, 5222, 6307,
9853, 10352, 11265	
MALICIOUS	3125, 4435
MALIGN	5844
MALT	4733
MAMA	3731
MAMMON	1170, 7529, 10771
MAN	238, 380, 381, 402,

491, 496, 596, 953, 1131, 1136, 1160, 1208, 1219,
1224, 1252, 1278, 1293, 1297, 1411, 1475, 1494,
1495, 1523, 1600, 1628, 1639, 1917, 2203, 2206,
2709, 2836, 3291, 3296, 3348, 3414, 3421, 3620,
3688, 3786, 3829, 4045, 4062, 4077, 4114, 4123,
4126, 4372, 4433, 4557, 4600, 4752, 4812, 4958,
5003, 5076, 5481, 5627, 5656, 5660, 5685, 5686,
5833, 5993, 5996, 6126, 6192, 6282, 6290, 6518,
6636, 6864, 6980, 7016, 7029, 7156, 7182, 7193,
7246, 7388, 7736, 7872, 8177, 8234, 8245, 8307,
8438, 8474, 8509, 8515, 8521, 8534, 8548, 8708,
8983, 9071, 9252, 9729, 9828, 9844, 9920, 9930,
9939, 10018, 10019, 10105, 10290, 10300, 10440,
10525, 10730, 10861, 10939, 10970, 11004, 11154,
11197, 11248, 11283, 11340, 11410, 11423, 11535,
11547, 11570, 11577, 11693, 11892, 12247, 12257,
12312, 12326, 12359, 12423, 12477, 12660, 12703,
12843, 12850

MAN-CHILD	2135
MAN-O'-WAR	5663
MANAGED	7609, 7777
MANAGEMENT	461, 9450
MANCHESTER	6545
MANDALAY	5664
MANFULLY	2071, 3617
MANGER	128, 7486, 11966
MANHATTAN	12623
MANHOOD	2863, 10177
MANIFESTO	10913
MANKIND	501, 958, 3347, 3874,

4940, 5120, 5527, 7040, 7289, 7295, 7297, 8174,
8411, 8757, 9987, 11454, 11653

MANLY	6954
MANNA	3021
MANNER	5956, 10109
MANNERS	557, 842, 1200, 2342,

3104, 3314, 3315, 3723, 3987, 4966, 7280, 7392,
7873, 8831, 8946, 10186, 10931, 12204, 12771

MANOEUVRE	11799
MANPOWER	8008
MANSION	7400
MANSION-HOUSE	7399
MANSIONS	1152
MANTLE	7483
MANURE	5337

MANUSCRIPT	5074
MANY	1186, 6311, 10822,
11623	
MANY-HEADED	8862
MAP	8678
MARATHON	1958, 4242
MARBLE	625, 1718, 7358,
10463, 11189	
MARBLE-CONSTANT	10081
MARBLE-HEARTED	10229
MARCH	9978, 10873, 11401
MARCHED	7239
MARCHES	8009
MARCHING	853, 7923
MARILYN	6831
MARINER	2420, 7766
MARK	6423, 7125, 10666
MARKET	3501, 12187
MARKSMEN	9241
MARLBOROUGH	9824
MARQUIS	6807
MARRED	10055
MARRIAGE	29, 408, 585, 788, 881,

1269, 1538, 1954, 2363, 2756, 3351, 3412, 3435,
3604, 3807, 3889, 4610, 5156, 5293, 5471, 5541,
6289, 6990, 7339, 7694, 7724, 7802, 7986, 8054,
8213, 8494, 8525, 8749, 9611, 9664, 9766, 9970,
10346, 10424, 10474, 10558, 10676, 10797, 11088,
11112, 11113, 11915, 12085, 12221, 12514, 12524,
12658

MARRIAGES	2755, 5096, 5830,
5984, 6667	
MARRIED	301, 561, 658, 1555,

1840, 1946, 2532, 2633, 2763, 2853, 3728, 3801,
4133, 4153, 5419, 6316, 6724, 7109, 7193, 7309,
7742, 8459, 8569, 9032, 9580, 10046, 10055, 10551,
10552, 10647, 11043, 11114, 11691, 11789, 12157,
12487

MARRIED LIFE	12525
MARRIES	1487, 1788, 9472,
10603	
MARRY	496, 740, 1045, 1898,

2203, 2212, 2319, 2664, 2717, 2878, 4500, 4545,
5082, 5583, 5912, 6437, 6992, 7195, 7700, 8268,
8684, 8724, 9210, 9609, 11009, 11497, 11551, 11555,
12612

MARRYING	2559, 2637, 6077,
11606	
MARTINI	78, 3505, 12666
MARTYR	9490
MARTYRDOM	844, 5108, 9882, 10531
MARTYRED	2490
MARTYRS	1597, 2938, 11541
MARVEL	1735, 6437

MEETINGS	3739, 11491	MERRIMENT	5112, 5150
MEGALOMANIA	575	MERRY	426, 1208, 1215, 1244,
MELANCHOLY	486, 1835, 1954, 4253,	3030, 9971, 10319	
5443, 5905, 7436, 7451, 7623, 8077, 9467, 10430		MERRY-GO-ROUND	6719, 11627
MELLOW	7754, 8627	MESS	3207, 3483, 4376,
MELODIES	5436, 5454	7219, 7459	
MELODIOUS	5361, 7491	MESSAGE	377, 666, 6583, 6701
MELODY	1823, 8895	MESSAGES	4170, 6118
MELONS	7012	MESSENGER	410
MELTING-POT	12858	MESSING	4230
MEMBER	6645, 7035	MET	817, 6196, 11384,
MEMBERS	1134	12795	
MEMOIRS	7223, 8599, 9491	METAL	1880
MEMORABLE	7018	METAPHOR	3650
MEMORANDUM	11, 2114	METAPHYSIC	1889
MEMORIAL	8583, 9563	METAPHYSICS	1945
MEMORIES	871, 2126, 7773,	METE	1163
10635, 10663, 11123		METEOR	7523, 11510
MEMORY	240, 1295, 2182, 3219,	METHOD	2964, 10118, 10518
5052, 5118, 5180, 5695, 5841, 7797, 7859, 8162,		METHODISM	8626
8229, 8344, 8432, 8884, 8888, 9033, 9074, 9265,		METRE	6382, 7633, 9260
9361, 9433, 9521, 9910, 10636, 10643, 11104, 11962		MEXICO	2770
MEN	42, 93, 175, 253, 312,	MICE	1822, 11185
322, 653, 733, 768, 1348, 1350, 1510, 1582, 1822,		MICHELANGELO	11862
2265, 2456, 2584, 3100, 3162, 3208, 3307, 3387,		MICHIGAN	258
3494, 3693, 4209, 4274, 4342, 4594, 4693, 4980,		MICKEY MOUSE	8895
5068, 5706, 5778, 6031, 6177, 6381, 7168, 7195,		MICROBE	988
7338, 7752, 8021, 8129, 8146, 8554, 8733, 8834,		MICROSCOPE	988
9152, 9226, 9350, 9351, 9446, 9523, 9724, 9789,		MICROSCOPIC	8835
9927, 9938, 9942, 10011, 10172, 10206, 10408,		MID-AIR	10846
10578, 11009, 11391, 11697, 11748, 12062, 12067,		MIDDAY	2563
12132, 12314, 12317, 12336, 12481, 12662, 12767,		MIDDLE	40, 194, 1114, 3934,
12842		6090	
MENACE	8593	MIDDLE AGE	24, 961, 2544, 8022,
MEND	238, 1006, 7826	8023, 9334, 9622	
MENDACITY	12544	MIDDLE AGES	1454
MENDIP	6737	MIDDLE CLASS	516, 994, 8325
MENTAL	7216	MIDDLE EAST	4624, 9336
MENTALITY	6227	MIDDLE WAY	8371
MENTION	5110	MIDDLE-AGED	4901, 5118, 9954,
MENTIONED	8655, 11771	11677	
MENTIONING	9341	MIDDLE-CLASS	7892, 9305, 11793,
MERCENARY	4736	12209	
MERCHANDISE	764	MIDDLESEX	1103, 6749
MERCIFUL	1165	MIDGE	1101, 9561
MERCURY	130, 6352	MIDNIGHT	599, 3815, 5388, 5451,
MERCY	1359, 1360, 1413,	6594, 8741, 9250, 10163, 10425, 12216	
1431, 1729, 2012, 3169, 3434, 6606, 6640, 7061,		MIDST	1183
7620, 7876, 8109, 8150, 8878, 9717, 10316, 10411		MIDWIFE	8689
MERIDIAN	1606	MIGHT	6301, 7747, 10415,
MERIT	2069, 3319, 8422,	12212, 12420	
8877, 9403, 10338		MIGHT-HAVE-BEEN	9568
MERITOCRACY	12848	MIGHTIER	6754
MERMAID	5434		

MISTRESSES	917
MISTRUST	8419
MISTS	1101
MISUNDERSTANDING	9411
MISUNDERSTOOD	3343, 4960
MISUSED	10905
MIX	8283, 11287
MOAN	5403, 11616
MOANDAY	5261
MOAT	10360
MOB	12124
MOBILIZED	7983
MOBS	4972
MOCCASINS	9015
MOCK	6666, 10074
MOCKERIES	8381
MOCKERY	10417
MOCKINGBIRD	6116, 12407
MODEL	3115, 8582
MODERATE	5915
MODERATION	244, 621, 4161, 5030, 5158, 5812, 6270, 6748, 6809, 8243, 11311
MODERN	511, 1010, 2044, 2324, 4367, 7952, 8925, 12467
MODERNNESS	3271
MODEST	4106, 4745, 9340, 11844
MODESTY	550, 1692, 7798, 8508, 9403, 10700
MOLOCH	7519
MOLTEN	1463
MOMENT	2538, 4062, 6190, 7311, 12114
MOMENTS	5391, 9574
MONARCH	794, 2576, 3589, 12107
MONARCHICAL	1459
MONARCHY	163, 784, 789, 796, 7810, 8331, 9697, 12569
MONASTERY	8662
MONEY	38, 75, 153, 181, 223, 243, 542, 647, 750, 818, 851, 980, 997, 1060, 1193, 1215, 1487, 1536, 1882, 2323, 2379, 2765, 2895, 3052, 3094, 3388, 3482, 3573, 3590, 3598, 3637, 3670, 3860, 4167, 4237, 4257, 4507, 4588, 4703, 4718, 4788, 4933, 4937, 4998, 5098, 5164, 5983, 6067, 6165, 6467, 6688, 6696, 6760, 7112, 7270, 7355, 8256, 8571, 8706, 9100, 9123, 9179, 9186, 9211, 9277, 9354, 9474, 9488, 9585, 9632, 9711, 9768, 9890, 10397, 10659, 10823, 10973, 10997, 11124, 11128, 11196, 11497, 11549, 11564, 11858, 11913, 11990, 12061, 12645, 12648, 12659
MONGRELS	3461
MONK	1490, 7818

MONKEY	1116, 3375, 3912, 4229, 11165, 12435
MONOGAMY	5177
MONOPOLY	2608, 4564, 6156
MONOTONOUS	6538
MONOTONY	3761, 9399, 11019
MONSTER	4205, 7779, 8183, 8862, 10345, 10416
MONSTROSITY	4454
MONSTROUS	3443
MONTEZUMA	6750
MONUMENT	2142, 3224, 4963, 6364, 6537, 9304
MOO	8032
MOOD	6891
MOON	185, 1449, 1548, 1920, 4097, 4991, 7581, 7651, 7745, 8223, 10078, 10390, 11436, 11524, 11677, 11843, 12545, 12671, 12708, 12812
MOON-STRUCK	7623
MOONLECHT	5999
MOONLIGHT	1080, 9935, 10318, 10330
MOONSHINE	9712
MOORED	3825
MOORISH	5286
MORAL	2105, 4066, 5334, 7992, 8996, 10549, 11661, 12502
MORALIST	677, 9691
MORALITY	35, 675, 1392, 5503, 6034, 6755, 7196, 8178, 8777, 9699, 10505, 10902, 11659, 12391
MORALS	1111, 1534, 2452, 3987, 7200, 9767, 10569, 11089
MORE	185, 321, 1624, 1644, 1728, 1856, 5674, 5874, 8155, 8843, 10113, 10263, 11071, 11669
MORIARTY	2960
MORN	7532
MORNING	327, 1653, 1661, 3406, 3484, 6000, 6344, 9198, 9422, 9472, 9949, 10588, 11609
MORON	308, 8252
MORTAL	2943, 4127, 4621, 6562, 6995, 7017, 7411, 7477, 8217, 8779, 11281, 11794, 12842
MORTALITY	4396, 4714, 4758, 5453
MORTALS	67, 6335, 6894, 10334
MORTIFIED	11096
MORTIFY	8862
MOSCOW	9237
MOSES	4792
MOSQUITO	8270
MOTH	3799

MUTE 6711, 9204
MY-LORDED 11556
MYRIADS 7505
MYRTLE 4090
MYSELF 669, 865, 2522, 3864, 7590, 7779, 10700, 11530, 11738
MYSTERIES 11868
MYSTERIOUS 9912
MYSTERY 523, 795, 820, 1508, 2171, 6437, 6448, 12461, 12682, 12698
MYSTIC 4770
MYTH 8702, 8882, 9576, 9767, 9805
MYTHICAL 4516
MYTHOLOGY 2892
NAIAD 8740
NAIL 6033, 8654, 9111
NAILED 4825
NAILING 11612
NAILS 6758, 10704
NAKED 1120, 1951, 2630, 6452, 7919, 10180, 10185, 12791
NAKEDNESS 1340, 2906, 8661, 12713
NAME 1183, 1438, 2784, 4366, 6550, 6702, 7598, 7861, 7866, 8368, 8591, 9411, 10336, 10344, 10366, 10388, 10883, 10945, 11180, 11205, 11285, 11760, 12054
NAMES 9547, 9835
NAPALM 3089
NAPOLEON 2960, 4839, 9978
NARCOTIC 5297
NARRATES 3568
NARRATIVE 1512, 4964, 8932
NARROW 7287, 10981
NARROW-SOULED 8868
NASAL 6146
NASTIEST 4099
NASTY 3888, 5018, 7736
NATION 320, 1696, 1751, 2289, 2875, 3789, 4584, 4828, 5502, 5520, 5661, 5697, 6309, 6811, 6865, 7050, 7396, 7642, 7955, 8010, 8460, 8754, 8969, 9357, 9363, 9526, 9542, 9708, 10677, 10816, 10943, 11810, 11912, 12009, 12046, 12587, 12588
NATIONAL 352, 6712
NATIONALISM 120, 3129
NATIONALITY 5266, 9377
NATIONS 62, 1227, 2288, 2883, 3100, 4095, 4594, 4909, 5506, 5625, 7429, 11718
NATIVE 5091, 6205, 7143, 8870, 8972, 10109
NATIVE LAND 9940
NATIVES 9975, 11238, 12350

NATIVITY 6929, 10326
NATO 4454
NATURAL 722, 4138, 6225, 6472, 8352, 8957, 9923
NATURALLY 7682
NATURE 55, 130, 347, 479, 493, 505, 506, 627, 638, 754, 774, 783, 800, 912, 939, 1282, 1375, 1603, 1806, 2095, 2445, 2669, 2706, 3309, 3360, 3761, 3830, 3887, 3938, 3985, 4043, 4339, 4508, 4634, 4652, 4735, 4865, 4898, 4917, 5221, 5771, 5862, 5935, 5954, 6137, 6180, 6366, 6496, 6518, 6665, 6835, 6949, 7240, 7408, 7432, 7615, 7905, 8118, 8119, 8138, 8350, 8468, 8547, 8814, 8817, 8838, 8850, 9007, 9025, 9076, 9140, 9145, 9149, 9150, 9318, 9803, 10048, 10141, 10214, 10234, 10259, 10418, 10790, 10906, 11375, 11465, 11827, 12062, 12327, 12343, 12344, 12347, 12537, 12699, 12702, 12838
NATURES 3317
NAUGHT 1621, 6464
NAUGHTY 11101
NAUSEATED 12653
NAVEL 9105
NAVIES 5679
NAVIGATE 9256
NAVIGATORS 3862
NAVY 1312, 2122, 3927, 3929, 6769, 10751
NAY 1139
NBC 12136
NEAERA 7475
NEAR 1645, 9029, 11477, 11492
NEARER 11409
NEARLY 6469
NEAT 3417, 4538, 11101
NECESSARY 300, 1409, 2297, 3335, 5599, 6556, 9261, 11715, 12079
NECESSITIES 17, 7102, 7954, 9772, 10237, 12759
NECESSITY 2615, 2708, 2710, 3160, 3602, 4666, 7601, 8677, 9207, 9587, 9895, 10359, 10906, 11641
NECK 2311, 2477, 7879, 8271, 12133
NECKLACE 6875
NEED 363, 2093, 4703, 4778, 5742, 6171, 8150, 9619, 9643, 9932, 10234, 11215, 11570
NEEDED 7726, 9242, 9907
NEEDLE 3722
NEEDS 1494, 6659, 7042, 7836, 12094
NEEDY 5965
NEGATION 4007

NEGATIVE 6618, 7219, 8649, 9672
NEGLECT 4284, 5196, 5502, 11628
NEGOTIATE 5522
NEGOTIATING 6352
NEGOTIATION 8
NEGRO 2677, 5591
NEIGH 187
NEIGHBOUR 2225, 4817, 9525
NEIGHBOURHOOD 5014, 9173
NEIGHBOURS 3236, 3637, 3671, 11571, 11656
NEITHER 1276
NELL 8574
NEPTUNE 7766
NERO 7202
NERVE 9606
NERVES 6467
NERVOUS 5356, 6103
NEST 4626, 5376, 11372
NET 2136, 6728
NETS 7635, 10632, 12231
NETTLE 10150
NETTLES 12118
NETWORK 5147
NEUROSES 16
NEUROSIS 9352, 11713, 11904
NEUROTIC 196, 1517, 3908, 7212, 10687
NEUROTICS 8994
NEUTER 11368
NEUTRAL 12589
NEUTRALITY 2644, 4627, 12591
NEVER 132, 468, 1655, 1802, 1908, 2022, 2298, 3923, 3924, 6249, 6520, 6708, 6814, 8274, 9397, 9477, 11156, 12142, 12174, 12207
NEVERMORE 8742
NEW 426, 1213, 3061, 4895, 5437, 5870, 6410, 8472, 8714, 11431, 11493, 12071, 12820
NEW ENGLAND 1023
NEW MAN 8497
NEW WORLD 3681
NEW YORK 1266, 2462, 2766, 5557, 7336, 7893, 7894, 8971, 9304, 9546
NEW YORKER 7357, 8972
NEW ZEALAND 6761
NEW-LAID 3913
NEWCASTLE 3848
NEWEST 10166
NEWS 1502, 3980, 4701, 4903, 6166, 6918, 7662, 8241, 8614, 8914, 11153, 11402, 11605, 12210

NEWSCASTERS 4546
NEWSPAPER 3401, 6963, 7327, 8536, 11153, 12854
NEWSPAPERS 5898, 8360, 8634, 11144, 12269
NEWTON 4870, 8814
NEXT 292, 8387
NIBBLES 6007
NICE 2141, 3084, 3854, 6000, 6626, 7709, 9246, 12572
NICEAN 8740
NICER 176, 2179, 12572
NICEST 4099, 6018, 7897
NICKNAME 4450, 8412
NIGGER 8282
NIGGERS 6512
NIGHT 606, 1320, 1474, 1542, 2788, 3484, 4583, 5218, 5260, 6419, 6427, 6451, 6596, 7319, 7406, 7651, 7679, 7859, 8106, 8279, 8893, 9275, 9734, 9982, 10214, 10271, 10322, 11270, 11578, 11601, 11639, 12768
NIGHTBLUE 5285
NIGHTINGALE 524, 5361, 5399, 6594, 7579
NIGHTMARE 5277
NIGHTS 6515
NILE 10066
NINETY 1096, 4661
NINETY-NINE 3138, 9377
NINEVEH 5679, 7058
NIP 9438
NO 118, 2046, 4211, 4552, 5256, 8159, 8552, 10957, 11568
NOAH 4870
NOBILITY 742, 743, 1924, 6230, 6898, 9790
NOBLE 1924, 2453, 5088, 5607, 9096, 10120, 10159, 11433
NOBLEMEN 3982
NOBLENESS 1563
NOBLER 10124
NOBLES 6754, 8963
NOBLESSE 6230, 11769
NOBLEST 1074, 4912
NOBLY 1647
NOBODY 377, 1491, 2628, 3591, 4482, 6743, 11000, 11860
NOISE 930, 2495, 2567, 2602, 5724, 6857, 7440, 7674, 8868, 9239, 11837
NOISELESS 4252, 5462
NOISY 12690
NOMADIC 12366
NON-BEING 11713

NON-COMBATANT	7763
NON-CONFORMISTS	7151
NON-CREATIVE	6697
NON-FICTION	673, 4795
NON-NEGOTIABLE	1316
NON-OBVIOUS	10917
NON-U	9548
NON-VIOLENCE	780, 2198, 3765, 5588
NONCONFORMITY	8322
NONE	40, 2111, 3821, 7228, 9060, 9900, 12830
NONSENSE	216, 583, 960, 1051, 1875, 4846, 7105, 9307, 9397, 11047
NOOKIE	4184
NOON	3500, 4757, 5016, 7650
NORFOLK	2564
NORMAL	8333
NORMAN	312, 674, 11433
NORTH	610, 6029, 6653
NORTH-WEST	11042
NORTHERN	1547, 5949
NORWAY	5088
NORWEGIAN	7517
NOSE	1668, 2428, 3714, 5653, 5802, 8476, 9577, 9886, 12288
NOSES	4428
NOSTALGIA	239, 834
NOT	740, 1001, 2402, 2866, 9148, 11993, 12618
NOTE	3886, 5485, 6142
NOTEBOOKS	12649
NOTES	9879, 9924
NOTHIN'	1283, 5647, 5754
NOTHING	141, 203, 375, 435, 494, 638, 653, 673, 1192, 1448, 1932, 2030, 2195, 2212, 2305, 2458, 2924, 3078, 3446, 3557, 3836, 3941, 4167, 4210, 4230, 4270, 4332, 4347, 4429, 4687, 4764, 5054, 5109, 5335, 5581, 5881, 5988, 6141, 6344, 6464, 6560, 7667, 7704, 7756, 7799, 8090, 8271, 8467, 8953, 9077, 9187, 9190, 9217, 9412, 9443, 9468, 9758, 10078, 10224, 10287, 10340, 10397, 10546, 10547, 10561, 10575, 10821, 10982, 11040, 11122, 11209, 11365, 11534, 11616, 11651, 11756, 11941, 12469, 12540, 12552, 12567, 12583, 12669
NOTHINGNESS	801, 5364
NOTHINGS	10590
NOTICES	3376
NOTICING	6621
NOTION	3682, 3958, 7757
NOUGHT	9570, 10608
NOUNS	7842
NOVEL	2034, 4386, 4964, 5419, 6023, 6033, 6037, 6689, 10991, 11015

NOVELIST	6034, 6105
NOVELS	2133, 2162, 6732, 7117
NOVELTY	7622
NOVEMBER	2535
NOWADAYS	6860
NOWHERE	5581, 5582, 12370
NOXIOUS	5578
NUBBLY	5656
NUCLEAR	1507, 7957
NUDE	5581
NUGGET	12649
NUISANCE	3262, 4742, 7299
NULL	8237
NUMBER	2330, 11856
NUMBERLESS	7435
NUMBERS	4810, 8794
NUMBING	6702
NUN	7437, 8291, 12739
NUNNERY	10127
NUPTIALS	5478
NURSE	992, 8191, 10083
NURSED	7471
NURSERIES	3440
NURSERY	1764
NURSES	739
NURSING	527
NURSLING	10594
NUTRITION	8841
NUTS	9080, 11572
NYMPH	7452, 7474
O'CLOCK	7352
OAK	2078, 5677, 6495
OAKS	1599, 3393, 5392, 6235
OAR	3833, 9049
OASES	8004
OATH	6302, 8732, 9100, 10570
OATHS	1894, 6604
OATS	5057
OBADIAH	6738
OBEDIENCE	1509, 3597, 6765, 7748
OBEDIENT	10685
OBEY	1037, 1109, 3018, 3112, 5639, 7269, 9528
OBEYED	4320, 7149, 8466
OBEYING	774
OBITUARY	971
OBJECT	532, 3959, 5321, 6287, 7236, 9801
OBJECTIVES	12386, 12639
OBJECTS	6664, 12730
OBLIGATION	5861

OBLIGATIONS 6230, 10738

OBLIVION 7244, 10416, 10598, 11842

OBLONG 6081

OBNOXIOUS 4776

OBOE 245

OBSCENITY 346, 9700, 12822

OBSCURE 7544

OBSCURITY 3881, 5311, 6651, 8029, 9266

OBSERVANCE 10109

OBSERVATION 2099, 3420, 8501, 9808

OBSERVE 1093, 2957, 8350

OBSERVED 10516

OBSERVER 605, 7224

OBSOLESCENCE 6326, 11049

OBSTACLES 2543, 11648

OBSTINACY 1604, 9898, 11036

OBSTRUCT 5311

OBSTRUCTION 10295

OBVIOUS 5728, 5737

OCCASION 6271, 12501

OCCASIONALLY 3925

OCCUPATION 2581, 8264, 10514

OCCUPATIONS 2779, 6318, 6419, 11032

OCCURRED 1057

OCCURRENCE 11329

OCCURRING 6079

OCEAN 1081, 1917, 5951, 6451, 6930, 7819, 7923, 8114, 10085, 10466, 12111, 12700

OCTAVE 11169

OCTOBER 3507

OCTOPUS 10740

ODD 256, 1594, 3395, 5719

ODES 11504

ODOROUS 10050

ODOURS 7485

OFF 8089

OFFENCE 1255, 4942, 7659, 7735, 8872

OFFENCES 1421

OFFEND 6797, 10456, 11187

OFFENDED 7880, 10337

OFFENDERS 3949, 10014

OFFENSIVE 1575, 5112, 8157, 9694, 12389, 12397

OFFER 3778, 4878, 8390, 9243

OFFERED 10693

OFFICE 14, 255, 1515, 3071, 4863, 5505, 5917, 8437, 9755, 12577

OFFICER 349, 7149

OFFICES 7430

OFFICIAL 4203, 4513, 10819

OFFICIALISM 3549

OFFICIOUS 5126

OFFSPRING 2756, 7583

OFTEN 1296, 7353

OGLE 6228

OIL 202, 405, 3581, 3963, 4135, 4624, 5213, 11165

OILED 6191

OILY 11630

OK 2402

OLD 24, 53, 91, 281, 689, 709, 885, 1099, 1298, 1401, 1735, 1827, 1982, 2103, 2135, 2276, 2442, 2863, 3082, 3186, 3268, 3844, 4133, 4160, 4555, 4662, 4665, 4895, 5118, 5623, 5688, 5809, 5986, 6088, 6154, 7029, 7105, 7126, 7291, 7990, 8332, 8938, 9010, 9058, 9552, 9622, 10537, 10829, 10890, 10984, 11119, 11174, 11219, 11263, 11750, 11883, 11996, 12167, 12443, 12457, 12815, 12849

OLD AGE 8049, 8761, 8806, 9398, 11166, 11796, 12813

OLD MAN 9784, 10049, 10281

OLD-FASHIONED 3468, 8339, 9800, 11049, 12467

OLDEN 8887

OLDER 81, 2555, 7780, 7935, 8354, 8504, 8619, 9858, 10944, 11958, 12761

OLIGARCHY 2224

OMEGA 1141

OMELETTE 984, 9069

OMENS 11213

OMINOUS 8930

OMIT 11093

OMNIBUS 4637

OMNIPOTENCE 2760

OMNIPOTENT 7503

OMNIPRESENT 8118

OMNISCIENCE 10813

ON GUARD 10504

ONCE 128, 6248, 6267, 8397, 11832, 12365

ONE 398, 1203, 1503, 3051, 7216, 7619, 9060, 9314, 9714, 10726, 11494

ONE UP 8907

ONE-AND-TWENTY 4740

ONE-EYED 3367, 4424

ONENESS 12827

ONESELF 3206, 7728, 7979, 8168

ONION 863, 10063, 10810

ONLY 9524, 9782

ONSET 8596

OUTCAST	10460
OUTLAST	4953
OUTLINE	2434, 11147, 11664
OUTLIVE	10463
OUTLIVED	2132
OUTPOSTS	5493
OUTRAGEOUS	11010
OUTRAGEOUSLY	10756
OUTSIDE	178, 3322, 6824, 8230
OUTSTRIPPED	5185
OUTWARD	7507
OUTWEIGHS	567
OUTWEPT	10586
OUTWORN	10617
OVAL	579
OVER	1095, 7313, 12315
OVER-CANOPIED	10331
OVER-PREPARED	8930
OVERARCHED	7518
OVERCARE	3595
OVERCOAT	6519, 9417
OVERCOME	430, 5295, 7508
OVERCOMES	3617, 7528
OVERDEVELOPED	3748
OVERDONE	1308
OVERFED	11775
OVERFLOWED	10808
OVERHEATS	4333
OVERLOADED	5610
OVERLOOK	4956, 4959, 5005
OVERMATCH	5068
OVERPAID	4513, 11775
OVERSEXED	11775
OVERTAXED	1067
OVERTHROW	3785, 10996
OVERTHROWN	12707
OVERTIME	370, 2120
OVERWHELM	10106
OVID	7760
OWE	7450, 10164
OWED	2309, 2638, 6688
OWES	2579, 8994
OWL	6096, 7364, 7376, 9220
OWN	139, 3452, 5872, 6272, 7904, 7987, 10306, 11354, 11749, 11828
OWNERSHIP	3540
OX	1325
OXEN	5140, 12793
OXFORD	779, 959, 3500, 3606, 3875, 4228, 4296, 4452, 5252, 6216, 9212, 10947, 10980, 11761
OXTAIL	5284

OXYGEN	415
OYSTER	1022, 2775, 4677, 7330, 10324, 10640, 11222
OYSTERS	9740
OZYMANDIAS	10614
PACE	11679
PACIFIC	5386
PACIFIST	12095
PACIFY	8401
PACK	534, 1569, 6237, 11797
PACK-HORSE	7925
PACT	1745
PADDINGTON	1330, 2050
PADDLE	5657, 6976
PADLOCK	8772, 8962
PAGAN	12857
PAGE	1695, 4663, 4924
PAID	1563, 1674, 5690, 8517, 8955, 12331
PAIL	12780
PAIN	329, 333, 524, 525, 1142, 1622, 1916, 3016, 3407, 3619, 4534, 5127, 5293, 5372, 6768, 7251, 7538, 8105, 8388, 8779, 9006, 9972, 10144, 10375, 10626, 10902, 11266, 11275, 11518, 11616, 11711, 12598
PAINFUL	722, 10930
PAINS	4540, 4868, 7147, 10676, 10926, 11077, 11187
PAINT	60, 341, 1374, 2612, 2641, 4710, 7947, 8639, 9366, 9661, 11950, 11951
PAINTED	957
PAINTER	6177, 6182, 7088, 8644, 9365, 9649, 10622, 11949, 12344
PAINTERS	2324
PAINTING	1270, 2539, 3396, 6844, 7688, 8475, 8641, 8642, 8643, 8985, 9589, 9825, 10686
PAIR	7584
PALACE	2899, 5409, 5410, 7402
PALACES	4884
PALATABLE	3538
PALATES	10350
PALE	3991, 10271, 11281
PALEONTOLOGY	10994
PALESTINE	7058
PALETTE	2159
PALL	8382
PALL MALL	7915, 11553
PALLADIUM	5302
PALLIATE	8667
PALM	5230, 11057
PALTERED	11500
PAMPER	3851

PAMPERED	6955	PARLIAMENTARY	4017, 4192
PANAMA	4420	PARLOUR	4760
PANDEMONIUM	7534	PAROCHIAL	4945, 5913, 7837
PANDORA	1127	PAROLE	5113
PANIC	1821	PARROT	2532
PANSIES	10140	PARSLEY	8027
PANTHER	8722	PARSON	2247, 2598, 2967,
PANTS	1281, 7030, 7316,	4119, 4598, 6359, 9971	
8042, 12088, 12186		PART	3798, 4162, 4556,
PANZER-MAN	8686	4969, 5566, 6711, 7928, 10089, 11384	
PAPACY	4592	PARTED	1477, 1541, 7618
PAPER	2716, 4627, 6592,	PARTHENIA	3811
6706, 6724, 6908, 7948, 8589, 10250, 10988		PARTIALITY	11315, 11866
PAPER WORK	8295	PARTICIPANTS	9452
PAPERS	72, 9492	PARTICULAR	3657
PAPIST	2378	PARTICULARS	220
PAR	11864	PARTIES	1754, 1980
PARABLE	7760	PARTING	217, 332, 3183, 9901,
PARACHUTE	2211	10392, 11491	
PARADISE	1351, 1844, 2749,	PARTNER	1079, 3797
3513, 5381, 5454, 5564, 5745, 5920, 6600, 7017,		PARTS	8837, 10030
7563, 7629, 7631, 7693, 9000, 9817, 11621		PARTY	299, 2463, 2837, 2846,
PARADOX	2303, 5728, 12455	3735, 5701, 6608, 6776, 8889, 9485, 9496, 12181,	
PARADOXICAL	3636	12567	
PARAGON	10120	PARTY-SPIRIT	8764
PARAGRAPHS	12291	PASS	1188, 1902, 3382,
PARALLEL	7007	4284, 5228, 6428, 7051, 7143, 12442	
PARALLELOGRAM	6081	PASSAGE	5069, 10662
PARALYZED	9683	PASSAGES	5433
PARAPETS	9420	PASSED	1142, 5295, 5412,
PARAPHRASE	8925	8524, 12795	
PARASITES	5217	PASSES	8448, 8744
PARCELS	12240	PASSING	6801
PARCHING	7547	PASSING-BELLS	8381
PARDON	1699, 3240, 4188,	PASSION	512, 525, 721, 1065,
4467, 10014		1774, 1953, 2166, 2376, 2951, 3029, 3032, 3545,	
PARELLELISM	34	3563, 4266, 4672, 5438, 5478, 6122, 6131, 6189,	
PARENT	2325, 8387, 12090,	6276, 6371, 6914, 7669, 7765, 8096, 8451, 8935,	
12486		9233, 9447, 9844, 10201, 11031, 11441, 11550,	
PARENTHESIS	11800	12297, 12856	
PARENTHOOD	11725	PASSIONATE	585, 11276, 12807
PARENTS	248, 1329, 2739, 3112,	PASSIONLESS	1618
3397, 4396, 5292, 5856, 8033, 8603, 9154, 10506,		PASSIONS	2219, 3104, 5008,
10914, 11824, 12631, 12635		5295, 5822, 5828, 6213, 7241, 8352, 9301, 9688,	
PARING	5269	10987, 11039, 11385	
PARIOLI	7968	PASSIVE	8464
PARIS	459, 1121, 4296, 4357,	PASSPORT	9290
4483, 4494, 4582, 8181, 9072, 11822, 11879		PAST	596, 954, 1425, 1687,
PARISH	5467, 12300	1757, 2661, 4405, 5161, 5547, 6288, 6330, 6843,	
PARKING LOT	7693	8338, 8657, 9279, 9305, 9546, 9781, 9813, 10383,	
PARKS	8675	10783, 11176, 11350, 11453, 11602, 12228, 12657,	
PARLIAMENT	2079, 8548, 9861,	12819	
10545, 11445		PASTEUR	8389
		PASTIME	6654

PASTNESS 3193
PASTORS 10107
PATE 8789
PATERNAL 8870
PATERNITY 9836
PATH 2514, 5752, 6324, 7794
PATHETIC 7379
PATHLESS 7441
PATHS 3509, 10953, 12441
PATIENCE 112, 1138, 1375, 1701, 2174, 2214, 3577, 4581, 4928, 5796, 6397, 7931, 8514, 9035, 9047, 9457, 9814, 10430, 11918, 12565
PATIENT 2999, 5857, 8345, 9994, 10155
PATIENTLY 3723, 11179
PATIENTS 7714
PATRICIAN 3933
PATRIOT 2998, 3893, 4149, 8408
PATRIOTIC 11861
PATRIOTISM 120, 2648, 3788, 4852, 5093, 6064, 10566, 11070
PATROL 7254
PATRON 5037
PATTER 3990
PATTERN 9327, 12392
PATTERNS 1584, 6491
PAUPER 8207
PAUSE 11869
PAUSES 9879
PAVED 2446
PAVEMENT 7529
PAY 1297, 1831, 3831, 4736, 5659, 5693, 5697, 6199, 9046, 9654, 11197
PAYING 5168, 9478, 9600, 12460
PAYROLL 10019
PEA-GREEN 6096
PEACE 66, 488, 611, 1097, 1271, 1360, 1405, 1418, 1531, 1532, 1544, 2357, 2373, 2444, 2881, 3048, 3049, 3152, 3313, 3424, 3431, 3516, 3601, 3845, 4082, 4383, 4527, 4535, 4948, 5002, 5004, 5272, 5397, 5519, 5591, 5769, 6109, 6164, 6197, 6200, 6338, 6538, 6574, 7438, 7540, 7627, 7740, 7995, 8109, 8136, 8580, 8581, 9363, 9363, 9615, 9705, 9805, 10169, 10184, 10937, 10953, 11313, 11405, 11482, 11942, 11966, 11985, 12125, 12582, 12590
PEACE OF MIND 8992
PEACE-MAKER 10040
PEACEABLE 9684
PEACEFUL 4941, 5510, 12585
PEACEFULLY 2683
PEACH 5204

PEACOCK 4210, 5408, 9684, 12445
PEACOCKS 9657
PEAL 4598
PEANUT 1022
PEAR 12651
PEARL 6937, 10329, 10352
PEARLS 3002, 10400, 10718, 12339
PEASANT 9178, 10674
PEASANTRY 11797
PEASANTS 11769
PEBBLE 8114
PECULIAR 4418, 10842
PEDANT 9785
PEDESTRIANS 2761
PEDIGREE 2791
PEEL 8244
PEEP 12722
PEEPERS 7221
PEEPING 4691
PEEPSHOW 6719
PEERAGE 8068, 8221, 12513
PEERING 7493
PEERLESS 6382, 7579
PEERS 3983, 6263, 6803, 6819
PEGASUS 5457
PELICAN 7256
PEN 1714, 1839, 4315, 5138, 6234, 6246, 6486, 11675, 11961
PENAL 7503
PENALISED 8938
PENALTY 4767
PENCE 1909, 6540, 11527
PENCILS 9462
PENETRATE 9418, 11943
PENETRATING 3436
PENNIES 9036
PENNSYLVANIA 4188
PENNY 2590, 6801, 12787
PENSION 6720
PEOPLE 261, 398, 418, 497, 1429, 1505, 1578, 1679, 1740, 1753, 1793, 2248, 2471, 2567, 2661, 2883, 3058, 3167, 3188, 3224, 3311, 3902, 3998, 4044, 4359, 4536, 4676, 4749, 4832, 5111, 5809, 5872, 5924, 5986, 6061, 6107, 6162, 6284, 6309, 6310, 6312, 6795, 7082, 7690, 7947, 7969, 8055, 8395, 8860, 8922, 9183, 9357, 9840, 9922, 10088, 10542, 10677, 10684, 11062, 12225, 12260, 12303, 12507, 12825
PEOPLED 1625, 7622, 9962
PERADVENTURE 4579
PERCEIVE 12701

676

PLATITUDES 12520

PLATO 3972, 6014, 7431, 7639, 11177, 12394

PLAY 498, 506, 985, 1092, 2489, 3128, 3185, 4324, 4702, 5776, 5914, 6214, 7398, 7796, 8045, 8087, 8088, 8694, 9249, 9613, 9899, 10123, 10422, 11056, 11211, 12517

PLAYBOY 11296

PLAYED 9384, 10434

PLAYER 11016

PLAYERS 10030

PLAYING 246, 5877, 7789, 7944

PLAYMATES 5909

PLAYS 3799

PLAYTHING 5051, 5910

PLAZA 3916

PLEASANT 2341, 4136, 6094, 7822, 8429, 9654, 11200, 11359, 12071

PLEASE 1354, 6975, 9957, 11289

PLEASED 64, 3705, 4448, 7597, 8090, 10028

PLEASES 8707, 10894

PLEASING 5794, 10930

PLEASURABLE 2339

PLEASURE 457, 645, 648, 695, 763, 785, 935, 976, 978, 997, 1260, 1855, 1949, 2003, 2479, 2596, 2611, 2703, 2969, 2986, 3016, 3512, 3826, 4496, 4667, 4723, 4842, 4992, 5073, 5317, 5383, 5444, 5781, 5837, 5911, 6147, 6316, 6768, 7013, 7201, 7305, 7439, 7719, 7860, 7877, 8848, 9065, 9169, 9248, 9306, 9375, 9676, 9823, 9972, 10670, 10865, 11554, 11711, 12047, 12213, 12505, 12769, 12821

PLEASURE-DOME 2417, 2418

PLEASURES 583, 642, 732, 1873, 2332, 2374, 2593, 2905, 4868, 5040, 5083, 7005, 7454, 7816, 9787, 10373, 11193, 11652

PLEDGE 5192, 9522

PLEDGED 819

PLENTY 1808, 5281, 8372

PLIANT 3814

PLOT 9249, 12012

PLOTS 2468, 2989

PLOTTING 3027, 9390

PLOUGH 2015, 9544, 10628, 11675

PLOUGHMAN 4248, 7457

PLOUGHSHARE 9646

PLOY 8908

PLUCK 9081

PLUCKING 2407

PLUMBER 155, 7155, 8941

PLUMS 3538

PLUNDER 6773, 8085

PLUNDERED 6650

PLURAL 6726

PLUTO 7444

PLUTOCRACY 12848

PM 571

PNEUMATIC 3234

POBBLE 6099

POCKET 5012, 9028, 12316, 12568

POCKETS 9417, 10735, 10997

POE 6521

POEM 1062, 3659, 5419, 5575, 6685, 7383, 7688, 8498, 11295, 11944, 12170, 12408

POEMS 262, 4236, 5576, 6418, 6785

POESY 700, 5446, 5456

POET 2087, 2169, 3010, 3196, 3197, 3198, 3503, 4005, 4965, 5278, 5382, 5458, 6182, 6781, 7142, 7902, 8380, 8790, 9238, 10335, 10336, 10618, 11051, 11058, 11254, 11338, 11442, 11664, 12104, 12262, 12686, 12787

POETIC 7985, 8765

POETRY 489, 520, 586, 603, 1299, 1374, 1892, 1974, 2397, 2429, 2496, 2927, 3028, 3199, 3658, 3661, 4086, 4237, 4401, 4755, 5346, 5413, 5428, 5431, 5432, 5514, 5939, 6106, 6654, 6752, 6756, 6962, 7292, 7431, 7690, 7842, 8379, 8683, 8796, 8924, 9599, 9771, 9780, 10597, 10686, 11055, 12597, 12704, 12784

POETS 484, 757, 1837, 2596, 3225, 3227, 3838, 4004, 4717, 4815, 7232, 7844, 8025, 8766, 8817, 9804, 10599, 12106, 12402, 12687, 12731, 12814

POINT 2296, 5672

POINT OF VIEW 8016

POINTLESS 8339

POINTS 1368, 10652

POISE 6501

POISED 6713

POISON 3511, 4240, 5444, 5990, 6565, 6941, 8098, 8429, 10313

POISONED 11246

POISONING 6853

POISONOUS 5441

POISONS 8449, 12193

POKER 8242, 12091

POLE 2861, 7600

POLECAT 3520

POLICE 609, 1108, 2813, 8128, 8237, 8295, 10565

POLICEMAN 3652, 3981, 8191, 8487, 9754

POLICEMEN	8294	POPULATION	884, 4153, 4629, 6159,
POLICY	1126, 1303, 4896,	6870, 9310	
9525, 9757, 10496, 12180, 12337		POPULISM	1471
POLISHED	2704, 3927	POPULOUS	7612, 10615
POLITE	1675	PORCELAIN	7234
POLITELY	3576	PORCUPINE	4303, 5565
POLITENESS	1988, 5722, 6474,	PORNOGRAPHY	6035, 7847, 9283,
9892, 10645, 10790		10854	
POLITICAL	491, 797, 3070, 4325,	PORPOISE	2106
4678, 4976, 4999, 6374, 6712, 6813, 6872, 6907,		PORT	1061, 5106, 10925,
7203, 7298, 8195, 8327, 8328, 8418, 8430, 8523,		12277	
8881, 9977, 10546, 11569		PORTALS	5282
POLITICIAN	1296, 1390, 2013,	PORTION	3292, 10828, 11453,
2360, 2627, 2723, 2728, 3819, 3893, 5558, 6351,		12697	
6969, 8174, 8262, 8754, 8875, 9535, 10098, 10244,		PORTIONED	6776
11815, 12150		PORTRAIT	2641, 5723, 9825, 9826
POLITICIANS	1301, 3860, 5559,	POSIES	6944
6911, 8056, 11180, 12191, 12556		POSITION	4323, 11596, 11874
POLITICS	28, 36, 40, 539, 656,	POSITIVE	1274, 6370, 7219, 8649
799, 1111, 1302, 1368, 2037, 2293, 2368, 2431, 2623,		POSSE	46
2733, 2826, 2864, 3316, 4260, 4569, 4571, 4755,		POSSESS	1422, 5815
5303, 5918, 6629, 6706, 6707, 6906, 7907, 7950,		POSSESSED	1759, 2412, 9312
8139, 8299, 8459, 8632, 9332, 9439, 9487, 9488,		POSSESSES	1991
9496, 9499, 9961, 10642, 11072, 11103, 11665,		POSSESSING	8785
11717, 11805, 11806, 11913, 11947, 12564, 12804		POSSESSION	124, 4273, 5212, 6368,
POLLUTION	3692, 5771, 10895	7236, 9680, 11159, 11954	
POLLY	3800	POSSESSIONS	10720
POLO	8246	POSSIBILITIES	6105
POLYGAMY	2988, 4766	POSSIBILITY	4881
POMP	5679, 7360, 8787	POSSIBLE	34, 1189, 1302, 3917,
POMPOUS	1600	7704, 9795, 12070, 12269	
POND	1564	POST	1069, 7662
PONDER	1443	POSTAL	5994
PONDERED	8741	POSTER	553
PONDERING	8075	POSTERITY	76, 1765, 2171, 2358,
PONDEROUS	8136	2845, 4239, 6364, 8344, 8944, 11574, 12601	
PONIES	4598, 5676	POSTHUMOUSLY	8182
PONY	336	POSTMAN	2000
POOH	7365	POSTPONED	4784
POOR	145, 649, 694, 3091,	POSTPONEMENT	7342
3239, 3544, 3570, 3823, 4122, 4256, 4292, 4615,		POSTSCRIPT	718, 10983
4867, 4902, 5063, 5134, 5323, 5373, 5521, 5854,		POT	254, 5275
5899, 5928, 5959, 6776, 7278, 8372, 8921, 9107,		POTATO	8357
9124, 9179, 9837, 9841, 10155, 10344, 11101, 11551		POTATO-GATHERER	5349
POORER	8061	POTENCY	3634, 7387
POOREST	8668, 9284	POTENT	2565
POP	1470, 6874	POTENTIAL	2058
POPE	1309, 6573, 10964	POTENTIALITY	9799
POPISH	8672	POUNCE	3773
POPPIES	6633, 6634	POUND	9194, 12568
POPULACE	12410	POUNDS	1909, 6499, 6540
POPULAR	5252, 7350		
POPULARITY	8551, 11842		

POVERTY 153, 786, 821, 979, 1528, 1734, 3409, 3496, 3529, 3996, 4006, 4986, 5134, 5310, 7804, 7810, 8277, 8543, 8553, 10508, 10803, 11538, 11875

POWDER 1310

POWER 15, 30, 31, 39, 183, 234, 334, 418, 537, 686, 734, 742, 771, 998, 1060, 1526, 1738, 1755, 1843, 2515, 2608, 2639, 2642, 2742, 2769, 2940, 2992, 3446, 4348, 4446, 4534, 4616, 4697, 4810, 4878, 4888, 5173, 5176, 5208, 5299, 5514, 5667, 5680, 5917, 6207, 6286, 6333, 6373, 6376, 6497, 6632, 7229, 7296, 7659, 8056, 8112, 8136, 8143, 8220, 8300, 8317, 8526, 8670, 8881, 8911, 9576, 9587, 9712, 10696, 10819, 10840, 10912, 10973, 11262, 11300, 11302, 11386, 11500, 11648, 11807, 12130, 12246, 12586, 12633, 12733, 12734, 12774

POWERFUL 2859, 3591, 7098, 7889, 10913, 12008

POWERLESS 9698, 11804

POWERLESSNESS 9670

POWERS 3269, 5035, 5071, 5476, 7596, 8395, 9263, 11942, 12740

PRACTICAL 2139, 4891, 5552, 6317

PRACTICE 3356, 9598, 9699, 10502

PRACTISE 8763, 10639

PRACTISED 1862, 7104

PRACTISES 2236

PRAGMATIST 10965

PRAISE 60, 604, 949, 1201, 2019, 3317, 3535, 3596, 3737, 4593, 5494, 5698, 5749, 5845, 5932, 6606, 6986, 7056, 7111, 7433, 7636, 8103, 8822, 9402, 10072, 10473, 10869, 10926, 11486, 12138

PRAISED 5936, 9057

PRAISING 1906, 3821, 7422, 10783, 10791

PRAM 2501

PRAY 90, 253, 304, 865, 950, 1275, 1359, 5315, 6306, 6971, 8399, 9503, 10802, 11432

PRAYER 49, 266, 1089, 4706, 5229, 5696, 6211, 6572, 7248, 9617, 11476, 11864, 11865

PRAYERS 1091, 1494, 4598, 4910, 7371, 8057, 12063

PRAYING 8355, 11299

PRAYS 2425, 9859, 11830

PREACH 9531, 9699, 12334

PREACHERS 6405, 9973

PREACHING 5089, 11539

PRECEDENCE 7429

PRECEDENCY 5136

PRECEDENT 9953

PRECIOUS 4087, 4680, 6157, 7530, 11183, 12371

PRECISIAN 7078

PREDATORY 9921

PREDECESSOR 1829, 3848

PREDICT 4919

PREDICTED 5337

PREDICTION 6281

PREFACES 6542

PREFER 11061

PREFERENCE 6256

PREFERMENT 510

PREGNANCY 6212, 7209

PREGNANT 5499

PREJUDICE 2809, 3984, 4440, 10792, 11871

PREJUDICES 2511, 5729, 5882, 7198, 7982, 10798

PRELATY 7647

PRELUDE 6846

PREMONITION 11745

PREOCCUPATION 9680

PREPARATION 648, 3682, 11103, 12781

PREPARE 1152, 8489, 8573

PREPARED 142, 2459, 3311, 8193

PREPAREDNESS 4038

PREROGATIVE 5667, 5871, 6376, 10483

PRESBYTER 7498

PRESENCE 2227, 3193, 4932, 9213, 12267, 12581, 12700

PRESENT 383, 2355, 2538, 2918, 5161, 5547, 6288, 6532, 6882, 7068, 7729, 9135

PRESENTED 188

PRESENTS 4932, 5880

PRESERVE 6372, 8290

PRESERVED 4613

PRESIDENCY 849, 2524, 3071, 6293, 9576

PRESIDENT 48, 2370, 2525, 4808, 5010, 5545, 5706, 7202, 8200, 8201, 11073, 11810, 11812, 11818, 12565

PRESIDENTIAL 12369

PRESIDING 7152

PRESS 4478, 4971, 8220, 8430, 9161, 11214, 11791

PRESSURE 3201, 6499, 8532

PRESTIGE 2720

PRESUME 10211, 10967

PRESUMPTION 11689

PRETEND 361, 2646

PRETENDER 1912

PRETENDING 6824, 12454

PRETEXTS 1756

PRETTIER 5875

PRETTY 1922, 2517, 3486, 8571, 8574, 8950, 8989, 12204

PREVAIL 3416, 6489

PREVENT 5601, 6632, 9702

PREVENTED 1125

PREVENTS 2455, 7084

PREVISION 12291

PREY 4260, 7562, 8839, 9163, 9640, 10606, 11254

PREYS 4958

PRICE 202, 270, 1013, 1041, 1232, 2357, 3700, 5165, 5312, 5520, 6661, 9065, 9640, 10544, 11137, 11708, 12132, 12339, 12499, 12563

PRICES 10733

PRICK 9366, 10153, 10313

PRICKING 10277, 10921

PRICKS 1128

PRIDE 1242, 1340, 2455, 2745, 3715, 3716, 3948, 4150, 4273, 5056, 5131, 6636, 7265, 8107, 8834, 8838, 9126, 9403, 9750, 9893, 10342, 10348, 12199, 12518

PRIEST 4497, 7498

PRIESTS 1664, 4813, 6754, 9804, 10882

PRIMAL 8352

PRIME 1046, 9552, 10455, 10892, 10929

PRIME MINISTER 545, 994, 4192, 7166, 10752

PRIME MINISTERS 828, 9749

PRIME MOVER 463

PRIMEVAL 6424

PRIMITIVE 75, 6076, 6614, 6833

PRIMROSE 5366, 7481, 10107

PRIMROSE HILL 1332

PRINCE 2178, 7149, 8017, 12199, 12296

PRINCIPALITY 6749

PRINCIPLE 640, 892, 1313, 2538, 2778, 2830, 3151, 5760, 6198, 6333, 6406, 6514, 7107, 7306, 9953, 12016

PRINCIPLES 1076, 2697, 2846, 5116, 6509, 8197, 9146, 11069, 11346

PRINT 7854, 8241, 11214, 11647, 12653

PRINTED 11741, 12261

PRINTING 2086, 5114, 7392

PRINTLESS 7426

PRIORITIES 1113

PRISM 3460

PRISON 1339, 1842, 6477, 7762, 9300, 9435, 11212, 12634, 12673

PRISONED 9847

PRISONER 5707, 7982, 10839

PRISONERS 12465, 12477

PRISONS 1587, 12465

PRIVACY 6699

PRIVATE 35, 322, 331, 607, 1883, 2765, 3058, 4468, 5243, 6513, 7167, 7658, 11300, 12561

PRIVATION 3746, 9595

PRIVILEDGED 2883

PRIVILEGE 660, 998, 2210, 3330, 3738, 3919, 12167

PRIVILEGES 5051, 7187

PRIZE 4254, 6828, 10413

PRIZES 10742

PROBABILITY 3157, 4200

PROBABLE 3917

PROBE 12330

PROBLEM 1695, 2764, 2956, 4581, 9733, 10689, 11007, 11062

PROBLEMS 4180, 4318, 4678, 5231, 6816, 7040

PROCEED 3356

PROCESSES 12383

PROCESSION 11850, 12611

PROCLAIM 7001, 7866

PROCRASTINATION 2750, 6965, 12840

PROCREANT 12412

PRODIGAL 2325

PRODUCE 4973, 9373, 12773

PRODUCEFUL 8025

PRODUCER 3325, 10734

PRODUCING 8307

PRODUCT 3528, 7264

PRODUCTION 55, 9856, 9857

PRODUCTIONS 9466

PRODUCTS 5490

PROFANITY 11865

PROFESSED 3752, 7640

PROFESSION 706, 9332, 9479, 11103

PROFESSIONAL 5329

PROFESSIONALS 5330

PROFESSIONS 28, 10488, 10535, 11683

PROFESSOR 589, 5284

PROFESSORS 6251

PROFILE 5236

PROFIT 1164, 1240, 3906, 6721, 7231, 10135, 12175

PROFITABILITY 2980

PROFITABLE 6968

PUBLIC 546, 607, 932, 2499, 2525, 2765, 3058, 3440, 4203, 5305, 7658, 8529, 8630, 11195, 11933, 11944, 11995, 12452, 12514
PUBLIC OPINION 9693
PUBLIC-SCHOOL 3542, 12207
PUBLICAN 10304
PUBLICATION 2006, 6699
PUBLICITY 971, 1041, 4362, 6106, 6278, 11563
PUBLISH 12272
PUBLISHED 242
PUBLISHER 2020, 8650
PUBLISHERS 76
PUBLISHES 7316
PUDDING 781, 8765
PUERILITY 4613
PUGNACIOUS 7905
PULL 4482, 7949, 11591
PULSE 7855, 8632, 11032, 12720
PULSE-LESS 6027
PUNCHES 9733
PUNCTILIO 7228
PUNCTUALITY 6474, 12203, 12471
PUNCTUATE 7828
PUNISH 1587, 2990, 3522
PUNISHED 2474, 4986
PUNISHMENT 225, 1053, 2941, 3529, 3959, 4471, 5214, 5779, 6789, 7870, 8144, 9323, 9668, 9769, 12052
PUNISHMENTS 4493, 4917, 8411
PUP 7348
PUPIL 3703, 4675
PURCHASER 11236, 11297
PURE 5468, 6002, 11400, 12485
PUREST 9644
PURGATORY 3513, 6289
PURIFIED 6925
PURIFIES 7391
PURIFYING 6629
PURITAN 6019, 6768
PURITANISM 7206
PURITY 2900, 3461, 8029
PURPLE 3195, 4490, 8432, 9505
PURPOSE 493, 1207, 2494, 3552, 4607, 5296, 6314, 6630, 9452, 10428, 10581, 11447, 11462
PURRING 7744
PURRS 6963
PURSE 5
PURSUE 3036, 4973
PURSUED 10448

PURSUIT 6104, 11327, 12466
PUSH 10706, 11116
PUSHED 9061
PUSHING 670
PUSSY 6096
PUT DOWN 116
PUT UP 2317
PUZZLE 5906, 11045
PUZZLED 4770
PYGMIES 839
PYJAMAS 6040
PYRAMID 7671, 8011
PYRENEES 6473
PYSCHOPATH 196
PYTHAGORAS 1602
QUAD 5719
QUAILS 3021
QUAKE 10668
QUAKER 4573
QUALIFICATION 2122
QUALIFIED 3890
QUALITIES 1675, 2279, 2726, 3049, 4154, 8242, 9821, 10542, 12375
QUALITY 4204, 5250, 7725, 10316, 10674, 10838, 12368
QUANGLE-WANGLE 6101
QUANTITY 5250
QUARKS 5262
QUARREL 3270, 3662, 4908, 9234, 9580, 10487, 10574
QUARRELLING 8216, 9098
QUARRELS 3817, 4715, 5810, 9537, 12048
QUARTER 23
QUARTERLY 11209
QUEBEC 5624
QUEEN 406, 3237, 4023, 5194, 6861, 7521, 10183, 10445, 10446, 10606, 11460
QUEENSBERRY 12123
QUEER 974, 3998, 8248, 8378, 10946, 12616
QUEERER 4327
QUENCH 10351
QUEST 806, 2552
QUESTING 6857
QUESTION 451, 592, 1554, 2025, 2808, 2809, 3625, 3978, 7265, 10124, 10715, 11767, 12607
QUESTION MARK 9677
QUESTIONING 5055
QUESTIONS 577, 982, 2860, 3683, 4795, 9803, 9878, 10776, 12293, 12482, 12861
QUEUE 7282

QUICK	382, 2761	RAINING	6485
QUICKER	7714	RAINS	2730, 8916
QUICKEST	7732, 8319	RAINY	2748
QUICKLY	9205, 10261	RAISE	700
QUIET	1008, 1927, 2200,	RAISED	11156, 12234
4564, 5272, 6054, 7010, 7271, 9355, 10566, 10691,		RAKE	2016, 6757
12596, 12739		RAMBLE	4315
QUIETEST	6612	RAMPART	12619
QUIETLY	7318	RAN	1329
QUILL	5885	RANG	3898
QUINCE	6098	RANK	1801, 5304
QUINTESSENCE	10120	RANKS	892, 6779
QUIT	7624, 7666	RANSACK	6924
QUITS	376, 7147	RAPE	2717, 8977
QUIXOTE	5084	RAPHAEL	12362
QUOTA	3776	RAPHAELS	4139
QUOTABLE	11138	RAPIDITY	2729
QUOTATION	5144	RAPPING	8741
QUOTATIONS	3318	RAPSCALLIONS	11886
QUOTE	3580, 7784, 10490,	RAPTURE	3954, 6919, 8262, 8821
12270, 12832		RAPTUROUS	6147
QUOTED	11178	RARE	5313, 5849, 7862,
RABBIT	331, 10577	10477, 12249	
RABBIT-LIKE	11751	RARER	5805
RABBITS	10699, 12201	RAREST	11684
RABBLE	8921	RASCALITY	10950
RACE	1209, 2699, 3279,	RASH	7615
5122, 5526, 7684, 8928, 9613, 9630, 9920, 10625,		RAT	1486, 9438, 11246
11290, 11449, 12554, 12827		RATHER	4195
RACES	5887, 6561, 12858	RATIOCINATION	1887
RACING	164, 9484	RATIONAL	643, 2945
RACK	10731	RATIONALISM	12829
RACKET	8336	RATIONED	6157
RADAR	4485	RATOMORPHIC	5740
RADIANCE	4352	RATS	1660, 8229, 8249
RADIANT	7414	RATTLE	6163, 8207, 8844
RADICAL	476, 3672, 12629	RAVEN	6521, 10260
RADICALISM	4610	RAVISH	2917
RADIO	599, 6534, 9830	RAVISHED	6923
RADIUS	7214	RAVISHING	975
RAG	5696, 12674, 12790	RAZOR	7755, 8866
RAG-BAG	352	RE-READ	9885
RAGE	1324, 2815, 8655,	REACH	2820, 3537, 5204,
11246, 11475, 11578, 11706		6943, 8024	
RAGES	10944, 11179	REACT	4984
RAGS	7722	REACTION	1066, 8122
RAILINGS	8424	REACTIONARIES	6908
RAIMENT	6739	READ	543, 755, 990, 1707,
RAIN	590, 1489, 3096, 5429,	1851, 2044, 3686, 4477, 4586, 5069, 5566, 5987,	
5997, 6194, 8561, 9002, 10316, 10595, 10704, 11411,		6542, 6848, 6986, 8530, 8760, 8826, 8911, 9222,	
11989, 12105		9466, 9673, 10327, 11573, 11770, 11841, 12210,	
RAINBOW	3, 399, 4371, 6533,	12269, 12815, 12860	
11411, 12693, 12708			

REFORMATION 3027, 12465

REFORMER 2257, 12096

REFORMERS 7835, 10510

REFRAIN 4345

REFRAINING 4855

REFRESHING 2015

REFUGEES 1696, 4329, 6722

REFUND 9325

REFUSE 407, 5249, 7204, 8390, 9243, 9845, 11780

REFUTE 8417

REGARD 8239

REGARDED 7210

REGIMEN 8987

REGIMENT 5638, 5717

REGION 7514

REGISTER 3867

REGRET 4330, 4447, 5622, 6901, 8250

REGRETS 9608

REGULAR 3497

REGULATED 11170

REHABILITATE 1587

REIGN 7516, 8017

REIGNED 3242

REIGNS 7556

REINCARNATION 7345

REINFORCEMENT 2047, 7512

REINS 107

REJECT 1000, 4930

REJECTED 1508, 3289

REJOICE 2292, 6581, 7628

REJOICING 7432

RELATED 2467, 8406

RELATION 11530, 11557, 11877, 12202

RELATIONS 2522, 4236, 4409, 5620, 7306, 8988

RELATIONSHIP 1540, 3549, 4741, 5293, 5425

RELATIONSHIPS 584, 1092, 8354, 11999

RELATIVE 1702

RELATIVITY 3126, 3140

RELAXATION 9628

RELAXES 1341

RELEASE 2685

RELENT 12035

RELIC 12233

RELICS 7671, 7861

RELIEF 698, 1358, 2656

RELIEVED 4115, 10134

RELIGION 58, 299, 712, 981, 1362, 1597, 1605, 1845, 1862, 1950, 2086, 2397, 2456, 2713, 2869, 3145, 3286, 3388, 3557, 3622, 4108, 4789, 4899, 4907, 5004, 5303, 5752, 5753, 6535, 6559, 6939, 7039, 7167, 7173, 7795, 8239, 8405, 8410, 8414, 8553, 8777, 8904, 9105, 9658, 9740, 9805, 10511, 10543, 10568, 10799, 10889, 10970, 11039, 11261, 11305, 11380, 12061

RELIGIONS 1537, 8994, 12053

RELIGIOUS 533, 1481, 1770, 3865, 7448, 8102, 12224, 12630

RELISHED 216, 3072, 12696

RELUCTANT 6436

RELUME 10351

RELY 5788, 6730

REMAIN 927, 11292

REMAINING 1503

REMAINS 5700, 8784, 9468

REMARKABLE 4891, 8490

REMARKS 2894, 10999, 11178

REMEDIES 736, 3619, 10054, 11298

REMEDY 751, 899, 2026, 3419, 5774, 9292, 12855

REMEMBER 240, 368, 535, 1197, 1298, 1382, 2409, 2545, 2807, 2942, 3712, 4203, 4691, 4826, 6196, 6224, 8920, 8990, 9037, 9553, 9813, 9979, 10176, 11180, 11278, 11286, 11342, 11856, 11873, 11882, 12023, 12626

REMEMBERED 597, 1432, 5038, 7838

REMEMBERING 2763, 9850, 11442

REMEMBRANCE 5431, 6038, 9862, 10140, 10462

REMIND 7024

REMINISCENCE 12407

REMORSE 78, 2588, 7569

REMORSELESS 7474

REMOTE 4114

RENDER 1187

RENDEZVOUS 9959

RENEW 10601

RENEWING 3118, 9361

RENOUNCE 3875

REPAIR 2056, 3297

REPAIRING 9541

REPAIRS 1315, 7482

REPARTEE 2234

REPAY 985, 1145

REPEAL 4232

REPEAT 2527, 4300, 5254, 9813

REPEATED 825

REPEL 560

REPENT 7628, 9964, 10351, 10616, 10888, 11359

REPENTANCE 1157, 1177, 3015, 3025, 3124, 9020, 9949, 12777

REPENTED 1967

REPENTING 11606

REPERTOIRE 7867

REPLACED 847

REPORTER 3632, 6744

REPORTS 11849

REPOSE 2260, 3329, 6409

REPREHEND 10646

REPRESENT 3083

REPRESENTATION 8353

REPRESENTATIVE 1739, 9794, 11810

REPRESSION 7307

REPROACH 6766, 8553, 9892

REPRODUCED 2508

REPROOF 5932

REPTILE 8801

REPUBLIC 59, 163, 787, 7701, 7810

REPUBLICAN 10677, 10901, 11719

REPUTATION 205, 4354, 6883, 7827, 8017, 9871, 10338, 10343, 10356, 11242

REPUTATIONS 3174

REQUEST 7876

REQUIRE 1350, 4463, 9829

REQUIRED 3439, 3578

REQUIREMENT 4686, 8190

REQUIREMENTS 5603

REQUISITE 65

REQUITED 8377

RESCUED 11961

RESEARCH 896, 1524, 3625, 4503, 5251, 6466, 7710

RESEMBLANCE 8475, 9332, 10975, 11344

RESEMBLE 1257, 10313, 12109

RESENT 2472, 11265

RESENTMENT 8097

RESERVATION 6302, 10580

RESERVED 2381

RESERVOIR 12555

RESIGN 12174

RESIGNATION 7035

RESIGNED 7318

RESIST 1168, 4227, 5708, 6018, 10524, 12311, 12470, 12497

RESISTANCE 160, 3597, 8144, 10963, 12179

RESISTIBLE 1525

RESISTING 5730

RESOLUTE 10278

RESOLUTION 1120, 7512, 7617, 8179, 10081, 10126

RESOLUTIONS 1891

RESOLVE 528, 3611, 12841

RESOLVED 6619

RESORTS 6206

RESOURCES 4015, 4719

RESPECT 361, 968, 1910, 2174, 2245, 6797, 8463, 8618, 9693, 10003, 11354, 11852, 12084

RESPECTABILITY 847, 8951, 9326, 10505

RESPECTABLE 1615, 1616, 4309, 4699, 7834, 8328, 9742

RESPECTED 912, 4213, 4303, 5331

RESPECTER 1129

RESPECTING 7364, 7978

RESPECTS 11857

RESPONSIBILITY 2741, 3113, 4355, 5724, 6286, 9730, 10557, 11142, 11644

RESPONSIBLE 6290

REST 427, 1027, 1179, 2581, 5558, 7631, 8109, 8120, 8535, 8731, 9190, 10145, 10602, 11987, 12205, 12525

RESTAURANT 562, 4100

RESTING 9633

RESTLESS 10749

RESTRAIN 6372

RESTRAINED 3259

RESTS 4253

RESULT 12468

RESULTS 3109, 8616, 9870

RESURRECTION 1413, 9901

RESUSCITATE 8924

RETAINER 993

RETENTIVE 10192

RETICULATED 5147

RETIRE 1046, 2464, 2876, 7635, 10578

RETIRED 2690, 11030

RETIREMENT 4323, 7611, 8247, 11633

RETIRING 5058

RETRACT 6625

RETREAT 173, 3782, 5807, 7991, 8007, 12768

RETREATING 3515, 8042

RETROGRADE 5205

RETURN 1223, 7472, 11129

RETURNED 1702, 7101

RETURNING 10839

RETURNS 3564, 5784

REVEAL 3892, 11471

REVELATION 6369

REVELATIONS 12511

REVENGE 721, 748, 749, 1948, 2810, 5317, 6793, 7508, 7953, 9189, 10136, 10313, 10498, 10852, 12066

REVERBERATION 6830

REVERE 5007

REVERENCE 789, 795, 4593

REVERSE 2620

REVERSED 4195

REVERSION 8782

REVIEW 6496, 7146, 9346

REVIEWERS 2413, 2427

REVIEWING 10798

REVIEWS 6262

REVISION 12291

REVIVALS 1901

REVOLT 3408, 6863, 6869

REVOLTED 7599

REVOLTING 8031

REVOLTS 7972, 11349

REVOLUTION 250, 476, 1764, 3088, 3263, 3680, 5510, 5560, 6868, 8317, 9489, 11986, 12224

REVOLUTIONARY 5563, 6325

REVOLUTIONIST 3795

REVOLUTIONISTS 7210

REVOLUTIONS 1713, 2047, 4906, 9718, 10012, 10563, 10837

REWARD 225, 3267, 3411, 4671, 6885, 7930, 9769, 10928, 11979

REWARDED 540

REWRITE 3686, 12495

RHETORIC 3792, 7431, 10672, 12784

RHETORICIAN 1888, 2870, 12797

RHEUMATISM 3377

RHINE 827

RHODESIA 10748

RHUBARB 5726

RHYME 4645, 7633, 7881, 7927, 8738, 8861

RHYMING 2191, 7634

RHYTHM 5000, 7055, 11169

RIB 9686

RIBS 1466, 7420

RICE 7370

RICH 108, 786, 1249, 1272, 2146, 2241, 3091, 3479, 3570, 3642, 4114, 4151, 5323, 5521, 5956, 7831, 7862, 8531, 8543, 9124, 9179, 9655, 9841, 10215, 10773, 10773, 10846, 11551, 11687, 11875, 12554

RICHER 8061

RICHES 138, 264, 704, 725, 1406, 3720, 6582, 6940, 7432, 7530, 11247

RICHESSE 6589

RICHEST 11652

RICHMOND HILL 6717

RID 4497, 10859, 11017

RIDDEN 6294, 6575

RIDDLE 2255, 2304, 5750, 8839

RIDDLES 2378, 6148

RIDE 314, 2462, 6948, 7133, 7359, 7360, 12090

RIDER 11210

RIDICULED 9896

RIDICULOUS 115, 2455, 4221, 5310, 6755, 6824, 7090, 7653, 8020, 8406, 8758, 9038

RIDING 1361, 12360

RIDLEY 5996

RIFLE 5700, 8381

RIFT 11424

RIGHT 148, 267, 286, 845, 1281, 1661, 1906, 2197, 2216, 2221, 2275, 2370, 2578, 2659, 2698, 3137, 3138, 3166, 4818, 4878, 4887, 4915, 5009, 5108, 5669, 6284, 6303, 6635, 6754, 7950, 8080, 8197, 8431, 8460, 8773, 8838, 9262, 9908, 10824, 10965, 11301, 11307, 11328, 11809, 11861, 12254, 12353, 12585, 12588

RIGHTEOUS 1177, 1370, 7963

RIGHTEOUSNESS 1171, 12296

RIGHTING 6381

RIGHTS 345, 453, 796, 1051, 2435, 2983, 3122, 4438, 4831, 4931, 4980, 6922, 7187, 9429, 10970

RIMBAUDS 8446

RIMINI 3975

RIND 7390

RING 786, 1434, 2622, 6097, 7274, 7491, 8370, 11493, 11727, 11970, 12131

RINGS 2000, 8705

RINKY-DINK 6831

RIOT 5597, 11377

RIPE 10029

RIPEN 3355

RIPENESS 10246

RISE 1525, 2366, 5218, 6284, 8526, 11515, 12031

RISEN 1040

RISER 4757

RISING 685

RISK 1677, 4779, 5160, 5352, 6064, 6630, 6800

RISKS 5500, 9926, 11073

RITZ 7085

RIVALRY 34

RIVER   631, 4011, 4358, 5559, 8088

RIVER-ROUNDED   4707

RIVERS   1206, 2987, 7760

ROAD   1796, 2238, 2724, 2788, 5687, 6001, 7064, 7220, 7712, 7892, 8035, 8850, 11108, 11621, 11783

ROADS   1321

ROAM   2582, 4148, 4149, 8520, 10749

ROAMING   6003

ROAR   2289, 3721, 3995

ROARS   4030

ROB   3435, 4315, 5195, 6740

ROBBED   8085, 8111, 10840

ROBBERY   1498

ROBBING   1535, 2750

ROBIN   1324

ROBS   10344, 10536

ROCK   2141, 3087, 7320, 11746, 12623, 12860

ROCK'N'ROLL   6161

ROCKET   3150, 8409, 12436

ROCKIES   3858

ROCKPILE   1590

ROCKS   4514, 9432

ROD   1239, 6377

RODE   11392, 11404, 11437

RODENTS   11154

ROGUE   2985, 7234

ROGUES   8951

ROLE   9, 2690

ROLL   3087

ROLLING   4358

ROLLS   12700

ROMAN   2247, 2344, 3865, 3883, 4592, 8940, 10062, 10210, 12078

ROMAN CONQUEST   9975

ROMANCE   585, 657, 1080, 2131, 2530, 5464, 10815, 12483, 12514

ROMANCES   11186

ROMANS   4461, 6776, 6778

ROMANTIC   3969, 6087, 9388, 11171

ROMANTICISM   12829

ROME   623, 1012, 1410, 5189, 5312, 8740, 10060, 10202, 11367, 12110

ROMEO   10387

ROOF   12543

ROOFS   12417

ROOKERY   8976

ROOKS   11472

ROOM   2896, 4276, 4291, 5930, 6658, 7685, 9534, 10657, 12230, 12659

ROOSEVELT   4165

ROOST   7335, 10875

ROOSTER   9174, 9193

ROOSTS   7663

ROOT   1193, 4946, 7015, 8411, 9143, 10255

ROOTAGE   12579

ROOTS   2129, 3172, 4512, 9460

ROSE   1567, 1668, 1823, 2063, 5377, 6717, 6962, 7088, 7572, 7864, 8435, 8726, 9164, 9505, 10073, 10249, 10388, 10929, 11001, 12109, 12810

ROSEBUD   11460

ROSEBUDS   4544

ROSEMARY   10140

ROSES   1657, 2952, 5016, 6120, 6944, 7021, 7022, 7036, 7852, 9552, 10844, 11113, 12219

ROSEWATER   1713

ROT   8595, 8841, 10029, 10295

ROTHSCHILD   3946

ROTTED   8036

ROTTEN   10110, 10305, 10689, 12821

ROTTENNESS   4975, 9326

ROUGH   4726, 7794, 10914

ROUGH-HEW   10143

ROUGHEST   10257

ROUGHLY   2104

ROUGHNESS   735

ROUGHNESSES   2612

ROUND   3641, 11627, 11630, 11693

ROUNDHEADS   9976

ROUSE   9951

ROUSSEAU   1084

ROUT   6739

ROUTINE   2164, 9257

ROVERS   1106

ROVING   326, 1984, 2921

ROW   1865, 3833, 9049

ROWE   2805

ROWS   11533

ROYAL   4625, 7535

ROYALTIES   538

ROYALTY   795, 2880, 6803, 7051

RUB   9632, 10125

RUBBISH   2945, 8297, 10864

RUBIES   1232

RUBS   7121

RUDE 3753, 12462, 12538
RUDENESS 4614
RUDIMENTS 10864
RUDOLPH 6920
RUDYARDS 11018
RUG 3599
RUGGED 1032, 4220, 5104
RUIN 663, 929, 1917, 3846, 5006, 7542, 7558, 10885, 11311, 12514
RUIN-TRACE 7819
RUINED 124, 1044, 1782, 2647, 7056, 7876, 12065
RUINS 2958, 6357, 10199
RUISLIP 1103
RULE 232, 1714, 2112, 2168, 2284, 2438, 3123, 5550, 7204, 7269, 7394, 7719, 8145, 8240, 8430, 8790, 8840, 11172, 11207, 11457, 11629, 12617, 12734
RULED 9868
RULER 4873
RULERS 1263, 7054, 7148
RULES 412, 1243, 4631, 7424, 8028, 8326, 9751, 9842, 9938, 11021, 12103
RULING 8811, 10963
RUM 11109, 12286
RUN 560, 1114, 2437, 3593, 5540, 6233, 6296, 6772, 8497, 8592, 10912, 10954, 11655
RUN-WAY 1099
RUNCIBLE 6095
RUNNING 2115, 2903, 7790, 8748
RUNS 313
RURAL 4824
RUSH 11642
RUSHED 9494
RUSHES 1812
RUSSELL 7743
RUSSIA 2304, 4095, 8127, 11916, 12818
RUSSIAN 317, 3234, 3932, 8066, 9237
RUSSIANS 11694, 11720
RUST 56, 10866, 12372
RUSTICS 4119
RUT 11846
RUTHERFORD 11901
RYE 1807, 8538
SABBATH 1160
SABIDIUS 6985
SABLE-VESTED 7557
SABOTAGE 11982
SABRINA 7425
SACK 10151

SACRAMENT 2658
SACRED 7478, 8777
SACRIFICE 3304, 3755, 5678, 6348, 7108, 7359, 7519, 11220
SACRIFICED 8396
SACRIFICES 1739, 3314, 4175, 7050, 7115, 12117
SAD 1636, 2562, 2736, 5734, 9170, 9400, 9553, 11033, 11273, 12420
SADDENS 1659
SADDER 1962
SADDEST 7203, 8948
SADDLING 10539
SADISTIC 9668
SADNESS 9462, 11396
SAFE 379, 540, 1479, 2758, 3547, 7882, 8206, 8375
SAFEGUARD 11136
SAFEGUARDS 3584
SAFELY 8371
SAFER 5486, 6794
SAFEST 3556
SAFETY 10150, 10171, 12027
SAFETY-PIN 352
SAGACITY 9626
SAGE 8461, 9819
SAGES 9264, 12742
SAID 69, 2272, 2526, 2982, 3580, 3931, 4435, 5485, 7311, 8472, 9984, 11071, 11255, 11534
SAIL 3268, 7065, 8084, 12356
SAILOR 2771, 11053, 11648
SAILORS 8079, 12105
SAILS 163, 3384, 7064, 10068
SAINT 7678, 8302, 8546, 8858, 9913
SAINTLY 7436
SAINTS 4673, 4902, 8329, 11091
SAKE 9967
SALAD 4135, 10067
SALARY 3876, 11705
SALESMAN 7331
SALIERI 852
SALISBURY 3945, 4999
SALLOWS 5359
SALLY 2065
SALMON-FISHERS 6998
SALT 1166, 8715, 8717, 11335, 12321
SALT WATER 11175
SALUTARY 8429

SALUTE	319, 341, 1911, 11190
SALVATION	617, 5586, 8541, 9299,
10544, 12756	
SAMARITAN	11564
SAMARKAND	3502
SAMARRA	6492
SAME	666, 2115, 2555, 3707,
4490, 5340, 5920, 6392, 7163, 9151, 9376, 9760,	
12277	
SAMSON	7666
SANCTIFIES	14
SANCTION	3582, 9797
SANCTUARY	828
SAND	338, 7320, 9857, 10005
SANDALS	7824, 9109
SANDALWOOD	7058
SANDS	2255, 6443
SANDWICHES	1496
SANE	10545, 11576
SANG	11579
SANGUINE	988, 4016
SANITY	3254, 3323, 10510
SANK	5518, 7069
SANS	3471
SANTA CLAUS	3421
SARCASM	2832
SARGENT	934
SASKATCHEWAN	6069
SAT	2613, 2627, 4322
SATAN	1181, 7534, 7535,
7552, 7598, 11852, 12195	
SATANIC	1344
SATIETY	716
SATIRE	3596, 5172, 5344,
7755, 7847, 9877, 11230, 12831	
SATIRIST	3874, 4575, 6611
SATISFACTION	3316, 3431, 3807,
4779, 6239, 11191	
SATISFACTORY	408
SATISFIED	2277, 3837, 4441,
5731, 8644, 10070, 10775, 11790, 12387, 12763	
SATISFY	11349, 12671
SATISFYING	2466
SATURDAY	2893, 5344, 8022
SATYR	8658
SATYRS	6934
SAUCE	8731, 9005
SAUCER	7745
SAUCES	12053
SAUNTERING	2016
SAUSAGE	4510
SAVAGE	2322, 3005, 3608,
6973, 10500, 11449	

SAVAGED	4455
SAVAGELY	12050
SAVAGES	2858
SAVE	598, 724, 1923, 2932,
3123, 8679, 11373, 12010, 12358	
SAVED	925, 2240, 3902, 6015
SAVES	3546, 9732
SAVING	5012
SAVINGS	6991
SAVIOUR	1911, 5694
SAVOUR	1166, 5864
SAW	2519, 3811, 3878,
8393, 12274, 12578	
SAXON	6431
SAY	37, 536, 2295, 2458,
2527, 3098, 3165, 3526, 3569, 4484, 5062, 6456,	
8258, 8650, 9434, 9973, 10240, 10710, 11317, 11366,	
11951, 12069, 12270, 12334	
SAYING	5505, 9810, 11022,
11028, 12595	
SAYS	6611, 8995, 10766,
11020	
SCABBARD	2356
SCAFFOLD	6524, 8633
SCALDED	3704
SCALE	3464, 8765
SCALES	6727
SCALPED	6740
SCAN	8757
SCANDAL	3409, 3441, 3523,
7735, 8614, 11516	
SCANDALOUS	349
SCAR	1645
SCARCE	10372, 10934
SCARE	4744
SCARECROW	10289
SCARED	3646, 8686, 9406
SCARF	10271
SCARFS	8845
SCARLET	990, 4688, 5206
SCARS	4763, 6758
SCATTER	2015, 10612
SCATTERS	7455
SCENE	4655, 10031, 10167
SCENERY	5417, 9651
SCENES	7097
SCENT	7852
SCEPTIC	4881
SCEPTICISM	1076, 3076, 6507,
8102, 9838	
SCEPTRED	5945
SCHEME	9754
SCHEMES	1822

SEDUCTIVE 12358

SEE 289, 467, 547, 1072, 1167, 1806, 1818, 1944, 2169, 2360, 2478, 2957, 3043, 3311, 3396, 3398, 3541, 4525, 5005, 5575, 6547, 7969, 8739, 8875, 9056, 9565, 9674, 10244, 10309, 10758, 11707, 12318, 12761, 12778

SEED 2015, 10629, 11541

SEED-TIME 6530

SEEDS 10162

SEEING 3713, 5129, 9103, 9660, 9802

SEEK 894, 1171, 1173, 1211, 3816, 8287, 8398, 8483, 8640, 9271, 11108, 12766

SEEKERS 9153

SEEKING 10028

SEEM 8114

SEEMED 7597

SEEN 105, 3037, 3040, 5100, 8097, 8117, 8340, 8642, 9780, 11309, 11605, 12398, 12523

SEES 2548, 5698, 7782, 8542

SEGREGATION 12099

SEIZE 5201

SELDOM 5926, 10147

SELECT 3331, 5424, 10598

SELF 737, 1068, 5860, 6573, 8482, 11011

SELF-ABUSE 2759

SELF-ACCEPTANCE 11217

SELF-BEGOTTEN 7664

SELF-COMMAND 3324

SELF-CONFIDENCE 5060

SELF-CONTAINED 12415

SELF-DEFEATING 89

SELF-DEFENCE 6921

SELF-DENIAL 6222

SELF-DISCIPLINE 5923, 6271

SELF-ENJOYMENT 12556

SELF-ESTEEM 1580, 4603

SELF-EVIDENT 9896

SELF-EXPRESSION 6662

SELF-GOVERNMENT 7935

SELF-HATE 8358

SELF-IMPOSED 4929

SELF-INDULGENCE 3764, 7108

SELF-LOVE 8847

SELF-MADE 4366, 10980

SELF-MASTERY 8138

SELF-PITY 1024

SELF-POSSESSION 8428

SELF-PROTECTION 7295

SELF-PUNISHMENT 837

SELF-REPROACH 12453

SELF-RESPECT 4552

SELF-RESTRAINT 3764

SELF-REVERENCE 11386

SELF-SAME 7471

SELF-SLAIN 11280

SELF-SLAUGHTER 10102

SELF-SUFFICING 12727

SELFISH 640, 6626, 11112

SELFISHNESS 4416

SELKIRK 5351

SELL 201, 5804, 6820, 10452

SELLING 6667, 11095

SELVES 4602, 9463, 12646

SEMINARY 3953

SENATE 2825, 6614

SENATOR 5013

SEND 5015, 5213, 6498, 11167

SENESCENCE 8023

SENILITY 8247

SENIOR 9308

SENIORS 6490

SENSATION 1916, 2785, 3955, 5416, 12182

SENSATIONAL 12491

SENSE 115, 862, 948, 1076, 1681, 2118, 2752, 5848, 5995, 6360, 6660, 7112, 7199, 7245, 7945, 8285, 9307, 9371, 9440, 9539, 10350, 10790, 10995, 11077, 12700

SENSELESS 3250, 4848

SENSES 7770, 12290

SENSIBILITY 9327, 9798

SENSIBLE 2869, 3321, 8710

SENSITIVE 4608

SENSORY 8118

SENSUAL 5078, 5436

SENSUOUS 7431

SENT 217

SENTENCE 2044, 2498, 3332, 6990, 7537, 8710, 8759, 11675, 12376

SENTENCED 12546

SENTIMENT 3755, 7055

SENTIMENTAL 3972, 4280, 5063

SENTIMENTALIST 12460, 12797

SENTIMENTALITY 6829, 7121

SENTIMENTS 5024, 8152, 11558

SENTINEL 4156, 6952

SEPARATE 1578, 4775, 7109

SEPARATELY 3605

SEPARATENESS 3665

SEPARATES 1689

SEPARATION 1861, 9262, 10654

SEPARATISM 3678
SEPULCHRE 2355
SEQUEL 113, 657
SEQUESTERED 4252
SERAPHIM 7490, 7673
SERENE 12720
SERENITY 193, 3581, 8137, 8900
SERGE 7030
SERIOUS 665, 2270, 2372, 2733, 3562, 4305, 4422, 4889, 10484, 11924
SERIOUS-MINDED 7789
SERIOUSIST 2757
SERIOUSLY 4818, 6103
SERMON 1508, 8550, 8559, 9268, 10508
SERMONS 1964, 10025
SERPENT 1221, 4464, 7502, 7610, 10066, 10582
SERVANT 410, 2728, 4222, 7599, 10094, 10539, 10698, 10721, 11723
SERVANTS 733, 872, 1481, 6213, 7669, 12013
SERVE 61, 1170, 1939, 5270, 6544, 7516, 7594, 7676, 7828, 9909, 10771, 12249, 12733
SERVED 10185, 12637
SERVES 12058
SERVICE 3139, 5601, 8408, 8618, 8754, 10866, 10952, 11020
SERVICES 1438, 2855, 12371
SERVING 10721
SERVING-MEN 5654
SERVITORS 7384
SESAME 465
SESSIONS 10462
SETTING 4438
SETTLE 3585, 5504, 5659, 6709
SETTLED 10660
SETTLEMENTS 4936
SETTLERS 6205, 12350
SEVEN 247, 671, 2813, 3579, 3937, 5174, 6131, 10030
SEVENTEEN 11594
SEVENTIES 11085
SEVENTY 442, 4660
SEVER 708, 10600
SEVERE 2060, 4117, 5568
SEVERED 7619
SEVERITY 735
SEW 1614
SEWER 4428, 6134, 7711, 12096
SEWING 1582

SEX 148, 150, 157, 452, 672, 818, 864, 1737, 2466, 2530, 2540, 2643, 2895, 3087, 3573, 4304, 4507, 4741, 4811, 6025, 6049, 6241, 6383, 6385, 6609, 6800, 6956, 7281, 7345, 7848, 8058, 8246, 9409, 9751, 9851, 10676, 10854, 11300, 12097, 12147
SEXES 2470, 4600, 10796, 12767
SEXLESS 12533
SEXTON 4689
SEXUAL 3623, 4199, 4267, 6228, 10970
SEXUALLY 367
SHACKLES 1015, 4102, 9596
SHADES 4112
SHADOW 1420, 3209, 3280, 3296, 5225, 5299, 7595, 8177, 10287, 10916, 10927, 11333, 11473, 11971
SHADOWS 6121, 10337, 11543, 11968
SHAFT 9461, 9943, 11405
SHAKE 3967, 12677
SHAKEN 3505, 10474
SHAKESPEARE 1957, 3842, 4443, 4809, 4870, 5080, 5182, 5209, 6032, 6043, 6650, 7464, 7671, 8263, 8859, 12119, 12735
SHAKING 7754
SHALLOW 252, 2085, 7641, 10433, 12461, 12463
SHAMBLES 3733
SHAME 2505, 3828, 5023, 6591, 7546, 10141, 10152, 10476, 12241
SHAMEFUL 5840
SHAMELESS 1771, 4035
SHANKS 478
SHAPE 816, 2278, 7520, 7550, 7551, 12282
SHAPED 2037
SHAPES 10336
SHARE 2124, 2179, 4754, 10658, 10942, 11933
SHARED 1693
SHARES 3946
SHARING 9793, 10835
SHARK 5690
SHARPENED 1954
SHAVE 2699, 12360
SHE 1561, 4320, 12604
SHEARS 7476, 10797
SHEATH 4523
SHEBA 10654, 12602
SHED 1224, 5963, 10207

SHEEP 97, 1151, 1174, 1415, 1429, 2318, 2929, 4455, 4908, 7489, 7883, 8527, 11019, 12193, 12736
SHEEP-HERDING 8915
SHEET 11581
SHELF LIFE 11773
SHELL 305
SHELLED 411
SHELTER 12200
SHELTERED 7920
SHELTERLESS 2535
SHEPHERD 526, 1151, 1419, 4275, 4528, 7457
SHEPHERDS 11343, 12082, 12105
SHERIDAN 9471
SHERIFF 6921
SHERRY 8721
SHIELD 227, 6578
SHIFTED 10563
SHILLING 6097, 8955
SHILLINGS 4292
SHINE 1167, 8223, 10463, 11262
SHINING 7020, 11964
SHIP 1842, 4520, 5059, 5633, 6417, 7065, 8064, 8079, 12623
SHIPS 93, 909, 3781, 4297, 6451, 6926, 11635
SHIPWRECK 699
SHIRAZ 1365
SHIRE 2976, 5606
SHIRK 11861
SHIRT 3945
SHIVER 1042
SHOCK 819, 2604, 3955, 4482, 7050, 9318, 10537, 11660
SHOCKING 8887
SHOCKS 8405, 9700
SHOE 10005
SHOEMAKER 47
SHOES 1216, 2110, 3285, 4108, 6656, 9965, 10438, 11587
SHOESTRING 12665
SHOOK 7818, 9343
SHOOT 403, 973, 2226, 2510, 3302, 4385, 4573, 4905, 8937, 10666, 11632, 12418, 12493
SHOOTING 8301, 9197
SHOOTS 11969
SHOPKEEPERS 8010
SHOPOCRACY 8219
SHOPPING 806, 4001, 7334

SHORE 5892, 6432, 7442, 10466
SHORT 1411, 4590, 5128, 8048, 8186, 8612, 11369
SHORT-LIVED 977
SHORTAGE 1119
SHORTCOMING 260, 6259
SHORTEN 1199, 1855
SHORTER 312, 3243, 8486, 9236
SHORTEST 2755, 9051, 9439
SHORTHAND 11733
SHORTNESS 10154
SHOT 2226, 3334, 6414, 6921, 9325, 9335
SHOULD 1802
SHOULDER-BLADE 3962
SHOULDERS 4736, 8117, 10890
SHOUT 4905, 12095
SHOUTED 5628
SHOVEL 9778
SHOW 676, 1078, 3430, 6368, 6680, 7337, 12186, 12608
SHOW BUSINESS 12097
SHOWED 5291
SHOWER 1556, 6644, 8333
SHOWERS 5964
SHOWERY 3257
SHOWING 146
SHRAPNEL 12397
SHREDS 10132
SHRIEKS 8876
SHRIMP 5561
SHRINES 4289
SHROUD 5443
SHRUG 11264
SHRUNK 10198
SHUFFLED 6384, 10125
SHUN 10238
SHUNTING 1829
SHUT 5687, 5975, 8791, 10410
SHUTTER 11544
SHUTTING 5460
SHUTTLE 11965
SHY 11366
SICILY 7336
SICK 3044, 3306, 5117, 5557, 5871, 8043, 8970, 10227, 10301, 10414, 10853, 11436, 11477, 11631, 11658, 11978, 12627
SICKER 4856
SICKLE 6446
SICKNESS 5895, 8761

SICKROOM 3830

SIDE 446, 620, 1852, 1867, 4337, 6283, 6523, 6773, 7302, 8629, 11843, 12562, 12645

SIDE-FALL 5349

SIDEARMS 4097

SIDEWAYS 2693

SIEVE 6092, 6093

SIGH 530, 4826, 8848, 10044, 11959

SIGHED 11636

SIGHS 10015

SIGHT 876, 3901, 5487, 5606, 6074, 10220, 11403, 11601, 12680

SIGHTED 7069

SIGN 154, 9187, 9231

SIGNAL 6451, 8073

SIGNALS 8064, 11308

SIGNATURE 3490

SIGNATURES 12516

SIGNIFICANCE 920, 931, 3891

SIGNIFY 11949

SIGNPOSTS 6240

SIGNS 1148, 2333, 11729, 12647

SILENCE 705, 1876, 2085, 2234, 2736, 3062, 3164, 4132, 4343, 4380, 4851, 4855, 5062, 5216, 5462, 6433, 6451, 6892, 7130, 7250, 7393, 7912, 8477, 9156, 9555, 9566, 9567, 10145, 10513, 10519, 10684, 10809, 11115, 11271, 11424, 11869, 12007

SILENCED 7910

SILENCING 7297

SILENT 551, 1980, 2374, 3845, 4121, 4445, 5369, 5725, 6684, 6685, 7076, 8153, 9088, 9553, 9777, 11155, 11822, 12717

SILENTLY 6421, 6426

SILK 4542, 9035

SILK-WORM 7276

SILLIER 2143

SILLIEST 5673, 9447

SILLY 670, 1304, 4729, 6073, 9436

SILVER 1115, 3534, 7410, 7491, 8244

SIMILAR 3194

SIMILIES 8959, 10146, 12683

SIMPLE 592, 3274, 3995, 4413, 8198, 8493, 8949, 12485, 12734

SIMPLEST 4387

SIMPLICITIES 2291

SIMPLICITY 5196, 8813

SIMPLIFY 2942, 11685

SIMPLY 11676

SIMULTANEOUSLY 8316

SIN 1033, 1149, 1202, 1417, 1649, 1727, 1949, 2032, 2416, 2658, 2954, 2988, 3025, 5290, 5410, 5693, 6379, 7628, 7735, 8285, 9147, 9323, 9605, 9744, 10215, 10411, 10530, 10888

SINCE 11906

SINCERE 3338, 5823, 9380, 11817

SINCERELY 12163

SINCERITY 1505, 7180, 8900, 9579, 10719, 12496

SINEWS 12139

SINEWY 6453

SINFUL 940, 8139

SING 1428, 3038, 4524, 5404, 9123, 9556, 10777, 11482, 12018, 12406, 12411

SINGE 10182

SINGEING 2972

SINGER 437, 4024, 7926

SINGERS 7867, 9573

SINGING 1477, 4746, 5944, 9847, 9848, 10624, 12645

SINGLE 661, 776, 4153, 4341, 6484

SINGLES 1105

SINGS 3770, 7321

SINGULARITY 2953

SINK 163, 7949, 8325

SINKS 2825

SINNED 2473

SINNER 1157, 6581, 8546

SINNERS 1177, 9633, 10127, 11091

SINNING 9020, 9633

SINS 1421, 2064, 4880, 6667, 9691, 10166, 10292, 10353, 10716, 11794, 12252

SION 1432

SIP 3855

SIPPING 12717

SIRE 7312

SIRENS 7672

SISSY 8723

SISTER 7825

SISTERHOOD 7889

SISTERS 3926, 5660, 9388

SIT 1033, 3140, 3205, 4488, 4809, 5655, 6456, 8219, 11876, 11948, 12270, 12683

SITS 9230

SITTING 5645, 5952, 7425

SITUATION 5164

SITWELLS	6106
SIX HUNDRED	11392
SIXPENCE	9217
SIXTEEN	11762
SIXTIES	6226, 7960
SIXTY	3187, 3859
SIXTY FOUR	6171
SIZE	3155, 6830
SKATING	3342
SKELETON	933, 6808
SKIES	6060, 10495, 11472
SKILL	334, 2667, 2767, 3832, 7931, 9642
SKILLED	903
SKIN	80, 97, 1228, 1230, 1267, 5916, 9052, 12546
SKIP	3478
SKIP-WORTHY	543
SKIRMISH	4242
SKITTLES	2010
SKUGG	3599
SKULL	3233
SKUNK	6278
SKY	613, 2686, 3212, 3300, 3473, 7947, 9236, 11323, 11662, 12477
SKYE	1473
SKYLINE	9304
SKYSCRAPERS	908, 4551
SLAB	8035
SLAG-HEAP	2968
SLAIN	2984, 6856
SLAMMING	996, 8336
SLANDER	5190, 11894
SLANG	1734, 9774
SLANTED	7143
SLAP	9620
SLASH	2510
SLASHING	11552
SLAUGHTERED	8085
SLAUGHTEROUS	10286
SLAVE	171, 1400, 1557, 2031, 2497, 3767, 6186, 6280, 6299, 7308, 8850
SLAVE-MORALITY	8185
SLAVERY	2621, 3997, 6753, 9993, 11133
SLAVES	1269, 2589, 5593, 7152, 7649, 8677, 11629, 12178
SLAY	6641, 6773
SLAYS	8897
SLEEP	151, 335, 589, 1611, 1724, 1925, 2354, 4434, 4682, 4856, 5194, 5453, 6110, 7067, 7175, 7406, 7584, 7588, 7800, 7861,

	8766, 9129, 9239, 9268, 9404, 9690, 10076, 10099, 10125, 10187, 10267, 10294, 10469, 10874, 10925, 11272, 11387, 11603, 12008, 12205, 12710, 12838
SLEEPING	600, 2196, 8083, 8169, 10268, 11590, 12213
SLEEPLESS	8766, 9569, 12736
SLEEPS	6980, 7855, 9092, 10095
SLEEVES	6615, 9774
SLEIGH	1082
SLEPT	7202, 8508, 11487
SLICE	12614
SLIMY	2421
SLINGS	10124
SLIP	4394
SLIPPED	4623
SLIPPERS	1614
SLIPPERY	12534
SLIPPING	6526
SLIT	5621
SLOGANS	1059
SLOP	10808
SLOP-PAIL	4706
SLOPPY	11808
SLOTH	7540, 10091
SLOUGH	1104, 1721
SLOVENLINESS	1531
SLOW	347, 1243, 6277, 6358, 9945, 10007
SLOW DOWN	9866
SLOWEST	5006, 10017
SLOWLY	624, 6886, 11188, 11446
SLUGGARD	12198
SLUM	105
SLUMBER	5174, 7859, 12741
SLUMBERED	10337
SLUT	3800
SMALL	518, 5318, 7301, 7636, 9128, 11216
SMALL TALK	7921
SMALL-ENDIANS	11240
SMALLER	200, 4382, 4404, 8437
SMALLEST	9346
SMALLPOX	9054
SMART	6009, 6613
SMART-ASSES	8744
SMARTED	6047
SMARTER	571, 3525
SMARTS	8792
SMASH	4345
SMASHED	3483

SMELL   2126, 3089, 5579, 6132, 9438, 9571, 10282, 10470, 11990

SMELLS   10174

SMELT   5721

SMILE   314, 324, 534, 2163, 2248, 4873, 5973, 9936, 12673

SMILED   5934

SMILES   1352, 1619, 2734, 5366, 7452, 8799

SMILY   6516

SMITE   1168

SMITH   4657

SMITHY   5271, 6453

SMOKE   850, 3170, 4370, 4397, 5374, 5634, 7401, 7925

SMOKED   5186, 5721, 11747

SMOKING   1465

SMOOTH   10327

SNAFFLE   2019

SNAKE   3450, 6040, 12040

SNAPPED   5294

SNAPPER-UP   10444

SNARE   11024

SNARES   8551

SNARL   3424

SNATCH   10354

SNEAK   5732

SNEAKY   8132

SNEER   8417

SNEERING   3948

SNEEZE   6030

SNIGGER   3457

SNOB   1689, 6602

SNOBBERY   11926

SNOBBISH   6398

SNOBS   106

SNORE   10091

SNORTED   2913

SNOTGREEN   5273

SNOW   1441, 2015, 2410, 4739, 5257, 5624, 7996, 8050, 8051, 9701, 10249, 12748

SNOW-LEOPARD   6029

SNOW-WHITE   12309, 12806

SNOWFLAKES   5479

SNOWS   12014

SNOWY   3257

SNUFF   2428, 4139

SNUFFED   9367

SNUG   969, 2772, 3599

SOAP   1737, 4916, 9225, 11888

SOAPBOXES   6459

SOAR   1776, 6772

SOARING   10624

SOBBED   3968

SOBER   3507, 4491, 7412, 7437, 7761, 10773, 11905, 11936

SOBERING   855, 6133

SOBERS   8815

SOCIAL   1881, 3664, 8322, 10939

SOCIALISM   1113, 2741, 3041, 8323, 10820, 11644, 12004

SOCIALIST   7940, 8322, 8324

SOCIETIES   6834, 12386, 12760

SOCIETY   44, 295, 492, 832, 1012, 1918, 1965, 2160, 3629, 3828, 4269, 5022, 5492, 5515, 5619, 6063, 6679, 6838, 6853, 7011, 7151, 7213, 7291, 7309, 7611, 7873, 8001, 9533, 9833, 9857, 10969, 10973, 11064, 11175, 11325, 11565, 11719, 12168, 12375, 12629, 12689, 12726

SOCKS   4178

SOCRATES   209, 8699

SODS   12620

SOFA   2594, 8722

SOFT   1241, 6086, 8584

SOFTNESS   6491, 7574

SOIL   7530, 11323

SOJOURN   629

SOJOURNER   12351

SOLACE   9994, 10711

SOLAR   2073

SOLD   1440, 2449, 11500

SOLDIER   3, 3353, 3394, 5103, 5700, 5708, 7366, 8408, 8467, 10078, 10291, 10532, 10534, 11048

SOLDIERS   423, 853, 3517, 5983, 7230, 9247, 9646, 9846

SOLE   12151

SOLECISM   1601

SOLICITING   10256

SOLICITOR   2874, 3914

SOLID   2228

SOLIDITY   8328

SOLITARY   1846, 5133, 7017

SOLITUDE   1625, 1918, 2491, 3147, 4243, 6506, 7011, 7091, 7130, 7607, 7611, 7739, 8212, 8521, 9004, 9416, 9772, 11012, 11666, 11709, 11946, 12727

SOLITUDES   9414

SOLOMON   2858, 5686, 8049, 10654

SOLUTION   2162, 7040, 10689

SOLUTIONS   6197

SOMEBODY   1519, 3922, 4189, 6970, 9497

SOMEONE   3335, 5925, 9472, 12558

SOMERSET HOUSE   10743

SOMETHING   1866, 2439, 3114, 3663, 7374, 11976, 12334, 12558

SOMETIMES   9230

SOMEWHERE   2115, 4371, 10580

SON   1236, 2990, 3237, 3879, 7484, 8963

SON-IN-LAW   9116

SONG   437, 1428, 2670, 3097, 3474, 3994, 4080, 4193, 4465, 5607, 6415, 7062, 7497, 8253, 9082, 9567, 9848, 10723, 11486, 11613

SONGS   5437, 8959, 9556, 10626

SONNET   5901, 8895, 9563

SONS   4835, 6812, 8257

SOON   9182

SOONER   644

SOONEST   10886

SOOTHE   2486

SOOTHES   8125

SOOTHSAYING   6269

SOPHISTICATION   6833

SOPHISTRY   691

SOPORIFIC   8902

SORBONNE   11059

SORDELLO   8918

SORE   2401, 6973

SOREST   9932

SORRINESS   4381

SORROW   601, 1214, 1222, 1358, 1981, 2339, 3250, 3512, 4803, 4929, 5443, 5445, 5674, 6396, 6425, 6815, 6855, 7092, 7482, 7913, 8447, 10063, 10233, 10392, 10856, 11213, 11336, 11442, 11483, 11740

SORROWS   6068, 9328, 10138, 10759, 11372

SORRY   1069, 1372, 5058, 6039, 8274, 9963, 10211, 11742

SOT   7960

SOUGHT   894, 9909

SOUL   90, 304, 425, 1164, 1393, 1413, 1629, 2067, 2176, 2348, 2414, 2704, 2793, 2795, 2821, 3010, 3310, 3994, 4326, 5127, 5224, 5239, 5247, 5257, 5427, 5459, 5468, 5960, 6140, 6440, 6585, 6928, 6930, 7015, 7061, 7231, 7387, 7465, 7629, 7739, 7786, 7804, 7855, 8637, 8653, 8762, 8788, 8837, 9249, 9503, 9563, 9805, 9863, 9940, 10175, 10221, 10370, 10570, 10581, 10749, 10893, 11471, 11506, 11703, 11756, 11762, 11919, 11948, 11966

SOULS   2404, 2914, 3238, 3894, 4078, 5671, 6484, 8785, 9562, 10772, 10825, 10961, 11078, 12783

SOUND   359, 4343, 5197, 7923, 8084, 8820, 8979, 10816, 11389, 12417, 12736

SOUNDED   10918

SOUNDS   2118, 5889, 6612, 8228, 9456, 11859

SOUP   1460, 9114

SOUR   10368

SOURCE   2023, 11176

SOUREST   10470

SOUTH   1442, 6029, 6653

SOUTH AFRICAN   10485

SOUTHERLY   10121

SOVEREIGN   733, 796, 1459, 3236, 11701, 12101

SOVEREIGNTY   2192, 7265

SOVIET   6155

SOW   5267, 7958, 9329

SOWN   1225

SOWS   11118, 11272

SPACE   1523, 1548, 3143, 3732, 3895, 4372, 4761, 5967, 7329, 10060, 11000, 12673

SPADE   1627, 1836, 5205

SPAGHETTI   7900

SPAIN   6194, 11517, 11518

SPANIARDS   752, 2970

SPANISH   7057

SPANKING   3081

SPARE   1239, 1893, 3997

SPARED   11265

SPARKLE   11390, 11504

SPARKLES   5365

SPARKS   1234, 10092

SPARTANS   10685

SPAT   12089

SPEAK   161, 1229, 1301, 2944, 3327, 3361, 4477, 5211, 5777, 5844, 6007, 6979, 7076, 8599, 9021, 10035, 10042, 10209, 10224, 10228, 10352, 10857, 10883, 11102, 11671

SPEAKER   2804, 4511

SPEAKERS   3326

SPEAKING   3714, 9197

SPEAKS   6122, 7783, 9165, 11995

SPEAR   1345, 7487, 7517

SPEARS   1936

SPECIALIST   3465

SPECIALITY   6455

SPECIALIZED   7070

SPECIES   4958, 7919

SPECIFICATION	12164
SPECTACLE	12522
SPECTATOR	4858, 12458
SPECTATORS	4713
SPECTRE	7045, 10727
SPECULATOR	11156
SPEECH	741, 2085, 3164, 3249, 3526, 4109, 4229, 4460, 4587, 4830, 5571, 5800, 5835, 6892, 7250, 8024, 8349, 8661, 9520, 9931, 10223, 10489, 10619, 10646, 10978, 11474, 12075
SPEECHES	1703, 2243, 4819, 10933
SPEECHLESS	2378
SPEED	1473, 3342, 4563, 4842, 8002
SPELL	9435, 9481, 11895
SPELLER	12154
SPELLING	7364, 7375, 7689
SPEND	4953, 5539
SPENDER	2326, 3670
SPENDING	725, 6207
SPENDTHRIFT	9865
SPENSER	5946
SPENT	3587, 5114, 7669, 11441
SPERMATOZOA	4870
SPHERE	7604
SPHERES	6927, 8511, 11971
SPHERICAL	6095
SPICE	2597, 10490
SPICY	7461
SPIDER	4760, 8836
SPIDER'S WEB	9191
SPIDERS	307
SPIES	10138
SPIN	11451
SPINACH	74
SPINE	6876
SPINOZA	9806
SPINSTER	7700
SPIRES	6216
SPIRIT	523, 713, 1950, 2232, 3904, 4079, 4364, 4451, 5966, 6562, 7259, 7536, 10079, 10192, 10476, 10589, 10623, 10725, 10862, 11523, 12181, 12700, 12827
SPIRITS	5357, 5459, 7879, 10479, 11440, 12433
SPIRITUAL	1987, 2924, 5596, 7071, 7582, 8691, 10652
SPIRITUALISTS	11143
SPIT	12089, 12101
SPITEFUL	6030
SPITS	9774

SPLENDID	1600
SPLENDOUR	12715
SPOIL	1893
SPOILED	1660, 12857
SPOILS	6827, 6911
SPOKE	9220, 11825
SPOKEN	2718, 7683, 10605
SPONGY	5201
SPONTANEITY	168
SPOONFED	4318
SPOONS	3213, 3337, 10550
SPORT	2057, 2593, 4241, 4715, 7127, 7453, 8301, 8326, 9613, 10147, 10241, 10841, 11202
SPORTS	1583, 7199, 12169
SPORTSMAN	5764, 6085
SPOT	4382, 6190, 7401, 10280
SPOTS	1228, 9792, 11844
SPOUTS	7602
SPREAD	750, 11706
SPRING	1016, 1483, 1558, 3229, 3887, 5366, 6504, 8495, 8623, 10612, 11268, 11439, 11585, 12357, 12682
SPRINGING	701
SPRINGLIKE	2
SPRINGS	5193, 12684
SPUNK	6027
SPUR	2453, 7476, 9136, 10136, 10262
SPURN	1594, 3936
SPURTS	11975
SPY	4760, 6055
SQUADRONS	7359
SQUANDERING	2996, 9759
SQUARES	5994
SQUEAK	3831
SQUEEZE	5201
SQUEEZED	3831
SQUEEZING	4142
SQUELCHING	9588
SQUIRE	2779
SQUIRM	8436
SQUIRRELS	8294
ST ANDREWS	5949
ST JOHN	8830
ST NICHOLAS	7829
ST PAUL'S	6761
STAB	7176, 10208
STABBED	3770
STABILITY	5144
STABLE	5426

STAFF 9299, 10404

STAG 6227

STAGE 2568, 3023, 4138, 7464, 10030, 10167, 10245, 10287, 10434, 12523

STAGECOACH 2694, 4452

STAGES 6326, 9896, 10633

STAGNATION 1786

STAID 7436

STAIN 613, 3706

STAINED 8384

STAINS 10593

STAIR 685, 7156

STAIRS 7352

STAKE 7949, 8633

STALK 9053

STALKING 12766

STALKS 3773

STAMP 9710

STAMPED 7132, 11416

STAMPS 8135

STAND 1161, 2671, 4633, 4806, 6204, 6577, 6775, 6922, 6935, 7594, 7974, 9112, 9884, 10273, 11984, 12211

STANDARD 2490

STANDARDS 1036, 9513, 11127

STANDING 4749

STANDS 5585, 11281

STANZA 7141

STAR 2233, 2677, 2925, 6729, 7532, 7626, 8077, 9723, 10052, 11358, 11484, 12600

STAR-CROSSED 10382

STAR-LED 7485

STAR-SPANGLED 5542

STARDOM 680

STARDUST 7692

STARE 11458

STARLIT 12789

STARS 392, 395, 907, 5394, 5421, 5953, 6096, 6426, 6928, 6929, 6931, 7007, 7243, 7273, 7488, 7565, 8432, 8726, 8889, 9559, 9720, 10189, 10932, 11361, 11428, 11604, 11959, 11966, 12036, 12239, 12414, 12498

START 932, 2282, 6255

STARTER 571

STARTLE 5428

STARTLED 4662

STARVATION 4615, 9693

STARVE 10301

STARVED 5406

STARVING 2787, 2828

STATE 609, 1123, 1763, 2168, 2991, 3836, 3957, 4459, 5162, 6160, 6468, 6776, 7008, 7301, 7304, 7790, 8976, 10963, 11196, 11615, 12223, 12600

STATELY 4480, 7106

STATELY HOMES 12652

STATEMENT 1384, 8913, 11885

STATES 981, 5385, 5940

STATESMAN 10, 47, 1748, 2727, 2995, 4137, 6351, 6502, 8754, 11066, 11815, 12149, 12785

STATESMEN 2859, 12127

STATION 1103, 2779, 3820, 6607, 10913, 12536

STATIONARY 4295

STATISTICALLY 3754

STATISTICIANS 11692

STATISTICS 1499, 2369, 2850, 4719, 5948

STATUE 208, 4636, 8311

STATUES 262, 5983

STATURE 7244, 7774, 9853

STATUS 6834, 11382

STATUS QUO 10959

STAY 3384, 5919, 6704, 7630, 8439, 8950

STAYING 4771, 6837, 12543

STAYING UP 11016

STAYS 9859

STEAL 809, 1498, 2386, 3225, 5398, 7710, 7865, 8871, 9097, 9244

STEALING 9855

STEALS 10344

STEALTH 4951, 5911

STEAM 7925

STEAMER 3943

STEED 5404

STEEL 495, 7417, 9709

STEEPED 9419

STEER 157, 7077, 10507, 11648

STEERING 6526

STEIN 262

STENDHAL 3905

STEP 501, 656, 4263, 6345, 8020, 8406, 8628, 9732, 11679, 12774

STEP-MOTHER 7670

STEPHEN 8050

STEPPED IN 10274

STEPPING-STONES 11470

STEPS 6736, 7402

STERILIZED 4422

STERN 6742

SWEAT 2305, 2673, 8419, 9250, 11614

SWEATS 10149

SWEET 1238, 1562, 1636, 1948, 2353, 2640, 5196, 5364, 5463, 5465, 5875, 6002, 6389, 6558, 6923, 7581, 7857, 8124, 8125, 10358, 10388, 11505, 11594, 11602

SWEETEN 10282

SWEETENERS 3441

SWEETER 9418

SWEETEST 723, 1812, 9456, 10470

SWEETHEART 9168

SWEETLY 10456

SWEETNESS 512, 7465, 11231

SWEETS 2611

SWELL 8889

SWELLS 12577

SWEPT 631

SWIFT 1209, 4575, 11620

SWIFT-FLOWING 2144

SWIFTER 393

SWILL 8306

SWIM 8787, 9167, 11175

SWIMMING 4011, 12021, 12574

SWIMMING POOL 9386

SWINDLES 4498

SWING 400, 10817

SWINGS 8636

SWISH 187

SWISS 3417

SWITZERLAND 12264

SWOONS 5939

SWORD 1198, 1346, 1714, 1839, 2356, 4523, 4756, 5943, 6234, 6854, 6858, 7858, 8202, 9646, 12478, 12787

SWORDS 6493, 6946

SWORE 1834, 6482, 11040

SYLLABLE 10287

SYLLOGISM 8233

SYMBOL 1071, 2074, 5274

SYMMETRY 1357

SYMPATHETIC 7196

SYMPATHIZE 4868

SYMPATHIZER 8523

SYMPATHY 3871, 6023, 7921, 9380

SYMPTOM 3371

SYMPTOMS 404, 2175, 8853

SYNTAX 2631, 4653

SYSTEM 6058, 6673, 8013, 8405, 8832

SYSTEMATICALLY 12583

SYSTEMS 8059, 11469

TABLE 2643

TABOOS 3259

TACITURN 7699

TACT 274, 1876

TAIL 5338, 5637, 5650, 7494

TAILOR 3141, 4927

TAINT 10349

TAKE 822, 1407, 2409, 2614, 3527, 3668, 3717, 3836, 3855, 4159, 9732, 12159, 12240

TAKEN 1231, 2209, 8529, 11453

TAKEN IN 9876

TAKES 1985

TAKING 2517

TALE 6016, 7457, 9260, 9924, 10029, 10218, 10287

TALENT 102, 169, 852, 1020, 1086, 1711, 1791, 2204, 2561, 2966, 3115, 4088, 4857, 5175, 6497, 7252, 10768, 10835, 12473

TALENTED 8947

TALENTS 2427, 4046, 5294, 8772, 9372, 9764

TALES 5038

TALK 257, 440, 730, 755, 1461, 2110, 2222, 2439, 2860, 2920, 2994, 3054, 3094, 4331, 4481, 4601, 5025, 5119, 5632, 5684, 5695, 6328, 6827, 7096, 8168, 8556, 8684, 8967, 9021, 9091, 10214, 10513, 11931, 12165

TALKATIVE 2331

TALKED 2272, 3374, 4139, 12428, 12503

TALKER 9368

TALKERS 4473

TALKING 574, 1518, 2200, 4166, 4899, 5109, 5233, 5925, 6334, 7327, 8697, 9032, 11207

TALKS 589

TALLER 4752

TAMBOURINE 3097

TAME 4519

TAMED 7019

TANGERINE 6726

TANGLE 12765

TANGLED 5279, 6475, 7635

TAPER 5374

TAPPED 2264

TARADIDDLES 6148

TARGET 2622

TARRED 6294

TARRY 4545

TARTS 6715

TARZAN 12256

TERRIBLE 3438, 6129, 10883, 11588

TERRIFIES 8477

TERRITORY 7331

TERROR 901, 1328, 1372, 2243, 2513, 4265, 5268, 6722, 6826, 7130, 9515, 10485, 11765, 12264

TERRORIST 11563

TERRORS 469, 3796

TEST 13, 965, 3723, 4399, 8040, 11346, 11767, 12324

TESTAMENT 1319, 10365

TESTED 11765

TESTING 6242

THAMES 1101, 1795, 7925, 11597, 12123

THANK 8071, 10394, 11356, 12229

THANKED 1572, 1816, 3451

THANKFUL 2570, 9478, 9558, 11851

THANKLESS 10230

THANKS 1431, 1433, 1699, 2145, 2873, 9433

THAT 7052

THAW 10102

THEATRE 101, 703, 1584, 3794, 4324, 4918, 7332, 9883, 9899, 11907

THEATRICAL 3301

THEE 4525, 5718

THEFT 3150, 8984

THEIST 677

THEME 10991

THEMSELVES 95, 4101, 12633

THEOLOGY 7903

THEORIES 5671

THEORIZE 2962

THEORY 2865, 3126, 4081, 4829, 8906, 11127

THERAPEUTIC 5731

THERAPIST 2052, 4732

THERAPY 6052, 12137

THERE 152, 279, 2354, 6851, 7156, 10992, 12761

THEREAFTER 5537

THEREFORE 2753

THERMODYNAMICS 3102

THERMOMETER 4638

THEY 5626

THICKENS 12012

THIEF 769, 2484, 2703, 7570, 7680, 10181, 12471, 12840

THIEVES 925, 2245

THIEVISH 7408

THIN 2494, 2503, 4025, 8311

THING 214, 1798, 2187, 6312, 8537, 8576, 9069, 11368

THINGS 1187, 3109, 3930, 5897, 7303, 7365, 8598, 8890, 9835, 11618, 12446

THINK 477, 1094, 2693, 2753, 2764, 2994, 3065, 3138, 3185, 3571, 4735, 4787, 4850, 4891, 5119, 5683, 5777, 5798, 5896, 6025, 6066, 6203, 6210, 6460, 6961, 7655, 8041, 8639, 8782, 9075, 9671, 9711, 10190, 10439, 10532, 10583, 10715, 10812, 10958, 11022, 11097, 11161, 11317, 11897, 11992, 12032, 12104, 12559, 12575, 12799

THINKER 2695, 5481

THINKING 2696, 2886, 3131, 3303, 3928, 4601, 4669, 4925, 5116, 5746, 6546, 7171, 8016, 8480, 8697, 8945, 9308, 9535, 9611, 9616, 10119, 10137, 10960, 12286

THINKS 394, 446, 5072, 5326, 6584, 8816, 9230

THINNER 6102, 6145

THIRD REICH 9337

THIRD-RATE 936

THIRST 5666, 9270, 9379, 11239

THIRTEEN 11831

THIRTY 427, 522, 2375, 3063, 7911

THIS 7052

THOMAS 670

THORN 4002, 5677, 7572, 9164

THORNS 10610

THORNTON WILDER 5328

THOROUGHNESS 6254

THOUGHT 37, 165, 229, 818, 1638, 1659, 2329, 2559, 2885, 3007, 3086, 3659, 3666, 3757, 4211, 4365, 4460, 4476, 4787, 5124, 5508, 5571, 5753, 5926, 5982, 6211, 6909, 7289, 8170, 8349, 8420, 8508, 8735, 8787, 8817, 8828, 8945, 9303, 9669, 9915, 10062, 10126, 10165, 10281, 10619, 11057, 11292, 11309, 11474, 11523, 11632, 12075, 12373, 12426, 12573

THOUGHTS 637, 5032, 5416, 5431, 6362, 6365, 6435, 6982, 7415, 7677, 7974, 8401, 8500, 9436, 9673, 10131, 10839, 10905, 11447, 11510, 11962, 12244, 12352, 12716

THOUSAND 1474, 2737, 11560

THOUSANDS 8810, 8897

THRALL 5405

THREAD 634, 8836, 10251, 11123

THREADS 10676

THREAT 3053, 7421

THREE 296, 1479, 2116, 2850, 3653, 3951, 3953, 6119, 6181, 7367

THREE-FOURTHS 513

THREE-PIPE 2956

THREE-SIDED 7814

THRESHOLD 12108

THRICE 10574

THRILLING 9502

THRIVE 2366, 6359

THROAT 983, 3661, 5621, 6537, 8351, 12785

THROATS 659, 4134

THRONE 3589, 5691, 6524, 7535, 8671, 10068, 10360

THRONES 7596

THROUGH 87, 3641, 4162, 4400, 4989, 11691, 12038

THROW 924, 986, 4646, 8588

THROWN 4349, 7052

THRUST 4469, 10431

THUMB 2156, 10277

THUMBSCREW 11518

THUMP 11582

THUNDER 5664, 5951, 7555, 9178, 9504, 10723, 11582

THUNDERBOLT 8713, 11397

THUNDERSTORM 4965, 6894

THURSDAY 7323

THUS 12156

THWACKUM 3434

THYME 7473

THYROID 7893

THYSELF 3292, 5238, 9102

TIBER 6778, 8940, 12033

TICK 12764

TICKET 1126, 6719

TICKLED 8844

TICKY-TACKY 9376

TIDE 1449, 1826, 1960, 7066, 10213, 11584

TIDILY 8376

TIE 7109, 9063

TIED 11323

TIGER 314, 985, 1357, 10169, 11812

TIGERS 2286, 9131, 11053

TILE 6575, 8337

TILLER 7766

TILLING 11194

TILT 1106

TIMBUCTOO 12434

TIME 6, 110, 272, 283, 376, 631, 632, 724, 742, 1087, 1207, 1418, 1513, 1601, 1826, 2165, 2463, 2871, 2879, 2891, 2926, 3030, 3077, 3108, 3189, 3598, 3882, 3903, 4009, 4191, 4212, 4225, 4354, 4544, 4826, 4913, 5202, 5741, 5744, 5864, 5872, 5977, 6009, 6042, 6196, 6310, 6406, 6441, 6725, 6882, 6886, 6891, 6894, 6895, 7200, 7374, 7492, 7580, 7680, 7720, 7819, 7927, 7993, 8182, 8230, 8338, 8374, 8451, 8457, 8461, 8723, 8738, 8924, 8934, 8991, 8997, 9144, 9157, 9171, 9181, 9240, 9293, 9652, 9950, 9996, 10114, 10154, 10196, 10216, 10257, 10339, 10368, 10369, 10372, 10416, 10419, 10453, 10472, 10491, 10696, 10709, 10858, 10898, 11094, 11163, 11359, 11373, 11450, 11478, 11504, 11579, 11628, 11681, 11686, 11971, 12045, 12086, 12281, 12353, 12471, 12539, 12545, 12812, 12823, 12840

TIME-TABLE 7117

TIMELINESS 5782

TIMES 17, 310, 793, 2342, 8408, 10887, 11317, 12067, 12089, 12814

TIMING 3492, 11805

TING-A-LING 421

TINGE 3882

TINKER 6727, 10653

TINKERING 3123

TINY 5317

TIP 11110

TIP-TOE 5463

TIPPERARY 5289, 12532

TIRE 9250

TIRED 655, 825, 1366, 1899, 4683, 5101, 6001, 8845, 9503, 9623

TIRESOME 12080

TIRING 4809, 7702

TITANIA 10330

TITANIC 7946

TITLE 2161, 2715, 8412, 12657

TITLED 8531

TITLES 10596, 10948

TITS 10694

TITWILLOW 3967, 3968

TO-MORROW 8068, 10287

TOAD 4228, 5670, 5990, 5991, 7585, 10025, 10346, 12049

TOAST 8260, 8519

TOASTED 263

TOBACCO 5187, 5891, 5907, 7717, 11747

TOBACCONIST 5186

TODAY 78, 1613, 3111, 3327, 3703, 6849, 6984, 8380, 9627, 12819, 12831

TOES 6099

TOGETHER 4403, 5479, 5733, 6170, 6724, 8146, 9357, 9737, 9901, 10600, 11515, 11744, 11912

TOGETHERNESS 3895

TOIL	5774, 6522, 7175,	TORY	266, 1112, 5116
9753, 10275, 12361		TOSSED	1461
TOILET	9883	TOTAL	82, 4039
TOILING	6434	TOTALITARIANISM	3766
TOLD	1356, 1962, 5652,	TOTEM	6722
10430		TOUCH	282, 7807, 10173,
TOLERANCE	2180, 4103, 6225,	11389	
12593		TOUCHED	6681, 11487
TOLERANT	6411, 12452	TOUCHES	12409
TOLERATE	9337	TOUCHING	11440
TOLERATES	1869	TOUCHSTONE	5514
TOLLS	2912	TOUGH	5528
TOMB	362, 9776, 9858,	TOUGHER	11958
10768, 11581		TOUGHEST	1077
TOMBSTONE	5668, 6438	TOUJOURS	6967
TOMMY	5694	TOULOUSE	7254
TOMORROW	1226, 1613, 1830,	TOURIST	961, 5578, 10850
2903, 3327, 4725, 5487, 6210, 6984, 7697, 9192,		TOURNAMENT	1105
9627, 12216, 12831		TOWER	8498
TOMORROWS	3111, 9846, 12676	TOWERED	7462
TONE	5436	TOWERS	519
TONGUE	275, 1198, 2189, 3360,	TOWERY	4707
3574, 4132, 4922, 6174, 8509, 9008, 9091, 9113,		TOWN	2595, 4747, 6411,
10104, 10252, 10933, 11336, 12835		6989, 7352, 7367, 7894, 12348	
TONGUES	7600, 7621, 10025	TOWNS	1379
TONIGHT	8018	TOY	6939
TONNAGE	7336	TOYS	2584, 3514, 6604,
TOOK	2066	8845, 11100	
TOOL	3101	TOYSHOP	7917
TOOLS	1888, 2310, 6522,	TRACES	223
11833		TRACK	11642
TOOTH	1218, 9008, 9162,	TRADE	2590, 3017, 3028,
11465		4513, 4897, 5633, 5825, 6841, 10733, 11092	
TOOTH-POINT	5670	TRADE UNIONISM	10551
TOOTHACHE	8091, 10051, 10095	TRADE UNIONIST	1124
TOOTHPASTE	4328	TRADES	4992, 9929
TOP	6384, 8895, 9393,	TRADITION	893, 2072, 2224, 2605
12230, 12757		TRADITIONS	473
TOP-BOOTS	9823	TRAGEDIES	10553, 11146
TORCH	5452, 5519, 6561,	TRAGEDY	55, 863, 1785, 1955,
6634, 10384		2077, 3480, 4392, 4453, 5350, 5503, 5759, 6026,	
TORIES	303, 1459, 1612, 5018,	6802, 7043, 7081, 7914, 8266, 8601, 11149, 12116,	
6742		12388, 12488	
TORMENT	820, 2685, 5409, 5775,	TRAGIC	6022, 7241, 9614
7173		TRAGICALLY	6022
TORMENTOR	11738	TRAIL	5598
TORMENTS	2328, 7541, 7988	TRAIN	160, 1103, 1247, 3859,
TORN	9089, 10914	4858, 6526, 7581, 11642, 12263, 12360, 12491	
TORONTONIAN	966	TRAINED	6243, 7090
TORRENT	4012	TRAINING	1066, 1277, 3610, 7922
TORRID	2061	TRAIT	3386, 12584
TORTURE	1929, 5072, 7257,	TRAITORS	10279
7346, 8110			
TORTURED	1372		

TRAMP 1478, 4402, 7145, 10954
TRAMPLE 11528, 11963
TRANCE 10590
TRANQUILIZE 10581
TRANQUILLITY 3286, 5046, 8447, 11690, 12705
TRANQUILLIZERS 6197
TRANSACTION 11561
TRANSCENDENT 7505
TRANSCENDENTAL 3971
TRANSFERRED 3539
TRANSFORMATION 637, 2729
TRANSFORMED 12455
TRANSFORMING 3369
TRANSGRESSING 412
TRANSGRESSION 1143
TRANSITORY 12678
TRANSLATE 2745
TRANSLATION 11295, 12338
TRANSLATOR 9232
TRANSMIT 12430
TRANSMUTATION 8119, 11375
TRANSPORT 12738
TRANSPORTED 11758
TRAPEZE 6261
TRAPPINGS 10101
TRASH 9857
TRAVEL 761, 1019, 1098, 1289, 3272, 3328, 3402, 4185, 9290, 9394, 11030, 11090, 11120, 11173, 11871, 12645
TRAVELLED 279, 918, 5385, 10633, 10910, 11668, 12745
TRAVELLER 779, 4858, 5353, 5857, 6429, 6761, 7408, 10096, 10613, 10620, 11227, 12720
TRAVELLERS 281, 10022
TRAVELLING 1789, 3718
TRAVELS 3042, 5691, 7836
TREACHEROUS 5826
TREAD 7426, 8827, 12816
TREADING 2106
TREASON 368, 2378, 2404, 2840, 3022, 3215, 4390, 10139, 10320
TREASURE 986, 3919, 7229, 10356
TREASURED 7389
TREASURES 1406, 5958
TREASURY 5551
TREAT 4056, 6850
TREATED 6793
TREATMENT 856, 7217, 12607
TREATY 3516

TREE 1337, 1981, 5363, 5575, 5576, 5719, 6089, 7570, 7916, 7920, 8041, 8812, 9143, 9184, 11229, 11323, 11467
TREE-TOPS 1082
TREES 509, 1251, 1599, 4488, 5617, 5677, 7571, 9504, 10457, 11599, 11758
TRELAWNY 4412
TREMBLE 8788
TREMBLING 5152, 5376
TRENCHES 10454
TRESSES 8874
TRIAL 3711, 5321, 6304, 7391
TRIALS 8356
TRIANGLE 315
TRIANGLES 7814
TRIBAL 5669
TRIBE 1264, 10352
TRIBES 1965
TRIBUNAL 1666
TRIBUTE 9936
TRICK 838, 996, 5794, 10156
TRICKS 5132, 10290
TRIED 1028, 1860, 2249, 2280, 6300, 8756, 10512, 12017, 12307
TRIFLE 10258
TRIFLES 832, 10347, 10444
TRIFLING 8344
TRIGGER 401
TRIMMING 7867
TRINKETS 5649
TRIP 7711, 11126, 11215
TRIPLE 5633
TRIUMPH 1529, 1541, 2607, 4415, 5320, 5503, 5683, 6739, 8143, 12003
TRIUMPHANT 567
TRIUMPHED 9293
TRIVIA 8013
TRIVIAL 5469, 6043, 8872
TRIVIALITY 1383, 7844
TROD 8051
TROIKA 4095
TROJAN 1127
TROJANS 12025
TROMBONE 4663
TROPHIES 8854, 12231
TROUBLE 360, 1080, 1423, 2664, 2705, 3752, 4704, 4748, 5324, 5712, 5731, 5906, 5922, 6241, 6964, 8388, 8586, 9483, 9636, 10276, 10518, 10658, 12024, 12158, 12285, 12440
TROUBLED 7841, 8564, 10682, 11745
TROUBLEMAKERS 6679

TROUBLES 132, 534, 4987, 8703, 9982, 10124, 12332

TROUBLESOME 5477, 7634

TROUSERS 1042, 4886

TROUT 4522, 11678

TROWEL 2481, 2880

TROY 1513, 9603, 12809

TRUANT 10152

TRUCK 5538

TRUCK DRIVERS 8615

TRUDGED 3007

TRUE 122, 517, 765, 773, 1632, 1845, 1895, 2116, 3865, 4160, 4435, 4650, 5190, 5827, 6511, 7323, 9108, 9818, 10108, 10956, 11288, 11416, 11418, 11464, 12437, 12506

TRULY 7851

TRUMPET 3034, 4139, 5524, 5717, 6825, 10918

TRUMPETS 5370, 6047

TRUMPS 5873

TRUST 39, 83, 1307, 1310, 1878, 3544, 3719, 5012, 5682, 6016, 6442, 8928, 9102, 10408, 10476, 11139, 11425, 11669, 12017, 12025, 12038, 12770, 12868

TRUSTED 7872

TRUSTY 1804

TRUTH 12, 85, 100, 222, 282, 283, 502, 521, 540, 661, 688, 696, 833, 1075, 1150, 1153, 1294, 1326, 1384, 1521, 1627, 1642, 2099, 2187, 2403, 2585, 2622, 2663, 3029, 3141, 3329, 3552, 3615, 3687, 3769, 4005, 4019, 4116, 4447, 4472, 4501, 4651, 4756, 4815, 4855, 4960, 5047, 5066, 5072, 5108, 5158, 5185, 5248, 5414, 5415, 5470, 5605, 5752, 5769, 5958, 6007, 6014, 6078, 6208, 6269, 6368, 6369, 6370, 6524, 6525, 6574, 6741, 6797, 7222, 7225, 7257, 7344, 7394, 7398, 7599, 7648, 7780, 7908, 8114, 8128, 8488, 8544, 8647, 8682, 8716, 8838, 9021, 9089, 9103, 9105, 9120, 9153, 9165, 9200, 9290, 9294, 9313, 9461, 9487, 9749, 9761, 9809, 9834, 9896, 9996, 10087, 10116, 10308, 10453, 10478, 10483, 10836, 10981, 11076, 11077, 11133, 11139, 11147, 11324, 11407, 11442, 11470, 11500, 11548, 11670, 11671, 11710, 11814, 11873, 11884, 11890, 12011, 12084, 12303, 12305, 12485, 12523, 12649, 12792

TRUTHFUL 11977

TRUTHS 345, 982, 1383, 1717, 2039, 4387, 4883, 4979, 4980, 6621, 10522, 11806, 12067

TRUTHTELLING 284

TRY 3854, 7731, 9516, 10158, 10680

TRYING 904, 7154, 11091, 11811

TUBE 4328

TUBERCULOSIS 9719

TUESDAY 7364, 8209

TUG 6124

TUMBLE 9302

TUMBLED 4221

TUMBLING 1881

TUMOUR 2, 31

TUMULT 1010, 1989, 5678, 5726, 12695, 12798

TUNE 1116, 1823, 2793, 5879

TUNES 4565

TUNING 246

TUNNEL 2805, 6526

TURBULENCE 2364

TURD 2191

TURF 12683

TURGENEV 4636

TURKEY 8126

TURKS 4013

TURN 1168, 6103, 12802

TURNED 76, 2423

TURNING 6083, 9296, 11562

TURNIP 5081, 6972

TURNPIKE 3117

TURTLE 2477

TUSCANY 6779

TUTORS 3698, 6377

TWENTIETH 6830

TWENTY 3587, 10879, 12679

TWENTY-TWENTY 12515

TWICE 2113, 2115, 5845, 7894, 11940, 12424

TWIG 5294, 8812

TWILIGHT 11396

TWIN 6150

TWINKLE 11358

TWINS 4220, 6802

TWIST 3814, 8901

TWO 34, 253, 1993, 2464, 4341, 6725, 6915, 7333

TWO-EDGED 7153

TYPE 8998, 11495

TYPING 2053

TYPIST 3230

TYRANNY 477, 1741, 4900, 7956, 7983, 8353, 8545, 9693, 10563, 12057

TYRANT 1259, 3863, 4894, 7149, 8058

TYRANTS 1756, 2706, 8677, 12859

UGLIER 4337

UGLINESSES 3350

713

UNFORTUNATE	1377
UNGAINED	10413
UNGAINLY	8205
UNHABITUAL	4950
UNHAPPILY	11149
UNHAPPINESS	6959, 8213, 9001, 9672, 9814, 11872
UNHAPPY	52, 807, 1048, 1377, 5099, 5276, 5778, 5852, 8996, 9380, 9518, 9690, 11094, 11528, 11735, 12609, 12612, 12833
UNHEARD	5436, 5597
UNHOLY	7451
UNICORN	5176
UNIFORM	4688, 5647
UNIMAGINATIVE	12448
UNIMPORTANT	7345, 8113
UNINTELLIGIBLE	1980, 12698
UNINTENTIONALLY	271
UNINTERESTING	12825
UNINTERRUPTED	6045
UNION	2755, 2803, 8141, 8396, 9792, 11371, 12226
UNIQUE	3194, 4557
UNITARIAN	7100
UNITE	3198, 6375, 7048
UNITED	2727, 7506
UNITED NATIONS	6388
UNITED STATES	195, 2770, 3679, 3743, 5513, 5747, 8229, 11719, 11802, 12408, 12578
UNITES	1689, 5268, 7356, 11730
UNITING	2802
UNITY	1468, 9615
UNIVERSAL	3173, 12451
UNIVERSE	464, 637, 920, 2036, 2758, 3133, 4327, 4413, 4630, 4854, 4968, 5169, 5257, 5787, 7903, 7951, 8555, 9723, 9806, 11601, 11641, 12389
UNIVERSITIES	691
UNIVERSITY	174, 1029, 1464, 2070, 2327, 2537, 2842, 3065, 3149, 8337, 8529, 10951
UNJUST	1489, 9429
UNKEMPT	1567
UNKINDEST	10208
UNKINDNESS	10349
UNKNOWABLE	7185
UNKNOWN	388, 545, 2724, 4408, 8663, 8825
UNLABELLED	4880
UNLAMENTED	8871
UNLEARN	11007
UNLEARN'D	8803
UNLIKE	12616

UNLOVE	2626
UNLOVELY	11463
UNLUCKILY	11149
UNLUCKY	6970
UNMARRIED	6323, 10552
UNMASK	10453
UNMOURNING	11597
UNMOVED	11321
UNMUZZLED	4880
UNNATURAL	657, 3623, 4339, 10284
UNNECESSARY	4391, 12762
UNOBTRUSIVE	5428
UNOBTRUSIVENESS	9738
UNOCCUPIED	9916
UNOFFICIAL	2965
UNORTHODOX	1035
UNPLEASANT	4055, 4457, 9341
UNPLEASANTNESS	8016
UNPOPULAR	959, 6900, 11064
UNPRECEDENTED	474
UNPREMEDITATED	9937
UNPREPARED	1398, 2536
UNPRINCIPLED	2054
UNPROFITABLE	10102
UNPUNISHED	1579
UNREAL	4559
UNREGENERATE	4673
UNREPRIEVED	7539
UNSAFE	6996, 8002
UNSAID	7339, 8746, 12595
UNSATISFIED	12505
UNSAVOURY	10146
UNSAYABLE	11793
UNSEEN	7582
UNSELFISHNESS	6241, 9793, 12826
UNSKILLED	8817
UNSOUGHT	6362, 10432
UNSOUNDNESS	6781
UNSPEAKABLE	12509
UNSPOILED	2566
UNSTUCK	352
UNSUCCESSFUL	1585
UNSUNG	9941
UNSUPPORTABLE	8354
UNSURE	10426
UNTALENTED	2054
UNTHOUGHT	3086
UNTIE	5240
UNTIMELY	12112
UNTOUCH'D	6938
UNTRAVELLED	4148

VERIFY 9598

VERLAINE 8446

VERMIN 1112, 11238

VERMONT 5723

VERSE 1940, 2687, 3660, 4543, 4723, 5937, 7737, 8802, 8948, 8960, 9209, 11017, 11293, 12687, 12730

VERSES 4948, 7146, 11165

VERSIONS 10568

VERTICAL 580, 2696

VERTIGO 6682

VESSEL 603

VESTAL 8786

VESTRY 10795

VETERANS 7741, 8806

VETOES 2981

VEXATION 12244

VEXES 5382, 11527

VEXING 10218

VIATICUM 4014

VIBRATES 12835

VIBRATION 4542

VICAR 5723

VICE 711, 1390, 1879, 2708, 3072, 3440, 4161, 4404, 4779, 5027, 5078, 5831, 7073, 7104, 7781, 7786, 7847, 7909, 8842, 9319, 10315, 10436, 10799, 11198, 11274, 11346, 11846, 11980, 12115, 12521

VICE-PRESIDENCY 3780

VICES 616, 1462, 1595, 2294, 2367, 5300, 5824, 7795, 7977, 8575, 9997, 10247, 12009, 12522

VICHYSSOISE 5354

VICIOUS 9745

VICISSITUDE 11033

VICTIM 3949, 4584

VICTIMS 588, 1482, 4255, 9545

VICTIS 6340

VICTOR 6911, 7507

VICTOR HUGO 2400

VICTORIA 4014, 8974

VICTORIAN 7749

VICTORIANS 12366

VICTORIES 3674, 7468, 11909

VICTORIOUS 6548

VICTORY 921, 941, 1133, 2306, 2321, 2377, 2560, 2931, 3089, 4771, 5622, 6298, 6610, 8048, 8780, 9832, 10869, 10917, 11942, 12590

VICTUALS 2010

VIENNA 1407, 7261

VIETNAM 10943

VIEW 1635, 2577, 4395, 7368, 9935

VIEWING 4094

VIGILANCE 7104

VIGILS 8766

VIGOROUS 3346, 6705

VIGOUR 560

VIKINGS 5612

VILE 5936, 10237

VILELY 10157

VILIFY 911

VILLA 7915, 9645

VILLAGE 4110, 4118

VILLAIN 7241, 8896, 10305, 10373

VILLAINY 11776, 11889

VILLON 11273

VINDICATE 8831

VINDICTIVE 7114

VINE 7473

VINES 5358

VINTAGE 4756

VIOLENCE 121, 285, 1586, 2533, 3235, 3792, 5997, 6620, 6698, 6748, 7258, 7992, 11732, 12223

VIOLENT 803, 3201, 3497, 5510

VIOLET 10174

VIOLETS 6485

VIOLIN 840, 1857, 8578

VIOLINS 11988

VIRGIN 6849, 7484, 7497

VIRGIN-CHOIR 5451

VIRGINITY 7004, 8970, 11763

VIRGINS 1923, 12357

VIRTUE 663, 682, 705, 711, 738, 1390, 1397, 1762, 1879, 1880, 2040, 3015, 3339, 4103, 4129, 4156, 4161, 5027, 5605, 5608, 5831, 5961, 6915, 6950, 7073, 7310, 7414, 7421, 7427, 7726, 7758, 7781, 7794, 7938, 8171, 8491, 8595, 8805, 9428, 9638, 10315, 10359, 10551, 10823, 10937, 11198, 11274, 11346, 11846, 11979, 11980, 12115, 12176

VIRTUES 2294, 3411, 4511, 4554, 4591, 5134, 5300, 5836, 6242, 7977, 8962, 10186, 10423, 11131, 11978, 12319, 12521, 12522

VIRTUOUS 1237, 1389, 4852, 10427, 11220, 12117, 12550

VISIBLE 1560, 5710, 8466, 12461

VISION 1258, 2680, 4918, 5450, 9721, 11067, 12797

VISIONARY 12711

VISIONS 1235, 10337, 10590

VISIT 779, 5893, 7917, 9935

VISITS 7845, 9169

VITAL 8343, 8779

WARMTH 5430, 8242

WARN 5623, 8380, 12181, 12721

WARNING 6692

WARNS 7208

WARRED 7632

WARRING 6949, 7566

WARRIOR 5512, 9934

WARS 6811, 7957, 8313, 8376, 8721, 8939, 9385, 9519, 9823, 10420, 12033

WARY 8956

WASH 2235, 3216

WASHED 2676

WASHES 8637

WASHING 6325, 11592

WASHING-DAY 8572

WASHINGTON 3737, 4884, 12101, 12577

WASHUP 5264

WASPS 11232

WASTE 204, 376, 3088, 6901, 7627, 9936, 10462, 11183, 12740

WASTE BASKET 10695

WASTE-PAPER 12221

WASTED 3197, 4514, 8998, 10369

WASTEFUL 10219

WASTEPAPER 1030

WASTING 9012, 12603

WATCH 1007, 1425, 2557, 4702, 5676, 6524, 7031, 8689, 10099, 12087

WATCHDOG 4113

WATCHER 5386

WATCHES 5021, 11397

WATCHING 1093, 8314, 9554

WATCHMAKER 2680

WATCHMAN 9944

WATCHWORD 8676

WATER 98, 378, 379, 2421, 3264, 4520, 4620, 4723, 5275, 5418, 6179, 6930, 7134, 8370, 8652, 9167, 9203, 10085, 10141, 10186, 10269, 10362, 10682, 10979, 12736

WATERFALL 6450

WATERGATE 4216

WATERLOO 8313, 8635, 11502, 12266

WATERMELONS 4001

WATERS 5260, 12021

WATERY 7482

WATSON 2954, 2960

WAVE 5689

WAVERS 9276

WAVES 3862, 7849, 8495, 10465

WAVING 10784

WAXES 3631

WAY 1153, 1533, 3786, 4431, 4656, 5011, 5633, 5971, 7995, 9253, 10239, 10726, 12608

WAYS 3054, 8103, 10001, 10953, 11428

WE 384, 5626, 11566

WEAK 1253, 2453, 4336, 4640, 5028, 5045, 5509, 5767, 5823, 6285, 7110, 7777, 10008, 11601

WEAK-MINDED 4322

WEAKEN 1690

WEAKENING 10915

WEAKER 1897

WEAKNESS 3967, 4616, 5822, 5890, 6680, 9998, 12007, 12048, 12217, 12246, 12429, 12831

WEAKNESSES 4129, 7124

WEALTH 1516, 2692, 2768, 3750, 3860, 4111, 5212, 5551, 6898, 6940, 7535, 8856, 9448, 9648, 10527, 10596, 10629, 11108, 11664, 11783, 11984, 12596

WEALTHY 494, 1445, 2379, 3746, 6224

WEANED 2913

WEAPON 85, 1253, 5515, 5588, 5735, 7159, 10752, 11741

WEAPONLESS 7653

WEAPONS 628, 12436

WEAR 3855, 4091, 6336, 7899, 12372, 12866

WEARINESS 5445, 8608, 10091

WEARING 838, 3042

WEARY 1614, 5715, 8741, 10192, 10602, 10920

WEASEL 3453, 6874, 8664

WEATHER 650, 5149, 5611, 5687, 6721, 11053, 11835

WEATHERED 1026

WEAVE 12231

WEAVES 11272

WEB 9063, 9946, 10056, 11438

WEBSTER 3233

WED 1434, 2350, 10039, 10052, 11474

WEDDED 7583

WEDDING 71

WEDDING NIGHT 8581

WEDDING-CAKE 590

WEDDING-DAY 5471

WICKED 303, 2154, 5816, 6787, 8231, 9221, 9964, 10151, 10277, 11589, 11695, 12454, 12472

WICKEDNESS 6792, 9428, 11353

WICKET 5649

WIDOW 4310, 7700, 8690, 10972

WIDOW-MAKER 5675

WIDOWED 6681

WIDOWHOOD 3802

WIFE 661, 738, 776, 1220, 2350, 2545, 2633, 2637, 3082, 3443, 3590, 4262, 4307, 4375, 4425, 4470, 4641, 4752, 5011, 5033, 5185, 6086, 6142, 6756, 6916, 7308, 8252, 8533, 8564, 8605, 8622, 10020, 10323, 10951, 11201, 11372, 11483, 11789, 12164

WIG 6758, 12206

WIGWAM 6432

WIL 334

WILD 131, 5652, 6039, 10112

WILD THYME 10331

WILDCAT 9131

WILDERNESS 1720, 4708, 7021, 11313

WILDNESS 4708

WILL 165, 669, 951, 2107, 3277, 3357, 3988, 4348, 4656, 6435, 6533, 6544, 7513, 7594, 7788, 8159, 8224, 8982, 9430, 9523, 9869, 9897, 9898, 10206, 10936

WILLIN' 2781

WILLINGNESS 3476, 6788, 8369, 10651

WILLOWS 11435

WILLS 6139, 10635

WILLY 6020

WIN 143, 1983, 2097, 4060, 4224, 6192, 6868, 7009, 7048, 7932, 8006, 8196, 11072

WINCED 4492

WIND 460, 506, 1225, 1374, 1854, 2771, 2975, 3095, 4649, 4836, 5359, 5421, 5612, 6042, 6062, 6519, 6588, 6712, 7923, 9183, 9969, 10032, 10442, 10609, 10612, 11026, 11505, 11620, 12674

WINDERS 12151

WINDOW 10386

WINDOW-PANE 8310

WINDOWS 219, 3238

WINDS 3862, 5641, 6558, 10235, 12710

WINDWARD 2269

WINDY 10435

WINE 98, 122, 569, 1215, 1250, 1964, 2546, 2952, 3804, 4543, 5192, 5365, 7661, 8361, 8627, 8693, 8716, 8936, 9167, 10037, 10270, 11516, 11759, 12474, 12794

WING 49, 2789, 3966, 4722, 7006, 7644, 9873, 10965

WINGS 1973, 2129, 4465, 5393, 11611

WINK 7194, 10168

WINNING 142, 1008, 4067, 6400, 8906, 9782

WINS 389, 6358

WINSTON 831

WINTER 57, 1483, 1542, 1971, 3211, 6396, 6503, 7486, 8044, 8916, 9022, 9312, 10371, 10471, 10587, 11098, 11784

WINTERS 10454

WIPES 11587

WIRELESS 377

WIRES 666

WISDOM 79, 166, 766, 1214, 1232, 1248, 1327, 1335, 1426, 1507, 2074, 2195, 2592, 3050, 3223, 3467, 3572, 3741, 4293, 4654, 4765, 4769, 5077, 6011, 6291, 6535, 7119, 7247, 7638, 7668, 8137, 8386, 8487, 8840, 9529, 9707, 11379, 11448, 11672, 11876

WISE 719, 740, 1233, 1236, 1261, 1337, 1338, 1528, 1654, 1749, 2081, 2947, 3009, 3389, 3492, 3574, 3591, 4207, 4209, 4213, 4588, 4740, 4956, 4959, 5126, 5138, 5217, 5813, 6378, 7165, 7605, 7675, 7782, 8349, 8567, 8964, 9123, 9130, 9220, 9261, 9529, 10377, 10412, 10415, 10492, 10934, 11066, 11096, 11221, 11344, 12799, 12834, 12839

WISECRACK 6218

WISECRACKING 8440

WISELY 3100, 9251

WISER 607, 752, 2426, 4059, 5545, 7105, 8752, 8867, 11411

WISEST 216, 7608, 7640, 9351, 11288

WISH 1089, 3575, 5091, 5934, 7179, 8093, 9303, 10165

WISHES 2320

WISTFUL 12477

WIT 227, 230, 483, 1683, 1889, 2181, 2806, 2930, 3995, 4430, 5990, 7113, 7119, 7225, 7647, 8187, 8440, 8771, 8789, 8828, 8849, 9707, 10016, 10115, 10209, 10604, 10975, 11338, 11834, 11877, 12438

WITH 1180, 6553

WITHDRAW 3363

WITHDRAWN 2274

WITHER 10070, 10814, 12792

WITHERS 3352, 5401